Fodor's 97

Canada

"When it comes to information on regional history, what to see and do, and shopping, these guides are exhaustive."

—*USAir Magazine*

"Usable, sophisticated restaurant coverage, with an emphasis on good value."

—Andy Birsh, *Gourmet Magazine* columnist

"Valuable because of their comprehensiveness."

—*Minneapolis Star-Tribune*

"Fodor's always delivers high quality...thoughtfully presented...thorough."

—*Houston Post*

"An excellent choice for those who want everything under one cover."

—*Washington Post*

Fodor's Travel Publications, Inc.
New York • Toronto • London • Sydney • Auckland
http://www.fodors.com/

Fodor's Canada

Editors: Anastasia Redmond Mills, Nancy van Itallie

Editorial Contributors: Rosemary Allerston, Steven K. Amsterdam, Robert Andrews, David Anger, David Brown, Susan Brown, Connie Bryson, Audra Epstein, Scott Inniss, Ed Kirby, Donna Nebenzahl, Jens Nielsen, Peter Oliver, Melissa Rivers, Heidi Sarna, Helayne Schiff, Linda K. Schmidt, Mary Ellen Schultz, M.T. Schwartzman (Gold Guide editor), Tina Sebert, Dinah Spritzer, Don Thacker, Paul A.R. Waters, Julie Watson, Ana Watts, Sara Waxman

Creative Director: Fabrizio La Rocca

Cartographer: David Lindroth

Cover Photograph: Peter Guttman

Text Design: Between the Covers

Copyright

Special Sales

CONTENTS

On the Road with Fodor's v

About Our Writers *v*
New This Year *v*
How to Use This Book *vi*
Don't Forget to Write *vi*

The Gold Guide x

Important Contacts A to Z *x*
Smart Travel Tips A to Z *xxii*

1 **Destination: Canada** 1

What's Where *2*
Pleasures and Pastimes *3*
New and Noteworthy *7*
Fodor's Choice *7*
Festivals and Seasonal Events *10*

2 **Vancouver** 14

3 **British Columbia** 66

4 **The Canadian Rockies** 116

5 **The Prairie Provinces** 166

Alberta, Saskatchewan, Manitoba

6 **Toronto** 227

7 **Province of Ontario** 283

Ottawa, Algonquin Park, Windsor, Niagara, London

8 **Montréal** 339

9 **Québec City** 403

10 **Province of Québec** 454

The Laurentians, l'Estrie, the Gaspé Peninsula

11 **New Brunswick** 492

12 **Prince Edward Island** 522

13 **Nova Scotia** 541

14 **Newfoundland and Labrador** 579

15 **Wilderness Canada** 604

Northwest Territories, Yukon

Canada *viii–ix*
Vancouver *16–17*
Downtown Vancouver *22*
Stanley Park *27*
Granville Island *30*
Downtown Vancouver Dining *35*
Greater Vancouver Dining *36*
Vancouver Lodging *44*
British Columbia *68–69*
Downtown Victoria *74*
Vancouver Island *86*
The Canadian Rockies *126–127*
Banff *128*
Alberta *170*
Downtown Calgary *172*
Greater Calgary *175*
Downtown Edmonton *185*
Saskatchewan *195*
Regina *196*
Saskatoon *206*
Manitoba *213*
Downtown Winnipeg *215*
Toronto *229*
Waterfront Toronto and the Financial District *234–235*
Inland Toronto *244–245*
Toronto Dining *252–253*
Toronto Lodging *264–265*
Lower Ontario Province *288–289*
Downtown Ottawa *293*
Greater Ottawa and Hull *293*
Niagara Falls *314*
Upper Ontario *328*
Montréal Exploring *342–343*

Vieux-Montréal *351*
Downtown Montréal *357*
Latin Quarter and Mount Royal Park *363*
Olympic Park and Botanical Garden *369*
Montréal Dining *372–373*
Montréal Lodging *380–381*
Montréal Métro *400*
Metropolitan Québec City *406–407*
Upper and Lower Towns *410–411*
Outside the City Walls *421*
Québec City Dining and Lodging *426–427*
Ile d'Orléans *445*
Lower Québec *456–457*
The Laurentians *462*
L'Estrie (Eastern Townships) and Montérégie *473*
Charlevoix *481*
Gaspé Peninsula *486*
New Brunswick *498–499*
Fredericton *501*
Downtown Saint John *508*
Greater Saint John *510*
Prince Edward Island *528*
Charlottetown *529*
Nova Scotia *548–549*
Halifax *550*
Newfoundland and Labrador *584–585*
Northwest Territories *614–615*
The Yukon *616*

ON THE ROAD WITH FODOR'S

WE'RE ALWAYS THRILLED to get letters from readers, especially one like this:

It took us an hour to decide what book to buy and we now know we picked the best one. Your book was wonderful, easy to follow, very accurate, and good on pointing out eating places, informal as well as formal. When we saw other people using your book, we would look at each other and smile.

Our editors and writers are deeply committed to making every Fodor's guide "the best one"—not only accurate but always charming, brimming with sound recommendations and solid ideas, right on the mark in describing restaurants and hotels, and full of fascinating facts that make you view what you've traveled to see in a rich new light.

About Our Writers

Our success in achieving our goals—and in helping to make your trip the best of all possible vacations—is a credit to the hard work of our extraordinary writers.

Travel junkie **Melissa Rivers,** updater of the British Columbia and Vancouver chapters, lives in Oregon and travels throughout the Pacific Northwest and eastern Mexico on assignments for Fodor's. In updating the Canadian Rockies chapter, Edmonton geographers **Connie Bryson** and **Don Thacker** traveled 7,000 kilometers (4,300 miles) and managed to escape numerous avalanches. **Jens Nielsen,** a travel writer based in Saskatoon, Saskatchewan, updated the Prairie Provinces chapter. Columnist and cookbook and restaurant guide author **Sara Waxman** shares insider's knowledge in the Toronto dining section.

The Québec chapters are the preserve of writers associated with *The Gazette* of Montréal. **Dorothy Guinan,** who wrote the Québec province chapter, does political research for the daily; **Donna Nebenzahl,** who edits the *Woman News* section, updated the Québec province and Québec City chapters. **Paul Waters,** the paper's travel editor, is the expert who handled the Montréal chapter. Award-winning Fredericton columnist **Ana Watts** updated the chapter on her province, New Brunswick. **Ed Kirby,** a Newfoundland and Labrador tourism writer who lives in St. John's, carefully combed through his chapter. Novelist, playwright, and sailor **Silver Donald Cameron,** who wrote the chapter on Nova Scotia, is one of Canada's most versatile authors. His books *Wind, Whales and Whisky: A Cape Breton Voyage* and *Sun, Sand and Strawberries: An Acadian Voyage* record cruises with his wife and son in the *Silversark,* a 27-foot sailboat they built themselves. Food and travel writer **Julie Watson,** who updated Nova Scotia and Prince Edward Island for this edition, lives on Prince Edward Island and tours the region researching articles and books such as her latest: *Ship Wrecks and Seafaring Tales* and *A Fine Catch Seafood Cookbook.* Editor of the magazine *Up here, Life in Canada's North* for the past 10 years, Yellowknife resident **Rosemary Allerston,** who updated the Northwest Territories section of the Wilderness Canada chapter, knows what's going on in the region. Award-winning writer and film scout **Tina Sebert,** updater of the Yukon section, lives in Whitehorse. She leads tours of the region and enjoys backpacking and rafting the Yukon River.

We'd also like to thank the Canadian Consulate General office in New York; Tourism Québec, particularly Pierre Tougas and Marie Dubé; and the Greater Québec Area Tourism and Convention Bureau, especially Richard Séguin and Monique Després.

New This Year

This year we've reformatted our guides to make them easier to use. Each chapter of *Canada* begins with brand-new recommended itineraries to help you decide what to see in the time you have; a section called When to Tour points out the optimal time of day, day of the week, and season for your journey. You may also notice our fresh graphics, new in 1996. More readable and more helpful than ever? We think so—and we hope you do, too.

Also check out Fodor's Web site (http://www.fodors.com/), where you'll find travel information on major destinations around the world and an ever-changing array of travel-savvy interactive features.

How to Use This Book

Organization

Up front is the **Gold Guide.** Its first section, **Important Contacts A to Z,** gives addresses and telephone numbers of organizations and companies that offer destination-related services and detailed information and publications. **Smart Travel Tips A to Z,** the Gold Guide's second section, gives specific information on how to accomplish what you need to in Canada as well as tips on savvy traveling. Both sections are in alphabetical order by topic.

Chapters in *Canada* are arranged geographically from west to east. Each city chapter begins with an Exploring section, which is subdivided by neighborhood; each subsection recommends a walking or driving tour and lists sights in alphabetical order. Each regional chapter is divided by geographical area; within each area, towns are covered in logical geographical order, and attractive stretches of road and minor points of interest between them are indicated by the designation *En Route.* Throughout, Off the Beaten Path sights appear after the places from which they are most easily accessible. And within town sections, all restaurants and lodgings are grouped together.

To help you decide what to visit in the time you have, all chapters begin with recommended itineraries; you can mix and match those from several chapters to create a complete vacation. The A to Z section that ends all chapters covers getting there, getting around, and helpful contacts and resources.

Icons and Symbols

★ Our special recommendations
✕ Restaurant
🏨 Lodging establishment
✕🏨 Lodging establishment whose restaurant warrants a detour
⛺ Campground
🦆 Rubber duckie (good for kids)
☞ Sends you to another section of the guide for more information
✉ Address
☎ Telephone number
⏲ Opening and closing times
🎟 Admission prices (those we give apply only to adults; substantially reduced fees are almost always available for children, students, and senior citizens)

Numbers in white and black circles—② and ❷, for example—that appear on the maps, in the margins, and within the tours correspond to one another.

Currency

Unless otherwise stated, prices are quoted in Canadian dollars.

Dining and Lodging

The restaurants and lodgings we list are the cream of the crop in each price range. Price charts appear in the Pleasures and Pastimes section that follows each chapter introduction.

Hotel Facilities

We always list the facilities that are available—but we don't specify whether they cost extra: When pricing accommodations, always ask what's included.

Assume that hotels operate on the **European Plan** (EP, with no meals) unless we note that they use the **American Plan** (AP, with all meals), the **Modified American Plan** (MAP, with breakfast and dinner daily), or the **Continental Plan** (CP, with a Continental breakfast daily).

Restaurant Reservations and Dress Codes

Reservations are always a good idea; we note only when they're essential or when they are not accepted. Book as far ahead as you can, and reconfirm when you get to town. Unless otherwise noted, the restaurants listed are open daily for lunch and dinner. We mention dress only when men are required to wear a jacket or a jacket and tie.

Credit Cards

The following abbreviations are used: **AE,** American Express; **DC,** Diners Club; **MC,** MasterCard; and **V,** Visa.

Don't Forget to Write

You can use this book in the confidence that all prices and opening times are based on information supplied to us at press time; Fodor's cannot accept responsibility for any errors. Time inevitably brings changes, so always confirm information when it matters—especially if you're making a detour to visit a specific place. In addition, when making reservations be sure to mention if you have a disability or are traveling with children, if you prefer a private bath or a certain type of bed, or if you have specific dietary needs or any other concerns.

Were the restaurants we recommended as described? Did our hotel picks exceed your expectations? Did you find a museum we recommended a waste of time? If you have complaints, we'll look into them and revise our entries when the facts warrant it. If you've discovered a special place that we haven't included, we'll pass the information along to our correspondents and have them check it out. So send your feedback, positive *and* negative, to the Canada Editor at 201 East 50th Street, New York, New York 10022—and have a wonderful trip!

Karen Cure
Editorial Director

Canada

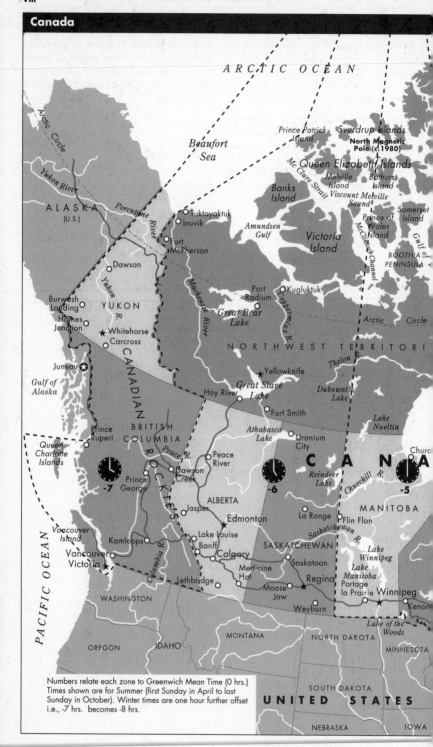

ARCTIC OCEAN

Beaufort
Sea

Prince Patrick
Island

Sverdrup Islands

**North Magnetic
Pole** (c.1980)

Queen Elizabeth Islands

Melville
Island

Bathurst
Island

Viscount Melville
Sound

Somerset
Island

Prince of
Wales
Island

BOOTHIA
PENINSULA

Gulf of

Mc Clure Strait

Banks
Island

McClintock Channel

Coppermine R.

Yukon River

Arctic Circle

Porcupine

River

ALASKA
(U.S.)

Tuktoyaktuk
Inuvik

Fort
McPherson

Amundsen
Gulf

Victoria
Island

Dawson

Yukon R.

Mackenzie River

Port
Radium

Kugluktuk

Great Bear
Lake

Arctic   Circle

Burwash
Landing

YUKON

Haines
Junction

Whitehorse
Carcross

NORTHWEST   TERRITORI

Yellowknife

Thelon R.

Juneau

Great Slave
Lake

Dubawnt
Lake

Lake
Nueltin

Gulf of
Alaska

CANADIAN

Hay River

Fort Smith

Prince
Rupert

BRITISH
COLUMBIA

Athabasca
Lake

Uranium
City

Queen
Charlotte
Islands

Peace R.

Peace
River

Dawson
Creek

C A N A D A

Churc

Prince
George

-7

ROCKIES

Reindeer
Lake

Churchill R.

-6

-5

Vancouver
Island

Jasper

ALBERTA

Edmonton

La Ronge

Flin Flon

MANITOBA

Kamloops

Lake Louise

Banff

Columbia R.

Calgary

SASKATCHEWAN

Saskatoon

Lake
Winnipeg

Vancouver
Victoria

Lethbridge

Medicine
Hat

Moose
Jaw

Regina

Lake
Manitoba

Portage
la Prairie

Winnipeg

Kenor

Weyburn

PACIFIC OCEAN

WASHINGTON

Lake of the
Woods

ORFGON   IDAHO

MONTANA

NORTH DAKOTA

MINNESOTA

Numbers relate each zone to Greenwich Mean Time (0 hrs.)
Times shown are for Summer (first Sunday in April to last
Sunday in October). Winter times are one hour further offset
i.e., -7 hrs. becomes -8 hrs.

SOUTH DAKOTA

UNITED   STATES

NEBRASKA   IOWA

ICELAND

GREENLAND
(Denmark)

Denmark Strait

Ellesmere Island

Devon Island

Lancaster Sound

Baffin Bay

Davis Strait

Baffin Island

Prince Charles Island

Foxe Basin

Lake Amadjuak

Iqaluit

Southampton Island

Lake Harbour

Hudson Strait

Cape Chidley

Labrador Sea

Coats Island

Mansel Island

Ivujivik

Ungava Bay

Nain

NEWFOUNDLAND

LABRADOR

Battle Harbour

Hudson Bay

D A

Belcher Islands

🕐 -4

Schefferville

Goose Bay

Labrador City

Gander

🕐 -2:30

John's

Fort Severn

Fort George

Q U E B E C

Sept-Iles

Anticosti Island

🕐 -3

Severn R.

James Bay

Lake Mistassini

GASPÉ PENINSULA

ST. PIERRE AND MIQUELON
(France)

Moosonee

PRINCE EDWARD ISLAND

Sydney

O N T A R I O

Rimouski

River

Chicoutimi

NEW BRUNSWICK

Charlottetown

Lake Nipigon

Québec City ★

Fredericton

NOVA SCOTIA

Cochrane

Ste.-Agathe-Des-Monts

Trois-Rivières

Saint John

Halifax ★

Thunder Bay

Timmins

Montréal

Bay of Fundy

Lake Superior

Sudbury

North Bay

St. Lawrence

MAINE

Sault Ste. Marie

Ottawa ☆

VT.

ATLANTIC OCEAN

Lake Huron

Toronto ★

Lake Ontario

N.H.

ISCONSIN

Lake Michigan

Niagara Falls

NEW YORK

MASSACHUSETTS

N

MICHIGAN

Lake Erie

CONN.

R.I.

0   400 miles

ILLINOIS   INDIANA   OHIO

PENNSYLVANIA

N.J.

0   600 km

IMPORTANT CONTACTS A TO Z

An Alphabetical Listing of Publications, Organizations, and Companies that Will Help You Before, During, and After Your Trip

A

AIR TRAVEL

Flying time to Montréal is 1½ hours from New York, 2 hours from Chicago, 6 hours from Los Angeles, 6½ hours from London. To Toronto: 1½ hours from New York and Chicago, 4½ hours from Los Angeles. To Vancouver: 6½ hours from Montréal, 4 hours from Chicago, 2½ hours from Los Angeles.

The major gateways to Canada are Montréal's **Dorval Airport** (☎ 514/633–3105), Toronto's **Pearson International Airport** (☎ 905/676–2275), and **Vancouver International Airport** (☎ 604/276–6101).

CARRIERS

To Montreal➤ Contact **Air Canada** (☎ 800/776–3000), **Continental** (☎ 800/525–0280), **Delta** (800/221–1212), **Northwest** (☎ 800/225–2525), **United** (☎ 800/722–5243), and **USAir** (☎ 800/428–4322).

To Toronto➤ Contact **Air Canada** (☎ 800/776–3000), **American** (☎ 800/433–7300), **Continental** (☎ 800/525–0280), **Delta** (800/221–1212), **Northwest** (☎ 800/225–2525), **TWA** (☎ 800/221–2000), **United** (☎ 800/722–5243), and **USAir** (☎ 800/428–4322).

To Vancouver➤ Contact **Air Canada** (☎ 800/776–3000), **Alaska Airlines** (☎ 800/426–0333), **American** (☎ 800/433–7300), **Delta** (800/221–1212), **Horizon Air** (☎ 800/547–9308), **Northwest** (☎ 800/225–2525), **Southwest** (☎ 800/435–9792), **United** (☎ 800/722–5243), and **USAir** (☎ 800/428–4322).

From the U.K.➤ Contact **Air Canada** (☎ 800/776–3000) or British Airways (☎ 0181/897–4000; outside London, 0345/222–111).

COMPLAINTS

To register complaints about charter and scheduled airlines, contact the U.S. Department of Transportation's **Aviation Consumer Protection Division** (⊠ C-75, Washington, DC 20590, ☎ 202/366–2220). Complaints about lost baggage or ticketing problems and safety concerns may also be logged with the **Federal Aviation Administration (FAA) Consumer Hotline** (☎ 800/322–7873).

CONSOLIDATORS

For the names of reputable air-ticket consolidators, contact the **United States Air Consolidators Association** (925 L St., Suite 220, Sacramento, CA 95814, ☎ 916/441–4166, fax 916/441–3520). For discount air-ticketing agencies, *see* Discounts & Deals, *below.*

PUBLICATIONS

For general information about charter carriers, ask for the Department of Transportation's free brochure **"Plane Talk: Public Charter Flights"** (⊠ Aviation Consumer Protection Division, C-75, Washington, DC 20590, ☎ 202/366–2220). The Department of Transportation also publishes a 58-page booklet, **"Fly Rights,"** available from the Consumer Information Center (⊠ Supt. of Documents, Dept. 136C, Pueblo, CO 81009; $1.75).

For other tips and hints, consult the Consumers Union's monthly **"Consumer Reports Travel Letter"** (⊠ Box 53629, Boulder, CO 80322, ☎ 800/234–1970; $39 1st year).

WITHIN CANADA

Air Canada (☎ 800/776–3000) operates in every province. The other major domestic carrier is **Canadian Airlines International** (☎ 800/426–7000). Regularly scheduled flights to every major city and to most smaller cities are available on Air Canada or Canadian Airlines International or the domestic carriers associated with them: **Air Alliance** (☎ 514/393–3333) serves Québec; **Air Atlantic** (☎ 902/427–5500) flies in the Atlantic region; **Air BC** (☎ 604/688–5515) serves British Columbia and Alberta with extended service out of Portland and Seattle; **Air Nova** (☎ 902/429–7111) serves Atlantic Canada; and **Air Ontario** (☎ 416/925–2311) serves the Ontario region. These airlines can also be contacted at local numbers within each of the many cities they serve. Check with the regional tourist agencies for charter companies and with the District Controller of Air Services in the territorial (and provincial) capitals for the locations of air bases that allow private flights and for regulations.

B

BETTER BUSINESS BUREAU

For local contacts in the hometown of a tour operator you may be considering, consult the **Council of Better Business Bureaus** (✉ 4200 Wilson Blvd., Suite 800, Arlington, VA 22203, ☎ 703/276–0100, FAX 703/525–8277).

BUS TRAVEL

Greyhound (☎ 800/231–2222) has the most widespread bus service to Canada, and you can get from almost any point in the United States to any point in Canada on its extensive network. One of the longest routes, from New York to Vancouver via Seattle, takes about 3½ days.

WITHIN CANADA

The bus is an essential form of transportation in Canada, especially if you want to visit out-of-the-way towns that do not have airports or rail lines. Two major bus companies, **Greyhound** (✉ 222 1st Ave. SW, Calgary, Alberta, T2P 0A6, ☎ 403/265–9111 or 800/231–2222) and **Voyageur** (✉ 505 E Boulevard Maisonneuve H2L 1Y4, Montréal, ☎ 514/843–4231), offer interprovincial service. In the United Kingdom, contact **Greyhound International** ✉ Sussex House, London Road, E. Grinstead, East Sussex, RHI9 1LD (☎ 01342/317317).

C

CAR RENTAL

The major car-rental companies represented in Canada are **Alamo** (☎ 800/327–9633; in the U.K., 0800/272–2000), **Avis** (☎ 800/331–1084; in Canada, 800/879–2847), **Budget** (☎ 800/527–0700; in the U.K., 0800/181181), **Dollar** (☎ 800/800–4000; in the U.K., 0990/565656, where it is known as Eurodollar), **Hertz** (☎ 800/654–3001; in Canada, 800/263–0600; in the U.K., 0345/555888), and **National InterRent** (sometimes known as Europcar InterRent outside North America; ☎ 800/227–3876; in the U.K., 01345/222–525). In Montréal, rates begin at $29 a day and $203 a week, not including 14% tax. In Toronto, rates begin at $27 a day and $169 a week, not including 14% tax. In Vancouver, rates begin at $22 a day and $148 a week, not including tax, which is 14%.

CHILDREN & TRAVEL

FLYING

Look into **"Flying with Baby"** (✉ Third Street Press, Box 261250, Littleton, CO 80163, ☎ 303/595–5959; $4.95 includes shipping), cowritten by a flight attendant. **"Kids and Teens in Flight,"** free from the U.S. Department of Transportation's Aviation Consumer Protection Division (✉ C-75, Washington, DC 20590, ☎ 202/366–2220), offers tips on children flying alone. Every two years the February issue of **Family Travel Times** (☞ Know-How, *below*) details children's services on three dozen airlines. **"Flying Alone, Handy Advice for Kids Traveling Solo"** is available free from the American Automobile Association (AAA) (✉ send stamped, self-addressed, legal-size envelope: Flying Alone, Mail Stop 800, 1000 AAA Dr., Heathrow, FL 32746).

KNOW-HOW

Family Travel Times, published quarterly by Travel with Your Children (✉ TWYCH, 40 5th Ave., New York, NY 10011, ☎ 212/477–5524; $40 per year), covers destinations, types of vacations, and modes of travel.

TOUR OPERATORS

If you're outdoorsy, look into the nature camps, called Conservation Summits, sponsored by the **National Wildlife Federation** (✉ 8925 Leesburg Pike,

THE GOLD GUIDE / IMPORTANT CONTACTS

Vienna, VA 22184, ☎ 703/790–4000 or 800/245–5484), as well as the family adventure tours, ranches, and lodges of **American Wilderness Experience** (✉ Box 1486, Boulder, CO 80306, ☎ 303/444–2622 or 800/444–0099).

CUSTOMS

IN THE U.S.

The **U.S. Customs Service** (✉ Box 7407, Washington, DC 20044, ☎ 202/927–6724) can answer questions on duty-free limits and publishes a helpful brochure, "Know Before You Go." For information on registering foreign-made articles, call 202/927–0540 or write U.S. Customs Service, Resource Management, 1301 Constitution Ave. NW, Washington DC, 20229.

COMPLAINTS➤ Note the inspector's badge number and write to the commissioner's office (✉ 1301 Constitution Ave. NW, Washington, DC 20229).

U.K. CITIZENS

HM Customs and Excise (✉ Dorset House, Stamford St., London SE1 9NG, ☎ 0171/202–4227) can answer questions about U.K. customs regulations and publishes a free pamphlet, **"A Guide for Travellers,"** detailing standard procedures and import rules.

D
DISABILITIES & ACCESSIBILITY

COMPLAINTS

To register complaints under the provisions of the Americans with Disabilities Act, contact the U.S. Department of Justice's **Disability Rights Section** (✉ Box 66738, Washington, DC 20035, ☎ 202/514–0301 or 800/514–0301, FAX 202/307–1198, TTY 202/514–0383 or 800/514–0383). For airline-related problems, contact the U.S. Department of Transportation's **Aviation Consumer Protection Division** (☞ Air Travel, *above*). For complaints about surface transportation, contact the Department of Transportation's **Civil Rights Office** (✉ 400 7th St., SW, Room 10215, Washington DC, 20590 ☎ 202/366–4648).

ORGANIZATIONS

The **Canadian Paraplegic Association National Office** (✉ 520 Sutherland Dr., Toronto, Ontario, M4G 3U9, ☎ 416/422–5640) provides information about touring in Canada.

TRAVELERS WITH HEARING IMPAIRMENTS➤ The **American Academy of Otolaryngology** (✉ 1 Prince St., Alexandria, VA 22314, ☎ 703/836–4444, FAX 703/683–5100, TTY 703/519–1585) publishes a brochure, "Travel Tips for Hearing Impaired People."

TRAVELERS WITH MOBILITY PROBLEMS➤ Contact the **Information Center for Individuals with Disabilities** (✉ Box 256, Boston, MA 02117, ☎ 617/450–9888; in MA, 800/462–5015; TTY 617/424–6855); **Mobility International USA** (✉ Box 10767, Eugene, OR 97440, ☎ and TTY 541/343–1284, FAX 541/343–6812), the U.S. branch of a Belgium-based organization (☞ *below*) with affiliates in 30 countries; **Moss-Rehab Hospital Travel Information Service** (☎ 215/456–9600, TTY 215/456–9602), a telephone information resource for travelers with physical disabilities; the **Society for the Advancement of Travel for the Handicapped** (✉ 347 5th Ave., Suite 610, New York, NY 10016, ☎ 212/447–7284, FAX 212/725–8253; membership $45); and **Travelin' Talk** (✉ Box 3534, Clarksville, TN 37043, ☎ 615/552–6670, FAX 615/552–1182) which provides local contacts worldwide for travelers with disabilities.

TRAVELERS WITH VISION IMPAIRMENTS➤ Contact the **American Council of the Blind** (✉ 1155 15th St. NW, Suite 720, Washington, DC 20005, ☎ 202/467–5081, FAX 202/467–5085) for a list of travelers' resources or the **American Foundation for the Blind** (✉ 11 Penn Plaza, Suite 300, New York, NY 10001, ☎ 212/502–7600 or 800/232–5463, TTY 212/502–7662), which provides general advice and publishes "Access to Art" ($19.95), a directory of museums that accommodate travelers with vision impairments.

IN THE U.K.

Contact the **Royal Association for Disability and Rehabilitation** (✉ RADAR, 12 City Forum, 250 City Rd., London EC1V 8AF, ☎ 0171/250–3222) or

Mobility International (✉ rue de Manchester 25, B-1080 Brussels, Belgium, ☎ 00–322–410–6297, FAX 00–322–410–6874), an international travel-information clearing-house for people with disabilities.

PUBLICATIONS

Several publications for travelers with disabilities are available from the **Consumer Information Center** (✉ Box 100, Pueblo, CO 81009, ☎ 719/948–3334). Call or write for its free catalog of current titles. The Society for the Advancement of Travel for the Handicapped (☞ Organizations, *above*) publishes the quarterly magazine **"Access to Travel"** ($13 for 1-year subscription).

The 500-page *Travelin' Talk Directory* (✉ Box 3534, Clarksville, TN 37043, ☎ 615/552–6670, FAX 615/552–1182; $35) lists people and organizations who help travelers with disabilities. For travel agents worldwide, consult the *Directory of Travel Agencies for the Disabled* (✉ Twin Peaks Press, Box 129, Vancouver, WA 98666, ☎ 360/694–2462 or 800/637–2256, FAX 360/696–3210; $19.95 plus $3 shipping).

Also check out **"Access to Travel"**, a quarterly magazine published by the Society for the Advancement of Travel for the Handicapped (✉ 347 Fifth Ave., New York, NY 10016 ☎ 212/447–7284); and the **"Handicapped Travel Newsletter"** (✉ Drawer 269, Athens, TX 75751, ☎ 903/677–1260).

TRAVEL AGENCIES & TOUR OPERATORS

The Americans with Disabilities Act requires that all travel firms serve the needs of all travelers. That said, you should note that some agencies and operators specialize in making travel arrangements for individuals and groups with disabilities, among them **Access Adventures** (✉ 206 Chestnut Ridge Rd., Rochester, NY 14624, ☎ 716/889–9096), run by a former physical-rehab counselor.

TRAVELERS WITH MOBILITY PROBLEMS➤ Contact **Hinsdale Travel Service** (✉ 201 E. Ogden Ave., Suite 100, Hinsdale, IL 60521, ☎ 708/325–1335), a travel agency that benefits from the advice of wheelchair traveler Janice Perkins; and **Wheelchair Journeys** (✉ 16979 Redmond Way, Redmond, WA 98052, ☎ 206/885–2210 or 800/313–4751), which can handle arrangements worldwide.

TRAVELERS WITH DEVELOPMENTAL DISABILITIES➤ Contact the nonprofit **New Directions** (✉ 5276 Hollister Ave., Suite 207, Santa Barbara, CA 93111, ☎ 805/967–2841).

TRAVEL GEAR

The **Magellan's** catalog (☎ 800/962–4943, FAX 805/568–5406), includes a section devoted to products designed for travelers with disabilities.

AIRFARES

For the lowest airfares to Canada, call 800/FLY–4–LESS.

CLUBS

Contact **Entertainment Travel Editions** (✉ Box 1068, Trumbull, CT 06611, ☎ 800/445–4137; $28–$53, depending on destination), **Great American Traveler** (✉ Box 27965, Salt Lake City, UT 84127, ☎ 800/548–2812; $49.95 per year), **Moment's Notice Discount Travel Club** (✉ 7301 New Utrecht Ave., Brooklyn, NY 11204, ☎ 718/234–6295; $25 per year, single or family), **Privilege Card** (✉ 3391 Peachtree Rd. NE, Suite 110, Atlanta, GA 30326, ☎ 404/262–0222 or 800/236–9732; $74.95 per year), **Travelers Advantage** (✉ CUC Travel Service, 49 Music Sq. W, Nashville, TN 37203, ☎ 800/548–1116 or 800/648–4037; $49 per year, single or family), or **Worldwide Discount Travel Club** (✉ 1674 Meridian Ave., Miami Beach, FL 33139, ☎ 305/534–2082; $50 per year for family, $40 single).

PASSES

☞ Train Travel, *below*.

STUDENTS

Members of Hostelling International–American Youth Hostels (☞ Students, *below*) are eligible for discounts on car rentals, admissions to attractions, and other selected travel expenses.

THE GOLD GUIDE / IMPORTANT CONTACTS

PUBLICATIONS

Consult *The Frugal Globetrotter,* by Bruce Northam (⊠ Fulcrum Publishing, 350 Indiana St., Suite 350, Golden, CO 80401, ☎ 800/992–2908; $16.95 plus $4 shipping).

DRIVING

AUTO CLUBS

Members of the Automobile Association of America (AAA) can contact the **Canadian Automobile Association** (⊠ 1775 Courtwood Crescent, Ottawa, Ontario K2C 3J2, ☎ 613/226–7631; emergency road service, ☎ 800/336–4357). Members of the Automobile Association of Great Britain, the Royal Automobile Club, the Royal Scottish Automobile Club, the Royal Irish Automobile Club and the automobile clubs of the Alliance Internationale de Tourisme (AIT) and Fédération Internationale de l'Automobile (FIA) are entitled to all the services of the CAA on presentation of a membership card.

INSURANCE

Drivers must have proof of insurance coverage, which is compulsory in Canada. The Canadian Non-Resident Inter-Provincial Motor Vehicle Liability Insurance Card, available from any U.S. insurance company, is accepted as evidence of financial responsibility anywhere in Canada. For more information, contact the Insurance Bureau of Canada (⊠ 181 University Ave., Toronto, Ontario, M5H 3M7, ☎ 416/362–2301).

F

FERRIES

Car ferries provide essential transportation on both the east and west coasts of Canada. **Marine Atlantic** (⊠ Box 250, North Sydney, NS B2A 3M3, ☎ 902/794–5700 or 800/341–7981 in the U.S. only) operates ferries between Nova Scotia and Newfoundland; New Brunswick and Prince Edward Island; New Brunswick and Nova Scotia; and also between Portland, Maine, and Nova Scotia. On the west coast, the **British Columbia Ferry Corporation** (⊠ 1112 Fort St., Victoria, BC V8V 4V2, ☎ 604/656–0757) has 42 ports of call. Other ferries also operate between the state of Washington and British Columbia's Vancouver Island.

G

GAY & LESBIAN TRAVEL

ORGANIZATIONS

The **International Gay Travel Association** (⊠ Box 4974, Key West, FL 33041, ☎ 800/448–8550, FAX 305/296–6633), a consortium of more than 1,000 travel companies, can supply names of gay-friendly travel agents, tour operators, and accommodations.

PUBLICATIONS

The premier international travel magazine for gays and lesbians is *Our World* (⊠ 1104 N. Nova Rd., Suite 251, Daytona Beach, FL 32117, ☎ 904/441–5367, FAX 904/441–5604; $35 for 10 issues). The 16-page monthly **"Out & About"** (☎ 212/645–6922 or 800/929–2268, FAX 800/929–2215; $49 for 10 issues and quarterly calendar) covers gay-friendly resorts, hotels, cruise lines, and airlines.

TOUR OPERATORS

Toto Tours (⊠ 1326 W. Albion Ave., Suite 3W, Chicago, IL 60626, ☎ 312/274–8686 or 800/565–1241, FAX 312/274–8695) offers group tours to worldwide destinations.

TRAVEL AGENCIES

The largest agencies serving gay travelers are **Advance Travel** (⊠ 10700 Northwest Fwy., Suite 160, Houston, TX 77092, ☎ 713/682–2002 or 800/292–0500), **Islanders/Kennedy Travel** (⊠ 183 W. 10th St., New York, NY 10014, ☎ 212/242–3222 or 800/988–1181), **Now Voyager** (⊠ 4406 18th St., San Francisco, CA 94114, ☎ 415/626–1169 or 800/255–6951), and **Yellowbrick Road** (⊠ 1500 W. Balmoral Ave., Chicago, IL 60640, ☎ 312/561–1800 or 800/642–2488). **Skylink Women's Travel** (⊠ 2460 W. 3rd St., Suite 215, Santa Rosa, CA 95401, ☎ 707/570–0105 or 800/225–5759) serves lesbian travelers.

I

INSURANCE

IN CANADA

Contact **Mutual of Omaha** (⊠ Travel Division, 500 University Ave., Toronto,

Ontario M5G 1V8, ☎ 800/465–0267 (in Canada) or 416/598–4083).

IN THE U.S.

Travel insurance covering baggage, health, and trip cancellation or interruptions is available from **Access America** (✉ 6600 W. Broad St., Richmond, VA 23230, ☎ 804/285–3300 or 800/334–7525), **Carefree Travel Insurance** (✉ Box 9366, 100 Garden City Plaza, Garden City, NY 11530, ☎ 516/294–0220 or 800/323–3149), **Near Travel Services** (✉ Box 1339, Calumet City, IL 60409, ☎ 708/868–6700 or 800/654–6700), **Tele-Trip** (✉ Mutual of Omaha Plaza, Box 31716, Omaha, NE 68131, ☎ 800/228–9792), **Travel Guard International** (✉ 1145 Clark St., Stevens Point, WI 54481, ☎ 715/345–0505 or 800/826–1300), **Travel Insured International** (✉ Box 280568, East Hartford, CT 06128, ☎ 203/528–7663 or 800/243–3174), and **Wallach & Company** (✉ 107 W. Federal St., Box 480, Middleburg, VA 22117, ☎ 540/687–3166 or 800/237–6615).

IN THE U.K.

The **Association of British Insurers** (✉ 51 Gresham St., London EC2V 7HQ, ☎ 0171/600–3333) gives advice by phone and publishes the free pamphlet *"Holiday Insurance and Motoring Abroad,"* which sets out typical policy provisions and costs.

L

LODGING

For information on hotel consolidators, *see* Discounts, *above.*

APARTMENT & VILLA RENTAL

Among the companies to contact are **Property Rentals International** (✉ 1008 Mansfield Crossing Rd., Richmond, VA 23236, ☎ 804/378–6054 or 800/220–3332, FAX 804/379–2073), and **Rent-a-Home International** (✉ 7200 34th Ave. NW, Seattle, WA 98117, ☎ 206/789–9377 or 800/488–7368, FAX 206/789–9379, rentahomeinternational £msn.com). Members of the travel club **Hideaways International** (✉ 767 Islington St., Portsmouth, NH 03801, ☎ 603/430–4433 or 800/843–4433, FAX 603/430–4444; $99 per year) receive two annual guides plus quarterly newsletters and arrange rentals among themselves.

FARM HOLIDAYS

For information about farm vacations, contact the **Canadian Country Vacations Association** (✉ 525 Kylemore Ave., Winnipeg, Manitoba R3L 1B5, ☎ 204/475–6624).

HOME EXCHANGE

Some of the principal clearinghouses are **HomeLink International/ Vacation Exchange Club** (✉ Box 650, Key West, FL 33041, ☎ 305/294–1448 or 800/638–3841, FAX 305/294–1148; $78 per year), which sends members five annual directories, with a listing in one, plus updates;

Intervac International (✉ Box 590504, San Francisco, CA 94159, ☎ 415/435–3497, FAX 415/435–7440; $65 per year), which publishes four annual directories.

HOTELS

The major hotel chains in Canada include **Best Western International** (☎ 800/528–1234, in the U.K., 0181/541–0033), **CP (Canadian Pacific) Hotels & Resorts** (☎ 800/828–7447, in the U.K., 0800/898852), **Choice Hotels International** (☎ 800/424–6423, in the U.K. 0800/444–4444), **Days Inns** (☎ 800/325–2525, in the U.K. 01483/440470), **Delta Hotels** (☎ 800/877–1133, in the U.K., 0171/937–8033), **Four Seasons Hotels** (☎ 800/332–3442, in the U.K., 0800/526648), **Holiday Inns** (☎ 800/465–4329, in the U.K., 0800/897121), **Hyatt Hotels** (☎ 800/223–1234, in the U.K. 0171/580–8197), **Marriott Hotels and Resorts** (☎ 800/228–9290, in the U.K., 0800/282811), **Radisson Hotels** (☎ 800/333–3333, in the U.K., 0800/891999), **Ramada** (☎ 800/228–2828, in the U.K., 0181/688–1418), **Relais & Châteaux** (☎ 800/743–8033; 800/677–3524 for reservations), **Sheraton** (☎ 800/325–3535, in the U.K., 0800/353535), **Travelodge** (☎ 800/255–3050, in the U.K., 0345/404040), and **Westin Hotels** (☎ 800/228–3000, in the U.K., 0171/408–0636).

M
MONEY

ATMS

For specific **Cirrus** locations in the United States and Canada, call 800/424–7787. For U.S. **Plus** locations, call 800/843–7587 and enter the area code and first three digits of the number from which you're calling (or of the calling area in which you want to locate an ATM).

CURRENCY EXCHANGE

If your bank doesn't exchange currency, contact **Thomas Cook Currency Services** (☎ 800/287–7362 for locations). **Ruesch International** (☎ 800/424–2923 for locations) can also provide you with foreign banknotes before you leave home and publishes a number of useful brochures, including a "Foreign Currency Guide" and "Foreign Exchange Tips."

WIRING FUNDS

Funds can be wired via **MoneyGram℠** (for locations and information in the U.S. and Canada, ☎ 800/926–9400) or **Western Union** (for agent locations or to send money using MasterCard or Visa, ☎ 800/325–6000; in Canada, 800/321–2923; in the U.K., 0800/833833; or visit the Western Union office at the nearest major post office).

P
PASSPORTS & VISAS

U.S. CITIZENS

Citizens and other legal residents of the United States do not need a passport or a visa to enter Canada, but proof of citizenship (a birth certificate, naturalization certificate, valid passport, voter registration card, or "green card") and proof of identity may be requested. U.S. residents entering Canada from a third country must have a valid passport, naturalization certificate, or "green card."

U.K. CITIZENS

For fees, documentation requirements, and to request an emergency passport, call the **London Passport Office** (☎ 0990/210410).

PHOTO HELP

The **Kodak Information Center** (☎ 800/242–2424) answers consumer questions about film and photography. The **Kodak Guide to Shooting Great Travel Pictures** (available in bookstores; or contact Fodor's Travel Publications, ☎ 800/533–6478; $16.50 plus $4 shipping) explains how to take expert travel photographs.

S
SAFETY

"Trouble-Free Travel," from the AAA, is a booklet of tips for protecting yourself and your belongings when away from home. Send a stamped, self-addressed, legal-size envelope to Trouble-Free Travel (⌧ Mail Stop 75, 1000 AAA Dr., Heathrow, FL 32746).

SENIOR CITIZENS

EDUCATIONAL TRAVEL

The nonprofit **Elderhostel** (⌧ 75 Federal St., 3rd Floor, Boston, MA 02110, ☎ 617/426–7788), for people 55 and older, has offered inexpensive study programs since 1975. Courses cover everything from marine science to Greek mythology and cowboy poetry. Fees for programs in the United States and Canada, which usually last one week, run about $300, not including transportation.

ORGANIZATIONS

Contact the **American Association of Retired Persons** (⌧ AARP, 601 E St. NW, Washington, DC 20049, ☎ 202/434–2277; annual dues $8 per person or couple). Its Purchase Privilege Program secures discounts for members on lodging, car rentals, and sightseeing, and the AARP Motoring Plan (☎ 800/334–3300) furnishes domestic trip-routing information and emergency road-service aid for an annual fee of $39.95 ($59.95 for a premium version). Senior citizen travelers can also join the AAA for emergency road service and other travel benefits (☞ Driving, *above, and* Discounts & Deals *in* Smart Travel Tips A to Z).

Additional sources for discounts on lodgings, car rentals, and other travel expenses, as well as helpful magazines and newsletters, are the **National Council of Senior Citizens** (⌧ 1331 F St. NW, Washington, DC 20004, ☎ 202/347–8800; annual membership $12) and Sears's **Mature Outlook**

(✉ Box 10448, Des Moines, IA 50306, ☎ 800/336–6330; annual membership $14.95).

CANOEING AND KAYAKING

Provincial **tourist offices** and the federal **Department of Northern Development and Indian Affairs** (✉ Ottawa, Ontario K1A OH4, ☎ 819/997–0002) can be of assistance, especially in locating an outfitter to suit your needs. You can also contact the **Canadian Recreational Canoeing Association** (✉ 5–1029 Hyde Park Rd., London, Ontario N0M 1Z0, ☎ 519/473–2109).

SCUBA DIVING

Contact **Dive B.C.** (✉ 707 Westminster Ave., Powell River, British Columbia V8A 1C5, ☎ 604/485–6267).

GROUPS

A major tour operator specializing in student travel is **Contiki Holidays** (✉ 300 Plaza Alicante, Suite 900, Garden Grove, CA 92640, ☎ 714/740–0808 or 800/266–8454).

HOSTELING

In the United States, contact **Hostelling International–American Youth Hostels** (✉ 733 15th St. NW, Suite 840, Washington, DC 20005, ☎ 202/783–6161, FAX 202/783–6171); in Canada, **Hostelling International–Canada** (✉ 205 Catherine St., Suite 400, Ottawa, Ontario K2P 1C3, ☎ 613/237–7884); and in the United Kingdom, the **Youth Hostel Association of England and Wales** (✉ Trevelyan House, 8 St. Stephen's Hill, St. Albans, Hertfordshire AL1 2DY, ☎ 01727/855215 or 01727/845047). Membership (in the U.S., $25; in Canada, C$26.75; in the U.K., £9.30) gives you access to 5,000 hostels in 77 countries that charge $5–$40 per person per night.

ORGANIZATIONS

A major contact is the **Council on International Educational Exchange** (✉ mail orders only: CIEE, 205 E. 42nd St., 16th Floor, New York, NY 10017, ☎ 212/661–1450), with walk-in locations throughout the U.S. and in the United Kingdom (✉ 28A Poland St., London W1V 3DB, ☎ 0171/437–7767). The CIEE's Council Travel Service is the exclusive U.S. agent for several student discount cards. The **Educational Travel Centre** (✉ 438 N. Frances St., Madison, WI 53703, ☎ 608/256–5551 or 800/747–5551, FAX 608/256–2042) offers rail passes and low-cost airline tickets, mostly for flights that depart from Chicago.

In Canada, contact **Travel Cuts** (✉ 187 College St., Toronto, Ontario M5T 1P7, ☎ 416/979–2406 or 800/667–2887), which sells student I.D. cards.

T

Among the companies that sell tours and packages to Canada, the following are nationally known, have a proven reputation, and offer plenty of options.

GROUP TOURS

DELUXE➤ **Globus** (✉ 5301 S. Federal Circle, Littleton, CO 80123-2980, ☎ 303/797–2800 or 800/221–0090, FAX 303/795–0962), **Maupintour** (✉ Box 807, 1515 St. Andrews Dr., Lawrence, KS 66047, ☎ 913/843–1211 or 800/255–4266, FAX 913/843–8351), and **Tauck Tours** (Box 5027, 276 Post Rd. W, Westport, CT 06881, ☎ 203/226–6911 or 800/468–2825, FAX 203/221–6828).

FIRST-CLASS➤ **Brendan Tours** (✉ 15137 Califa St., Van Nuys, CA 91411, ☎ 818/785–9696 or 800/421–8446, FAX 818/902–9876), **Caravan Tours** (✉ 401 N. Michigan Ave., Chicago, IL 60611, ☎ 312/321–9800 or 800/227–2826), **Collette Tours** (✉ 162 Middle St., Pawtucket, RI 02860, ☎ 401/728–3805 or 800/832–4656), **Gadabout Tours** (✉ 700 E. Tahquitz Canyon Way, Palm Springs, CA 92262, ☎ 619/325–5556 or 800/952–5068), and **Mayflower Tours** (✉ Box 490, 1225 Warren Ave., Downers Grove, IL 60515, ☎ 708/960–3793 or 800/323–7604, FAX 708/960–3575).

BUDGET➤ **Cosmos** (☞ Globus, *above*).

PACKAGES

Independent vacation packages are available from major tour operators and airlines. Contact **Adventure Vacations** (✉ 10612 Beaver Dam Rd., Hunt Valley, MD 21030-2205, ☎ 410/

785–3500 or 800/638–9040, FAX 410/584–2771), **Air Canada Vacations** (☎ 514/876–4141), **Delta Dream Vacations** (☎ 800/872–7786), **United Vacations** (☎ 800/328–6877), and **USAir Vacations** (☎ 800/455–0123). **Gogo Tours,** based in Ramsey, New Jersey, sells Canada packages only through travel agents.

FROM THE U.K.➢ Travel agencies that offer cheap fares to Canada include **Trailfinders** (✉ 42–50 Earl's Court Rd., London W8 6FT, ☎ 0171/937–5400), **Travel Cuts** (✉ 295A Regent St., London W1R 7YA, ☎ 0171/637–3161; ☞ Students, *above*), and **Flightfile** (✉ 49 Tottenham Court Rd., London W1P 9RE, ☎ 0171/700–2722).

THEME TRIPS

ADVENTURE➢ **American Wilderness Experience** (✉ Box 1486, Boulder, CO 80306, ☎ 303/444–2622 or 800/444–3833, FAX 303/444–3999) runs sea-kayaking, canoeing, hiking, and camping trips. **Canadian Adventure Tours** (✉ Box 929, Whistler, British Columbia, Canada VON 1BO, ☎ FAX 604/938–0727) gives beginners and experts the chance to hike, horseback ride, rock climb, mountain bike, river raft, and canoe in western Canada. **Canadian Helicopters** (✉ Box 3186, Station B, Calgary, Alberta, Canada T2H 4L7, ☎ 403/295–2183 or FAX 403/274–1723) operates multiday heli-

copter tours in western Canada that provide hiking, fishing, and skiing opportunities. **Mountain Travel-Sobek** (✉ 6420 Fairmount Ave., El Cerrito, CA 94530, ☎ 510/527–8100 or 800/227–2384, FAX 510/525–7710) has hiking, heli-hiking, rafting, and horseback-riding trips throughout the Canadian Rockies. **OARS** (✉ Box 67, Angels Camp, CA 95222, ☎ 209/736–4677 or 800/346–6277, FAX 209/736–2902) has rafting and sea-kayaking trips. **Touch the Arctic Adventure Tours** (✉ Yellowknife International Airport, PS 9000 SCII, Yellowknife, NWT, XIA 2R3, ☎ 800/661–0894, FAX 403/873–4274) has been arranging dog-sledding, rafting, camping, fishing, sailing, and cultural trips to the Northwest Territories for 30 years. **Trek America** (✉ Box 189, Rockaway, NJ 07866, ☎ 201/983–1144 or 800/221–0596, FAX 201/983–8551) includes biking, hiking, kayaking, and camping in its Canadian tours. Hut-to-hut skiing, hiking, and canoeing tours in British Columbia's Wells Gray Park are sold by **Wells Gray Park Backcountry Chalets** (✉ Box 188, Clearwater, British Columbia, Canada VOE 1NO, ☎ 604/587–6444, FAX 604/587–6446).

BICYCLING➢ **Backroads** (✉ 1516 5th St., Berkeley, CA 94710-1740, ☎ 510/527–1555 or 800/462–2848,

FAX 510/527–1444) and **Timberline** (✉ 7975 E. Harvard, #J, Denver, CO 80231, ☎ 303/759–3804 or 800/417–2453, FAX 303/368–1651) have trips throughout Canada. **Bike Riders** (✉ Box 254, Boston, MA 02113, ☎ 617/723–2354 or 800/473–7040, FAX 617/723–2355) focuses on Prince Edward Island, Iles de-la-Madeleine, and Nova Scotia, while **Bicycle Adventures** (✉ Box 7875, Olympia, WA 98507, ☎ 360/786–0989 or 800/443–6060, FAX 360/786–9661) runs biking and hiking vacations in British Columbia. For biking and kayaking in Nova Scotia, try **Butterfield & Robinson** (✉ 70 Bond St., Toronto, Ontario, Canada M5B 1X3, ☎ 416/864–1354 or 800/387–1147). For bike tours of the Canadian Rockies, contact **Rocky Mountain Worldwide Cycle Tours** (✉ Box 1978, Canmore, Alberta, Canada TOL OMO, ☎ 403/678–6770 or 800/661–2453, FAX 403/678–4451).

CROSS-COUNTRY SKIING➢ Try **Backroads** (☞ *above*) for trips in the Canadian Rockies.

CULTURAL➢ Immerse yourself in the lifestyles of native peoples with **Creeway Wilderness Experiences** (✉ Box 347, Moose Factory, Ontario, Canada POL 1WO, ☎ FAX 705/658–4390).

DRIVING➢ Custom-tailored itineraries for independent travelers can be arranged by **Off**

The Beaten Path (✉ 109 E. Main St., Bozeman, MT 59715, ☎ 406/586–1311 or 800/445–2995, FAX 406/587–4147).

FISHING➤ For fishing throughout Canada, contact **Anglers Travel** (✉ 3100 Mill St., #206, Reno, NV 89502, ☎ 702/324–0580 or 800/624–8429, FAX 702/324–0583), **Cutting Loose Expeditions** (✉ Box 447, Winter Park, FL 32790-0447, ☎ 407/629–4700 or 800/533–4746), **Fishing International** (✉ Box 2132, Santa Rosa, CA 95405, ☎ 800/950–4242, FAX 707/539–1320), and **Rod & Reel Adventures** (✉ 3507 Tully Rd., #B6, Modesto, CA 95356-1052, ☎ 209/524–7775 or 800/356–6982, FAX 209/524–1220).

GOLF➤ **ITC Golf Tours** (✉ 4134 Atlantic Ave., #205, Long Beach, CA 90807, ☎ 310/595–6905 or 800/257–4981) arranges customized itineraries.

HEALTH➤ Contact **Spa-Finders** (✉ 91 5th Ave., #301, New York, NY 10003-3039, ☎ 212/924–6800 or 800/255–7727).

HIKING➤ (☞ Back-roads, *above*).

HORSEBACK RIDING➤ Riding trips that include deluxe camping or lodge accommodations are offered by **American Wilderness Experience** (☞ Adventure, *above*). **FITS Equestrian** (✉ 685 Lateen Rd., Solvang, CA 93463, ☎ 805/688–9494 or 800/600–3487) is a leading

horseback-riding operator.

LEARNING➤ Contact **Earthwatch** (✉ Box 403, 680 Mount Auburn St., Watertown, MA 02272, ☎ 617/926–8200 or 800/776–0188, FAX 617/926–8532), **Natural Habitat Adventures** (✉ 2945 Center Green Ct., Boulder, CO 80301, ☎ 303/449–3711 or 800/543–8917, FAX 303/449–3712), **Oceanic Society Expeditions** (✉ Fort Mason Center, Bldg. E, San Francisco, CA 94123-1394, ☎ 415/441–1106 or 800/326–7491, FAX 415/474–3395), **Questers** (✉ 381 Park Ave. S, New York, NY 10016, ☎ 212/251–0444 or 800/468–8668, FAX 212/251–0890), and **Smithsonian Study Tours and Seminars** (✉ 1100 Jefferson Dr., SW, Room 3045, MRC 702, Washington, DC 20560, ☎ 202/357–4700, FAX 202/633–9250).

WALKING➤ A slow-pace journey through the Canadian Arctic or Nova Scotia can be arranged by **Country Walkers** (✉ Box 180, Waterbury, VT 05676-0180, ☎ 802/244–1387 or 800/464–9255, FAX 802/244–5661).

YACHT CHARTERS➤ Contact **Ocean Voyages** (✉ 1709 Bridgeway, Sausalito, CA 94965, ☎ 415/332–4681, FAX 415/332–7460).

ORGANIZATIONS

The **National Tour Association** (✉ NTA, 546 E. Main St., Lexington, KY 40508, ☎ 606/226–4444 or 800/755–8687) and the **United States Tour**

Operators Association (✉ USTOA, 211 E. 51st St., Suite 12B, New York, NY 10022, ☎ 212/750–7371) can provide lists of members and information on booking tours.

PUBLICATIONS

Contact the USTOA (☞ Organizations, *above*) for its **"Smart Traveler's Planning Kit."** Pamphlets in the kit include the "Worldwide Tour and Vacation Package Finder," "How to Select a Tour or Vacation Package," and information on the organization's consumer protection plan. Also get copy of the Better Business Bureau's **"Tips on Travel Packages"** (✉ Publication 24-195, 4200 Wilson Blvd., Arlington, VA 22203; $2). The National Tour Association will send you **"On Tour,"** a listing of its member operators, and a personalized package of information on group travel in North America.

TRAIN TRAVEL

Amtrak (☎ 800/872–7245) currently has service from New York to Montréal, New York and Buffalo to Toronto, Chicago to Toronto, and Seattle to Vancouver, providing connections between Amtrak's U.S.-wide network and VIA Rail's Canadian routes.

Transcontinental rail service is provided by **VIA Rail Canada** (☎ 800/665–0200). **Rocky Mountaineer Railtours** (☎ 800/665–7245) operates spectacular two-day, all-daylight rail trips through the Canadian Rockies to the west coast. In the United Kingdom, **Long-Haul Leisurail** (⊠ Box 113, Peterborough, PE3 8HY, ☎ 01733/335599) represents both VIA Rail and Rocky Mountaineer Railtours.

DISCOUNT PASSES

The **Canrailpass** allows 12 days of coach-class travel within a 30-day period; sleeping cars are available, but they sell out very early and must be reserved at least a month in advance during the high season (June 1–Sept. 30), when the pass is C$510 for adults age 25–60, C$460 for travelers under 25 or over 60. Low-season rates (Oct. 1–Dec. 14 and Jan. 6–May 31) are C$349 for adults and C$319 for youth and senior citizens. The pass is not valid during the Christmas period (Dec. 15–Jan. 5). The Canrailpass must be purchased prior to arrival in Canada; for more information and reservations, contact VIA Rail in the U.S. or **Long-Haul Leisurail** in the U.K.

TRAVEL AGENCIES

For names of reputable agencies in your area, contact the **American Society of Travel Agents** (⊠ ASTA, 1101 King St., Suite 200, Alexandria, VA 22314, ☎ 703/739–2782), the **Association of Canadian Travel Agents** (⊠ Suite 201, 1729 Bank St., Ottawa, Ontario K1V 7Z5, ☎ 613/521–0474, FAX 613/521–0805) or the **Association of British Travel Agents**

(⊠ 55-57 Newman St., London W1P 4AH, ☎ 0171/637–2444, FAX 0171/637–0713).

U

U.S. GOVERNMENT TRAVEL BRIEFINGS

The U.S. Department of State's American Citizens Services office (⊠ Room 4811, Washington, DC 20520; enclose SASE) issues **Consular Information Sheets** on all foreign countries. These cover issues such as crime, security, political climate, and health risks as well as listing embassy locations, entry requirements, currency regulations, and providing other useful information. For the latest information, stop in at any U.S. passport office, consulate, or embassy; call the interactive hot line (☎ 202/647–5225, FAX 202/647–3000); or, with your PC's modem, tap into the department's computer bulletin board (☎ 202/647–9225).

V

VISITOR INFORMATION

Contact the tourism department of the province or territory you plan to visit: **Discover British Columbia** (⊠ Parliament Buildings, Victoria, BC V8V 1X4, ☎ 800/663–6000), **Alberta Tourism** (⊠ Box 2500, Edmonton, AB T5J 2Z4, ☎ 800/661–8888), **Tourism Saskatchewan** (⊠ 500–1900 Albert St., Regina, SK S4P 4L9, ☎ 800/667–7191), **Travel Manitoba** (⊠ Dept. 20, 155

Carlton St., 7th floor, Winnipeg, MB R3C 3H8, ☎ 800/665–0040, ext. 20), **Ontario Ministry of Culture, Tourism, and Recreation** (☎ 77 Bloor St. W., 9th floor, Toronto, Ont. M7A 2R9, 800/668–2746), **Tourisme Québec** (☎ 60 Rue D'Auteuil, Québec, PQ G1R 4C4, ☎ 800/363–7777), **Tourism New Brunswick** (⊠ Box 12345, Fredericton, NB E3B 5C3, ☎ 800/561–0123), **Nova Scotia Dept. of Tourism and Culture** (⊠ Box 130, Halifax, NS B3J 2M7, ☎ 800/565–0000), **Prince Edward Island Dept. Of Tourism, Parks and Recreation** (⊠ Visitors Services Division, Box 940, Charlottetown, PEI C1A 7M5, ☎ 800/463–4734), **Newfoundland and Labrador Dept. of Tourism and Culture,** ⊠ Box 8300, St. John's, NF A1B 4J6, ☎ 800/563–6353), **Tourism Yukon** (⊠ Box 2703, Whitehorse, YK Y1A 2C6, ☎ 403/667–5340), and **Northwest Territories Tourism** (⊠ Box 1320, Yellowknife, NWT X1A 2L0, ☎ 800/661–0788).

IN THE U.K.

Contact the **Visit Canada Center** (⊠ 62–65 Trafalgar Sq., London, WC2 5DT, ☎ 0891/715–000) or **Québec Tourism** (⊠ 59 Pall Mall, London SW1Y 5JH, ☎ 0171/930–8314).

W

WEATHER

For current conditions and forecasts, plus the local time and helpful travel tips, call the **Weather Channel Con-**

nection (☎ 900/932–8437; 95¢ per minute) from a Touch-Tone phone.

In larger cities and towns across Canada, Environment Canada's local weather offices can provide forecasts and weather reports over the telephone.

The *International Traveler's Weather Guide* (✉ Weather Press, Box 660606, Sacramento, CA 95866, ☎ 916/974–0201 or 800/972–0201; $10.95 includes shipping), written by two meteorologists, provides month-by-month information on temperature, humidity, and precipitation in more than 175 cities worldwide.

The Gold Guide / SMART TRAVEL TIPS

SMART TRAVEL TIPS A TO Z

Basic Information on Traveling in Canada and Savvy Tips to Make Your Trip a Breeze

A
AIR TRAVEL

If time is an issue, **always look for nonstop flights,** which require no change of plane. If possible, **avoid connecting flights,** which stop at least once and can involve a change of plane, even though the flight number remains the same; if the first leg is late, the second waits.

For better service, **fly smaller or regional carriers,** which often have higher passenger satisfaction ratings. Sometimes they have such in-flight amenities as leather seats or greater legroom and they often have better food.

CUTTING COSTS

The Sunday travel section of most newspapers is a good place to look for deals.

MAJOR AIRLINES➤ The least-expensive airfares from the major airlines are priced for round-trip travel and are subject to restrictions. Usually, you must **book in advance and buy the ticket within 24 hours** to get cheaper fares, and you may have to **stay over a Saturday night.** The lowest fare is subject to availability, and only a small percentage of the plane's total seats is sold at that price. It's smart to **call a number of airlines, and when you are quoted a good price,** **book it on the spot**—the same fare may not be available on the same flight the next day. Airlines generally allow you to change your return date for a $25 to $50 fee. If you don't use your ticket, you can apply the cost toward the purchase of a new ticket, again for a small charge. However, most low-fare tickets are nonrefundable. To get the lowest airfare, **check different routings.** If your destination has more than one gateway, **compare prices to different airports.**

FROM THE U.K.➤ To save money on flights, **look into an APEX or Super-Pex ticket.** APEX tickets must be booked in advance and have certain restrictions. Super-PEX tickets can be purchased right at the airport.

CONSOLIDATORS➤ Consolidators buy tickets for scheduled flights at reduced rates from the airlines, then sell them at prices below the lowest available from the airlines directly—usually without advance restrictions. Sometimes you can even get your money back if you need to return the ticket. Carefully read the fine print detailing penalties for changes and cancellations. If you doubt the reliability of a consolidator, **confirm your reservation with the airline.**

ALOFT

AIRLINE FOOD➤ If you hate airline food, **ask for special meals when booking.** These can be vegetarian, low-cholesterol, or kosher, for example; commonly prepared to order in smaller quantities than standard fare, they can be tastier.

SMOKING➤ Smoking is not allowed on flights of six hours or less within the continental United States. Smoking is also prohibited on flights within Canada. For U.S. flights longer than six hours or international flights, **contact your carrier regarding their smoking policy.** Some carriers have prohibited smoking throughout their system; others allow smoking only on certain routes or even certain departures of that route.

B
BOOKS AND MOVIES

FICTION

Mordecai Richler's *St. Urbain's Horseman* and *The Apprenticeship of Duddy Kravitz* (made into a movie starring Richard Dreyfus) are classics about growing up Jewish in Montréal. Margaret Atwood, a prolific poet and novelist, is regarded as a stateswoman of sorts in her native Canada. Her novel *Cat's Eye* is set in northern Canada and

Toronto. Alice Munro writes about small-town life in Ontario in *The Progress of Love.* The mordant wit of Robertson Davies lovingly skewers Canadian academic life in works such as *The Deptford Trilogy* and *The Lyre of Orpheus. Northern Lights,* by Howard Norman, focuses on a child's experiences growing up in Manitoba and, later, Toronto. Howard Engel's mystery series follows the adventures of Bennie Cooperman, a Toronto-based detective; *The Suicide Murders* is especially compelling. Jack Hodgin's *Spit Delaney's Island* is peopled with loggers, construction workers, and other rural Canadians. Joy Kogawa's first novel, *Obasan,* tells about the Japanese community of Canada during World War II. *Medicine River* is a collection of short stories by Native American writer Thomas King. For an excellent view of New Brunswick, especially the famed salmon-fishing region called the Miramichi, look for the humorous books *The Americans Are Coming* and *The Last Tasmanian* by local author Herb Curtis.

NONFICTION

Canada North is a more recent title by Farley Mowat, whose *Never Cry Wolf* is a humorous account of a naturalist who goes to a remote part of Canada to commune with wolves. Andrew Malcolm gives a cultural and historical overview of the country in *The Canadians.* Stephen Brook's *The Maple Leaf Rag* is a

collection of idiosyncratic travel essays. *Why We Act Like Canadians: A Personal Exploration of Our National Character,* is one of Pierre Berton's many popular nonfiction books focusing on Canada's history and culture. *Klondike,* one of Berton's best books, recounts the sensational history of the Klondike Gold Rush. *Short History of Canada,* by Desmond Morton, is a recent historical account of the country. *Local Colour—Writers Discovering Canada,* edited by Carol Marin, is a series of articles about Canadian places by leading travel writers. Thomas King, Cheryl Calver, and Helen Hoy collaborated on *The Native in Literature,* about the literary treatment of Native Americans.

MOVIES

Black Robe (1991) evokes 17th-century Québec in the story of a missionary priest. *Jesus of Montréal* (1989) is a perceptive observation of French Canadian society; it focuses on the conflict between the Church and an actor chosen to play Christ in a religious performance. In the witty *Decline of the American Empire* (1986) intellectuals explore their concepts of gender, sex, and love. The wry comedy *My Uncle Antoine* (1971) focuses on Québec village life.

BUSINESS HOURS

Stores, shops, and supermarkets are usually open Monday through Saturday from 9 to 6—although in

major cities, supermarkets are often open from 7:30 AM until 9 PM. Blue laws are in effect in much of Canada, but a growing number of provinces have stores with limited Sunday hours, usually from noon to 5 (shops in areas highly frequented by tourists are usually open on Sunday). Retail stores are generally open on Thursday and Friday evenings, most shopping malls until 9 PM. Most banks in Canada are open Monday through Thursday from 10 to 3, and from 10 to 5 or 6 on Friday. Some banks are open longer hours and also on Saturday morning. All banks are closed on national holidays. Drugstores in major cities are often open until 11 PM, and convenience stores are often open 24 hours a day, seven days a week.

NATIONAL HOLIDAYS

National holidays for 1997 are: New Year's Day, Good Friday (March 28), Easter Monday (March 31), Victoria Day (May 19), Canada Day (July 1), Labor Day (September 1), Thanksgiving (October 13), Remembrance Day (November 11), Christmas, and Boxing Day (December 26).

PROVINCIAL HOLIDAYS

Alberta: Family Day (February 17), Heritage Day (August 4). **British Columbia:** British Columbia Day (August 4). **New Brunswick:** New Brunswick Day (August 4). **Newfoundland:** St. Patrick's Day

(March 17), St. George's Day (April 23), Discovery Day (June 27), Memorial Day (July 7). **Manitoba, Northwest Territories, Ontario, Saskatchewan,** and **Nova Scotia:** Civic Holiday (August 4). **Québec:** St. Jean Baptiste Day (June 24). **Yukon:** Discovery Day (August 18).

C

CAMERAS, CAMCORDERS, & COMPUTERS

IN TRANSIT

Always **keep your film, tape, or disks out of the sun;** never put these on the dashboard of a car. Carry an extra supply of batteries, and **be prepared to turn on your camera, camcorder, or laptop computer for security personnel** to prove that it's real.

X-RAYS

Always **ask for hand inspection at security.** Such requests are virtually always honored at U.S. airports, and are usually accommodated abroad. Photographic film becomes clouded after successive exposure to airport x-ray machines. Videotape and computer disks are not by X-rays, but **keep your tapes and disks away from metal detectors.**

CUSTOMS

Before departing, **register your foreign-made camera or laptop with U.S. Customs.** If your equipment is U.S.-made, call the consulate of the country you'll be visiting to find out whether it should be registered

with local customs upon arrival.

CAR RENTAL

CUTTING COSTS

To get the best deal, **book through a travel agent who is willing to shop around.** Ask your agent to **look for fly-drive packages,** which also save you money, and **ask if local taxes are included** in the rental or fly-drive price. These can be as high as 20% in some destinations. Don't forget to find out about required deposits, cancellation penalties, drop-off charges, and the cost of any required insurance coverage.

Also **ask your travel agent about a company's customer-service record.** How has it responded to late plane arrivals and vehicle mishaps? Are there often lines at the rental counter, and—if you're traveling during a holiday period—does a confirmed reservation guarantee you a car?

Always **find out what equipment is standard** at your destination before specifying what you want; automatic transmission and air-conditioning are usually optional—and very expensive.

INSURANCE

When driving a rented car, you are generally responsible for any damage to or loss of the rental vehicle, as well as any property damage or personal injury that you cause. Before you rent, **see what coverage you already have** under the terms of your personal auto insurance policy and credit cards.

If you do not have auto insurance or an umbrella insurance policy that covers damage to third parties, purchasing CDW or LDW is highly recommended.

LICENSE REQUIREMENTS

In Canada your own driver's license is acceptable. If you have rented in the United States, be sure to keep the rental contract with you to indicate that use in Canada is authorized by the rental agency.

SURCHARGES

Before you pick up a car in one city and leave it in another, **ask about drop-off charges or one-way service fees,** which can be substantial. Note, too, that some rental agencies charge extra if you return the car before the time specified on your contract. To avoid a hefty refueling fee, **fill the tank just before you turn in the car**—but be aware that gas stations near the rental outlet may overcharge.

CHILDREN & TRAVEL

When traveling with children, **plan ahead** and **involve your youngsters** as you outline your trip. When packing, **include a supply of things to keep them busy** en route. On sightseeing days, try to **schedule activities of special interest to your children,** like a trip to a zoo or a playground. If you **plan your itinerary around seasonal festivals,** you'll never lack for things to do. In addition, **check local newspapers for special events** mounted by public libraries, museums, and parks.

BABY-SITTING

For recommended local sitters, **check with your hotel desk.**

DRIVING

If you are renting a car, don't forget to **arrange for a car seat when you reserve.** Sometimes they're free.

FLYING

As a general rule, infants under two not occupying a seat fly at greatly reduced fares and occasionally for free. If your children are two or older **ask about special children's fares.** Age limits for these fares vary among carriers. Rules also vary regarding unaccompanied minors, so again, check with your airline.

BAGGAGE➤ In general, the adult baggage allowance applies to children paying half or more of the adult fare. If you are traveling with an infant, **ask about carry-on allowances** before departure. In general, for infants charged 10% of the adult fare you are allowed one carry-on bag and a collapsible stroller, which may have to be checked; you may be limited to less if the flight is full.

SAFETY SEATS➤ According to the FAA, it's a good idea to **use safety seats aloft** for children weighing less than 40 pounds. Airline policies vary. U.S. carriers allow FAA-approved models but usually require that you buy a ticket, even if your child would otherwise ride free, since the seats must be strapped

into regular seats. However, some U.S. and foreign-flag airlines may require you to hold your baby during takeoff and landing—defeating the seat's purpose. Other foreign carriers may not allow infant seats at all, or may charge a child rather than an infant fare for their use.

FACILITIES➤ When making your reservation, **request for children's meals or freestanding bassinets** if you need them; the latter are available only to those seated at the bulkhead, where there's enough legroom. If you don't need a bassinet, **think twice before requesting bulkhead seats**—the only storage space for in-flight necessities is in inconveniently distant overhead bins.

GAMES

In local toy stores, look for travel versions of popular games such as Trouble, Sorry, and Monopoly ($5 to $8).

LODGING

Most hotels allow children under a certain age to stay in their parents' room at no extra charge; others charge them as extra adults. Be sure to **ask about the cutoff age.** In addition, priority for connecting rooms is often given to families. Inquire about programs and discounts when you make your reservation.

CUSTOMS & DUTIES

To speed your clearance through customs, **keep receipts for all your purchases abroad** and **be ready to show the inspector what**

you've bought. If you feel that you've been incorrectly or unfairly charged a duty, you can **appeal assessments in dispute.** First ask to see a supervisor. If you are still unsatisfied, **write to the port director** your point of entry, sending your customs receipt and any other appropriate documentation. The address will be listed on your receipt. If you still don't get satisfaction, you can take your case to customs headquarters in Washington.

IN CANADA

American and British visitors may bring in the following items duty-free: 200 cigarettes, 50 cigars, and 14 ounces of tobacco; 1 bottle (1.1 liters or 40 imperial ounces) of liquor or wine, or 24 355-milliliter (12-ounce) bottles or cans of beer for personal consumption; gifts up to the value of C$60 per gift. A deposit is sometimes required for trailers (refunded upon return). Cats and dogs must have a certificate issued by a licensed veterinarian that clearly identifies the animal and certifies that it has been vaccinated against rabies during the preceding 36 months. Plant material must be declared and inspected. With certain restrictions (some fruits and vegetables), visitors may bring food with them for their own use, providing the quantity is consistent with the duration of the visit.

Canada's firearms laws are significantly stricter than the U.S.'s. All handguns, semi-automatic, and fully automatic weapons are prohibited and cannot be brought into the country. Sporting rifles and shotguns may be imported provided they are to be used for sporting, hunting, or competition while in Canada. All firearms must be declared to Canada Customs at the first point of entry. Failure to declare firearms will result in their seizure, and criminal charges may be made.

Check with customs about bringing mace or pepper spray into Canada; in most cases, these are prohibited (although in some provinces you can purchase pepper spray in sporting goods stores for use as dog- or bear-repellent).

IN THE U.S.

You may bring home $400 worth of foreign goods duty-free if you've been out of the country for at least 48 hours and haven't already used the $400 allowance, or any part of it, in the past 30 days.

Travelers 21 or older may bring back 1 liter of alcohol duty-free, provided the beverage laws of the state through which they reenter the United States allow it. In addition, regardless of their age, they are allowed 100 non-Cuban cigars and 200 cigarettes. Antiques, which the U.S. Customs Service defines as objects more than 100 years old, are duty-free. Original works of art done entirely by hand are also duty-free.

These include, but are not limited to, paintings, drawings, and sculptures.

Duty-free, travelers may mail packages valued at up to $200 to themselves and up to $100 to others, with a limit of one parcel per addressee per day (and no alcohol or tobacco products or perfume valued at more than $5); on the outside, the package must be labeled as being either for personal use or an unsolicited gift, and a list of its contents and their retail value must be attached. Mailed items do not affect your duty-free allowance on your return.

IN THE U.K.

From countries outside the EU, including Canada, you may import, duty-free, 200 cigarettes, 100 cigarillos, 50 cigars, or 250 grams of tobacco; 1 liter of spirits or 2 liters of fortified or sparkling wine or liqueurs; 2 liters of still table wine; 60 milliliters of perfume; 250 milliliters of toilet water; plus £136 worth of other goods, including gifts and souvenirs.

D

DISABILITIES & ACCESSIBILITY

When discussing accessibility with an operator or reservationist, **ask hard questions.** Are there any stairs, inside *or* out? Are there grab bars next to the toilet *and* in the shower/tub? How wide is the doorway to the room? To the bathroom? For the most extensive facilities,

meeting the latest legal specifications, **opt for newer accommodations,** which more often have been designed with access in mind. Older properties or ships must usually be retrofitted and may offer more limited facilities as a result. Be sure to **discuss your needs before booking.**

DISCOUNTS & DEALS

You shouldn't have to pay for a discount. In fact, you may already be eligible for all kinds of savings. Here are some time-honored strategies for getting the best deal.

LOOK IN YOUR WALLET

When you **use your credit card to make travel purchases,** you may get free travel-accident insurance, collision damage insurance, medical or legal assistance, depending on the card and bank that issued it. Visa and MasterCard provide one or more of these services, so **get a copy of your card's travel benefits.** If you are a member of the AAA or an oil-company-sponsored road-assistance plan, always **ask hotel or car-rental reservationists for auto-club discounts.** Some clubs offer additional discounts on tours, cruises, or admission to attractions. And don't forget that auto-club membership entitles you to free maps and trip-planning services.

SENIORS CITIZENS & STUDENTS

As a senior-citizen traveler, you may be

eligible for special rates, but you should mention your senior-citizen status up front. If you're a students or under 26 can also get discounts, especially if you have an official ID card (☞ Senior-Citizen Discounts *and* Students on the Road, *below*).

DIAL FOR DOLLARS

Look into "1-800" discount reservations services, which often have lower rates. These services use their buying power to get a better price on hotels, airline tickets, and sometimes even car rentals. When booking a room, always **call the hotel's local toll-free number** rather than the central reservations number—you'll often get a better price. Ask the reservationist about special packages or corporate rates, which are usually available even if you're not traveling on business.

JOIN A CLUB?

Discount clubs can be a legitimate source of savings, but you must use the participating hotels and visit the participating attractions in order to realize any benefits. Remember, too, that you have to pay a fee to join, so **determine if you'll save enough to warrant your membership fee.** Before booking with a club, **make sure the hotel or other supplier isn't offering a better deal.**

GET A GUARANTEE

When shopping for the best deal on hotels and car rentals, **look for guaranteed exchange rates,** which protect you against a falling dollar. With your rate locked in, you won't pay more even if the price goes up in the local currency.

DRIVING

Canada's highway system is excellent. It includes the Trans-Canada Highway, the longest highway in the world, which runs about 5,000 miles from Victoria, British Columbia, to St. John's, Newfoundland, using ferries to bridge coastal waters at each end. The second-longest Canadian highway, the Yellowhead Highway, follows the old Indian route from the Pacific Coast and over the Rockies to the prairies. North of the population centers, roads become fewer and less developed.

By law, you are required to **wear seat belts** (and use infant seats). Some provinces have a statutory requirement to drive with vehicle headlights on for extended periods after dawn and before sunset. In the Yukon, the law requires that you **drive with your headlights on** when using territory highways.

Speed limits vary from province to province, but they are usually within the 90–100 kph (50–60 mph) range outside the cities. The price of gasoline costs from 44¢ to 63¢ a liter. (There are 3.8 liters in a U.S. gallon, 4.5 liters in a Canadian Imperial gallon.) Distances are always shown in kilometers, and gasoline is always sold in liters. The Imperial gallon is seldom used.

FROM THE U.S.

Drivers must have proper owner registration and proof of insurance coverage, which is compulsory in Canada. The Canadian Non-Resident Inter-Provincial Motor Vehicle Liability Insurance Card, available from any U.S. insurance company, is accepted as evidence of financial responsibility anywhere in Canada. The minimum liability coverage in Canada is $200,000, except in Québec where the minimum is $50,000. If you are driving a car that is not registered in your name, carry a letter from the owner that authorizes your use of the vehicle.

The U.S. Interstate Highway System leads directly into Canada: I–95 from Maine to New Brunswick; I–91 and I–89 from Vermont to Québec; I–87 from New York to Québec; I–81 and a spur off I–90 from New York to Ontario; I–94, I–96, and I–75 from Michigan to Ontario; I–29 from North Dakota to Manitoba; I–15 from Montana to Alberta; and I–5 from Washington state to British Columbia. Most of these connections hook up with the Trans-Canada Highway within a few miles. There are many smaller highway crossings between the two countries as well. From Alaska, take the Alaska Highway (from Fairbanks), the Klondike Highway (from Skagway), and the Top of the World Highway (to Dawson City).

THE GOLD GUIDE / SMART TRAVEL TIPS

I
INSURANCE

Travel insurance can protect your monetary investment, replace your luggage and its contents, or provide for medical coverage should you fall ill during your trip. Most tour operators, travel agents, and insurance agents sell specialized health-and-accident, flight, trip-cancellation, and luggage insurance as well as comprehensive policies with some or all of these coverages. Comprehensive policies may also reimburse you for delays due to weather—an important consideration if you're traveling during the winter months. Some health-insurance policies do not cover preexisting conditions, but waivers may be available in specific cases. Coverage is sold by the companies listed in Important Contacts A to Z; these companies act as the policy's administrators. The actual insurance is usually underwritten by a well-known name, such as The Travelers or Continental Insurance.

Before you make any purchase, **review your existing health and homeowner's policies** to find out whether they cover expenses incurred while traveling.

BAGGAGE

Airline liability for baggage is limited to $1,250 per person on domestic flights. On international flights, it amounts to $9.07 per pound or $20 per kilogram for checked baggage (roughly $640 per 70-pound bag) and $400 per passenger for unchecked baggage. Insurance for losses exceeding the terms of your airline ticket can be bought directly from the airline at check-in for about $10 per $1,000 of coverage; note that it excludes a rather extensive list of items, shown on your airline ticket.

COMPREHENSIVE

Comprehensive insurance policies include all the coverages described above plus some that may not be available in more specific policies. If you have purchased an expensive vacation, especially one that involves travel abroad, comprehensive insurance is a must; **look for policies that include trip delay insurance,** which will protect you in the event that weather problems cause you to miss your flight, tour, or cruise. A few insurers will also sell you a waiver for preexisting medical conditions. Some of the companies that offer both these features are Access America, Carefree Travel, Travel Insured International, and TravelGuard (☞ Important Contacts A to Z).

FLIGHT

You should **think twice before buying flight insurance.** Often purchased as a last-minute impulse at the airport, it pays a lump sum when a plane crashes, either to a beneficiary if the insured dies or sometimes to a surviving passenger who loses his or her eyesight or a limb. Supplementing the airlines' coverage de-scribed in the limits-of-liability paragraphs on your ticket, it's expensive and basically unnecessary. Charging an airline ticket to a major credit card often automatically provides you with coverage that may also extend to travel by bus, train, and ship.

HEALTH

Medicare generally does not cover health care costs outside the United States; nor do many privately issued policies. If your own health insurance policy does not cover you outside the United States, **consider buying supplemental medical coverage.** It can reimburse you for $1,000–$150,000 worth of medical and/or dental expenses incurred as a result of an accident or illness during a trip. These policies also may include a personal-accident, or death-and-dismemberment, provision, which pays a lump sum ranging from $15,000 to $500,000 to your beneficiaries if you die or to you if you lose one or more limbs or your eyesight, and a medical-assistance provision, which may either reimburse you for the cost of referrals, evacuation, or repatriation and other services, or automatically enroll you as a member of a particular medical-assistance company.

U.K. TRAVELERS

You can buy an annual travel insurance policy valid for most vacations during the year in which it's purchased. If you are pregnant or have a preexisting medical condition make sure you're covered before buying such a policy.

TRIP

Without insurance, you will lose all or most of your money if you cancel your trip regardless of the reason. Especially if your airline ticket, cruise, or package tour is nonrefundable and cannot be changed, it's essential that you **buy trip-cancellation-and-interruption insurance.** When considering how much coverage you need, look for a policy that will cover the cost of your trip plus the nondiscounted price of a one-way airline ticket should you need to return home early. Read the fine print carefully, especially sections that define "family member" and "preexisting medical conditions." Also **consider default or bankruptcy insurance,** which protects you against a supplier's failure to deliver. Be aware, however, that if you buy such a policy from a travel agency, tour operator, airline, or cruise line, it may not cover default by the firm in question.

L

Canada's two official languages are English and French. Though English is widely spoken, it may be useful to **learn a few French phrases** if you plan to travel to the province of Québec or to the French Canadian communities in the Maritimes (Nova Scotia, New Brunswick, and Prince Edward Island), northern Manitoba, and Ontario.

Canadian French, known as Québecois or *joual,* is a colorful language often quite different from that spoken in France.

LODGING

Aside from the quaint hotels of Québec, Canada's range of accommodations more closely resembles that of the United States than of Europe. In the cities you'll have a choice of luxury hotels, moderately priced modern properties, and smaller older hotels with perhaps fewer conveniences but more charm. Options in smaller towns and in the country include large, full-service resorts; small, privately owned hotels; roadside motels; and bed-and-breakfasts. Even though Canada is as attuned to automobile travel, you won't find motels frequently. Even here you'll need to make reservations at least on the day on which you're planning to pull into town.

There is no national government rating system for hotels, but many provinces rate their accommodations. For example, in British Columbia and Alberta, a blue Approved Accommodation decal on the window or door of a hotel or motel indicates that it has met provincial hotel association standards for courtesy, comfort, and cleanliness. Ontario's voluntary rating system includes about 1,000 Ontario properties.

Expect accommodations to cost more in summer than in the off-season. When making reservations, **ask about special deals** and packages when reserving. Big city hotels that cater to business travelers often offer weekend packages, and many city hotels offer rooms at up to 50% off in winter. If you're planning to visit a major city or resort area in high season, **book well in advance.** Also be aware of any special events or festivals that may coincide with your visit and fill every room for miles around. For resorts and lodges, consider the winter ski-season high as well and plan accordingly.

APARTMENT & VILLA RENTAL

If you want a home base that's roomy enough for a family and comes with cooking facilities, **consider taking a furnished rental.** This can also save you money, but not always—some rentals are luxury properties (economical only when your party is large). Home-exchange directories list rentals—often second homes owned by prospective house swappers—and some services search for a house or apartment for you (even a castle if that's your fancy) and handle the paperwork. Some send an illustrated catalog; others send photographs only of specific properties, sometimes at a charge; up-front registration fees may apply.

B&BS

Bed and breakfasts can be found in both the country and the cities. Every provincial tourist

SMART TRAVEL TIPS / THE GOLD GUIDE

board either has a listing of B&Bs or can refer you to an association that will help you secure reservations. Rates range from $20 to upwards of $70 a night and include a Continental or a full breakfast. Some B&B hosts lock up early; be sure to ask. Room quality varies from house to house as well, so don't be bashful about asking to see a room before making a choice. **Fodor's** *Canada's Great Country Inns* lists places to stay from coast to coast. You can buy it in most bookstores or ask to have it ordered.

DORMS AND HOSTELS

There are a few alternatives to camping if you're on a budget. Among them are hostels, which are open to young and old, families and singles (☞ Students on the Road, *below*), and university campuses, which open their dorms to travelers for overnight stays from May through August.

HOME EXCHANGE

If you would like to find a house, an apartment, or some other type of vacation property to exchange for your own while on holiday, **become a member of a home-exchange organization,** which will send you its updated listings of available exchanges for a year, and will include your own listing in at least one of them. Arrangements for the actual exchange are made by the two parties involved, not by the organization.

M
MAIL

In Canada you can buy stamps at the post office or from automatic vending machines in most hotel lobbies, railway stations, airports, bus terminals, many retail outlets, and some newsstands. Within Canada, postcards and letters up to 30 grams cost 46¢; between 30 grams and a kilogram, the cost is $3.75. Letters and postcards to the United States cost 52¢ for up to 30 grams, and $3.40 for up to 250 grams. Prices include GST.

International mail and postcards run 92¢ for up to 30 grams, and $2.10 for up to 100 grams.

Telepost is a fast "next day or sooner" service that combines the CN/CP Telecommunications network with letter-carrier delivery service. Messages may be telephoned to the nearest CN/CP Public Message Centre for delivery anywhere in Canada or the United States. Telepost service is available 24 hours a day, seven days a week, and billing arrangements may be made at the time the message is called in. Intelpost allows you to send documents or photographs via satellite to many Canadian, American, and European destinations. This service is available at main postal facilities in Canada, and is paid for in cash.

RECEIVING MAIL

Visitors may have mail sent to them c/o General Delivery in the town they are visiting, for pickup in person within 15 days, after which it will be returned to the sender.

MONEY

American money is accepted in much of Canada (especially in communities near the border). However, visitors are encouraged to exchange at least some of their money into Canadian funds at a bank or other financial institution in order to get the most favorable exchange rate. Traveler's checks (some are available in Canadian dollars) and major U.S. credit cards are accepted in most areas.

The units of currency in Canada are the Canadian dollar (C$) and the cent, in almost the same denominations as U.S. currency ($5, $10, $20, 1¢, 5¢, 10¢, 25¢, etc.). The $1 and $2 bill are no longer used; they have been replaced by $1 and $2 coins. At press time the exchange rate was C$1.35 to US$1 and C$2.15 to £1.

ATMS

CASH ADVANCES➢ Before leaving home, **make sure that your credit cards have been programmed for ATM use.** in Canada. Note that Discover is accepted mostly in the United States. Local bank cards often do not work overseas either; **ask your bank about a Visa debit card,** which works like a bank card but can be used at any ATM displaying a Visa logo.

TRANSACTION FEES➢ Although fees charged for ATM transactions may be higher abroad than at home, Cirrus and Plus exchange rates are excellent, because they are based on wholesale rates offered only by major banks.

COSTS

The following prices are for Toronto (prices in other cities and regions are often lower): A soda (pop) costs $1–$1.25; a glass of beer, $3–$6; a sandwich, $3.50–$6; a taxi, as soon as the meter is turned on, $2.20, and $1 for every kilometer; a movie, about $8.

EXCHANGING CURRENCY

For the most favorable rates, **change money at banks.** You won't do as well at exchange booths in airports or rail and bus stations, in hotels, in restaurants, or in stores, although you may find their hours more convenient. To avoid lines at airport exchange booths, **get a small amount of the local currency before you leave home.**

TAXES

A goods and services tax of 7% (GST) applies on virtually every transaction in Canada except for the purchase of basic groceries.

HOTEL➤ Alberta and Ontario charge 5% tax on hotel rooms; British Columbia adds 8% to 10%; Québec adds 6.5% and New Brunswick, 11%.

SALES➤ In addition to the GST, all provinces except Alberta, the Northwest Territories, and the Yukon levy a sales tax from 4% to 12% on most items purchased in shops, on restaurant meals, and sometimes on hotel rooms. Manitoba, Québec, Nova Scotia, and Newfoundland offer a sales-tax rebate system similar to the federal one; call the provincial toll-free information lines for details (☞ Important Contacts A to Z). Most provinces do not tax goods shipped directly by the vendor to the visitor's home address.

VAT➤ You **can get a full GST refund** on any purchase taken out of the country and on short-term accommodations (but not on food, drink, tobacco, car or motorhome rentals, or transportation); rebate forms, which must be submitted within 60 days of leaving Canada, may be obtained from certain retailers, duty-free shops, customs officials or from Revenue Canada (✉ Visitor's Rebate Program, Ottawa, Ontario K1A 1J5, ☎ 800/668-4748 in Canada). Instant rebates are provided by some duty-free shops when leaving Canada, and most provinces do not tax goods that are shipped directly by the vendor to the purchaser's home. You'll need your receipts.

TRAVELER'S CHECKS

Whether or not to buy traveler's checks depends on where you are headed; **take cash to rural areas and small towns, traveler's checks to cities.** The most widely recognized checks are issued by American Express, Citicorp, Thomas Cook, and Visa. These are sold by major commercial banks for 1%–3% of the checks' face value—it pays to **shop around.** Both American Express and Thomas Cook issue checks that can be countersigned and used by either you or your traveling companion. So you won't be left with excess foreign currency, **buy a few checks in small denominations** to cash toward the end of your trip. Before leaving home, **contact your issuer for information on where to cash your checks** without a incurring a transaction fee. Record the numbers of all your checks, and keep this listing in a separate place, crossing off the numbers of checks you have cashed.

WIRING MONEY

For a fee of 3%–10%, depending on the amount of the transaction, you can have money sent to you from home through Money-Gram^{SM} or Western Union (☞ Money Matters *in* Important Contacts A to Z). The transferred funds and the service fee can be charged to a Master-Card or Visa account.

P

PACKING FOR CANADA

How you pack will depend on when you go and what you plan to do. Layering is the best defense against Canada's cold winters;

a hat, scarf, and gloves are essential. For summer travel, loose-fitting natural-fiber clothes are best; bring a wool sweater and light jacket. If you're planning to spend time in Canada's larger cities, pack both casual clothes for day touring and more formal wear for evenings out.

If you plan on camping or hiking in the deep woods during the summer, particularly in northern Canada, insect repellent is a must, especially in June, which is blackfly season. Bring an extra pair of eyeglasses or contact lenses in your carry-on luggage, and if you have a health problem, **pack enough medication** to last the trip or have your doctor write you a prescription using the drug's generic name, because brand names vary from country to country (you'll then need a duplicate prescription from a local doctor). It's important that you **don't put prescription drugs or valuables in luggage to be checked,** for it could go astray. To avoid problems with customs officials, carry medications in the original packaging. Also, don't forget the addresses of offices that handle refunds of lost traveler's checks.

LUGGAGE

Airline baggage allowances depend on the airline, the route, and the class of your ticket; ask in advance. In general, on domestic flights and on international flights between

the United States and foreign destinations, you are entitled to check two bags. A third piece may be brought on board, but it must fit easily under the seat in front of you or in the overhead compartment. In the United States, the FAA gives airlines broad latitude regarding carry-on allowances, and they tend to tailor them to different aircraft and operational conditions. Charges for excess, oversize, or overweight pieces vary.

If you are flying between two foreign destinations, note that baggage allowances may be determined not by piece but by weight—generally 88 pounds (40 kilograms) in first class, 66 pounds (30 kilograms) in business class, and 44 pounds (20 kilograms) in economy. If your flight between two cities abroad *connects* with your transatlantic or transpacific flight, the piece method still applies.

SAFEGUARDING YOUR LUGGAGE➤ Before leaving home, **itemize your bags' contents** and their worth, and label them with your name, address, and phone number. (If you use your home address, cover it so that potential thieves can't see it readily.) Inside each bag, **pack a copy of your itinerary.** At check-in, **make sure that each bag is correctly tagged** with the destination airport's three-letter code. If your bags arrive damaged—or fail to arrive at all—file a written report with the airline before leaving the airport.

IN THE U.S.

Citizens and legal residents of the United States do not need a passport or a visa to enter Canada, but proof of citizenship (a birth certificate or valid passport) and proof of identity may be requested. Naturalized U.S. residents should carry their naturalization certificate or "green card." U.S. residents entering Canada from a third country must have a valid passport, naturalization certificate, or "green card."

U.K. CITIZENS

Citizens of the United Kingdom need only a valid passport to enter Canada for stays of up to six months. Applications for new and renewal passports are available from main post offices and at the passport offices in Belfast, Glasgow, Liverpool, London, Newport, and Peterborough. You may apply in person at all passport offices, or by mail to all except the London office. Children under 16 may travel on an accompanying parent's passport. All passports are valid for 10 years. Allow a month for processing.

It is advisable that you **leave one photocopy of your passport's data page** with someone at home and keep another with you, separated from your passport, while traveling. If you lose your passport, promptly call the nearest embassy or consulate and the local police; having the data page information can speed replacement.

S

SENIOR-CITIZEN DISCOUNTS

VIA Rail Canada (☞ Rail Travel *in* Important Contacts A to Z) offers those 60 and over a 10% discount on basic transportation for travel any time and with no advance-purchase requirement. This 10% discount can also apply to off-peak reduced fares that have advance-purchase requirements.

To qualify for age-related discounts, **mention your senior-citizen status up front** when booking hotel reservations, not when checking out, and before you're seated in restaurants, not when paying the bill. Note that discounts may be limited to certain menus, days, or hours. When renting a car, **ask about promotional car-rental discounts**—they can net even lower costs than your senior-citizen discount.

STUDENTS ON THE ROAD

Persons under 18 years of age who are not accompanied by their parents should bring a letter from a parent or guardian giving them permission to travel to Canada.

To save money, **look into deals available through student-oriented travel agencies.** To qualify, you'll need to have a bona fide

student ID card. Members of international student groups are also eligible (☞ Students *in* Important Contacts A to Z).

T

TELEPHONES

LONG-DISTANCE

The long-distance services of AT&T, MCI, and Sprint make calling home relatively convenient and let you avoid hotel surcharges; typically, you dial an 800 number in the United States.

TIPPING

Tips and service charges are not usually added to a bill in Canada. In general, tip 15% of the total bill. This goes for waiters, waitresses, barbers and hairdressers, taxi drivers, etc. Porters and doormen should get about 50¢–$1 a bag ($1 or more in a luxury hotel). For maid service, $1 a day is sufficient ($2 in luxury hotels).

TOUR OPERATORS

A package or tour to Canada can make your vacation less expensive and more hassle-free. Firms that sell tours and packages reserve airline seats, hotel rooms, and rental cars in bulk and pass some of the savings on to you. In addition, the best operators have local representatives available to help you at your destination.

A GOOD DEAL?

The more your package or tour includes, the better you can predict the ultimate cost of your vacation. Make sure you know exactly

what is covered, and **beware of hidden costs.** Are taxes, tips, and service charges included? Transfers and baggage handling? Entertainment and excursions? These can add up.

Most packages and tours are rated deluxe, first-class superior, first class, tourist, or budget. The key difference is usually accommodations. If the package or tour you are considering is priced lower than in your wildest dreams, **be skeptical.** Also, **make sure your travel agent knows the accommodations** and other services. Ask about the hotel's location, room size, beds, and whether it has a pool, room service, or programs for children, if you care about these. Has your agent been there in person or sent others you can contact?

BUYER BEWARE

Each year a number of consumers are stranded or lose their money when operators—even very large ones with excellent reputations—go out of business. To avoid becoming one of them, take the time to **check out the operator**—find out how long the company has been in business and ask several agents about its reputation. Next, **don't book unless the firm has a consumer-protection program.** Members of the USTOA and the NTA are required to set aside funds for the sole purpose of covering your payments and travel arrangements in case of default. Nonmember operators

THE GOLD GUIDE / SMART TRAVEL TIPS

may instead carry insurance; look for the details in the operator's brochure—and for the name of an underwriter with a solid reputation. Note: When it comes to tour operators, **don't trust escrow accounts.** Although there are laws governing those of charter-flight operators, no governmental body prevents tour operators from raiding the till.

Next, **contact your local Better Business Bureau and the attorney general's offices** in both your own state and the operator's; have any complaints been filed? Finally, **pay with a major credit card.** Then you can cancel payment, provided that you can document your complaint. Always **consider trip-cancellation insurance** (☞ Insurance, *above*).

BIG VS. SMALL➤ Operators that handle several hundred thousand travelers per year can use their purchasing power to give you a good price. Their high volume may also indicate financial stability. But some small companies provide more personalized service; because they tend to specialize, they may also be more knowledgeable about a given area.

USING AN AGENT

Travel agents are excellent resources. In fact, large operators accept bookings made only through travel agents. But it's good to **collect brochures from several agencies** because some agents' suggestions may be skewed by promotional relationships with tour and package firms that reward them for volume sales. If you have a special interest, **find an agent with expertise in that area;** ASTA can provide leads in the United States. (Don't rely solely on your agent, though; agents may be unaware of small-niche operators, and some special-interest travel companies only sell direct.)

SINGLE TRAVELERS

Prices are usually quoted per person, based on two sharing a room. If traveling solo, you may be required to pay the full double-occupancy rate. Some operators eliminate this surcharge if you agree to be matched up with a roommate of the same sex, even if one is not found by departure time.

TRAIN TRAVEL

To save money, **look into rail passes** (☞ Important Contacts A to Z). But be aware that if you don't plan to cover many miles, you may come out ahead by buying individual tickets.

Many travelers assume that rail passes guarantee them seats on the trains they wish to ride. Not so. You need to **book seats ahead even if you are using a rail pass;** seat reservations are required on some European trains, particularly high-speed trains, and are a good idea on trains that may be crowded—particularly in summer on popular routes. You will also need a reservation if you purchase sleeping accommodations.

U

U.S.
GOVERNMENT

The U.S. government can be an excellent source of travel information. Some of this is free and some is available for a nominal charge. When planning your trip, **find out what government materials are available.** For a small charge, you can **order publications from the Consumer Information Center** in Pueblo, Colorado. Free brochures are also available from the Department of Transportation, the U.S. Customs Service, and other government agencies. For specific titles, see the appropriate publications entry in Important Contacts A to Z, *above*.

W

WHEN TO GO

When to go will depend on your itinerary and your interests. In the maritime provinces of Nova Scotia, New Brunswick, and Prince Edward Island, the weather is relatively mild, though snow can remain on the ground well into spring and fog is common year-round. In Newfoundland and Labrador temperatures vary widely; winter days can be about 32°F (0°C) in St. John's—and as low as −50°F (−45°C) in Labrador and on the west coast. Québec and Ontario have hot, steamy summers and severe winters, with snow lasting from mid-

December to mid-March. The whole of eastern Canada enjoys blooming springs and brilliant autumns.

Farther west, in Manitoba, Saskatchewan, and Alberta, summers are short but sunny, and marked by an occasional heavy shower. In winter, snowfall here is light, but temperatures stay low. Southern British Columbia has warmer winters and mild summers. Though the weather fluctuates because of the mountain ranges—the Coast Mountains and the eastern chain of the Rockies—the coastal region has the country's mildest winters, with rainfall almost inevitable. Summers here are fairly sunny, but seldom oppressively hot. The best time to visit northern Canada is during its short but surprisingly warm summer. The area—which includes the northern parts of the provinces of British Columbia, Alberta, Saskatchewan, Manitoba, Ontario, and Québec, as well as the Yukon and Northwest Territories—is like Siberia in winter, with devastating cold and dangerous wind chill.

Climate in Canada

The following are average daily maximum and minimum temperatures for some of Canada's major cities.

CALGARY

Jan.	23F	− 5C	May	61F	16C	Sept.	63F	17C
	2	−17		37	3		39	4
Feb.	29F	− 2C	June	67F	19C	Oct.	54F	12C
	8	−13		44	7		30	− 1
Mar.	34F	1C	July	74F	23C	Nov.	38F	3C
	14	−10		49	9		17	− 8
Apr.	49F	9C	Aug.	72F	22C	Dec.	29F	− 2C
	27	− 3		47	8		8	−13

EDMONTON

Jan.	14F	−10C	May	63F	17C	Sept.	62F	17C
	− 3	−19		41	5		41	5
Feb.	22F	− 6C	June	69F	21C	Oct.	52F	11C
	4	−16		48	9		32	0
Mar.	31F	− 1C	July	74F	23C	Nov.	32F	0C
	13	−11		53	12		17	− 8
Apr.	49F	9C	Aug.	71F	22C	Dec.	21F	− 6C
	29	− 2		50	10		5	−15

HALIFAX

Jan.	33F	1C	May	58F	14C	Sept.	67F	19C
	20	− 7		41	5		53	12
Feb.	33F	1C	June	67F	19C	Oct.	58F	14C
	19	− 7		50	10		44	7
Mar.	39F	4C	July	73F	23C	Nov.	48F	9C
	26	− 3		57	14		36	2
Apr.	48F	9C	Aug.	73F	24C	Dec.	37F	3C
	33	1		58	13		25	4

MONTRÉAL

Jan.	23F	− 5C	May	65F	18C	Sept.	68F	20C
	9	−13		48	9		53	12
Feb.	25F	− 4C	June	74F	23C	Oct.	57F	14C
	12	−11		58	14		43	6
Mar.	36F	2C	July	79F	26C	Nov.	42F	6C
	23	− 5		63	17		32	0
Apr.	52F	11C	Aug.	76F	24C	Dec.	27F	− 3C
	36	2		61	16		16	− 9

OTTAWA

Jan.	20F	− 7C	May	65F	18C	Sept.	68F	20C
	4	−16		44	7		49	9
Feb.	23F	− 5C	June	75F	24C	Oct.	57F	14C
	6	−14		54	12		39	4
Mar.	34F	1C	July	80F	27C	Nov.	41F	5C
	18	− 8		58	14		29	− 2
Apr.	51F	11C	Aug.	77F	25C	Dec.	25F	− 4C
	33	1		56	13		12	−11

QUÉBEC CITY

Jan.	20F	− 7C	May	62F	17C	Sept.	66F	19C
	6	−14		43	6		49	9
Feb.	23F	− 5C	June	72F	22C	Oct.	53F	12C
	8	−13		53	12		39	4
Mar.	33F	1C	July	78F	26C	Nov.	39F	4C
	19	− 7		58	14		28	− 2
Apr.	47F	8C	Aug.	75F	24C	Dec.	24F	− 4C
	32	0		56	13		12	−11

TORONTO

Jan.	30F	− 1C	May	64F	18C	Sept.	71F	22C
	18	− 8		47	8		54	12
Feb.	32F	0C	June	76F	24C	Oct.	60F	16C
	19	− 7		57	14		45	7
Mar.	40F	4C	July	80F	27C	Nov.	46F	8C
	27	− 3		62	17		35	2
Apr.	53F	12C	Aug.	79F	26C	Dec.	34F	1C
	38	3		61	16		23	− 5

VANCOUVER

Jan.	42F	6C	May	60F	16C	Sept.	65F	8C
	33	1		47	8		52	11
Feb.	45F	7C	June	65F	18C	Oct.	56F	13C
	36	2		52	11		45	7
Mar.	48F	9C	July	70F	1C	Nov.	48F	9C
	37	3		55	13		39	4
Apr.	54F	12C	Aug.	70F	21C	Dec.	43F	6C
	41	5		55	13		35	2

1 Destination: Canada

WHAT'S WHERE

The sections below correspond to regional chapters in this book; major cities that have their own chapters are indicated below in boldface type.

British Columbia

Canada's westernmost province harbors Pacific beaches, forested islands, year-round skiing, world-class fishing—a wealth of outdoor action and beauty. Its towns and cities, from Anglophile Victoria to the re-created Native American village of 'Ksan reflect the diversity of its inhabitants. Cosmopolitan **Vancouver,** Canada's answer to San Francisco, enjoys a spectacular setting. Tall fir trees stand practically downtown, rock spires tower close by, the ocean is at your doorstep, and people from every corner of the earth create a young and vibrant atmosphere.

Canadian Rockies

The series of ranges that form the Canadian Rockies straddles the British Columbia–Alberta line from the U.S. border in the south to the Yukon in the north. Their beauty has been preserved in provincial and national parks; in these mountains you can fish, ski, hike, mountain climb, boat, and horseback ride, as well as enjoy some of the best resort facilities anywhere.

New Brunswick

New Brunswick is where the great Canadian forest, sliced by sweeping river valleys and modern highways, meets the Atlantic. To the north and east, the gentle, warm Gulf Stream washes quiet beaches. Besides the seacoast, there are pure inland streams, pretty towns, and historic cities. The province's dual heritage (35% of its population is Acadian French) provides added spice.

Newfoundland and Labrador

Canada's easternmost province, Newfoundland, was a center of the world's cod fishing industry for 400 years until the supply ran out in 1992. In summer, Newfoundland's stark cliffs, bogs, and meadows become a riot of wildflowers and greenery, and the sea is dotted with boats and buoys. St. John's, the capital, is a classic harbor city.

Nova Scotia

This little province on the Atlantic coast, compact and distinctive, has a capital city, Halifax, the same size as Christopher Marlowe's London. The days when Nova Scotians were prosperous shipwrights and merchants trading with the world left Victorian mansions in all the salty little ports that dot the coastline and created a uniquely Nova Scotian outlook: worldly, approachable, and sturdily independent.

Ontario

With shorelines on four of the five Great Lakes, Ontario is Canada's second-largest and most urbanized province, but only 10 million people live in this vast area, and 90% of them are within a narrow strip just north of the U.S. border. A bit north of the strip, Ottawa, Canada's capital, gathers government workers and parliamentarians. **Toronto** thrives on ethnic diversity, filled as it is with Italians, Chinese, Portuguese, and other groups in a vibrant mix of cultures. This cosmopolitan, world-class city, established by Scots who set up banks and built churches, is Canada's center of culture, commerce, and communications.

Prairie Provinces

Between the eastern slopes of the Rockies and the wilds of western Ontario lie Canada's three prairie provinces: Alberta, Saskatchewan, and Manitoba. The northern parts of this region are sparsely populated expanses of lakes, rivers, and forests. The fertile plains of the south support farms and ranches—interspersed with wide river valleys, lakes, rolling hills, badlands, dry hills of sand, and oil wells—as well as five busy cities: Calgary, Edmonton, Saskatoon, Regina, and Winnipeg.

Prince Edward Island

In the Gulf of St. Lawrence north of Nova Scotia and New Brunswick, Prince Edward Island seems too good to be true, with its crisply painted farmhouses, manicured green fields rolling down to sandy beaches, the warmest ocean water north of Florida, lobster boats in trim little harbors, and a vest-pocket capital city, Charlottetown, packed with architectural heritage.

Québec

Québec is set apart by its strong French heritage, a matter not only of language but of customs, religion, and political structure. Defining the land outside the cities are innumerable lakes, streams, and rivers; farmlands and villages; great mountains, such as the Laurentians with their ski resorts, and deep forests; and a rugged coastline along the Gulf of St. Lawrence. **Québec City,** which enjoys one of the most beautiful natural settings in North America, perched on a cliff above a narrow point in the St. Lawrence River, is the capital of, as well as the oldest municipality in, Québec province. **Montréal** is Canada's most romantic metropolis, an island city that seems to favor grace and elegance over order and even prosperity—a city full of music, art, and joie de vivre.

Wilderness Canada

Life above the 60th parallel in the mountainous, river-threaded Yukon and the flat, lake-dotted Northwest Territories is strange and wonderful. The landscape is austere and beautiful in ways unlike anywhere else in North America: tundra plains that reach to the Arctic Ocean; remote ice fields of the St. Elias Mountains; and white-water rivers snaking through mountain ranges and deep canyons. This is also the last region of North America where Native peoples have managed to sustain traditional cultures relatively undisturbed.

PLEASURES AND PASTIMES

Baseball

If you're missing a bit of Americana, don't fret. Baseball has been a favorite in Canada since the major leagues expanded into Montréal in 1969 with the Montréal Expos, and the Toronto Blue Jays formed a World Series–caliber club. The Toronto Blue Jays won the World Series in 1992 (the first time a non–U.S. team played in and won the baseball championship) and again in 1993. Minor league teams compete in Vancouver, Edmonton, Calgary, Lethbridge, and Medicine Hat.

Biking

Eastern and western Canada offer some of the best bicycling terrain. In the east, bikers favor the Gaspé Peninsula in Québec and the surrounding Atlantic provinces. The terrain is very hilly around the Gaspé and varied in Prince Edward Island, New Brunswick, and Nova Scotia. A western tour might include the area around the Rocky Mountains and on through British Columbia. Some cities, such as Vancouver and Ottawa, have bike trails marked throughout town. Write to the provincial tourist boards for road maps (which are more detailed than the maps available at gas stations) and information on local cycling associations.

Boating

With so much coastline—on the Atlantic and Pacific, the Great Lakes, major rivers, and thousands of smaller lakes—boating is extremely popular throughout Canada. Boat rentals are widely available, and provincial tourism departments can provide lists of sources.

Camping

Canada's 2,000-plus campgrounds range from simple roadside turnoffs with sweeping mountain vistas to fully equipped facilities with groomed sites, trailer hookups, recreational facilities, and vacation village atmosphere. Many of the best sites are in Canada's national and provincial parks, with nominal overnight fees. Commercial campgrounds offer more amenities, such as electrical and water hookups, showers, and even game rooms and grocery stores. They cost more and are—some think—antithetical to the point of camping: getting a little closer to nature. Contact tourist offices for listings.

Canoeing and Kayaking

Your degree of expertise and experience will dictate where you canoe. Beginners can try waterways in more settled areas; pros head north to the streams and rivers that flow into the Arctic Ocean. *See* Important Contacts A to Z for names of organizations that can supply more information.

Curling

For a true taste of Canadian sportsmanship you might want to watch a curling match, which is not unlike a shuffleboard game on ice. Two teams of four players each compete by sliding large polished granite stones toward the center of a bullseye, or "house."

Dining

The earliest European settlers of Canada—the British and the French—bequeathed a rather bland diet of meat and potatoes. But though there are few really distinct national dishes here, except in Québec, the strong ethnic presence in Canada makes it difficult not to have a good meal. This is especially true in the larger cities, where Greek, Italian, Chinese, Indian, and other immigrants operate restaurants. In addition, each province is well known for various specialties. **Ontario** is famous for its cheeses, while seafood usually heads the menu at restaurants in **British Columbia, Newfoundland, Nova Scotia, New Brunswick,** and **Prince Edward Island.** Fiddleheads, curled young fern fronds picked in the spring, often accompany dishes in the Maritime Provinces of New Brunswick, Nova Scotia, and Prince Edward Island. In **Alberta** and **Saskatchewan,** the meals invariably center on thick steaks and roasts. In some areas of Canada, especially in the plains, you may be lucky enough to find some Native treats, such as venison, pheasant, and buffalo meat accompanied by fiddlehead ferns in the spring or wild rice. Vestiges of what the European settlers learned from the Native Americans are also evident in the hearty ingredients that make up the French-Canadian cuisine, which thrives in **Québec.** To enjoy the best of the province's hearty meat pies and pâtés, head to Québec City; Montréal dining tends to be more classic French than French-Canadian.

Fishing

Anglers can find their catch in virtually any region of the country, though restrictions, seasons, license requirements, and catch limits vary from province to province. In addition, a special fishing permit is required to fish in all national parks; it can be obtained at any national park site, for a nominal fee. **Newfoundland** offers mackerel, salmon, and sea trout in the Atlantic and speckled trout and rainbow trout in its fresh waters. The waters surrounding **Prince Edward Island** have some of the best deep-sea tuna fishing. **Nova Scotia** has some of the most stringent freshwater restrictions in Canada, but the availability of Atlantic salmon, speckled trout, and striped bass makes the effort worthwhile. Salmon, trout, and black bass are abundant in the waters of **New Brunswick,** and although many salmon pools in the streams and rivers are leased to private freeholders, either individuals or clubs, fly fishing is still readily available for visitors. The lakes of **Québec** hold trout, bass, pike, and landlocked salmon, called ouananiche (pronounced *wah*-nah-nish). Just about every kind of North American freshwater game fish is available in some part of **Ontario. Manitoba** and **Saskatchewan** offer lake trout, brook trout, pike, grayling, walleye, Hudson Bay salmon, and smallmouth bass. They also offer a winter fishing season, but some areas require a guide. **Alberta** is considered a paradise for sportfishers, with its trout in streams; its pike, walleye, and perch in lakes; and its grayling, goldeye, and whitefish in rivers. **British Columbia** is unparalleled for salmon, but only two of the five species may be taken in nontidal waters. **Northwest Territories** has Arctic char, lake trout, and grayling in Great Bear and Great Slave lakes.

Football

The Canadian Football League, which dates from the 1800s, plays with three downs, a 110-yard field, and 12 players per side. Teams are in Toronto, Montréal, Ottawa, Hamilton, Winnipeg, Regina, Calgary, Edmonton, and Vancouver. The Grey Cup, which Canadians take as seriously as we do our Super Bowl, is played every November.

Golf

Every province has something for the duffer, but British Columbia and Ontario dominate the golf scene. Ontario has nearly 400 golf courses. British Columbia also has many golf courses, and Victoria's mild weather makes it especially appealing to golfers. Because public courses are often overcrowded, if you are a member of a golf club, check to see if it has a reciprocal playing arrangement with any of the private clubs in the areas that you will be visiting. Prince Edward Island has focused on course development and now has challenging, scenic, and affordable courses.

Hiking

Miles and miles of trails weave through all of Canada's national and provincial parks as well as along the Trans-Canada Trail or Confederation Trail system, a network of trails which will, when completed, allow people to walk from the Atlantic to the Pacific and to the Arctic. Write to provincial tourist offices or the Inquiry Center for the National Parks Department (☞ National Parks, *below*).

Hockey

Officially, Canada's national sport is lacrosse, but ice hockey is the national favorite. It's played by children and professionals alike, with leagues and teams organized everywhere. The National Hockey League teams in Canada include the Vancouver Canucks, Calgary Flames, Winnipeg Jets, Edmonton Oilers, Toronto Maple Leafs, Ottawa Senators, Montréal Canadiens, and Québec Nordiques. The season runs from October to April.

Horseback Riding

This sport is popular out West, especially in places like Banff National Park in Alberta, which has many outfitters that can arrange week-long trips on the park's trails. A growing number of working ranches in Alberta and British Columbia offer horseback vacations.

Mountain Climbing

Mountain climbers find challenge on the summits of Banff and Jasper national parks in Alberta and the provincial park of Mt. Robson and Yoho National Park in British Columbia. Mountain climbing should not be undertaken lightly. Write to the Inquiry Center (☞ National Parks, *below*) for more information about these parks or contact mountaineering organizations listed in individual chapters.

National Parks

Banff, the country's first national park, was established in 1887, and since then the national park system has grown to encompass 34 national parks and 112 national historic sites. Because of Canada's eagerness to preserve its environment, new lands are continually being added to this network. Almost every park offers camping—either primitive camping or campsites with various facilities that can accommodate recreational vehicles. Hiking trails weave their way through each of the parks. Among the most popular preserves are Fundy National Park in New Brunswick and several Rocky Mountain parks.

Rodeos and Horse Racing

Alberta is rodeo country. The biggest and most famous event is the Calgary Stampede, held every year in July. Thoroughbred racing during the spring, summer, and fall takes place in Ontario, Manitoba, Saskatchewan, Alberta, and British Columbia. Harness racing dominates the east and is popular in other areas of the country.

Scuba Diving

More than 3,000 shipwrecks lie off the coast of Nova Scotia, making it particularly attractive to divers. The provincial Department of Tourism can provide details on the location of wrecks and where to buy or rent equipment. The famed *Marco Polo* sank off the north shore of Prince Edward Island—just one of a hundred wrecks off its shores. In Ontario, the Fathom Five National Marine Park, at the tip of Georgian Bay's Bruce Peninsula, has 20 known wrecks you can explore in exceptionally clear waters. A wealth of sea life makes diving in coastal areas of British Columbia particularly attractive.

Shopping

ANTIQUES➤ On the whole, prices for antiques are lower in Canada than in the United States. Shops along Montréal's rue Sherbrooke Ouest stock everything from ancient maps to fine crystal; Vieux-Montréal and the rue Notre-Dame sell antiques and collectibles ranging from Napoléonic-period furniture to 1950s bric-a-brac. Toronto's offerings are equally eclectic, although priced higher than elsewhere in Canada. The Yorkville area, with its European collections, caters to interior designers; the markets at Lansdowne and Harbourfront are livelier and have wider selections. Antiques shopping is a respectable pastime in Vancouver as well, and Victoria offers some of the best buys in antique silver in the shops clustered on Fort Street.

ARTS AND CRAFTS➤ Sweaters, silver objects, pottery, and Acadian crafts can be found in abundance in the Maritimes. For pewter, head for Fredericton, New Brunswick, or Pugwash, Nova Scotia. For woven items, visit the village of St. Andrews, New Brunswick. In Québec province, check out the wood carvings. The Mennonite communities of Ontario sell their handmade quilts each May at the Mennonite Relief sale.

MAPLE SYRUP➤ Eastern Canada is famous for its sugar maples. The trees are tapped in early spring, and the sap is collected in buckets to be boiled down into maple syrup. This natural confection is sold all year. Avoid the tourist shops and department stores; for the best prices, stop at farm stands and markets in the provinces of Québec, Ontario, and New Brunswick. A small can of syrup costs between $6 and $9.

NATIVE CANADIAN ART➤ Interest has grown in the highly collectible art and sculpture of the Inuit, usually rendered in soapstone. For the best price and a guarantee of authenticity, purchase Inuit and other native crafts in the province where they originate. Many styles are now attributed to certain tribes and are mass-produced for sale in galleries and shops miles away from their regions of origin. At the very top galleries you can be assured of getting pieces done by individual artists, though the prices will be higher than in the provinces of origin. The Canadian government has registered the symbol of an igloo as a mark of a work's authenticity. Be sure this Canadian government sticker or tag is attached before you make your purchase. Many galleries and shops in the west also carry work done by Native Canadians of the Northwest, who have revived their ancient art. They are known for their highly stylized masks, totem poles, and canoes. Themes and images from nature, such as whales, bears, wolves, and eagles, are prominent in their work. Bright colors and geometric patterns distinguish their woven products—blankets, wall hangings, and clothing.

In and around Calgary you can find ceremonial headdresses, clothing, and tools made by the nomadic Plains tribes. Algonkian and Iroquoian art survives mainly in the museums of eastern Canada and in the gift shops of some of the reservations in Ontario.

Skiing

Skiing is probably the most popular winter sport in Canada. For downhill skiing there are slopes in every province, but those in Québec, Alberta, and British Columbia are the best. The Whistler-Blackcomb ski area, north of Vancouver, has been rated by several major ski magazines as the best ski resort in the world. Alberta and British Columbia also offer heli-skiing trips. For cross-country skiing, almost any provincial or national park will do.

Whale-Watching

The shores off British Columbia are among the best places to observe whales, seals, and other natural wildlife. Daylong and sometimes week-long boat trips are offered. In the Pacific Ocean, along Vancouver Island, migrating whales pass on their way to California breeding grounds in the fall and come back in the spring. Resident pods of Killer (Orca) whales are frequently seen along the British Columbia coast. On the Atlantic coast, the waters around Newfoundland offer excellent whale watching, and giant humpback, right whales, finback, and minke whales can be seen in the Bay of Fundy. Boat trips are available from New Brunswick and Nova Scotia. The St. Lawrence River estuary, particularly near the mouth of the Saguenay River, is another important whale-watching area.

White-Water Rafting

There are opportunities for rafting in almost every province, but the white waters of Ontario and British Columbia are especially inviting for thrill seekers. Commercial rafting companies offer a variety of trip packages.

Winter Sports

Canadians flourish in winter, as the range of winter sports attests. In addition to the sports already mentioned, at the first drop of a snowflake Canadians will head outside to ice skate, toboggan, snowmobile, dogsled, snowshoe, and ice fish. A network of 6,000 kilometers (3,720 miles) of snowmobile trails are being developed in Atlantic Canada.

NEW AND NOTEWORTHY

BRITISH COLUMBIA➤ Island Highway 19, which runs along the east coast of Vancouver Island, is being expanded from two to four lanes. Scheduled for completion in 1997, the expansion is expected to smooth the flow of traffic between Victoria and Campbell River and shorten travel time between the two cities.

CANADIAN ROCKIES➤ **Rocky Mountaineer Rail Tours** added a bi-level, state-of-the-art dome coach to its service through the spectacular mountains between towns in the Alberta Rockies and Vancouver. The **Banff Springs Hotel** opened a $16 million spa.

MONTRÉAL➤ In October 1995, Montréal survived yet another **referendum** on the independence of Québec. Separatists lost by the narrowest possible margins with more than 49% of the vote, and so the city faces at least one more nerve-wracking debate in the future. But this island city has never let politics get in the way of a good time. Its summer **festivals** of jazz, film, fireworks, and comedy are among the most important in the world. And the Canadiens hockey team moved into a brand-new downtown home, **Centre Molson.**

NEWFOUNDLAND AND LABRADOR➤ A year-long celebration in Newfoundland and Labrador in 1997 marks the **500th anniversary of John Cabot's voyage** from England that launched European exploration of North America.

PRINCE EDWARD ISLAND➤ Travelers coming to Prince Edward Island via New Brunswick will see the completion of the Island's newest attraction: the longest continuous multispan **bridge** in the world, linking the Island with the mainland, due to open in the summer.

VANCOUVER➤ **Airport** expansion was due for completion by the end of 1996.

FODOR'S CHOICE

No two people will agree on what makes a perfect vacation, but it's fun and helpful to know what others think. We hope you'll have a chance to experience some of Fodor's Choices yourself in Canada. For detailed information about each entry, refer to the appropriate chapter.

Historic Sites

★ **Basilique Notre-Dame de Montréal, Montréal.** The enormous (3,800-seat) rectangular neo-Gothic church, opened in 1829 and has a medieval-style interior with stained-glass windows, a stunning vaulted blue ceiling, and pine and walnut-wood carving.

★ **Basilica of Ste-Anne de Beaupré, Québec City.** The monumental and inspiring church is an important shrine that draws hordes of pilgrims. According to local legend, St. Anne was responsible over the years for saving voyagers from shipwrecks in the harsh waters of the St. Lawrence; she is also believed to have healing powers.

★ **Vieille Ville, Québec City.** The Old Town is small and dense, steeped in four centuries of history and French tradition. Immaculately preserved as the only fortified city in North America, it is a UNESCO World Heritage Site.

★ **Plains of Abraham, Québec City.** The site of the famous 1759 battle between the French and the British that decided the fate of New France is now part of a large park overlooking the St. Lawrence River.

★ **Kings Landing Historical Settlement, New Brunswick.** This reconstructed village—more than 60 buildings, including homes, an inn, a forge, a store, a church, a school, working farms, and a sawmill—illustrates life in the central St. John River valley between 1790 and 1900.

★ **Klondike National Historic Sites, Dawson City, Wilderness Canada.** Dredge No. 4 was used to dig up the creek bed during the height of Bonanza Creek's gold-bearing largesse. The two writers most closely associated with the Yukon Territory are honored at the Jack London Interpretive Center and the Robert W. Service Cabin.

Parks and Gardens

★ **Butchart Gardens, Victoria, British Columbia.** This world-class horticultural collection grows more than 700 varieties of flowers and has Italian, Japanese, and English rose gardens.

★**Pacific Rim National Park, Vancouver Island, British Columbia.** The first national marine park in Canada comprises a hard-packed white sand beach, a group of islands, and a demanding coastal hiking trail where you'll find panoramic views of the sea, the rain forest, sandstone cliffs, and wildlife.

★**Banff National Park, Canadian Rockies.** Canada's first national park was officially established in 1887. Its spectacular mountain peaks, forests, and wildlife remain relatively untouched by human development, protected by strict laws.

★**Jardin Botanique de Montréal** (Botanical Gardens), **Montréal.** This park, with 181 acres of gardens in summer and 10 greenhouses open all year, has one of the best bonsai collections in the West and the largest Ming-style garden outside Asia.

★**Cape Breton Highlands National Park, Nova Scotia.** A wilderness of wooded valleys, plateau barrens, and steep cliffs, it stretches across the northern peninsula of Nova Scotia's Cape Breton Island.

★**Prince Edward Island National Park, Prince Edward Island.** Along the north shore of the island on the Gulf of St. Lawrence, sky and sea meet red sandstone cliffs, rolling dunes, and long stretches of sand.

★**Nahanni National Park, Wilderness Canada.** Access to the mountainous park is possible only by helicopter or plane; inside the park, canoes and rafts are the principal means of travel.

Views to Remember

★**The view from the Jasper Tramway, Canadian Rockies.** From the steep flank of Whistlers Mountain you can see the summit of Mt. Robson (the Canadian Rockies' highest mountain), the Miette valley to the west, and Athabasca valley to the east.

★**View of Niagara Falls by helicopter, Ontario.** The flight takes you over the Giant Whirlpool, up the Niagara Gorge, and past the American Falls and then banks around the curve of the Horseshoe Falls.

★**Peggy's Cove, Nova Scotia.** At the mouth of a bay facing the open Atlantic, the cove, with its houses huddled around the narrow slit in the boulders, has the only Canadian post office in a lighthouse.

★**Signal Hill, St. John's, Newfoundland.** Overlooking the snug, punch-bowl harbor of St. John's and the sea, this hilltop was taken and retaken by opposing forces in the 17th century.

Restaurants

★**Star Anise, Vancouver.** Pacific Rim cuisine with French flair shines in this intimate restaurant on the west side of town. *$$$*

★**Emerald Lake Lodge, Yoho, Canadian Rockies.** The eclectic menu of this glass-enclosed dining room at the edge of a secluded, glacier-fed lake in Yoho National Park, joins traditional Canadian and American fare with nouvelle sauces. *$$$$*

★**Toqué, Montréal.** This is the most fashionable and the most zany restaurant in Montréal. The menu depends on what the two chefs found fresh that day and on which way their ever-creative spirit moved them. *$$$*

★**North 44, Toronto.** A steel compass highlighting Toronto's latitude embedded in a gorgeous marble floor and textured walls hung with mirrored sconces set the scene for sophisticated dishes such as crisp tortilla spring rolls plump with barbecued chicken and vegetables or spaghettini with seared scallops. *$$$–$$$$*

★**Aux Anciens Canadiens, Québec City.** The house, dating from 1675, has four dining rooms with varying historical themes. The cooking is authentic, hearty French-Canadian. *$$$*

★**L'Eau à la Bouche, Ste-Adèle, Québec.** At this Bavarian-style property you'll find a superb marriage of nouvelle cuisine and traditional Québec cooking in such dishes as roast partridge stuffed with oyster mushrooms and cream sauce. *$$$$*

★**Lobster suppers in New Glasgow, St. Anne's, and North Rustico, Prince Edward Island.** Whether commercial or put on by church or civic groups, these meals feature lobster, rolls, salad, and mountains of sweet, home-baked goodies. *$$*

Hotels

★**English Bay Inn, Vancouver.** In this 1930s Tudor house a block from the ocean, the guest rooms have wonderful sleigh beds with matching armoires. A small, sunny English country garden brightens the back of the inn. $$

★**King Edward, Toronto.** The grande dame of downtown Toronto hotels, built in 1903, has an air of understated elegance, with its vaulted ceiling, marble pillars, and palm trees. $$$$

★**Auberge les Passants du Sans Soucy, Montréal.** A tiny gem, the only inn in Vieux-Montréal, has rooms with brass beds, bare stone walls, exposed beams, soft lighting, and lots of fresh-cut flowers. $$

★**Hostellerie Les Trois Tilleuls, St-Marc-sur-Richelieu, Québec.** This romantic little inn on a quiet country road near Montréal has modern rooms, each with a balcony or terrace facing the lovely Rivière Richelieu. $$$–$$$$

★**West Point Lighthouse, West Point, Prince Edward Island.** A functioning lighthouse in a provincial park, this small inn sits next to the beach. $$

FESTIVALS AND SEASONAL EVENTS

Contact tourist boards for more information about these and other festivals.

WINTER

DECEMBER➤ **British Columbia:** The **Carol Ships,** sailboats full of carolers and decorated with colored lights, ply the waters of the Vancouver harbor.

Newfoundland and Labrador: In St. John's, New Year's revelers pour out of downtown pubs to gather on the waterfront to ring in the new year.

JANUARY➤ **Alberta: Jasper Winter Festival** in Jasper and Marmot Basin presents dog sledding, skating, ice sculpting, and other events.

British Columbia: The **Polar Bear Swim** on New Year's Day in Vancouver, is said to bring good luck all year. **Skiing competitions** take place at most alpine ski resorts throughout the province (through February).

Ontario: The **Niagara Falls Festival of Lights** is an extravaganza of colored lights in the parks surrounding the Falls.

FEBRUARY➤ **Alberta: Calgary Winter Festival** is a 10-day celebration of Calgary's Olympic spirit, with winter sports and ice sculpting.

Manitoba: Festival du Voyageur, in St. Boniface, Winnipeg, celebrates the history of the region's early fur traders.

Ontario: Ontario Winter Carnival Bon Soo animates Sault Ste. Marie. Ottawa's **Winterlude** encourages ice sculpting, snowshoe races, ice boating, and other winter action.

Québec: *La Fête des Neiges* is winter carnival in Montréal. **Winter Carnival** in Québec City is an 11-day festival of winter sports competitions, ice-sculpture contests, and parades. Cross-country skiers race between Lachute and Gatineau in the **Canadian Ski Marathon.**

Yukon: The **Yukon Sourdough Rendezvous,** in Whitehorse, has dog-team races, leg wrestling, log sawing, snowshoe races, local arts and crafts, and talent contests.

SPRING

MARCH➤ **British Columbia:** The **Pacific Rim Whale Festival** on Vancouver Island's west coast celebrates the spring migration of gray whales with guided tours by whale experts and accompanying music and dancing. The **Vancouver International Wine Festival** is held at this time.

Manitoba: The **Royal Manitoba Winter Fair** takes place in Brandon.

Northwest Territories: The **Caribou Carnival** fills three days with traditional Inuit and Dene northern games, ice sculpting, cultural exhibits, and races in Yellowknife.

APRIL➤ **Alberta: Silver Buckle Rodeo** at Red Deer attracts cowboys from all over North America.

British Columbia: TerrifVic Jazz Party, in Victoria, has top international Dixieland bands.

Ontario: The **Maple Syrup Festival** sweetens Elmira. **Shaw Festival** in Niagara-on-the-Lake (through November) presents plays by George Bernard Shaw and his contemporaries.

Québec: Sugaring-off parties celebrate the beginning of the maple syrup season.

MAY➤ **Alberta:** The **International Children's Festival** in Calgary and Edmonton draws professional musicians, mimes, jugglers, clowns, puppeteers, and singers worldwide. At the **Red Deer Annual Westerner Spring Quarter Horse Show,** horses from western Canada and the United States compete.

British Columbia: Cloverdale Rodeo in Surrey is rated sixth in the world by the Pro Rodeo Association. **Vancouver Children's Festival** provides free open-air stage performances.

Nova Scotia: In the Annapolis Valley, the **Apple Blossom Festival** includes dancing, parades, and entertainment.

Ontario: Stratford Festival, in Stratford, presents many of Shakespeare's plays (through early November). **Folk Arts Festival** draws artists to St. Catharines. The **Canadian Tulip Festival,** in Ottawa, celebrates spring with 3 million blossoming tulips.

Saskatchewan: The **International Band and Choral Festival,** in Moose Jaw, attracts 7,000 musicians, 100 bands, and 25 choral groups. **Vesna Festival,** in Saskatoon, is the world's largest Ukrainian cabaret, with traditional Ukrainian food and crafts.

SUMMER

JUNE➤ **Alberta: Jazz City International Festival** in Edmonton has 10 days of jazz concerts, workshops, club dates, and free outdoor events. **Ponoka Annual Stampede** professional rodeo attracts participants from across the continent. **Banff Festival of the Arts** (through August) showcases nearly 1,000 young artists in music, opera, dance, drama, comedy, and visual arts.

British Columbia: Canadian International Dragon Boat Festival, in Vancouver, includes entertainment, exotic foods, and the ancient "awakening the dragons" ritual of long, slender boats decorated with huge dragon heads. **Whistler Summer Festivals,** through September, present daily street entertainment and a variety of music festivals at the international ski and summer resort.

Manitoba: Winnipeg's **Red River Exhibition** features lumberjack contests, bodybuilding shows, and an international band festival. **Winnipeg International Children's Festival** provides top national and international children's entertainment and activities.

New Brunswick: St. John's Day commemorates the city's birthday and includes a parade, street dance, concerts, and sporting and cultural events.

Nova Scotia: The **International Blues Festival** draws music lovers to Halifax.

Ontario: Toronto's **Metro International Caravan** is an ethnic fair. **Changing of the Guard** begins at Ottawa's Parliament Buildings (through August).

Prince Edward Island: Charlottetown Festival Theatre offers concerts and musicals (through September). In Summerside the annual **Summerside Highland Gathering** kicks off a summer of concerts and "Come to the Ceilidh" evenings.

Québec: Some of the world's best drivers compete in the **Molson Grand Prix** in Montréal. Québec City hops with the **International Jazz Festival.** Beauport hosts the **International Children's Folklore Festival.**

Saskatchewan: Frontier Days Regional Fair and Rodeo, in Swift Current, is a community fair with parades, a horse show, and a rodeo. **Mosaic,** in Regina, celebrates cultures from around the world.

Yukon: The **Yukon International Festival of Storytelling,** in Whitehorse, draws storytellers from all over the circumpolar North.

Northwest Territories: The **Midnight Classic Golf Tournament** in Yellowknife tees off at midnight on the first day of summer.

JULY➤ **Alberta: Ukrainian Pysanka Festival** in Vegreville celebrates with costumes and traditional singing and dancing. **Calgary Exhibition and Stampede** is one of the most popular Canadian events and includes 10 days of Western showmanship, hot-air balloon races, chuckwagon races, agricultural shows, crafts exhibits, and Indian dancing. **Edmonton's Klondike Days** celebrate the town's early frontier community with pancake breakfasts, gambling casinos, gold panning, and raft races.

British Columbia: Harrison Festival of the Arts focuses on different ethnic music, dance, and theater, such as African, Caribbean, or Central American. **Vancouver Sea Festival** celebrates the city's nautical heritage with the World Championship Bathtub Race, sailing regattas, and windsurfing races.

Manitoba: At the **Winnipeg Folk Festival,** in Birds Hill Park, 24 kilometers (15 miles) northeast of Winnipeg, country, bluegrass, folk, Acadian music, and jazz can be heard on 10 stages. **Manitoba Stampede and Exhibition** in Morris is an agricultural fair with rodeos and chuckwagon races.

New Brunswick: Loyalist City Festival, in St. John, celebrates the town's founding with parades, dancing, and sidewalk festivities. The **Shediac Lobster Festival** takes place in the town that calls itself the Lobster Capital of the World. There's an **Irish Festival** in Miramichi. The **New Brunswick Highland Games & Scottish Festival** is in Fredericton.

Newfoundland and Labrador: The **Hangashore Folk Festival** is in Corner Brook, the **Exploits Valley Salmon Festival** in the Grand Falls area, the **Fish, Fun and Folk Festival** in Twillingate, and the **Conception Bay Folk Festival** in Carbonear. **Musicfest** in Stephenville celebrates music from rock and roll to traditional Newfoundland music. **Signal Hill Tattoo** in St. John's (through August) reenacts the final, 1762 battle of the Seven Years' War between the British and the French. The **Burin Peninsula Festival of Folk Song and Dance** features traditional Newfoundland entertainment.

Nova Scotia: Antigonish Highland Games, staged annually since 1861, has Scottish music, dance, and such ancient sporting events as the caber toss. Halifax hosts both the **Nova Scotia International Tattoo** and the **Atlantic Jazz Festival.**

Ontario: Ottawa celebrates **Canada Day** with entertainment and fireworks. The **Queen's Plate** Thoroughbred horse race takes place in Toronto. There's a **Blueberry Festival** in Sudbury. The **Molson INDY** race roars through Toronto. **Caribana** festival celebrates Toronto's West Indian community. The **Glengarry Highland Games,** in Maxville, is North America's largest Highland gathering.

Prince Edward Island: The **Annual Outdoor Scottish Fiddle and Dance Festival** skirls through Richmond. Rollo Bay hosts a **Fiddle Festival.** Summerside's **Lobster Carnival** is a weeklong feast of lobster.

Canada Day Festivities abound in even the smallest community on the first of the month.

Québec: Festival International de Jazz de Montréal draws more than 2,000 musicians from all over the world for this 11-day series. **Québec International Summer Festival** offers entertainment in the streets and parks of old Québec City. Montréal's **Juste pour Rire** (Just for Laughs) comedy festival features comics from around the world, in French and English. Drummondville **World Folklore Festival** brings troupes from more than 20 countries to perform in the streets and parks. At **Festival Orford** international artists perform in Orford Park's music center (through August). **Matinée Ltd. International** spotlights the best male tennis players in Montréal.

Saskatchewan: *The Trial of Louis Riel,* in Regina, one of Canada's longest running stage shows, reenacts the events surrounding the North West Rebellion of 1885 (late July through August). **Shakespeare on the Saskatchewan Festival,** in Saskatoon, has productions in tents on the banks of the South Saskatchewan River (early July–late August).

Northwest Territories: The **Annual Great Northern Arts Festival** in Inuvik presents displays, workshops, live performances, and artist demonstrations for the region's premiere cultural event.

AUGUST➤ **Alberta:** The **Fringe Theatre Festival,** in Edmonton, is one of the major festivals for alternative theater in North America. The **Golden Walleye Classic** in High Prairie is a three-day fishing tournament with $90,000 in prizes.

British Columbia: Squamish Days Loggers Sports Festival draws loggers from around the world to compete in a series of incredible logging feats. The **Abbotsford International Airshow** is three days of flight performances and a large-aircraft display. **Pacific National Exhibition** in Vancouver has parades, exhibits, sports, entertainment, and logging contests.

Manitoba: Folklorama, the largest multicultural festival in the world, sets up more than 40 pavilions throughout Winnipeg. The **National Ukrainian Festival,** in Dauphin, offers costumes, artifacts, exhibits, fiddling contests, dancing, and workshops. The **Icelandic Festival,** in Gimli, gathers the largest Icelandic community outside of Iceland. **Pioneer Days,** in Steinbach, celebrates the heritage of the Mennonites with demonstrations of threshing and baking, a parade, a horse show, a barbecue, and Mennonite foods.

New Brunswick: The **Miramichi Folk Song Festival** features traditional and contemorary folk songs steeped in Maritime lore. **Acadian Festival,** at Caraquet, celebrates the region's Acadian heritage with folk singing and indigenous food. The **Chocolate Festival** in St. Stephen includes suppers, displays, and children's events.

Newfoundland and Labrador: Gander's **Festi-**

val of Flight celebrates this town as the aviation "Crossroads of the World," with dances, parades, and a folk festival. *Une Longue Veillée* folk festival, celebrating western Newfoundland's French heritage, brings traditional musicians, singers, and dancers to Cape St. George.

Nova Scotia: There's Lunenburg's **Nova Scotia Fisheries Exhibition and Fishermen's Reunion.** The **Nova Scotia Gaelic Mod** in St. Ann's celebrates Scottish culture on the grounds of the only Gaelic college in North America. The **Halifax International Buskerfest** has daily outdoor shows by street performers, a food festival, and stage entertainment.

Ontario: Brantford's **Six Nations Native Pageant** celebrates Iroquois culture and history. **Royal Canadian Henley Regatta,** in St. Catharines, is the largest rowing regatta in North America.

Prince Edward Island: Eldon's **Highland Games** gathers Scotsmen and women. The **Annual Community Harvest Festival** animates Kensington. **Old Home Week** fills Charlottetown with nostalgia. An **International Hydroplane Regatta** brings speed to the Summerside waterfront.

Québec: Montréal hosts a **World Film Festival.** St-Jean-sur-Richelieu's **Hot Air Balloon Festival** is the largest gathering of hot air balloons in Canada.

Saskatchewan: Buffalo Days Exhibition, in Regina, features rides, a grandstand show, dancing, livestock judging, and horse racing.

AUTUMN

SEPTEMBER➤ **Alberta: Spruce Meadows Masters' Tournament,** in Calgary, is an international horse-jumping competition at one of North America's leading equestrian centers.

British Columbia: Cars speed through downtown Vancouver in the **Molson Indy Formula 1 race.**

Newfoundland and Labrador: Deer Lake hosts the **Humber Valley Agricultural Home and Handicraft Exhibition.**

Ontario: The **Canadian Open Golf Championship** plays through Oakville. Toronto's **Festival of Festivals** salutes international film. St. Catharines toasts the **Niagara Grape and Wine Festival.**

Prince Edward Island: Festival Acadien de la Region Evangeline is an

agricultural fair with Acadian music, a parade, and lobster suppers, at Wellington Station.

Québec: Québec International Film Festival screens in Québec City. The **Gatineau Hot Air Balloon Festival** brings together hot air balloons from across Canada, the United States, and Europe.

OCTOBER➤ **British Columbia:** The **Vancouver International Film Festival** is held. **Okanagan Wine Festivals** take place in the Okanagan-Similkameen area.

Nova Scotia: There's the **Shearwater International Air Show.**

Ontario: Kitchener–Waterloo's **Oktoberfest** attracts more than half a million enthusiasts to its many beer halls and tents.

Québec: Festival of Colors celebrates foliage throughout the province.

NOVEMBER➤ **Ontario:** Toronto's **Royal Agricultural Winter Fair** draws exhibitors and contestants to the largest indoor agricultural fair and equestrian competition in the world.

Prince Edward Island: The Prince Edward Island Crafts Council **Annual Christmas Craft Fair** brings juried producers to Charlottetown for the largest event of its kind on the Island.

2 Vancouver

Cosmopolitan Vancouver, Canada's answer to San Francisco, enjoys a spectacular setting. Tall fir trees stand practically downtown, rock spires tower close by, the ocean laps at your doorstep, and people from every corner of the earth create a youthful and vibrant atmosphere.

VANCOUVER IS A YOUNG CITY, even by North American standards. Although 300 to 400 years of settlement may make cities like Québec and Halifax historically interesting to travelers, Vancouver's youthful vigor attracts visitors to its powerful elements that have not yet been ground down by time. Vancouver is just over 100 years old; it was not yet a town in 1870, when British Columbia became part of the Canadian confederation. The city's history, such as it is, remains visible to the naked eye: Eras are stacked east to west along the waterfront like some century-old archaeological dig—from cobblestoned, late-Victorian Gastown to shiny postmodern glass cathedrals of commerce grazing the sunset.

Updated by
Melissa Rivers

The Chinese were among the first to recognize the possibilities of Vancouver's setting. They came to British Columbia during the 1850s seeking the gold that inspired them to name the province Gum-shan, or Gold Mountain. As laborers they built the Canadian Pacific Railway, giving Vancouver's original townsite a purpose—one beyond the natural splendor that Royal Navy captain George Vancouver admired during his lunchtime cruise around its harbor on June 13, 1792. The transcontinental railway, along with the city's Great White Fleet of clipper ships, gave Vancouver a full week's edge over the California ports in shipping tea and silk to New York at the dawn of the 20th century.

Vancouver's natural charms are less scattered than those in other cities. On clear days, the mountains appear close enough to touch. Two 1,000-acre wilderness parks lie within the city limits. The salt water of the Pacific and fresh water direct from the Rocky Mountain Trench form the city's northern and southern boundaries.

Bring a healthy sense of reverence when you visit: Vancouver is a spiritual place. For its original inhabitants, the Coast Salish peoples, it was the sacred spot where the mythical Thunderbird and Killer Whale flung wind and rain all about the heavens during their epic battles—how else to explain the coast's occasional fits of meteorological temper? Devotees of a later religious tradition might worship in the sepulchre of Stanley Park or in the polished, incense-filled quiet of St. James Anglican Church, designed by English architect Sir Adrian Gilbert Scott and perhaps Vancouver's finest building.

Vancouver has a level of nightlife possible only in a place where the finer things in life have never been driven out to the suburbs and where sidewalks have never rolled up at 5 PM. There is no shortage of excellent hotels and restaurants here, either. But you can find good theater, accommodations, and dining almost anywhere these days. Vancouver's real culture consists of its tall fir trees practically downtown and its towering rock spires close by, the ocean at your doorstep, and people from every corner of the earth all around you.

Pleasures and Pastimes

Dining

Vancouver offers the visitor a diverse gastronomical experience; restaurants—from the bustling downtown area to trendy beachside neighborhoods—have enticing locales in addition to succulent cuisine. A new wave of Asian immigration and tourism has brought a proliferation of upscale Asian (Chinese, Japanese, Korean, Thai, and Vietnamese) restaurants, offering dishes that would be at home in their own leading cities. Cutting-edge restaurants currently perfecting and defining

Vancouver *(Boxes Refer to Detail Maps)*

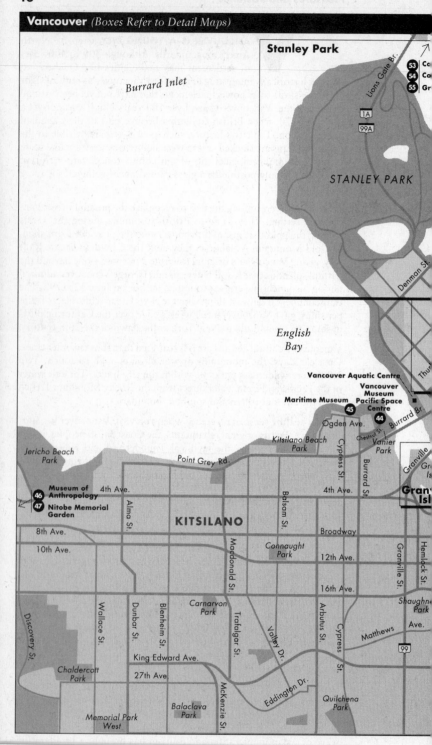

Stanley Park

53 Co
54 Ca
55 Gr

Burrard Inlet

1A
99A

Lions Gate Br.

STANLEY PARK

Denman St.

English Bay

Vancouver Aquatic Centre

Vancouver Museum
Pacific Space Centre

Maritime Museum

45

Ogden Ave.

Kitsilano Beach Park

Chestnut St.

Vanier Park

Thur

Burrard Br.

Jericho Beach Park

Point Grey Rd.

Cypress St.

Burrard St.

Granville

Gr
Is

Museum of Anthropology
46

4th Ave.

4th Ave.

**Gran
Isl**

47 **Nitobe Memorial Garden**

Alma St.

Balsam St.

8th Ave.

KITSILANO

Broadway

10th Ave.

Macdonald St.

Connaught Park

12th Ave.

Granville St.

Hemlock St.

16th Ave.

*Shaughn
Park*

Carnarvon Park

Discovery St.

Wallace St.

Dunbar St.

Blenheim St.

Trafalgar St.

Valley Dr.

Arbutus St.

Cypress St.

Matthews

Ave.

99

King Edward Ave.

Chaldercott Park

27th Ave

McKenzie St.

Eddington Dr.

Quilchena Park

Balaclava Park

Memorial Park West

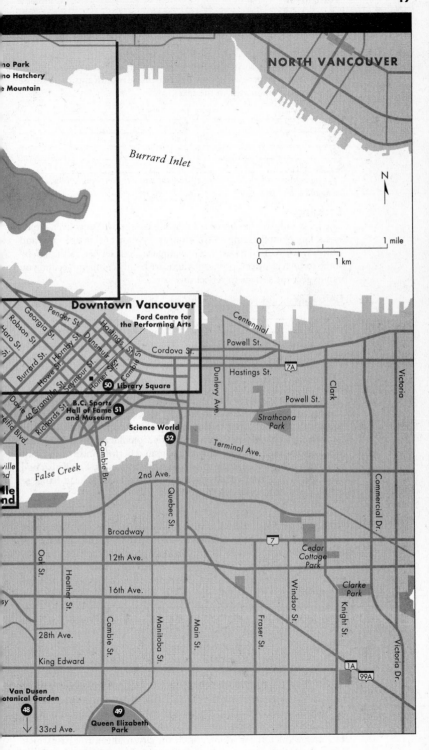

no Park
no Hatchery
e Mountain

Burrard Inlet

NORTH VANCOUVER

N

0   1 mile
0   1 km

Downtown Vancouver

Ford Centre for the Performing Arts

Pender St.
Georgia St.
Robson St.
Haro St.
Hastings St.
Dunsmuir St.
Cordova St.
Burrard St.
Howe St.
Hornby St.
Seymour St.
Homer St.
Cambie St.
Richards St.
Granville St.
Davie St.
elia Blvd.

Centennial
Powell St.
7A
Hastings St.
Powell St.
Clark
Victoria

50 Library Square

B.C. Sports Hall of Fame and Museum **51**

Science World **52**

Dunlevy Ave.

Strathcona Park

ville
nd

False Creek

le
nd

Cambie Br.

2nd Ave.

Quebec St.

Terminal Ave.

Commercial Dr.

Broadway

7

Cedar Cottage Park

Oak St.

12th Ave.

Heather St.

16th Ave.

Cambie St.

Manitoba St.

Main St.

Fraser St.

Windsor St.

Clarke Park

Knight St.

28th Ave.

sy

King Edward

1A

99A

Victoria Dr.

Van Dusen otanical Garden

48

↓ 33rd Ave.

Queen Elizabeth Park **49**

Pacific Northwest fare—including such homegrown regional favorites as salmon and oysters, accompanied by British Columbia and Washington State wines—have become some of the city's leading attractions.

Vancouver dining is usually fairly informal; casual but neat dress is appropriate everywhere except the few expensive restaurants that require jacket and tie (indicated in the text).

CATEGORY	COST*
$$$$	over $40
$$$	$30–$40
$$	$20–$30
$	under $20

*per person, including appetizer, entrée, and dessert; excluding drinks, service, and sales tax

Lodging
The hotel industry has become a major business for Vancouver, which hosts large numbers of conventioneers, Asian businesspeople, and others who are used to an above-average level of service. Although by some standards pricey, properties here are highly competitive, and you can expect the service to reflect this.

CATEGORY	COST*
$$$$	over $200
$$$	$150–$200
$$	$100–$150
$	under $100

*All prices are for a standard double room for two, excluding 10% provincial accommodation tax, 15% service charge, and 7% GST.

Nightlife and the Arts
Vancouver compares favorably to New York or London when it comes to its range of nightlife and arts venues. The arts are enthusiastically supported, so you'll find everything here, from nationally touring musicals to off-off Broadway shows to film and performing arts festivals to renowned symphonic, opera, and ballet companies. You'll also find the city a hotbed for live music—from jazz and blues to head-bangers' heavy metal and everything in between.

Shopping
Unlike many cities where suburban malls have taken over, Vancouver has a downtown that is still lined with individual boutiques and specialty shops. A multitude of antiques stores, ethnic markets, art galleries, high-fashion outlets, and fine department stores dots the city. Stores are usually open daily, Thursday and Friday nights, and Sunday noon to 5.

EXPLORING VANCOUVER

Vancouver may be small when compared to New York or San Francisco, but it still takes time to explore. Many sights of interest are concentrated in the hemmed-in peninsula of Downtown Vancouver. The heart of Vancouver—which includes the downtown area, Stanley Park, and the West End high-rise residential neighborhood—sits on this peninsula bordered by English Bay and the Pacific Ocean to the west; by False Creek, the inlet home to Granville Island, to the south; and by Burrard Inlet, the working port of the city, to the north, past which loom the North Shore mountains. The oldest part of the city—Gastown and Chinatown—lies at the edge of Burrard Inlet, around Main Street, which runs north–south and is roughly the dividing line between the east side and the west side. All the avenues, which are numbered, have east and west designations. You'll also find places of interest elsewhere in the city, either on the North Shore across Burrard Inlet or south of downtown in the Kitsilano area across English Bay or in the Granville Island area across False Creek. Then, too, there's Whistler, a renowned winter and summer resort a few hours' drive north of Vancouver.

Great Itineraries

Numbers in the text below correspond to numbers in the margin and on the Vancouver Exploring, Downtown Vancouver, Stanley Park, and Granville Island maps.

IF YOU HAVE 1–2 DAYS

If you have only one day in Vancouver, start with an early morning drive through **Stanley Park** to see the **Vancouver Aquarium** ㉝; **Lost Lagoon** ㉔; the **Royal Vancouver Yacht Club** ㉗; **Deadman's Island** ㉘, a former burial ground for the local Salish Indians and the early settlers; the lighthouse at **Brockton Point** ㉚; **Lumberman's Arch** ㉜; **Lions Gate Bridge**; **Prospect Point** ㉞; **Siwash Rock** ㉟; and **Second Beach** ㊱ on **English Bay.** Allow at least two hours to take in the wonderful marine exhibits at the aquarium and another hour or two for a driving tour through the park. In the early afternoon, your tour of the park will end in the West End; head northeast on Denman Street to **Robson Street** ① to lunch and meander on foot through the abundance of trendy shops lining the street between Denman and Burrard, then walk northeast on Burrard Street to view the many buildings of architectural interest—the copper-roofed **Hotel Vancouver** ④, the gothic-style **Christ Church Cathedral** ⑥, the Art Deco **Marine Building** ⑧, and the soaring, postmodern canopies of **Canada Place** ⑩. Stops along the way at the **Vancouver Art Gallery** ③, the **Canadian Craft Museum** ⑦, and the tiny **Sri Lankan Gem Museum** will make for a very full day of sightseeing.

Day two can follow a more leisurely paced walking tour of the shops, eateries, and cobblestone streets of **Gastown,** the original townsite of Vancouver, and **Chinatown** ⑲, the second-largest Chinatown in North America. Take a camera to capture **Blood Alley, Goaler's Mews,** the false-front buildings, and the steam powered clock in Gastown and the brightly painted buildings, Chinese gates, and the classical **Dr. Sun Yat-sen Gardens** ㉓ in Chinatown. There are plenty of places to eat and shop in both districts.

IF YOU HAVE 3–4 DAYS

If you have another day to tour Vancouver following your exploration of **Stanley Park** ㉔–㊱, **Robson Street** ①, **Gastown,** and **Chinatown** ⑲ in the downtown core, head to the south side of False Creek and English Bay on day three to delve into the many boutiques, dining outlets, theaters, and lively public market of **Granville Island** ㊲–㊸. Buses and ferries provide easy transit, and there is plenty of parking if you prefer to drive; touring Granville Island is best accomplished on foot.

On day four, you'll need a car to tour the far-flung sights south of downtown Vancouver. Museum and history buffs will want to tour the **Museum of Anthropology** ㊻ (housing fantastic totem poles, canoes, jewelry, costumes, and other art of Pacific Northwest natives and other aboriginal groups) on the campus of the University of British Columbia, and the **Vancouver Museum** ㊹ (showcasing the city's history in cheerful, life-size displays), **Pacific Space Centre** ㊹ (a new high-tech museum focusing on outer space), and the **Maritime Museum** ㊺ (tracing the maritime history of the West Coast), all just south of downtown in the Kitsilano area. Gardening and outdoor enthusiasts may prefer to spend day four touring **Nitobe Memorial Garden** ㊼ (a traditional Japanese strolling garden on the campus of the University of British Columbia), **Van Dusen Botanical Garden** ㊽ (55 ornamental acres showcasing the abundant plantlife of the Pacific Northwest), and **Queen Elizabeth Park** ㊾ (the highest point in southern Vancouver affording scenic views of downtown), all situated south of downtown in the residential section of Vancouver.

If you still have a couple of daylight hours left, make your way back through downtown Vancouver to the **Lions Gate Bridge** and follow the signs into the mountains of the North Shore to see the **Capilano Suspension Bridge and Park** ㊼, a park built around a cedar plank suspension footbridge that swings high above the Capilano River, or the less touristy **Lynn Canyon Suspension Bridge and Park** (the bridge is not quite as high, but the setting is far more natural and admission is free) before heading to the peak of **Grouse Mountain** ㊽ to enjoy the splendid panorama of Vancouver highlighted by the rich colors of the setting sun.

IF YOU HAVE 5-7 DAYS

★ ★ ★ If you have another two days to explore and you've already seen **Stanley Park** ㉔–㊱, **Robson Street** ①, **Gastown, Chinatown** ⑲, **Granville Island** ㊲–㊸, and the museums ㊹–㊻ and gardens ㊼–㊾ of Vancouver and parks on the North Shore ㊼–㊽, don't miss a side trip to beauti-
★ ful **Whistler** (☞ British Columbia *in* Chapter 3), in the mountains north of the city. Although it's ranked as one of the top ski destinations in the world, this growing resort offering an ever-expanding array of outdoor activities and festivals is worth a visit any time of year. The 2½-hour drive there on the scenic Sea to Sky Highway takes you from glorious seaside vistas into the heart of lush alpine.

Robson to the Waterfront

Museums and buildings of architectural and historical interest are the primary drawing cards in downtown Vancouver. There's also plenty of fine shopping to provide breaks (or to distract, depending on your perspective) along the way. It's a new city, when compared to others, but still highly rich in culture and diversity.

Numbers in the text and margin below correspond to points of interest on the Downtown Vancouver map.

A Good Walk

If you're a shopaholic, coffee junkie, and/or people watcher, begin your tour of Vancouver on **Robson Street** ① (☞ Shopping, *below*), also referred to as Vancouver's Rodeo Drive because of the sheer number of see-and-be-seen sidewalk cafes and high-end boutiques, and as Robson Strasse because of its European flavor. Start at the northwest end near the cross streets of Bute or Thurlow and follow Robson southeast to Horby to reach **Robson Square** ②, a central park area that encompasses landscaped walkways, government office buildings, and the **Vancouver Art Gallery** ③, which houses the city's finest art collection. On the north side of the gallery across Hornby Street sits the **Hotel Vancouver** ④, its copper, chateau-style roof making it one of the city's best-known landmarks. **Cathedral Place** ⑤, a spectacular office tower, stands across the street on the corner of Hornby and Georgia. Three large sculptures of nurses at the corners of the building are replicas of the statues that ornamented the Art Deco Georgia Medical-Dental Building, the site's previous structure. If you're fascinated by gemstones, pop inside to visit the **Sri Lankan Gem Museum**. To the left of Cathedral Place is the Gothic-style **Christ Church Cathedral** ⑥, the oldest church in Vancouver. Head east up Burrard and you'll see on your right a restored terra-cotta arch—formerly the front entrance to the medical building—and frieze panels showing scenes of individuals administering care; these decorate the **Canadian Craft Museum** ⑦, one of the first national cultural facilities dedicated to crafts. Farther still up Burrard, on the opposite side of the street, is the **Marine Building** ⑧, its intriguing terra-cotta bas-reliefs making it one of Canada's best examples of Art Deco architecture.

Across the street (due east, on the corner of Burrard and Hastings) is the elaborate **Vancouver Club** ⑨, the private haunt of the city's top business movers and shakers. This marks the start of the old financial district, which runs southeast along Hastings, where temple-style banks, investment houses, and businesspeople's clubs survive as evidence of the city's sophisticated architectural advances prior to World War I. Until the period between 1966 and 1972, when the first of the bank towers and underground malls on West Georgia Street were developed, this was Canada's westernmost business terminus. **Sinclair Centre** ⑪, at Hastings and Howe streets, is a painstakingly restored complex of government buildings that now houses offices and retail shops; among the four terrazzo structures are the 1905 **Post Office** with its elegant clock tower and the 1913 **Winch Building.** Near Granville Street you'll find the former headquarters (1906–1908) of the **Canadian Imperial Bank of Commerce (CIBC)** ⑫, one of Vancouver's oldest and most powerful chartered banks; the columns, arches, and details are of typically Roman influence. The more Gothic **Royal Bank** ⑬ stands directly across the street. It was intended to be half of a symmetrical building that was never completed, due to the Depression. Striking, though, is the magnificent hall, reminiscent of a European cathedral. The **Toronto–Dominion Bank** ⑭, one block east at the corner of Hastings and Seymour, is of the same style as the CIBC but was built in 1920.

Head northeast up Seymour toward Burrard Inlet and you'll run into the **Canadian Pacific Station** ⑮, the third and most pretentious of three Canadian Pacific Railway passenger terminals. From here, you can either meander through the station and the courtyards to its left or turn north up Cordova, take a right on Howe, and you'll face the soaring canopies of **Canada Place** ⑩, site of Vancouver's primary **cruise ship pier,** the **Trade and Convention Center,** and the luxurious **Pan Pacific Hotel** (☞ Lodging, *below*), with its spectacular three-story lobby, waterfall, and totem poles. Here you can stop for a snack in one of the dining outlets on the water or catch a film at the IMAX theater. Stop off at **Tourism Vancouver Infocentre** across the street (next door to the Waterfront Centre Hotel) to pick up brochures on other Vancouver attractions and events before leaving the area.

TIMING

This walking tour, with time factored in to soak in the intriguing architecture along the route, will take approximately two to three hours if you're not drawn into all the shops along the way. Allow about an hour at the Craft Museum, and another two to three to see the collections at the Art Gallery.

Sights to See

⑩ **Canada Place.** Originally built on an old cargo pier to be the off-site Canadian pavilion in Expo '86, Canada Place was later converted into Vancouver's **Trade and Convention Center.** It is dominated at the shore end by the luxurious **Pan Pacific Hotel** (☞ Lodging, *below*) with its spectacular three-story lobby and waterfall. The fabric roof shaped like 10 sails that covers the convention space has become a landmark of Vancouver's skyline. Below is a cruise-ship facility, and at the north end are an Imax theater, a restaurant, and an outdoor performance space. A prom-

Downtown Vancouver

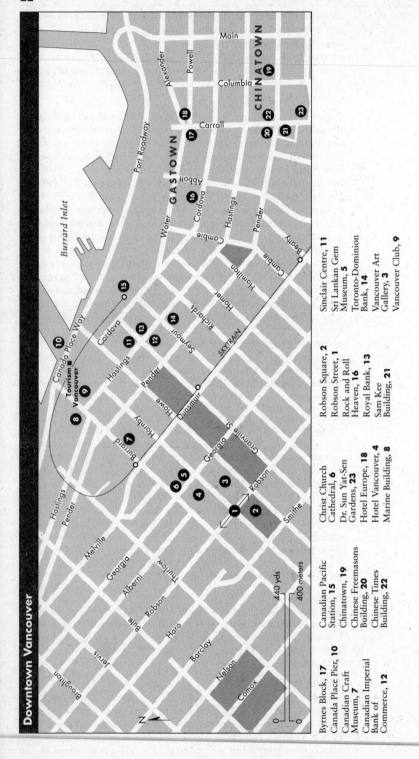

Byrnes Block, **17**
Canada Place Pier, **10**
Canadian Craft Museum, **7**
Canadian Imperial Bank of Commerce, **12**

Canadian Pacific Station, **15**
Chinatown, **19**
Chinese Freemasons Building, **20**
Chinese Times Building, **22**

Christ Church Cathedral, **6**
Dr. Sun Yat-Sen Gardens, **23**
Hotel Europe, **18**
Hotel Vancouver, **4**
Marine Building, **8**

Robson Square, **2**
Robson Street, **1**
Rock and Roll Heaven, **16**
Royal Bank, **13**
Sam Kee Building, **21**

Sinclair Centre, **11**
Sri Lankan Gem Museum, **5**
Toronto-Dominion Bank, **14**
Vancouver Art Gallery, **3**
Vancouver Club, **9**

enade runs along the pier's west side, affording views of the Burrard Inlet harbor and Stanley Park. ⊠ *999 Canada Pl., ☎ 604/775–8687.*

7 Canadian Craft Museum. The Craft Museum, which opened in 1992, is one of the first national cultural facilities dedicated to crafts—historical and contemporary, functional and decorative. Craft embodies the human need for artistic expression in everyday life, and examples here range from elegantly carved utensils with decorative handles to colorful hand-spun and handwoven garments. The two-level museum offers exhibits, lectures, and the Museum Shop, which specializes, of course, in Canadian crafts. The structure was once a medical building, still evident outside in the restored terra-cotta arch and frieze panels showing scenes of individuals administering care. The restful courtyard is a quiet place to take a break. ⊠ *639 Hornby St., ☎ 604/ 687–8266. ☞ $4. ⊙ Apr.–Oct., Mon.–Sat. 10–5, Sun. and holidays noon–5; Nov.–Mar., Mon. and Wed.–Sat. 10–5, Sun. and holidays noon–5.*

15 Canadian Pacific Station. This is the third and most imposing of three Canadian Pacific Railway passenger terminals. Constructed from 1912 to 1914, this terminal replaced the other two as the western terminus for Canada's transcontinental railway. After Canada's railways merged, the station became obsolete until a 1978 renovation turned it into an office-retail complex and SeaBus terminal. Murals in the waiting rooms (now used by Skytrain, SeaBus, and BC Transit passengers) show the scenery passengers once saw on their journeys across Canada. ⊠ *Foot of Granville St., ☎ 604/521–0400 (BC Transit).*

6 Christ Church Cathedral. This tiny church, built in 1895, is the oldest in Vancouver. Constructed in Gothic style with buttresses and pointed-arch windows, it looks like the parish church of an English village. By contrast, the cathedral's rough-hewn interior is that of a frontier town, with Douglas-fir beams and ornate woodwork that offers excellent acoustics for the vespers, carols, and Gregorian chants frequently sung here. ⊠ *690 Burrard St., ☎ 604/682–3848. ⊙ Weekdays 10–4.*

4 Hotel Vancouver. Built in 1939, this is one of the last of the railway-built hotels (the last was the Chateau Whistler, in 1989). Reminiscent of a medieval French castle, this château style has been incorporated into hotels in almost every major Canadian city. With the onset of the Depression, construction was halted here, and the hotel was finished only in time for the visit of King George VI in 1939. It has been renovated twice: During the 1960s it was unfortunately modernized, but the more recent refurbishment is more in keeping with the spirit of what is the most recognizable roof on Vancouver's skyline. The exterior of the building has carvings of malevolent-looking gargoyles at the corners, an ornate chimney, Indian chiefs on the Hornby Street side, and an assortment of grotesque mythological figures. (☞ Lodging, *below.*) ⊠ *900 W. Georgia St., ☎ 604/684–3131.*

8 Marine Building. Constructed in 1931, this Art Deco building is ornamented with terra-cotta bas-reliefs depicting the history of transportation: airships, biplanes, steamships, locomotives, and submarines. These motifs were once considered radical and modernistic adornments, because most buildings were still using classical or Gothic ornamentation. From the east, the Marine Building is reflected in bronze by 999 West Hastings, and from the southeast it is mirrored in silver by the Canadian Imperial Bank of Commerce. Stand on the corner of Hastings and Hornby streets for the best view of the building. ⊠ *355 Burrard St.*

2 Robson Square. Built in 1975 and designed by architect Arthur Erickson to be the gathering place of downtown Vancouver, Robson Square functions from the outside as a park. It encompasses the Vancouver Art Gallery, government offices, and law courts woven together by landscaped walkways, as well as a block-long glass canopy over one of the walkways and a waterfall that helps mask traffic noise. An ice-skating rink and restaurants occupy the below-street level. ⊠ *800 Robson St.*

❶ Robson Street. If you're in for a day of shopping, amble down this street (☞ Shopping, *below*), where you'll find any item from souvenirs to high fashions, and espresso to sushi.

⓫ Sinclair Centre. Outstanding Vancouver architect Richard Henriquez has knitted four government office buildings (built between 1905 and 1939) into Sinclair Centre, an office-retail complex. The two Hastings Street buildings—the 1905 **Post Office** with the elegant clock tower and the 1913 **Winch Building**—are linked with the **Post Office Extension** and **Customs Examining Warehouse** to the north. Painstaking and very costly restoration involved finding master masons—the original terrazzo suppliers in Europe—and uncovering and refurbishing the pressed-metal ceilings. ⊠ *757 W. Hastings St.,* ☏ *604/666–4438.*

❺ Sri Lankan Gem Museum. This museum, housed in a jewelry store with a floor of 9,000 polished Brazilian agates set in pyrite, opened in Cathedral Place in 1993. It has some $5 million worth of gemstones, including moonstones, rubies, lapis, garnets, jade, and emeralds. Many of the gems are from Sri Lanka. Admission proceeds benefit the Vancouver Symphony Orchestra. ⊠ *925 W. Georgia St.,* ☏ *604/688–8528.* 🎟 *$3.50.* ◷ *Mon.–Sat. 10:30–5:30.*

Tourism Vancouver Infocentre. Here you'll find brochures and personnel to answer questions, as well as an attractive Northwest Coast native art collection. ⊠ *200 Burrard St.,* ☏ *604/683–2000.*

❸ Vancouver Art Gallery. This gallery was a classical-style 1912 courthouse until architect Arthur Erickson converted it to a spacious gallery in 1980. Notice the detail: lions that guard the majestic front steps and the use of columns and domes—features borrowed from ancient Roman architecture. Behind the old courthouse, a more modest staircase now serves as a speakers' corner. ⊠ *750 Hornby St.,* ☏ *604/682–5621.* 🎟 *$6, free Thurs. after 5.* ◷ *Mon.–Wed. 10–6, Thurs. and Fri. 10–9, Sat. 10–5, Sun. and holidays noon–5.*

❾ Vancouver Club. Built between 1912 and 1914, this was a gathering place for the city's elite. Its architecture evokes that of private clubs in England inspired by Italian Renaissance palaces. The Vancouver Club is still the private haunt of city business people. ⊠ *915 W. Hastings St.,* ☏ *604/685–9321.*

Chinatown and Gastown

Gastown is where Vancouver originated after Jack Deighton arrived at Burrard Inlet in 1867 with his Indian wife, a barrel of whiskey, and few amenities and set up a saloon to entertain the scattered loggers and trappers living in the area. When the transcontinental train arrived in 1887, Gastown became the transfer point for trade with the Orient and was soon crowded with hotels and warehouses. The Klondike gold rush encouraged further development until 1912, when the "Golden Years" ended. From the 1930s to the 1950s hotels were converted into rooming houses, and the warehouse district shifted elsewhere. The neglected area gradually became run-down. However, both Gastown and Chinatown were declared historic districts in the late 1970s and have been revitalized. Gastown is now chock-a-block with boutiques, cafes, and souvenir shops.

The Chinese were among the first inhabitants of Vancouver, and some of the oldest buildings in the city are in Chinatown. There was already a sizable Chinese community in British Columbia because of the 1858 Cariboo gold rush in central British Columbia, but the greatest influx from China came in the 1880s, during construction of the Canadian Pacific Railway, when 15,000 laborers were imported. Even while doing the hazardous work of blasting the rail bed through the Rocky Mountains, the Chinese were discriminated against. The Anti-Asiatic Riots of 1907 stopped growth in Chinatown for 50 years, and immigration from China was discouraged by more and more restrictive policies, climaxing in a $500 head tax during the 1920s. In the 1960s the city council planned bulldozer urban renewal for Strathcona, the residential part of Chinatown, as well as freeway connections through the most historic blocks of the district. Fortunately, the project was halted, and today Chinatown is an expanding, vital neighborhood fueled by investment from Vancouver's most notable newcomers—immigrants from Hong Kong. It is best to view the buildings in Chinatown from the south side of Pender Street, where the Chinese Cultural Center stands. From here you'll see important details that adorn the upper stories. The style of architecture in Vancouver's Chinatown is patterned on that of Canton and won't be seen in any other Canadian cities.

A Good Walk

★ Pick up Water Street at Richards Street and head east into **Gastown,** named for the original townsite saloon keeper, "Gassy" Jack Deighton. A **statue** of Gassy Jack stands on the west side of Maple Tree Square, at the intersection of Water, Powell, Alexander, and Carrall streets, where he built his first saloon. Along the way you'll pass **Blood Alley** and **Gaoler's Mews,** which are tucked behind 12 Water Street, and **Rock and Roll Heaven** ⑯, a museum devoted to the legends of rock music. At the corner of Water and Cambie streets, you can see and hear the world's first **steam powered clock** (it chimes on the quarter hour). Two buildings of historical and architectural note are the **Byrnes Block** ⑰ on the corner of Water and Carrall streets and the **Hotel Europe** ⑱ (1908–1909) at Powell and Alexander streets.

From Maple Tree Square, walk three blocks south on Carrall Street to ★ Pender Street, where **Chinatown** ⑲ begins. The corner of Carrall and Pender streets, now the western boundary of Chinatown, is one of the neighborhood's most historic spots. It's here that you'll find the **Chinese Freemasons Building** ⑳ (circa 1901) and the **Sam Kee Building** ㉑ (circa 1913), and, directly across Carrall Street, the **Chinese Times Building** ㉒ (circa 1902). Across Pender are the first living classical Chinese gardens built outside China, **Dr. Sun Yat-sen Gardens** ㉓, tucked behind the **Chinese Cultural Center,** which houses exhibition space, classrooms, and the occasional mah-jongg tournament. Finish up by poking around in the open-front markets and import shops that line several blocks of Pender running east.

TIMING

The walk itself will take from two to three hours depending on your pace; allow extra time for the guided tour of the garden in Gastown. Daylight hours are best (though shops and restaurants are open into the night in both areas); there are few traffic signals for safe crossings in Gastown, so avoid commuter rush hours.

Sights to See

Blood Alley and **Gaoler's Mews.** Once the site of the city's first civic buildings—the constable's cabin and courthouse, and a two-cell log jail—today the cobblestone street with antique lighting is home to architectural offices. ⊠ *Behind 12 Water St.*

⑰ Byrnes Block. This building was constructed on the site of Gassy Jack's second saloon after the 1886 Great Fire. The date is just visible at the top of the building above the door where it says "Herman Block," which was its name for a short time. ⊠ *Water and Carrall Sts.*

⑳ Chinese Freemasons Building. This fascinating structure has two completely different styles of facade: The side facing Chinatown presents a fine example of Cantonese-imported recessed balconies; the Carrall Street side displays the standard Victorian style common throughout the British Empire. It was in this building that Dr. Sun Yat-sen hid for months from the agents of the Manchu dynasty while he raised funds for its overthrow, which he accomplished in 1911. ⊠ *1 W. Pender St.*

㉒ Chinese Times Building. Police officers could hear the clicking sounds of clandestine mah-jongg games played after sunset on the building's hidden mezzanine floor. Attempts by vice squads to enforce restrictive policies against the Chinese gamblers proved fruitless, because police were unable to find the players. The building dates to 1902.

㉓ Dr. Sun Yat-sen Gardens. The gardens were built in the 1980s by 52 artisans from Suzhou, the Garden City of the People's Republic. The gardens incorporate design elements and traditional materials from several of that city's centuries-old private gardens. As you walk through the gardens, remember that no power tools, screws, or nails were used in the construction. Free guided tours are offered throughout the day; telephone for times. ⊠ *578 Carrall St.,* ☎ *604/689–7133.* ▨ *$5.* ☽ *Daily 10–6.*

⑱ Hotel Europe. Once billed as the best hotel in the city, this circa 1908–1909 flatiron building was Vancouver's first reinforced concrete structure. Designed as a functional commercial building, the hotel lacks ornamentation and fine detail, a style unusually utilitarian for the time. ⊠ *Alexander and Powell Sts.*

⑯ Rock and Roll Heaven. Formerly the Beatles Museum, Rock and Roll Heaven exhibits memorabilia from Jimi Hendrix, Jim Morrison, the Beatles, and other rock icons. ⊠ *19 Water St.,* ☎ *604/685–8841.* ▨ *$4.* ☽ *Mon.–Sat. 11–7, Sun. noon–7.*

㉑ Sam Kee Building. Constructed in 1913, this building is recognized by *Ripley's Believe It or Not!* as the narrowest building in the world, at just 6 feet wide. Its bay windows overhang the street and the basement burrows under the sidewalk. ⊠ *8 W. Pender St.*

Stanley Park

★ A 1,000-acre wilderness park just blocks from the downtown section of a major city is a rarity. In the 1860s, due to a threat of American invasion, the area that is now **Stanley Park** was designated a military reserve (though it was never needed). When the city of Vancouver was incorporated in 1886, the council's first act was to request that the land be set aside for a park. In 1888 permission was granted and the grounds were named Stanley Park after Lord Stanley, then governor general of Canada.

An afternoon in Stanley Park gives you a capsule tour of Vancouver that includes beaches, the ocean, the harbor, Douglas fir and cedar forests, and a good look at the North Shore mountains. The park sits on a peninsula, and along the shore is a pathway 9 kilometers (5½ miles) long called the seawall. You can drive or bicycle all the way around. Bicy-

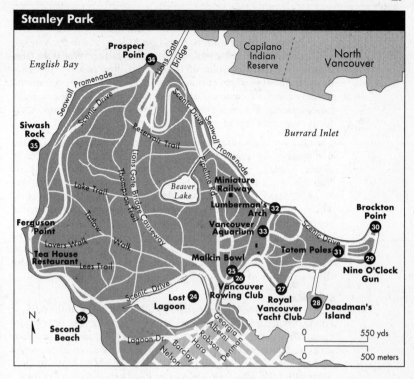

Stanley Park

cles are for rent at the foot of Georgia Street near the park entrance. Cyclists must ride in a counterclockwise direction and stay on their side of the path.

Numbers in the text and margin correspond to points of interest on the Stanley Park map.

A Good Biking or Driving Tour

A good place to start is at the foot of Alberni Street beside **Lost Lagoon** ㉔. Go through the underpass and veer right to the seawall past **Malkin Bowl** ㉕, an open amphitheater. Just past the amphitheater is a cutoff to the left that leads to the renowned **Vancouver Aquarium** ㉝, while the main road continues on to the rest of the park's sights. The old wood structure that you pass next is the **Vancouver Rowing Club** ㉖, a private athletic club established in 1903; a bit farther along is the **Royal Vancouver Yacht Club** ㉗. About ½ kilometer (⅓ mile) away is the causeway to **Deadman's Island** ㉘, a former burial ground for the local Salish Indians and the early settlers. It is now a small naval training base, called H.M.C.S. *Discovery,* that is not open to the public.

Just ahead is the **Nine O'Clock Gun** ㉙, a cannonlike apparatus at the water's edge. Originally it was used to alert fishermen to a curfew ending weekend fishing; now it signals 9 o'clock every night. Just to the north is **Brockton Point** ㉚ and its small but functional lighthouse and foghorn. The **totem poles** ㉛, which are a bit farther down the road and slightly inland on your left, make a popular photo stop for visitors. Continue on and you'll pass the **miniature steam train,** just five minutes northwest of the aquarium; it's a big hit with children as it chugs through the forest. The **children's water park** across the road is also popular throughout the summer.

At kilometer 3 (mile 2) is **Lumberman's Arch** ㉜, a huge log archway dedicated to the workers in Vancouver's first industry. Beside the arch is an asphalt path that leads back to Lost Lagoon and to the Vancouver Aquarium. About 2 kilometers (1¼ miles) farther is the **Lions Gate Bridge**—the halfway point of the seawall. Just past the bridge is **Prospect Point** ㉞, where cormorants build nests. Continuing around the seawall, you'll come to the **English Bay** side and the beginning of sandy beaches. The imposing rock just offshore is **Siwash Rock** ㉟, the focus of a native legend.

The next attraction along the seawall is the large saltwater pool at **Second Beach** ㊱. In summer it is a children's pool with lifeguards, but in winter, when the pool is drained, skateboarders perform stunts here. You can take a shortcut from here back to Lost Lagoon by walking along the perpendicular road behind the pool, which cuts into the park. The wood footbridge that's ahead will lead you to a path along the south side of the lagoon to your starting point at the foot of Alberni or Georgia street. If you continue along the seawall, you will emerge from the park into a high-rise residential neighborhood, the **West End.** You can walk back to Alberni Street along Denman Street, where there are plenty of places to stop for coffee, ice cream, or a drink.

TIMING

You'll find parking lots near virtually all of the sights of the park; if you're driving, take the time to park and get a better look or take pictures. With that advice in mind, expect a driving tour to take about an hour. Biking will depend on your speed, but with stops to see the sights, expect it to take several hours. Add at least two hours to thoroughly tour the aquarium, and you've filled a half- to full-day tour.

Sights to See

㉕ **Malkin Bowl.** This open amphitheater becomes a theater under the stars during the summer. ⊠ *1st right off Pipeline Rd. past park entrance,* ☎ *604/687–0174.*

㉞ **Prospect Point.** Here cormorants build their seaweed nests along the cliff's ledges. The large black diving birds are distinguished by their long necks and beaks; when not nesting, they often perch atop floating logs or boulders. Another remarkable bird found along the park's shore is the beautiful great blue heron, which reaches up to 4 feet tall and has a wing span of 6 feet. The heron preys on passing fish in the waters here; the oldest heron rookery in British Columbia is in the trees near the aquarium.

㉟ **Siwash Rock.** Legend tells of a young Indian who, about to become a father, bathed persistently to wash his sins away so that his son could be born pure; for his devotion he was blessed by the gods and immortalized in the shape of Siwash Rock. Two small rocks, said to be his wife and child, are up on the cliff just above the site.

㉛ **Totem poles.** Totem poles were not made in the Vancouver area; these, carved of cedar by the Kwakiutl and Haida peoples late in the last century, were brought to the park from the north coast of British Columbia. The carved animals, fish, birds, and mythological creatures were like family coats-of-arms or crests.

★ ㉝ **Vancouver Aquarium.** The humid Amazon rain-forest gallery has piranhas, giant cockroaches, alligators, tropical birds, and jungle vegetation. Other displays show the underwater life of coastal British Columbia, the Canadian arctic, and other areas of the world. There are also huge tanks (populated with orca and beluga whales and playful sea otters) that have large windows for underwater viewing. ☎ *604/*

682–1118. 🎫 $11. ⏲ July–Labor Day, daily 9–8; Labor Day–June, daily 10–5:30.

Granville Island

★ **Granville Island** was just a sandbar until World War I, when the federal government dredged False Creek for access to the sawmills that lined the shore. The sludge from the creek was heaped up onto the sandbar to create the island and to house much-needed industrial- and logging-equipment plants. By the late 1960s, however, many of the businesses that had once flourished on Granville Island had deteriorated. Buildings were rotted, rat-infested, and dangerous. In 1971, the federal government bought up leases from businesses that wanted to leave and offered an imaginative plan to refurbish the island with a public market, marine activities, and artisans' studios. The opposite shore of False Creek was the site of the 1986 World's Fair and is now part of the largest urban redevelopment plan in North America.

The small island has no residents except for a small houseboat community. Most of the former industrial buildings and tin sheds have been retained but are painted in upbeat reds, yellows, and blues. Through a committee of community representatives, the government regulates the types of businesses that settle on Granville Island; most of the businesses permitted here involve food, crafts, marine activities, and the arts.

Numbers in the text and margin correspond to points of interest on the Granville Island map.

A Good Walk

To reach Granville Island on foot, make the 15-minute walk from downtown Vancouver to the south end of Hornby Street. Aquabuses (☎ 604/689–5858) depart here and deliver passengers across False Creek to Granville Island Public Market. Another option is the Granville Island Ferries (☎ 604/684–7781), which leave every five minutes from a dock behind the Vancouver Aquatic Centre. Still another way to reach the island is to take a 20-minute ride on a B.C. Transit (☎ 604/261–5100) bus; to do this take a University of British Columbia (U.B.C.), Granville, Arbutus, Cambie, or Oak bus from downtown to Granville and Broadway, and transfer to Granville Island Bus 51 or False Creek Bus 50 from Gastown or stops on Granville Street for direct service to Granville Island. Parking is free for one to three hours; paid parking is available in garages on the island.

The ferry will drop you off at the **Granville Island Public Market** ㊲, where fast food outlets and fruit and vegetable, meat, coffee, liquor, and flower stalls are enclosed in the 50,000-square-foot building. At the **Granville Island Information Centre** ㊳, catercorner to the market, stop to pick up a map of the island.

Walk south on Johnston Street to begin a clockwise loop tour of the island. **Ocean Cement** is one of the last of the island's former industries; its lease does not expire until the year 2004. Next door is the **Emily Carr Institute of Art and Design** ㊴. Past the art school, on the left, is **Sea Village,** one of the only houseboat communities in Vancouver. Take the boardwalk that starts at the houseboats and continues partway around the island.

As you circle around to Cartwright Street, stop in **Kakali** at number 1249, where you can watch the fabrication of fine handmade paper from such materials as blue jeans, herbs, and sequins. Another unusual artisan on the island is the glassblower at the **Small Sterling Glass Studio** (✉ 1404 Old Bridge St.), around the corner. The next two attrac-

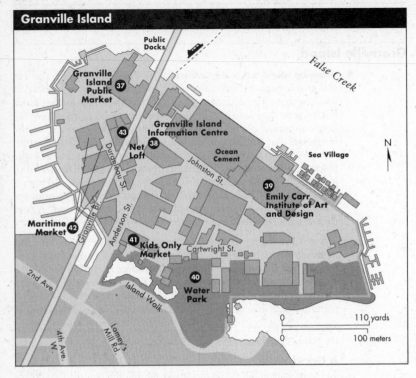

Granville Island

tions will make any child's visit to Granville Island a thrill. First, on Cartwright Street, is the children's **Water Park** ㊵. A bit farther down, beside Isadora's restaurant, is the **Kids Only Market** ㊶, selling anything and everything a child could desire. Cross Anderson Street and walk down Duranleau Street. On your left are the seafaring stores of the **Maritime Market** ㊷. The last place to explore on Granville Island is the **Net Loft** ㊸, a collection of small, high-quality stores. Once you have come full circle, you can either take the ferry back to downtown Vancouver or stay for dinner and catch a play at the **Arts Club** (☎ 604/687–1644) or the **Waterfront Theater** (☎ 604/685–6217).

TIMING

If your schedule is tight, you can complete a tour of Granville Island in three to four hours; if you're a shopping fanatic, plan for a full day here.

Sights to See

㊴ **Emily Carr Institute of Art and Design.** Just inside the front door of the institute, to your right, is the **Charles H. Scott Gallery**, which hosts contemporary multimedia exhibits. ⊠ *1399 Johnston St.,* ☎ *604/687–2345.* ☜ *Free.* ⊗ *Daily noon–5.*

㊳ **Granville Island Information Centre.** Maps are available here, and a slide show depicts the evolution of Granville Island. Ask about special-events days; perhaps there's a boat show, an outdoor concert, a dance performance, or some other happening. ⊠ *1592 Johnston St.,* ☎ *604/666–5784.* ⊗ *Daily 8–6.*

㊲ **Granville Island Public Market.** As the government allows no chain stores, each outlet here is unique, and most are of good quality. You probably won't be able to leave the market without a snack, espresso, or fixings for a lunch out on the wharf. Year-round you'll see mounds of raspberries, strawberries, blueberries, and more exotic fruits like persimmons and litchis. You'll find plenty of outdoor seating on the water side of the market. ⊠ *1669 Johnston St., under Granville Street bridge, 2nd floor,* ☎ *604/666–6477.* ☉ *Memorial Day–Labor, daily 9–6; Labor Day–Memorial Day, Tues.–Sun. 9–6.*

40 **The Granville Island Water Park.** This kid's paradise offers a wading pool, sprinklers, and a fire hydrant made for children to shower one another. ⊠ *1318 Cartwright St.,* ☎ *604/665–3425.* ☞ *Free.* ☉ *June–Aug., daily 10–6.*

41 **Kids Only Market.** Yet another slice of kid's heaven on Granville Island, the Kids Only Market has two floors of small shops selling toys, arts-and-crafts materials, dolls, records and tapes, chemistry sets, and other good kids stuff. ⊠ *1496 Cartwright St.,* ☎ *604/689–8447.* ☉ *Daily 10–6.*

42 **Maritime Market.** These businesses are all geared to the sea. The first walkway to the left, Maritime Mews, leads to marinas and dry docks. ⊠ *1650 Duranleau St.,* ☎ *604/687–1556.*

43 **The Net Loft.** In this blue building is a collection of small, high-quality stores, including a bookstore, a crafts store-gallery, a kitchenware shop, a postcard shop, a custom-made hat shop, a handmade paper store, a British Columbian native Indian gallery, and a do-it-yourself jewelry store. ⊠ *1666 Johnston St., across from Public Market,* ☎ *604/ 876–6637.*

Greater Vancouver

The metropolis of Vancouver includes North Vancouver across Burrard Inlet and the larger, more residential peninsula south of downtown bordered by English Bay to the north, the Strait of Georgia to the west, and the Fraser River to the south. There are wonderful museums, gardens, and natural sights sprinkled throughout Greater Vancouver, but you'll need a car to maximize your time and cover as much ground as your itinerary allows.

Numbers in the margin correspond to points of interest on the Vancouver Exploring map.

A Good Drive

This tour includes numerous museums, so start out early and head south across the Burrard Bridge to Vanier Park. Here you'll find the **Vancouver Museum** ㊹ (showcasing the city's history in cheerful, life-size displays), the **Pacific Space Centre** ㊹ (a high-tech museum focusing on outer space), and the **Maritime Museum** ㊺ (tracing the maritime history of the West Coast). There are hands-on exhibits to attract the kids at each of these. Next, follow Ogden Avenue out of the park to Fourth Avenue, then go west to the University of British Columbia to visit the **Museum of Anthropology** ㊻, housing an amazing collection of totem poles and other Native American artifacts, and **Nitobe Memorial Garden** ㊼, a Japanese-style strolling garden.

For more gardens, follow Southwest Marine Drive through the U.B.C. grounds and turn left onto 41st Avenue. Turn left again on Oak Street to reach the entrance of the **Van Dusen Botanical Garden** ㊽ (it'll be on your left); this 55-acre complex is planted with English-style mazes, water gardens, herb gardens, and more. Return to 41st Avenue, continue farther east, and then turn left on Cambie Street to reach **Queen Elizabeth Park** ㊾, which overlooks the city.

You can head back downtown across the Cambie bridge (stay in the right lane), which flows onto Smithe Street. Turn right on Homer and look for parking within the next few blocks so that you can stop to see **Library Square** ⑩, the city's new multimillion dollar central library project that resembles Rome's coliseum. From there it's only three more blocks to B.C. Place, where you'll find the **B.C. Sports Hall of Fame and Museum** ⑪, devoted to British Columbia's favorite sons who made a name for themselves in sports. Turn south on Cambie and follow it to Pacific Boulevard (don't cross the Cambie Bridge), which winds east around False Creek and turns into Quebec Street at the head of the Creek. Turn right here, and right again into the parking lot of **Science World** ⑫, a hands-on museum. After a science lesson, head straight across Quebec to Main Street, turn left, and make a second left at the Georgia Viaduct, which leads onto Dunsmuir. Follow it for eight or so city blocks, turn left on Howe Street, then right onto Georgia, which will take you through town and Stanley Park and across the Lions Gate Bridge to North Vancouver. Follow the signs into the mountains of the North Shore to see the **Capilano Suspension Bridge and Park** ⑬, where a cedar plank footbridge swings high above the Capilano River. Nearby in the Capilano Regional Park, the **Capilano Salmon Hatchery** ⑭ is another good spot to visit. Up the hill a bit farther, at the end of the Nancy Greene Highway, is **Grouse Mountain** ⑮, where you can ride a funicular to see Vancouver views.

TIMING

To cover all the sights of Greater Vancouver, taking sufficient time at each of the museums and gardens, could easily take two days. Either pick and choose those you really want to see (skipping a few along the route), or limit yourself to the sights south of the city one day and save the remaining sights downtown and on the North Shore for another day.

Sights to See

⑪ **B.C. Sports Hall of Fame and Museum.** Part of the B.C. Place Stadium complex, this museum shows video documentaries and has photographs, costumes, and an array of sporting equipment on display. Bring tennis shoes to wear in the high-tech, hands-on participation gallery. ⊠ B.C. Place, 777 Pacific Blvd. S, ☎ 604/687–5523. ☞ $2. ☾ Wed.– Sun. 9–5.

⑭ **Capilano Salmon Hatchery.** In the Capilano Regional Park, the hatchery has viewing areas and exhibits about the life cycle of the salmon. ⊠ 4500 Capilano Park Rd., ☎ 604/666–1790. ☾ Call for seasonal hours. ☞ Free.

⑬ **Capilano Suspension Bridge and Park.** At this, Vancouver's oldest tourist attraction, you can get a taste of the mountains and test your mettle on the swaying, 450-foot cedar plank suspension bridge that hangs 230 feet above the rushing Capilano River. The amusement park also has viewing decks, nature trails amid tall firs and cedars, a gift shop, a totem carving shed, and displays for the kids. ⊠ 3735 Capilano Rd., North Vancouver, ☎ 604/987–7474. ☞ Call for admission fees. ☾ Call for seasonal hours.

⑮ **Grouse Mountain.** The Skyride to the top is a great way to take in stunning city, sea, and mountain vistas. In the theater at the peak you can catch a film on Vancouver's transformation from a string of scattered native, trapper, and logger settlements to a bustling, modern metropolis. ⊠ 6400 Nancy Greene Way, North Vancouver, ☎ 604/984–0661. ☾ Call for seasonal hours. ☞ Gondola $15, theater $3.

⑩ **Library Square.** Built to evoke images of the coliseum in Rome, the spiraling library building, open plazas, frescoed waterfall, and shaded atriums of the new Library Square were completed in 1995. This architectural stunner is a favorite backdrop for current movie productions, so you may see it at the movies or on television before you actually visit it. The book collection is moved about on motorized shelving systems in the ultra-high-tech library that fills the core of the structure; the outer edge of the spiral houses trendy boutiques, coffee shops, and a fine book and gift shop that benefits the library. ⊠ *350 W. Georgia St.,* ☎ *604/331–3600.* ☉ *Mon.–Wed. 10–9, Thur.–Sat. 10–6; also Oct.–Apr., Sun. 1–5.*

🖑 ㊺ **Maritime Museum.** This museum on English Bay traces the history of marine activities on the West Coast. Permanent exhibits depict the port of Vancouver, the fishing industry, and early explorers; the model ships on display are a delight. Traveling exhibits vary but always have a maritime theme. Guided tours are led through the double-masted schooner *St. Roch,* the first ship to sail in both directions through the treacherous Northwest Passage. A changing variety of restored heritage boats from different cultures is moored behind the museum, and a huge Kwakiutl totem pole stands out front. ⊠ *1905 Ogden Ave., north end of Cypress St., via Granville Island Ferry,* ☎ *604/257–8300.* ⊞ *$5.* ☉ *May–Aug., daily 10–5; Sept.–Apr., Tues.–Sun. 10–5.*

★ ㊻ **Museum of Anthropology.** The MOA is Vancouver's most spectacular museum, focusing on the arts of the Pacific Northwest natives and aboriginals from around the world, including the works of Bill Reid, Canada's most respected Haida Indian carver. His *The Raven and the First Men,* which took five carvers more than three years to complete, is its centerpiece. Reid's Pacific Northwest Coast artworks are world renowned. On the campus of the University of British Columbia, the museum is housed in an award-winning glass-and-concrete structure designed by Arthur Erickson. In the Great Hall are large and dramatic totem poles, ceremonial archways, and dugout canoes—all adorned with carvings of frogs, eagles, ravens, bears, and salmon. Also showcased are exquisite carvings of gold, silver, and argillite (a black stone found in the Queen Charlotte Islands), as well as masks, tools, and costumes from many other cultures. The museum contains a ceramics wing, which houses about 600 pieces from 15th- to 19th-century Europe. ⊠ *6393 N.W. Marine Dr.,* ☎ *604/822–3825.* ⊞ *$5, free Tues.* ☉ *Tues. 11–9, Wed.–Sun. 11–5.*

㊼ **Nitobe Memorial Garden.** This 2½-acre garden is considered the most authentic Japanese garden outside Japan. The circular path around the park symbolizes the cycle of life and provides a tranquil view from every direction. In April and May cherry blossoms are the highlight, and in June the irises are magnificent. ⊠ *1903 West Mall, University of British Columbia,* ☎ *604/822–6038.* ⊞ *$3.* ☉ *Summer, daily 10–6; winter, weekdays 10–3.*

🖑 ㊹ **Pacific Space Centre.** At press time, the facility was undergoing expansion scheduled for completion in the spring of 1997. The new facility, called Pacific Space Centre, will contain interactive exhibits and high-tech learning systems—a virtual reality Cyberwalk, a kinetic space ride simulator, and a theater showcasing Canada's achievements in space—advanced enough to qualify it for NASA Teacher Resource Center status. During the day, catch the astronomy show at the **H.R. MacMillan Planetarium** on site. If the sky is clear, the half-meter telescope at the **Gordon MacMillan Southam Observatory** is focused on whatever stars or planets are worth watching that night. ⊠ *1100 Chestnut St., Vanier Park,* ☎ *604/738–7827; special-events schedule, 604/738–2855.* ⊞ *Observatory free, planetarium shows vary.* ☉ *Observatory daily 7 PM–11 PM; planetarium July–early Sept., daily 11–4.*

49 **Queen Elizabeth Park.** This park has lavish gardens brimming with roses and other flowers, an abundance of grassy picnicking spots, and illuminated fountains. In the **Bloedel Conservatory,** you can see tropical and desert plants and 35 species of free-flying tropical birds. Other park facilities include 20 tennis courts, lawn bowling, pitch and putt, and a restaurant. ⊠ *Cambie St. and 33rd Ave.,* ☎ *604/872–5513.* ⊑ *Conservatory $3.* ☉ *Apr.–Sept., weekdays 9–8, weekends 10–9; Oct.–Mar., daily 10–5.*

52 **Science World.** In a gigantic shiny dome built over an Omnimax Theater for Expo '86, this hands-on museum encourages visitors to touch and participate in the theme exhibits. The special Search Gallery is aimed at younger children, as are the fun-filled demonstrations given in Center Stage. ⊠ *1455 Quebec St.,* ☎ *604/268–6363.* ⊑ *Science World $8, Omnimax $9.* ☉ *Weekdays 10–5, weekends 10–6.*

44 **Vancouver Museum.** This museum's permanent exhibits focus on the city's early history and native art and culture. Life-size replicas of an 1897 Canadian Pacific Railway passenger car, a trading post, and a Victorian parlor, as well as a real dugout canoe, are highlights. ⊠ *1100 Chestnut St., Vanier Park,* ☎ *604/736–4431.* ⊑ *$5, extra charge for special exhibitions.* ☉ *Summer, daily 10–5; winter, Tues.–Sun. 10–5.*

48 **Van Dusen Botanical Garden.** On what was a 55-acre golf course now grows one of the largest collections of ornamental plants in Canada. Native and exotic plant displays include a shrubbery maze; rhododendrons bloom in May and June. For a bite to eat, stop in Sprinklers Restaurant (☎ *604/261–0011*), on the grounds. ⊠ *5251 Oak St., at 37th Ave.,* ☎ *604/266–7194.* ⊑ *$4.50.* ☉ *July and Aug., daily 10–9; Oct.–Apr., daily 10–4; May, June, and Sept., daily 10–6.*

DINING

American

$$ ✕ **Griffin's.** The Sunday brunch ambience here is cheerful, energetic, and kid-oriented: Kids in miniature chef's hats (provided by the restaurant) whip up their own pancakes and take turns churning ice cream for dessert. The rest of the week the emphasis is on the adult crowd. This brasserie uniquely blends the charm of old Italy with sophisticated design and fresh, regional ingredients. Squash-yellow walls, bold black-and-white tiles, and splashy food art keep it lively. The open kitchen prepares inspired cuisine, including such buffet selections as convict bread (a round loaf stuffed with goat cheese, olives, tomatoes, and peppers in olive oil), smoked salmon, chicken pasta al pesto, and baked Pacific cod. ⊠ *900 W. Georgia St.,* ☎ *604/662–1900. Reservations essential. AE, D, DC, MC, V.*

$ ✕ **Isadora's.** Not only does Isadora's offer good coffee and a "West Coast–fresh" menu that ranges from lox and bagels to vegetarian pastas and seafood platters, but it also has children's specials and an inside play area packed with toys. Rest rooms with changing-tables accommodate families. In summer, the restaurant opens onto Granville Island's water park. Service can be slow, but Isadora's staff is friendly. The restaurant is no-smoking. ⊠ *1540 Old Bridge St., Granville Island,* ☎ *604/681–8816. DC, MC, V. Closed dinner Mon. Sept.–May.*

Chinese

$$–$$$ ✕ **Imperial Chinese Seafood.** This elegant Cantonese restaurant in the
★ Art Deco Marine Building offers stupendous views through two-story floor-to-ceiling windows of Stanley Park and the North Shore mountains across Coal Harbour. Any dish featuring lobster, crab, or shrimp from the live tanks is recommended, as is the dim sum served every day from

Downtown Vancouver Dining

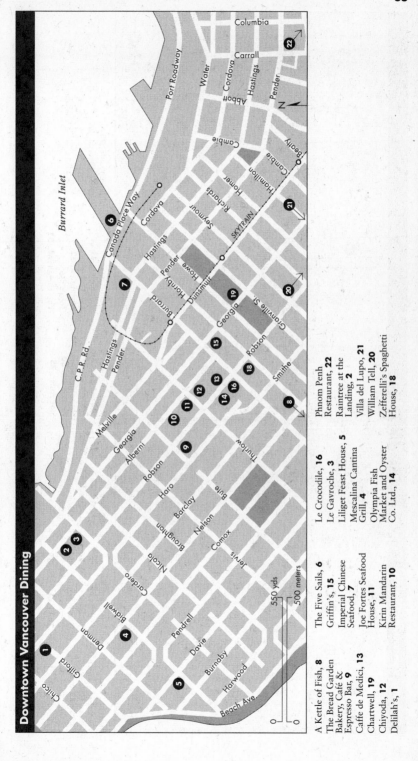

Burrard Inlet

A Kettle of Fish, **8**
The Bread Garden Bakery, Café & Espresso Bar, **9**
Caffe de Medici, **13**
Chartwell, **19**
Chiyoda, **12**
Delilah's, **1**

The Five Sails, **6**
Griffin's, **15**
Imperial Chinese Seafood, **7**
Joe Fortes Seafood House, **11**
Kirin Mandarin Restaurant, **10**

Le Crocodile, **16**
Le Gavroche, **3**
Liliget Feast House, **5**
Mescalina Cantina Grill, **4**
Olympia Fish Market and Oyster Co. Ltd, **14**

Phnom Penh Restaurant, **22**
Raintree at the Landing, **2**
Villa del Lupo, **21**
William Tell, **20**
Zefferelli's Spaghetti House, **18**

Greater Vancouver Dining

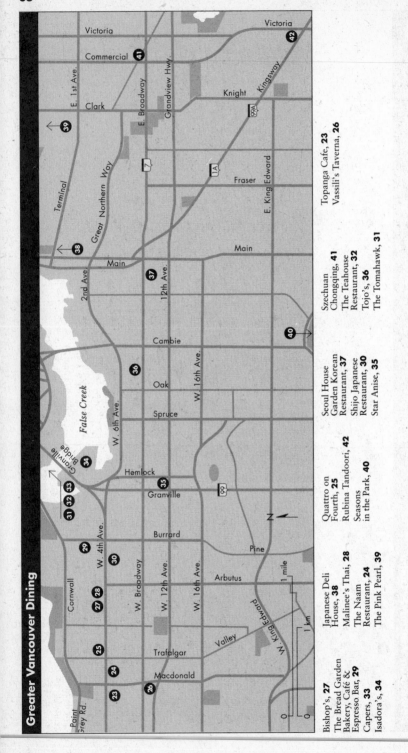

Victoria

Commercial **41**

Victoria **42**

E. 1st Ave.

Clark

E. Broadway

Grandview Hwy.

Knight

Kingsway

39 ←

Great Northern Way

Terminal

7

1A

Fraser

E. King Edward

99A

38 ←

2nd Ave.

Main

Main

12th Ave.

37

False Creek

Cambie

40 →

W. 16th Ave.

Oak

36

Spruce

W. 6th Ave.

W. 16th Ave.

Granville Bridge

34

Hemlock

35

33

31 32

Granville

99

Burrard

N ←

Pine

W. 4th Ave.

29

30

W. Broadway

Arbutus

W. 12th Ave.

W. 16th Ave.

W. King Edward

Cornwall

27 28

Valley

25

W. King Edward

24

Trafalgar

Macdonald

23

26

Point Grey Rd.

0   1 km

0   1 mile

Bishop's, **27**
The Bread Garden
Bakery, Café &
Espresso Bar, **29**
Capers, **33**
Isadora's, **34**

Japanese Deli
House, **38**
Malinee's Thai, **28**
The Naam
Restaurant, **24**
The Pink Pearl, **39**

Quattro on
Fourth, **25**
Rubina Tandoori, **42**
Seasons
in the Park, **40**

Seoul House
Garden Korean
Restaurant, **37**
Shijo Japanese
Restaurant, **30**
Star Anise, **35**

Szechuan
Chongqing, **41**
The Teahouse
Restaurant, **32**
Tojo's, **36**
The Tomahawk, **31**

Topanga Cafe, **23**
Vassili's Taverna, **26**

11 to 2:30. Portions tend to be small and pricey (especially the abalone, shark's fin, and bird's nest delicacies) but never fail to please. ✉ *355 Burrard St.,* ☎ *604/688–8191. Reservations essential. AE, MC, V.*

$$ ✕ **Kirin Mandarin Restaurant.** Fish swim in tanks set into the slate-green walls, part of the lavish decorations of this restaurant serving a smattering of northern Chinese cuisines. Dishes include Shanghai-style smoked eel, Peking duck, and Szechuan hot-and-spicy scallops. Kirin is just two blocks from most of the major downtown hotels. A second location at Cambie focuses on milder Cantonese creations. ✉ *1166 Alberni St., 102,* ☎ *604/682–8833;* ✉ *555 W. 12th Ave.,* ☎ *604/879–8038. Reservations essential. AE, DC, MC, V.*

$$ ✕ **Pink Pearl.** This noisy, 650-seat Cantonese restaurant has tanks of live seafood—crab, shrimp, geoduck, oysters, abalone, rock cod, lobsters, and scallops. Menu highlights include clams in black-bean sauce, crab sautéed with five spices (a spicy dish sometimes translated as crab with peppery salt), and Pink Pearl's version of crisp-skinned chicken. Arrive early for dim sum on the weekend if you don't want to be caught in the lineup. ✉ *1132 E. Hastings St.,* ☎ *604/253–4316. Reservations essential. AE, DC, MC, V.*

$ ✕ **Szechuan Chongqing.** At this unpretentious, white-tablecloth restaurant, try the Szechuan-style crunchy green beans tossed with garlic and ground pork or the Chongqing chicken—a boneless chicken served on a bed of spinach cooked in dry heat until crisp, giving it the texture of dried seaweed and a salty, rich, and nutty taste. ✉ *1668 W. Broadway,* ☎ *604/734–1668. Reservations essential. AE, MC, V.*

Continental

$$$–$$$$ ✕ **Chartwell.** Named after Sir Winston Churchill's country home (a
★ painting of which hangs over the green marble fireplace), the flagship dining room at the Four Seasons hotel (☞ Lodging, *below*) looks like an upper-class British club. Floor-to-ceiling dark wood paneling, deep leather chairs, and a quiet setting make this the city's top spot for a power lunch. The chefs cook robust, inventive Continental food as well as lighter offerings and a variety of low-calorie, low-fat entrées. Favorites include tomato basil soup with gin, rack of lamb, and a variety of salmon offerings. ✉ *791 W. Georgia St.,* ☎ *604/844–6715. Reservations essential. Jacket and tie. AE, DC, MC, V.*

$$$–$$$$ ✕ **William Tell.** Silver service plates, embossed linen napkins, and a silver vase on each table set the tone of Swiss luxury. The William Tell serves excellent Continental food on the main floor of the Georgian Court Hotel. Chef Christian Lindner offers sautéed veal sweetbreads with red onion marmalade and marsala sauce and such Swiss specialties as *Zürcher Geschnezeltes* (thinly sliced veal with mushrooms in a light white wine sauce) and *Bündnerfleisch* (paper-thin slices of air-dried beef). Reserve in advance for the all-you-can-eat "Swiss Farmer's Buffet" on Sunday night. ✉ *765 Beatty St.,* ☎ *604/688–3504. Reservations essential. Jacket and tie. AE, DC, MC, V.*

$$$ ✕ **Seasons in the Park.** Seasons has a commanding view over the park gardens to the city lights and the mountains beyond. In a comfortable room with lots of light wood and white tablecloths, this restaurant in Queen Elizabeth Park serves a conservative Continental menu with such standards as grilled salmon with fresh mint and roast duck with sun-dried cranberry sauce. ✉ *Queen Elizabeth Park at 33rd and Cambie St.,* ☎ *604/874–8008. Reservations essential. AE, MC, V. Closed Dec. 25.*

$$$ ✕ **Teahouse Restaurant.** The best of the Stanley Park restaurants is perfectly poised for watching sunsets over the water, especially from its glassed-in conservatorylike wing. Although the Teahouse has a less innovative menu than its sister restaurant, Seasons in the Park, certain specialties, such as the cream of carrot soup, lamb with herb crust, and the perfectly grilled fish, don't need any meddling. ⊠ *7501 Stanley Park Dr., at Ferguson Point, Stanley Park,* ☎ *604/669–3281. Reservations essential. AE, MC, V. Closed Dec. 25.*

Deli/Bakery

$ ✕ **Bread Garden Bakery, Café & Espresso Bar.** Once a croissant bakery, this is now the ultimate Kitsilano 24-hour hangout. Salads, quiches, elaborate cakes and pies, giant muffins, and cappuccino draw a steady stream of the young and fashionable. The wait in line may be long here or at any of its other locations. Reports indicate that quality has suffered with the rapid expansion, but the Garden's following is still strong. ⊠ *2996 Granville St.,* ☎ *604/736–6465;* ⊠ *1880 W. 1st Ave.,* ☎ *604/738–6684;* ⊠ *812 Bute St.,* ☎ *604/688–3213. AE, MC, V.*

East Indian

$$ ✕ **Rubina Tandoori.** For the best East Indian food in the city, try Ru-
★ bina Tandoori, 20 minutes from downtown. The large menu spans most of the subcontinent's cuisines, and the especially popular *chevda* (an East Indian salty snack) is shipped to fans all over North America. Non-smokers sit in the smaller, funkier back room with the paintings of coupling gods and goddesses; smokers have the slightly more subdued front room. ⊠ *1962 Kingsway,* ☎ *604/874–3621. Reservations essential. DC, MC, V. Closed Sun.*

French

$$$ ✕ **Le Gavroche.** At this charming, somewhat formal turn-of-the-century house, a woman dining with a man will be offered a menu without prices. The classic French cooking, lightened—but by no means reduced—to nouvelle cuisine, on the menu also includes such simple dishes as smoked salmon with blini and sour cream. Other options may be as complex as sea bass with white beans, garlic confit, and parsley and lemon jus or grilled veal tenderloin with chanterelles and lobster sauce. The excellent wine list stresses Bordeaux. Tables by the front window promise mountains-and-water views. ⊠ *1616 Alberni St.,* ☎ *604/685–3924. Reservations essential. AE, DC, MC, V. No lunch weekends. Closed holidays.*

$$ ✕ **Le Crocodile.** In a roomy location off Burrard Street, Chef Michael Jacob serves extremely well-cooked, simple food at reasonable prices. His Alsatian background shines with the caramel-sweet onion tart. Anything that involves innards is superb, and even such old standards as duck à l'orange are worth ordering here. Sadly, the quality is not what it was years ago in the smaller incarnation of this well-known restaurant. ⊠ *100–909 Burrard St.,* ☎ *604/669–4298. Reservations essential. AE, DC, MC, V. No Sat. lunch. Closed Sun. and holidays.*

Greek

$$ ✕ **Vassili's Taverna.** The menu in this family-run restaurant in the heart of the city's small Greek community is almost as conventional as the decor: checked tablecloths and mandatory paintings of white fishing villages and the blue Aegean Sea. At Vassili's, though, even standards become memorable due to the flawless preparation. The house specialty is a deceptively simple *kotopoulo* (a half chicken, pounded flat, herbed, and charbroiled). ⊠ *2884 W. Broadway,* ☎ *604/733–3231. Reservations essential. AE, DC, MC, V. No lunch weekends. Closed Mon.*

Health Food

$ ✕ **Capers.** Hidden in the back of the most lavish health food store in
★ the Lower Mainland, Capers drips with earth-mother chic: wood tables, potted plants, and heady aromas from the store's bakery. Breakfast starts at 8: free-range eggs and bacon with no additives, or
feather-light blueberry pancakes. Top choices from the lunch and dinner menu include roasted squash soup and local mushrooms with
capellini. The newer 4th Avenue location, with its dining room above
the store, is by far the nicer of the two; the West Vancouver store is
somewhat old and dingy. ✉ *2496 Marine Dr., W. Vancouver,* ☎ *604/*
925–3374; ✉ *2285 W. 4th Ave.,* ☎ *604/739–6685. MC, V. No Sun.*
dinner at Marine Dr.

$ ✕ **Naam Restaurant.** Vancouver's oldest alternative restaurant is open
24 hours, so if you need to satisfy a late-night tofu-burger craving, rest
easy. The Naam also serves wine, beer, cappuccino, and wicked chocolate desserts, along with the vegetarian stir-fries. Wood tables and
kitchen chairs provide a homey atmosphere. On warm summer evenings,
try the outdoor courtyard at the back of the restaurant. ✉ *2724 W.*
4th Ave., ☎ *604/738–7151. MC, V.*

Italian

$$$ ✕ **Caffè de Medici.** This elegant, somewhat formal restaurant has or-
nate molded ceilings, rich green velvet curtains and chair coverings,
portraits of the Medici family, and a courtly, peaceful atmosphere. Al-
though an enticing antipasto table sits in the center of the room, con-
sider the *bresaola* (air-dried beef marinated in olive oil, lemon, and
pepper) as a worthwhile appetizer. Try the rack of lamb in a mint, mus-
tard, and vermouth sauce. Any of the pastas is a safe bet. ✉ *1025 Rob-*
son St., ☎ *604/669–9322. Reservations essential. AE, D, DC, MC,*
V. No lunch weekends.

$$$ ✕ **Villa del Lupo.** Ask the top chefs in town where they go for Italian,
★ and Villa del Lupo is the answer more often than not. Country-house
elegant decor sets a romantic tone, but come prepared to roll up the
sleeves and mop up the sauce with a chunk of crusty bread. Agnolotti
pasta stuffed with roasted duck, veggies, and ricotta cheese; rabbit loin
with mushrooms, black olives, and thyme; and braised lamb osso buco
in a sauce of tomatoes, red wine, cinnamon, and lemon are favorites
here. ✉ *869 Hamilton St.,* ☎ *604/688–7436. Reservations essential.*
AE, MC, V. No lunch weekends.

$$ ✕ **Quattro on Fourth.** This new kid on the block in Kitsilano shot to
stardom quickly. Mosaic floor, mustard-colored walls with stark green
and mauve stenciled borders, cherry-stained tables, and a wraparound
covered porch for al fresco dining set the Mediterranean atmosphere.
Mushroom lovers usually jump at the truffle fettuccine, but if you can't
make up your mind, there's the antipasto platter and *combinazione* (a
plate for two featuring the five most popular pastas and sauces). The
gelato trio is a perfect topper. ✉ *2611 W. 4th Ave.,* ☎ *604/734–4444.*
Reservations essential. AE, DC, MC, V. No lunch. Closed Dec. 25.

$$ ✕ **Zefferelli's Spaghetti House.** As one might guess from the name,
spaghetti, penne, fusilli, tortellini, and fettuccine dressed in creative but
subtle sauces—from roasted garlic, broccoli, feta cheese, and tomatoes
sauce to traditional meat sauce—play first string at Zefferelli's, but osso
buco (braised veal with veggies served over pesto orzo), grilled prawns,
and chicken saltimbocca (with prosciutto and sage finished in marsala
wine) are strong competition. Done up in forest green, mustard, and

persimmon, the trendy, somewhat rushed dining room has an open kitchen at one end and a wall of windows overlooking busy Robson Street at the other. ⊠ *1136 Robson St.,* ☎ *604/687–0655. Reservations essential. AE, DC, MC, V. No lunch weekends.*

Japanese

$$$ ✕ **Tojo's.** Hidekazu Tojo is a sushi-making legend here. His handsome
★ blond-wood tatami rooms, on the second floor of a modern green-glass tower on West Broadway, provide proper ambience for intimate dining, but Tojo's 10-seat sushi bar stands as the centerpiece. With Tojo presiding, it offers a convivial ringside seat for watching the creation of edible art. Although tempura and teriyaki dinners will satisfy, the seasonal menu is more exciting. In fall, ask for *dobin mushi*, a soup made from pine mushrooms that's served in a teapot. In spring, try salad made from scallops and pink cherry blossoms. ⊠ *777 W. Broadway, 202,* ☎ *604/872–8050. Reservations essential. AE, DC, MC, V. No lunch. Closed Sun.; Dec. 24–26; and Jan. 1 and 2.*

$$ ✕ **Chiyoda.** The *robata* (grill) bar curves through Chiyoda's main room: On one side are the customers and an array of flat baskets full of the day's offerings; on the other side are the chefs and grills. There are 35 choices of things to grill, from squid, snapper, and oysters to eggplant, mushrooms, onions, and potatoes. The finished dishes, dressed with sake, soy, or *ponzu* (vinegar and soy sauce), are dramatically passed over on the end of a long wooden paddle. ⊠ *1050 Alberni St., 200,* ☎ *604/688–5050. AE, DC, MC, V. No lunch Sat. Closed Sun.*

$$ ✕ **Shijo Japanese Restaurant.** Shijo has an excellent and very large sushi bar, a smaller *robata* (grill) bar, tatami rooms, and a row of tables overlooking bustling Fourth Avenue. The epitome of modern urban Japanese chic is conveyed through the jazz music, handsome lamps with a bronze finish, and lots of black wood. Count on creatively prepared sushi in generous proportions, eggplant *dengaku* (topped with light and dark miso paste and broiled), and shiitake foil *yaki* (fresh shiitake mushrooms cooked in foil with lemony *ponzu* sauce). ⊠ *1926 W. 4th Ave.,* ☎ *604/732–4676. Reservations essential. AE, MC, V. No lunch weekends.*

$ ✕ **Japanese Deli House.** The least expensive sushi in town is served in the high-ceilinged main-floor room of a turn-of-the-century building on Powell Street, once the heart of Vancouver's Japantown. The food is especially fresh and good if you can make it an early lunch: sushi rectangles and rolls are made at 11 AM for the 11:30 opening, and there are all-you-can-eat sushi and tempura lunch specials on weekdays. ⊠ *381 Powell St.,* ☎ *604/681–6484. No credit cards. No dinner Sun. and Mon.*

Korean

$ ✕ **Seoul House Garden Korean Restaurant.** This bright, popular restaurant, decorated in Japanese style, serves a full menu of Japanese and Korean food, including sushi. The best bet is the Korean barbecue, which you cook at your table; the dinner of marinated beef, pork, chicken, or fish comes complete with a half dozen side dishes—kimchi, salads, stir-fried rice, and pickled vegetables—as well as soup and rice. Service can be chaotic. ⊠ *36 E. Broadway,* ☎ *604/874–4131. Reservations essential. MC, V. No lunch Sun.*

Mexican/Spanish

$$–$$$ ✕ **Mescalero Cantina Grill.** Here you find the look and feel of a Santa
★ Fe cocina, from stucco walls and leather chairs inside to a charming greenery-draped patio for open-air dining. The amazingly young and attractive waitstaff are appropriately clad in denim. Tapas are the main draw—Cajun beef and black bean tostada; panfried blue cornmeal-crusted oysters; roast chicken and chorizo chimichangas; and grilled

salmon, asparagus, and goat cheese burritos—but dinner selections such as blackened red snapper with avocado, corn, black bean, vodka salsa with crème fraîche are equally good. ⊠ *1215 Bidwell St.,* ☎ *604/669–2399. Reservations essential. AE, MC, V. Closed Dec. 25 and 26.*

$ ✕ **Topanga Cafe.** Arrive before 6:30 or after 8 PM to avoid waiting in line for this 40-seat Kitsilano classic. The Tex-Mex food hasn't changed much since 1978, when the Topanga started dishing up fresh salsa and homemade tortilla chips. Quantities are still huge and prices low. Kids can color blank menu covers while waiting for food; a hundred or more of the clientele's best efforts are framed on the walls. ⊠ *2904 W. 4th Ave.,* ☎ *604/733–3713. Reservations not accepted. MC, V. Closed Sun.*

Nouvelle

$$$ ✕ **Bishop's.** John Bishop established this restaurant as a favorite in 1985 by serving West Coast Continental cuisine with an emphasis on British Columbia seafood. Linguine tossed with fresh acorn squash, roasted shallots, and walnuts cohabit on the seasonal menu with medallions of venison, smoked Alaskan black cod, seared lamb loin, and roast rabbit leg. The small white rooms—their only ornament some splashy expressionist paintings—are favored by Pierre Trudeau and by Robert De Niro when he's on location in Vancouver. ⊠ *2183 W. 4th Ave.,* ☎ *604/738–2025. Reservations essential. AE, DC, MC, V. No lunch. Closed Dec. 24–26 and 1st week in Jan.*

$$$ ✕ **Five Sails.** On the fourth floor of the Pan Pacific Hotel, this special-occasion restaurant affords a stunning panoramic view of Canada Place, Lions Gate Bridge, and the lights of the north shore across the bay. Austrian chef Ernst Dorfler has a special flair for presentation, from the swan-shape butter served with breads early in the meal to the chocolate ice-cream bonbon served at the end. The broad-reaching, seasonally changing Pacific Rim menu often includes caramelized swordfish, spicy Mongolian-style chicken, and such old favorites as medallions of British Columbia salmon or lamb from Salt Spring Island. ⊠ *Pan Pacific Hotel, 300–999 Canada Pl.,* ☎ *604/662–8211. Reservations essential. AE, DC, MC, V. No lunch. Closed Dec. 24 and 26 and Jan. 1.*

$$$ ✕ **Star Anise.** When Sammy Lalji and Adam Busby, top performers from
★ the highly regarded Bishop's (☞ *above*), left to open their own restaurant, they built a faithful following in record time. Their superior skills in attentive service, imaginative presentation, and excellent preparation of Pacific Rim cuisine with French flair shine in this intimate, no-smoking location just off Granville. Don't miss the cilantro and Dungeness crab cakes with fried ginger threads, rouille, and potatoes that are often on the seasonal menu; spot prawn ravioli, grilled pork chops, and carrot and ginger mousse are also good choices. ⊠ *1485 W. 12th Ave.,* ☎ *604/737–1485. Reservations essential. AE, D, DC, MC, V. Closed Dec. 25 and 26 and Jan. 1.*

$$ ✕ **Delilah's.** Cherubs dance on the ceiling, candles flicker on the ta-
★ bles, and martini glasses clink in toasts at this incredibly popular restaurant. Under the direction of chef Peg Montgomery, the nouvelle California cuisine is delicious, innovative, and beautifully presented. The menu, which changes seasonally, lets you choose two- or five-course prix-fixe dinners. Try the salmon in strawberry peppercorn sauce and the pecan-crusted pork loin if they're available. Patrons have been known to line up before the restaurant even opens for dinner. ⊠ *1739 Comox St.,* ☎ *604/687–3424. Reservations not accepted. DC, MC, V. No lunch. Closed Dec. 24–27.*

Pacific Northwest

$$ ✕ **Liliget Feast House.** Only a few blocks from English Bay, this downstairs "longhouse" serves the original Northwest Coast cuisine: bannock bread, baked sweet potato with hazelnuts, alder-grilled salmon, and soapberries for dessert. Try the authentic but odd dish—"oolichan grease"—that's prepared from candlefish. Native music is piped in, and Northwest Coast Indian masks (for sale) peer from the walls. ✉ *1724 Davie St.,* ☎ *604/681–7044. Reservations essential. AE, MC, V. No lunch.*

$$ ✕ Raintree at the Landing. In a beautifully renovated heritage building in busy Gastown, this cool, spacious restaurant has a local menu and a wine list that offers local vintages. The kitchen, focusing on healthy cuisine, teeters between willfully eccentric and exceedingly simple; it bakes its own bread and makes luxurious soups. Main courses, which change daily depending on market availability, may include salmon and crab gnocchi; smoked Fraser Valley duck breast; and rabbit terrine. Recent reports indicate problems with slow, surly service. ✉ *1630 Alberni St.,* ☎ *604/688–5570. Reservations essential. AE, DC, MC, V. No lunch weekends. Closed Dec. 24–26.*

$ ✕ The Tomahawk. North Vancouver was mostly trees in 1926, when the Tomahawk first opened. Over the years, the original hamburger stand grew and mutated into part Northwest Coast Indian kitsch museum, part gift shop, and part restaurant. Renowned for its Yukon breakfast—five slices of back bacon, two eggs, hash browns, and toast—the Tomahawk also serves gigantic muffins, excellent French toast, and pancakes. The menu switches to oysters, trout, and burgers named for Indian chiefs at lunch and dinner. ✉ *1550 Philip Ave.,* ☎ *604/988–2612. AE, MC, V.*

Seafood

$$ ✕ Joe Fortes Seafood House. Reserve a table on the second-floor bal-
★ cony at this Vancouver seafood hot spot to take in the view of the broad wall murals, the mounted blue marlins, and, most especially, the ever-entertaining boy-meets-girl scene at the noisy bar downstairs. The signature panfried Cajun oysters, clam and corn fritters, salmon with smoked apple and cider chutney, and seared sea scallops in sesame and oyster glaze are tasty and filling, but often overlooked in favor of the reasonably priced daily special. ✉ *777 Thurlow St.,* ☎ *604/669–1940. Reservations essential. AE, D, DC, MC, V.*

$$ ✕ A Kettle of Fish. Since opening in 1979, this family-run restaurant at the northeast end of Burrard Bridge has attracted a strong local following; count on getting top-quality seafood here. The menu varies daily according to market availability, but there are generally 15 kinds of fresh seafood to choose from that are either grilled, sautéed, poached, barbecued, or blackened Cajun-style according to your preference. The British Columbia salmon and the seafood combo plate are always good choices. ✉ *900 Pacific Blvd.,* ☎ *604/682–6661. AE, DC, MC, V. No lunch weekends.*

$ ✕ Olympia Fish Market and Oyster Co. Ltd. Owner Carlo Sorace fries up some of the city's best fish-and-chips in this tiny shop behind a fish store in the middle of the Robson Street shopping district. The choice is halibut, cod, prawns, calamari, and whatever's on special in the store, served with homemade coleslaw and genuine—never frozen—french fries. It's funky and fun. ✉ *1094 Robson St.,* ☎ *604/685–0716. Reservations not accepted. DC, MC, V.*

Southeast Asian

$$ ✕ Malinee's Thai. The city's most consistently interesting Thai food
★ can be found in this typically Southeast Asian–style room hung with tapestries. The owners, two Canadians who lived for several years in Thailand, can give you detailed descriptions of every dish. Steamed fish with ginger, pickled plums, and red chili sauce is on the regular menu; steamed whole red snapper marinated in oyster sauce, ginger, cilantro, red pepper, and lime juice is a special worth ordering when it's avail-

able. ✉ *2153 W. 4th Ave.,* ☎ *604/737–0097. Reservations essential. AE, DC, MC, V. No lunch Sat. Closed Sun. and Dec. 24–26.*

$ ✕ **Phnom Penh Restaurant.** Part of a small cluster of Southeast Asian
★ shops on the fringes of Chinatown, it has potted plants and framed
views of Angkor Wat. The hospitable staff serves unusually robust Vietnamese and Cambodian fare, including crisp, peppery garlic prawns
fried in the shell and slices of beef crusted with ground salt and pepper mixed in the warm beef salad. The decor in the Broadway location is fancier, but the food is every bit as good as at East Georgia Street.
✉ *244 E. Georgia St.,* ☎ *604/682–5777;* ✉ *955 W. Broadway,*
☎ *604/734–8898. AE, MC. Closed Tues.*

LODGING

$$$$ ▦ **Four Seasons.** This bustling 28-story hotel adjacent to the Vancouver Stock Exchange is attached to the Pacific Centre shopping mall. Standard rooms are average in size; roomier corner rooms are recommended.
Decor in the rooms and hallways is tasteful and stylish. As expected of
an award-winning hotel of this caliber, service is top notch, attention
to detail is outstanding, and it has all the amenities. The formal dining
room, Chartwell (☞ *Dining, above*), is one of the best in the city. Even
pets receive red carpet treatment here—they're served Evian and pet treats
in silver bowls. ✉ *791 W. Georgia St., V6C 2T4,* ☎ *604/689–9333;
in Canada, 800/268–6282; in the U.S., 800/332–3442;* ℻ *604/844–
6744. 274 rooms, 111 suites. 2 dining rooms, bar, lobby lounge, minibars, no-smoking floors, room service, indoor-outdoor pool, hot tub
massage, sauna, aerobics, exercise room, shuffleboard, shops, piano,
baby-sitting, laundry service and dry cleaning, concierge, business services, meeting rooms, parking (fee). AE, DC, MC, V.*

$$$$ ▦ **Pan Pacific Hotel.** Sprawling Canada Place, on a pier right by the
financial district, houses the luxurious Pan Pacific (built in 1986 for
the Expo), the Vancouver Trade and Convention Centre, and a cruise-
ship terminal. The three-story atrium lobby (once you locate it) has a
dramatic totem pole and waterfall, and the lounge, the restaurant, and
the café all have huge expanses of glass offering harbor views and mountain backdrops. Earth tones and Japanese detail give the rooms an understated elegance. The hotel's fine dining restaurant, the Five Sails (☞
Dining, above), offers what is arguably the best panoramic view in town
and an imaginative menu to match. The busy hotel seems better suited
to conventions than an intimate weekend getaway, but they do have
pampering down to a science. ✉ *300–999 Canada Pl., V6C 3B5,* ☎
*604/662–8111; in Canada, 800/663–1515; in the U.S., 800/937–
1515;* ℻ *604/685–8690. 467 rooms, 39 suites. 3 restaurants, coffee
shop, lobby lounge, in-room modem lines, in-room safes, kitchenettes
in some suites, minibars, no-smoking floors, in-room VCRs, outdoor
pool, barber/beauty salon, hot tubs, massage, saunas, steam rooms, aerobics, health club, indoor track, paddle tennis, racquetball, squash, shops,
baby-sitting, laundry service and dry cleaning, concierge, business services, convention center, meeting rooms, travel services, parking (fee).
AE, DC, MC, V.*

$$$$ ▦ **Sutton Place.** The feel here is more exclusive guest house than large
★ hotel: The lobby has sumptuously thick carpets, enormous displays of
flowers, and elegant European furniture. The rooms are furnished
with rich, dark woods reminiscent of 19th-century France. Bathrobes,
slippers, and umbrellas come with the room. Despite its size, this hotel
achieves and maintains a significant level of intimacy and exclusivity.
The Café Fleuri serves one of the best Sunday brunches in town; Le
Club, a fine Continental restaurant, is for special occasions. Leather,
dark wood, wingback chairs, and a fireplace give the Gérard Lounge

Vancouver Lodging

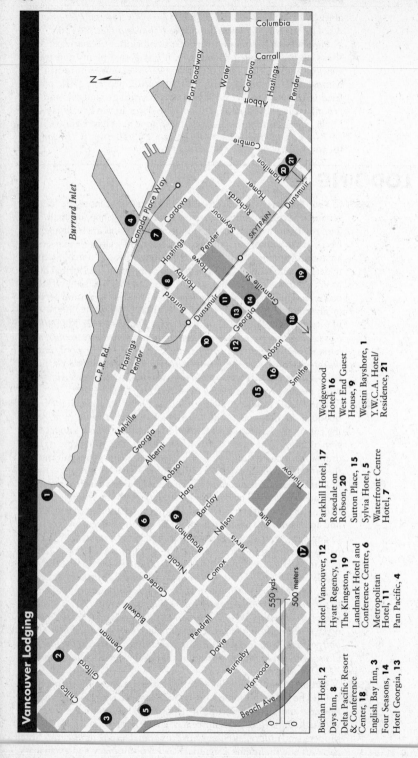

Buchan Hotel, **2**
Days Inn, **8**
Delta Pacific Resort & Conference Center, **18**
English Bay Inn, **3**
Four Seasons, **14**
Hotel Georgia, **13**

Hotel Vancouver, **12**
Hyatt Regency, **10**
The Kingston, **19**
Landmark Hotel and Conference Centre, **6**
Metropolitan Hotel, **11**
Pan Pacific, **4**

Parkhill Hotel, **17**
Rosedale on Robson, **20**
Sutton Place, **15**
Sylvia Hotel, **5**
Waterfront Centre Hotel, **7**

Wedgewood Hotel, **16**
West End Guest House, **9**
Westin Bayshore, **1**
Y.W.C.A. Hotel/Residence, **21**

the feel of a refined gentlemen's club. The tiny La Boulangerie Bakery, added in 1993, is a hit. Le Grande Residence, a luxury travel apartment hotel suitable for extended stays, adjoins the hotel. ⊠ *845 Burrard St., V6Z 2K6,* ☎ *604/682–5511 or 800/961–7555,* FAX *604/682–5513. 350 rooms, 47 suites. Restaurant, bar, café, lobby lounge, kitchenettes, minibars, no-smoking floors, room service, indoor pool, beauty salon, massage, sauna, steam room, health club, spa, bicycles, piano, laundry service and dry cleaning, concierge, business services, meeting rooms, complimentary breakfast and limo service for business guests, parking (fee). AE, D, DC, MC, V.*

$$$–$$$$ ★ 🏨 **Rosedale on Robson.** If you're planning to be in town a while and want to keep expenses down by doing some of your own cooking, look into a room at the all-suite Rosedale on Robson, opened in 1995. Rooms in shades of peach and light green are generous in size and have European kitchens, bleached hemlock furniture, and private garden patios or balconies overlooking the city. Rooms on upper floors on the north side have views of Coal Harbour. You'll find charming gardens with strolling paths on the second and third floors of the complex. ⊠ *838 Hamilton St., V6B 5W4,* ☎ *604/689–8033 or 800/661–8870,* FAX *604/689–4426. 275 suites. Restaurant, bar, in-room video games, kitchenettes, minibars, no-smoking floors, refrigerators, limited room service, indoor lap pool, hot tub, massage, sauna, steam room, exercise room, convenience store, coin laundry, laundry service and dry cleaning, business services, meeting rooms, parking (fee). AE, DC, MC, V.*

$$$–$$$$ 🏨 **Westin Bayshore.** The closest thing to a resort in the downtown area, the Bayshore is perched right on the best part of the harbor. Because it is only a five-minute walk from Stanley Park, because of the truly fabulous view, and because of its huge outdoor pool, sun deck, and grassy areas, it is the perfect place to stay in summer, especially for a family. The tower, renovated in 1995, has rooms with the best views of the water; rooms in the main wing were updated in 1993 in contemporary style. The café is unpretentious, and Trader Vic's, the hotel's dining room, is a pleasant, Polynesian-style experience. ⊠ *1601 W. Georgia St., V6G 2V4,* ☎ *604/682–3377 or 800/228–3000,* FAX *604/687–3102. 484 rooms, 33 suites. Restaurant, café, 2 bars, in-room modem lines and safes in tower rooms, minibars, no-smoking floors, room service, indoor and outdoor pools, barbershop/beauty salon, massage, steam rooms, exercise room, boating, fishing, bicycles, billiards, piano, laundry service and dry cleaning, concierge, business services, meeting rooms, travel services, downtown shuttle, car rental, float plane dock, parking (fee). AE, D, DC, MC, V.*

$$$ 🏨 **Delta Pacific Resort & Conference Center.** It's not a view or a shoreline that makes this place a resort, it's the facilities on the 14-acre site: swimming pools (one indoor, with a three-story tubular water slide), tennis courts with a pro (matching list for partners), an outdoor fitness circuit, aqua-exercise classes, outdoor volleyball nets, a play center and summer camps for children, and a playground. In spite of the hotel's size, the atmosphere is casual and friendly. Guest rooms are modern with contemporary decor and a pleasant blue and green color scheme. The Japanese restaurant is expensive and not the best value. ⊠ *10251 St. Edwards Dr., Richmond, V6X 2M9,* ☎ *604/278–9611; in Canada, 800/268–1133; in the U.S., 800/877–1133;* FAX *604/276–1121. 453 rooms, 5 suites. 2 restaurants, lobby lounge, in-room modem lines, minibars, no-smoking floors, room service, 3 indoor and outdoor pools, barbershop, beauty salon, hot tub, massage, saunas, 4 tennis courts, golf putting, squash, volleyball, bicycles, baby-sitting, children's programs (ages 5–12), laundry service and dry cleaning, busi-*

ness services, convention center, meeting rooms, travel services, car rental, free parking. AE, DC, MC, V.

$$$ 🏨 **Hotel Vancouver.** The copper roof of this grand château-style hotel
★ dominates Vancouver's skyline. Opened in 1939 by the Canadian National Railway, the hotel commands a regal position in the center of town. Even the standard guest rooms have an air of prestige with mahogany furniture, TVs in armoires, attractive linens, and the original, deep bathtubs. Suites, with French doors, graceful wingback chairs, and fine mahogany furniture, take up two floors and come with extra services and amenities. Afternoon tea in the lobby lounge is a real treat. A major renovation in 1996 added a restaurant and saw the elegant lobby completely redone in marble. ⊠ *900 W. Georgia St., V6C 2W6, ☎ 604/684–3131 or 800/441–1414, FAX 604/662–1937. 504 rooms, 46 suites. 3 restaurants, lobby lounge, in-room modem lines, minibars, no-smoking rooms, room service, indoor lap pool, hot tub, exercise room, massage, spa, steam rooms, shops, piano, baby-sitting, laundry service and dry cleaning, concierge, concierge floor, business services, meeting rooms, travel services, car rental, parking (fee). AE, D, DC, MC, V.*

$$$ 🏨 **Hyatt Regency.** The 34-story hotel opened in 1973. The standard rooms are spacious and decorated in deep, dramatic colors and dark wood; all are equipped with irons and ironing boards, coffeemakers, modem lines, and voice mail. Ask for a corner room with a balcony on the north or west side. The lobby, with its four-story atrium, can't escape the convention hotel feel. For a small fee, the Regency Club gives you the exclusivity of a floor accessed by keyed elevators, your own concierge, a private lounge with a stereo and large TV, complimentary breakfast, 5 PM hors d'oeuvres, and evening pastries. ⊠ *655 Burrard St., V6C 2R7, ☎ 604/683–1234 or 800/233–1234, FAX 604/689–3707. 612 rooms, 34 suites. Restaurant, 2 bars, café, in-room modem lines, in-room safes, minibars, no-smoking floors, room service, outdoor heated pool, sauna, exercise room, shops, baby-sitting, children's programs (ages 6–12), laundry service and dry cleaning, concierge, concierge floor, business services, meeting rooms, travel services, car rental, parking (fee). AE, D, DC, MC, V.*

$$$ 🏨 **Metropolitan Hotel.** This 18-story hotel built in 1984 by the Hong Kong Mandarin chain is now a member of the Preferred Hotels group. Although the rates went down, the surroundings did not change: The lobby is still restrained and tasteful—one has to look for the registration desk, which is tucked off to the left as you walk in. A slight Oriental theme touches the rich dark-mahogany furnishings. Most rooms have narrow balconettes, and the studio suites—roomier, and only slightly more expensive than a standard room—are recommended. ⊠ *645 Howe St., V6C 2Y9, ☎ 604/687–1122 or 800/667–2300, FAX 604/689–7044. 179 rooms, 18 suites. Restaurant, piano bar, juice bar, in-room fax, printer, and modem lines in business rooms, minibars, no-smoking floors, room service, indoor lap pool, massage, men's steam room, exercise room, racquetball, squash, laundry service and dry cleaning, concierge, business services, meeting rooms, parking (fee). AE, DC, MC, V.*

$$$ 🏨 **Waterfront Centre Hotel.** Dramatically elegant, the 23-story glass
★ hotel opened in 1991 across from Canada Place, which can be reached from the hotel by an enclosed walkway. Views from the caramel-color lobby and 70% of the guest rooms are of Burrard Inlet. The rooms are attractively furnished with contemporary artwork, minibars, and armoires concealing the TV. Large corner rooms offer the best views. A live string quartet entertains in the lobby restaurant, Herons, during the lavish Sunday brunch. ⊠ *900 Canada Place Way, V6C 3L5, ☎ 604/691–1991 or 800/441–1414, FAX 604/691–1999. 460 rooms, 29 suites. Restaurant, minibars, no-smoking rooms, room service, heated outdoor pool, massage, steam rooms, shops, baby-sitting, laun-*

dry service and dry cleaning, concierge, business services, meeting rooms, travel services, car rental, parking (fee). AE, D, DC, MC, V.

$$$ ★ ⊞ **Wedgewood Hotel.** This small, elegant property is run by an owner who cares fervently about her guests. The intimate lobby is decorated in fine detail with polished brass, beveled glass, a fireplace, tasteful artwork, and fine antiques. All the extra touches are here, too: nightly turndown service, afternoon ice delivery, dark-out drapes, flowers on the balcony, robes, and a morning newspaper. No tour groups or conventions stop here; the Wedgewood's clients are almost exclusively corporate, except on weekends, when the place turns into a couples' retreat. ⊠ *845 Hornby St., V6Z 1V1,* ☎ *604/689–7777 or 800/663–0666,* FAX *604/688–3074. 59 rooms, 34 suites. Restaurant, bar, some in-room modems, in-room safes, minibars, no-smoking floor, room service, massage, sauna, exercise room, piano, baby-sitting, laundry service and dry cleaning, concierge, business services, meeting rooms, travel services, parking (fee). AE, D, DC, MC, V.*

$$–$$$ ⊞ **Landmark Hotel and Conference Center.** The towering Landmark is still the tallest hotel in downtown Vancouver and contains some of the prettiest guest rooms in town. The bold jewel tones (emerald, sapphire, and ruby) of paintings by British Columbia's beloved Emily Carr (whose works hang in every room) are repeated on walls and furnishings. All rooms enjoy a fine view, but the Cloud Nine revolving restaurant on the top floor is a great place for an unobstructed view of Vancouver over an early breakfast buffet (go elsewhere for dinner). ⊠ *1400 Robson St., V6G 1B9,* ☎ *604/687–0511 or 800/325–3535,* FAX *604/687–2801. 351 rooms, 7 suites. Restaurant, café, sports bar, minibars, no-smoking rooms, saunas, exercise room, laundry service and dry cleaning, business services, meeting rooms, travel services, parking (fee). AE, DC, MC, V.*

$$–$$$ ⊞ **Parkhill Hotel.** Cool pastel shades echo the colors of Impressionist prints decorating the surprisingly spacious rooms in this West End hotel just a block from the seawall and sandy Sunset Beach. Large, comfortable sitting areas, half-moon balconies with city or bay views, minifridges, hair dryers, and complimentary downtown shuttle services are part of the package. ⊠ *1160 Davie St., V6E 1N1,* ☎ *604/685–1311 or 800/663–1525,* FAX *604/681–0208. 191 rooms. 2 restaurants, lounge, in-room safes, minibars, no-smoking rooms, pool, sauna, exercise room, laundry service and dry cleaning, business services, meeting rooms, travel services, car rental, parking (fee). AE, D, DC, MC, V.*

$$ ⊞ **Days Inn.** For the business traveler looking for a bargain, this location is tops. The six-story hotel, which opened as the Abbotsford in 1920, is the only moderately priced hotel in the business core. Recent renovations of the guest rooms and the lobby have made it even more agreeable. Rooms are bright, clean, and functional; standard units are very large, but there is no room service and few amenities. Suites 310, 410, 510, and 610 have a harbor view. ⊠ *921 W. Pender St., V6C 1M2,* ☎ *604/681–4335,* FAX *604/681–7808. 74 rooms, 11 suites. Restaurant, 2 bars, in-room safes, no-smoking rooms, billiards, coin laundry, laundry service and dry cleaning, free offsite parking. AE, D, DC, MC, V.*

$$ ★ ⊞ **English Bay Inn.** This renovated 1930s Tudor house is one block from the ocean and Stanley Park. The guest rooms—each with a private bath—have wonderful sleigh beds (in all but one room) with matching armoires and Ralph Lauren linen. The common areas of this no-smoking inn are elegantly furnished with museum-quality antiques: The sophisticated but cozy parlor has wingback chairs, a fireplace, a gilt Louis XIV clock and candelabras, and French doors overlooking the front garden. Breakfast is served in a rather formal room with a Gothic dining room suite, a fireplace, and a 17th-century grandfather clock.

✉ *1968 Comox St., V6G 1R4,* ☎ *604/683–8002. 4 rooms, 1 suite. Free parking. AE, MC, V.*

$$ 🏨 **Hotel Georgia.** Built in 1927, this handsome 12-story hotel has such Old World features as a dark-wood-paneled lobby, ornate brass elevators, and a subdued, genteel atmosphere. Rooms are small but well furnished, with nothing worn around the edges. Executive rooms have an almost separate seating area; rooms facing the art gallery have the best views. From this hotel it's a five-minute walk to the business district. Kids under 16 stay free in their parents' room. ✉ *801 W. Georgia St., V6C 1P7,* ☎ *604/682– 5566 or 800/663– 1111,* FAX *604/682–8192. 310 rooms, 3 suites. Restaurant, 3 bars, minibars in deluxe rooms, limited room service, barber/beauty shop, laundry service and dry cleaning, business services, meeting rooms, travel services, parking (fee). AE, D, DC, MC, V.*

$$ 🏨 **West End Guest House.** This lovely Victorian house, built in 1906,
★ is a true "painted lady," from its gracious front parlor, cozy fireplace, and early 1900s furniture to its white-trimmed teal exterior. Most of the small but handsome rooms have high brass beds, antiques, gorgeous linens, and dozens of old framed pictures of Vancouver. The basement suite has a sitting area and a side garden view. The inn's genial host, Evan Penner, adds small touches such as a pre-dinner glass of sherry, duvets and feather mattress pads, terry bathrobes, and turndown service. The inn is in a residential neighborhood two minutes from Robson Street. Room rates include a full breakfast at this no-smoking establishment. ✉ *1362 Haro St., V6E 1G2,* ☎ *604/681–2889,* FAX *604/ 688–8812. 6 rooms. Bicycles, free parking. AE, D, MC, V.*

$ 🏨 **Buchan Hotel.** The three-story 1930s building is conveniently set in a tree-lined residential street a block from Stanley Park. For the budget price, guests rent tiny, institutional rooms with very basic furnishings, ceiling fans, and color TV, but no telephone or air-conditioning. Fresh paint and bedding came with a change in management in 1994. The pension-style rooms with shared bath down the hall are perhaps the most affordable accommodations in downtown. This is a no-smoking hotel. ✉ *1906 Haro St., V6G 1H7,* ☎ *604/685–5354 or 800/668– 6654,* FAX *604/685–5367. 60 rooms, 30 with private bath. TV lounge, public telephone, coin laundry, bike and ski storage, parking (fee). AE, DC, MC, V.*

$ 🏨 **The Kingston.** The Kingston is a small budget hotel convenient for shopping. It is an old-style, four-story building, with no elevator—the type of establishment you'd find in Europe. The Spartan rooms, renovated in 1995, are small and immaculate and share a bathroom down the hall. All rooms have phones and a few have TVs and private baths. Rooms on the south side are brighter. Continental breakfast is included. ✉ *757 Richards St., V6B 3A6,* ☎ *604/684–9024,* FAX *604/684– 9917. 60 rooms, 7 with bath. TV lounge, sauna, coin laundry, free overnight parking (fee charged during the day). AE, MC, V.*

$ 🏨 **Sylvia Hotel.** To stay at the Sylvia Hotel from June through August you'll need to book six months ahead. What make this older hotel so popular are its low rates and near-perfect location: about 25 feet from the beach (with good views), 200 feet from Stanley Park, and a 20-minute walk from Robson Street. The unadorned rooms have worn, plain furnishings. Suites are huge, and all have kitchens, making this a fine family accommodation. One drawback is an unfriendly staff. ✉ *1154 Gilford St., V6G 2P6,* ☎ *604/681–9321. 97 rooms, 18 suites. Restaurant, bistro, lounge, laundry service and dry cleaning, parking (fee). AE, DC, MC, V.*

$ 🏨 **Y.W.C.A. Hotel/Residence.** Opened in the heart of the entertainment
★ district in late 1995, the secured 12-story building has bright, airy, and very comfortable rooms. All are equipped with cheery floral bed-

spreads, framed floral prints on the wall, white laminated nightstands and desk, a minifridge, and a phone. Some have sinks in the room and share a bath down the hall, others share a bath between two rooms, and still others have private baths. The hotel is open to both men and women and offers discounts for seniors, students, and YWCA members. ⊠ *733 Beatty St.,* ☎ *604/895–5830; in British Columbia and Alberta, 800/663–1424;* FAX *604/681–2550. 155 rooms. No-smoking floors, refrigerators, 3 shared kitchens, 2 shared kitchenettes, 3 shared TV lounges, 2 coin laundries, meeting rooms, parking (fee). MC, V.*

NIGHTLIFE AND THE ARTS

For information on events, pick up a free copy of the *Georgia Straight* (available at cafés and bookstores around town), or look in the entertainment section of the *Vancouver Sun* (Thursday's paper has listings in the "What's On" column). Call the **Arts Hotline** (☎ 604/684–2787) for the lastest lineups in entertainment. For tickets, book through **Ticketmaster** (☎ 604/280–3311).

The Arts

Dance

Watch for **Ballet British Columbia**'s (☎ 604/669–5954) Dance Alive! series September through April, presenting visiting or local ballet companies (from the Kirov to Ballet British Columbia). Local modern dance companies worth seeing are **Karen Jamison, Judith Marcuse, and JumpStart**. Most performances by these companies can be seen at the Queen Elizabeth Theatre (☞ Music, *below*).

Film

Ridge Theatre (⊠ 3131 Arbutus St., ☎ 604/738–6311) generally plays foreign films and rerun double bills. **Pacific Cinématèque** (⊠ 1131 Howe St., ☎ 604/688–3456) shows esoteric foreign and art films. The **Vancouver International Film Festival** (☎ 604/685–0260) is held during September and October in several theaters around town.

Music

The **Vancouver Symphony Orchestra** (☎ 604/684–9100) and the **CBC Orchestra** (☎ 604/662–6000) play at the restored **Orpheum Theatre** (⊠ 601 Smithe St.). Choral groups like the **Bach Choir** (☎ 604/921–8012), the **Cantata Singers** (no phone), and the **Vancouver Chamber Choir** (☎ 604/738–6822) play a major role in Vancouver's classical music scene. The **Early Music Society** (☎ 604/732–1610) performs medieval, Renaissance, and baroque music throughout the year and hosts the Vancouver Early Music Summer Festival, one of the most important early music festivals in North America. Concerts by the **Friends of Chamber Music** (no phone) and the **Vancouver Recital Society** (☎ 604/736–6034) are always of excellent quality.

Vancouver Opera (☎ 604/682–2871) stages five high-caliber productions a year, usually in October, November, February, March, and June, at the **Queen Elizabeth Theatre** (⊠ 600 Hamilton St.). This theater is also a major venue in Vancouver for traveling Broadway musicals.

Theater

The **Vancouver Playhouse** (⊠ Hamilton St. at Dunsmuir, ☎ 604/872–6622) is the best-established venue in Vancouver for mainstream theatrical shows. The newly completed **Ford Centre for the Performing Arts** (⊠ 771 Homer St., ☎ 604/844–2808) was built to showcase major productions and attract top touring companies. The **Arts Club Theatre** (⊠ 1585 Johnston St., ☎ 604/687–1644), has two stages on Granville

Island and theatrical performances all year. **Carousel Theatre** (☎ 604/669–3410) performs off-off Broadway shows at the Waterfront Theatre (✉ 1405 Anderson St.) on Granville Island. **Touchstone** (☎ 604/687–8737), at the Firehall Theatre (✉ 280 E. Cordova St.), is a small but lively company. The **Back Alley Theatre** (✉ 751 Thurlow St., ☎ 604/688–7013) hosts *Theatresports*, a hilarious improv event. The **Vancouver East Cultural Centre** (✉ 1895 Venables St., ☎ 604/254–9578) is a multipurpose performance space that always hosts high-caliber shows. The **Starlight Theatre** (✉ West End, ☎ 604/689–0096) is the latest of Vancouver's live performance venues to be refurbished.

Bard on the Beach (☎ 604/875–1533) is a summer series of Shakespeare's plays performed under a huge tent on the beach at Vanier Park. **The Fringe** (☎ 604/873–3646), Vancouver's annual live theatrical arts festival, is staged in September at churches, dance studios, and theater halls around town.

Nightlife

Bars and Lounges

The **Gérard Lounge** (✉ 845 Burrard St., ☎ 604/682–5511) at The Sutton Place Hotel is probably the nicest in the city because of its fireplaces, wingback chairs, dark wood, and leather. For spectacular views, head up to the **Roof Lounge** (✉ 900 W. Georgia St., ☎ 604/684–3131) in the Hotel Vancouver, where a band plays contemporary dance music nightly. The **Bacchus Lounge** (✉ 845 Hornby St., ☎ 604/689–7777) in the Wedgewood Hotel is stylish and sophisticated. The **Garden Terrace** (✉ 791 W. Georgia St., ☎ 604/689–9333) in the Four Seasons is bright and airy with greenery and a waterfall, plus big soft chairs you won't want to get out of; a pianist plays here on the weekends.

For a more lively atmosphere, try **Joe Fortes** (✉ 777 Thurlow St., 604/669–1940), known in town as the local "meet market." Billiards is now tremendously popular in Vancouver, and the **Soho Café and Billiards** (✉ 1144 Homer, ☎ 604/688–1180) is the place to go. Another "hot" pool hall is the **Automotive Billiards Club** (✉ 1095 Homer, ☎ 604/682–0040).

Microbreweries have finally hit Vancouver, a few of them taking off in a big way. At **Steam Works** (✉ 375 Water St., ☎ 604/689–2739) on the edge of bustling Gastown, they use an age-old steam brewing process and large copper kettles (visible through glass walls in the dining room downstairs) to whip up six to nine brews; the espresso ale is interesting. The **Yaletown Brewing Company** (✉ 1111 Mainland St., ☎ 604/681–2739) is based in a huge renovated warehouse with a glassed-in brewery turning out eight tasty microbrews; it also has a darts and billiards pub and a restaurant with an open-grill kitchen.

On Granville Island, the after-work crowd heads to **Bridges** (☎ 604/687–4400) near the Public Market overlooking False Creek. Slightly more upscale is **Pelican Bay** (☎ 604/683–7373), the lounge in the Granville Island Hotel, at the other end of the island. The **Backstage Lounge** (✉ 1585 Johnston St., ☎ 604/687–1354), behind the main stage at the Arts Club Theatre, stocks one of the largest selections of scotches in town and is the hangout for local and touring musicians and actors.

Casinos

A few casinos have been licensed recently in Vancouver; proceeds go to local charities and arts groups. No alcohol is served. A good bet is the **Royal Diamond Casino** (✉ 535 Davie St., ☎ 604/685–2340) downtown. The **Great Canadian Casino** (✉ 2477 Heather St., ☎ 604/872–5543), in the Holiday Inn, is an option for gamblers in downtown Vancouver.

Comedy

Yuk Yuks (✉ 750 Pacific Blvd., ☎ 604/687–5233) is good for a few laughs. The cheerful **Punchlines Comedy Theatre** (✉ 15 Water St., ☎ 604/684–3015) is in Gastown.

Music

DISCOS

Although discos come and go, lines still form every weekend at **Richard's on Richards** (✉ 1036 Richards St., ☎ 604/687–6794) for live and taped dance tunes. **Graceland** (✉ 1250 Richards St., ☎ 604/688–2648) attracts a slightly younger dance crowd. The go-go dancers at **Mars** (✉ 1320 Richards St., ☎ 604/662–7707) are supposed to be there to get dancers into the swing of things.

JAZZ

A jazz and blues hot line (☎ 604/682–0706) gives you current information on concerts and clubs. The **Alma Street Café** (✉ 2505 Alma St., ☎ 604/222–2244), a restaurant, is a traditional venue with good mainstream jazz; live performances have the spotlight Wednesday through Saturday. The **Glass Slipper** (✉ 185 E. 11th Ave., ☎ 604/877–0066) has mainstream to contemporary jazz with a more underground atmosphere.

ROCK

The **Town Pump** (✉ 66 Water St., ☎ 604/683–6695) is the main venue for local and touring rock bands. You'll find taped classic rock and roll, plenty of music memorabilia, and specialty salads and sandwiches dished up at the **Hard Rock Cafe** (✉ 686 W. Hastings, ☎ 604/687–7625). The **86th Street Music Hall** (✉ 750 Pacific Blvd., ☎ 604/683–8687) serves up big-name bands. The **Commodore Ballroom** (✉ 870 Granville St., ☎ 604/681–7838), a Vancouver institution, has been restored to its original Art Deco style and offers live music ranging from B.B. King to zydeco bands.

OUTDOOR ACTIVITIES AND SPORTS

Beaches

An almost continuous string of beaches runs from Stanley Park to the University of British Columbia. The water is cool, but the beaches are sandy, edged by grass. Liquor is prohibited in parks and on beaches. For information, call the **Vancouver Board of Parks and Recreation** (☎ 604/257–8400).

Kitsilano Beach. Kits Beach, with a lifeguard, is the busiest—transistor radios, volleyball games, and sleek young people are ever present. The part of the beach nearest the Maritime Museum is the quietest. Facilities include a playground, tennis courts, a heated saltwater pool, concession stands, and nearby restaurants and cafés.

Point Grey Beaches. Jericho, Locarno, and Spanish Banks, which begin at the end of Point Grey Road, offer a huge expanse of sand, especially in summer and at low tide. The shallow water here, warmed slightly by sun and sand, is best for swimming. Farther out, toward Spanish Banks, you'll find the beach less crowded, but the last concession stand and washrooms are at Locarno. If you keep walking along the beach just past Point Grey, you'll hit Wreck Beach, Vancouver's nude beach.

West End Beaches. Second Beach and Third Beach, along Beach Drive in Stanley Park, draw families. Second Beach has a guarded saltwater pool. Both have concession stands and washrooms. The liveliest of the West End beaches is English Bay Beach, at the foot of Denman Street. A water slide, live music, a windsurfing outlet, and other concessions here stay jumping all summer long. Farther along Beach Drive, Sunset Beach, surprisingly quiet considering the location, has a lifeguard but no facilities.

Participant Sports

Biking

Stanley Park (☞ Stanley Park, *above*) is the most popular spot for family cycling. Rentals are available here from **Bayshore Bicycles** (⊠ 745 Denman St., ☎ 604/688–2453) or **Stanley Park Rentals** (⊠ 1798 W. Georgia, ☎ 604/681–5581).

Another popular summer biking route is along the north or south shores of **False Creek.** For bikes, try **Granville Island Bike Rentals** (⊠ 1496 Cartwright, ☎ 604/669–2453) or **Granville Island Water Sports** (⊠ Charter Boat Dock, ☎ 604/662–7245).

Boating

Several charter companies offer a cruise-and-learn vacation, usually to the Gulf Islands. **Sea Wing Sailing Group, Ltd.** (⊠ Granville Island, ☎ 604/669–0840) offers a five-day trip teaching the ins and outs of sailing. If you'd rather just rent a speedboat to zip around the bay for a day, contact **Granville Island Boat Rentals** (☎ 604/682–6287) or **Granville Island Water Sports** (☎ 604/662–7245); the latter also rents jet skis and offers para-sailing for the more adventurous.

Fishing

You can fish for salmon all year in coastal British Columbia. **Sewell's Marina Horseshoe Bay** (⊠ 6695 Nelson St., Horseshoe Bay, ☎ 604/ 921–3474) organizes a daily four-hour trip on Howe Sound or has hourly rates on U-drives. **Bayshore Yacht Charters** (⊠ 1601 W. Georgia St., ☎ 604/691–6936) offers fishing charters.

Golf

Lower Mainland golf courses are open all year. Spacious **Fraserview Golf Course** (⊠ 7800 Vivian St., ☎ 604/280–8633), with fairways well defined by hills and mature conifers and deciduous trees, is the busiest in the country. **Seymour Golf and Country Club** (⊠ 3723 Mt. Seymour Parkway, ☎ 604/929–5491), on the south side of Mt. Seymour, on the North Shore, is a semiprivate club open to the public on Monday and Friday. One of the finest public courses in the country is **Peace Portal** (⊠ 6900 4th Ave., ☎ 604/538–4818), near White Rock, a 45-minute drive from downtown.

Health and Fitness Clubs

Both the **YMCA** (⊠ 955 Burrard St., ☎ 604/681–0221) and the **YWCA** (⊠ 580 Burrard St., ☎ 604/662–8188) downtown have drop-in rates that let you participate in all activities for the day. Both have pools, weight rooms, and fitness classes; the YMCA has racquetball, squash, and handball courts. **The Bentall Centre Athletic Club** (⊠ 1055 Dunsmuir St., lower level, ☎ 604/689–4424), has racquetball and squash courts, weight rooms, and aerobics.

Hiking

Pacific Spirit Park (⊠ 4915 W. 16th Ave., ☎ 604/224–5739), more rugged than Stanley Park, has 61 kilometers (38 miles) of trails, a few washrooms, and a couple of signboard maps. Go for a wonderful walk in the West-Coast arbutus and evergreen woods only 15 minutes from downtown Vancouver. The **Capilano Regional Park** (☞ Greater Vancouver, *above*), on the North Shore, provides a scenic hike.

Jogging

The seawall around **Stanley Park** (☞ Stanley Park, *above*) is 9 kilometers (5½ miles) long and gives an excellent minitour of the city. You can take a shorter run of 4 kilometers (2½ miles) in the park around **Lost Lagoon.**

Skiing

CROSS-COUNTRY

The best cross-country skiing is at **Cypress Bowl Ski Area** (⊠ Cypress Bowl Ski Area Rd., Exit 8 off Hwy. 1 westbound, ☎ 604/922–0825).

DOWNHILL

Vancouver is two hours from **Whistler/Blackcomb** (☞ Side Trip to Whistler, *below*), one of the top-ranked ski destinations in the world.

There are three ski areas on the North Shore mountains, close to Vancouver, with night skiing. The snow is not as good as at Whistler, and the runs are generally used by novice, junior, and family skiers or those who want a quick ski after work. **Cypress Bowl** (⊠ End of Cypress Bowl Ski Area Rd., Exit 8 off Hwy. 1 westbound, ☎ 604/926–5612; snow report, 604/926–6007) has a large number of runs, and most are long. **Grouse Mountain** (⊠ 6400 Nancy Greene Way, ☎ 604/984–0661; snow report, 604/986–6262) has extensive night skiing, restaurants, and bars. **Mt. Seymour** (⊠ 1700 Mt. Seymour Rd., ☎ 604/986–2261; snow report, 604/879–3999) is high and gets a good snow cover.

Tennis

Stanley Park has several well-surfaced outdoor courts near English Bay Beach; many of the other city parks have public courts as well. Contact the **Vancouver Board of Parks and Recreation** (☎ 604/257–8400) for other locations. There are no fees for use of public tennis courts.

Water Sports

KAYAKING

Rent a kayak from **Ecomarine Ocean Kayak Center** (⊠ 1668 Duranleau St., ☎ 604/689–7575) on Granville Island to explore the waters of False Creek and the shoreline of English Bay.

WINDSURFING

Sailboards and lessons are available at **Windsure Windsurfing School** (⊠ Jericho Beach, ☎ 604/224–0615) and **Windmaster** (⊠ English Bay Beach, ☎ 604/685–7245).

Spectator Sports

The **Vancouver Canucks** (☎ 604/899–4635) of the National Hockey League play in the Coliseum October–April. The Pacific Coast League **Canadians** (☎ 604/872–5232) play baseball in an old-time outdoor stadium; their season runs April–September. The **B.C. Lions** (☎ 604/583–7747) football team scrimmages at the B.C. Place Stadium downtown June–November. The **Vancouver Eighty-Sixers** (☎ 604/299–0086) play soccer in Swangard Stadium from late April through early September. The **Vancouver Grizzlies** (☎ 604/899–4666), members of the National Basketball Association, hoop it up at the new G.M. Place arena near B.C. Place. Tickets are available from Ticketmaster (☎ 604/280–4444).

SHOPPING

Unlike many cities where suburban malls have taken over, Vancouver has a downtown that is still lined with individual boutiques and specialty shops. Stores are usually open daily and on Thursday and Friday nights, and Sunday noon to 5.

Auctions

On Wednesday at noon and 7 PM, art and antiques auctions are held at **Love's** (⊠ 1635 W. Broadway, ☎ 604/733–1157). **Maynard's** (⊠ 415 W. 2nd Ave., ☎ 604/876–6787) has home furnishings auctions on Wednesday at 7 PM.

Shopping Districts

The immense **Pacific Centre Mall** (⊠ 550–750 W. Georgia St., ☎ 604/688–7236), on two levels and mostly underground, in the heart of downtown, connects Eaton's and the Bay department stores, which stand at opposite corners of Georgia and Granville streets. A commercial center has developed around **Sinclair Centre** (⊠ 757 W. Hastings St., ☎ 604/666–4438; ☞ Robson to the Waterfront *in* Exploring Vancouver, *above*), which caters to sophisticated and upscale tastes. **Robson Street,** stretching from Burrard to Bute streets, is chockablock with small boutiques and cafés. Vancouver's liveliest street is not only for the fashion-conscious; it also provides many excellent corners for people-watching and attracts an array of street performers. **Fourth Avenue,** from Burrard to Balsam streets, has an eclectic mix of stores (from sophisticated women's clothing to surfboards). **Oakridge Shopping Centre** (⊠ 650 W. 41st Ave., at Cambie St., ☎ 604/261–2511) has chic, expensive stores that are fun to browse.

Ethnic Districts

Chinatown (☞ Gastown and Chinatown *in* Exploring Vancouver, *above*)—centered on Pender and Main streets—is an exciting and animated place for restaurants, exotic foods, and distinctive architecture. Commercial Drive (around East 1st Avenue) is the heart of the Italian community, here called **Little Italy.** You can sip cappuccino in coffee bars where you may be the only one speaking English, or buy sun-dried tomatoes, real Parmesan, or an espresso machine. The **East Indian shopping district** is on Main Street around 50th Avenue. Curry houses, sweetshops, grocery stores, and sari shops abound. A small **Japantown** on Powell Street at Dunlevy Street is made up of grocery stores, fish stores, and a few restaurants.

Department Stores

Among Vancouver's top department stores is **Eaton's** (⊠ 701 Granville St., ☎ 604/685–7112), which carries everything: clothing, appliances, furniture, jewelry, accessories, and souvenirs. **Holt Renfrew** (⊠ Pacific Centre, Granville at Georgia, ☎ 604/681–3121) is smaller, focusing more exclusively on high fashion for men and women. Both are Canadian-owned and have stores at most malls as well as downtown.

Flea Market

A huge **flea market** (⊠ 703 Terminal Ave., ☎ 604/685–0666), with more than 360 stalls, is held weekends and holidays from 9 to 5. It is easily accessible from downtown on the SkyTrain, if you exit at the Main Street station.

Specialty Stores

Antiques

A stretch of antiques stores runs along Main Street from 19th to 35th avenues. **Folkart Interiors** (✉ 3715 W. 10th Ave., ☎ 604/228–1011) specializes in whimsical British Columbia folk art and Western Canadian antiques. The Vancouver Antique Center (✉ 422 Richards St., 204, ☎ 604/681–3248) has two floors of antiques and collectibles dealers under one roof. For Oriental rugs, go to **Granville Street** between 7th and 14th avenues.

Art Galleries

There are many private galleries throughout Vancouver. **Buschlen/Mowatt** (✉ 1445 W. Georgia St., 111, ☎ 604/682–1234), among the best of them, is a showcase for Canadian and international artists. **Diane Farris** (✉ 1565 W. 7th Ave., ☎ 604/737–2629; call first), also very good, often spotlights hot new artists.

Books

Bollum's Books (✉ 710 Granville St., ☎ 604/689–1802) carries 250,000 books and CD rom titles, all nicely displayed and well lit, with several comfortable sitting areas, including a little café, for browsers. **Duthie's** (✉ 919 Robson St., ☎ 604/684–4496; ✉ 4444 W. 10th Ave., ☎ 604/224–7012), downtown and near the university, is a booklovers' favorite in Vancouver. **World Wide Books and Maps** (✉ 736A Granville St., downstairs, ☎ 604/687–3320), one of several specialty bookstores in town, offers travel books and maps that cover the world.

Clothing

Fashion is big business in Vancouver, and there are clothing boutiques on almost every corner downtown. If your tastes are traditional, don't miss **George Straith** (✉ 900 W. Georgia St., ☎ 604/685–3301) in the Hotel Vancouver, offering tailored designer fashions for both sexes. Handmade Italian suits, cashmere, and leather for men are sold at stylish **E.A. Lee** (✉ 466 Howe St., ☎ 604/683–2457); there are also a few women's items to browse through. Buttoned-down businesswomen usually shop at **Wear Else?** (✉ 789 W. Pender St., ☎ 604/662–7890), focusing on career women's fashions. For truly unique women's clothing, try **Dorothy Grant** (✉ Sinclair Centre at Hastings and Granville, ☎ 604/681–0201), where traditional Haida native designs meld with modern fashion in a boutique that looks more like an art gallery.

At the architecturally stunning **Versus** (✉ 1008 W. Georgia St., ☎ 604/688–8938) boutique, ladies and gents sip espresso as they browse through the fashionable Italian designs of Gianni Versace. **Leone** (✉ 757 W. Hastings St., ☎ 604/683–1133) is yet another ultrachic boutique, dividing designer collections in themed areas. Trendy men's and women's casual wear by Ralph Lauren is available at **The Polo Store** (✉ 375 Water St., ☎ 604/682–7656).

Gifts

Want something special to take home from British Columbia? One of the best places in Vancouver for good-quality souvenirs (West Coast native art, books, music, jewelry, and so on) is the **Clamshell Gift Shop** (✉ Vancouver Aquarium, ☎ 604/685–5911) in Stanley Park. The **Salmon Shop** (☎ 604/666–6477) in the Granville Island Public Market will wrap smoked salmon for travel. In Gastown, Haida, Inuit, and Salish native art is available at **Images for a Canadian Heritage** (✉ 164

Water St., ☎ 604/685–7046), as is a selection of fine Canadian crafts. Near Granville Island, **Leona Lattimer's** shop (✉ 1590 W. 2nd Ave., ☎ 604/732–4556), built like an Indian longhouse, is full of Indian arts and crafts ranging from cheap to priceless.

SIDE TRIP

If you think of skiing when you hear mention of Whistler, British Columbia, you're thinking on track. Whistler and Blackcomb mountains, part of **Whistler Resort** (☎ 800/944–7853), are the two largest ski mountains in North America and are consistently ranked the first- or second-best ski destinations on the continent. There's winter and summer glacier skiing, the longest vertical drop in North America, and one of the most advanced lift systems in the world. It has also grown in popularity as a summer destination, with a range of outdoor activities and events filling the warm, sunny months.

Adjacent to the area is the 78,000-acre **Garibaldi Provincial Park** (☎ 604/898–3678), with dense mountainous forests splashed with hospitable lakes and streams. Even if you don't want to roam much farther than the village, there are five lakes for canoeing, fishing, swimming, and windsurfing, and many nearby hiking and mountain-bike trails.

En Route The **Coast Mountain Circle** links Vancouver to Cariboo Country. This 702-kilometer (435-mile) route takes in spectacular Howe Sound, the deep-water port of Squamish, Whistler Resort, and Pemberton Valley before heading back to Vancouver through scenic Fraser Canyon and Harrison Hot Springs (☞ Chapter 3). The loop makes a comfortable two- to three-day journey. For more information contact the **Coast & Mountains Tourism Association** (✉ 204-1755 W. Broadway, Vancouver V6J 4S5, ☎ 604/739–9011 or 800/667–3306, FAX 604/739–0153).

Whistler

At the base of the mountains are **Whistler Village, Village North,** and **Upper Village**—a rapidly expanding, interconnected community of lodgings, restaurants, pubs, gift shops, and boutiques. With dozens of hotels and condos within a five-minute walk of the mountains, the site is frenzied with activity. Culinary options in the resort range from burgers to French, Japanese to deli cuisine; and nightly entertainment runs the gamut from sophisticated piano bars to casual pubs.

Whistler Village is a pedestrian-only community. Anywhere you want to go within the resort is at most five minutes away, and parking lots are just outside the village. The bases of Whistler and Blackcomb mountains are also just at the edge; in fact, you can ski right into the lower level of the Chateau Whistler Hotel. At last count, 16,800 bed units in Whistler were within 400 yards of the lifts (which means about 52% of all accommodations are considered ski-in/ski-out).

In winter, the village buzzes with skiers taking to the slopes, but as the scenery changes from winter's snow-white to summer's lush-green landscapes, the mood of Whistler changes, too. Things seem to slow down a bit, and the resort sheds some of its competitive edge and relaxes to a slower pace. Even the local golf tournaments and the triathlon are interspersed with Mozart and bluegrass festivals.

Dining and Lodging

DINING

Dining at Whistler is informal; casual dress is appropriate everywhere. At press time, there were record numbers of promising new restaurants coming on the scene in Whistler, so you're bound to find something worthwhile to suit virtually any craving.

For price categories, *see* the dining price chart *in* Pleasures and Pastimes, *above.*

$$$ ✗ **Il Caminetto di Umberto, Trattoria di Umberto.** Umberto offers home-style Italian cooking in a relaxed atmosphere; he specializes in such pasta dishes as crab-stuffed cannelloni or a four-cheese lasagna. The Trattoria has a Tuscan-style rotisserie, highlighting a pasta dish served with a tray of chopped tomatoes, hot pepper, basil, olive oil, anchovies, and Parmesan so that you can mix it as spicy and flavorful as you like. Il Caminetto is known for its veal, osso buco, and zabaglione. ⊠ *Il Caminetto, 4242 Village Stroll,* ☎ *604/932–4442.* ⊠ *Trattoria, Mountainside Lodge, 4417 Sundial Pl.,* ☎ *604/932–5858. Reservations essential. AE, DC, MC, V.*

$$$ ✗ **Les Deux Gros.** The name means "the two fat guys," which may ex-
★ plain the restaurant's motto, "Never trust a skinny chef." Portions of the country French cuisine are generous indeed. The Alsatian onion pie, steak tartare, juicy rack of lamb, and salmon Wellington are all superbly crafted and presented, and the service is friendly but unobtrusive. Just southwest of the village, this is the spot for a special romantic dinner; request one of the prime tables by the massive stone fireplace. ⊠ *1200 Alta Lake Rd.,* ☎ *604/932–4611. Reservations essential. AE, MC, V. No lunch.*

$$$ ✗ **Wildflower Cafe.** The main dining room of the Chateau Whistler is an informal, comfortable restaurant. Huge windows overlook the ski slopes. The rustic effect of the Chateau lobby continues in the Wildflower—more than 100 antique wood birdhouses decorate the room, and chairs and tables have a farmhouse look. An à la carte menu focuses on Northern Italian cuisine and fresh seafood; the restaurant also offers terrific breakfast, lunch, and dinner buffets that may include fresh crêpes and omelets, sweet-potato-and-parsnip soup, barbecued salmon, smoked halibut, artichoke-and-mushroom salad, pepper salad, seafood pâté, pasta in spicy tomato sauce, and cold meats. ⊠ *Chateau Whistler Resort, 4599 Chateau Blvd.,* ☎ *604/938–2033. Reservations essential. AE, D, DC, MC, V.*

$$ ✗ **La Rúa.** One of the brightest lights on the Whistler dining scene is
★ on the ground floor of Le Chamois (☞ Lodging, *below*). Reddish flagstone floors and sponge-painted walls, a wine cellar behind a wrought-iron door, modern oil paintings, and sconce lighting give the restaurant an intimate, Mediterranean ambience. Favorites from the Continental menu include Asian prawns, rack of lamb, and baked sea bass with fresh herbs. ⊠ *4557 Blackcomb Way,* ☎ *604/932–5011. Reservations essential. AE, DC, MC, V. No lunch.*

$ ✗ **Hard Rock Cafe.** You know you're in a big-time tourist destination when you see a Hard Rock Cafe, and Whistler joined the ranks when H.R.C. opened its doors here in late 1995. Guitars and gold records adorn the walls, but the incredible mural of rock icons on the ceiling of the main dining room is the main attraction. Steaks, sandwiches, and salads are tasty and filling if rather uninventive at this cheerful, tremendously popular diner. ⊠ *4295 Blackcomb Way,* ☎ *604/938–9922. Reservations essential. AE, DC, MC, V.*

$ ✗ **Zeuski's.** This cozy taverna tucked in a corner of the Delta Resort
★ complex introduced tasty, inexpensive Greek fare to Whistler. Tile floors, stucco walls with stenciled trim, candlelit tables for two, and hanging baskets of greenery provide an intimate, slightly Mediterranean atmosphere. It's hard to pass on the spanikopita, souvlaki, and other standards, but the house special, katapoulo (chicken breast rolled in pistachios and roasted), is not to be missed, nor are the tender, del-

icately herb-battered calamari. ✉ *3174 Springs La.,* ☎ *604/932–6009. Reservations essential. AE, MC, V. Closed Dec. 25.*

LODGING

At press time, Whistler was undergoing a tremendous building boom, much of it centered around new lodging complexes, including the **Holiday Inn SunSpree Resort** (☎ 800/565–4329) in Whistler Village Center, the **Sheraton** (☎ 800/325–3535) in Whistler Village Plaza, and several condotels (time-share condo complexes run like hotels) to be managed by **Marriott** (☎ 800/228–9290) and **Radisson** (☎ 800/777–0185). All lodgings can be booked through the **Whistler Resort Association** (☎ 604/932–3928 or 800/944–7853); summer rates are greatly discounted.

CATEGORY	COST*
$$$$	over $300
$$$	$200–$300
$$	$100–$200
$	under $100

All prices are for a standard double room for two, excluding 10% provincial accommodation tax, 15% service charge, and 7% GST.

$$$$　🏨 **Chateau Whistler.** Whistler's most extravagant hotel is a large and friendly-looking fortress in the Upper Village. It was built and is run by Canadian Pacific. The marvelous lobby is filled with rustic Canadiana, handmade Mennonite rugs, enormous fireplaces, and enticing overstuffed sofas. Floor-to-ceiling windows in the lounge, the health club, and the café overlook the base of Blackcomb Mountain. The standard rooms are average, but the suites are fit for royalty, with specially commissioned quilts and artwork, complemented by antique furnishings. Both the Wildflower Cafe (☞ Dining, *above*) and La Fiesta, a tapas bar, are very good choices for a meal. The resort added an extensive spa facility in late 1993. Ask about summer rates that drop by 50%. ✉ *4599 Chateau Blvd., Box 100, V0N 1B0,* ☎ *604/938–8000; in the U.S. and Canada, 800/441–1414;* FAX *604/938–2055. 307 rooms, 36 suites. Restaurant, tapas bar, lobby lounge, minibars, no-smoking floors, room service, indoor-outdoor pool, hot tub, massage, saunas, steam rooms, 18-hole golf course, 3 tennis courts, exercise room, mountain bicycles, downhill skiing, ski shop, ski storage, shops, piano, laundry service and dry cleaning, concierge, business services, meeting rooms, travel services, parking (fee). AE, D, DC, MC, V.*

$$$$　🏨 **Delta Whistler Resort.** The resort, at the base of Whistler Mountain, kitty-corner to the Whistler Village Gondola and adjacent to the Whistler Golf Club, is a large complex, complete with shopping, dining, and fitness amenities. Rooms in the north tower, decorated in soothing shades of burgundy and forest green, and the newer south tower, which was closed for renovation at press time, are very generous in size (almost every room will easily sleep four). There are a few standard rooms, but most have fireplaces, whirlpool bathtubs, balconies, and/or kitchens. ✉ *4050 Whistler Way, Box 550, V0N 1B0,* ☎ *604/932–1982; in the U.S., 800/877–1133; in Canada, 800/268–1133;* FAX *604/932–7318. 268 rooms, 24 suites. Restaurant, sports bar, seasonal pool bar, kitchenettes, minibars, no-smoking rooms, room service, pool, massage, indoor and outdoor hot tubs, steam room, 2 indoor/outdoor (changes seasonally) tennis courts, exercise room, mountain bikes, bike and ski storage, downhill skiing, shops, video games, coin laundries, laundry service and dry cleaning, concierge, business services, meeting rooms, parking (fee). AE, DC, MC, V.*

$$$–$$$$　🏨 **Le Chamois.** Sharing the prime ski-in, ski-out location at the base
★　of the Blackcomb runs is this elegant luxury hotel. Of the 62 spacious

guest rooms with convenience kitchens, the most popular are the studios with Jacuzzi tubs set in front of the living room's bay windows overlooking the slopes and lifts. Guests can keep an eye on the action also from the glass elevators and the heated outdoor pool. ⊠ *4557 Blackcomb Way, V0N 1B0,* ☎ *604/932–8700; in the U.S. and Canada, 800/777–0185;* FAX *604/938–1888. 62 suites and studios. 2 restaurants, kitchenettes, minibars, refrigerators, limited room service, pool, hot tub, exercise room, mountain bikes, downhill skiing, ski storage, coin laundry, meeting room, parking (fee). AE, DC, MC, V.*

$$$ ⌂ **Edgewater.** Next to pretty little Green Lake nestles this intimate new cedar lodge. In traditional Canadiana shades of olive, crimson, pale corn yellow, and cloudy blue, the interior is simple and relaxing, a true country retreat. You can do everything here from sleigh riding and singing around a campfire to canoeing, bird-watching, and cross-country skiing. An extended Continental breakfast (juice, granola, fruit, and breakfast breads) is included in the tariff at this nonsmoking establishment. ⊠ *Off Hwy. 99, 2.5 km (1½ mi) north of village, Box 369, V0N 1B0,* ☎ *604/932–0688,* FAX *604/932–0686. 6 rooms, 6 suites. Dining room, fireside lounge with bar, outdoor hot tub, bird-watching gear, hiking, boating, cross-country skiing, ski storage. MC, V.*

$$ ⌂ **Pension Edelweiss.** The Edelweiss, one of several charming and very European bed-and-breakfasts around Whistler, is within walking distance of Whistler Village. Rooms have a crisp, spic-and-span feel, in keeping with the Bavarian chalet style of the house; all have private baths and some have balconies and telephones. Each morning a different breakfast (included in the room rate) is served: Scandinavian, American, French, German. A bus stop just outside provides easy access to Whistler Village. Smoking is not permitted here. ⊠ *7162 Nancy Greene Way, Box 850, V0N 1B0,* ☎ *604/932–3641 or 800/665–1892,* FAX *604/938–1746. 8 rooms, 1 suite. Hot tub, sauna, bicycles, ski storage, bus and train stations shuttle. AE, MC, V.*

$ ⌂ **Hostelling International Whistler Youth Hostel.** While it's nothing to write home about, it is the cheapest sleep in town. Bunks in men's or women's dorms, a few private couple's rooms, a shared kitchen, and a game room make up the basic accommodations of this hostel overlooking Alta Lake. The train passes by twice a day. ⊠ *Alta Lake Rd., V0N 1B0,* ☎ *604/932–5492,* FAX *604/932–4687. 2 dorms, 3 private rooms, all with shared baths. Kitchen, game room, ski storage. No credit cards.*

Outdoor Activities and Sports

CANOEING, KAYAKING, AND WINDSURFING

You'll see canoes, kayaks, and sailboards at the many lakes and rivers near Whistler. If you want to get in on the fun, rentals are available at **Alta Lake** at both **Lakeside Park** and **Wayside Park.** Another spot that's perfect for canoeing is the **River of Golden Dreams,** either from Meadow Park to Green Lake or upstream to Twin Bridges. Kayakers looking for a thrill may want to try **Green River** from Green Lake to Pemberton. You'll find the breezes reliable for windsurfing on **Alpha, Alta,** and **Green** lakes. Call **Whistler Outdoor Experience** (☎ 604/932–3389), **Whistler Sailing and Water Sports** (☎ 604/932–7245), **Whistler Windsurfing** (☎ 604/932–3589), or **Sea to Sea Kayaking** (☎ 604/898–5498) for equipment or guided trips.

FISHING

Whistler Backcountry Adventures (⊠ No. 36, 4314 Main St., ☎ 604/938–1410) or **Whistler Fishing Guides** (⊠ Carlton Lodge, 4218 Mountain Sq. [base of both gondolas], ☎ 604/932–4267) will take care of anything you need—equipment, guides, and transportation. All five of the lakes around Whistler are stocked with trout, but the area around

Dream River Park is one of the most popular fishing spots. Slightly far-ther afield, try **Cheakamus Lake, Daisy Lake,** and **Callaghan Lake.**

GOLF

Arnold Palmer designed the par-72 championship **Whistler Golf Course** (⌧ 4010 Whistler Way, ☎ 604/932–4544). **Chateau Whistler Golf Club** (4612 Blackcomb Way, ☎ 604/938–2092), designed by Robert Tren Jones II, was ranked the best new course in Canada by Golf Digest in 1993. The summer of 1995 saw the introduction of **Nicklaus North Golf Course** (Hwy. 99, ☎ 604/938–9898), a challenging 18-hole course designed by Jack Nicklaus.

SKIING

Cross-Country: The meandering trail around the **Whistler Golf Course** in the village is an ideal beginners' route. For more advanced skiing try the 28 kilometers (17½ miles) of track-set trails that wind around scenic **Lost Lake, Chateau Whistler Golf Course,** and the new **Nick-laus North Golf Course** and **Green Lake.** Cross-country trail maps and equipment rental information is available at the **Whistler Activity and Information Center** (☎ 604/932–2394) in the village.

Downhill: The vertical drops and elevations at **Blackcomb** (☎ 604/932–3141, FAX 604/932–3141) and **Whistler** (☎ 604/932–3434, FAX 604/938–9174) mountains are, perhaps, the most impressive features to skiers here. The resort covers 6,998 acres of skiable terrain in 12 alpine bowls, on three glaciers, and over 200 marked trails, served by the most advanced high-speed lift system on the continent. Blackcomb has a 5,280-foot vertical drop, North America's longest, while Whistler comes in second, with a 5,020-foot drop. The top elevation is 7,494 feet on Blackcomb and 7,160 on Whistler. Blackcomb and Whistler have more than 100 marked trails each and receive an average of 360 inches of snow per year; Blackcomb is open June–August for summer glacier skiing. **Whistler Ski School** and **Blackcomb Ski School** offer lessons to skiers of all levels.

Heli-Skiing: In Whistler, **Mountain Heli-Sports** (☎ 604/932–2070), **Tyax Heli-Skiing** (☎ 604/932–2500 or 800/663–8126), and **Whistler Heli-Skiing** (☎ 604/932–4105) have guided day trips with up to four glacier runs, or 12,000 vertical feet of skiing, for experienced skiers; the cost is about $350.

SPORTS CENTER

Meadow Park Sports Centre (☎ 604/938–3133) has a six-lane pool, a children's wading pool, a hockey/ice skating rink, a hot tub, a sauna, a steam room, and two squash courts.

Whistler A to Z

ARRIVING AND DEPARTING

By Bus: Maverick Coach Lines (☎ 604/255–1171, FAX 604/255–5770) has buses leaving every couple of hours for Whistler Village from the depot in downtown Vancouver. The fare is approximately $26 round-trip. During ski season, the last bus leaves Whistler at 9:45 PM. **Perime-ter Bus Transportation** (☎ 604/266–5386, FAX 604/266–1628) has daily service, November–April and June–September from Vancouver International Airport to Whistler. Prepaid reservations are necessary 24 hours in advance; the ticket booth is on Level One of the airport. The fare is around $32 one way.

By Car: Driving time from Seattle to Vancouver is about three hours. Whistler is 75 miles (120 kilometers), or 2½ hours, north of Vancouver on Route 99, the Sea-to-Sky Highway.

By Train: B.C. Rail (☎ 604/984–5246, FAX 604/984–5505) travels north from Vancouver to Whistler along a beautiful route. The Vancouver Bus Terminal and the North Vancouver Station are connected by bus shuttle. Rates are $52 round-trip for the train only.

GETTING AROUND

Streets in Whistler Village, Village North, and Upper Village are clearly marked and easy to negotiate by car, and pay parking is readily available. However, there's really no reason to use a car in Whistler because the resort association operates a free public transit system that loops throughout the resort; call ☎ 604/932–4020 for information and schedules.

CONTACTS AND RESOURCES

B&B Reservation Agencies: Whistler Bed and Breakfast Inns (☎ 604/932–3282 or 800/665–1892) represents the leading inns of Whistler.

Car Rentals: Budget Rent-A-Car (☎ 604/932–1236, FAX 604/932-3026) and **Thrifty Car Rental** (☎ 604/938–0302 or 800/367–2277, FAX 604/938–1228) have rental outlets in the village.

Emergencies: Dial 0 for **police, ambulance,** or **poison control.**

Guided Tours: If you are interested in a tour of the area, **Alpine Adventure Tours** (☎ 604/683–0209) has a Whistler history tour of the valley and a Squamish day trip. If four-wheel drive and ATV tours of the backcountry have more appeal for you, contact **Whistler Backcountry Adventures** (☎ 604/938–1410). **Whistler Nature Guides** (☎ 604/932–4595) provides guided alpine hiking tours. Budget-priced, guided camping trips out of Vancouver are available through **Bigfoots Backpacker Adventure Express** (☎ 604/739–1025).

Visitor Information: Contact the **Whistler Resort Association** (4010 Whistler Way, Whistler V0N 1B4, ☎ 604/932–4222 or 800/944–7853; in the U.S. and Canada, FAX 604/932–7231). There is an **information booth** (☎ 604/932–2394) in Whistler Village at the front door of the Conference Center; hours fluctuate, so call before visiting.

A provincial government **Travel Infocentre** (☎ 604/932–5528) is on the main highway, about 1½ kilometers (1 mile) south of Whistler.

VANCOUVER A TO Z

Arriving and Departing

By Bus

Greyhound Lines (☎ 604/662–3222 or 800/661–8747) is the largest bus line serving Vancouver. The Pacific Central Station (✉ 1150 Station St.) is the depot. **Quick Shuttle** (☎ 604/244–3744; in the U.S., 800/665–2122) bus service runs between Vancouver and Seattle five times a day in winter and up to eight times a day in summer.

By Car

From the south, I–5 from Seattle becomes **Route 99** at the U.S.–Canada border. Vancouver is a three-hour drive (226 kilometers, or 140 miles) from Seattle. Avoid border crossings during peak times such as holidays and weekends.

Route 1, the **Trans-Canada Highway,** enters Vancouver from the east. To avoid traffic, arrive after rush hour (8:30 AM).

By Ferry

B.C. Ferries (24-hour recorded schedule information, ☎ 604/277–0277; reservations, 604/669–1211) operates two major ferry terminals outside Vancouver. From Tsawwassen to the south (an hour's drive from downtown), ferries sail to Victoria and Nanaimo on Vancouver Island and to the Gulf Islands (the small islands between the mainland and Vancouver Island). From Horseshoe Bay (30 minutes north of downtown), ferries sail a short distance across the strait and up the coast to Nanaimo on Vancouver Island.

By Plane

Vancouver International Airport is on an island about 14 kilometers (9 miles) south of downtown. Current expansion of the airport facilities was due for completion in 1996; all departing passengers are charged a $10 improvement fee for international departures (including U.S.) and $8 for departures to Canadian destinations. **American Airlines** (☎ 800/433–7300), **Delta** (☎ 604/221–1212), **Horizon Air** (☎ 800/547–9308), and **United** (☎ 800/241–6522) fly into the airport. The two major domestic airlines are **Air Canada** (☎ 604/688–5515 or 800/776–3000) and **Canadian Airlines** (☎ 604/279–6611 or 800/426–7000).

Air B.C. (☎ 604/688–5515 or 800/776–3000) offers 30-minute harbor-to-harbor service (downtown Vancouver to downtown Victoria) several times a day. Planes leave from near the Westin Bayshore Hotel. **Helijet Airways** (☎ 604/273–1414) has helicopter service from downtown Vancouver to downtown Victoria. The heliport is near Vancouver's Pan Pacific Hotel.

BETWEEN THE AIRPORT AND DOWNTOWN

The drive from the airport to downtown takes 20 to 45 minutes, depending on the time of day. Airport hotels offer free shuttle service to and from the airport.

The **Vancouver Airporter Service** (☎ 604/244–9888) bus leaves the international and domestic arrivals levels of the terminal building approximately every half hour, stopping at major downtown hotels. It operates from 6 AM until midnight. The fare is $9 one way and $15 round-trip.

Taxi stands are in front of the terminal building on domestic and international arrivals levels. Taxi fare to downtown is about $22. Area cab companies are **Yellow** (☎ 604/681–3311) and **Black Top** (☎ 604/681–2181).

Limousine service from **Airlimo** (☎ 604/273–1331) costs a bit more than the taxi fare to downtown: The current rate is about $30.

By Train

The **Pacific Central Station** (✉ 1150 Station St.) is the hub for rail, bus, and SkyTrain service. The **VIA Rail** (☎ 800/561–8630) station is at Main Street and Terminal Avenue. VIA provides trans-continental service through Jasper to Toronto three times a week. Passenger trains leave the **B.C. Rail** (☎ 604/631–3500) station in North Vancouver for Whistler and the interior of British Columbia. **Amtrak** (☎ 800/835–8725 or 800/872–7245) reinstated train service between Seattle and Vancouver in May 1995; at press time one round-trip was available per day.

Getting Around

By Bus

Exact change is needed to ride **B.C. Transit** (☎ 604/261–5100) buses: $1.50. Books of 25 tickets are sold at convenience stores and newsstands; look for a red, white, and blue "Fare Dealer" sign. Day passes, good for unlimited travel after 9:30 AM, cost $4.50 for adults. They are available from fare dealers and any SeaBus or SkyTrain station. Transfers are valid for 90 minutes and allow travel in both directions. Because of traffic and overcrowding, this mode can be time-consuming and uncomfortable; however, you can get just about anywhere you need to go in the city by bus.

By Car

Because no freeways cross Vancouver, rush-hour traffic still tends to be horrendous. The worst bottlenecks outside the city center are the North Shore bridges, the George Massey Tunnel on Route 99 south of Vancouver, and Route 1 through Coquitlam and Surrey. Parking downtown is both expensive and tricky to find.

By Rapid Transit

Vancouver has a one-line, 25-kilometer (15-mile) rapid transit system called **SkyTrain,** which travels underground downtown and is elevated for the rest of its route to New Westminster and Surrey. Trains leave about every five minutes. Tickets, sold at each station from machines (correct change is not necessary), must be carried with you as proof of payment. You may use transfers from SkyTrain to SeaBus (☞ *below*) and B.C. Transit buses and vice versa. The skytrain is convenient for transit between Gastown and Science World, but that's about it for points of interest.

By SeaBus

The **SeaBus** is a 400-passenger commuter ferry that crosses Burrard Inlet from the foot of Lonsdale (North Vancouver) to downtown. The ride takes 13 minutes and costs the same as the transit bus (and it's much faster). With a transfer, connection can be made with any B.C. Transit bus or SkyTrain.

By Taxi

It is difficult to hail a cab in Vancouver; unless you're near a hotel, you'd have better luck calling a taxi service. Try **Yellow** (☎ 604/681–3311) or **Black Top** (☎ 604/681–2181).

Opening and Closing Times

Banks traditionally are open Monday through Thursday 10 to 3 and Friday 10 to 6, but many banks have extended hours and are open on Saturday, particularly outside of downtown. **Museums** are generally open 10–5, including Saturday and Sunday. Most are open one evening a week as well. **Department store** hours are Monday through Wednesday and Saturday 9:30 to 6, Thursday and Friday 9:30 to 9, and Sunday noon to 5. Many smaller stores are also open Sunday.

Contacts and Resources

B&B Reservation Agencies

A Home Away From Home (✉ 1441 Howard Ave., V5B 3S2, ☎ 604/294–1760, FAX 604/294–0799), **Town & Country Bed and Breakfast** (✉ 2803 W. 4th Ave., V6K 1K2, ☎ 604/731–5942).

Car Rentals

Avis Rent A Car (☎ 604/689–2847 or 800/879–2847), **Budget Rent A Car** (☎ 604/668–7000; in the U.S., 800/527–0700), **Thrifty Car Rental** (☎ 604/688–2207 or 800/367–2277).

Consulates

United States (✉ 1075 W. Pender St., ☎ 604/685–4311), **United Kingdom** (✉ 800–1111 Melville St., ☎ 604/683–4421).

Doctors and Dentists

Doctors are on call through the emergency ward at **St. Paul's Hospital** (⊠ 1081 Burrard St., ☎ 604/682–2344), a downtown facility open around the clock. **Medicentre** (⊠ 1055 Dunsmuir St., lower level, ☎ 604/683–8138), a drop-in clinic in the Bentall Centre, is open weekdays. The counterpart to Medicentre is **Dentacentre** (⊠ 1055 Dunsmuir St., lower level, ☎ 604/669–6700), which is next door and is also open weekdays.

Emergencies

Call 911 for **police, fire** department, and **ambulance.**

Guided Tours

Tour prices tend to fluctuate, so inquire about current rates when booking tours. Kids are generally charged half the adult fare.

AIR TOURS

Tour the mountains and fjords of the North Shore by helicopter for around $200 per person (minimum of three people) for 50 minutes: **Vancouver Helicopters** (☎ 604/270–1484) flies from the Harbour Heliport downtown. Or see Vancouver from the air for $70 for 30 minutes: **Harbour Air**'s (☎ 604/688–1277) seaplanes leave from beside the Westin Bayshore Hotel.

BOAT TOURS

The Royal Hudson, Canada's only functioning steam train, heads along the mountainous coast up Howe Sound to the logging town of Squamish. After a break here, you sail back to Vancouver on the M.V. *Britannia*. This excellent excursion costs about $60, takes 6½ hours, and is organized by **Harbour Ferries** (⊠ 1 N. Foot Denman St., ☎ 604/688–7246). Reservations are advised.

Harbour Ferries (☞ *above*) also operates a 1½-hour narrated tour of Burrard Inlet aboard the paddlewheeler M.V. *Constitution*; the tour operates Wednesday–Sunday and costs $16. Sunset cruises are also available.

Fraser River Connection (⊠ 810 Quayside Dr., in Information Centre at Westminster Quay, ☎ 604/525–4465) will take you on a seven-hour tour of a fascinating working river—past log booms, tugs, and houseboats. Between May and October, ride from New Westminster to Fort Langley aboard a convincing replica of an 1800s-era paddlewheeler for under $45.

ORIENTATION

Gray Line (☎ 604/879–3363), the largest tour operator, offers the 3½-hour Grand City bus tour year-round. Departing from the Sandman Inn in winter and the Plaza of Nations in summer, the tour includes Stanley Park, Chinatown, Gastown, English Bay, and Queen Elizabeth Park and costs about $31. During the spring, summer, and fall, **Westcoast City and Nature Sightseeing** (☎ 604/451–5581) accommodates up to 24 people in vans that run a 3½-hour City Highlights Tour for about $30 (pickup available from any downtown location). Using minibuses departing from downtown hotels and transit stations, **Vance Tours** (☎ 604/941–5660) offers a similar tour (3½ hours, $33) that includes a visit to the University of British Columbia, and a shorter city tour (2½ hours, $30).

The **Vancouver Trolley Company** (☎ 604/451–5581) runs turn-of-the-century–style trolleys through Vancouver from April to October on a 2-hour narrated tour of Stanley Park, Gastown, English Bay, Granville Island, and Chinatown, among other sights. A day pass allows you to complete one full circuit, getting off and on as often as you like. Start the trip at any of the sights and buy a ticket on board. Adult fare is under $20. During the rest of the year, the trolley runs the same circuit on a 2½-hour trip, but no on-off option is available. Between June and September, **Gray Line** (☎ 604/879–3363) offers a similar narrated tour aboard double-decker buses; passengers get on and off as they choose and are allowed to ride free the following day if they haven't had their fill. Adult fare is about $20.

North Shore tours usually include any or several of the following: a gondola ride up Grouse Mountain, a walk across the Capilano Suspension Bridge, a stop at a salmon hatchery, the Lonsdale Quay Market, and a ride back to town on the SeaBus. Half-day tours cost anywhere from $45–$55 and are offered by **Landsea Tours** (☎ 604/255–7272), **Harbour Ferries** (☎ 604/687–9558), **Gray Line** (☎ 604/879–3363), and **Pacific Coach Lines** (☎ 604/662–7575).

PERSONAL GUIDES

Early Motion Tours (☎ 604/687–5088) will pick you up for a tour of Vancouver in a Model-A Ford convertible. For about $70–$80, up to four people can take an hour-long trip around downtown, Chinatown, and Stanley Park. **AAA Horse & Carriage** (☎ 604/681–5115) offers a one-hour tour of Stanley Park, along the waterfront, and through a cedar forest and a rose garden for about $10; the tour departs from the information booth near the zoo. Individualized V.I.P. tours are available from personal guide **Marcel Jonker** (☎ 604/261–9169).

WALKING TOURS

The Gastown Business Improvement Society (☎ 604/683–5650) sponsors free 90-minute historical and architectural walking tours daily June–August. Meet the guide at 2 PM at the statue of Gassy Jack in Maple Tree Square.

Late-Night Pharmacy

Shopper's Drug Mart (✉ 1125 Davie St., ☎ 604/685–6445) offers 24-hour service daily.

Road Emergencies

BCAA (☎ 604/293–2222) has 24-hour emergency road service for members of AAA or CAA.

Travel Agencies

American Express Travel Service (✉ 1040 W. Georgia St., ☎ 604/669–2813), **Mirage Holidays** (✉ 14–200 Burrard St., ☎ 604/685–4008), **P. Lawson Travel** (✉ 409 Granville St., Suite 150, ☎ 604/682–4272).

Visitor Information

Vancouver Tourist Info Centre (✉ 200 Burrard St., ☎ 604/683–2000) provides maps and information about the city and is open July and August daily 8 to 6; the remainder of the year, weekdays 8:30 to 5, Saturday 9 to 5. A kiosk in Pacific Centre Mall is open Tuesday through Friday only; hours are 10 to 6 in summer, 10 to 5 in winter. Eaton's department store downtown also has a tourist information counter that is open all year. **Discover B.C.** (☎ 800/663–6000) is available year-round to assist with tourist information and reservations.

3 British Columbia

In Canada's westernmost province you'll find a wealth of outdoor beauty and action—on Pacific beaches and forested islands or in year-round skiing and world-class fishing. Its towns and cities, from Anglophile Victoria to the re-created Native American village of 'Ksan, reflect the diversity of its inhabitants.

Updated by
Melissa Rivers

BRITISH COLUMBIA, CANADA'S WESTERNMOST province, harbors Pacific beaches, forested islands, year-round skiing, world-class fishing—a wealth of outdoor action and beauty. The people of the province are a similarly heterogeneous mix: descendants of the original Native American peoples and 19th-century British and European settlers and more recent immigrants from Asia and Eastern Europe. From Anglophile Victoria to the re-created Native American village of 'Ksan, British Columbia's towns reflect the vigor of its inhabitants.

Canada's third-largest province (only Québec and Ontario are bigger), British Columbia occupies almost 10% of Canada's total surface area, stretching from the Pacific Ocean eastward to the province of Alberta, and from the U.S. border north to the Yukon and Northwest Territories. It spans more than 360,000 square miles, making it larger than every American state except Alaska.

British Columbia's popularity as a vacation destination stems from its status as the most spectacular part of the nation, with salmon-rich waters, abundant coastal scenery, and stretches of snow-capped peaks. The region's natural splendor has ironically become the source of conflict. For more than a century, logging companies have depended on the abundant supply of British Columbia timber, and whole towns are still centered on the industry. But environmentalists and many residents see the logging industry as a threat to the natural surroundings. Compromises have been achieved in recent years, but the issue is far from resolved.

The province used to be very British and predictable, reflecting its colonial heritage; but no longer. Vancouver (☞ Chapter 2) is an international city whose relaxed lifestyle is spiced by a rich and varied cultural scene embracing large Chinese, Japanese, Italian, and Greek communities. Even Vancouver Island's Victoria, which clings with restrained passion to British traditions and lifestyles, has undergone an international metamorphosis in recent years.

No matter how modern the province may appear, evidence remains of the earliest settlers: Pacific Coast natives (Haida, Kwakiutl, Nootka, Salish, and others) who occupied the land for more than 12,000 years before the first Europeans arrived en masse in the late 19th century. Today's native residents often face social barriers that have kept them from the mainstream of the province's rich economy. Although some have gained university educations and have fashioned careers, many are just now beginning to make demands on the nonnative population. In dispute are thousands of square miles of land claimed as aboriginal territory, some of which is within such major cities as Vancouver, Prince George, and Prince Rupert. Although the issue of ownership remains undecided, British Columbia's roots show throughout the province, from such native arts as wood-carved objects and etched-silver jewelry in small-town boutiques to authentic culinary delights from traditional recipes in big-city dining establishments.

Pleasures and Pastimes

Dining

Throughout British Columbia you'll find a variety of cuisines, from Vancouver Island's seafood places to interior British Columbia's wild game–oriented menus. Prices vary from location to location, but ratings reflect the categories listed on the dining chart.

British Columbia

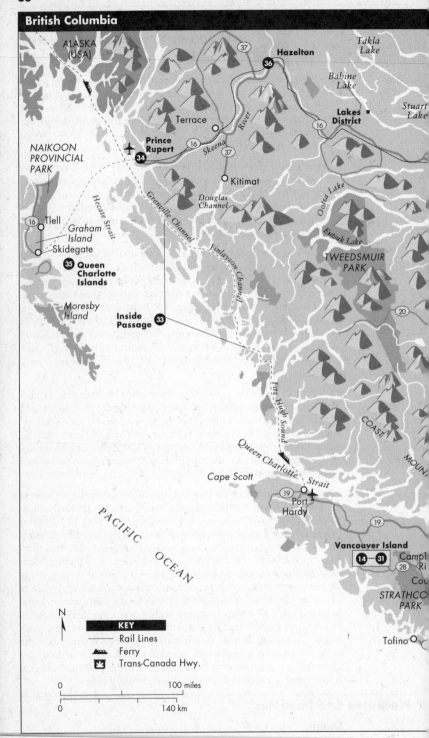

ALASKA (USA)

Takla Lake

37

Hazelton

36

Babine Lake

Terrace

River

Skeena

Prince Rupert

34

16

37

16

Lakes District

Stuart Lake

Kitimat

Douglas Channel

Oosta Lake

NAIKOON PROVINCIAL PARK

Hecate Strait

Grenville Channel

Finlayson Channel

Eutsuk Lake

TWEEDSMUIR PARK

16 Tell

Graham Island

Skidegate

35 **Queen Charlotte Islands**

20

Moresby Island

Inside Passage 33

Fitz Hugh Sound

COAST

Queen Charlotte

Cape Scott

Strait

19

Port Hardy

19

MOUNT

Vancouver Island

14 — 31

Camp Ri

28

Cou

STRATHCO PARK

PACIFIC OCEAN

Tofino

N

KEY

— Rail Lines

⚓ Ferry

🔽 Trans-Canada Hwy.

0   100 miles

0   140 km

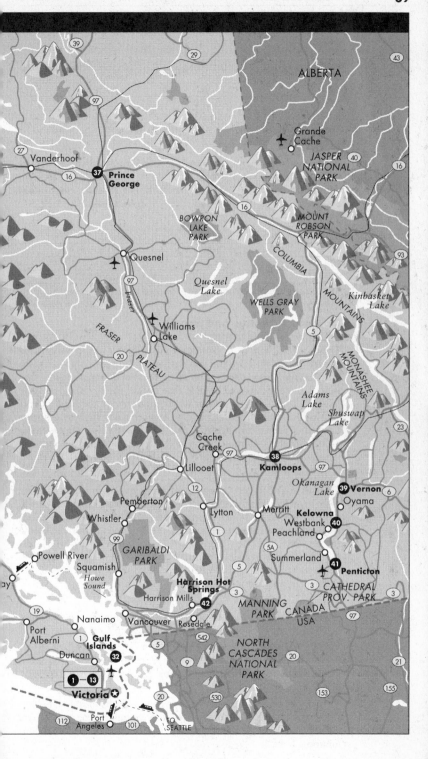

Restaurants are generally casual in the region; if a restaurant requires jacket or jacket and tie, it is noted in the service information of the review.

CATEGORY	VICTORIA*	OTHER AREAS*
$$$$	over $40	over $35
$$$	$30–$40	$25–$35
$$	$20–$30	$15–$25
$	under $20	under $15

per person, excluding drinks, service, and 7% GST, in Canadian dollars

Lodging

Accommodations across the province range from bed-and-breakfasts and rustic cabins to deluxe chain hotels. In the cities, you'll find an abundance of lodgings, but once you get off the beaten track, guest rooms are often a rare commodity and usually require advance booking.

CATEGORY	VICTORIA*	OTHER AREAS*
$$$$	over $180	over $125
$$$	$110–$180	$90–$125
$$	$70–$110	$50–$90
$	under $70	under $50

All prices are for a standard double room, excluding 10% provincial accommodation tax, service charge, and 7% GST. Prices are in Canadian dollars.

Outdoor Activities and Sports

CANOEING AND KAYAKING

These are favorite ways to explore the miles of extended, interconnected waterways and the breathtaking coastline of British Columbia. The **Inside Passage, Queen Charlotte Strait,** the **Strait of Georgia,** and the other island-dotted straits and sounds that border the mainland provide fairly protected sea-going from Washington state to the Alaskan border, with numerous marine parks to explore along the way. Another particular favorite among paddlers is the **Powell Forest Canoe Route,** a 60-kilometer (45-mile) circuit of 12 lakes connected by streams, rivers, and well-maintained portage trails along the Powell River.

FISHING

Miles of coastline and thousands of lakes, rivers, and streams bring more than 750,000 fishermen to British Columbia each year. The waters of the province hold 74 species of fish (25 of them sport fish), including Chinook salmon and rainbow trout. A saltwater-fishing license for one day costs $3.75 for both Canadian residents and non-Canadians and is available at virtually every fishing lodge and sporting-goods outlet along the coast. Annual licenses are about $11 for non–British Columbia Canadians and $38 for non-Canadians.

GOLF

There are more than 225 golf courses in British Columbia, and the number is growing. The province is now an Official Golf Destination of both the Canadian and American PGA tours. Greens fees are about $25–$50. The topography here tends to be mountainous, and many courses have fine views as well as treacherous approaches to greens.

HIKING

Virtually all of British Columbia's provincial parks have fine hiking-trail networks. Heli-hiking is also very popular here; helicopters deliver hikers to high alpine meadows and verdant, untouched mountaintops.

RAFTING

With such beautiful rivers as the Adams, Chilcotin, Chilliwack, Fraser, Illecillewaet, Nahatlach, and Thompson lacing British Columbia, you can choose from a wide range of rafting trips.

SKIING

British Columbia has hundreds of kilometers of groomed **cross-country** (Nordic) ski trails in the provincial parks and more than 40 cross-country resorts. Most downhill destinations have carved out Nordic routes along the valleys, and there are literally thousands more trails in unmanaged areas of British Columbia.

With more than half the province higher than 4,200 feet above sea level, new **downhill** areas are constantly opening. Currently, more than 40 major resorts in the province have downhill facilities.

Heli-skiing on a large scale was invented in British Columbia over three decades ago and has grown in popularity ever since. Heli-skiing operators often serve well-established resorts, taking clients into otherwise inaccessible deep-powder regions of the mountains. **Snow-cats**—which are modified slope-grooming machines—can also transport skiers to pristine, powdery runs.

WHALE-WATCHING

Three resident and several transient pods of orca (killer) whales travel in the waters around Vancouver Island and are the primary focus of nature-watching charter boat tours that depart Victoria from May to October. June and July are actually the best time to see the whales, and harbor seal, sea lion, porpoise, and marine bird sightings are a safe bet anytime. Numerous outfitters in Victoria and other Vancouver Island cities offer outings for a closer look.

Exploring British Columbia

When you travel by car, keep in mind that more than three-quarters of British Columbia is mountainous terrain. Trips that appear relatively short may take longer, especially in the northern regions and along the coast, where roads are often narrow and winding. In certain areas—most of the uninhabited west coast of Vancouver Island, for example—roads do not exist.

British Columbia encompasses a vast range of climates, largely a result of the province's size, its mountainous topography, and its border on the Pacific. Vancouver Island, surrounded by Pacific waters, has relatively mild winters and summers (usually above 32°F winter, below 80°F summer), although winter brings frequent rains. Likewise, the northern coast around Prince Rupert and the Queen Charlotte Islands has wet winter months and few extremes in temperature. As you move inland, especially toward the Peace River region in the north, the climate becomes much colder. In the southern interior, the Okanagan Valley is arid, with temperatures dropping below freezing in winter and sometimes reaching 90°F in summer.

Numbers in the text below correspond to numbers in the margin and on the British Columbia, Downtown Victoria, and Vancouver Island maps.

Great Itineraries

IF YOU HAVE 1–3 DAYS

See **Victoria** ①–⑬, as British a city as you'll find outside England. There's a great deal to explore in the city itself, from the picturesque, flower-fringed Inner Harbour and all the museums and attractions surrounding it to the cobblestoned streets of Bastion Square and the red gates of Chinatown, all towered over by majestic Craigdarroch Castle. World-famous Butchart Gardens is only half an hour away by car, and you'll want another full day to explore the beautiful grounds. On day three, head out to **Sooke** ⑭ or to one of the **Gulf Islands** ㉜ to stay at a romantic country inn for a night. Another three-day option is to fly to **Prince Rupert** ㉞ to tour the region north of Vancouver Island, including the abandoned Haida villages of the **Queen Charlotte Islands** ㉟ for a day or so before spending a day aboard a ferry cruising the breathtaking **Inside Passage** ㉝ on the way to **Port Hardy** ㉚ on Vancouver Island and a plane home from there.

IF YOU HAVE 4–6 DAYS

A brief stay in **Victoria** ①–⑬ can be followed by a leisurely tour of Vancouver Island and perhaps a portion of the mainland coast if you have more time. Assuming you plan to stay on Vancouver Island, day four allows time to stop to see the Native Heritage Center in **Duncan** ⑮, the murals of **Chemainus** ⑯, and the petroglyphs in **Nanaimo** ⑰. On day five, a decision is necessary concerning whether to trek across island to the scenic west coast to visit **Tofino** ㉒ and **Ucluelet** ㉑ and spend some time whale watching or hiking around **Pacific Rim National Park** ㉓ or to continue up the east coast to do some salmon fishing in **Campbell River** ㉙ or **Port Hardy** ㉚. If you want to go on to the **Queen Charlotte Islands** ㉟ by boat, you'll have a full day of cruising the Inside Passage, but little time to actually tour the islands. If you've gone the eastern route, day six will take you by ferry from **Comox/Courtenay** ㉗ across the Strait of Georgia to **Powell River** ㉘ on the Sunshine Coast, a paradise for outdoors lovers. Ferries and short highway jaunts will carry you down the scenic coast to Vancouver. If you've crossed to the west coast, you can spend day six backtracking to **Victoria** or making your way to **Nanaimo** to catch the ferry to Vancouver and the mainland.

IF YOU HAVE 7–10 DAYS

After visiting Vancouver Island and the upper mainland, tour British Columbia's lower mainland. Day seven takes you through the rolling lowlands of southwestern British Columbia to **Harrison Hot Springs** ㊷ for some deep relaxation in the natural springs. Points of interest in the vicinity include Hell's Gate on the Fraser River, Minter Gardens, and the Kilby Historical Store and Farm. Days eight through ten are best spent making the loop through the Okanagan Valley (the fruit-growing capital of the province), with stops in **Penticton** ㊶ to see the Kettle Valley Railway and Cathedral Provincial Park, **Kelowna** ㊵ to tour the vineyards, **Vernon** ㊴ for the O'Keefe Historic Ranch, and **Kamloops** ㊳ to fish in one of the many lakes or visit the wildlife preserves.

When to Tour British Columbia

Victoria is at its peak each year from late spring to early fall, but high summer is the prettiest time in this city adorned with flower baskets and colorful gardens. Rooms can be hard to come by, so book well in advance if you plan to visit from June through August. Summer and fall are the best seasons to tour the islands of the province (frequent ferry service to the Gulf Islands, the Queen Charlottes, and Prince Rupert drops off in slower winter and spring months). Vancouver Island also booms with tourism during the summer and fall (especially during the fishing derbys and to see the fall leaves); the winter resorts draw more locals than visitors, so the crowds are much smaller than on the mainland. High Country and the Okanagan Valley have something to appeal to visitors year-round. Winter brings snow for downhill and cross-country skiing, spring is filled with blossoms on fruit trees, and summer affords warm, dry temperatures conducive to all the outdoor activities. Fall harvest time is a particular favorite; pears, apples, and other produce are readily available, harvest festivals are frequent, and the turning leaves add their color.

VICTORIA

71 km (44 mi) on land and 24 nautical mi south of Vancouver; approximately 1 hour by ferry, ½ hour by air; 2½ hours by direct ferry from Seattle.

Victoria, originally Fort Victoria, was the first European settlement on Vancouver Island and is the oldest city on Canada's west coast. It was chosen in 1843 by James Douglas to be the Hudson's Bay Company's westernmost outpost, and it became the capital of British Columbia in 1868. Today it's a compact seaside town laced with tea shops and gardens. Though it's quite touristy during the high summer season, it's also at its prettiest, with flowers hanging from turn-of-the-century lampposts and strollers feasting on the beauty of Victoria's natural harbor.

Numbers in the text and margin correspond to points of interest on the Downtown Victoria map.

A Good Walk

Begin your tour of Victoria on the waterfront at the **Visitors Information Centre** ①. Just across the way is the **Empress Hotel** ②, originally opened in 1908. A short walk around the harbor leads you to the **Royal London Wax Museum** ③. Next to the wax museum are the **Pacific Undersea Gardens** ④, with more than 5,000 marine specimens. Across Belleville Street is the **Parliament Buildings** ⑤ complex. Follow Belleville Street one block east to reach the **Royal British Columbia Museum** ⑥, where you can spend hours wandering through the centuries, back 12,000 years. Just behind the museum and bordering Douglas Street is **Thunderbird Park,** where totem poles and a ceremonial longhouse stand in one corner of the garden of **Helmcken House,** the oldest house in British Columbia. A walk east on Superior Street to Douglas Street will lead you to **Beacon Hill Park** ⑦, a haven for joggers, walkers, and cyclists. From the park, go north on Douglas Street and stop off at the glass-roof **Crystal Gardens** ⑧, where you can see 75 varieties of birds, hundreds of flowers, and monkeys. From Crystal Gardens, continue north on Douglas Street to View Street, then west to **Bastion Square** ⑨, with its gas lamps, restaurants, cobblestone streets, and small shops. While you're here, you can stop in at the **Maritime Museum of British Columbia** ⑩. West of Government Street, between Pandora Avenue and Johnson Street, is **Market Square** ⑪, one of the most picturesque shopping districts in the city. Just around the corner from Market Square is Fisgard Street, the heart of **Chinatown** ⑫. A 15-minute walk or a short drive east on Fort Street will take you to Joan Crescent and lavish **Craigdarroch Castle** ⑬. From downtown Victoria, you can take the Munro bus to **Anne Hathaway's Cottage,** a full-size replica of the original thatched home in Stratford-Upon-Avon, England.

Sights to See

☙ **Anne Hathaway's Cottage.** Tucked away in a unique English village complex in Victoria is a full-size replica of the original thatched home of Shakespeare's wife in Stratford-Upon-Avon, England. The building and the 16th-century antiques inside are typical of Shakespeare's era. The Olde England Inn, on the grounds, is a pleasant spot for tea or a traditional English-style meal. You can also stay ($$–$$$$; AE, DC, MC, V) in one of the 50 antiques-furnished rooms, some complete with four-poster beds. Guided tours leave from the inn in winter and from

Downtown Victoria

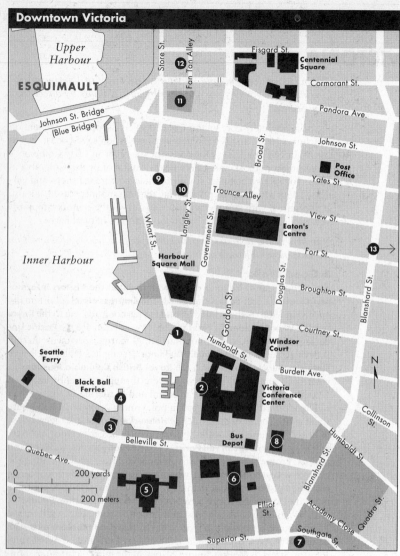

Upper Harbour

ESQUIMAULT

Johnson St. Bridge (Blue Bridge)

Store St.

Fan Tan Alley

12

11

Fisgard St.

Centennial Square

Cormorant St.

Pandora Ave.

Broad St.

Johnson St.

Post Office

Yates St.

9

10

Trounce Alley

Langley St.

Government St.

View St.

Eaton's Centre

Fort St.

13

Inner Harbour

Wharf St.

Harbour Square Mall

Gordon St.

Douglas St.

Broughton St.

Blanshard St.

Courtney St.

1

Humboldt St.

Windsor Court

Seattle Ferry

Black Ball Ferries

4

2

Victoria Conference Center

Burdett Ave.

Collinson St.

3

Belleville St.

Bus Depot

8

Humboldt St.

Blanshard St.

Quebec Ave.

0   200 yards

0   200 meters

5

6

Elliot St.

Academy Close

Quadra St.

7

Superior St.

Southgate St.

N

Bastion Square, **9**
Beacon Hill Park, **7**
Chinatown, **12**
Craigdarroch Castle, **13**
Crystal Gardens, **8**
Empress Hotel, **2**
Maritime Museum of British Columbia, **10**

Market Square, **11**
Pacific Undersea Gardens, **4**
Parliament Buildings, **5**
Royal British Columbia Museum, **6**
Royal London Wax Museum, **3**

Visitors Information Centre, **1**

the cottage in summer. ✉ *429 Lampson St., V9A 5Y9,* ☎ *250/388–4353.* 🎫 *$6.50.* 🕐 *June–Sept., daily 9–8; Oct.–May, daily 10–4.*

❾ Bastion Square. This is the spot James Douglas chose as the original Fort Victoria in 1843 and the original Hudson's Bay Company trading post. Today fashion boutiques and restaurants occupy the old buildings. The cobblestone streets are lighted by gas lamps.

❼ Beacon Hill Park. In this haven for joggers, walkers, and cyclists, the southern lawns offer one of the best views of the Olympic Mountains and the Strait of Juan de Fuca. There are also lakes, walking paths, abundant flowers, a wading pool, a petting zoo, and an outdoor amphitheater for Sunday afternoon concerts.

❷ Chinatown. The Chinese were responsible for building much of the Canadian Pacific Railway in the 19th century, and their influences still mark the region. If you enter Chinatown (one of the oldest in Canada) from Government Street, you'll walk under the elaborate **Gate of Harmonious Interest,** made from Taiwanese ceramic tiles and decorative panels. Along the street, merchants display fragile paper lanterns, embroidered silks, imported fruits, and vegetables. **Fan Tan Alley,** just off Fisgard Street, holds claim not only to being the narrowest street in Canada but also to having been the gambling and opium center of Chinatown, where mah-jongg, fan-tan, and dominoes games were played.

❸ Craigdarroch Castle. This lavish mansion was built as the home of British Columbia's first millionaire, Robert Dunsmuir, who oversaw coal mining for the Hudson's Bay Company. He died before the castle's completion in about 1890. Converted into a museum depicting turn-of-the-century life, the castle is strikingly authentic, with elaborately framed landscape paintings, stained-glass windows, carved woodwork—precut in Chicago for Dunsmuir and sent by rail—and rooms for billiards and smoking. There's a wonderful view of downtown Victoria from the fourth-floor tower. ✉ *1050 Joan Crescent,* ☎ *250/592–5323.* 🎫 *$6.* 🕐 *Mid-June–early Sept., daily 9–7:30; mid-Sept.–mid-June, daily 10–4:30.*

❽ Crystal Gardens. Opened in 1925 as the largest saltwater swimming pool in the British Empire, this glass-roof building—owned by the provincial government—is now home to flamingos, macaws, 75 varieties of other birds, hundreds of blooming flowers, and monkeys. At street level there are several boutiques and Rattenbury's Restaurant, one of Victoria's well-frequented establishments. ✉ *713 Douglas St.,* ☎ *250/381–1213.* 🎫 *$6.50.* 🕐 *Dec.–Apr., daily 10–4:30; May–Aug., daily 8–8; Sept.–Nov., daily 9–6; closed Dec. 25.*

❷ Empress Hotel. Originally opened in 1908, it is a symbol of both the city and the Canadian Pacific Railway. Designed by Francis Rattenbury, whose works dot Victoria, the property is another of the great châteaus built by Canadian Pacific, still the owners. The ingredients that made the 483-room hotel a tourist attraction in the past are still here. Stop in for high tea—served at hour-and-a-half intervals during the afternoon (no jeans, shorts, or T-shirts are permitted in the tea lobby). ✉ *721 Government St.,* ☎ *250/384–8111.*

Helmcken House. The oldest house in British Columbia was built in 1852 by pioneer doctor and statesman John Sebastian Helmcken. It is a treasure trove of history, from the early Victorian furnishings to an intriguing collection of 19th-century medical tools. Audio tours last 20 minutes. **Thunderbird Park,** with totem poles and a ceremonial longhouse constructed by Kwakiutl Chief Mungo Martin, occupies one corner of the garden. For further information on these and other heritage attractions in Victoria (Craigflower Farm and Schoolhouse, Emily Carr House, and Point Ellice House), call ☎ 250/387–4697. ✉ *Helmecken House, 10 Elliot St.,* ☎ *250/361–0021.* 🎫 *$4.* ☉ *May–Sept., daily 10–5; call for winter hours.*

⑩ Maritime Museum of British Columbia. In Victoria's original courthouse dugout canoes, model ships, Royal Navy charts, photographs, uniforms, and ship's bells chronicle Victoria's seafaring history. A seldom-used 100-year-old cage lift, believed to be the oldest in North America, ascends to the third floor. ✉ *28 Bastion Sq.,* ☎ *250/385–4222.* 🎫 *$5.* ☉ *Daily 9:30–4:30; closed Dec. 25.*

⑪ Market Square. One of the most picturesque shopping districts in the city offers a variety of specialty shops and boutiques. At the turn of the century this area—once part of Chinatown—provided everything a visitor desired: food, lodging, entertainment. Today the square has been restored to its original, pre-1900s character.

④ Pacific Undersea Gardens. Here you can see more than 5,000 marine specimens in their natural habitat. You'll also see a short, rather hokey show of performing scuba divers and a giant Pacific octopus. Unfortunately, there are no washrooms, and the site is not wheelchair accessible. This one is usually a disappointment to all but the youngest tourists. ✉ *490 Belleville St.,* ☎ *250/382–5717.* 🎫 *$6.75.* ☉ *Oct.–May, daily 10–5; June–Sept., daily 9–9; shows every 35 min; closed Dec. 25.*

⑤ Parliament Buildings. The stone structures, completed in 1897, dominate the Inner Harbour and are flanked by statues of two men: Sir James Douglas, who chose the site where Victoria was built, and Sir Matthew Baille Begbie, the man in charge of law and order during the gold-rush era. Atop the central dome is a gilded statue of Captain George Vancouver, the first European to sail around Vancouver Island; a statue of Queen Victoria stands in front of the complex; and outlining the buildings at night are more than 3,000 lights. Another of Rattenbury's creations, the complex is a good example of the rigid symmetry and European elegance that characterize much of the city's architecture. Tours, several times daily, are conducted in at least four languages in summer and three in winter. ✉ *501 Belleville St.,* ☎ *250/387–3046.* 🎫 *Free.* ☉ *Sept.–May, weekdays 8:30–5; June–Aug., daily 9–5; closed holidays.*

⑥ Royal British Columbia Museum. This is easily the best attraction in Victoria. Here you can spend hours wandering through the centuries, back 12,000 years. In the prehistoric exhibit, you can actually smell the pines and hear the calls of mammoths and other ancient wildlife. Other exhibits allow you to explore a turn-of-the-century town, with trains rumbling past. In the Kwakiutl Indian longhouse, the smell of cedar envelops you, while piped-in potlatch songs tell the origins of the genuine ceremonial house before you. ✉ *675 Belleville St.,* ☎ *250/387–3014.* 🎫 *$5; free Mon. Oct.–Apr.* ☉ *Sept.–June, daily 10–5:30; July and Aug., daily 9:30–7; closed Dec. 25 and Jan. 1.*

③ Royal London Wax Museum. This museum is in the old CPR Steamship Terminal, also designed by Rattenbury, completed in 1924. Today it houses some 300 wax figures, including replicas of Queen Victoria, Elvis, and Marilyn Monroe. ✉ *470 Belleville St.,* ☎ *250/388–4461.* 🎫 *$7.* ☉ *May–Aug., daily 9–9; Sept.–Apr., daily 9:30–5.*

① Visitors Information Centre. It's conveniently placed on the waterfront. The bridge immediately to the south affords a grand view of the Inner Harbour and, across the water on Songhees Point, the 182½-foot **Welcome Totem** (now the tallest totem pole in the world) erected in 1994 for the Commonwealth Games. ⊠ *812 Wharf St.,* ☎ *250/953–2033.* ⊙ *July and Aug., Mon.–Sat. 9–9, Sun. 9–7; May, June, and Sept., daily 9–7; Oct.–Apr., daily 9–5.*

Dining and Lodging

$$$–$$$$ ✕ **Empress Room.** For that special-occasion dinner, reserve a fireside table in the elegant Empress Room. Innovative and beautifully presented Pacific Northwest cuisine vies for attention with the setting when candlelight dances on the tapestried walls beneath an intricately carved mahogany ceiling. Fresh local ingredients go into imaginative seasonal dishes such as house-cured Pacific salmon with wild blackberry-ginger butter, pan-roasted Arctic char with wild-rice polenta and gooseberry chutney, or peppered Vancouver Island venison with black currant sauce, all perfectly complemented by wines from the Empress Hotel's extensive cellar. The dining room is no-smoking. ⊠ *721 Government St.,* ☎ *250/381-8111. Reservations essential. AE, D, DC, MC, V. No lunch.*

$$$ ✕ **Chez Daniel.** One of Victoria's old standbys, Chez Daniel offers dishes that are rich, though the nouvelle influence has found its way into some creations. The interior, following a burgundy color scheme, seems to match the traditional caloric cuisine. The award-winning wine list is varied, and the menu has a wide selection of basic dishes including rabbit, salmon, duck, and steak. The romantic atmosphere here encourages you to linger. ⊠ *2524 Estevan Ave.,* ☎ *250/592-7424. Reservations essential. AE, MC, V. No lunch. Closed Sun. and Mon.*

$$–$$$ ✕ **Marina Restaurant.** This lovely, round restaurant overlooking the
★ Oak Bay Marina is so popular with the locals that it's always crowded and a bit noisy. While seasonings and presentation often change, the best bets on the imaginative menu are warm salmon salad, grilled marlin in citrus sesame vinaigrette, rack of lamb in port glaze, and crab served with drawn butter and Indonesian hot-and-sour sauce. Choose from more than 500 wines to complement the meal. If you don't have reservations and the dining room and sushi bar are full, head downstairs to the Café Deli for Mediterranean picnic foods prepared by the chefs upstairs; go early for the best selection. ⊠ *1327 Beach Dr.,* ☎ *250/598-8555. Reservations essential. AE, DC, MC, V. Closed Dec. 25.*

$$–$$$ ✕ **Pescatore's Fish House and Oyster Bar.** Conveniently situated across from the Inner Harbour, upbeat Pescatore's specializes in fresh seafood (grilled wild Coho salmon, fresh spinach, and smoked gruyère on Italian flatbread) and Pacific Northwest specialties (rosemary and garlic marinated lamb and oyster mushrooms on angel hair pasta). Daily blue plate specials tend to be both reasonably priced and creative—pan-seared chicken breast in chanterelle sauce with crushed potatoes and vegetables. A favorite of downtown business people, this popular spot is frequently too crowded and noisy to be considered romantic. ⊠ *614 Humboldt St.,* ☎ *250/385-4512. Reservations essential. AE, MC, V. Closed Dec. 25.*

$$ ✕ **Camilles.** This restaurant is romantic, intimate, and one of the few West Coast–cuisine restaurants in Victoria. Such house specialties as carrot and smoked gruyère cheese cake (an appetizer), roast loin of venison with wild mushroom risotto, rack of lamb stuffed with mint pesto, and hazelnut crêpes are all served in generous portions. Camilles also has an extensive wine cellar. ⊠ *45 Bastion Sq.,* ☎ *250/381-3433. Reservations essential. AE, MC, V. No lunch.*

$$ ✕ **Il Terrazzo.** A charming redbrick terrace edged by potted greenery,
★ lit by flickering candles, and warmed by fireplaces and overhead heaters make Il Terrazzo, tucked away off Waddington Alley, and not visible

from the street, the locals' choice for romantic al fresco dining in Victoria. Baked garlic served with warm cambozola cheese and focaccia; scallops dipped in roasted pistachios garnished with arugula, Belgian endive, and mango salsa; grilled lamb chops on angel hair pasta with tomatoes, garlic, mint, and black pepper; and other hearty Northern Italian dishes come piping hot from the restaurant's authentic wood oven. Anything from the daily fresh sheet is worth a try here. ⊠ *555 Johnson St., off Waddington Alley (call for directions),* ☎ *250/361–0028. Reservations essential. AE, MC, V. No lunch Sun.*

$$ ✕ **Pagliacci's.** Another fine Italian bistro, Pagliacci's is a must. Dozens of pasta dishes, quiches, veal, and chicken in marsala sauce with fettuccine are standard. The pastas are freshly made in-house. You'll dine surrounded by orange walls covered with photos of Hollywood movie stars. ⊠ *1011 Broad St.,* ☎ *250/386–1662. Reservations not accepted. AE, MC, V.*

$–$$ ✕ **Don Mee's.** A large neon sign invites guests inside this traditional Chinese restaurant. The long, red staircase leads to an expansive, comfortable dining room for Szechuan and Cantonese entrées such as sweet-and-sour chicken, almond duck, and bean curd with broccoli. Dim sum is served daily during lunch hours. ⊠ *538 Fisgard St.,* ☎ *250/383–1032. AE, DC, MC, V.*

$–$$ ✕ **Le Petit Saigon.** This intimate café-style restaurant offers quiet dining with beautifully presented meals and fare that is primarily Vietnamese, with a touch of French. The crab, asparagus, and egg swirl soup is a specialty of the house, and combination meals are cheap and tasty. ⊠ *1010 Langley St.,* ☎ *250/386–1412. AE, MC, V. No lunch Sat.*

$ ✕ **Barb's Place.** This funky, blue-painted take-out shack is on Fisherman's Wharf, on the south side of Victoria Harbour west of the Inner Harbour just off Marine Drive, where fishing boats come in. It has become an institution in Victoria, and the locals consider the authentic fish and chips to be the best. Pick up an order before taking a quick ride on the little harbor ferry across the bay to Songhees Point for a picnic. ⊠ *310 Lawrence St.,* ☎ *250/384–6515. No credit cards.*

$ ✕ **Cafe Mexico.** Hearty portions of Mexican food, such as *pollo chipotle* (grilled chicken with melted cheddar and spicy sauce on a bed of rice) are served at this spacious, redbrick dining establishment just off the waterfront. Colorful bullfight ads and cactus plants provide a suitably Mexican atmosphere. ⊠ *1425 Store St.,* ☎ *250/386–5454. AE, DC, MC, V. Closed Dec. 25.*

$ ✕ **Periklis.** Standard Greek cuisine is offered in this warm, taverna-style restaurant, but there are also steaks and ribs on the menu. The dolma and the baklava are especially good. You can enjoy Greek and belly dancing, but brace yourself for the hordes of people who come for the nightly entertainment. ⊠ *531 Yates St.,* ☎ *250/386–3313. Reservations essential. AE, MC, V. No lunch weekends.*

$ ✕ **Siam.** The Thai chefs at Siam work wonders with both hot and mild Thai dishes. The *phad Thai goong* (fried rice noodles with prawns, tofu, peanuts, eggs, bean sprouts and green onions) and *panang* (choice of meat in curry and coconut milk) are particularly good options. The restaurant is spacious and conveniently near the Inner Harbour. The well-stocked bar has a variety of beers suited to the spices used here. ⊠ *512 Fort St.,* ☎ *250/383–9911. Reservations essential. MC, V. No lunch Sun.*

$ ✕ **Six-Mile-House.** Although it's a bit of a drive from downtown, this 1855 carriage house is a Victoria landmark. The brass, carved oak moldings, and stained glass set a festive mood for the evening. The menu constantly changes but always includes seafood selections and burgers. Try the cider or one of the many international beers offered. ⊠ *494 Island Hwy.,* ☎ *250/478–3121. DC, MC, V.*

$$$$ ✕🏨 **The Aerie.** The million-dollar view of Finlayson Arm and the
★ Gulf Islands persuaded Leo and Maria Schuster to build their small,
luxury resort here, 30 kilometers (19 miles) north of Victoria. In the
Mediterranean-style villa, some plush rooms have a patio; others have
fireplaces and whirlpool tubs tucked into window nooks to take advantage of the scenery. The dining room is open to the public for stunning dinner views and outstanding cuisine. The maple-smoked salmon,
pheasant consommé, medallions of venison in morel sauce, and crème
brûlée with fruit sorbet are more than worth the drive from Victoria.
A full gourmet breakfast is included in the tariff. ✉ *600 Ebedora La.,
Malahat V0R 2L0,* ☎ *250/743–7115 or 250/743–4055,* 📠 *250/743–
4766. 10 rooms, 10 suites. Dining room, no-smoking rooms, indoor
pool, indoor and outdoor hot tubs, sauna, spa, tennis court, exercise
room, library, meeting room, helipad. AE, MC, V.*

$$$$ 🏨 **Bedford Regency.** This European-style hotel in the heart of downtown is reminiscent of San Francisco's small hotels, with personalized
service and strict attention to details. Rooms are in earth colors, and
many have goose-down comforters, fireplaces, and whirlpool bathtubs.
Meeting rooms and small conference facilities are also available, making this a good business traveler's lodging. ✉ *1140 Government St.,
V8W 1Y2,* ☎ *250/384–6835 or 800/665–6500,* 📠 *250/386–8930.
40 rooms. Restaurant, pub, no-smoking rooms, laundry service and
dry cleaning, business services, free parking. AE, MC, V.*

$$$$ 🏨 **Chateau Victoria.** Wonderful views can be had from the upper
rooms and rooftop restaurant of this 19-story hotel across from Victoria's new Conference Centre, near the Inner Harbour and the Royal
British Columbia Museum. Rooms are fairly standard in size, and
some have balconies or sitting areas and kitchenettes. ✉ *740 Burdett
Ave., V8W 1B2,* ☎ *250/382–4221 or 800/663–5891,* 📠 *250/380–
1950. 71 rooms, 107 suites. Restaurant, lounge, no-smoking rooms,
room service, indoor pool, laundry service and dry cleaning, concierge,
business services, meeting rooms, ferry shuttle, free parking. AE, D,
DC, MC, V.*

$$$$ 🏨 **Empress Hotel.** This is Victoria's dowager queen with a face-lift. First
opened in 1908, the hotel underwent a major renovation in 1989 that
enhanced its Edwardian charm, updated existing guest rooms, and added
some 45 new ones (opt for one of the new rooms for more space). Stained
glass, carved archways, and hardwood floors are used effectively.
Dominating the Inner Harbour area, the Empress is the city's primary
meeting place for politicians, locals, and tourists. Afternoon tea has
been a tradition here since 1908, but it's so popular today that reservations are a must. The **Bengal Lounge** is full of colonial charm from
British India, including a stuffed Bengal tiger, overhead fans, and
mosquito netting. Award-winning Pacific Northwest cuisine is served
in the elegant **Empress Room** (☞ *Dining, above*). ✉ *721 Government
St., V8W 1W5,* ☎ *250/384–8111; in Canada, 800/441–1414;* 📠
*250/381–4334. 466 rooms, 17 suites. Restaurant, café, 2 lounges, no-
smoking rooms, room service, indoor pool, sauna, health club, laundry service and dry cleaning, concierge, business services, convention
center, parking (fee). AE, D, DC, MC, V.*

$$$–$$$$ 🏨 **Abigail's.** A Tudor country inn with gardens and crystal chande-
★ liers, Abigail's is not only lovely but also convenient—four blocks east
of downtown. The guest rooms are prettily detailed in contemporary
colors. Down comforters, together with Jacuzzis and fireplaces in
some, add to the pampering atmosphere. The elegant informality in
this no-smoking hotel is noticeable especially in the guest library and
sitting room, where hors d'oeuvres are served each evening. Breakfast,
included in the room rate, is served from 7:30 to 9 in the downstairs

dining room. ⊠ *906 McClure St., V8V 3E7,* ☎ *250/388–5363,* FAX
250/388–7787. 16 rooms. Breakfast room, no-smoking rooms, library, concierge, free parking. MC, V.

$$$–$$$$ 🏨 **Beaconsfield Inn.** Built in 1875 and restored in 1984, the Beaconsfield has retained its Old World charm. Dark mahogany wood appears throughout the house; down comforters and some canopy beds adorn the rooms, reinforcing its Edwardian style. Some of the rooms have fireplaces and whirlpool bathtubs. Added pluses are the guest library and the conservatory/sun room. Full breakfast, with homemade croissants or scones, and afternoon tea as well as evening sherry are included in the room rates. ⊠ *998 Humboldt St., V8V 2Z8,* ☎ *250/384–4044,* FAX *250/721–2442. 6 rooms, 3 suites. Breakfast room, no-smoking rooms, library. MC, V.*

$$$–$$$$ 🏨 **Oak Bay Beach Hotel.** This Tudor-style hotel beside the ocean in Oak Bay, on the southwest side of the Saanich Peninsula, is just 10 minutes from the bustle of downtown. The hotel overlooks the Haro Strait and catches the setting sun; antiques and flower prints decorating the rooms echo the dreamy landscaped grounds above the pebble beach. The restaurant, Bentley's on the Bay, is a good spot for a romantic dinner, and the pub, with its cozy fireplace, is fun for sipping a brew with the locals. ⊠ *1175 Beach Dr., V8S 2N2,* ☎ *250/598–4556 or 800/668–7758,* FAX *250/598–6180. 51 rooms. Restaurant, pub, no-smoking rooms, limited room service, boating, marina, meeting room, downtown shuttle, free parking. AE, DC, MC, V.*

$$$ 🏨 **Clarion Hotel Grand Pacific.** This is one of Victoria's newest and finest hotels, with mahogany woodwork and an elegant ambience. Overlooking the harbor, and adjacent to the legislative buildings, the hotel accommodates business travelers and vacationers looking for comfort, convenience, and great scenery; all rooms have terraces, with views of either the harbor or the Olympic Mountains. The elaborate health club is one of the best in the city. ⊠ *450 Québec St., V8V 1W5,* ☎ *250/386–0450 or 800/663–7550,* FAX *250/386–8779. 130 rooms, 19 suites. Dining room, lounge, no-smoking rooms, room service, indoor pool, massage, sauna, aerobics, racquetball, squash, bicycles, laundry service and dry cleaning, business services, convention center, meeting rooms, downtown shuttle, free parking. AE, D, DC, MC, V.*

$$$ 🏨 **Holland House Inn.** Two blocks from the Inner Harbour, legislative buildings, and ferry terminals, this no-smoking hotel surrounded by a picket fence has a sense of casual elegance. Some of the individually designed rooms have original fine art created by local artists, and some have four-poster beds and fireplaces. All rooms have private baths, and all but two have their own balconies. A lavish breakfast is included in room rates. ⊠ *595 Michigan St., V8V 1S7,* ☎ *250/384–6644,* FAX *250/384–6117. 10 rooms. No-smoking rooms. AE, MC, V.*

$$$ 🏨 **Mulberry Manor.** This Tudor-style mansion is the last building designed by Victoria architect Samuel McClure, and it has been restored and decorated to magazine-cover perfection with antiques, sumptuous linens, and tile baths. The manor sits behind a high stone wall on an acre of carefully manicured, landscaped grounds. Charming hosts Susan and Tony Temple provide sumptuous breakfasts with homemade jams and great coffee. ⊠ *611 Foul Bay Rd., V8S 1H2,* ☎ *250/370–1918,* FAX *250/370–1968. 3 rooms, 1 suite. Breakfast room, no-smoking rooms. MC, V.*

$$$ 🏨 **Ocean Pointe Resort.** Across the "blue bridge" (Johnson Street
★ Bridge) from downtown Victoria, the resort opened in the summer of
1992 on the site of an old shingle mill in an area once claimed by the Songhees natives. From here you have the best possible view of the twinkling lights of the Parliament buildings across the Inner Harbour. Public rooms and half of the guest rooms offer romantic evening views of

downtown Victoria. Guest rooms are spacious; some come with floor-to-ceiling windows. Amenities include the only full European aesthetics spa in Western Canada. ⊠ *45 Songhees Rd., V9A 6T3,* ☎ *250/360–2999 or 800/667–4677,* FAX *250/360–5856. 213 rooms, 37 suites. 2 restaurants, lounge, kitchenettes, no-smoking rooms, indoor pool, sauna, spa, 2 tennis courts, exercise room, racquetball, squash, laundry service and dry cleaning, business services, meeting rooms, free parking. AE, DC, MC, V.*

$$$ ⊞ **Victoria Regent Hotel.** Originally built as an apartment house, this is now a posh, condo-living hotel that offers views of the harbor or city. The outside is plain, with a glass facade, but the interior is sumptuously decorated with warm earth tones and modern furnishings; each suite has a living room, a dining room, a deck, a kitchen, and one or two bedrooms with bath. It's a good choice for families. ⊠ *1234 Wharf St., V8W 3H9,* ☎ *250/386–2211 or 800/663–7472,* FAX *250/386–2622. 15 rooms, 32 suites. Restaurant, kitchenettes, no-smoking rooms, refrigerators, coin laundry, meeting room, free parking. AE, D, DC, MC, V.*

$$–$$$ ⊞ **Borthwick Country Manor.** Flower boxes and awnings trim the windows of this Tudor-style house, built in 1979 on the Saanich Peninsula in the quiet countryside not far from Butchart Gardens or Victoria. Owners Susan and Michael Siems provide afternoon tea and a gourmet four-course breakfast. Rooms are cheerful, with coordinated English floral duvets, shams, and curtains. French doors lead to the backyard, with gardens to admire and a hot tub to enjoy; on sunny summer mornings, you may enjoy an al fresco breakfast on the patio. ⊠ *9750 Ardmore Dr., R.R. 2, V8L 5H5,* ☎ FAX *250/656–9498. 5 rooms. Breakfast room, no-smoking rooms, library, hot tub, fishing, bicycles. AE, MC, V.*

$$–$$$ ⊞ **Coast Victoria Harbourside.** Built in 1991 on the more residential
★ section of the harbor front next to Fisherman's Wharf (west of the Inner Harbour) the hotel enjoys water views while staying removed from the bustling traffic and crowds on Government Street. Serene relaxation in modern comfort is a theme here, from the warm mahogany-paneled lobby and soothing shades of blue-gray and pale pink in average-size guest rooms to an extensive health club. Fishing and whale-watching charters and the pudgy little harbor ferries stop at the hotel's marina just outside, and the action of the Inner Harbour is a leisurely stroll or quick shuttle ride away. ⊠ *146 Kingston St., V8V 1V4,* ☎ *250/360–1211 or 800/663–1144,* FAX *250/360–1418. 125 rooms, 7 suites. Restaurant, lounge, no-smoking rooms, room service, indoor/outdoor pool, hot tub, sauna, health club, business services, meeting rooms, downtown shuttle, free parking. AE, DC, MC, V.*

$–$$ ⊞ **Admiral Motel.** On Victoria harbor along the tourist strip, this small, modern motel is in the center of things, although it is relatively quiet in the evening. If you're looking for basic, clean lodging, the Admiral is just that. The amiable owners take good care of the rooms, and small pets are permitted. Kids under 12 stay free in their parents' room. ⊠ *257 Belleville St., V8V 1X1,* ☎ FAX *250/388–6267. 32 rooms, 23 with kitchens. Kitchenettes, no-smoking rooms, coin laundry, free parking. AE, D, MC, V.*

$ ⊞ **Cats Meow.** If you're on a tight budget, you may appreciate this small youth hostel operated by bubbly Daphne Cuthill and resident meow Rufus. The hostel offers a dorm room and two private rooms, as well as two kitchens and a TV room. Laundry service is available at nominal extra cost; Daphne also arranges discounted day trips. It's only a 15-minute walk east of downtown in the quiet Fernwood neighborhood, not far from Craigdarroch Castle. ⊠ *1316 Grant St., V8R 1M3,* ☎ FAX *250/595–8878. 1 dorm with 6 beds shares 1 bath, 2 private rooms share 1 bath. No credit cards.*

Nightlife and the Arts

The Arts

GALLERIES

The **Art Gallery of Greater Victoria,** one of Canada's finest art museums, is home both to large collections of Chinese and Japanese ceramics and other art and to the only authentic Shinto shrine in North America. The gallery also hosts a permanent Emily Carr exhibit and numerous temporary exhibitions yearly. ⊠ *1040 Moss St.,* ☎ *250/384–4101.* ✉ *$5; free Thurs. after 5, although donations are accepted.* ☉ *Mon.–Wed., Fri., and Sat. 10–5; Thurs. 10–9; Sun. 1–5.*

The **Fran Willis North Park Gallery** (⊠ 1619 Store St., ☎ 250/381–3422) is in a gorgeously restored warehouse near the waterfront; it shows contemporary paintings and sculpture by local artists. **Eagle's Moon Gallery** (⊠ 1010 Government St., ☎ 250/361–4184) showcases the totems, serigraphs, and original paintings of Tsimishian artist Roy Henry Vickers. Original art and fine Canadian crafts are the focus at the **Northern Passage Gallery** (⊠ 1020 Government St., ☎ 250/381–3380).

MUSIC

The **Victoria Symphony** has a winter schedule and a summer season, playing in the recently refurbished **Royal Theatre** (⊠ 805 Broughton St., ☎ 250/386–6121) and at the **University Centre Auditorium** (⊠ Finnerty Rd., ☎ 250/721–8480). The **Pacific Opera Victoria** performs three productions a year in the 900-seat **McPherson Playhouse** (⊠ 3 Centennial Sq., ☎ 250/386–6121), adjoining the Victoria City Hall. The **Victoria International Music Festival** (☎ 250/736–2119) features internationally acclaimed musicians each summer from the first week in July through late August.

The **Victoria Jazz Society** (☎ 250/388–4423) organizes an annual **JazzFest International** in late June, which in the past has featured such jazz, blues, and world-beat artists as Dizzy Gillespie, Frank Morgan, and Ellis Marsalis. For listings of clubs and restaurants featuring jazz during the year, call **Jazz Hotline** (☎ 250/658–5255).

THEATER

Live productions can be seen at the **Belfry Theatre** (⊠ 1291 Gladstone Ave., ☎ 250/385–6815), the **Phoenix Theatre** (⊠ Finnerty Rd., ☎ 250/721–8000) at the University of Victoria, **Langham Court Theatre** (⊠ 805 Langham Ct., ☎ 250/384–2142), and **McPherson Playhouse** (⊠ 3 Centennial Sq., ☎ 250/386–6121).

Nightlife

In addition to live music, darts, and brewery tours, **Spinnakers Brew Pub** (⊠ 308 Catherine St., ☎ 250/386–2739) pours plenty of British Columbian microbrewery beer. **Harpo's** (⊠ 15 Bastion Sq., ☎ 250/385–5333) has live rock, blues, and jazz, with visits from internationally recognized bands. For dancing, head to **Sweetwater's** (⊠ 27-560 Johnson St., ☎ 250/383–7844), where a younger crowd moves on two dance floors to taped techno and Top-40.

Outdoor Activities and Sports

Golf

Although **Victoria Golf Club** (⊠ 1110 Beach Dr., ☎ 250/598–4321) is private, it's open to other private-club members; the windy course is the oldest (built in 1893) in British Columbia and has spectacular views. The **Cordova Bay Golf Course** (⊠ 5333 Cordova Bay Rd., ☎ 250/658–4444), Victoria's newest public course, is an 18-hole, par-

72 course set on the shoreline. The **Olympic View Golf Club** (✉ 643 Latoria Rd., ☎ 250/474–3673), 20 minutes from downtown, offers both challenging and forgiving tees and stunning views.

Hiking

Swan Lake Christmas Hill Nature Sanctuary. This 23-acre lake, in 110 acres of open fields and wetlands, is 10 minutes from downtown Victoria. From the 1½-mile chip trail and floating boardwalk, birders can spot a variety of waterfowl even in winter, as well as nesting birds in the tall grass. ✉ *3873 Swan Lake Rd. (Bus 70 or 75),* ☎ *250/479–0211.* 🎫 *Free.* 🕐 *Nature House open weekdays 8:30–4, weekends and holidays noon–4.*

Whale-Watching

To see the pods of orca (killer whales) that travel in the waters around Vancouver Island, you can take charter boat tours from Victoria between May and October. These three-hour Zodiac (motor-powered inflatable boat) excursions cost about $70 per person. **Five Star Charters** (☎ 250/388–7223) and **Seacoast Expeditions** (✉ Ocean Pointe Resort, ☎ 250/383–2254) are the top operators. For a longer trip, contact the **Canadian Outback Adventure Company** (✉ 1110 Hamilton St., 206, Vancouver, ☎ 604/688–7206) to learn more about their week-long sea kayaking trips among the orca in Johnston Strait off the north coast of Vancouver Island.

Shopping

Shopping in Victoria is easy: Virtually everything can be found in the downtown area on or near Government Street stretching north from the Empress. **Beautiful B.C.** (✉ 910 Government St., ☎ 384–7773) focuses on products produced in British Columbia, from maple syrup to original art. The **Cowichan Trading Co., Ltd.** (✉ 1328 Government St., ☎ 250/383–0321) sells native jewelry, moccasins, and Cowichan Indian sweaters. **Hill's Indian Crafts** (✉ 1008 Government St., ☎ 250/385–3911) has a mixture; you'll have to plow through some schlocky souvenirs to find the good-quality West Coast native art. The **House of Traditions** (✉ 910 Government St., ☎ 250/361–3020) offers frilly lace blouses and skirts, some Victorian in fashion. As the name would suggest, **Irish Linen Stores** (✉ 1090 Government St., ☎ 250/383–6812) offers fine linen and lace items—hankies, napkins, tablecloths, and place mats. The high ceiling, elaborate moldings, and murals at **Munro's Books** (✉ 1108 Government St., ☎ 250/382–2464) are worth a peek. If the British spirit of Victoria has you searching for fine teas, head next door to **Murchie's** (✉ 1110 Government St., ☎ 250/383–3112) for a choice of 40 varieties, plus blended coffees, tarts, and cakes. Men's designer clothes by Ralph Lauren are available at **The Polo Store** (✉ 1200 Government St., ☎ 250/381–7656). You'll smell the sweets well before you get to **Roger's Chocolates** (✉ 913 Government St., ☎ 250/384–7021).

For a wide selection, head to the larger shopping centers downtown. **Eaton Centre** (✉ 1 Victoria Eaton Centre, at Government and Fort Sts., ☎ 250/382–7141) is a department store and mall with around 100 boutiques and restaurants. **Market Square** (✉ 560 Johnson St., ☎ 250/386–2441) has three stories of specialty shops and offbeat stores; there's everything from fudge, music, and comic books to jewelry, local arts, and New Age accoutrements.

A 10-minute drive (or Bus 1 or 2) from downtown out Fort Street to Oak Bay Avenue will take you to one of the few residential shopping areas that is not a mall. **Oak Bay Village** is great for browsing, buying, or an afternoon cuppa'. Start at the corner of Oak Bay and Foul Bay and work your way east toward the water.

At last count, Victoria had 60-plus antiques shops specializing in coins, stamps, estate jewelry, rare books, crystal, china, furniture, or paintings and other works of art. A short walk on Fort Street going away from the harbor will take you to Antique Row between Blanshard and Cook streets. You will also find antiques on the west side of Government Street near the Old Town.

Side Trip

Butchart Gardens. This 50-acre garden about 21 kilometers (13 miles) north of downtown Victoria grows more than 700 varieties of flowers and has Italian, Japanese, and English rose gardens. In summer, many of the exhibits are illuminated at night, and fireworks light the sky over the gardens every Saturday night. Also on the premises are a teahouse and restaurants. ⊠ *800 Benvenuto Ave., Brentwood Bay,* ☎ *250/652–5256 or 250/652–4422.* ☞ *$13, excluding GST; discounted rates in winter.* ⊙ *Hours vary seasonally; call ahead.*

Victoria A to Z

Arriving and Departing

BY BOAT

There is year-round passenger service (closed Christmas) between Victoria and Seattle on the *Victoria Clipper* (☎ 250/382–8100; in the U.S., 800/888–2535).

Washington State Ferries (☎ 250/381–1551; in the U.S., 206/464–6400) cross daily, year-round, between Sidney, just north of Victoria, and Anacortes, Washington. **Black Ball Transport** (☎ 250/386–2202; in the U.S., 206/457–4491) operates between Victoria and Port Angeles, Washington. Direct passenger and vehicle service between Seattle and Victoria is available May 21–September 18 on the *Royal Victorian,* operated by **Victoria Line** (☎ 250/480–5555). Reservations are advised if you're traveling with a vehicle.

BY HELICOPTER

Helijet Airways (☎ 604/273–1414 or 250/382–6222) helicopter service is available from downtown Vancouver to downtown Victoria.

BY PLANE

Air B.C. (☎ 604/688–5515 or 250/360–9074; in the U.S., 800/776–3000), the major regional line, and **Horizon Air** (☎ 800/547–9308) both provide service between Seattle and Victoria airports (☞ British Columbia A to Z, *below*).

Getting Around

BY BUS

The **B.C. Transit System** (☎ 250/382–6161) runs a fairly extensive service in Victoria and the surrounding areas, with an all-day pass that costs $4 for adults, $3 for students and senior citizens.

BY TAXI

Taxis are available from **Empress Taxi** (☎ 250/381–2222) and **Victoria Taxi** (☎ 250/383–7111).

Contacts and Resources

CAR RENTALS

A good local rental agent in Victoria is **ABC Rent a Car** (☎ 250/388–3153, FAX 250/388–0111).

EMERGENCIES
Dial 911.

GUIDED TOURS
Tally-Ho Horsedrawn Tours (☎ 250/479–1113) offers visitors a get-acquainted session with downtown Victoria that includes Beacon Hill Park. **Victoria's Carriage Tours** (☎ 250/383–2207) is another option for horse-drawn tours. From April through September it's possible to tour downtown Victoria by pedicab; contact **Kabuki Kabs** (☎ 250/385–4243). The best way to see the sights of the Inner Harbour is by **Harbour Gondola** (☎ 250/361–3511), complete with an authentically garbed gondolier to narrate the tour. **Gray Line** (☎ 250/388–5248) offers city tours on double-decker buses that visit the city center, Chinatown, Antique Row, Oak Bay, and Beacon Hill Park; a combination tour stops at Butchart Gardens as well. History buffs may prefer looking into Victoria's background on the intriguing guided cemetery tours put together by the **Old Cemeteries Society** (☎ 250/384–0045).

HOSPITAL
Victoria General Hospital (⊠ 35 Helmcken Rd., ☎ 250/727–4212).

LATE-NIGHT PHARMACY
McGill and Orme Pharmacies (⊠ 649 Fort St., ☎ 250/384–1195).

LODGING RESERVATION SERVICE
Tourism Victoria has a lodging reservations service; call ☎ 800/663–3883.

VISITOR INFORMATION
For Victoria, contact **Tourism Victoria** (⊠ 1175 Douglas St., Suite 710, V8W 2E1, ☎ 250/953–2033, FAX 250/361–9733).

VANCOUVER ISLAND

Vancouver Island, the largest island on Canada's west coast, stretches 450 kilometers (280 miles) from Victoria in the south to Cape Scott in the north. Some 97% of the island's population live between Victoria and Campbell River (halfway up the island); 50% of them live in Victoria itself. The western side is wild, often inhospitable, with just a handful of small settlements. Nevertheless, the west coast is invaded every summer by fishermen, kayakers, scuba divers, and hikers. The west-coast towns of Ucluelet and Tofino are the whale-watching capitals of Canada, if not of the whole west coast of North America. The two towns are quite different in character, though both are relaxed in winter and swell to several times their sizes in summer. Virtually all of the island's permanent human habitation is on the eastern coast, where the weather is gentler and the topography is low-lying.

The cultural heritage of the island is from the Kwakiutl, Nootka, and Coastal Salish native groups. Native art and cultural centers flourish throughout the region, especially in the lower end of the island, enabling visitors to catch a glimpse of contemporary native culture.

Mining, logging, and tourism are the important island industries. Environmental issues, such as the logging practices of British Columbia's lumber companies, are becoming important to islanders—both native and nonnative. Residents are working to establish a balance between the island's wilderness and its economy.

Numbers in the margin correspond to points of interest on the Vancouver Island map.

Vancouver Island

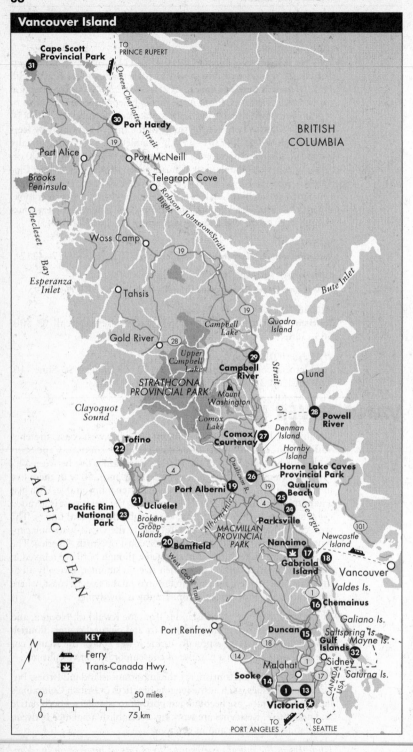

TO PRINCE RUPERT

Cape Scott Provincial Park 31

30 **Port Hardy**

Port Alice

Brooks Peninsula

Port McNeill

Telegraph Cove

Queen Charlotte Strait

Robson Bight

Johnstone Strait

BRITISH COLUMBIA

Woss Camp

19

Tahsis

Cheslacet Bay

Esperanza Inlet

Gold River 28

Campbell Lake

19

Upper Campbell Lake

Quadra Island

Bute Inlet

STRATHCONA PROVINCIAL PARK

▲ Mount Washington

29 **Campbell River**

Lund

Strait of Georgia

Clayoquot Sound

Comox Lake

28 **Powell River**

Tofino 22

27 **Comox/ Courtenay**

Denman Island

Hornby Island

4

Horne Lake Caves Provincial Park

26

Port Alberni 19

19

Qualicum Beach 25

21 **Ucluelet**

Pacific Rim National Park 23

Broken Group Islands

Alberni Inlet

4

24 **Parksville**

MACMILLAN PROVINCIAL PARK

Qualicum R.

101

20 **Bamfield**

West Coast Trail

Nanaimo 17

Gabriola Island

Newcastle Island

18

Vancouver

Valdes Is.

1

16 **Chemainus**

Galiano Is.

Port Renfrew

Duncan 15

18

Saltspring Is.

Gulf Islands

Mayne Is.

32

14

Malahat

Sidney

1

Saturna Is.

17

Sooke 14

1 – 13

CANADA USA

Victoria ★

PACIFIC OCEAN

KEY
⚓ Ferry
🍁 Trans-Canada Hwy.

0 —— 50 miles
0 —— 75 km

TO PORT ANGELES

TO SEATTLE

Sooke

⑭ *42 km (26 mi) west of Victoria on Rte. 14.*

Sooke is a logging, fishing, and farming community. **East Sooke Park,** on the east side of the harbor, has 3,500 acres of beaches, hiking trails, and wildflower-dotted meadows. You can also visit the **Sooke Region Museum and Travel Infocentre,** where displays of Salish and Nootka crafts and artifacts from 19th-century Sooke occasionally compete with barbecued salmon and strawberry shortcake on the front lawn in summer. ⊠ *2070 Phillips Rd., Box 774, V0S 1N0,* ☎ *250/642–6351.* 🎟 *Free; donations accepted.* ☉ *June–Aug., daily 9–6; Sept.–May, Tues.–Sun. 9–5.*

Dining and Lodging

$ ✕ **Seventeen Mile House.** Stop here on the road between Sooke and Victoria for British pub fare, a beer, or fresh local seafood. Built as a hotel, the house is an education in turn-of-the-century island architecture. ⊠ *5121 Sooke Rd.,* ☎ *250/642–5942. MC, V.*

$$$$ ✕🏠 **Sooke Harbour House.** This 1931 clapboard farmhouse-turned-
★ country inn has three suites, a 10-room addition, and a dining room—all of which exude elegance. One of the finest restaurants in British Columbia, it is well worth the trip to Sooke from Victoria. The seafood is just-caught fresh, and the herbs are grown on the property. Four chefs in the kitchen guarantee an abundance of creative dishes. In the romantic guest rooms, natural wood and white finishes add to each unit's unique theme. Rooms range from the Herb Garden Room—decorated in shades of mint, with French doors opening onto a private patio—to the Longhouse Room, complete with Native American furnishings. All units have fireplaces and either ocean or mountain views. Breakfast and lunch are included in room rates, but you must make a reservation for your meals. Nonguests must make reservations for dinner. ⊠ *1528 Whiffen Spit Rd., R.R. 4, V0S 1N0,* ☎ *250/642–3421 or 250/642–4944,* ⅻ *250/642–6988. 13 rooms. Restaurant, no-smoking rooms, beach, meeting room. AE, MC, V.*

$$-$$$ ✕🏠 **Ocean Wilderness.** This large 1940s log cabin sits on five forested, beachfront acres, 13 kilometers (8 miles) west of Sooke. Auction-buff owner Marion Rolston built a rough cedar addition in 1990 and has furnished her home with a fine collection of Victorian antiques. Romantic canopies and ruffled linens on high beds dominate the spacious guest rooms, which have sitting areas with views of either the Strait of Juan de Fuca or the pretty gardens in the back, as well as private decks or patios. The dining room fare is innovative West Coast treatments of fresh local fish and meats. ⊠ *109 W. Coast Rd., R.R. 2, V0S 1N0,* ☎ ⅻ *250/646–2116. 9 rooms. Dining room, no-smoking rooms, hot tub, hiking trails. MC, V.*

Shopping

Watercolor artist and author **Sue Coleman** (☎ 250/478–0380) in Metchosin, 35 minutes west of Victoria on the road to Sooke, invites visitors to the island to tour her studio by appointment.

Duncan

⑮ *60 km (37 mi) north of Victoria on the Trans-Canada Hwy.*

Duncan is nicknamed City of Totems for the many totem poles that dot the small community. The two carvings behind the City Hall are worth a short trip off the main road.

Duncan is also home to the **Native Heritage Centre.** Covering 13 acres on the banks of the Cowichan River, the center includes a native long-house, a theater, occasional interpretive dance presentations, an arts-and-crafts gallery that focuses on carvings and weaving traditions, and native fare served in the Bighouse Restaurant. ⊠ *200 Cowichan Way,* ☎ *250/746–8119.* ☞ *$6.75.* ⊙ *Mid-May–mid Oct., daily 9:30–5:30; mid-Oct.–mid-May, daily 10–4:30.*

Also in Duncan is the **British Columbia Forest Museum.** More a park than a museum, it spans some 100 acres, combining indoor and out-door exhibits that focus on the history of forestry in British Columbia. You ride an original steam locomotive around the property and over an old wood trestle bridge. The exhibits show logging and milling equip-ment. ⊠ *R.R. 4, Trans-Canada Hwy.,* ☎ *250/746–1251,* FAX *250/746–1487.* ☞ *$7.* ⊙ *May–Sept., daily 9:30–6; Oct.–Apr. by appointment.*

Shopping

Duncan is the home of Cowichan wool sweaters, hand knitted by the Cowichan people. A large selection is available from **Hills Indian Crafts** (☎ 250/746–6731) on the main highway, about 1½ kilometers (1 mile) south of Duncan. **Modeste Wool Carding** (⊠ 2615 Modeste Rd., Duncan, ☎ 250/748–8983), about a half mile off the highway, also carries a selection of handmade knitwear.

Chemainus

⓰   *85 km (53 mi) north of Victoria, 27 km (17 mi) south of Nanaimo.*

Chemainus is known for the bold epic murals that decorate its town-scape. Once dependent on the lumber industry, the small community began to revitalize itself in the early 1980s when its mill closed down. Since then, the town has brought in international artists to paint more than 30 murals depicting local historical events around town. Foot-prints on the sidewalk lead you on a self-guided tour of the murals. Restaurants, shops, tea rooms, coffee bars, art galleries, antiques deal-ers, and the new Chemainus Theater (☎ 250/246–9820 or 800/565–7738) have added to the town's growth.

Nanaimo

⓱   *113 km (70 mi) northwest of Victoria, 115 km (71 mi) southeast of Comox, 155 km (96 mi) southeast of Campbell River, 23 km (14 mi) on land plus 38 nautical mi west of Vancouver.*

Throughout the Nanaimo region, there are petroglyphs (rock carvings) representing humans, birds, wolves, lizards, sea monsters, and super-natural creatures. The **Nanaimo District Museum** (⊠ 100 Cameron St., ☎ 250/753–1821) will give you information about local carvings. Eight kilometers (5 miles) south of town at **Petroglyph Provincial Park,** you can follow marked trails that begin at the parking lot to see designs carved thousands of years ago.

Dining and Lodging

$$ ✕ **Mahle House.** This casually elegant place serves innovative North-
★   west cuisine, such as braised rabbit with Dijon mustard and red wine sauce. Among the items on the regular menu are a succulent carrot and ginger soup and a catch of the day. Care for detail, an intimate setting, and three country-style rooms make this one of the finest dining ex-periences in the region. ⊠ *Cedar and Heemer Rds.,* ☎ *250/722–3621. MC, V. No lunch. Closed Mon. and Tues.*

$–$$ ✕ **The Grotto.** A Nanaimo institution that specializes in a variety of
★   seafood, this casual restaurant has a waterfront setting. Try oysters on

the half shell, the spareribs, garlic prawn pasta, or the seafood platter that's big enough for two. The Kitchen Sink, a heaping bowl of clams, shrimp, and salmon steamed in white wine, herbs, and butter, is a favorite here. ⊠ *1511 Stewart Ave.,* ☎ *250/753–3303. AE, MC, V. No lunch. Closed Dec. 25.*

$$$–$$$$ ✕⊞ **La Coast Bastion Inn.** This convenient hotel is downtown near the ferry terminal and train and bus stations. Rooms with balconies and modern furnishings have views of the old Hudson's Bay fort and the ocean. ⊠ *11 Bastion St., V9R 2Z9,* ☎ *250/753–6601; in the U.S., 800/663–1144,* ℻ *250/753–4155. 179 rooms. Restaurant, lounge, Irish deli/pub, no-smoking rooms, room service, hot tub, sauna, exercise room, laundry service and dry cleaning, meeting rooms. AE, DC, MC, V.*

$–$$$ ✕⊞ **Yellow Point Lodge.** Yellow Point is a very popular resort area on
  ★   a spit of land south of Nanaimo, east of Ladysmith. Rebuilt in 1986 after a fire destroyed the original, the lodge lost almost nothing in ambience. Nine large lodge rooms and a range of cottages all have private baths; most are available year-round. Perched on a rocky knoll overlooking the Stuart Channel are beach cabins, field cabins, and beach barracks for the hardy, which are closed mid-October to mid-April, have no running water, and share a central bathhouse. You can stroll the lodge's 180 acres of land, and there are plenty of canoes and kayaks available for exploring the shoreline. Three full meals and snacks are included in the rate. ⊠ *Yellow Point Rd., R.R. 3, Ladysmith V0R 2E0,* ☎ *250/245–7422,* ℻ *250/245–7411. 50 rooms. Restaurant (for guests only), no-smoking rooms, saltwater pool, hot tub, sauna, 2 tennis courts, badminton, jogging, volleyball, boating, mountain bikes. MC, V.*

$$$ ⊞ **Best Western Dorchester Hotel.** Upbeat Mediterranean tones of champagne, ochre, and teal brighten the exterior of the Dorchester. Once the Nanaimo Opera House, this elegant hotel in the city center overlooking the harbor has a distinctive character, with gold knockers on each of the doors, winding hallways, and a rooftop patio. The rooms are small but exceptionally comfortable, and most have views of the harbor. ⊠ *70 Church St., V9R 5H4,* ☎ *250/754–6835 or 800/528–1234,* ℻ *250/754–2638. 64 rooms. Restaurant, lounge, no-smoking rooms, room service, library, laundry service and dry cleaning, meeting rooms. AE, D, DC, MC, V.*

Outdoor Activities and Sports

CANOEING AND KAYAKING
For multiple-day, guided sea-kayak expeditions, contact **Wild Heart Adventures** (⊠ Site P, C-5, R.R. 4, Nanaimo, V9R 5X9, ☎ 250/722–3683, ℻ 250/722–2175).

GOLF
Fairwinds Golf and Country Club (⊠ 3730 Fairwinds Dr., Nanoose Bay, ☎ 250/468–7666 or 800/930–4622).

Gabriola Island

⓲ *3.7 nautical mi (20-minute ferry ride) east of Nanaimo.*

From rustic, rural Gabriola Island, which has lodging, you can take a further 10-minute ferry ride to **Newcastle Island,** where you can picnic, ride your bicycle, walk on trails leading past old mines and quarries, and catch glimpses of deer, rabbits, and eagles.

Port Alberni

⑲ *80 km (49 mi) from Nanaimo north on Route 19 and west on Route 4.*

Port Alberni is mainly a pulp- and sawmill town and a stopover on the way to Ucluelet and Tofino. The salmon-rich waters attract fishermen.

From here, you can take a breathtaking trip to towns along the Alberni Inlet and Barkley Sound aboard the **Lady Rose,** a Scottish ship built in 1937. ⊠ *Argyle St. dock,* ☎ *250/723–8313; reservations Apr.–Sept., 800/663–7192.* ✉ *Bamfield $36, Broken Group Islands $38, Ucluelet $40.* ☉ *Sailings daily 8 AM.*

Bamfield

⑳ *95 nautical mi (4-hour cruise) south of Port Alberni.*

In Bamfield, a remote village of about 200, the seaside boardwalk affords an uninterrupted view of ships heading up the inlet to Port Alberni. The town is well equipped to handle overnight visitors. Bamfield is also a good base for boating trips to the Broken Group Islands and hikes along the West Coast Trail (☞ *below*).

Ucluelet

㉑ *160 km (100 mi) by car west of Port Alberni.*

Ucluelet, which in the native language means "people with a safe landing place," is totally focused on the sea. Fishing, water tours, and whale watching are the primary activities. A variety of charter companies take tourist boats to greet the 20,000 gray whales that pass close to Ucluelet on their migration to the Bering Sea every March through May. Sometimes you can even see the migrating whales from the Ucluelet shore.

Dining and Lodging

$$ ✕ **Whale's Tale.** At this no-frills, dark but warmly decorated down-to-earth place, the cooking and the rustic decor go hand-in-hand. The view isn't much, but the cedar-shingle building, set on pilings, shakes with a good gust of wind. The menu is highlighted by prime rib and a variety of local seafood. ⊠ *1861 Peninsula Rd.,* ☎ *250/726–4621. MC, V. No lunch. Closed Nov.–Jan.*

$$ ✕ **Wickaninnish Restaurant.** Before the Canadian government ac-
★ quired this wonderful wood building for its interpretive center, it was a unique inn. It is still a restaurant, with an ambience—the beach setting, combined with the building's glass exterior and stone-and-beam interior, accented by a stone fireplace—that cannot be matched anywhere else in the area. Seafood is the primary choice here—especially the West Coast chowder—but if you order the stir-fry, you won't be disappointed. ⊠ *Long Beach, 16 km (11 mi) north of Ucluelet,* ☎ *250/726–7706. AE, MC, V. Closed mid-Oct.–mid-Feb.*

$$–$$$ 🏨 **Canadian Princess Fishing Resort.** If vintage ships are to your liking, book a cabin on this converted 230-foot survey ship, which has 36 comfortable, but hardly opulent, staterooms. Each offers one to four berths, and all share washrooms. Roomier than the ship cabins, the resort's deluxe shoreside rooms come complete with more contemporary furnishings; a few feature fireplaces. This unique resort provides the bare necessities—mostly to nature enthusiasts and fishermen. ⊠ *Boat Basin, Box 939, V0R 3A0,* ☎ *250/726–7771 or 800/663–7090,* FAX *250/726–7121. 46 shoreside and 30 shipboard sleeping units. 2 bars, dining room, no-smoking rooms, boating, fishing. AE, DC, MC, V.*

Tofino

㉒ *321 km (199 mi) northwest of Victoria, 208 km (129 mi) west of Nanaimo, 126 km (78 mi) west of Port Alberni, 42 km (26 mi) northwest of Ucluelet.*

Tofino is commercial, with beachfront resorts, motels, and several unique B&Bs. The surrounding area remains natural; you can walk along the beach discovering caves, cruise around the ancient forests of Meares Island, or take an hour-long water taxi ride to the hot springs north of town.

Lodging

$$$$ **Chesterman's Beach Bed and Breakfast.** This small, romantic bed-
★ and-breakfast on the beach has rolling ocean surf for a front yard. You can walk the beach, search the tidal pools, or—from March to October—watch whales migrate. The self-contained suite in the main house (complete with sauna and full kitchen) and the separate Lookout Suite are romantic and cozy; both have a fireplace, comfortable beds, and a view of the beach. The self-sufficient one-bedroom garden cottage offers no ocean view but accommodates up to four; it's a good option for a family vacation. ⊠ *1345 Chesterman's Beach Rd., V0R 2Z0,* ☎ FAX *250/725–3726. 1 room, 2 suites. Beach, no-smoking rooms, kitchenettes, refrigerators. MC, V.*

$$$–$$$$ **Pacific Sands Beach Resort.** Just a mile north of Pacific Rim National Park, this beachside resort has motel suites and individual two-bedroom cottages, each with a beautiful bay view. The motel rooms have modern furnishings, and fireplaces make them seem cozy. Some of the specialty suites in the three-story addition have hot tubs outside on the deck. Dangerous currents and riptides off the beach in front of the resort make it unsuitable for swimming. ⊠ *1421 Pacific Rim Hwy., Box 237, V0R 2Z0,* ☎ *250/725–3322 or 800/565–2322,* FAX *250/725–3155. 54 rooms, 10 cottages. Kitchenettes, no-smoking rooms, beach, coin laundry. AE, MC, V.*

Outdoor Activities and Sports

CANOEING AND KAYAKING

You can rent canoes and kayaks from **Tofino Sea-Kayaking Company** (⊠ Box 620, V0N 3J0, ☎ 250/928–3117 or 250/725–4222).

GOLF

Long Beach Golf Course (⊠ Pacific Rim Hwy., ☎ 250/725–3332).

Pacific Rim National Park★

㉓ *85 km (53 mi) west of Port Alberni.*

Pacific Rim National Park (⊠ Box 280, Ucluelet, V0R 3A0, ☎ 250/726–7721, FAX 250/726–4720) is the first national marine park in Canada. It comprises three separate areas—Long Beach, the Broken Group Islands, and the West Coast Trail for a combined area of 49,962 hectares (20,243 acres). Each section accommodates a specific interest.

The **Long Beach** unit gets its name from an 11-kilometer (7-mile) strip of hard-packed white sand strewn with twisted driftwood, shells, and the occasional Japanese glass fishing float. It is a favorite spot in summer, and you often have to fight heavy traffic along the twisting Route 4 from Port Alberni.

The 100 **Broken Group Islands** can be reached only by boat. Many commercial charter tours are available from Ucluelet, at the southern end of Long Beach, and from Bamfield and Port Alberni. The islands and their waters are alive with sea lions, seals, and whales. The sheltered lagoons of Gibraltar, Jacques, and Hand islands offer protection and good boating conditions, but go with a guide.

The third element of the park, the **West Coast Trail** (☞ Hiking, *below*), stretches along the coast from Bamfield to Port Renfrew. After the S.S. *Valencia* ran aground in 1906, killing all but 30 of the crew and passengers, the Canadian government constructed the lifesaving trail to help future victims of shipwrecks reach safe ground. The trail remains, with demanding bogs, steep slopes and gullies, cliffs (with ladders), slippery boardwalks, and insects. The rewards of a hike here are the panoramic views of the sea, the dense rain forest, sandstone cliffs with waterfalls, and wildlife that includes gray whales and seals.

Outdoor Activities and Sports

HIKING

One of the most challenging hikes in British Columbia is along the **West Coast Trail** (☞ Exploring, *above*). The demanding 77-kilometer (47-mile) trail is for experienced hikers and follows part of the coast known as the "Graveyard of the Pacific" because of the large number of shipwrecks that have occurred there. It can be traveled only on foot, takes an average of six days to complete, and is open from May to late September. A permit is necessary to hike this trail; reservations are available from March through September.

En Route   Heading back to the east coast from Port Alberni, stop off at **Cathedral Grove** in MacMillan Provincial Park on Route 4. Walking trails lead you past Douglas fir trees and western red cedars, some as much as 800 years old. Their remarkable height creates a spiritual effect, as though you were gazing at a cathedral ceiling. Another stop along the way is **Butterfly World** (⊠ Rte. 4, Box 36, Coombs, V0R 1M0, ☏ 250/248–7026), an enclosed tropical garden housing an amazing collection of exotic, free-flying tropical butterflies.

Parksville

㉔   *38 km (24 mi) northwest of Nanaimo, 47 km (29 mi) east of Port Alberni, 72 km (45 mi) southeast of Courtenay, 151 km (94 mi) northwest of Victoria, at junction of Routes 4 and 19.*

Parksville is one of the east island's primary resort areas, where lodges and waterfront motels cater to families, campers, and boaters. In **Rathtrevor Provincial Park** (☏ 250/248–9449), 1½ kilometers (about 1 mile) south of Parksville, high tide brings ashore the warmest ocean water in British Columbia, so plan to swim here.

Lodging

$$–$$$ 🏨 **Holiday Inn Express.** Across the street from the pretty beach in Parksville, this hotel opened in 1994. Kids under 19 stay free with their parents in the motel-modern rooms outfitted with two queen-size beds. King-size rooms have whirlpool tubs. ⊠ *424 W. Island Hwy., V9P 1K8,* ☏ *250/248–2232 or 800/661–3110,* FAX *250/248–3273. 87 rooms, 3 suites. No-smoking rooms, indoor pool, hot tub, exercise room. AE, DC, MC, V.*

$–$$ 🏨 **Roadhouse Inn.** This small Swiss-style chalet, set on 3 acres, is central to four of the region's golf courses. The rooms, on the second floor, are comfortable, with basic furnishings. ⊠ *1223 Smithers Rd., V9P 2C1,* ☏ *250/248–2912. 6 rooms. Restaurant. MC, V.*

Outdoor Activities and Sports

GOLF

Morningstar Golf Course (⊠ 525 Lowery Rd., Parksville, ☎ 250/248–8161).

Qualicum Beach

㉕ *12 km (7 mi) north of Parksville.*

Qualicum Beach is known largely for its salmon fishing and opportunities for beachcombing. The nonprofit **Old School House Gallery and Art Centre** (⊠ 122 Fern Rd. W, ☎ 250/752–6133), with seven working studios, shows and sells the work of local artists and artisans.

Horne Lake

㉖ *25 km (16 mi) north of Parksville, then 15 km (9 mi) west off Hwy. 19.*

At Horne Lake you'll find the **Horne Lake Caves Provincial Park.** Three of the six caves are open at all times. If you decide to venture in, bring along a flashlight, warm clothes, and a hard hat, and be prepared to bend and even crawl. Riverbend Cave, 1,260 feet long, requires ladders and ropes in some parts, and can only be explored with a guided tour. Spelunking lessons and tours are offered for all levels, from beginner to advanced. Make reservations for tours. ☎ 250/248–7829. ▨ *Fees for tours vary depending on ability.*

En Route Between the Horne Lake turnoff and the twin cities of Comox and Courtenay is tiny Buckley Bay, where ferries leave for **Denman Island,** with connecting service to **Hornby Island.** Denman offers old-growth forests and long sandy beaches, while Hornby's spectacular beaches have earned it the nickname the Undiscovered Hawaii of British Columbia. Many artists have settled on the islands, establishing studios for pottery, jewelry, wood carving, and sculpture.

Comox and Courtenay

㉗ *220 km (136 mi) northwest of Victoria, 17 nautical mi west of Powell River, 46 km (29 mi) southeast of Campbell River.*

Comox and Courtenay are near **Strathcona Provincial Park** and commonly provide a base for Mt. Washington skiers in winter. Strathcona, the largest provincial park on Vancouver Island, encompasses **Mt. Golden Hinde,** at 7,220 feet the island's highest mountain; and **Della Falls,** Canada's highest waterfall, reaching 1,440 feet. The park's multitude of lakes and 161 campsites attract summer canoers, fishermen, and wilderness campers, and the **Strathcona Park Lodge and Outdoor Education Center,** well known for its wilderness-skills programs, has information on the park's facilities. ⊠ *Education Center, Rte. 28, Upper Campbell Lake, about 45 km (28 mi) west of Rte. 19, Box 2160, Campbell River, V9W 5C9,* ☎ *250/286–3122.* ☉ *Hours vary; call ahead.*

Dining and Lodging

$$ ✕ **Old House Restaurant.** This bilevel restaurant offers casual dining
★ in a restored 1938 house with large cedar beams and a stone fireplace. People flock here for the West Coast home-style cuisine—pastas, salads, and sandwiches, along with fancier, more innovative dishes (rack of lamb, panfried flounder, California cioppino)—on the fresh-daily sheet. ⊠ *1760 Riverside La., Courtenay,* ☎ *250/338–5406. AE, DC, MC, V.*

$$ ▥ **Greystone Manor.** This no-smoking bed-and-breakfast, set in a 1918 house with period furnishings, looks out on Comox Harbor, where

a playful colony of seals is often visible. The antiques, wood stove, and wood paneling add to the hospitable, cozy feel here. Breakfast, which includes fresh fruit, muffins, and fruit pancakes, is enough to keep you filled most of the day. You can walk in the English garden and on trails nearby. ⊠ *4014 Haas Rd., Site 684–C2, R.R. 6, Courtenay V9N 8H9,* ☎ *250/338–1422. 3 rooms with bath. Breakfast room, no-smoking rooms, hiking. MC, V.*

$$ 🏨 **Kingfisher.** Ten minutes south of Courtenay, this hotel stands among
★ trees and overlooks the Strait of Georgia. Solid furnishings, clean white stucco walls, a bright lobby with lots of greenery, and rooms with mountain and ocean views make this place special. ⊠ *4330 S. Island Hwy. (Site 672, R.R. 6), Courtenay V9N 8H9,* ☎ *250/338–1323; in British Columbia, OR, and WA, 800/663–7929;* FAX *250/338–0058. 30 units. Restaurant, lounge, pool, tennis court. AE, D, DC, MC, V.*

Outdoor Activities and Sports

SKIING

Cross-Country. Mt. Washington (☞ *below*) has 36 kilometers (22 miles) of double track–set Nordic trails.

Downhill. Mt. Washington Ski Resort Ltd. (⊠ Box 3069, Courtenay V9N 5N3, ☎ 250/338–1386), with nearly 50 runs and an elevation of 5,200 feet, is the largest ski area on the island, and the third-largest in terms of visitors in the province. It's a modern, well-organized mountain with snowpack averaging 472 inches a year. **Forbidden Plateau** (⊠ Box 3268, Courtenay V9N 5N4, ☎ 250/334–4744), near Mt. Washington, has 15 runs and a vertical drop of 1,150 feet.

Powell River

㉘ *17 nautical mi (75-minute ferry ride) east across Strait of Georgia from Comox, 121 km (76 mi) plus 12.5 nautical mi northwest of Vancouver.*

Powell River was established around the MacMillan pulp-and-paper mill, which opened in 1912. Renowned as a year-round salmon-fishing destination, the mainland Sunshine Coast town has 30 regional lakes that offer exceptional trout fishing, as well. For information contact **Powell River Travel Info Center** (⊠ 4690 Marine Ave., ☎ 250/485–4701).

Campbell River

㉙ *266 km (165 mi) northwest of Victoria, 155 km (96 mi) northwest of Nanaimo, 225 km (140 mi) southeast of Port Hardy.*

Campbell River is ringed by shopping centers that make it look like a free-zoned mess. But people come for the fish; some of the biggest salmon ever caught on a line have been landed just off the coast here. At the mouth of the town's namesake, you can try for membership in Campbell River's Tyee Club, which would allow you to fish in a specific area and possibly land a giant chinook. Requirements for membership in the club include registering and landing a tyee (a spring salmon weighing 30 pounds or more). Coho salmon and cutthroat trout are also plentiful in the river. For information contact **Campbell River Tourism** (⊠ 1235 Island Hwy., Box 482, Campbell River, V9W 5C1, ☎ 250/286–1616 or 800/463–4386).

Dining and Lodging

$–$$ ✕ **Royal Coachman Inn.** Informal, blackboard-menu restaurants like
★ this one dot the landscape of the island. The menu, which changes daily, is surprisingly daring for what is essentially a high-end pub, and the inn draws crowds nightly, especially on Tuesday and Saturday (prime

rib nights). Come early for both lunch and dinner to avoid a wait. ⊠ *84 Dogwood St.,* ☎ *250/286–0231. AE, MC, V.*

$$$–$$$$ ✕⬚ **April Point Lodge and Fishing Resort.** Operated for 50 years by
★ the friendly Peterson family, the lodge has developed a tremendous reputation. The 1944 cedar lodge is surrounded by refurbished fishermen's cabins and guest houses that spread across a point of Quadra Island and stretch into Discovery Passage across from Campbell River. The accommodations are tidy and comfortable; most have kitchen facilities, fireplaces, and sun decks. Kwakiutl and Haida art adorn the comfortable lounge and dining room, where fine regional cuisine is served. Native feasts on the beach on warm summer nights are especially memorable, with spitted salmon roasted over an open fire; fresh steamed scallops, prawns, and clams; and wine from the extensive cellar. ⊠ *1000 April Point Rd., Box 1, V9W 4Z9,* ☎ *250/285–2222,* FAX *250/285–2411. 33 units. 2 bars, breakfast room, coffee shop, dining room, lobby lounge, picnic area, sushi bar, tea shop, no-smoking rooms, saltwater pool, exercise room, hiking, diving, dock, snorkeling, marina, fishing (salt and freshwater), bicycles, piano, baby-sitting, coin laundry, laundry service, business services, meeting rooms, airport shuttle, helipad. AE, D, DC, MC, V. Some units closed Nov.–Mar.*

$$$–$$$$ ⬚ **Tsa-Kwa-Luten Lodge.** This resort, operated by members of the Kwakiutl tribe, offers authentic Pacific Coast native food and cultural activities. It stands on a high bluff amid 1,100 acres of forest on Quadra Island, a 10-minute ferry ride from Campbell River. Each room in the main lodge has a sea view from a deck or patio; many have a fireplace and loft. Four beachfront cabins have fireplaces, whirlpool tubs, kitchen facilities, and private verandas. Guests can take part in traditional dances in the resort's lounge, which resembles a longhouse, and visit nearby petroglyphs to make rubbings. ⊠ *Lighthouse Rd., Box 460, Quathiaski Cove, V0P 1N0,* ☎ *250/285–2042 or 800/665–7745,* FAX *250/285–2532. 26 rooms, 4 cabins. Restaurant, lounge, no-smoking rooms, room service, hot tub, sauna, exercise room, fishing, mountain bikes, laundry service, business services, meeting rooms. AE, DC, MC, V.*

Outdoor Activities and Sports

CANOEING AND KAYAKING

Island Sauvage (⊠ 131 Beach St., Campbell River, V9W 5G4, ☎ 250/286–0205, FAX 250/287–8840) has canoes and kayaks for rent.

GOLF

Storey Creek Golf Club (⊠ Box 727, Campbell River, ☎ 250/923–3673).

HIKING

Island Sauvage (⊠ 131 Beach St., Campbell River, V9W 5G4, ☎ 250/286–0205; in Canada, 800/667–4354) can arrange heli-hiking.

En Route Pods of resident orcas live year-round in **Johnstone Strait;** in **Robson Bight** they like using the beaches to rub against. Because of their presence, Robson Bight has been made into an ecological preserve: Whales there must not be disturbed by human observers. Some of the island's best whale-watching tours, however, are conducted nearby, out of **Telegraph Cove,** a village built on pilings over water. In Telegraph Cove, you can rent canoes and kayaks from **Stubbs Island Charters** (☎ 250/928–3185). Half-day whale-watching expeditions are available through **Stubbs Island Whale Watching** (⊠ Box 7, Telegraph Cove, ☎ 250/928–3185) on the west coast of Johnstone Strait and **Seasmoke Tours** (⊠ Box 483, Alert Bay, ☎ 250/974–5225) on the east coast. For a longer trip, contact the **Canadian Outback Adventure Company** (⊠

1110 Hamilton St., 206, Vancouver, ☏ 250/688–7206) to learn more about their week-long sea kayaking trips among the orca (killer whales) in Johnstone Strait.

Port Hardy

㉚ *499 km (310 mi) northwest of Victoria, 274 nautical mi southeast of Prince Rupert, 238 km (148 mi) northwest of Campbell River, 284 km (176 mi) northwest of Courtenay, 391 km (243 mi) northwest of Nanaimo.*

Port Hardy is the departure and arrival point for B.C. Ferries going through the Inside Passage to and from Prince Rupert, the coastal port serving the Queen Charlotte Islands. In summer the town can be crowded, so book your accommodations well in advance. Ferry reservations for the trip between Port Hardy and Prince Rupert should also be made well in advance.

Lodging

$$ 🏨 **Glen Lyon Inn.** The rooms have a full ocean view of Hardy Bay and, like most area motels, have clean, modern amenities. Eagles can often be spotted eyeing the water for fish to prey on. The inn is a short ride from the ferry terminal. ⊠ *6435 Hardy Bay Rd., Box 103, V0N 2P0,* ☏ *250/949–7115,* ℻ *250/949–7415. 29 rooms. Restaurant, lounge, no-smoking rooms. AE, D, DC, MC, V.*

Cape Scott

㉛ *60 km (37 mi) on logging roads northwest of Port Hardy.*

The northernmost point on Vancouver Island is in **Cape Scott Provincial Park,** a wilderness camping region designed for well-equipped and experienced hikers. At Sand Neck, a strip of land that joins the cape to the mainland of the island, you can see both the eastern and the western shores at once.

THE GULF ISLANDS

Traveling up the northeastern coastline of Vancouver Island in the late 1790s, Captain George Vancouver dubbed the expansive body of water on which he sailed the Gulf of Georgia, thinking that it led to open sea. While the name of the waterway was later changed to the Strait of Georgia when further exploration revealed that the British Columbia mainland lay to the east, the islands dotting the strait con-
㉜ tinue to be known as the **Gulf Islands.**

Of the hundreds of islands in this strait, the most popular are Galiano, Mayne, North and South Pender, Saturna, and Salt Spring. A temperate Mediterranean climate (warmer, with half the rainfall of Vancouver), scenic beaches, towering promontories, rolling pasturelands, and virgin forests are common to all, but each also has its unique flavor. Marine birds are numerous, and unusual vegetation such as arbutus trees (also known as madrones, a leafy evergreen with red peeling bark) and Garry oaks differentiate the islands from other areas around Vancouver. Writers, artists, craftspeople, weekend cottagers, and retirees take full advantage of the undeveloped islands.

For a first visit to the Gulf Islands, make a stopover on Salt Spring Island, the most commercialized of the southern islands, or on more subdued, pastoral Mayne Island. Their proximity to Vancouver makes each feasible for a one- or two-day trip. Free maps are available on the ferry or in island stores.

Mayne Island

28 nautical mi from Swartz Bay (32 km, or 20 mi, north of Victoria),
22 nautical mi from Tsawwassen (39 km, or 24 mi, south of Vancouver).

Middens of clam and oyster shells give evidence that tiny **Mayne Island**—only 21 square kilometers (8½ square miles)—was inhabited as early as 5,000 years ago. It later became the stopover point for miners headed from Victoria to the gold fields of Fraser River and Barkersville, and by the mid-1800s had developed into the communal center of the inhabited Gulf Islands, with the first school, post office, police lockup, church, and hotel. Farm tracts and orchards established in the 1930s and 1940s and worked by Japanese farmers until their internment during World War II continue to thrive today, and a farmer's market is open each Saturday during harvest season. There are few stores, restaurants, or historic sites here, but Mayne's manageable size (even if you're on a bicycle) and slower pace make it very popular.

Starting at the ferry dock at **Village Bay,** head toward Miners Bay on Village Bay Road. About half a mile from the ferry landing on the left is the unmarked path to **Helen Point** (pull off on the shoulder near the grouping of power lines that cross the road), previously a native reservation, which currently has no inhabitants. You'll pass middens by the bay and log cabin remains in the woods on the hour-long hike out to Helen Point, where you can look out across Active Pass (named for the turbulent waters).

A quarter mile farther on the right side of Village Bay Road is the entrance to **Mount Parke,** declared a wilderness park in 1989. Drive as far as the gate and the sign that reads NO VEHICLES PAST THIS POINT. From here it's a 15- to 20-minute hike to the highest point on the island and a stunning, almost 360-degree view of Vancouver, Active Pass, and Vancouver Island.

Continue on Village Bay Road toward **Miners Bay,** a little town 2 kilometers (1¼ miles) away. Here, you'll find **Plumbers Pass Lockup,** built in 1896 as a jail and now a minuscule museum chronicling the island's history (closed Sept.–June).

From Miners Bay head east on Georgia Point Road to **St. Mary Magdalene Church,** a pretty stone chapel built in 1898 that now doubles as an Anglican and United church. The graveyard beyond is also interesting; generations of islanders—the Bennets, Georgesons, Maudes, and Deacons (whose names are all over the Mayne Island map)—are buried here. Across the road, a stairway leads down to the beach.

At the end of Georgia Point Road is the **Active Pass Lighthouse,** built in 1855, which still signals ships into the busy waterway. The grassy grounds, open to the public every day from 1 to 3, are great for picnicking.

Head Back down Georgia Point Road and turn left on Waugh Road, which turns into Campbell Bay Road. There's a great pebble beach for beachcombing at shallow (and therefore warmer) **Campbell Bay.** Look for a pull-out on the left just past the bottom of the hairpin turn. A fence post marks the entrance to the path leading to the beach. Campbell Bay Road ends at Fernhill Road; turn right here and you'll end up back in Miners Bay.

Dining and Lodging

$$$$　✕🏠 **Fernhill Lodge.** Constructed of wood from the property, this 1983 West Coast cedar contemporary is host to fantastical theme rooms— Moroccan, East Indian, Edwardian, Japanese, Colonial, Jacobean, and French. Two of them have outdoor hot tubs. Outside on the five-acre grounds are a rustic gazebo with a meditation loft, an Elizabethan knot garden, and a medieval "garden of physic." To complete the unique experience, hosts Mary and Brian Crumblehulme offer historical dinners (Roman, Chaucer, and Cleopatra to name a few) several nights a week; non-guests must reserve in advance. Breakfasts, which are included in the room rate, are rather less exotic. This is a no-smoking inn, and pets are not allowed. ⊠ *Fernhill Rd., R.R. 1 C–4, Mayne Island, V0N 2J0,* ☎ *250/539–2544. 7 rooms. Dining room, no-smoking rooms, sauna, bicycles, library. MC, V.*

\$\$\$\$ ✕ ⛰ **Oceanwood Country Inn.** This Tudor-style house on 10 quiet,
★ forested acres overlooking Navy Channel has English country decor throughout. The inn was expanded in 1995. Fireplaces, ocean view balconies, and whirlpool or soaking tubs make several rooms deluxe; all are inviting, with cozy down comforters on comfortable beds, cheerful wall stenciling, and cushioned chairs in brightly lit reading areas. For dinner, the waterfront dining room, which is open to the public, offers award-winning regional cuisine emphasizing fresh local ingredients including fruit, vegetables, and herbs from the inn's extensive garden. You may find grilled salmon, tomato and Dungeness crab soup, or wild mushroom and goat cheese ravioli on the prix-fixe, fresh daily menu. Afternoon tea and breakfast are included in the room rates. There is a guest pay phone, no children or pets are allowed, and smoking is restricted to the library and outdoors. ⊠ *630 Dinner Bay Rd., Mayne Island, V0N 2J0,* ☎ *250/539–5074,* ℻ *250/539–3002. 12 rooms. Restaurant, no-smoking rooms, hot tub, sauna, hiking, jogging, beach, bicycles, game room, library, meeting room with VCR and movie library. MC, V.*

Salt Spring

28 nautical mi from Swartz Bay (32 km, or 20 mi, north of Victoria), 22 nautical mi from Tsawwassen (39 km, or 24 mi, south of Vancouver).

Named for the saltwater springs at its north end, Salt Spring is the largest and most developed of the Gulf Islands. Among its first nonnative settlers were black Americans who came here to escape slavery in the 1850s. The agrarian tradition they and other immigrants established remains strong, but tourism and art now support the local economy. A government wharf, two marinas, and a waterfront shopping complex at Ganges serve a community of more than 8,500 residents.

In **Ganges,** a pedestrian-oriented seaside village and the island's cultural and commercial center, you'll find dozens of smart boutiques, galleries, and restaurants. **Mouat's Trading Company** (Fulford–Ganges Road), built in 1912 and still functioning as a community store, is worth a peek. Ganges is also the site of **ArtCraft,** a summer-long art, crafts, theater, music, and dance festival. Dozens of working **artists' studios** are open to the public here; pick up a studio tour map at the Chamber of Commerce on Lower Ganges Road.

From Ganges, you can circle the northern tip of the island by bike or car (on Vesuvius Bay Road, Sunset Road, North End and North Beach Roads, Walker Hook Road, and Robson Road) past fields and peek-a-boo marine views. You can take a shortcut on North End Road past **St. Mary Lake,** your best bet for warm-water swimming.

The summit of **Mt. Maxwell Provincial Park,** near the center of Salt Spring, affords spectacular views of south Salt Spring, Vancouver Island, and other Gulf Islands. It's also a great picnic spot. The last portion of the drive is steep, winding, and unpaved. ⊠ *Mt. Maxwell Rd.,* *off Fulford–Ganges Rd.*

From Mt. Maxwell, follow Fulford–Ganges Road south, then turn east on Beaver Point Road to reach **Ruckle Provincial Park,** site of an 1872 heritage homestead and extensive fields still being farmed by the Ruckle family. The park also has camping and picnic spots and trails leading to rocky headlands.

Dining and Lodging

$$ ✕ **House Piccolo.** Blue and white tablecloths and framed pastel prints on whitewashed walls give this cozy restaurant a casual feel. Broiled sea scallop brochette, roasted British Columbia venison with juniper berries, and the salmon du jour are good choices from the dinner menu, but save room for homemade ice cream or the signature chocolate terrine. ⊠ *108 Hereford Ave., Ganges,* ☎ *250/537–1844. Reservations essential. AE, DC, MC, V. No lunch. Closed Dec. 25 and 26 and Jan.*

$–$$ ✕ **Pomodori.** This local favorite is set in a heritage farmhouse warmed
★ by woodburning fireplaces and overlooking Chemainus across the water. Earthenware pots with dried flowers, antique farm implements, battered wooden tables, bent willow chairs, and international folk music set an eclectic tone for an eatery with a unique menu that changes daily. Roasted tomato, red pepper, and Italian feta in balsamic-vinegar and olive-oil dressing with home-baked focaccia for dipping, chicken, prawn, and mussel jambalaya, and fresh vegetable and herb stew appear often. ⊠ *Booth Bay Resort, 375 Baker Rd., Ganges,* ☎ *250/537–2247. Reservations essential. MC, V. No lunch Mon.–Sat.*

$$$$ ✕🔟 **Hastings House.** One of the finest country inns in North Amer-
★ ica and a member of the Relais et Châteaux group, Hastings House knows how to pamper its guests. The centerpiece of this luxurious 30-acre seaside resort is a Tudor-style manor built in 1940. Guest quarters are in the manor or the farmhouse, in cliff-side or garden cottages, and in lovely suites in the reconstructed barn. All are furnished with fine antiques (primarily English) and follow an English country theme, with such extras as eiderdowns, fireplaces, covered porches or decks, and idyllic views of gardens, pastures, or the harbor. Elegant dinners in the manor house are formal and open to the public: The prix-fixe menu may include grilled eggplant with goat cheese, plum tomato and roasted garlic soup, peppered sea bass on wilted spinach with nasturtium butter, Salt Spring lamb loin with rosemary, and mille-feuille of raspberries with framboise cream. ⊠ *160 Upper Ganges Rd., Box 1110, Ganges, V0S 1E0,* ☎ *250/537–2362 or 800/661–9255,* 📠 *250/537–5333. 3 rooms, 7 suites, 2 2-bedroom suites. Restaurant, minibars, no-smoking rooms, beach, croquet, nature trails, mountain bikes. AE, MC, V. Closed Thanksgiving–mid-Mar.*

$$$$ 🔟 **Old Farmhouse Bed and Breakfast.** Gerti Fuss operates this delightful bed-and-breakfast with the assistance of her husband, Karl. Their gray-and-white saltbox farmhouse sits in a quiet meadow edged by towering trees. The style of the main house, a registered historic property built in 1895, is echoed in the four-room wing added by Karl in 1989, which has country-comfortable guest rooms furnished with pine bedsteads, down comforters, lace curtains, floral chintz fabrics, and wicker chairs. Breakfast in the dining room begins with Gerti's fresh-daily baked goods, followed by a hot entrée such as smoked salmon soufflé. ⊠ *1077 Northend Rd., V8K 1L9,* ☎ *250/537–4113,* 📠 *250/537–4969. 4 rooms. Breakfast room, no-smoking rooms, boating, ferry pick-up service. MC, V.*

$$$$ ⊞ **Salty Springs Resort.** Perched on a 50-foot bluff on the northern shore
of Salt Spring, this is the only property to take advantage of the natural mineral springs of the island. The one-, two-, and three-bedroom
Ponderosa pine cabins have Gothic arch ceilings, fireplaces, kitchenettes, and therapeutic whirlpool massage bathtubs tapped into the
mineral springs. Outside are flower boxes, gas grills, picnic tables, and
unobstructed ocean or forest views. ⊠ *1460 N. Beach Rd., V8K 1J4,*
☎ *250/537–4111,* ℻ *250/537–2939. 12 units. Picnic areas, kitchenettes, refrigerators, gas grills, boating, bicycles, game/music room,
coin laundry. MC, V.*

Shopping

There are bargains galore at both of the island's **Saturday markets,**
held each year between April and October. Fresh produce, seafood, crafts,
clothing, herbs and aromatherapy mixtures, candles, toys, home-
canned items, and more are available at the two markets; one is at the
top of the hill (next to the Harbour House) overlooking Ganges Harbour, the other in the center of town between Fulford–Ganges Road
and Centennial Park.

NORTH OF VANCOUVER ISLAND

Gateway to Alaska and the Yukon, this vast, rugged region is marked
by soaring, snowcapped mountain ranges, scenic fjords, primordial islands, and towering rain forests. Once the center of a vast trading network, the "North by Northwest Region" is home to Haida natives who
have lived here for 10,000 years and more recent immigrants drawn
by the natural resources of fur, fish, and forest. Visitors come to explore the ancient native villages of the Queen Charlotte Islands and
Hazelton, to fish for rainbow trout or giant halibut, and to tour cities
such as Prince Rupert and Prince George, cities that grew out of important fur trading posts.

*Numbers in the margin correspond to points of interest on the British
Columbia map.*

㉝ The 507-km (274-nautical-mile) **Inside Passage,** between Port Hardy
on northern Vancouver Island and Prince Rupert, is a sheltered marine highway that follows a series of natural channels behind protective islands along the green-and-blue shaded British Columbia coast.
The undisturbed landscape of rising mountains and humpbacked islands has a striking, prehistoric look. The comfortable **Queen of the
North,** carrying up to 800 passengers and 157 vehicles, takes 15 hours
(almost all in daylight during summer sailings) to make the Port Hardy
to Prince Rupert trip. Reservations are required for the cruise and advised for hotel accommodations at ports of call. ⊠ *B.C. Ferries, 1112
Fort St., Victoria V8V 4V2,* ☎ *250/386–3431.* 🚢 *Cost varies according
to cabin, vehicle, and season.* ☉ *Oct.–Apr., sailings once weekly; May,
sailings twice-weekly; June–Sept., sailings daily, departing on alternate
days from Port Hardy and Prince Rupert; departure time 7:30 AM, arrival time 10:30 PM. Schedule and fares subject to change.*

An alternative to the ferry cruise along the Inside Passage is one of the
more expensive luxury-liners that sail along the British Columbia coast
(☞ Chapter 1) from Vancouver to Alaska.

Prince Rupert

㉞ *1,502 km (931 mi) by highway and 750 km (465 mi) by air northwest
of Vancouver; 15 hours by ferry northwest of Port Hardy on Vancouver
Island.*

Prince Rupert, the final stop on the B.C. Ferries route through the In-side Passage, has a mild but wet climate, so take rain gear. The town lives off fishing, fish processing, logging, saw- and pulp-mill operations, and deep-sea shipping.

The **Museum of Northern British Columbia** has one of the province's finest collections of coastal native art, some artifacts dating back 10,000 years. Native artisans work on totem poles in the carving shed and, in summer, the museum runs a 2½-hour boat tour of the harbor and Metlakatla native village. ⊠ *1st Ave. and McBride St., Prince Rupert,* ☎ *250/624–3207.* 🖃 *Free; donations accepted.* ⊙ *Sept.–May, Mon.–Sat. 10–5; June–Aug., Mon–Sat. 9–9, Sun. 9–5.*

Dining and Lodging

$$ ✕ **Smile's Seafood Café.** If you don't mind walking among the fish-processing plants by the railway, you'll find this place a real change of pace. It has been a mainstay of Prince Rupert since 1935 and has suc-ceeded because it provides small-town friendly service along with its seafood menu. Favorites include the halibut cheeks and the fisherman's platter. ⊠ *113 George Hills Way,* ☎ *250/624–3072. MC, V.*

$$$$ ✕🖼 **Crest Motor Hotel.** This warm, modern hotel is a block from the
★ two shopping centers but stands on a bluff overlooking the harbor. The restaurant, pleasantly decorated with brass rails and beam ceilings, has a waterfront view and specializes in seafood; particularly outstanding are the salmon dishes. ⊠ *222 1st Ave. W, V8J 3P6,* ☎ *250/624–6771 or 800/663–8150,* 🖷 *250/627–7666. 103 rooms. Restaurant, coffee shop, lounge, in-room modem lines, minibars and whirlpool tubs in some rooms, no-smoking floor, room service, outdoor hot tub, steam room, exercise room, fishing, baby-sitting, dry cleaning, business ser-vices, meeting rooms. AE, D, DC, MC, V.*

$$$ 🖼 **Best Western Highliner Inn.** This modern high rise near the water-front is conveniently situated and relatively well priced. It's in the heart of the downtown shopping district only one block from the air-line terminal building. Ask for a room with a private balcony and view of the harbor. ⊠ *815 1st Ave. W, V8J 1B3,* ☎ *250/624–9060 or 800/668–3115,* 🖷 *250/627–7759. 96 rooms. Restaurant, lounge, beauty salon, coin laundry. AE, DC, MC, V.*

Shopping

Native art and other local crafts are available at **Studio 9** (⊠ 516 3rd Ave. W, ☎ 250/624–2366).

Queen Charlotte Islands

㉟ *93 nautical mi southwest of Prince Rupert, 367 nautical mi northwest of Port Hardy.*

A popular vacation destination, the Queen Charlotte Islands, or Misty Islands, though once the remote preserve of the Haida natives, are now easily accessible by ferry. Today the Haida make up only one sixth of the population, but they continue to infuse the island with a sense of the Haida past and contribute to the logging and fishing industries, as well as to tourism. Haida elders lead tours—an essential service if you want to reach the isolated, abandoned villages. Limited accommoda-tions make it necessary to reserve guest rooms well in advance.

In the Queen Charlottes, 150 kilometers (93 miles) of paved road, most of it on **Graham Island** (the northernmost and largest of the group of 150), connect Queen Charlotte in the south to Masset in the north. Some of the other islands are laced with gravel roads. The rugged, rocky west coast of the archipelago faces the ocean; the east coast has many broad sandy beaches. Throughout, the mountains and shores are often shrouded in fog and rain-laden clouds, adding to the islands' mystery.

★ **Naikoon Provincial Park,** in the northeast corner of Graham, preserves a large section of unique wilderness, where low-lying swamps, pine and cedar forests, lakes, beaches, trails, and wildlife combine to create an intriguing environment. Take the 5-kilometer (3-mile) walk from the Tlell Picnic Site to the beach, and on to the bow section of the old wooden shipwreck of the *Pezuta*, a 1928 log-hauling vessel. ☎ 250/557–4390.

On the southern end of Graham Island, the **Queen Charlotte Islands Museum** has a small but impressive display of Haida totem poles, masks, and carvings of both silver and argillite (hard black slate). A natural-history exhibit gives interesting background on the wildlife of the islands. ✉ *Box 1373, Skidegate V0T 1S1,* ☎ *250/559–4643.* ⊠ *$2.50.* ☉ *Apr.–late Oct., weekdays 9–5, weekends 1–5; Nov.–Mar., Wed.–Sun. 1–5.*

Also on Graham Island, the **Ed Jones Haida Museum,** in Old Masset on the northern coast, exhibits totems and artifacts. Nearby, artists sell their work from their homes. South of Graham, in and around **South Moresby National Park Reserve,** lie most of the better-known abandoned Haida villages, which are accessible by water. Visiting some of the villages requires at least several days' travel time and careful planning for the wilderness. ✉ *Parks Canada,* ☎ *250/559–8818.*

Dining and Lodging

$$ ✕▥ **Tlell River House.** The smell of fresh-cut wood welcomes you into this secluded lodge in the woods overlooking the Tlell River. The beach (and the shipwreck of the *Pezuta*) is only a few hundred feet away. The rooms have wood paneling, floral curtains, and thick down comforters. In the restaurant, you'll find excellent seafood and deliciously rich cheesecakes. ✉ *Beitush Rd. south of Tlell River Bridge, Rte. 16, Box 56, Tlell V0T 1Y0,* ☎ *250/557–4211; in Canada, 800/667–8906;* ℻ *250/557–4622. 10 rooms. Restaurant, lounge, fishing, meeting room. AE, MC, V.*

$$ ▥ **Alaska View Lodge.** On a clear day, you can see the mountains of Alaska from the porch of this bed-and-breakfast. A long stretch of sandy beach borders the lodge on one side and woods on the other. With advance notice and at an additional cost, the owner makes a three-course dinner, using classical recipes based on Queen Charlotte fare, such as home-smoked salmon, scallops, and Dungeness crab. ✉ *Tow Hill Rd., Box 227, Masset V0T 1M0,* ☎ *250/626–3333; in Canada, 800/661–0019,* ℻ *250/626–3858. 4 rooms. Dining room, no-smoking rooms. MC, V.*

$–$$ ▥ **Spruce Point Lodge.** This cedar-sided building, encircled by a balcony, attracts families and couples because of its low rates and down-home feel. Like most Queen Charlotte accommodations, this one tends to the rustic and has locally made pine furnishings. For the money you get a Continental breakfast and an occasional seafood barbecue, with a menu that depends on the daily catch. Bunk rooms are usually available at a low nightly rate. ✉ *609 6th Ave., Queen Charlotte V0T 1S0,* ☎ ℻ *250/559–8234. 7 rooms. Breakfast room, occasional dinners, boating, fishing. MC, V.*

Shopping

The Haida of the region carve valuable figurines from a variety of hard, black slate called argillite found only on the islands. Their works are sold at the **Adams Family House of Silver** (☎ 250/626–3215), in Old Masset, behind the Ed Jones Haida Museum. **Joy's Island Jewellers**

(☎ 250/559–4742) in Queen Charlotte also carries a good selection. Other island specialties are silk-screen prints and silver jewelry.

En Route   To see interior British Columbia, take Route 16 east from Prince Rupert. On the way you'll pass through or near such communities as **Terrace,** with a hot-springs complex at the Mt. Layton Resort, skiing at Shames Mountain, and excellent fishing in the Skeena River; and **Kitimat** (Route 37 south of Terrace), at the head of the Douglas Channel, where the fishing is superb.

Hazelton

㊱ *293 km (182 mi) northeast of Prince Rupert, 439 km (273 mi) northwest of Prince George, 1,217 km (756 mi) northwest of Vancouver.*

At Hazelton, a town rich in the culture of the Gitksan and Wet'-suwet'en peoples, you must visit **'Ksan,** just outside town, a re-created Gitksan village. The elaborately painted community of seven longhouses is a replica of the one that stood on the same site when the first European explorers arrived in the 19th century. The carving shed, often used by 'Ksan artists, is open to the public, and three other longhouses can be visited: One displays contemporary masks and robes, another has song-and-dance dramas in the summer, and the third exhibits pre-European tools of bone, sinew, stone, and wood. ✉ *Box 326, V0J 1Y0,* ☎ *250/842–5544.* 🎫 *$7.* ☉ *Apr.–Sept., daily 9–6; Oct.–Mar., Thurs.–Mon. 9–5; tours May–mid-Oct. on the hour.*

The **'Ksan Museum** displays works and artifacts from the Upper Skeena River region as well as modern-day regalia kept at the museum by local natives. ✉ *Box 333, V0J 1Y0,* ☎ *250/842–5723.* 🎫 *Donation.* ☉ *Mid-Apr.–Sept., daily.*

Prince George

㊲ *721 km (447 mi) from Prince Rupert, 786 km (487 mi) from Vancouver.*

At the crossroads of two railways and two highways, Prince George has grown to become the capital of Northern British Columbia and the third largest city in the province. Nestled on the edge of a vast forested plateau, it has an economy fueled by forest industries, from tree farms to logging to lumber and paper processing. **Canadian Forest Products Ltd.** (☎ 250/561–3947) provides free tours of the area's pulp and sawmills.

In Ft. George Park, you can visit the **Fraser–Ft. George Regional Museum** to see the fine collection of artifacts illustrating local history. ✉ *Box 1779, V2L 4O7,* ☎ *250/562–1612.* 🎫 *$3.* ☉ *May–Sept., daily 9–5; Sept.–Apr., Tues.–Sun. noon–5.*

A collection of photos, rail cars, and logging and sawmilling equipment at the **Central B.C. Railway and Forest Industry Museum** traces the town's origin to the building of the railway and the development of logging. ✉ *Box 2408, V2N 2S6,* ☎ *250/563–7351.* 🎫 *$3.50.* ☉ *May–Sept., Thurs.–Mon. 9–5.*

The **Prince George Native Art Gallery** displays traditional and contemporary works (carvings, sculpture, jewelry, and literature) by the region's native peoples. ✉ *144 George. St., V2L 1P9,* ☎ *250/562–7385.* 🎫 *Free.* ☉ *June–Sept., daily 9–5; Oct.–May, Tues.–Sat. 9–5.*

Gold Rush Trail

Begins at Prince George and ends at Lilloet, 170 km (106 mi) west of Kamloops, 131 km (81 mi) northeast of Whistler.

From Prince George you can turn south on Route 97 toward Kamloops and the Okanagan Valley, following the 640-kilometer (400-mile) **Gold Rush Trail,** along which frontiersmen traveled in search of gold in the 19th and early 20th centuries. It takes you through Quesnel, Williams Lake, Wells, and Barkerville and along the Fraser Canyon and Cache Creek. Most towns and communities through which the trail passes have re-created villages, history museums, or historic sites that help to tell the story of the gold-rush era. For more information contact the **Cariboo Chilcotin Coast Tourist Association** (⊠ Box 4900, Williams Lake V2G 2V8, ☎ 250/392–2226; in the U.S. 800/663–5885; FAX 250/392–2838) and **Heritage Attractions of British Columbia** (⊠ Ministry of Small Business, Tourism, and Culture, 800 Johnson St., Victoria, V8V 1X4, ☎ 250/387–5129).

Alternatively, you can continue on Route 16 to Route 5 for a longer (some say even more spectacular) route through High Country (☞ *below*) to the same place.

OKANAGAN VALLEY AND ENVIRONS

Including High Country and Southwestern British Columbia

Diversity of setting differentiates High Country from the other regions of British Columbia. This roughly triangular territory, stretching from Valemount in the north just past Revelstoke in the southeast to Merritt, farther south and west, presents a spectacular array of scenery, from deep canyons carved by the Thompson and Fraser rivers to the towering ranges of the Rockies, Monashees, and Selkirks. Skiing, white-water rafting, heli-skiing, and other challenging outdoor activities can be a focus of any High Country tour. The Okanagan Valley region, four hours east of Vancouver by car, or one hour by air, is part of a highland plateau between the Cascade range of mountains on the west and the lower Monashees on the east. Though small in size (only 3% of the province's total land mass), the area contains the interior's largest concentration of people. Dominating the valley is Okanagan Lake, a vacation magnet for tourists from both the west coast and Alberta. In summer rooms can be scarce here. The largest towns along the lake, bordered by Route 97—Vernon at the north end, Kelowna in the middle, and Penticton to the south—are actually one large unit. Okanagan Lake is their glue, offering recreation, lodging, and restaurants. Between, and along the lake, are the recreational and resort communities of Summerland, Peachland, Westbank, and Oyama, which are popular tourist destinations and have camping facilities, motels, and cabins. The valley is the fruit-growing capital of Canada, producing apricots, pears, cherries, plums, apples, grapes, and peaches, plus clouds of fragrant blossoms from mid-April through early June.

Kamloops

38 *355 km (220 mi) northeast of Vancouver, 163 km (102 mi) northwest of Kelowna.*

Kamloops, officially a part of High Country, is a convenient passageway into the Okanagan Valley from Fraser Canyon and Thompson Valley, and a stop on the Canadian Pacific Railroad. The town is surrounded by 500 lakes, which provide an abundance of trout, Dolly Varden, and kokanee. In late September and October, however, attention turns to the sockeye salmon, when thousands of these fish, intent on breeding, return home to the waters where they were spawned, in Adams River

(65 kilometers, or 40 miles, east of Kamloops off the Trans-Canada Highway).

Once every four years—the last time was 1994—the sockeye run reaches a massive scale, as more than a million salmon pack the waters and up to 500,000 visitors come to observe. The **Roderick Haig-Brown Conservation Area,** which protects the 11-kilometer (7-mile) stretch of Adams River, is the best vantage point. ⊠ *66 mi east of Kamloops; B.C. Parks district office,* ☎ *604/851–3000.*

The **Kamloops Wildlife Park** houses 71 species in fairly natural habitats on 55 acres. Canyon hiking trails, a miniature railway, and adjacent water slides provide something for everyone. ⊠ *Box 698, V2C 5L7,* ☎ *250/573–3242.* ⊠ *$5.50.* ☉ *Call for seasonal hours; closed Dec. 25.*

Dining and Lodging

$$$ ✕🏨 **Lac le Jeune Resort.** With 160 kilometers (99 miles) of cross-country skiing, a lake stocked with trout, and a restaurant that serves robust helpings, this resort lets you enjoy the outdoors. The rustic, self-sufficient cabins have ample space and amenities for families, and pets are permitted. In the large, comfortable rooms in the main lodge, no phones or televisions distract from the beauty of the setting. ⊠ *Off Coquihala Hwy., 29 km (18 mi) southwest of Kamloops, Box 3215, Kamloops V2C 6B8,* ☎ *250/372–2722 or 800/561–5253,* 🅵🅰🆇 *250/372–8755. 28 rooms, 4-plex chalet, 6 cabins. Restaurant, lounge, no-smoking rooms, sauna, boating, fishing, cross-country skiing, theater, meeting room. AE, D, DC, MC, V.*

$$ ✕🏨 **Corbett Lake Country Inn.** In Merritt, south of Kamloops off ★ Route 5A, this restaurant presents a different fixed menu every night; favorites include rack of lamb and chateaubriand. The single (with extra beds) and duplex cabins are comfortable and basic, as are rooms in the main lodge. Fly-fishing for rainbow trout on the private lake is a big attraction here, and no fishing license is required. Small pets are allowed. ⊠ *Off Rte. 5A, 11 km (7 mi) south of town, Box 327, Merritt V0K 2B0,* ☎ *250/378–4334. 3 rooms, 10 cabins. Restaurant, boating, fishing. V. Closed mid-Jan.–Apr. and mid-Oct.–Dec. 23.*

Outdoor Activities and Sports

CANOEING AND KAYAKING

Mount Robson Adventure Holidays (⊠ Box 687, Valemount V0E 2Z0, ☎ 250/566–4386, 🅵🅰🆇 250/566–4351) arranges canoe trips at the northern end of the High Country near Mount Robson Park.

GOLF

Rivershore Golf Club (⊠ off Old Shuswap Rd., Kamloops, ☎ 250/573–4211), a Robert Trent Jones–designed course, is one of British Columbia's longest, at 7,007 yards.

RAFTING

Regional operators include **Mount Robson Adventure Holidays** (⊠ Box 687, Valemount V0E 2Z0, ☎ 250/566–4386, 🅵🅰🆇 250/566–4351) and **Fraser River Raft Expeditions Ltd.** (⊠ Box 10, Yale V0K 2S0, ☎ 250/863–2336; in Canada, 800/363–7238; 🅵🅰🆇 250/863–2355).

SKIING

With 3,100 feet of vertical drop, **Sun Peaks Resort** (⊠ Box 869, Kamloops V2C 5M8, ☎ 250/578–7222 or 800/807–3257, 🅵🅰🆇 250/578–7223) has 63 runs. **Mt. Mackenzie** (⊠ Box 1000, Revelstoke V0E 2S0, ☎ 250/837–5268) has 26 runs and offers deep-powder skiing.

For High Country heli-skiing, contact **Mike Wiegle Helicopter Skiing** (⊠ Box 159, Blue River, V0E 1J0, ☎ 250/673–8381 or 800/661–9170,

FAX 250/673–8464) and **Robson Heli Magic** (✉ Box 18, Valemount, V0E 2Z0, ☎ 250/566–4700, FAX 250/566–4333).

Vernon

39 *117 km (73 mi) southeast of Kamloops.*

Vernon is organized around forestry and agriculture. The city borders on two other lakes besides Okanagan, the more enticing of which is Kalamalka Lake. The **Kalamalka Lake Provincial Park** has warm-water beaches and some of the most scenic viewpoints and hiking trails in the region. It is also the town closest to the ski area and gaslight-era-theme village resort atop Silver Star Mountain.

★ Twelve kilometers (7½ miles) north of Vernon, the **O'Keefe Historic Ranch** gives visitors a window on cattle-ranch life at the turn of the century. The late-19th-century Victorian mansion is opulently furnished with original antiques. On the 50 acres are a Chinese cooks' house, St. Ann's Church, a blacksmith shop, a reconstructed general store, a display of the old Shuswap and Okanagan Railroad, and a contemporary restaurant. ✉ *9830 Rte. 97, 12 km (7½ mi) north of Vernon,* ☎ *250/542–7868.* ☞ *$5.* ☉ *Mid-May–mid-Oct., daily 9–5.*

Dining and Lodging

$$ ✕ **Craigellachie Dining Room.** The home-cooked meals in the dining room of the Putnam Station Hotel are filling rather than fancy. Soups and sandwiches are on the lunch menu, while old favorites like barbecue ribs, lasagne, pork chops, steaks, and pastas are offered in the evenings. The daily three-course special is generally a good deal. ✉ *Silver Star Mountain Resort,* ☎ *250/542–2459. Reservations essential. AE, MC, V.*

$$$ ✕▦ **Vance Creek Hotel.** Looking more like the set of a spaghetti West-
★ ern than a modern hotel, the Vance Creek enjoys a prime location in the heart of the resort. Rooms are simple, with coordinated decor and boxy bathrooms. Those on the first floor are equipped with kitchenettes, bunk beds, and private outside entrances. Willow furniture and fireplaces add a touch more comfort to suites in the 1993 annex. ✉ *Silver Star Mountain Resort, Box 3, Silver Star Mountain, BC V0E 1G0,* ☎ *250/549–5191,* FAX *250/549–5177. 84 rooms. Bar, dining room, lobby lounge, kitchenettes, no-smoking rooms, refrigerators, bicycles, cross-country and downhill skiing, ski storage, coin laundry, meeting rooms. AE, D, MC, V. Closed mid-Apr.–mid-May.*

$$–$$$ ✕▦ **Silver Lode Inn.** Owners Max Schlaepfer and Trudi Amstutz serve
★ hearty helpings of real raclette or fondue in their cheerful Silver Lode Restaurant. The inn's no-frills rooms offering the basic comforts are the most reasonably priced in the village. ✉ *Silver Star Mountain Resort, Box 5, Silver Star Mountain, BC V0E 1G0,* ☎ *250/549–5105,* FAX *250/549–2163. Restaurant, bar, lobby lounge, indoor pool, hot tub, bicycles, ski storage, meeting room. AE, MC, V.*

Outdoor Activities and Sports

GOLF

Predator Ridge Golf Resort (✉ 360 Commonage Rd., Vernon, ☎ 250/542–3436).

SKIING

Silver Star Mountain Resort (✉ Box 2, Silver Star Mountain V0E 1G0, ☎ 250/542–0224; in the U.S., 800/663-4431; FAX 250/542–1236), near Vernon, with more than 80 runs, offers the extra of well-lighted night downhill skiing.

Kelowna

40 *46 km (29 mi) south of Vernon, 68 km (42 mi) north of Penticton.*

Kelowna, the largest city in the Okanagan, is home to **Father Pandosy's Mission,** the first nonnative settlement in the region, founded in 1859. ✉ *3685 Benvoulin Rd.,* ☎ *250/860–8369.* 🎫 *Free; donations accepted.* ☉ *Daily 8–dusk.*

Kelowna is the geographic center of the valley's wine industry, with **Calona Wines Ltd.** (✉ 1125 Richter St., ☎ 250/762–3332), British Columbia's oldest and largest winemaker. Also around Kelowna are smaller but more intimate wineries, including **Gray Monk Estate Winery** (✉ 1055 Camp Rd., 8 km, or 5 mi, west of Winfield, off Rte. 97, ☎ 250/766–3168) and **Cedarcreek Estate Winery** (✉ 5445 Lakeshore Rd., 12 km, or 7½ mi, south of Kelowna, off Rte. 97, Pandosy and Lakeshore Rds., ☎ 250/764–8866).

Dining and Lodging

$$–$$$ ✕ **Papillon.** This contemporary-looking restaurant has a Continental menu that offers pasta, seafood, and steak. The Prawns and Scallops Caribbean is outstanding. The wine list includes a wide selection of imported and local wines. ✉ *375 Leon Ave.,* ☎ *250/763–3833. Reservations essential. AE, DC, MC, V. No lunch weekends.*

$$$$ ✕▥ **Lake Okanagan Resort.** A Hotels and Resorts property, it is self-
★ contained on the west side of Okanagan Lake. The rooms have either kitchens or kitchenettes and range in size from one-room suites in the main hotel to spacious three-room chalets spread around the 300 acres. Large rooms, functional furnishings, wood-burning fireplaces, perfect views of the lake, and all the resort activities, including nature and dinner cruises, make this a good choice. ✉ *2751 Westside Rd., V1Y 8B2,* ☎ *250/769–3511 or 800/663–3273,* ℻ *250/769–6665. 150 rooms. Restaurant, café, poolside lounge, no-smoking rooms, refrigerators, 3 pools, hot tub, sauna, 9-hole golf course, 7 tennis courts, badminton, basketball, exercise room, hiking, horseback riding, horseshoes, Ping-Pong, volleyball, beach, dock, snorkeling, boating, jet skiing, waterskiing, bicycles, video games, children's programs (ages 6–12), playground, coin laundry, laundry service and dry cleaning, meeting rooms, helipad. AE, DC, MC, V.*

$$$–$$$$ ✕▥ **Hotel Eldorado.** Rebuilt in the style of the 1926-vintage Eldorado Arms, which burned down in the early 1990s, the new Eldorado has much of the original's charm intact. Rooms tend to be small and cozy, with light carpets, floral patterns, and Canadian heritage furnishings; many have balconies affording superb views of Okanagan Lake. The Eldorado Dining Room serves fresh rack of lamb and seafood dishes. Full breakfast is included in the room rate. ✉ *500 Cook Rd., V1W 3G9,* ☎ *250/763–7500,* ℻ *250/861–4779. 20 rooms. Restaurant, lounge, no-smoking rooms, boating. AE, DC, MC, V.*

Outdoor Activities and Sports

CANOEING AND KAYAKING

Numerous waterways run through the region. For guided trips, try **Okanagan Canoe Holidays** (✉ R.R. 1, 2910 N. Glenmore Rd., V1Y 7P9, ☎ ℻ 250/762–8156).

GOLF

Gallaghers Canyon Golf and Country Club (✉ 4320 McCulloch Rd., Kelowna, ☎ 250/861–4240). **Harvest Golf Club** (✉ 2725 KLO Rd., East Kelowna, ☎ 250/862–3103).

HIKING

You can hike the rail bed of the **Kettle Valley Railway** network along Lake Okanagan between Penticton and Kelowna. The Visitors Bureau for Kelowna (☎ 250/861–1515) can provide maps and information.

SKIING

Cross-Country. Postill Lake Lodge (✉ Box 854, V1Y 7P5, ☎ 250/860–1655) has excellent trails just east of Kelowna.

Downhill. Big White Ski Resort (✉ Box 2039, Station R, V1X 4K5, ☎ 250/765–3101 or 800/663-2772, FAX 250/765–8200) is the highest ski area in British Columbia, at 7,606 feet. The Big White has almost 70 runs, and is expanding rapidly.

Shopping

At **Geert Maas Sculpture Gardens, Gallery, and Studio** (✉ R.R. 1250, Reynolds Rd., V1Y 7P9, ☎ 250/860–7012), in the hills above Kelowna, world-class sculptor Geert Maas exhibits his distinctive bronze, stoneware, and mixed media abstract figures in an indoor gallery and a garden. He also sells medallions, original paintings, and etchings. The **Okanagan Pottery Studio** (☎ 250/767–2010), on Route 97 in Peachland, south of Kelowna, sells handcrafted ceramics.

Penticton

41 *395 km (245 mi) east of Vancouver.*

Although Penticton's winter population is about 25,000, its summer population nears 130,000. Sixteen kilometers (10 miles) north of town, you can take a ride on the historic **Kettle Valley Steam Railway** (✉ 10112 S. Victoria Rd., Summerland, ☎ 250/494–8422), reopened in 1995, which passes through 10 kilometers (6 miles) of orchards, vineyards, and wooded mountain terrain along the 1915 line that opened up the interior of British Columbia by connecting Vancouver with the Kootenays.

An 11-kilometer (7-mile) drive south from Penticton on Route 97 takes you to the **Okanagan Game Farm** (☎ 250/497–5405), with more than 650 species of wild animals from around the world.

West of Penticton is British Columbia's Kootenay Country, named for one of the mountain ranges that fill it.

Dining and Lodging

$$–$$$ ★ ✕ **Granny Bogner's.** The theme is determinedly homey: flowing lace curtains, Oriental rugs, wood chairs, cloth-covered tables, and waitresses in long skirts. But the food at this mostly Continental restaurant is excellent. The poached halibut and roasted duck have contributed to the widely held belief that this is the best restaurant in the Okanagan. ✉ *302 Eckhardt Ave. W,* ☎ *250/493–2711. Reservations essential. AE, MC, V. No lunch. Closed Sun., Mon., and Jan.*

$$$$ **Clarion Lakeside Resort and Conference Center** (formerly the Coast Lakeside Resort). On the shore of Okanagan Lake, this resort is both a peaceful retreat and right in the center of the action. Vancouver businesspeople love this place for its comfort and conference facilities. The rooms are bright and airy, and half of them have lake views; whirlpool bathtubs were added to some in 1994, and all units were redecorated in 1995. ✉ *21 Lakeshore Dr. W, V2A 7M5,* ☎ *250/493–8221; in the U.S., 800/252–7466; in Canada, 800/458–6262;* FAX *250/493–0607. 204 rooms. Coffee shop, dining room, outdoor café, in-room modem lines, minibars in some rooms, no-smoking floor, room service, indoor pool, beauty salon, hot tub, massage, sauna, 2 tennis courts, aerobics,*

health club, jogging, shuffleboard, volleyball, beach, dock, snorkeling, windsurfing, jet skiing, parasailing, waterskiing, bicycles, billiards, comedy club/nightclub, recreation room, video games, baby-sitting, children's programs (ages 5–12), dry cleaning, concierge, business services, convention center, meeting rooms. AE, DC, MC, V.

$$ ☒ **Riordan House.** John and Donna Ortiz didn't expect to give guided tours to their newly spiffed-up 1921 house. But people seemed to like the place, built by a Prohibition rum-runner and furnished now with family antiques, so the Ortizes bowed to the inevitable and opened it as a bed-and-breakfast. One bedroom has a fireplace and one a sitting area; all look out on the surrounding hills. The Continental breakfast stars home-baked croissants, scones, muffins, and a selection of seasonal fruit; box lunches are packed on request. ☒ *689 Winnipeg St., V2A 5N1,* ☎ ℻ *250/493–5997. 3 rooms share 3 baths. Breakfast room, no-smoking rooms, in-room VCR, bicycles, airport and beach shuttle. MC, V.*

Outdoor Activities and Sports

GOLF

Osoyoos Golf and Country Club (☒ 12300 46th Ave., off Hwy. 97 south, Osoyoos, ☎ 250/495–7003).

SKIING

Apex Resort (☒ Box 1060, Penticton, V2A 7N7, ☎ 250/492–2880 or 800/387–2739, ℻ 250/292–8622) has 56 trails, a vertical rise of 2,000 feet, and a peak elevation of 7,187 feet.

In Kootenay Country (☞ Chapter 4) are two major ski areas: **Whitewater** (☒ Box 60, Nelson V1L 5P7, ☎ 250/354–4944), with 28 runs and plenty of powder skiing, and **Red Mountain Resorts** (☒ Box 670, Rossland V0G 1Y0, ☎ 250/362–7700), which spans two mountains and three mountain faces and has 30 marked runs. Also in Kootenay Country, try **Kootenay Helicopter Skiing** (☒ Box 717, Nakusp V0G 1R0, ☎ 250/265–4447 or 800/663–0100). With accommodations at the Tenderfoot Lodge, they run three- to seven-day all-inclusive packages in the Selkirks and Monashees.

Cathedral Provincial Park

75 km (47 mi) southwest of Penticton.

Off Route 3 along the U.S. border, **Cathedral Provincial Park** (☎ 250/494–6500) preserves 82,000 acres of lakes and rolling meadows, teeming with mule deer, mountain goats, and California bighorn sheep. To reach the main part of the park, either take the steep, eight-hour hike, or arrange (and pay in advance) for the **Cathedral Lakes Lodge** (☎ 250/499–5848, ℻ 250/499–5266) to transport you by four-wheel-drive vehicle. There are 16 campsites in the park, which is open mid-June through early October.

Outdoor Activities and Sports

SKIING

Manning Park Resort (☒ Box 1480, Hope, V0X 1L0, ☎ 604/840–8822), west of Cathedral Provincial Park, has excellent cross-country trails and downhill facilities.

En Route Winding farther west, Route 3 connects with the Trans-Canada Highway (Highway 1), which parallels the Fraser River. To the north, a glimpse through the mists above roiling **Hell's Gate**, off Highway 1 in Fraser Canyon, hints at how the region got its name. An airtram (cable car) carries visitors across the foaming canyon above the fishway, where millions of sockeye salmon fight their way upriver to spawning grounds four times a year—April, July, August, and October. In addition to interpretive displays on the life cycle of the salmon, you'll find a fudge factory, a gift shop, and a restaurant at the lower air-tram terminal. ⊠ *Box 129, Hope,* ☎ *604/867–9277.* ⊠ *$8.50.* ☉ *Mid-Apr.–mid-Oct. daily 9 AM; closing time seasonal (between 5 and 7 PM).*

Harrison Hot Springs

㊷ *128 km (79 mi) northeast of Vancouver.*

The small resort community of Harrison Hot Springs lies at the southern tip of picturesque Harrison Lake. Vacationers flock here to relax in this almost pristine natural setting. Mountains surround the 64-kilometer-long (40-mile-long) lake, which, ringed by pretty beaches, provides a broad range of outdoor activities, in addition to the hot springs. Across from the beach in the **Harrison Hot Springs Resort** is a spring-fed public pool. ⊠ *100 Esplanade, Harrison Hot Springs,* ☎ *604/796–2244.* ⊠ *$5.50.* ☉ *Sun.–Thurs. 8 AM–9 PM, Fri. and Sat. 8 AM–10 PM.*

★ ☺ A tour of **Kilby Historic Store and Farm,** a heritage attraction in nearby Harrison Mills, takes you back in time to the British Columbia of the 1920s. Visitors tour the general store and farm buildings of T. Kilby and other pioneers of the area, chat with the shopkeeper, sniff whatever is simmering on the wood-burning stove, and tramp through the orchards, stockroom, fueling station, barn, and dairy house on the grounds. The kids can enjoy feeding the farm animals. You can sample 1920s-style home cooking in the **Harrison River Tearoom.** This is a fine slice of living history. ⊠ *215 Kilby Rd. (1½ km, or 1 mi, off Hwy. 7 on north shore of Fraer River; follow signs), Harrison Mills,* ☎ *604/796–9576.* ⊠ *$4.50.* ☉ *Mid-Apr.–June and Sept.–Nov., Thurs.–Mon. 11–5; July and Aug., daily 11–5.*

Rosedale

8 km (5 mi) southwest of Harrison Hot Springs, 120 km (75 mi) east of Vancouver.

★ The well-signed **Minter Gardens** is a 27-acre compound containing 11 beautifully presented theme gardens—Chinese, rose, English, fern, fragrance, and more—along with aviaries and ponds. There are playgrounds and a giant evergreen maze. ⊠ *Exit 135 off Hwy. 1, 52892 Bunker Rd., Rosedale,* ☎ *604/794–7191; in Canada, 800/661–3919.* ⊠ *$9.* ☉ *Apr.–Oct., daily 9–dusk.*

☺ It's hard to miss the **Trans-Canada Waterslides,** a tremendously popular water park that has slides with such names as Kamikaze, Cannonball, Super Heroes, Black Hole, and Flash Flood, along with wave and soaking pools, snack bars, and sunbathing areas to provide plenty of warm-weather fun. ⊠ *Bridal Falls Rd., Rosedale,* ☎ *604/794–7455.* ⊠ *$12.* ☉ *Mid-May–mid-June, weekends 10–8; mid-June–early Sept., daily 10–9.*

Dining and Lodging

$$–$$$ ✕ **Black Forest.** Ask the locals where to dine and they'll send you here, to a charming Bavarian dining room on Harrison Village Esplanade, overlooking the lake. It comes as no surprise that the specialties here are German standards, from schnitzels to Black Forest cake, with a few Continental dishes (mainly steaks and seafood) thrown in for good measure. Hearty German beer and an array of wines round out the selection. ⊠ *180 Esplanade,* ☎ *604/796–9343. AE, MC, V. No lunch.*

$$$–$$$$ ✕🏨 **Harrison Hot Springs Hotel.** Ever since fur traders and gold miners discovered the soothing hot springs in the late 1800s, Harrison has been a favored stopover spot. Built beside the lake in the 1920s, the Harrison Hot Springs Hotel has continued to grow over the decades. The most reasonably priced rooms, in the original building and the west tower, have an old English look, with Edwardian furnishings and ceiling moldings; those in the east tower (added in 1989) are more modern and plush, with a heftier price tag. All rooms were renovated in 1994 and have new carpet, wallpaper, drapes, and bedspreads in lighter, brighter tones. Amenities include a PGA-rated nine-hole golf course and, of course, hot spring–fed pools. ✉ *100 Esplanade, Harrison Hot Springs V0M 1K0,* ☎ *604/796–2244 or 800/663–2266,* FAX *604/796–9374. 290 rooms, 16 cottages. 2 restaurants, lounge, no-smoking floors, room service, 2 indoor pools, outdoor pool, beauty salon, 2 saunas, 9-hole golf course, 1 indoor and 2 outdoor tennis courts, health club, hiking, bicycles, playground, laundry service and dry cleaning, business services, meeting rooms. AE, DC, MC, V.*

BRITISH COLUMBIA A TO Z

Arriving and Departing

By Boat
☞ Victoria, *above.*

By Bus
Greyhound (☎ 604/662–3222; in Canada, 800/661–8747; in the U.S., 800/231–2222) connects destinations throughout British Columbia with cities and towns all along the Pacific North Coast.

By Car
Driving time from Seattle to Vancouver is about 3 hours. From other Canadian regions, three main routes lead into British Columbia: through Sparwood, in the south, take Route 3; from Jasper and Banff, in the central region, travel on Highway 1 or Route 5; and through Dawson Creek, in the north, follow Routes 2 and 97.

By Plane
British Columbia is served by **Victoria International Airport** and **Vancouver International Airport.** Domestic airports are in most cities. **Air Canada** (☎ 604/688–5515; in the U.S., 800/776–3000) and **Canadian Airlines International** (☎ 604/279–6611; in the U.S., 800/426–7000) are the two dominant carriers. **Kenmore Air** (☎ 206/486–1257 or 800/543–9595) offers direct daily flights from Seattle to Victoria, Nanaimo, Campbell River, and Northeast Vancouver Island.

Getting Around

By Bicycle
GULF ISLANDS
Because Mayne Island is so small (only 21 square kilometers, or 8 square miles), with mild hills and wonderful scenery, it is great territory for a vigorous bike ride. At 100 kilometers (62 miles) on the circular route, Salt Spring offers more of a challenge. Some bed-and-breakfasts have bicycles; ask that they be set aside for you when you make your reservations. On Mayne, you can rent bikes at the **Miner's Bay gas station;** on Salt Spring, try **Island Spoke Folk** (☎ 250/537–4664) at the Trading Company Building in Ganges.

By Bus

Pacific Coach Lines (☎ 800/661–1725) operates daily connecting service between Victoria and Vancouver on B.C. Ferries. **Island Coach Lines** (☎ 250/385–4411) serves the Vancouver Island area. **Maverick Coach Lines** (☎ 250/662–8051) serves Nanaimo from Vancouver on B.C. Ferries (☞ *below*).

Greyhound Lines of Canada (☎ 604/662–3222; in Canada, 800/231–2222) serves the area north of Vancouver. Among its hundreds of stops in the province are Prince Rupert, Terrace, and Smithers.

By Car

Major roads in British Columbia, and most secondary roads, are paved and well engineered. Mountain driving is slower but more scenic. There are no roads on the mainland coast once you leave the populated areas of the southwest corner near Vancouver.

Route 17 connects the Swartz Bay ferry terminal on the Saanich Peninsula with downtown Victoria. The Trans-Canada Highway (Highway 1) runs south from Nanaimo to Victoria. Route 14 connects Sooke to Port Renfrew, on the west coast of Vancouver Island, with Victoria.

The roads on both islands are narrow and winding. Exercise extreme caution around the many cyclists, especially thick on the roads in summer.

By Ferry

B.C. Ferries (in Vancouver, ☎ 604/277–0277; in Victoria, 250/656–0757; reservations, 604/669–1211 or 250/629–3215; in Nanaimo, 250/753–6626) provides frequent year-round passenger and vehicle service between Vancouver and Vancouver Island, from Tsawwassen (south of Vancouver) to Swartz Bay (30 minutes by car north of Victoria); Tsawwassen to Nanaimo; and Horseshoe Bay (north of Vancouver) to Nanaimo. B.C. Ferries also provides service from outside Vancouver and Victoria to the northern and southern Gulf Islands (reserve ahead), the Sunshine Coast, Nanaimo, through the Inside Passage between Port Hardy and Prince Rupert, and from Prince Rupert to the Queen Charlotte Islands. When you travel with a vehicle in summer, plan to arrive at the terminal well in advance of the scheduled sailing time.

Mayne and Salt Spring Islands are an hour to an hour and a half via ferry from Swartz Bay and Tsawwassen.

The *Queen of Prince Rupert* (☎ 250/386–3431), a B.C. Ferries ship, sails six times a week between late May and September (three times a week the rest of the year), and can easily accommodate recreational vehicles. The crossing from Prince Rupert to Skidegate, near Queen Charlotte on Graham Island, takes about six hours. Schedules vary and reservations are required. The M.V. *Kwuna,* another B.C. Ferries ship, connects Skidegate Landing to Alliford Bay on Moresby Island. Access to smaller islands is by boat or air; plans should be made in advance through a travel agent.

By Plane

Harbour Air Ltd. (☎ 250/537–5525 or 800/665–0212; in British Columbia, 800/665–0212) and **Hanna Air Saltspring** (☎ 250/537–9359; in British Columbia, 800/665–2359) provide several regularly scheduled 20- to 30-minute daily floatplane flights from Ganges on Salt Spring Island to Coal Harbour in downtown Vancouver and to Vancouver Airport. **Air B.C.** (☎ 800/776-3000) provides both airport-to-airport and harbor-to-harbor service from Vancouver to Victoria at least hourly. Both flights take about 35 minutes.

QUEEN CHARLOTTE ISLANDS

Harbour Air (☎ 250/627–1341 or 250/637–5355) runs scheduled floatplanes between Sandspit, Masset, Queen Charlotte City, and Prince Rupert daily except December 25 and 26 and January 1.

By Train

MAINLAND

B.C. Rail (☎ 604/984–5246, 604/631–3500, or 800/663–8238) travels from Vancouver to Prince George, a route of 747 kilometers (463 miles), and offers daily service to Whistler. **Via Rail** (in British Columbia, ☎ 800/561–8630) provides service between Prince Rupert and Prince George.

VANCOUVER ISLAND

Esquimalt & Nanaimo Rail Liner (✉ 450 Pandora Ave., Victoria V8W 3L5, ☎ 250/383–4324; in British Columbia, 800/561–8630) makes the round-trip from Victoria's Pandora Avenue Station to Courtenay; schedules vary seasonally.

Contacts and Resources

B&B Reservation Agencies

Garden City Reservation Service (✉ 660 Jones Terr., Victoria, V8Z 2L7, ☎ 250/479–1986, ℻ 250/479–9999) specializes in Victoria but can book bed-and-breakfast accommodations throughout British Columbia.

Car Rentals

Most major agencies, including **Avis, Budget,** and **Hertz,** serve cities throughout the province (☞ Renting and Leasing Cars *in* the Gold Guide). Car rentals are available on Salt Spring through **Heritage Rentals** (☎ 250/537–4225, ℻ 250/537–4226).

Emergencies

Except in Vancouver and Victoria (☞ Chapter 2 *and* Victoria, *above*) dial 0 for **police, ambulance,** or **poison control.** On the Gulf Islands, dial 911 for **police, fire,** or **ambulance service.**

HOSPITALS

British Columbia has hospitals in virtually every town, including: on the Gulf Islands, **Lady Minto Hospital** (☎ 250/537–5545) in Ganges on Salt Spring Island; in Prince George, **Prince George Regional Hospital** (✉ 2000 15th Ave., ☎ 250/565–2000; emergencies, 250/565–2444); in Chilliwack, **Chilliwack General Hospital** (✉ 45600 Menholm Rd., ☎ 250/795–4141); in Kamloops, **Royal Inland Hospital** (✉ 311 Columbia St., ☎ 250/374–5111); in Kelowna, **Kelowna General Hospital** (✉ 2268 Pandosy St., ☎ 250/862–4000).

LATE-NIGHT PHARMACIES

In Prince George, **Hart Drugs** (✉ 3789 W. Austin Rd., ☎ 250/962–9666); in Kamloops, **Kipp-Mallery I.D.A. Pharmacy** (✉ 273 Victoria St., ☎ 250/372–2531); in Hope, **Pharmasave Drugs** (✉ 235 Wallace St., ☎ 604/869–2486).

Guided Tours

ORIENTATION

Classic Holidays Tour & Travel (102–75 W. Broadway, Vancouver V5Y 1P1, ☎ 604/875–6377) and **Sea to Sky** (1928 Nelson Ave., West Vancouver V7V 2P4, ☎ 604/922–7339) offer tours throughout the province.

SPECIAL-INTEREST

A few Vancouver Island–based companies that conduct whale-watching tours are: **Jamie's Whaling Station** (✉ Box 590, Tofino V0R 2Z0, ☎ 250/725–3919; in Canada, 800/667–9913), **Tofino Sea-Kayaking Company** (✉ Box 620, Tofino, V0R 2Z0, ☎ 250/725–4222) on the west coast, **Robson Bight Charters** (✉ Box 99, Sayward V0P 1R0, ☎ 250/282–3833) near Campbell River, and, near Port Hardy, **Stubbs Island Charters** (✉ Box 7, Telegraph Cove V0N 3J0, ☎ 250/928–3185).

Ecosummer Expeditions (✉ 1516 Duranleau St., Vancouver V6H 3S4, ☎ 604/669–7741 or 800/688–8605, FAX 604/669–3244) and the **Canadian Outback Adventure Company** (✉ 1110 Hamilton St., 206, Vancouver, ☎ 604/688–7206) run ecological tours of the Queen Charlotte and Gulf Islands.

The history and culture of the First Nations (native) people of the region are the focus of new summer tours including **Lheit-Lit'en Nation Elders Salmon Camp Tours** (✉ Lheit-Lit'en Native Heritage Society, R.R. 1, Site 27, Compartment 60, Prince George, V2N 2H8, ☎ 250/963–8451, FAX 250/963–8324) on the mainland and **Yuquot History Tours** (✉ Ahaminaquis Tourist Centre, Box 459, Gold River, V0P 1G0, ☎ 250/283–7464, FAX 250/283–2335) on Vancouver Island. The **Canadian Outback Adventure Company** (✉ 1110 Hamilton St., 206, Vancouver, ☎ 604/688–7206) runs a unique summer tour of the abandoned Queen Charlotte Islands villages of the Haida Gwai, including the United Nations–designated world heritage site at Ninstints.

Outdoor Activities and Sports

FISHING

For updated fishing information and regulations, contact the **B.C. Fish Branch** (✉ Ministry of Environment, Parliament Buildings, Victoria V8V 1X4, ☎ 250/387–9688). For a guide to saltwater fishing, contact the **Department of Fisheries and Oceans** (✉ Recreational Fisheries Division, 555 W. Hastings St., Vancouver V6B 5G3, ☎ 604/666–3545).

GOLF

Tee-Time Central Booking Service, for out-of-town golfers, lists courses throughout Vancouver Island and mainland British Columbia. ✉ *412–4004 Bluebird Rd., Kelowna, V1W 1X3,* ☎ *250/764–4118 or 800/930–4622.* ⊙ *May 15–Oct. 15, weekdays 9–5.*

HIKING

B.C. Parks (✉ 800 Johnson St., 2nd floor, Victoria, V8V 1X4, ☎ 250/387–5002) offers detailed information.

For heli-hiking, **Highland Helicopter** (✉ 1685 Tranmer, Agassiz V0M 1K0, ☎ 604/796–9610) and **Mount Robson Adventure Holidays** (✉ Box 687, Valemount V0E 2Z0, ☎ 250/566–4386) on the mainland can provide further information.

RAFTING

Hyak Wilderness Adventures (✉ 204B–1975, Maple St., Vancouver V6J 3S9, ☎ 604/734–8622; in Canada, 800/663–7238; FAX 604/734–5718), **Canadian River Expeditions** (✉ 301–3524 W. 16th Ave., Vancouver, V6R 3C1, ☎ 604/938–6651; in Canada, 800/898–7238), and **Alpine Rafting Company** (⊠ Box 1409, Golden V0A 1H0, ☎ 250/344–5016 or 800/663–7080, ℻ 250/344–7102) provide options ranging from lazy half-day floats to exhilarating white-water journeys of up to a week.

SKIING

The **Canada West Ski Areas Association** (⊠ 3313 32nd Ave., Vernon, V1T 2M8, ☎ 250/542–9020, ℻ 250/542–5070) can provide information about the top heli- and snow-cat ski operators in British Columbia.

Visitor Information

For information concerning the province contact **Discover British Columbia** (⊠ Ministry of Tourism, Parliament Buildings, Victoria V8V 1X4, ☎ 250/663–6000 or 800/663–6000). More than 140 communities in the province have **Travel Infocentres.**

For Prince George, contact Tourism Prince George (⊠ 1198 Victoria St., V2L 2L2, ☎ 250/562–3700, ℻ 250/563–3584).

The principal regional tourist offices are: **Tourism Association of Southwestern B.C.** (⊠ 204–1755 W. Broadway, Vancouver V6J 4S5, ☎ 604/739–9011 or 800/667–3306, ℻ 604/739–0153), **Tourism Association of Vancouver Island** (⊠ 302–45 Bastion Sq., Victoria V8W 1J1, ☎ 250/382–3551, ℻ 250/382–3532), **Okanagan–Similkameen Tourist Association** (⊠ 104–515 Rte. 97 S, Kelowna V1Z 3J2, ☎ 250/769–5959, ℻ 250/861–7493), **High Country Tourist Association** (⊠ 2–1490 Pearson Pl., Kamloops V2C 6H1, ☎ 250/372–7770 or 800/567–2275, ℻ 250/828–4656), **North By Northwest Tourism** (⊠ 3840 Alfred Ave., Box 1030, Smithers V0J 2N0, ☎ 250/847–5227, ℻ 250/847–7585), **Rocky Mountain Visitors Association** (⊠ 495 Wallinger Ave., Box 10, Kimberley V1A 2Y5, ☎ 250/427–4838, ℻ 250/427–3344), **Prince Rupert Convention and Visitors Bureau** (⊠ 100 McBride St., Box 669 CMG, Prince Rupert V8J 3S1, ☎ 250/624–5637 or 800/667–1994), **Kootenay Country Tourist Association** (⊠ 610 Railway St., Nelson V1L 1H4, ☎ 250/352–6033, ℻ 250/352–1656), **Cariboo Chilcotin Coast Tourist Association** (⊠ 190 Yorston St., Box 4900, Williams Lake V2G 2V8, ☎ 250/392–2226 or 800/663–5885, ℻ 250/392–2838), **Peace River Alaska Highway Tourist Association** (⊠ 9908 106th Ave., Box 6850, Fort St. John V1J 4J3, ☎ 250/785–2544, ℻ 250/785–4424). **Salt Spring Island Chamber of Commerce** (⊠ 121 Lower Ganges Rd., Box 111, Ganges, V0S 1E0, ☎ 250/537–5252, ℻ 250/537–4276) and **Mayne Island Chamber of Commerce** (⊠ General Delivery, Mayne Island, V0N 2J0, no phone) provide information on the Gulf Islands. For information on the Queen Charlotte Islands, contact the **Queen Charlotte Islands Travel Information Centre** (⊠ Box 337, Queen Charlotte V0T 1S0, ☎ 250/559–4742, ℻ 250/559–8188).

4 The Canadian Rockies

The ranges that form the Canadian Rockies straddle the British Columbia–Alberta line from the U.S. border in the south to the Yukon Territory in the north. Their beauty has been preserved in provincial and national parks; in these mountains you can fish, ski, hike, climb, boat, and ride, as well as enjoy some of the best resort facilities anywhere.

By Peter Oliver

Updated by
Don Thacker

COMPARING MOUNTAINS IS A SUBJECTIVE and imprecise business. Yet few would argue that the 640-kilometer (400-mile) stretch of the Canadian Rockies easily ranks as one of the most extravagantly beautiful ranges on earth. Approaching the mountains from the east, you are struck by the wall of rock on the western horizon, made more dramatic by the white snowfields that cling to the upper slopes until well into the summer. First visible from about 100 kilometers (about 60 miles) away, the mountains become progressively more imposing with each passing mile. Near the south end of the range (Waterton Lakes National Park), the view is particularly dramatic as gently rolling prairie butts up abruptly against the edge of the mountains. Farther north, in Banff and Jasper national parks, tree-covered foothills roll out of the mountains.

It is obvious how the Rockies got their name. Wildly folded sedimentary and metamorphic rocks have been thrust up to form ragged peaks and high cliffs; you can't help but be awed by the forces of nature that operated here. Add glaciers and snowfields to the high peaks, carpet the valleys with forests, mix in a generous helping of large mammals, wildflowers, rivers, and lakes, and you've got the recipe for the Canadian Rockies.

The peaks of the Rockies are aligned in long, closely spaced ranges that run in approximately a north-south direction. From east to west these can be grouped into the foothills, front ranges, main ranges, and a small area of west ranges. Apart from forming distinct sets of mountains, these groupings differ somewhat in geology and age—which increases from 40 to 50 million years in the foothills to 110 to 120 million years in the west ranges. The main ranges have the highest peaks.

The Columbia Mountains, a series of parallel ranges just west of the Rockies, are often grouped with the Rockies. Many recreational activities that are prohibited in the national parks of the Rockies (notably helicopter-assisted skiing and heli-hiking) are allowed in the Columbias. The Columbias were formed about 180 million years ago and consist of four subranges: the Cariboos to the north and, farther south, the Purcells, Selkirks, and Monashees, from east to west, respectively.

Recognizing early the region's exceptional natural beauty, the Canadian government began shielding the area from human development and resource exploitation in the 1880s. In 1885, the government created a park preserve around the Cave and Basin Hot Springs in Banff. Two years later, Canada's first national park, Rocky Mountain Park (later Banff National Park), was officially established. Lands that would later become Yoho National Park and Glacier National Park in the Columbias were first set aside in 1886.

Today, approximately 25,000 square kilometers (roughly 10,000 square miles)—an area larger than the state of New Hampshire—are protected in seven national parks in the Rockies and the Columbias. Because they were protected early on, the parks of the Rockies—Waterton Lakes, Banff, Kootenay, Yoho, and Jasper—have remained relatively untouched by human development. The only significant clusters of human settlement are in the town centers of Banff, Jasper, and Waterton Lakes, and the area around Lake Louise. Several thousand more square kilometers are also protected as wilderness areas and provincial parks, most notably Mt. Robson and Mt. Assiniboine provincial parks and Kananaskis Country.

Most of the facilities and roads of the Rockies are concentrated in the valleys, where the elevations are only about 1,000 feet higher than in the major prairie cities to the east. Banff has an elevation of 4,600 feet; Jasper, 3,500 feet. Consequently, temperatures in the mountain towns are rather similar to those in the major cities in Alberta. The mountains themselves rise to elevations above 10,000 feet, and the alpine areas (above tree line) may be whitened by snowfalls even in midsummer.

The Icefields Parkway runs down the heart of the Rockies for 230 kilometers (143 miles) from Jasper to Lake Louise. While all roads in the Rockies offer stunning scenery, the Icefields Parkway is without doubt the most impressive. More than 100 glaciers show off their blue ice along this drive; at the Columbia Icefields, the Athabasca Glacier reaches almost to the roadway (a short walk takes you right up to the ice). Large animals such as elk, moose, deer, and bighorn sheep, occasionally even bears and mountain goats, are fairly common along this route. Two high passes, the Bow Pass in the south and the Sunwapta Pass about halfway along the route, rise almost to tree line, offering a chance to see carpets of alpine wildflowers in summer. Hiking trails abound along the route if you want to explore the land more closely. Even if you're on a tight schedule, make a point of driving at least part of the Icefields Parkway.

Pleasures and Pastimes

See individual towns or Contacts and Resources *in* Canadian Rockies A to Z, *below,* for addresses and telephone numbers.

Biking

Biking is a popular pastime in the Rockies, whether for a short spin around town or on a multiday guided tour. Around Banff, the **Vermilion Lakes loop** and the more strenuous **loop over Tunnel Mountain** are popular half-day bike tours. For a longer ride, **Route 1A** between Banff and Lake Louise is a good choice. For a rugged workout you can test lungs and legs on the steep switchbacks leading up to **Mt. Norquay** ski area. **Highway 93** is a long and strenuous route for cycling but is becoming increasingly popular because of the wide paved shoulders along most of the way and, of course, the beautiful scenery. The **Overlander Bike Trail** in Jasper National Park takes you through four different scenic zones: marshland, river, meadow, and mountain.

Mountain biking has become increasingly popular in recent years, leading to controversy in the Canadian Rockies. Park officials have reported problems resulting from breakdowns (flat tires, broken frames, and so on) in remote areas, occasionally requiring rescue. Problems have also been reported with mountain bikers unwittingly breaking scent lines between bear mothers and cubs. As a result, although mountain bikes provide good access to the backcountry, they are restricted to relatively few trails, primarily fire roads in the parks. Check with the nearest park warden or bike store before heading off-road. Mountain bikers may find Kananaskis Country, with its more lenient restrictions, preferable.

Camping

Of the more than 40 public **campgrounds** within the national parks (not including backcountry sites for backpackers and climbers), most operate on a first-come, first-served basis, though some allow reservations a few days in advance. The season generally runs from mid-May to October, although at least one campground in each park remains open year-round. Hookups are available at most of the 40 national park campgrounds and at four of the 30 Kananaskis campgrounds. Prices for a one-night stay range from $15 to $20 at hook-up sites and from $10 to $14 at sites without hookups.

Numerous privately run campgrounds, which usually take reservations, offer sites outside park boundaries.

Climbing

Except for Waterton Lakes, where the rock is generally crumbly, the Canadian Rockies is one of the world's great **climbing** regions. Among the classic ascents are **Mt. Assiniboine,** the "Matterhorn of the Rockies"; glacier-cloaked **Mt. Athabasca; Mt. Sir Donald,** in Glacier National Park; the daunting **Mt. Robson;** and, in the Purcells, the spires of the **Bugaboos.** Climbing and mountaineering are year-round activities in the Canadian Rockies, although October and November—after the summer and before ice-falls are solid enough for winter climbing—are the least desirable months.

Climbing permits are required within the parks and can be obtained at park warden offices. Except for very experienced mountaineers, guide and instruction services are essential for climbers here.

Dining

Dining in the Canadian Rockies is, for the most part, a casual affair. Given the general mix of travelers to the region—families and active outdoorspeople—emphasis is on good food served in large quantities, at slightly inflated prices. This is not the place for the traveler who expects haute service and cuisine; there is only a handful of top-caliber restaurants in the region. However, people who like fresh game and fish will not be disappointed. Trout, venison, elk, moose, quail, and other game are items that even modest dining establishments feature on their menus.

CATEGORY	COST*
$$$$	over $35
$$$	$25–$35
$$	$15–$25
$	under $15

per person, excluding drinks, service, and sales tax

Fishing

The principal game **fish** in the Canadian Rockies is trout—cutthroat and rainbow are the most common varieties. The best fishing tends to be in streams, rivers, and lakes in the valleys, rather than in waters from glacial sources. Fishing is usually better outside the national parks where fish stocking programs are more common. The **Bow River,** the **lakes of British Columbia,** and the streams of **Crowsnest Pass** are prime fishing spots outside the national parks.

You need a fishing license, which you can buy at information centers and sports shops throughout the region. A British Columbia license is good only in British Columbia; an Alberta license is good only in Alberta. If you are fishing in the national parks only, then you must have a national parks fishing license (but not provincial licenses).

Golf

The **golf** season is short, running from about mid-May through mid-October. Given the abundance of water in the region, golf courses are generally in excellent playing condition, with lush grasses and well-kept greens. If hole lengths seem long, keep in mind that at the elevation of Canadian Rockies courses (above 4,000 feet), a golf ball tends to travel 10% farther than at sea level.

Courses here, on the relatively flat valley floors, are not difficult to walk if you're so inclined; the mountains simply provide dramatic backdrops. All courses offer full pro-shop services, including cart rentals. Most courses enforce a standard dress code, requiring shirts with collars and Bermuda-length shorts or long pants.

The area between Golden and Kimberley in British Columbia is growing as a golfing hotbed: Golfers here can now choose from ten 18-hole courses and two nine-hole courses.

Hiking

The four contiguous parks (Banff, Jasper, Kootenay, and Yoho) have 2,900 kilometers (1,750 miles) of **hiking** trails. In Waterton Lakes there are 183 kilometers (114 miles) of trails, with further access to more than 1,200 kilometers (750 miles) of trails in adjacent Glacier National Park in the United States. Kananaskis Country offers numerous hiking and backpacking opportunities (water can be in short supply, especially in late summer and fall), while Revelstoke and Glacier parks in British Columbia are generally best for shorter day hikes.

The hiking season runs from early April to early November for trails in the valleys, and mid-June to mid- or late September for trails that extend into alpine areas. Though most trails are restricted to foot traffic, horses and mountain bikes are permitted in some areas. Check with the park warden for selected trails.

For backpacking you need to register with the nearest park warden for permits. This is principally for safety reasons—so that you can be tracked down in case of emergency—as well as for trail-usage records. The fee is $5 per person per night (to a maximum of $25 per person per trip or $35 annually) for the use of backcountry campsites. You can make reservations up to three weeks in advance by contacting the park office. The office can also supply trail and topographical maps and information on current trail status.

If you're interested in hiking or backpacking, check out several good books that describe various routes and route combinations. One of the best, *The Canadian Rockies Trail Guide,* by Brian Patton and Bart Robinson (Summerthought Ltd., $14.95), is available in most bookstores in Banff, Lake Louise, and Jasper.

Horseback Riding

One of the most satisfying ways to explore the Canadian Rockies is on **horseback.** Horses are prohibited on many trails within the national parks, but there are still some opportunities; among the most attractive areas for pack trips within the parks is Tonquin Valley in Jasper. Restrictions are far fewer in Kananaskis Country, the provincial parks, and the British Columbia Rockies region.

Lodging

The **hotels, inns, and lodges** of the Canadian Rockies comprise an eclectic list, ranging from rustic, backcountry lodges without electricity or running water to a growing number of standard roadside motels to hotels of supreme luxury. With just a few exceptions, however, they share one common trait—room rates that are considerably higher in the summer than during the rest of the year. The week between Christmas and New Year's often commands a higher rate as well. For this reason, flexibility in travel planning can mean considerable savings—a room that goes for $150 a night in summer may well drop to $75 from late September through May. Lodgings are categorized according to their off-peak rates. High-season rate increases are noted within each listing. High-season rates generally run from sometime in June to late September, but this varies with the lodging, so check in advance for off-season rates. Over the past few years the Rockies have become busier, and the period considered "peak-season" has been gradually lengthening.

Backcountry lodges have been an integral part of Canadian Rockies travel since the '20s. They vary considerably in terms of accommodations and accessibility. At the luxurious end are lodges with private rooms, private baths, full electricity, telephones, and restaurant-style dining; at the rugged extreme are lodges with bunk beds, kerosene lamps for evening light, and outhouses. A few are accessible by car in summer, some can be reached only by hiking or by skiing in winter, or by helicopter. Note that most backcountry lodges are priced on a per-person basis (the price generally includes meals) rather than the double-room rate used for more standard accommodations. Guest ranches, mainly in the ranching area just east of Kananaskis Country, are another alternative accommodation. These offer comfortable accommodations with a definite ranching theme; horseback riding and pack trips are standard visitor activities.

CATEGORY	COST*
$$$$	over $120
$$$	$80–$120
$$	$50–$80
$	under $50

All prices are for a standard double room (or an equivalent, where not applicable), are in Canadian dollars, and do not include the 7% goods and services tax, a 5% room tax in Alberta, an 8% room tax in British Columbia, and in some areas, a small municipal tax.

Rafting

Rafting opportunities range from gentle floats along the Bow River near Banff to rollicking white-water rides on the Kicking Horse River near Golden. Most trips are half- or full-day. The season runs from May through October; if you want white water at its frothiest, June is usually the best month, when rivers are still swollen with the snowmelt, but not dangerously so.

Shopping

When **shopping** in the Canadian Rockies, you'll find the best selection in Banff. Malls at the **Rimrock** and **Banff Springs Hotel** and shops on **Banff Avenue** have souvenirs, as well as native crafts, sporting gear, landscape paintings, woolens, and outdoor wear. In Jasper the stores are concentrated on **Patricia Street** and **Connaught Drive,** and at the **Jasper Park Lodge.** In general, expect to pay a resort premium for most goods.

Skiing

There are 11 lift-service **ski areas** in the region, five of which are within an hour's drive of Banff; daily lift tickets cost between $25 and $50. Cross-country opportunities are also plentiful, and many backcountry lodges are winterized and offer guide services for backcountry touring. Numerous tour operators feature ski packages designed to a fit a variety of interests, abilities, and budgets.

Heli-skiing was once considered an activity exclusively for experienced, well-conditioned skiers. But in recent years, heli-ski operators also have introduced programs for intermediate skiers with little or no powder-skiing experience. Daily tours start above $200 per person, and weekly packages (including meals and lodging but not airfare) begin at about $2,000 off season and climb up to $5,000 in the busy months.

Water Sports

Swimmers generally avoid the icy, glacial-fed waters of the Rockies. However, several lakes near Jasper can become relatively temperate during spells of warm summer weather. **Pyramid Lake** has a large beach, although it would be unusual for the water to warm above 20°C

(68°F). **Lake Annette** and **Lake Edith,** near Jasper Park Lodge, also have beaches and somewhat warmer water that reaches the low 20s°C (low 70s°F) during warm spells. These waters are among the clearest anywhere—crystalline views of the lake bottom fool swimmers into trying to put a foot onto rocks that are hopelessly beyond their reach.

Motorized boats are not allowed on most lakes in the parks, but rowboat and canoe rentals are available at **Lake Louise** and **Moraine Lake** in Banff National Park, at **Emerald Lake** and **Lake O'Hara** in Yoho, and at **Lac Beauvert, Pyramid Lake,** and **Patricia Lake** in Jasper National Park.

Spray Lakes Reservoir and **Kananaskis Lake** are the main sites of boating activity in Kananaskis Country—where motorized boating is allowed. **Lake Windermere,** in British Columbia, is popular among sailors, board sailors, and water-skiers and is pleasant for swimming in the midsummer months. To the north, the long, dam-controlled **Kinbasket** and **Revelstoke** lakes give boaters, canoeists, and fishermen more of a wilderness experience. There are several boat ramps on the lakes but few services.

For sailors and board sailors who like strong winds, Waterton Lakes, with winds from the Alberta prairies often exceeding 50 kilometers (30 miles) per hour, is the place to be. The water is numbingly cold, though, so be sure to wear a wetsuit. The **Athabasca, Bow, Kicking Horse,** and **Maligne rivers** provide various levels of river-running challenges for canoeists and kayakers—from relatively still water to roaring white water.

For scuba divers **Patricia Lake,** near Jasper, is a popular spot to explore the remains of the *Habakkuk.* This was a ship made of ice: a military prototype, secretly designed during World War II to take advantage of the fact that the plastic nature of ice (maintained by a cooling system) could absorb an impact without major structural damage to the vessel. What remains is mostly a skeleton of cooling pipes, but it makes for an interesting historical dive.

Exploring the Canadian Rockies

The Canadian Rockies can be divided into four broad regions. The **Banff and Lake Louise** area is the main hub of tourism and makes a convenient reference point for the other regions.

North and west of Banff lie the spectacular Icefields Parkway and Jasper National Park (north), and the smaller Kootenay, Yoho, and Glacier National Parks (west). Jasper National Park includes the townsite of Jasper—a smaller and more relaxed version of Banff. Kootenay, Yoho, and Glacier parks have comparatively few visitor facilities but make good destinations to escape the crowds of Banff and Jasper National Parks.

The region **South of Banff** includes Kananaskis Country and tiny Waterton Lakes National Park. Kananaskis Country, adjacent to Banff National Park but outside the national park system, allows many activities—for example, snowmobiling and hunting—that are prohibited in the national parks. Waterton, a small park along the United States border contiguous with Glacier National Park in Montana, offers character different from the main parks of the Canadian Rockies.

The **British Columbia Rockies** region, west of the main Rocky Mountains, consists of a series of parallel, somewhat more weathered mountain ranges. The parks here are smaller and more scattered, interspersed with functional rather than tourist towns.

Great Itineraries

The Canadian Rockies region is a sizable chunk of real estate, about twice the area of New York State. You could easily spend a month and still just skim the surface. The heart of the Canadian Rockies—the adjoining national parks of Banff, Jasper, Kootenay, and Yoho—puts the major attractions relatively close together. Ten days would allow for a leisurely tour of the main parks, with time left over for hiking or exploring some of the outlying regions of the Rockies. Five days would be sufficient for a visit to the major attractions in both Banff and Jasper parks, but there wouldn't be much time spent sitting about. A weekend would be time enough to get a flavor for Banff and Lake Louise, the hub of the region.

Numbers in the text below correspond to numbers in the margin and on the maps.

IF YOU HAVE 2 DAYS

The best option is to visit the Banff/Lake Louise region. One day could be spent in and around **Banff** ①–⑪—exploring, shopping, or just relaxing, perhaps with visits to one or two of the attractions on the outskirts of town—the **Upper Hot Springs** ⑤, the **Cave and Basin Centre** ⑦, the **Sulphur Mountain Gondola** ⑥, or one of the short drives near town. The second day would allow a visit to the **Lake Louise** ⑫ area, including scenic Moraine Lake, where you can hike, rent a boat, or just sightsee.

Alternatively, you could choose to make **Jasper** ⑮ your destination, and spend one day in and around the town (shopping, the **Jasper Tramway** ⑯, **Pyramid and Patricia lakes** ⑰). The second day could be filled with a visit to one or two of the scenic attractions within an hour's drive of Jasper—**Athabasca Falls** ⑱, **Mt. Edith Cavell** ⑲, **Maligne Lake** ⑳, **Miette Hot Springs** ㉑, or **Mt. Robson** ㉖.

IF YOU HAVE 5 DAYS

More days allow either a more vigorous or a more relaxed schedule. If you are feeling energetic, an ideal option would be a two-day visit to the **Banff** ①–⑪/**Lake Louise** ⑫ area, a day spent exploring the Icefields Parkway between Lake Louise and Jasper, and a two-day visit to the **Jasper** ⑮ area.

IF YOU HAVE 10 DAYS

This is enough time to do some serious exploring. You could spend five days touring the **Banff** ①–⑪/**Lake Louise** ⑫ area, the Icefields Parkway, and **Jasper** ⑮ and environs. Then you have the option of either spending the additional five days just relaxing to break up the hectic schedule or focusing on a specific activity such as hiking (which could easily fill up the remaining time).

If you aren't one to sit around in the same spot for too long, spend the extra five days visiting the out-of-the-way regions—Yoho (perhaps visiting the famous **Burgess Shale** ㉘ fossil beds), **Mt. Revelstoke** ㊱, **Glacier** ㉟, or **Waterton Lakes** ㉜ national parks, or the British Columbia Rockies.

When to Tour the Canadian Rockies

The main places of interest in the Rockies attract crowds in the peak summer season, so try to reach them early if you want seclusion. If hiking is your passion, remember that high-altitude trails may be snow covered until well into June. Animals are more common before the July crowds arrive, although mid-summer visitors are still certain to see plenty. Wildflowers, especially in the alpine meadows, reach their peak from early July to mid-August.

Although the weather is best during the mid-June to mid-September period, you can avoid crowds and make substantial savings on lodgings by scheduling your visit just outside this period. Check on rates, though, as many hotel operators are waking up to the fact that they can keep rates high to the end of September and still fill their rooms.

BANFF AND LAKE LOUISE

Most people who come to the Canadian Rockies make the Banff and Lake Louise area their first destination, perhaps their only destination. Banff is the largest town in the parks, and at just over an hour's drive west of Calgary it is a logical first stop in the mountains. Banff has enough lodging, dining, recreation, and shopping opportunities to keep visitors entertained around the townsite, but most people also make a point of visiting smaller, but majestic, Lake Louise, a half hour's drive north of Banff. For visitors on a tight schedule, the Banff–Lake Louise area offers just about every type of activity and scenic highlight available in the Canadian Rockies.

From Banff, the most popular excursions are the spectacular drive north along the Icefields Parkway (Route 93) to Jasper, 280 kilometers (180 miles) away, and the short trip immediately south into Kananaskis Country. Excursions into the less frequented Yoho and Kootenay parks offer the same magnificent scenery, without the crowds.

Hiking

The trails of Banff National Park tend to get a lot of traffic during the summer peak season. The most interesting **hikes** are north of Banff townsite. The most popular day-hiking areas, both accessible and scenic, are around **Lake Louise** and **Moraine Lake**.

Banff

128 km (79 mi) west of Calgary.

Numbers in the margin correspond to points of interest on the Canadian Rockies and Banff maps.

❶ Banff is a town of unlikely contrasts: Amid the bustle of commercialism, elk regularly wander into town to graze the lush grass on the town common; tour-bus sightseers carrying souvenir-stuffed bags mix on Banff Avenue (the main drag) with rugged outdoors people, among them some of the world's most accomplished mountaineers. For almost all who come to the Canadian Rockies, Banff is the central depot in their travel.

Banff straddles a thin line between mountain resort town and tourist trap. The town was governed by Parks Canada until January of 1990, when the residents voted to become an autonomous municipality (a move rejected by the residents of Jasper to the north). This allowed Banff to reduce the strict and vigilant zoning laws the park authorities had in place. An expansion of both commercial and residential properties has followed. Thus Banff is certainly no quaint little western outpost; except for the oft-photographed Banff Springs Hotel, its architecture is mostly modern, simple, and undistinguished. But the park authorities placed limits on the acreage of the town and so, instead of expanding, Banff has compressed itself. The result is a hub of hyperactivity, especially during the summer—a hub that seems all the more hectic in contrast to the surrounding wilderness.

❷ An amazing number of shops and restaurants have been crammed together on the short stretch of **Banff Avenue** that composes the core of downtown. Clustered together in about a half-dozen indoor malls are art galleries, clothing stores, photo shops, bookstores, and confectioners whose fudge and cookie output makes Banff Avenue a minefield for anyone with a sweet tooth. Items sold in the galleries range from trinkets to kitsch to genuine art; price does not necessarily indicate real value.

The Victorian **Banff Park Museum** houses a taxidermy collection of animals indigenous to Banff National Park, as well as wildlife art and a library on natural history. ✉ *92 Banff Ave.,* ☎ *403/762–1558.* ☜ *$2.25.* ◷ *June–Labor Day, daily 10–6; Sept.–May, daily 1–5.*

The **Whyte Museum** displays art, photography, historical artifacts, and exhibits about life in the Canadian Rockies. The museum hosts special events for families in summer. ✉ *111 Bear St.,* ☎ *403/762–2291.* ☜ *$3.* ◷ *Mid-May–mid-Oct., daily 10–6; off-season hours vary.*

❸ For a pleasant after-dinner walk, stroll to the **Parks Administration Building** with its splendid summertime flower gardens at the rear. It stands at the south end of Banff Avenue, across a stone bridge over the Bow River. For park information, such as maps, park regulations, and so on, the **Information Centre** can provide a wealth of help. ✉ *224 Banff Avenue,* ☎ *403/762–1550.* ◷ *Mid-May–Sept., daily 8–8; Oct.–mid-May, daily 9–5.*

★ ❹ The **Banff Springs Hotel** (☞ Dining and Lodging, *below*) is the architectural highlight of Banff and can at times resemble a year-round three-ring circus. Built in 1888, the hotel is easily recognized by its castlelike exterior; inside, the visitor can expect to get lost in the crazy-quilt network of restaurants, shops, salons, and ballrooms. Even renovators got confused; evidently, the hotel has a hidden room—one that was accidentally sealed off by an overzealous plasterer. It was left that way to add a chapter to the hotel lore. ✉ *Spray Ave., 2 km (1¼ mi) south of downtown Banff.*

❺ The **Upper Hot Springs** is a sulphur pool that can be soothing, invigorating, or both. The hot spring water is especially inviting on a dull, cold day. Lockers, period bathing suits, and towels are available to rent. ✉ *Mountain Ave., 3 km (2 mi) south of downtown Banff; or via 20-min hike up steep trail from Banff Springs Hotel parking area,* ☎ *403/762–1515.* ☜ *$5.*

❻ Great vistas can be had from the **Sulphur Mountain Gondola.** Views during the steep eight-minute ride to and from the 7,500-foot summit are spectacular, but they are hardly private. The observation decks and short summit trails are well visited, especially in summer. From the main deck you can hike the short distance to the summit of Samson Peak and frolic among the lazy Rocky Mountain bighorn sheep that graze there or visit the gift shop or the reasonably priced restaurant. ✉ *Mountain Ave., 3 km (2 mi) south of downtown Banff, lower terminal next to Upper Hot Springs.* ☎ *403/762–5438 or 403/762–2523.* ☜ *$10.*

❼ The **Cave and Basin National Historic Site** became the birthplace of the Canadian Rockies park system when the region was given national park protection in 1885. Two interpretive trails provide good insight into geology and plant life here, with half-hour and one-hour ranger-guided tours available. Cave and Basin also includes hands-on interpretive displays on the wildlife and history of the national park. A prize exhibit is a huge wood-and-metal reconstruction of a 19th-century Canadian Pacific locomotive, complete with a life-size model of Lady Agnes Macdonald (wife of Canada's first prime minister, Sir John A. Macdonald) sitting, as was her wont, on a specially constructed seat attached to the cowcatcher in front of the train! The **Cave and Basin Centre**

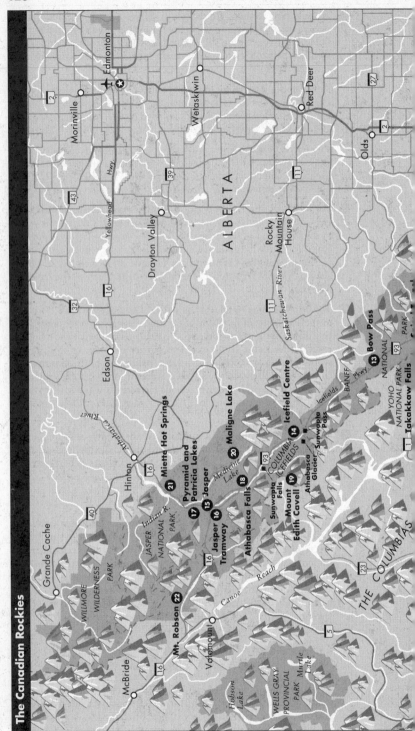

Banff

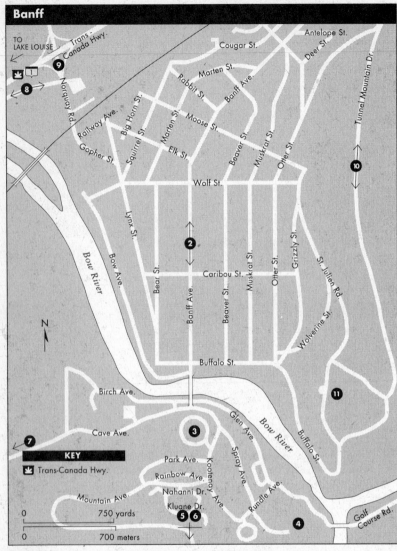

TO
LAKE LOUISE

Trans-Canada Hwy.

Norquay Rd.

Railway Ave.

Gopher St.

Big Horn St.

Squirrel St.

Lynx St.

Bear St.

Bow River

Bow Ave.

N

Cougar St.

Antelope St.

Deer St.

Marten St.

Rabbit St.

Banff Ave.

Moose St.

Marten St.

Elk St.

Beaver St.

Muskrat St.

Otter St.

Tunnel Mountain Dr.

Wolf St.

Caribou St.

Banff Ave.

Beaver St.

Muskrat St.

Otter St.

Grizzly St.

St. Julien Rd.

Wolverine St.

Buffalo St.

Birch Ave.

Cave Ave.

Park Ave.

Rainbow Ave.

Nahanni Dr.

Kluane Dr.

Mountain Ave.

Glen Ave.

Kootenay Ave.

Spray Ave.

Rundle Ave.

Bow River

Buffalo St.

Golf Course Rd.

KEY

Trans-Canada Hwy.

0   750 yards

0   700 meters

Banff Avenue, **2**
Banff Centre, **11**
Banff Springs
Hotel, **4**
Cave and Basin
Centennial Centre, **7**

Norquay Road, **9**
Parks Administration
Building, **3**
Sulphur Mountain
Gondola, **6**

Tunnel Mountain
Drive, **10**
Upper Hot Springs, **5**
Vermilion Lakes
Drive, **8**

Pool is no longer open for swimming, but guided tours are offered. A boardwalk leads to a marsh where the warm water supports a variety of tropical fish. ⊠ *Cave Ave., 2 km (1¼ mi) west of downtown Banff,* ☎ *403/762–1557.* ☞ *$2.25.* ☉ *June–early Sept., daily 9–6; Sept.–May, daily 9:30–5.*

❽ For a pleasant, short expedition near Banff townsite, try the **Vermilion Lakes Drive,** just off the west Banff exit from Highway 1. It offers excellent opportunities for wildlife sightings: elk, bighorn sheep, muskrat, and the occasional moose. Dawn and dusk are the best times.

❾ The short trip up the steep **Norquay Road** leads to a car park with a prize view of Banff townsite and the Bow River valley. Just below, bighorn sheep, deer, goats, elk, and Columbian ground squirrels negotiate their pastoral existence on some extremely treacherous slopes.

❿ **Tunnel Mountain Drive** (east side of Banff) makes a scenic 5-kilometer (3-mile) loop. The drive is closed in winter, but just off the drive, the Hoodoos—fingerlike rock formations caused by erosion—are accessible year-round.

⓫ The **Banff Centre,** a 50-year-old, highly renowned training center for musicians, artists, and writers, is *the* place in town and in the parks for performances ranging from poetry readings to rock concerts. The Banff Festival of the Arts is held here every summer. Within the Centre, the **Walter Philips Gallery** focuses on contemporary works by Canadian and international artists. ⊠ *St. Julien Rd.,* ☎ *403/762–6300; gallery,* ☎ *403/762–6281.* ☞ *Free.* ☉ *Tues.–Sun. noon–5.*

Dining and Lodging

$$$$ ✕ **Le Beaujolais.** Elegantly decorated in neoclassical style, this restau-
★ rant is strikingly out of place in casual Banff. Tapestries on the wall lend a hint of baronial splendor, and the richness of the food is a suitable match. Traditional French preparations of beef, veal, and lamb are menu highlights. Fish and seafood specialties include halibut, salmon, sea bass, and lobster. For dessert, spoil yourself with the Raspberry Balloon—a mixture of fresh raspberries, raspberry-flavored ice cream, and raspberry liqueur, all smothered in whipped cream. The wine cellar is lavishly and imaginatively stocked. ⊠ *212 Buffalo St., at Banff Ave.,* ☎ *403/762–2712. Reservations essential. AE, MC, V. No lunch.*

$$$$ ✕ **Ristorante Classico.** The Rimrock hotel's restaurant juxtaposes
★ northern Italian cuisine with a backdrop of the Bow Valley. The dining room—complete with abstract paintings and intricate moldings on the high ceiling—is divided into three cozy sections. Tables are surrounded by grand old armchairs. Chef Hans Sauter creates such originals as the appetizer *fagottini ripieni di ragu ai funghi e gorgonzol* (phyllo pastry filled with mushroom ragout on a tomato coulis, enhanced with gorgonzola). The entrées are no less daring, with such dishes as *roulade di salmone picante* (seared peppered salmon roulade with gazpacho), *cotoletta di vitello ai ferri al rosmarino* (grilled veal chop with rosemary), and rack of lamb baked in an aromatic crust. Fresh fruit desserts and an extensive wine list will complete your epicurean evening. ⊠ *Rimrock Resort Hotel, Mountain Ave.,* ☎ *403/762–3356. Reservations essential. AE, D, DC, MC, V. No lunch.*

$$–$$$$ ✕ **Banff Springs Hotel.** This hotel houses restaurants, bars, and lounges of varying formality and cuisine—from coffeehouses to a grand dining room—that create a miniculinary universe in the heart of the Rockies. **Samurai,** a Japanese restaurant, may have the best food—the standard of its sushi and *shabu-shabu* (thin strips of beef, chicken, or fish that are cooked in a copper bowl full of boiling water) must be high enough to satisfy the hotel's large Japanese clientele. The best over-

all dining experience may be at the **Waldhaus,** where a Bavarian-style meal—they specialize in fondues—is often followed by a Bavarian-style sing-along. The **Grapes Wine Bar,** which serves a light-fare menu, including adventurous salads, pâtés, and a choice selection of cheeses, is tucked away in a small, quiet room on the mezzanine level. Big windows provide nice views here. The **Alhambra,** open in summer only, specializes in Spanish cuisine in a grottolike setting (jacket and tie required). A hotel highlight in summer is the barbecue on the **Red Terrace.** The flavor of the traditional barbecue fare—steaks, corn on the cob, roast potatoes—seems greatly enhanced by the view of Rundle Mountain and the Bow River. ⊠ *Spray Ave.,* ☎ *403/762–2211. Reservations essential. AE, D, DC, MC, V.*

$$$ ✕ **Buffalo Mountain Lodge.** An exposed, rough-hewn post-and-beam interior gives the dining room a comfortable likeness to a converted barn. This is a woodcrafter's showcase, highlighted by the large polished wine cabinet that separates the dining and bar areas. The menu offers Rocky Mountain cuisine—fish, meat, and game dishes with sweet nouvelle sauces supplemented by hearty soups, fresh-baked breads, and a very extensive and frequently updated wine list. ⊠ *Tunnel Mountain Rd.,* ☎ *403/762–2400. AE, DC, MC, V.*

$$$ ✕ **Caboose.** In the railway depot, the Caboose is reminiscent of the bygone train era. Old train-engine, rail-car, and train-depot paraphernalia fills the dining room; dim lighting adds to the spirit of nostalgia. The Continental dishes, served with salad, are good but basic: simply prepared prime rib and beef, plus crab legs, salmon, lobster, prawns, and trout. ⊠ *Elk and Lynx Sts.,* ☎ *403/762–3622. AE, MC, V. No lunch.*

$$$ ✕ **Ticino.** This stucco-and-wood-beam dining room has Swiss-Italian fare. There are numerous standard pasta and meat dishes, as well as more adventurous Alpine cuisine. Fondue is a house specialty; the *mar-e-mont* (Italian for "ocean and mountain") is a beef-and-shrimp fondue you cook yourself in hot broth. Baked salmon, beef medallions, and panfried veal are among the other entrées. ⊠ *High Country Inn, 415 Banff Ave.,* ☎ *403/762–3848. AE, MC, V. No lunch.*

$$ ✕ **Balkan Restaurant.** The bright blue-and-white decor, with tile trim, cane-back chairs, and plants, evokes the Mediterranean. The menu lists classic Greek dishes, such as moussaka and souvlaki, as well as creative ethnic mixes, such as Greek stir-fry (rice and veggies with feta cheese). ⊠ *120 Banff Ave.,* ☎ *403/762–3454. AE, MC, V.*

$$ ✕ **Giorgio's Trattoria.** This split-level eatery serves high-quality Italian food that is immensely popular with the local crowd, so you might have to wait a bit during the busy hours for a table. Philippine mahogany tables and bar, Tuscany-style sponged walls, a beamed ceiling, and detailed wrought-iron work on the stairway give it an elegant look. The menu consists mainly of pizzas—try the exotic pizza *mare* with tiger shrimp, mussels, cilantro, sun-dried tomatoes, and roast garlic topping—and such pasta dishes as the ricotta ravioli *con gamberetti* (ravioli tossed with baby shrimps in oregano butter and virgin olive oil). ⊠ *219 Banff Ave.,* ☎ *403/762–5114. AE, MC, V. No lunch.*

$–$$ ✕ **Barbary Coast.** This sports-theme restaurant with neo-California cuisine is a local favorite. The plant-filled, skylighted dining room is decorated with paraphernalia from all manner of sport, from baseball to bobsledding. Prime rib is a house specialty, pizzas with pesto sauce are always a favorite, and the menu also includes a variety of pastas. Live blues bands play in the bar after 10 PM daily. ⊠ *119 Banff Ave.,* ☎ *403/762–4616. AE, MC, V.*

$ ✕ **Joe Btfsplk's Diner.** This place, named for an Al Capp cartoon character, is fun, camp, or overbearing, depending on your taste. It's a re-created '50s-style diner, with red vinyl banquettes, chrome-trimmed tables with individual jukeboxes, and waitresses dressed in vintage '50s attire. The menu is taken straight from a true-Americana cookbook: burgers, meat loaf, mashed potatoes, and apple pie for lunch or dinner, and eggs and bacon for breakfast. Fresh-baked cookies and muffins, available for take-out, are the culinary highlight. ⊠ *221 Banff Ave.,* ☎ *403/762–5529. Reservations not accepted. AE, DC, MC, V.*

$$$$ ☆ **Buffalo Mountain Lodge.** Part of the Canadian Rocky Mountain Resorts group, along with Emerald Lake Lodge in Yoho and Deer Lodge in Lake Louise, this complex shares their ambience and style. The lobby of the main lodge, warm with polished pine and exposed rough-hewn beams, is dominated by a large stone hearth with a buffalo head over the mantel. There is a hotel-condo cluster built in 1987, as well as an older group of chalet buildings. Newer rooms are dressed in pastel shades and have small fireplaces, wicker chairs, and pine cabinetry. Older chalet units are larger, with two bedrooms, and are similarly decorated. Rates increase by 40% June–September. ⊠ *Tunnel Mountain Rd., Box 1326, T0L 0C0,* ☎ *403/762–2400 or 800/661–1367,* ℻ *403/762–4495. 40 rooms, 20 studios, 11 lofts, 14 chalets. 2 restaurants, lobby lounge, hot tub, steam room. AE, DC, MC, V.*

$$$$ ☆ **Rimrock Resort Hotel.** Perched atop Sulphur Mountain, flanked by the gondola and hot pools, the hotel looks deceptively small and simple from the front. But the mountain-modern–style structure, clad in broken-face Tyndall stone with forest-green stucco and a green slate roof, and built into the steeply sloping mountain, is eight stories high. The huge lobby has a 25-foot ceiling, giant windows facing the Rockies, and an oversize marble fireplace. Nearly all rooms have views of the Bow Valley; each is decorated individually, but all share a certain formal elegance, with dark color schemes of burgundy, brown, and blue, and plush leather and velvet furnishings. Rates increase by 60% June–September. ⊠ *Mountain Ave., Box 1110, T0L 0C0,* ☎ *403/762–3356 or 800/661–1587,* ℻ *403/762–4132. 304 rooms, 41 suites. 2 restaurants, lobby lounge, indoor pool, sauna, exercise room, squash, shuttle downtown. AE, DC, MC, V.*

$$$–$$$$ ☆ **Banff Springs Hotel.** Built in 1888 to house wealthy Europeans who had come on Canadian Pacific trains to take the waters, this castlelike hotel marked the beginning of Banff's tourism boom. The massive, stone hotel has a seemingly endless maze of hallways and stairwells, huge sitting areas, and banquet rooms, complemented by dark wood furnishings and chandeliers. The complexity of the hotel's floor plan can be disorienting—some say, bring a compass—and the seasonally decorated lobby is surprisingly small, contributing to traffic jams during checkout time—use the express checkout. The guest rooms, most of which have mountain views, come in all shapes and sizes. The 87 different types of interior are linked by their blue, burgundy, and green color schemes and such old-hotel characteristics as high ceilings, tapestries and oil paintings on the walls, antique furniture, and marble sinks. A world-class spa, opened in the summer of 1995, is an oasis of pampering and luxury. Guest rooms are not soundproof, and often noises carry. Overbooking can be a problem; confirm your reservation. Rates increase about 25% mid-May–mid-Oct. ⊠ *Spray Ave., Box 960, T0L 0C0,* ☎ *403/762–2211 or 800/441–1414,* ℻ *403/762–5755. 804 rooms, 80 suites. 12 restaurants, 3 bars, indoor pool, spa, 27-hole golf course, 5 tennis courts, bowling, health club, horseback riding, nightclub, convention center. AE, D, DC, MC, V.*

$$$ ☆ **Banff Park Lodge.** The high, slanted ceiling and dark-cedar paneling, in addition to the lean, modern, and unembellished style, exude a Scandinavian feeling. On a quiet street in downtown Banff, the lodge is within walking distance of shops and restaurants. The rooms are bright, with lots of beige and ecru. Rates double June–September. ⊠ *222 Lynx St., Box 2200, T0L 0C0,* ☎ *403/762–4433 or 800/661–9266,* FAX *403/762–3553. 211 rooms. 2 restaurants, indoor pool, sauna. AE, DC, MC, V.*

$$$ 🏨 **Banff Rocky Mountain Resort.** Five kilometers (3 miles) east of Banff, this resort, with chalet-style buildings and numerous outdoor facilities, is the place for active people. Inside, rooms are bright, with white walls, wall-to-wall carpeting, and lots of blond-wood trim. Many rooms have fireplaces and kitchens with microwave ovens. Rates increase by 75% mid-June–September and late December–early January. ⊠ *Banff Ave. and Tunnel Mountain Rd., Box 100, T0L 0C0,* ☎ *403/762–5531 or 800/661–9563,* FAX *403/762–5166. 170 studio, 1-bedroom, and 2-bedroom units. Indoor pool, 2 tennis courts, exercise room, squash, shuttle to downtown. AE, DC, MC, V.*

$$$ 🏨 **Storm Mountain Lodge.** This is one of the original Canadian Pacific
★   Railway backcountry lodges, built in 1922. Not nearly as back-country today, it is on Route 93, just east of Vermilion Pass. The sitting area of the main, log cabin–style lodge is dominated by a large fireplace that is crowned by the head of a bighorn sheep. The dining area embodies the elegance of simplicity: straight-back wood chairs and white tablecloths on an enclosed porch with big glass windows overlooking the Pass. Sleeping cabins, tucked in the woods, are smallish but cozy, made so by fireplaces, old lamps, and down comforters. ⊠ *Rte. 93, 5 km (3 mi) west of Hwy. 1, Box 670, T0L 0C0,* ☎ FAX *403/762–4155. 12 cabins. Restaurant, lounge, hiking. AE, MC, V. Closed late Sept.–late May.*

$$ 🏨 **Castle Mountain Village.** The Village, about halfway between Banff and Lake Louise, consists of six different chalet styles to suit most budgets. The smallest have kitchens, bathrooms, and sleeping areas with fireplaces. Although cramped and on the dark side, they are clean and quiet. Larger and newer pine-log chalets, which make up the vast majority of the units, have two bedrooms, Jacuzzis, and sleep up to six. For four people, the large chalets are a comfortable, economical choice. Request a cabin with a view of Castle Mountain. Rates increase by 60% mid-June–late September; pets are $10 extra each. ⊠ *Rte. 1A between Banff and Lake Louise, Box 1655, T0L 0C0,* ☎ *403/762–3868,* FAX *403/762–8629. 21 chalets. Exercise room, coin laundry. MC, V.*

$$ 🏨 **High Country Inn.** There is nothing fancy here—just clean, simple, comfortable motel rooms. The units are of standard size, cedar-covered walls give some rooms a touch of regional character, and many rooms have a balcony. Ask for a room in the back, away from the heavy traffic on Banff Avenue. Rates increase by 75% June–September. ⊠ *419 Banff Ave., Box 700, T0L 0C0,* ☎ *403/762–2236; in Canada, 800/661–1244;* FAX *403/762–5084. 69 rooms. Restaurant, indoor pool, heated parking. AE, MC, V.*

$–$$ 🏨 **Red Carpet Inn.** Under the same management as the High Country Inn next door, Red Carpet offers one of the few moderately priced lodging options in downtown Banff. It is basically no-frills, with small motel-style rooms decorated in pastel shades, right down to the pastel-painted wooden furnishings. Front rooms, on Banff Avenue, get traffic noise. Rates double May–September. ⊠ *425 Banff Ave., Box 1800, T0L 0C0,* ☎ *403/762–4184; in Canada, 800/563–4609;* FAX *403/762–4894. 52 rooms. Hot tub. AE, MC, V.*

Nightlife and the Arts
THE ARTS

Most of the cultural activity in the Canadian Rockies is in and around Banff, and unquestionably the hub of this activity is the **Banff Centre** (⊠ St. Julien Rd., ☎ 403/762–6300; in Alberta and British Columbia, 800/413–8368). Presenting a performing-arts grab bag throughout the year, with pop and classical music, theater, and dance, the center peaks in summer with the three-month Banff Festival of the Arts.

The **Lux Cinema** (⊠ Wolf and Bear Mall, ☎ 403/762–8595) plays major releases.

NIGHTLIFE

For cocktails and socializing, the Banff Springs Hotel (☞ Dining and Lodging, *above*) has lounges and dining rooms with entertainment and dancing. **Wild Bill's** (⊠ Banff Ave. and Caribou St., ☎ 403/762–0333) is a cowboy bar with live music where two-steppers can strut their stuff. If you prefer rock and roll with your drink, try **Back Alley** (⊠ 137 Banff Ave., ☎ 403/762–8434) and **Barbary Coast** (⊠ 119 Banff Ave., ☎ 403/762–4616).

Outdoor Activities and Sports

BIKING

Bikes can be rented from **Park and Pedal Bike Shop** (⊠ 229 Wolf St., ☎ 403/762–3190).

BOATING

Lake Minnewanka Boat Tours (⊠ Box 2189, T0L 0C0, ☎ 403/762–3473) offers 1½-hour tours in summer on Lake Minnewanka, near town. The cost is $20.

GOLF

The **Banff Springs Hotel** (☎ 403/762–6801) has a 27-hole course (advance bookings required).

HORSEBACK RIDING

Arrangements for hourly or daily rides, as well as lessons, can be made through the concierge at the **Banff Springs Hotel. Brewster Stables** (⊠ Box 2280, T0L 0C0, ☎ 403/762–2832) and **Brewster's Kananaskis Guest Ranch** (☎ 403/673–3737), on the Bow River 30 minutes east of Banff, have horses to rent.

RAFTING

Rocky Mountain Raft Tours (⊠ Box 1771, T0L 0C0, ☎ 403/762–3632) has one- to three-hour trips on the Bow River and also offers canoe rentals.

SKIING

Cross-country. Banff Alpine Guides (⊠ Box 1025, T0L 0C0, ☎ 403/678–6091) leads backcountry ski tours.

Downhill. Mt. Norquay (⊠ Box 1258, T0L 0C0, ☎ 403/762–4421) runs generally short and steep with a growing range of expert terrain. At **Sunshine Village** (⊠ Box 1510, T0L 0C0, ☎ 403/762–6500 or 800/661–1363) the terrain is mostly intermediate and above the tree line. These resorts and Lake Louise (☞ *below*) have dining options, ski schools, day-care facilities, and licensed day lodges. A good bargain is the $46.50 day pass (three-day minimum) from Ski Banff/Lake Louise (⊠ Box 1805, T0L 0C0, ☎ 403/762–4561), which allows you to ski at the three areas and includes free shuttle service to the slopes.

Heli-skiing. Mike Wiegele Helicopter Skiing (⊠ Box 249, T0L 0C0, ☎ 403/762–5548 or 800/661–9170) serves the Banff region. *See also* Skiing *in* Contacts and Resources, *below*.

SPORTING GEAR

Mountain Magic (⊠ 224 Bear St., ☎ 403/762–2591) has three floors of hiking, climbing, skiing, running, and biking equipment, and a 30-foot indoor climbing wall for gear testing. **Monod's** (⊠ 111 Banff Ave.,

☎ 403/762–3725; ⊠ 129 Banff Ave., ☎ 403/762–4571) offers a wide array of sports equipment and clothing.

Shopping

Of the numerous galleries and shops along Banff Avenue, perhaps the best for crafts and other art items, principally by Canadian craftspeople, is **The Quest for Handcrafts** (⊠ 105 Banff Ave., ☎ 403/762–2722). For arts and crafts, including handmade jewelry and watercolor paintings, check out the **Canadian House Gallery** (⊠ Caribou and Bear Sts., ☎ 403/762–3757). The **Banff Indian Trading Post** (⊠ Birch and Cave Aves., ☎ 403/762–2456) has a good selection.

If you have a sweet tooth, one place too good to miss is **Welch's Chocolate Shop** (⊠ 126 Banff Ave., near Wolf St., ☎ 403/762–3737). Its selection of homemade candies includes licorice jelly beans and chocolate and sugar sculptures of local wildlife.

Lake Louise

56 km (35 mi) north of Banff.

Numbers in the margin correspond to points of interest on the Banff map.

★ ⑫ Ask visitors what pops to mind when they think of the Canadian Rockies and they are as likely to say **Lake Louise** as Banff. What they are really thinking of is the lake itself, with the impressive Victoria Glacier flowing off the mountain at the lake's end, and the hotel located at the lakeshore—the classy Chateau Lake Louise. The scenery here is among the most spectacular in all of Banff National Park, and the Chateau Lake Louise is comparable in quality to the Banff Springs Hotel in Banff—both are owned and operated by the Canadian Pacific chain of luxury hotels.

The town of Lake Louise, though, is another story—blink and you'll miss it on your way through. That's not to say there aren't hotels, restaurants, shopping, and other services here—there are (☞ Dining and Lodging, *below*), and some very good ones at that.

Most people traveling from Banff to Lake Louise take Highway 1 for about 56 kilometers (35 miles) north along the Bow River. But if you aren't in a hurry, the two-lane Route 1A, running approximately parallel to Highway 1, is the more scenic option.

The Lake Louise ski area at Mount Whitehorn is generally regarded as one of Canada's best and frequent home to World Cup downhill races. In summer, you can ride the **Lake Louise Summer Sightseeing Lift** (known as the "Friendly Giant" to winter skiers) to the summit, where the stunning view—including over a dozen glaciers—is augmented by interpretive guides who give free tours of mountain flora and fauna. In good weather, the sun deck of the Whitehorn Tea House, at the top of the lift, is a good place to break for lunch. ⊠ *Lake Louise exit, Hwy. 1,* ☎ *403/522–3555.* ⚏ *$9.50.* ☉ *June–Sept., daily.*

The **Chateau Lake Louise,** built in 1923, overlooks blue-green Lake Louise and the Victoria Glacier at the far end of the lake. The hotel's setting is as scenic as it is popular. Canoe rentals are available at the boat house. The château is also a departure point for several short, moderately strenuous, well-traveled hiking routes. The most popular hike (about 3½ kilometers, or 2¼ miles) is to Lake Agnes. The tiny lake hangs on a mountain-surrounded shelf that opens to the east with a distant view of the Bow River valley. ⊠ *6 km (4 mi) south of junction of Hwys. 93 and 1, 6 km (4 mi) northwest of junction of Hwy. 1 and Bow Valley Pkwy.; follow signs.*

Moraine Lake is a photographic highlight in Banff National Park. In an area dubbed the "Valley of the Ten Peaks," the lake reflects in deep blue the peaks of sedimentary rock that rise abruptly around it. As beautiful as it is, don't expect Moraine Lake necessarily to offer an escape from the Lake Louise crowd; it is one of the two main stops that tour buses make in Lake Louise (the other is Lake Louise itself), as well as a popular departure point for hikers. However, a hiking path that runs along the lakeshore will quickly take you away from the crowds. ⊠ *11 km (7 mi) south of Lake Louise.*

If you are seeking solitude, several moderate **hiking trails** lead from Moraine Lake into some spectacular country. A popular day hike is the trek over Sentinel Pass and through Paradise Valley to Lake Louise. For great views, the short (3-kilometer, or 2-mile) but steep hike from Moraine Lake to Larch Valley is well worth the effort. Another option is to rent a canoe, available from the office of Moraine Lake Lodge. ⊠ *Moraine Lake Lodge Office, Box 70, T0L 1E0,* ☎ *403/522–3733.* ☺ *June–Sept., daily.*

Dining and Lodging

$$$$ ✕ **Post Hotel.** Here is one of the true epicurean experiences in the Canadian Rockies. A low, exposed-beam ceiling and a stone, wood-burning hearth in the corner lend a warm, in-from-the-cold atmosphere; white tablecloths and fanned napkins provide an elegant touch. Daring European cuisine is combined with a lighter, California influence. The house specialty is Alberta rack of lamb; veal and venison are also good choices. Or try the free-range duck sausage served with gnocchi and mango-lime salsa, or salmon with one of the house specialty sauces, which change twice a year. Homemade pastries and desserts cap off the meal. Although the food is excellent, service can be stuffy. ⊠ *200 Pipestone Rd.,* ☎ *403/522–3989. Reservations essential. AE, MC, V.*

$$–$$$$ ✕ **Chateau Lake Louise.** Several restaurants and pubs in this hotel present an array of options, from light snacking in the **Chateau Deli** to night-on-the-town elegance in the **Edelweiss Dining Room** (jacket required for dinner). Regardless of choice, dining inevitably defers to the view through the 10-foot-high windows. The size of the **Victoria Dining Room,** with seating for more than 300, is nicely tempered by plush carpeting, upholstered chairs, and standing plants. The food and atmosphere are European hotel-style—croissants and jam for breakfast, Continental fare for lunch and dinner—with white cotton tablecloths and polished silver. For simpler, less expensive, coffee shop–style eating throughout the day, there is the **Poppy Room.** From early June to early September, afternoon tea in the **Lakeside Lounge** is a culinary highlight that usually includes fresh scones, pastries, or croissants—along with coffee and tea—served on high-tea silver. In summer you can sample Continental cuisine at the **Tom Wilson dining room.** Dinner reservations are necessary in summer for most of the restaurants. ⊠ *Lake Louise Dr.,* ☎ *403/522–3511, Ext. 1818. AE, D, DC, MC, V.*

$$$ ✕ **The Station.** Housed in a lovingly restored master's office and two early 20th-century burgundy Canadian Pacific rail cars, this restaurant stands on the site of the original railway station in Lake Louise. The narrow cars are decorated with period furnishings, paintings, and photographs. After your meal you can retire to the original observation room, with its brocade tapestry and deep upholstered couch, for coffee or tea. The centerpiece of the master's office is a huge three-sided fireplace that faces out onto each of three small dining rooms. The fresh fare on the menu is expertly prepared but quite predictable, with Alberta beef, chicken, and fish dishes dominating. ⊠ *Sentinel Rd.,* ☎ *403/522–2386. Reservations essential. MC, V.*

$ ✕ **Laggan's Mountain Bakery and Deli.** This six-table coffee shop in the Samson Mall is where the local work crews, mountain guides, and park wardens come for an early-morning muffin and a cup of coffee. Laggan's has excellent baked goods, especially the sweet poppy-seed breads. You can pick up a sandwich here if you're driving north on the Icefields Parkway. ✉ *Samson Mall, off Hwy. 1,* ☎ *403/522–2017. Reservations not accepted. No credit cards.*

$$$$ 🏨 **Château Lake Louise.** There's a good chance that no hotel—any-
★ where—has a more dramatic view out its back door than this château. Terraces and lawns reach to the famous aquamarine lake, backed up by the Victoria Glacier. The impressive stone facade opens to a simi-larly grand interior, with lobby and sitting areas that convey a stadi-umlike sense of spaciousness. In the public areas, off-white walls, polished wood and brass, and burgundy carpeting blend well with the lake view, seen through large, horseshoe-shape windows. Guest rooms have bright, floral-pattern wallpaper and neo-colonial furnishings; some have terraces. In spite of all the space, though, the hotel can be-come very crowded with bus tours, hikers, and day-trippers from Banff, and rooms can be noisy. There is a minimal rate increase dur-ing peak season. ✉ *Lake Louise Dr., Lake Louise T0L 1E0,* ☎ *403/522–3511 or 800/441–1414,* 🖷 *403/522–3834. 511 rooms, 66 suites. 5 restaurants, indoor pool, steam room, exercise room, horse-back riding, boating. AE, D, DC, MC, V.*

$$$$ 🏨 **Post Hotel.** The location, next to a small shopping mall just off
★ Highway 1, is rather ordinary, but this red-roofed hotel makes up for it in other ways. Amber-color wood dominates the decor, giving the hotel an atmosphere of muted elegance—a modern interpretation of the country-lodge concept. Rooms come in 15 different configurations, from standard doubles to units with sleeping lofts, balconies, and fire-places. The wood theme extends to the furniture, made of solid Cana-dian pine. Bathrooms are large, most equipped with whirlpool tubs. Two streamside log cabins—each intended for two people—date back to the original Post Hotel, built in 1938, and evoke a mood of old-fashioned, in-the-mountains romance. Seven deluxe, two-level suites come with a king-size bed and a large living room with a river-stone fireplace. The restaurant is regularly rated as one of the best in the Canadian Rock-ies. Rates increase by 75% June–September. ✉ *Box 69, T0L 1E0,* ☎ *403/522–3989 or 800/661–1586,* 🖷 *403/522–3966. 98 units. Restau-rant, lounge, pub, indoor pool, steam room. AE, MC, V. Closed late Oct.–early Dec.*

$$$ 🏨 **Paradise Lodge & Bungalows.** Only 2 kilometers (1¼ miles) down the access road from the lake, this lodge has one- and two-bedroom suites with wood furnishings and oak paneling in the two main log build-ings. One-bedroom units come with a full kitchen and a fireplace, while the two-bedroom option includes a balcony. The bungalows, or log-sided cabins (some with kitchenettes), are more rustic from the out-side than on the inside. Set in a spruce and pine grove, they can be somewhat dark and feel cramped, but they are well maintained. ✉ *Box 7, T0L 1E0,* ☎ *403/522–3595,* 🖷 *403/522–3987. 24 suites, 21 1- and 2-room bungalows. Playground, coin laundry. MC. V. Closed mid-Oct.–mid-May.*

$$$ 🏨 **Skoki Lodge.** An 11-kilometer (6½-mile) hike or ski from the Lake Louise ski area, Skoki is the kind of backcountry lodge you must work to get to. The high-alpine scenery of Skoki Valley makes the trek well worthwhile, as does the small log-cabin lodge itself, built in 1930. The log walls, big stone fireplace, and mantel cluttered with old ski gear make Skoki seem the epitome of backcountry coziness. So, too, do the rooms upstairs in the main lodge, with beds tucked tightly under the

wood eaves. Some of the cabins have wood-burning stoves. All together it can accommodate 22 guests. Don't expect such luxuries as private baths, running water, or electricity. Meals are included in the rates. An afternoon tea, with freshly baked bread and sweets, is also served to lodge guests and day-trippers. Reserve far in advance. ⌧ *Box 5, T0L 1E0,* ☎ *403/522–3555,* ⸬ *403/522–2095. 4 lodge rooms, 3 cabins. Dining room. AE, MC, V. Closed late Sept.–Dec. 23, Easter–late June.*

$$ ⚏ **Lake Louise Inn.** This five-building complex offers a variety of accommodations, from small one-bedrooms to two-bedroom condo units, some with a balcony, a fireplace, and/or a kitchenette. A three-story building, completed in 1991, adds to the wide array of lodging options with 12 one-room suites and 24 motel-style rooms with private entrances. Catch the morning sun in the lobby, with its wood and stone-wall decor. For economy-minded travelers, the Pinery, a separate 56-room building, offers spare but comfortable accommodations. In winter, there's a shuttle to the mountain and multiday ski packages. Rates increase 70% during peak season. ⌧ *210 Village Rd., Box 209, T0L 1E0,* ☎ *403/522–3791 or 800/661–9237,* ⸬ *403/522–2018. 222 rooms and condo units. Restaurant, pizzeria, pub, indoor pool, hot tub, sauna, ice skating. AE, DC, MC, V.*

Nightlife

If you don't want to spend the evening outdoors, the **Chateau Lake Louise** has lounges and dining rooms with entertainment and dancing.

Outdoor Activities and Sports

HORSEBACK RIDING

The concierge at **Chateau Lake Louise** can arrange for trail rides and lessons.

SKIING

At **Lake Louise** (⌧ Box 5, Lake Louise, T0L 1E0, ☎ 403/522–3555) the downhill terrain is large and varied, with a fairly even spread of novice, intermediate, and expert runs (☞ Skiing *in* Banff, *above*).

SPORTING GEAR

Monod's (⌧ Chateau Lake Louise, ☎ 403/522–3837) has a wide selection of gear and clothing.

NORTH AND WEST OF BANFF

Just north of Lake Louise, Routes 1 and 93 diverge. Route 93, the **Icefields Parkway,** continues northward for 230 kilometers (143 miles) to Jasper. Highway 1 bears west over Kicking Horse Pass—named, according to local lore, after an unpleasant encounter between a pack animal and a member of an exploratory expedition in the mid-1800s—into Yoho National Park and British Columbia (to continue in this direction, *see* the British Columbia Rockies, *below*).

Hiking

BANFF NATIONAL PARK

The short (2½-kilometer, or 1½-mile), steep **Parker Ridge Trail** at the northern end of the park along the Icefields Parkway is one of the easiest hikes in the National Parks to bring the hiker into the alpine world above tree line. It provides an excellent view of the Saskatchewan Glacier, where the river of the same name begins. Snowbanks can persist into early summer, but sunshine lays intricate carpets of wildflowers across the trail in late July and August.

JASPER NATIONAL PARK

Jasper, with the most extensive trail network (nearly 1,000 kilometers, or 600 miles), is popular for hikers who want to go deep into the wilderness for several days at a time. Be aware that, in an effort to minimize environmental impact, park officials in Jasper set quotas for some of the park's most popular backpacking routes. In the height of the summer season, be prepared to encounter filled quotas for such areas as the Skyline Trail and Tonquin Valley. About a third of each trail's quota is pre-booked by reservations, which can be made up to three weeks in advance by contacting the Jasper National Park Information Centre (☞ Contacts and Resources, *below*). **Tonquin Valley,** near Mt. Edith Cavell, is one of Canada's classic backpacking areas. Its high mountain lakes, bounded by a series of steep, rocky peaks known as the Ramparts, attract many visitors in the height of summer. The **Skyline Trail** wanders for 44 kilometers (28 miles), at or above the tree line, past some of the park's most spectacular scenery. Good day-hiking areas in Jasper are around **Maligne Lake, Mt. Edith Cavell,** and **Miette Hot Springs.**

KOOTENAY NATIONAL PARK

The trail that best characterizes the hiking in Kootenay is the strenuous **Rockwall Trail,** which runs along the series of steep rock facades that are the predominant feature of the park. **Floe Lake,** sitting at the base of a sheer 3,300-foot wall, is a trail highlight. Several long dayhike spurs connect the trail with Route 93.

YOHO NATIONAL PARK

Yoho is divided into two parts: the popular hiking area around **Lake O'Hara,** dotted with high-alpine lakes, and the less-traveled **Yoho River valley,** terminating at the Yoho Glacier. Access to the Lake O'Hara region is somewhat restricted by the long, rather uneventful fire road from Highway 1. Most hikers and climbers take the Lake O'Hara Lodge shuttle bus. Entry into the Yoho River valley is more immediate, either from Takakkaw Falls or from Emerald Lake.

The Icefields Parkway

231 km (143 mi) between Lake Louise and Jasper.

For the best views of the spectacular scenery, try to choose a clear day to drive the Icefields Parkway. There aren't many facilities along the route, so be sure to check the gas gauge and pack some food if you plan to drive its entire length. The road rises to near tree line at several points, and it can be chilly at these high elevations even in midsummer—bring some warmer clothing along. The most dramatic scenery is in the north end of Banff National Park and the south end of Jasper National Park, where ice fields and glaciers become common on the high mountains surrounding the route (ice fields are massive reservoirs of ice; glaciers are the slow-moving rivers of ice that flow from the ice fields). Scenic overlooks and hiking trails of varying length abound along the route.

★ ⓭ **Bow Pass,** at 6,787 feet the highest drivable pass in the national parks of the Canadian Rockies, may be covered with snow as late as May and as early as September. On the south side of the pass is Bow Lake, source of the Bow River, which flows through Banff. Above Bow Lake hangs the edge of Crowfoot Glacier; to the south, across the lake, is the beginning of the Waputik Icefield. Around the lake are stubby trees and underbrush—this is where the tree line ends and high-alpine country begins. On the north side of the pass is **Peyto Lake**; its startlingly deep aqua blue color comes from the minerals in glacier runoff. ⊠ *41 km (25 mi) north of Lake Louise; 190 km (118 mi) south of Jasper.*

Sunwapta Pass marks the juncture of Banff and Jasper national parks. At 6,675 feet, it is the second highest drivable pass in the national parks of the Canadian Rockies. Regardless of whether you approach it from the north or south, be prepared for a series of hairpin turns as you switch-back your way up to the pass summit. Wildlife abounds in this area and is most visible in spring and autumn after a snowfall, when herds of bighorn sheep come to the road to lick up the salt used to melt snow and ice. Drive cautiously. ⊠ *122 km (76 mi) north of Lake Louise; 108 km (67 mi) south of Jasper.*

The **Athabasca Glacier** is a 7-kilometer (4½-mile) tongue of ice flow-ing from the immense Columbia Icefield almost to the highway. This is the most popular stop on the Icefields Parkway. Several other glaciers are visible from here; they all originate from the Columbia Icefield—a giant alpine lake of ice covering 325 square kilometers (130 square miles), whose edge is visible from the highway. You can take a trip onto the Athabasca Glacier on buses (called snow-coaches) modified to drive on ice. Hikers can also walk onto the tongue of the glacier, but venturing very far without a trained guide is dangerous due to hidden crevasses and slippery, sharp ice. ⊠ *127 km (79 mi) north of Lake Louise; 103 km (64 mi) south of Jasper. Bus tours: Brewster Tours,* ☎ *403/762–6700; 1½-hr tour,* 🖃 *$21.50;* ⊙ *May–mid-Oct. Guided half-day walk-ing tours:* ⊠ *Athabasca Glacier Ice Walks, Box 216, Revelstoke, BC, V0E 2S0,* ☎ *604/837–3542;* 🖃 *about $40; tickets also available at Columbia Icefields or from agencies in Banff, Lake Louise, and Jasper.*

⓮ The **Icefield Centre** is the interpretive center for the Athabasca Glacier and Columbia Icefields. In summer you can stock up on gas and food. The center provides interpretive exhibits, including a model of the en-tire ice field and an audiovisual presentation. Keep in mind that the summer midday rush (between 11 and 3) can be so intense that even the Icefield Centre's promotional materials suggest you choose another time of day to come. ⊠ *Opposite Athabasca Glacier on Rte. 93; 127 km (79 mi) north of Lake Louise; 103 km (64 mi) south of Jasper; sum-mer,* ☎ *403/852–7030; winter, 403/852–6176.* ⊙ *Mid-May–mid-June and Sept., daily 9–4; mid-June–early Sept., daily 9–6.*

Jasper

287 km (178 mi) north of Banff, 362 km (224 mi) west of Edmonton.

⓯ The town of **Jasper** is at the edge of a broad, open valley where the Athabasca and Miette rivers converge. The modest but attractive town came into being in 1911–1912, with the arrival of the railroad.

The shopping and dining scene in Jasper is even more casual than Banff's. The center of town is full of space for adults to hang out and for kids to play. In the past, Jasper was used by most visitors as a stepping-off point for the vast, surrounding backcountry, not as a destination in it-self. That is changing as the town grows. Nonetheless, Jasper remains a quiet, relaxed, and less commercialized place to stay in the parks.

Jasper is among the preeminent backpacking areas in North America. Multiday loops of more than 160 kilometers (100 miles) are possible on well-maintained trails. Backpacking and horse-packing trips in the northern half of the park offer legitimate wilderness seclusion, if not the dramatic glacial scenery of the park's southern half. However, day trips are much more common, especially around Mt. Edith Cavell, Pyra-mid Lake, Jasper Park Lodge, and Maligne Lake (☞ Hiking, *above*).

The main drag in Jasper is **Connaught Drive**; railroad tracks border one side of the road, a dense collection of shops, restaurants, and motels line the other. This strip gets crowded with tourists; drive it with an eye out for pedestrians.

◔ In the center of Jasper stands a scale model of a **19th-century locomotive;** children can climb around and sound the steam whistle. This simple pleasure is immensely popular with young kids.

★ ⓰ The **Jasper Tramway** whisks riders 3,191 vertical feet up the steep flank of Whistlers Mountain to an impressive overlook of the town of Jasper. You can see stunning views of the summit of Mt. Robson (when that mountain is clear) and the Miette valley to the west and the Athabasca valley to the east. On the seven-minute ride, the lift operator doubles as a guide, revealing the geological and historical secrets of key elements in the surrounding landscape. The upper station is above tree line (be sure to bring warm clothes). From it, a 20-minute scramble will take you to the summit, where you can sign a register to prove you were there. ⊠ *Whistlers Mountain Rd., 3 km (2 mi) south of Jasper off Rte. 93,* ☎ *403/852–3093.* ☏ *$10.* ☉ *Mid-Apr.–mid-June and early Sept.–mid-Oct., daily 9:30–5; mid-June–early Sept., daily 8 AM–10 PM.*

Jasper-Yellowhead Museum has historical exhibits showing what life in the area was like when prospectors, surveyors, settlers, and others arrived more than a century ago. ⊠ *400 Pyramid Lake Rd.,* ☎ *403/ 852–3013.* ☏ *Donations accepted.* ☉ *Mid-May–early Sept., daily 10–9; early Sept.–mid-May, Tues.–Sun. 2–4.*

◔ **Jasper Aquatic Center** pleases children with an indoor water slide, the Kidspool, and a huge regular pool. ⊠ *Pyramid Lake Rd.,* ☎ *403/852– 3663.* ☏ *$4.* ☉ *Public swim, Mon.–Thurs. 6 PM–8:30 PM, Fri. 4–9:30, weekends 2–9:30; call for other hours.*

⓱ **Pyramid** and **Patricia lakes** are on the outskirts of Jasper. Motorboats, sailboats, rowboats, canoes, kayaks, catamarans, and 4-seater pedal boats can be rented from Pyramid Lake Resort. Pyramid Lake is one of only two lakes in Jasper National Park where boat motors are allowed (the other is a section of Maligne Lake). There are picnic tables and a sandy beach at Pyramid Lake, but you're likely to find the water too cold for swimming even in mid-summer. At Patricia Lake Bungalows, you can rent from a small selection of canoes and rowboats. ⊠ *Pyramid Lake Resort, Pyramid Lake Rd., 6 km (4 mi) north of Jasper,* ☎ *403/852–4900.* ☏ *Boat rentals start at $10 per hr per boat.* ☉ *May–Oct., approximately 8 AM–10 PM.* ⊠ *Patricia Lake Bungalows, Pyramid Lake Rd., 5 km (3 mi) north of Jasper,* ☎ *403/852–3560.* ☏ *Boat rentals $6 per hr.*

Dining and Lodging

$$$$ ✕ **Becker's Gourmet Restaurant.** French cuisine is served in this small
★   mountain-lodge retreat with panoramic views of the Athabasca River from a glass-enclosed dining room. The menu is creatively assembled from French classics such as brie baked in puff pastry or veal with wild mushrooms. Breakfast begins at 8 AM. ⊠ *Near Becker's Chalets, 8 km (5 mi) south of Jasper on Rte. 93,* ☎ *403/852–3535. Reservations essential. MC, V. No lunch. Closed mid-Oct.–Apr.*

$$$$ ✕ **Jasper Park Lodge.** For fancy dining and a wide-ranging Continental menu, the **Beauvert Room** is the place to go around Jasper. The huge dining room, with its stone pillars and hard angles, conveys a big-hotel–style ambience. Menu favorites include the warm artichoke pâté with water biscuits and garden crudités, and the slow-roasted loin of Alberta pork, honey-glazed and served with apricot chutney. The **Edith Cavell Dining Room** overlooks a mountain of the same name and is slightly smaller and more private than the Beauvert Room, with tall wooden pillars, wall tapestries, and live classical piano music. The menu is very French, with a few local nuances. The chowder of wild mushrooms and mixed grains and the hearts of romaine lettuce with roast

garlic in anchovy dressing are each meals in themselves. **Moose's Nook,** more intimate but retaining a modern coolness, offers imaginative Continental dishes, including pastas and Alberta prime rib of beef, as well as a popular salad and dessert bar. Beauvert and Moose's Nook are open for breakfast; the Edith Cavell Dining Room is open for dinner only. ⊠ *Jasper Park Lodge, 4 km (2½ mi) northeast of Jasper, off Rte. 16,* ☎ *403/852–3301 or 800/441–1414. Reservations essential. AE, D, DC, MC, V.*

$$$–$$$$ ✕ **Le Beauvallon.** This is often the restaurant of choice for Jasperites
★   going out for a special meal. Upholstered chairs, blue tablecloths, and wood-trimmed crimson walls give the dining room an air of elegance that is enhanced by the strains of a world-class harpist playing in the nearby lounge. The menu has some seafood items, but meat and game dishes are the highlight, including rack of spring lamb, caribou Normandy, and venison Yorkshire. The giant Sunday-brunch buffet has epic feast potential for active outdoorspeople. Try Le Beauvallon for breakfast, too. ⊠ *Chateau Jasper, 96 Giekie St.,* ☎ *403/852–5644. Reservations essential. AE, DC, MC, V.*

$$ ✕ **Palisades.** A surprisingly rich Greek streak runs through Jasper, and this restaurant is a good place to get a feel for it. Bright white walls, a greenhouse ceiling over part of the dining room, and numerous plants evoke a sunny Mediterranean mood. The walls are adorned with more than 2,000 works (for sale) by local artists. Moussaka and souvlaki, along with baklava for dessert, are the characteristic Greek items, and pizzas are available, too. ⊠ *Cedar Ave. near Connaught Dr.,* ☎ *403/852–5222. AE, DC, MC, V.*

$ ✕ **Mountain Foods.** This is a good place to pick up a morning cup of coffee or sandwiches for a picnic lunch. The café has a health-food store in the back and a deli counter up front. Though the emphasis is on health foods, you can still get an old-fashioned three-meat hero to eat in or take out. The tabbouleh salad is especially good. Browse through the store's book rack while waiting for your sandwich to be made. ⊠ *606 Connaught Dr.,* ☎ *403/852–4050. MC, V.*

$$$$ 🏨 **Jasper Park Lodge.** Jasper's original resort, a lakeside village northeast of town, hums with on-site recreational amenities. The main lodge, with large windows overlooking Beauvert Lake (busy year-round with either ice skaters or canoes and paddleboats) and the mountains, has polished-stone floors, carved totem-pole pillars, and high ceilings that convey a cool, open atmosphere. The rooms vary: Some are done in modern, hotel-room style; others have an exposed-log, rustic character, with fireplaces; but most are arranged in one-story three-, five-, six-, and eight-bedroom cottages, and all have brightly patterned, light-as-a-feather down comforters covering the beds, plus a porch, a patio, or a balcony. Room service is delivered by staff who skillfully negotiate the paved paths between cottages on bicycles in summer. Reader feedback has suggested that tour groups may receive substantially better deals and service than individual travelers. Overbooking can be a problem during peak season; confirm your reservation. Rates nearly double June–September. ⊠ *4 km (2½ mi) northeast of Jasper, off Rte. 16, Box 40, T0E 1E0,* ☎ *403/852–3301 or 800/441–1414,* ℻ *403/852–5107. 442 rooms. 4 restaurants, coffee shop, 3 bars, 18-hole golf course, 4 tennis courts, horseback riding, boating, fishing, bicycles, ice skating, sleigh rides. AE, D, DC, MC, V.*

$$$ 🏨 **Chateau Jasper.** Large wood beams cantilevered over the front door of this two-story inn suggest a Scandinavian interior, but rooms are of the American motel style with Colonial motif, most notable in the Colonial-style headboards. Burgundy carpets and low ceilings add

coziness to largish rooms. The hotel's restaurant, Le Beauvallon, is excellent. Rates more than double June–September. ⊠ *96 Giekie St., T0E 1E0,* ☎ *403/852–5644,* FAX *403/852–4860. 119 rooms. Restaurant, indoor pool, heated indoor parking. AE, DC, MC, V.*

$$ 🏨 **Alpine Village.** Just south of town, this is one of Jasper's bargains.
★   Logs in many cabins are left exposed on interior walls, adding to the warm, rustic feeling of this family-run operation. Rooms have pinewood furnishings, fieldstone fireplaces, and beamed ceilings. Most units have sun decks; two-bedroom cabins have full kitchens. Mt. Edith Cavell rises in the distance, and the Athabasca River runs just out front, though you must cross a small road to reach it. Rates increase 50% mid-June–mid-September. ⊠ *Rte. 93A, 1 km (⅔ mi) south of Jasper, Box 610, T0E 1E0,* ☎ *403/852–3285. 42 units. Outdoor hot tub. MC, V. Closed mid-Oct.–Apr.*

$$ 🏨 **Jasper Inn.** A modern interpretation of chalet-style architecture, this inn has lots of oblique angles and hard edges, with sleek, low-slung furniture to match. The angular coolness is warmed by slanted cedar ceilings and redbrick fireplaces. During breakfast, the sky-lighted dining area can be as bright as the beach on a sunny day. Accommodations are arranged in a variety of ways, but living areas in condo-style units are particularly spacious. Most units have kitchenettes and fireplaces. Rates more than double June–September; children stay free in their parents' room. ⊠ *Giekie St. and Bonhomme Ave., Box 879, T0E 1E0,* ☎ *403/852–4461,* FAX *403/852–5916. 129 rooms, 14 suites. Restaurant, lobby lounge, indoor pool, sauna, steam bath. AE, DC, MC, V.*

$–$$ 🏨 **Patricia Lake Bungalows.** On the shores of Patricia Lake, this is a great place for peace and quiet, just a short drive from Jasper. Patricia Lake is too cold for swimming, but wonderful for canoeing, especially early in the day when the surrounding mountains are reflected in the calm waters. The clean, bright, and roomy cabins have basic furnishings—queen-size beds, dressers and tables, kitchen facilities, and TV. Shower stalls are the rule here, not bathtubs. This is one of the few remaining bargain accommodations in Jasper. Ask for a cabin; the half-dozen motel-style units look a bit dingy. Rates increase 25% June–September. ⊠ *Pyramid Lake Rd., 5 km (3 mi) from Jasper. Box 657, Jasper, T0E 1E0,* ☎ *403/852–3560,* FAX *403/852–4060. 7 rooms, 29 cabins. Boating, bicycles, coin laundry. Closed mid-Oct–Apr.*

Nightlife and the Arts

FILM

The **Chaba Movie Theatre** (⊠ Connaught Dr., ☎ 403/852–4749) plays major releases.

NIGHTLIFE

The **Astoria Hotel** (⊠ 404 Connaught Dr., ☎ 403/852–3351) is a popular spot that can become crowded and raucous. The **Athabasca Hotel**'s nightclub (⊠ 510 Patricia St., ☎ 403/852–3386) has dancing to Top-40 music and live bands. For cocktails and socializing, the **Jasper Park Lodge** offers lounges and dining rooms with entertainment and dancing. The **Whistle Stop** (⊠ Whistlers Inn, Connaught Dr., ☎ 403/852–3361) is a local haunt with the decor and ambience of a British pub.

PERFORMING ARTS

The **Jasper Activity Centre** (⊠ 303 Pyramid Ave., ☎ 403/852–3381) hosts local theater, music, and dance troupes throughout the year. The **Jasper Folk Festival,** on the first weekend in August, presents Canadian folk music in the town center and at other venues.

Outdoor Activities and Sports

BIKING

Bikes can be rented from **Freewheel Cycle** (✉ 611 Patricia St., ☎ 403/852–3898).

CLIMBING

The **Jasper Climbing School and Mountaineering Service** (✉ Box 452, T0E 1E0, ☎ 403/852–3964) offers daylong guided trips as well as climbing instruction.

GOLF

Jasper Park Lodge (☎ 403/852–6090) has an 18-hole course.

HIKING

For information on Skyline and Tonquin Valley trail quotas, contact: **Information Centre,** Jasper National Park (✉ 500 Connaught Dr., T0E 1E0, ☎ 403/852–6177). **Rocky Mountain Hiking** (✉ Box 2623, T0E 1E0, ☎ 403/852–5015) has trained backcountry guides to take visitors on customized multiday hikes and also offers interpretive programs, day hikes, and some caving.

HORSEBACK RIDING

For trail rides or lessons contact the concierge at **Jasper Park Lodge** or **Pyramid Riding Stables** (✉ Box 787, T0E 1E0, ☎ 403/852–3562).

RAFTING

Jasper Raft Tours (✉ Box 398, T0E 1E0, ☎ 403/852–3613) runs half-day float trips on the Athabasca. **Maligne River Adventures** (✉ Box 280, T0E 1E0, ☎ 403/852–3370) runs half-day white-water trips on the Maligne. Prices begin at $50.

SKIING

Cross-Country. Jasper has excellent groomed trails at Pyramid and Patricia lakes and on the Icefields Parkway near town. Maligne Lake has a range of moderate-to-challenging lakeside and forest cross-country ski trails. Reservations for backcountry huts in Tonquin Valley can be made through **Tonquin Valley Pack and Ski Trips** (✉ Box 550, T0E 1E0, ☎ 403/852–3909).

Downhill. Marmot Basin (✉ Box 1300, Jasper T0E 1E0, ☎ 403/852–3816), near Jasper, has a wide mix of terrain, and slopes are a little less crowded than those around Banff.

SPORTING GEAR

Totem Ski Shop (✉ 408 Connaught Dr., ☎ 800/363–3078 or 403/852–3078) is the major sporting goods outlet.

Shopping

You'll find a large selection of native arts and crafts at **E&A Studio** (✉ 609B Patricia St., ☎ 403/852–3606). **Jasper Originals** (✉ Beauvert Promenade, Jasper Park Lodge, ☎ 403/852–5378) has regional arts and crafts.

Jasper National Park

South border of Park: 178 km (111 mi) north of Banff townsite, 152 km (94 mi) south of Jasper townsite. East border of Park: 323 km (201 mi) west of Edmonton, 50 km (31 mi) east of Jasper townsite.

Apart from the innumerable scenic vistas and hiking trails, a number of special attractions in Jasper National Park make for easy half-day trips south, east, north, or west from the Jasper townsite. Don't expect much in the way of accommodation, though; apart from a single motel at Miette Hot Springs, and two cabin-type facilities near the east gate, all the accommodation in this huge park—almost as large as the entire state of Connecticut—is clustered in the townsite.

⑱ At **Athabasca Falls,** the Athabasca River is compressed through a narrow gorge, producing a violent torrent of water. The falls are especially dramatic in early summer, when the river is swollen by snowmelt. Trails and overlooks provide numerous vantage points to view the falls and the nearby montane forest. ⊠ *31 km (19 mi) south of Jasper.*

⑲ **Mount Edith Cavell** is the highest mountain in the vicinity of Jasper townsite. Named after a heroic nurse who was shot by the Germans during the First World War, it towers above the surroundings at 11,033 feet and shows off its permanently snow-clad north face to the town of Jasper. From highway 93A, a narrow, winding 14½-kilometer (9-mile) road (often closed until the beginning of June) leads to the base of the mountain. Trailers are not permitted on this road, but they can be dropped off at a parking lot near the junction with 93A. There are several pullouts along the road that offer spectacular views, as well as access to trails leading up the **Tonquin Valley,** one of the premier hiking (as well as horse-packing and backcountry skiing) areas in the park.

The mountain itself is arguably the most spectacular site in Jasper National Park reachable by automobile. From the parking lot—which can become quite congested—there is a short paved trail that leads up to the base of an imposing mile-high cliff. The Angel Glacier drips out of a valley partway up the cliff, adding to the drama of the scene. If you feel ambitious, a steep 3-kilometer (2-mile) trail climbs up the valley opposite the mountain, opening into an alpine meadow—**Cavell Meadows.** The meadow is carpeted with wildflowers from mid-July to mid- or late-August and affords an excellent view of the Angel Glacier on the opposite slope. ⊠ *27 km (17 mi) south of Jasper.*

★ ⑳ You can explore **Maligne Lake,** 22 kilometers (14 miles) long, one of the largest glacier-fed lakes in the world, on a 1½-hour guided cruise or in a rented boat. Several day hikes (approximately 4 hours roundtrip), some with steep sections, lead to alpine meadows offering panoramas of the lake and the surrounding mountain ranges. You can also take horseback riding and fishing trips, and there's an excellent cafeteria here. ⊠ *Maligne Lake Rd., 44 km (28 mi) southeast of Jasper. Book tours,* ⊠ *Maligne Lake Scenic Cruises, 626 Connaught Dr.,* ☎ *403/852–3370.* 🈺 *Boat tours $31.* ⊘ *Mid-May–Oct., daily 10–5, every hr on the hr.*

En Route   Along the way to Maligne Lake, you'll pass **Maligne Canyon,** where the Maligne River cuts a narrow 50-meter-deep gorge through limestone bedrock. An interpretive trail winds its way from a picnic area across six bridges where you can catch the spray from the thundering Maligne River. It is an impressive sight, but the 4-kilometer (2½-mile) trail along the canyon can be crowded, so it's best saved for evening, when the crowds thin out. Along the trail, you'll find a restaurant and Indian crafts store at the Maligne Canyon Chalet.

Also on the Maligne Lake Road is **Medicine Lake.** A complex, underground drainage system causes the lake to empty almost completely at times, leading early Indians to suspect that spirits were responsible for the dramatic fluctuations in the level of the placid waters.

㉑ **Miette Hot Springs** is a relaxing spot, especially when the weather turns inclement. Visitors come here to soak in naturally heated mineral waters originating from three springs that reach 54°C (129°F) and have to be cooled to 40°C (104°F) to allow bathing. A short walk leads to the remnants of the original hot spring facility, where several springs still pour heated sulphurous water into the adjacent creek. Day passes and suit, locker, and towel rentals are available. ⊠ *Miette Hot Springs Rd. off Rte. 16, 58 km (36 mi) northeast of Jasper,* ☎ *403/866–3939.* ⌦ *$4.* ⊙ *Late May–early Oct., daily 8 AM–11 PM.*

㉒ At 12,972 feet, towering **Mt. Robson** is the highest mountain in the Canadian Rockies. The peak was not successfully scaled until 1913, despite numerous attempts. Certain routes on Robson are still considered by experienced mountaineers to be among the world's most challenging. Mt. Robson's weather is notoriously bad even when the weather elsewhere is perfectly fine; it is a rare day that the summit is not encircled by clouds. A favorite backpacking trip on the mountain is the strenuous 18-kilometer (11-mile) hike to **Berg Lake,** through the wonderfully named Valley of a Thousand Falls. Berg Lake is no tranquil body of water; the grunt and splash as Robson's glaciers calve chunks of ice into the lake are regular sounds in summer. The 5-kilometer (3-mile) mostly level hike to **Kinney Lake,** along the Berg Lake trail, is a good option for day hikers. ⊠ *Rte. 16, 80 km (50 mi) west of Jasper.*

Kootenay National Park

34 km (21 mi) west of Banff townsite.

Kootenay National Park, named for the Kootenai Indians who settled in the area, is just over the border in British Columbia and touches the west side of Banff National Park and the south end of Yoho National Park. When the tourist population of Banff swells during the busy summer months, Kootenay park remains surprisingly quiet, although not for lack of natural beauty; the scenery can certainly match that of Banff and Jasper parks. Facilities are few here, so most visitors tend to see the park only as they drive through on Highway 93, which traverses the length of the park, while on their way to other points in British Columbia.

㉓ **Vermilion Pass** is at the juncture of Banff and Kootenay national parks. At 5,416 feet, this is not one of the highest passes in the Canadian Rockies, but it marks the boundary between Alberta and British Columbia and the Continental Divide—rivers east of here flow east, eventually to the Atlantic Ocean; rivers to the west flow to the Pacific Ocean.

Just beyond the Vermilion Pass summit is the head of the **Stanley Glacier trail,** one of the fine choices for a day hike in the park. The trail climbs easily for 4 kilometers (2½ miles) through fire remnants and new growth, across rock debris and glacial moraine, ending in the giant amphitheater of the Stanley Glacier basin. ⊠ *3 km (2 mi) from east gate of Kootenay park.*

㉔ **Floe Lake** sits at the base of a 3,300-foot-high cliff—the Rockwall. The lake is one of the most popular hiking destinations in Kootenay National Park. The 10-kilometer (6-mile) trail from the highway passes through characteristic Kootenay backcountry terrain. Plan a full day for this one. ⊠ *Trailhead, 22 km (14 mi) from east gate of Kootenay park.*

En Route Along the stretch of highway 93 that leads through Kootenay National Park from Banff National Park to Radium Hot Springs, 63 kilometers (39 miles) to the south, the only service area is at **Vermilion Crossing,** the approximate halfway point. Here, you'll find fuel and basic groceries (summer only). Between Vermilion Crossing and Radium, the mountains open up gradually, their flanks covered by thick stands of Douglas fir, as the Vermilion River joins with the wider Kootenay

River. The highway then heads west, winding through the narrow limestone canyon cut by the Sinclair River.

Yoho National Park

57 km (36 mi) northwest of Banff townsite.

Yoho National Park abuts Banff National Park to the east and Kootenay National Park to the south. The name "Yoho" is an Indian word that translates, approximately, to "awe inspiring." Indeed, the park is awe inspiring, containing some of the most outstanding scenery in the Canadian Rockies. It is also quieter than Banff park to the east.

Yoho is divided by Highway 1 into the northern half, which includes Takakkaw Falls, the Yoho River Valley, and Emerald Lake, and the southern half, of which Lake O'Hara is the physical and spiritual epicenter.

㉕ The **Spiral Tunnels,** train tunnels cut through the flanks of Mount Ogden and Cathedral Crags, make figure-eight loops on each side of Highway 1. These tunnels were the engineering answer to the problem of getting trains up and down the steep grade of the Rockies' western slope. Many trains use the tunnels, and Rocky Mountaineer RailTours (☎ 800/665–7245) and Canadian Pacific Railroad (CPR; ☎ 403/762–3722) provide schedules so you can time your arrival at the roadside observation deck off Highway 1 for when a train is passing through. Without a train, the tunnels simply look like holes in the mountainside; but when a train goes through, its engine emerges from one tunnel while its caboose disappears into the other, almost directly above the engine. ✉ *9 km (5½ mi) west of Banff National Park.*

㉖ In the northern half of Yoho park, **Takakkaw Falls,** 833 feet high, is the highest waterfall in all of Canada, let alone the Rockies. The falls are spectacular in early summer when melting snow and ice provide ample runoff. (The flow of the falls can also increase during summer hot spells, which speed the melt of glacial ice.) But the falls are just a taste of what lies ahead for day hikers and backpackers who choose to explore the region's trail network through the Yoho River Valley with its ice fields and high cliffs. ✉ *Access from 13-km (8-mi) Yoho Valley Rd., off Hwy. 1, 13 km (8 mi) west of Banff National Park.*

㉗ **Emerald Lake** is a vivid turquoise shimmer at the base of the President Range, where you can rent a canoe, have a cup of tea at the teahouse by the lodge, or take a stroll around the lake. The lake also is a trailhead for hikers, as well as a frequent haunt of cross-country and backcountry skiers in winter. ✉ *Access from 8-km (5-mi) road off Hwy. 1, 19 km (12 mi) west of Banff National Park.*

㉘ The **Burgess Shale site,** halfway between the Takakkaw Falls road and the Emerald Lake Lodge road, contains the fossilized remains of 120 marine species dating back 515 million years. Burgess Shale was designated a World Heritage Site in 1981; guided hikes are the only way to see the actual fossil sites, and they're popular, so make reservations. The hikes are conducted July through mid-September, and the going is fairly strenuous; the round-trip distance is 20 kilometers (12 miles). There is a shorter, steeper hike to the Mt. Stevens trilobite fossil beds. Guided hikes are also offered to extensions of the Burgess Shale fossils in Kootenay and Banff national parks. Allow a full day for any of the hikes. ✉ *Trailhead, 16 km (10 mi) west of Banff National Park. Reservations for guided hikes, ✉ Canadian Wilderness Tours, Box 3060, Canmore, Alberta, T0L 0M0, ☎ 403/678–3795. ✑ $25–$45.*

㉙ **Lake O'Hara,** in Yoho's other half, is widely regarded as one of *the* places for outdoor enthusiasts to go in the Canadian Rockies. For summer, Lake O'Hara Lodge (☞ Dining and Lodging, *below*) is booked months in advance. Although the forest-lined fire road between Highway 1 and the lake can be hiked, it makes more sense to ride the lodge-run bus even if you aren't staying at the lodge. (Call the lodge for times and space availability.) Save your legs for hiking any of several moderately strenuous trails that radiate from the lodge into a spectacular, high-alpine world of small lakes surrounded by escarpments of rock and permanent snowpack. Keep in mind, however, that the bus makes the Lake O'Hara area accessible to many other people, too. If you're looking for a true wilderness experience, other places (notably Kootenay) are better choices. ⊠ *Access from 11-km (6-mi) Lake O'Hara Fire Rd. off Lake Louise/Great Divide Dr., 3 km (2 mi) west of Banff National Park.*

Dining and Lodging

$$$$ ✕▦ **Emerald Lake Lodge.** This enchanted place at the edge of a secluded,
★ glacier-fed lake is only a 20-minute drive from Lake Louise and an hour from Banff. You can get light meals in a comfortable sitting area by the large stone hearth in the log-cabin main lodge. Guest rooms have fireplaces and balconies. The dining room is a glass-enclosed terrace, with views of the lake through tall stands of evergreens. The menu mixes traditional Canadian and American fare—steaks, game, and fish—with such nouvelle sauces as ginger-tangerine glaze. **Cilantro-on-the-Lake,** opened in 1995, offers cafe-style light meals (summer only). Rates increase about 70% during peak season. ⊠ *Yoho National Park, 9½ km (6 mi) north of Field, BC, Box 10, Field, BC V0A 1G0,* ☎ *604/343–6321 or 800/663–6336,* ✉ *604/343–6724. 85 units in 2- and 4-room cottages. 2 restaurants, bar, tea shop, sauna, outdoor hot tub, exercise room, horseback riding, boating. AE, DC, MC, V.*

$$$$ ▦ **Lake O'Hara Lodge.** In summer, guests are ferried by a lodge-operated bus along an 11-kilometer (7-mile) fire road between Highway 1 and the grounds. In winter, guests must ski the distance. The lodge and lakeside cabins offer fairly luxurious backcountry living, including private rooms with baths and a dining room that serves three meals a day (included in the room rates). Avoid the smaller, cramped, noisy rooms near the gentlemen's bathroom. Reservations for the high summer season (mid-June–Sept.) should be booked several months in advance. ⊠ *Off Hwy. 1, Yoho National Park, Box 55, Lake Louise, Alberta T0L 1E0,* ☎ *604/343–6418; off-season, 403/678–4110. 23 units in lodge and cabins. Dining room, hiking, boating. No credit cards. Closed mid-Apr.–mid-June and Oct.–mid-Feb.*

Outdoor Activities and Sports

HORSEBACK RIDING
The concierge at **Emerald Lake Lodge** can arrange for horseback riding expeditions and lessons.

SOUTH OF BANFF

The region immediately southeast of Banff—the town of Canmore and, south of it, the group of provincial parks and recreation areas jointly known as Kananaskis Country—attracted mostly locals from Calgary and Banff until the 1988 Olympics brought brand-new facilities—ski jumps, cross-country trails, and other sports installations, as well as hotels and restaurants—to the region. Farther south, Waterton Lakes National Park marks the meeting of the prairie and the mountains as well as the two countries it straddles.

Canmore

24 km (15 mi) southeast of Banff townsite, 106 km (66 mi) west of Calgary.

㉚ **Canmore** has become a modern boomtown, attracting high-end tourism developments and residents who crave a mountain lifestyle. The attractive, boutique-lined Main Street and several good restaurants are indications that Canmore is no longer strictly a locals' town. It's become the regional center for the active outdoor life—with streets full of young, robust types who live for climbing, hiking, and mountain-biking in summer, cross-country and alpine skiing in winter. Several outfitters, climbing schools, and guide services operate out of Canmore. Many tourists make Canmore their base for exploring the national parks or Kananaskis Country. This modern version of Canmore didn't really emerge until the 1988 Winter Olympics, when new facilities around Canmore and Kananaskis Country gave this area widespread appeal.

The **Canadian Museum of Rail Travel** (⊠ 1 Van Horne St., North Canmore, ☎ 403/852–3918), housed in restored Canadian Pacific Railway cars, presents a good picture of rail travel in the 1920s.

Dining and Lodging

$$–$$$ ✕ **Pepper Mill.** The small dining room is simply adorned with off-white
★ walls, green tablecloths, and cloth-covered hanging lamps. Reputed for its pepper steak, the restaurant also serves well-prepared pasta dishes, fish, and seafood. ⊠ *726 9th St.,* ☎ *403/678–2292. AE, MC, V. No lunch.*

$$ ✕ **Faro's.** Colorful drawings of Canmore hung against white walls and blond-wood tabletops contribute to a bright, casual environment. The menu is eclectic, listing barbecued dishes, pizzas, and steaks, but such Greek entrées as souvlaki are the house specialties. ⊠ *8th St. and 8th Ave.,* ☎ *403/678–2234. AE, MC, V.*

$$$ ▥ **Mt. Assiniboine Lodge.** Built by the Canadian Pacific Railroad in 1928, the handsome, log-sided main lodge appears to have changed little in more than 60 years. The backcountry lodge's setting is classically alpine—in the southeast corner of Banff National Park at the edge of mile-long Lake Magog, with the rocky pyramid of Mt. Assiniboine in full view. Guests can hike in from Sunshine Village or hike (or ski) in from Spray Lakes Reservoir, the distance ranging between 20 and 30 kilometers (12 and 18 miles) depending on the route chosen. Guests can also fly in by helicopter from Canmore, saving their hiking legs for high-country jaunts from the lodge. Among the lodge's noteworthy amenities are large down comforters on the beds and hearty meals served family-style. There are cabins that sleep two to four people, as well as rooms in the lodge. The lodge has some electricity and running water, but guests should be prepared to use outhouses. Room rates include all meals and hiking (or skiing) guide service. Rates increase about 15% during peak season. ⊠ *Box 1527, T0L 0N0,* ☎ *403/678–2883,* FAX *403/678–4877. 6 lodge rooms, 6 cabins. Dining room. MC, V. Closed Oct.–mid-Feb. and mid-Apr.–late June.*

$$ ▥ **Rocky Mountain Ski Lodge.** Several motels in Canmore provide lower-price alternatives to Banff accommodations. Of these, Rocky Mountain Ski Lodge is a notch above the rest. It's really three separate motel properties rolled into one. Slanting, exposed wood-and-beam ceilings give a chaletlike feel to otherwise simple motel rooms. Rooms in the older section have kitchenettes, but the decor is more '60s American than Swiss-chalet. Rates increase about 75% June–September. ⊠ *Hwy. 1A, Box 3000, T0L 0N0,* ☎ *403/678–5445; in Canada, 800/665–*

6111; ℻ 403/678–6484. *82 units, some with kitchen, kitchenette, and/or fireplace. Sauna, playground. AE, MC, V.*

$ 🖭 **Bow Valley Motel.** In the center of Canmore, this two-story, few-frills motel is enhanced by the friendliness of its management. If you put a premium on being able to walk to dining and shopping, this is the place to stay. Rooms are clean and simply furnished, with a bed, a dresser, a small fridge, and a 20-inch TV. Five rooms have kitchens. Rates increase about 75% early June–late September. ⊠ *610 8th St., Box 231, T0L 0M0,* ☎ *403/678–5085,* ℻ *403/678–6560. 25 rooms. Outdoor hot tub, coin laundry. MC, V.*

Nightlife and the Arts

Join Canmore's local folk and kick back at **Sherwood House** (⊠ 738 8th St., ☎ 403/678–5211), which occasionally has live bands on weekends.

Stonecrop Studio (⊠ 8th Ave. and Main St., T0L 0M0, ☎ 403/678–4151), now in its 20th year, displays the works in progress of local artists using bronze, ceramics, pottery, and silver, among other media.

Outdoor Activities and Sports

GOLF

Canmore Golf Course (off Hwy 1, Canmore, ☎ 403/678–4785) has 18 holes.

SKIING

Cross-country. The Canmore Nordic Centre (⊠ Box 1979, T0L 0M0, ☎ 403/678–2400) has 70 kilometers (44 miles) of groomed trails. The **Canadian School of Mountaineering** (⊠ Box 723, T0L 0M0, ☎ 403/678–4134) leads backcountry tours.

Kananaskis Country

North entrance: 26 km (16 mi) southeast of Canmore, 80 km (50 mi) west of Calgary.

③① **Kananaskis Country** is a 4,200-square-kilometer (1,600-square-mile) recreational region made up of three provincial parks. It has spectacular mountain scenery, although it's not quite as awesome as that in the adjacent national parks. It offers a multitude of outdoor activities, some of which are prohibited or discouraged in the national parks. Camping, hiking, bicycling, fishing, hunting, golfing, boating, all-terrain vehicles, canoeing, and horseback riding predominate in spring, summer, and fall. Downhill skiing, cross-country skiing, snowshoeing, ice skating, snowmobiling, dogsledding, ice fishing, and camping predominate in winter.

The main highway through Kananaskis Country is Route 40, also known as the **Kananaskis Trail.** It runs north-south through the impressive scenery of the front ranges of the Rockies. Only the northern 40 kilometers (25 miles) of the road remain open from December 1 to June 15, in part because of the extreme conditions of the **Highwood Pass** (at 7,280 feet, the highest drivable pass in Canada), and in part to protect winter wildlife habitat in **Peter Lougheed Provincial Park** and southward. Highway 40 continues south to join Route 541, west of Longview. Access to East Kananaskis Country, a popular area for horseback-riding trips, is on Route 66, which heads west from Priddis.

The **Canmore Nordic Centre,** built for the 1988 Olympic Nordic skiing events, is one of the region's most popular attractions. This state-of-the-art facility in the northwest corner of Kananaskis Country, just south of Canmore, has an extensive groomed cross-country network. Some trails are lighted for night skiing, and a 1½-kilometer (1-mile) paved trail is open in summer for roller skiing and in-line skating. Lessons and rentals are available. ✉ *Box 1979, Canmore T0L 0M0,* ☎ *403/678–2400.* *No trail fee.* ⏲ *Lodge daily 9–5:30; some trails until 9* PM.

Kananaskis Village (☞ Dining and Lodging, *below*), a full-service resort built for the 1988 Olympics, brings first-class lodging, dining, and golf to Kananaskis Country. A lodge, a hotel, and an inn cluster next to an attractively landscaped artificial pond on a small plateau between the Nakiska ski area and two 18-hole golf courses. Many visitors to the region stay at one of the several campgrounds, most of which can accommodate recreational vehicles.

The **William Watson Lodge** is unique in the Canadian Rockies, in that it is designed exclusively for people who have disabilities and senior citizens. Access points have been built along Mt. Lorette Ponds north of Kananaskis Village to accommodate anglers using wheelchairs, and many hiking trails near the village have been cut wide and gentle enough for wheelchair travel. Overnight and day-use facilities, including cabins, are available to people with disabilities and Alberta senior citizens. Albertans get preference; people with disabilities from out of province must book 60 days in advance. ✉ *30 km (18 mi) south of Kananaskis Village on Rte. 40, Box 130, Kananaskis T0L 2H0,* ☎ *403/591–7227.* ⏲ *Office weekdays 8* AM*–9* PM.

Dining and Lodging

$$$$ ✕ **L'Escapade.** This is the signature dining room of the Hotel at Kananaskis. The atmosphere is intimate and the service attentive. The menu offers innovative Canadian dishes such as Brome Lake duck, Arctic musk ox, Yukon char, and desserts flambéed at the table. Soft, live music plays nightly for dancing. ✉ *Hotel at Kananaskis, Hwy. 40, Kananaskis Village,* ☎ *403/591–7711 or 800/441–1414. Reservations essential. AE, D, DC, MC, V.*

$$$$ ✕🏨 **Hotel and Lodge at Kananaskis.** The Hotel and the Lodge are part of Canadian Pacific's chain of luxury hotels. The tastefully designed and decorated rooms are large and even lavish, some with rosewood furnishings, ceramic-base lamps, half-bay windows, and rustic wood armoires to hide TV sets. Many of the Hotel's rooms have fireplaces, Jacuzzi tubs, and large sitting areas. Several restaurants, skewed toward high-end elegance, serve food ranging from Spanish tapas to haute cuisine. For casual dining, try the **Peaks Dining Room** in the Lodge, offering family favorites, including burgers for lunch or dinner and a buffet-style breakfast, plus nightly family entertainment. Premium rates apply May–October. ✉ *Rte. 40, 28 km (17 mi) south of Hwy. 1, Kananaskis Village T0L 2H0,* ☎ *403/591–7711 or 800/441–1414,* FAX *403/591–7770. 243 rooms, 78 suites. 3 restaurants, 2 lounges, indoor pool, sauna, steam room, 2 18-hole golf courses, health club, heated indoor parking. AE, D, DC, MC, V.*

$$$ 🏨 **Kananaskis Guest Ranch.** Near the Bow River at the edge of Kananaskis Country, the main lodge, with a restaurant and a lounge, is surrounded by cabins and larger "chalets." Cedar walls and, in some units, cedar-beamed ceilings give a rustic flavor to otherwise plain, double-bed bedrooms. The Donut Tent—a log-and-wood-roofed "tent" with a large hole in the middle, where bonfires are built for family-style barbecues—is the ranch's claim to fame. In addition to the obligatory horseback riding, the ranch also offers jet-boat trips on the Bow River. ✉ *Ranch Rd., from Seebe-Exshaw exit on Hwy. 1 east of Canmore, General Delivery, Seebe T0L 1X0,* ☎ *403/673–3737 or 800/691–*

5085, FAX *403/673–2100. 33 units in cabins and chalets. Dining room, lounge, whirlpool. AE, MC, V. Closed mid-Oct–Apr.*

$$$ 🏨 **Kananaskis Inn.** Part of the complex built for the 1988 Olympics, and overlooking the resort's pond, the Inn has log pillars and an inviting redwood exterior. Inside, the rooms are motel-style, some with private balconies, kitchenettes, or fireplaces. Premium rates apply June–September. ⊠ *Hwy. 40, 28 km (17 mi) south of Hwy. 1, Box 10, Kananaskis Village T0L 2H0,* ☎ *403/591–7500,* FAX *403/591–7633. 94 rooms. Restaurant, bar, indoor pool, hot tub, steam room, coin laundry. AE, MC, V.*

$$$ 🏨 **Mt. Engadine Lodge.** Hiking and cross-country skiing trails lead out
★ the back door of this backcountry lodge to the mountains and lakes of Kananaskis Country. The lodge's use of wood—exterior cedar walls and interior white-pine ceilings and furnishings—keeps guests feeling close to nature. Rooms (shared as well as private) have a scrubbed simplicity to them, as do the common areas. Mediocre meals, served family-style, are included in the rate. The lodge operators are also backcountry guides, and hiking packages are available. ⊠ *At Mt. Shark, turn off on Spray Trail, 38 km (22 mi) south of Canmore, Box 1679, Canmore T0L 0M0,* ☎ *403/678–4080,* FAX *403/678–2109. 10 rooms in lodge and 2 cabins, all with shared baths. Restaurant, sauna. MC, V. Closed May–mid-June, Oct.–Dec. 25, and weekdays Jan.–Apr.*

$$–$$$ 🏨 **Homeplace Ranch.** Just east of the Kananaskis Country foothills, the guest ranch is what its name suggests: homey. It is secluded, reached over several miles of gravel roads, surrounded by other working ranches. Bedrooms have tiny, private baths (unusual for ranch accommodations), and the small living-dining area is cluttered with books and magazines that provide good reading, the principal evening activity. A "south ranch," 1½ hours away, opened in 1995. It is very similar to the main ranch, except that accommodation is in 6 cabin units. During the day, the activity is riding over the rolling land through the aspen groves and open meadows near the ranch. You can also take extended, multiday pack trips into Kananaskis Country. Meals, included in the guest rate, are served family-style, and such is the homey atmosphere that you might find yourself wanting to pitch in and help with the cooking or the dishes. Packages, including 3- to 5-day pack trips, are available in summer. Rates increase about 40% during peak season. ⊠ *Main ranch, off Hwy. 2, 10 km (6 mi) west of Priddis; south ranch, 30 km (20 mi) south of Longview; R.R. 1, Box 6, Priddis, Alberta T0L 1W0;* ☎ FAX *403/931–3245. Main ranch, 7 rooms; south ranch, 6 cabins. Dining room. No credit cards.*

Nightlife

For the most part, nightlife in Kananaskis is of the do-it-yourself variety, but the **Lodge at Kananaskis** (☞ Dining and Lodging, *above*) has lounges and dining rooms with entertainment and dancing.

Outdoor Activities and Sports

GOLF

Kananaskis Country Course (☎ 403/591–7070) has two 18-hole links.

HORSEBACK RIDING

Boundary Stables (⊠ Box 44, Kananaskis Village T0L 2H0, ☎ 403/591–7171) has horses to rent for trail rides.

SKIING

Nakiska (⊠ Box 1988, Kananaskis Village T0L 0M0, ☎ 403/591–7777), about 45 minutes southeast of Banff, was the site of the 1988 Olympic Alpine events and has wide-trail intermediate skiing and not always reliable snow.

Waterton Lakes National Park

354 km (220 mi) south of Banff townsite, 267 km (166 mi) south of Calgary.

㉜ Waterton Lakes National Park lies near the southern end of the Canadian Rockies. Geologically, it is closely related to the main mountain parks to the north, but geographically it is separated by several hundred kilometers of highway. As a result, Waterton is a rare side trip from Banff—people who visit Waterton Lakes generally make it their principal destination or combine it with a vacation in Glacier National Park across the U.S. border in Montana.

Waterton is the meeting of two worlds—the flatlands of the prairie and the abrupt upthrust of the mountains. Chief Mountain, the squared-off peak on the eastern end of the stand of mountains visible as you approach from the north, juts up from the prairie, dominating the horizon. In this juncture of worlds, the park squeezes into a relatively small area (525 square kilometers, or 200 square miles) an unusual mix of wildlife, flora, and climate zones.

The common denominator in the park is wind. Although the mountains and canyon walls provide protection in some areas, the wind blows powerfully and regularly from the prairie, often at speeds of more than 50 kilometers (30 miles) per hour. Trees along the lakesides bear evidence of this, as they grow at about an 80-degree angle, rather than straight up.

Politically, too, Waterton represents a meeting of worlds. Although the park was officially established in 1895, it was joined in 1932 with Glacier National Park in Montana to form **Waterton/Glacier International Peace Park**—a symbol of friendship and peaceful coexistence between Canada and the United States. In fact, some services in the park, including the Prince of Wales Hotel—perhaps the park's most recognizable landmark—are under Glacier Park management in the United States. In 1995, this park was designated a World Heritage Site by UNESCO.

Whether it is a pervading spirit of international peace or the park's isolation, Waterton is a decidedly low-key place. The townsite of Waterton Park is a small, quiet community, located in roughly the geographical center of the park. In winter the town essentially closes down; in summer several hundred residents call the park home. Hiking, horseback riding, and boating are the main activities. The park contains numerous short hikes for day-trippers and some longer treks for backpackers. Boats (nonmotorized) can be rented at Upper Waterton Lake or Cameron Lake. For windsurfing enthusiasts, the winds that rake across Upper Waterton Lake create an exciting ride. Bring a wetsuit, though; the water remains numbingly cold throughout the summer.

Because of Waterton's proximity to the U.S. border and its bond with Glacier National Park, many visitors come to the park from the south. You can fly into Great Falls or Kalispell, Montana, and drive to Waterton. If you drive from Calgary (via Routes 2, 3, and 6), you can take an interesting side trip to **Crowsnest Pass** (☞ Off the Beaten Path, *below*).

Red Rock Canyon is one of the more popular natural attractions in Waterton park. "Canyon" is stretching the term, as it is little more than a gully carved into the rock by a mountain stream. But "red rock" is appropriate; the exposed rock throughout the canyon displays a remarkably red hue. This is a popular spot for a picnic and a stroll along the paths that line the canyon. ⊠ *10 km (6 mi) north of Waterton Park townsite.*

Cameron Lake is the jewel of Waterton. It sits in a land of high basins and glacially carved cirques, filled in summer with hundreds of varieties of alpine wild flowers, including 22 varieties of wild orchids. You also can rent canoes and paddleboats to explore Cameron Lake. ⊠ *Akima Pkwy, 13 km (8 mi) southwest of Waterton Park townsite.*

One of the park's most popular activities is the two-hour cruise on Upper Waterton Lake from the town of Waterton Park south to **Goat Haunt,** where there are shelters, a ranger station, and a boat dock. From here, several short, easy hikes are possible before you return to Waterton; properly equipped overnighters can also camp out at Goat Haunt. (Because Goat Haunt is in the United States, travelers going to and from must clear Customs.) ⊠ *Waterton International Shoreline Cruise Company, Box 126, Waterton Park, Alberta T0K 2M0,* ☎ *403/859–2362.* ⊡ *$17.* ⊙ *Mid-May–mid-Sept.*

Lodging

$$–$$$ ★ 🏨 **Kilmorey Lodge.** The 60-year-old inn with a log-cabin facade sits at the edge of the Waterton Park townsite. Rooms are steeped in country-cottage atmosphere, with pine-wood walls, eiderdown comforters, sloped floors, and homespun antique furnishings. Some rooms have additional sleeping or sitting areas. ⊠ *Box 100, Waterton Park, Alberta T0K 2M0,* ☎ *403/859–2334,* 𝔽𝔸𝕏 *403/859–2342. 23 rooms. Restaurant, lounge. AE, D, DC, MC, V.*

$$–$$$ ★ 🏨 **Prince of Wales Hotel.** Perched between two lakes, the hotel has breathtaking views of both a mountain backdrop and a lake-and-prairie setting. Fantastically ornamented with eaves, balconies, and turrets, it's crowned by a high steeple. The baronial, dark-paneled interior evokes the feeling of a royal Scottish hunting lodge. Expect creaks and rattles at night—the old hotel (built in the 1920s) is exposed to rough winds. Children under 12 stay free in their parents' room. Rates increase about 50% mid-June–September. ⊠ *Waterton Park townsite; reservations, Station 0928, Phoenix, AZ 85077,* ☎ *602/207–6000 or 406/226–5551. 81 rooms. Restaurant. MC, V. Closed late-Sept.–mid-May.*

$$ 🏨 **Bayshore Inn.** As the name suggests, this two-story inn is on the lakeside, and rooms with balconies take full advantage of the setting. Otherwise, the inn's common areas and motel-style rooms are rather ordinary. The lakeside patio is a great spot for light meals and drinks. Rates increase 40% late May–September. ⊠ *Main St., Box 38, Waterton Park, Alberta T0K 2M0,* ☎ *403/859–2211; off-season, 403/238–4847;* 𝔽𝔸𝕏 *403/859–2291. 62 rooms, 8 suites. Restaurant, bar, coffee shop, lounge, pizzeria. AE, D, MC, V. Closed mid-Oct.–late Mar.*

Outdoor Activities and Sports

GOLF

Waterton Golf Course (2 km, or 1 mi, east of Waterton Park townsite, ☎ 403/859–2114) has 18 holes.

HORSEBACK RIDING

Alpine Stables (⊠ Box 53, Waterton Park, Alberta T0K 2M0, ☎ 403/859–2462).

OFF THE
BEATEN PATH

Crowsnest Pass. Between Calgary or Banff and Waterton, you can take a side trip to the site of a turn-of-the-century coal-mining settlement. From the outset, the industry here was ill-fated. In April of 1903, some 90 million tons of rock from Turtle Mountain buried a portion of the town of Frank, killing about 70 people. Then in 1914 a massive mine explosion killed 189 people, and a few years later the coal-mining industry all but collapsed. The story of the slide and the history of coal mining in the region are well recorded at the **Frank Slide Interpretive Center.** ⊠ *Crowsnest Pass, Rte. 3, 35 km (22 mi) west of Rte. 6 intersection,*

☎ 403/562-7388. 🎟 $4. ⊙ May 16–Labor Day, daily 9–8; Labor
Day–May 15, daily 10–4.

THE BRITISH COLUMBIA ROCKIES

"British Columbia Rockies" is in part a misnomer. It is a term often
used to refer to the Columbia Mountains of southeastern British
Columbia, which flank the western slope of the Rockies, but which
technically (and geologically) are not a part of the Rockies.

If differentiating the Columbias from the Rockies seems confusing, at
least their separation is made obvious by the broad, low valley of the
Columbia River, known colloquially as the Columbia River trench. Four
separate ranges form the Columbias themselves: To the north are the
Cariboos, west of Jasper and Mt. Robson parks; reaching south like
three long talons from the Cariboos are (west to east) the Monashees,
the Selkirks, and the Purcells. Finally, there are the Bugaboos—a few
dramatic peaks in the Purcells that are often thought of as encompassing
the entire region.

The British Columbia Rockies are a bit older than the true Rockies. Numerous peaks exceed 10,000 feet in height, the upper slopes have extensive areas of alpine meadows above tree line, evergreen forests cover
the valleys and lower slopes, and glaciers and snowfields are not uncommon (especially in Glacier National Park, not to be confused with
the U.S. Glacier National Park, in Montana). However, only a relatively
small portion of the British Columbia Rockies is protected from development by national or provincial park status. Human encroachment
from residential and commercial development, farming, mining, and lum-
bering is rather common in the accessible portions of these ranges. The
towns reflect this difference—tourism is a secondary pursuit; their primary function is to serve the local residents and industry.

This is not to suggest that the British Columbia Rockies lack drama
or beauty—the protected areas offer a sense of isolation and grandeur
easily rivaling that found in the parks to the east. For enthusiasts of
activities such as motorboating, heli-skiing/hiking, or hunting, there
are opportunities in the British Columbia Rockies that are severely restricted in the protected parks elsewhere in the region. As the first ranges
to capture storms moving from the west across the plains of interior
British Columbia, the Columbias get much more rain and snow than
do the Rockies. Annual precipitation in many areas exceeds 60 inches,
and in the Monashees, the most westerly of the subranges, annual snowfalls can exceed 65 feet.

Such precipitation has helped to create the large, deep glaciers that add
to the high-alpine beauty of the Columbias. Lower down, the moist
climate has contributed to much lusher forests than those found in the
Rockies to the east. In winter, the deep snows have made the Columbias
a magnet for deep-powder and helicopter skiers.

From Banff, there are two main routes through the British Columbia
Rockies. The first follows the Trans-Canada Highway (Highway 1),
northwest from Banff to Lake Louise, then almost due west, through
Golden, Glacier National Park, Mt. Revelstoke National Park, and finally the town of Revelstoke. The second route follows the Trans-Canada
from Banff halfway to Lake Louise, then cuts south on Highway 93
through the southern British Columbia Rockies and Kootenay National
Park (☞ North and West of Banff, *above*), then through Radium Hot
Springs, Invermere, Fairmont Hot Springs, Fort Steele, Cranbrook, Kim-

berley (a small side trip), and finally through Fernie on a return swing to southern Alberta through the Crowsnest Pass.

Golden

80 km (50 mi) west of Lake Louise, 105 km (65 mi) north of Radium Hot Springs.

For the most part, the towns of the Columbia River trench are not beautiful, nor do they aspire to be. For example, **Golden**—a town best described as a service center—is the epitome of this unassuming character. Primarily a stopping-off point for anyone journeying elsewhere, Golden is a base for several river runners, outfitters, and guide services.

Lodging

$ ☒ **Swiss Village.** A combination motel and campground, this complex has a little more modern polish than some of its Golden neighbors. There is nothing special here, just basic motel rooms—bed, bathroom, TV— at a fair price. The RV sites have electrical hookups and water. Rates increase about 60% mid-June–September. ☒ *Off Hwy. 1, west end of Golden, Box 765, V0A 1H0,* ☎ *604/344–2276,* FAX *604/344–5259. 40 rooms, 10 RV sites. Sauna. AE, MC, V.*

Outdoor Activities and Sports

RAFTING

Alpine Rafting Company (☒ Box 1409, V0A 1H0, ☎ 604/344–5016) runs a variety of white-water trips on the Kicking Horse and the Illecillewaet, between Glacier National Park and Revelstoke, including multi-day trips.

En Route The 105 kilometers (65 miles) south from Golden to Radium Hot Springs, where Route 93 joins Route 95, ramble along the rolling flood plain of the Columbia River. To the right are the river and the Purcell Mountains; more immediately to the left are the Rockies, although the major peaks are hidden by the ranges in the foreground. Resorts catering to RVs—hard to find in the parks—abound here.

Climbers and hikers in search of solitude can find it in the **Bugaboo Recreation Area.** The Bugaboos are especially popular among experienced rock climbers. Rock "spires" that rise from glaciers like giant rocket cones are both dramatic to look at and challenging to climb. This is wild country: Except for the Bugaboo Lodge—reserved mainly for heli-hiking and heli-skiing guests—and remote alpine huts, there are no facilities in this area. ☒ *Access on unpaved roads out of Spillimacheen and Brisco, between 65 and 77 km (41 and 48 mi) south of Golden.*

Glacier National Park

58 km (36 mi) west of Golden, 45 km (28 mi) east of Revelstoke.

Relatively small **Glacier National Park** is marked by rugged mountains and, not surprisingly, an abundance of glaciers (more than 400). The glaciers result not because of the exceptionally high elevation—although some peaks here do exceed 10,000 feet—but because of the exceptionally high winter snowfalls in the park. Many of the glaciers can be seen from the highway, but to fully appreciate Glacier National Park, you must take to the trail.

At **Rogers Pass,** near the center of Glacier National Park, the heavy winter snowfalls made rail and road construction particularly difficult. Avalanches claimed the lives of hundreds of railway-construction workers in the early 1900s and continued to be a threat during highway construction in the 1950s.

Today, the Rogers Pass war against avalanches is both active and passive. Heavy artillery—105mm howitzers—is used to shoot down snow buildups before they can become so severe as to threaten a major avalanche. (If you're traveling in the backcountry, even in summer, be alert to unexploded howitzer shells that pose a potential hazard.) On the passive side, train tunnels and long snow sheds along the highway shield travelers from major slide paths.

From the **Illecillewaet Campground,** a few kilometers west of the park's **Rogers Pass Centre** (off Highway 1), several trails lead to good overlooks and glacier tongues, offering day-hiking opportunities. One of the best, although fairly strenuous, is the **Asulkan Valley trail.** This 13-kilometer (8-mile) loop passes waterfalls and yields views of the Asulkan Glacier and three massifs—the Ramparts, the Dome, and Mt. Jupiter. A much easier hike is the 1½-kilometer (1-mile) loop **Brook trail** (6 kilometers, or 3½ miles, west of the Rogers Pass Centre), with views of the glaciers of Mt. Bonney.

Glacier National Park's history is well documented at the **Rogers Pass Centre**—worth a visit whether you're staying in Glacier or just passing through. Open year-round, the center displays geology and wildlife and offers 30-minute movies on subjects ranging from avalanches to bears. ⊠ *Hwy. 1,* ☎ *604/837–6274.* 🎫 *Free with park pass ($4).* ☉ *May–June 15 and Sept. 15–Oct., daily 9–5; June 16–Sept. 14, daily 7–7; Nov.–Apr., Thurs.–Mon. 9–5.*

Lodging

$$ 🏨 **Glacier Park Lodge.** This modern, two-floor Best Western at the top of Rogers Pass—the only lodging within Glacier National Park boundaries—offers ambience in the chain's familiar format: wood-veneer tables and chairs, maroon wall-to-wall carpeting, and undecorated walls. The steep-sloping A-frame roof is a design concession to the heavy winter snows. On Highway 1, the lodge accommodates long-distance travelers with its 24-hour service station, 24-hour coffee shop, and gift shop. Rates double mid-June–September. ⊠ *The Summit, Rogers Pass, BC V0E 2S0,* ☎ *604/837–2126 or 800/528–1234,* 📠 *604/837–2126. 51 rooms. Restaurant, coffee shop, outdoor hot tub, heated outdoor pool in summer. AE, D, DC, MC, V.*

Mt. Revelstoke National Park

Western edge, Revelstoke; eastern edge, 20 km (12 mi) west of Glacier National Park.

36 Conceived primarily as a day-use park, **Mt. Revelstoke National Park** covers just 260 square kilometers (100 square miles). The park's principal attraction is the 26-kilometer (16-mile) **Summit Road** to the top of the mountain, at 6,395 feet. The gravel road begins from Highway 1, 2 kilometers (1¼ miles) before the turnoff to the town of Revelstoke, and its last few kilometers may be closed off by melting snows until well into July. You can choose among several easy hikes from the summit parking lot that meander past small lakes and offer views of the Selkirk and Monashee ranges as well as mountain meadows full of wildflowers.

Revelstoke Dam is a large hydroelectric and flood-control project that offers a free, self-guided tour and a short film about the dam and water power. Lake Revelstoke, a reservoir created by the dam on the Columbia River, is popular for boating in summer, primarily along its southern reaches. ⊠ *Rte. 23, 4 km (2½ mi) north of Revelstoke; visitor center,* ☎ *604/837–6515.* ☜ *Self-guided tours free.* ☉ *Mid-Mar.–mid-June and mid-Sept.–mid-Oct., daily 9–5; mid-June–mid-Sept., daily 8–8.*

Revelstoke

❸⓻ *148 km (92 mi) west of Golden, on western edge of Mt. Revelstoke National Park.*

The town of Revelstoke is a skiers' headquarters in winter. The downtown district, an attractive, authentic turn-of-the-century renovation, today houses modern shops, restaurants, and businesses.

Dining and Lodging

$$$$ ✕ **One-Twelve.** In the Regent Inn (☞ *below*), this restaurant is the real
★ star of the British Columbia Rockies. Low, cedar ceilings and an abundance of historic photos lend warmth to the atmosphere. Continental dishes, such as salmon, chicken Cordon Bleu, and beef brochette, are the basic fare, but the blue ribbon of the menu is the lamb broiled with rosemary and red wine. ⊠ *Regent Inn, 112 1st St. E,* ☎ *604/837–2107. Reservations essential. AE, D, DC, MC, V.*

$$$ 🏨 **Regent Inn.** The inn mixes many styles: colonial, with its brick-arcade facade; true Canadian, in its pine-trimmed lobby area and restaurant; and Scandinavian, in the angular, low-slung wood furnishings of the guest rooms. Rooms are on the large side but have no spectacular views. Continental breakfast is complimentary. ⊠ *112 Victoria Rd., Box 450, Revelstoke, BC V0E 2S0,* ☎ *604/837–2107,* 🖷 *604/837–9669. 38 rooms. Restaurant, pub, sauna, outdoor Jacuzzi. AE, D, DC, MC, V.*

Outdoor Activities and Sports

BIKING
In Revelstoke, try **Spoketacular** (⊠ 11 Mackenzie Ave., ☎ 604/837–2220) for rentals.

SKIING
Selkirk Tangiers Helicopter Skiing (⊠ Box 1409, Golden V0A 1H0, ☎ 250/344–5016 or 800/663–7080, 🖷 250/344–7012) runs three-, five-, and seven-day all-inclusive packages in the Selkirk and Monashee mountains from their base in Revelstoke. **Cat Powder Skiing** (⊠ Box 1479, Revelstoke V0E 2S0, ☎ 250/837–5151) organizes two-, three-, and five-day all-inclusive packages that run into the Selkirks and on the upper slopes of Mt. MacKenzie in Revelstoke.

Radium Hot Springs

❸⓼ *127 km (79 mi) southwest of Banff, 103 km (64 mi) south of Golden, at junction of Hwys. 93 and 95.*

Radium Hot Springs is little more than a service town for the highway traffic passing through it. Prices here are less steep than those in the parks. The town also offers a convenient access point for Kootenay National Park.

Radium Hot Springs, the springs that give the town its name, are the town's longest-standing attraction, and the summer lifeblood for the numerous motels in the area. There are two outdoor pools tucked beneath the walls of Sinclair Canyon. The hot pool is maintained at 41°C (106°F); in a cooler pool the hot mineral water is diluted to 28°C (82°F). Lockers, towels, and suits are available to rent. ⊠ *Rte. 93, 2 km (1¼ mi) northeast of Rte. 95,* ☎ *604/347–9485 or 800/767–1611.* ☜ *$4,* *day passes available.* ☉ *Hot pool, daily 9* AM–*10:30* PM, *cooler pool schedule varies.*

Lodging

$$$ 🏨 **Radium Hot Springs Resort.** The recreational facilities and activities are what bring this resort to life. Accommodations are in hotel rooms or one-, two-, or three-bedroom condo units. Rooms are modern, with hardwood furnishings and sponge-painted walls, and each has a sun deck, a wet bar, and a view overlooking the golf fairways. Condos have full kitchens. Big windows fill the main dining room with sunlight. Golf and ski packages are available. Rates increase 30% May–October and Christmas week. ✉ *Off Rte. 93, south of Radium Hot Springs, Box 310, Radium Hot Springs, BC V0A 1M0,* ☎ *604/347–9311 or 800/665–3585,* FAX *604/347–9588. 90 rooms, 30 condo units. Dining room, indoor pool, hot tub, sauna, 18-hole golf course, 2 tennis courts, exercise room, racquetball, squash, mountain bikes, cross-country skiing. AE, DC, MC, V.*

$$ 🏨 **The Chalet.** The hotel sits on a crest above town; all rooms have expansive views of the Columbia River valley. The decor is nothing special—lots of browns, navy blue, and wood veneer—but each room comes with a sitting area and minikitchen (microwave, refrigerator, sink), and all have balconies. Rates increase 30% mid-June–September. ✉ *Madsen Rd., Box 456, Radium Hot Springs, British Columbia V0A 1M0,* ☎ *604/347–9305,* FAX *604/347–9306. 17 suites. Sauna, hot tub. AE, DC, MC, V.*

Outdoor Activities and Sports

GOLF

Arrangements for golfing can be made through **Fairmont Hot Springs Resort** (☎ 800/663–4979 or 604/345–6514), with two 18-hole courses on site (☞ *below*), or **Radium Hot Springs Resort** (☎ 604/347–9652), with one 18-hole course on site (☞ *above*).

Invermere

18 km (11 mi) south of Radium Hot Springs.

Invermere is another of the many highway-service towns in the British Columbia Rockies. It is the central access point for Windermere Lake, Panorama Resort, and the Purcell Wilderness area.

For summer water sports, **Windermere Lake**—actually an extra-wide stretch of the Columbia River—is popular among swimmers, boaters, and board sailers. The town of Invermere has a good beach on the lake.

If you're visiting the Invermere area between May and September, one of the best museums in the area is the **Windermere Valley Pioneer Museum** (✉ 622 3rd St., ☎ 604/342–9769), which depicts the life of 19th-century settlers through artifacts and memorabilia.

Panorama (☞ Dining and Lodging *and* Skiing, *below*) is a year-round resort known best for skiing in winter. For summer visitors it has tennis courts, an outdoor pool, and hiking and biking trails. The resort is on the edge of the **Purcell Wilderness**—a large section of the southern British Columbia Rockies devoted to backcountry hiking, camping, and fishing, with relatively few facilities.

Dining and Lodging

$$$$ ✕ **Toby Creek Dining Lounge.** The restaurant, part of a 1960s-era ski lodge, has cedar walls, a slanted ceiling, and—in winter—a big roaring fire in the central fireplace. In summer, the outside deck offers fresh air, though not much of a view. The varied menu lists salads, steaks, stir-fry, and chicken dishes, as well as breakfast in summer. ✉ *Panorama*

Resort, 18 km (11 mi) west of Invermere, ☎ *604/342–6941. Reservations essential. AE, D, MC, V.*

$$–$$$ ✕ **Chalet Edelweis.** This little chalet really looks as if it could have been
★   transplanted from a hillock in the Swiss countryside. The interior is refreshingly simple—a few blond-wood tables, scrubbed white walls, and a small bar. The atmosphere inspires you to try the fondue, but schnitzels and fettuccine are also good. ⊠ *934 7th Ave.,* ☎ *604/342– 3525. Reservations essential. AE, MC, V.*

$$$ 🏨 **Panorama Resort.** At the edge of the Purcell Wilderness, this resort has a wide variety of accommodations and activities. All units have complete cooking facilities. The lodge at the base of the ski lifts is more casual and conveys a college-dorm atmosphere. Inside, rooms are large, with yellow walls and lots of mirrors. The other accommodations are in condo villas that look to be part of a mountainside suburb. Attractively decorated, many have fireplaces, patios, or balconies. Panorama has a fine ski area, but mountain biking and hiking trails, in addition to an outdoor pool and tennis courts, make this a rich year-round destination. Only the **Toby Creek Dining Lounge** (☞ *above*) is open in summer. Rates increase 35% Christmas week and February break and 20% late June–early September.⊠ *18 km (11 mi) west of Invermere, BC V0A 1T0,* ☎ *604/342–6941 or 800/663–2929,* 🅵🅰🆇 *604/342–3395. 105 lodge rooms, 250 condo units. 3 restaurants, cafeteria, 3 bars, outdoor pool, sauna, 8 tennis courts, downhill skiing, nightclub. AE, D, MC, V.*

$$ 🏨 **Delphine Lodge.** Originally built in 1899, the hotel has been restored
★   and now feels like a cozy bed-and-breakfast. Big, lace-curtained windows shed lots of light on a living-dining area distinguished by its polished, wide-board floors, huge stone hearth, and antique straight-back chairs and wicker rockers. Handcrafted pine furnishings and down comforters fill the smallish, pastel-shade bedrooms. Full breakfast is served every morning. ⊠ *Main St., 5 km (3 mi) west of town, Box 2797, Invermere, British Columbia V0A 1K0,* ☎ *604/342–6851. 6 rooms, 1 with private bath, 5 sharing 2 baths. No-smoking rooms. V.*

Outdoor Activities and Sports

SKIING

Downhill. Panorama (☞ Dining and Lodging, *above*), in the Purcells, has the second-highest lift-served vertical rise (4,300 feet) in North America.

Heli-skiing. R.K. Heli-Ski (⊠ Box 695, Invermere, British Columbia V0A 1K0, ☎ 604/342–3889 or 800/661–6060), based at the Panorama ski area, offers daily tours as well as multiday packages.

Fairmont Hot Springs

39   *20 km (12 mi) south of Invermere, 94 km (58 mi) north of Fort Steele.*

Fairmont Hot Springs is named for the hot springs and the resort that has sprouted around it. The "town" is little more than a service strip along the highway, but turn in to the resort and things become considerably more impressive. The town is also close to Columbia Lake, which is popular with boaters and board sailers. Golf is a growing attraction at several fine courses in the area.

Lodging

$$–$$$ 🏨 **Fairmont Hot Springs Resort.** With a wide selection of activities from golf to heli-hiking, vacationing at this resort is like being at camp. In addition to the recreational facilities, Fairmont also has hot springs, a spa, and an airport. Inside the attractive, low-slung bungalow-style structure, rooms are contemporary, many with wood paneling. Some rooms are equipped with kitchens and have balconies or patios. Golf, ski, and spa packages are available. Rates increase 75% mid-June–September. ✉ *Rte. 93/95, Box 10, V0B 1L0,* ☎ *604/345–6311; in Canada, 800/663– 4979;* ⓕⒶⓍ *604/345–6616. 140 lodge rooms, 300 RV sites. 7 restaurants, lobby lounge, snack bar, 4 outdoor pools, 2 18-hole golf courses, 2 tennis courts, hot springs, spa, private airstrip. AE, D, DC, MC, V.*

Fort Steele

🏵 *94 km (58 mi) south of Fairmont Hot Springs.*

Fort Steele and nearby Kimberley are historically significant because they were home to many German and Swiss immigrants who arrived in the late 19th century to work as miners and loggers. Southeastern British Columbia was not unlike the Tyrol region they had left, so it was easy to settle here. Later, a demand for experienced alpinists to guide and teach hikers, climbers, and skiers brought more settlers from the Alpine countries, and Tyrolean influence is evident throughout southeastern British Columbia. Schnitzels and fondues appear on menus as often as burgers and fries.

★ **Fort Steele Heritage Town,** a reconstructed 19th-century mining outpost, consisting of more than 60 buildings, is a step back to silver-lead mining days. Its theater, milliner's, barbershop, and dry-goods store breathe authenticity, helping to preserve the 1890s flavor. Plan a half-day or more; there is enough here to hold the interest of children and adults alike. ✉ *3 km (2 mi) south of Fort Steele on Hwy 93/95,* ☎ *604/426–6923.* ⓣ *2 consecutive days $5.50; grounds free Sept.–mid-June, weather permitting.* ☉ *Concessions and museum mid-June–early Sept., daily 9:30–8; grounds mid-June–early Sept., daily 9:30–dusk.*

The Arts

At the **Wild Horse Theater** (✉ Fort Steele, V0B 1N0, ☎ 604/426–6923), college presentations are staged from late June to mid-September.

Cranbrook

16 km (10 mi) southwest of Fort Steele, 27 km (17 mi) southeast of Kimberley.

Cranbrook is primarily a service center for motorists and the surrounding mining and logging industries. As one of the largest towns in the region, it has correspondingly more choice in the way of moderately priced basic motels and restaurants.

Dining

$$–$$$ ✕ **City Cafe.** If you find yourself stuck for lunch in the fast-food world of Cranbrook, City Cafe will be a breath of fresh air. The low ceilings and pine banquettes give the small dining room a French country-bistro air. Sandwiches served on fresh, crusty French bread are tasty and very reasonably priced. A German side to the menu lists schnitzel, a popular choice. ✉ *1015 Baker St.,* ☎ *604/489–5413. DC, MC, V.*

Kimberley

🏵 *40 km (25 mi) west of Fort Steele, 98 km (61 mi) south of Fairmont Hot Springs.*

Kimberley, a cross between quaint and kitschy, is rich with Tyrolean character. The Platzl ("small plaza," in German), a walking mall of shops and restaurants styled after a Bavarian village, is crowned by what is reputed to be the world's largest cuckoo clock. Chalet-style buildings are as common here as log cabins are in the national parks. In summer Kimberley plays its alpine theme to the hilt: Merchants dress up in lederhosen and dirndls, and promotional gimmicks abound.

Dining and Lodging

$$–$$$ ✕ **Chef Bernard's Kitchen.** Dining in this small, homey storefront
★ restaurant on the Kimberley pedestrian mall is like dining in someone's pantry. The decor is alpine—goat horns, cowbells, and photos fill the walls. The menu is international, ranging from German to Thai to Cajun. Homemade desserts are always a favorite. Breakfast is served in summer. ⊠ *170 Spokane St.,* ☎ *604/427–4820. Reservations essential. AE, D, DC, MC, V.*

$$ 🏨 **Inn of the Rockies.** In keeping with downtown Kimberley's Bavarian theme, the hotel's exterior is exposed-wood beams and stucco. Large rooms have a small sitting area and are plainly furnished with dark brown wood–veneer furniture, including a bed, a bureau, and a TV. The restaurant serves good, reasonably priced food. Just a block from the Platzl, this is *the* hotel in Kimberley. There is a minimal rate increase during peak season. ⊠ *300 Wallinger Ave., V1A 1Z4,* ☎ *604/ 427–2266 or 800/661–7559,* ℻ *604/427–7621. 41 rooms. Restaurant, lounge, hot tubs, exercise room, game room, coin laundry. AE, DC, MC, V.*

The Arts

In summer, Bavarian bands in Kimberley strike up with oompah music on the Platzl, especially when festivals are in swing. The **Old Time Accordion Championships,** in early July, is a Kimberley highlight.

Outdoor Activities and Sports

SKIING

Kimberley Ski Resort (⊠ Box 40, Kimberley, BC V1A 2Y5, ☎ 604/427–4881) has a vertical drop of more than 2,000 feet and on-mountain facilities.

Fernie

96 km (60 mi) east of Fort Steele, 331 km (206 mi) southwest of Calgary.

Fernie is largely a winter destination, serving skiers at the **Fernie Snow Valley** ski area. One of the largest towns between Cranbrook and Calgary, it offers a wider selection of motels and restaurants than the other centers along this route.

Skiing

Fernie Snow Valley (⊠ Ski Area Rd., Fernie, British Columbia V0A 1M1, ☎ 604/423–4655) has a vertical rise of more than 2,000 feet and on-mountain facilities.

CANADIAN ROCKIES A TO Z

Arriving and Departing

By Bus

Greyhound Lines (call local listing) provides regular service to Calgary, Edmonton, and Vancouver, with connecting service to Jasper and Banff. **Brewster Transportation and Tours** (☎ 800/661–1152) offers service between the Calgary International Airport and Banff, Jasper, and Lake Louise. **Laidlaw Transportation** (☎ 403/762–9102) also operates between Calgary Airport and the Banff–Lake Louise area.

By Car

Highway 1, the Trans-Canada Highway, is the principal east–west route into the region. Banff is 128 kilometers (80 miles) west of Calgary on Route 1 and 858 kilometers (515 miles) east of Vancouver. The other major east–west routes are Route 16 to the north, the main highway between Edmonton and Jasper, and Route 3 to the south. The main routes from the south are Route 89 (Highway 2 in Canada), which enters Canada east of Alberta's Waterton Lakes National Park from Montana, and Route 93, also from Montana, which provides access to the British Columbia Rockies.

By Plane

Calgary is the most common gateway for travelers arriving by plane. If you plan to visit only Jasper and northern park regions, you may prefer to use Edmonton as a gateway city. Both cities have international airports served by several major carriers; the Calgary flight schedule is somewhat more extensive.

Calgary International Airport and **Edmonton International Airport** serve the Rockies region. (For airline information, *see* Calgary A to Z *and* Edmonton A to Z *in* Chapter 5.)

Air Canada and **Canadian Airlines** have daily flights to and from many points in southern British Columbia; most of these flights connect with flights through Vancouver International Airport and the airports in Calgary and Edmonton.

By Train

VIA Rail (☎ 800/561–8630) trains stop in Jasper, with connecting overnight runs to and from Toronto, Edmonton, and Vancouver. A specialty train-tour service, **Rocky Mountaineer RailTours** (☎ 800/665–7245, FAX 604/984–2883) connects Vancouver, Kamloops, Banff, Jasper, and Calgary. Dome cars allow panoramic mountain views, and friendly staff provide excellent food and service. In 1995 they added a new luxury coach to their service, catering specifically to people accustomed to five-star hotels and luxury resorts. This bi-level, glass-enclosed dome coach features two spiral staircases, a private dining area, an open-air observation platform, on-board hosts, and a personal chef. The RailTour coaches travel through the Rockies during daylight only.

Getting Around

The national parks system has a complex fee structure. Different annual and day pass fees apply depending on which parks you plan to visit. In general, an annual pass costs around $35 per person and a day pass costs about $5 per person.

By Car

Automobile is the way to travel in the Canadian Rockies, though some guided tour operators offer good sightseeing trips by bus and train. Unless you plan to go off the beaten path (in Kananaskis Country or in the Columbias only; vehicles aren't permitted off major roadways in the national parks), a four-wheel-drive vehicle is not necessary. Major roadways are well maintained. Keep in mind, however, that snow arrives in early fall and remains until late spring. When traveling between October and April, stay informed of local road conditions, especially if you're traveling over mountain passes or along the Icefields Parkway (Route 93). A few roads, such as Route 40 over Highwood Pass in Kananaskis Country, are closed in winter.

Car-rental outlets are at the Calgary and Edmonton airports, as well as in Banff and Jasper, Alberta, and Cranbrook, British Columbia. Daily rentals for sightseeing are available but should be reserved well ahead of time, especially in summer.

Contacts and Resources

Emergencies
Ambulance (☎ 911). **Police** (☎ 911).

Guided Tours
AUTO TOURS
Audiocassette tapes for self-guided auto tours of the parks are produced by **Auto Tape Tours** (☎ 201/236–1666) and **Rocky Mountain Tape Tours.** Tapes can be rented or purchased at news or gift shops in Banff, Lake Louise, and Jasper.

BICYCLE TOURS
Several operators offer guided on-road and off-road bicycle tours. **Rocky Mountain Cycle Tours** (✉ Box 1978, Canmore, Alberta T0L 0M0, ☎ 403/678–6770 or 800/661–2453) runs one- to seven-day tours in the Banff area and in British Columbia. Prices begin at $80.

BUS TOURS
Brewster Transportation and Tours (✉ Box 1140, Banff, Alberta T0L 0C0, ☎ in Banff, 403/762–6700; in Jasper, 403/852–3332; in Calgary, 403/221–8242; or 800/661–1152) offers half-, full-, and multiday sightseeing tours of the parks. Prices start at about $33 per person.

Tauck Tours (✉ 276 Post Rd. W, Box 5027, Westport, CT 06880, ☎ 800/468–2825) conducts multiday bus tours through the region.

HELI-TOURS
Alpine Helicopters (✉ Box 2069, Canmore, Alberta T0L 0M0, ☎ 403/678–4802) is 20 minutes southeast of Banff and provides year-round, guided "flightseeing" tours (20–60 minutes) above the Banff and Kananaskis valleys. They also offer half- or full-day heli-hiking tours. Prices begin at $85.

SEASONAL TOURS
Challenge Enterprises (✉ Box 2008, Canmore, Alberta T0L 0M0, ☎ 403/678–2628) specializes in half-day to multiday guided snowmobile tours. Prices start at $75 per person.

Kingmik Expeditions (✉ Box 227, Lake Louise, Alberta T0L 1E0, ☎ 604/344–5298) specializes in dogsledding tours through the mountains and across the frozen waters of Lake Louise. You can even have a go at being the musher; tours range from half- to five-day outings with prices starting around $60 per sled (2 adults per sled).

Mountain Fly Fishers (✉ Box 2414, Canmore, Alberta T0L 0M0, ☎ 403/678–2915) offers fly-fishing instruction, guide services, float-fishing tours, and equipment rentals. "Hike and wade" programs start at $110 per person, two people per guide.

Outdoor Activities and Sports
CAMPING
Campground information is available from the **Canadian Parks Service** (✉ Information Services, Box 2989, Station M, Calgary, Alberta T2P 3H8, ☎ 403/292–4401 or 800/651–7959, FAX 403/292–6004) and from **Kananaskis Country** (✉ #100, 3115-12th St. NE, Calgary,

Alberta T2E 7J2, ☎ 403/297–3362, FAX 403/297–2180). Contact **Discover British Columbia** or **Alberta Tourism** for special camping publications.

CLIMBING
Banff Alpine Guides (✉ Box 1025, Banff, Alberta T0L 0C0, ☎ 403/ 678–6091), the **Canadian School of Mountaineering** (✉ 629 10th St., Box 723, Canmore, Alberta T0L 0M0, ☎ 403/678–4134), and **Yamnuska Mountain Adventures** (✉ Box 1920, 1316 Railway Ave., Canmore, AB, T0L 0M0, ☎ 403/678–4164, FAX 403/678–4450), catering to all ability levels, lead trips throughout the parks. Climbing gear can be rented at outdoor stores in Banff.

Climbers or backpackers interested in extended stays of more than three or four days might consider membership in the **Alpine Club of Canada** (✉ Box 2040, Indian Flats Rd., Canmore, Alberta T0L 0M0, ☎ 403/ 678–3200). The club maintains several mountain huts in the parks.

FISHING
In Alberta, the fee for an annual license for nonresident Canadians is $18 and for non-Canadians $36. Non-Canadians can also purchase a 5-day license for $24. In British Columbia, the fees for one-day, eight-day, and annual licenses for nonresident Canadians are $10, $20, and $28, respectively; for non-Canadians the fees are $10, $25, and $40. The fee for a 7-day national park license is $6; an annual license is $13.

GOLF
In Alberta parks, peak-season greens fees range from $35 to $55 and cart rental costs from $20 to $30. Carts are mandatory on some courses.

HORSEBACK RIDING
Alberta Tourism and Tourism British Columbia can provide listings of pack-trip outfitters and guest ranchers, which proliferate on the fringes of the national parks. In British Columbia, further information is also available from the **Guide-Outfitters Association** (✉ Box 759, 100 Mile House, British Columbia V0K 2E0, ☎ 604/278–2688).

SKIING
Cross-Country. Groomed trails (and rental equipment) can be found near the Banff Springs Hotel, Chateau Lake Louise, Jasper Park Lodge, Fairmont Hot Springs Resort, and Mt. Engadine Lodge. Lake O'Hara Lodge, Mt. Assiniboine Lodge, and Skoki Lodge offer guided backcountry ski touring (☞ individual towns, *above*).

Downhill. ☞ individual towns, *above*.

Heli-Skiing. The original, and by far the largest, heli-skiing operator in the region is **Canadian Mountain Holidays** (✉ Box 1660, Banff, Alberta T0L 0C0, ☎ 403/762–7100 or 800/661–0252). They offer heli-skiing (and in summer, heli-hiking) packages in the Cariboo and Purcell Ranges in the British Columbia Rockies, with accommodation at their relatively luxurious but remote lodges. Reserve several months in advance.

Safety
Visitors to the backcountry must register with the nearest park warden's office. Very few of the natural hazards in the Rockies are marked with warning signs. Be wary of slippery rocks and vegetation near rivers and canyons, snow-covered crevasses on glaciers, avalanche conditions in winter, and potentially aggressive animals. Each year there are several fatalities from natural hazards in the Rockies.

Visitor Information

The region's three major sources of visitor information are **Alberta Tourism** (✉ 3rd floor, Commerce Pl., 10155 102 St., Edmonton, Alberta T5J 4L6, ☎ 800/661–8888), **Discover British Columbia** (✉ Parliament Bldgs., Victoria, British Columbia V8V 1X4, ☎ 800/663–6000), and **Parks Canada** (✉ Information Services, Box 2989, Station M, Calgary, Alberta T2P 3H8, ☎ 403/292–4401 or 800/651–7959). Parks Canada information is also available at the **Parks Information Centre** (✉ Box 900, 224 Banff Ave., Banff, Alberta T0L 0C0, ☎ 403/762–1550).

You can contact individual offices of the four contiguous Rockies parks directly: **Banff** (☎ 403/762–1550), **Jasper** (☎ 403/852–6176), **Kootenay** (in summer, ☎ 604/347–9505; in winter, 604/347–9551), or **Yoho** (☎ 604/343–6783). For local information, contact: **Banff–Lake Louise Tourism Bureau** (✉ 224 Banff Ave., Banff, Alberta T0L 0C0, ☎ 403/762–8421), **Lake Louise Visitor Centre** (✉ Village Rd. beside Samson Mall, Box 213, Lake Louise, Alberta T0L 1E0, ☎ 403/522–3833), **Jasper Tourism and Commerce** (✉ Box 98, 632 Connaught Dr., Jasper, Alberta T0E 1E0, ☎ 403/852–3858), **Kananaskis Country** (✉ #100, 3115-12th St. NE, Calgary, Alberta T2E 7J2, ☎ 403/297–3362), **Waterton Lakes National Park** (✉ Superintendent, Waterton Park, Alberta T0K 2M0, ☎ 403/859–2224), **Waterton Park Chamber of Commerce** (✉ Box 55, Waterton Park, Alberta T0K 2M0, ☎ 403/859–2203), **Mount Revelstoke and Glacier National Parks** (✉ Visitor Centre, Box 350, Revelstoke, British Columbia V0E 2S0, ☎ 604/837–6274), and **Rocky Mountain Visitors Association** (✉ Box 10, Kimberley, British Columbia V1A 2Y5, ☎ 604/427–4838).

5 The Prairie Provinces

Alberta, Saskatchewan, Manitoba

*Between the eastern slopes of the
Rockies and the wilds of western
Ontario lie Canada's three prairie
provinces: Alberta, Saskatchewan, and
Manitoba. The northern parts of this
region are sparsely populated expanses
of lakes, rivers, and forests. The fertile
plains of the south support farms and
ranches—interspersed with wide river
valleys, lakes, rolling hills, badlands,
dry hills of sand, and oil wells—as well
as five busy cities: Calgary, Edmonton,
Saskatoon, Regina, and Winnipeg.*

ALBERTA, SASKATCHEWAN, AND MANITOBA contain Canada's heartland: the principal source of such solid commodities as wheat, oil, and beef. These provinces are also the home of a rich stew of ethnic communities that make the area unexpectedly colorful and cosmopolitan.

By Theodore Fischer

Updated by Jens Nielsen

The term "prairie provinces" is a bit of a misnomer, as most of this region (the northern half of Alberta and Saskatchewan, and the northern two-thirds of Manitoba) consists of sparsely populated expanses of lakes, rivers, and forests. Most of northern Saskatchewan and Manitoba belongs to the Canadian Shield, with a foundation of Precambrian rock that is some of the oldest in the world. On the fertile plains of the south, wheat is still king, but other crops, as well as livestock, help boost the economy. The landscape is quite diverse, with farms and ranches interspersed with wide river valleys, lakes, rolling hills, badlands, and even dry hills of sand.

Early milestones in the history of this region include the period when dinosaurs roamed what was then semitropical swampland 75 million years ago and the epoch when the first human settlers crossed the Bering Strait from Asia 12,000 years ago. Later, Plains Indians of the Athapaskan, Algonquian, and Siouan language groups developed a culture and hunted buffalo here. In the 17th century European fur traders began arriving, and in 1670 the British Crown granted the Hudson's Bay Company administrative and trading rights to "Rupert's Land," a vast territory whose waters drained into Hudson Bay. A hundred years later, the North West Company went into direct competition by building outposts throughout the area. From this fur-trading tradition arose the Métis—mostly French-speaking offspring of Indian women and European traders who followed the Roman Catholic religion but adhered to a traditional Indian lifestyle.

By 1873 the North West Mounted Police was established in Manitoba, just six years after the formation of the Canadian government. In 1874, the Mounties began their march west: Their first chores included resolving conflicts between the Indians and American whiskey traders and overseeing the orderly distribution of the free homesteads granted by the Dominion Lands Act of 1872. The Mounties played a role in the North West Rebellion—a revolt by Métis, who feared that the encroachment of western settlement would threaten their traditions and freedom. Although the Métis eventually succumbed, and their leader, Louis Riel, was hanged in 1885, Riel is now hailed as a martyr of the Métis and a statue of him stands on the grounds of Manitoba's Legislature Building.

Railroads arrived in the 1880s and with them a torrent of immigrants seeking free government land. An influx of farmers from the British Isles, Scandinavia, Holland, Germany, Eastern Europe, Russia, and especially Ukraine, plus persecuted religious groups, such as the Mennonites, Hutterites, Mormons, and Jews, transformed the prairies into a rich wheat-growing breadbasket and cultural mosaic that is still very much in evidence today. In 1947, a big oil strike transformed Edmonton and Calgary into gleaming metropolises full of western oil barons.

The people of the prairie provinces are relaxed, reserved, and irascibly independent. They maintain equal suspicion toward "Ottawa" (big government) and "Toronto" (big media and big business). To visitors, the people of this region convey a combination of Western openness and Canadian-style courtesy: no fawning, but no rudeness. Visitors also find exceptional outdoor recreational facilities—a spectrum of historical attractions that focuses on Mounties, Métis, dinosaurs, and railroads; excellent accommodations and cuisine at reasonable (but not low) prices; and quiet, crowdless expanses of extraordinarily wide-open spaces.

Pleasures and Pastimes

Dining

Although places specializing in generous helpings of Canadian beef still dominate the scene, restaurants throughout the prairie provinces now tastily reflect the region's ethnic makeup and offer a wide variety of cuisine to fit every price range.

WHAT TO WEAR

Dress in the prairie cities tends to formality in expensive restaurants and is casual in moderate and inexpensive restaurants. In the reviews below, if a restaurant requires men to wear a jacket or a jacket and tie, the service information indicates it.

CATEGORY	COST*
$$$$	over $25
$$$	$20–$25
$$	$15–$20
$	under $15

*three-course dinner, per person, excluding drinks, service, and taxes

Lodging

Although lodging has never been a problem in the major cities in the prairies, there's been a welcome improvement at many of the lakes and parks in recent years. Prince Albert National Park, for instance, once essentially a summer getaway, has in recent years, with the addition of several excellent properties, become a legitimate four-season resort.

CATEGORY	COST*
$$$$	over $150
$$$	$75–$150
$$	$50–$75
$	under $50

*All prices are for a standard double room, excluding taxes.

Exploring the Prairie Provinces

As one leaves the Rockies, the landscape becomes dramatically flatter. From the foothills of Alberta to the Great Lakes, you can explore the Prairies from west to east, with visits to the region's five major cities, Calgary, Edmonton, Regina, Saskatoon, and Winnipeg.

Great Itineraries

Enormous distances separate many of the region's major attractions. If you're ambitious and want to include all three prairie provinces, you will need considerable time.

IF YOU HAVE 2 DAYS

If you're interested in the rich history of the Plains Indians, take the time to delve into the area around Saskatoon known as the Heart of the Old Northwest. Start in **Saskatoon** ㊸–㊹ and use it as the base for day trips. On the first day, you can go to nearby **Wanuskewin** ㊿ to view **Wanuskewin Heritage Park**, a wonderfully cerebral onetime buffalo hunting ground. Less than an hour's drive away is **Batoche** ㊶ and **Batoche National Historic Site**, where Louis Riel fought his last battle against the North West Mounted Police. **Duck Lake** ⑤②, 30 minutes north of Batoche, along Highway 11, a series of colorful murals on town buildings depict the 1885 Northwest Rebellion. **Fort Carlton Provincial Park**, another 15 minutes west, is a reconstructed stockade from the fur-trade days. On the second day, go to **North Battleford** ⑤④, 138 kilometers (86 miles) northwest of Saskatoon, for the **Fort Battleford National Historic Site**, also dealing with the North West Mounted Police.

IF YOU HAVE 4 DAYS

If you're particularly interested in dinosaurs and fossil hunting, travel from ⌖ **Calgary** ①–⑯, Alberta, to ⌖ **Regina** ㉘–㉞, Saskatchewan, by way of Drumheller, Alberta, and Eastend, Saskatchewan. In ⌖ **Drumheller** ⑰, just over an hour east of Calgary on the Trans-Canada Highway, you can spend an entire day at the world-class **Royal Tyrell Museum of Paleontology**. East on the Trans-Canada en route to Dinosaur Provincial Park near Brooks, you pass through the unique Badlands areas, where rivers flowed more than 70 million years ago. South along the Trans-Canada, the thriving oil-rich city of ⌖ **Medicine Hat** ⑱ is a good choice for an overnight stop. Farther east, south of the Trans-Canada, you come to the small community of **Eastend** ㊴, where you can view a recently discovered, fully preserved Tyrannosaurus rex skeleton in a working lab—the **Eastend Fossil Research Station**.

IF YOU HAVE 12 DAYS

You can choose between two major routes westward from ⌖ **Winnipeg** ㊳–⑦⓪—north on the Yellowhead (Highway 16) to ⌖ **Edmonton** ㉑–㉕ via ⌖ **Saskatoon** ㊸–㊹, or south on the Trans-Canada to ⌖ **Calgary** ①–⑯ via ⌖ **Regina** ㉘–㉞. Either is approximately 1,370 grueling kilometers (850 miles). On the Yellowhead route, you can stop for one or two nights in ⌖ **Riding Mountain National Park** (a half hour north of Highway 16 on Highway 10). Here you'll find forested landscape and sparkling clear lakes, as well as comfortable amenities. Langenburg, just inside the Saskatchewan border, offers the quirky Gopherville exhibit as part of the provincial tourism information center. Less than an hour away at the junction of highways 9 and 16, is ⌖ **Yorkton,** a bustling farming community, home of a Western Development Museum and good lodgings. About three hours north you come to Saskatoon, Saskatchewan's largest city. Plan on staying at least two nights. A further 90 minutes westward is the historic community of ⌖ **North Battleford** ⑤④, where the **Western Development Museum** and **Fort Battleford National Historic Site** rate as the two must-see attractions. Lloydminster, which straddles the border of Alberta and Saskatchewan, was the home of the Barr Colonists and today houses a museum paying tribute to those times. In its modern state, it is a headquarters for the oil industry. From here it is approximately two hours to Edmonton.

If you take the more southerly Trans-Canada route, you'll stop in such major centers as ⌖ **Brandon** ㊱, ⌖ **Regina** ㉘–㉞, ⌖ **Swift Current** ㊱, and ⌖ **Medicine Hat** ⑱ en route to Calgary. All offer interesting diversions and adequate facilities for dining and accommodation.

When to Tour the Prairie Provinces

Unless you enjoy bone-chilling cold temperatures, you would be well-advised to skip winter and opt for summer, when the nights are long and the temperatures are usually hot in this area dominated by continental climate patterns.

CALGARY

With the eastern face of the Rockies as its backdrop, the crisp concrete-and-steel skyline of Calgary, Alberta, seems to rise from the plains as

Alberta

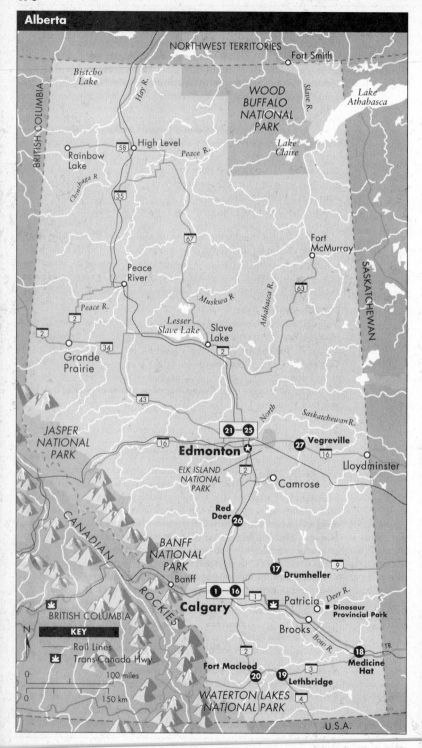

NORTHWEST TERRITORIES

Fort Smith

Bistcho Lake

Hay R.

WOOD
BUFFALO
NATIONAL
PARK

Slave R.

Lake
Athabasca

BRITISH COLUMBIA

58 High Level

Rainbow
Lake

Peace R.

Chinchaga R

35

*Lake
Claire*

67

Fort
McMurray

63

Peace
River

Peace R.

2

2

Muskwa R.

Athabasca R.

SASKATCHEWAN

34

*Lesser
Slave Lake*

Slave
Lake

2

Grande
Prairie

43

North

Saskatchewan R.

JASPER
NATIONAL
PARK

16

Edmonton

21 — 25

27 **Vegreville**

16

Lloydminster

ELK ISLAND
NATIONAL
PARK

2

Camrose

**Red
Deer**

26

CANADIAN

BANFF
NATIONAL
PARK

Banff

1 — 16

17 **Drumheller**

9

1

Patricia

Deer R.

■ **Dinosaur
Provincial Park**

ROCKIES

Calgary

BRITISH COLUMBIA

Brooks

Bow R.

N

KEY

Rail Lines
Trans-Canada Hwy.

2

18 **Medicine
Hat**

TR

0   100 miles

Fort Macleod

20

19 **Lethbridge**

3

0   150 km

*WATERTON LAKES
NATIONAL PARK*

4

U.S.A.

if by sheer force of will. In fact, all the elements in the great saga of the Canadian West—Mounties, Indians, railroads, cowboys, oil—have converged to create a city with a brand-new face and a surprisingly traditional soul.

Calgary, Gaelic for "preserved pasture at the harbor," was founded in 1875 at the junction of the Bow and Elbow rivers as a North West Mounted Police post. The Canadian Pacific Railroad arrived in 1883, and ranchers established major spreads on the plains surrounding the town. Incorporated as a city in 1894, Calgary grew quickly, and by 1911 its population had reached 43,000.

The major growth came with the oil boom in the 1960s and 1970s, when most Canadian oil companies established their head offices in the city. Today, Calgary is a city of more than 740,000 mostly easy-going and downright neighborly people. It is Canada's second-largest center for corporate head offices. Downtown is still evolving, but Calgary's planners have made life during winter pleasanter by connecting most of the buildings with Plus 15, a network of enclosed walkways 15 feet above street level.

Calgary supports professional football and hockey teams. It is also the perfect starting point for one of the preeminent dinosaur-exploration sites in the world. Glenbow Museum is one of the top four museums in Canada, and the Calgary Centre for the Performing Arts is a showcase for the arts. Calaway Park, on the western edge of Calgary, is a playground for children of all ages.

Downtown Calgary

In the Calgary grid pattern, numbered streets run north–south in both directions from Centre Street, and numbered avenues run east–west in both directions from Centre Avenue.

Numbers in the text and margin below correspond to numbers on the Downtown Calgary map.

A Good Walk

Start at **Calgary Tower** ① for a bird's-eye view of the city. Take the Plus 15 walkway over 9th Avenue Southeast to **Glenbow Museum** ②, a major showcase of art and history. Next take the Plus 15 walkway above 1st Street Southeast to join a walking tour of the **Calgary Centre for the Performing Arts** ③ theater complex. You can step outside on **Olympic Plaza** ④, where Olympic medals were presented in 1988. Nearby, you'll see the **Municipal Building** ⑤, whose mirror-glass walls reflect other city landmarks. Hop on the C-Train, Calgary's light rail system, for a free ride (along 7th Avenue downtown only) to the center of the downtown shopping district. Here, the top attraction is **Devonian Gardens** ⑥, an enclosed roof garden above Toronto Dominion Square. On 8th Avenue, between Macleod Trail and 4th Street Southwest, you'll find **Stephen Avenue Mall** ⑦, for shopping in the ground floors of Calgary's oldest structures. Head north on 1st Street Southwest to the ornate **Calgary Chinese Cultural Centre** ⑧ to take in the architecture and the museum.

TIMING

Allow the better part of a day. Saturday would be best in order to get into all the places of interest, because some are closed on some weekdays.

Sights to See

❸ The **Calgary Centre for the Performing Arts** (⊠ Plus 15 walkway above 1st St. SE, ☎ 403/294–7444). This complex of three theater spaces, a concert hall, and a shopping area was pieced together with the his-

Calgary Centre for the Performing Arts, **3**

Calgary Chinese Cultural Centre, **8**

Calgary Tower, **1**

Devonian Gardens, **6**

Glenbow Museum, **2**

Municipal Building, **5**

Olympic Plaza, **4**

Stephen Avenue Mall, **7**

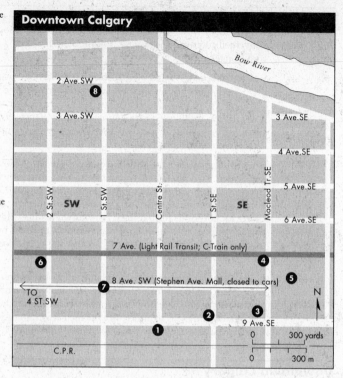

Downtown Calgary

toric **Calgary Public Building** (1930) and the **Burns Building** (1913). Come at night for a performance, or take a one-hour walking tour at noon most weekdays.

8 The ornate **Calgary Chinese Cultural Centre** is in the heart of Chinatown beside the Bow River. Its focal point is the Hall of Prayers of the **Temple of Heaven**; the column details and paintings include 561 dragons and 40 phoenixes. The center also houses a cultural museum, a craft store, an herbal medicine store, and a 330-seat Chinese restaurant. ✉ *197 1st St. SW,* ☎ *403/262–5071.* 🏛 *Centre free, museum $2.* ☼ *Daily 9:30–9.*

1 **Calgary Tower.** The 626-foot, scepter-shape edifice affords great views of the city's layout, the surrounding plains, and the face of the Rockies rising 80 kilometers (50 miles) west. A flame on top is lit for special occasions; the revolving **Panorama Dining Room** provides refreshment. ✉ *9th Ave. and Centre St. S,* ☎ *403/266–7171.* 🏛 *$4.95.* ☼ *Weekdays and Sat. 7:30 AM–11:30 PM, Sun. 7:30 AM–10:30 PM.*

6 **Devonian Gardens.** Above Toronto Dominion Square is a 2½-acre enclosed roof garden with 20,000 mostly tropical plants, nearly a mile of lush walkways, a sculpture court, and a playground. Reached by a glass-enclosed elevator just inside the 8th Avenue door, the Devonian Gardens has a reflecting pool that turns into a skating rink in winter and a small stage for musical performances year-round. ✉ *Between 2nd and 3rd Sts. and 7th and 8th Aves. SW.* 🏛 *Free.* ☼ *Daily 9–9.*

2 **Glenbow Museum.** Calgary's premier showcase of both art and history is ranked among the top four museums in Canada. Along with traveling exhibits, the Glenbow has comprehensive displays devoted to Alberta's native (Indian and Inuit) inhabitants, early European settlers, and latter-day pioneers. The mineralogy collection and the cache of arms and armor are superb. ⊠ *130 9th Ave. SE,* ☎ *403/264–8300 or 403/237–8988.* ⊡ *$5.* ☉ *Sept.–May, Tues.–Sun. 10–6; June–Aug., daily 9–5.*

❺ The Municipal Building (⊠ 8th Ave. SE and Macleod Trail SE). Among the city landmarks reflected in the angular, mirror-walled structure is the stunning **City Hall,** a stately 1911 sandstone building that still houses the mayor's office and some city offices.

❹ Olympic Plaza (⊠ 7th Ave. SE and Macleod Trail SE). The site of the Olympic medals presentation, the plaza is a popular year-round venue for city festivals, arts, and entertainment. You can go skating here in winter.

❼ Stephen Avenue Mall. In this pedestrian-only shopping area, shops, nightclubs, and restaurants occupy the ground floors of Calgary's oldest structures, mostly sandstone buildings erected after an 1886 fire destroyed almost everything older.

Greater Calgary

Numbers in the text and margin below correspond to numbers on the Greater Calgary map.

A Good Drive

From Chinatown, continue by car about half a mile to **Fort Calgary Interpretive Centre** ⑨, at the confluence of the Bow and Elbow rivers, to learn the history of the region. Directly across the 9th Avenue Bridge is the **Deane House** ⑩, dating from 1906. Continue east on 9th Avenue, turn north on 12th Street, and cross the bridge to St. George's Island and the **Calgary Zoo, Botanical Gardens,** and **Prehistoric Park** ⑪. Next head south and west to Olympic Way and **Stampede Park** ⑫ for tours of the grounds and a visit to the Grain Academy museum. Follow Macleod Trail south and go west on Heritage Drive to **Heritage Park** ⑬, where you can see authentic historic structures from all over western Canada. East across Glenmore Reservoir, turn north on Crowchild Trail to reach the **Museum of the Regiments** ⑭ and the **Naval Museum of Alberta.** Continuing north on Crowchild Trail, turn east on 9th Avenue Southwest and then north again on 11th Street Southwest to the **Science Centre and Planetarium** ⑮ for hands-on exhibits and star shows. Another drive from Chinatown takes you west on 6th Avenue, following signs to Crowchild Trail, which you take north to 16th Avenue Northwest (Highway 1) and then head west on it about 8 kilometers (5 miles) to **Canada Olympic Park** ⑯, site of the 1988 Winter Olympics, where you can visit ski jumps and try the bobsled and luge rides. Just past the Olympic Park is **Calaway Park,** western Canada's largest amusement park.

TIMING
Because of the distances, allow a full day, with the zoo as main component in the morning, leaving Calaway Park for the afternoon and evening.

Sights to See

Calaway Park. Western Canada's largest outdoor amusement park, also has live entertainment, miniature golf, a driving range, a maze, a petting farm, food outlets, and shops. ⊠ *Hwy. 1, 10 km (6 mi) west of Calgary,* ☎ *403/240–3822.*

⑪ Calgary Zoo, Botanical Gardens, and Prehistoric Park. On St. George's Island, in the middle of the Bow River, the zoo houses more than 1,400 animals in natural settings. The Canadian Wilds section replicates endangered Canadian ecosystems. The Prehistoric Park displays dinosaur replicas in a re-creation of their bygone natural habitat. ⊠ *1300 Zoo Rd. NE, ☎ 403/232–9372. ⊠ $7.50. ⊘ Apr.–June, week-days 9–4, weekends and holidays 9–6; July–Sept., daily 9–6; Sept.–Mar., daily 9–4.*

🖐 **⑯ Canada Olympic Park.** The site of the 1988 Winter Olympics is today a year-round attraction. A one-hour bus tour goes over, under, around, and through the 70- and 90-meter ski jumps and the bobsled and luge tracks (in summer you have the option of walking down the slopes). In winter the slopes are open to the public (lessons available). Visitors can try Olympic-size thrills on the scarifying one-minute bobsled sim-ulator—the Bobsled Bullet ($39)—and the slightly briefer Tourist Luge Ride ($12); safety equipment is provided. On the premises are a day lodge with a cafeteria and the **Olympic Hall of Fame,** a collection of Olympic memorabilia and video displays. ⊠ *88 Olympic Rd. SW, ☎ 403/286–2632. ⊠ Bus or self-guided tour $6, tour and Hall of Fame $8. ⊘ Park mid-June–Sept. 2, daily 7 AM–9 PM; Sept. 3–mid-June, daily 8 AM–9 PM; Hall of Fame daily 10–5.*

⑩ The Deane House. Once part of Fort Calgary, this is the restored 1906 post commander's house; it has free tours and a tearoom serving light meals. ⊠ *809 9th Ave. SE, ☎ 403/269–7747.*

⑨ Fort Calgary Interpretive Centre. At the confluence of the Bow and Elbow rivers, the fort established in 1875 by the North West Mounted Police was to subdue Montana whiskey traders, who were raising havoc among the Indians. The original fort is being rebuilt by a group of vol-unteers. An ultracontemporary interpretive center traces the history of area aboriginal peoples, Mounties, and European settlers. ⊠ *750 9th Ave. SE, ☎ 403/290–1875. ⊠ $2. ⊘ Daily 9–5.*

🖐 **⑬ Heritage Park.** More than 100 authentic structures have been col-lected from all over western Canada and relocated here beside Glen-more Reservoir. The "neighborhoods," inhabited by costumed staff, range from an 1850s fur-trading post to a 1910-era town. Steam trains, horse-drawn buses, and paddle-wheel steamers provide transportation, and North America's only antique amusement park re-creates bygone thrills. Theme snacks—sarsaparilla, beef jerky, fresh apple pie—abound. ⊠ *1900 Heritage Dr. SW, ☎ 403/259–1900. ⊠ $7.50. ⊘ Late May–June, weekdays 10–4, weekends 10–6; July–Sept. 2, daily 10–6; Sept. 3–early Oct., weekends and holidays 10–5.*

⑭ Museum of the Regiments. The collection depicts the history of Cal-gary-based regiments dating back to 1900. ⊠ *4520 Crowchild Trail SW, ☎ 403/240–7674. ⊠ Free. ⊘ July–Labor Day, daily 10–6; Labor Day–June, daily 10–4.*

Naval Museum of Alberta. Canada's second-largest naval museum fo-cuses on the unlikely role of the Prairie Provinces in the Navy. ⊠ *1820 24th St. SW, ☎ 403/242–0002. ⊠ Free. ⊘ July–Labor Day, daily 10–6; Labor Day–June, daily 10–4.*

🖐 **⑮ Science Centre and Planetarium.** More than 35 hands-on exhibits of scientific marvels, such as holograms, frozen shadows, and laser beams, fascinate visitors; user-friendly demonstrations are given Friday through Sunday. Up in the planetarium, the 360-degree Star Chamber presents educational star shows with children's matinees on weekends and laser shows on Friday through Sunday nights. Imaginative combinations of special effects, magic tricks, and old-time show-biz make performances appealing to all ages. ⊠ *701 11th St. SW, ☎ 403/221–3700. ⊠ Sci-ence Centre $6.75, Science Centre and Planetarium $8. ⊘ Tues.–Fri. 9–5, weekends 10–5.*

Calgary Zoo, Botanical Gardens, and Prehistoric Park **11**

Canada Olympic Park, **16**

Deane House, **10**

Fort Calgary Interpretive Centre, **9**

Heritage Park, **13**

Museum of the Regiments, **14**

Science Centre and Planetarium, **15**

Stampede Park, **12**

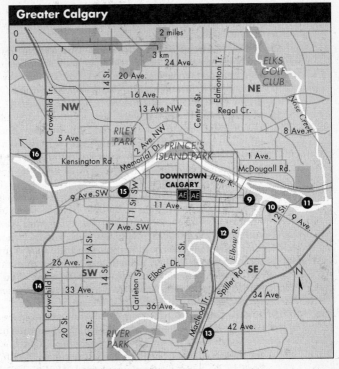

Greater Calgary

⓬ **Stampede Park.** International attention focuses here each July for the Calgary Exhibition and Stampede (☞ Festivals and Seasonal Events *in* Chapter 1). Throughout the year, the Roundup Centre, Big Four Building, and Agriculture Building host trade shows; the **Olympic Saddledome** (☎ 403/261–0400) has concerts and Calgary Flames hockey games; and the Grandstand holds Thoroughbred and harness racing (☞ Spectator Sports, *below*). Visitors can wander the grounds, take free one-hour tours of the Saddledome, and visit the free **Grain Academy** in Roundup Centre, an interesting little museum that proudly proclaims itself "Canada's only grain interpretive centre." ⊠ *17th Ave. and 2nd St. SE,* ☎ *403/261–0101; Grain Academy in Stampede Park,* ☎ *403/263–4594.* 🎟 *Free.* ☉ *Weekdays 10–4, Sat. noon–4.*

Dining and Lodging

$$$$ ✗ **Owl's Nest Dining Room.** Plush armchairs and dark-wood booths
★ express the subdued confidence of a restaurant long proclaimed the best in town. Standards are maintained, and all dishes are served with impeccable Continental flair. Alberta beef entrées are ample and tender; British Columbia salmon is memorably fresh; the wine list is still exhaustive. ⊠ *Westin Hotel, 320 4th Ave. SW,* ☎ *403/266–1611. Reservations essential. AE, DC, MC, V.*

$$$ ✗ **Grand Isle Seafood Restaurant.** This large second-floor restaurant offers a riverfront view and modern and very appealing decor. Dim sum is featured. ⊠ *128 2nd Ave. SE,* ☎ *403/269–7783. AE, D, DC, MC, V.*

$$$ ✗ **Hy's Steak House.** This is where Calgary (and Edmonton, Winnipeg, Toronto, and more) goes for immense portions of charcoal-broiled steaks, fresh seafood, chicken, and a huge selection of wines. Wood paneling and earthy decor are components of a sedate Victorian ambience. ⊠ *316 4th Ave. SW,* ☎ *403/263–2222. Reservations essential. AE, DC, MC, V. Closed Sun.*

$$ ✕ **Billy MacIntyre's Cattle Company.** This Western restaurant chain serves up authentic Alberta-style home cooking, following the recipes used by Alberta ranchers in the early 1900s. Try the baby-back ribs. ⊠ *No. 500, 3630 Brentwood Rd. NW,* ☎ *403/282–6614;* ⊠ *7104 Macleod Trail S,* ☎ *403/252–2260. Reservations not accepted. AE, DC, MC, V.*

$$ ✕ **Mescalero.** The casual dining here is influenced by the *cocina rustica* of the American southwest and Latin America. The apple-wood grill turns out tapas. The daily menu is full of freshness and creativity. In the restaurant's Crazy Horse Bar you can sip margaritas and order from a café menu. ⊠ *1315 1st St. SW,* ☎ *403/266–3339. Reservations essential. AE, MC, V.*

$ ✕ **Buzzards Café.** This lively European-style downtown café serves
★   70 wines by the bottle or glass and the exclusive home brew, Buzzard Breath Ale. Wine-theme prints and posters adorning the walls remind you of the original attraction to this place. Food selections include 8-ounce Alberta beef Buzzard Burgers, pub grub, and low-priced entrées, such as teriyaki chicken and fettuccine Alfredo. In summer, dine out on the patio. Adjoining the café is Bottlescrew Bill's Old English Pub. ⊠ *140 10th Ave. SW,* ☎ *403/264–6959. Reservations not accepted. AE, DC, MC, V.*

$ ✕ **Kaos Café.** Rapidly becoming Calgary's premiere jazz club, this relaxed New York–style café specializes in a jazzy selection of entrées, coffees, and desserts. The large outdoor patio is a pleasant choice in summer, and the Saturday and Sunday brunches are popular. ⊠ *718 17 Ave. SW,* ☎ *403/228–9997. Reservations essential. AE, DC, MC, V.*

$$$$ ▥ **Delta Bow Valley.** The bright, 24-story high rise occupies a relatively quiet street on the southern edge of downtown. Decent-size contemporary rooms, with rose-and-green furnishings, have good views from upper floors. For the brightest and most colorful units, request a room with a northern exposure. The sunny lobby—decorated in pink tones and with lush foliage—is an uplifting addition to an already lively setting. ⊠ *209 4th Ave. SE, T2G 0C6,* ☎ *403/266–1980 or 800/268–1133,* ℻ *403/266–0007. 400 rooms. 2 restaurants, bar, no-smoking floors, indoor pool, sauna, exercise room. AE, DC, MC, V.*

$$$$ ▥ **The Palliser.** The downtown area of every Canadian city has a grand
★   old railroad hotel, and the Palliser is Calgary's. This landmark, built in 1914, was restored in the early 1990s. Guest rooms are tastefully appointed with classic furnishings, ornate moldings, and high ceilings. ⊠ *133 9th Ave. SW, T2P 2M3,* ☎ *403/262–1234 or 800/268–9411,* ℻ *403/260–1260. 406 rooms. Restaurant, bar, no-smoking floor, exercise room. AE, DC, MC, V.*

$$$$ ▥ **Radisson Plaza Hotel.** This is a business-class hotel with a convenient location in the heart of downtown, connected to the Calgary Convention Centre. Nearby are the Glenbow Museum and the Calgary Centre for Performing Arts. The warm, inviting lobby leads to the clean pastel-and-maroon-tone rooms. ⊠ *110 9th Ave., T2G 5A6,* ☎ *403/266–7331 or 800/661–7776,* ℻ *403/262–8442. 387 rooms. 2 restaurants, 2 bars, no-smoking floors, indoor pool, sauna, health club. AE, DC, MC, V.*

$$$$ ▥ **Sheraton Cavalier.** In northeast Calgary, the hotel has a lobby decorated with pale colors, a multitude of plants, and a large marble water fountain. **Barlow's Lounge** hosts live entertainment from Thursday through Saturday. For sports fans, **Henry's Pub,** the hotel's sports bar, has large TV screens. **Oasis River Country,** on the second floor of the hotel, has two 200-foot water slides and a recreation and exercise area. ⊠ *2620 32nd Ave. NE, T1Y 6B8,* ☎ *403/291–0107 or 800/325–*

3535, FAX *403/291–2834. 307 rooms. Restaurant, bar, no-smoking rooms, indoor pool. AE, DC, MC, V.*

$$$$ 🏨 **Westin Hotel.** Calgary's Plus 15 pedway (walkway) system connects
★   this luxury high rise in the midst of downtown to most other important nearby structures. Rooms in the Tower Section, especially, are large and decorated with tasteful contemporary furniture and pastel and neutral tones. The rooftop pool is one of this lodging's unique attractions. The Owl's Nest restaurant (☞ *above*) is one of the best dining spots in town. For lighter meals stop in at the Lobby Court, which features Fitness Buffet breakfasts. ✉ *320 4th Ave. SW, T2P 2S6,* ☎ *403/266–1611 or 800/228–3000,* FAX *403/265–7908. 525 rooms. 2 restaurants, 2 bars, no-smoking rooms, indoor pool, sauna, health club. AE, DC, MC, V.*

$$$ 🏨 **Carriage House.** This unique, locally owned property, almost 10 kilometers (6 miles) south of City Centre, has a lobby with fish tanks, caged songbirds, and a waterfall. Room decor is comfortably mismatched. Nighttime entertainment options include a disco and rock club, a country and rock saloon, and an English pub. Guests receive discounts at the nearby Family Leisure Centre (☞ Outdoor Activities and Sports, *below*). ✉ *9030 Macleod Trail S, T2H 0M4,* ☎ *403/253–1101 (call collect from the U.S.); in Canada, 800/661–9566;* FAX *403/259–2414. 175 rooms. 2 restaurants, 3 bars, no-smoking rooms, outdoor pool, sauna. AE, DC, MC, V.*

$$ 🏨 **Prince Royal Inn.** Calgary's bargain inn has a great deal going for it within its 28 floors: a downtown and convenient location, all-suite (studios, one-, and two-bedroom) accommodations with fully equipped kitchens, free parking, free Continental breakfast, and a health club. It's a great deal for families. ✉ *618 5th Ave. SW, T2P 0M7,* ☎ *403/263–0520; in Canada, 800/661–1592;* FAX *403/262–9991. 300 suites. Restaurant, bar, no-smoking floors, sauna, health club. AE, DC, MC, V.*

$$ 🏨 **Ramada Inn Airport.** This convenient and comfortable property is on the northeast side of town a few minutes from Calgary International Airport. Bright rooms are large, with standard furnishings, and are tastefully decorated with a rose-and-mauve scheme. ✉ *1250 McKinnon Dr. NE, T2E 7T7,* ☎ *403/230–1999 or 800/661–5095,* FAX *403/277–2623. 168 rooms. Restaurant, bar, no-smoking rooms, indoor pool, sauna, sun deck. AE, DC, MC, V.*

Nightlife and the Arts

Tickets for events at the Calgary Centre for the Performing Arts, Jubilee Auditorium, and Olympic Saddledome are available at Ticketmaster outlets at Calgary Centre box office, The Bay, and Sears (☞ Shopping, *below*), or can be charged over the phone (☎ 403/270–6700 or 403/266–8888).

The Arts

MUSIC AND DANCE

Calgary Philharmonic Orchestra (☎ 403/294–7420) concerts, chamber groups, and a broad spectrum of music and dance shows are presented in the 1,755-seat Jack Singer Concert Hall in the **Calgary Centre for the Performing Arts** (✉ 205 8th Ave. SE, ☎ 403/294–7455). The larger **Jubilee Auditorium** (✉ 1415 14th Ave. NW, ☎ 403/297–8000) hosts the Alberta Ballet company and a variety of classical music, opera, dance, pop, and rock concerts. Concerts are also performed at **University of Calgary Theatres** (✉ 2500 University Dr. NW, ☎ 403/220–4900).

THEATER

Calgary's showcase theater facility is the **Calgary Centre for the Performing Arts** (✉ 205 8th Ave. SE, ☎ 403/294–7455), with three modern auditoriums in two contiguous historic buildings. Productions by resident Alberta Theatre Projects (ATP) of works by principally Canadian playwrights are highly recommended. More than 20 local companies use the stage of the **Pumphouse Theatre** (⊠ 2140 9th Ave. SW, ☎ 403/263–0079). The **University of Calgary Theatre** (⊠ Reeve Theatre, 2500 University Dr. NW, ☎ 403/220–4900) stages classic and contemporary works. **Loose Moose** (⊠ 2003 McKnight Blvd. NE, Calgary, ☎ 403/291–5682) features competitive "Theatresports" and all sorts of fun and games.

Nightlife

BARS AND CLUBS

Gargoyle's (1213 1st St. SW, ☎ 403/263–4810) caters to an older, upscale crowd. The club atmosphere at **Republik** (219-17th Ave. SW, ☎ 403/244–1884) attracts a young crowd for alternative rock. The Mexican accent at **Señor Frog's** (739 2nd Ave. SW, 403/264–5100) is popular with all ages.

CASINOS

In Calgary, play blackjack, roulette, and wheel of fortune at **River Park Casino** (⊠ 1919 Macleod Trail S, ☎ 403/269–6771). **Cash Casino Place** (⊠ 4040B Blackfoot Trail SE, ☎ 403/287–1635) has games of chance. At **Tower Casino** in Tower Centre you can place wagers. **Frontier Casino** in the Big Four Building in Stampede Park is another place to play.

COMEDY

The Calgary outpost of **Yuk Yuk's** (⊠ Blackfoot Inn, 5940 Blackfoot Trail, ☎ 403/258–2028), Canada's comedy chain, has name performers from Canada and the United States. **Jester's** (⊠ 239 10th Ave. SE, ☎ 403/269–6669) has comedians and Wednesday night open mikes.

MUSIC

For Western sights and sounds, head for **Ranchman's** (⊠ 9615 Macleod Trail S, ☎ 403/253–1100). The **Longhorn Dance Hall** (⊠ 9631 Macleod Trail S, ☎ 403/258–0528) is another Western hangout. The **Rocking Horse Saloon** (⊠ 24 7400 Macleod Trail S, ☎ 403/255–4646) features country music every night but Sunday. **Sole Luna** (⊠ 739 2nd Ave. SW, ☎ 403/264–5100) has nightly dancing amid Mediterranean-style decor.

Outdoor Activities and Sports

Participant Sports

BICYCLING AND JOGGING

Calgary has about 200 kilometers (120 miles) of bicycling and jogging paths, most of which wind along rivers and through city parks. Maps are available at visitor centers and bike shops. You can rent bikes at **Sports Rent** (⊠ 4424 16th Ave. NW, Calgary, ☎ 403/292–0077) and from **Budget Rent-A-Car** (⊠ 140 6th Ave. SE, ☎ 403/264–5212).

HEALTH AND FITNESS CLUBS

Three **Leisure Centre** water parks in Calgary have wave pools and water slides, plus gymnasiums and training facilities; Southland and Family have racquetball and squash courts. ⊠ *Village Square Leisure Centre, 2623 56th St. NE,* ☎ *403/280–9714;* ⊠ *Family Leisure Centre, 11150 Bonaventure Dr. SE,* ☎ *403/278–7542;* ⊠ *Southland Leisure Centre, 2000 Southland Dr. SW,* ☎ *403/251–3505. Rates and hours vary.*

Just south of downtown, the striking white-dome **Lindsay Park Sports Centre** (⊠ 2225 Macleod Trail SW, ☎ 403/233–8393) encompasses a 50-meter natatorium, a 200-meter track, racquetball and squash courts, and a weight room.

Spectator Sports

FOOTBALL

The **Calgary Stampeders** of the Canadian Football League play home games in **McMahon Stadium** (✉ 1817 Crowchild Trail NW, ☎ 403/289–0205) throughout the season, which runs July through November.

HOCKEY

The **Calgary Flames** play National Hockey League matches October–April at the **Olympic Saddledome** (17th Ave. and 2nd St. SE, ☎ 403/261–0475) in Stampede Park.

HORSE RACING

There's racing year-round (except March) in **Stampede Park** (✉ 17th Ave. and 2nd St. SE, ☎ 403/261–0101). Thoroughbreds race April–May and September–November; trotters May–September and December–February. **Spruce Meadows** (✉ southwest of Calgary city boundary, ☎ 403/974–4200) is one of the world's finest show-jumping facilities, with major competitions held June–September.

Shopping

Calgary's best shopping is in the center of the downtown district, where you can wander through various shopping centers connected by indoor walkways. **Bankers Hall** has exclusive specialty shops, restaurants, and cinemas. **Scotia Centre** has fashion, accessory, and other retail outlets. **Penny Lane Mall** is in renovated, early 20th-century buildings. **Toronto Dominion Centre** is home to the indoor park—Devonian Gardens—as well as more than 100 stores. The **Eaton Centre** has more than 500 stores. For outdoor shopping, the six-block stretch of 8th Avenue Southwest between 3rd Street Southwest and Macleod Trail Southeast has been turned into the traffic-free **Stephen Avenue Mall** (although traffic is allowed during the evenings). **Uptown 17** and **Kensington** are trendy shopping districts northwest of the city center on 10th Street and Kensington Road, respectively; here you'll find craft shops, antiques stores, boutiques, galleries, cafés, and coffee shops.

Side Trips

Numbers in the margin correspond to places of interest on the Alberta map.

Drumheller

🕥 *20 km (12 mi) east of Calgary on Trans-Canada Highway (Hwy. 1), then 120 km (75 mi) north on Route 9.*

The road to Drumheller takes you through the vast Canadian prairie of seemingly endless expanses of flat country in every direction. Once a coal-mining center, the town lies in the rugged valley of the Red Deer River, where millions of years of wind and water erosion exposed the "strike" that produced what amounts to present-day Drumheller's major industry: dinosaurs.

The barren lunar terrain of stark badlands and eerie rock cylinders (called hoodoos) may seem an ideal setting for the herds of dinosaurs that stalked the countryside 75 million years ago, but in fact, when the dinosaurs were here the area had a semitropical climate and verdant marshlands not unlike the Florida Everglades. You learn this and more geological and paleontological history of Alberta at the **Royal Tyrrell Museum of Paleontology.** Participate in hands-on exhibits and meet the local hero, *Albertosaurus,* a smaller, fiercer version of *Tyrannosaurus rex,* the first dinosaur discovered around here. ✉ *Rte. 838, 6 km (4 mi) west of Drumheller,* ☎ *403/823–7707; in Calgary, 403/294–1992.* ✉

$6.50. ☉ *Mid-May–early Sept., daily 9–9; mid-Sept.–mid-May, Tues.–Sun. 10–5.*

Capitalizing on its rich paleontological past, Drumheller has a number of dinosaur-related businesses. **Reptile World** (⊠ Rte. 9, ☎ 403/823–8623) has a crowd-pleasing collection of poisonous snakes. The **Homestead Antique Museum** (⊠ Rte. 838, ☎ 403/823–2600) packs 4,000 Indian artifacts, medical instruments, pieces of period clothing, and other items of Canadiana into a roadside Quonset hut. **Prehistoric Park** (⊠ off Rte. 575, ☎ 403/823–7625) depicts life-size dinosaurs in a badlands setting and sells a vast selection of fossils, bones, rocks, and petrified wood. No visit to Drumheller is complete without a family portrait beside the comic-book *Tyrannosaurus rex* guarding the Route 9 bridge over the Red Deer River.

Dinosaur Provincial Park

142 km (90 mi) south of Drumheller on Route 56 to Trans-Canada Highway (Hwy. 1) east, north at Brooks on Route 873, east on Route 544, and follow signs.

Dinosaur Provincial Park encompasses 15,000 acres of Canada's baddest badlands. Soft sedimentary rock was deposited by rivers 72 million years ago and sculpted into starkly fascinating shapes by melting waters of the Ice Age that occurred a mere 14,000 years ago. Incessant wind, water, and frost erosion have exposed one of the world's most important collections of fossilized bones. Roads lead in to some *in situ* fossil sites; two looped interpretive trails lead to more, with guided tours on weekends. In summer, 90-minute bus tours explore backcountry areas from which visitors are otherwise restricted. The cacti bloom from June through August. The **Royal Tyrrell Museum of Paleontology Field Station** in the park offers a concise orientation to the prehistoric world. Note: Concessions are limited; bring a lunch to eat in one of the picnic areas. ⊠ *Rte. 544, Patricia, 48 km (30 mi) northeast of Brooks,* ☎ *403/378–4587.* 🎫 *Free.* ☉ *Tyrrell Field Station mid-May–early Sept., daily 9–9; Sept.–mid-May, Wed.–Sun. 10–5.*

Medicine Hat

⑱ *95 km (60 mi) southeast of Patricia, 293 km (182 mi) southeast of Calgary on Trans-Canada Highway.*

Roadside views on the way to Medicine Hat consist of small well pumps and storage tanks amid endless expanses of "prairie wool," principally spear and blue grama grass. Much local lore concerns the origin of the name Medicine Hat, but one legend tells of a battle waged between Cree and Blackfoot Indians: The Cree fought bravely until their medicine man deserted, losing his headdress in the South Saskatchewan River. The site's name, *Saamis,* meaning "medicine man's hat," was later translated by white settlers into Medicine Hat.

Medicine Hat is a prosperous and scenic city built on high banks overlooking the South Saskatchewan River. Alberta's fifth-largest city's wealth derives from vast deposits of natural gas below, some of which is piped up to fuel quaint gas lamps in the turn-of-the-century downtown area. Prosperity is embodied in the striking, glass-sided **Medicine Hat City Hall,** which won the Canadian Architectural Award in 1986. Guided group and self-guided tours are available. ⊠ *1st St. SE and 6th Ave. SE,* ☎ *403/529–8100.* ☉ *Weekdays 8:30–4:30.*

Medicine Hat's greatest achievement was turning the land alongside the South Saskatchewan River and Seven Persons Creek into parkland and environmental preserves interconnected by 15 kilometers (9⅓ miles) of walking, biking, and cross-country ski trails. Detailed trail maps are available at the **Tourist Information Centre** (⊠ 8 Gehring Rd. SW, ☎ 403/527–6422). There is a half mile of falling water at **Riverside Amusement Park** (⊠ Hwy. 1 and Power House Rd., ☎ 403/529–6218), with water slides, go-carts, and inner tubing. **Echo Dale Regional Park** (⊠ Holsom Rd. off Rte. 3, ☎ 403/529–6225) provides a riverside setting for swimming, boating, fishing, a 1900s farm, and a historic coal mine.

DINING AND LODGING

$$ ✕🔃 **Medicine Hat Lodge.** On the edge of town adjacent to a shopping mall, this hotel has several rooms with inward views of the indoor pool, the whirlpool, and the huge, curving water slide. The Atrium Dining Room serves fine Continental meals. J.D.'s is a hotel country-and-western club with live music. ⊠ *1051 Ross Glen Dr. SE, T1B 3T8,* ☎ *403/529–2222 or 800/661–8095. 190 rooms. 2 restaurants, 2 bars, no-smoking rooms, indoor pool, steam room. AE, DC, MC, V.*

Lethbridge

⑲ *164 km (102 mi) west of Medicine Hat on Crowsnest Highway (Rte. 3); 217 km (135 mi) south of Calgary via Hwy. 2 and Rte. 3.*

Lethbridge, Alberta's third-largest city, is an 1870s coal boomtown that is now a center of agriculture, oil, and gas. The main attraction, **Fort Whoop-Up,** part of the **Indian Battle Park,** is a reconstruction of a southern Alberta whiskey fort. Along with weapons, relics, and a 15-minute audiovisual historical presentation, Fort Whoop-Up has wagon-train tours of the river valley and other points of local historical interest. ⊠ *Indian Battle Park, Whoop-Up Dr. and Oldman River,* ☎ *403/329–0444.* ⊠ *Fort Whoop-Up $2.50.* ☯ *Late May–Labor Day, Mon.–Sat. 10–6, Sun. 2–8; off-season, call for hours.*

Henderson Lake Park, 3 kilometers (2 miles) east of downtown Lethbridge, is filled with lush trees, a golf course, a baseball stadium, tennis courts, a swimming pool, and a 60-acre man-made lake. Alongside the lake, **Nikka Yuko Japanese Gardens** is a tranquil setting for manicured trees and shrubs, miniature pools and waterfalls, a teahouse, and pebble designs originally constructed in Japan and reassembled alongside Henderson Lake. ⊠ *Henderson Lake Park, Mayor Magrath Dr. and S. Parkside Dr.,* ☎ *403/320–3020; gardens,* ☎ *403/328–3511.* ⊠ *$3.* ☯ *Mid-May–mid-June, daily 9–5; mid-June–Aug., daily 9–8; Sept.–early Oct., daily 9–5.*

DINING AND LODGING

$$$ ✕ **Cafe Martinique.** This locally renowned fine dining spot, in the El Rancho Motor Hotel, specializes in aged steaks and chateaubriand made with tender Alberta beef. For something lighter in a more informal setting, try the El Rancho coffee shop, on the same property. Live music and dancing take place most nights. ⊠ *526 Mayor Magrath Dr.,* ☎ *403/327–5701. Reservations essential. AE, DC, MC, V.*

$$ ✕ **Sven Eriksen's Family Restaurant.** Tasty versions of Canadian prairie standards, including chicken and an especially good prime rib, are cooked up at this homey, colonial-style eatery. "Family Restaurant" label notwithstanding, there's a full bar. ⊠ *1715 Mayor Magrath Dr.,* ☎ *403/328–7756. Reservations essential. AE, MC, V.*

$$ 🔃 **Lethbridge Lodge Hotel.** This modern-day lodge has great Oldman River views and a pleasant tropical indoor courtyard filled with exotic plants, a swimming pool, a whirlpool, a waterfall, and chairs for lounging. The hotel contains two restaurants: At the more formal **Anton's,** the waiters are dressed in tuxedos, and reservations are needed. ⊠ *320 Scenic Dr., T1J 4B4,* ☎ *800/661–1232 or 403/328–*

1123. 190 rooms. Restaurant, bar, no-smoking rooms, indoor pool, whirlpool. AE, MC, V.

$ ☷ **Parkside Inn.** This comfortable, nearly 40-year-old hotel is a good bargain, conveniently situated across the street from a golf course and within walking distance of Henderson Lake Park and the Japanese Gardens. The lobby is done in muted burgundies and blues, while rooms are styled in grays and rusts. The hotel's tavern has live country-and-western music on weekends and the lounge has video lottery machines. ⊠ *1009 Mayor Magrath Dr., T1K 2P7,* ☎ *403/328–2366. 65 rooms. Restaurant, bar, no-smoking rooms. AE, MC, V.*

Fort Macleod

❷⓿ *50 km (31 mi) west of Lethbridge on Route 3.*

Fort Macleod, southern Alberta's oldest town, was founded by the Mounties in 1874 to maintain order among the farmers, Indians, whiskey vendors, and ranchers beginning to settle here. The pre-1900 wood-frame buildings and the more recent sandstone-and-brick buildings have established this as Alberta's first historic area. For information about guided and self-guided tours, visit the information booth (☎ 403/553–2500) beside **Fort Macleod Museum.** An authentic reconstruction of the 1874 fort, this museum grants almost equal exhibitory weight to settlers, Indians, old North West Mounted Police, and today's Royal Canadian Mounted Police. ⊠ *25th St.,* ☎ *403/553–4703.* ☷ *$6.50.* ☉ *May–mid-June and early Sept.–mid-Oct., daily 9–5; mid-June–early Sept., daily 9–8:30.*

Head-Smashed-In Buffalo Jump is about a 15-minute drive from Fort Macleod. At the large, seven-level interpretive center built into the side of a cliff, you can learn how Plains Indians herded buffalo over the edge to their death in order to harvest meat and fur from the carcasses. Museum displays describe the tradition and offer some insight into the life and customs of the Plains Indians, especially the Blackfoot. Guided walks and audiovisual exhibits are presented. ⊠ *18 km (11 mi) northwest of Fort Macleod on Rte. 785 (off Hwy. 2),* ☎ *403/553–2731.* ☷ *$6.50.* ☉ *May 16–Labor Day, daily 9–8; Labor Day–May 15, daily 9–5.*

Calgary A to Z

Arriving and Departing

BY CAR

The Trans-Canada Highway (Highway 1) runs west to southeast across Alberta, through Calgary. Highway 2 passes through Calgary on its way from the U.S. border to Edmonton and points north. Calgary is 690 kilometers (425 miles) northwest of Helena, Montana; it's 670 kilometers (419 miles) northeast of Seattle, via the Trans-Canada Highway.

BY PLANE

Calgary International Airport is 20 minutes northeast of the city center. Airlines serving Calgary include Air Canada, Canadian Airlines International, Air BC, American, Delta, United, and KLM.

Between the Airport and Downtown: Taxis make the trip for about $18.

Getting Around

BY BUS AND LRT

Calgary Transit (⊠ 206 7th Ave. SW, ☎ 403/276–7801) operates a comprehensive bus system and light rail transit system (the C-Train or LRT) throughout the area. Fares on both are $1.50. Books of 10 tickets are $12. A Calgary Transit (CT) Day Pass good for unlimited rides costs $4. The C-Train has lines running northwest (Brentwood), northeast (Whitehorn), and south (Anderson) from downtown. The C-Train is free to ride within the downtown core.

BY CAR

Although many attractions are in the downtown area and can be reached on foot, a car is useful for visiting outlying attractions.

BY TAXI

Taxis are fairly expensive, at $2.05 for the drop and about $1 for each additional mile. Major taxi services are **Checker** (☎ 403/299–9999), **Yellow Cab** (☎ 403/974–1111), **Red Top** (☎ 403/974–4444), **Associated Cabs** (☎ 403/299–1111), and **Co-op** (☎ 403/531–8294).

Contacts and Resources

EMERGENCIES

Dial 911 for all emergencies; **police,** ☎ 403/266–1234; **poison center,** ☎ 403/670–1414.

GUIDED TOURS

Several companies offer tours of Calgary and environs, although none operate on regular schedules. Call the **Calgary Convention and Visitors Bureau** (☎ 800/661–1678) for up-to-date information.

HOSPITALS

Emergency rooms are at **General Hospital** (✉ 841 Centre Ave. E, ☎ 403/268–9111), **Foothills Hospital** (✉ 1403 29th Ave. NW, ☎ 403/670–1110), **Alberta Children's Hospital** (✉ 1820 Richmond Rd. SW, ☎ 403/229–7211), and **Rocky View Hospital** (✉ 7007 14th St. SW, ☎ 403/541–3000).

LATE-NIGHT PHARMACY

The **Super Drug Mart** (✉ 504 Elbow Dr. SW, ☎ 403/228–3338) is open daily until midnight.

VISITOR INFORMATION

The main **Calgary Convention and Visitors Bureau** (✉ 237 8th Ave. SE, T2G 0K8, ☎ 403/263–8510 or 800/661–1678) is open daily 8–5. There are also walk-in visitor service centers at the base of the Calgary Tower and at the Calgary International Airport.

EDMONTON

Lucky Edmonton is a recidivist boomtown that never seems to go bust. The first boom arrived in 1795, when the North West Company and Hudson's Bay Company both established fur-trading posts in the area. Boom II came in 1897, when Edmonton became principal outfitter on the overland "All Canadian Route" to the Yukon goldfields; as a result, Edmonton was named capital when the province of Alberta was formed in 1905. The latest and greatest of booms began on February 13, 1947, when oil was discovered in Leduc, 40 kilometers (25 miles) to the southwest. More than 10,000 wells were eventually drilled within 100 kilometers (62 miles) of the city and with them came fields of refineries and supply depots. By 1965 Edmonton had solidified its role as the "oil capital of Canada."

More interesting is how wisely Edmonton has spread the wealth to create a beautiful and livable city. Shunning the uncontrolled development of some other oil boomtowns, Edmonton turned its great natural resource, the North Saskatchewan River valley, into a 27-kilometer (17-mile) greenbelt of parks and recreational facilities. With a population of 875,000, Edmonton is the largest northerly city in the Americas and the fifth-largest city in Canada. It is also Canada's second-largest city in land area—270 square miles. As the seat of the Alberta government and home to the University of Alberta, Edmonton has an unusually sophisticated atmosphere that has generated many fine restaurants and a thriving arts community. One of its attractions, the West Edmonton Mall, is a year-round drawing card for shoppers and families, complete with facilities ranging from an amusement park to a shopping center and hotel, and from a cinema complex to a water park. The city also has professional football and hockey teams.

Downtown Edmonton

The Edmonton street system is a straight grid with numbered streets running north–south (numbers decrease as you go south) and numbered avenues running east–west (numbers decrease as you go east). Edmontonians often use the last digit or two of large numbers as shorthand for the complete number: The Inn on 7th is on 107th Street; the 9th Street Bistro can be found on 109th Street. Edmonton's "main drag" is Jasper Avenue, which runs east–west through the center of downtown.

The city's striking physical feature, where most recreational facilities are located, is the broad green valley of the North Saskatchewan River, running diagonally northeast to southwest through the city center. The downtown area lies just north of the river, between 95th and 109th streets.

Numbers in the text and margin below correspond to numbers on the Downtown Edmonton map.

A Good Walk and Ride

Start at the **Edmonton Convention Centre** ㉑, an architecturally inventive space built into a hillside with terraced levels accessed by glass-enclosed escalators. Head west along Jasper Avenue and turn north on 99th Street to **Sir Winston Churchill Square** ㉒, where you'll find many of the city's major cultural institutions. Across 99th Street is the **Edmonton Art Gallery** ㉓. Directly west of Churchill Square begins a maze of multilevel shopping malls, department stores, cinemas, and office buildings—all climatically controlled and interconnected by a network of tunnels and second-floor pedways (☞ Shopping, *below*). Enter the LRT station on Jasper Avenue at 103rd or 104th Street for the ride to Grandin Station and the **Alberta Government Centre** ㉔, where you can tour the **Alberta Legislature Building** ㉕.

TIMING
You can do this tour in just a few hours any day of the week.

Sights to See

㉔ **Alberta Government Centre.** The seat of Alberta's government, this complex encompasses several acres of carefully manicured gardens and fountains open for strolling. ⌧ *109th St. and 97th Ave.*

㉕ **Alberta Legislature Building.** The stately 1912 Edwardian structure overlooks the river on the site of an early trading post. Frequent free tours of the building help to explain the intricacies of the Albertan and Canadian systems of government. ⌧ *109th St. and 97th Ave.,* ☎ *403/ 427–7362.* ⌧ *Tours free.* ⊘ *Daily; phone for exact times.*

㉓ **Edmonton Art Gallery.** More than 30 annual exhibits of classical and contemporary art from Canada and the rest of the world take place here. ⌧ *2 Sir Winston Churchill Sq.,* ☎ *403/422–6223.* ⌧ *$3, free Thurs. after 4.* ⊘ *Mon.–Wed. 10:30–5, Thurs. and Fri. 10:30–8, weekends and holidays 11–5.*

Downtown Edmonton

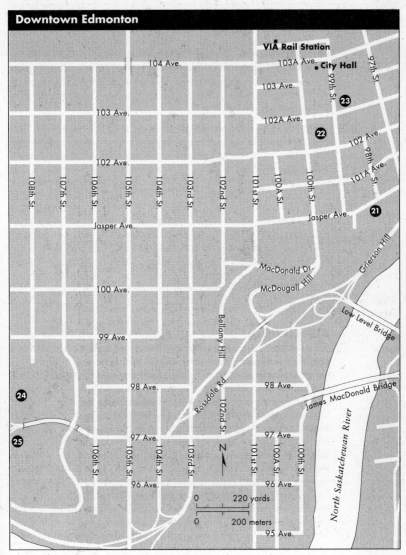

VIA Rail Station
103A Ave.
City Hall
104 Ave.
103 Ave.
103 Ave.
102A Ave.
102 Ave.
102 Ave.
Jasper Ave.
Jasper Ave.
MacDonald Dr.
McDougall Hill
Low Level Bridge
100 Ave.
99 Ave.
Bellamy Hill
Rossdale Rd.
98 Ave.
98 Ave.
James MacDonald Bridge
97 Ave.
97 Ave.
N
96 Ave.
96 Ave.
North Saskatchewan River
95 Ave.

104 Ave., 103 Ave., 102 Ave., Jasper Ave., 100 Ave., 99 Ave., 98 Ave., 97 Ave., 96 Ave.

108th St., 107th St., 106th St., 105th St., 104th St., 103rd St., 102nd St., 101st St., 100A St., 100th St., 99th St., 97th St., 98th St., 101A Ave.

0   220 yards
0   200 meters

Alberta Government
Centre, **24**

Alberta Legislature
Building, **25**

Edmonton Art
Gallery, **23**

Edmonton Convention
Centre, **21**

Sir Winston Churchill
Square, **22**

㉑   **Edmonton Convention Centre.** This most unconventional building is filled
with surprises. The center has been built onto a slope with various terraced levels reached by glass-enclosed escalators with great views of
the North Saskatchewan River valley. On the Pedway (walkway) Level
check out the **Canadian Country Music Hall of Honor,** actually a wall
filled with plaques memorializing such good old boys as Hank Snow,
Wilf Carter, and Orval "The Canadian Plowboy" Prophet. ⊠ 9797
Jasper Ave., ☎ *403/421–9797.*

㉒   **Sir Winston Churchill Square** is the focus of the Civic Centre, a six-block
area that incorporates many of Edmonton's major institutions. Among
them, the largest theater complex in Canada, the **Citadel Theatre,**
houses five different venues (plus workshops and classrooms) and an
indoor garden with a waterfall. The **Edmonton Public Library** (⊠ 7
Sir Winston Churchill Sq., ☎ 403/423–2331) augments books and art
exhibits with a lively round of activities in the Children's Department.
The **Chinatown Gate** is a symbol of friendship between Edmonton and
its sister city, Harbin, China; it spans the portal to Edmonton's meager Chinatown. Nearby, the **City Hall** (⊠ 1 Sir Winston Churchill Sq.,
☎ 403/496–8200) is more than a place for civic government. This architectural showcase contains a grand stairway, a large art exhibition
space, and a 200-foot tower with an enormous 23-bell carillon.

Greater Edmonton

A Good Drive

To make a circuit, start northwest of city center at the **Edmonton Space
and Science Centre,** where you can play with high-tech equipment in
hands-on displays. On the western edge of the city is the **Wild Waters
Waterslide Park,** a great place to cool off the kids. Moving toward the
center again, you can visit the **West Edmonton Mall,** the world's largest,
for entertainment or even shopping. On the south side of the North
Saskatchewan River, just off Whitemud Drive, is **Fort Edmonton Park,**
where costumed interpreters take you back in time. Still on the south
side of the river, but around a few bends just off Groat Road, is **William
Hawrelak Park,** a perfect place for kids to fish. After fishing, you can
visit the **Valley Zoo,** just across the river, also geared to children. A few
blocks north is the **Provincial Museum of Alberta,** which focuses on
natural and human history. Across the river again, via the 109th Street
Bridge, you'll come to the **Old Strathcona Historic Area,** the **Old Strathcona Model and Toy Museum,** and the **Telephone Historical Museum,**
all within a few blocks of one another. To the northeast, still on the
south side of the river, lies **Muttart Conservatory,** an important botanical facility. Finally, you can end your tour with thrills at the **Whitemud Drive Amusement Park,** toward the southeastern side of the city.

TIMING

You can spend several days taking in places of interest outside Edmonton's downtown neighborhood, depending on how much time you
want to devote to shopping or playing in the amusement parks.

Sights to See

Edmonton Space and Science Centre. Explore the heavens using a stunning variety of high-tech techniques. Standing exhibits and a fascinating
science shop are always of interest, but the star attractions include laser-
light concerts and IMAX films of an appropriately celestial nature.
⊠ *11211 142nd St.,* ☎ *403/451–3344.* ⊒ *$12.* ☉ *mid-June–early
Sept., daily 10–10, IMAX shows Mon.–Sat. hourly 11–9, Sun. 10–
10; early Sept.–mid-June, Tues.–Sun. 10–10, IMAX shows Tues.–Sun.
hourly 11–9.*

☺ **Fort Edmonton Park.** Canada's largest historical park (158 acres) is home
to an authentic re-creation of several periods in Edmonton history. There
is a fur press (an apparatus for bundling pelts for shipping) in the 1846
Hudson's Bay Company fort; a blacksmith shop, a saloon, and a jail
along 1885 Street; photo studios and a firehouse on 1905 Street; and
relatively modern conveniences on 1920 Street. Horse wagon, streetcar, stagecoach, and pony rides are available as well as a short trip on
a steam-powered train. ⊠ *Whitemud and Fox Drs.,* ☎ *403/496–
8787.* ☜ *$6.50.* ☉ *Mid-May–June, daily 10–4; July–early Sept., daily
10–6; Sept., Mon.–Sat. 11–2, Sun. and holidays 10–6.*

Muttart Conservatory. At one of North America's most important
botanical facilities, separate greenhouses each contain flora of a different climate: arid, tropical, and temperate. A show pavilion features
special seasonal floral displays. ⊠ *9626 96A St.,* ☎ *403/496–8755.*
☜ *$4.25.* ☉ *Sun.–Wed. 11–9, Thurs.–Sat. 11–6.*

Old Strathcona Historic Area. The area surrounding 104th Street and
Whyte (82nd) Avenue on the south side of the river is a district of restored houses and shops built mainly when Strathcona Town amalga-
mated with Edmonton, in 1912. The low buildings and wide streets
have a decidedly Old West air, and Old Strathcona is a good place to
get out and wander. For a more determined exploration, pick up a walking tour map at the **Old Strathcona Foundation.** ⊠ *8331 104th St.,*
☎ *403/433–5866.* ☉ *Weekdays 8:30–4:30.*

☺ **Old Strathcona Model and Toy Museum.** Here you'll find intricate
models of planes, buildings, wildlife, and much more, all made of
paper. ⊠ *8603 104th St.,* ☎ *403/433–4512.*

Provincial Museum of Alberta. At the province's foremost natural and
human history museum, four main galleries depict Alberta's heritage.
The new People's Gallery (scheduled to open in fall 1996) contains a
collection of native artifacts that is among the finest in North America. ⊠ *12845 102nd Ave.,* ☎ *403/453–9100.* ☜ *$5.* ☉ *May–Sept.,
daily 9–8; Oct.–Apr., Tues.–Sun. 9–5.*

☺ **Telephone Historical Center.** The largest telephone museum in Canada
is filled with hands-on exhibits. ⊠ *10437 83 Ave.,* ☎ *403/441–2077.*

☺ **Valley Zoo.** This small but imaginative zoo in riverside Laurier Park
places exotic species in well-known storybook settings. ⊠ *134th St.
and Buena Vista Rd.,* ☎ *403/496–6911.*

West Edmonton Mall. Listed in the *Guinness Book of World Records*
as the world's largest mall, this is Edmonton's preeminent shopping
attraction. Its sheer magnitude and variety transform it from a mere
shopping center to an indoor city with high-rent districts, blue-collar
strips, and hidden byways waiting to be discovered. There are 800 stores
and services, including six major department stores, 19 movie theaters,
and 90 places to eat; the mall also contains an amusement park, an
ice-skating rink, a replica of Columbus's ship the *Santa Maria,* an 18-
hole miniature-golf course, the "Deep Sea Adventure" submarine ride
and dolphin show, the 5-acre World Waterpark water amusement
park, Fantasyland Hotel (☞ Lodging, *below*), a playhouse, a chapel,
a bingo parlor, and a casino. If you don't feel like walking the mall,
rent an electric scooter or hitch a ride on a rickshaw. ⊠ *8770 170th
St.,* ☎ *403/444–5300.* ☜ *Amusement-park day pass $22.95, individual
ride tickets $1 (rides cost 1–7 tickets), World Waterpark day pass $22.95,
Deep Sea Adventure $12.* ☉ *Weekdays 10–9, Sat. 10–6, Sun. noon–5.*

↺ **Whitemud Drive Amusement Park.** Here you can enjoy go-carts, bumper-boats, miniature golf, and batting cages. ⊠ *7411 51st Ave.,* ☎ *403/465–1190.*

↺ **Wild Waters Waterslide Park.** For plenty of wet fun, try the equipment at this facility. ⊠ *21515 103rd Ave.,* ☎ *403/447–4476.*

↺ **William Hawrelak Park.** Children only—or adults in their company—may fish in this rainbow trout-stocked pond. The park includes paddleboats and an adventure playground. ⊠ *Off Groat Rd., south of North Saskatchewan River,* ☎ *403/496–7275.*

Dining and Lodging

$$$$ ✕ **La Boheme.** On the historic east-side Gibbard Block, this fittingly splendid restaurant presents classic French cuisine, prepared with invention and served with solicitous care. Edwardian pressed-tin ceilings and a French provincial fireplace surrounded by Voltaire chairs enhance the setting. Specialties include lamb sausages, pâté maison, and daily concoctions of fresh fish. The restaurant is part of a bed-and-breakfast. ⊠ *6427 112th Ave.,* ☎ *403/474–5693. Reservations essential. AE, MC, V.*

$$$$ ✕ **Unheardof Dining Lounge.** Hardly "unheard-of" any longer, this is
★ an extremely popular restaurant in an antiques-filled old house. The seven-course prix-fixe dinner changes weekly but is likely to include game in autumn, and poultry or beef the rest of the year. Dinners begin with a light pâté and are punctuated by surprising salads and refreshing sorbets. Desserts, especially the Danish cream-cheese cheesecake, are light and delicious. ⊠ *9602 82nd Ave.,* ☎ *403/432–0480. Reservations essential. AE, MC, V. No lunch Tues.–Sat.*

$$$ ✕ **Bistro Praha.** Table lamps and paintings of Prague street scenes make this European-style café feel as homey as Grandma's living room. The background music is classical, the clientele mainly urban young professional. The menu includes such Eastern European favorites as cabbage soup and Wiener schnitzel. A rich selection of desserts and a choice from 12 brands of tea make this a perfect stop for snacks. ⊠ *10168 100A St., at Jasper Ave.,* ☎ *403/424–4218. AE, DC, MC, V.*

$$$ ✕ **Bourbon Street.** This is actually an assemblage of moderately priced restaurants around a cul-de-sac on the main floor of West Edmonton Mall. "Exterior" decor features New Orleans street lamps and wrought-iron balconies. **Café Orleans** serves such Cajun/Creole dishes as jambalaya and oysters. **Sherlock Holmes** is an English pub with imported draft beer and such dishes as Mrs. Hudson's Home Made Pies. **Albert's** has deli fare including the Montréal favorite, smoked meat. Other spots include **Kokomo's California Bar and Grill, Hard Rock Cafe,** and, for belly-up-to-the-bar drinking, the **Bourbon Street Saloon.** ⊠ *West Edmonton Mall, 8770 170th St., Entrance 6. AE, MC, V.*

$$$ ✕ **La Spiga.** Admirable Northern Italian cuisine is served in a flower-filled 1913 house that feels more like Montréal than the western plains. Menu highlights include rack of lamb with grappa, breast of chicken with fresh tomato, and various renditions of veal. Portions are large and accompanied by fettuccine; the wine list is long. ⊠ *10133 125 St., at 102nd Ave.,* ☎ *403/482–3100. Reservations essential. AE, MC, V. No lunch. Closed Sun.*

$$ ✕ **Pacific Fish Company.** This restaurant satisfies landlocked Edmonton's appetite for fresh seafood with daily fly-ins. Order oysters Rockefeller and whiskey shrimp as appetizers, and anything charbroiled over mesquite turns out fine. Decor runs to deck flooring, corrugated walls, and nets dangling overhead. ⊠ *10020 101A Ave.,* ☎ *403/422–0282. Reservations essential. AE, MC, V.*

$ ✕ **Chianti Café.** This extremely popular spot occupies part of the main
★ floor of Strathcona Square, a converted post office in the lively Old
Strathcona District. A mostly young crowd gathers for square meals
with tasty shellfish appetizers, more than 20 varieties of pasta, a couple of dozen veal dishes, and a discriminating selection of desserts. Be
prepared to wait for seating on weekend evenings. ⊠ *10501 82nd Ave.,*
☎ *403/439–9829. AE, DC, MC, V.*

$ ✕ **Vi's.** In summer, this old house has outdoor seating on a deck over-
looking the river; in winter, patrons are warmed by a blazing fire. All
year the menu emphasizes the basics: hearty soups, fresh salads, extravagant sandwiches, and desserts—with special mention for chocolate pecan pie. Try Vi's for Sunday brunch. ⊠ *9712 111th St.,* ☎ *403/
482–6402. AE, MC, V.*

$$$ ✕🏨 **Westin Hotel.** This brown block structure in the heart of down-
town has an atrium lobby with a decorative mobile, trees, and plants
that convey comfort and luxury. The large, comfortable beige-and-pas-
tel rooms are tastefully decorated with attractive artwork. The expe-
rienced staff speaks a total of 29 languages. Some of the finest food in
the downtown area can be found in the **Carvery.** ⊠ *10135 100th St.,
T5J 0Z1,* ☎ *403/426–3636 or 800/228–3000,* FAX *403/428–6060. 420
rooms. 2 restaurants, 2 bars, no-smoking floors, indoor pool, sauna.
AE, DC, MC, V.*

$$$$ 🏨 **Edmonton Hilton.** This financial-district luxury high rise connects
★ by second-level passageways to five major office buildings and two shop-
ping centers. Rooms—all with bay windows and blue-and-gray color
schemes—are decorated with sophistication and include marble table-
tops, walnut furniture, and accents of brass. The **Rose and Crown** is
an authentic English pub, perfect for throwing darts and drinking
draft beers. ⊠ *10235 101st St., T5J 3E9,* ☎ *403/428–7111 or
800/268–9275,* FAX *403/441–3098. 313 rooms. 3 restaurants, 2 bars,
no-smoking floors, indoor pool, sauna. AE, DC, MC, V.*

$$$ 🏨 **Edmonton House.** The building's cylindrical design creates oddly
★ shaped but large and comfortable one- and two-bedroom and execu-
tive suites. All units have balconies with views of the skyline or the river
valley, and kitchens are fully equipped (down to a toaster). A small mez-
zanine-level convenience store supplies basics. Weekend and long-term
rates are available. ⊠ *10205 100th Ave., T5J 4B5,* ☎ *403/424–5555
or 800/661–6562,* FAX *403/425–5485. 293 suites. Restaurant, bar, no-
smoking floors, indoor pool, sauna, exercise room, underground parking. AE, DC, MC, V.*

$$$ 🏨 **Fantasyland Hotel.** This important component of massive West Ed-
monton Mall (☞ Greater Edmonton, *above*) has regular and theme
rooms; the latter include Victorian coach rooms, where guests sleep in
open carriages; Roman rooms, with classic round beds; truck rooms,
where the bed is the back of a pickup; and Polynesian rooms, with cata-
maran beds and waterfalls. All theme rooms have Jacuzzis, and non-
theme quarters are comfortable and tidy. ⊠ *17700 87th Ave., T5T 4V4,*
☎ *403/444–3000 or 800/661–6454,* FAX *403/444–3294. 334 rooms,
125 theme rooms. 2 restaurants, bar. AE, DC, MC, V.*

$$$ 🏨 **Howard Johnson Plaza Hotel.** At the renovated property on a quiet
street a few blocks from downtown the lobby and the fair-size guest
rooms have old-style flair: richly appointed cherry-wood furniture and
a warm, cozy ambience. Some rooms have balconies, and almost all
have a unit that includes TV, VCR, minibar, and snacks. A selection
of videotapes is for rent in the lobby. Room rates include breakfast buffet. ⊠ *10010 104th St., T5J 0Z1,* ☎ *403/423–2450. 138 rooms.*

Restaurant, bar, no-smoking floors, indoor pool, sauna, exercise room. AE, DC, MC, V.

$$$ 🏨 **Inn on 7th.** Edmonton shorthand provides the name for this cheerful property on 107th Street. In the foliage-filled lobby stand Paul Bunyan–size easy chairs. Run by the Courtyard Inn chain, this hotel caters to tourists and government employees. Rooms are comfortably modern, and the location is convenient. ✉ *10001 107th St., T5J 1J1,* ☎ *403/429–2861 or 800/661–7327,* ℻ *403/426–7225. 180 rooms. Restaurant, bar, deli, no-smoking floors. AE, DC, MC, V.*

$$ 🏨 **West Harvest Inn.** This clean, modern three-story hotel catering to families is on the western edge of town, only five minutes from West Edmonton Mall. Rooms in the new wing are slightly larger and more expensive than those in the older wing, but all are comfortable. **Grainfield's** family restaurant is located on the premises. ✉ *17803 Stony Plain Rd. (Rte. 16), T5S 1B4,* ☎ *403/484–8000 or 800/661–6993,* ℻ *403/486–6060. 162 rooms. Restaurant, bar. AE, MC, V.*

$ 🏨 **Travelodge.** This budget chain operates two clean and functional motels in Edmonton: Travelodge West is on the edge of town, not far from West Edmonton Mall, while Travelodge South is on the road to the airport. ✉ *18320 Stony Plain Rd., T5S 1A7,* ☎ *403/483–6031 or 800/661–9563,* ℻ *403/484–2358. 227 rooms. 10320 45th Ave. S, T6H 5K3,* ☎ *403/436–9770. 222 rooms. Restaurant, bar, no-smoking rooms, indoor pool. AE, DC, MC, V.*

$ 🏨 **YMCA of Edmonton.** This Y has an outstanding location: in the heart of downtown adjacent to Edmonton Centre shopping mall. Rooms are small and spare but carpeted and cheerfully furnished. Singles and couples are invited to stay for $30 to $50 a night; families are accommodated as well. All the Y's facilities are available to overnight guests. ✉ *10030 102A Ave., T5J 0G5,* ☎ *403/421–9622,* ℻ *403/428–9469. 113 rooms, 30 with bath. Cafeteria, indoor pool, health club, jogging, racquetball. MC, V.*

Nightlife and the Arts

Tickets for events in Edmonton are available from TicketMaster (☎ 403/451–8000) at various locations, as well as at Champions in West Edmonton Mall and at Sears stores.

The Arts

FILM

Edmonton's **Metro Cinema** (✉ NFB Theatre, Canada Place, ✉ 9700 Jasper Ave., ☎ 403/425–9212) presents classics, imports, and brave new films on weekend nights. The **Edmonton Film Society** screens an ambitious program at a theater in the **Provincial Museum of Alberta** (✉ 12845 102nd Ave., ☎ 403/453–9100). The **Princess Theatre** (✉ 10337 Whyte Ave., ☎ 403/433–5785), an old-time movie house in the Old Strathcona district, presents revivals, experiments, and foreign films.

MUSIC AND DANCE

The **Edmonton Opera** (☎ 403/424–4040), **Edmonton Symphony Orchestra** (☎ 403/428–1414), and **Alberta Ballet Company** (☎ 403/428–6839) all perform in the **Northern Alberta Jubilee Auditorium** (✉ 87th Ave. and 114th St., ☎ 403/427–9622) at the University of Alberta.

THEATER

Edmonton has 13 professional theater companies. The paramount facility is the glass-clad downtown **Citadel Theatre Complex** (✉ 99th St. and 101A Ave., ☎ 403/425–1820), where four theaters mingle esoteric works and classics. **Northern Light Theater** (✉ Kaasa Theatre, Jubilee Auditorium, 87th Ave. and 114th St., ☎ 403/471–1586) takes chances on avant-garde productions that usually succeed.

Nightlife

BARS AND CLUBS
The **Rose & Crown** English-style pub in the Edmonton Hilton (✉ 10235 101st St., ☎ 403/428–7111) is a popular downtown gathering place with dart boards and a huge selection of beers. **Elephant & Castle Pubs** are pleasant watering holes in downtown Edmonton's Eaton Centre (☎ 403/424–4555) and the West Edmonton Mall (☎ 403/444–3555).

CASINOS
Roulette, blackjack, and wheel of fortune action usually takes place in Edmonton between noon and midnight daily except Sunday at the **Casino ABS Downtown** (✉ 10549 102 St., ☎ 403/424–9461). For games of chance you can also go to **Casino ABS South** (✉ 7055 Argyll Rd., ☎ 403/466–0199). The **Palace Casino** at the West Edmonton Mall (☎ 403/444–2112) offers shoppers another way to part with their money.

COMEDY
Edmonton has a branch of **Yuk Yuk's,** Canada's comedy chain, at West Edmonton Mall (☎ 403/481–9857).

MUSIC
The **Sidetrack Cafe** (✉ 10333 112th St., ☎ 403/421–1326) has top-name entertainers, big-screen telecasts of sports events, Variety Night on Sunday, and the Monday-night Comedy Bowl. **Yardbird Suite** (✉ 10203 86th Ave., ☎ 403/432–0428) is Edmonton's premiere jazz showcase. **Club Malibu** (✉ 10310 85th Ave., ☎ 403/432–7300) blasts out Top 40 hits in a converted armory. **Thunderdome** (✉ 9920 63rd Ave., ☎ 403/433–3661) has classic rock. **Cook County Saloon** (✉ 8010 103rd St., ☎ 403/432–2665) has a mellow honky-tonk ambience and country-and-western music.

Outdoor Activities and Sports

Participant Sports

BICYCLING AND JOGGING
The North Saskatchewan River valley is the longest stretch of urban parkland in Canada. For information about jogging and cycling trails call the **River Valley Outdoor Centre** (✉ 10125 97th Ave., ☎ 403/496–7275).

HEALTH AND FITNESS CLUBS
The **Kinsmen Sports Centre** (✉ 9100 Walterdale Rd., ☎ 403/496–7300) and **Mill Woods Recreation Centre** (✉ 7207 28th Ave., ☎ 403/496–2929) have swimming pools and a variety of facilities for the entire family.

Spectator Sports

AUTO RACING
Capital Raceway (✉ Rte. 19, 2 km west of Hwy. 2S, on way to Devon, ☎ 403/462–8901), a multi-use motor-sport complex, has events most weekends from May to October.

HOCKEY
The **Edmonton Oilers** play National Hockey League hockey October—April at the **Edmonton Coliseum** (✉ 118th Ave. and 74th St., ☎ 403/471–2191 or 403/451–8000).

HORSE RACING
Northlands Park (✉ 112th Ave. and 74th St., ☎ 403/471–7379) hosts harness racing from early March to mid-May and from mid-Septem-

ber through December. Thoroughbred racing occupies the summer months, mid-May through early September.

Shopping

In the heart of **downtown,** between 100th and 103rd streets, is a complex of shopping centers—Eaton Centre (⌧ 102nd Ave.), ManuLife Place (⌧ 102nd Ave.), and Edmonton Centre (⌧ 100th St.)—and department stores (the Bay, Eaton's) connected by tunnels or second-level pedways. **West Edmonton Mall** (⌧ 87th Ave. and 170th St.) has 800 retail establishments, including such department stores as Sears, the Bay, Eaton's, Zeller's, and Canadian Tire (☞ Greater Edmonton, *above*). **Old Strathcona Historic Area** (⌧ Whyte [82nd] Ave. and 104th St.) has restaurants and enticing boutiques. **High Street/124th Street** (⌧ along 124th and 125th Sts. between 102nd and 109th Aves.) is an outdoor shopping area full of boutiques, bistros, bookstores, and galleries.

Side Trips

Numbers in the margin correpond to places of interest on the Alberta map.

Red Deer

26 *149 km (92 mi) south of Edmonton, 145 km (90 mi) north of Calgary.*

Red Deer, midway between Calgary and Edmonton on Highway 2, is on the Red Deer River. Along the riverbank winds **Waskasoo Park,** with nearly 30 miles of pedestrian and bike paths, equestrian trails, and canoeing and fishing. At the **Red Deer and District Museum,** you can see a pioneer home and other historic items. ⌧ 4525 47A Ave., ☎ 403/343–6844. 🖾 *Donation.* ☿ *Weekdays noon–5 and 7–9, weekends 1–5.*

Elk Island National Park

48 km (30 mi) east of Edmonton on Rte. 16.

Elk Island National Park, probably Canada's least-known national park, was established in 1906 as the country's first federal wildlife sanctuary for large mammals. It covers 194 square kilometers (75 square miles) and is dedicated to protecting the environment. A herd of 850 plains and 350 wood bison roam the park, as well as elk, moose, whitetail deer and more than 240 species of birds, including herons. There are an interpretive center, a nine-hole golf course, a lake, and 80 campsites. ⌧ *Rte. 16,* ☎ *403/922–5790 or 403/992–6380.* ☿ *Daily.*

The **Ukrainian Cultural Heritage Village** consists of 34 historic buildings from around the province that have been assembled to typify the lifestyle of a pre-1930s village of Ukrainian settlers. Guides in period dress interpret the displays. ⌧ *Rte. 16, 3km (2 mi) east of Elk Island National Park,* ☎ *403/662–3640.* 🖾 *$6.50.* ☿ *Mid-May–Labor Day, daily 10–6.*

Vegreville

27 *101 km (63 mi) east of Edmonton on Rte. 16.*

Vegreville is the center of eastern Alberta's Ukrainian culture and home of the "world's largest Easter egg" (*pysanka*), measuring 30 feet high, at the east end of the town's main street. Colorfully decorated, it consists of more than 3,500 pieces of aluminum. A Ukrainian festival takes place here annually the first weekend in July. ⌧ *Rte. 16., 101 km (62 mi) east of Edmonton.*

Edmonton A to Z

Arriving and Departing

BY CAR

Edmonton is situated on the Yellowhead Highway (Highway 16), which runs from Winnipeg through the central parts of Saskatchewan and Alberta. This highway is four lanes and divided through most of Alberta and intersects with the four-lane divided Highway 2, which runs south to Calgary.

BY PLANE

Most international flights and long-haul domestic flights use **Edmonton International Airport.** Along with the major Canadian airlines (Air Canada, Canadian Airlines International, Air BC, NWT Air), Edmonton is served by American, Delta, and Northwest.

Between the Airport and Downtown. Taxi rides from Edmonton International cost approximately $28 to city center, but **The Grey Goose Airporter** (☎ 403/463–7520) provides frequent service between the airport and major downtown hotels. Fare is $11 one way, $18 round-trip.

Getting Around

BY BUS AND LRT

Edmonton Transit (☎ 403/496–1611) operates a comprehensive system of buses throughout the area and a light rail transit (LRT) line from downtown to the northeast side of the city. The fare is $1.65; transfers are free. Buses operate from 5:30 AM to 2 AM. The LRT is free in the downtown area (between Churchill and Grandin stations) weekdays 9–3 and Saturday 9–6. The **Downtown Information Centre** above Central LRT Station (⊠ 100A St. and Jasper Ave.) provides free information, timetables, and maps, weekdays 9–5.

BY TAXI

Taxis tend to be costly: $2 for the first 105 meters, and 10¢ for each additional 105 meters. Cabs may be hailed on the street, but phoning is recommended. Call **Alberta Co-op Taxi** (☎ 403/425–8310), **Checker** (☎ 403/455–2211), or **Yellow** (☎ 403/462–3456).

Contacts and Resources

DENTISTS

For 24-hour dental care, contact **Denta Care** (⊠ 472 Southgate Shopping Centre, 111th St. and 51st Ave., ☎ 403/434–9566).

EMERGENCIES

Dial 911 for police, fire, ambulance, and poison center.

GUIDED TOURS

From early May to early October three **Royal Tours** (☎ 403/488–9090) itineraries hit the high points of Edmonton. **Klondike Jet Boats** (☎ 403/486–0896) ply the North Saskatchewan River, May–October.

HOSPITALS

Emergency rooms are at the **Royal Alexandra Hospital** (⊠ 10240 Kingsway Ave., ☎ 403/477–4111) and **University of Alberta Hospitals** (⊠ 8440 112th St., ☎ 403/492–8822).

LATE-NIGHT PHARMACIES

Mid-Niter Drugs (⊠ 11408 Jasper Ave., ☎ 403/482–1171) is open until midnight. **Shoppers Drug Mart** (⊠ 8210 109 St., ☎ 403/433–3121) is open 24 hours.

Edmonton Tourism Information Centres are at Gateway Park (✉ Hwy. 2, ☎ 403/496–8400 or 800/463–4667) and City Hall. Other offices are open around Edmonton; for locations and times call the above number.

REGINA

Regina, Saskatchewan, was originally dubbed Pile O'Bones, in reference to the remnants left by years of buffalo hunting by Indians and later European hunters, but it was renamed after the Latin title of Queen Victoria, the reigning monarch in 1883. It was at this time that the railroad arrived and the city became the capital of the Northwest Territories. The Mounties made it their headquarters. When the province of Saskatchewan was formed in 1905, Regina was chosen as its capital. At the beginning of the 20th century, immigrants from the British Isles, Eastern Europe, and East Asia rushed in to claim parcels of riverfed prairie land for $1 per lot. Oil and potash were discovered in the 1950s and 1960s, and Regina became a major agricultural and industrial distribution center as well as the head office of the world's largest grain-handling cooperative.

The centerpiece of this city of 185,000 is Wascana Centre, created by expanding meager Wascana Creek into the broad Wascana Lake and surrounding it with 2,000 acres of parkland. This unique multipurpose site contains the city's major museums, the Saskatchewan legislature, the University of Regina campus, and all the amenities of a big-city park and natural-habitat waterfowl sanctuary.

Downtown Regina

Streets in Regina run north–south; avenues, east–west. The most important north–south artery is Albert Street (Route 6); Victoria Avenue is the main east–west thoroughfare. The Trans-Canada Highway (Highway 1) bypasses the city to the south and east.

Numbers in the text and margin below correspond to numbers on the Regina map.

A Good Drive

Begin at the northwest corner of Wascana Centre, at the **Royal Saskatchewan Museum** ㉘ and check out the Earth Sciences Gallery and the First Nations Gallery. Continue south on Albert Street past **Speakers Corner,** where, as in London's Hyde Park, free speech is volubly expressed. Turn left on Legislative Drive to the **Legislative Building** ㉙, for a tour of its marble interior. Take Saskatchewan Road (west on Legislature) south to the **MacKenzie Art Gallery** ㉚, which displays European and Canadian art. Continuing along Saskatchewan Road, turn north on Avenue G and then east on Lakeshore Drive to the **Wascana Waterfowl Park Display Ponds** ㉛ to see the many breeds of migratory birds that stop here. Return to Broad Street (Wascana Parkway), cross the bridge to Wascana Drive, and head toward Winnipeg Street and the **Saskatchewan Science Centre** ㉜ for hands-on exhibits demonstrating various scientific phenomena. Next, take a car or bike to Broad Street and follow it north to Dewdney Avenue, then head west to **Government House** ㉝, once the residence of Saskatchewan's lieutenant governors. Continue west on Dewdney Avenue to the **Royal Canadian Mounted Police Training Academy** ㉞, the Mounties' national training center.

Saskatchewan

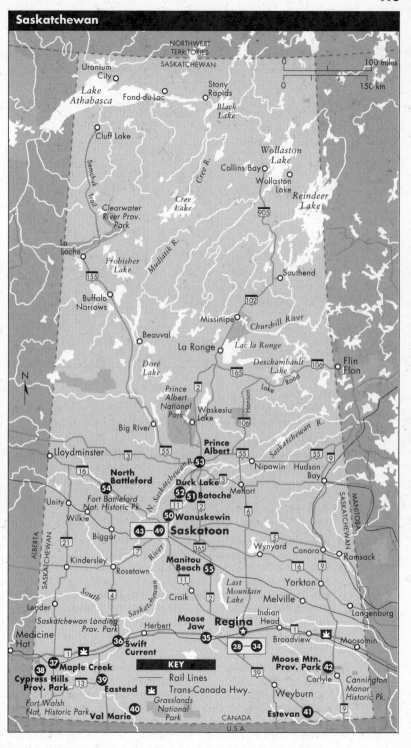

NORTHWEST TERRITORIES
SASKATCHEWAN

100 miles
150 km

Uranium City
Lake Athabasca
Fond-du-Lac
Stony Rapids
Black Lake
Cluff Lake
Wollaston Lake
Collins Bay
Wollaston Lake
Reindeer Lake
Cree R.
905
Semchuk Trail
Clearwater River Prov. Park
Cree Lake
La Loche
155
Frobisher Lake
Mudiatik R.
Southend
102
Buffalo Narrows
Missinipe
Churchill River
Beauval
La Ronge
Lac la Ronge
Flin Flon
Doré Lake
165
Deschambault Lake
106
2
Hanson Lake Road
Prince Albert National Park
Waskesiu Lake
106
Big River
N
Prince Albert
Saskatchewan R.
Lloydminster
3
55
53
55
55
9
North Battleford
54
N. Saskatchewan R.
Duck Lake
52 51 Batoche
Nipawin
Hudson Bay
Unity
Fort Battleford Nat. Historic Pk.
11
Melfort
2
MANITOBA SASKATCHEWAN
Wilkie
50 Wanuskewin
6
Biggar
43 49 Saskatoon
ALBERTA SASKATCHEWAN
21
Kindersley
7
365
5
Wynyard
Canora
Kamsack
Rosetown
4
Manitou Beach
55
11
16
9
Leader
South
Saskatchewan
Craik
2
Last Mountain Lake
Yorkton
Medicine Hat
Saskatchewan Landing Prov. Park
Herbert
Moose Jaw
Regina
Melville
Langenburg
36
Swift Current
35
Indian Head
1
Broadview
Moosomin
1
28 34
37
Maple Creek
Moose Mtn. Prov. Park
42
38
39
39
Carlyle
Cannington Manor Historic Pk.
Cypress Hills Prov. Park
13
Eastend
Grasslands National Park
Weyburn
9
Fort Walsh Nat. Historic Park
40 Val Marie
CANADA
Estevan 41
U.S.A.

KEY

—— Rail Lines

Trans-Canada Hwy.

196

Government House, **33**

Legislative Building, **29**

Mackenzie Art Gallery, **30**

Royal Canadian Mounted Police Academy, **34**

Royal Saskatchewan Museum, **28**

Saskatchewan Science Centre, **32**

Wascana Waterfowl Park Display Ponds, **31**

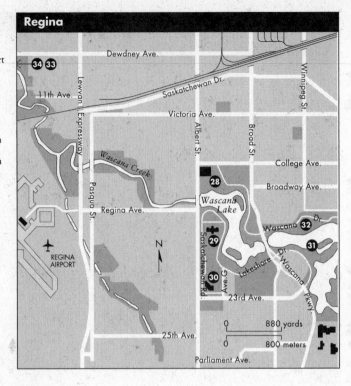

Regina

TIMING

While the tour will take most of the day, time your visit to catch the RCMP training academy's daily drill parade at 1 PM.

Sights to See

33 **Government House.** Between 1891 and 1945 this was the lavish home of Saskatchewan's lieutenant governors. It has been restored with period furnishings and mementos of the governors and their families. ⊠ 4607 Dewdney Ave., ☎ 306/787–5726. ☞ Free. ☉ Oct.–Mar., Tues.–Fri. 1–4, Sun. 1–5; Apr.–June and Sept., Tues.–Sat. 1–4, Sun. 1–5; July and Aug., Tues.–Fri. 1–4, Sun. 1–5.

29 **Legislative Building.** Dominating the skyline in the provincial capital is the dome of this quasi-Versailles–style structure. "The Ledge" was built in 1908–12, with Tyndall stone from Manitoba on the exterior and 34 types of marble from all over the world in the interior. As you tour the Legislative Assembly Chamber, note the huge picture of Queen Elizabeth—a reminder that Canada retains a technical allegiance to the monarchy. Free tours leave on the half hour. ⊠ Legislature Dr., ☎ 306/787–5357. ☞ Free. ☉ Victoria Day–Labor Day, daily 8–9; winter, daily 8–5.

30 **MacKenzie Art Gallery.** Here you will find 19th- and 20th-century European art and Canadian historical and contemporary works, with a special emphasis on western Canadian art. The popular Prairie Artists Series allows emerging Saskatchewan artists to display recent work. For three nights a week in August, a stage becomes the courtroom setting for The Trial of Louis Riel. Riel led rebellions of the Métis against the new Canadian government in the 1870s and 1880s and was tried in Regina (and ultimately hanged) for treason. ⊠ 3475 Albert St., ☎ 306/522–4242. ☞ Free. ☉ Fri.–Tues. 11–6, Wed. and Thurs. 11–10.

③④ Royal Canadian Mounted Police Training Academy. This is the Mounties' only training center. Visitors can tour the grounds and the non-denominational RCMP Chapel, a converted cookhouse originally built in 1883 and considered Regina's oldest building. In July and August, the spectacular Sunset Retreat Ceremony takes place Tuesday evening; try to arrive by 6:30. On the grounds is the **Centennial Museum,** which has exhibits and mementos of the Mounties (originally the North West Mounted Police). The order's proud history is revealed by weaponry, uniforms, photos, and oddities, such as Sitting Bull's rifle case and tobacco pouch. ⊠ *11th Ave. W,* ☎ *306/780–5838.* ☞ *Free.* ☉ *June–mid-Sept., daily 8–6:45; mid-Sept.–May, daily 10–4:45.*

② ② Royal Saskatchewan Museum. Here a time line traces local history from before the dinosaur era to today. The Earth Sciences Gallery depicts 2 billion years of Saskatchewan geological history, while the First Nations Gallery highlights aspects of native life and history. The museum is home to Canada's first animated dinosaur, "Megamunch." ⊠ *College Ave. and Albert St.,* ☎ *306/787–2815.* ☞ *Free.* ☉ *May–Sept. 2, daily 9–8:30; Sept. 3–Apr., daily 9–4:30.*

② ③② Saskatchewan Science Centre. Housed in the refurbished City of Regina powerhouse, now called the Powerhouse of Discovery, the museum has hands-on exhibits that encourage visitors to build bubbles, juggle hot-air balloons, make voice prints, and take apart models of human bodies. Demonstrations of biological, geological, and astronomical phenomena begin on the hour. The Kramer IMAX Theatre shows breathtaking films several times daily on a five-story screen. ⊠ *Science center, Winnipeg St. and Wascana Dr.,* ☎ *306/352–5811; IMAX, 306/522–4629.* ☞ *$5.50.* ☉ *May and June, Mon.–Thurs. 9–6, Fri. 9–8, Sat. 10–8, Sun. 10–6; July and Aug., daily 10–8; Sept.–Apr., Tues.–Fri. 9–4, Sat. noon–8, Sun. noon–6. Closed holidays.*

③① Wascana Waterfowl Park Display Ponds. The serenity and beauty of the park attract nature lovers. A boardwalk constructed over a marsh is accompanied by display panels that help identify the more than 60 breeds of migrating waterfowl found here. ⊠ *Lakeshore Dr.,* ☎ *306/522–3661.* ☞ *Free.* ☉ *Daily 9–9.* ☉ *Guided tours (if there is a group) June–Sept., daily 3.*

Dining and Lodging

$$$$ ✕ **The Diplomat.** Downtown in an old brick building, one of Regina's most elegant restaurants is an upscale, traditional steak house. The decor suggests the Victorian era, with paintings of Canada's prime ministers on the walls and dusty-rose cloths and candles on the tables. It offers an extensive selection of seafood and steaks and an outstanding rack of lamb, as well as a high-quality wine list. ⊠ *2302 Broad St.,* ☎ *306/359–3366. Reservations essential. AE, D, MC, V.*

$$ ✕ **Bartleby's.** This good-time downtown "dining emporium and gathering place" is a veritable museum of Western memorabilia, musical instruments, and old-time carnival games. Victorian lampshades and heavy leather armchairs further convey the whimsical tone. Karaoke music at night adds a bit of fun. The menu runs to big sandwiches and western beef, especially prime rib. ⊠ *1920 Broad St.,* ☎ *306/565–0040. Reservations essential. AE, DC, MC, V.*

$$ ✕ **C.C. Lloyd's.** Locals esteem the fine service and casual elegance of the dining room in the downtown Chelton Inn. The decor evokes the atmosphere of Manhattan circa 1930, and the menu features such international classics as rack of lamb, chicken en croûte dijonnaise (in a mustard crust), fillet of beef Madeira, shrimp Provençal, and a variety of tasty steaks. ⊠ *1907 11th Ave.,* ☎ *306/569–4650. Reservations essential. AE, MC, V.*

$ ✕ **Brewsters.** The copper kettle and shiny fermentation tanks are proudly prominent in Saskatchewan's first brew pub. This full-mash brewery has 11 in-house concoctions on tap, as well as a large selection of imports and domestic beers, wine, and spirits. The menu consists of pub snacks and full meals. ⊠ *Victoria East Plaza, 1832 Victoria Ave. E,* ☎ *306/761–1500. Reservations not accepted. AE, MC, V.*

$ ✕ **Simply Delicious.** Everything is homemade in this small country-style café. Offerings include cinnamon buns, fresh pies, chicken noodle and vegetable soups, several salads, and specialty coffees. ⊠ *826 Victoria Ave.,* ☎ *306/352–4929. Reservations not accepted. No credit cards.*

$$$ ⊡ **Hotel Saskatchewan Radisson Plaza.** This one-time railway hotel built in 1927 has been restored. Rooms are decorated in an early 1930s style, with lots of wood and lace curtains. Every afternoon in the Victoria Room high tea is served, and fine dining is offered every evening in the Cortlandt Hall Dining Room. For a light lunch or evening cocktails visit the cozy and casually elegant Monarch Lounge. ⊠ *2125 Victoria Ave., S4P 0S3,* ☎ *306/522–7691 or 800/333–3333,* FAX *306/757–5521. 215 rooms. 2 restaurants, bar, no-smoking rooms, health club. AE, DC, MC, V.*

$$$ ⊡ **Ramada Hotel.** The tallest building in Saskatchewan, Regina's newest and most luxurious hotel rises 25 stories over the city and is attached to the Saskatchewan Trade & Convention Centre. Rooms are furnished in subtle pastels and have modern amenities. The pool has a three-story water slide, and there's a Tourism Saskatchewan information center in the lobby. ⊠ *1919 Saskatchewan Dr., S4P 4H2,* ☎ *306/525–5255 or 800/268–8998,* FAX *306/781–7188. 255 rooms. 2 restaurants, bar, no-smoking rooms, indoor pool. AE, DC, MC, V.*

$$$ ⊡ **Regina Inn.** A plant-filled lobby welcomes you into this modern downtown hotel, where all the guest rooms—decorated with blues, grays, and browns—have balconies overlooking either Broad or Victoria street. On the ground floor is the Lauderdale Bar and Grill, the local hot spot. ⊠ *1975 Broad St., at Victoria Ave., S4P 1Y2,* ☎ *306/525–6767 or 800/667–8162,* FAX *306/352–1858. 237 rooms. 2 restaurants, bar, 2 outdoor hot tubs, exercise room, nightclub, indoor parking. AE, DC, MC, V.*

$$$ ⊡ **Regina Travelodge Hotel.** The hotel's convenient location, on Regina's main thoroughfare and close to downtown, is the biggest draw for its guests. The other feature is the well-known water-slide complex on the property. In the evenings the pub, the Blarney Stone, is a cheerful place to grab a beer or soda. ⊠ *4177 Albert St., S4S 3R6,* ☎ *306/586–3443 or 800/255–3050,* FAX *306/586–9311. 200 rooms. Restaurant, pub, indoor pool, hot tub. AE, DC, MC, V.*

$$$ ⊡ **Sands Hotel and Resort.** This modern downtown property has a dra-
★   matic multilevel, sun-filled lobby enhanced by abundant foliage and a charming waterfall. A second-floor oasis is the perfect setting for such water-theme pastimes as a soothing soak in the whirlpool or, for the children, a dip in either the kiddie or the standard pool. The modern rooms are airy and furnished in light colors and dusty-rose tones. ⊠ *1818 Victoria Ave., S4P 0R1,* ☎ *306/569–1666 or 800/268–1133,* FAX *306/525–3550. 251 rooms. 2 restaurants, bar, pub, indoor pool, sauna, free parking. AE, DC, MC, V.*

$$ ⊡ **Chelton Inn.** This older hotel in the heart of downtown is one of Regina's biggest bargains. Its modernized rooms are downright huge. Contemporary, light-wood furnishings match the earth tones that are used in the draperies and upholstery. Service is particularly friendly. The cuisine in C.C. Lloyd's (☞ *Dining, above*) is among the best in

town. ⊠ *1907 11th Ave., S4P 0J2,* ☎ *306/569–4600 or 800/667–
9922,* FAX *306/569–3531. 56 rooms. Restaurant, bar, coffee shop. AE,
DC, MC, V.*

$$ 🏨 **Landmark Inn.** Three stories high, on the south side of town, it has
★ a unique indoor-outdoor water slide. Rooms, in pastel greens and
white, are large, light, and airy, with modern furnishings. ⊠ *4150 Al-
bert St. (Rte. 6), S4S 3R8,* ☎ *306/586–5363; in Saskatchewan,
800/667–9811; elsewhere in Canada, 800/667–8191;* FAX *306/586–
0901. 188 rooms. Restaurant, bar, no-smoking rooms, indoor pool,
sauna. AE, DC, MC, V.*

$ 🏨 **West Harvest Inn.** Rebuilt and refurbished in 1995, this five-story
★ brick 1960s-vintage hotel is dependable. The average-size rooms have
low-key beige-patterned drapes and spreads and modern, dark-cherry
furniture. ⊠ *4025 Albert St. (Rte. 6), S4S 3R6,* ☎ *306/586–6755 or
800/667–3529,* FAX *306/584–1345. 105 rooms. Restaurant, bar, 2 hot
tubs, sauna, exercise room. AE, DC, MC, V.*

Nightlife and the Arts

The Arts

MUSIC AND DANCE

The Saskatchewan Centre (⊠ Wascana Centre, 200 Lakeshore Dr., ☎
306/565–0404) is the venue for the **Regina Symphony** (Canada's
longest-running symphony orchestra), pop concerts, dance perfor-
mances, and Broadway musicals and plays.

THEATER

On a theater-in-the-round stage inside the old Regina City Hall, the
Globe Theatre (⊠ 1801 Scarth St., ☎ 306/525–9553) offers classic
and contemporary Saskatchewan works from October to April. **Regina
Little Theatre** (⊠ Regina Performing Arts Centre, 1077 Angus St.,
☎ 306/352–5535 or 306/543–7292) presents lighthearted original
productions.

Nightlife

BARS AND CLUBS

Caper's, in the Ramada Hotel (⊠ 1919 Saskatchewan Dr., ☎ 306/525–
5255), is where local movers and shakers mingle with visitors from the
convention center next door.

CASINO

The city's newest marquee attraction, the posh **Casino Regina** (⊠ 1880
Saskatchewan Dr., ☎ 800/555–3189) in the extensively refurbished
former Union Station railroad passenger terminal, has slot machines
and table games such as blackjack, roulette, and baccarat.

MUSIC

The Pump (⊠ 641 Victoria Ave. E, ☎ 306/522–0977) features Cana-
dian and American country-and-western bands. **Delbert's** (⊠ 1433
Hamilton St., ☎ 306/757–7625) is known for high-energy rock and
roll. **Longbranch Saloon** (⊠ 1400 McIntyre St., ☎ 306/525–8336) spe-
cializes in country-and-western music.

Outdoor Activities and Sports

Participant Sports

BICYCLING AND JOGGING

Wascana Place (⊠ 2900 Wascana Dr., ☎ 306/522–3661) provides maps
of the many jogging, biking, and hiking trails in Wascana Centre. The
Devonian Pathway—8 kilometers (about 5 miles) of paved trails that
follow Wascana Creek and pass through six city parks—is a favorite
of walkers, joggers, and cyclists.

HEALTH AND FITNESS CLUBS

The **Regina Sportplex & Lawson Aquatic Centre** (⊠ 1717 Elphinstone St., ☎ 306/777–7156 or 306/777–7323) encompasses a pool and diving well, a 200-meter track, tennis and badminton courts, weight rooms, a sauna, a whirlpool, and drop-in aerobic and aqua exercise sessions.

Spectator Sports

CURLING

Check out this incredibly popular local sport at the **Caledonian Curling Club** (⊠ 2225 Empress Rd., near airport, ☎ 306/525–8171).

FOOTBALL

The **Saskatchewan Roughriders** (☎ 306/525–2181) of the Canadian Football League play their home games at Taylor Field.

HOCKEY

The **Regina Pats** play other Western Hockey League (minor league) teams in the Agridome (⊠ Exhibition Park, Lewvan Expressway and 11th Ave., Regina, ☎ 306/522–5604).

HORSE RACING

Queensbury Downs Raceway (⊠ Exhibition Park, Lewvan Expressway and 11th Ave., Regina, ☎ 306/781–9310) hosts Standardbred racing in summer and televised racing year-round.

Shopping

Art and Antiques

The **Strathdee Shoppes** (⊠ Dewdney Ave. and Cornwall St.) consist of arts, crafts, antiques, and specialty stores—plus a food court. The **Antique Mall** (⊠ 1175 Rose St., ☎ 306/525–9688) encompasses 28 antiques, art, and collectibles sellers. **Patchworks** (⊠ 3026 13th Ave., ☎ 306/522–0664), features arts and crafts. **Sarah's Corner** (⊠ 1853 Hamilton St., ☎ 306/565–2200), has craft and artwork. **Affinity's Antiques** (⊠ 1178 Albert St., ☎ 306/757–4265) sells vintage collectibles.

Malls

Cornwall Centre (⊠ 11th Ave. and Saskatchewan Dr.), downtown, is an indoor mall with more than 100 shops, including Eaton's and Sears. Indoor passages connect to the **Galleria** (⊠ 11th Ave. and Saskatchewan Dr.), an indoor mall with more than 50 stores. **Victoria Square Mall** (⊠ 223 Victoria Ave. E) has some 30 stores. **Northgate Mall** (⊠ Albert St. N and 9th Ave. N) has more than 80 stores. **Southland Mall** (⊠ Albert St. S and Gordon Rd.) has more than 80 stores. **Golden Mile Centre** (⊠ 3806 Albert. St.) has about 60 stores.

Side Trips

Numbers in the margin correspond to places of interest on the Saskatchewan map.

Moose Jaw
③⑤ *71 km (44 mi) west of Regina.*

Saskatchewan's third-largest city, Moose Jaw is a prosperous railroad and industrial center, renowned as a wide-open Roaring-'20s haven for American gangsters. It is said that Al Capone visited here from Chicago. Today, Moose Jaw's most prominent citizen stands right on the Trans-Canada Highway: Mac the Moose, an immense sculpture that greets travelers from beside the **visitor information center** (⊠ Hwy. 1 east of Hwy. 2, ☎ 306/692–6414).

The **Western Development Museum** (✉ 50 Diefenbaker Dr., ☎ 306/693–6556), which focuses on air, land, water, and rail transportation, houses the Snowbirds Gallery, filled with memorabilia, including vintage airplanes, of Canada's air demonstration team, the Snowbirds, who are stationed at the nearby Armed Forces base. **The Moose Jaw Art Museum** (✉ Crescent Park, Athabasca St. and Langdon Crescent, ☎ 306/692–4471) displays Indian art and small farm implements. While you're here, pick up *A Walking Tour of Downtown Moose Jaw* ($1.50), a guide to the city's notable and notorious landmarks. As you drive around, notice the historical murals on the walls of many downtown buildings.

At the offbeat **Pioneer Village and Museum,** 13 kilometers (8 miles) south of Moose Jaw on Highway 2, in addition to a series of old buildings and cars, you can see the *Sukanen,* a large, unfinished ship made by a Finnish settler between 1928 and 1941 and patterned after a 17th-century Finnish fishing vessel. ✉ *Hwy. 2,* ☎ *306/693–7315.* *$2.50.* ⏲ *June–Sept., daily 9–5.*

Swift Current

㊱ *174 km (108 mi) west of Regina on the Trans-Canada Highway.*

West of Regina, the square townships and straight roads of the grain-belt prairie farms gradually give way to the arid rolling hills of the upland plains ranches. The highway skirts the edge of the Missouri Coteau—glacial hills that divide the prairie from the dry western plain—on its way west to Swift Current (population 16,000). The town cultivates its Western image during Frontier Days Regional Fair and Rodeo (☞ Festivals and Seasonal Events *in* Chapter 1). Further depicting Swift Current are the exhibits at the **Swift Current Museum,** where pioneer and Indian artifacts and exhibits of local natural history are displayed. ✉ *105 Chaplin St.,* ☎ *306/778–2775.* *Free.* ⏲ *May–Aug., weekdays 1:30–4:30 and 7–9, weekends 1:30–4:30; Sept.–Apr., weekdays 1:30–4:30.*

A 50-kilometer (31-mile) drive north from Swift Current on Highway 4 will bring you to **Saskatchewan Landing Provincial Park.** The 54-square-kilometer (21-square-mile) natural preserve lies at the point where Indians and pioneers forded the South Saskatchewan River en route to northern Saskatchewan. It has campsites, picnic facilities, and an interpretive center. ✉ *Rte. 4,* ☎ *306/375–2434.* *$6 per day per car; camping mid-Sept.–mid-May, $8 with electricity, $7 without electricity; mid-May–mid-Sept., $14 with electricity, $12 without electricity.* ⏲ *Daily.*

DINING AND LODGING

$$ ✕ **Wong's Kitchen.** This longtime Swift Current favorite serves fine Canadian food and an even better Oriental menu: Dry garlic ribs are the star attraction. Count on live entertainment nightly. ✉ *Hwy. 1, S. Service Rd.,* ☎ *306/773–6244. Reservations essential. AE, MC, V.*

$ **Horseshoe Lodge.** It's conveniently situated along the Trans-Canada Highway service road, yet the rooms still have fine views of the surrounding countryside. The cocktail lounge is a popular meeting spot, and the restaurant offers solid Canadian cooking. ✉ *Mobile Rte. 35, S9H 3X6,* ☎ *306/773–4643,* FAX *306/773–0309. 49 rooms. 2 restaurants, bar, outdoor pool. AE, DC, MC, V.*

Maple Creek

㊲ *128 km (80 mi) west of Swift Current just south of the Trans-Canada Highway on Route 21.*

The highway skirts the southern edge of the Great Sand Hills. These desertlike remnants of a huge glacial lake now abound with such native wildlife as pronghorn, mule deer, coyote, jackrabbit, and kangaroo rats. Maple Creek, a self-styled "old cow town," has a number of preserved Old West storefronts. Saskatchewan's oldest museum, the **Old Timer's Museum,** displays pictures and artifacts of Mounties, early ranchers, and Indians. ⊠ *218 Jasper St.,* ☎ *306/662–2474.* ☞ *$2.* ☉ *June–Sept., daily 9–5; Oct., Apr., and May, weekdays 1–4.*

Cypress Hills Provincial Park

38 *27 kilometers (17 miles) south of Maple Creek on Route 21.*

Cypress Hills Provincial Park consists of two sections, a Centre Block and a West Block, which are about 25 kilometers (16 miles) apart and separated by nonpark land. The larger West Block abuts the border with Alberta and is connected to Alberta's Cypress Hills Provincial Park. Within the Centre Block, the Cypress Hills plateau, rising more than 4,000 feet above sea level, is covered with spruce, aspen, and lodgepole pines erroneously identified as cypress by early European explorers. From Lookout Point you have an 80-kilometer (50-mile) view of Maple Creek and the hills beyond. In addition to the wildlife and flora that abound in the park, there is Cypress Four Seasons Resort (☞ Dining and Lodging, *below*). Maps are available at the Administrative Building near the park entrance. ⊠ *Cypress Hills Provincial Park, Rte. 21,* ☎ *306/662–4411.* ☞ *$6 per day per car.* ☉ *Daily.*

A rough gravel road connects the Cypress Hills Centre Block plateau with the West Block plateau. During wet weather, take Route 21 north to Maple Creek and Route 271 southwest to the West Block. Here, you'll find **Fort Walsh National Historic Park.** The original fort was built by the Mounties in 1875 to establish order between the "wolfers" (whiskey traders) and the Assiniboine Indians. Fort Walsh remained the center of local commerce until its abandonment in 1883. Today, free bus service links the Visitor Reception Centre and the reconstructed fort itself, Farwell's Trading Post, and a picnic area. No private vehicles are permitted beyond the parking area. ⊠ *Ft. Walsh, Rte. 271, 55 km (34 mi) southwest of Maple Creek,* ☎ *306/662–2645.* ☞ *Free.* ☉ *Mid-May–mid-Oct., daily 9–5.*

DINING AND LODGING

$$ ⊞ **Cypress Four Seasons Resort.** This resort in the Centre Block of Cypress Hills Provincial Park is not part of the Four Seasons chain, but the rooms here are new, comfortable, modern, and right in the middle of a lodgepole-pine forest. Either pastels or earth tones adorn the contemporary rooms. The restaurant is a bright and woodsy place with picture windows that overlook the forest. The standard Canadian fare is more successful than the Chinese dishes on the menu. ⊠ *Box 1480, Maple Creek, S0N 1N0,* ☎ *306/662–4477,* FAX *306/662–3238. 31 rooms, 15 cabins, 10 condos. Restaurant, bar, indoor pool. MC, V.*

Eastend

39 *120 km (80 mi) east of Cypress Hills on Rte. 13.*

In the tiny town of Eastend in the Frenchman River valley, paleontologists in 1994 found one of only 12 *Tyrannosaurus rex* fossils unearthed thus far anywhere in the world. The fossil, believed to be 65 million years old, is one of a number of fossils that have been found in the area. You can visit a fully operational laboratory in Eastend (with a viewing area), the **Eastend Fossil Research Station** (⊠ 118 Maple Ave. S, ☎ 306/295–4009), where paleontologists are working on the T-rex fossil. There are also trips on which you can dig for fossils yourself; contact the **Eastend Tourism Authority** (☎ 306/295–4009).

Val Marie

40 *152 km (94 mi) south of Swift Current, 37 km (23 mi) north of U.S. border.*

Grasslands National Park is between Val Marie and Killdeer in southwestern Saskatchewan. The Frenchman River valley, part of which is within the Grasslands, was the first portion of mixed-grass prairie in North America to be set aside as a park, and is marked by strange land formations and badlands. Colonies of black-tailed prairie dogs are the most numerous of the many animal species found here. Interpretive and visitor services are limited. Tent camping is permitted, and electrical hookups are provided; all sites cost $10 per night. ⊠ *Box 150, S0N 2T0,* ☎ *306/298–2257.* ⊘ *Park office June–Aug., daily 8–6, and Sept.–May, weekdays 8–4:30; information center late May–early Sept., daily 8–6.*

Estevan

41 *205 kilometers (127 miles) southeast of Regina on Route 39.*

Estevan, within 16 kilometers (10 miles) of the U.S. border, has a rich history dating back to Prohibition days in the United States, when rum-running was popular here. In summer, the town hosts popular stage plays in an outdoor tent setting. For information, call **Estevan Tourism** (☎ 306/634–6044).

Moose Mountain Provincial Park

42 *139 km (86 mi) east of Weyburn, which is 115 km (71 mi) southeast of Regina via Routes 6 and 39.*

Moose Mountain Provincial Park is 401 square kilometers (155 square miles) of rolling poplar and birch forest that forms a natural refuge for moose and elk and a wide variety of birds. A 24-kilometer (15-mile) gravel road goes in to moose and elk grazing areas (best times: early morning and early evening). The park supplements wildlife experiences with beaches, golf, tennis, and riding horses. Of the 330 campsites, ⅓ have electric hookups. The Kenosee Inn (⊠ Kenosee Village, Saskatchewan S0C 2S0, ☎ 306/577–2099) is a 30-room accommodation on the park grounds. ⊠ *Rtes. 9 and 209,* ☎ *306/577–2131; camping reservations, 306/577–2144.* ⊠ *$6 per day per car; camping fees $14 per night with electricity; $12 without electricity.* ⊘ *Daily.*

Cannington Manor Historic Park, just south of Moose Mountain Provincial Park, preserves the 1880s lifestyle of this experimental Victorian settlement that attempted to re-create upper-class life in England and was abandoned after only 15 years when the railway bypassed the town. What remain to be seen are the original manor house, a church, shops, and a museum in the original schoolhouse. ⊠ *Rte. 603, 16 km (10 mi) northeast of Manor,* ☎ *306/787–9573.* ⊠ *Donations accepted.* ⊘ *Late May–early Sept., daily 10–6.*

Regina A to Z

Arriving and Departing

BY CAR
Regina stands at the crossroads of the Trans-Canada Highway (Highway 1) and Highway 11, which goes north to Saskatoon.

BY PLANE
Regina Airport, 8 kilometers (5 miles) southwest of downtown, is served by Air Canada, Canadian Airlines International, Northwest Airlines, and several Canadian commuter airlines.

Between the Airport and Downtown. Cabs charge about $7 for the 10-
to 15-minute ride downtown.

Getting Around

BY BUS

Regina Transit's (☎ 306/777–7433) 19 bus routes serve the metropolitan area daily except Sunday. The fare is $1.10.

BY TAXI

Taxis are easy to find outside major hotels, or they can be summoned
by phone. Call **Regina Cabs** (☎ 306/543–3333), **Capital Cab** (☎ 306/
781–7777), or **Co-op Taxis** (☎ 306/586–6555).

Contacts and Resources

EMERGENCIES

Dial 911 for emergency fire, police, or ambulance service.

GUIDED TOURS

Classic Carriage Service (☎ 306/543–9155) offers horse-drawn carriage rides around the city in summer and horse-drawn sleigh and
hayrides around Wascana Centre in winter. Both tours accommodate
15 to 20 people and cost $60 to $75 per hour.

HOSPITALS

Emergency rooms are located at **Regina General Hospital** (⊠ 1140 14th
Ave., ☎ 306/766-4444), **Plains Health Centre** (⊠ 4500 Wascana Pkwy.,
☎ 306/766–6211), and **Pasqua Hospital** (⊠ 4101 Dewdney Ave.,
☎ 306/766–2222).

LATE-NIGHT PHARMACY

Shopper's Drug Marts (⊠ Northgate Mall, ☎ 306/777–8010; ⊠
Broad St. and 14th Ave., ☎ 306/757–8100; ⊠ Gordon Rd. and Albert St., ☎ 306/777–8040; and ⊠ Victoria Sq., ☎ 306/777–8060)
are open until midnight.

VISITOR INFORMATION

Tourism Regina (⊠ Box 3355, S4P 3H1, ☎ 306/789–5099) has an information center on the Trans-Canada Highway (Highway 1) on the
eastern approach to the city and is open Victoria Day (late May) to
Labor Day, 8–6; Labor Day to Victoria Day, weekdays 8:30–4:30. The
Tourism Saskatchewan information center (⊠ 500-1900 Albert St.,
☎ 306/787–2300) is open weekdays 8–5.

SASKATOON

Saskatchewan's largest city is Saskatoon (population 200,000), nicknamed "City of Bridges" because it has seven spans across the South
Saskatchewan River, which cuts the city in half diagonally. Saskatoon
was founded in 1882 when a group of Ontario Methodists was granted
200,000 acres to form a temperance colony. Teetotaling Methodists
controlled only half the land, however, and eventually the influence of
those who controlled the other half turned the town wet. The coming
of the railroad in 1890 made it the major regional transportation hub,
but during the 20th century it became known for its three major resources: potash, oil, and wheat. Saskatoon today is the high-tech hub
of Saskatchewan's agricultural industry and is also home to the University of Saskatchewan—a major presence in all aspects of local life.

Downtown Saskatoon

Reasonably compact for a Western city, Saskatoon proper is easily accessible to drivers and cyclists. Idylwyld Drive divides the city into east
and west; 22nd Street divides the city into north and south. The down-

town area and the Spadina Crescent are located on the west side of the South Saskatchewan River.

Numbers in the text and margin below correspond to numbers on the Saskatoon map.

A Good Drive

Begin exploring at **Meewasin Valley Centre** 43, a small museum that traces Saskatoon history back to temperance-colony days. Follow Spadina Crescent north along the river to the **Ukrainian Museum of Canada** 44. Just north of the museum is **Kinsmen Park** 45, with riverside amusements. From Spadina Crescent, head east over the river on the University Bridge to the picturesque **University of Saskatchewan** 46 campus. You can detour into the northeastern part of the city to the **Forestry Farm Park and Zoo** 47 for animals and hiking trails. Return to the university campus, head west on College Drive, and then pick up University Drive, lined with grand old houses. University Drive eventually joins Broadway Avenue, the city's oldest business district. Follow Broadway Avenue south to 8th Street; head west to Lorne Avenue and then south to the **Western Development Museum** 48, on the **Saskatoon Prairieland Exhibition Grounds** 49, to see a re-creation of a 1910 boomtown. To return to downtown Saskatoon, take the scenic route: Head north on Lorne Avenue, then west on Ruth Street to the river. Follow St. Henry Avenue, Taylor Street, Herman Avenue, and Saskatchewan Crescent past the fine old homes that overlook one of the prettier stretches of the South Saskatchewan River. Cross over the 19th Street Bridge.

TIMING

By car this tour can easily be done without stops in a morning or afternoon. If you want to explore museums or take a hike, leave more time and choose any day except Monday, when the Ukrainian Museum is closed.

Sights to See

🖐 47 **Forestry Farm Park and Zoo.** More than 300 animals live here. The zoo spotlights such species native to Saskatchewan as deer, wolf, bear, coyote, and fox. The park offers barbecue areas, nature displays, cross-country ski trails, and sports fields. It also has a trout pond for fishing and train rides in the zoo area. ⊠ *Off Attridge Dr., northeast Saskatoon,* ☎ *306/975–3382.* 🎟 *May 1–Labor Day, $3; Labor Day–May 1, free; vehicle charge, $2.* ☉ *May 1–Labor Day, daily 9–9; Labor Day–May 1, daily 10–4.*

🖐 45 **Kinsmen Park.** This riverside amusement park includes a children's play village. ⊠ *Spadina Crescent and 25th St.,* ☎ *306/975–3366.*

43 **Meewasin Valley Centre.** This small museum traces Saskatoon history back to temperance-colony days. Meewasin is Cree for "beautiful valley," and this is a fitting place to embark upon the **Meewasin Valley Trail,** a 19-kilometer (12-mile) biking and hiking trail along both banks of the beautiful South Saskatchewan River. ⊠ *402 3rd Ave. S,* ☎ *306/665–6888.* 🎟 *Free.* ☉ *Weekdays 9–5, weekends 10:30–5.*

49 **Saskatoon Prairieland Exhibition Grounds** (☎ *306/931–7149*) is a vast plot that encompasses space for agricultural shows, rodeos, and horse races, and the Western Development Museum (☞ *below*).

44 **Ukrainian Museum of Canada.** This collection celebrates—through photos, costumes, textiles, and of course the famous *pysanky* (Easter eggs)—the rich history of the Ukrainian people who make up 10% of

206

Forestry
Farm Park and
Zoo, **47**

Kinsmen
Park, **45**

Meewasin
Valley
Centre, **43**

Saskatoon
Prairieland
Exhibition
Grounds, **49**

Ukrainian
Museum of
Canada, **44**

University of
Saskatchewan, **46**

Western
Development
Museum, **48**

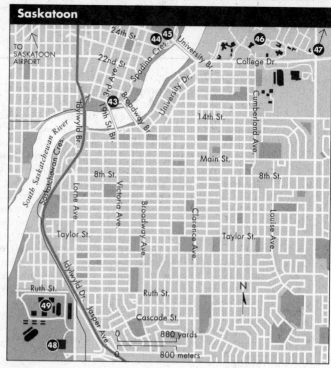

Saskatchewan's population. ✉ *910 Spadina Crescent E,* ☎ *306/244–3800.* 🎫 *$2.* ☉ *Tues.–Sat. 10–5, Sun. 1–5.*

46 **University of Saskatchewan.** The parklike riverside campus occupies a 2,550-acre site on the east bank of the river. The university grounds, among the most picturesque in Canada, house several museums and galleries, including the **Natural Sciences Museum,** the **Little Stone School House,** the **Museum of Antiquities,** the **Biology Museum,** and the **Gordon Snelgrove Gallery.** A highlight is the **Diefenbaker Canada Centre,** a museum, art gallery, and research center in Canadian studies commemorating Canada's 13th prime minister. The center explores John Diefenbaker's life and times. Two replica rooms represent the Privy Council Chamber and the prime minister's Ottawa office where he served in the late 1950s and early 1960s. ✉ *Diefenbaker Canada Centre,* ☎ *306/966–8384.* ☉ *Weekdays 9:30–4:30, weekends and holidays 12:30–5.*

48 **Western Development Museum.** One of four such museums in Saskatchewan, the Saskatoon branch is called "1910 Boomtown" and re-creates early 20th-century life in the Canadian west. ✉ *2610 Lorne Ave. S,* ☎ *306/931–1910.* 🎫 *$4.50.* ☉ *Daily 9–5.*

Dining and Lodging

$$$ ✕ **Jamieson Street.** Marvelously renovated, this former railway station is lined with rich wood throughout. The menu includes such seafood entrées as paella, prawns, and scallop fricassee; meat dishes include prairie bison. The wine list is reasonable. ✉ *No. 3, 305 Idylwyld Dr. N,* ☎ *306/664–9555. Reservations essential. AE, MC, V.*

$$$ ✕ **R.J. Willoughby's.** The lush, tropical, pink-and-green color scheme of the Holiday Inn's main dining room is enhanced by copious groves of bamboo and foliage. The menu offers Continental preparations plus themed evenings with specialty buffets (prime rib on Wednesday, pasta on Friday, seafood on Sunday). The Sunday Brunch, which features an impressive array, including custom-made omelets and flambéed fruit, is very popular. ⊠ *Holiday Inn, 90 22nd St. E,* ☎ *306/665–7576. Reservations essential. AE, DC, MC, V.*

$$ ✕ **St. Tropez Bistro.** This sophisticated spot a short stroll from downtown hotels offers intimate French-bistro decor, with blue-and-pink florals, candlelit tables, and imaginative preparations that change daily. Veal, fish, pasta, quiche, and outstanding homemade bread are often on the menu. A tasty specialty is the blackened chicken. For dessert, try the chocolate fondue. ⊠ *243 3rd Ave. S,* ☎ *306/652–1250. Reservations essential. AE, MC, V. Closed Sun.*

$$ ✕ **Saskatoon Station Place.** The station is newly built, but the vintage railroad cars and decorative antiques are fascinatingly authentic. The newspaper-style menu headlines Canadian prime rib and steaks, seafood, and Greek specialties, such as Greek ribs and souvlaki. ⊠ *221 Idylwyld Dr. N,* ☎ *306/244–7777. Reservations essential. AE, MC, V.*

$ ✕ **Lydia's.** This Broadway Avenue–neighborhood pub offers a wide selection of international beers and has a full menu, including beef and chicken kebabs as well as Cajun chicken, Caesar salad, and a variety of pasta dishes. There's music every weekend. ⊠ *650 Broadway Ave.,* ☎ *306/652–8595. DC, MC, V.*

$ ✕ **Taunte Maria's.** This is a Mennonite restaurant, where you're served hearty soups, huge farmer's sausages, potato salad, homemade bread, and noodles steeped in gravy. The decor, too, reflects the Mennonite tradition: simple, functional, and comfortable. Try to save room for Ho-Ho Cake (chocolate cake with cream filling and chocolate icing) or bread pudding with ice cream. ⊠ *51st St. and Faithfull Ave.,* ☎ *306/931–3212. Reservations not accepted. MC, V. Closed Sun.*

$$$ 🏨 **Delta Bessborough.** Saskatoon's grand old landmark, opened in 1935, ★ looks like a castle and dominates the skyline from its riverfront setting. The hotel has recently been restored and upgraded with modern amenities, but it still retains the grand appearance. ⊠ *601 Spadina Crescent E, S7K 3G8,* ☎ *306/244–5521 or 800/268–1133,* FAX *306/653–2458. 227 rooms. 2 restaurants, 2 bars, no-smoking rooms, indoor and outdoor pools, sauna. AE, DC, MC, V.*

$$$ 🏨 **Radisson Hotel Saskatoon.** One of Saskatoon's newest luxury properties has a prime riverfront location downtown and 19 floors of classically styled, ample-size rooms. Units are large, and the peach, gray, and pastel colors make them bright and airy; for still more atmosphere, request a river view. The elaborate Waterworks Recreation Complex encompasses an indoor pool, a whirlpool, a sauna, and two three-story water slides. ⊠ *405 20th St. E, S7K 6X6,* ☎ *306/665–3322 or 800/228–9898,* FAX *306/665–5531. 291 rooms. 2 restaurants, bar, no-smoking rooms, indoor pool, sauna. AE, DC, MC, V.*

$$$ 🏨 **Sheraton Cavalier.** Downtown, opposite Kiwanis Park, this eight-story property has unusually large rooms that face either the city or the river, and an elaborate water-sports complex. Benedict's Dining Room is the place for elegant dining, while Windows Café is more informal and offers a view of the river from every table. Lorenzo's Lounge, a piano bar, has nightly music. The Barley Bin is a sophisticated but chummy pub. ⊠ *612 Spadina Crescent E, S7K 3G9,* ☎ *306/652–6770 or 800/325–3535,* FAX *306/244–1739. 250 rooms. 2 restaurants, pub, no-smoking rooms, 2 indoor pools, sauna. AE, DC, MC, V.*

$$ 🏨 **Travelodge.** This sprawling property near the airport has two flora-filled indoor pool complexes. Rooms come in a great variety of sizes and shapes, and many may have balconies overlooking the pool. The Aloha Gardens offers informal poolside dining; the Heritage Dining Room is the place for fine dining. ⊠ *106 Circle Dr. W, S7L 4L6,* ☎ *306/242–*

8881 or 800/255–3050, FAX 306/665–7378. 220 rooms. 2 restaurants, 2 bars, no-smoking rooms, 2 indoor pools, sauna. AE, DC, MC, V.

$ ▦ **Colonial Square Motel.** This pink-stucco, two-story motel opened in 1989, east of the river, along a fast-food strip. Rooms are furnished in pastel colors and have two queen-size beds or a double bed plus a pullout sofa. Across the parking lot is the Venice Pizza House and Lounge. ⊠ 1301 8th St. E, S7H 0S7, ☎ 306/343–1676 or 800/667–3939, FAX 306/956–1313. 80 rooms. Restaurant, bar, no-smoking rooms. AE, MC, V.

$ ▦ **Patricia Hotel.** Conveniently located in the center of downtown, this
★ older hotel is appealing if you're looking for a bargain. Some rooms are also available as a youth hostel. There's a dining room, Karz Kafe, and a lounge. ⊠ 345 2nd Ave. N, ☎ 306/242–8861, FAX 306/242–8861. 45 rooms. Restaurant, bar. MC, V.

Nightlife and the Arts

The Arts

MUSIC AND DANCE

The **Saskatoon Symphony** (☎ 306/665–6414) performs an October–April season at **Saskatoon Centennial Auditorium** (⊠ 35 22nd St. E, ☎ 306/644–9777). When the symphony isn't in concert, the 2,003-seat auditorium hosts ballet, rock and pop concerts, comedians, musical comedies, and opera. The **Mendel Art Gallery** (⊠ 950 Spadina Crescent E, ☎ 306/975–7610) has a regular concert program. The **Saskatoon Jazz Society** performs in its permanent space, **The Bassment** (⊠ 245 3rd Ave. S, ☎ 306/652–1421). Each summer Saskatoon is home to the popular **Saskatchewan Jazz Festival,** when jazz musicians from around the world play more than 125 performances throughout the city.

THEATER

Saskatoon's oldest professional theater, **25th Street Theatre Centre** (⊠ 420 Duchess St., ☎ 306/664–2239), produces mostly works by Saskatchewan playwrights, as well as **The Fringe Festival** every summer. **Persephone Theatre** (⊠ 2802 Rusholme Rd., ☎ 306/384–7727) presents six plays and musicals a year. **Gateway Players** (⊠ 709 Cumberland St., ☎ 306/653–1200) presents five productions from October through April. **Nightcap Productions** (☎ 306/653–2300) offers "Shakespeare on the Saskatchewan" in a riverside tent in July and August. **Saskatoon Soaps** present midnight improvisational comedy at the Broadway Theatre (⊠ 715 Broadway Ave., ☎ 306/652–6556).

Nightlife

BARS AND CLUBS

One Up (⊠ 410 22nd St. E, ☎ 306/244–7770) is a civilized rooftop place with great river views. Saskatoon's businesspeople interface with traveling executives at **Caper's Lounge** (⊠ 405 20th St. E, ☎ 306/665–3322) in the Radisson Hotel Saskatoon. See top rock groups at **Bud's On Broadway** (⊠ 817 Broadway Ave., ☎ 306/244–4155). **Amigos** (⊠ 632 10th St. E, ☎ 306/652–4912) is a rock hangout. The **Artful Dodger** (⊠ 100–119 4th Ave. S, ☎ 306/653–2577) pub has live entertainment. Go out to **Texas T** (⊠ 3331 8th St. E, ☎ 306/373–8080) for country sights and sounds around the city's largest dance floor.

Outdoor Activities and Sports

Participant Sports

BICYCLING AND JOGGING

The **Meewasin Valley Trail** (☎ 306/665–6888) is a gorgeous 19-kilometer (12-mile) biking and jogging trail along both banks of the South Saskatchewan River in Saskatoon.

The **Riverraquet Athletic Club** (✉ 322 Saguenay Dr., ☎ 306/242–0010) has racquetball and squash courts, a weight room, aerobics classes, miniature golf, and beach volleyball in summer. The **Saskatoon Field House** (✉ University of Saskatchewan, 2020 College Dr., ☎ 306/975–3354) has tennis courts, a weight room, a gymnastics area, an indoor track, a fitness dance area, and drop-in fitness classes.

Spectator Sports

HOCKEY
The **Saskatoon Blades** play major junior hockey league action in the Western Hockey League at **Saskatchewan Place** (✉ 3515 Thatcher Ave., ☎ 306/938–7800).

HORSE RACING
Marquis Downs Racetrack (✉ Prairieland Exhibition Centre, enter on Ruth St., ☎ 306/242–6100) has Thoroughbred racing from early May through mid-October.

Shopping

Malls and Shopping Districts
Midtown Plaza (✉ 22nd St. and 1st Ave., ☎ 306/652–9366) and **Scotia Centre Mall** (✉ 123 2nd Ave., ☎ 306/665–6120) are enclosed malls downtown. If you enjoy funkier, smaller boutiques and restaurants, head to **Broadway Avenue** (✉ between 8th and 12th Sts. east of river), the city's oldest business district and location of more than 150 shops and restaurants and a cinema.

Specialty Stores
Trading Post Limited (✉ 226 2nd Ave. S, ☎ 306/653–1769) carries an extensive and reasonably priced selection of Inuit and Indian crafts and Canadian foodstuffs—including Saskatoon berry products. Local crafts are available at **Handmade House** (✉ 710 Broadway Ave., ☎ 306/665–5542). The **Homespun Craft Emporium** (✉ 250A 2nd Ave. S, ☎ 306/652–3585) has crafts.

Side Trips

Numbers in the margin correspond to places of interest on the Saskatchewan map.

Wanuskewin
50 *5 km (3 mi) north of Saskatoon just off Hwy. 11 on Rte. 4.*

Wanuskewin Heritage Park portrays 6,000 years of Northern Plains Indian culture. The Interpretive Centre has an archaeological laboratory, displays, films, and hands-on activities. Outside, walking trails take you to archaeological sites, including a medicine wheel, tipi rings, bison kills and pounds, habitation sites, and stone cairns. ✉ *R.R. 4, Saskatoon, S7K 3J7,* ☎ *306/931–6767.* 🎟 *$6.* ☼ *June–Sept., daily 9–9; Sept.–May, daily 9–5.*

Batoche
51 *100 km (60 mi) northeast of Saskatoon off Hwy. 11 (follow signs).*

Batoche National Historic Site is the center of Métis heritage. It was here that the Métis under Louis Riel fought and lost their last battle against the Canadian militia in 1885. The large historical park includes a visitor center, displays, a historic church and rectory, and walking trails that take you by many of the battle sites. ✉ *Batoche,* ☎ *306/423–6227.* 🎟 *$3.* ☼ *July and Aug., daily 10–6; May, June, Sept., and Oct., daily 9–5.*

Duck Lake

52 *20 km (12 mi), or 30 minutes, north of Batoche along Hwy. 11.*

Duck Lake lies between the North and South Saskatchewan rivers. Town buildings are decorated with life-size murals depicting regional history, including the 1885 Northwest Rebellion. The **Regional Interpretive Centre** has more than 2,000 artifacts from this period. ☎ *306/467–2057.* ⌨ *$2.50.* ☉ *Mid-May–Labor Day, daily 9–6.*

Twenty-four kilometers (15 miles) west of Duck Lake on Route 212 is **Fort Carlton Provincial Historic Park,** with a reconstructed stockade and buildings from the mid-1800s fur-trade days. ☎ *306/787–9573.* ⌨ *$2.50.* ☉ *Daily 10–6.*

Prince Albert

53 *141 km (88 mi) north of Saskatoon on Hwy. 11 and Rte. 2.*

Prince Albert is Saskatchewan's fourth-largest city (population 34,000), the center of the lumber industry, and the self-proclaimed "Gateway to the North." The prosperous modern city straddles the North Saskatchewan River; its most interesting attractions are downtown. Pick up a walking-tours pamphlet at the **Prince Albert Historical Museum,** housed in an old firehouse. ⊠ *River St. and Central Ave.,* ☎ *306/764–2992.* ⌨ *$1.* ☉ *Mid-May–Aug., Mon.–Sat. 10–6, Sun. 10–9.*

Prince Albert National Park, 80 kilometers (50 miles) north of Prince Albert, encompasses nearly a million acres of wilderness and waterways and is divided into three landscapes: wide-open fescue grassland, rolling wooded parkland, and dense boreal forest. In addition to hiking trails, the park has three major campgrounds, with more than 500 sites, plus rustic campgrounds and primitive sites in the backcountry. Pick up maps and information at the **Waskesiu Lake Visitor Centre** in Waskesiu, a townsite with restaurants, motels, and stores, and a golf course within the park. The **Nature Centre,** inside the visitor center, can help to orient you to the plant and animal life of the area. Hiking along the marked trails, you have a good chance of spotting moose, deer, bear, elk, and red fox. Canoes, rowboats, and powerboats can be rented from Waskesiu Lake Marina. Lodging in Waskesiu includes **Chateau Park Chalets** (☎ *306/663–5556),* the **Hawood Inn** (☎ *306/663–5911),* **Waskesiu Lake Lodge** (☎ *306/663–5975),* and the **Lakeview Hotel** (☎ *306/663–5311);* all offer year-round accommodation. ⊠ *Prince Albert National Park, off Rte. 2,* ☎ *306/663–5322;* ⊠ *Waskesiu Lake Visitor Centre, Rtes. 263 and 264,* ☎ *306/663–5322.* ⌨ *Free.* ☉ *Park daily; visitor center May–Sept., daily 8 AM–10 PM, and Oct.–Apr., weekdays 8–4:30.*

North Battleford

54 *138 km (86 mi) northwest of Saskatoon on Rte. 16.*

The **Western Development Museum** in North Battleford presents a re-created 1920s farming village, complete with homes, offices, churches, and a Mountie post. The museum also exhibits vintage farming tools and provides demonstrations of agricultural skills used. ⊠ *Rtes. 16 and 40,* ☎ *306/445–8033.* ⌨ *$4.50.* ☉ *Call for hrs.*

While you're in North Battleford, visit the **Allen Sapp Gallery,** which features the paintings of Cree Indian artist Allen Sapp. ⊠ *1901 100th St.,* ☎ *306/445–3304.* ⌨ *Free.* ☉ *May–Sept., daily 1–5; Sept.–May, Wed.–Sun. 1–5.*

Fort Battleford National Historic Site pays tribute to the role of mounted police in the development of the Canadian west. The fort was established in 1876 as the North West Mounted Police headquarters for the

District of Saskatchewan. Costumed guides explain day-to-day life at the post, and an interpretive center has exhibits relating to the history of the Mounted Police and ways of life of Indians and settlers. ⊠ *Central Ave.,* ☎ *306/937–2621.* 🎟 *Free.* ☉ *July and Aug., daily 9–6; May, June, Sept., and Oct., daily 9–5.*

Manitou Beach

⑤⑤ *124 km (77 mi) southeast of Saskatoon, via Rtes. 16 and 365.*

Fifty years ago the town of Manitou Beach was a world-famous spa nicknamed the "Carlsbad of Canada." The mineral water in Little Manitou Lake is said to be three times saltier than the ocean and dense enough to make anyone float. Today, **Manitou Springs Mineral Spa** attracts vacationers as well as sufferers from arthritis, rheumatism, and skin disorders to the spa resort (☞ *below*). ⊠ *Rte. 365,* ☎ *306/946–3949.*

DINING AND LODGING

✕🏨 **Manitou Springs Resort.** On the lake shore, it has rooms and suites with balconies and good views. The rooms are comfortable, with cushy fabrics in muted pastels. The spa is lined with cedar. There's Continental cuisine, including a small selection of seafood, as well as prairie fare—steaks and roasts—in the light and airy dining room overlooking the lake. ⊠ *Box 610, Watrous, SK S0K 4T0,* ☎ *306/946–2233 or 800/667–7672 (in Canada only). 56 rooms, 4 suites. Dining room, massage, mineral spa, exercise room, bicycles, shops, meeting rooms. MC, V.*

Saskatoon A to Z

Arriving and Departing

BY CAR

The two-lane Yellowhead Highway (Route 16) passes though Saskatoon on its journey from Winnipeg through to Edmonton and west. There is also access to Saskatoon along Highway 11 from Regina.

BY PLANE

Saskatoon Airport, 7 kilometers (4½ miles) northwest of downtown, is served by Canadian Airlines International, Air Canada, Northwest Airlines, and Canadian commuter carriers.

Between the Airport and Downtown. Taxis to the downtown area cost about $9.

Getting Around

BY BUS

Saskatoon Transit (☎ 306/975–3100) buses offer convenient service to points around the city. Tickets cost $1.25.

BY TAXI

Taxis are plentiful, especially outside downtown hotels, but they are fairly expensive. For service, call **United Yellow Cab** (☎ 306/652–2222), **Blueline Taxi** (☎ 306/653–3333), or **Saskatoon Radio Cab** (☎ 306/242–1221).

Contacts and Resources

EMERGENCIES

Dial 911 for police, fire, ambulance, poison, and emergency services.

GUIDED TOURS

W.W. Northcote River Cruises (☎ 306/665–1818) depart on the hour for 11-kilometer (7-mile) tours of the South Saskatchewan River. Cruises run June–August, daily 10–8.

HOSPITALS
Emergency rooms include **City Hospital** (⊠ Queen St. and 6th Ave. N, ☎ 306/655–8230), **Royal University Hospital** (⊠ University Grounds, ☎ 306/655–1362), and **St. Paul's Hospital** (⊠ 1702 20th St. W, ☎ 306/665–5113).

LATE-NIGHT PHARMACY
Shoppers Drug Mart (⊠ 610 Taylor St. E, at Broadway Ave., ☎ 306/343–1608) is open till midnight; another branch (⊠ 2410 22nd St. W, ☎ 306/382–5005) is open 24 hours.

VISITOR INFORMATION
Tourism Saskatoon (⊠ 6-305 Idylwyld Dr. N, S7L OZ1, ☎ 306/242–1206) is open weekdays 8:30–5 during most of the year and 8:30–7 mid-May–early September. In summer, visitor information centers open at various points along the highway.

WINNIPEG

With a population of more than 650,000, Winnipeg, Manitoba, ranks as Canada's seventh-largest city and the largest population center between Toronto and Calgary. Though geographically isolated, this provincial capital has become a center for both commerce and culture, home to a symphony orchestra, ballet and opera companies, a lively theater scene, and a thriving community of local and native artists.

The first stop on the great Canadian land rush of the late 19th century, Winnipeg still counts among its citizens descendants of the original French and British settlers, and it has distinct neighborhoods of Ukrainians, Jews, Italians, Mennonites, Hungarians, Portuguese, Poles, and Chinese. Unlike the boom-and-bust towns farther west, Winnipeg has enjoyed steady growth, with a diversified economy based on manufacturing, banking, transportation, and agriculture. Winnipeg looks like the cosmopolitan centers of midwestern America—Minneapolis, Milwaukee, Chicago—with a downtown area filled with cast-iron buildings and established neighborhoods of older homes along curving, tree-lined streets.

Originally, buffalo-hunting Plains Indians were the only inhabitants of the area, which was franchised by the British Crown to the Hudson's Bay Company. That was until 1738, when Pierre Gaultier de Varennes established a North West Company fur-trading post at the junction of the Red and Assiniboine rivers. Lord Selkirk, a Scot, brought a permanent agricultural settlement in 1812; Winnipeg was incorporated as a city in 1873; and soon after, in 1886, the Canadian Pacific Railroad arrived, bringing a rush of European immigrants. Winnipeg boomed as a railroad hub, a center of the livestock and grain industries, and a principal market city of western Canada.

Downtown Winnipeg

It's somewhat difficult to get your bearings in Winnipeg. The downtown area lies just north of the junction of the Red and Assiniboine rivers, and its streets interconnect at skewed angles with the curving rivers, creating diagonal streets in all directions. Much of downtown Winnipeg is linked by a network of enclosed pedestrian overpasses and underground concourses. The intersection of Portage Avenue and Main Street is the focal point of the city, with Portage Avenue (Highway 1) the principal artery heading west and Main Street (Route 52) heading north. South of Winnipeg, the main drag is Pembina Highway (Route

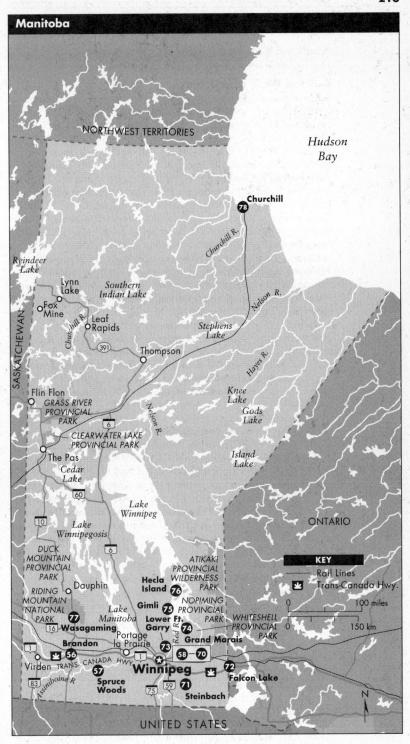

Hudson Bay

NORTHWEST TERRITORIES

Churchill 78

Churchill R.

Reindeer Lake

Lynn Lake ○

○ Fox Mine

Southern Indian Lake

○ Leaf Rapids

Churchill R.

Nelson R.

Stephens Lake

391

Thompson ○

Hayes R.

SASKATCHEWAN

Flin Flon ○

GRASS RIVER PROVINCIAL PARK

6

CLEARWATER LAKE PROVINCIAL PARK

Nelson R.

Knee Lake

Gods Lake

The Pas ○

Cedar Lake

60

Island Lake

10

Lake Winnipegosis

6

Lake Winnipeg

ONTARIO

DUCK MOUNTAIN PROVINCIAL PARK

● Dauphin

ATIKAKI PROVINCIAL WILDERNESS PARK

KEY

Rail Lines

Trans-Canada Hwy.

0 ———— 100 miles

0 ———— 150 km

RIDING MOUNTAIN NATIONAL PARK

Hecla Island 76

Gimli 75

NOPIMING PROVINCIAL PARK

WHITESHELL PROVINCIAL PARK

77

16 **Wasagaming**

Lake Manitoba

Lower Ft. Garry 74

Red R.

Brandon

Portage la Prairie ●

73

Grand Marais

1

56

58 — 70

Winnipeg ✪

72 **Falcon Lake**

Virden ○

TRANS-CANADA HWY

83

Assiniboine R.

57

Spruce Woods

75

59

71

Steinbach

N

UNITED STATES

42). Streets in St. Boniface, east of the Red River, are labeled in French—evidence of the community's ethnic heritage.

Numbers in the text and margin below correspond to numbers on the Downtown Winnipeg map.

A Good Walk and Drive

Begin at the southeast corner of downtown Winnipeg at the tourist information center (☞ Contacts and Resources, *below*), housed in the **Legislative Building** 58. Walk east on Broadway and south on Carlton Street to tour **Dalnavert** 59, the 1895 house built for Manitoba's premier. Back at the Legislature, head north on Osborne Street past the stately The Bay store (the legacy of the Hudson's Bay Company) to the **Winnipeg Art Gallery** 60 to view Inuit sculpture and art. Turn east at the north end of the Winnipeg Art Gallery to Portage Avenue for a look at the shopping district (☞ Shopping, *below*). Continue east on Portage Avenue to Main Street and what's reputed to be the windiest intersection in the world. Five floors above the breeze, visit the **Winnipeg Commodity Exchange** 61, the oldest and largest futures exchange in Canada. Belowground is **Winnipeg Square,** a concourse with shops and fast-food stores. Emerge to street level on the north side of Portage Avenue and into the **Exchange District** 62—a concentration of renovated warehouses, banks, and insurance companies now thriving as a nightlife center and Sunday open-air market. Continue north on Main Street to Rupert Avenue and **Centennial Centre** 63, site of a concert hall, a natural history museum, and a planetarium. **St. Boniface,** about 2½ kilometers (1½ miles) away, can be reached by crossing the Provencher Bridge east over the Red River and turning right onto avenue Taché. Here you can visit the **St. Boniface Cathedral** 64, in whose churchyard Louis Riel is buried, and the **St. Boniface Museum** 65, which focuses on French and Métis history and culture in Manitoba. Follow avenue Taché south to Goulet Stet, turn right, and follow it onto Norwood Bridge, which takes you to the **Forks National Historic Site** 66 and the Forks complex, at the junction of the Assiniboine and Red rivers. A longer drive—left on River Avenue, left on Donald Street, and right on Corydon Avenue—will bring you to **Assiniboine Park** 67, where the zoo and several lovely gardens are. South of the park, you can follow Shaftsbury Boulevard past Assiniboine Forest across Wilkes Avenue to McCreary Road, where the **Fort Whyte Center for Environmental Education** 68 re-creates natural habitats of Manitoba in a former cement quarry. To see where Canadian money is made, drive 6½ kilometers (4 miles) southeast of downtown off Highway 1 or take Bus 50 (available on the east side of Fort Street between Portage and Graham avenues on weekdays) to the **Royal Canadian Mint** 69. Also southeast of the center off Highway 1 is **Fun Mountain Waterslide Park** 70.

TIMING

This makes for a pleasant, leisurely day's tour in summer.

Sights to See

🌸 67 **Assiniboine Park.** West of town along the river of the same name, the park encompasses 376 acres of cycling paths, picnic areas, playgrounds, a miniature railway, formal English and French gardens, a conservatory, and a cricket pitch. **Assiniboine Zoo,** also on the grounds, houses more than 1,200 species in reasonably natural settings. ☎ 204/986–6921, 204/986–3050. ⬛ Zoo $3, free Tues. ☉ Zoo Oct.–Mar., daily 10–4, Apr., May, and Sept., daily 10–7; June and July, daily 10–9; Aug., daily 10–8; park daily 7–10.

63 **Centennial Centre.** A concert hall, the **Manitoba Museum of Man and Nature,** and the dazzling **Manitoba Planetarium** are the focal points

Assiniboine
Park, **67**

Centennial
Centre, **63**

Dalnavert, **59**

Exchange
District, **62**

The Forks
National
Historic Site, **66**

Fort Whyte
Center for
Environmental
Education, **68**

Fun Mountain
Waterslide
Park, **70**

Legislative
Building, **58**

Royal
Canadian
Mint, **69**

St. Boniface
Cathedral, **64**

St. Boniface
Museum, **65**

Winnipeg Art
Gallery, **60**

Winnipeg
Commodity
Exchange, **61**

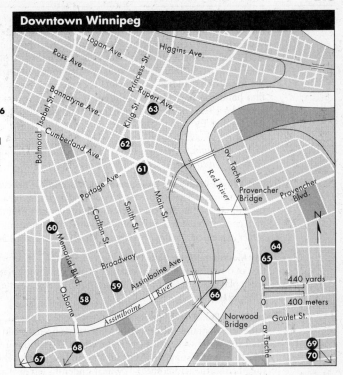

Downtown Winnipeg

of this complex. Exhibits at the museum focus on prehistoric Manitoba, local wildlife, the native peoples of the region, and the exploration of Hudson Bay. Downstairs, the planetarium presents a variety of cosmic adventures in the multimedia Star Theater; 60 interactive multisensory exhibits in Touch the Universe explain laws of nature. ⌧ *190 Rupert Ave.,* ☎ *204/943–3139 or 204/943–3142.* ⌧ *Museum $4, planetarium $3.50, science gallery $3.50, Omni pass (3-day, all-inclusive) $9.* ⊙ *Mid-May–early Sept., daily 10–6; Sept.–mid-May, Tues.–Thurs. 10–6, weekends noon–6.*

⑤⑨ Dalnavert. This Queen Anne Revival–style house was built in 1895 for Sir Hugh John Macdonald, who became premier of Manitoba. Costumed guides escort visitors around the premises. ⌧ *61 Carlton St.,* ☎ *204/943–2835.* ⌧ *$3.21.* ⊙ *Jan. and Feb., weekends noon–4; Mar.–May, weekends and Tues.–Thurs. noon–4:30; June–Aug., weekends and Tues.–Thurs. 10–5:30; Sept.–Dec., weekends and Tues.–Thurs. noon–4:30.*

⑥② Exchange District. A concentration of renovated warehouses, banks, and insurance companies built during Winnipeg's turn-of-the-century boom period now stands as a thriving nightlife spot. On Sunday, from May through October, attention focuses on **Old Market Square Park** (⌧ King St. and Bannatyne Ave.), a new marketplace bursting with fresh produce, fish, crafts, and street performers. ⌧ *Bordered by Portage Ave. and Main St.*

⑥⑥ Forks National Historic Site. Winnipeg began here, at the junction of the Red and Assiniboine rivers, 6,000 years ago. On 10 landscaped acres, you can learn about the region's history through interpretive displays as you stroll paths or rest on benches overlooking the river. The Historic Site also has a playground and an amphitheater. Interpretive programs are presented as well; check at the Historic Site information center at the back of the Manitoba Children's Museum (☞ *below*). Next to the Historic Site and sharing the 2-mile riverside promenade with it is **The Forks,** a 56-acre complex of renovated railway buildings and parkland now hosting a public market in former stables; a playground; a small boat dock; Johnston terminal, with shops and restaurants; and the **Manitoba Children's Museum.** The museum is western Canada's first hands-on museum for children. In five galleries, kids can climb aboard a 1952-vintage steam engine and passenger car, try out a fully functioning TV studio, and more. ⊠ *Forks Market Rd. off Main St., Historic Site,* ☎ *204/983–2007; The Forks, 204/943–7752; Children's Museum, 204/956–1888.* ☉ *Victoria Day–Labor Day, daily 9:30–6; Labor Day–Victoria Day, weekdays 8–4:30.*

☝ ⑥⑧ **Fort Whyte Center for Environmental Education.** This center, on 200 acres of land in the southwest corner of the city, re-creates the natural habitats of Manitoba's lakes and rivers in and around several former cement quarries. Self-guided nature trails and an interpretive center explain all. ⊠ *1961 McCreary Rd., Winnipeg,* ☎ *204/989–8355.*

☝ ⑦⓿ **Fun Mountain Water Slide Park,** located about 13 kilometers (8 miles) east of downtown, includes bumper boats, a mammoth hot tub, rides, and a playground. ⊠ *Hwy. 1, east at Murdock Rd., Winnipeg,* ☎ *204/ 255–3910.*

⑤⑧ **Legislative Building.** The classic Greek-style structure made of local Tyndall stone contains the offices of Manitoba's premier and members of the cabinet, as well as the chamber where the legislature meets. The 240-foot dome supports Manitoba's symbol, Golden Boy—a gold-sheathed statue with a sheaf of wheat under his left arm and the torch of progress in his right hand. In the grounds fronting the river stand statues that celebrate Manitoba's ethnic diversity, including Scotland's Robert Burns, Iceland's Jon Sigurdson, Ukrainian poet Taras Ahevchenko, and Métis leader and "Father of Manitoba" Louis Riel. ⊠ *450 Broadway at Osborne St.,* ☎ *204/945–5813.*

⑥⑨ **Royal Canadian Mint.** You can see Canadian coins rolling off the presses at this facility. ⊠ *520 Lagimodière Blvd. (at Trans-Canada Hwy.),* ☎ *204/257–3359.* 🎟 *$2.* ☉ *Tours May–Aug., weekdays 9–5, Sat. noon–5.*

⑥④ **St. Boniface Cathedral.** The largest French community in western Canada was founded as Fort Rouge in 1783 and became an important fur-trading outpost for the North West Company. Upon the arrival of Roman Catholic priests, the settlement was renamed St. Boniface. Remnants of a 1908 basilica that survived a 1968 fire can be seen outside the perimeter of the present cathedral, built in 1972. The grave of Louis Riel, the St. Boniface native son who led the Métis rebellion, is in the churchyard. ⊠ *Av. de la Cathedral and av. Taché,* ☎ *204/233–7304.*

⑥⑤ **St. Boniface Museum.** Housed in the oldest (1846) structure in Winnipeg and the largest oak log building in North America, the museum tells the French and Métis side of Manitoba history. Artifacts include an altar crafted from papier-mâché, the first church bell in western Canada, and a host of innovative household gadgets. ⊠ *494 av. Tache,* ☎ *204/237–4500.* 🎟 *$2.14.* ☉ *Mid-May–mid-June, weekdays 9–5, weekends 10–5; mid-June–Aug., Sun. 10–8, Mon.–Thurs. 9–8, Fri. and Sat. 9–5; Sept., weekdays 9–5, weekends and holidays 10–5; Oct.–mid-May, weekdays 9–5.*

⑥⓿ **Winnipeg Art Gallery.** The gallery, which owns the world's largest collection of Inuit sculpture and art, also houses contemporary Canadian art and sculpture. ⊠ *300 Memorial Blvd.,* ☎ *204/786–6641.* 🖃 *$3, free Wed.* 🕤 *Mid-June–Labor Day, Thurs.–Tues. 10–5, Wed. 10–9; Sept.–early June, Tues. and Thurs.–Sun. 11–5, Wed. 11–9.*

🖲 **Winnipeg Commodity Exchange.** At the oldest and largest futures exchange in Canada, you can observe the controlled chaos of wild men (and a few women) involved in the buying and selling of grains, cooking oils, gold, and silver. ⊠ *360 Main St.,* ☎ *204/949–0495.* 🕤 *Weekdays 9:30–1:20.*

Dining and Lodging

$$$$ ✕ **Le Beaujolais.** This sophisticated, bright spot in the French St. Boni-
★ face district presents waiters in black tie; a softly lit ambience with French blue, coral, and burgundy decor; fresh-cut flowers; and a menu that combines classic French with lighter nouvelle cuisine. Fresh salmon with herb vinaigrette is the recommended seafood; tournedos with green peppercorns, veal with Roquefort and leeks, and rack of lamb are other entrée suggestions. Save room for dessert. ⊠ *131 Provencher Blvd.,* ☎ *204/237–6306. Reservations essential. AE, DC, MC, V.*

$$$ ✕ **Restaurant Dubrovnik.** The setting is a romantic Victorian town house, with seating on an enclosed veranda overlooking the Assiniboine River. An extensive menu blends Continental specialties, such as rack of lamb, breast of duck, and pheasant, with southern Yugoslavian dishes. Two good choices are *gibanica* (feta cheese in phyllo pastry) and *muckalica* (pork, lamb, chicken, and sausage casserole). A lengthy wine list is available. ⊠ *390 Assiniboine Ave.,* ☎ *204/944–0594. Reservations essential. Jacket required. AE, MC, V. Closed Sun.*

$$$ ✕ **Victor's.** In the Marlborough Inn (☞ *below*), with its rich wood paneling and chandeliers, Victor's serves Continental cuisine in a stylish, upscale atmosphere. **Joanna's Café,** in the same hotel, is a more casual dining spot appropriate for before- or after-dinner drinks. In both restaurants, poppy-seed cake is a must for dessert. ⊠ *331 Smith St.,* ☎ *204/947–2751. Reservations essential. AE, DC, MC, V. Closed Sun.*

$$ ✕ **Amici.** The sophisticated and posh downtown *ristorante* is the local avatar of *cucina nuova,* the Italian version of nouvelle cuisine. Clever pastas and such dishes as roast quail on radicchio and chicken stuffed with goat cheese are served in a second-floor dining room that's divided by partitions of frosted glass. Downstairs, the Bombolini Wine Bar serves many simpler dishes at lower prices. ⊠ *326 Broadway,* ☎ *204/943–4997. Reservations essential. AE, DC, MC, V. Closed Sun.*

$$ ✕ **Bistro Dansk.** Wood tables, bright red chairs, and strains of classi-
★ cal music convey a cozy European air. Dinner entrée selections mingle Danish specialties like *frikadeller* (meat patties), and salmon topped with crab, with such dishes as roast chicken. A less expensive lunch menu features a vast variety of open-face sandwiches. ⊠ *63 Sherbrook St.,* ☎ *204/775–5662. Reservations essential. DC, V. Closed Sun.*

$$ ✕ **Picasso's.** It may be named for a Spanish painter, but this is a Portuguese restaurant that serves outstanding seafood. On the street level it's a bustling neighborhood café; upstairs there's a subdued atmosphere where white tablecloths, candlelight, and soft music prevail. Try the salmon or Arctic char; Portuguese favorites are paella, octopus stew, and steak Picasso. ⊠ *615 Sargent Ave.,* ☎ *204/775–2469. Reservations essential. AE, DC, MC, V.*

$ ✕ **d'8 Schtove.** The name is Mennonite for "the eating room," and,
★ true to its name, the menu features heavyweight servings of soup, salads, and Mennonite concoctions, usually involving meat, potatoes, onions, and vegetables. Try the *klopz* (ground-beef-and-pork meatballs) or *wrenikje* (cottage-cheese pierogi). The south-side location is bright and immaculately clean, and the restaurant looks spacious, although

you may still have to wait for a table. Service is quick and friendly. ⊠ *1842 Pembina Rte.,* ☎ *204/275–2294. Reservations not accepted. AE, DC, MC, V.*

$ ✕ **Homer's.** This good-time, downtown place, with a definite Mediterranean atmosphere, has been one of the city's favorite Greek restaurants for more than 15 years. Greek specialties include roast leg of lamb and moussaka, but Homer's is also famous for ribs, steak, seafood, pasta, and fresh hot bread. In the summer ask to be seated outdoors on the patio. ⊠ *520 Ellice Ave.,* ☎ *204/788–4858. Reservations essential. AE, DC, MC, V.*

$ ✕ **Kelekis.** This north-end shrine has purveyed legendary burgers, hot dogs, and fries for more than 60 years. Decor includes a photo montage of family history and autographed photos of celebrities. Breakfast, lunch, and dinner are served daily. ⊠ *1100 Main St.,* ☎ *204/ 582–1786. Reservations not accepted. No credit cards.*

$ ✕ **Mandarin.** The Sargent Avenue Mandarin is a crowded, 12-table, west-side place with unique and reasonably exotic northern Chinese dishes. Complete Gourmet Delight Dinners include soup, dumplings, entrées, and dessert. Wine is the only alcohol served. The River Mandarin, a spin-off, has a slightly different menu, a calmer pace, and a full liquor license. ⊠ *Mandarin, 613 Sargent Ave.,* ☎ *204/775–7819; River Mandarin,* ⊠ *252 River Ave.,* ☎ *204/284–8963. Reservations essential. AE, MC, V.*

$$$ ⌧ **Crowne Plaza Winnipeg Downtown.** Winnipeg's largest hotel, this Holiday Inn is 17 stories high and connects to the convention center. Rooms are decorated in pastels and have pleasant modern furnishings— some rooms overlook the skylighted pool. Ticker's lobby bar is a lively spot for a rendezvous. ⊠ *350 St. Mary Ave., R3C 3J2,* ☎ *204/942– 0551 or 800/465–4329,* ℻ *204/943–8702. 406 rooms. 3 restaurants, no-smoking rooms, indoor and outdoor pools, sauna, exercise room, cabaret. AE, DC, MC, V.*

$$$ ⌧ **Holiday Inn Airport/West.** This bright and sumptuous modern prop-
★   erty stands next to the Trans-Canada Highway's western approach to Winnipeg, near the airport, the racetrack, and shopping areas. Rooms are large, with modern earth-tone furnishings. Executive suites, decorated in blue and green, are a bit fancier than standard units. The atrium is a lush setting for the pool and poolside lounge. ⊠ *2520 Portage Ave., R3J 3T6,* ☎ *204/885–4478 or 800/465–4329,* ℻ *204/831–5734. 210 rooms. 2 restaurants, indoor pool, sauna, exercise room. AE, DC, MC, V.*

$$$ ⌧ **Hotel Fort Garry.** Built in 1913 and known far and wide as the Grand Castle, the old railroad hotel is one of Winnipeg's gathering places. On the south edge of downtown, near Union Station, the hotel and its hushed, spacious lobby are furnished with inviting armchairs and original marble, brass, and crystal finishes. Large guest rooms still have classic, dark-wood furnishings and floral wallpapers. ⊠ *222 Broadway, R3C 0R3,* ☎ *204/942–8251 or 800/665–8088,* ℻ *204/956–2351. 246 rooms. 2 restaurants, cabaret. AE, DC, MC, V.*

$$$ ⌧ **Place Louis Riel.** This luxury-class bargain is a converted apartment
★   building that has 255 contemporary suites with living rooms, dining areas, and fully equipped kitchens. Though all rooms are up-to-date, the suites on the upper floors facing west are preferred because of their view of the Legislative Building. The supreme downtown location— adjacent to Eaton Place mall—is only one of the hotel's advantages. ⊠ *190 Smith St., R3C 1J8,* ☎ *204/947–6961; in Canada, 800/665– 0569;* ℻ *204/947–3029. 255 suites. Restaurant, lounge, no-smoking rooms, free parking. AE, DC, MC, V.*

$$$ 🏨 **Travelodge Hotel Downtown Winnipeg.** This high-rise venture of Canada's oldest budget chain is in a strategically desirable location, next to the bus depot and adjacent to the Bay and Winnipeg Art Gallery. Rooms on the south side look out on the Legislative Building, and north-side rooms overlook the city. Guest rooms have subdued modern furnishings in either neutral or pastel colors. ⊠ *360 Colony St., R3B 2P3,* ☎ *204/786–7011 or 800/661–9563,* 📠 *204/772–1443. 157 rooms. Restaurant, no-smoking rooms, indoor pool. AE, DC, MC, V.*

$$$ 🏨 **Westin Hotel Winnipeg.** The top luxury hotel in town is near Win-
★ nipeg's hub—Portage and Main streets—and is connected by the sky-walk to office buildings and Portage Place Mall. The 21st-floor rooftop indoor pool makes a dramatic setting for a swim. Chimes offers a contemporary atmosphere for light meals. Other restaurants include the elegant Velvet Glove Dining Room and Café Express for quick meals at affordable prices. ⊠ *2 Lombard Pl., R3B 0Y3,* ☎ *204/957–1350 or 800/228–3000,* 📠 *204/956–1791. 350 rooms. 3 restaurants, no-smoking rooms, indoor pool, sauna, exercise room. AE, DC, MC, V.*

$$ 🏨 **Charter House.** Half the rooms in this five-story low-rise on the south
★ side of downtown have balconies. Furnishings are contemporary motel style, and the atmosphere is friendly. The Rib Room is a popular, moderately priced place for dinner. ⊠ *330 York Ave., R3C 0N9,* ☎ *204/942–0101; 800/782–0175 in Manitoba;* 📠 *204/956–0665. 90 rooms. 2 restaurants, no-smoking rooms, pool. AE, DC, MC, V.*

$$ 🏨 **Gordon Downtowner Motor Hotel.** There's nothing fancy here, but it's a good deal on the edge of downtown, a block from the Portage Place mall. Most rooms are decorated in dusty rose with gray carpeting. Modern two-room suites are the best bargains. ⊠ *330 Kennedy St., R3B 2M6,* ☎ *204/943–5581,* 📠 *204/947–3041. 40 rooms. Restaurant, pub, free parking. AE, DC, MC, V.*

$$ 🏨 **Journey's End.** This south-side lodging is a reliable choice. The rooms are an adequate size and are furnished in contemporary style, with rose or beige carpets, dusty-rose and earth-tone accessories. There is no charge for local phone calls, and morning coffee is free. ⊠ *3109 Pembina Hwy., R3T 4R6,* ☎ *204/269–7390 or 800/668–4200,* 📠 *204/261–7565. 80 rooms. Restaurant. AE, DC, MC, V.*

$$ 🏨 **Ramada Marlborough.** This ornate, 1914 gothic structure in the Financial District has vaulted ceilings and a stained-glass window and is home to Joanna's Café and Victor's (☞ *above*). The public areas and guest rooms are freshly decorated. The lounge provides an intimate setting for guests. In the spacious lobby, with its marble floors, high ceilings, and wood paneling, there are soft and comfortable sofas. ⊠ *331 Smith St., R3B 2G9,* ☎ *204/942–6411, 204/942–2017 or 800/667–7666,* 📠 *204/942–2017. 121 rooms. 2 restaurants. AE, DC, MC, V.*

$ 🏨 **Assiniboine Gordon Inn on the Park.** This two-story hotel and motor inn is adjacent to a park on the west side, not far from the airport. Rooms are modern and large, albeit somewhat overwrought, with masculine dark wood and bold designs. ⊠ *1975 Portage Ave., R3J 0J9,* ☎ *204/888–4806. 48 rooms. Restaurant, lounge, disco. AE, MC, V.*

Nightlife and the Arts

The Arts

FILM

In Winnipeg, the best places to find imports, art films, oldies, and midnight cult classics are at **Cinémathèque** (⊠ 100 Arthur St., ☎ 204/942–6795) and **Cinema 3** (⊠ 585 Ellice Ave., ☎ 204/783–1097). The **Winnipeg Art Gallery,** (⊠ 300 Memorial Blvd., ☎ 204/786–6641) also has a cinema series.

MUSIC AND DANCE

Winnipeg's principal venue for serious music, dance, and pop concerts is the magnificent 2,263-seat Centennial Concert Hall in the **Manitoba Centennial Centre** (⊠ 555 Main St., ☎ 204/956–1360). From September to mid-May it is the home of the **Winnipeg Symphony Orchestra** (☎ 204/949–3999); the **Royal Winnipeg Ballet** (☎ 204/956–2792 or 800/667–4792) performs here in October, December, March, and May; and the **Manitoba Opera** (☎ 204/942–7479) presents three operas a year—in November, February, and May. Throughout the year, pop concerts take place at the center.

The **Winnipeg Art Gallery** (⊠ 300 Memorial Blvd., ☎ 204/786–6641) hosts jazz, blues, chamber music, and contemporary groups. For contemporary dance and new music, check out **Le Rendez-Vous** (⊠ 768 av. Tache, ☎ 204/233–9214 or 204/237–7692) in St. Boniface. Other performance spaces include **Pantages Playhouse Theatre** (⊠ 180 Market Ave. E, ☎ 204/986–3003) and the **Winnipeg Convention Centre** (⊠ 375 York Ave., ☎ 204/956–1720).

THEATER

One of Canada's most acclaimed regional theaters, the **Manitoba Theatre Centre,** produces serious plays from many sources at the 785-seat **Mainstage** (⊠ 174 Market Ave., ☎ 204/942–6537) and more experimental work in the **MTC Warehouse Theatre** (⊠ 140 Rupert Ave., ☎ 204/942–6537). The **Prairie Theatre Exchange** focuses on local playwrights in an attractive facility in the Portage Place mall (⊠ Portage Ave. and Carlton St., ☎ 204/942–5483).

Nightlife

BARS AND CLUBS

Hy's Steak Loft (⊠ 216 Kennedy St., ☎ 204/942–1000) is convenient for cocktails and has a late-evening piano bar. A most convincingly British pub in the Exchange District is **The King's Head** (⊠ 120 King St., ☎ 204/957–1479).

CASINOS

Play blackjack, baccarat, la boule, and roulette at the **Crystal Casino** (⊠ 7th floor, Hotel Fort Garry, 222 Broadway Ave., ☎ 204/957–2600). There's state-of-the-art gaming at **McPhillips Street Station** (⊠ 484 McPhillips St., ☎ 204/957–3900). You can also try your luck at **Club Regent** (⊠ 1425 Regent Ave., ☎ 204/957–2700).

COMEDY

Try **Rumors Comedy Club** (⊠ 2025 Corydon Ave., ☎ 204/488–4520). The **Comedy Oasis** (⊠ 531 St. Mary's Rd., ☎ 204/231–1463) is also good for laughs.

MUSIC

The **Palomino Club** (⊠ 1133 Portage Ave., ☎ 204/772–0454) is a country-and-western hangout. Rhythm-and-blues fans can check out **Mustang Sally's** (⊠ 114 Market Ave., ☎ 204/957–2700). A somewhat sedate dance floor comes alive after 9 PM in **Windows Lounge** in the Sheraton Winnipeg (⊠ 161 Donald St., ☎ 204/942–5300).

Outdoor Activities and Sports

Participant Sports

BICYCLING AND JOGGING

Most public parks in Manitoba have marked biking and jogging paths. For information on routes, pick up maps from **Travel Manitoba** (☞ Visitor Information *in* Manitoba, *below*).

HEALTH AND FITNESS CLUBS

Drop-in rates and a full slate of classes and equipment are available at **Body Options** (⊠ 1604 St. Mary's Rd., ☎ 204/255–6600) and **Bodyworks** (⊠ 2 Donald St., ☎ 204/477–1691).

Spectator Sports

FOOTBALL

The **Winnipeg Blue Bombers** (☎ 204/784–2583) of the Canadian Football League play home games at the Winnipeg Arena.

HORSE RACING

Assiniboia Downs (⊠ 3975 Portage Ave., at Perimeter Hwy. W, ☎ 204/885–3330) hosts Thoroughbred racing May–October.

Shopping

Art and Crafts

The **Crafts Guild of Manitoba** (⊠ 183 Kennedy St., ☎ 204/943–1190) displays works by Manitoba carvers, weavers, and jewelers. **Northern Images** (⊠ 216 Portage Place Mall, 393 Portage Ave., ☎ 204/942–5501; Airport Executive Centre, 1790 Wellington Ave., ☎ 204/788–4806) markets the work of the Inuit and Déné members of the North Territories Co-operative, which owns the stores. For more Indian art, check out the **Great Canadian Print Company** (⊠ 75 Albert St., ☎ 204/942–1002). **The Upstairs Gallery** (⊠ 266 Edmonton St., ☎ 204/943–2734) has prints, drawings, wall hangings, and sculpture.

Malls and Shopping Districts

Downtown shopping is dominated by **Portage Place** (⊠ Portage Ave. between Balmoral and Carlton Sts.) and **Eaton Place** (⊠ bounded by Graham Ave., Hargrave St., St. Mary Ave., and Donald St.), two malls with numerous stores, fast-food joints, and movie theaters.

Across the Assiniboine River, the **Osborne Village** area (⊠ Osborne St. between River and Corydon Aves.) has 150 trendy boutiques and specialty shops, cafés, restaurants, and crafts shops.

Side Trips

Numbers in the margin correspond to places of interest on the Manitoba map.

Brandon

56 *197 km (122 mi) west of Winnipeg.*

Brandon, Manitoba's second-largest city (population 40,000), is west of Winnipeg, along the Trans-Canada Highway. It is home to the **Commonwealth Air Training Plan Museum,** which contains historic pre–World War II aircraft from the time when the Royal Canadian Air Force had a major training school here. ⊠ *Airport, Hangar 1, Brandon Airport,* ☎ *204/727–2444.* 🎫 *$3.* ☉ *May–Oct., daily 10–4; Nov.–Apr., daily 1–4.*

Spruce Woods

57 *180 km (114 mi) west of Winnipeg.*

In **Spruce Woods Provincial Heritage Park,** among rolling hills covered with spruce and basswood, lies the desertlike **Spirit Sands,** a 16-square-kilometer (7-square-mile) tract of cactus-filled sand dunes. Walk the self-guided trail through the dunes, but keep your eyes peeled for lizards and snakes! Your final destination will be **Devil's Punch Bowl,** a dramatic pit dug out by an underground stream. You can also tour the park in a horse-drawn covered wagon. ⊠ *Rte. 5,* ☎ *204/827–2543.* ☉ *May–Sept., daily.*

Steinbach
71 *48 km (30 mi) southeast of Winnipeg.*

The town of Steinbach is populated with nearly 10,000 descendants of Mennonites who fled religious persecution in late-19th-century Europe. Note the large number of automobile dealerships: Manitoban car buyers flock here because of the Mennonite reputation for making square deals.

In the **Mennonite Heritage Village,** a 40-acre museum, guides demonstrate blacksmithing, wheat grinding, and old-time housekeeping chores while conversing in the Mennonite German dialect. During the Pioneer Days festival in early August, everyone wears costumes and demonstrates homespun crafts. An authentic and extremely low-priced restaurant serves Mennonite specialties, such as borscht, pierogi, and *ukrenky* (cheese or potato torte). ⊠ *Rte. 12, 2 km (1¼ mi) north of Steinbach,* ☎ *204/326–9661.* ☞ *$3.50.* ☉ *May and Sept., Mon.–Sat. 10–7, Sun. noon–7; June–Aug., Mon.–Sat. 10–7, Sun. noon–7.*

Falcon Lake
72 *143 km (89 mi) east of Winnipeg.*

Whiteshell Provincial Park, a 2,590-square-kilometer (984-square-mile) tract on the edge of the Canadian Shield, has 200 lakes that offer some of the best northern-pike, perch, walleye, and lake-trout fishing in western Canada. The Falcon Lake townsite has a shopping center, a golf course, tennis courts, a very good beach, a sailing club, and top-grade accommodations in the 34-room **Falcon Lake Resort & Club** (☎ 204/349–8400). **Beaver Creek** trail is a short walk to such wilderness denizens as beaver and deer. Farther on, **West Hawk Lake** (or Crater Lake)—formed a few thousand years ago by a falling meteor—is 365 feet deep and full of feisty smallmouth bass. Scuba divers love it. ⊠ *Hwy. 1E,* ☎ *204/369–5232.* ☉ *Daily 8 AM–11 PM.*

Lower Fort Garry
73 *32 km (20 mi) north of Winnipeg.*

Lower Fort Garry, built in 1830, is the oldest stone fort remaining from the Hudson's Bay Company fur-trading days. Nowadays, costumed employees describe daily tasks and recount thrilling journeys by York boat, the "boat that won the west." Beaver, raccoon, fox, and wolf pelts hang in the fur loft as a reminder of the bygone days. ⊠ *Rte. 9,* ☎ *204/785–6050.* ☞ *$5.* ☉ *Grounds year-round in daylight hours; buildings mid-May–Sept. 2, daily 10–6.*

Grand Marais
74 *87 km (54 mi) northeast of Winnipeg.*

Grand Beach Provincial Park is on the eastern shore of Lake Winnipeg, the seventh-largest lake in North America. On summer weekends, crowds flock here from Winnipeg for the white-powder sand, the grass-crowned 30-foot dunes, and a lagoon that makes bird-watchers' dreams come true. Grand Marais is the service area at the southern portal to the park. ⊠ *Rte. 12,* ☎ *204/754–2212.* ☉ *May–Sept., daily.*

Gimli
75 *76 km (47 mi) north of Winnipeg.*

Gimli, the largest Icelandic community outside the homeland, was once the center of the independent state of New Iceland. A giant Viking statue proclaims allegiance to the far-off island; the **Gimli Historical Museum,** on the Gimli harbor waterfront, preserves the ethnic heritage of early Ukrainian and Icelandic settlers and records the history of the Lake Winnipeg commercial fishing industry. ⊠ *Rte. 9, Gimli harbor*

area, ☎ *204/642–5317.* ☑ *$2.* ☉ *Mid-May–June, Wed.–Sun. 10–5;*
July and Aug., daily 10–6.

Hecla Island

76 *175 km (109 mi) north of Winnipeg.*

Hecla Provincial Park, about a 2½-hour drive from Winnipeg, is a densely
wooded archipelago named for the Icelandic volcano that drove the
area's original settlers to Canada. The park is on the central North American flyway, and 50,000 waterfowl summer here. **Moose Tower** is a
good spot in the early morning and evening to view moose and other
wildlife. The original 1880s **Hecla Icelandic Fishing Village** is restored
near **Gull Harbour,** the tourist center of the park and site of the luxurious **Gull Harbour Resort** (☎ 204/475–2354), complete with a marina, hiking trails, and a devilishly difficult golf course. ☑ *Rte. 8,* ☎
204/378–2945. ☉ *May–Sept., daily.*

Wasagaming

77 *304 km (190 mi) northwest of Winnipeg via Routes 1 and 10.*

Riding Mountain National Park lies among rolling hills south of Dauphin
in the western part of the province. Manitoba's only national park covers 3,026 square kilometers (1,150 square miles) and comprises forests
and grasslands that support a herd of bison. The townsite of Wasagaming is on Clear Lake, which is ideal for fishing and boating and offers
supervised swimming. The **Elkhorn Ranch and Resort** (☑ Box 40, Rte.
10, Dauphin, R0J 2H0, ☎ 204/848–2802) offers an 18-hole golf
course, tennis, and trail rides. There is also plenty of camping, as well
as other hotels and cabins nearby. ☑ *Riding Mountain National Park,*
Wasagaming ROJ 2HO, ☎ *204/848–2811.*

Churchill

78 *1,600 km (1,000 mi) north of Winnipeg.*

Churchill is Canada's northernmost seaport, on the shore of Hudson
Bay. It has become a mecca for international travelers wanting to see
polar bears up close. **Tundra Buggy Tours** (☎ 204/675–2212 or
800/544–5049) has specially designed vehicles that go out on the tundra for better viewing. Half-day tours, offered July–September, cost $74;
full-day tours, offered in October and early November, cost $162. You
can also ride a Tundra Buggy to the **Tundra Buggy Lodge** ($312.50 per
person per night, including meals), similar to a train, with viewing balconies, berths, and a dining car, which is stationed in the Churchill wilderness wherever wildlife viewing is best.

Winnipeg A to Z

Arriving and Departing

BY CAR

Two main east–west highways link Winnipeg with the prairie provinces.
The Trans-Canada Highway (Highway 1) runs through Winnipeg,
Regina, and Calgary. West of Winnipeg the Yellowhead Highway
(Route 16) branches off the Trans-Canada and heads northwest toward
Saskatoon and Edmonton.

Travelers from the United States can reach the Manitoba capital from
Minneapolis along I–94 and I–29, connecting to Route 75 at the Canadian border. The driving distance between Minneapolis and Winnipeg
is 691 kilometers (432 miles).

Winnipeg International Airport, 8 kilometers (5 miles) from the city, is served by Northwest, Air Canada, Canadian Airlines International, and several commuter airlines.

Between the Airport and Downtown. Taxi fare downtown runs about $10–$12. Some airport-area hotels provide complimentary airport shuttles.

Getting Around

BY BUS

The **City of Winnipeg Transit System** (☎ 204/986–5700) operates an extensive network of buses throughout the city and metropolitan area. Adult fare is $1.35, and it's 75¢ for senior citizens and children over four; exact change is required and transfers are free.

BY TAXI

Taxis—relatively expensive by U.S. standards—can be found outside downtown hotels or summoned by phone. Car services are **Unicity** (☎ 204/947–6611) and **Duffy's Taxi** (☎ 204/775–0101).

Contacts and Resources

EMERGENCIES

Dial 911 for fire, police, ambulance, or poison control.

GUIDED TOURS

Several lines ply the Red and Assiniboine rivers between May and mid-October. The **Paddlewheel River Rouge** (☎ 204/942–4500) offers a variety of cruises (dining, dinner-dance, evening), combining sailings with double-decker bus tours.

The **Prairie Dog Central Steam Train** (☎ 204/832–5259) follows a 58-kilometer (36-mile) route from the Canadian National Railways (CNR) St. James Station (⊠ 1661 Portage Ave.) to Grosse Isle on Sunday, from mid-May through September, departing at 11 AM and 3 PM.

Walking tours of the turn-of-the-century Exchange District begin at the Manitoba Museum of Man & Nature (⊠ 190 Rupert Ave., ☎ 204/943–3139 or 204/956–2830) during July and August.

HOSPITALS

Emergency rooms are located at the **Health Sciences Centre** (⊠ 700 William Ave., ☎ 204/787–3167 or 204/787–2306), **Riverview Health Centre** (⊠ 1 Morley Ave., ☎ 204/452–3411), and **Misericordia General Hospital** (⊠ 99 Cornish Ave., ☎ 204/788–8188).

LATE-NIGHT PHARMACY

Shopper's Drug Mart (⊠ 471 River Ave., ☎ 204/950–7000) is open 24 hours.

VISITOR INFORMATION

The **Government Tourist Reception Office** (⊠ Broadway and Osborne St., ☎ 204/945–3777 or 800/665–0040), housed in the Manitoba Legislative Building, is open May–Labor Day, daily 8:30 AM–9 PM; Labor Day–April, weekdays 8:30–4:30. **Tourism Winnipeg** (⊠ 320-25 The Forks Market Rd., ☎ 204/943–1970) is open weekdays 8:30–4:30; and there's an airport location (☎ 800/665–0204) that's open 8 AM–9:45 PM.

THE PRAIRIE PROVINCES A TO Z

Arriving and Departing

By Bus
Greyhound Lines (consult local directory) and local bus companies provide service from the United States, other parts of Canada, and throughout the prairie provinces.

By Plane
Air Canada and **Canadian Airlines International** have direct or connecting service from Boston, New York, Chicago, San Francisco, and Los Angeles to Winnipeg, Regina, Saskatoon, Calgary, and Edmonton. Commuter affiliates serve other U.S. and Canadian destinations. U.S. airlines serving the prairie provinces include **Northwest** to Winnipeg; **American, Delta,** and **United** to Calgary; **American, Delta,** and **Northwest** to Edmonton.

By Train
There is no direct rail service between the United States and the prairie provinces. **VIA Rail** trains (from New York and Connecticut, ☎ 800/361–3677; from the Atlantic seaboard, 800/561–3949; from the Midwest, 800/387–1144; from the western United States, 800/665–0200) connect eastern Canada and the West Coast through Winnipeg–Saskatoon–Edmonton.

Getting Around

By Car
Two main east–west highways link the major cities of the prairie provinces. The Trans-Canada Highway (Highway 1), mostly a four-lane divided freeway, runs through Winnipeg, Regina, and Calgary on its nationwide course. The two-lane Yellowhead Highway (Route 16) branches off the Trans-Canada Highway west of Winnipeg and heads northwest toward Saskatoon, Saskatchewan, and Edmonton, Alberta. Traveling north–south, four-lane divided freeways connect Saskatoon–Regina (Highway 11) and Edmonton–Calgary (Highway 2).

From the United States, interstate highways cross the Canadian border, and two-lane highways continue on to major cities of the prairie provinces. From Minneapolis, I–94 and then I–29 connect to Route 75 at the Manitoba border south of Winnipeg. A main route to Alberta is I–15 north of Helena, Montana, which connects to Highway 2 and Routes 3 and 4 to Calgary.

By Plane
Canadian Airlines International (☎ 204/632–1250) offers flights to cities and towns throughout the Prairie Provinces.

By Train
VIA Rail (☎ 800/561–8630) operates train service between major cities and towns on two east–west routes through the Prairie Provinces.

Visitor Information

Alberta Tourism (✉ Box 2500, Edmonton T5J 2Z4, ☎ 403/427–4321; in Alberta, 800/222–6501; in the U.S. and Canada, 800/661–8888) distributes extremely comprehensive and useful free promotional literature. The office is open weekdays 9 to 4:30. **Travel Manitoba** (✉ Dept. 2036, 7th floor, 155 Carlton St., Winnipeg R3C 3H8, ☎ 204/945–3777 or 800/665–0040) distributes a free road map and several useful brochures. The office is open weekdays 8:30 to 4:30. **Man-**

itoba Travel Idea Centre (⊠ 21 Forks Market Rd., Winnipeg R3C 4T7, ☎ 204/945–3777) is intended primarily for walk-in traffic and is open Monday through Thursday, 10 to 6 and Friday, 10 to 8. **Manitoba Travel Information Centres,** just inside the Manitoba border along major routes, are open mid-May through early September, 8 AM to 9 PM. **Tourism Saskatchewan** (⊠ Suite 500, 199 Albert St., Regina S4P 4Z9, ☎ 800/667–7191) can provide you with brochures and maps of attractions, accommodations, and parks inside and outside the province. The main office is open weekdays 8 to 7, Saturday 10 to 4. **Information centers,** in cities throughout the province, also open in summer along major highways leading into the province.

6 Toronto

Toronto thrives on ethnic diversity, filled as it is with Italians, Chinese, Portuguese, and other groups in a vibrant mix of cultures. This cosmopolitan, world-class city, established by Scots who set up banks and built churches, is Canada's center of culture, commerce, and communications.

MUCH OF TORONTO'S EXCITEMENT is explained by its ethnic diversity. Nearly two-thirds of the 3.2 million people who now live in the metropolitan area were born and raised somewhere else. Half a million Italians live here, as do the largest Chinese community in Canada and the biggest Portuguese colony in North America. What this has meant to Toronto is the rather rapid creation of a mix of cultures that has echoes of turn-of-the-century New York City—but without the slums, crowding, disease, and tensions.

By Allan Gould

Updated by David Anger

Still, to give to its burgeoning ethnic population all, or even most, of the credit for Toronto's becoming a cosmopolitan, world-class city in just a few decades would be a kind of reverse racism, and not totally correct, either. Much of the thanks must be given to the so-called dour Scots who set up the banks, built the churches, and created the kind of solid base for a community that would come to such a healthy fruition in the four decades following World War II. Toronto is clearly this country's center of culture, commerce, and communications—"New York run by the Swiss," according to Peter Ustinov.

Toronto has gained the nickname Hollywood North, because dozens of major films have been made in this city, especially over the past decade, from *Moonstruck* to *Used People,* and from David Cronenberg's *Dead Ringers* and *Naked Lunch* to such TV series as *Top Cops, Class of '96, Road to Avalon,* and many more. Indeed, it is hard to walk about the city nowadays without tripping over a movie crew and a number of famous people. But as this is Canada—and Toronto—you'll probably all apologize sweetly.

Toronto's roots go back to 1615, when a French explorer named Etienne Brûlé was led by Hurons to the land between the Humber and Don rivers, which was known to the Indians as Toronto ("a place of meetings"). Over the ensuing two centuries it became a busy Indian village named Teiaiagon, a French trading post, and a British town named York. Finally, on March 6, 1834, the city was officially named Toronto again.

Pleasures and Pastimes

Dining

The restaurant scene is in a state of perpetual motion. Is it the reluctant economy that causes all those openings and closings, or is everyone searching for that elusive, perfect little restaurant? Still, more new restaurants opened than closed this year in Toronto.

The formal haute cuisine establishments have all but faded into Toronto's gastronomic history, making way for bistros, cantinas, tavernas, trattorias, tapas bars, noodle bars, wine bars, and smart cafés. Steak houses are proliferating, and the cuisines of the world have appeared on Toronto's doorstep. Recipes need no passports to cross borders. The restaurants of Little Italy, a half dozen individual Chinatowns, urban and suburban, and Little India, have long served up some of the best cooking from their countries. Now, a tidal wave of restaurants specializing in the cuisines of Southeast Asia has hit. Korean, Vietnamese, Laotian, Thai, and Malaysian dishes are taking our taste buds by storm with their assertive, clean flavors: chili, ginger, lemongrass, coconut, lime, and tamarind.

Toronto's brilliant young chefs recognize that when most customers start requesting "sauce on the side," the public's collective taste is chang-

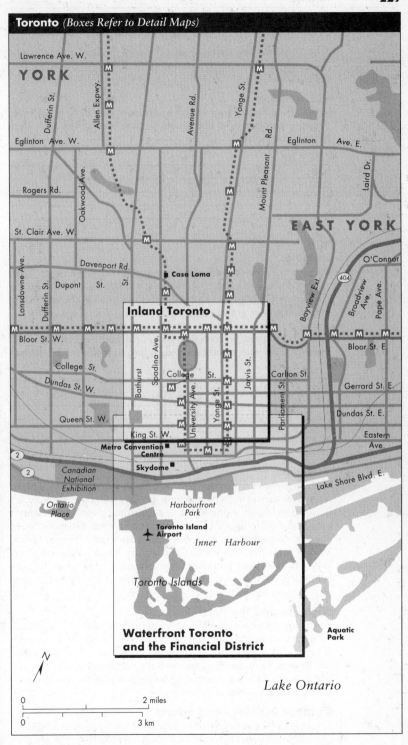

Toronto *(Boxes Refer to Detail Maps)*

Lawrence Ave. W.

Y O R K

Dufferin St.

Allen Expwy.

Avenue Rd.

Yonge St.

Eglinton Ave. W.

Mount Pleasant Rd.

Eglinton Ave. E.

Laird Dr.

Rogers Rd.

Oakwood Ave.

E A S T   Y O R K

St. Clair Ave. W.

O'Connor

Lansdowne Ave.

Dufferin St.

Davenport Rd.

Bayview Ext.

404

Broadview Ave.

Pape Ave.

Dupont St.

St.

■ Casa Loma

Inland Toronto

Bloor St. W.

Spadina Ave.

Bloor St. E.

College St.

Bathurst

College St.

University Ave.

Yonge St.

Jarvis St.

Carlton St.

Gerrard St. E.

Dundas St. W.

Parliament St.

Dundas St. E.

Queen St. W.

King St. W.

Eastern Ave.

2

■ Metro Convention Centre

■ Skydome

Lake Shore Blvd. E.

2

Canadian National Exhibition

Ontario Place

Harbourfront Park

✈ Toronto Island Airport

Inner   Harbour

Toronto Islands

Waterfront Toronto and the Financial District

Aquatic Park

Lake Ontario

0 — 2 miles

0 — 3 km

ing; those with vision are looking over their shoulders toward California for a more creative marriage of fresh-market ingredients.

All restaurants have smoking and nonsmoking sections, and some maintain a totally smoke-free environment. If this is important to you, call to check.

WHAT TO WEAR

Unless noted below, dress in Toronto is casual but neat. In the more elegant and/or expensive restaurants, men are likely to feel more comfortable in a jacket.

CATEGORY	COST*
$$$$	over $40
$$$	$30–$40
$$	$20–$30
$	under $20

*per person without 7% Goods and Services Tax (GST) and 8% provincial sales tax, tip, or drinks

Lodging

Places to stay in this cosmopolitan city range, as one might expect, from luxurious hotels to budget motels to a few dozen bed-and-breakfasts. Prices are cut over weekends and during quiet times of the year (many Toronto hotels drop their rates a full 50% in January and February). Wherever you stay in Toronto, try to bargain for a lower-than-standard rate. You can insist on corporate prices or demand special deals, and you should get your request granted, as long as rooms are available.

CATEGORY	COST*
$$$$	over $175
$$$	$125–$175
$$	$70–$125
$	under $70

All prices are for a standard double room, excluding 7% GST, 5% room tax, and optional service charge

Museums

There may not be a museum mile here, but this metropolis by the lake certainly possesses miles of museums. The Royal Ontario Museum, affectionately known as the ROM, is a sprawling giant that presents a brilliant and wildly diverse collection from mummies to televisions, totem poles to shopping bags. Its period rooms are superb. For art lovers, Toronto is the place to explore Canadian art, which is definitely overlooked by most American and European curators. Then, too, Toronto boasts offbeat museums devoted to the study of hockey, design, history, science, and even shoes.

Nightlife and the Arts

Toronto is not only Canada's capital of the lively arts; it has also become the third most important theater city in the English-speaking world, after New York and London. True, Winnipeg has a very fine ballet, and Montréal's orchestra is superb. But no other city in Canada, and few in North America, can compete with the variety of music, opera, dance, and theater found in Toronto.

Outdoor Activities and Sports

In Canada's largest city, sports are more of a religion than a pastime. The big professional baseball, basketball, and hockey teams are considered civic treasures. Even the fledgling Canadian pro-football franchise commands a loyal audience. When Toronto residents aren't watching a match, they're enjoying lifetime fitness pursuits. In the warmer months, the streets and lakefront brim with bikers, runners, and walkers. When the cold takes over, it seems as if every hardy soul is skating outdoors.

Shopping

Toronto prides itself on having some of the finest shopping in North America; and, indeed, most of the world's name boutiques can be found here. There's also a large artistic and crafts community, with many art galleries, custom jewelers, clothing designers, and artisans selling everything from sophisticated glass sculpture to Native art, traditional crafts, antiques, quilts, wood carvings, and pine furniture. Local food items include wild rice, available in bulk or in gift packages, and maple syrup in jars or cans.

EXPLORING TORONTO

Imagine the downtown area of Toronto as a large rectangle. The southern boundary is Lake Ontario. The western edge, shooting north to Bloor Street (the northern edge) and beyond, is Spadina Avenue, near the foot of which stands the CN (Canadian National) Tower, Harbourfront, and the spectacular SkyDome Stadium. Just west of the rectangle along the waterfront are the Canadian National Exhibition (CNE) grounds, site of the enormous annual fair, and Ontario Place, an upscale amusement park built on man-made islands. Toward the east side of downtown, running from the lakefront north for hundreds of miles (believe it or not), is Yonge Street, which divides the city in half. University Avenue, a major road that parallels Yonge Street, for some reason changes its name to Avenue Road at the corner of Bloor Street, next to the Royal Ontario Museum. A further note: College Street, legitimately named, as many of the University of Toronto's buildings run along it, becomes Carlton Street where it intersects Yonge Street, then heads east.

Great Itineraries

IF YOU HAVE 3 DAYS

Start at the grandiose **Union Station** and glance upward at the romantic roof of the famed **Royal York Hotel,** which has defined Toronto's cityscape since 1928. Head north on Yonge, surveying the towering edifices of pride and progress above, before arriving at **Eaton Centre.** Conquering this vast consumer emporium could take nearly a day for the shopping enthusiast, but there's a whole city to see. So, exit on Queen Street West and behold the magnificent **New City Hall** of 1965. Three decades after its completion, Viljo Revell's monumentally sculpted twin towers and plaza stand as one of North America's best examples of modern design. Cold weather permitting, rent skates and glide across **Nathan Phillips Square.** The next day, ride the subway to Bloor and Yonge. Walk west along Bloor Street—a dazzling upscale shopping thoroughfare—to Avenue Road, where the **Royal Ontario Museum** awaits. The ROM is no lightweight, so plan on spending two to four hours here. Exit the ROM on University Avenue, walking south to **Queen's Park,** home of Ontario's rambling, Romanesque-inspired **Provincial Parliament Building** of 1886. On day three, visit the impressive **Art Gallery of Ontario,** which contains the largest collection in the world of Henry Moore sculptures. Then stroll along the waterfront, stopping at the Queen's Quay Terminal in **Harbourfront** and passing by the **Skydome.** On a clear day, ride to the peak of the **CN Tower,** the world's tallest freestanding structure.

IF YOU HAVE 5 DAYS

Extra time offers the opportunity to experience the city as locals live it. Besides the attractions mentioned in the three-day tour, you might try these: On a Saturday, conquer either the **Kensington** or **St. Lawrence**

Market (☞ Shopping, *below*). Both are vibrant ventures, although the St. Lawrence at Front and Jarvis streets is larger and indoors. In summer, buy fresh ingredients for a picnic lunch before cruising across Lake Ontario on a ferry boat to the **Toronto Islands.** Plan to either walk or bike on the islands—no automobiles are permitted. In the late afternoon, you can explore **Queen Street West**—Toronto's version of Soho. On day five, return to the **Yorkville** district, the epicenter for affluent Toronto. Beyond the tony designer boutiques and elegant restaurants, check out the **Bata Shoe Museum** and **Casa Loma.** Admission to these cultural landmarks is the best deal in Yorkville.

IF YOU HAVE 7 DAYS

Follow the three- and five-day itineraries above; then, on day six, rent a car. Approximately 45 minutes north of Toronto on Islington Avenue sits the stunning **McMichael Canadian Art Collection** on over 100 acres of blissful meadows and woodlands. Its 5,000-piece collection champions Canada's landscape artists known as the Group of Seven, including Tom Thomson. These works are augmented by many Native and contemporary Canadian artworks. Plan on taking in a first-rate lunch at the McMichael's restaurant. Next, travel to the **Ontario Science Centre** and the **Toronto Zoo,** especially if there are little ones along. Day seven is ripe for exploring overlooked neighborhoods and sites, such as the **Design Exchange** and the **Hockey Hall of Fame.** Both are rescued historic buildings from the wrecking ball: The Design Exchange is in the old Toronto Stock Exchange, and the Hockey Hall of Fame is in the original Bank of Montréal. Whether you're a hockey devotee or not, a visit to the Hall of Fame is demanded, if only because it's encased in Spanish architect Santiago Calatrava's incredible six-story galleria.

Numbers in the text correspond to numbers in the margin and on the Toronto, Waterfront Toronto and the Financial District, and Inland Toronto maps.

The Toronto Islands

The islands form a pleasant park with numerous attractions, including a stunning view of the Toronto skyline. The four thin, curved, tree-lined islands—Centre, Ward's, Algonquin, and Olympic—have been attracting visitors since 1833, four years before Victoria became queen and just a year before the town of York changed its name to Toronto.

A Good Walk

Just behind the giant Westin Harbour Castle is the debarkation point for ferries to the **Toronto Islands** ①. It takes only eight minutes for the quaint little ferries to chug across the tiny bay. On these islands, all transportation comes to you compliments of your feet: No cars are allowed anywhere. Your nostrils will wonder at the lack of exhaust fumes, while your feet will wonder why you insist on walking all the way along the boardwalk from Centre to Ward's Island (2½ kilometers, or 1½ miles). You'll be wise to rent a bike for an hour or more and work your way across the interconnected islands. If you are traveling with children, Centre Island is certainly the one to check out first. A few hundred yards from the ferry docks lies **Centreville,** an amusement park that's supposed to be a turn-of-the-century children's village. Perhaps most enjoyable for children is **Far Enough Farm,** which is near enough to walk to.

TIMING

Take the earliest possible ferry and return at your leisure. Plan on, at least, staying for a picnic lunch. Families may want to stay longer. If you love the outdoors plan for the entire day.

Sights to See

Numbers in the margin correspond to points of interest on the Waterfront Toronto and the Financial District map.

❶ Toronto Islands. These are surely among the highlights of any trip to the city—especially from May to October. The more than 550 acres of parkland are irresistible for renting a bike, hiking, snowshoeing, or skiing cross-country with downtown Toronto over your shoulder. Encircling the islands are sandy beaches; the best are on the southeast tip of Ward's Island, the southernmost edge of Centre Island, and the west side of Hanlan's Point. ⊠ *Island information,* ☎ *416/392–8195. Ferries, Foot of Bay St.,* ☎ *416/392–8193 or 416/392–8186.* 🖪 *$3.* ☉ *Winter, daily every ½ hr or so until 10 or 11 AM, every hr or so thereafter; summer, daily 3 times per hr.*

🐾 Beaches. There are free changing rooms near each area, but no facilities for checking your clothes. Swimming in the various lagoons and channels is prohibited. Yet there are great swimming areas at Hanlon's Point, Manitou Beach, and Ward Island. The beaches on Ward tend to be the least crowded. They're also the cleanest; there have been problems with the cleanliness of Lake Ontario's water over the past decade. Except for the hottest days in August, the Great Lake tends to be uncomfortably chilly, so bring appropriate clothing.

🐾 Centreville. The concept works wondrously well: True, the pizza, fries, and hot dogs are barely edible—pack a lunch!—but on the little Main Street there are charming shops, a town hall, a little railroad station, and more than a dozen rides, including a restored 1890s merry-go-round with more than four dozen hand-carved animals. There's no entrance fee to the modest, 14-acre amusement park, although you'll have to pay a nominal charge for each ride or buy an all-day pass. ⊠ *Centre Island,* ☎ *416/203–0405.* 🖪 *95¢ per ride.* ☉ *Mid-May–Labor Day, weekdays 10:30–6, weekends 10:30–8; Labor Day–Oct., weekends 10:30–6 weather permitting.*

🐾 Far Enough Farm. It has all kinds of animals to pet and feed, ranging from piglets to geese, cows to birds. This is a great treat for youngsters, especially the wee ones. ⊠ *Centre Island,* ☎ *416/393–8195.* 🖪 *Free.* ☉ *Daily, dawn–dusk.*

🐾 Gibraltar Lighthouse. Built in 1808 near the southeastern tip of Ward's Island, it is the oldest monument in the city still standing on its original site, but it cannot be entered. Right next to it is a pond stocked with rainbow trout and a concession for buying bait and renting rods. ⊠ *Gibraltar Point.*

Harbourfront

Until the early 1980s, Toronto was notoriously negligent about its waterfront. The Gardiner Expressway, Lakeshore Boulevard, and a network of rusty rail yards stood as hideous barriers to the natural beauty of Lake Ontario. Some 15 years ago the various levels of government began a struggle to change this unfortunate situation. First came the very handsome Westin Harbour Castle Hotel and an attractive tower of condominiums at the foot of Yonge Street on Harbourfront. Nowadays these buildings are just part of a phalanx of hotels, condominiums, shopping malls, and recreational and cultural attractions that stretch for almost a mile along the lakefront west of Yonge Street.

A Good Walk

Back at the ferry docks on the mainland, your next move should be to **Harbourfront** ②, within walking distance of Union Station. If you're

234

Waterfront Toronto and the Financial District

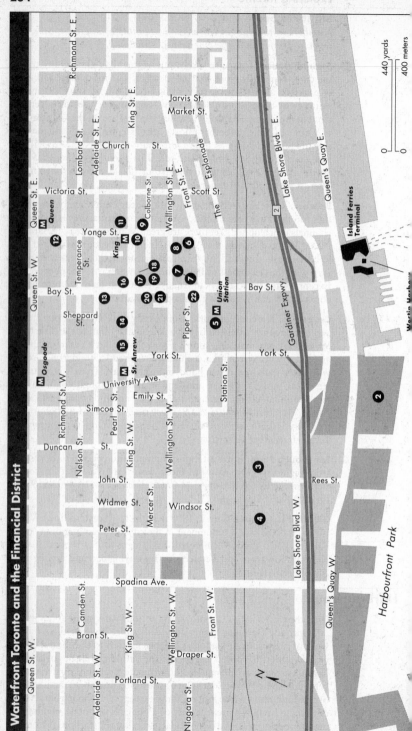

Richmond St. E.

King St. E.

Jarvis St.
Market St.

Lombard St.

Adelaide St. E.

Church St.

Wellington St. E.

Front St. E.

The Esplanade

Scott St.

Lake Shore Blvd. E.

Queen's Quay E.

Island Ferries Terminal

Westin Harbour

Queen St. E.

M Queen

Victoria St.

Colborne St.

11

9

Yonge St.

12

Temperance St.

M King

10

10

8

6

Queen St. W.

16

17

18

19

7

7

Bay St.

13

20

21

22

Bay St.

M Union Station

5

Sheppard St.

14

Piper St.

15

M St. Andrew

York St.

York St.

M Osgoode

Richmond St. W.

University Ave.

Emily St.

Simcoe St.

Station St.

Gardiner Expwy.

Pearl St.

King St. W.

Wellington St. W.

2

Duncan St.

Nelson St.

John St.

Rees St.

3

Widmer St.

Mercer St.

Windsor St.

Lake Shore Blvd. W.

4

Peter St.

Queen's Quay W.

Spadina Ave.

Camden St.

King St. W.

Wellington St. W.

Front St. W.

Harbourfront Park

Brant St.

Adelaide St. W.

Draper St.

N

Portland St.

Niagara St.

Queen St. W.

440 yards

400 meters

0

0

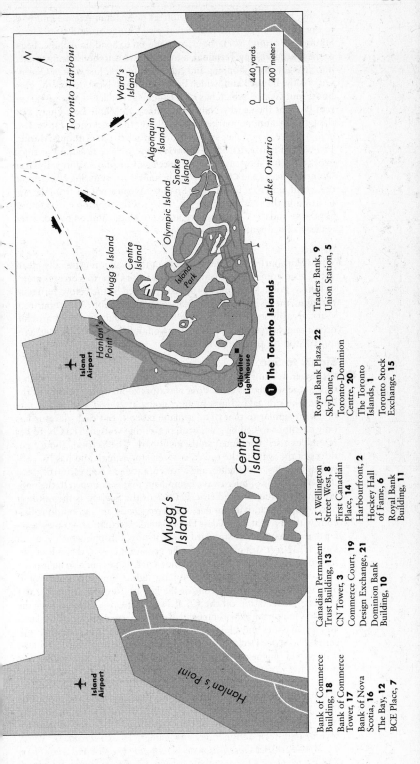

1 The Toronto Islands

Bank of Commerce Building, **18**
Bank of Commerce Tower, **17**
Bank of Nova Scotia, **16**
The Bay, **12**
BCE Place, **7**

Canadian Permanent Trust Building, **13**
CN Tower, **3**
Commerce Court, **19**
Design Exchange, **21**
Dominion Bank Building, **10**

15 Wellington Street West, **8**
First Canadian Place, **14**
Harbourfront, **2**
Hockey Hall of Fame, **6**
Royal Bank Building, **11**

Royal Bank Plaza, **22**
SkyDome, **4**
Toronto-Dominion Centre, **20**
The Toronto Islands, **1**
Toronto Stock Exchange, **15**

Traders Bank, **9**
Union Station, **5**

driving, head for the foot of Bay Street or Spadina Avenue and park in one of the many lots. A streetcar also swings around from Union Station (☞ *below*) to Harbourfront and on to Spadina Avenue. Begin at the **Queen's Quay Terminal,** a former food warehouse transformed into an eight-story shopping and cultural complex. Just west of Queen's Quay is the **Power Plant,** which hosts art shows. Next door is the **HarbourFront Centre,** which has arts, canoeing, and ice-skating. You can rent boats at the nearby **Nautical Centre.** On **Maple Leaf Quay,** visit the outdoor antique market, especially on the weekends. Otherwise, enjoy the very popular and indoor **Harbourfront Antique Market.** Just west of Harbourfront is **Ontario Place,** a 96-acre family-oriented experience that showcases the province and Canada. A short walk from Ontario Place is the **CN Tower** ③, the tallest freestanding structure in the world, on Front Street, near Spadina Avenue, not far from the waterfront. In the shadow of the CN Tower is the **SkyDome** ④ stadium. SkyDome and the CN Tower are linked to Union Station by a covered walkway lined with fast-food outlets.

TIMING

While Harbourfront buzzes throughout the year, it is especially pleasant to visit from May to October, when Lake Ontario's breezes aren't so bitterly cold. As the natives are barely fazed by the below-zero temperatures, the district remains a year-round destination. A Harbourfront visit can easily stretch across an entire day, particularly if there are children along. Set aside at least one to two hours for the CN Tower, a required stop for first-time visitors.

Sights to See

☺ ③ **CN Tower.** It's fully 1,815 feet, 5 inches high, and it really is worth a visit, if the weather is clear. Four elevators zoom up the outside of the tower. The ride takes but a minute, going at 20 feet a second, a rate of ascent similar to that of a jet-plane takeoff. But each elevator has only one floor-to-ceiling glass wall, preventing vertigo. The CN Tower resembles a self-contained amusement park. The **Skypod,** about two-thirds of the way up the tower, is seven stories high and has two observation decks, a nightclub, and a restaurant that revolves 360 degrees. It also has loads of microwave equipment that is not open to the public but is its true raison d'être. Level 2 of the Skypod is the **outdoor observation deck,** with an enclosed promenade and an outdoor balcony with a breathtaking **Glass Floor**—solid glass that is five times heavier than demanded for standard construction, through which you can look 1,122 feet straight down to the ground. Level 3, the **indoor observation deck,** has not only conventional telescopes but also high-powered periscopes that almost simulate flight. A unique Tour Wand System provides an audio tour of the city of Toronto. A minitheater shows a presentation on the CN Tower. Here you can also visit the **EcoDek,** multimedia environmental displays that explore air, water, land, and urban issues and a large-screen theater that focuses on global concerns. The **Space Deck,** 33 stories higher, at an elevation of 1,465 feet, is the world's highest public observation gallery. But even from the Skypod below, you can often see Lake Simcoe to the north and the mist rising from Niagara Falls to the south. All the decks provide spectacular panoramic views of Toronto, Lake Ontario, and the Toronto Islands. Peak visiting hours are 11–4, particularly on weekends; you may wish to work around them. At the base of the CN Tower, you can try several high-tech action rides and games. ⊠ *301 Front St. W,* ☎ *416/360–8500.* ▱ *Observation deck, including EcoDek and Glass Floor, $12; Space Deck $15; action attractions $7–$8.* ☉ *Summer, daily 10 AM–midnight; fall–spring times vary by up to an hr, so call ahead.*

★ ❷ **Harbourfront.** This 100-acre waterfront culture and recreation center draws more than 3 million visitors each year. It stretches along Queen's Quay from York Street for nearly a mile to Bathurst Street. The trip is well worth planning for: Check *Now* magazine, *Eye Weekly* magazine, the Thursday edition of the *Toronto Star,* and Saturday's *Globe and Mail* to see what concerts, dances, art shows, and festivals are taking place, and build your visit around them. More than 100 dealers crowd the **HarbourFront Antique Market** (⊠ 390 Queen's Quay W, ☎ 416/260–2626) in a sprawling warehouse, peddling everything from Victorian candlesticks to 18th-century furniture, modern collectibles to vintage jewelry. At **HarbourFront Centre** (⊠ 235 Queen's Quay W, ☎ 416/973–3000) craftspeople—working in glass, metal, ceramics, and textiles—create in full view of the public. There are also concerts, live theater, and readings here. The Centre's York Quay Gallery presents crafts as well as fine arts, while the Bounty gift shop showcases contemporary craft goods. A shallow pond at the south end is used for canoe lessons in warmer months and as the largest artificial ice-skating rink in North America in more wintry times. The **Nautical Centre** (⊠ 283 Queen's Quay W, ☎ 416/973–4094) has many private firms renting vessels and offering sailing and canoeing lessons. On **Maple Leaf Quay,** an outdoor antiques market of 70 or so dealers doubles in size on Sunday. The **Queen's Quay Terminal** (⊠ 207 Queen's Quay W, ☎ 416/203–0501) is a 57-year-old food warehouse transformed in 1983 into a magnificent eight-story structure with delightful (though pricey) specialty shops, eateries, and the handsome 450-seat Premiere Dance Theatre. The **Power Plant** (⊠ 231 Queen's Quay W, ☎ 416/973–4949), in a 1927 building with a tall red smokestack, hosts exhibitions of contemporary arts—painting, sculpture, architecture, video, photography, design, installation, file, and performance art.

☺ **Ontario Place.** This waterfront entertainment complex is built on three man-made islands that offer something for everyone. Its architectural centerpiece is the **Cinesphere,** an homage to Buckminster Fuller's acclaimed geodesic dome at Expo '67. Inside the dome a six-story movie screen shows IMAX and 70mm films. You can explore the *Haida,* a World War II destroyer. At the outdoor **Forum,** nightly concerts take place. **Children's Village** has water games, slides, puppet shows, clowns, magicians, and a children's theater. From mid-May to September, Ontario Place brims with people and concerts. ⊠ *South of Lakeshore Blvd.,* ☎ *416/314–9900.* ☞ *Free; charge for some individual attractions, including events at the Forum.* ☼ *Mid-May–mid-Sept., daily 10 AM–midnight.*

☺ ❹ **SkyDome.** One of Toronto's newest—and already one of its most famous—landmarks is the home of the Blue Jays. It is the world's only stadium with a fully retractable roof. Toronto has lost no opportunity to honor its World Series–winning baseball team—the official address of SkyDome is 1 Blue Jays Way. One way to see the huge 52,000-seat stadium is to buy tickets for a Blue Jays game or one of the many other events that take place here. These may include cricket matches, Wrestlemania, monster truck races, Peter Pan on ice, and even the opera *Aïda.* You can take a one-hour walking tour (including a 15-minute film). The tours are not available, however, when daytime events are scheduled. ⊠ *Tour entrance: Front and John Sts., between Gates 1 and 2, northeast corner of SkyDome,* ☎ *416/341–2770.* ☞ *Tour $9.* ☼ *Tour leaves daily on the hr 10–3 or 4; call ahead.*

The Financial District

This is the epicenter of Canada's commercial life. To prove it, the nation's leading banks have erected handsome and modern monuments to their achievements by way of towering skyscrapers. Many of the 20th century's best and brightest architects have contributed to Toronto's especially modern attitude, including I.M. Pei, Edward Durrell Stone, Mies van der Rohe, and Santiago Calatrava, among others. Running below all of this design splendor is the Underground City, a dazzling maze of tunnels that links the Financial District and keeps the business people warm during the city's long cold season.

A Good Walk

On the south side of Front Street, between Bay and York streets across from the handsome Royal York Hotel, stands monumental **Union Station** ⑤. From here, walk back along Front Street to the northwest corner of Yonge Street, where you'll find the **Hockey Hall of Fame** ⑥ in a former branch of the Bank of Montréal. In a dramatic contrast of old and new, the original Bank of Montréal building has been incorporated into the striking **BCE Place** ⑦ with its huge, sophisticated galleria. Just steps north is a shabby row of shops, among the oldest surviving commercial buildings in the city, which give a sense of the scale of buildings from the 1850s, when Toronto was new. Continue up Yonge from Front Street and take a left at the first intersection. At **15 Wellington Street West** ⑧ is an elegant stone bank. Head back a few steps to Yonge Street and go north again. On the northeast corner of Yonge and Colborne streets is the 1905–06 **Traders Bank** ⑨, the first "skyscraper" of the city. The next building to the north, built in 1913, is owned by **Canadian Pacific,** the famous company whose transcontinental railroad literally helped build a country. At the southwest corner of King and Yonge streets is the **Dominion Bank Building** ⑩, erected in 1913. Diagonally across the intersection is the original **Royal Bank Building** ⑪. Farther north along Yonge Street, at Richmond Street West, is the original Simpsons department store, now **The Bay** ⑫. Outside, continue a few steps west to Bay Street, a name synonymous with finance and power in Canada, as Wall Street is in the United States. Head south (left), back toward the lakefront. Just south of Adelaide Street, on the west side of Bay Street, is the **Canada Permanent Trust Building** ⑬. Turn right (west) along King Street, and on your right stands the first of the towering bank buildings that have defined Toronto's skyline over the past two decades. Here is **First Canadian Place** ⑭, built in the early 1970s. Farther along you come to the second phase of the project, opened in 1983, which houses the ultramodern **Toronto Stock Exchange** ⑮. On the northeast corner of King and Bay streets is the **Bank of Nova Scotia** ⑯, built between 1949 and 1951, and partially replaced by the modern **Scotia Tower** just to the east. On the southeast corner of King and Bay streets is the "old" **Bank of Commerce Tower** ⑰, which for a third of a century was the tallest building in the British Commonwealth. Tucked behind this tower is the **Bank of Commerce Building** ⑱, built between 1929 and 1931 and one of Toronto's premiere bank buildings. The company's 57-story glass and stainless steel **Commerce Court** ⑲ is just south of the "old tower." Due west, across Bay Street, also on the south side of King Street, are the five black towers of the **Toronto-Dominion Centre** ⑳, the first International-style skyscrapers built in Toronto, which houses the Toronto-Dominion Bank's **Gallery of Inuit Art,** one of the finest of its kind in Canada. Immediately to the south of the Toronto-Dominion Centre towers is the fabulous **Design Exchange** ㉑, an exposition complex housed in the former Toronto Stock Exchange Building of 1937. Walk south another block to the northwest corner of Bay and Front streets: Here, in all its golden glory, is the **Royal Bank Plaza** ㉒. Running beneath the financial district is Toronto's **Underground City,** a sprawling maze of convenience shops, lobbies, and even trees.

TIMING

Plan on spending an entire day in the Financial District, especially if you stop at the various museums and shops along the way. Since many of these acclaimed buildings are closed on Saturday and Sunday, schedule this walk during the work week. Be aware, of course, that during the cold season these marvelous edifices create chilling wind tunnels; dress appropriately.

Sights to See

18 **Bank of Commerce Building.** Nearly 70 years after its completion in 1931, this ranks as the best office tower in the financial district, combining monumentality and grace in a stunning 34-story structure. The Romanesque exterior is awe-inspiring, as is the equally compelling interior of marble floors, limestone walls, and bronze vestibule doors decorated with masks, owls, and animals. In the alcoves on each side of the entrance, murals trace the history of transportation. The bronze elevator doors are richly decorated; the vaulted banking hall is illuminated by period chandeliers. It's so beautiful that visitors are inclined to snap a photo, but bank officials forbid it. ⊠ *25 King St. W.*

17 **Bank of Commerce Tower.** For 30 years the tallest building in the British Commonwealth, it has a set-back top; huge, carved human heads adorn all four sides. The base has bas-relief carvings, and there is marvelous animal and floral ornamentation around the vaulted entrance. ⊠ *King and Bay Sts.*

16 **Bank of Nova Scotia and Scotia Plaza.** This 25-story 1949 building by architect John Lyle has successfully been joined to a 68-story 1989 postmodern tower. The original building is in neoclassical beaux-arts style. Above the large exterior windows, it has sculptural panels inspired by Greek mythology. In the lobby, reliefs symbolizing four regions of Canada fill the walls below a brightly colored, gilded plaster ceiling. The north wall relief depicts some of the industries and enterprises financed by the bank. The original stainless-steel-and-glass stairway decorated with marine motifs leads up from the marble counters and floors. All this opens graciously onto the recent Scotia Plaza building. ⊠ *30–44 King St. W.*

12 **The Bay.** Built in 1895 as Simpson's department store, it was one of the city's first buildings with a steel-frame construction. Later bought by The Bay, the department store no longer possesses the allure that Robert Simpson's emporium did, but the **Thompson Gallery** (☎ 416/861–4571) on the top floor is worth the circuitous climb of elevators and escalators. This emporium's melange of buildings blankets an entire block. The most stunning is the six-story 1907 structure at Queen and Yonge streets, with attractive terra-cotta decorations. The Art Deco section along Richmond Street, near Bay Street, was added in 1928. In 1971, an aluminum and glass office tower went up at the corner of Queen and Bay. The Bay is owned by Hudson's Bay Company, North America's oldest company, which received a fur-trading charter from King Charles II of England in 1670. ⊠ *160–184 Yonge St.*

7 **BCE Place.** Completed in 1990, this granite and glass mixed-use complex, in a dramatic contrast of old and new, represents the last hurrah of Toronto's 1980s building boom. But what a triumph! Two towers—51 and 44 stories—incorporate 12 historic buildings, including the original Bank of Montréal building, plus a magnificent six-story galleria atrium designed by Santiago Calatrava. ⊠ *161 Bay St.*

13 **Canadian Permanent Trust Building.** Built in the very year of the stock market crash (and we don't mean the 1987 one), it's a stout skyscraper in the New York wedding-cake style. Ornate stone carvings decorate both the lower stories and the top, where carved, stylized faces peer down to the street below. The imposing vaulted entrance has polished brass doors, and even the elevator doors in the foyer are embossed brass. The spacious banking hall has a vaulted ceiling, marble walls and pillars, and a marble floor with mosaic borders. ⊠ *320 Bay St.*

⑲ Commerce Court. The Bank of Commerce's sister structure is the 57-story glass and stainless steel tower built in 1968. ⊠ *243 Bay St.*

㉑ Design Exchange. Since its opening in 1994, the DX has emerged as North America's most innovative design exposition and promotion center, encompassing architecture, decorative arts, graphics, and interiors. All this glory stands in a stunning Art Deco structure of polished pink granite and smooth buff limestone that once housed the Toronto Stock Exchange. The Toronto-based architectural firm of KPMB Associates gracefully blended the past with the present here, preserving Charles Comfort's famed murals above the historic trading floor. ⊠ *234 Bay St.,* ☎ *416/363–6121.* ▭ *$5.* ☉ *Tues.–Fri. 10–6, weekends noon–5.*

⑩ Dominion Bank Building. Erected in 1913 by the same architects who designed the Bank of Montréal (☞ *above*), this classic Chicago-style skyscraper has a marble and bronze stairway leading to the second floor. Upstairs, the opulent banking hall has a marble floor and marble walls. On the ornate plaster ceiling are reproduced the coats of arms of the nine Canadian provinces in existence at the time it was built. ⊠ *King and Yonge Sts., southwest corner.*

⑧ 15 Wellington Street West. The oldest building on this walk, it is an elegant stone Greek Revival structure that houses a bank. ⊠ *15 Wellington St. W.*

⑭ First Canadian Place. This 72-story office tower is difficult to miss. Designed in the early 1970s by Edward Durrell Stone for the Bank of Montréal, the edifice is covered in Italian white marble. He deliberately faced it with white to contrast with the black of the Toronto-Dominion Centre, to the south, and with the silver of the Commerce Court tower, diagonally opposite. The marble theme continues inside the glamorous lobby. ⊠ *50 King St. W.*

⑥ Hockey Hall of Fame. Writer John Robert Columbo observed that the two distinctly Canadian institutions are the United Church of Canada and the National Hockey League. So, it is appropriate that in this hockey capital of the world sits a first-rate tribute to the fast and furious winter sport. In addition to showcasing the coveted Stanley Cup trophy, the Hall of Fame contains 13 zones, including one where visitors can take shots at a computer-generated goalie; another is a precise replica (right down to the trainer's whirlpool) of the Montréal Canadiens' dressing room. There's also a store that carries an array of hockey jerseys, skates, and other apparel, as well as souvenirs. Even non-hockey fans marvel at this multimedia exhibition, which is inventively based in a historic branch of the Bank of Montréal from 1893. An archive and resource library is also available by appointment. ⊠ *BCE Place, Concourse Level,* ☎ *416/360–7765.* ▭ *$8.75.* ☉ *Weekdays and Sun. 10–5, Sat. 9:30–6.*

⑪ Royal Bank Building. Built in 1913 for the Royal Bank, it has a distinctive cornice, an overhanging roof, a decorative pattern of sculpted ox skulls above the ground-floor windows, and classically detailed leaves at the top of the Corinthian columns. ⊠ *King and Yonge Sts., northeast corner.*

㉒ Royal Bank Plaza. Built in 1976, it is already a classic of its kind. Be sure to go into the 120-foot-high banking hall to see the lovely hanging sculpture by Jesus Raphael Soto. ⊠ *Bay and Front Sts., northwest corner.*

20 **Toronto-Dominion Centre.** Mies van der Rohe, the guiding light of modern architecture, designed this austere four-building masterwork, even though he died in 1969 before it was fully realized. As he did with his acclaimed Seagram Building on New York's Park Avenue, Mies stripped these buildings to their skin and bones of bronze-color glass and black metal I-beams. The tallest tower reaches 56 stories. The only decoration consists of geometric repetition, and the only extravagance is the use of rich materials, such as marble counters and leather-covered furniture. Walk inside the low-rise square banking pavilion at King and Bay to experience a virtually intact Mies interior. Here you can visit the **Gallery of Inuit Art,** one of the few galleries in North America devoted to Inuit art. This space holds the Toronto-Dominion Bank's incredible collection, which equals that of the Smithsonian Institution. The gallery focuses attention on Canada's huge and unexplored Northern frontier. ⊠ *Centre: 55 King St. W.* ⊠ *Gallery: 79 Wellington St.,* ☎ *416/982–8473.* 🎟 *Free.* ☉ *Weekdays 8–6, weekends 10–4.*

15 **Toronto Stock Exchange.** At North America's second-largest stock exchange, go to the fourth-floor visitor center, where you can learn about the securities industry through colorful displays, or even join in daily presentations. The attractions are many: a 140-seat auditorium, an educational audiovisual presentation, a real-time stock-quotation terminal, and avant-garde artworks by General Idea and Robert Longo. ⊠ *Exchange Tower, 2 First Canadian Pl.,* ☎ *416/947–4700.* 🎟 *Free.* ☉ *Tues.–Thurs. 10–2, hourly; Fri. 2.*

9 **Traders Bank.** Built in 1905–06, the first "skyscraper" in the city, 15 stories high, came complete with an observation deck, now closed. The building has been dwarfed by 50-story giants. ⊠ *67 Yonge St.*

Underground City. The origins of what is purportedly the largest pedestrian walkway in the world go back over a generation. One can walk—and shop, eat, and browse—without ever seeing the light of day, from beneath Union Station to the Royal York Hotel, the Toronto-Dominion Centre, First Canadian Place, the Sheraton Centre, the Eaton Centre, and the Atrium-on-Bay. Altogether, it extends through nearly 5 kilometers (3 miles) of tunnels and seven subway stops. If you become disoriented (and many newcomers do), head for a subway station: maps of the underground area are posted near the turnstiles. Enter the subterranean community from anywhere between Dundas Street on the north and Union Station on the south, and you'll encounter art exhibitions, buskers, fountains, and trees growing as much as two stories high, as well as crowds of business men and women on breaks from their offices in the towers above.

5 **Union Station.** Designed in 1907, when trains were still as exciting as space shuttles are today, it was opened in 1927 by the Prince of Wales. If any building in Toronto can be called monumental, this is it. Over 750 feet long and set well back along its Front Street block, this landmark borrows from Classical architecture to create a magnificently powerful yet simple structure. Walk along the lengthy concourse and study the mellow reflection in its walls. Bask in the light flooding through the high, arched windows at each end of the mammoth hall. Try to imagine the awe of the immigrants who poured into Toronto between the wars by the tens of thousands, staring up at the towering ceiling of Italian tile or leaning against one of the 22 pillars, each 40 feet tall and weighing 75 tons. ⊠ *65–75 Front St. W.*

Central Toronto

This walk highlights Toronto's commercial and cultural diversity. It begins at Eaton Centre on Yonge Street and extends westward to Spadina Avenue, the city's bustling discount thoroughfare. In between lie the New City Hall and the Art Gallery of Ontario. A walk through Chinatown provides a sense of the city's ethnic diversity.

A Good Walk

Start at **Eaton Centre** ㉓, a 3-million-square-foot shopping complex extending along the west side of Yonge Street all the way from Queen Street up to Dundas Street (with subway stops at each end) that has become the number-one tourist attraction of Toronto. Exit the Eaton Centre at Queen Street and walk just one long block west to Toronto's city halls. The **Old City Hall** ㉔ is the very beautiful building at the northeast corner of Queen and Bay streets, sweetly coexisting with the futuristic **New City Hall** ㉕, just across the street, on the west side. West of University Avenue on Queen Street stands **Campbell House** ㉖, a living museum. Just north of the New City Hall begins Toronto's main **Chinatown.** Huge Chinese characters hang over the **52nd Division police station** ㉗, on the west side of Simcoe Street, just south of Dundas Street. Turn left off Dundas Street onto McCaul Street for the **Ontario College of Art** ㉘. Directly across the street is **Village by the Grange** ㉙, an apartment and shopping complex. Return to Dundas Street and head west to the **Art Gallery of Ontario** ㉚. The stretch of **Spadina Avenue** from Queen Street to College Street has never been fashionable, but on it you'll find a treasure trove of offbeat stores. **Kensington Market** ㉛ is a delightful side tour off Spadina Avenue, where you'll find bargains of the more edible kind. Afterward, you can rest in **Bellevue Square.**

TIMING

Set aside at least half a day for this tour. It is an excellent weekend adventure, although the New City Hall is closed on Saturday and Sunday. One of the best times to explore Chinatown is on a Sunday, when business booms. You can plan an entire sojourn around Eaton Centre. A visit to the AGO can easily extend from two to four hours.

Sights to See

Numbers in the margin correspond to points of interest on the Inland Toronto map.

㉚ **Art Gallery of Ontario.** The Henry Moore Sculpture Centre has the largest public collection of Moore's sculpture in the world. The **Canadian Wing** includes major works by such northern lights as Emily Carr, Cornelius Krieghoff, David Milne, and Homer Watson. Visitors of any age can drop by the **Anne Tannenbaum Gallery School** on Sunday and explore painting, printmaking, and sculpture in Toronto's most spectacular studio space. The museum arranges numerous other workshops and special activities. The AGO also has a growing collection of works by Rembrandt, Hals, Van Dyck, Hogarth, Reynolds, Chardin, Renoir, de Kooning, Rothko, Oldenburg, Picasso, Rodin, Degas, Matisse, and many others. The **Grange,** a historic house just behind the AGO, is a perfect place to browse, either before or after a visit to the gallery. From extremely modest beginnings in 1900, the AGO is now in the big leagues in terms of exhibits and support. A 1992 renovation has won international acclaim and put the AGO among North America's top 10 art galleries. ✉ *317 Dundas St. W, 3 blocks west of St. Patrick station on University subway line,* ☎ *416/979–6648.* ▣ *$7.50, Wed. evening free.* ☉ *Wed. 10–10, Thurs.–Sun., 10–5:30.*

⏱ **Bellevue Square.** In this lovely little park with shady trees, benches, and a wading pool and playground for children you can rest after a visit to Kensington Market (☞ *below*). ⊠ *Denison Sq. and Augusta Pl.*

㉖ **Campbell House.** Built in 1822 and tastefully restored with elegant 18th- and early 19th-century furniture, it is one of Toronto's most charming living museums. Costumed hostesses will tell you about the social life of the upper class of the period. Guided tours are available. ⊠ *160 Queen St. W,* ☎ *416/597–0227.* ⊜ *$3.50.* ⊘ *Oct.–mid-May, weekdays 9:30–4:30; mid-May–Oct., weekdays 9:30–4:30, weekends noon–4:30.*

⏱ **Chinatown.** It's diverse, exciting, and lively. You'll pass shops selling reasonably priced silk blouses and antique porcelain, silk kimonos for less than half the price elsewhere, lovely sake sets, and women's silk suits. It is the largest Chinatown in Canada and one of the largest in North America. There are more than 100,000 Chinese living in the city; just over a century ago there was only one—Sam Ching, who ran a hand laundry on Adelaide Street. Today, Chinatown covers much of the area bounded by Queen Street, Spadina Avenue, Dundas Street, and Bay Street. Many of the banks still have abacuses, for those who prefer the 4,000-year-old hand-held calculators to modern electronic ones. On Sundays, up and down Spadina Avenue and along Dundas Street, Chinese music blasts from storefronts, cash registers ring, abacuses clack, and bakeries, markets, herbalists, and restaurants do their best business of the week.

⏱ ㉓ **Eaton Centre.** Even if you rank shopping with the flu, you may be charmed, possibly dazzled, by this impressive environment. From its graceful glass roof, arching 127 feet above the lowest of the mall levels, to Michael Snow's exquisite flock of fiberglass Canada geese floating poetically in the open space of the galleria, to the glass-enclosed elevators, porthole windows, and nearly two dozen long and graceful escalators, there are plenty of good reasons for visiting the Eaton Centre. Galleria Level 1 contains two food courts; popularly priced fashions; photo, electronics, and record stores; and much "convenience" merchandise. Level 2 is directed to the middle-income shopper, while Level 3, suitably, has the highest elevation, fashion, and prices. **Eaton's,** one of Canada's classic department-store chains, has a nine-floor branch here. At the southern end of Level 3 is a skywalk that connects the center to the seven-floor **The Bay** department store across Queen Street. Dozens of restaurants, from snack to full-service, can be found here. A 17-theater cinema complex is at the Dundas Street entrance. ⊠ *220 Yonge St.,* ☎ *416/598–2322.* ⊘ *Weekdays 10–9, Sat. 9:30–6, Sun. noon–5.*

㉗ **52nd Division Police Station.** Even the large police station building in Chinatown has a Chinese flavor. Large Chinese characters identify it, demonstrating the Asian community's strong influence here. Otherwise, the postmodern building of 1977 recalls the Art Deco craze of the 1930s. ⊠ *225 Dundas St. W,* ☎ *416/808–2222.*

㉛ **Kensington Market.** This old, steamy, smelly, raucous, colorful, European-style marketplace titillates all the senses. Go and explore, especially during warmer weather, when the goods pour out into the narrow streets: Russian rye breads, barrels of dill pickles, fresh fish on ice, mountains of cheese, bushels of ripe fruit, and crates of chickens and rabbits that will have your children both giggling and horrified. Jewish and Eastern European stores sit side by side with Portuguese, Caribbean, Latin American, and East Indian stores—with Vietnamese, Japanese, and Chinese establishments sprinkled throughout. Most shops are open every

244

Central Toronto
Art Gallery of
Ontario, **30**
Campbell House, **26**
Eaton Centre, **23**
52nd Division
police station, **27**
Kensington
Market, **31**
New City
Hall, **25**
Old City Hall, **24**
Ontario College
of Art, **28**
Village by the
Grange, **29**

**North-Central
Toronto**
Bata Shoe Museum
Collection, **41**
Black Creek Pioneer
Village, **43**
Casa Loma, **42**
George R. Gardiner
Museum of Ceramic
Art, **38**
McMichael Canadian
Art Collection, **44**
Metro Toronto
Zoo, **46**
Metropolitan Toronto
Reference Library, **40**
Ontario Legislative
Bulding, **36**
Ontario Science
Centre, **45**
Provincial Parliament
Buildings, **35**
Queen's Park, **34**
Royal Ontario
Museum, **37**
Sigmund Samuel
Canadiana
Collection, **33**
University of
Toronto, **32**
Yorkville, **39**

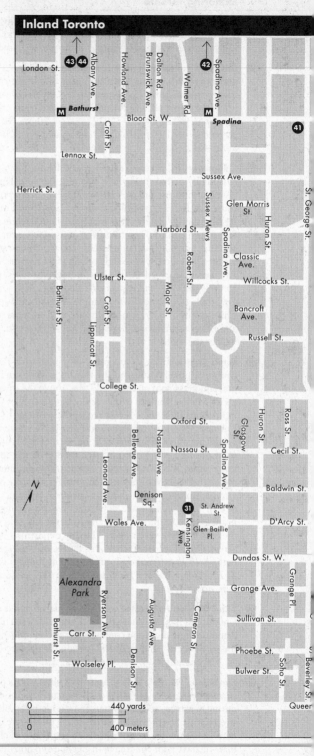

Inland Toronto

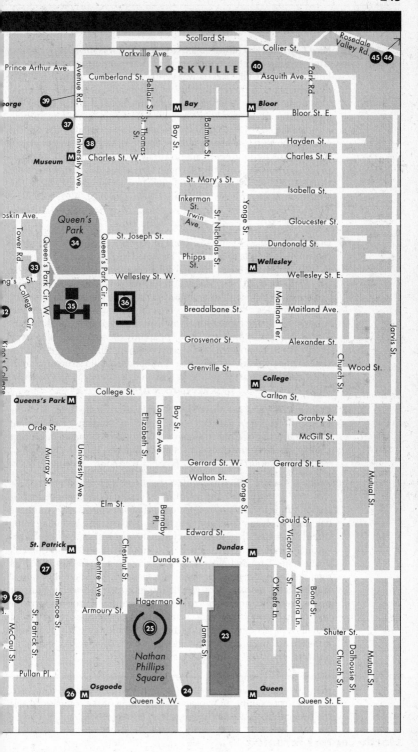

day except Sunday, from as early as 6 AM. ⊠ *Northwest of Dundas St. and Spadina Ave.,* ☎ *416/979–3757.* ⊙ *6 AM–6 PM; hrs. may vary.*

㉕ New City Hall. The futuristic-looking complex was the result of a massive international competition in 1958. The winning presentation, by Finnish architect Viljo Revell, was very controversial: two towers of differing height, and curved! But there was and is a logic to it all: An aerial view of the New City Hall shows a circular council chamber sitting like an eye between the two tower "eyelids." Within months of its opening in 1965, the New City Hall became a symbol of a thriving city. Annual events at the New City Hall include the Spring Flower Show in late March; the Toronto Outdoor Art Exhibition early each July, and the Cavalcade of Lights from late November through Christmas each year, when more than 100,000 sparkling lights are illuminated across both city halls. The underground garage holds 2,400 cars. ⊠ *100 Queen St. W,* ☎ *416/392–9111; TDD 416/392–7354.* 🎟 *Tour free.* ⊙ *Weekdays 8:30–4:30; cafeteria daily 7:30–4; guided tour weekdays 10, 11, and 2.*

㉔ Old City Hall. It was considered one of North America's most impressive municipal halls in its heyday. Designed by E. J. Lennox, it opened in 1899. When the New City Hall debuted in 1965, the Friends of Old City Hall organized to ensure its preservation, while also heightening Toronto's awareness of its architectural heritage. Since the opening of its younger sister, Old City Hall has been the site for the provincial courts, county offices, and thousands of low-cost marriages. The fabulous gargoyles above the front steps were apparently the architect's witty way of mocking certain turn-of-the-century politicians. There is a great stained-glass window as you enter. The handsome old structure stands in delightful contrast to its daring and unique sibling. ⊠ *60 Queen St. W,* ☎ *416/327–5828.* ⊙ *Weekdays 8:30–4:45.*

㉘ Ontario College of Art and Design Gallery. Across the street from the OGA, the college's gallery shows works by students, faculty, and alumni. It is one of Canada's major art institutions, and an important exhibit space for emerging artists and designers. ⊠ *291 Dundas St.,* ☎ *416/977–6000, ext. 262.* 🎟 *Free.* ⊙ *Wed.–Sat. 10–6.*

Spadina Avenue. Toronto's widest street has been pronounced "Spa-*dye*-nah" for a century and a half. For decades it has contained a collection of inexpensive stores, factories that sell wholesale if you have connections, ethnic food and fruit stores, and eateries, including some often first-class, if modest-looking, Chinese restaurants sprinkled throughout the area. Each new wave of immigrants—Jewish, Chinese, Portuguese, East and West Indian, South American—has added its own flavor to the mix, but Spadina-Kensington's basic bill of fare is still bargains galore. Here you'll find gourmet cheeses at gourmet prices, fresh (no, not fresh-frozen) ocean fish, fine European kitchenware at half the price of that in stores in the Yorkville area, yards of remnants piled high in bins, designer clothes minus the labels, and the occasional rock-and-roll night spot and interesting greasy spoon. ⊠ *Spadina, between College and Queen Sts.*

㉙ Village by the Grange. This apartment and shopping complex has more than 100 shops selling everything from ethnic fast food to serious art. It's a perfect example of wise, careful blending of the commercial and the residential. ⊠ *89 McCaul St.,* ☎ *416/598–1414.*

North-Central Toronto

The competing interests of academia, culture, and commerce all converge at the corner of University Avenue and Bloor Street. Before reaching this landmark intersection—where the Royal Ontario Mu-

seum stands across the street from a brand-new Club Monaco shop—
the major forces of Toronto metropolitan life unfold: government, industry, and the University of Toronto. Even though all these sites lie
in the middle of a busy city, the area is surprisingly tranquil, particularly on weekends.

A Good Tour

University Avenue runs from downtown Toronto at Front Street to Bloor,
where it becomes Avenue Road and runs to the city's northern fringes.
West of the avenue, north of College Street, lies the **University of Toronto** ㉜. Follow King's College Road north from College Street to King's
College Circle. At the top of the circle is **Hart House**, the Gothic-style
student center. Continue around the circle to the Romanesque **University College.** Next is **Knox College,** whose Scottish origins are evident
in the bagpipe music that escapes from the building at odd hours. On
the west side of the circle, the **Medical Sciences Building** is a giant assemblage of Brutalist architecture. Return to College Avenue and walk
west to St. George, where you can proceed north to the **Forestry Building** and **Sidney Smith Hall.** At the crossroads of Hardord and Hoskin
Avenue, turn right onto Hoskin and walk past **Massey College.** From
Massey, follow Queen's Park Circle south to the **Sigmund Samuel Canadiana Collection** ㉝, displaying 18th- and 19th-century Canadian household objects and arts. It overlooks **Queen's Park** ㉞, on Queen's Park
Circle. The **Provincial Parliament Buildings** ㉟ sit in the middle of the
park. East of the park is the **Ontario Legislative Building** ㊱. Just to the
north of Queen's Park is the revered **Royal Ontario Museum** ㊲ (ROM).
Across University Avenue stands the **George R. Gardiner Museum of
Ceramic Art** ㊳, home to a rarefied $25-million collection of European
ceramics. Next you can visit the upscale neighborhood of **Yorkville** ㊴.
A block north of Bloor and Yonge streets, just east of Yorkville, stands
the magnificent **Metropolitan Toronto Reference Library** ㊵. Several
blocks west, across the street from the St. George subway station near
Bloor Street, is the **Bata Shoe Museum Collection** ㊶. You'll need transportation to reach **Casa Loma** ㊷, a spectacular mansion north of the
center just off Spadina Avenue. Farther north and a bit west, in North
Yorkville, is the **Black Creek Pioneer Village** ㊸ living history site. The
excellent **McMichael Canadian Art Collection** ㊹ is 45 minutes north and
a bit west in the village of Kleinburg. On the other side of town, you
can try a host of technical marvels at the **Ontario Science Centre** ㊺, just
south of Eglinton Avenue in East York. The sprawling **Metro Toronto
Zoo** ㊻ is beyond the Science Center, 30 minutes northeast of downtown
in Scarborough.

TIMING

Schedule your tour between Tuesday and Saturday, when the museums and shops are open. As this city offers something for everyone,
plan on setting aside at least a couple of days. Remember that even a
highly abbreviated visit to the ROM takes a minimum of two hours.

Sights to See

㊶ **Bata Shoe Museum Collection.** Opened in April 1995, the collection,
the only one of its kind in North America, contains more than 10,000
items of footwear from nearly every country in the world, some dating back more than 4,000 years. Items such as pressurized sky-diving
boots, iron-spiked shoes used for crushing chestnuts, and smugglers'
clogs are just a few of the pieces in this collection. ✉ *327 Bloor St. W,*
☎ *416/979–7799.* 💲 *$6, free 1st Tues. of month.* ⊘ *Tues., Wed., Fri.,
and Sat. 10–5, Thurs. 10–8, and Sun. noon–5.*

㊸ **Black Creek Pioneer Village.** This living history site is as good a reproduction as you'll find of a rural Victorian community in the 1860s.

Roblin's Mill, powered by a big wooden water wheel, grinds wheat as it was done 130 years ago. At the weaver's shop, a costumed interpreter explains the magic of the loom. At other artisans' shops scattered around the village, you can watch blacksmiths, clock makers, gunsmiths, and broom makers at their trades. ☒ *1000 Murray Ross Pkwy., near Jane St. and Steeles Ave., North York,* ☎ *416/736–1733.* ▧ *$7.50.* ☉ *Mid-Mar.–late Dec., Wed.–Sun. 10–5.*

🖐 ㊷ **Casa Loma.** The architect E. J. Lennox, who also designed Toronto's Old City Hall and the King Edward Hotel, created a 20th-century castle here, with 98 rooms; two towers; secret panels; long, creepy passageways; and some of the best views of Toronto. The medieval-style castle cost over $3 million to build shortly before World War I. You tour it at your own speed guided by a tape recording. You'll have walked a good mile by the time you're done, so wear sensible shoes. ☒ *1 Austin Terr., Spadina Ave. south of St. Clair Ave., near St. Clair W subway stop,* ☎ *416/923–1171.* ▧ *$8.* ☉ *Daily 9:30–4.*

㊳ **George R. Gardiner Museum of Ceramic Art.** The collection focuses on 17th-century English delftware and 18th-century yellow European porcelain. Don't miss the museum's gift shop, which stocks many unusual items. It is also part of the ROM, meaning that it costs not a penny more to visit if you go to the ROM as well. ☒ *111 Queen's Park, across University Ave. from ROM,* ☎ *416/586–8000.* ▧ *$8 (includes admission to ROM).* ☉ *Tues.–Sat. 10–5, Sun. 11–5.*

㊹ **McMichael Canadian Art Collection.** A 45-minute drive north of downtown, in the village of Kleinburg, this celebrated institution is superb. The landscape paintings of Canada's Group of Seven artists and extensive collections of Inuit and Native art are only part of the McMichael's charm. The gallery is set in 100 acres of woodland, with strategically placed windows so that visitors can appreciate the scenery even as they admire the art. ☒ *10365 Islington Ave., west of Rte. 400 and north of Major Mackenzie Dr., Kleinburg,* ☎ *905/893–1121.* ▧ *$7.* ☉ *Mid-Oct.–mid-May, Tues.–Sat. 10–4, Sun. 10–5; mid-May–mid-Oct., daily 10–5.*

㊵ **Metropolitan Toronto Reference Library.** This well-situated resource was designed by one of Canada's most admired architects, Raymond Moriyama, who also created the Ontario Science Centre. Arranged around a tall, wide interior atrium, the library gives a delightful sense of open space. Fully one-third of the more than 1.3 million books—spread across 28 miles of shelves—are available to the public. In the many headphone-equipped audio carrels, you may listen to any one of more than 10,000 albums. Open on Saturdays from 2 to 4 and by appointment, the **Arthur Conan Doyle Room** houses the finest public collection of Holmesiana anywhere, with records, films, photos, books, manuscripts, and letters. ☒ *789 Yonge St., north of Bloor St.,* ☎ *416/393–7000 or 416/393–7131.* ▧ *Free.* ☉ *Mon.–Thurs. 10–8, Fri. and Sat. 10–5, Sun. 1:30–5.*

🖐 ㊻ **Metro Toronto Zoo.** The 710 acres were developed for animals, not people. The Rouge Valley, just east of Toronto, was an inspired choice of site when it was built in the 1960s, with its varied terrain, from river valley to dense forest, where mammals, birds, reptiles, and fish have been grouped according to where they live in the wild. In most of the regions, you'll find remarkable botanical exhibits in enclosed, climate-controlled pavilions. Don't miss the 3-ton banyan tree in the **Indo-Malayan Pavilion,** the fan-shape traveler's palm from Madagascar in the **African Pavilion,** or the perfumed flowers of the jasmine vines in the **Eurasian Pavilion.** The "round-the-world tour" takes about three hours and is suitable for any kind of weather, because most of the time is spent inside pavilions. It's been estimated that it would take four full days to see everything in the Metro Zoo, so study the map you'll get at the zoo entrance and decide in advance what you wish to see most. For younger children, there is the delightful **Littlefootland,** a special area that allows contact with tame animals, such as rabbits and sheep. In winter, cross-country skiers follow groomed trails that skirt the animal exhibits; lessons and rentals are available. An electrically powered train moves silently among the animals without frightening them. It can accommodate wheelchairs (available free inside the main gate), and all pavilions have ramp access. If you're on a very tight budget, the zoo is free if you show up the last hour of the day, which is enough time to give you a taste of this very impressive, world-class institution. ✉ *Meadowvale Rd. north of Rte. 401, 30-min drive from downtown, or take Bus 86A from Kennedy subway station, Scarborough,* ☎ *416/392–5900.* 💷 *$9.95; parking in winter free, parking Mar.–Oct. $4.* ◷ *Daily 9:30–4:30.*

❸❻ Ontario Legislative Building. The mammoth building, which opened in 1893, is also referred to as Queen's Park. It is home to the provincial government offices. Its extraordinary architecture includes rectangular towers, triangular roofs, and circular and oval glass. ✉ *50 Queen's Park.*

⟲ ❹❺ The Ontario Science Centre. Built to commemorate Canada's centennial in 1967, the Science Centre is a stunningly successful blend of education and entertainment that should not be missed. It has free movies and thrilling space, communications, laser, nutrition, and electricity exhibits. Also, be sure to check out the marvelous permanent exhibit called "the Sport Show." ✉ *770 Don Mills Rd. (about 11 km, or 7 mi, from downtown; Yonge St. subway from downtown to Eglinton station and Eglinton East bus to Don Mills Pkwy. stop), North York,* ☎ *416/696–3127 or 416/429–4100.* 💷 *$7.50, parking $2.* ◷ *Daily 10–6.*

⟲ ❸❺ Provincial Parliament Buildings. Surrounded by Queen's Park, the pink, 1889 buildings have a heavy, almost Romanesque quality. A closer look reveals beautifully complex detail carved in the stone. Inside are huge, lovely halls that echo half a millennium of English architecture. The long hallways are hung with hundreds of oils by Canadian artists, most of which capture scenes of the province's natural beauty. Should you choose to take one of the frequent (and free) tours, you will see the chamber where the 130 elected representatives from across Ontario, called MPPs (Members of Provincial Parliament), meet on a regular basis. There are two heritage rooms—one each for the parliamentary histories of Great Britain and Ontario—filled with old newspapers, periodicals, and pictures. The lobby holds a fine collection of minerals and rocks of the province. On the lawn in front of the Parliament Buildings, facing College Street, stand many statues, including one of Queen Victoria and one of Canada's first prime minister, Sir John A. Macdonald. ✉ *1 Queen's Park, University Ave. subway, Queen's Park stop,* ☎ *416/325–7500.* 💷 *Free.* ◷ *Guided tour mid-May–Labor Day, daily on the hr 9–4, weekends every ½ hr 9–11:30 and 1:30–4; frequent tours rest of the year; also at 6:45 PM when evening sessions are held.*

❸❹ Queen's Park. Many visitors consider this to be the soul of Toronto. Surrounding the large oval-shaped patch of land are medical facilities to the south, the University of Toronto to the west, and the Royal Ontario Museum to the north. To most natives, Queen's Park is chiefly synonymous with politics, as the Provincial Parliament Building (☞ *above*) sits in the middle of this charming urban oasis. ✉ *Queen's Park Circle, between College St. and Bloor St. W.*

⊙ ㊲ **Royal Ontario Museum** (ROM). Once labeled "Canada's single great-est cultural asset" by the Canada Council, the museum floundered throughout its early existence, which began in 1912 (on the day the *Titanic* sank). By the 1970s, the monstrous building had leaky roofs, no climate control, and little space to display its glorious treasures. It never stopped collecting—always with brilliance—reaching more than 6 million items altogether. Even though drastic government cutbacks prompted the museum to close the beloved McLaughlin Planetarium, the ROM remains a crowd pleaser that artfully interprets everything from science to pop culture for a mass audience. Today, thanks to a major fund-raising effort, the museum has the space it needs, and when expansion is completed sometime before the end of the century, the ROM will be the second-largest museum in North America, after New York's Metropolitan Museum of Art. What makes the ROM unique is the fact that science, art, and archaeology exhibits are all under one roof. **The Dinosaur Collection** absorbs children and adults alike. The **Evolution Gallery** has an ongoing audiovisual program on Darwin's theories of evolution. The **Roman Gallery** has the most extensive col-lection of Roman artifacts in Canada. And the **European Musical In-struments Gallery** has a revolutionary audio system and more than 1,200 instruments dating back to the late 16th century. The **Discovery Gallery** allows children (over age six) to handle objects from the ROM's col-lections and to study them, using microscopes, ultraviolet light, and magnifying glasses. **The Bat Cave** contains 4,000 freeze-dried and ar-tificial bats in a lifelike presentation; piped-in narration directs visi-tors on a 15-minute walk through a dimly lit replica of an 8-foot-high limestone tunnel in Jamaica, filled with sounds of dripping water and bat squeaks. The brilliant **Ancient Egypt Gallery** is connected with the newer **Nubia Gallery**; both exhibit artifacts that illuminate the ancient cultures. ⊠ *110 Queen's Park, University Ave. subway to Museum stop,* ☎ *416/586–5549.* ▣ *$8, free Tues. after 4:30.* ☉ *Mon. and Wed.–Sat. 10–6, Tues. 10–8, Sun. 11–6; Discovery Gallery hrs vary, so call ahead.*

㉝ **Sigmund Samuel Canadiana Collection.** This worthy assemblage of 18th-and 19th-century Canadian furnishings, glassware, silver, and period rooms is maintained by the ROM. ⊠ *14 Queen's Park Crescent W, northwest corner of University Ave. and College St.* ▣ *Free.* ☉ *Tues.–Thurs. 1–4:30.*

㉜ **University of Toronto.** One of Canada's largest and most revered in-stitutions of higher learning began in 1827, when King George IV signed a charter for a "King's College in the Town of York, Capital of Upper Canada." The Church of England had control then, but by 1850 the college was proclaimed nondenominational, renamed the University of Toronto, and put under the control of the province. Then, in a spirit of good Christian competition, the Anglicans started Trinity College, the Methodists began Victoria, and the Roman Catholics begat St. Michael's; by the time the Presbyterians founded Knox College, the whole thing was almost out of hand. The 17 schools and faculties are now united, and they welcome anyone who can pass the entrance exams and afford the tuition. Like that of most large universities built over several decades, the quality of the institution's vast architecture catalog is mixed. There is much to see and do around the main cam-pus of the University of Toronto. One highlight is **Hart House** (⊠ 7 Hart House Circle), the Gothic-style student center built in the second decade of this century; the dining hall has stained glass windows and cheap and rather good food. The ravishing **Rosebrugh Building** (⊠ 4 Taddle Creek Rd.) of 1921 features an eye-catching display of ener-getic brickwork, making it one of the university's most delightful struc-tures. Romanesque **University College** (⊠ 15 King's College Circle) was built in 1859. **Knox College** (⌧ 59 St. George St.) has been training ministers since 1844, although the building was erected in 1915. On the site of the **Medical Sciences Building** (⌧ 1 King's College Circle), Drs. Banting, Best, and others discovered the insulin that has saved the lives of tens of millions of diabetics around the world. The handsome redbrick **Forestry Building** (⌧ 45 St. George St.) and the modern and massive **Sidney Smith Hall** (⌧ 100 St. George St.), with its two wings, are also worth a look. **Massey College** (⌧ 4 Devonshire Pl.), of 1963, blends medieval ideas and forms into a modern architectural idiom. ⌧ *Public and Community Relations Office, 27 King's College Circle, Room 133S,* ☎ *416/978–2021; tour information, 416/978– 5000.* ⊙ *Guided 1-hour walking tour leaves from map room of Hart House, summer, weekdays 10:30, 12:30, and 2:30.*

㊴ Yorkville. This is one of the most dynamic and expensive areas of Toronto; some call it Toronto's Rodeo Drive, others call it Toronto's Fifth Avenue. One thing is certain: These blocks are packed with specialty shops, ritzy restaurants, and high-price stores specializing in designer clothes, furs, and jewels. ⌧ *Bordered by Avenue Rd., Yonge and Bloor Sts., and Yorkville Ave.* []

DINING

Cafés

By Sara Waxman

$ ✕ **Future Bakery & Café.** A European-style bakery has blossomed into a small chain of cafeterias supplied by their own dairy. Old European recipes have remained: beef borscht, buckwheat cabbage rolls, and potato-cheese *varenycky* slathered with thick sour cream. This place is beloved by students for its generous portions, by homesick Europeans hungry for goulash and knishes, by the cheesecake-and-coffee crowd, by health-conscious foodies looking for fruit salad with homemade yogurt and honey, and by people-watchers looking for people worth watching from 7 AM to 2 AM. ⌧ *1535 Yonge St.,* ☎ *416/944–1253;* ⌧ *438 Bloor St. W,* ☎ *416/922–5875;* ⌧ *2199 Bloor St. W,* ☎ *416/769–5020;* ⌧ *739 Queen St. W,* ☎ *416/504–4235;* ⌧ *St. Lawrence Market, 95 Front St. E,* ☎ *416/366–7259. Reservations not accepted. MC, V.*

$ ✕ **Marché.** This self-service restaurant has created the atmosphere of a vast old-world market square. Herbs grow in pots; fresh fruits and vegetables are piled high; an enormous snowbank holds bright-eyed fish and fresh seafood; oysters await shucking; fresh pasta spews from pasta makers, ready to be cooked to order. A rotisserie roasts lacquer-crisp game birds and European sausages. At the grill, a chef is at the ready with steaks and chops. Bread and croissants are mixed, placed on racks to rise, and baked before your eyes. Pizza is prepared to order and *rosti* (a superior Euro-latke served with sour cream and smoked salmon) is fried to order. Choose your food, then sit under a tree or in a cozy cottage. There's a daunting list of wines by the glass, but servers are friendly and eager to advise. So popular is this high-concept, low-price dining adventure, open 7:30 AM to 2 AM Wednesday through Saturday and 7:30 AM to 1 AM Sunday through Tuesday, that smaller versions have sprouted up all over town. ⌧ *42 Yonge St.,* ☎ *416/366–8986. Reservations not accepted. AE, DC, MC, V.*

$ ✕ **Masquerade Caffè Bar.** An eclectic array of red, yellow, blue, and green sofas, chairs, and banquettes fills this Felliniesque environment. The Harlequin pattern of the bar is echoed in the red-on-red walls. Murano glass mosaics add sparkle to the huge primary-color stoves. The Italian menu, which changes daily, may include roasted onion soup with

Bistro 990, **17**
Boba, **21**
Borgo Antico, **20**
Canoe, **8**
Centro, **29**
Cuisine of
India, **25**
Future Bakery
& Café, **27**
Grano, **28**
Il Fornello, **6**
Joso's, **23**
Jump Café & Bar, **11**
KitKat Bar & Grill, **3**
Lai Wah Heen, **15**
Lotus, **1**
Marché, **10**
Marketta, **24**
Masquerade
Caffè Bar, **12**
Mövenpick, **7**
Nami, **13**
North 44, **30**
Prego de la Piazza, **19**
Pronto, **31**
Rodney's Oyster Bar, **14**
Splendido, **18**
Thai Magic, **26**
Thai Thai Cafe, **9**
Tiger Lily's Noodle
House, **5**
Vanipha Lanna, **22**
Verona, **2**
Wah Sing, **16**
Xango, **4**

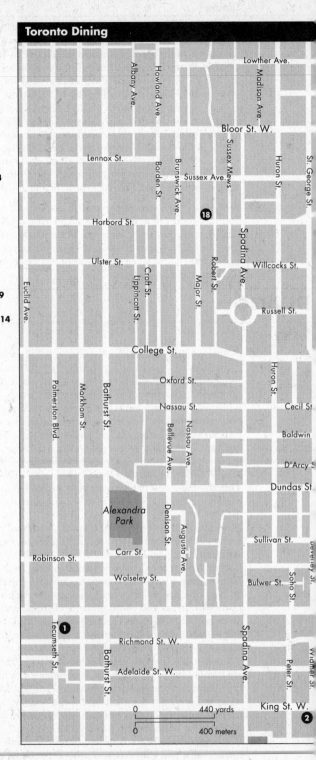

Toronto Dining

pesto croutons; exotic lettuce salad with tuna, cheese, olives, and marinated mushrooms; a seafood or vegetable antipasto; saffron and porcini risotto; divine mushroom-filled ravioli; or a choice of *panini*—Italian sandwiches on homemade breads with scrumptious meat, cheese, and veggie fillings. Zabaglione—eggs, marsala wine, and a bit of sugar whipped to a thick, frothy cream and poured over fresh berries—is a knockout dessert. ⊠ *BCE Place, Front and Yonge Sts.*, ☎ *416/363–8971. Reservations not accepted. AE, MC, V. Closed Sun.*

Canadian

$$$ ✕ **Canoe.** A delicious homage to Canadian foods is filtered through the world's finest cuisines. The kitchen complements the breathtaking view of the Toronto Islands through the huge windows on the 54th floor of the Toronto Dominion Bank Tower. The understated decor does not distract from views of the sparkling lake afloat with sailboats in summer or the inspirational presentations at table. Fiddlehead and Fundy Bay sea scallop soup is an outstanding testament to the Maritimes, and Québec foie gras and artichoke terrine with herbed pumpernickel crust constitutes an ode to French Canada. The adventurous meat eater can savor hay-roasted rack of lamb in a buckwheat, honey, and sunflower seed crust, or braised venison osso buco with hearty vegetables. Aged Alberta beef is given fine treatment here. Canadiana courses right through the menu to desserts such as a golden, melting, tall butter tart with a glass of Ontario's ice wine. There is a wine cellar of great breadth, and a sommelier whose knowledge and panache makes ordering a bottle a delight. ⊠ *Toronto Dominion Center, 66 Wellington St. W, 54th floor,* ☎ *416/364–0054. Reservations essential. AE, DC, MC, V. Closed weekends.*

Chinese

$$$ ✕ **Lai Wah Heen.** If you are in the mood for Cantonese culinary fireworks, phone and preorder Lustrous Peacock as your first dish. This extravagant presentation, complete with an explosion of white vapor curling and rolling across the table, is a feathery yet robust salad of melon, barbecued duck, chicken, honeyed walnuts, and more exotic ingredients that make this a feast for the mouth as well as the eye. Whole roast suckling pig marinated in Hoisin sauce is presented whole and carved at your table, but preorder one day in advance. If you are a fan of Peking duck, you will love this two-course showbiz presentation. The mahogany-color lacquer-crisp duck is wheeled in on a trolley, where it is sliced and diced and presented with panache. Some excellent choices from the hundred-dish inventory are wok-fried shredded beef and vegetables in a crisp potato nest; filet of sole done two ways in one dish—steamed with asparagus and fenced in by crisply crumbed and fried sole fingers. A real crowd pleaser are the crunchy egg noodles that come topped with tasty tidbits from land and sea. At lunch, the dim sum is divine. Translucent dumplings and pouches bursting with juicy fillings of shark's fin sprinkled with bright red lobster roe; shrimp dumplings with green tops that look like baby bok choy; dumplings with scallops; crystal shrimp; and a minisize baked barbecued pork pie that has everyone begging for more. The service is French in an elegant room with a sculptured ceiling, etched glass turntables, and silver serving dishes and domes. ⊠ *Metropolitan Hotel, 118 Chestnut St., 2nd floor,* ☎ *416/977–9899. AE, DC, MC, V.*

$ ✕ **Tiger Lily's Noodle House.** Always on the cutting edge of what our
★ taste buds crave, the doyenne of Toronto caterers, Dinah Koo, has brought her Asian spices to this clean and bright hand-painted storefront café. If you want to know what real egg rolls taste like, you'll find them

here: they make fresh egg pancakes, wrap them tightly around seasoned shredded vegetables, and deep-fry them for seconds—till the pancake is puffy and golden. Shrimp dumplings—iridescent packets bulging with crunchy nubbins—come four to an order with a pungent dipping sauce. But most people come for the noodles, cooked in many ways and combinations: bowls of translucent vermicelli with slices of perfectly cooked duck breast and vegetables in a bowl of clear, flavorful duck broth—combinations with choices of noodles or wontons, meat or vegetable broth, and garnishes of barbecued pork, Shanghai chicken, or veggies. Vegetarian noodle cake will make vegans smile, and if you want your Chinese food steeped in tradition, not grease, you'll find double happiness here. ⊠ *257 Queen St. W,* ☎ *416/977–5499. AE, MC, V.*

$ ✕ **Wah Sing.** Just one of a jumble of Asian restaurants clustered on tiny Kensington Market street, this meticulously clean and spacious restaurant has two-for-the-price-of-one lobsters (in season, which is almost always). Chopped, shell on, and fried with black-bean sauce or ginger and green onion, they're scrumptious and tender. Or try giant shrimp Szechuan-style, or choose one of the lively queen crabs from the tank. Chicken and vegetarian dishes for landlubbers are good, too. Service is pleasant, and at the end of your meal there's a juicy sliced orange for dessert. ⊠ *41 Baldwin St.,* ☎ *416/596–1628. AE, MC, V.*

Fish and Seafood

$$$–$$$$ ✕ **Joso's.** Joso Spralja—artist, musician, and restaurateur—has filled
★ his two-story midtown restaurant with objets d'art: sensual paintings of nudes and the sea, stylized busts of women, signed celebrity photos, and intriguing wall hangings. The kitchen prepares dishes of the Dalmatian side of the Adriatic Sea, and the international artistic community that frequents the place adores the magnificent, unusual, and healthy array of seafood and fish. *Risotto carajoi* is Joso's own creation of rice and sea snails simmered in an aggressively seasoned tomato sauce. Try tiger prawns from Vietnam, porgy from Boston, salmon trout from northern Ontario, or baby clams from New Zealand. The dish that seems most often carried aloft by speed-walking servers is flame-grilled prawns, their charred tails pointing skyward. ⊠ *202 Davenport Rd.,* ☎ *416/925–1903. Reservations essential. AE, DC, MC, V. Closed Sun. No lunch Sat.*

$$$ ✕ **Rodney's Oyster Bar.** This playful, basement raw bar is a hotbed of bivalve variety frequented by table-for-one diners, showbiz, and agency types. The offerings include salty Lewis Islands from Cape Breton, perfect Malpeques from Rodney Clark's own oyster beds in Prince Edward Island, and New York Pine Islands—described by some as being like a walk in the woods rather than the sea. Eat a mature five-inch-long Malpeque, turn the shell upside down, and count the rings (like a tree) that appear as the oyster grows each year. A zap of Rodney's own line of condiments or a splash of vodka and freshly grated horseradish are certain eye-openers. State-of-the-art equipment turns out soft-shell steamers, Quahogs, oyster slapjack chowder, and an array of oceanic delights. "Sharing and half-orders are okay here," says Rodney. Ask for the daily "white plate specials." ⊠ *209 Adelaide St. E,* ☎ *416/363– 8105. AE, DC, MC, V. Closed Sun.*

French

$$$ ✕ **Bistro 990.** A superior kitchen combined with bistro informality makes this a favorite restaurant for the '90s. Start dinner with steamed Prince Edward Island string-cultured mussels, with a red tomato curry and cilantro, or Provençal fish soup with rouille and garlic croutons. Move on to traditional steak, grilled rare and served with French fries and

bordelaise or Roquefort sauce, or pan-roasted half chicken with garlic, mashed potatoes, and rosemary. The pasta might be fusilli with peppers, tomatoes, olives, basil, and Parmesan. The purist kitchen uses artesian spring water for all stocks and homemade breads. Country-style desserts such as lemon tart and apple and sun-dried cherry crumble are not grand, just wonderful. Faux stone walls stenciled with Cocteauesque designs, sturdily upholstered chairs, and a tiled floor create an ambience where a jacket and tie is easily as acceptable as casual clothes. ⊠ *990 Bay St.,* ☎ *416/921–9990. AE, DC, MC, V. Closed Sun. No lunch Sat.*

Indian

$$ ✕ **Cuisine of India.** It's fascinating to see Chef Shishir Sharma at work in the glass-walled, open kitchen of his casually styled, unassuming suburban restaurant. He slaps a ball of dough with his hands, thrusts it onto a smooth, round rock, and lowers it into the depths of the tandoor oven. Moments later, the puffy, crusty, buttery-center nan is ready to eat. Sharma has mastered the art of blending spices, herbs, and roots with other ingredients and achieves a delicate balance of flavors and visual appeal. He lifts a whole salmon trout from its marinade, fits it onto a forged steel skewer, and plunges it deep into the tandoor. A whole leg of lamb for two, halved chicken breasts, and giant shrimp can all be ordered oven-baked, too. Vegans can also enjoy elaborate dinners here. The vegetable dishes are diverse in their seasonings and come with fragrant basmati rice. It's worth the 20-minute taxi ride from the city center to enjoy this exquisite cuisine. ⊠ *5222 Yonge St.,* ☎ *416/229–0377. Reservations required. AE, DC, MC, V.*

Italian

$$$–$$$$ ✕ **Centro.** The facade of etched glass, granite, and marble shouts hard-
★ edge. But inside it's as warm as the folksy blowups of owner Franco Prevedello's home town of Asolo, in northern Italy. Massive columns that seem to hold up a bright blue ceiling combine with salmon-color walls lined with comfortable banquettes to create an intimate space in this 182-seat restaurant. This is Toronto's trendsetter restaurant. Every detail—from the variety of homemade breads to the incredible desserts, from the coat check to the valet parking—is overseen by Franco. You can be sure that he's tasted the ricotta-and-spinach gnocchi with a ragout of scallion and herb-seasoned sweetbreads, and he's approved the peppered linguine with clams, basil, and pancetta. The 2-inch-thick veal chop grilled over mesquite tingles with Sicilian seasoning; poached Atlantic salmon nestles gently in a bowl of elegant risotto and asparagus. The menu doesn't just change with each season, it seems to get better. ⊠ *2472 Yonge St.,* ☎ *416/483–2211. Reservations essential. AE, DC, MC, V. Closed Sun.*

$$$ ✕ **Borgo Antico.** Simple and dramatic, like the unassuming wooden windowpane facade, describes owner/chef Pino Posterero's Mediterranean food ensembles: baby artichoke salad ringed with black truffle wearing a cap of sliced parmesan; the finest carpaccio in the city rubbed with a dry marinade and aged for ten days; and seared giant scallops glazed with balsamico on a turban mold of couscous. Domestic vegetables have never tasted so good. Having the time of his life, Pino cooks turnip in a stock made with honey, coriander, and orange juice. It is heartening to read the creative pasta selections on the menu: gnocchetti sardi with potatoes, sautéed mushrooms, sage, and chili oil; orcchiette with shrimp, asparagus, scallops—and the list goes on. Black Angus steak is superbly glazed with Asian five-spice and foie gras; half lobsters are draped with fresh tagliolini. Desserts, too, are outstanding;

Pino bakes the best biscotti in town. ✉ *29 Yorkville Ave.,* ☎ *416/969–9982. AE, MC, V.*

$$$ ✕ **Prego de la Piazza.** Tucked into a chic shopping passage between the glitz of the Renaissance Plaza and the timeworn stones of the gracefully aging Church of the Redeemer, this see-and-be-seen Italian eatery is a busy spot. Come summer, when the outdoor patio is in full bloom, it's filled with the who's who of the city's highly visible film and television industry, which has earned Toronto the name "Hollywood North." The menu has evolved into a concise litany of everyone's favorites: stone-roast half chicken with herbs; homemade *agnolotti* (round ravioli) with stuffings like beet with burned butter sauce or butternut squash with tomato and fresh basil; and pasta with sauces that are oil-based, tomato-based, or cream-based. And there's a vast display of cold antipasti including marinated vegetables and savory tortes. Chef Massimo strolls through the contemporary room, checking to see who's eating what. Next door at Enoteca della Piazza, a design award–winning wine bar, the chic and cheerful sip wine from a list of several hundred labels and nibble on *affettati misti* (thin slices of dry cured meats), smoked chicken, and marinated eggplant. The third separate and distinct room is called Black and Blue, a tribute to fine steaks, cigars, and tippling. ✉ *150 Bloor St. W,* ☎ *416/920–9900. AE, DC, MC, V. Closed Sun.*

$$$ ✕ **Pronto.** On the cutting edge of innovative, modern Italian cuisine, this glitzy black, mirror-and-chrome restaurant has the look of Milan. The menu marries the sunny flavors of California with solid Italian tradition and includes pan-fried oyster mushrooms on red oak lettuce laced with white-truffle olive oil, and sophisticated pastas like lemon fettuccine with mussels and roast garlic. A brace of boneless jumbo quails, charred to the color of mahogany, comes with whole roast cloves of garlic, sweet and crisp snow pea vines, and drunk sour sun-dried cherries. But the kitchen, not losing sight of rustic tradition, shines with homey dishes such as braised lamb shank served in a massive bowl with flageolets and greens. The trend of the future, using vegetable purées as sauces, has, not surprisingly, come from Pronto. ✉ *692 Mt. Pleasant Rd.,* ☎ *416/486–1111. Reservations essential. AE, D, MC, V.*

$$$ ✕ **Splendido.** This latest in a series of slick, upbeat Italian restaurants is immensely popular with television-, music-, and film-industry types. Chef-partner Arpi Magyar presents a sparkling Cal-Ital contemporary menu. The chef coaxes ricotta and potato into plump gnocchi and serves them with splashes of white truffle oil and chives as an appetizer or main course; he roasts farm-raised chicken in a wood-burning oven and perches it on a bread salad textured with currants and pine nuts. Rack of lamb is baked with honey mustard and partnered with homey garlic potato purée. Casual, sophisticated good taste meets the eye at every turn. Walls in warm shades of orange and blue are hung with artist Helen Lucas's glorious, oversize flower paintings, mirrors are anything but square, and a glass wall marked "Cucina" separates the open kitchen from the dining room. The bar is popular for nightcaps. ✉ *88 Harbord St.,* ☎ *416/929–7788. AE, DC, MC, V.*

$$ ✕ **Grano.** ★ What started as a bakery and takeout antipasto bar has grown into a joyful collage of the Martella family's Italy. Come for animated talk, good food, and great bread in these lively rooms with faux ancient plaster walls, wooden tables, and bright chairs. There's a small espresso bar to perch at while you wait for a table or takeout. Choose, if you can, from 40 delectable vegetarian dishes and numerous meat and fish antipasti. Lucia's homemade gnocchi and ravioli are divine, as are the tiramisù or the white chocolate and raspberry pie. ✉ *2035 Yonge St.,* ☎ *416/440–1986. AE, DC, MC, V. Closed Sun.*

$$ ✕ **KitKat Bar & Grill.** Walls are crammed with autographed memorabilia, and the kitchen is built around a massive tree. It all seems quite natural in this eclectic and eccentric Southern Italian eatery. As it's in the middle of the theater district, pre- and post-theater hours are really busy. Choose from window tables in the front, perch at the long bar, enjoy the privacy of an old-fashioned wooden booth, or sit at a picnic table in the rear. Portions are enormous. An antipasto platter for two is a meal; pastas, seafood, roast chicken, and grilled steak are all delectable. Owner Al Carbone welcomes everyone like long-lost family. ⊠ *297 King St. W,* ☎ *416/977–4461. AE, DC, MC, V. Closed Sun. No lunch Sat.*

$$ ✕ **Verona.** The kitchen sends over homemade savories as soon as you're seated: diced marinated vegetables in olive oil, lush olive spread, and a basket of fresh breads. This gives you the chance to appreciate the casual, yet sophisticated surroundings and the professional service. The wine list is reasonable, the menu offers well-known traditional dishes, and the ingredients are the finest quality. You might start with an opulent mix of salad greens piled high on the plate, tossed with sun-dried-tomato *crostini,* slicked with balsamic vinegar and virgin olive oil dressing, and crowned by grilled oyster mushrooms. Or try the made-from-scratch soups: cream of smoked salmon afloat with spinach, herbs and tomato is a favorite. For pasta-holics there's fresh linguine tangled around juicy slices of lamb tenderloin, portobello mushrooms, and red onions in a sauce perfumed with cilantro. You can also have grilled New York steak, carefully cooked Atlantic salmon, and a variety of pizzas from the woodburning oven. Zabaglione—eggs, marsala wine, and sugar whipped up for two and poured over freshly sliced berries—makes a perfect grand finale. ⊠ *335 King St. W,* ☎ *416/593–7771. AE, DC, MC, V. Closed Sun. No lunch Sat.*

$ ✕ **Il Fornello.** Pizza aficionados especially love Il Fornello's 10-inch,
★   thin-crust pie, baked in a wood-burning oven. Orchestrate your own medley from over 100 traditional and exotic toppings that include braised onion, *capicolla* (spicy Italian sausage), pancetta, provolone, calamari, escargots, mussels, eggplant, and anchovies. A bottle of extra-virgin, herbal olive oil sits on each table. Pastas, veal dishes, and salads are available, too. Wheat-free pizza crust and dairy-free cappuccino are now on the menu—your taste buds won't know the difference. Customer clamor prompted the opening of more venues. ⊠ *55 Eglinton Ave. E,* ☎ *416/486–2130;* ⊠ *86 Bloor St. W,* ☎ *416/588–5658;* ⊠ *214 King St. W,* ☎ *416/977–2855;* ⊠ *1560 Yonge St.,* ☎ *416/920– 8291;* ⊠ *486 Bloor St. W,* ☎ *416/588–9358;* ⊠ *1968 Queen St. E,* ☎ *416/691–8377;* ⊠ *1218 St. Clair Ave. W,* ☎ *416/658–8511;* ⊠ *35 Elm St.,* ☎ *416/598–1766;* ⊠ *576 Danforth Ave.,* ☎ *416/466– 2931. AE, MC, V.*

Japanese

$$$ ✕ **Nami.** In this large, attractive, downtown restaurant, diners can choose to eat at the sushi bar, in tatami rooms with nontraditional wells under the tables, or at the *robatayaki* (a cooking grill surrounded by an eating counter). Watch the chef douse soft-shell crabs with a special sauce and put them on the grill. Scallops, shrimp, Atlantic salmon, mackerel, and ocean perch sizzle on skewers. At the sushi bar, it's a thrill to watch the chef at work: He slaps a bit of rice on his palm, tops it with a spicy condiment, a shred of vegetable, and a cap of toro, yellowtail, or maguro tuna. In seconds, he hand-rolls cornets of salmon skin, and if sea urchin is at hand, he ties it into a neat packet with a ribbon of green onion. Each sushi design is as personal as a signature. Special $22 dinner combos at a table or booth include soup, salad, tempura, yakitori (skewers of chicken) or a beef or salmon teriyaki dish, rice, and dessert. ✉ *55 Adelaide St. E,* ☎ *416/362–7373. AE, DC, MC, V. Closed Sun. No lunch Sat.*

Mixed Menu

$$$–$$$$ ✕ **North 44.** A foyer decorated with brushed-steel nuggets outlined in
★ black, a steel compass embedded in a gorgeous marble floor, textured walls hung with mirrored sconces holding exotic arrangements of fresh ginger and lilies—can Chef Marc McEwen's dishes meet the standards of this singular decor? Yes. Awaken your taste buds with such appetizers as grilled mahogany quails with gingered couscous, barbecue honey balsamic leeks, and smoky tomato plum sauce; and who could decline a nibble of crisp tortilla spring rolls plump with barbecued chicken, vegetables, and plum mustard chili dip? The kitchen grills Atlantic salmon to perfection, tops it with a honey mustard crust, and partners it with sesame bok choy greens and crisp leeks. Winning combinations are spaghettini with seared scallops; grilled calamari, shrimp, and sweet tomato fondue; or pan-fried gnocchi. Caramelized apple-pecan layer cake and crème brûlée with berries are worth every luscious calorie. In the rear, a delightful private dining room seating 12 to 15 people has a wraparound mural of the view from a Venetian canal. ✉ *2537 Yonge St.,* ☎ *416/487–4897. AE, DC, MC, V. No dinner Sun.*

$$$ ✕ **Boba.** "If there is a hard way to do something," says owner Bob Bermann, "we'll find it," explaining how they ferment apples for two weeks to make their apple sourdough bread. Barbara Gordon and Bob Bermann are a sophisticated culinary couple who've been on the cutting edge of the restaurant scene since they arrived here about a decade ago. Currently ensconced in a charming brick house, they've put their own stamp on the place with a decor of robust and gorgeous color. The dishes they've dreamed up are original and delicious; their flamboyant presentations bring to mind gourmet chefs at play. Steak gets the royal treatment: Filet mignon is grilled, set on a bed of sautéed spinach, and tucked alongside a generous slab of ethereal roast garlic–studded bread pudding. A splash of rich pinot noir glaze and a handful of frizzled red onion rings finish the dish. Grilled salmon comes surrounded by bright red beet risotto, chunky with tiny diced beets, made festive with brilliant greens of baby bok choy and sugar snap peas. ✉ *90 Avenue Rd.,* ☎ *416/961–2622. AE, MC, V. No lunch weekdays.*

$$$ ✕ **Jump Café & Bar.** Look up through the atrium and you'll see that you're surrounded by towering skyscrapers and big city ambience. Try to get a table at the glass wall that abuts the interior courtyard, which, from May to September, becomes a vast flower- and fountain-filled patio. The East-meets-West menu with Italian top notes is refreshing, with appetizers such as Mediterranean octopus with Tuscan bean salad, charred artichokes and leeks in spiced olive oil, and crisp duck spring rolls with cucumber noodles. The chef's pasta of the moment is gnocchi malfatti with roast garlic, spinach, and ricotta, pan-fried in sage brown butter and tossed in a tomato cream sauce. From 5 PM to 7 PM, a smartly dressed, downtown office crowd packs the bar. ✉ *Commerce Court E, Yonge and Wellington Sts., Court Level,* ☎ *416/363–3400. AE, DC, MC, V. Closed Sun. No lunch Sat.*

$$ ✕ **Marketta.** The clientele includes cyclists, foot soldiers, and the anonymous-but-hungry in chauffeur-driven limos. The warmth of natural brick walls and wood furniture, refreshed by massive pots of seasonal blooms and greens, has an inviting casual charm. At the antipasto counter, sense-thrilling riffs of East-meets-West with Mediterranean visions are displayed like jewels at Tiffany's. Three choices just aren't enough when trays of honey-mustard salmon, grilled spring rolls, rose-

mary quail, jicama mango salad, scallops and lemon-grass skewers, and
the like flaunt their charms. At your table, you can indulge in risotto
with sweet peas, grilled corn, and fresh herbs and parmesan. From the
grill-meister you can order focaccia with peppered veal, eggplant,
arugula, and roasted red pepper aioli served with sweet potato fries;
grilled sirloin burger with Monterey Jack; or grilled duck sausage with
fava beans and barley risotto. Among the treasury of desserts, individual
lemon meringue pie is sensational. ⊠ *138 Avenue Rd.,* ☎ *416/924–
4447. AE, DC, MC, V.*

Pacific Rim

$$$ ✕ **Lotus.** In a tiny, unpretentious restaurant on a downtown side street,
chef Susur Lee creates outstanding Pacific Rim cuisine filtered through
classic French traditions. Rack of lamb arrives with an extravaganza
of savories and sauces. Calamari and shrimp are crisp and juicy in a
five-spice tempura batter. If tuna done three ways is on the menu, in-
dulge yourself. The dazzling cuisine is in direct contrast to the plain
but comfortable interior. ⊠ *96 Tecumseth St.,* ☎ *416/504–7620.
Reservations essential. AE, MC, V.*

South American

$$–$$$ ✕ **Xango.** A jet-setting multilingual bevy of South Americans and the
local nomadic kiss-kiss crowd are just some of the beautiful people who
know that the discreet red capital X on a black tile is where the action
is. A contemporary menu is introduced on a three-tiered rack of appe-
tizers: oysters Ecuadorian-style with lime, chilies, tomatoes, and crisp
curried onions; empanadas filled with grilled onions and served with sliced
pears, crumbled Spanish blue cheese, and walnut vinaigrette; and Chilean
sweet corn tamales with chorizo sausage and olive salsa. Guatemalan
chicken perched on saffron mashed potatoes or seafood loaded into a
crisp plantain basket give us blasts of flavor and eye-catching presenta-
tions. Coco Cabana, a luscious coconut custard in a coconut, and flan
Borracho are dazzling scene-stealing desserts. Upstairs, tango and tapas
fans can enjoy flamenco dancers and live guitar, conga, and vocalists. If
you're looking for quiet intimacy, Xango is not for you. ⊠ *106 John St.,*
☎ *416/593–4407. AE, MC, V. Closed Sun. and Mon. No lunch.*

Swiss

$$ ✕ **Mövenpick.** Swiss hospitality, an eager-to-please staff, and a cosmopolitan atmosphere make this downtown restaurant all things to
all people. Among the dinner specialties are *Zürcher G'Schnatzlets,*
the famous Swiss dish of thinly sliced veal and mushrooms in a creamy
white wine sauce served with *rosti* (pan-fried) potatoes; *Kasseler,* a
thick, smoked, juicy pork chop grilled to perfection and served with
braised savoy cabbage; and red wine herring from Iceland marinated
in wine and selected spices. The Swiss Farmers Sunday Brunch ($24.80
per person), a vast buffet of food stations, is particularly popular. You
can have your eggs with ham, sausage, bacon, or rosti potatoes.
Cheeses, breads, juices, cereals, and accompaniments are displayed in
abundance. You can also sample more salads than you bargained for,
with raw and marinated vegetables, and a variety of smoked fish and
soup. Cold cuts include traditional smoked turkey and Black Forest
ham as well as *Bündnerfleisch,* a Swiss salt-cured, air-dried beef.
Roast chicken, leg of lamb, and beef roasts are complemented by sautéed
vegetables and fresh pastas. A dessert table with fresh fruits, Swiss cakes,
tarts, and flans satisfies your sweet tooth. ⊠ *165 York St.,* ☎ *416/366–
5234. AE, DC, MC, V.*

Thai

$$ ✕ **Thai Magic.** Bamboo trellises, cascading vines, fish and animal carvings, and a shrine to a voluptuous mermaid goddess make a magical setting for coolly saronged waiters and hot-and-spicy Thai food. Hurricane Kettle is a dramatic presentation of fiery seafood soup. Whole coriander lobster sparkles with flavor, while chicken with cashews and whole dried chilies is for the adventurous. If you're in the mood for Thai, this is certainly a pretty place to indulge. ✉ *1118 Yonge St.,* ☎ *416/968–7366. Reservations essential. AE, MC, V. Closed Sun. No lunch Sat.*

$ ✕ **Thai Thai Cafe.** The downtown casual café branch of Thai Magic invites browsing and grazing through an exciting showcase of hot and cold original and traditional Thai dishes. Basil beef with bamboo shoots, chili chicken with cashew nuts, and the exuberant black bean mango chicken can intrigue the taste buds. The special seafood kettle, a ceramic pot plump with shrimp, fish, crab, and mussels, serves two. Here you'll find all the fun, flavor, aromas, and color of a Thai market at giveaway prices. You can eat in or take out. ✉ *92 King St. E,* ☎ *416/364–8424. MC, V. Closed Sun.*

$ ✕ **Vanipha Lanna.** Every night this tidy, colorful restaurant is crowded
★ with people who don't care if they're sitting almost cheek to cheek with strangers, or how long they have to wait for their food. They can't get enough of the clean, bright flavors, grease-free cooking (everything's made from scratch), and lovingly garnished Lao-Thai presentations. The bamboo steamer of dumplings with minced chicken and seafood, sticky rice in a raffia cylinder, and chicken and green beans stir-fried in lime sauce are exceptional. Rice is served from a huge silver tureen. ✉ *471 Eglinton Ave. W,* ☎ *416/484–0895. MC, V. Closed Sun.*

LODGING

$$$$ 🏨 **Four Seasons Toronto.** It's hard to imagine a hotel more exclusive
★ than the Four Seasons. The location is ideal: on the edge of Yorkville, a few meters from the Royal Ontario Museum. The 380 units are tastefully appointed. Maids come twice a day, and there are comfortable bathrobes, oversize towels, fresh flowers, and a fine indoor/outdoor pool. Although special rates will not drop the cost much below $200 a night, the hotel does offer some inventive packages. Its restaurants include the Studio Café, the Lobby Bar, La Serre, for dinner only, and the formal dining room, Truffles. ✉ *21 Avenue Rd., 1 block north of Bloor St., M5R 2G1,* ☎ *416/964–0411 or 800/332–3442,* 🆇 *416/964–1489. 380 rooms. 4 restaurants, indoor-outdoor pool, sauna, health club, meeting rooms. AE, DC, MC, V.*

$$$$ 🏨 **King Edward.** The grande dame of downtown Toronto hotels is this beauty built in 1903 and entirely remodeled in the early '80s. The "King Eddie," a member of the worldwide Forte chain, still has an air of understated elegance, with its vaulted ceiling, marble pillars, and palm trees. Among its guests have been the Duke of Edinburgh, Margaret Thatcher, and Charles de Gaulle. A highlight of the King Eddie is the Chef's Table: for $100 per person, executive chef John Higgins will prepare an eight-course meal for up to eight people, at a table right next to the stoves in his kitchen. After the meal, he'll give you a full kitchen tour. If you'd rather not eat in the kitchen, the hotel's two restaurants, Chiaro's and the Café Victoria, are favorites among Toronto power brokers. For a genteel afternoon pastime, take in teas in the lobby lounge from 3 to 5. But be warned, at the King Eddie neither the accommodation nor the food comes cheap. ✉ *37 King St. E, M5C 1E9,* ☎ *416/863–9700 or 800/225–5843,* 🆇 *416/367–5515. 315 rooms. 2* restaurants, spa, health club, business services, meeting rooms. AE, DC, MC, V.

$$$$ 🖭 **Park Plaza Hotel.** It may lack a pool, but this hotel has one of the
★ best locations in the city: a short distance from the Royal Ontario Museum, Queen's Park, and the Yorkville shopping district. The 350 units are well appointed in a plush, old-fashioned way, and they seem to coast by on their old-shoe familiarity to regular Toronto visitors who have been staying in them since the days when there was much less choice of accommodation. Request a south-facing room in the older tower; the cityscape views—with glimpses of Lake Ontario—are stunning. The Roof Restaurant was once described by novelist Mordecai Richler as "the only civilized place in Toronto." Additions include a 550-seat ballroom, a business center, a palm court café, and a restaurant off the lobby (the Prince Arthur Room), all designed by Zeidler Roberts Partnership, the architects who were responsible for the Eaton Centre and Ontario Place. ⊠ 4 Avenue Rd., at Bloor St. W, M5R 2E8, ☎ 416/924–5471 or 800/268–4927, FAX 416/924–4933. 350 rooms. 2 restaurants, lounge, ballroom, business services. AE, DC, MC, V.

$$$$ 🖭 **Westin Harbour Castle.** A favorite with conventioneers, this hotel
★ is just steps from Harbourfront and the Toronto Islands ferry. It's a bit inconvenient to the city's amenities, except for those directly on the lakeshore, but it offers the best views of any hotel in the city. A free shuttle bus service and frequent public transportation links it to downtown business and shopping. The swimming pool, squash courts, and health club are among the best in town. Its 980 rooms are well appointed and tastefully modern, and the frequent family and weekend rates help bring its regular price down by as much as a third. The revolving Lighthouse restaurant, atop the 37th floor, has a spectacular view. ⊠ 1 Harbour Sq., M5J 1A6, ☎ 416/869–1600 or 800/228–3000, FAX 416/869–0573. 980 rooms. 2 restaurants, pool, health club, squash. AE, DC, MC, V.

$$$ 🖭 **Metropolitan Hotel.** In this handsome 16-story hotel the glass-en-
★ closed atrium lobby could hardly be more convenient: just steps behind City Hall and a few short blocks from Eaton Centre. The guest rooms, which include 16 for travelers with disabilities, are all well decorated with finely crafted furniture and desks; many have queen- and king-size beds. Its restaurant, The Tapestry, is open for all meals. In addition, it is connected by a walkway from the mezzanine level to the Museum of Textiles, where some 15,000 textiles from around the world are displayed in the only museum of its kind in Canada. ⊠ 108 Chestnut St., north of Nathan Phillips Sq., M5G 1R3, ☎ 416/977–5000, FAX 416/977–9513. 491 rooms. 3 restaurants, 2 bars, indoor pool, sauna, hot tub, health club, children's programs. AE, DC, MC, V.

$$$ 🖭 **Royal York Hotel.** One of Canada's famous railway hotels, this grand
★ hostelry was built in 1928 by the Canadian Pacific Railway for the convenience of passengers passing through the nearby train station. The Royal York, with its romantic skyscraper-cum-chateau profile, is a Toronto landmark. Inside are a bustling lobby and spacious corridors. The outstanding health club offers picturesque views of Toronto's architecture. The restaurants include the Royal Tea Room, which serves a full afternoon tea on weekdays noon–5 and weekends 2:30–5. Besides being just across Front Street from Union Station, it is convenient to all downtown attractions and is linked to the Underground City. ⊠ 100 Front St. W, M5J IE3, ☎ 416/368–2511 or 800/441–1414, FAX 416/368–9040. 1,408 rooms. 3 restaurants, 4 bars, room service, indoor lap pool, sauna, massage, fitness center. AE, DC, MC, V.

$$$ 🖭 **Sheraton Centre.** This busy conventioneer's favorite is across from the New City Hall, just a block from Eaton Centre, which is accessible through an underground passage. The belowground level is part

of Toronto's labyrinth of shop-lined corridors, and there are more shops on the ground and second floors. The restaurants' reach seems to exceed their grasp, but the Long Bar, overlooking Nathan Phillips Square, is a great place to meet friends for a drink. A plus here are the outstanding athletic facilities, especially the 25-meter pool. ⊠ *123 Queen St. W, M5H 2M9,* ☎ *416/361–1000 or 800/325–3535,* FAX *416/947–4854. 1,382 rooms. 2 restaurants, 2 bars, no-smoking floors, indoor-outdoor pool, hot tub, sauna, exercise room. AE, DC, MC, V.*

$$$ 🏨 **Toronto Hilton International.** In the financial district close to New City Hall, major businesses, and other attractions, it is a convenient base for visitors. Despite its bland contemporary decor, the top three floors of executive rooms shine with such extras as minibars, clothing pressers, and coffee/tea makers. Executive-floor guests also have privileges in the executive lounge, which sits atop the hotel on the 32nd floor overlooking the New City Hall. The indoor-outdoor pool is modest, but the view of the city from the glass-enclosed elevators on the outside of the building is a thrill. ⊠ *145 Richmond St. W, at University Ave., M5H 3M6,* ☎ *416/869–3456 or 800/267–2281* FAX *416/869–3187. 600 rooms. Restaurant, pool. AE, DC, MC, V.*

$$ 🏨 **Delta Chelsea Inn.** This 1,600-room giant is Toronto's largest hotel. Especially popular with tour groups and out-of-town business people on a tight budget, it features a year-round activity center with supervised children's programs. The hotel is a couple of short blocks north of the Eaton Centre and half a block from the busy Bay Street bus route. However, it is a little farther from a subway station than most other downtown hotels. ⊠ *33 Gerrard St. W, M5G 1Z4,* ☎ *416/595–1975 or 800/877–1133,* FAX *416/585–4302. 1,600 rooms. 2 restaurants, 3 lounges, 2 pools, hot tub, sauna, fitness center. AE, DC, MC, V.*

$$ 🏨 **Guild Inn.** One of the most historic hotels in Canada dates from 1914, when Gen. Harold C. Bickford called it home. The smaller European-style rooms in the original building are augmented by standard rooms in a new wing that have balconies overlooking the Inn's beautiful garden. Throughout the hotel, photographs and bibelots of the Guild's past abound. All the historical artifacts, including the grounds, are overseen by a curator. It sits among 95 acres of English country gardens above the Scarborough bluffs, 20 minutes from downtown. There's no inn more romantic than this one, and the view from here at sunset is extraordinary. ⊠ *201 Guildwood Pkwy., Scarborough M1E 1P6,* ☎ *416/261–3331,* FAX *416/261–5675. 95 rooms. Restaurant, outdoor pool, tennis court. AE, MC, V.*

$$ 🏨 **Novotel Toronto Centre.** This moderately priced hotel—part of a popular French chain—opened in the late '80s. These nine floors in the heart of downtown offer modest, modern rooms within walking distance of Harbourfront and the CN Tower. ⊠ *45 The Esplanade, M5E 1W2,* ☎ *416/367–8900 or 800/668–6635,* FAX *416/360–8285. 266 rooms. Restaurant, indoor pool, sauna, exercise room. AE, DC, MC, V.*

$$ 🏨 **Radisson Markham.** If you prefer a suburban setting, where hotels typically offer greater value for money than downtown hotels can, this one, on Route 7 in the town of Markham, is a 35-minute drive north of downtown. The hotel has a resortlike setting complete with an enclosed garden courtyard. Many of the rooms overlook this area and its grove of trees. The guest rooms are embellished with such specials as lighted mirrors, minibars, hair dryers, and coffee/tea makers. All guests enjoy a complimentary Continental breakfast. It is a good base for visits to the McMichael Collection (☞ North-Central Toronto, *above*) and Cottage Country (☞ Chapter 7). ⊠ *50 E. Valhalla Dr., Markham L3R 0A3,* ☎ *905/477–2010,* FAX *905/477–2026. 202 rooms. Restaurant, pool, sauna, fitness center. AE, DC, MC, V.*

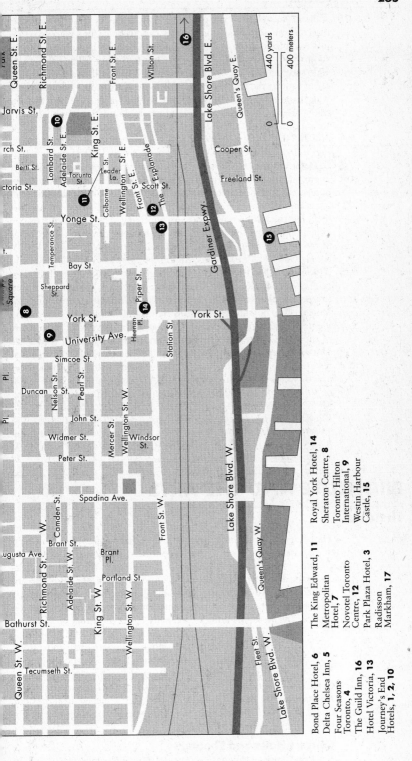

Bond Place Hotel, **6**
Delta Chelsea Inn, **5**
Four Seasons
Toronto, **4**
The Guild Inn, **16**
Hotel Victoria, **13**
Journey's End
Hotels, **1, 2, 10**

The King Edward, **11**
Metropolitan
Hotel, **7**
Novotel Toronto
Centre, **12**
Park Plaza Hotel, **3**
Radisson
Markham, **17**

Royal York Hotel, **14**
Sheraton Centre, **8**
Toronto Hilton
International, **9**
Westin Harbour
Castle, **15**

$ 🏨 **Bond Place Hotel.** If you plan to spend your money on shopping rather than on your accommodation, this is a good choice for a place to stay—just two blocks from the Eaton Centre. The hotel has clean, spacious rooms with color TVs and phones, but few other frills. The Garden Café serves breakfast, lunch, and dinner, but you'll find a wider variety of food at the Eaton Centre. The Bond Place is also a few minutes' walk from the Elgin, Pantages, and Winter Garden theaters. Several floors are set aside for nonsmoking guests. Lower rates apply in winter months. ✉ *65 Dundas St. E, M5B 2G8,* ☎ *416/362–6061 or 800/268–9390,* 𝖥𝖠𝖷 *416/360–6406. 286 rooms. Restaurant, no-smoking floors. AE, DC, MC, V.*

$ 🏨 **Hotel Victoria.** Business travelers on skimpy expense accounts may
★   appreciate the personal service and quiet atmosphere of this Yonge Street hotel a block east of Union Station. The eight-story Victorian-era building is appointed with standard hotel furnishings. There are few luxuries here, but the location and price are appealing. The hotel maintains an affiliation with the Toronto Athletic Club for guest privileges. ✉ *56 Yonge St., M5E 1G5,* ☎ *416/363–1666; in Canada and NY, 800/363–8228;* 𝖥𝖠𝖷 *416/365–7327. 28 rooms. Restaurant, lobby bar. AE, DC, MC, V.*

$ 🏨 **Journey's End Hotels.** This rapidly growing chain offers three convenient Toronto locations. The airport hotel costs about $100 for up to four people, with 10% off for corporate travelers and senior citizens; the two downtown locations charge only about $60 on weekend nights. These latter-mentioned lodgings are an easy walk from many of the sights. Don't expect original antiques here, but all rooms are spotlessly clean and quite pleasant, and each location has an informal restaurant. No pools or saunas or convention rooms, but the prices are so low, how can you complain? ✉ *All locations,* ☎ *905/624–8200 or 800/668–4200,* ✉ *262 Carlingview Dr., near Rte. 427 and airport, M9W 5G1,* ☎ *416/674–8442,* 𝖥𝖠𝖷 *416/674–3088; 258 rooms.* ✉ *280 Bloor St. W, a few blocks west of Avenue Rd. and University Ave., M5S 1V8,* ☎ *416/968–0010,* 𝖥𝖠𝖷 *416/968–7765; 214 rooms.* ✉ *111 Lombard St., near Queen and Jarvis Sts., M5C 2T9,* ☎ *416/367–5555,* 𝖥𝖠𝖷 *416/367–3470; 196 rooms. Restaurant. AE, DC, MC, V.*

NIGHTLIFE AND THE ARTS

The Arts

The best places to get information on cultural happenings are in the Thursday editions of the *Toronto Star,* the Saturday *Globe and Mail,* the free weeklies *Now* and *Eye Weekly,* and *Toronto Life.* For half-price tickets on the day of a performance, don't forget the **Five Star Tickets booth,** located in the Royal Ontario Museum lobby during the winter and, at other times, at the corner of Yonge and Dundas streets, outside the Eaton Centre. The museum booth is open daily 10–7, the Yonge and Dundas booth is open (in good weather) Monday–Saturday noon–7:30 and Sunday 11–3. Tickets are sold for cash only, all sales are final, and a small service charge is added to the price of each ticket. The booth outside the Eaton Centre also gives out piles of superb brochures and pamphlets on the city. Tickets for almost any event in the city can be obtained through **Ticketmaster** (☎ 416/872–2222). Tickets can be picked up at the door on the night of the event or at any Ticketmaster location; note that a service charge applies to all orders.

Concert Halls and Theaters

The **Roy Thomson Hall** has become the most important concert hall in Toronto. It is the home of the Toronto Symphony and the Toronto Mendelssohn Choir, one of the world's finest choral groups. It also hosts orchestras from around the world and popular entertainers. The best seats are in Rows H and J in the orchestra and Row L upstairs. Rush seats are sold two hours before curtain. ⊠ *60 Simcoe St., at King St. W, 1 block west of University Ave.,* ☎ *416/593–4828.* ⌨ *Tickets $20–$60, theater tour $3, organ tour $5.* ☉ *Theater tour Mon., Tues., and Thurs. 12:30; organ tour Wed. 12:30.*

Massey Hall has always been cramped and dingy, but its near-perfect acoustics and its handsome, U-shape tiers sloping down to the stage have made it a happy place to hear the Toronto Symphony, or anyone else in the world of music, for almost a century. The nearly 2,800 seats are not terribly comfortable, but it remains a venerable place to catch the greats and near-greats. The best seats are in Rows G–M center and Rows 32–50 in the balcony. ⊠ *178 Victoria St., at Shuster, east of Eaton Centre,* ☎ *416/593–4828.* ⌨ *Tickets $20–$60.*

The **O'Keefe Centre** is the home of the Canadian Opera Company and the National Ballet of Canada. It also hosts visiting comedians, pre-Broadway musicals, rock stars, and almost anyone else who can fill it. When it was built in 1960, it was the largest concert hall on the continent, with 3,167 seats. Avoid the extreme front rows (lettered AA, BB, and so on). ⊠ *1 Front St. E, 1 block east of Union Station,* ☎ *416/872–2262.* ⌨ *Tickets $20–$50.*

Since 1970, the **St. Lawrence Centre for the Arts** has been presenting everything from live theater to string quartets and forums on city issues. The main hall, the luxuriously appointed **Bluma Appel Theatre,** hosts the often brilliant productions of the **Canadian Stage Company** and **Theatre Plus.** Classical and contemporary plays are often on a level with the best of Broadway and London's West End. The best seats are Rows E–N, Seats 1–10. ⊠ *Front St. and Scott St.,* ☎ *416/366–7723.* ⌨ *Tickets $20–$45.*

The **Royal Alexandra** has been the place to be seen in Toronto since its opening in 1907. The plush red seats, gold brocade, and baroque swirls and curlicues all make theatergoing a refined experience here. All this magnificence was almost torn down in the 1960s but was rescued by none other than "Honest Ed" Mirvish, locally famous in the discount-store game. He not only restored the theater but also made it profitable. The best seats are in Rows C–L center; avoid Rows A and B; for musicals try the first rows of the first balcony. ⊠ *260 King St. W,* ☎ *416/872–3333 or 416/872–1212.* ⌨ *Tickets $35–$75 (more for major musicals); student tickets $15 and up.*

Classical Concerts

The Toronto Symphony, which just celebrated its 75th season, is not about to retire. Since 1922, with conductors of the quality of Seiji Ozawa, Walter Susskind, Sir Thomas Beecham, and Andrew Davis, it has achieved world acclaim. Maestro Jukka-Pekka Sarasti replaced Gunther Herbig in the 1994/95 season, reinvigorating the repertory with 20th-century pieces to complement older masterworks. When the Toronto Symphony is home, it presents about three concerts weekly from September to May in Roy Thomson Hall (☞ *above*). ⌨ *Tickets $19–$50.*

The **Toronto Mendelssohn Choir** (☎ 416/598–0422) often performs with the Toronto Symphony. This 180-singer group, going since 1894, has been applauded worldwide, and its *Messiah* is handled well every Christmas. For tickets, call Roy Thomson Hall (☞ *above*).

Dance

The **National Ballet of Canada** made its official debut in 1951. In less than four decades, the company has done some extraordinary things, with such principal dancers as Karen Kain, Rex Harrington, Kimberly Glasco, and Jeremy Ramson all wowing audiences. ⊠ *O'Keefe Centre,* ☎ *416/362–1041 or 416/872–1111.* 🎫 *Tickets $15–$55.* ☉ *Performances Nov., Dec., Feb., and May.*

Toronto Dance Theatre, its roots in the Martha Graham tradition, tours Canada and has played major festivals in England, Europe, and the United States. ⊠ *Premiere Dance Theatre, Harbourfront, 235 Queen's Quay W,* ☎ *416/973–4000.* 🎫 *Tickets $19–$31.*

Film

Every September since 1976, Toronto has held a world-class film festival, called—with no great modesty—the **Festival of Festivals** (☎ 416/967–7371 or 416/968–3456). Whether retrospectives of the films of Marguerite Duras, Jean-Luc Godard, and Max Ophuls, or tributes to the careers of Martin Scorsese, Robert Duvall, and John Schlesinger, this is the time for lovers of film.

Toronto is one of the film capitals of the world, and you can often catch a movie here that is not showing anywhere else—or even available on video.

Carlton Cinemas shows rare, important films from Canada and around the world in nearly a dozen screening rooms. ⊠ *20 Carlton St., east of College St. subway,* ☎ *416/598–2309.*

Opera

Since its founding in 1950, the **Canadian Opera Company** (☎ 416/363–8231) has grown into the largest producer of opera in Canada. Each year, at Toronto's O'Keefe Centre (☞ *above*), more than 150,000 people attend the season of seven operas, with such world-class performers as Joan Sutherland, Grace Bumbry, Martina Arroyo, Marilyn Horne, and Canada's own Louis Quilico and Maureen Forrester. The COC also performs free outdoor concerts during the summer at Harbourfront.

Theater

There are more than four dozen performing spaces in Toronto; the following are among the most prominent:

The **Young People's Theatre,** the only theater center in the country devoted solely to children, does not condescend or compromise its dramatic integrity. ⊠ *165 Front St. E, near Sherbourne,* ☎ *416/862–2222.*

The **Elgin** and **Winter Garden theaters** are two recently renovated old vaudeville palaces, stacked upon one another. The Elgin, downstairs, has about 1,500 seats; the Winter Garden is some 500 seats smaller; both are stunningly attractive. These landmark theaters of 1913 overcame tawdry stints as movie houses to showcase traveling as well as locally based artistic productions. ⊠ *189 Yonge St., north of Queen St. W,* ☎ *416/870–8000.*

Second City, just east of the heart of downtown, has been providing some of the best comedy in North America since its owner Andrew Alexander bought the rights to the name for one dollar. Among those who have cut their teeth on the Toronto stage are the late Gilda Radner, Dan Aykroyd, Martin Short, Andrea Martin, Catherine O'Hara, and the late John Candy. Shows can be seen alone or in a dinner-theater package. ⊠ *Old Firehall Theatre, 110 Lombard St., at Jarvis,* ☎ *416/863–1111.*

When planning your trip to Toronto, consider contacting the **Ford Centre for the Performing Arts** (⊠ 5040 Yonge St., ☎ 416/872–2222 or 416/733–9388), less than a half-hour's drive north of the waterfront, close to the North York subway stop, to see the wildly acclaimed Hal Prince production of the classic American musical *Show Boat. The Phan-*

tom of the Opera has been running forever at the stunning **Pantages Theatre** (☎ 416/872–2222) downtown. *Beauty and the Beast* should run a long time at the new **Prince of Wales Theatre** (☎ 416/872–1212) next to the Royal Alex. Expect good seats to run close to $100 each, but these Broadway-quality productions are worth paying for.

Next to Second City, **Yuk-Yuk's Komedy Kabaret** has always been the major place for comedy in Toronto. This is where the zany comedian Howie Mandel and the inspired impressionist Jim Carey got their starts, and where such comic luminaries as George Carlin, Rodney Dangerfield, Robin Williams, and Mort Sahl have presented their best routines. ⊠ *2335 Yonge St., north of Eglinton Ave.;* ⊠ *5165 Dixie St.;* ☎ *416/967–6425.* ☉ *Thurs.–Sun.* ⌳ *Cover $6 and up.*

Mysteriously Yours . . . should be of special interest to murder-mystery buffs. On Thursday, Friday, and Saturday evenings, a "despicable crime" is perpetrated at the Royal York Hotel (☞ Lodging, *above*). The mystery begins to unravel during dinner at 6:30 and show at $7:30 and is solved by 9:30. The complete dinner and mystery costs $50–$65 per person, including tax and tip. Tickets for the show only run $15 to $30. Call Brian Caws (☎ 416/486–7469 or 800/668–3323).

Nightlife

The area bounded by Front, Adelaide, Peter, and John streets has become the center of Toronto's club and bar scene in recent years.

Bars

The **Loose Moose Tap & Grill** (⊠ 220 Adelaide St. W, ☎ 416/971–5252) is a popular bar. In 1993, hockey superstar Wayne Gretzky opened **Wayne Gretzky's** (⊠ 99 Blue Jay Way, ☎ 416/979–7825), a sports bar and restaurant.

Dancing

Barracuda (⊠ 21 Scollard St., ☎ 416/921–4496), on a gigantic warehouse site, has music and dancing, indoor batting cages, indoor beach volleyball, and weekend live local radio broadcasts. At **Big Bop** (⊠ 651 Queen St. W, ☎ 416/504–6699), DJs play '60s music downstairs and '90s music upstairs in a four-story, century-old fun house. **Club Energy** (⊠ 41 Constellation Ct., ☎ 416/675–2500), in an old warehouse near the airport, has a giant dance floor with an amazing laser-light show synchronized with the music. At **Fluid** (⊠ 217 Richmond St. W, ☎ 416/593–6116), which caters to a Yorkville-ish older (25–35) crowd, the decor is metallic and modular, with custom-made furnishings. **RPM** (⊠ 132 Queen's Quay, ☎ 416/869–1462), a popular dance club near Harbourfront, draws lovers of dance, rock, and alternative music, while professional dancers perform in cages above the crowd.

Gay and Lesbian Clubs

Fab and *X-Extra* chronicle the gay and lesbian scene here. These free publications can be readily found in the Church and Wellesley district, Toronto's burgeoning gay epicenter. Near or along Church Street are several nightlife options. **Woody's** (⊠ 467 Church St., ☎ 416/972–0887) is fashionable yet neighborly. **Crews** (⊠ 508 Church St., ☎ 416/972–1662) is youthful. The Sunday night window drag show at **Bar 501** (⊠ 501 Church St., ☎ 416/944–3272) is an institution not to be missed. For the aspiring Versace-model crowd, **Boots** (⊠ 592 Sherbourne, ☎ 416/921–0665) rocks in a fabulous warehouse space.

Jazz Clubs

Chick 'n Deli (⊠ 744 Mt. Pleasant Rd., near Eglinton Ave., ☎ 416/489–3363 or 416/489–7931), long one of the great jazz places in Toronto, now has jazz only on Saturdays; there's a dance floor, and dark wood everywhere gives it a casual, neighborhood-pub feel. **Top O' The Senator** (⊠ 249 Victoria St., ☎ 416/364–7517), this city's first club exclusively for jazz and cabaret, has the atmosphere of a 1930s lounge.

Lounges

Up on the 51st floor of the ManuLife Centre, the romantic **Aquarius Lounge** (⊠ 55 Bloor St. W, at Bay St., ☎ 416/967–5225) is the highest piano lounge in the city. The **Consort Bar** (⊠ 37 King St. East, ☎ 416/863–9700), in the King Edward Hotel, features swing on Thursday, Friday, and Saturday evenings, and Sunday afternoons. In the classy Four Seasons Hotel, **La Serre** (⊠ Avenue Rd. and Yorkville Ave., ☎ 416/964–0411), which looks like a library in a mansion, has a stand-up piano bar and a pianist worth standing for. The gorgeous and tasteful **Park Plaza Roof Lounge** (⊠ Avenue Rd. and Bloor St., ☎ 416/924–5471) has been used as a setting in the writings of such Canadian literary luminaries as Margaret Atwood and Mordecai Richler.

Rhythm and Blues

The modern—brass, black, polished oak—**Network** (⊠ 138 Pears Ave., near Davenport Rd., ☎ 416/323–0164) entertainment lounge is a supper club and show specializing in name acts such as the Stylistics, Junior Walker, and Goodman and Brown.

Rock and Popular Music

Most major international recording companies have offices in Toronto, so the city is a regular stop for top musical performers of today, such as the Rolling Stones, Genesis, Billy Joel, Whitney Houston, Sting, and Bruce Springsteen. Tickets ($15–$40) can usually be booked through **Ticketmaster** (☎ 416/872–1111).

Major venues include the **SkyDome** (⊠ 1 Blue Jays Way, Front St. W and Peter St., ☎ 416/341–3663), **Maple Leaf Gardens** (⊠ 60 Carlton St., ☎ 416/977–1641), the **O'Keefe Centre** (⊠ 1 Front St. E, ☎ 416/872–2262), and **Exhibition Stadium** (⊠ CNE grounds, Dufferin St. at waterfront, ☎ 416/393–6000). **Ontario Place** (⊠ Lakeshore Blvd. W between Dufferin and Bathurst Sts., ☎ 416/314–9900) has pop, rock, and jazz concerts all summer at a nominal cost. We say "nominal" because you may pay around $10 to see/hear a fabulous singer or group (or orchestra or ballet corps) that would cost you $25–$50 elsewhere. This is one of the loveliest and least expensive places for concerts in all of Toronto. **Kingswood Music Theatre** (⊠ Rte. 400, 10 min north of Rte. 401, ☎ 905/832–8131) has important rock and pop concerts during the warmer months. **The Phoenix Concert Theatre** (⊠ 410 Sherbourne St., ☎ 416/323–1251) has a wide variety of music, with DJs from local radio stations broadcasting live on Monday (classic rock) and Saturday (alternative music). A major showcase for more daring arts in Toronto has long been the **Rivoli** (⊠ 332 Queen St. W, west of University Ave., ☎ 416/597–0794), where the back room functions as a club, with theater happenings, progressive rock and jazz music, and comedy troupes with very funny improvisations.

OUTDOOR ACTIVITIES AND SPORTS

Participant Sports

Contact the **Ministry of Tourism and Recreation** (⊠ Queen's Park, M7A 2R2) for pamphlets on various activities. For information on sports in the province, call ☎ 800/668–2746 from anywhere in the continental United States and Canada (except the Northwest Territories and the Yukon). In Toronto, contact Ontario Travel (☎ 416/314–0944).

A number of fine **conservation areas** circle metropolitan Toronto, many less than a half hour from downtown. Most have large swimming areas, sledding, and cross-country skiing, as well as skating, fishing, and boating. For information on summer or winter sports in conservation areas around Toronto, call **Metro Region Conservation** (☎ 416//661–6600).

Bicycling
More than 29 kilometers (18 miles) of street bike routes cut across the city and dozens more follow safer paths through Toronto's many parks. Bikes can be rented on the Toronto Islands. The 19-kilometer (12-mile) **Martin Goodman Trail** runs along the waterfront all the way from the Balmy Beach Club in the east end out past the western beaches southwest of High Park.

Metro Parks Department (✉ 55 John St., ☎ 416/392–8186) has maps that show bike (and jogging) routes that run through Toronto parkland. **Ontario Cycling** (✉ 1185 Eglinton Ave. E, ☎ 416/426–7242) has maps, booklets, and information. Maps are available at most local bike shops.

Boating
You can rent canoes, punts, and/or sailboats at Grenadier Pond in High Park, at Centre Island, at Ontario Place, at Harbourfront, and at most of the conservation areas surrounding metro Toronto.

Fishing
You don't have to go very far from downtown Toronto to catch trout, perch, bass, walleye, salmon, muskie, pike, and whitefish. Contact Communication Services, Wildlife Information, **Ministry of Natural Resources** (✉ Queen's Park, M7A 1W3, ☎ 416/314–2225).

Within metro Toronto itself, fishing is permitted in the trout pond at Hanlan's Point on Toronto Island, as well as in Grenadier Pond in High Park. The salmon fishing just off the Scarborough Bluffs, in Toronto's east end, is extraordinary.

There are more than 100 charter boats (about $60 for a half-day) on Lake Ontario; contact **Ontario Travel** (☎ 416/314–0944). Be warned, though: Some fish caught in this province have such high levels of mercury in them that you can take your temperature at the same time that you eat them. It's sad, but water pollution (including acid rain) has taken its toll upon the edibility of many fish in Ontario.

Fitness Facilities
Nearly every major hotel in metro Toronto has a decent indoor swimming pool; some even have indoor/outdoor swimming pools. Among the best are those at the **Sheraton Centre** (✉ 123 Queen St. W, at Bay St., ☎ 416/361–1000) and the **Inn on the Park** (✉ Eglinton Ave. near Leslie St., ☎ 416/444–2561). Many also have health clubs, with saunas and Nautilus equipment; be sure to call ahead to inquire about availability and fees, particularly if you're not a guest.

Golf
The season lasts only from April to late October. The top course is **Glen Abbey** (✉ 1333 Dorval Dr., Oakville, ☎ 905/844–1800), where the **Canadian Open Championship** is held in late summer; cart and greens fees will cost up to $75 on weekends, but this 18-hole course is a real beauty. Less challenging, but much closer to the heart of the city, is the nine-hole **Don Valley Golf Course** (✉ 4200 Yonge St., ☎ 416/392–2465),

just south of Route 401. The **Flemingdon Park Golf Club** (⊠ Don Mills Rd. and Eglinton Ave., ☎ 416/429–1740) has nine holes not far from the city. For other courses, contact **Metro Parks** (☎ 416/392–8186) or **Ontario Travel** (☎ 416/314–0944).

Horseback Riding

Sunnybrook Stables (⊠ Leslie St. and Eglinton Ave., ☎ 416/444–4044), in Sunnybrook Park, has an indoor arena, an outdoor ring, and about 19 kilometers (nearly 12 miles) of bridle trails through the Don valley.

Ice-Skating

Toronto operates some 30 outdoor artificial rinks and 100 natural-ice rinks—and all are free. Among the most popular are those in Nathan Phillips Square, in front of the New City Hall at Queen and Bay streets; down at Harbourfront, which has Canada's largest outdoor artificial ice rink; College Park, at Yonge and College streets; Grenadier Pond, within High Park, at Bloor and Keele streets; and inside Hazelton Lanes, the classy shopping mall on the edge of Yorkville, on Avenue Road, just above Bloor Street. You need to bring your own skates to most outdoor rinks; one exception is Nathan Phillips Square, where equipment can be rented. For details on any city rink, call ☎ 416/392–1111.

Jogging

The Martin Goodman Trail (☞ Bicycling, *above*) is ideal. Also try the boardwalk of The Beaches in the east end, High Park in the west end, the Toronto Islands, or any of Toronto's parks. Some hotels will provide maps of popular jogging routes.

Sailing

This can be a breeze, especially between April and October. Contact the **Ontario Sailing Association** (⊠ 1185 Eglinton Ave., North York M3C 3C3, ☎ 416/426–7271). The **Royal Canadian Yacht Club** (⊠ 1441 St. George St., ☎ 416/967–7245) has its summer headquarters in a beautiful Victorian mansion on Centre Island.

Skiing

CROSS-COUNTRY

Try Toronto's parks and ravines; High Park; the lakefront along the southern edge of the city; Tommy Thompson Park; Toronto Islands; and Centennial Park, in the western borough of Etobicoke, only a 20-minute drive from downtown.

DOWNHILL

You can get a taste of this sport within metro Toronto at the small **Earl Bales Park** (⊠ Bathurst St. south of Sheppard Ave.) and **Centennial Park Ski Hill** (Etobicoke, ☎ 416/394–8754). The best alpine hills are a good 45 to 60 minutes north of the city (☞ Chapter 7, Barrie, Collingwood, and Huntsville).

Sleigh Riding and Tobogganing

Black Creek Pioneer Village (⊠ North of 401 along Rte. 400, at Steeles Ave., ☎ 416/736–1733) is open winter weekends 10–5 for skating, tobogganing, and horse-drawn sleigh rides. The best parks for tobogganing include **High Park,** in the west end, and **Winston Churchill Park,** at Spadina and St. Clair avenues, just two blocks from Casa Loma: It is sheer terror.

Tennis

The city provides dozens of courts, all free, and many of them floodlit. Parks with courts open from 7 AM to 11 PM, in season, include the famous High Park, off Bloor Street at Keele Street, in the west end; Stanley Park, on King Street West, three blocks west of Bathurst Street; and Eglinton Park, on Eglinton Avenue West, just east of Avenue Road.

A number of indoor courts are open throughout the winter months. Call the **Ontario Tennis Association** (☏ 416/426–7135).

Spectator Sports

Auto Racing

For the past several years, the **Molson Indy** has been roaring around the Canadian National Exhibition grounds, including the major thoroughfare of Lakeshore Boulevard, for three days in mid-July. You'll pay more than $85 for a three-day "red" reserved seat, but general admission for the qualifying rounds, the practice rounds, and the Indy itself can be as cheap as $10–$20, depending upon the day. For tickets and information call Ticketmaster (☏ 416/872–4639).

Less than a half-hour drive away is the **Cayuga International Speedway** (☏ 705/743–6671), where international stock-car races are held from May through September.

Baseball

The **Toronto Blue Jays** (☏ 416/341–1111), whose home is the Sky-Dome (☞ Harbourfront, *above*), have developed into one of baseball's most dynamic teams. Indeed, their back-to-back World Series wins in 1992 and 1993 still have the whole city buzzing. The Jays have the most costly tickets in the major leagues, ranging from rotten $5 seats (the nose-bleeds) up to ones that cost $11, $15, and $19.50, and they usually sell out every single home game, so plan way ahead of your Toronto visit.

Canoeing and Rowing

One of the world's largest **canoeing and rowing regattas** is held every July 1, as it has been for more than a century, on Toronto Island's Long Pond. ✉ *Canoe Ontario*, ☏ 416/426–7170.

Football

The Canadian Football League has teetered near extinction in recent years, but it continues to draw fans. The **Toronto Argonauts** (☏ 416/341–5151), which are partly owned by hockey superstar Wayne Gretzky, have been as erratic as the league itself. The Argos play their home games at the SkyDome (☞ Harbourfront, *above*).

Golf

The permanent site of the **Canadian Open Golf Championship** is Glen Abbey (☞ *above*), a course designed by Jack Nicklaus. This tournament is one of golf's Big Five and is always played in late summer.

Hockey

The **Toronto Maple Leafs** (box office: ✉ 60 Carlton at Church St., ☏ 416/977–1641 at 9 AM sharp on day of game you wish to see) play 40 home games each season (Oct.–Apr.), usually on Wednesday and Saturday nights, in the big, ugly Maple Leaf Gardens. There are always tickets available at each game—at least from scalpers in front of the stadium on Carlton Street, a half block east of the corner of Yonge and College streets.

Horse Racing

HARNESS AND THOROUGHBRED RACING

The **Ontario Jockey Club** (☏ 416/675–6110) operates three major racetracks. **Woodbine Race Track** (✉ Rte. 27 and Rexdale Blvd., 30 min northwest of downtown Toronto, near airport, ☏ 416/675–6110) is the showplace of Thoroughbred and harness racing in Canada. Horses run late April through late October. **Mohawk** (✉ Rte. 401, 30 min west of Toronto, beyond Milton, ☏ 905/854–7820), in the heart of Ontario's Standardbred breeding country, has a glass-enclosed, climate-controlled grandstand and other attractive facilities. **Fort Erie** (✉ 230 Catherine St., ☎ 905/871–3200), in the Niagara tourist region, is one of the most picturesque racetracks in the world, with willows, manicured hedges, and flower-bordered infield lakes.

ROYAL HORSE SHOW
This highlight of Canada's equestrian season is part of the Royal Winter Fair each November. ✉ *CNE grounds, Dufferin St. at waterfront,* ☎ *416/393–6400.*

Soccer

Although Toronto keeps getting and losing and getting a professional soccer team, one can catch this exciting sport, as well as collegiate football, in the very handy **Varsity Stadium** (✉ Bloor St. W at Bedford, 1 block west of Royal Ontario Museum and University Ave., ☎ 416/978–7388).

SHOPPING

Toronto is the shopping capital of Canada. There's a fine selection of British Isles imports and Canadiana, as well as everything from Gianni Versace suits to Ikea furnishings. Books, antiques, and clothing are plentiful and interesting. The biggest sale day of the year is Boxing Day, the first business day after Christmas, when nearly everything in the city is half price. As winter fades, clothing prices tend to drop even further. Summer sales start in late June and continue through August. Keep your receipts; federal (GST) and provincial (PST) tax are refundable at the trip's conclusion.

Bargaining

Shoppers can haggle at flea markets, including the Harbourfront Antique Market, and perhaps in the Chinatown and Kensington Market/Spadina Avenue areas. In some small boutiques, where the owner is in attendance, you may be able to negotiate for a better price than what you see on the ticket.

Refund Information

Visitors, including Canadians from other provinces, can receive a refund on the 7% GST and on the 8% PST for purchases over $100 (☞ GST and Sales Tax *in* Smart Travel Tips A to Z).

Opening Times

Most shops are open Monday through Friday 10 to 6, and Thursday until 8. Most shops are closed on Sunday and many stores close on major holidays, including Good Friday, Easter Monday, and Victoria Day (third Monday in May).

Shopping Districts

The **Yorkville Avenue/Bloor Street area** is where you'll find the big fashion names, fine leather goods, important jewelers, some of the top private art galleries, upscale shoe stores, and discount china and glassware. Streets to explore include Yorkville Avenue, Cumberland Street, and Scollard Street, all running parallel to Bloor Street, and Hazelton Avenue, running north from Yorkville Avenue near Avenue Road. **Hazelton Lanes,** between Hazelton Avenue and Avenue Road, and the adjacent **York Square** are among the most chichi shopping areas in Canada, and they are headquarters for café society during the brief annual spell of warm weather.

On **Bloor Street** you'll find such wonderful stores as **Zoe,** with haute couture designs; **The Bay,** a department store with clothes for men and women; **Holt Renfrew,** possibly the most stunning store in Toronto, with marble, chrome, glass, and glittering fashions for both sexes; **Harry Rosen** for men; and such shoe shops as **Boutique Quinto** and **David's.** In **The Colonnade,** on the south side of Bloor Street, a few doors east of University Avenue, is another upscale cluster of stores. Even with the invasion of such American chains as The Gap and Banana Republic, the tone is très expensive, and très good.

The **Eaton Centre** is a very large galleria-style shopping center downtown, on Yonge Street between Queen and Dundas streets. With scores of large and small stores and restaurants, all sheltered from the weather, it's one of the city's major tourist attractions. Generally speaking, the lower levels are lower priced and the higher levels are more expensive. ✉ *220 Yonge St.,* ☎ *416/598–2322.*

Queen Street West, starting just west of University Avenue and continuing past Spadina Avenue, creeping ever westward past Bathurst Street, is a trendy area near the Ontario College of Art. Here, you'll find young, hip designers; new- and used-book bookstores; vintage clothes; two comic-book stores, including the biggest in North America (Silver Snail, No. 367; also check out the Dragon Lady Comic Shop at No. 200); and the more progressive private galleries.

Harbourfront includes an antiques market (✉ 390 Queen's Quay W, ☎ 416/260–2626) that is Canada's biggest on Sunday, when it draws about 200 dealers. The market is open Tuesday–Friday 11–5, Saturday 10–6, and Sunday 8–6. The **Queen's Quay Terminal** (✉ 207 Queen's Quay W, ☎ 416/203–0501) is a renovated warehouse that now houses a collection of unique boutiques, craft stalls, patisseries, and so on; it's a great place to buy gifts. There's frequent streetcar service from Union Station, but it's a fairly easy walk. Parking is expensive.

Spadina Avenue, from Wellington Street north to College Street, has plenty of low-price clothing for the whole family, as well as fur and leather factory outlets. **Winner's** (✉ South of King St., ☎ 416/585–2052) is a good discount outlet for women and children. **Evex Luggage Centre** (✉ 369 Spadina Ave., ☎ 416/966–1422), south of College, has good discount luggage, handbags, and leather accessories.

Downtown Toronto has a vast underground maze of shopping warrens that burrow in between and underneath the office towers. The tenants of the **Underground City** are mostly chain and convenience stores, and the shopping is rather dull. The network runs roughly from the Royal York Hotel near Union Station north to the Eaton Centre.

Department Stores

The major department stores have branches around the city and flagship stores downtown. They accept major credit cards and have liberal return policies. However, service tends to be very slow and uninformed compared with that of boutiques. The exclusive **Holt Renfrew** (☞ *above*) on Bloor Street sings with élan and quality. The bigger names are **Eaton's,** in the Eaton Centre (☞ *above*), and **The Bay,** on Yonge Street between Queen and Richmond streets and at Yonge and Bloor streets (☞ *above*).

Specialty Shops

Antiques and Galleries

Yorkville is the headquarters of establishment antiques dealers. There are several other pockets around town, including a strip along Queen Street East, roughly between Sherbourne and George streets.

The Allery (⊠ 322½ Queen St. W, ☎ 416/593–0853) specializes in antique prints and maps. **Art Metropole** (⊠ 788 King St. W, ☎ 416/703–4400) specializes in limited-edition, small-press, or self-published artists' books from around the world. **Ballenford Architectural Books** (⊠ 98 Scollard St., ☎ 416/588–0800) has Canada's largest selection of architectural titles and a gallery with usually interesting exhibits of architectural drawings and related work. **Jane Corkin Gallery** (⊠ 179 John St., north of Queen St., ☎ 416/979–1980) specializes in photography. In the same building is **Isaacs Gallery** (☎ 416/421–9985), owned by Av Isaacs, godfather of many of the established Canadian artists. For more avant-garde works, look in **Cold City** (⊠ 30 Duncan St., ☎ 416/504–6681). **YYZ** (⊠ 1087 Queen St. W, ☎ 416/531–7869) has a good collection of unusual contemporary pieces. **Mercer Union** (⊠ 333 Adelaide St. W, ☎ 416/977–1412) is in the forefront of the arts. Also check out **Toronto Photographers Workshop** (⊠ 80 Spadina Ave., ☎ 416/504–4242). At the galleries at 80 Spadina Avenue you'll usually find at least one opening on a Saturday afternoon. **Prime Canadian Gallery** (⊠ 52 McCaul St., ☎ 416/593–5750) has an ever-changing array of merchandise. **Quasi Modo** (⊠ 789 Queen St. W, next door to Dufflet Pastries, ☎ 416/703–8300) has a quirky collection of 20th-century furniture and design; you never know what will be on display: vintage bicycles, Noguchi lamps, or a corrugated cardboard table by Frank Gehry. **20th Century** (⊠ 23 Beverley St., north of Queen St., ☎ 416/598–2172) is for serious collectors of 20th-century design, particularly furniture, lamps, jewelry, and decorative arts. Many of the pieces are museum quality, and the owners are extremely erudite.

Books

Toronto is rich in bookstores selling new books, used books, best-sellers, and remainders. If you just need a current magazine or a paperback for the plane, there are the ubiquitous chains—Coles and SmithBooks. Otherwise, try the following:

Albert Britnell Book Shop (⊠ 765 Yonge St., north of Bloor St., ☎ 416/924–3321) has been a Toronto legend since 1893, with a marvelous British ambience and great browsing. **Another Man's Poison** (⊠ 29 McCaul St., ☎ 416/593–6451) showcases an eclectic collection of rare design books plus an interesting hodgepodge of offbeat decorative pieces. **Book Cellar** (⊠ 1560 Yonge St., north of St. Clair Ave., ☎ 416/967–5577) offers a fine choice of classical records, as well as international political and intellectual journals. An entirely separate venture is the literarily centered **Book Cellar** (⊠ 142 Yorkville Ave., near Avenue Rd., ☎ 416/925–9953) in Yorkville. **Edward's Books and Art** (⊠ 356 Queen St. W, near Spadina Ave., ☎ 416/593–0126; ⊠ 2179 Queen St. E, the Beaches, ☎ 416/698–1442; ⊠ Park Plaza Hotel, 170 Bloor St. W, ☎ 416/961–2428; ⊠ 2200 Yonge St., south of Eglinton Ave., ☎ 416/487–5431), one of the nicest local bookstore chains in the city, now at four locations, advertises huge discounts on bestsellers and remainders in every Saturday's *Globe and Mail*. In addition, the stores carry an impressive catalog of current and rare artists' monographs. All are open Sunday. **Glad Day Books** (⊠ 598 Yonge St., ☎ 416/961-4161), one block north of the Church and Wellesley gay mecca, holds the distinction of being Canada's first specialty bookstore for lesbian and gay titles. **Bob Miller Book Room** (⊠ 180 Bloor St. W, northwest of ROM, ☎ 416/922–3557) has the best literature and philosophy section in the city and a staff that has been with Bob for decades. **Pages Books and Magazines** (⊠ 256 Queen St. W, ☎ 416/598–1447) has a wide selection of international and small-press literature; fashion and design books and magazines; and books on film, art, and literary criticism. This is one astoundingly intellectual bookstore. **This Ain't the Rosedale Library** (⌂ 483 Church St., south of Wellesley Ave., ☎ 416/929–9912) stocks the largest selection of baseball books in Canada, as well as a good range of fiction, poetry, photography, design, rock, and jazz books. **The World's Biggest Book Store** (⌂ 20 Edward St., 1 block north of Eaton Centre, ☎ 416/977–7009) is equipped with over 65,000 square feet of selling floor, making this leviathan Canada's largest book shop. Its 160,000 titles are particularly strong in business, computers, and travel. In addition to encyclopedic magazine and video sections, the store showcases the city's best array of Canadian books. **Writers & Co.** (⌂ 2005 Yonge St., near Davisville, a few blocks south of Eglinton, ☎ 416/481–8432) is arguably Canada's finest literary bookstore, with hard-to-find poets, essayists, and world novelists. If you have been looking for a rare Caribbean poetry collection, a Swedish play in translation, or an Asian novella, this is the store to visit.

Clothing

Queen Street West is well known for its stores catering to the young, hip, and zany. Among those in the neighborhood are **Boomer** (⌂ No. 309, ☎ 416/598–0013), **Due West** (⌂ No. 431, ☎ 416/593–6267), **No. 6 Clothing Company** (⌂ No. 290A, ☎ 416/593–2745), and **Rag Tag** (⌂ No. 359, ☎ 416/979–3939). Yonge Street is also a popular area for clothes shopping; try **Soul Underground** (⌂ No. 673, ☎ 416/924–4119).

Brown's (⌂ 1975 Avenue Rd., south of Rte. 401, ☎ 416/489–1975) provides classic clothing for short men and women. There's a **Brown's** store for men only (⌂ 545 Queen St. W, ☎ 416/507–5937). **Muskat & Brown** (⌂ 2528 Yonge St., ☎ 416/489–4005) is for petite women. **Fetoun** (⌂ Four Seasons Hotel, 162 Cumberland St., ☎ 416/923–3434) is a high-fashion emporium for the nouveau riche. If you go to a lot of charity balls, this is the place to shop. **Linda Lundstrom** (⌂ 2507 Yonge St., ☎ 416/480–1602; ⌂ 136 Cumberland St., ☎ 416/927–9009) is an award-winning designer of high-fashion winter clothing. This is the place to buy an eye-catching parka. **Venni** (⌂ 274 Queen St. W, ☎ 416/597–9360; 2638 Yonge St., ☎ 416/489–9561; ⌂ Bayview Village Shopping Centre, ☎ 416/223–4304) highlights trendy Canadian-designed clothing at three locations.

Food Markets

Kensington Market (⌂ Northwest of Dundas St. and Spadina Ave.) is an outdoor market, open daily, with a vibrant ethnic mix. Saturday is the best day to go, preferably by public transit, because parking is difficult. **St. Lawrence Market** (⌂ Front and Jarvis Sts., ☎ 416/392–7219) is best early on Saturday, when, in addition to the permanent indoor market on the south side of Front Street, there's a farmer's market in the building on the north side. The historic south market was once Toronto's city hall, and it fronted the lake before extensive landfill projects were undertaken.

Gifts

The Guild Shop (⌂ 118 Cumberland St., ☎ 416/921–1721) is an outlet for a wide variety of Canadian artists, in the broadest sense of the word. Soapstone carvings from Inuit communities in the Arctic, aboriginal paintings from British Columbia and Ontario, and even woolen ties from Nova Scotia are among the items for sale. Whether or not you buy anything, the Guild Shop is worth a visit for an appreciation of indigenous Canadian arts and crafts. **Arts-on-King** (⌂ 169 King St. E, ☎ 416/777–9617) is a bright and spacious store with a varied selection of glass, ceramic, wood, and other creations. Established artists have exhibits in their Loft Galleries. **Filigree** (⊠ 1210 Yonge St., ☎ 416/961–5223) has a good assortment of linens, as well as drawer liners, silver frames, and other Victorian pleasures. In the neighborhood are other gift shops selling fine glass and antiques.

Robin Kay Home and Style (⊠ Eaton Centre, ☎ 416/977–6540) is this country's answer to Martha Stewart, featuring lovely Canadian products to enliven any interior, from bibelots to linens.

Jewelry
Secrett Jewel Salon (⊠ 150 Bloor St. W, ☎ 416/967–7500) is a reputable source of unusual gemstones and fine new and estate jewelry; local gemologists consider it the best in town.

SIDE TRIP

Whitby

🐦 **Cullen Gardens and Miniature Village.** The village, stretching across 25 acres of carefully tended gardens, showcases a collection of miniature reproductions—built to ½ scale—of more than 140 historic and contemporary Ontario buildings. A 35-minute drive east of downtown Toronto along Route 401, the village is owned by the family that runs one of Toronto's best-known garden-store chains. Activities continue throughout the year, from a tulip festival in May to a rose festival in June and July and a winter carnival in late December and early January. ⊠ 300 Taunton Rd. W, L1N 5R5, ☎ 905/668–6606. ☑ $9.95. ☉ Easter–late June and Labor Day–mid-Nov., daily 10–6; late June–Labor Day, daily 9–9; mid-Nov.–early Jan., daily 10–10.

TORONTO A TO Z

Arriving and Departing

By Bus
The bus terminal (⊠ 610 Bay St., north of Dundas St., ☎ 416/393–7911) serves a number of lines. **Greyhound** (☎ 416/367–8747 or 800/231–2222) has regular bus service into Toronto from all over the United States and Canada. From Detroit, the trip takes five hours; from Buffalo, two to three hours; from Chicago and New York City, 11 hours. Several other bus companies, such as **Trentway-Wagar** and **Voyageur,** offer service to many of the same destinations.

By Car
Detroit–Windsor and Buffalo–Fort Erie crossings can be slow, especially on weekends and holidays. The wonderfully wide Highway 401—reaching up to 16 lanes as it slashes across metro Toronto from the airport on the west almost as far as the zoo on the east—is the major link between Windsor, Ontario (and Detroit), and Montréal. It's also known as the Macdonald-Cartier Freeway but is really never called anything other than "the 401." There are no tolls, but be warned: In weekday rush hours the 401 can become dreadfully crowded, even stop-and-go. Plan your trips to avoid these times.

If you're driving from Buffalo or Niagara Falls, take the Queen Elizabeth Way, which curves up along the western shore of Lake Ontario, eventually turns into the Gardiner Expressway, and flows right into the downtown core.

Yonge Street, which begins at the lakefront, is called Route 11 once you get north of Toronto and continues all the way to the Ontario–Minnesota border, at Rainy River. At 1,896 kilometers (1,178 miles), it is the longest street in the world.

By Plane

Flights into Toronto land at the **Lester B. Pearson International Airport,** so named in 1984 to honor Canada's Nobel Peace Prize–winning prime minister of nearly three decades earlier. It's commonly called "the Toronto airport" or "Malton" (after the once-small town where it was built, just northwest of the city). The cavernous Terminal 3, which opened in 1991 and is used mainly by Canadian Airlines International, American Airlines, and United Airlines, is seldom congested. Terminal 2, the home of Air Canada and USAir, among others, has also undergone a face-lift. Terminal 1, which was built in 1964, shows its age; but at least the peak-hour pandemonium is a thing of the past. Airlines using Terminal 1 include Northwest and Delta.

Toronto is served by **American** (☎ 800/433–7300), **Delta** (☎ 800/843–9378), **Northwest** (☎ 800/225–2525), **United** (☎ 800/241–6522), **USAir** (☎ 800/428–4322), **Air Canada** (☎ 416/925–2311 or 800/268–7240), **Canadian Airlines International** (☎ 416/798–2211 or 800/665–1177), as well as more than a dozen European and Asian carriers with easy connections to many U.S. cities. **Air Ontario,** affiliated with Air Canada (☎ 416/925–2311), flies from the small, downtown Island Airport to and from Ottawa, Montréal, London (Ontario), and Newark. It is a convenient alternative to Pearson International if you're staying downtown and making trips to these cities.

BETWEEN THE AIRPORT AND CENTER CITY

Although Pearson is not far from the downtown area (about 32 kilometers, or 18 miles), the drive can take well over an hour during Toronto's weekday rush hours. Taxis and limos to a hotel or attraction near the lake typically cost $30 or more. Airport cabs have fixed rates to different parts of the city. You have little choice but to pay the full fare from the airport, but it is often possible to negotiate a lower fare from downtown, where airport cabs have to compete with regular city cabs for business. It is illegal for city cabs to pick up passengers at the airport, unless they are specifically called—a time-consuming process, but sometimes worth the wait.

Pacific Western (☎ 905/564–6333) offers express coach service linking the airport to three subway stops in the southwest and north-central areas of the city. Buses depart several times each hour from 8 AM to 11:30 PM. Fares average $6–$7. The service to and from several downtown hotels operates every 20 minutes from 6:25 AM to 12:45 AM daily and costs approximately $12. Some airport and downtown hotels offer free shuttle bus service from the three terminals.

Should you be renting a car at the airport, be sure to ask for a street map of the city. Route 427 runs south some 6 kilometers (4 miles) to the lakeshore. Here you pick up the Queen Elizabeth Way (QEW or Queen E) east to the Gardiner Expressway, which runs east into the heart of downtown. If you take the QEW west, you'll find yourself swinging around Lake Ontario, toward Hamilton, Niagara-on-the-Lake, and Niagara Falls.

By Train

Amtrak (☎ 800/872–7245) runs a daily train to Toronto from Chicago (a 12-hour trip), and another from New York City (12 hours). From Union Station (✉ Front St. between Bay and York Sts.) you can walk underground to many hotels—a real boon in inclement weather. There is a cab stand outside the main entrance of the station.

Getting Around

Most of Toronto is laid out on a grid pattern. The key street to remember is Yonge Street (pronounced "young"), the main north–south artery. Most major cross streets are numbered east and west of Yonge Street. In other words, if you are looking for 180 St. Clair Avenue West, you want a building a few blocks *west* of Yonge Street; 75 Queen Street East is a block or so *east* of Yonge Street.

At press time, the fare for buses, streetcars, and trolleys was $2 in exact change, but 10 adult tickets/tokens cost $15. Two-fare tickets are available for $3.50 for adults. If you plan to stay in Toronto for more than a month consider the **Metropass,** a photo-identity card that currently costs $78 for adults plus $3 extra for the photo.

Families can take advantage of the **Day Pass.** It costs $6 and is good for unlimited travel for one person, Monday–Friday after 9:30 AM, and all day Saturday. On Sundays and holidays, it's good for up to six persons (maximum two adults) for unlimited travel. Call the Toronto Transit Commission (TTC; ☎ 416/393–4636) from 7 AM to 11:30 PM for information on how to take public transit to any street or attraction in the city. The TTC publishes a very useful **Ride Guide** each year. It shows nearly every major place of interest and how to reach it by public transit. These guides are available in most subways and many other places around the city. The subways stop running at 2 AM, but the TTC has bus service from 1 to 5:30 AM on many major streets, including Queen, College, Bloor, Yonge, part of Dufferin, and as far north as Finch and Eglinton.

By Bus

All buses and streetcars accept exact change, tickets, or tokens. Paper transfers are free; pick one up from the driver when you pay your fare.

By Car

Pedestrian crosswalks are sprinkled throughout the city; they are marked clearly by yellow overhead signs and very large painted Xs. All a pedestrian has to do is stick out a hand, and cars (you hope!) screech to a halt in both directions. Right turns on red lights are nearly always permitted, except where otherwise posted. You must come to a complete stop before making the turn.

By Subway

The TTC runs one of the safest, cleanest, most trustworthy systems of its kind anywhere. There are two major subway lines, with 60 stations along the way: the **Bloor/Danforth Line,** which crosses Toronto about 5 kilometers (3 miles) north of the lakefront, from east to west, and the **Yonge/University/Spadina Line,** which loops north and south, like a giant "U," with the bottom of the "U" at Union Station. Tokens and tickets are sold in each subway station and at hundreds of convenience stores along the many routes of the TTC. Get your transfers just after you pay your fare and enter the subway; you'll find them in machines on your way down to the trains.

By Taxi

The meter begins at $2.50 and includes the first .2 kilometer (roughly .1 mile). Each additional .235 kilometer (.145 mile) is 25¢—as is each passenger in excess of four. The waiting time "while under engagement" is 25¢ for every 33 seconds—and in one of the horrible traffic jams, this could add up. Still, it's possible to take a cab across downtown Toronto for $8 to $9. The largest companies are **Beck** (☎ 416/461–1131), **Co-op** (☎ 416/504–2667), **Diamond** (☎ 416/366–6868), **Metro** (☎ 416/504–8294), and **Royal** (☎ 416/785–3322). For more information, call the Metro Licensing Commission (☎ 416/392–3000).

Contacts and Resources

B&B Reservation Services

More than two dozen private homes are affiliated with **Toronto Bed & Breakfast** (✉ 21 Kingswood Rd., M4E 3N4, ☎ 416/596–1118, FAX 416/690–5089), most of them scattered around metro Toronto. Rooms cost as little as $50 a night and include breakfast. You might also try the **Metropolitan Bed & Breakfast** (✉ 615 Mt. Pleasant Rd., Suite 269, M4S 3C5, ☎ 416/964–2566, FAX 416/537–0233) registry service, which has about 30 city and suburban homes on its books. Another 15 to 20 homes in various parts of the city have signed up with **Bed and Breakfast Homes of Toronto** (✉ Box 46093, College Park, M5B 2L8, ☎ 416/363–6362)—you can write for a brochure detailing individual homes.

Consulates

The **Consulate General of the United States** (✉ 360 University Ave., north of Queen St., M56 1S4, ☎ 416/595–0228).

The **British Consulate General** (✉ 777 Bay St., at College St., M56 2G2, ☎ 416/593–1267).

Doctors and Dentists

Ask at your hotel desk or call **Dial-a-Doctor** (☎ 416/756–6259) or the **Dental Emergency Service** (☎ 416/967–5649).

Emergencies

Dial 911 for **police** and **ambulance.**

Guided Tours

ORIENTATION

You can take tours of the Toronto harbor and islands on comfortably equipped **Toronto Tours** (☎ 416/869–1372) boats, for about $15. The hourly tour passes the Toronto Islands, with lovely views of the Toronto cityscape. Boats leave from the Pier Six Building next to Queen's Quay Terminal from early May through mid-October, daily 10–6. Tours leave as late as 7:15 PM in summer. Other boats depart from the Westin Harbour Castle hotel at the foot of Yonge Street.

Greyhound Sightseeing Bus Tours (☎ 416/367–8747) runs tours from April through November. The 2½-hour tours start at the bus terminal (✉ Bay and Dundas Sts.) and include the Eaton Centre, the old and new city halls, Queen's Park, the University of Toronto, Yorkville, Ontario Place, and Casa Loma—the latter, for a full hour. The fare is $18.

In winter, city bus tours are provided by **Niagara Tours** (☎ 416/868–0400). These tours, lasting a full day, make a circuit of the city's high points. Pickups are made at all major downtown hotels between 9:30 and 10 AM, returning around 6. The fare is $98.

Downtown Toronto Walking Tour (☎ 416/922–7606) is just that—the closest look possible at central Toronto, with the emphasis on architecture. The 2- to 2½-hour tours take place daily Tuesday–Sunday between May and October, starting in front of Old City Hall on the northeast corner of Bay and Queen streets. Starting times vary, so call in advance. The cost is $10.

Mosaic Environ Excursion Toronto (☎ 416/778–9686) offers a five-hour tour that visits some of the ethnic neighborhoods and green spaces that give Toronto its special character. This tour, which starts at Union Station, goes beyond the downtown area to include Cabbagetown, Little Italy, and the picturesque area around the Humber River. The cost is $34.95 and includes a picnic lunch.

SPECIAL-INTEREST

Ghost Walk (☎ 416/501–0615) takes you on a walking tour of the haunted places in Toronto. This first-rate adventure is available from mid-May to October. The cost of the tour is $10.

Underground City Tours (☎ 905/886–9111), Marius Frederick's fascinating 2½-hour tour full of tidbits about the city's life and history, meets at the south door of the Eaton Centre across from the Bay on Queen Street Tuesday and Wednesday at 10 and 1:30. The cost is $15.

The **Bruce Trail Association** (☎ 416/690–4453 or 800/665–4453) arranges day and overnight hikes around Toronto and its environs.

Hotel Reservation Service
Accommodation Toronto (☎ 905/629–3800), a service of the Hotel Association of Toronto, is an excellent source for finding the room and price you want. Ask about family deals and special packages.

Late-Night Pharmacies
Pharma Plus Drugmart (✉ Church St. and Wellesley Ave., ☎ 416/924–7760). **Shoppers Drug Mart** (✉ 700 Bay St., ☎ 416/979–2424; ✉ 2500 Hurontario St., Mississauga, ☎ 905/896–2500).

Road Emergencies
The **Canadian Automobile Association** (☎ 416/222–5222) has 24-hour road service; membership benefits are extended to U.S. AAA members.

The following gas stations and auto-repair shops are open 24 hours: several **Texaco** stations (✉ 153 Dundas St. W, behind New City Hall; ✉ 333 Davenport, south of Casa Loma; ✉ 601 Eglinton Ave. E, west of Ontario Science Center); **Cross Town Service Center** (✉ 1467 Bathurst St., at St. Clair Ave. W); **Jim McCormack Esso** (✉ 2901 Sheppard Ave. E), in the Scarborough area, heading toward the Metro Zoo; **Guido's Esso** (✉ 1104 Albion Rd.), not far from the airport; and **Bill's Service Station** (✉ 2272 Lakeshore Blvd. W), close to the QEW.

Visitor Information
The **Metropolitan Toronto Convention & Visitors Association** (✉ 207 Queen's Quay W, Suite 509, M5J 1A7, ☎ 416/203–2500 or 800/363–1990) has its office at Queen's Quay Terminal. Booths providing brochures and pamphlets about the city and its attractions, as well as accommodations, are set up in the summer outside the Eaton Centre, on Yonge Street just below Dundas Street, and outside the Royal Ontario Museum.

The **Traveller's Aid Society** recommends restaurants and hotels and distributes subway maps and Ontario sales tax rebate forms. ✉ *Union Station, arrivals level and basement level, Room B23,* ☎ *416/366–7788;* ✉ *Pearson Airport, Terminal I, arrivals level, past Customs, near Area B,* ☎ *905/676–2868; Pearson Airport, Terminal 2, between international and domestic arrivals;* ☎ *905/676–2869;* ✉ *Pearson Airport, Terminal 3, arrivals level, near international side,* ☎ *905/612–5890.*

7 Province of Ontario

Ottawa, Algonquin Park, Windsor, Niagara, London

With shorelines on four of the five Great Lakes, Ontario is Canada's second-largest and most urbanized province, but only 10 million people live in this vast area, and 90% of them are within a narrow strip just north of the U.S. border. A bit north of the strip, Ottawa, Canada's capital, gathers government workers and parliamentarians.

By David E.
Scott

Updated by
David Anger

ONTARIO IS AN IROQUOIAN WORD variously in-
terpreted as: beautiful lake, beautiful water, or
rocks standing high beside the water (the last an
apparent reference to Niagara Falls). Ontario is Canada's second-
largest province—from east to west the traveler will cross 2,080 kilometers (1,300 miles) and one time zone. However, only 10 million people
live in this vast area, and 90% of them are within a narrow strip just
north of the U.S. border.

Ontario is Canada's most urban province; half of its population lives
in four cities whose boundaries have spread to such an extent that they
almost adjoin. Metropolitan Toronto has more than 2 million people.
To the east, Oshawa has 175,000 people and heavily populated suburbs. South and west of Toronto are Hamilton with 550,000 people
and St. Catharines with 290,000. Half of Ontario's population is of
British stock, but successive waves of immigrants over the past century have turned the province into a mini-United Nations. Thunder Bay
contains the largest settlement of Finns outside Finland. Toronto has
half a million Italians, the largest Chinese community in Canada, and
the most numerous Portuguese colony in North America. More recent
arrivals include thousands of West Indians, Vietnamese, Somalis, South
Africans, and east Europeans, giving Ontario—Toronto in particular—
a cosmopolitan flavor rivaling New York or Chicago's.

The towns and cities of northern Ontario are strung along the railway
lines that brought them into being. The discovery of immense deposits
of gold, silver, uranium, and other minerals by railway construction
gangs sparked mining booms that established such communities as Sudbury, Cobalt, and Timmins, which continue to owe their existence to
mining.

Ontario has the most varied landscape of any Canadian province. The
most conspicuous topographical feature is the Niagara Escarpment,
which runs from Niagara to Tobermory at the tip of the Bruce Peninsula in Lake Huron. The northern 90% of Ontario is covered by the
Canadian Shield, worn-down mountain ranges of the world's oldest
rock, reaching only 2,183 feet above sea level at their highest point.

East of Hamilton toward Niagara Falls is a narrow strip along the south
shore of Lake Ontario in a partial rain shadow of the Niagara Escarpment. The climate, moderated in winter by Lakes Ontario and Erie,
allows the growing of tender fruits and grapes, making it Canada's largest
wine-producing area.

Pleasures and Pastimes

The Arts
By combining public and private resources, Ontario has fostered one
of North America's most supportive environments for the arts. Each
year thousands flock to see great Shakespeare at the Stratford Festival
and top-notch music at the Shaw Festival. Better still, each city claims
an arts prize. In Hamilton it's the Hamilton Opera, while in Ottawa
it's the National Arts Centre Orchestra. Beyond these stalwarts, there
are plenty of upstart dance, music, and theater companies.

Dining
The cuisine of this vast province runs the gamut from fresh-caught fish
in cottage country to French-influenced dishes in Ottawa and great home-
style Canadian fare such as maple-syrup pie in southern Ontario. Given
the enormous British influence here, menus feature plenty of roast beef,

shepherd's pie, and rice pudding, especially in the English-dominated enclaves of London, Stratford, and Hamilton. Ontarians crave Tim Horton's doughnuts, found at franchise shops in virtually every city.

WHAT TO WEAR

Dress is relaxed throughout the province. Casual sportswear and jeans are acceptable almost everywhere; shorts and T-shirts are much less acceptable. In the more elegant dining rooms, men are likely to feel more comfortable in jacket and tie; women may prefer dress pants or a skirt. If a jacket and/or a tie is required, it's noted in individual reviews.

Unless noted otherwise, reservations are not necessary.

CATEGORY	COST*
$$$$	over $50
$$$	$35–$50
$$	$15–$35
$	under $15

*per person, excluding drinks, service, 7% GST, 8% food tax, and 10% bar tax

Lodging

Reservations are strongly recommended anywhere in Ontario during summer months. Generally you get what you pay for at Ontario hotels and motels, though rates are often double those charged in the United States for comparable accommodation. Bed-and-breakfast associations exist in most cities, but, again, many of those rates exceed what you'd pay for a good hotel or motel room south of the border. In Niagara Falls, the closer the hotel is to the falls, or the better the view is of them, the higher the rate.

CATEGORY	COST*
$$$$	over $100
$$$	$75–$100
$$	$35–$75
$	under $35

*All prices are for a standard double room, excluding taxes.

Museums

The diverse museums of Canada's most populous province document Ontario's evolution from a rough-hewn outpost to a lively cosmopolitan society. Living history museums, such as Upper Canada Village, reveal the early years. Numerous institutions, particularly in southern Ontario, chronicle the War of 1812. The National Gallery of Canada in Ottawa, among others, is the place to examine the region's fascinating artistic tradition.

Outdoor Activities and Sports

Bicycling along Colonel By Drive in Ottawa, camping in the mammoth Polar Bear Provincial Park, dogsledding through the wilderness, cross-country skiing in a grove of birch tress, and fishing, of course, on brilliantly clear lakes—these are just a few of Ontario's favorite pursuits.

CAMPING

There are 261 provincial parks in Ontario and hundreds of other parks that are privately owned and operated as businesses. The provincial parks are owned, maintained, and protected by the province, and they range in size from only a few acres to massive areas of land such as Polar Bear Provincial Park, which, at 15,000 square kilometers (9,300 square miles), is just a tad smaller than the 15,498-square-kilometer (9,609-square-mile) state of Vermont. Algonquin, created in 1893, is Ontario's oldest park.

Most of the provincial parks offer a variety of services for campers, from electrical outlets and sturdy, covered picnic shelters to laundry facilities and camp stores for provisions. Some also have cottages for rent. Additionally, many sponsor educational programs that teach children wilderness survival techniques and aim to offer a better understanding of nature.

In southern Ontario most provincial parks operate from mid-May until Labor Day weekend; in northern Ontario provincial parks open from early June until Labor Day weekend. Even when "closed," however, the parks never completely shut down, and visitors are welcome in the off-season, though few facilities are maintained. Some parks may be gated to prevent vehicular entry, but all are accessible to pedestrians from sunrise to sunset. Expect vault privies to be open, fireplace grates should be available, and fees usually will be collected through self-serve registration. Winter camping, which is becoming a popular pastime, is allowed in some provincial parks, though most are unsupervised and facilities are limited. During the fall and winter months reservations are not required at most parks.

DOGSLEDDING
In northwestern Ontario, near Kenora, you can take dogsled tours into the wilderness.

FISHING
Ontario has about 250,000 lakes and 150,000 rivers that contain myriad species of fish. The favorite trophies of most anglers are salmon and trout, but others lust after pike or muskie and still others swear that battling a frenzied black bass on light tackle is life's ultimate piscatorial challenge.

Ice Fishing. In winter most of Ontario's lakes freeze, providing good fishing for hardy souls who want to drill a hole through the ice and drop down a baited hook and line. The best ice-fishing spots in Ontario are Mitchell's Bay off Lake St. Clair, Lake Simcoe, Lake Nipissing, and lakes between and around North Bay and Temagami. Licenses are required for any fishing in Ontario, and they may be purchased from the Ministry of Natural Resources district offices, and most sporting goods stores, tourist outfitters, and resorts. Seasons and catch limits change annually and there are closed seasons in some districts. Regulations are published in the *Summary of the Fishing Regulations* (☞ Fishing *in* Ontario A to Z, *below*).

HIKING
Hiking trails are signposted along all Ontario highways, and usually there's parking, trail information, and comfort stations.

RAFTING
For thrills (and perhaps a few spills), few sports can beat white-water rafting. Eastern Ontario has many rivers suitable for the sport.

SKIING
Cross-Country. Nordic ski trails exist just about anywhere in the province where you find snow and accommodations for skiers.

Downhill. Ontario has hundreds of alpine slopes, although most are under 660 feet in vertical drop. All major Ontario ski centers have high-tech snow-making equipment, which in average years has guaranteed good skiing from late November through early April.

SNOWMOBILING

Ontario is crisscrossed by thousands of miles of snowmobile trails, most of which are kept groomed by enthusiastic members of dozens of snowmobile clubs. For many trails a permit must be purchased.

Shopping

Visitors from the States often relish Ontario's handsome inventory of things British, scooping up everything from china teacups and cashmere clothing to crumpet tins. Others marvel at the province's rich handicraft tradition. Ottawa, Sault Ste. Marie, Midland, and Thunder Bay have museum shops and galleries that specialize in native and Inuit crafts. Antiques stores abound. Some of the best antiques can be found at small shops in Bayfield (north of London), Cobourg (east of Toronto, near Lake Ontario), Meaford (on the north coast of Georgian Bay), Peterborough, Shakespeare (near Stratford), and St. Jacobs (near Kitchener/Waterloo).

Exploring Ontario

You could spend a lifetime exploring this enormous province and still not see it all. But by using three cities—Ottawa, Sault Ste. Marie, and Toronto—as bases for one- and two-day excursions, you can visit all the major sights and some special little corners that even many Ontarians don't know about.

Numbers in the text correspond to numbers in the margin and on the Eastern Ontario Province, Downtown Ottawa, Greater Ottawa and Hull, Niagara Falls, and Upper Ontario maps.

Great Itineraries

IF YOU HAVE 3 DAYS

Spend two days in **Ottawa** ①–⑲. In Canada's capital city, begin on **Parliament Hill** ①; weather and season permitting, catch the colorful Changing of the Guard ceremony. Also visit the lush **Garden of the Provinces** ④ and **Confederation Square** ⑦, with the **National War Memorial.** History buffs must see the **National Archives of Canada** and the **National Library of Canada** ⑤, which is replete with government ephemera, maps, and photographs. Ottawa's oldest building—the **Bytown Museum** ⑨—offers a great lesson in early Canada. The **Museum of Contemporary Photography** ⑪ and the **National Gallery of Canada** ⑬ survey the country's vast treasure trove of visual arts. The dinosaur exhibit at the **Canadian Museum of Nature** ⑱ really appeals to youngsters, while the beautiful **Canadian Museum of Civilization** ⑲ claims everyone's attention through its stunning chronicle of Canada's evolution. On Day 3, plan on more history lessons. Drive to **Upper Canada Village** ⑳, which captures the spirit of the United Empire Loyalists' struggle to sustain Canadian independence during the War of 1812. Afterward, cruise the Heritage Highway, stopping at historic **Kingston** ㉒, the country's capital from 1841 to 1844. Besides the massive Fort Henry, Kingston is home to the International Hockey Hall of Fame. Consider taking a jaunt to **Picton** ㉓, a Loyalist enclave with strong ties to Sir John A. MacDonald, Canada's first prime minister. If you're ambitious, you can try to make it to 🏨 **Peterborough** ㉖ by nightfall.

IF YOU HAVE 5 DAYS

After spending three days in **Ottawa** ①–⑲, **Kingston** ㉒, and **Picton** ㉓, you can use **Peterborough** ㉖ as a springboard to Ontario's "cottage country." Native rock carvings can be found at the **Petroglyphs Provincial Park** ㉗, northeast of Peterborough on Route 26. To the west via Routes 12 and 93, dash to the towns of **Penetanguishene** ㉙, known locally as Pentang, and **Midland** ㉚, on the shores of Georgian Bay. To

Lower Ontario Province

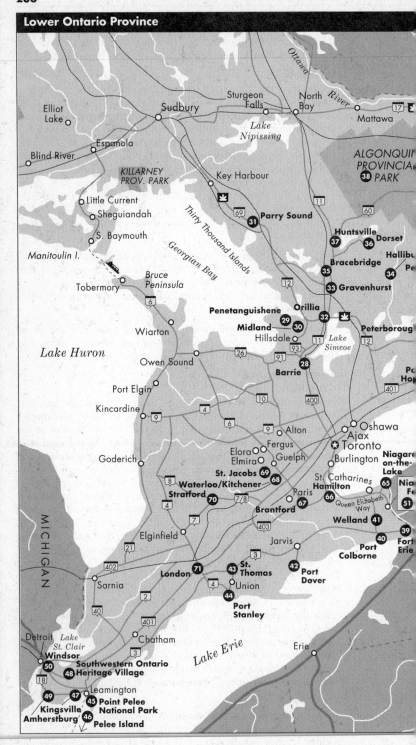

Elliot Lake

Blind River

Espanola

Sudbury

Sturgeon Falls

North Bay

Mattawa

17

Ottawa River

Lake Nipissing

ALGONQUIN PROVINCIA PARK

38

KILLARNEY PROV. PARK

Key Harbour

Little Current

Sheguiandah

S. Baymouth

Manitoulin I.

69

Parry Sound

31

11

Huntsville

37

Dorset

36

Halliburton

Pe

34

Thirty Thousand Islands

60

Tobermory

Bruce Peninsula

Georgian Bay

Bracebridge

35

33 Gravenhurst

6

Wiarton

12

Penetanguishene

Orillia

29 30

32

Lake Simcoe

Peterborough

Midland

Hillsdale

11

12

Lake Huron

Owen Sound

26

93

91

28 Barrie

Port Elgin

Kincardine

9

4

10

400

401

Po
Ho

6

9

Alton

Oshawa

Ajax

Toronto

Goderich

Elora

Elmira

Fergus

Guelph

Burlington

Niagare on-the-Lake

St. Jacobs

69

68

St. Catharines

65

Nia
Fe

Waterloo/Kitchener

Hamilton

Stratford

70

7/8

Paris

67

66

Queen Elizabeth Way

51

8

4

Brantford

403

Welland

41

40 39 Fort Erie

7

Elginfield

Jarvis

3

Port Colborne

21

MICHIGAN

London

71

43 St. Thomas

42 Port Dover

402

Sarnia

4

Union

2

44 Port Stanley

40

401

Lake St. Clair

Detroit

Chatham

3

Lake Erie

Erie

Windsor

50

48 Southwestern Ontario Heritage Village

18

49 47

Leamington

45 Point Pelee National Park

Kingsville

Amherstburg

46 Pelee Island

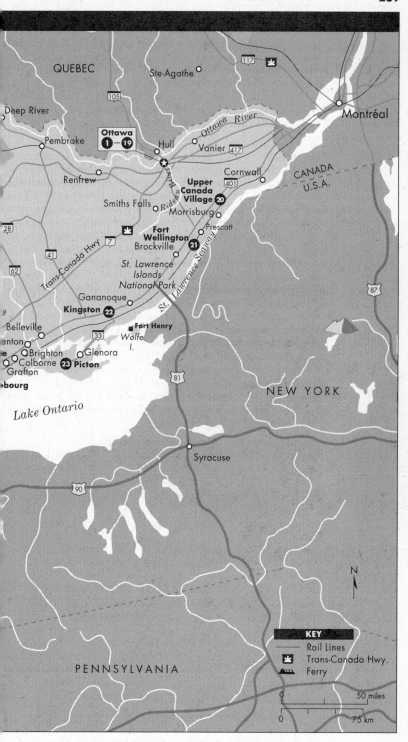

QUEBEC

Ste-Agathe

[117]

Deep River

[105]

Pembroke

Ottawa **1** — **19**

Hull

Vanier [417]

Montréal

Ottawa River

Renfrew

Cornwall

CANADA
U.S.A.

Smiths Falls

Upper Canada Village **20**

[401]

Rideau River

Morrisburg

[28]

[62]

[41]

[7]

Trans-Canada Hwy

Fort Wellington **21**

Prescott

Brockville

St. Lawrence Islands National Park

St. Lawrence Seaway

[87]

Gananoque

Kingston **22**

[33]

y

Belleville

Fort Henry

Wolfe I.

enton

Brighton

Glenora

NEW YORK

Colborne

23 **Picton**

Grafton

bourg

Lake Ontario

[81]

Syracuse

[90]

N

PENNSYLVANIA

KEY

— Rail Lines

Trans-Canada Hwy.

Ferry

0 _____ 50 miles

0 _____ 75 km

experience its beauty, take a cruise from either town. Afterward, whiz through **Barrie** ㉘ along Route 93 to 91, where you'll drive southbound to **St. Jacobs** (69) and **Elmira.** Both villages are in the heart of Mennonite and Hutterite country. On day five, travel to **Kitchener/Waterloo** (68). The **Kitchener Market** is stellar. You can also visit the **Woodside Historic Park,** former home of William Lyon MacKenzie King, prime minister of Canada from 1921 to 1948. **Stratford** (70) is home to the acclaimed Stratford Festival, a centerpiece of Canada's rich artistic landscape.

IF YOU HAVE 7 DAYS

After five days of visits to **Ottawa** ①–⑲, **Kingston** ㉒, the towns around Georgian Bay ㉙–㉜, **Kitchener/Waterloo** (69), and **Stratford** (70), head for the large, staid city of **London** (71) via Routes 7 and 4. Here, **Storybook Gardens** is one of the least expensive theme parks around. The **London Regional Art and Historical Museums** mount interesting exhibitions within their modern building. Next, drive along Route 3 through United Empire Loyalist territory—the villages of **Port Stanley** ㊹, **St. Thomas** ㊸, **Port Dover** ㊷, and **Port Colborne** ㊵. By nightfall on Day 6, you will have reached **Niagara Falls** (51)–(64), which offers every sort of accommodation from upscale hotels to family-run motels. Upriver is **Niagara-on-the-Lake** (65), home to several first-rate inns. Devote the last day to taking in the Falls and its environs, where high- and low-brow attractions flourish, including the neat-and-tidy **Greenhouse and Plant Conservatory** (59) and the **floral clock** (52). You can take a ride on the ***Maid of the Mist*** (57), which edges so close to both falls that hooded rain slickers are required attire. In addition to this thriller, Niagara Falls spotlights a dazzle of attractions from the wacky tourist mecca on **Clifton Hill** (64) to **Marineland** (60). In Niagara-on-the-Lake, you can go to the **Niagara Apothecary,** a pharmacy museum, and the the British **Fort George.** In summer, the Shaw Festival is the place to catch a Pinter play, or perhaps a work by Mahler.

When to Tour the Province of Ontario

In winter, Ontario's weather veers toward the very severe, making road travel difficult, and many museums and attractions are either closed or have limited hours. Plan to visit between April and October, when most sites are open longer hours. Try to avoid touring over the crazy July 1 Canada Day weekend. The warm months also offer travelers the chance to catch some of the province's many cultural highlights, especially the Stratford and Shaw festivals, as well as to enjoy outdoor action such as boating and hiking, or even just resting on a beach.

OTTAWA

Canadians are taught in school that it was Queen Victoria's fault their capital is inconveniently situated off the main east–west corridor along the U.S. border. But the facts are that politicians of the day were no more capable of making an unpopular decision than many who have followed them. They dithered, from 1841 to 1857, trying to decide among five possible sites, including Québec City, Montréal, Cobourg, Kingston, and Ottawa. In 1857 they passed the buck to Buckingham Palace, and Queen Victoria got them off the hook.

She chose Ottawa for five reasons, all valid at the time: The site was politically acceptable to both Canada east and Canada west. It was also centrally located, reassuringly remote from the hostile United States, and industrially prosperous. And it had a naturally beautiful setting at the confluence of the Ottawa and Rideau rivers.

Three decades earlier, when Colonel John By and his Royal Engineers arrived to build a canal from Ottawa to Kingston, only a few scattered settlers lived at what is now Ottawa. The waterway was to ensure a protected supply route from Montréal to the Great Lakes in the event of a repeat of the War of 1812 against the Americans. Between 1826 and 1832 the canal was hacked through 200 kilometers (125 miles) of swamp, rock, and lakes whose different levels were overcome by locks.

By established his canal headquarters at what is now Ottawa, and the population growth was immediate as men arrived with their families, seeking employment on the largest construction project on the continent. The settlement, then called Bytown, grew rapidly and fast became a rowdy, rough-and-tumble backwoods town. The Ottawa River then was used for floating timber to Montréal—each spring lumberjacks tied their rafts of timber to the shore and celebrated their release from isolated lumber camps in the taverns and brothels of Bytown.

By 1837, when its population had reached 2,400, Bytown was declared by the attorney general of Upper Canada to be a town. Government moved slowly even then, and it was not legally incorporated until 1850. Five years later, when the population had reached 10,000, Bytown became a city and was farsightedly given the name Ottawa, an Indian name meaning "a place for buying and selling."

Construction started on the Parliament Buildings in 1859. The buildings are magnificent, but their location in the mid-1850s earned Ottawa the nickname "Westminster in the Wilderness." More recently, perhaps because of their neo-Gothic towers and spires—or possibly because of legislation passed inside them—some refer to Parliament Hill as "Disneyland on the Rideau."

As early as 1899, federal politicians were concerned with more than just the grounds around the Parliament Buildings, known as "the Hill." A variety of commissions and committees and plans have become today's National Capital Commission (NCC). The NCC works with all municipalities within the 2,903-square-kilometer (1,800-square-mile) National Capital Region, which includes neighboring Hull and a big chunk of Québec, to coordinate development in the best interests of the region. The result is a profusion of beautiful parks, bicycle paths, jogging trails, and the world's longest skating rink, a 6-kilometer (4-mile) stretch of the Rideau Canal kept cleared and smooth from January to March and provided with heated huts, food concessions, and skate-sharpening and rental services.

A Good Tour

Given Ottawa's architectural beauty and the fact that parking is at premium here, one of the best ways to see many of the gems in this metropolis of 600,000 is on foot. Begin at the **Parliament Buildings** ①. The Centre Block and the **Peace Tower** are surrounded by 29 acres of lawn, punctuated by statues of celebrated Canadians. Turn right onto Wellington Street and walk past Bank Street to the **Bank of Canada** ②, inside which is the **Currency Museum,** where seven galleries chronicle the evolution of notes and coins within the context of Canadian history. Now turn right onto Kent Street to the **Supreme Court** ③, housed in a stunning Art Deco edifice. At the end of Wellington Street is the **Garden of the Provinces** ④. Across from the park are the **National Archives of Canada** ⑤ and the **National Library of Canada.** Return toward Parliament Hill via the friendly **Sparks Street Pedestrian Mall** ⑥. Emerging from the mall, you'll face **Confederation Square** ⑦ and the

National War Memorial. Adjacent to the square stands the **National Arts Centre** ⑧, a huge theater complex designed around repeated hexagon motifs. Walk northward along the Rideau Canal to Ottawa's older buildings: The **Bytown Museum** ⑨ houses a collection of 3,500 artifacts of Colonel By. Next door are the **Rideau Locks** ⑩ between the Hill and Ottawa's beautiful and grand landmark hotel, the **Château Laurier Hotel** (☞ Dining and Lodging, *below*), named for the country's first French Canadian prime minister. Between the hotel and the canal is the **Museum of Contemporary Photography** ⑪, which opened in 1992. Several blocks away, between George and York Streets, is **Byward Market** ⑫, a farmers' market and center for boutiques and cafés. About a five-minute walk up Sussex Drive, the **National Gallery of Canada** ⑬ reflects the Parliament Buildings in its modern mirror-and-granite facade.

To conquer the rest of Ottawa's highlights, it's time to hop in a car and continue on Sussex Drive, Ottawa's embassy row. Take a glimpse at the entrance to 24 Sussex Drive—the **residence of the prime minster** ⑭—before finding the Governor General's home, called **Rideau Hall** ⑮, at 1 Sussex Drive. Follow Sussex Drive past Rideau Hall to the Rockcliffe Driveway and then watch for the signs that proclaim 4 kilometers (2½ miles) to the **National Aviation Museum** ⑯. It's worth the drive to the **National Museum of Science and Technology** ⑰, where children, in particular, will enjoy the institution's hands-on or "minds-on" exhibits. You'll find the **Canadian Museum of Nature**'s ⑱ fabulous dinosaur display across the Ottawa River in Hull, Quebec. While you're in Hull, stop by the **Canadian Museum of Civilization** ⑲, a stunning collection that documents the country's history.

Timing
You'll need at least a day to visit the sights in the walking portion of the tour and a day to drive to the more distant attractions. Between Wednesday and Sunday are the best days to find the places open.

Sights to See

❷ **Bank of Canada Currency Museum.** The ancestors of the credit card are all here: bracelets made from elephant hair, cowrie shells, whale's teeth, and what is believed to be the world's largest coin. Here, too, of course, is the country's most complete collection of Canadian notes and coins. ⊠ *245 Sparks St.,* ☎ *613/782–8914.* ☞ *$2, free Tues.* ☉ *May–Sept., Mon.–Sat. 10:30–5, Sun. 1–5; Oct.–Apr., Tues.–Sat. 10:30–5, Sun. 1–5.*

❾ **Bytown Museum.** In the former commissariat used by the Royal Engineers and Lt. Col. John By during the building of the Rideau Canal—the oldest stone masonry building in the city—you'll find exhibits that record the life and times of Bytown and Ottawa. ⊠ *Wellington St. at bottom of Ottawa Locks, behind Chateau Laurier Hotel,* ☎ *613/234–4570.* ☞ *$2.25.* ☉ *Mid-May–mid-Oct., Mon. and Wed.–Sat. 10–4, Sun. 2–5; Apr.–mid-May and mid-Oct.–Nov., weekdays 10–4.*

⑫ **Byward Market.** A farmers' market has been on this site since 1840. Surrounding the market stalls are permanent specialty food shops, some well over 100 years old, as well as cafés and boutiques. ⊠ *Between George and York Sts.*

☞ ⑲ **Canadian Museum of Civilization.** Across the Ottawa River in Hull, Quebec, is one of the area's most architecturally stunning museums. Here, visitors can trace Canada's history from prehistoric times to the present. In the Grand Hall, six native longhouses, towering totem poles, and life-size reconstructions of Canadian historic scenes help you travel

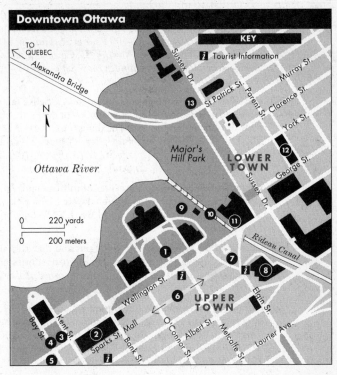

Bank of
Canada
Currency
Museum, **2**

Bytown
Museum, **9**

Byward
Market, **12**

Confederation
Square, **7**

Garden of the
Provinces, **4**

Museum of
Contemporary
Photography, **11**

National
Archives of
Canada/
National
Library of
Canada, **5**

National Arts
Centre, **8**

National
Gallery of
Canada, **13**

The Parliament
Buildings, **1**

Rideau
Locks, **10**

Sparks Street
Pedestrian
Mall, **6**

Supreme
Court, **3**

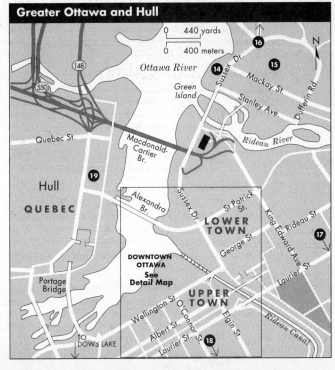

Canadian
Museum of
Civilization, **19**

Canadian
Museum of
Nature, **18**

National
Aviation
Museum, **16**

National
Museum of
Science and
Technology, **17**

Residence of
the Prime
Minister, **14**

Rideau
Hall, **15**

through time. Kids can enjoy hands-on activities in the newly expanded Children's Museum. In the Cineplus, you'll find the larger-than-life IMAX and Omnimax. ⊠ *100 Laurier St., Hull,* ☎ *819/776–7000; Cineplus, 819/776–7010.* ☞ *Museum $5; Cineplus usually $7, but prices change depending on program.* ☉ *May–Sept., daily 9–5, Thurs. 9–9; Oct.–Apr., Tues.–Sun. 9–5, Thurs. 9–9.*

⑱ **Canadian Museum of Nature.** Housed in a castlelike building, the museum and its exhibits explore the evolution of the Earth, birds and mammals of Canada, and plants. The dinosaur collection is outstanding. The Viola MacMillan Mineral Gallery displays a world-class collection. ⊠ *McLeod St. at Metcalfe St.,* ☎ *613/996–3102.* ☞ *$4; ½-price Thurs. until 5, free 5–8.* ☉ *Daily 10–5, Thurs. until 8.*

❼ **Confederation Square.** In the center of this triangular junction in the heart of the city stands the **National War Memorial,** which honors the 66,651 Canadian dead of World War I. ⊠ *Wellington, Sparks, and Elgin Sts.*

❹ **Garden of the Provinces.** Two fountains and the arms and floral emblems of Canada's 10 provinces and two territories commemorate confederation in this park. ⊠ *Southwest corner of Bay and Wellington Sts.*

⑪ **Museum of Contemporary Photography.** Opened in 1992, the museum holds more than 158,000 images, spotlighted in changing exhibitions. There are also a 50-seat theater and a boutique. ⊠ *1 Rideau Canal,* ☎ *613/990–8257.* ☞ *Free.* ☉ *Wed., Fri., Sat, and Sun. 11–5, Thurs. 11–8; closed Wed. and Thurs. in winter.*

❺ **National Archives of Canada** and **National Library of Canada.** The archives, Canada's oldest cultural institution, contain more than 60 million manuscripts and government records, 1 million maps, and about 11 million photographs. The National Library collects, preserves, and promotes the published heritage of Canada and exhibits books, paintings, maps, and photographs. Both institutions mount interesting exhibitions on a regular basis. ⊠ *395 Wellington St. at Bay St.; archives,* ☎ *613/995–5138; library, 613/992–9988.* ☞ *Free.* ☉ *Daily 9 AM–10:30 PM.*

❽ **National Arts Centre.** Completed in 1969, the complex includes an opera hall, a theater, a studio theater, and a salon for readings and concerts. The grounds are populated with sculptures by Canadian artists, most notably "Balancing" by John Hooper. The canal-side café, **Le Café,** spills outside in warm weather and is popular for a meal or drink. ⊠ *53 Elgin St.,* ☎ *613/996–5051.* ☞ *Free.* ☉ *30- to 40-min tours depart from main lobby May–Aug., daily; Sept.–Apr., Tues., Thurs., and Sat. (also Sun. to end of Oct.) at noon, 1:30, and 3.*

⑯ **National Aviation Museum.** Among the more than 100 aircraft here are a replica of the Silver Dart that made the first powered flight in Canada as well as World War I Sopwiths. Engines, propellers, and other aeronautical antiques complete the collection. ⊠ *Rockcliffe and Aviation parkways,* ☎ *613/993–2010 or 800/463–2038.* ☞ *$5, free Thurs. 5–9.* ☉ *Mon. holidays and Tues.–Sun. 9–5 (Thurs. until 9); Sept.–Apr., Thurs. 9–8.*

⑬ **National Gallery of Canada.** In addition to being housed in one of the best pieces of contemporary architecture in the country, if not North America—a magnificent, glass-towered temple to art by Canadian architect Moshe Safdie—the gallery contains one of the premier collections of Canadian art in the world. Inside is the reconstructed Rideau Convent Chapel, a classic example of French Canadian 19th-century architecture with the only neo-Gothic fan-vaulted ceiling on the continent. The building has three restaurants and a large bookstore with publications on the arts. ⊠ *380 Sussex Dr.,* ☎ *613/990–1985.* ☜ *Free, except special events.* ☉ *Mon.–Wed. 10–5, Thurs. 10–8, Fri.–Sun. 10–5; closed Mon., Tues., and holidays in winter.*

🖐 ⑰ **National Museum of Science and Technology.** Canada's largest museum spotlights permanent displays of printing presses, antique cars, steam locomotives, and agricultural machinery, as well as ever-changing exhibits, many of which are hands-on, or "minds-on." The evening "Discover the Universe" program uses the largest refracting telescope in Canada to stargaze into the world of astronomy. A picnic area, a gift shop, and a free parking lot are useful for families. ⊠ *1867 St. Laurent Blvd.,* ☎ *613/991–3044.* ☜ *$5, free Thurs. 5–9.* ☉ *Mon. holidays and Tues.–Sun. 9–5 (Thurs. until 9); Sept.–Apr., Thurs. 9–8.*

🖐 ❶ **Parliament Buildings.** Three beloved Gothic-style buildings with green copper roofs dominate the nation's capital from Parliament Hill on a promontory overlooking the Ottawa River, though none faces it. Originally built in 1867, they were destroyed by fire and rebuilt in 1916. The **Centre Block** is where the Senate and House of Commons, the two houses of Parliament, work to shape the laws of the land. The central **Peace Tower** houses a Memorial Chamber with an Altar of Sacrifice, which bears the names of 66,651 Canadians killed during active service in World War I and 44,895 Canadians who died in World War II.

★ There's plenty of room to stand and no charge for the colorful **Changing of the Guard ceremony** that takes place in front of the Peace Tower at 10 AM daily, June 22–August 25, weather permitting. The Ceremonial Guard brings together two of Canada's most historic regiments, the Canadian Grenadier Guards and the Governor General's Foot Guards. The bells of the 53-bell **carillon** range individually from 10 pounds to 11 tons, and together weigh 60 tons. Concerts are performed by the **Dominion Carillonneur** (☎ 613/992–4793) daily from 12:30 to 12:45.

North (toward the river) of the Centre Block and reached from it is the **Library of Parliament,** which escaped the fire of 1916 but was damaged in its own fire in 1952. A statue of a young Queen Victoria is the centerpiece of the many-sided chamber, whose walls are lined with books, many of them priceless, and carved wooden galleries restored from the 1952 fire.

In front of, and to either side of, the Centre Block are the **East Block** and the **West Block.** The East Block has four historic rooms open to the public: the original Governor General's office restored to the period of Lord Dufferin, 1872–1878; the offices of Sir John A. Macdonald and Sir George-Étienne Cartier, Fathers of the Confederation in 1867; and the Privy Council Chamber. The West Block, originally designed to house the civil service, has been converted to offices for parliamentarians and is not open to the public.

Against the backdrop of the imposing Parliament Buildings, a free half-hour lazer **Sound and Light Show** highlights Canada's history. There's bleacher seating. ⊠ *Parliament Hill,* ☎ *613/992–4793 or 613/996–0896.* ☜ *Free.* ☉ *Mid-May–Labor Day, daily 9–8:30; Labor Day–mid-May, daily 9–4:30; 20-min tours in English or French every ½ hr.; same-day reservations for tours available at white Infotent east of Centre Block; sound-and-light shows early July–Labor Day, twice (1 in English, 1 in French) daily; May–June and Sept., 4 nights per wk.*

❶④ **Residence of the Prime Minister.** It has been home to men named Laurier, Massey, and Trudeau, among others. Unlike the White House, it is not open for public inspection. Lacking an invitation, you can hope only for a drive-by glimpse of a couple of roof gables and some expensive landscaping. Don't even try parking near the mansion; security is tight. ⊠ 24 Sussex Dr.

⑮ Rideau Hall. The official residence of the governor-general of Canada since 1865 houses visiting heads of state, royalty, and the monarch when any of them are here on official business. The 1830 mansion has a ballroom, a skating rink, and a cricket pitch. Sentries of the Canadian Grenadier Guards and the Governor General's Foot Guards are posted outside the main gate of Rideau Hall from late June through August. Free walking tours of the grounds are conducted year-round, but days and times change frequently according to season. ⊠ 1 Sussex Dr., ☎ 613/993–0311.

⑩ Rideau Locks. On the Rideau Canal, which runs southward through the city from the Ottawa River, the locks are a downtown landmark. ⊠ Junction of Rideau Canal and Wellington St., where Wellington becomes Rideau St.

❻ Sparks Street Pedestrian Mall. Here, the automobile has been banished and browsers wander in warm weather among fountains, rock gardens, sculptures, and outdoor cafés. ⊠ 1 block south of Wellington St., between Confederation Square and Kent St.

❸ Supreme Court. Established in 1875, this body became the ultimate court of appeal in the land in 1949. The nine judges sit in their stately Art Deco building for three sessions each year. ⊠ Kent and Wellington Sts., ☎ 613/995–4406, Ext. 327. 🎫 Free. ☉ Tours May–Aug., daily 9–5; Sept.–Apr., by appointment.

Dining and Lodging

$$$ ✕ **Flippers.** As the name suggests, this is a seafood restaurant, and the specialties change almost daily as different kinds of fresh fish and seafood are available. The decor in the old building on Bank Street includes marine artifacts and model ships. ⊠ 823 Bank St., 2nd floor, ☎ 613/232–2703. Reservations essential. AE, MC, V.

$$ ✕ **Chequers.** In this three-story, Gothic-style 1868 country inn 25 kilometers (16 miles) southwest of Ottawa, the specialties are French and Spanish haute cuisine. The service is European and so is the decor. ⊠ 816 Hazeldean Rd., Stittsville, ☎ 613/836–1665. Reservations essential. AE, MC, V.

$$ ✕ **Courtyard Restaurant.** Fine French cuisine is served in this lovely, historic limestone building on a quiet cul-de-sac near Byward Market, a five-minute stroll from the Parliament Buildings. The forerunner of today's elegant dining establishment was a log tavern built in 1827, probably to take advantage of the construction of the nearby Rideau Canal. The humble tavern was replaced by the limestone Ottawa Hotel a decade later. Extensive renovations created the Courtyard Restaurant, and its cuisine and ambience attracted a dedicated following. ⊠ 21 George St., ☎ 613/241–1516. Reservations essential. AE, MC, V.

$$ ✕ **Fresco.** The cozy Italian restaurant's dominant feature is a mural of mountains on the back wall, although the dizzying number of food options is impressive, too. You can choose from 10 sauces to accompany such house specialties as scallops, salmon, and veal. ⊠ 354 Elgin St., ☎ 613/235–7541. AE, MC, V.

$$$$ 🏨 **Château Laurier Hotel.** Ottawa has all kinds of posh new hotels with
★ great service and food, but this grand hotel is an institution. It's one of Canada's great railroad hotels, built in 1916 and named for Sir Wilfrid Laurier, who served as prime minister from 1896 to 1911. Many

of its rooms are unfortunately a little on the small side. The Château, as it's known, is part of the Ottawa experience. ⊠ *1 Rideau St., K1N 8S7,* ☎ *613/241–1414,* ℻ *613/562–7030. 430 rooms. Restaurant, lounge, bar, indoor pool. AE, MC, V.*

$$$–$$$$ 🏨 **Minto Place Suite Hotel.** One- and two-bedroom suites in this 31-story hotel, which is within strolling distance of Sparks Street Mall, have full kitchen and laundry facilities. ⊠ *433 Laurier Ave. W, K1R 7Y1,* ☎ *613/232–2200,* ℻ *613/232–6962. 418 suites. Lounge, indoor pool, sauna, whirlpool, health club, indoor parking. AE, MC, V.*

$$$–$$$$ 🏨 **Westin Hotel.** Adjacent to the Rideau Centre shopping mall and convention hall, this hotel in the heart of Ottawa showcases elegant rooms within a modern 24-story tower. In winter, guests can cross the street to the Rideau Canal for a windswept Canadian skating adventure. ⊠ *11 Colonel By Dr., K1N–9H4,* ☎ *613/560–7000,* ℻ *613/234–5396. 484 rooms. 2 restaurants, lounge, indoor pool, 2 saunas, whirlpool, exercise room, 3 squash courts. AE, MC, V.*

Nightlife and the Arts

The Arts

More than 900 performances are showcased at the **National Arts Centre** (⊠ 53 Elgin St., ☎ 613/996–5051; ☞ *above*) annually, and it is the home of the National Arts Centre Orchestra. In summer, the Centre is one of the hosts of the **Ottawa International Jazz Festival, Cultures Canada,** and the biennial **Canada Dance Festival.**

Nightlife

Barrymore's (⊠ 323 Bank St., ☎ 613/233–0307) has transformed the Imperial Theatre of 1914, strategically situated on Ottawa's hopping Bank Street promenade, into one of the city's most energetic nightclubs. It draws a twenty- to thirty-something crowd. Live musicians take center stage from Monday through Saturday until midnight, after which dance music thumps through the three-tiered hall until 2 AM.

Outdoor Activities and Sports

Biking

Ottawa has 114 kilometers (65 miles) of **bicycle paths.** On Sunday, **Queen Elizabeth Drive** and **Colonel By Drive** are closed to traffic until noon for cyclists. Rent A Bike (in the Château Laurier Hotel; ☞ Dining and Lodging, *above*) rents a variety of bicycles, including tandems and children's models.

Hiking

The **Rideau Trail** runs 406 kilometers (241 miles) along the Rideau Canal from Kingston to Ottawa. Access points from the highway are marked with orange triangles. Contact Rideau Trail Association (⊠ Box 15, Kingston, K7L 4V6).

Shopping

Antiques

John Coles at the **Astrolabe Gallery** (⊠ 90 Sparks St., Ottawa, ☎ 613/234–2348) is a good source for 19th-century prints of Ottawa scenes or antique maps of North America.

Market

Byward Market (⊠ between George and York Sts.), site of a farmers' market since 1840, has fresh produce, maple products, and flowers. Surrounding the market stalls are permanent specialty food shops, some well over 100 years old, as well as cafés and boutiques.

Shopping Centers and Malls

Rideau Centre (⊠ Rideau St. and Colonel By Dr.) has more than 200 stores, including The Bay, Ogilvy's, and Eaton department stores.

Ottawa A to Z

Arriving and Departing

BY BUS

Voyageur Colonial Bus Lines (⊠ 265 Catherine St., ☎ 613/238–5900) offers frequent service from Montréal and Toronto to Ottawa, including some express buses.

BY CAR

Highway 417 links Ottawa to Quebec from the east; Route 16 connects Ottawa with the Trans-Canada Highway to the south.

BY PLANE

Ottawa International Airport (☎ 613/998–3151), 18 kilometers (12 miles) from downtown, is served by **Air Canada** (☎ 613/247–5000 or 800/268–7240), **First Air** (☎ 613/839–1247 or 800/267–1247), **Canadian Airlines International** (☎ 613/237–1380 or 800/665–1177), **Delta Airlines** (☎ 800/363–2857 or 800/843–9378), **KLM** (☎ 613/567–4747 or 800/361–5073), and **USAir** (☎ 800/428–4322).

BY TRAIN

Trans-Canada **ViaRail** serves the Ottawa rail station (⊠ 200 Tremblay Rd., ☎ 613/244–8289) at the southeastern end of town.

Getting Around

BY BUS

OC Transpo (☎ 613/741–4390) serves the metropolitan region of Ottawa–Carleton on the Ontario side of the Ottawa River. It operates buses on city streets and on the Transitway, a system of bus-only roads. All bus routes in downtown Ottawa meet at the Rideau Centre (⊠ Rideau St. between Nicholas and Sussex and the Mackenzie King Bridge).

BY TAXI

Major cab companies such as **Blue Line** (☎ 613/238–1111) and **Diamond** (☎ 613/741–5330) operate in and around Ottawa.

Contacts and Resources

EMERGENCIES

Dial 911.

Hospitals. The main hospitals in Ottawa are **Ottawa General Hospital** (☎ 613/737–7777) and **Ottawa Civic Hospital** (☎ 613/761–4000).

Late Night Pharmacy. Shoppers Drug Mart (⊠ 1460 Merivale Rd., ☎ 613/224–7270) is open 24 hours.

GUIDED TOURS

By Boat. Paul's Boat Lines Limited (☎ 613/225–6781) offers seven 75-minute cruises daily on the Rideau Canal and four 90-minute cruises daily on the Ottawa River from mid-May to mid-October. Canal boats dock across from the National Arts Centre; river cruise boats dock at the Bytown Museum at the foot of the Ottawa Locks on the Rideau Canal. **Ottawa Riverboat Company** (☎ 613/562–4888) operates two-hour sightseeing tours on the Ottawa River from May through October. The SS **Bytown Pumper** (☎ 613/737–6601) is a wood-burning steamboat that offers tours on the Rideau River from mid-May to mid-October. It has an 1897 engine in a 1903 hull. Cruises depart daily at 10, noon, 2, and 4 from Hog's Back Marina Park; dinner cruises are available (call ahead—the boat is sometimes chartered for the evening).

By Bus. Gray Line (☎ 613/748–4426) operates frequent, two-hour, 50-kilometer (31-mile) orientation tours ($16) from mid-May through October. **Picadilly Bus Tours** (☎ 613/820–6745) has a regular schedule of 1¼-hour tours in double-decker London buses to Ottawa's major sites, May through October.

VISITOR INFORMATION

Ottawa Tourism and Convention Authority (⊠ Ottawa–Carleton Centre, 111 Lisgar St., 2nd floor, Ottawa, Ontario K2P 2L7, ☎ 613/237–5150); **National Capital Visitors Association** (☎ 800/465–1867).

THE HERITAGE HIGHWAY

Upper Canada Village

★ ⓴ *86 km (53 mi) southeast of Ottawa on Rtes. 2 and 401.*

Eight villages disappeared under rising waters when the St. Lawrence Seaway opened in 1959, but their best historic buildings were moved to a new site, called Upper Canada Village, a faithful re-creation of an Ontario community from the 1800s. The village occupies 66 acres of the 2,000-acre **Crysler's Farm Battlefield Memorial Park,** which figured prominently in the War of 1812. Such anachronisms as radios and tape players are banned in this throwback to the days of the United Empire Loyalists. The village has three mills, two farms, two churches, two hotels, and 25 other buildings. A leisurely tour takes three to four hours. More than 150 staff people are on site, all in early 1800s costume, to answer questions. The Village Store sells Canadian crafts and village-made bread, cheese, and flour. Willard's Hotel serves lunches, full-course meals, and teas. ⊠ *Rte. 2E, Morrisburg,* ☎ *613/543–3704.* 🖼 *$9 ($13.75 for 2 days).* ⊙ *Mid-May–mid-Oct., daily 9:30–5; mid-Oct.–mid-May, special events only.*

Fort Wellington

★ ㉑ *40 km (25 mi) west of Morrisburg on Rte. 2.*

Fort Wellington was built by the British in 1813 to protect goods and troops moving between Montréal and Upper Canada after the outbreak of the War of 1812. The fort, never attacked, was completed in 1814, the year the war ended. The Ottawa–Kingston Rideau Canal eliminated its need and the fort was abandoned. In 1837 rebellion broke out in Upper and Lower Canada, and the British built a new and stronger Fort Wellington on the site. The buildings are furnished in 1846 period style. ⊠ *370 Vankoughnet St.,* ☎ *613/925–2896.* 🖼 *$2.25.* ⊙ *Mid-May–Aug., daily 10–6; Sept.–mid-Oct., daily 10–5; mid-Oct–mid-May, by reservation only.*

Ontario's oldest barracks building is one block west of Fort Wellington and open in summer as a museum. Lunches and dinners at **Stockade Barracks and Hospital Museum** feature historic menus year-round. By prior arrangement, groups of 15–40 can have five- or six-course meals of 1812-style dishes served by mess waiters in military uniforms. ⊠ *356 East St.,* ☎ *613/925–4894.* 🖼 *$2.* ⊙ *June–Sept., weekends 10–5.*

Kingston

㉒ *100 km (75 mi) southwest of Prescott on Rte. 401.*

Kingston's imposing architecture has been impressing visitors since 1673, when La Salle chose the location as the site for a meeting between Governor Frontenac and the Iroquois. Before the meeting, Frontenac built a stockaded fort to impress the Indians and thus tap into the fur trade. Thanks to misguided American strategy, Kingston survived the War of 1812 almost totally unscathed. Many of its beautiful limestone buildings remain in mint condition today. From 1841 to 1844, Kingston was the capital of the province of Canada; today the gorgeous, cut-limestone **city hall** (⊠ 216 Ontario St., ☎ 613/546–4291) dominates the downtown core, facing a riverfront park. Tours are given weekdays in summer, but you can wander through the lobby any time of year.

The city occupied a strategic site at the junction of the St. Lawrence River and the Rideau Canal system, and four Martello towers still guard the harbor. The **Royal Military College of Canada** has a museum in Fort Frederick, the largest of the Martello towers. The museum contains the internationally renowned Douglas Arms Collection, which includes the small arms owned by General Porfirio Díaz, president of Mexico from 1886 to 1912. ⊠ *Off Rte. 2, east of Kingston,* ☎ *613/5613/541–6000, Ext. 6652.* ☞ *Free.* ☉ *Last weekend in June–Labor Day, daily 10–5.*

★ The massive **Fort Henry** was built during the War of 1812 to repel a possible American invasion, which never came. Students in period military costume guide visitors, hold parades, and re-create the pomp and pageantry of an era past. ⊠ *Rtes. 2 and 15,* ☎ *613/542–7388.* ☞ *Late May–mid-Oct., $9.50.* ☉ *Daily 10–5.*

Locals nicknamed it Tea Caddy Castle, Molasses Hall, and Pekoe Pagoda, but Canada's first prime minister, Sir John A. Macdonald, who lived in the house for a year, called it **Bellevue** because of its view of the St. Lawrence River. Today the 1840 house is a National Historic Park site restored and furnished in the style of 1848, when Macdonald lived here. ⊠ *35 Centre St.,* ☎ *613/545–8666.* ☞ *$2.50.* ☉ *June–Labor Day, daily 9–6; Apr., May, Sept., and Oct., daily 10–5.*

The lore of steam engines and their history is on display in the **Pump House Steam Museum** (⊠ 23 Ontario St., ☎ 613/546–4696), the restored Victorian-style 1849 municipal water-pumping station. All the exhibits run on steam (only between June and Labor Day); models range from miniature equipment to an 1897-model Toronto-built engine with a 9-ton flywheel. The rambling display area at the **Marine Museum of the Great Lakes at Kingston,** at the historic former Kingston dry dock, traces Great Lakes shipping since 1678. A 3,000-ton, 210-foot retired icebreaker, the *Alexander Henry,* is also open for tours in summer. Summer visitors can rent a stateroom and sleep aboard. ⊠ *55 Ontario St.,* ☎ *613/542–2261).* ☞ *$3.75 for 1 museum, $5.25 for both.* ☉ *Museums Apr.–Dec., daily 10–5; Jan.–Mar., weekdays 10–4. Icebreaker mid-May–mid-Oct.*

Kingston is the birthplace of organized ice hockey—the first league game was played in the city in 1885. So it seems fitting that the city is also home to an **International Hockey Hall of Fame,** a shrine to puck-chasing. (Canada's other Hockey Hall of Fame opened at a larger venue in Toronto in 1993.) ⊠ *York and Alfred Sts., 1 block north of Princess St. (Rte. 2),* ☎ *613/544–2355.* ☞ *$2.* ☉ *Mid-June–mid-Sept., daily 10–5; late Sept.–early June, weekends by appointment.*

Lodging

$$$ 🏨 **Hochelaga Inn.** This Victorian inn, built more than a century ago, is in a quiet residential and historic neighborhood, but still only a five-minute walk from downtown. All the rooms have private baths, and all but one have a queen-size bed. The inn has no bar or restaurant,

but a Continental breakfast, served in a small dining room, is included in the room rate. Guests have the use of a cozy living room. ⌂ *24 Sydenham St. S, K7L 3G9,* ☎ ☏ *613/549–5534. 23 rooms. AE, MC, V.*

En Route   Route 33 will take you south past Kingston's Gothic-style penitentiary at Collins Bay to the island county of **Prince Edward.** A free, 10-minute ferry ride (every 15 minutes in summer) lands you at Glenora, and it's 9 kilometers (6 miles) to Picton, the county seat. New Englanders wandering the island may find themselves wondering if they've ever left home—so similar are the scenery and the pages of history that brought both regions into being. The island was one of the earliest parts of Ontario to be settled after the American Revolution, and the Loyalist influence remained dominant for generations. The first of these settlers landed at Adolphustown Reach from Bateaux on June 16, 1784, and village locals nicknamed the landing area the Plymouth Rock of Ontario. The earliest burial ground in the district is located here, and the Loyalist church erected in 1822 is still used as a parish meeting hall.

Picton

㉓   *60 km (45 mi) southwest of Kingston on Rte. 33.*

Picton is a serene town of 4,300 with fine old buildings and strong associations with Sir John A. Macdonald, Canada's first prime minister, who practiced law at the 1834 county courthouse, which is still in use. Within the town is the **Macaulay Heritage Park,** which sits on about 15 acres of land and includes picnic facilities, the **Macaulay House,** and the **County Museum.** Tours of the park and the town's attractions are available by prior arrangement and may include a visit to the jail, where a double gallows is kept handy (although it hasn't been used since 1884). ⌂ *1 block south of Rte. 33 at Union and Church Sts.,* ☎ *613/476–3833.* ⌸ *Macaulay house $2.* ☾ *Weekdays 10–4:30.*

Dining and Lodging

$$$–$$$$ ✕⌂ **Isaiah Tubbs Resort.** A dozen kilometers west of Picton, this posh 60-room property has rooms and suites with fireplaces as well as 12 seasonal cottages. There's fine dining in the Restaurant on the Knoll Overlooking the Sandbanks at West Lake. (That's the correct name of the restaurant and that's what it overlooks!) ⌂ *R.R. 1, K0K 2T0,* ☎ *613/393–2090 or 800/267–0525,* ☏ *613/393–1291. 60 rooms. Restaurant, indoor pool, outdoor pool, sauna, whirlpool, exercise room. AE, MC, V.*

$$$ ⌂ **Merrill Inn.** This beautiful 1870 house is a short stroll from the heart of downtown Picton. It has been converted to a cozy 15-room inn by the same folks who created Idlewylde Inn at London (☞ *below*). The refrigerator is stocked with soft drinks and the sideboard with croissants, muffins, tea, and coffee 24 hours a day, but no meals are served. ⌂ *343 Main St. E, K0K 2T0,* ☎ *613/476–7451 or 800/567–5969. 14 rooms. AE, D, MC, V.*

Cobourg

㉔   *75 km (50 mi) west of Picton on Hwy. 401 or Rte. 2.*

Cobourg once expected to be chosen as the provincial capital. It was passed over, but not before the town just about bankrupted itself building the magnificent **Victoria Hall,** officially opened in 1860 by the young Prince of Wales, later King Edward VII. A courtroom modeled after London's Old Bailey was on the ground floor, and town council meetings, formal balls, and concerts were held on the second floor. Today you can tour some of the building's 41 rooms. ⊠ *5 King St. W,* ☎ *905/372–5831.* ⊠ *Free.* ⊙ *Guided tours in summer or by prior arrangement.*

Keene

㉕ *27 km (17 mi) north of Port Hope via Rtes. 28 and 2.*

The town of Keene has several attractions, especially **Serpent Mounds Provincial Park.** About 2,000 years ago a nomadic native tribe buried its dead in nine earth mounds, the largest of which is shaped like a 200-foot-long serpent. An interpretation center explains the site and displays artifacts. ⊠ *R.R. 3, Rte. 34, Keene,* ☎ *705/295–6879.* ⊠ *$5 per vehicle.* ⊙ *Mid-May–mid-Oct., daily.*

About 3 kilometers (2 miles) north of the village of Keene is the well-signed **Lang Pioneer Village,** with its museum and 26 pioneer buildings. You can see displays and demonstrations of pioneer arts and crafts in summer. ⊠ *Off Rte. 34, Lang,* ☎ *705/295–6694.* ⊠ *$5.* ⊙ *June–Labor Day, weekdays 11–5, Sat. 1–5, Sun. noon–5; visitor center only Labor Day–May, weekdays 9–4.*

Peterborough

㉖ *13 km (9 mi) northeast of Keene via Rtes. 34 and 7.*

The small city of Peterborough is home to Trent University and 70,000 people. High notes here are the **Centennial Fountain** in Little Lake, at 250 feet the highest jet fountain in Canada, and the lift locks on the **Trent-Severn Waterway,** which are among the world's highest. Built in 1904, the lift lock floats boats 65 feet straight up in less than 10 minutes. The lock and the Trent Canal operate mid-May–mid-October; you can see slides and films at the **Peterborough Lift and Lock Visitor Center.** ⊠ *Hunter St. E,* ☎ *705/7450–4950.* ⊙ *May–Oct., daily 10–5.*

Dining and Lodging

$$$ ✕🏨 **Ramada Inn.** This hotel is connected to the city's largest downtown indoor shopping complex. Guest rooms are comfortably furnished. Sir William's restaurant offers Continental fare and lighter meals (be sure to reserve), and snacks are served at the Garden Cafe in the pool area. ⊠ *100 Charlotte St., Peterborough, K9J 7L4,* ☎ *705/743–7272,* FAX *705/749–0845. 170 rooms. 2 restaurants, indoor pool, sauna, whirlpool, free parking. AE, D, MC, V.*

Petroglyphs Provincial Park

㉗ *50 km (31 mi) northeast of Peterborough on Rte. 28.*

Canada's largest concentration of native rock carvings was found at the east end of Stony Lake, outside the hamlet of Stonyridge, in 1954. The site is now within **Petroglyphs Provincial Park.** The well-preserved symbols and figures, which are carved on a flat expanse of white marble almost 70 feet wide, are encased in a protective building. The more than 900 carvings are believed to be of Algonquin spirit figures. ⊠ *East of Rte. 28 on Northey's Bay Rd., Stonyridge,* ☎ *705/877–2552.* ⊠ *$6 per vehicle.* ⊙ *Mid-May–mid-Oct., daily.*

Stony Lake is also one of Ontario's most popular locations for weekend "cottages." Drive along the lakeside roads for a glimpse of what Canadians call cottages, but which, in some cases, look more like mansions.

NORTH OF TORONTO TO THE LAKES

There are several ways to explore this picturesque area, known to Torontonians as "Cottage Country." You can take a day trip from Toronto, driving through the area and perhaps stopping for a picnic lunch at one of the lakes or at one of numerous roadside restaurants. Alternatively, spend up to a week exploring the district from one of many lakeside resorts near towns such as Orillia, Gravenhurst, Bracebridge, and Huntsville. A cheaper—but equally satisfying choice—is to rent a cottage for a week or two. "Cottages" range from log cabins to palatial homes that would not look out of place in a wealthy urban neighborhood. Rentals are available through local real estate agents.

Barrie

28 *75 km (46 mi) north of Toronto on Rte. 400.*

Barrie is a city of almost 80,000 on the shores of Lake Simcoe. A winter carnival attracts ice fishermen, dogsled racers, and ice motorcyclists. From late June through Labor Day, there's informal drama in **Gryphon Theatre** at Georgian College and harness racing at **Barrie Raceway.**

More than a dozen artists have studios in the Barrie area; most of the work spaces are attached to their homes. For studio tour maps, call tour organizer Chris Symes (☎ 705/329–0842). Among those studios worth a visit is the home of **Henni Stoffregen,** who sells lampshades, place mats, cards, and numerous other items made from pressed wildflowers, leaves, and grasses. ⊠ *Mill St. and Mt. St. Louis Rd. near Hillsdale,* ☎ *705/835–3296.*

Dining and Lodging

$$$$ ✕☟ **Inn at Horseshoe.** On the ski hill at the resort near Barrie, this top-drawer lodge is well equipped. The modern guest rooms come with down comforters. Many suites have sunken living rooms, woodburning fireplaces, and whirlpools. Dining options range from the distinctive Continental menu of the formal Silks restaurant to the informal fare at the Santa Fe–style Go West Grill. When the snow melts, you can tee off on the 18-hole or the nine-hole golf courses. ⊠ *Horse Valley Rd., L4M 4Y8,* ☎ *705/835–2790,* FAX *705/835–5932. 57 rooms, 53 suites. 2 restaurants, lounge, 1 indoor and 2 outdoor pools, hot tub, 27-hole golf course, 2 tennis courts, fitness center, squash, mountain biking. AE, MC, V.*

$$$–$$$$ ✕☟ **Blue Mountain Resort.** In addition to owning the largest ski resort in Ontario, this acclaimed lodge at the base of the slopes has an outstanding 18-hole golf course. The guest rooms are fairly standard, and suites as well as condominium units have kitchens and fireplaces. At the Pottery dining room, you'll find Continental interpretations of Canadian standards, or you can opt for the Mexican-influenced Montero Pavilion restaurant. ⊠ *RR 3, Collingwood L9Y 3Z2,* ☎ *705/445–0231,* FAX *705/444–1751. 98 rooms, 2 suites, 100 condominiums. 2 restaurants, lounge, indoor and outdoor pools, sauna, golf course, 9 tennis courts, beach. AE, MC, V.*

Outdoor Activities and Sports

SKIING

Blue Mountain (☎ 705/445–0231 or 416/869–3799), near Collingwood, west of Barrie on Route 26, is Ontario's most extensively developed and heavily trafficked ski area, with a vertical drop of 720 feet. It has 31 pistes served by a high-speed quad lift, three triple chairs, eight double chairs, two pomas, and a rope tow. **Horseshoe Valley Resort** (☎ 705/835–2790) near Barrie is among the few resorts that offer both

Nordic and downhill skiing facilities. It has 22 trails served by a quad and two triple and three double lifts. The vertical drop is only 309 feet, but seven of the runs are rated for advanced skiers.

Penetanguishene and Midland

㉙ ㉚ *80 km (50 mi) north of Barrie on Rtes. 400 and 93.*

The quiet towns of Penetanguishene (known locally as Penetang) and Midland occupy a small corner of northern Simcoe County known as Huronia. This 30-by-60-kilometer (20-by-40-mile) area was the scene of some of the most grisly episodes in North American history. Each town sits on a snug, safe harbor at the foot of a bay that leads out to Georgian Bay.

Just 5 kilometers (3 miles) east of Midland on Route 12, visitors can explore a complete reconstruction of **Ste-Marie among the Hurons.** Jesuit missionaries built the Ste-Marie mission at this spot in 1639. The Jesuits preached Christianity, and the Hurons—also called Wendat—taught the French settlers how to survive in the harsh climate. By 1648 the mission was home to one-fifth of the European population of New France. The villagers built Ontario's first hospital, farm, school, and social service center here and constructed a canal from the Wye River. A combination of disease and Iroquois attacks led to the mission's demise. Twenty-two structures, faithfully reproduced from a scientific excavation, including a native longhouse and a wigwam, can now be toured. The canal is working again; staff in period costume saw timber, repair shoes, sew clothes, and grow vegetables. ⌂ *Rte. 12,* ☎ *705/526–7838.* 🖾 *$7.25.* ☼ *May–mid-Oct., daily 10–4:30; mid-Oct.–Apr., by appointment.*

On a hill overlooking Ste-Marie is **Martyrs' Shrine,** a twin-spired stone cathedral built in 1926 to honor the eight missionaries who died in Huronia; in 1930 five of the priests were canonized by the Roman Catholic church. The grounds include a theater, a souvenir shop, a cafeteria, and a picnic area. ⌂ *Off Rte. 12,* ☎ *705/526–3788.* ☼ *Mid-May–mid-Oct., daily 9–9.*

The best artifacts from several hundred archaeological digs in the area are displayed at **Huronia Museum and Gallery of Historic Huronia** in Little Lake Park in Midland. Behind the museum and gallery building is **Huron Indian Village,** a full-scale replica of a 16th-century Huron settlement. ⌂ *Little Lake park,* ☎ *705/526–2844.* 🖾 *Museum and village $5.* ☼ *Oct.–late Apr., weekdays 9–5; May–Sept., Mon.–Sat. 9–5:30, Sun. 10–5.*

Cruises leave from the town docks of both Midland and Penetang to explore the 30,000 Islands region of Georgian Bay from May to Thanksgiving (the second Monday in October). From Midland town dock the 250-passenger MS *Miss Midland* (☎ 705/526–0161; in Ontario, 800/461–1767) offers one to four 2½-hour sightseeing cruises daily. From the Penetang town dock, the 200-passenger MS *Georgian Queen* (☎ 705/549–7795) takes passengers on three-hour tours of the islands, from late May through mid–October. The cruises leave once daily at 2 PM. Call ahead.

Parry Sound

㉛ *110 km (68 mi) north of Penetang or Midland on Rtes. 12 and 69.*

Parry Sound is home to Canada's largest sightseeing cruise ship, the **Island Queen,** which offers an extensive three-hour cruise of Georgian Bay once or twice daily, depending on season. There's free parking at the town dock. ⊠ *9 Bay St.,* ☎ *705/746–2311.* 🖃 *$15.* ☉ *June–Thanksgiving (mid-Oct.).*

From mid-July to mid-August, the **Festival of the Sound** (☎ 705/746–2410) fills the auditorium of Parry Sound High School and the decks of the *Island Queen* with jazz, popular music, classical piano, and show tunes.

Lodging

$$ 🏨 **Highland Inn.** An enormous atrium anchors this completely self-contained hotel/motel/resort. Honeymoon suites have heart-shape tubs or sunken Jacuzzis. Sunday brunches by the pool in the Garden Cafe are popular; there are three other dining areas (reserve ahead) as well. ⊠ *Box 515, King St. and Rte. 12, L4R 4L3,* ☎ *705/526–9307 or 800/461–4265,* 🖷 *705/526–0099. 119 rooms, 13 suites. 4 restaurants, indoor pool, sauna, exercise room. AE, MC, V.*

Orillia

32 *35 km (21 mi) northeast of Barrie on Hwy. 11.*

Orillia will be recognized by readers of Canada's great humorist, Stephen Leacock, as Mariposa, the "little town" he described in *Sunshine Sketches of a Little Town.* The writer's former summer home is now a museum, the **Stephen Leacock Memorial Home.** In the Mariposa Room, characters from the book are matched with the Orillia residents who inspired them. ⊠ *Off Rte. 12B in east end of Orillia,* ☎ *705/326–9357.* 🖃 *$7.50.* ☉ *Daily 10–5.*

Gravenhurst

33 *39 km (24 mi) northeast of Barrie on Hwy. 11.*

North along Highway 11, rolling farmland suddenly changes to lakes and pine trees amid granite outcrops of the Canadian Shield. This region, called Muskoka, is the playground of people who live in the highly urbanized areas around Toronto. Gravenhurst is a town of fewer than 6,000 and the birthplace of Canada's least-known hero—least known in Canada, that is. In China, Norman Bethune's name is almost as well known as Wayne Gretzky's is in Canada. Bethune is remembered for his heroic work in China as a field surgeon and medical educator. The **Bethune Memorial House,** an 1880-vintage frame structure, has become a shrine of sorts to Chinese diplomats visiting North America. ⊠ *235 John St. N,* ☎ *705/687–4261.* 🖃 *$2.25.* ☉ *June–Labor Day, weekdays 10–6; Labor Day–May, daily 10–5; closed winter holidays.*

The RMS **Segwun** (the initials stand for Royal Mail Ship) is the sole survivor of a fleet of steamships that once provided transportation through the Muskoka Lakes. The 128-foot boat, built in Scotland and assembled in Gravenhurst in 1887, carries 99 passengers on cruises from mid-June to mid-October. Cruises range from 90 minutes to two days in length (passengers dine aboard but sleep in one of Muskoka's grand resorts). ⊠ *Muskoka Lakes Navigation and Hotel Company Limited, 820 Bay St., Sagama Park, Gravenhurst P1P 1G7,* ☎ *705/687–6667.*

Haliburton

34 *60 km (37 mi) northeast of Gravenhurst via Hwy. 11 and Rte. 118; 250 km (156 mi) northeast of Toronto.*

Haliburton, close to huge Algonquin Provincial Park, is a Nordic skiing and winter sports base in winter. In summer the self-guided trails of **Leslie Frost Natural Resources Center** (⊠ Rte. 35 at St. Nora's Lake, ☎ 705/766–2451) offer a great primer in Ontario's wildlife.

Outdoor Activities and Sports

SKIING LODGE-TO-LODGE

From the town of Haliburton, three- and four-night guided lodge-to-lodge cross-country ski packages are available along the Haliburton Nordic Trail system. There are groups for skiers of all levels, and the trips cover 8–25 kilometers (5–16 miles) per day, depending on the group's abilities. Eight lodges participate in the program and skiers stay and dine at a different lodge each night; by the time skiers come off the trail, luggage will be in their rooms. Packages include all meals, trail passes, and a guide. Contact John Teljeur of the **Haliburton Nordic Trail Association** (⊠ Box 670, Haliburton, Ontario K0M 160, ☎ 705/457–3133 or 800/461–7677).

SNOWMOBILING

C Mac Snow Tours (⊠ R.R. 3, Walton, Ontario N0K 1Z0, ☎ 519/887–6686 or 800/225–4258) has three- and five-night all-inclusive excursions in Haliburton Highlands/Algonquin Park.

Bracebridge

③⑤   *11 km (8 mi) north of Gravenhurst via Hwy. 11.*

🄲 🄲   In Bracebridge are the well-signposted **Santa's Village** and **Mister Rudolph's Funland.** After letting Santa know what they'd like to find under the Christmas tree, youngsters can ride the Kris Kringle Riverboat, the Candy Cane Express Train, minibikes, bumper boats, paddleboats, pony rides, and more. Mister Rudolph's Funland, for children 12 and older, offers go-carts, batting cages, in-line skating, 18-hole mini-putt, and an indoor activity center with video games. ⊠ *Santa's Village Rd. (west of Bracebridge),* ☎ 705/645–2512. 🎫 *Santa's Village: Unlimited rides for 1 day $13.98. Rudolph's Funland: 10 tickets, $20 (2–3 tickets per ride).* ☉ *Santa's village: Mid-June–Labor Day, daily 10–6. Mister Rudolph's Funland: late May–mid-June and Labor Day–Thanksgiving, weekends 10–10; mid-June–Labor Day, daily 10–10.*

Dining and Lodging

$$$ ✕🏨 **Inn at the Falls.** This Victorian inn and its annex of motel-style
★   rooms command a magnificent view of the pretty Bracebridge Falls on the Muskoka River. Accommodations include rooms, cottages, and suites; six of the units have fireplaces. The outdoor pool is heated. The main dining room (reserve ahead) and pub-lounge offer food and live entertainment; there's an outdoor patio for dining and sipping as well. Try the steak-and-kidney pie. ⊠ *17 Dominion St., Box 1139, P0B 1C0,* ☎ *705/645–2245,* 🆇 *705/645–5093. 32 rooms, 2 cottages, 6 suites. Dining room, pub, outdoor pool. AE, MC, V.*

Dorset

③⑥   *48 km (30 mi) northeast of Bracebridge via Hwy. 11 and Rte. 117.*

Dorset is a pretty village on a narrows between two bays of the Lake of Bays. The village is home to **Robinson's General Store** (☎ 705/766–2415), which, with the exception of the World War II years, has been continuously owned and operated by a Robinson since it opened in 1921. You'll find everything here from moose-fur hats to stoves and pine furniture. You can circle back to Toronto on scenic Route 35 or make Dorset a stop on a circle tour from Huntsville (☞ *below*) around the Lake of Bays.

Huntsville

③⑦ *34 km (21 mi) north of Bracebridge on Hwy. 11; 215 km (134 mi) north of Toronto via Hwys. 400 and 11.*

The Huntsville region is filled with lakes and streams, stands of virgin birch and pine, and deer and smaller forest dwellers that browse along the trails. Because the area is Toronto's summer playground, too, there is no shortage of year-round resorts.

Dining and Lodging

$$$$ ✕🏠 **Deerhurst Resort.** This spectacular, ultra-deluxe Canadian Pacific resort is a self-contained community on 800 acres. The flavor is largely modern, although the main lodge, complete with dining room and Cypress Lounge, dates from 1886 and is appointed with a rustic flair. The menu offers such delicacies as Ontario game—buffalo and caribou—as well as Mediterranean dishes. ✉ *1235 Deerhurst Dr., Huntsville P1B 2E8,* ☎ *705/789–6411. 400 rooms, indoor pool, 2 18-hole golf courses, tennis court, exercise room, racquetball, squash, nature trail. AE, MC, V.*

$$$ ✕🏠 **Walker Lake Resort.** In winter, the rustic cottages here overlook deer-feeding stations on either side of the frozen lake. The **Norseman Restaurant** is marvelous for formal Continental meals. ✉ *R.R. 4, Huntsville P1B 2J6,* ☎ *705/635–2473. 7 cottages. Restaurant. MC, V.*

Outdoor Activities and Sports

CROSS-COUNTRY SKIING

In southern Ontario, the Huntsville area is usually the cross-country skier's best bet for an abundance of natural snow. Both Deerhurst and Walker Lake resorts (☞ *above*) have trails.

Alqonquin Park

③⑧ *50 km (34 mi) northeast of Huntsville on Rte. 60.*

Algonquin Provincial Park stretches across 7,600 square kilometers (3,040 sq mi) of lakes, forests, rivers, and cliffs. It is a hiker's, canoeist's, and camper's paradise. But don't be put off if you're not the athletic or rough-outdoors sort. About a third of all visitors to Algonquin come for the day to visit a museum, walk one of the 14 interpretive trails, or enjoy a swim or a picnic. Swimming is especially good at Lake of Two Rivers, about halfway between the west and east gates along Route 60. A morning drive through the park in May or June is often rewarded by a sighting of moose, which are attracted to the highway by the slightly salty water in roadside ditches. Wolf-howling expeditions, led by a park naturalist, take place in August. Two newly added attractions near the east side of the park are the **visitor center,** which includes a bookstore, a restaurant, and a viewing deck, and the **Algonquin Logging Museum,** which depicts life at an early Canadian logging camp. The drive back to Toronto takes about four hours. Alternatively, once you reach the east gate of the park, you're only two to three hours northwest of Ottawa. ✉ *Box 219, Whitney K0J 2M0,* ☎ *705/633–5572.* 💳 *$6 per vehicle.* ☉ *Park daily 8 AM–10 PM. Museum mid-June–Labor Day, daily 10–6; Labor Day–Oct., weekends 10–5.*

Outdoor Activities and Sports

SKIING

Downhill. Mount Madawaska ski area (☎ 613/756–2931), near Barry's Bay, south of the park on Route 60, has a vertical drop of 400 feet.

FORT ERIE AND WEST TO WINDSOR

Fort Erie

39 *155 km (95 mi) south of Toronto via the Queen Elizabeth Way.*

Fort Erie, at the extreme southeast tip of the Niagara Peninsula, is a drab, boom-or-bust town of fast-food chains, taverns, and gas stations whose profits rise or fall with the exchange rate between Canadian and U.S. dollars. The heavy American influx to the area is not without historic irony; the last American presence on Canadian soil arrived here at the end of the War of 1812.

Old Fort Erie, at the south end of Fort Erie, has been reconstructed as it existed before it was destroyed at the end of the War of 1812. The Old Fort's colorful and bloody history reveals that thousands of soldiers lost their lives within sight of the earthworks, drawbridges, and palisades. The fort itself was destroyed in 1779 and again in 1803 by spectacular storms that drove masses of ice ashore at the foot of Lake Erie. Visitors are conducted through the display rooms by guards in period British army uniforms. In summer the guards stand sentry duty, fire the cannon, and demonstrate drill and musket practice. ⊠ *350 Lakeshore Rd.,* ☎ *905/871–0540.* ⊠ *$3.50.* ☉ *May, weekdays 10–4, weekends 9:30–6; June–early Oct., daily 9:30–6.*

The town's other major attraction, the **Fort Erie Race Track,** opened in 1897, but it is one of the most modern—and picturesque—tracks in North America. Glass-enclosed dining lounges overlook a 1-mile dirt track and a seven-furlong turf course. Also in view are gardens, ponds, and waterways. ⊠ *Bertie St. and Queen Elizabeth Way,* ☎ *905/871–3200.* ☉ *May–Sept., Fri.–Mon. at 1; Oct., Fri.–Sun. at 1.*

Port Colborne

40 *30 km (20 mi) west of Fort Erie on Rte. 3.*

The Lake Erie town of Port Colborne (population 18,800) remains an enclave for descendants of United Empire Loyalist stock. Chronicling this rich history is the **Port Colborne Historical and Marine Museum,** a six-building complex where afternoon tea is served (at a price) at Arabella's Tea Room. ⊠ *280 King St.,* ☎ *905/834–7604.* ⊠ *Free.* ☉ *May–Dec., daily noon–5.*

Welland

41 *10 km (6 mi) north of Port Colborne on Rte. 58 or 140.*

Because the industrial town of Welland had been bypassed by the 14 million to 16 million tourists who visit Niagara Falls annually, in 1988 Welland staged a Festival of Arts Murals. Thirty giant murals now decorate downtown buildings; the longest is 130 feet, and the tallest is three stories high. You can pick up a free mural tour map from **Welland Tourism** (⊠ 32 E. Main St., ☎ 905/735–8696) or from brochure racks at City Hall and in local restaurants and hotels. Welland is also the home of the annual **Niagara Food Festival.** Held in the downtown Market Square around the end of September or early October, this festival brings together an array of local farmers, wineries, and restaurants to provide the food.

Port Dover

42 *107 km (66 mi) west of Welland via Rtes. 58, 23, 3, and 6.*

Port Dover is the home of the world's largest fleet of freshwater fishing boats. It's a pretty beach resort town where freshwater fish is served up steamy and golden at a number of restaurants.

St. Thomas

43 *75 km (50 mi) west of Port Dover on Rte. 3 and 28 km (17 mi) east of London on Rte. 3.*

St. Thomas's first buildings went up in 1810, over a decade and a half ahead of the first building in London (Ontario, not England). However, while St. Thomas's population has leveled at 29,000, London's has hit 310,000. Note the **statue of Jumbo,** the Barnum and Bailey circus elephant, killed here in a freak railway accident in 1885. The monument is a 10%-larger-than-life-size statue of the largest elephant ever in captivity. ⊠ *555 Talbot St.*

Adjacent to the Jumbo monument are a railway caboose, the St. Thomas Chamber of Commerce and **tourist office,** and a gift shop for Jumbo kitsch. *St. Thomas–Elgin Tourist Association,* ⊠ *555 Talbot St.,* ☎ *519/631–1981.* ☉ *May–Labor Day, daily 9–9.*

Port Stanley

44 *15 km (10 mi) south of St. Thomas on Rte. 4.*

The summer resort town of Port Stanley has a fine brown sand beach and the boutiques, snack bars, and kitsch stands that survive on vacationers following the sun.

It isn't hauled by a steam engine anymore, but the **London and Port Stanley Railroad** (L&PS) still packs in travelers. The operation has proven so popular—particularly with children—that the little novelty train ride now runs year-round and its trackage has been doubled. The railroad, built in 1856, was intended as a main trade link between Canada and the United States. The trade didn't materialize, but the railroad survived on excursion traffic until 1957. Railroad buffs later restored some passenger cars and repaired the line as far as Union, in 1992 extending it to St. Thomas. You can take a 45-minute excursion to Union year-round, or—from June through October—a two-hour round-trip to St. Thomas. ⊠ *Port Stanley Railway Station,* ☎ *519/782–3730.* ☜ *Round-trip fare to Union $8, to St. Thomas $11.* ☉ *Call ahead.*

Dining and Lodging

$$–$$$$ ✕☶ **Kettle Creek Inn.** This small, elegant country inn with a cleverly
★ designed modern annex offers fine food and a friendly pub ambience. Some rooms have whirlpool baths and gas fireplaces. There are other nice touches, such as old-fashioned pedestal sinks, interesting local artwork, and views from all the rooms and suites of a landscaped courtyard and a gazebo. Continental breakfast is included in the room rates. The three dining rooms (reserve ahead) in the original inn offer daily specials, including fresh Lake Erie fish just brought ashore by the local fishing fleet and fresh Ontario lamb and pork tenderloin. ⊠ *216 Joseph St., N5L 1C4,* ☎ *519/782–3388,* ☒ *519/782–4747. 10 rooms, 5 suites. 3 dining rooms. AE, D, DC, MC, V.*

Point Pelee National Park

★ **45** *150 km (95 mi) west of Port Stanley/St. Thomas on Hwy. 401 or Rte. 3, near Leamington on Rte. 33.*

Point Pelee juts into Lake Erie, serving as a rest stop for migrating birds and butterflies. The southern tip of the point, Point Pelee National Park, has the smallest dry land area of any Canadian national park, yet it manages to draw more than half a million visitors every year. There's no overnight camping, but there are many rules and regulations to observe because the park is home to a number of endangered species of plants and reptiles. Drive slowly to the visitor center, 5 kilometers (3 miles) inside the park, where you'll find exhibits, slide shows, and a keen, knowledgeable staff to answer questions. Seven hundred kinds of plants and 347 species of birds have been recorded here. A propane-powered, open-sided train operates from the center to the tip of Point Pelee, the southernmost part of the Canadian mainland. September in Pelee is the best time to see monarch butterflies resting before they head 3,350 kilometers (2,100 miles) south to winter in the Sierra Madre of Mexico. It is also among the best locations in North America for birdwatching, especially during spring and fall migrations. In September, groups of birders bedecked with camera lenses the size of rocket launchers and clanking with binoculars, tape recorders, video equipment, and even CB radios converge on the park and on the hotels, highways, motels, and restaurants of nearby Leamington, an otherwise quiet town of 23,000. ⊠ *R.R. 1, Point Pelee,* ☎ *519/322–2365.* ⊠ *Apr.–Labor Day $5 per vehicle, Labor Day–Mar. free.* ☉ *Daily 6 AM–10 PM.*

Pelee Island

46 *25 km (15 mi) and 90 minutes by ferry from Point Pelee via Rte. 33 and Leamington ferry.*

Pelee is a small, flat island, roughly 13 by 6 kilometers (8 by 4 miles), at the west end of Lake Erie, served spring through fall by ferry boats that link it with Kingsville and Leamington in Ontario and Sandusky in Ohio. In winter there are scheduled flights from Windsor. Ferries land at either West Dock or Scudder Dock, the main communities on the island. The permanent population is 270, but in summer that quadruples as vacationers, mostly from Ohio, cram into 200 private cottages. At the end of October and beginning of November, 700 hunters arrive to fill 18,000 pheasants with buckshot. The island has raised pheasants for hunters since 1932, a business that helps reduce taxes. There's usually someone to inform visitors about Pelee's biggest industry, the pheasant farm in the middle of the island, and explain why the chicks wear what look like sunglasses. (It's so they can't peck one another's eyes out.) Pelee Island is not the most southerly place in Canada—that honor belongs to neighboring Little Middle Island—but Pelee *is* south; it's on the same latitude as northern California and northern Spain.

From the community of **West Dock,** you can see **Perry's Victory and International Peace Monument,** 12 miles away on North Bass Island in Ohio. The 352-foot-high monument commemorates American commander Captain Oliver Hazard Perry, who won control of Lake Erie at Put-in-Bay Island, Ohio, in 1813 by sailing straight into the British fleet while firing broadside, succinctly reporting: "We have met the enemy and they are ours."

Kingsville

47 *10 km (7 mi) west of Leamington on Rte. 18.*

In Kingsville, one of the southernmost towns in Ontario, **Jack Miner's Bird Sanctuary** is well signposted. Jack Miner was an avid hunter who realized no species could survive both its natural enemies *and* man. In 1904 he dug ponds, planted trees, and introduced four Canada geese with clipped wings to the ponds. That number grew to the 50,000 that now winter here. From 1910 to 1940 Miner lectured on conservation and convinced kings and presidents of its need, thus earning him the Order of the British Empire in 1943. His former home is now a trust, open year-round except Sunday. No admission is charged and nothing is sold on the grounds. A two-story museum in the former stables has a wealth of Miner memorabilia, and at a pond beside the house you can feed far-from-shy geese and ducks with free feed. At 3 and 4 PM daily, including Sunday, the birds are flushed for "air shows," and circle wildly overhead until they feel it's safe to land. The best times to view migrations are late March, October, and November. ⊠ *Essex County Rd. 29, 5 km (3 mi) north of Kingsville,* ☎ *519/733–4034.* ⊠ *Free.* ☉ *Mid-Mar.–Dec., Mon.–Sat. 9–5.*

The **John R. Park Homestead and Conservation Area,** 8 kilometers (5 miles) west of Kingsville, is a pioneer village anchored by one of Ontario's few examples of American Greek Revival architecture, an 1842 home. The 10 buildings include the house of John R. Park, a shed built with no nails, a smokehouse, an icehouse, an outhouse, a blacksmith shop, a sawmill, and a livestock stable. ⊠ *County Rd. 50 at Iler Rd.,* ☎ *519/738–2029.* ⊠ *$3.* ☉ *July–Labor Day, daily 11–5; Oct.–mid-May, call ahead.*

Southwestern Ontario Heritage Village

48 *About 10 km (6 mi) north of Kingsville on Rte. 23.*

The turn-of-the-century Southwestern Ontario Heritage Village has 20 historic buildings on 54 wooded acres. Volunteers in period dress show visitors how pioneers baked, operated looms, and dipped candles. The **Transportation Museum** of the Historic Vehicle Society of Ontario, Windsor Branch, also on the grounds, displays a fine collection of travel artifacts, from snowshoes to buggies to vintage automobiles. The gem of the collection is the world's only 1893 Shamrock. This adorable two-seater was the second effort at a workable prototype built by the Mira Brothers. When this one didn't run properly, either, the brothers abandoned their brief career as auto manufacturers. ⊠ *County Rd. 23,* ☎ *519/776–6909.* ⊠ *$3.50.* ☉ *Village and museum Apr.–Nov., Wed.–Sun. 11–5; July and Aug., daily 11–5.*

Amherstburg

49 *25 km (15 mi) west of Kingsville on Rte. 18.*

The riverside parks in the quiet town of Amherstburg are great places to watch the procession of Great Lakes shipping. **Navy Yard Park,** with flower beds ringed by old anchor chains, has benches overlooking Bois Blanc Island and the narrow main shipping channel.

Fort Malden was the British base in the War of 1812 from which Detroit was captured, though the site dates back to 1727, when a Jesuit mission began occupying lands in the area. Now the fort is an 11-acre National Historic Park, which includes remains of the original earthworks, restored barracks, a military pensioner's cottage, two exhibit buildings, and picnic facilities. ⊠ *100 Laird Ave.,* ☎ *519/736–5416.* ⊠ *$2.* ☉ *Jan.–May, daily 1–5; May–Dec., daily 10–5; closed holidays.*

The **North American Black Historical Museum** tells of daring escapes by U.S. slaves and the Underground Railroad system many used to flee to Canada. Between 1800 and 1860, 30,000 to 50,000 slaves made the pilgrimage to Canada, the Promised Land, and many of those crossed the Detroit River at Amherstburg because it was the narrowest point. An 1848-vintage church and log cabin contain exhibits, artifacts, and biographies. ⊠ *277 King St.,* ☎ *519/736–5433.* 🎟 *$3.50.* ⊙ *Wed.–Fri. 10–5, weekends 1–5.*

Windsor

🔟   *30 km (20 mi) north of Amherstburg on Rte. 18 and 150 km (100 mi) west of London on Rte. 401.*

Windsor, long an unattractive industrial city that hosted Ford, General Motors, and Chrysler manufacturing plants, has become a pleasant place to visit. The riverfront has pretty parks, some with fountains and statues, all overlooking the spectacular Detroit skyline. The cities are linked by the Ambassador Bridge and the Windsor–Detroit Tunnel. If you're traveling by car, start your visit at the **Convention and Visitors Bureau** (⊠ 80 Chatham St. E), where you can get a free date-stamped parking pass for use during your stay.

The **Art Gallery of Windsor** mounts changing displays of contemporary and historic Canadian and foreign art. However, a strange thing happened to the gallery in 1993: Its exhibits were temporarily moved from its usual riverside location to a local shopping mall, to make way for Ontario's first casino. The Art Gallery moves back to its own building when a permanent site for the casino is completed, possibly sometime in 1996. ⊠ *Devonshire Mall, 3100 Howard Ave., Windsor,* ☎ *519/969–4494.* 🎟 *Free.* ⊙ *Tues–Fri. 10–7, Sat. 10–5, Sun. noon–5.*

The **Francois Baby House: Windsor's Community House** is a collection of area artifacts displayed in the 1812 house where the Battle of Windsor, the final incident in the Upper Canada Rebellion, was fought in 1838. ⊠ *254 Pitt St. W,* ☎ *519/253–1812.* 🎟 *Free.* ⊙ *Tues.–Sat. 10–5, Sun. 2–5.*

Farmers, butchers, and bakers from southwestern Ontario sell their fresh produce at **Windsor City Market,** which rents space to more than 100 permanent vendors. ⊠ *Chatham St. E between MacDougall and Market Sts.,* ☎ *519/255–6260.* ⊙ *Tues.–Thurs. 7–4, Fri. 7–6, Sat. 5–4.*

Willistead Manor is the former home of Edward Chandler Walker, second son of Hiram, who founded Walker's Distillery in 1858. The 15-acre estate is now a city park. Work on the 36-room Tudor-Jacobean–style mansion was completed in 1906; no expense was spared in its construction. Call ahead: the manor is open by appointment only, and tours are by reservation only. ⊠ *Niagara St. and Kildare Rd.,* ☎ *519/253–2365.* 🎟 *$3.50.* ⊙ *Tour Sept.–Nov., 1st and 3rd Sun. of each month 1–4:30; Aug.–Dec., Sun. and Wed. 1–4.*

Since 1959, Windsor and Detroit have combined their national birthday parties (Canada Day, July 1; and Independence Day, July 4) into a massive bash called **International Freedom Festival.** The two-week party includes nonstop entertainment with more than 100 special events on both sides of the river and a spectacular fireworks display, billed as the largest in North America. For information, call the Convention and Visitors Bureau (☎ 519/255–6530).

Dining and Lodging

$$ ✕ **Brigantino's.** This popular establishment with traditional red-and-white check tablecloths is outstanding for home-style Italian cooking and melt-in-your-mouth pasta. ⊠ *851 Erie St. E,* ☎ *519/254–7041. Reservations essential. AE, D, DC, MC, V.*

$$ ✕ **Old Fish Market.** A wonderful ambience is created here with hanging plants, brass railings, and lovely woodwork. The menu, predictably, is heavy on seafood. It has a deserved reputation of excellence. ✉ *1063 Chatham St. W,* ☎ *519/253–7417. Reservations essential. AE, DC, MC, V.*

$$$$ 🏨 **Hilton International Windsor.** Each of the guest rooms in this 22-story, downtown riverbank hotel has a view of Detroit's impressive skyline and the shipping activity on the world's busiest inland waterway. The Park Terrace Restaurant and Lounge offers a wide menu and a spectacular river view. In the River Runner Bar and Grill, there's music and dancing. ✉ *277 Riverside Dr. W, N9A 5K4,* ☎ *519/973–5555 or 800/463–6655,* 🖷 *519/973–1600. 303 rooms. 2 restaurants, bar, room service, indoor pool, sauna, whirlpool, meeting rooms. AE, MC, V.*

NIAGARA AND WEST TO LONDON

Niagara Falls

★ *130 km (80 mi) south of Toronto via the Queen Elizabeth Way.*

There is probably no natural attraction exploited as thoroughly as Niagara Falls. You can fly above the falls in a helicopter; get almost directly underneath them by boat; go around them on bridges; or go behind them in a tunnel. The falls are illuminated in colors 365 nights a year. More than 300 years ago, the first travel writer to visit Niagara Falls, Father Louis Hennepin, wrote, "The universe does not afford its parallel. The roar of them can be heard 15 leagues away" (a distance of 72 kilometers, or 45 miles). Hennepin, an explorer and missionary, described their height as 600 feet—when in fact they are 176 feet high. When Europeans read Hennepin's 1678 accounts, they ranked Niagara among the Seven Wonders of the World. Despite Hennepin's gross exaggerations and the crass commercialism that is much in evidence, few have ever been disappointed by a visit to the falls. About 12 million tourists visit each year. Daredevils have been drawn to Niagara Falls since 1828: Eight people have survived plunging over the falls in a variety of contraptions, and the list of those who perished in the attempt is a long one. Fines for performing illegal stunts on property owned by the Niagara Parks Commission (NPC) have been raised to $10,000, but the stunt-lovers keep on coming.

The NPC was formed in 1885 to preserve the area around the falls. Beginning with a small block of land, the NPC gradually acquired most of the land fronting on the Canadian side of the Niagara River, from Niagara-on-the-Lake to Fort Erie. This 56-kilometer (35-mile) riverside drive is a 3,000-acre ribbon of parkland lined with parking overlooks, picnic tables, and barbecue pits, and the public is welcome to use the facilities at no charge.

A Festival of Lights runs in the area from the end of November to the third week of February. It started in Niagara Falls, Ontario, in 1981 and now stretches the length of the Niagara Parkway between Fort Erie and Niagara-on-the-Lake. The city claims a multitude of superlatives during this period: world's largest Christmas tree (the Skylon Tower), world's largest gift (Your Host Motor Inn decorated to look like a giant gift-wrapped box), world's largest candle (the Minolta Tower), and so on. The festival started with massive corporate displays, but the idea caught on with smaller businesses and private residents. There are now so many displays that tours are offered ranging from 2½ to 3½ hours.

Niagara Falls

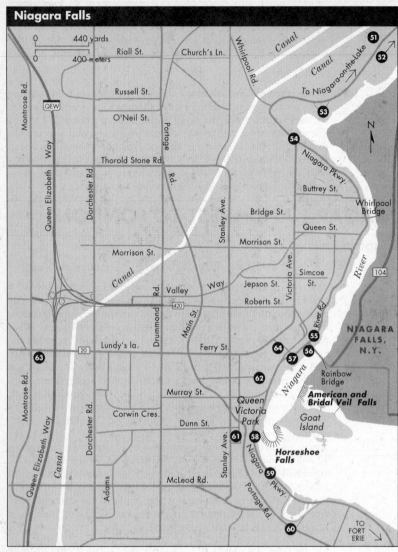

0   440 yards
0   400 meters

Riall St.
Church's Ln.
Whirlpool Rd.
Canal
Canal
To Niagara-on-the-Lake
Russell St.
O'Neil St.
QEW
Queen Elizabeth Way
Montrose Rd.
Portage Rd.
Dorchester Rd.
Thorold Stone Rd.
Niagara Pkwy.
Buttrey St.
Whirlpool Bridge
Bridge St.
Stanley Ave.
Queen St.
Morrison St.
Morrison St.
Victoria Ave.
Simcoe St.
River
104
Canal
Valley   Way
Jepson St.
Roberts St.
Drummond Rd.
Main St.
420
River Rd.
NIAGARA FALLS, N.Y.
Lundy's la.
Ferry St.
20
63
Montrose Rd.
Murray St.
Niagara
Rainbow Bridge
Skylon Tower, 62
Queen Victoria Park
American and Bridal Veil Falls
Corwin Cres.
Dorchester Rd.
Dunn St.
Goat Island
Stanley Ave.
Horseshoe Falls
Adams
McLeod Rd.
Niagara Pkwy.
Portage Rd.
TO FORT ERIE

N

51
52
53
54
55
56
57
58
59
60
61
62
63
64

Clifton Hill, **64**
Floral clock, **52**
Greenhouse and Plant Conservatory, **59**
Maid of the Mist boats, **57**
Marineland, **60**
Minolta Tower, **61**

Niagara Falls Museum, **55**
Niagara Glen, **53**
Niagara Spanish Aero Car, **54**
NPC School of Horticulture, **51**
Ride Niagara, **56**

Skylon Tower, **62**
Table Rock Scenic Tunnels, **58**
White Water Park, **63**

51 You can visit the **NPC School of Horticulture,** several miles north of (downriver from) the falls, on the Niagara Parkway. The school has been graduating professional gardeners since 1936, and students display their expertise with flowers and shrubbery.

52 From the school it's a short distance (downriver) to one of the world's largest **floral clock**s. Its 40-foot-wide "living" face is planted in a different design each year.

53 Heading back upriver, you'll find trails maintained by the NPC in the **Niagara Glen.** A bicycle trail that parallels the Niagara Parkway from Fort Erie to Niagara-on-the-Lake winds between beautiful homes on one side and the river, with its abundant bird life, on the other.

54 The **Niagara Spanish Aero Car,** a cable car that crosses the Whirlpool Basin in the Niagara Gorge, has been operating since 1918. This trip is not for the fainthearted; when you're swinging high above the roiling whirlpool, those cables seem awfully thin. The **Great Gorge Adventure** involves taking an elevator to the bottom of the Niagara Gorge, where you can walk a boardwalk beside the roaring torrent of the Niagara River. There the gorge is rimmed by sheer cliffs as it enters the Giant Whirlpool. ⊠ *River Rd., 3 km (2 mi) north of falls,* ☎ *905/354–5711.* ▨ *Aero Car $4.50, Great Gorge Adventure $4.25, NPC Explorer Passport $12.60 (discount admission to Table Rock Scenic Tunnels, Spanish Aero Car, and Great Gorge Adventure).* ◔ *June–Labor Day, daily 9–9; Labor Day–mid-Oct., shorter hrs, weather permitting.*

55 The **Niagara Falls Museum** claims to be North America's oldest museum and is chockablock with everything from stuffed birds to an excellent collection of Egyptian mummies. It houses the Daredevil Hall of Fame and displays barrels and other contraptions in which people have gone over the falls. There are 26 galleries on four floors and 700,000 exhibits, so gauge your time accordingly—this museum is well worth two hours of browsing. ⊠ *5651 River Rd.,* ☎ *905/356–2151.* ▨ *$6.75.* ◔ *Mid-June–Labor Day, daily 8:30–11; Labor Day–mid-June, daily 10–5.*

56 **Ride Niagara** is divided into three portions: a theater presentation, an elevator ride down to the tunnel, and the shuttle that's located near the falls and simulates plunging down the rapids in a barrel. The entire event takes about 20–25 minutes. Children under 3 are not admitted. ⊠ *5755 River Rd.,* ☎ *905/374–7433.* ▨ *$7.95.* ◔ *Daily; call for hrs.*

57 **Maid of the Mist boats** have been operating since 1846, when they were wooden-hulled, coal-fired steamboats. Nowadays, passengers are issued hooded rain slickers for the 30-minute trip because the three modern boats get so close to both falls that the spray is heavy. ⊠ *Boats leave from foot of Clifton Hill,* ☎ *905/358–5781.* ▨ *$8.65.* ◔ *Mid-May–late June and Labor Day–late Oct., daily 9:45–4:45, every 30 mins; late June–Labor Day, daily 9:45–7:45, as often as every 15 mins; late Oct.–mid-May, weekdays 9:45–7:45, every 30 mins.*

58 At **Table Rock Scenic Tunnels** your admission ticket includes use of rubber boots and a hooded rain slicker. You walk to an observation plaza just under the lip of the falls, and from there a tunnel takes you almost to the middle of the falls and behind the wall of crashing water. ⊠ *Tours begin at Table Rock House, Queen Victoria Park,* ☎ *905/354–1551.* ▨ *$5.50.* ◔ *Mid-June–Labor Day, daily 9–10:30; Labor Day–early June, daily 9–5; closed Dec. 25.*

⑤⑨ The NPC's enormous **Greenhouse and Plant Conservatory** (☎ 905/356–4699), just south of the Horseshoe Falls, is open daily. Here you can see myriad plants and flowers year-round.

🖐 ⑥⓪ **Marineland,** a theme park with a marine show, wildlife displays, and rides, is 1½ kilometers (1 mile) south of the falls. The daily marine show includes performing dolphins, harbor seals, and sea lions. Children can pet and feed members of a herd of 500 deer and get nose-to-nose with North American freshwater fish. Among the many rides is the world's largest steel roller coaster. Marineland is signposted from Niagara Parkway or reached from the Queen Elizabeth Way by exiting at McLeod Road (Exit 27). ⊠ *7657 Portage Rd.,* ☎ *905/356–8250 or 905/356–9565.* ⎚ *$21.95.* ⊙ *Apr.–June and Sept., daily 10–5; June–Aug., daily 9–6.*

Two towers offer panoramic views of the Horseshoe Falls and the surrounding area: the **Minolta Tower** (325 feet above ground level), at the base of which is a reptile display and an aquarium, which have separate entrance fees, and the **Skylon Tower** (520 feet high). ⊠ *Minolta Tower, 6732 Oakes Dr.,* ☎ *905/356–1501.* ⎚ *Tower $5.95.* ⊠ *Skylon Tower, 5200 Robinson St., above Horseshoe Falls,* ☎ *905/356–2651.* ⎚ *$6.95, elevator to dining area $2.* ⊙ *Mid-June–Labor Day, daily 8–1; Labor Day–early June, daily 10–9.*

🖐 ⑥③ **White Water Park** offers just about every means of getting wet there is, including Canada's biggest water slide, two hot tubs, and a wave pool. If you arrive within the first hour of the day, you'll receive $1 off the admission price. ⊠ *7430 Lundy's La.,* ☎ *905/357–3380.* ⎚ *$13.95.* ⊙ *June–Labor Day, daily 10–8.*

🖐 ⑥④ **Clifton Hill,** almost directly opposite the American Falls, is probably the most crassly commercial district of Niagara Falls. Sometimes referred to as "Museum Alley," this area encompasses the Guinness World of Records Museum, Ripley's Believe It Or Not Museum, Louis Tussaud's Waxworks Museum, the Haunted House, the Funhouse, the House of Frankenstein and Super Star Recording (where you can record the musical number of your choice), Movieland Wax Museum, Criminals Hall of Fame Wax Museum, the Elvis Presley Museum, and the That's Incredible Museum.

Dining and Lodging

$$ ✕ **Capri Restaurant.** Soft chairs and a softly tinkling piano create an elegant mood here. The combination of good steak, seafood, and Italian dishes makes this one of the better Niagara dining spots. ⊠ *5438 Ferry St.,* ☎ *905/354–7519. Reservations essential. AE, MC, V.*

$$ ✕ **Queenston Heights Restaurant.** This is one of four restaurants operated by the Niagara Parks Commission, which ensures good food at fair prices. It is a few kilometers north of (downriver from) the falls, and you can have a relaxed lunch or dinner overlooking a golf course or, if you're lucky, the Niagara Gorge. The Sunday brunch here is especially good. ⊠ *14184 Niagara Pkwy., Queenston Heights Park,* ☎ *905/262–4274. Reservations essential. AE, DC, MC, V.*

$$ ✕ **Skylon Tower's Revolving Dining Room and Summit Suite Restaurant.** If you have just one night for dining at the falls, make a reservation at the Skylon Tower's Revolving Dining Room. It makes a full circle every hour, and the view of the illuminated falls at night—at any time of the year—is a sight long remembered. The Canadian and Continental cuisine is usually excellent. The Skylon's Summit Suite Restaurant serves buffet breakfasts, plus lunch and dinner, and it has dancing, but it doesn't revolve. ⊠ *Skylon Tower,* ☎ *905/356–2651. Reservations essential. AE, DC, MC, V.*

$$$$ 🏨 **Skyline Brock Hotel, Skyline Foxhead Hotel, Skyline Village Inn.** The former Sheraton-Foxhead Hotel has been renovated and divided into three separate hotels under one management. The rates at the Foxhead start lower than those at the other two but climb to as high as $209. Many guest-room windows overlook the falls and some have particularly splendid views; rates are based to some extent on the view. Marilyn Monroe walked through the large, classic 1920s-style Skyline Brock Hotel in the film *Niagara*, while the Skyline Foxhead Hotel is a prosaic 1960s high rise, and the Village Inn is a typical motel. ✉ *5685 Falls Ave., L2E 6W7,* ☎ *905/374–4444,* FAX *905/357–4804. Skyline Brock Hotel, 232 rooms; Skyline Foxhead Hotel, 395 rooms; Skyline Village Inn, 208 rooms. 5 restaurants, 3 bars, 3 coffee shops, lounge. AE, MC, V.*

$$ 🏨 **Michael's Inn.** If you're on a first, second, third, or even fourth honeymoon, consider something fun and romantic. Michael's Inn has a number of theme rooms, all of which overlook the American falls and the gorge. Carry your mate across the threshold into deepest Africa, the Old South, or the Orient. The "Midnight at the Oasis" room has a Jacuzzi for two surrounded by mirrors, a 6½-foot-high stuffed tiger, palm-leaf wallpaper, and bamboo trees. The indoor pool has a slide. ✉ *5599 River Rd., L2E 3H3,* ☎ *905/354–2727 or 800/263–9390,* FAX *905/374–7706. 130 rooms. Dining room, lounge, indoor pool, sauna, whirlpool. AE, MC, V.*

Guided Tours

BY BUS

Double Deck Tours (☎ 905/295–3051), in 4½- to 5-hour tours in double-decker English buses, includes most of the major sights of Niagara Falls. The tours operate daily from mid-May through October. The fare of $34.90 includes GST and admissions to Table Rock Scenic Tunnels, Maid of the Mist, and a trip in the Niagara Spanish Aero Car. A shorter tour does not stop at attractions to which admission is charged, and costs $14.

The **Niagara Parks Commission** operates a People Mover System, consisting of air-conditioned buses, on a loop route between its public parking lot above the falls at Rapids View Terminal (well marked) and the Niagara Spanish Aero Car parking lot about 8 kilometers (5 miles) downriver. With a day's pass (available at any booth on the system: $3) you can get on and off as many times as you wish at the well-marked stops along the route.

BY HELICOPTER

Niagara Helicopters Ltd. takes you on a nine-minute flight over the Giant Whirlpool, up the Niagara Gorge, and past the American Falls and then banks around the curve of the Horseshoe Falls for a never-to-beforgotten thrill—if you dare to keep your eyes open. ☎ *905/357–5672.* 🎫 *$70 per person.* ☉ *Daily 9 AM–½ hr after sunset.*

Nightlife and the Arts

There are free band concerts on summer Sundays at **Queenston Heights Park, Queen Victoria Park,** and **Old Fort Erie** (☞ Fort Erie and West to Windsor, *above*), as well as **Rainbow Bridge Carillon** recitals.

Outdoor Activities and Sports

BIKING

The NPC (☎ 905/356–2241) operates 55 kilometers (30 miles) of **bicycle trails** along the Niagara River between Fort Erie and Niagaraon-the-Lake.

WINE REGION

Some of the Niagara Peninsula's 13 wineries are on the Niagara Parkway between Niagara Falls and Niagara-on-the-Lake, or on Route 55 from the Queen Elizabeth Way. As the quality of Ontario wines has improved in recent years, winemakers have stepped up their marketing and promotional activities. Look for the **Wine Regions Welcome Centre** (⊠ Casablanca Blvd., Grimsby), just off Queen Elizabeth Way East. The center is open in July, Friday 3–8, Saturday 9–5, and Sunday 10–3.

For a map of the wine region, including locations of individual wineries and details of summer events, write: **Wine Council of Ontario** (⊠ 110 Hanover Dr., Suite B205, St. Catharines, Ontario L2W 1A4, ☎ 905/684–8070). Several wineries offer tours, and the product may be sampled and bought; for exact times, call ahead. The best-known wineries include **Château des Charmes Wines Ltd.** (☎ 905/262–4219), **Hillebrand Estates Winery** (☎ 905/468–7123), **Iniskillin Wines** (☎ 905/468–3554), **Konzelmann Winery** (☎ 905/935–2866), **Reif Winery** (☎ 905/468–7738), and **Willowbank Estate Wines** (☎ 905/468–4219).

Niagara-on-the-Lake

⊛ *15 km (10 mi) north of (downriver from) Niagara Falls.*

The Victorian town of Niagara-on-the-Lake is one of Ontario's show-places. Stately homes sit back from tree-shaded streets, well apart from their neighbors. Though most are at least a century old, their owners maintain their original charm by keeping rose trellises freshly painted and brass door knockers gleaming. A dozen lovely inns here, some a century and a half old, make this a perfect getaway for Torontonians and travelers worn down by the neon of this village's southern neighbor. Any proposed new business is screened by the village council to ensure that no chrome, glass, or neon-girdled atrocity will mar the Victorian character. There's no room on these tiny roads for the invasion of motor homes, campers, and buses that occurs each summer, so be prepared for long traffic snarls. The best way to enjoy the town at any time of year is to stroll.

The **Niagara Apothecary,** a pharmacy museum on the main street across from the 1848 courthouse, replicates the pharmacy that first opened here in 1866. The serving counters are solid planks of walnut, and the crystal chandeliers are reproductions of original gasoliers. ⊠ *5 Queen St.,* ☎ *905/468–3845.* ⊡ *Free.* ⊙ *Mid-May–Labor Day, daily noon–6.*

The **Niagara Historical Society Museum,** built in 1906, houses a collection of artifacts from prehistory through the arrival of the Loyalists and the War of 1812. ⊠ *43 Castlereagh St.,* ☎ *905/468–3912.* ⊡ *$2.50.* ⊙ *May–Oct., daily 10–5; Jan. and Feb., weekends 1–5; Mar., Apr., Nov., and Dec., daily 1–5.*

The British **Fort George** was fully restored in 1939. Today soldiers in period dress perform drills and musical programs on the parade square. ⊠ *Niagara Pkwy.,* ☎ *905/468–4257.* ⊡ *$4.* ⊙ *Apr.–June, daily 9:30–4:30; July–Labor Day, daily 10–5; Labor Day–Nov., daily 9:30–4:30.*

The Arts

The event that has really put Niagara-on-the-Lake on the map is the

★ **Shaw Festival.** A stagestruck Toronto lawyer's dream in 1961 now has an impressive track record and a world-class reputation. Brian

Doherty started the festival in 1961 with a few Shaw plays produced on weekends in the old town courthouse. The performances were well received, and the company drew continuing support, mainly from Toronto. The government helped to finance the building of the 863-seat Shaw Festival Theatre, which opened in 1973. This is the only festival in the world specializing in the works of George Bernard Shaw and his contemporaries. Besides the modern Festival Theatre, the original Court House Theatre and the cozier Royal George Theatre also stage plays. The festival starts at the end of April and runs through mid-November. ⌧ *Shaw Festival Box Office, Box 774, Niagara-on-the-Lake, Ontario, Canada L0S 1J0; in the U.S., ☎ 800/724–2934; in Canada, 800/267–4759.*

Dining and Lodging

Restaurants abound in and around the center of Niagara-on-the-Lake, but most are overpriced and of mediocre quality. It is best to stick to one of the better-known hotels, or the many informal (and more reasonably priced) coffee shops.

$$$$ ✕🏨 **Prince of Wales.** The Wiens family has been dispensing gracious
★ hospitality here since 1975, when they turned a 16-room inn into a 105-room hotel. The original section of the inn was built as Long's Hotel in 1864. The additions over the years now make the hotel a block long, but the changes (inside and out) have been so sensitively wrought that only an expert could guess where most of them were made. An exception is the modern Greenhouse Patio Restaurant, particularly popular with the local lunch crowd, where tables sit under a canopy of hanging plants and behind glass walls overlooking the main street. Guests may also dine in the dining room, the Queen's Royal Lounge, or the Three Feathers Cafe. Reserve ahead for any of the restaurants, which serve traditional English fare of pork, duck, and salmon. Guest rooms are furnished in reproduction French provincial or traditional English furniture; some have fireplaces. ⌧ *6 Picton St., L0S 1J0, ☎ 905/468–3246 or 800/263–2452, ℻ 905/468–13310. 90 rooms, 11 suites. 3 dining rooms, lounge, indoor pool, sauna, whirlpool, tennis, health club. AE, MC, V.*

$$$ ✕🏨 **Oban Inn.** This elegant, historic country inn has a view of Lake Ontario. Each room is distinct, embellished with antiques in an old-world English tone. Some have fireplaces. You can also enjoy the library and the garden. The popular dining room spotlights Canadian beef favorites with a fresh twist of vegetables and fruits (reserve ahead). ⌧ *160 Front St., L0S 1J0, ☎ 905/468–2165, ℻ 905/468–4165. 22 rooms. Dining room, lounge. AE, DC, MC, V.*

$$$ ✕🏨 **Queen's Landing.** The owner of this remarkable property—who
★ also runs the Pillar & Post hotel and restaurant—has placed antique furnishings and fireplaces in 78 rooms and Jacuzzis in 44 rooms. Located at the mouth of the Niagara River, right across from historic Fort Niagara, the hotel has knockout views. The formal dining room has recently won acclaim for its spicy, inventive cuisine. Local wines also top the menu; note—no jeans are permitted here. Tennis and golf are available nearby. ⌧ *Melville and Bryon Sts., Box 1180, L0S 1J0, ☎ 905/468–2195 or 800/361–6645, ℻ 905/468–2227. 137 rooms. Dining room, lounge, lap pool, indoor pool, sauna, whirlpool, exercise room, baby-sitting. AE, DC, MC, V.*

Guided Tours

Antours (☎ 416/424–4403) provides several tours of Niagara-on-the-Lake, which include lunch and major performances at the Shaw Festival.

En Route   The **Niagara Peninsula** is Ontario's fruit basket. From mid-summer to late fall, fruit and vegetable stands proliferate along the highways and byways, and there are several farmers' markets along the Queen Elizabeth Way between Niagara Falls and Hamilton. Some of the best displays of fruits and vegetables are on Lincoln County Road 55, between Niagara-on-the-Lake and the Queen Elizabeth Way. **Harvest Barn Market** (⊠ RR3, Rte. 55, Niagara-on-the-Lake, ☎ 905/468–3224), marked by a red-and-white-striped awning, not only features regional fruits and vegetables but also tempts with a bakery offering sausage rolls, tiny loaves of bread, and fruit pies. You can test the market's wares at the picnic tables, where knowledgeable locals have lunch.

Hamilton

66 *75 km (50 mi) west of Niagara Falls on the Queen Elizabeth Way.*

Hamilton is Canada's steel capital—the Dofasco and Stelco mills produce 60% of the country's iron and steel. This isn't the sort of city where you'd expect to find 2,700 acres of gardens and exotic plants, a symphony orchestra, a modern and active theater, 45 parks, a 100-voice choir, and an opera company. But they're all here in Hamilton, Ontario's second-largest city and Canada's third-busiest port.

The city's downtown is on a plain between the harbor and the base of "the mountain," a 250-foot-high section of the Niagara Escarpment. Downtown Hamilton is a potpourri of glass-walled high rises, century-old mansions, a convention center, a coliseum, and a shopping complex.

Hamilton is also home to Canada's largest indoor **farmers' market**—176 stalls spread over more than 20,000 square feet—started in 1837. ⊠ *Adjoining Jackson Square and new Eaton Centre,* ☎ *905/546–2096.* ☉ *Tues. and Thurs. 7–6, Fri. 9–6, Sat. 6–6.*

The Art Gallery of Hamilton houses 7,500 art objects in an acclaimed three-level modern structure in the central business district. It is particularly strong in 20th-century Canadian art. ⊠ *123 King St. W,* ☎ *905/527–6610.* ☒ *Donations accepted.* ☉ *Wed., Fri., and Sat. 10–5; Thurs. 10–9; Sun. 1–5.*

The **Royal Botanical Gardens,** opened in 1932, encompass five major gardens and 48 kilometers (30 miles) of trails that wind across marshes and ravines, past the world's largest collection of lilacs, 2 acres of roses, and all manner of shrubs, trees, plants, hedges, and flowers. Two teahouses are open May 1 to Thanksgiving (mid-October). ⊠ *Plains Rd. (Rte. 2), Burlington, accessible from Queen Elizabeth Way and Rtes. 6 and 403,* ☎ *905/527–1158; in Ontario and Québec, 800/668–9449.* ☒ *Mid-May–Labor Day, $5.25; Labor Day–mid-May, grounds free, greenhouse $2.* ☉ *Main building daily 9–5, outdoor garden daily 9:30–6; closed Dec. 25.*

Plant lovers can marvel at **Gage Park**'s 70-acre botanical greens, a beautiful oasis in the center of the city. Its rose garden, growing more than 30 varieties, is especially stunning. ⊠ *Main St. E and Gage Ave., east of downtown.*

★   Sir Allan Napier MacNab, a War of 1812 hero and Upper Canada's pre-confederation prime minister, built a 35-room mansion called **Dundurn Castle** in 1832–35. Now a museum, it has been furnished to reflect the opulence in which MacNab lived at the height of his political career. ⊠ *Dundurn Park and York Blvd.,* ☎ *905/546–2872.* ☒ *$5.* ☉ *June–Labor Day, daily 11–4; Labor Day–May, Tues.–Sun. 1–4; closed nonholiday Mon.*

Flamboro Downs harness racing track, just west of Hamilton, has matinee and evening races year-round, though not on a daily basis. The clubhouse has two dining areas that overlook the track. ⊠ *Rte. 5.,* ☎ *905/627–3561.*

☺ At **African Lion Safari,** lions, tigers, cheetahs, elephants, and zebras abound. You can drive your own car or take an air-conditioned tram over a 9-kilometer (6-mile) safari trail through the wildlife park. ⊠ *Rockton, near Hamilton, off Rte. 8, south of Cambridge,* ☎ *519/623–2620.* ⊡ *$14.50.* ☉ *Grounds early Apr.–Oct., daily 9–6:30; tour weekdays 9–4, weekends 9–5.*

Dining and Lodging

$$ ✕ **Ancaster Old Mill.** This historic mill is just outside Hamilton and
★ worth the trip if only to sample the bread, baked daily with flour ground at the mill on millstones installed in 1863. The dining rooms are light and bright with hanging plants. Try to get a table overlooking the mill stream and a waterfall. ⊠ *548 Old Dundas Rd., Ancaster,* ☎ *905/648–1827. Reservations essential. AE, DC, MC, V.*

$$$$ ✕▥ **Langdon Hall.** This magnificent colonial-revival-style mansion on
★ 40 landscaped acres has grand public rooms and huge fireplaces. It was built in 1898 as a summer home for a great-grandson of John Jacob Astor and has been sensitively converted to a grand country hotel with 13 guest rooms in the original building and 28 in a modern annex. The house has a billiard room, a conservatory, a card room, and a drawing room. The dining room (reserve ahead) menu offers delectable variations on French and Continental dishes. Call for directions. ⊠ *R.R. 33, Cambridge, N3H 4R8,* ☎ *519/740–2100,* ℻ *519/740–8161. 41 rooms. Dining room, room service, pool, sauna, hot tub, boating, 2 tennis courts, croquet, exercise room, billiards, meeting rooms. AE, MC, V.*

$$$ ✕▥ **Royal Connaught Hotel.** This venerable 1914 hotel in the heart of downtown Hamilton is a grand old place complete with a ballroom. The indoor swimming pool has one of Canada's longest water slides. The Grill is the hotel's very popular dining room (reserve ahead). Meat is broiled over an open mesquite fire. There's a marble floor and, after you've eaten—or while you're waiting for your entrée to be flamed—you can dance in the gazebo. ⊠ *112 King St. E., L8N 1A8,* ☎ *905/546–8111,* ℻ *905/546–8144. 206 rooms, 21 suites. Restaurant, lounge, indoor pool, sauna, whirlpool, comedy, cabaret. AE, MC, V.*

Nightlife and the Arts

Opera Hamilton (⊠ Summers Lane, opposite Art Gallery of Hamilton, ☎ 905/527–7627) holds performances in the Great Hall of Hamilton Place from September through April. Its repertory embraces works from *Aida* to *Nixon in China.*

Outdoor Activities and Sports

HIKING

The 680-kilometer (430-mile) **Bruce Trail** stretches northwest along the limestone Niagara Escarpment from the orchards of the Niagara Peninsula to the cliffs and bluffs at Tobermory, at the end of the Bruce Peninsula. You can access the Bruce Trail at just about any point along the route, so your hike can be as long or as short as you wish. Contact the Bruce Trail Association (⊠ Box 857, Hamilton, Ontario L8N 3N9, ☎ 905/592–6821).

The **Canadian Experience** (⊠ R.R. 1, Ravenna, Ontario N0H 2E0, ☎ ℻ 519/599–7465) offers a number of hiking and sightseeing excursions with overnight accommodation on a farm adjacent to the Bruce Trail.

Shopping

Hess Village, in two blocks between Main and King streets, is crammed with interesting boutiques, cafés, and pubs.

Brantford

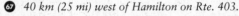

67   *40 km (25 mi) west of Hamilton on Rte. 403.*

Brantford is named for Joseph Brant, the Loyalist Mohawk chief who brought members of the Six Nations Confederacy into Canada after the American Revolution. King George III showed gratitude to Chief Brant and his loyal Indian subjects by building the **Mohawk Church.** In 1904, by royal assent, it was given the name His Majesty's Chapel of the Mohawks (now changed to Her Majesty's). It is the oldest Protestant church in Ontario and the only one that may suggest Royal in its name. The simple, white-painted frame building has eight stained-glass windows depicting the colorful history of the Six Nations people. A guide is available. ✉ *292 Mohawk St.,* ☎ *519/445–4528.* 🎟 *$1.* ⊙ *Daily 1–5.*

Woodland Indian Cultural Educational Centre is a museum of sorts that aims to preserve and promote the culture and heritage of the native people of the First Nation. The modern building contains displays and exhibits showing early Woodland Indian culture. ✉ *184 Mohawk St., near Mohawk Chapel,* ☎ *519/759–2650.* 🎟 *$3.* ⊙ *Weekdays 8:30–4, weekends 10–5.*

Although Brantford is the hometown of hockey star Wayne Gretzky, it is better known as "the Telephone City" because Alexander Graham Bell invented the device here and made the first long-distance call from his parents' home to nearby Paris, Ontario, in 1874. The **Bell Homestead** is now a National Historic Site. Next door is the house of the Reverend Thomas Henderson, a Baptist minister who left the church when he recognized the profit potential in telephones. His home was the first telephone office and now is a museum of telephone artifacts and displays. Guided tours can be arranged. ✉ *94 Tutela Heights Rd.,* ☎ *519/756–6220.* 🎟 *$2.50.* ⊙ *Mid-Mar.–Thanksgiving, Tues.–Sun. 9:30–4:30.*

Outdoor Activities and Sports

BIKING

Brantford is protected by a flood-control dam on top of which is a **bicycle trail** that passes most of the city's many interesting tourist attractions.

HIKING

The **Grand Valley Trail** runs 128 kilometers (80 miles) between Elora and Brantford. Contact the Grand Valley Trail Association (✉ Box 1233, Kitchener, Ontario N2G 4G8).

Kitchener and Waterloo

68   *Approximately 27 km (18 mi) north of Brantford on Rte. 24.*

Kitchener and Waterloo merge into one another and are usually referred to as K–W. The region was settled around 1800 by Swiss-German Mennonites from Pennsylvania. The German origins remain obvious: There's a huge glockenspiel downtown by Speakers' Corner, and each October since 1967 the city has hosted Oktoberfest. The event now draws more than 600,000 people, who swarm to more than a dozen festival halls where they dance, gorge on German-style food, listen to oompah bands, and drink with a fervor that seems driven by an irrational fear that all Canadian breweries are about to go on strike.

Farmers' markets thrive everywhere in Ontario, but the **Kitchener Market** is particularly well known. It isn't the oldest or the largest, but it's been around since 1869 and since 1986 has been housed in spacious quarters at Market Square. The block-long complex is wrapped in green-tinted glass and contains 70 shops and snack bars and an Eaton's department store. ⊠ *Frederick and Duke Sts.,* ☎ *519/741–2287.* ⊗ *Sat. 6–2.*

William Lyon Mackenzie King, who was prime minister of Canada for almost 22 of the years between 1921 and 1948, spent his teenage years in a rented 10-room house called Woodside, now **Woodside National Historic Park.** There's no particular imprint here of the bachelor prime minister whose diaries reveal his belief in mysticism, portents, and communications with the dead, but the house has been furnished to reflect the period of the King family's occupancy. ⊠ *528 Wellington St., Kitchener,* ☎ *519/571–5684.* ⊡ *$2.50.* ⊗ *May–Dec., daily 10–5; Jan.–Apr., by appointment only.*

The **Seagram Museum** is a shrine to booze, and every exhibit in the enormous former barrel warehouses and new exhibition building relates to the product. Tour guides are available, and if you develop a powerful thirst while browsing, a specialty liquor store sells Seagram products and gift items. Lunch and dinner are available in a fine dining room on the premises. ⊠ *57 Erb St. W, Waterloo,* ☎ *519/885–1857.* ⊡ *Free.* ⊗ *May–Dec., daily 10–6; Jan.–Apr., Tues.–Sun. 10–6.*

Doon Heritage Crossroads is a complete pioneer village just north of Route 401, a few kilometers south and west of Kitchener. The village tranquilly recalls the lifestyle of a people who lived near the main highway of the early 1800s—the Huron Road. You can wander tree-shaded roadways where neither automobiles nor the noises of the urban complex to the north intrude. Staff at the village wear period costumes; some work at old-time crafts. ⊠ *R.R. 2 north of Hwy. 401, Kitchener,* ☎ *519/748–1914.* ⊡ *$5.* ⊗ *May–Labor Day, daily 10–4:30; Labor Day–Dec., weekdays 10–4:30.*

Dining and Lodging

$$$ ✕▦ **Valhalla Inn.** This modern hotel has a major sports complex in its basement and is connected by a glassed-in skywalk to the Market Square shopping mall and Farmers' Market. Shatz's, the main, more formal restaurant (reserve ahead), is candlelit and decorated in earth tones. Continental fare dominates the menu. A smaller cafe is fine for casual meals. ⊠ *105 King St. E, N2G 2K8,* ☎ *519/744–4141,* ℻ *519/578–6889. 203 rooms. Café, dining room, lounge, indoor pool, sauna, whirlpool, miniature golf, bowling. AE, MC, V.*

$$$ ▦ **Best Western Walper Terrace Hotel.** This rejuvenated 1893 hotel sustains a Kitchener tradition started in 1820 by Phineas Varnum, who built what was then called the Varnum Inn. The current owners have kept at least one piece of period cherry-wood furniture in each of the guest rooms. The wooden-trim moldings, carved marble pillars, and the ornate brass banister of the main staircase have been preserved, along with the ballroom. The Bismarck Cafe has an art deco floor, vaulted ceilings, marble pillars, stained-glass windows, and a view of one of the city's major intersections. The setting is romantic, and meals are moderately priced (reserve ahead). ⊠ *1 King St. W, N2G 1A1,* ☎

519/745–4321, FAX *519/745–3625. 60 rooms, 20 suites. Restaurant, lounge. AE, MC, V.*

Nightlife

Lulu's Roadhouse (⊠ 4263 King St. E, Rte. 8, ☎ 519/650–0000 or 800/561–5858), a unique spot located in a former Kmart store just south of Kitchener, is Canada's largest bar. It can seat 2,000 customers at 450 tables and on bar stools, and there's room for another 1,000 standing along the longest (333 feet) and second-longest (310 feet) bars in the world. Since Lulu's opened in 1984, it's been packing 'em in to watch performances by big-name rock-and-roll entertainers.

St. Jacobs

★ ⑥⑨ *10 km (6 mi) north of Kitchener and Waterloo on Rte. 8.*

The villages of St. Jacobs and Elmira (10 kilometers, or 6 miles, north of St. Jacobs via Route 86 and County Road 21) are in the heart of Mennonite and Hutterite country. These are peaceful people who live off the land, refuse to fight in wars, and have a strict moral code. They also resist modern conveniences, such as cars, electricity, and the internal combustion engine. The region is a shopper's paradise, with many stands selling all manner of fresh and preserved foods and gift items handcrafted by the Mennonites. **Crafts By Us** (⊠ 42 Arthur St. S, ☎ 519/669–8480) is one of several stores found in the Elmira Olde Town Village at the main intersection in Elmira.

Dining and Lodging

$$$$ ✕▥ **Millcroft Inn.** This 19th-century stone knitting mill has been con-
★ verted to an exquisite full-service country inn beside the millpond. About 40 kilometers (25 miles) northeast of Elmira (80 kilometers, or 50 miles, northwest of Toronto) in Alton, it is one of Canada's finest hostelries and a member of the Relais & Châteaux Association. Some large suites have fireplaces. Rooms are available in both the older inn and a more modern annex, where they tend to be more spacious. In addition to sports facilities, there's a year-round outdoor whirlpool. The dining room menu offers a relatively limited choice of traditional Continental dishes, but quality more than makes up for the lack of variety (reserve ahead). ⊠ *John St., Alton, L0N 1A0,* ☎ *519/941–8111,* FAX *519/941–9192. 43 rooms, 9 suites. Dining room, outdoor pool, 2 saunas, whirlpool, 2 tennis courts, exercise room. AE, DC, MC, V.*

$$$ ✕▥ **Benjamins.** This is a lovely re-creation of the original 1852 Farmer's Inn. Nine guest rooms on the second floor are furnished in antiques, and every bed is covered with a locally made Mennonite quilt. The licensed, 120-seat restaurant (reserve ahead) has pine ceiling beams, an open-hearth fireplace, lots of greenery, and imaginative French cuisine. ⊠ *17 King St., St. Jacobs, N0B 2N0,* ☎ *519/664–3731,* FAX *519/664–2218. 9 rooms. Restaurant. AE, MC, V.*

$$$ ✕▥ **Elora Mill.** This is one of Canada's few remaining five-story grist-
★ mills. It has been converted to luxury accommodations and offers superb dining. There are 16 guest rooms in the 1859 mill building and 16 more in four other historic stone buildings in the immediate vicinity of the mill. The inn is in the heart of a village about 15 kilometers (9 miles) north of Elmira full of stone buildings that could have been lifted from England's Cotswolds or southern France. The cuisine is a mix of imaginative Canadian and European dishes (reserve ahead), and live music sometimes accompanies dining. ⊠ *77 Mill St. W, Elora,* ☎ *519/846–5356,* FAX *519/846–9180. 32 rooms. Dining room. AE, MC, V.*

Outdoor Activities and Sports

BIKING

Two popular bike routes can be reached from **Fergus,** 18 kilometers (11 miles) northwest of Elmira: One is a 32-kilometer (20-mile) tour around Lake Belwood, the other a 40-kilometer (25-mile) loop around Eramosa Township. There is little traffic on these scenic routes, and restaurants are few and far between, so take a picnic lunch.

HIKING

A popular minihike in southern Ontario (part of the Grand Valley Trail) is the 5-kilometer (3-mile) pathway along the Elora Gorge between Fergus and Elora, 15 kilometers (9 miles) north of Elmira. Among the features are a whirlpool at Templin Gardens, a restored English garden, and a bridge across the gorge at Mirror Basin, where there are excellent views up and down the gorge. This hike should not be attempted in street shoes.

Stratford

70 *46 km (28 mi) west of Kitchener on Rtes. 7 and 8.*

The city of Stratford was named by homesick English settlers; all that the town had in common with England's Stratford was a river called Avon meandering through rolling countryside—and not even particularly similar countryside. Nowadays the village is famous for hosting the annual Stratford Festival, which welcomes more than 400,000 people to its acclaimed performances of music, opera, and drama.

The Arts

★ The **Stratford Festival** hosts music, opera, and drama annually. It all started in 1953, in a massive tent, with Sir Alec Guinness playing Richard III. The next year, musical programs were added to supplement Shakespeare's plays. The venture was a huge success, and the 1957 season opened in a permanent home with 2,262 seats, none of which is more than 65 feet from the stage. The 1901-vintage, 1,107-seat Avon Theatre became a partner in the festival in 1967, and the Tom Patterson Theatre, seating 496, opened in 1971. The Stratford Festival now starts around the beginning of May and runs until late October. ⊠ *Tourism Stratford, Box 818, 88 Wellington St., N5A 6W1,* ☎ *519/271–5140 or 800/561–7926,* FAX *519/273–1818.*

Dining and Lodging

$$$$ ✕ **Church Restaurant and Belfry.** One block from the Avon Theatre, this church—complete with organ pipes and stained-glass windows—has been converted into a restaurant that offers such French favorites as onion soup, quiches, and cassoulet. There's even an old pew outside the washroom. The Belfry restaurant and bar upstairs is more casual and less expensive. ⊠ *Brunswick and Waterloo Sts.,* ☎ *519/273–3424. Reservations essential. AE, DC, MC, V.*

$$$ ✕🛏 **Queen's Inn at Stratford.** In this beautifully restored 1853 hotel, guests can enjoy traditional Canadian food in the dining room (reserve ahead) while listening to tinkling music from a baby grand piano. Light fare is served in one half of the divided room, and there are also a popular pub-lounge and two function rooms. ⊠ *161 Ontario St., N5A 3H3,* ☎ *519/271–1400,* FAX *519/271–7373. 30 rooms. Restaurant, lounge. AE, MC, V.*

$$ ✕🛏 **La Brassine.** Near the edge of Lake Huron northwest of Stratford,
★ this large farm home–cum–country inn has a kitchen that produces some of the finest French cuisine west of the Québec border. You must book ahead at least 24 hours for Wednesday–Saturday dinners or daily if you're a resident of one of the guest rooms in the inn. Everything served

is created in-house; the linen-covered tables are set with crystal and silver. There is no liquor license. The management accepts the credit cards noted below, but prefers cash or check payment if possible. Call for directions. ⊠ *R.R. 2, Goderich,* ☎ *519/524–6300. 5 rooms. MC, V.*

$$ 🏠 **Woods Villa Bed and Breakfast.** Owner Ken Vinen has restored this elegant 1875 home of a wealthy magistrate to 19th-century grandeur. Vinen uses the public rooms to display his astonishing collection of restored vintage jukeboxes, music boxes, and player pianos. In summer, a full breakfast is served on an outside patio beside an enormous, ceramic-tile swimming pool. Some of the five rooms have fireplaces. Woods Villa does not accept children or pets; the latter might ruffle the feathers of Vinen's five macaws. Note that while the credit cards listed below are accepted, cash is preferred. ⊠ *62 John St. N, Stratford, N5A 6K7,* ☎ *519/271–4576. 5 rooms. Outdoor pool. MC, V.*

London

71 *75 km (46 mi) southwest of Stratford on Rtes. 7 and 4.*

London is a quiet, provincial city where old money rules the arts and development projects. Its nickname is Forest City—it has more than 50,000 trees on city property and 1,500 acres of parks, including 1,000 acres along the Thames River. It has also become famous for its hospitals, which specialize in organ-transplant and other intricate operations. This low-key city has been called a microcosm of Canadian life; it is so "typically Canadian," it's often used as a test market for new products—if something will sell in London, it will probably sell anywhere in Canada.

Because **Storybook Gardens** is owned and operated by the city's Public Utility Commission, this is one of the least expensive children's theme parks in the country. It's on the Thames River in the 281-acre Springbank Park. You'll see a castle, storybook characters, and a zoo with foreign and indigenous animals, including some from Old MacDonald's Farm. Children can slide down Jack and Jill's hill and the throat of Willie the Whale. ⊠ *929 Springbank Dr.,* ☎ *519/661–5770.* 🎟 *$5.* ☉ *May–Labor Day, daily 10–8; Labor Day–Thanksgiving (mid-Oct.), weekdays 10–5, weekends 10–6.*

London Regional Art and Historical Museum is as interesting from the outside as its exhibits are on the inside. The gallery is contained in six joined, glass-covered structures whose ends are the shape of croquet hoops. ⊠ *Forks of the Thames,* ☎ *519/672–4580.* 🎟 *Donation requested.* ☉ *Tues.–Sun. noon–5.*

The **London Museum of Archaeology** houses more than 40,000 native artifacts and a gallery of artists' conceptions of the lives of the Attawandaron natives who lived on the Lawson site, a nearby archaeological dig, some 500 years ago. Nearby is a reconstructed multifamily longhouse on its original site. ⊠ *1600 Attawandaron Rd., south of Rte. 22,* ☎ *519/473–1360.* 🎟 *$3.50.* ☉ *May–Labor Day, daily 10–5; Labor Day–Oct., Tues.–Sun. 10–5; Jan.–Apr., Wed.–Sun. 1–4.*

London's oldest building is also one of its most impressive. The wrecker's ball came awfully close to the **Old Courthouse Building,** and it got one wall of the former Middlesex County Gaol. But a citizens' group prevailed, and the Old Courthouse, modeled after Malahide Castle in England, reopened as the home of the Middlesex County council. ⊠ *399 Ridout St. N,* ☎ *519/434–7321.* 🎟 *Free.* ☉ *June–Aug., weekdays 8:30-noon and 1–4:30.*

Dining and Lodging

$$ ✕ **Marienbad and Chaucer's Pub.** Reasonably priced Czech fare is served in surroundings that will remind you of your Eastern European vacation (if you had one). Great goulash, schnitzels, and sauerbraten are among the choices. ⊠ *122 Carling St.,* ☎ *519/679–9940. AE, MC, V.*

$$ ✕ **Michael's on the Thames.** This popular lunch and dinner spot overlooking the Thames River offers flambéed dishes. The Canadian and Continental cuisine also includes fresh seafood, chateaubriand, and flaming desserts and coffees. ⊠ *1 York St., at Thames River,* ☎ *519/672–0111. Reservations essential. AE, MC, V, DC.*

$$$$ 🏨 **Delta London Armouries.** This 20-story, silver-mirrored tower rises from the center of the 1905 London Armoury. The lobby is a greenhouse of vines, trees, plants, and fountains, wrapped in marble and accented by rich woods and old yellow brick. The architects left as much of the original armory intact as possible. A set of steps through manicured jungle takes you to the indoor swimming pool, sauna, and whirlpool. Guest rooms are spacious and decorated in pastel shades. Suites vary in size and grandeur—the Middlesex Suite has a grand piano. ⊠ *325 Dundas St., N6B 1T9,* ☎ *519/679-6111,* ℻ *519/679–3957. 242 rooms, 8 suites. Restaurant, indoor pool, sauna, racquetball, squash. AE, MC, V.*

$$$$ 🏨 **Idlewylde Inn.** Though an elevator was installed in this converted 1878 mansion, the architects succeeded in keeping many original features in the 27 luxurious guest rooms and suites and in the public rooms. Some rooms have a Jacuzzi. Complimentary breakfast and snacks are included in the rate. ⊠ *36 Grand Ave., N6C 1K8,* ☎ ℻ *519/433–2891. 27 rooms. AE, DC, MC, V.*

London also has a strip of motels on Wellington Road north of Hwy. 401 and on Dundas Street East, out toward the airport.

Guided Tours

BY BOAT

From mid-May through October you can get another view of London by cruising on the Thames River in a 60-passenger boat. Afternoon cruises (⊠ Spring Bank Park, ☎ 519/473–0363) depart every hour from Storybook Gardens.

BY BUS

The easiest way to get an overview of the town is to take a tour on a big, red, double-decker—what else?—London bus. They operate from City Hall, July 1 to Labor Day (at 10 and 2).

Outdoor Activities and Sports

BIKING

Scenic **Springbank Park** has miles of pretty bicycle trails.

SAULT STE. MARIE AND WEST TO THUNDER BAY

Sault Ste. Marie

Numbers in the margin correspond to points of interest on the Upper Ontario Province map.

72 *700 km (434 mi) northwest of Toronto.*

Sault Ste. Marie has always been a natural meeting place and cultural melting pot. Long before Etienne Brulé "discovered" the rapids in

Upper Ontario

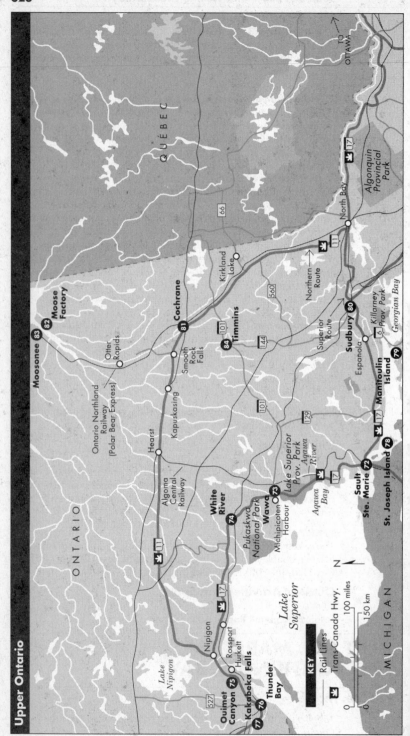

QUÉBEC

TO OTTAWA

Algonquin Provincial Park

North Bay

17

11

Kirkland Lake

66

560

Northern Route

Superior Route

81 Cochrane

101 Timmins

84

144

80 Sudbury

Espanola

Killarney Prov. Park 6

79 Manitoulin Island

Georgian Bay

82 Moose Factory

83 Moosonee

Otter Rapids

Smooth Rock Falls

101

Kapuskasing

Ontario Northland Railway (Polar Bear Express)

Hearst

129

17

28

72 Sault Ste. Marie

St. Joseph Island

ONTARIO

Algoma Central Railway

White River 74

73 Wawa

Michipicoten Harbour

Lake Superior Prov. Park

Agawa River

17

Agawa Bay

Pukaskwa National Park

11

17

Nipigon

Rossport

Hurkett

75 Ouimet Canyon

Kakabeka Falls

527

76 Thunder Bay

77

Lake Nipigon

Lake Superior

MICHIGAN

N

100 miles

150 km

KEY

Rail Lines
Trans-Canada Hwy.

0

1622, Ojibwa tribes gathered here. Whitefish, their staple food, could easily be caught year-round, and the rapids in the St. Mary's River linking lakes Huron and Superior were often the only open water for miles during the winter. When Father Jacques Marquette opened a mission in 1668, he named it Sainte Marie de Sault. Today everybody but tourists call the city simply "the Sault," and the smaller city across the river in Michigan is called "the Soo." Different spelling, identical pronunciation.

The elegant **Ermatinger Stone House** was built by Montréal fur trader Charles Oakes Ermatinger in 1814 and is the oldest building in Canada west of Toronto. Ermatinger married Charlotte, a daughter of influential Indian chief Katawebeda, a move that didn't hurt his business. Today, costumed interpreters show visitors through the house and demonstrate cooking, baking, and crafts. ⊠ *831 Queen St. E,* ☎ *705/759–5443.* ✈ *Donation requested.* ⊙ *Apr. and May, weekdays 10–5; June–Sept., daily 10–5; Oct. and Nov., weekdays 1–5.*

One of the Sault's most-touted sights is a boat tour through the **Soo Locks,** the 16th and final lift for ships bound for Lake Superior from the St. Lawrence River, 600 feet lower and 3,200 kilometers (2,000 miles) downstream. Your cruise boat will be lifted only 21 feet through one of the four locks on the U.S. side, but if you haven't been through a lock before it's an interesting experience. (☞ Guided Tours, *below.*)

The **Algoma Central Railway** not only operates main line track between the Sault and iron mines at Hearst and Michipicoten Harbor but also runs a lucrative sideline of tour trains to and from scenic Agawa Canyon, through which their main line passes (☞ Guided Tours, ★ *below*). In summer the train stops for two hours in **Agawa Canyon,** a deep valley 19 kilometers (12 miles) long with cliff walls up to 800 feet high through which the Agawa River flows. During the stopover, passengers can lunch in a park, hike to their choice of three waterfalls, or climb to a lookout 250 feet above the train. Dining car service is continuous 7 AM–3:45 PM.

Dining and Lodging

$$$ ✕🏠 **Quality Inn Bayfront.** If you're planning to take the Agawa Canyon Train Tour (☞ Guided Tours, *below*), book a room at this popular hotel. The rooms and suites are clean and modern with many creature comforts, and the inn has a sauna and in-house movies. Most important— because the train leaves at 8 AM and you should be at the station by 7:30 AM at the latest—the hotel is directly across the street from the Algoma Central Railroad station. When you return at night, the hotel's swimming pool and dining room await you. Gran Sesta Ristorante (reserve ahead) in the hotel offers good prices, friendly service, and southern Italian dishes garnished with edible flowers. The dining area is bright and airy with lots of brass and greenery. ⊠ *180 Bay St., P6A 6S2,* ☎ *705/945–9264 or 800/228–5151,* FAX *705/945–9766. 109 rooms, 13 suites. Dining room, indoor pool, sauna, whirlpool, exercise room, meeting rooms. AE, MC, V.*

Guided Tours

BY BOAT

Lock Tours Canada runs two-hour excursions through the 21-foot-high Soo Locks, the 16th and final lift for ships bound for Lake Superior from the St. Lawrence River. Tours aboard the 200-passenger MV *Chief Shingwauk* or 156-passenger MV *Bon Soo* leave from the Norgoma Dock just downriver from the Holiday Inn, May 15–October 15, and up to eight times daily July 1–Labor Day. ⊠ *Roberta Bondar Dock and Foster Dr.,* ☎ *705/253–9850.* ✈ *$14.*

BY BUS AND VAN

Hiawathaland Tours (☎ 705/759–6200) operates three city tours by double-decker bus and a wilderness tour by minivan to Aubrey Falls from June 15 to October 15. A 75-minute evening tour is also available.

BY TRAIN

The **Agawa Canyon Train** or the **Snow Train**—the name varies with the seasons—runs from Sault Ste. Marie for a scenic day trip up the Agawa Canyon and back. ⊠ *129 Bay St.,* ☎ *705/946–7300.* 🎫 *Agawa trip $46, Snow Train $45.* ☉ *Tour trains June 5–mid-Oct., daily; Jan.–Mar., weekends; trains depart 8 AM and return at 5 in warmer seasons and 4 in cooler weather.*

Wawa

73 *225 km (131 mi) north of Sault Ste. Marie on Trans-Canada Rte. 17.*

Wawa is the first town north of the Lake Superior Provincial Park. It is an Ojibwa word meaning "wild goose," and the 3,700 residents of Wawa have erected a massive goose monument at the entrance to town from Route 17. Next door is the town's new log-cabin tourist information office.

White River

74 *90 km (56 mi) north of Wawa on Trans-Canada Rte. 17.*

White River is marked by a huge thermometer indicating 72 degrees below zero and a sign that advises: "White River—coldest place in Canada." The town has another claim to fame: It was the home of Winnie-the-Pooh, the black bear immortalized in the Christopher Robin children's stories by British author A. A. Milne. A 25-foot-high statue honoring Winnie was put up in 1992, and each August the town holds a three-day Winnie's Homecoming Festival, with parades, street dances, and a community barbecue.

Dining and Lodging

$$ ✕🖬 **Rossport Inn.** The hamlet of Rossport, about 200 km (125 mi) west of White River, on a harbor off Lake Superior, is about as close as you can get to an unspoiled outpost on the Great Lakes. The inn was built in 1884 as a railroad hotel and now has six small guest rooms sharing two bathrooms. This is one of the nicest country inns in the province. It's cozy and down-home—the nightlife consists of swapping lies with the innkeepers and other guests about the fish that got away. Breakfast is included in the room rate. The dining room's home-style cooking of locally caught fish, as well as of steak, chicken, pork chops, and lobster, is irresistible. ⊠ *Rossport Loop, ½ mi from Trans-Canada Hwy., Bowman St., P0T 2R0,* ☎ *807/824–3213. 6 rooms. Dining room. MC, V. Closed Nov.–May.*

Ouimet Canyon

★ **75** *300 km (200 mi) west of White River on Trans-Canada Rte. 17.*

Just past the town of Hurkett, west of Nipigon, watch for signs to Ouimet Canyon. This geological anomaly is a midget compared to Agawa Canyon but, because of the vantage point, it is more spectacular. At Ouimet, the visitor strolls a wide path and suddenly comes to the edge of the canyon. Viewing platforms extend over the edge so you can look straight down 329 feet. The far wall is only 492 feet away, and the chasm is only 2½ kilometers (1½ miles) long. Geologists believe the canyon could be a gigantic fault in the earth's surface, or it could have been carved by a glacier. ⊠ *Off Rte. 17, 10 km (6 mi) west of Hurkett.* ☎ *Free.* ⊙ *Mid-May–Thanksgiving (mid-Oct.), daily 9–5.*

En Route   If legend is to be believed, wearing an amethyst will protect you from hangovers. Ontario's gemstone is an imperfect quartz, tinted violet or purple by the impurity of iron atoms mixing with the original liquid rock. There are five amethyst mines between Sleeping Giant Provincial Park and Ouimet Canyon, a distance of 50 kilometers (31 miles) along Routes 11 and 17 east of Thunder Bay. All are signposted from the highway, and each offers the opportunity to hand-pick some samples (you pay for them by the pound). **Amethyst Mine Panorama** is closest to Thunder Bay (☞ *below*). Also on the site is a gift shop and custom-jewelry store. Tours of the mine run four times daily at 11, 12:30, 3, and 5. Follow Loon Lake Road from Routes 11 and 17, east of Thunder Bay. ⊠ *E. Loon Rd.,* ☎ *807/622–6908.* ☎ *Tour $1.* ⊙ *Mid-May–June and Sept.–mid-Oct., daily 10–5; July and Aug., daily 10–7.*

Thunder Bay

⓻   *67 km (42 mi) southwest of Ouimet Canyon on Trans-Canada Rte. 17.*

Although they amalgamated into one city of 110,000 in 1970, there are still Port Arthur and Fort William sections of Thunder Bay. The city is one of the world's largest grain-handling centers. It has an extraordinary ethnic mix, with 42 nationalities clearly represented, 110 churches, and the largest Finnish population outside Finland. The area has Ontario's best skiing and longest ski season, superb fishing and hunting, unlimited canoe and boating routes, and even mountain climbing. Several amethyst mines have shops in the city. There are also an art gallery, dozens of restaurants, nine shopping malls, and **Old Fort William,** a reconstructed fur-trading fort with 42 historic buildings on a 125-acre site. ⊠ *Broadway Av.,* ☎ *807/577–8461.* ☎ *$10.* ⊙ *mid-May–mid-Oct., daily 10–5.*

Dining and Lodging

$$–$$$ ✕☷ **Valhalla Inn.** The warm lobby is based on old Scandinavian design, with plenty of wood and brass. The large guest rooms have queen-size beds and commissioned prints by area artists. The Nordic dining room offers signature Scandinavian dishes, including smoked salmon and Swedish fish chowder. ⊠ *1 Valhalla Inn Rd., Thunder Bay P7E 6J1,* ☎ *807/577–1121 or 800/964–1121,* ℻ *807/475–4723. 220 rooms. Dining room, indoor pool, sauna, whirlpool, exercise room. AE, D, MC, V.*

Outdoor Activities and Sports

ICE CLIMBING

Alpamayo Exploration and Adventure Services Co. (⊠ Box 2204, Thunder Bay, Ontario P7B 5E8, ☎ 807/344–9636) has one-day trips or expeditions up to five days in length in the Thunder Bay area. Deluxe accommodations in rustic cabins or motels are provided, but meals are not included.

SKIING

Downhill. The highest ski slopes in Ontario are **Candy Mountain Resort** (☎ 807/475–5250) and **Loch Lomond** (☎ 807/475–7787), both just outside Thunder Bay and both with 750 feet of vertical drop. Lift tickets are interchangeable between the two areas. Also close to Thunder Bay are **Big Thunder National Ski Centre** (☎ 807/475–4402), with a vertical drop of 660 feet and a 5-kilometer (3-mile) lighted trail, and served by a double chair and a T-bar; and **Mount Baldy Ski Area** (☎ 807/683–8441), with a vertical drop of 650 feet and served by a double chair and a T-bar.

Kakabeka Falls

(77) *40 km (25 mi) northwest of Thunder Bay off Rtes. 11 and 17.*

Kakabeka Falls, on the Kaministikwia River, drops 154 feet over a limestone ledge into a deep gorge. The falls can be seen from either side and there are large, free parking lots.

EAST ALONG GEORGIAN BAY AND SOUTH TO MANITOULIN ISLAND

On a half-day journey by car you can see the stunning beauty of Georgian Bay and the stark landscape of industrial Sudbury. Highlights include the wildflowers on St. Joseph Island, the rugged simplicity of Matiloulin Island, and the Big Nickel Mine Tour in Sudbury.

St. Joseph Island

(78) *40 km (25 mi) southeast of Sault Ste. Marie via Rte. 17.*

St. Joseph Island is a sparsely settled bit of land about 24 by 30 kilometers (16 by 20 miles) in the mouth of the St. Mary's River connected by causeway and bridge to the mainland. In spring the island is a scented riot of wild lilac, and you're likely to see moose and deer along the quiet side roads. In fur-trading days, **Fort St. Joseph,** established by the British at the southeast tip of the island, guarded the trade route from Montréal to the upper Great Lakes. Today visitors can wander the national historic park on the rounded peninsula on which the fort and commercial buildings once stood and see the outlines and a few aboveground stone ruins of the 42 building sites that have been identified. Free walking tours and a free booklet are available at the visitor center, which is about 30 minutes by car southeast of the Gilbertson Bridge. Call ahead for directions. ☎ *705/246–2664.* ⏲ *Late May–Thanksgiving (mid-Oct.), daily 10–5.*

Manitoulin Island

(79) *149 km (92 mi) east of St. Joseph Island and south of Espanola via Rtes. 17 and 6.*

Manitoulin Island, the world's largest freshwater island, which sits at the top of Lake Huron plugging the mouth of Georgian Bay, is 160 kilometers (100 miles) long and varies in width from 3 to 64 kilometers (2 to 40 miles). The island is pretty and rugged, with granite outcrops, forests, meadows, rivers, and rolling countryside. Only 20% of the land is arable, and much of the rest is used for grazing sheep and cattle. Yachters rate the waters around the islands among the best in the world, and hunters and fishermen have taken advantage of the island's riches for generations. Hikes and exploration could easily turn this "side trip" into a week-long stay. For the most part it has not been ravaged by time and human incursions. Archaeological digs on Manitoulin Island have produced traces of human habitation that are more than 30,000 years old, making them the oldest on the North American continent. There is no interim record of people living on the island until explorer Samuel de Champlain met some island residents in 1650. The towns on the island, such as Little Current (closest to the mainland), Sheguiandah, and Wikwemikong, are simple and picturesque.

Little Current–Howland Centennial Museum, about 18 kilometers (12 miles) south of Little Current, in the village of Sheguiandah on Route 6, displays local native and pioneer artifacts. ✉ *Rte. 6,* ☎ *705/368–*

2367. ☒ $1.50. ⊙ June–mid-Sept., daily 10–4:30; Thanksgiving (mid-Oct.), Sat.–Mon. 10–4:30.

At the extreme eastern end of the island is the Indian settlement of **Wikwemikong.** One of Manitoulin's most colorful events is the Wikwemikong Pow Wow, held on Civic Holiday (the first Monday in August) weekend. Dancers accompanied by drummers and singers compete for prizes while performing the steps of their ancestors.

You can also reach Manitoulin Island, especially if you are heading up the Bruce Peninsula from southern Ontario, by ferry. The **MV Chi-Cheemaun,** connects the picturesque town of Tobermory, at the northern tip of the peninsula, with South Baymouth on the island. The trip takes 2 hours, 45 minutes each way. There are four sailings in each direction daily between mid-June and Labor Day, and three during the spring and fall. Reservations are advised. ☒ Ontario Northland Marine Services, 343 8th St. E, Owen Sounds, N4K 1L3, ☎ 519/596–2511 or 800/265–3163. ☒ One-way $10.50, plus $23 per car.

Sudbury

80 60 km (40 mi) east of Espanola on Trans-Canada Rte. 17.

The mining town of Sudbury used to bear the brunt of frequent unkind jokes. After all, didn't the U.S. astronauts go there to train in the type of terrain they were likely to encounter on the moon? Today, the Greening of Sudbury, a student planting project, and other renovations have given this clean city of 110,000 a face-lift. There are concerts in the park, art centers, and cruises on Lake Ramsey, the largest freshwater lake inside city limits in North America. Despite these attractions, Sudbury remains a mining town. The western world's two largest nickel producers, International Nickel Company (Inco) and Falconbridge, are the mainstays of the local economy.

Northern Ontario's greatest tourism magnet, **Science North,** opened in 1984. This hands-on science museum is housed in two snowflake-shape buildings that cling to a rocky ledge of the shore of Lake Ramsey. Lie on a bed of nails, create a soapstone carving, or make your own hurricane or snowstorm. At every turn, eager museum staff answer questions and encourage participation in the dozens of laboratories. ☒ 100 Ramsey Lake Rd., ☎ 705/522–3701 or 800/461-4898. ☒ Museum and IMAX theater $8.50. ⊙ Daily 10–5.

The **Big Nickel,** a 30-foot replica of the 1951 Canadian commemorative coin, has been synonymous with Sudbury for almost three decades. It stands on a barren hillside on the west side of the city, overlooking Inco's smokestacks. Near the Big Nickel is the entrance to the **Big Nickel Mine.** At 73 feet, it is one of the shallowest mines in the area. Science North (☞ above) offers tours of the mine in summer. Visitors are given hard hats, coats, and boots and lowered into the mine shaft in a "cage" elevator. In the 437-yard-long drifts, or tunnels, miners demonstrate mining techniques. ☒ Rte. 17 and Big Nickel Mine Rd., ☎ 705/673–5659 or 705/522–3701. ☒ $8.50; admission package to Science North, the IMAX theater, and Big Nickel Mine available. ⊙ Tour May–Labor Day, daily 9–6.

The 2½-hour **Path of Discovery Tour** bus leaves from the Big Nickel and Science North several times daily. It stops at the spot where a railroad worker discovered copper and nickel ores 4 kilometers (2½ miles) west of the townsite in 1884. The tour also goes to the edge of the Sudbury Basin, a massive indentation in the landscape created 2 billion years ago by a meteorite, a volcanic eruption, or a combination of the two.

The event created an elliptical depression 59 kilometers (40 miles) long and 27 kilometers (18 miles) wide. The tour visits Sudbury's oldest mine, historic sites in Copper Cliff, and the smelter and super stack at Inco, the world's largest integrated nickel mining, smelting, and refining complex. ☎ *705/673–5659 or 705/522–3701.* ✉ *$11.* ☉ *Daily 10–5.*

FROM COCHRANE TO MOOSONEE AND MOOSE FACTORY ISLAND

For many people, these northern outposts of Moosonee and Moose Factory are simply flyover land, but you can find undiscovered Canada here. The terrain is densely packed with pines; moose and bear are common. Nearby lies the expansive, awe-inspiring James Bay.

Cochrane

㉛ *400 km (250 mi) north of Sudbury via Rtes. 17 east and 11 north.*

Cochrane is the connection point for reaching Ontario's gateway to the Arctic, Moose Factory and Moosonee, at the southern end of James Bay. There's train service to Cochrane from Toronto or North Bay. Although you can fly to Moosonee via Air Creebec (✉ Timmons Airport, R.R. 4, Timmons, Ontario P4N 7C3, ☎ 705/264–9521 or 800/567–6567), which has service from Timmins, Ontario Northland's (✉ 65 Front St. W, Toronto, Ontario M5J 1E6, ☎ 416/314–

★ 3750) *Polar Bear Express* train is the more popular and more nostalgia-inducing option. Every day except Friday from late June to Labor Day, the *Polar Bear* leaves Cochrane at 8:30 AM and arrives at Moosonee just before 1 PM and departs Moosonee at 5:15 PM and returns to Cochrane by 9:20 PM. Meals, light lunches, and snacks are available in the snack car. It's a 20-minute boat ride from Moosonee aboard the *Polar Princess* to Moose Factory Island. Passengers then transfer to a bus for a guided island tour (☞ *below*).

Dining and Lodging

If you plan to take the *Polar Bear Express* train, you'll probably need to stay over in Cochrane. There are seven motels in and around the town. Not all have restaurant facilities, but they are geared to early wake-up calls for guests taking the train and late check-ins for those returning from the excursion. The three largest are 🏨 **Westway Motor Motel** (✉ 21 1st St., Cochrane, POL 1CO, ☎ 705/272–4285, FAX 705/272–4429), 🏨 **Cochrane Station Inn** (✉ 200 Railway St., Cochrane, POL 1CO, ☎ 705/272–3500, FAX 705/272–5713), and 🏨 **Chimo Motel** (✉ Box 2326, Cochrane, POL 1CO, ☎ 705/272–6555, FAX 705/272–5666).

Moose Factory

㉜ *300 km (200 mi) north of Cochrane via Rtes. 11 and 634.*

Moose Factory Island, one of a number in the delta of the Moose River, is 8 kilometers (5 miles) long and just over a kilometer wide. The island was the site of the second Hudson's Bay Company trading post, established in 1672 on what was then called Hayes Island, 24 kilometers (16 miles) up the Moose River from James Bay. It was captured by the French in 1686 and renamed Fort St. Louis. Contrary to popular myth, the holes in the floor of **St. Thomas Anglican Church** (✉ Front Rd., ☎ 705/658–4800) are to let floodwater *out* and to ventilate the foundation. When the church was being built in 1864, the foundation floated a short distance in a spring flood, but the church itself has never floated anywhere. The altar cloths and lectern hangings are of moose hide decorated with beads.

The Hudson's Bay—now known as the North West Company after the group of fur traders who competed against the Bay in the 19th century—post is a modern building. Beside it is the 1850 **Hudson's Bay Staff House** in which are sold animal pelts, carvings, snowshoes, gloves, slippers, and beadwork.

The **Blacksmith's Shop** in Centennial Park on Moose Factory Island isn't the oldest wooden building in Ontario, but the stone forge inside it may be the oldest "structure" in the province. The original shop was built in the late 1600s but moved back from the riverbank in 1820. The forge stones had to be transported a long distance and were disassembled and rebuilt at the present location. In summer an apprentice smith runs the forge and explains its operation.

Moosonee

83 *2 km (1 mi) from Moose Factory; 24 km (14 mi) from James Bay.*

Moosonee is Ontario's only tidal port; summer tides average 5 feet. The community came into existence only in 1903, when the Revillon Frères Trading Company of France established a post to compete with the Hudson's Bay Company. It wasn't until the Ontario Northland Railway arrived in 1932 that the region's population began to catch up to that of Moose Factory. The **Moosonee visitor center** (⊠ Ferguson Rd. at 1st St., ☎ 705/336–2364) is in a small, one-story office building. Next door is a theater in which free videos on wildlife and natural and cultural history are shown. Down Revillon Road is the modern **Ministry of Natural Resources Interpretive Centre** (☎ 705/336–2489), offering exhibits of regional wildlife and of the area's geological and geographical history. During tourist season, natives open stalls on Revillon Road to sell handcrafts ranging from moccasins and buckskin vests to jewelry, beadwork, and wood and stone carvings.

Dining and Lodging

$$$ ✕🏨 **Polar Bear Lodge, Moosonee Lodge.** Both face the Moose River. Their rates are high for the caliber of accommodation offered, but these are the only choices. Both hotels serve meals, but alcohol is available only during the dinner hour, and only to those dining at the hotel. ⊠ *mailing address for both, 65 Enterprise Rd., Rexdale, Ontario M9W 1C4; Moosonee Lodge, ⊠ Revillon St., Moosonee, ☎ 705/336–2351, FAX 705/336–2773; Polar Bear Lodge, ☎ 705/336–2345, FAX 705/336–2185. Polar Bear Lodge, 28 rooms; Moosonee Lodge, 21 rooms. Restaurant. MC, V.*

Timmins

84 *144 km (90 mi) southwest of Cochrane on Rtes. 11 and 101.*

The mining center of **Timmins** (population 46,600) prides itself on being the largest city in Canada (in area, that is, not population). Despite its vastness, there's not much to see in Timmins, except for one of Canada's few underground mine tours. Visitors dress in full mining attire for the 2½-hour tour of the old Hollinger gold workings. Surface attractions include a headframe, a prospector's trail with a view of mineral outcrops and ore samples, and a refurbished miners' house. The road to the tour site, near downtown Timmins, is well marked. ⊠ *Timmins Underground Gold Mine Tour, Park Rd. off Hwy. 101, ☎ 705/267–6222. ☜ $16; winter rates reduced up to 50%; discount coupons* *available.* ☉ *Tours mid-May–late Oct., daily at 10:30 and 1:30; Nov.–May, Wed.–Sun., call for precise times.*

ONTARIO A TO Z

Arriving and Departing

By Car

The **Macdonald–Cartier Freeway,** known as Highway 401, is Ontario's major highway link. It runs from Windsor in the southwest through Toronto, along the north shore of Lake Ontario, and along the north shore of the St. Lawrence River to the Québec border west of Montréal. The **Trans-Canada Highway** follows the west bank of the Ottawa River from Montréal to Ottawa and on to North Bay. From North Bay to Nipigon at the northern tip of Lake Superior, there are two Trans-Canada highways, and from just west of Thunder Bay to Kenora, near the Manitoba border, another two. For 24-hour road-condition information anywhere in Ontario, call ☎ 416/235–1110.

By Plane

Toronto, the area's chief city, is served by most major international airlines. (☞ Chapter 6.)

By Train

Ontario is served by cross-Canada **VIA Rail** (☎ 416/366–8411; outside Toronto, Kingston, London, Windsor, Hamilton, 800/361–1235; within those cities check local listings) and connects with **Amtrak** (☎ 800/872–7245) service at Windsor (Detroit) and Fort Erie (Buffalo).

Getting Around

For information on Toronto travel options, *see* Chapter 6.

By Car

Ontario is a no-fault province, and minimum liability insurance is $200,000. If you're driving across the Ontario border, either bring the policy or the vehicle registration forms and a free Canadian Non-Resident Insurance Card from your insurance agent. If you're driving a borrowed car, also bring a letter of permission signed by the owner. Driving motorized vehicles (including boats, all-terrain vehicles, and motorbikes) while impaired by alcohol is taken seriously in Ontario and results in heavy fines or imprisonment, or both. You can be convicted for refusing to take a Breathalyzer test. Radar warning devices are not permitted in Ontario even if they are turned off. Police can seize them on the spot, and heavy fines may be imposed. Seat belts must be worn by adults and children weighing more than 40 pounds, if the car is designed with them; infants from birth to 20 pounds must travel in a rear-facing child restraint system; children 20–40 pounds must travel in a safety seat.

Studded tires and window coatings that do not allow a clear view of the vehicle interior are forbidden in Ontario. Right turns on red lights are permitted unless otherwise noted. Pedestrians crossing at designated crosswalks have the right of way.

By Taxi

Cabs are plentiful in Ontario's major cities.

Contacts and Resources

B&B Listing

A comprehensive bed-and-breakfast guide listing about 200 establishments is published by the **Federation of Ontario Bed and Breakfast Accommodation** (✉ Box 437, 253 College St., Toronto, Ontario M5T 1R5, ☎ 416/964–2566).

Emergencies

Dial 911 for **police, fire,** or **ambulance** anywhere in Ontario.

Outdoor Activities and Sports

CAMPING

Peak season in Ontario's parks is June through August, and it is advised that you reserve a campsite, if reservations are accepted, by phone (☎ 416/314–0998 or 800/668–2746), by mail, or in person; sites can be guaranteed by using a Visa or MasterCard credit card. All provincial parks have some sites available on a first-come, first-served basis. In an effort to avoid overcrowding on canoe routes and hiking or backpacking trails in such major canoeing parks as Algonquin, Quetico, Killarney, and Frontenac, daily quotas have been established governing the number of people permitted in the parks. In these parks interior permits can be reserved ahead of time. In the four above-mentioned parks and in Lake Superior Provincial Park, cans and bottles are permitted only in the organized car campground areas. For more detailed information on parks and campgrounds in Ontario, write to the **Ministry of Culture, Tourism and Recreation** (☞ Contacts and Resources *in* Ontario A to Z, *below*) for a free camping guide.

DOGSLEDDING

Burton Penner (✉ Box 151, Vermilion Bay, Ontario POV 2VO, ☎ 807/227–5593) of Vermilion Bay, 91 kilometers (57 miles) east of Kenora (490 kilometers, or 300 miles, west of Thunder Bay), offers guided dogsled tours into the wilderness, overnighting in an outpost cabin or heated wall tent. Rates run from $300 per person for a one-night trip, everything included, but are reduced to $250 per person for a group of three. Longer trips are also available.

FISHING

Licenses are required for fishing in Ontario and may be purchased from the Ministry of Natural Resources district offices and from most sporting goods stores, outfitters, and resorts. Seasons and catch limits change annually and some districts infringe closed seasons. Restrictions are published in *Summary of the Fishing Regulations,* free from the Ministry of Natural Resources (✉ Public Information Centre, Macdonald Block, Room M1-73, 900 Bay St., Toronto, Ontario M7A 1W3, ☎ 416/314–2000).

Fishing Lodges. There are about 500 fishing resorts and lodges listed in the current catalogue of fishing packages available free from the **Ministry of Culture, Tourism and Recreation** (☞ Visitor Information, *below*). The establishments listed are not hotels that happen to be located near bodies of water that contain fish, but businesses designed to make sport fishing available to their guests. To that end, each property offers all the accoutrements of the modern fisherman, including boats, motors, guides, float planes, and freezers. Rates at these lodges are hefty.

HIKING

Call ☎ 800/665–4453 or **Hike Ontario** (☎ 416/462–7362) for information about hiking in the province.

RAFTING

A growing number of companies in Eastern Ontario offer packages ranging from half-day to week-long trips between May and September. **River-Run** (⊠ Box 179, Beachburg, Ontario K0J 1C0, ☎ 800/267–8504), a 90-minute drive west of Ottawa, has a one-day tour on the Ottawa River. **Owl Rafting** (⊠ Box 29, Forester's Falls, Ontario K0J 1V0, ☎ 613/646–2263 or 613/238–7238) offers half-day excursions on the nearby Ottawa and Madawaska rivers. **Esprit Rafting Adventures** (⊠ Box 463, Pembroke, Ontario K8A 6X7, ☎ 819/683–3241) offers trips such as rafting on the Ottawa River, canoeing in Algonquin Park, or mountain biking in the Upper Ottawa Valley.

SKIING

For a recorded snow report, call ☎ 416/314–0998.

SNOWMOBILING

Overnight guided excursions are available in Haliburton Highlands/Algonquin Park (☞ Haliburton, *above*) and out of Kenora. At Kenora, **Halley's Camps** (⊠ Box 608, Kenora, Ontario P9N 3X6, ☎ 807/224–6531; in Ontario and Manitoba, 800/465–3325) has guided all-inclusive excursions on wilderness trails to outpost camps for three to six nights.

Visitor Information

Ontario has a wealth of excellent and free tourist information. The best source is the **Ministry of Culture, Tourism and Recreation** (⊠ 77 Bloor St. W, Toronto, Ontario M7A 2R9; in Canada and the U.S., except the Yukon, Northwest Territories, and AK, ☎ 800/668–2746).

Ontario's principal regional and municipal tourist offices are: **Greater Hamilton, Regional Municipality of Hamilton–Wentworth** (⊠ 127 King St. E, Hamilton, Ontario L8N 1B1, ☎ 905/546–2666 or 800/263–8590), **Kingston District Chamber of Commerce** (⊠ 209 Wellington St., Kingston, Ontario K7K 2Y6, ☎ 613/548–4453 or 613/548–4415), **Kitchener and Waterloo Chamber of Commerce** (⊠ Box 2367, 67 King St. E, Kitchener, Ontario N2H 6L4, ☎ 519/576–5000, FAX 519/742–4760), **Midland Chamber of Commerce** (⊠ 208 King St., Box 158, Midland, Ontario L4R 4K8, ☎ 705/526–7884), **Niagara Falls, Canada Visitor and Convention Bureau** (⊠ 5433 Victoria Ave., Niagara Falls, Ontario L2G 3L1, ☎ 905/356–6061 or 800/563–2557), **Ontario Northland** (⊠ 65 Front St. W, Toronto, Ontario M5J 1E6, ☎ 416/314–3750), **Greater Peterborough Chamber of Commerce** (⊠ 175 George St. N, Peterborough, Ontario K9J 3G6, ☎ 705/748–9771), **Peterborough Kawarthas Tourist Bureau** (☎ 705/742–2201), **Sault Ste. Marie Economic Development Corporation** (⊠ 99 Foster Dr., 3rd floor, Sault Ste. Marie, Ontario P6A 5N1, ☎ 705/759–5432), **Tourism Thunder Bay** (⊠ 500 E. Donald St., Thunder Bay, Ontario P7E 5V3, ☎ 807/625–2149), **Convention and Visitors Bureau of Windsor, Essex County, and Pelee Island** (⊠ 333 Riverside Dr. W, Suite 103, Windsor, Ontario N9A 5K4, ☎ 519/255–6530 or 800/265–3633).

8 Montréal

*Montréal is Canada's most romantic
metropolis, an island city that seems to
favor grace and elegance over order
and even prosperity; a city full of
music, art, and joie de vivre.*

By Patricia
Lowe

Updated by
Paul and Julie
Waters

MONTRÉAL IS CANADA'S MOST ROMANTIC
metropolis, an island city that seems to favor
grace and elegance over order and even pros-
perity; a city full of music, art, and joie de vivre. It is rather like the
European capital Vienna—past its peak of power and glory, perhaps,
but still a vibrant and beautiful place full of memories, dreams, and
festivals.

That's not to say Montréal is ready to fade away. It may not be so young
anymore—it celebrated its 350th birthday in 1992—but it remains
Québec's largest city and an important port and financial center. Its
office towers are full of young Québécois entrepreneurs, members of
a new breed who are ready and eager to take on the world.

Montréal is the only French-speaking metropolis in North America and
the second-largest French-speaking city in the world, but it's a toler-
ant place that over the years has made room for millions of immigrants
who speak dozens of languages. Today about 15% of the 3.1 million
people who live in the metropolitan area claim English as their mother
tongue and another 15% claim a language that's neither English nor
French. The city's gentle tolerance has won recognition: Several times
it has been voted one of the world's most livable cities.

The city's grace, however, has been sorely tested in recent decades. Since
1976, Montréal has twice weathered the election of a separatist provincial government, a law banning all languages but French on virtually
all public signs and billboards, and four referendums on the future of
Québec and Canada.

The latest chapter in this long constitutional drama was the cliffhanger
referendum on Québec independence on October 30, 1995. In that show-
down between federalists and independents, Québécois voters chose
to remain part of Canada, but by the thinnest of possible margins. More
than 98% of eligible voters participated, and the final province-wide
result was 49.42% in favor of independence and 50.58% against. In
fact, 60% of the province's francophones voted in favor of establishing an independent Québec. But Montréal, where most of the province's
anglophones and immigrants live, bucked the separatist trend. Voters
in the metropolitan region voted nearly 70% against independence. And
the drama continues. The separatist Parti-Québécois still controls the
provincial government and has a new and revered leader in Lucien
Bouchard, so it's likely there will be another referendum in 1997. And
there's no respite in Ottawa. The Bloc-Québécois, an allied separatist
party that Mr. Bouchard founded, dominates the official opposition
in Canada's federal parliament. All this has prompted some Montrealers to begin talking about seceding from Québec and forming their
own province or city-state.

But in spite of uncertainty about the future, most Montrealers still delight in their city, which has weathered all these storms with aplomb.
It is, after all, a city that's used to turmoil. It was founded by the French,
conquered by the British, and occupied by the Americans. It has a long
history of reconciling contradictions, and even today is a city of contrasts. The flamboyant glass office tower of La Maison des Coopérants,
for example, soars above a Gothic-style Anglican cathedral that squats
gracefully in its shadow. The neo-Gothic facade of the Basilique Notre-
Dame-de-Montréal glares across Place d'Armes at the pagan temple
that is the head office of the Bank of Montréal. And while pilgrims
still climb the steps to the Oratoire St-Joseph's on their knees on one

side of the mountain, thousands of their fellow Catholics line up to get into the very chic Casino de Montréal on the other side—certainly not what the earnest French settlers who founded Montréal envisioned when they landed on the island in May 1642.

Those 54 pious men and women under the leadership of Paul Chomedy Sieur de Maisonneuve, hoped to do nothing less than create a new Christian society. They named their settlement Ville-Marie in honor of the mother of Christ and set out to convert the Indians. Those early years were marked by the heroism of two remarkable women—Jeanne Mance, a French noblewoman who arrived with de Maisonneuve, and Marguerite Bourgeoys, who came 11 years later. Jeanne Mance, working alone, established the Hôpital Hôtel Dieu de St-Joseph, still one of the city's major hospitals. In 1659, she invited members of a French order of nuns to help her in her efforts. That order, the Religieuses Hospitalières de St-Joseph, now has its motherhouse in Montréal and is the oldest nursing group in the Americas. Marguerite Bourgeoys, with Jeanne Mance's help, established the colony's first school and taught both French and Indian children how to read and write. Bourgeoys founded the Congrégation de Notre Dame, a teaching order that still has schools in Montréal, across Canada, and around the world. She was canonized a saint by the Roman Catholic church in 1982.

Piety wasn't the settlement's only raison d'être, however. Ville Marie was ideally located to be a commercial success, as well. It was at the confluence of two major transportation routes—the St. Lawrence and Ottawa rivers—and fur trappers used the town as a staging point for their expeditions. But the city's religious roots were never forgotten. Until 1854, long after the French lost possession of the city, the island of Montréal remained the property of the Sulpicians, an aristocratic order of French priests. The Sulpicians were responsible for administering the colony and for recruiting colonists. They still run the Basilique Notre-Dame-de-Montréal, and are still responsible for training priests for the Roman Catholic archdiocese.

The French regime in Canada ended with the Seven Years' War—what Americans call the French and Indian Wars. British troops took Québec City in 1759 and Montréal fell less than a year later. The Treaty of Paris ceded all New France to Britain in 1763, and soon English and Scottish settlers poured into Montréal to take advantage of the city's geography and economic potential. By 1832, Montréal was a leading colonial capital of business, finance, and transportation, and had grown far beyond the walls of the old settlement. Much of that business and financial leadership has since moved to Toronto, the upstream rival Montrealers love to hate.

Pleasures and Pastimes

Churches

Montréal's two most popular and most enduring attractions are a pair of monuments dedicated to a Jewish couple who lived 2,000 years ago—the oratory dedicated to St. Joseph on the north side of Mont-Royal and the Basilique Notre-Dame-de-Montréal dedicated to his wife in the heart of the old city. But these are just two of the dozens of beautiful churches built in the days when the Québécois were among the most devout adherents to the Roman Catholic church. In fact, Mark Twain, novelist and anticleric, once complained (or perhaps boasted) that you couldn't throw a rock in Montréal without breaking a church window. Other gems of ecclesiastical architecture are St. Patrick's Basilica, the Jesuit-run Le Gésu, the Chapelle Notre Dame des Lourdes,

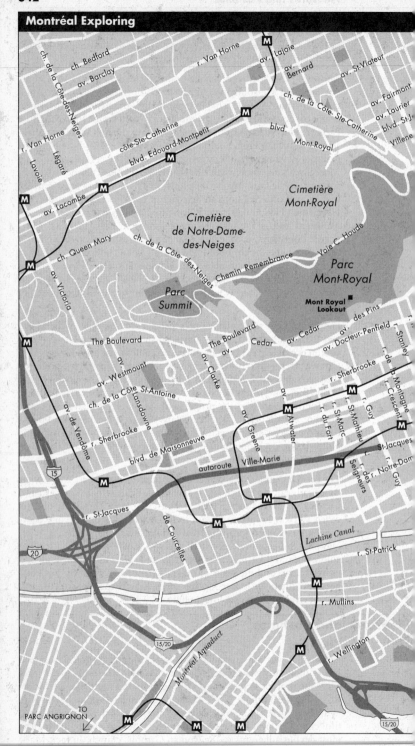

ch. Bedford
ch. de la Côte-des-Neiges
av. Barclay
r. Van Horne
av. Lajoie
av. St-Viateur
av. Bernard
r. Van Horne
Légaré
Lavoie
ch. de la Côte-Ste-Catherine
av. Fairmont
av. Laurier
blvd. St-J
côte-Ste-Catherine
blvd. Edouard-Montpetit
blvd. Mont-Royal
Villene
av. Lacombe
Cimetière Mont-Royal
av. Victoria
ch. Queen Mary
ch. de la Côte-des-Neiges
Cimetière de Notre-Dame-des-Neiges
Chemin Remembrance
Voie C. Houde
Parc Mont-Royal
Parc Summit
Mont Royal Lookout
The Boulevard
The Boulevard
av. Cedar
av. des Pins
av. Cedar
Cedar
av. Docteur-Penfield
r. Stanley
av. Westmount
av. Clarke
r. Sherbrooke
r. de la Montagne
ch. de la Côte St-Antoine
Lansdowne
r. Guy
r. Crescent
av. de Vendôme
r. Sherbrooke
av. Greene
r. St-Mathieu
r. St-Marc
r. du Fort
blvd. de Maisonneuve
av. Atwater
autoroute Ville-Marie
r. des Seigneurs
St-Jacques
r. Notre-Dam
r. St-Jacques
de Courcelles
Lachine Canal
r. St-Patrick
15
20
r. Mullins
15/20
Montréal Aquaduct
r. Wellington
TO PARC ANGRIGNON
15/20

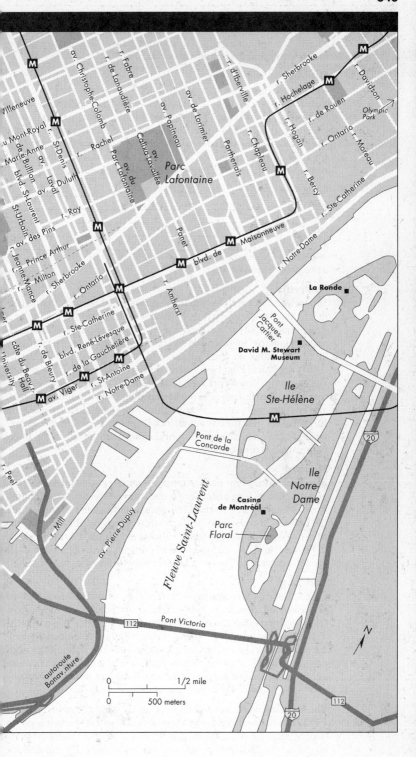

and in the distant north end of the city, the Église de la Visitation, the oldest extant church on the island and a jewel box of baroque decoration. But even humble parish churches in working-class neighborhoods are as grand as some cathedrals.

Dining

Montrealers are passionate about food. They love to dine on classic dishes in restaurants like Les Halles and the Beaver Club, or swoon over culinary innovations in places like Toqué, but they can get equally passionate about humbler fare. They'll argue with some heat about where to get the juiciest smoked meat, the crispiest barbecued chicken, and the soggiest *stimés* (steamed hot dogs). The city has more than 4,500 restaurants, representing more than 75 ethnic groups.

CATEGORY	COST*
$$$$	over $30
$$$	$20–$30
$$	$10–$20
$	$5–$10

per person without tax (combined GST of 7% and provincial tax of 4% on all meals), service, or drinks

Festivals

Summer and fall are just one long succession of festivals that begins in late June with a 10-day Jazz Festival when as many as a million fans descend on the city to hear more than 1,000 musicians, including giants like guitarist John Scofield and tenor saxophonist Joe Lovano, play in concert halls, on street stages, and on the sidewalks. In August there's the World Film Festival and the lively Just for Laughs Comedy Festival in the Vieux-Port area. Other festivals celebrate beer, alternative films, French-language music and song from around the world, and international cuisine. Every Saturday in June and every Sunday in July the skies over the city waterfront erupt in color and flame as fireworks teams from around the world compete for prizes in the International Fireworks Competition.

History

Montréal is one of the oldest European settlements in North America, and traces of its long history are found everywhere. Some buildings in Vieux-Montréal date to the 17th century. Other parts of the city are full of wonderful examples of Victorian architecture. Museums like the McCord Museum of Canadian History, the Musée d'Archéologie de la Pointe-à-Callière, and the Stewart Museum in the Old Fort on Ile Ste-Hélène attest to the city's fascination with its past.

Lodging

On the island of Montréal alone there are rooms available in every type of accommodation, from world-class luxury hotels to youth hostels, from student dormitories to budget executive motels. Keep in mind that during peak season (May–August) it may be difficult to find a bed without reserving, and most, but not all, hotels raise their prices. Rates often drop from mid-November to early April. Throughout the year a number of the better hotels have two-night, three-day, double-occupancy packages that offer substantial discounts.

The Ritz-Carlton Kempinski has been setting standards of luxury since 1912, and the nearby Westin Mont-Royal is one of the best modern luxury hotels in the country. But the city also offers more intimate charm, at the Château Versailles on rue Sherbrooke, for example, or the tiny Auberge les Passants du Sans Soucy in the heart of Vieux-Montréal.

CATEGORY	COST*
$$$$	over $160
$$$	$120–$160
$$	$85–$120
$	under $85

All prices are for a standard double room, excluding an optional service charge.

Nightlife

Montréal's reputation as a fun place to visit for a night on the town dates at least to Prohibition days in the United States, when hordes of thirsty Americans would flood the city every weekend to eat, drink, and be merry. The city has dozens of discos, bistros, show-bars, and jazz clubs, not to mention hundreds of bars where you can go to argue about sports, politics, and religion until the early hours of the morning. Much of the action takes place along rue St-Denis and adjacent streets in the eastern part of the city or rues Bishop, Crescent, and de la Montagne in the downtown area. The night scene is constantly shifting—last year's hot spot can quickly become this year's dive. The best and easiest way to figure out what's in is to stroll down rue St-Denis or rue Bishop at about 10:30 and look for the place with the longest lineup and the rudest doorman.

Shopping

The development of the Underground City has made shopping a year-round sport in Montréal. That vast complex linked by underground passageways and the Métro includes two major department stores, at least a dozen huge shopping malls, and more than 1,000 boutiques. Add to this Montréal's status as one of the fur capitals of the world, and you have a city that was born to be shopped.

EXPLORING MONTRÉAL

The Ile de Montréal is an island in the St. Lawrence River, roughly equidistant (256 kilometers, or 160 miles) from Lake Ontario and the point where the river widens into the Gulf of St. Lawrence. The island is 51 kilometers (32 miles) long and 14 kilometers (9 miles) wide and is bounded on the north by the narrow Rivière des Prairies and on the south by the St. Lawrence. The only rise in the landscape is the 764-foot Mont-Royal, which gave the island its name and which residents call simply "the mountain." The city of Montréal is the oldest and by far the largest of the 24 municipalities on the island, which together make up the Communauté Urbaine de Montréal (the Montréal Urban Community), the regional government that runs, among other things, the police department and the transit system. There is a belt of off-island suburbs on the South Shore of the St. Lawrence and just to the north across the narrow Rivière-des Prairies, on an island of its own, is Laval, a suburb that has grown to be the second-largest city in the province. But the countryside is never far away. The pastoral Eastern Townships, first settled by Loyalists fleeing the American Revolution, are less than an hour's drive away, and the Laurentians, an all-season playground full of lakes and ski hills, are even closer.

For a good overview of the city, head for the lookout at the Chalet du Mont-Royal. You can drive most of the way, park, and walk ½ kilometer (¼ mile) or hike all the way up from chemin de la Côte-des-Neiges or avenue des Pins. If you look directly out—southeast—from the belvedere, at the foot of the hill will be the McGill University campus and, surrounding it, the skyscrapers of downtown Montréal. Just beyond, along the banks of the river, are the stone houses of Vieux-

Montréal. Hugging the South Shore on the other side of the river are the Iles Ste-Hélène and Notre-Dame, sites of La Ronde amusement park, the Biosphere, the Casino de Montréal, acres of parkland, and the Lac de l'Ile Notre-Dame public beach—all popular excursions. To the east is rue St-Denis and the Latin Quarter with its rows of French and ethnic restaurants, bistros, chess hangouts, designer boutiques, antiques shops, and art galleries. Even farther east you can see the flying-saucer-shaped Olympic Stadium with its leaning tower.

Montréal is easy to explore. Streets, subways, and bus lines are clearly marked. The city is divided by a grid of streets roughly aligned east–west and north–south. (This grid is tilted about 40 degrees off—to the left of—true north, so west is actually southwest and so on.) North–south street numbers begin at the St. Lawrence River and increase as you head north. East–west street numbers begin at boulevard St-Laurent, which divides Montréal into east and west halves. The city is not so large that seasoned walkers can't see all the districts around the base of Mont-Royal on foot. Nearly everything else is easily accessible by the city's quiet, clean, and very safe bus and Métro (subway) system.

Great Itineraries

In Prohibition days, thirsty Americans often came to Montréal for one-night jaunts, and were happy with the experience, but getting any real feel for this bilingual, multicultural city takes a lot longer. An ideal stay would be seven days, but a modern visitor should spend at least three days walking and soaking up the atmosphere. That's enough time to visit Mont-Royal, explore Vieux-Montréal, do some shopping downtown, and perhaps visit the Parc Olympique. It also includes enough nights for an evening of bar-hopping on rue St-Denis or rue Crescent and another for a long, luxurious dinner at a restaurant like Nuances or Toqué.

IF YOU HAVE 3 DAYS
Any visit to Montréal should start with Mont-Royal. The mountain is Montréal's most enduring symbol and the view from the big, flag-stoned terrace in front of the Chalet du Mont-Royal is both magnificent and helpful for orientation. Afterward wander down to avenue des Pins and then through McGill University to the Centre-Ville (downtown). Make an effort to stop at the Musée des Beaux-Arts and St. Patrick's Basilica. Day 2 should be spent exploring Vieux-Montréal, with special emphasis on the Basilique Notre-Dame-de-Montréal and the Musée d'Archéologie de Pointe de la Pointe-à-Callière. On Day 3 you can either visit the Parc Olympique (recommended for children) or stroll through the Quartier Latin (Latin Quarter).

IF YOU HAVE 5 DAYS
Once again start with a visit to Parc Mont-Royal, but instead of going downtown after you've viewed the city from the Chalet du Mont-Royal, visit the Oratoire St-Joseph. You should still have enough time to visit the Musée des Beaux-Arts before dinner. That will leave time on Day 2 to get in more shopping as you explore downtown with perhaps a visit to the Centre Canadien d'Architecture. Spend all of Day 3 in Vieux-Montréal, and on Day 4 stroll through the Quartier Latin. On Day 5, visit the Parc Olympique and then do one of three things: visit the islands, take a ride on the Lachine Rapids, or revisit some of the sights you missed in Vieux-Montréal or downtown.

IF YOU HAVE 7 DAYS
A week will give you enough time to do the five-day itinerary, expanding your Vieux-Montréal explorations to two days and adding a shopping spree on rue Chabanel and a visit to the Casino.

Vieux-Montréal (Old Montréal)

Numbers in the text below correspond to numbers in the margin and on the maps.

When Montréal's first European settlers arrived by river in 1642 they stopped to build their houses just below the treacherous Lachine Rapids that blocked the way upstream. They picked a site near an old Iroquois settlement on the bank of the river nearest Mont-Royal. In the mid-17th century Montréal consisted of a handful of wood houses clustered around a pair of stone buildings, all flimsily fortified by a wood stockade. For the next three centuries this district—bounded by rues Berri and McGill on the east and west, rue St-Jacques on the north, and the river to the south—was the financial and political heart of the city. Government buildings, the largest church, the stock exchange, the main market, and the port were there. The narrow but relatively straight streets were cobblestone and lined with solid, occasionally elegant houses, office buildings, and warehouses—also made of stone. Exiting the city meant using one of four gates through the thick stone wall that protected against native people and marauding European powers. Montréal quickly grew past the bounds of its fortifications, however, and by World War I the center of the city had moved toward Mont-Royal. The new heart of Montréal became Dominion Square (now Square Dorchester). For the next two decades Vieux-Montréal, as it became known, was gradually abandoned, the warehouses and offices emptied. In 1962 the city began studying ways to revitalize Vieux-Montréal, and a decade of renovations and restorations began.

Today, Vieux-Montréal is a center of cultural life and municipal government. Most of the summer activities revolve around Place Jacques-Cartier, which becomes a pedestrian mall with street performers and outdoor cafés. This lovely square is a good place to view the annual fireworks festival at La Ronde, and it's adjacent to the Vieux-Port, one of the city's most popular recreation grounds. Classical music concerts are staged all year long at Basilique Notre-Dame, which has one of the finest organs in North America, and English-language plays are staged in the Centaur Theatre in the old stock-exchange building. This district has six museums devoted to history, religion, and arts.

A Good Walk

Take the Métro to the Square-Victoria Station and follow the signs to the **Centre de Commerce Mondial de Montréal** ①, one of the most pleasant enclosed spaces in Montréal, with a fountain and frequent art exhibits. Exit on the east side of the complex and turn right on rue St-Pierre, walk south to rue St-Jacques, and turn left. This was once the financial heart, not just of Montréal, but of Canada. As you walk east, note the fine decorative stone flourishes—grapevines, nymphs, angels, and goddesses—on the Victorian office buildings. This part of Vieux-Montréal can seem almost tomblike on weekends when the business and legal offices in the district close down, but don't worry, things get livelier as you get closer to the waterfront.

Stop at **Place d'Armes** ②, a square that was the site of battles with the Iroquois in the 1600s and later became the center of Montréal's "Upper Town." There are calèches at the south end of the square; the north side is dominated by the **Bank of Montréal** ③, an impressive building with Corinthian columns, built in 1847 and remodeled by renowned architects McKim, Mead & White in 1905. The soaring towers of the **Basilique Notre-Dame-de-Montréal** ④, one of the most beautiful and ornate churches in North America, dominate the south end of Place d'Armes. The low, more retiring stone building behind a wall to the west of the basilica is the **Vieux Séminaire** ⑤, Montréal's oldest building. This elegant example of 17th-century Québec architecture is unfortunately closed to the public. Moving back toward the basilica, visit **rue St-Sulpice,** one of the the first streets in Montréal. On the eastern side of the street a plaque marks the spot where Jeanne Mance built Hôpital Hôtel-Dieu, the city's first hospital, in 1644. Now cross rue St-Sulpice—the Art Deco **Aldred Building** sits on the far left corner—and take rue Notre-Dame Est. One block farther, just past boulevard St-Laurent, on the left, rises the black-glass-sheathed **Palais de Justice** (1971), the main courthouse for the judicial district of Montréal. The large domed building at 155 rue Notre-Dame Est, is the Classical Revival–style **Old Courthouse** ⑥ (1857), now municipal offices. Across the street, at 160 rue Notre-Dame Est, is the **Maison de la Sauvegarde** (1811), one of the oldest houses in the city and now home to the European sausage restaurant, Chez Better (☞ Dining, *below*). The Old Courthouse abuts the small **Place Vauquelin** ⑦, named after the 18th-century naval hero who is memorialized by a statue in its center. North of this square is **Champs-de-Mars,** the former site of a colonial military parade ground and now a public park. The ornate building on the east side of Place Vauquelin is the Second Empire–style **Hôtel de Ville** ⑧, or City Hall, built in 1878. On July 24, 1967, President Charles de Gaulle of France stood on the central balcony here and made his famous *"Vive le Québec libre"* speech.

You are in a perfect spot to explore **Place Jacques-Cartier** ⑨, the square that is the heart of Vieux-Montréal. At the western corner of rue Notre-Dame is the **Greater Montréal Convention and Tourism Bureau** ⑩. Both sides of the square are lined with two- and three-story stone buildings that were originally homes or hotels. In the summer, the one-block **rue St-Amable** ⑪ near the bottom of the square becomes a marketplace for local jewelers, artists, and craftspeople.

Retrace your steps to the north end of Place Jacques-Cartier and continue east on rue Notre-Dame. On the right, at the corner of rue St-Claude, is **Château Ramezay** ⑫, built as the residence of the 11th governor of Montréal, Claude de Ramezay, and now a museum. Continue east to rue Berri. On the corner are two houses from the mid-19th century that have been transformed into the **George-Étienne Cartier Museum** ⑬, honoring the most important French-Canadian statesman of his day and one of the leading figures in founding the Canadian federation in 1867.

When you come out of the museum, walk south on rue Berri to rue St. Paul and then start walking west again toward the center of the city. The first street on your right is rue Bonsecours, one of the oldest in the city. On the corner is the charming Maison du Calvet, now a restaurant and small bed-and-breakfast. Opposite it is the small but beautiful **Chapelle Notre-Dame-de-Bonsecours** ⑭, built by St. Marguerite Bourgeoys, Montréal's first schoolteacher. The long, domed building to the west of the chapel is the **Marché Bonsecours** ⑮ (1845), for many years Montréal's main produce, meat, and fish market, and now municipal offices. The market has been transformed into a cultural center with exhibits on Montréal.

Rue St-Paul is the most fashionable street in Vieux-Montréal. For almost 20 blocks it is lined with restaurants, shops filled with Québécois handicrafts, and nightclubs. In an old stone building on rue St-Paul Ouest is an exhibit that focuses on the very new: **Images du Futur** ⑯ is devoted to interactive art and the information superhighway. Eight blocks west of Place Jacques-Cartier, rue St-Paul leads to **Place Royale** ⑰, the site of the first permanent settlement in Montréal.

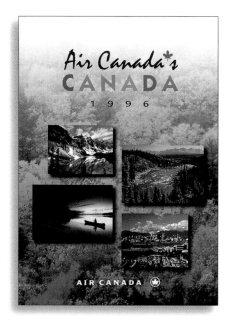

All the best trips start with Fodor's.

Behind the Old Customs House you will find **Pointe-à-Callière** ⑱, a small park that commemorates the settlers' first landing and is the site of **Musée d'Archéologie Pointe-à-Callière,** Montréal's dazzling museum of history and archeology. A 1½-block walk down rue William takes you to the **Youville Stables** ⑲ on the left. These low stone buildings enclosing a garden were originally built as warehouses in 1825 (they never were stables). They now house offices, shops, and Gibby's restaurant (☞ Dining, *below*).

Across rue William from the stables is the old fire station that houses the **Centre d'Histoire de Montréal** ⑳, a museum that chronicles the day-to-day life of Montrealers throughout the years. Now walk back east on rue William and turn right down rue du Port to rue de la Commune. Across the street is the **Vieux-Port-de-Montréal** ㉑. This once seedy area has been transformed into a very pleasant and popular waterfront park, and makes a fitting close to any walk in Vieux-Montréal. If you have time, you can arrange for a harbor excursion or a daring ride on the Lachine Rapids. The Vieux-Port is also home to the **Cinéma IMAX** ㉒, which shows films on a seven-story screen. The impact can be more terrifying than the rapids.

TIMING

If you walk briskly and don't stop, you could get through this route in under an hour. A more realistic and leisurely pace would take about 90 minutes—still without stopping—longer in winter when the streets are icy. The Basilique Notre-Dame is one of Montréal's most famous landmarks and deserves at least a 45-minute visit; Château de Ramezay deserves the same. Pointe-à-Callière could keep an enthusiastic history buff occupied for a whole day, but give it at least two hours.

Sights to See

Numbers in the margin correspond to points of interest on the Vieux Montréal map.

❹ **Basilique Notre-Dame-de-Montréal** (Notre-Dame Basilica). The first church called Notre-Dame was a bark-covered structure built in 1642, the year the first settlers arrived. Three times it was torn down and rebuilt, each time in a different spot, each time larger and more ornate. The present church is an enormous (3,800-seat), neo-Gothic structure that opened in 1829. Its architect was an American Protestant named James O'Donnell, who converted to Catholicism during construction and is buried in the church crypt. The twin towers are 228 feet high, and the western one holds one of North America's largest bells. The interior of the church is neo-Gothic, with stained-glass windows, a stunning vaulted blue ceiling studded with thousands of 24-carat gold stars, and pine and walnut wood carving in traditional Québec style. If the church interior looks familiar, that might be because you've seen it on television. In 1978, Luciano Pavarotti sang a program of Christmas music in the church, which is still often rebroadcast in December in the U.S. With more than 7,000 pipes, the pipe organ is one of the largest on the continent. If you just want to hear the organ roar, drop in for the 11 AM solemn Mass on Sunday and pay special attention to the recessional. Behind the main altar is the Sacré-Coeur Chapel, which was destroyed by fire in 1978 and rebuilt in five different styles. The chapel is often called the Wedding Chapel because of the hundreds of Montrealers who get married in it every year. When pop star Céline Dion married her manager in 1994, however, the lavish and elaborate ceremony was in the main church. Also in the back of the church is a small museum of religious paintings and historical objects. Please note: Notre-Dame is an active house of worship and visitors should dress accordingly. Also, it is advisable to plan your visit around the daily 12:15

PM Mass in the chapel and the 5 PM Mass in the main church. ⊠ *116 rue Notre-Dame Ouest; basilica,* ☎ *514/849–1070; museum, 514/842–2925.* ⊡ *Basilica donation requested, tour free; museum $1.* ☉ *Basilica Labor Day–June 24, daily 7–6, and June 25–Labor Day, daily 7 AM–8 PM; guided tour daily (except Sun. morning) May–June 24, daily 9–4, and June 25–Labor Day, daily 8:30–4:30, and Labor Day–mid-Oct., daily 9–4; museum weekends 9:30–5.*

❶ Centre de Commerce Mondial de Montréal (Montréal World Trade Center). This is one of the most pleasant enclosed spaces in Montréal, with a fountain, frequent art exhibits, and some surprisingly comfortable benches. It also has Montréal's own chunk of the Berlin Wall, complete with colorful grafitti. The center covers a block of the rundown ruelle des Fortifications, a narrow lane that marks the place where the city walls once stood. Developers glassed it in and sandblasted and restored 11 of the 19th-century buildings that lined it. It's home to the Hôtel Inter-Continental (☞ Lodging, *below*), a growing number of boutiques and restaurants, and an imaginative food court. *Métro: Square-Victoria Station and follow signs.*

⓴ Centre d'Histoire de Montréal. This museum uses video games, soundtracks, models, and more than 300 artifacts to re-create the day-to-day life of the ordinary men and women who have lived in Montréal, from the Indians of precolonial time to modern factory workers. Some of the most touching exhibits are the ones depicting family life in Montréal's working-class tenements in the 20th century. ⊠ *335 Place d'Youville,* ☎ *514/872–3207.* ⊡ *$4.50.* ☉ *Tues.–Sun. 10–5.*

⓮ Chapelle Notre-Dame-de-Bonsecours. The indomitable Marguerite Bourgeoys dedicated this chapel to the Virgin Mary in 1657. It became known as a sailor's church, and small wood models of sailing ships hang from the ceiling. In the basement there's a small museum that tells the story of the saint's life with a series of little tableaux. A gift shop sells Marguerite Bourgeoys souvenirs. From the museum you can climb to the rather precarious bell tower (beware of the slippery metal steps in winter) for a fine view of Vieux-Montréal and the port. ⊠ *400 rue St-Paul Est,* ☎ *514/845–9991.* ⊡ *Museum $2.* ☉ *Museum May–Nov., Tues.–Sat. 9–4:30, Sun. 11:30–4:30, and Dec.–Apr., Tues.–Fri. 10:30–2:30, Sat. 10–4:30, Sun. 11:30–4:30; chapel May–Nov., daily 9–5, and Dec.–Apr., daily 10–3.*

⓬ Château Ramezay. This charming little castle is one of the most elegant colonial buildings in Montréal. It was built as the residence of the 11th governor of Montréal, Claude de Ramezay. In 1775–76 it was the headquarters for American troops seeking to conquer Canada; Benjamin Franklin stayed here during that winter occupation. The château became a museum of city and provincial history in 1895, and it has been restored to the style of Governor de Ramezay's day. ⊠ *280 rue Notre-Dame Est,* ☎ *514/861–3708.* ⊡ *$5.* ☉ *June–Sept., daily 10–6; Oct.– May, Tues.–Sun. 10–4:30.*

NEED A
BREAK?

In summer there are few places in the city that are lovelier and livelier than Place Jacques Cartier. You could stop at a *terasse* (sidewalk café) for a beer or a coffee or just sit on a bench amid the flower vendors and listen to the street musicians or watch a juggler perform. If you're peckish, there are several snack bars and ice cream stands. If you're really daring, you could try *poutine,* Québec's very own contribution to junk-food culture. It consists of french fries covered with cheese curds and smothered in gravy—an acquired taste.

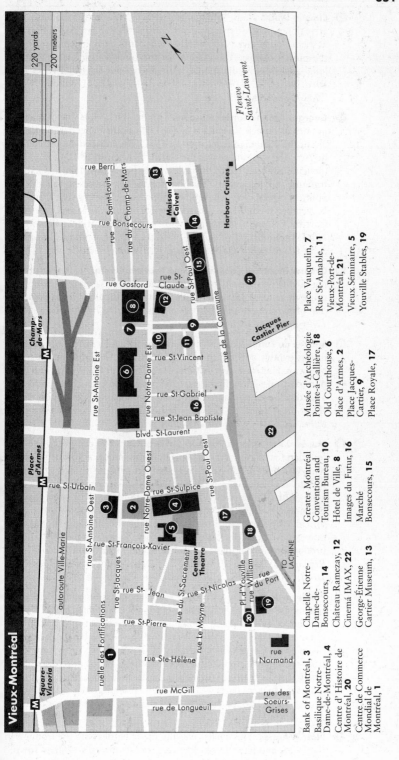

Vieux-Montréal

220 yards
200 meters

Fleuve Saint-Laurent

Harbour Cruises

Maison du Calvet

rue Berri
rue Saint-Louis
rue du Champ-de-Mars
rue Bonsecours
rue St-Paul Oest
rue Gosford
rue St-Claude
rue St-Antoine Est
rue Notre-Dame Est
rue St-Vincent
rue St-Gabriel
rue St-Jean Baptiste
blvd. St-Laurent
rue de la Commune

Champ-de-Mars

Jacques Castier Pier

Place-d'Armes

rue St-Urbain
rue St-Sulpice
rue Notre-Dame Ouest
rue St-Paul Oest

autoroute Ville-Marie

rue St-Antoine Oest

rue St-Jacques
rue St-François-Xavier
rue St- Jean
rue du St-Sacrement
Centaur Theatre
rue St-Nicolas
Pl. d'Youville
rue William
rue du Port

Square-Victoria

ruelle des Fortifications

rue St-Pierre
rue Le Moyne
rue Ste-Hélène
rue McGill
rue de Longueuil

rue Normand
rue des Soeurs-Grises

TO LACHINE

Bank of Montréal, **3**
Basilique Notre-Dame-de-Montréal, **4**
Centre d' Histoire de Montréal, **20**
Centre de Commerce Mondial de Montréal, **1**

Chapelle Notre-Dame-de-Bonsecours, **14**
Château Ramezay, **12**
Cinemá IMAX, **22**
George-Étienne Cartier Museum, **13**

Greater Montréal Convention and Tourism Bureau, **10**
Hôtel de Ville, **8**
Images du Futur, **16**
Marché Bonsecours, **15**

Musée d'Archéologie Pointe-à-Callière, **18**
Old Courthouse, **6**
Place d'Armes, **2**
Place Jacques-Cartier, **9**
Place Royale, **17**

Place Vauquelin, **7**
Rue St-Amable, **11**
Vieux-Port-de-Montréal, **21**
Vieux Séminaire, **5**
Youville Stables, **19**

🖐 ㉒ **Cinéma IMAX.** Nausea, panic, and vertigo are some of the more negative things people experience the first time they see an IMAX film roar at them from a seven-story screen. Wonder and excitement are among the more positive. The content of the films—most under an hour long—is decidedly educational. It's best to reserve ahead. ⊠ *Vieux-Port, Shed No. 7,* ☎ *514/496–3519 or 514/790–1245.* ⊞ *$11.75.* ⊙ *Tues.–Sun. from 9:45 AM.*

⓮ **Georges-Étienne Cartier Museum.** This exhibit honors one of the most important French Canadians of the 19th century, a leader in bringing about the Canadian federation in 1867. The museum comprises two houses. The west house was the Cartiers's home in 1862 and has been meticulously restored to the style of that period, with plush Victorian furniture and decorations. The house on the east focuses on Sir Georges's political career. One delightful exhibit that runs every year from mid-November to mid-December is the Victorian Christmas, when the Cartiers's home is festooned with period decorations. ⊠ *458 rue Notre-Dame Est,* ☎ *514/283–2282.* ⊞ *$3.* ⊙ *Late May–Labor Day, daily 10–6; Labor Day–mid-May, Wed.–Sun. 10–noon and 1–5.*

⓾ **Greater Montréal Convention and Tourism Bureau.** This small building (1811) was the site of the old Silver Dollar Saloon, so named because there were 350 silver dollars nailed to the floor. Today it's now one of two tourist information offices operated by Info-Touriste. ⊠ *174 rue Notre-Dame Est,* ☎ *514/873–2015.*

⓰ **Images du Futur.** Make a virtual dog growl and a virtual jungle grow in this exhibit devoted to interactive art and the information superhighway. There are also exhibits of the latest in CD-ROMs and computerized animation. In the electronic café, visitors can have coffee and a sandwich and plug into the Internet on one of 40 computers. ⊠ *85 rue St-Paul Ouest,* ☎ *514/849–1612.* ⊞ *$11.75.* ⊙ *Sun.–Thurs. 10–6, Fri.–Sat. 10–9; call for show times.*

🖐 ⓲ **Musée d'Archéologie Pointe-à-Callière.** Here you can get to the very foundations of New France. This museum in the ☞ **Pointe-à-Callière** park was built around the excavated remains of structures dating to Montréal's beginnings, including the city's first Catholic cemetery. It's a labyrinth of stone walls and corridors, illuminated by spotlights and holograms of figures from the past. An audiovisual show gives a historical overview of the area. It also has an excellent gift shop, full of interesting books on Montréal's history, as well as pictures and reproductions of old maps, engravings, and other artifacts. ⊠ *350 pl. Royale,* ☎ *514/872–9150.* ⊞ *$7.* ⊙ *June 24–Labor Day, Tues.–Sun. 10–8; Sept. 6–June 23, Tues. and Thur.–Sun. 10–5, Wed. 10–8.*

Palais de Justice. Built in 1971, this black glass building is the main courthouse for the judicial district of Montréal. Criminal law in Canada falls under federal jurisdiction and is based on British common law, but civil law is a provincial matter and Québec's is based on France's Napoleonic Code, which governs all the minutiae of private life—from setting up a company and negotiating a mortgage to drawing up a marriage contract and registering the names of children. Lawyers and judges in Québec courts wear the same elaborate gowns as their British counterparts, but not the wigs. This building is not open for tours. ⊠ *1 rue Notre-Dame Est.*

❷ **Place d'Armes.** This square was the site of battles with the Iroquois in the 1600s and later became the center of Montréal's "Upper Town." In the middle of the square is a statue of Paul de Chomedey, the founder of Montréal. In 1644 he was wounded here in a battle with Indians. There are tunnels beneath the square, which protected the colonists from the extremes of winter weather and provided an escape route. Unfortunately, the tunnels are too small and dangerous to visit. ⊠ *Bordered by rues Notre-Dame Ouest and St-Jacques.*

❾ Place Jacques-Cartier. This two-block-long square, at the heart of Vieux-Montréal, opened in 1804 as a municipal market, and every summer it is transformed into a flower market. The 1809 monument at the top of the square celebrates Lord Nelson's victory over Napoléon Bonaparte's French navy at Trafalgar. It was built, not as you might expect, by patriotic British residents of Montréal, but by the Sulpician priests, who didn't have much love for the Corsican emperor, either.⊠ *Bordered by rues Notre-Dame Est and de la Commune.*

⓲ Pointe-à-Callière. This small park commemorates the settlers' first landing and is the site of ☞ **Musée d'Archéologie Pointe-à-Callière,** Montréal's dazzling museum of history and archeology. A small stream used to flow into the St. Lawrence here, and it was on the point of land between the two waters that the colonists landed their four boats on May 17, 1642. The settlement was almost washed away the next Christmas by a flood. When it was spared, de Maisonneuve placed a cross on top of Mont-Royal as thanks to God. ⊠ *Bordered by rues de la Commune and William.*

㉑ Vieux-Port-de-Montréal. This port was once the very heart and soul of the city's commercial life. But bigger ships and a longer shipping season made the port obsolete. Now the area is a popular waterfront park with a promenade and benches with views of the river. In summer, there's a giant flea market (☞ Shopping, *below*) in one of the warehouses. Several companies offer boat excursions on the river (☞ Outdoor Activities and Sports, *below*). Cruise ships dock here and so do visiting naval vessels. The port also marks the start of one of the city's most popular bicycle paths. Every weekend, hundreds of Montrealers follow the route of the old Lachine Canal (built in 1825 to bypass the Lachine Rapids and rendered obsolete by the St. Lawrence Seaway) to Parc René Lévesque in Lachine, a narrow spit of land with a great views of Lac St-Louis.

❺ Vieux Séminaire. This is Montréal's oldest building, which is considered the finest, most elegant example of 17th-century Québec architecture. It was built in 1685 as a headquarters for the Sulpician priests who owned the island of Montréal until 1854, and it is still a residence the Sulpicians who administer the basilica. The clock on the roof over the main doorway is the oldest (pre-1701) public timepiece in North America. Behind the seminary building is a small but beautiful garden, which is unfortunately closed to the public as is the seminary itself. ⊠ *116 rue Notre-Dame Ouest, behind wall west of Basilique Notre-Dame-de-Montréal.*

Centre-Ville (Downtown)

On the surface, Montréal's Centre-Ville is much like the downtown core of many other major cities—full of life and noisy traffic, its streets lined with department stores, boutiques, bars, restaurants, strip clubs, amusement arcades, and bookstores. But, in fact, much of the area's activity goes on beneath the surface, in Montréal's Underground City. Development of this unique endeavor began in 1966 when the Métro opened. Now it includes (at last count) seven hotels, 1,500 offices, 30 movie theaters, more than 1,600 boutiques, 200 restaurants, three universities, two colleges, two train stations, a skating rink, 40 banks, a bus terminal, an art museum, a complex of concert halls, the home ice of the Montréal Canadiens, and a church. All this is linked by Métro lines and more than 30 kilometers (19 miles) of well-lit, boutique-lined passages that protect shoppers and workers from the hardships of winter and the sweltering heat of summer. A traveler arriving by train could book into a fine hotel and spend a week in Montréal shopping, dining, and going to a long list of movies, plays, concerts, sports events, and discos, without once stepping outside.

Aboveground, the downtown core is a sprawling 30-by-8-block area bounded by avenue Atwater and boulevard St-Laurent on the west and east, respectively, avenue des Pins on the north, and rue St-Antoine on the south. In the early days of European settlement, this area was a patchwork of farms, pastures, and woodlots. After 1700, however, Montréal was growing too big for the walled confines of Vieux-Montréal. In 1701 the French administration signed a peace treaty with the Iroquois, and the colonists began to feel safe about building outside Montréal's fortifications. The city inched northward, toward Mont-Royal, particularly after the British conquest in 1760. By the end of the 19th century, rue Ste-Catherine was the main commercial thoroughfare, and the city's elite built mansions on the slope of the mountain. Since 1960 city planners have made a concerted effort to move the focus eastward. With the opening of Place des Arts (1963) and the Complexe Desjardins (1976), the city center shifted in that direction.

A Good Walk

Numbers in the text below correspond to numbers in the margin and on the maps.

Our downtown walk begins underground at the McGill Métro station, one of the central points in the Underground City. It's linked to half a dozen office towers and two of the "Big Three" department stores, **Eaton** ㉓ and La Baie (the other is Ogilvy). Passages also link the station to such major shopping malls as Le Centre Eaton, Les Promenades de la Cathédrale, and Les Cours Mont-Royal.

A tunnel links the Centre Eaton to **Place Ville-Marie** ㉔. This 1962 office tower was Montréal's first modern skyscraper and the mall complex underneath it was the first link in the Underground City. From here head south via the passageways toward **Le Reine Elizabeth** ㉕, or Queen Elizabeth, hotel. The **Gare Centrale** (Central Railway Station), just behind the hotel, is where most trains from the United States and the rest of Canada arrive. Follow the signs marked "Métro/Place Bonaventure" to **Place Bonaventure** ㉖. On the lower floors of this building are shops, restaurants, and offices, which are topped by the Bonaventure Hilton International and 2½ acres of gardens.

When you've finished exploring Place Bonaventure, go to the northwest corner of the building and descend the escalator into the Underground City. This time follow the signs for **Le 1000 rue de la Gauchetière** ㉗, a skyscraper that's home to the Amphithéâtre Bell, a $5-million indoor ice rink that's open year-round. Return to the tunnels, and follow signs to the Bonaventure Métro station and then to the Canadian Pacific Railway Company's **Windsor Station** ㉘, with its massive stone exterior and amazing steel-and-glass roof. The rail station and the Place Bonaventure métro station below it are all linked to **Centre Molson** ㉙, the new home of the Montréal Canadiens.

Exit the Underground City at the north end of Windsor Station and cross rue de la Gauchetière to **St. George's** ㉚ (1872), a jewel of neo-Gothic architecture and the prettiest Anglican church in the city. Just to the east across rue Peel is **Place du Canada** ㉛, a park with a statue of Sir John A. Macdonald, Canada's first prime minister. Cross the park and rue de la Cathédrale to **Mary Queen of the World Cathedral** ㉜, which is modeled after St. Peter's Basilica in Rome. People sometimes call the massive gray granite building across boulevard René-Lévesque from the cathedral the "Wedding Cake," because it rises in tiers of decreasing size and has lots of columns, but its real name is the **Sun Life Building** ㉝ (1914). At one time it was the largest building in the British Commonwealth. During World War II, much of England's financial reserves and national treasures were stored in Sun Life's vaults. The park that faces the Sun Life Building just north of boulevard René-Lévesque is **Square Dorchester** ㉞, for many years the heart of Montréal. Walk east along boulevard René-Lévesque to **St. Patrick's Basilica** ㉟ (1847). This beautiful old church is to Montréal's English-speaking Catholics what Notre-Dame is to the city's French-speaking Catholics.

After visiting the church, backtrack a half block, cross boulevard René-Lévesque, and walk north on rue Phillips (which becomes rue Aylmer) to rue **Ste-Catherine,** the main retail shopping street of Montréal. Here you'll see the exteriors of some of the places you've already visited underground. At the northwest corner of rues Ste-Catherine and Aylmer is **La Baie** department store. The church just west of La Baie is **Christ Church Cathedral** ㊱ (1859), the main church of the Anglican diocese of Montréal.

As you continue your walk west, pause briefly to admire the **view** at the corner of rue Ste-Catherine and avenue McGill College. Look north up this broad boulevard and you can see the Victorian-era buildings of the McGill University campus with Mont-Royal looming in the background. The grim-looking gray castle you can see high on the slopes to the right is the Royal Victoria Hospital.

Another six blocks farther west is **Ogilvy** ㊲, the last of the Big Three department stores. **Rue de la Montagne,** and rues **Crescent** and **Bishop,** the two streets just west of it, constitute the heart of Montréal's downtown nightlife and restaurant scene. This area once formed the playing fields of the Montréal Lacrosse and Cricket Grounds, and later it became an exclusive suburb lined with millionaires' row houses. Since then these three streets between rues Sherbrooke and Ste-Catherine have become fertile ground for trendy bars, restaurants, and shops ensconced in those old row houses.

While you're in the vicinity, take in **Le Centre Canadien d'Architecture** ㊳, the Canadian Center for Architecture, just four blocks west at rue St-Marc on rue Baile. Walk north on rue Fort three blocks to rue Sherbrooke. On the north side of the street you will see a complex of fine neoclassical buildings in a shady garden. This is the **Grand Séminaire de Montréal** ㊴, a former seminary and girls' school.

Three blocks east at rue Bishop you'll enter a very different environment: the exclusive neighborhood known as the **Golden Square Mile** ㊵. In the heart of this district at the corner of rues Sherbrooke and de Musée is the **Musée des Beaux-Arts de Montréal** ㊶, the Museum of Fine Arts. The oldest museum in the country, it was founded by a group of Anglophone Montrealers in 1860 and has a large collection of art, artifacts, and decorative art from around the world. Walking east on rue Sherbrooke brings you to the small and exclusive **Holt Renfrew** ㊷ department store, perhaps the city's fanciest, at the corner of rue de la Montagne. One block farther east at rue Drummond stands the **Ritz-Carlton** ㊸, the grande dame of Montréal hotels.

The grassy campus of **McGill University** ㊹ is on the north side of rue Sherbrooke just three blocks west of the Ritz-Carlton. Just across rue

Sherbrooke from the campus is the **McCord Museum of Canadian History** ㊺, one of the best history museums in Canada. Turn right on rue University and walk a block to the McGill Métro station. Take the train one stop in the direction of Honoré-Beaugrand to the **Place des Arts** ㊻ station and follow the signs to the theater complex of the same name. The **Musée d'Art Contemporain** ㊼, the city's modern art museum, is in Place des Arts. While still in Place des Arts, follow the signs to the **Complexe Desjardins** ㊽, an office building, hotel, and mall along the lines of Place Ville-Marie (☞ *above*). The next development south is the **Complexe Guy-Favreau,** a huge federal office building named after the Canadian minister of justice in the early '60s. If you continue in a straight line, you will hit the **Palais des Congrès de Montréal Convention Centre** ㊾ above the Place d'Armes Métro stop. But if you take a left out of Guy-Favreau onto rue de la Gauchetière, you will be in **Chinatown** ㊿, a relief after all that enclosed retail space.

TIMING

Just to walk this route briskly will take a minimum of two hours, even on a fine day. Several of the musuems along the route—the McCord, the Centre Canadien d'Architecture, the Musée d'Art Contemporain, and the Musée des Beaux-Arts—are worthy of visits of at least two hours each. So if you want to see everything, it would be wise to spread the tour of downtown over two days, stopping the first day after the Musée des Beaux-Arts. Another possibility is to walk the route in one day, stopping briefly at places like St. Patrick's Basilica and perhaps going for a skate at the Amphithéâtre Bell, and then doing the museums on another day.

Sights to See

Numbers in the margin correspond to points of interest on the Downtown Montréal map.

Amphithéâtre Bell. Skating is a passion in Montréal and you can do it year-round in this $5-million indoor ice rink on the ground floor of the skyscraper Le 1000 rue de la Gauchetière. The rink is bathed in natural light and surrounded by cafés, a food court, and a winter garden. It's open to skaters of all levels of experience; skate rentals and lockers are available. There are also skating lessons, Saturday-night skating to rock music, and scheduled ice shows. To find the rink once you're inside the building, remember the French word for skating rink is *patinoire.* ⊠ *1000 rue de la Gauchetière,* ☎ *514/395–0555, Ext. 237.* ⊠ *$5, skate rental $4.* ☉ *Weekdays 11:30–10, Sat. 11:30–7, Sun. 11:30–6; dancing on ice for those 18 or over, Sat. 7 PM—midnight.*

NEED A BREAK?

The formerly grim passageways at the back of Central Station just below the escalators leading to Place Ville-Marie have been transformed into one of Montréal's trendiest food courts, Les Halles de la Gare. This is not a burger-and-fried-chicken emporium—the dining area is set up like a library with wooden tables and trompe l'oeil bookshelves. The food available includes some of the best bread and baked goods in the city, salads, sandwiches made with fresh terrine and pâté, and homemade pastries and ice cream. If it's nice out, you can take your snack and go up the escalator to the mall under Place Ville-Marie and then up the stairs in the middle of its food court to the terrace, a wide area with a fine view much favored by office workers on their lunch break or coffee break.

Centre Molson. Opened in Spring 1996, this arena is the new home of the Montréal Canadiens, the hockey team devoted hometown fans call simply *les Glorieux.* The brown-brick building replaces the old Forum that had been the Canadiens's home since 1917. The new

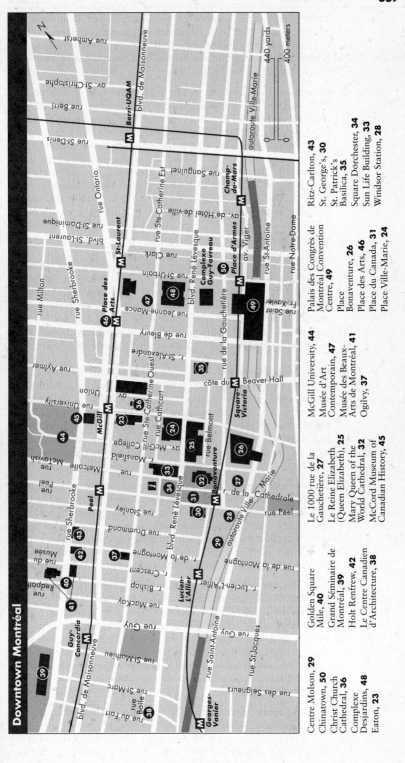

Downtown Montréal

Centre Molson, **29**
Chinatown, **50**
Christ Church Cathedral, **36**
Complexe Desjardins, **48**
Eaton, **23**

Golden Square Mile, **40**
Grand Séminaire de Montréal, **39**
Holt Renfrew, **42**
Le Centre Canadien d'Architecture, **38**

Le 1000 rue de la Gauchetière, **27**
Le Reine Elizabeth (Queen Elizabeth), **25**
Mary Queen of the World Cathedral, **32**
McCord Museum of Canadian History, **45**

McGill University, **44**
Musée d'Art Contemporain, **47**
Musée des Beaux-Arts de Montréal, **41**
Ogilvy, **37**

Palais des Congrès de Montréal Convention Centre, **49**
Place Bonaventure, **26**
Place des Arts, **46**
Place du Canada, **31**
Place Ville-Marie, **24**

Ritz-Carlton, **43**
St. George's, **30**
St. Patrick's Basilica, **35**
Square Dorchester, **34**
Sun Life Building, **33**
Windsor Station, **28**

name refers to the Molson family who established Montréal's first brewery in the 18th century and whose present company, Molson-O'Keefe, owns the hockey team. So far, however, Montrealers stubbornly call the place the New Forum. ⊠ *1260 rue de la Gauchetière Ouest,* ☎ *517/932–2582.*

50 **Chinatown.** The Chinese first came to Montréal in large numbers after 1880, following the construction of the transcontinental railroad. They settled in an 18-block area between boulevard René-Lévesque and avenue Viger to the north and south, and near rues Hôtel de Ville and Bleury on the west and east, an area that became known as Chinatown, where there are many restaurants, food stores, and gift shops. If you have enough energy you may want to stroll south on rue St-Urbain for a block to rue St-Antoine. Half a block east is **Steve's Music Store** (⊠ 51 rue St-Antoine Ouest), a shabby warren of five storefronts jammed with just about everything you need to be a rock star except talent. Sooner or later every musician and wanna-be musician in the city wanders through it.

NEED A BREAK?　　For a huge bowl of beef soup full of noodles, vegetables, and big slices of beef, stop at **Pho Bang New York** (⊠ 970 blvd. St-Laurent, ☎ 514/954–2032), a Vietnamese restaurant on the edge of Chinatown. This small-white-tiled place specializes in traditional Vietnamese soups that are served in bowls big enough to bathe a small dog. And it's cheap, too—for less than $5, you get soup, a plate of crispy vegetables, and a small pot of tea. The restaurant does not accept credit cards.

36 **Christ Church Cathedral.** This is the main church (1859) of the Anglican diocese of Montréal. In early 1988, the diocese leased the land and air rights to a consortium of developers for 99 years. The consortium then built **La Maison des Coopérants,** a 34-story office tower, behind the cathedral, and a huge retail complex, **Les Promenades de la Cathédrale,** under it. The church has a quiet graceful interior and frequent organ recitals and concerts. ⊠ *535 rue Ste-Catherine Ouest.* ⊙ *Daily 8–6.*

48 **Complexe Desjardins.** Built in 1976, this is an office building, hotel, and mall development along the lines of Place Ville-Marie. The luxurious **Le Meridien** hotel (☞ Lodging, *below*) rises from its northwest corner. The large galleria space is the scene of all types of performances, from lectures on Japanese massage techniques to pop music, as well as avid shopping in the dozens of stores. ⊠ *Bounded by rues Ste.-Catherine, Jeanne-Mance, and St.-Urbain and blvd. René Lévesque.*

40 **Golden Square Mile.** This was once the richest neighborhood in Canada. At the turn of the century, the people who lived here—mostly of Scottish descent—controlled 70 percent of the country's wealth. Their baronial homes filled an area that stretched from avenue Atwater in the west to rue de Bleury in the east and from rue de la Gauchetière in the south to avenue des Pins halfway up the mountain. Most of those palatial homes have been leveled to make way for high rises and office towers, and the few left are either consulates or conference centers associated with McGill University.

39 **Grand Séminaire de Montréal.** This seminary run by the Sulpicians, is housed in buildings that date to 1860; two squat towers in the extensive gardens date to the 17th century. It was in one of these that St. Marguerite Bourgeoys set up her first school for native girls. The towers, which are among the oldest buildings on the island, are visible from the street; there is a little area just by the gates with three plaques that explain towers and their history in French. The seminary is private, but the public can go to Mass at 10:30 on Sunday morning from September to June in the newly restored chapel. This is a lovely example of 19th-century neoclassical design with choir seating and a magnificent French-style organ. ⊠ *2065 rue Sherbrooke Ouest.*

㊳ Le Centre Canadien d'Architecture (Canadian Center for Architecture). Architect Phyllis Lambert transformed one of the city's grand old mansions into the centerpiece of what is probably the world's premier architectural collection. The center traces the history and development of all architecture (not just Canadian), with exhibits that include blueprints, photographs, scale models, and hands-on demonstrations. The main exhibit is in the Shaughnessy Mansion, a grand 19th-century home that gave its name to Shaughnessy Village, the surrounding neighborhood of homes and apartments. ⊠ *1920 rue Baile,* ☎ *514/939–7000.* ⊡ *$5.* ⊙ *Wed. and Fri. 11–6, Thurs. 11–8, weekends 11–5.*

㉜ Mary Queen of the World Cathedral. Seat of the Roman Catholic archbishop of Montréal, this church (1894), is modeled after St. Peter's Basilica in Rome. Victor Bourgeau, the same architect who did the interior of Notre-Dame in Vieux-Montréal, thought the idea of the cathedral's design terrible but completed it after the original architect proved incompetent. Inside there is even a canopy over the altar that is a miniature copy of Bernini's *baldacchino* in St. Peter's. ⊠ *1085 rue Cathédral; through main doors on blvd. René Lévesque.*

☝ **㊺ McCord Museum of Canadian History.** A grand, eclectic attic of a museum, the McCord documents the life of ordinary Canadians, using costumes and textiles, decorative arts, paintings, prints and drawings, and the 700,000-print-and-negative Notman Photographic Archives, which highlights 19th-century life in Montréal. The McCord is the only museum in Canada with a permanent costume gallery. There are guided tours (call for times), a reading room and documentation center, a gift shop and bookstore, and a tearoom. ⊠ *690 rue Sherbrooke Ouest,* ☎ *514/398–7100.* ⊡ *$5.* ⊙ *Tues., Wed., and Fri. 10–6; Thurs. 10–9; weekends 10–5; closed Mon. except statutory holidays.*

㊹ McGill University. James McGill, a wealthy Scottish fur trader, bequeathed the money and the land for this institution, which opened in 1828 and is perhaps the finest English-language university in the nation. The student body numbers 15,000, and the university is best known for its medical and engineering schools. Most of the campus buildings are fine examples of Victorian architecture. ⊠ *845 rue Sherbrooke Ouest.*

NEED A BREAK? — The McGill University campus is an island of green in a sea of traffic and skyscrapers. On a fine day you can sit on the grass in the shade of a 100-year-old tree and just let the world drift by.

☝ **㊼ Musée d'Art Contemporain.** The museum's large permanent collection of modern art represents works by Québécois, Canadian, and international artists in every medium. The museum often has weekend programs, with many child-oriented activities, and almost all are free. There are guided tours; hours vary. ⊠ *185 rue Ste-Catherine Ouest,* ☎ *514/847–6226.* ⊡ *$5, Wed. evening free.* ⊙ *Tues. and Thurs.–Sun. 11–6, Wed. 11–9.*

㊶ Musée des Beaux-Arts de Montréal (Museum of Fine Arts). Montréal's main art museum houses its permanent collection and displays its special exhibits in the older Benaiah-Gibb Pavilion on the north side of rue Sherbrooke and in the glittering Pavilion Jean-Noël-Desmarais right across the street. The newer pavilion, with a dramatic glass front that incorporates the redbrick facade of a former apartment building, was designed by architect Moshe Safdie, and more than doubles the size of the museum. The two buildings are connected by underground tunnels and hold a large collection of European and North American fine and decorative art; ancient treasures from Europe, the Near East, Asia, Africa, and America; art from Québec and Canada; and Native American and Eskimo artifacts. The museum has a gift shop, an art-book store, a restaurant, a cafeteria, and a gallery from which you can buy or rent paintings by local artists. ⊠ *1380 rue Sherbrooke Ouest,* ☎ *514/285–1600.* ⊑ *Permanent collection free, special exhibitions* *$10.* ⊙ *Tues. and Thurs.–Sun. 11–6, Wed. 11–9.*

46 **Place des Arts.** The Place des Arts theater complex, which opened in 1963, is reminiscent of New York's Lincoln Center in that it is a government-subsidized complex of three very modern theaters. Guided tours of the halls and backstage are available. The **Musée d'Art Contemporain,** the city's modern art museum, moved here in 1991 (☞ *above*). ⊠ *183 rue Ste.-Catherine Ouest,* ☎ *514/842–2112; guided tour, 514/285–4275.*

31 **Place du Canada.** This park has a statue of Sir John A. Macdonald, Canada's first prime minister. In October 1995, this area was the site of a huge rally for Canadian unity that drew more than 300,000 participants from across the country. That patriotic demonstration was at least partly responsible for blunting the separatist drive and preserving a slim victory for the pro-unity forces in the subsequent referendum on independence for Québec. At the south end of Place du Canada is **Le Château Champlain** (☞ Lodging, *below*), known as the Cheese Grater because of its rows and rows of half-moon-shape windows. ⊠ *Bordered by blvd. Réne Lévesque and rue de la Gauchetière.*

35 **St. Patrick's Basilica.** This basilica (1847), is one of the purest examples of the Gothic Revival style in Canada. St. Patrick's is off the tourist trail and lacks some of Notre-Dame's grandeur, but it makes up for it in warmth. The colors are soft and the vaulted ceiling over the sanctuary glows with green and gold mosaics. The old pulpit has panels depicting the Apostles and the huge lamp is decorated with six 6-foot-high angels that hangs over the main altar. If you're named after some obscure saint, you might find his or her portrait in one of the 150 painted panels that decorate the oak wainscoting along the walls of the nave. The church has a strong musical tradition: solemn Mass is sung every Sunday at 11 AM (in Latin, the third week of every month) from September to June. ⊠ *460 blvd. René-Lévesque Ouest,* ☎ *514/866–0491.* ⊙ *Daily 8:30–6.*

34 **Square Dorchester.** Until 1870, a Catholic burial ground occupied this block (and there are still bodies buried beneath the grass); but with the rapid development of the area, the city decided to turn it into a park. The statuary includes a monument to the Boer War in the center and a statue of the Scottish poet Robert Burns near rue Peel. ⊠ *Bordered by rues Peel and Metcalfe McTavish.*

Quartier Latin (Latin Quarter)

Numbers in the text below correspond to numbers in the margin and on the maps.

Early in this century, rue St-Denis cut through a bourgeois neighborhood of large, comfortable residences. The Université de Montréal was established here in 1893, and the students and academics who moved into the area dubbed it the Quartier Latin, or Latin Quarter. The university eventually moved to a larger campus on the north side of Mont-Royal, and the area went into decline. It revived in the early 1970s, and then boomed, largely as a result of the 1969 opening of the Université du Québec à Montréal and the launch of the International Jazz Festival in the summer of 1980. Plateau Mont-Royal, the neighborhood just north of the Quartier Latin, shared in this revival. Its residents are now a mix of immigrants, working-class Francophones, and young professionals eager to find a home they can renovate close to the city center. The Quartier Latin and Plateau Montréal are home to rows of French and ethnic restaurants, charming bistros, coffee shops, designer boutiques, antiques shops, and art galleries. When night falls, these streets are always full of omnilingual hordes—young and not so young, rich and poor, established and still studying.

Many of the older residences in this area have graceful wrought-iron balconies and twisting staircases that are typical of Montréal. They were built that way for practical reasons. The buildings are what Montrealers call duplexes or triplexes, that is, two or three residences stacked on top of each other. To save interior space, the stairs to reach the upper floors were put outside. The stairs and balconies are treacherous in winter, but in summer they are often full of families and couples, gossiping, picnicking, and partying. If Montrealers tell you they spend the summer in Balconville, they mean they don't have the money or the time to leave town and won't get any farther than their balcony.

A Good Walk

Begin at the **Berri-UQAM** Métro stop, perhaps the most important in the whole city, because three lines intersect here. The "UQAM" in the subway name is pronounced "oo-kam" by local Francophones and "you-kwam" by local Anglophones. It refers to the **Université du Québec à Montréal** ⑤①, which has no traditional campus. It has some splendid fragments of Gothic grandeur you can see sprouting up among the modern brick hulks, and the ornate **Chapelle Notre-Dame-de-Lourdes** ⑤②.

Rue St-Denis is lined with cafés, bistros, and restaurants that attract the academic crowd. On rue Ste-Catherine there are a number of low-rent nightclubs popular with avant-garde rock-and-roll types. Just west of rue St-Denis you find the **Cinémathèque Québécoise** ⑤③, which houses one of the largest cinematic reference libraries in the world.

Around the corner and a half block north on rue St-Denis stands the 2,500-seat **Théâtre St-Denis** ⑤④, the second-largest auditorium in Montréal (after Salle Wilfrid Pelletier in Place des Arts). Sarah Bernhardt and many other famous actors have graced its stage. On the next block north you see the Beaux-Arts **Bibliothèque Nationale du Québec** (1915), a library that houses Québec's official archives (✉ 1700 rue St-Denis, ☎ 514/873–1100), which are open Tuesday–Saturday 9–5.

Turn left on Sherbrooke and left again on boulevard St-Laurent for the **Musée Juste pour Rire** ⑤⑤, the world's first museum of humor. Backtrack east on rue Sherbrooke and turn left on rue St-Denis. Above the Sherbrooke Métro station is the **Institut de Tourisme et d'Hôtellerie du Québec,** where students learn the art of cooking and serving food, mixing drinks, and managing a hotel in a singularly ugly building that overlooks **Square St-Louis** ⑤⑥, one of the most graceful green spaces in Montréal.

The stretch of **rue Prince Arthur** ⑤⑦, beginning at the western end of ☞ Square St-Louis and continuing several blocks west, is a center of youth culture. When you reach **boulevard St-Laurent** ⑤⑧, take a right and stroll north on the street that cuts through Montréal life in a number of ways. First, this is the east–west dividing street; like the Greenwich meridian, boulevard St-Laurent is where all the numbers begin.

The street is also lined with shops and restaurants that represent the ethnic diversity of Montréal.

This area was still partly rural in the mid-19th century, with lots of open space and fresh air, which made it healthier than overcrowded Vieux-Montréal. So in 1861, the Hôpital Hôtel-Dieu, the hospital Jeanne Mance founded in the 17th century, moved into a new building at what is now the corner of avenue des Pins and rue St-Urbain, just a block west of boulevard St-Laurent. Hôtel-Dieu, one of the city's major hospitals, is still there, and right next to it is the **Musée des Hospitalières** ⑤⑨, which gives a remarkable picture of the early days of colonization.

Just 30 years after the hospital moved, the first electric tramway that could climb the slope to Plâteau Mont-Royal was installed on boulevard St-Laurent. Working-class families, who couldn't afford a horse and buggy to pull them up the hill, began to move in. In the 1880s the first of many waves of Russian-Jewish immigrants escaping the pogroms arrived and settled here. Boulevard St-Laurent became known as the Main, as in "Main Street," and Yiddish was the primary language spoken along some stretches. The Russian Jews were followed by Greeks, Eastern Europeans, Portuguese, and, most recently, Latin Americans.

The 10 blocks north of rue Sherbrooke are filled with delis, junk stores, restaurants, luncheonettes, and clothing stores, as well as fashionable boutiques, bistros, cafés, bars, nightclubs, bookstores, and galleries exhibiting the work of the latest wave of "immigrants" to the area—gentrifiers and artists. The block between rues Roy and Napoléon is particularly rich in delights.

Merchants are attempting to re-create rue Prince Arthur on **rue Duluth** ⑥⓪. Turn right and walk four blocks east to rue St-Denis, where you will find Greek and Vietnamese restaurants and boutiques and art galleries on either side of the street. Walk east another nine blocks and you come to **Parc Lafontaine.** At about 100 acres, it's the smallest of Montréal's three major parks, but it's a lively place and is much loved by area residents.

After exploring the park, walk south to rue Sherbrooke Est and then turn right and walk west on rues Sherbrooke and Cherrier to the Sherbrooke Métro station to complete the walk. Or head west to begin the Parc du Mont-Royal tour (☞ *below*).

TIMING

This is a comfortable afternoon walk, lasting perhaps two hours, longer if you linger for an hour or so in the Musée des Hospitallières and spend some time shopping. There's a bit of a climb from boulevard de Maisonneuve to rue Sherbrooke.

Sights to See
Numbers in the margin correspond to points of interest on the Latin Quarter and Mount Royal Park map.

⑤② **Chapelle Notre-Dame-de-Lourdes.** This tiny Roman Catholic chapel is one of the most ornate pieces of religious architecture in the city. It was built in 1876 and decorated with brightly colored murals by artist Napoléon Bourassa, who lived nearby. It's a mixture of Roman and Byzantine styles, and its beautifully restored interior is a must-see, despite the panhandlers that cluster at its doors and the somewhat eccentric devotees it attracts. ⊠ *430 rue Ste-Catherine Est.* ⊙ *Daily 8–5.*

⑤③ **Cinémathèque Québécoise.** This museum and repertory movie house is one of Montréal's great bargains. For $3 you can visit the perma-

Boulevard
St-Laurent, **58**

Chalet du
Mont-Royal, **62**

Chapelle Notre-Dame-
de-Lourdes, **52**

Cinémathèque
Mont-Royal, **64**

Cimetière Notre-Dame-
des-Neiges, **65**

Cinémathèque
Québécoise, **53**

Collège Notre
Dame, **67**

Lac aux Castors
(Beaver Lake), **63**

Musée des
Hospitalières, **59**

Musée Juste
pour Rire, **55**

Observatoire
de l'Est, **61**

Oratoire St-Joseph, **66**

Rue Duluth, **60**

Rue Prince Arthur, **57**

Square St-Louis, **56**

Théâtre St-Denis, **54**

Université du Québec à
Montréal (UQÀM) **51**

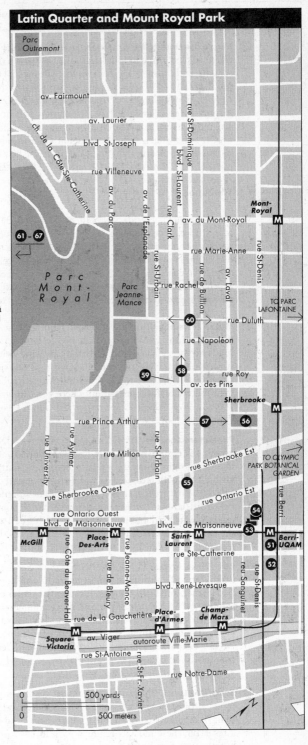

Latin Quarter and Mount Royal Park

nent exhibition on the history of filmmaking equipment and see two movies. ✉ *335 blvd. de Maisonneuve Ouest,* ☎ *514/842–9763.*

59 **Musée des Hospitalières.** France in the 17th century was consumed with religious fervor, and aristocratic men and women often built hospitals, schools, and churches in distant lands. The nuns of the Religieuses Hospitalières de St-Joseph who came to Montréal in the mid-17th century to help Jeanne Mance run the Hôpital Hôtel Dieu were good examples of this fervor, and much of their spirit is evident in the letters, books, and religious artifacts displayed here. Pay special attention to the beautiful wooden stairway in the museum's entrance hall. There's a fascinating and sometimes chilling exhibit on the history of medicine and nursing. ✉ *201 av. des Pins Ouest,* ☎ *514/849–2919.* 🎫 *$5.* ☉ *Mid-June–mid-Oct., Tues.–Fri. 10–5, weekends 1–5; mid-Oct.–mid-June, Wed.–Sun. 1–5.*

NEED A BREAK?

Café Santropol (✉ 3990 St-Urbain, ☎ 514/842–3110) serves hearty soups, cake, salads, a huge selection of teas, and unusual high-rise sandwiches garnished with fruit (the Jeanne Mance mixes pineapples and chives in cream cheese). The atmosphere is, well, homey, with a molded tin ceiling and a private little *terasse* out back—all under the watchful eye of a plaster statue of St. Francis of Assisi. One percent of the profits go to charity. Credit cards are not accepted.

55 **Musée Juste pour Rire** (International Humor Museum). This is the first museum in the world to be dedicated to laughter. Its multimedia exhibits explore and celebrate humor by drawing visitors into their plots. And some of the visiting exhibits have a serious side. There is a large collection of humor videos, a cabaret where budding comics can test their material, and a restaurant where you can watch old tapes while you eat. ✉ *2111 blvd. St-Laurent,* ☎ *514/845–4000,* 🎫 *$9.95.* ☉ *Tues.–Sun. 1–8.*

Parc Lafontaine. Montréal's two main cultures are reflected in this park's layout: the eastern half is pure French with paths, gardens, and lawns laid out in rigid geometric shapes; the western half is based on the English model with meandering paths and irregularly shaped ponds that follow the natural contours of the land. For summer visitors there are two artificial lakes where you can rent paddleboats, bowling greens, tennis courts, and an open-air theater with free arts events. In winter, the two artificial lakes form a large skating rink. ✉ *3933 av. Parc Lafontaine,* ☎ *514/872–6211.* ☉ *Daily 9 AM–10 PM.*

57 **Rue Prince Arthur.** In the 1960s, the young people who moved to the neighborhood transformed this street into a small hippie bazaar of clothing, leather, and smoke shops. It remains a center of youth culture, although it's now much tamer and more commercial. The city turned the blocks between avenue Laval and boulevard St-Laurent into a pedestrian mall. Hippie shops have metamorphosed into inexpensive Greek, Vietnamese, Italian, Polish, and Chinese restaurants and little neighborhood bars. ✉ *Beginning at western end of sq. St-Louis and stretching a few blocks west.*

56 **Square St-Louis.** This is one of the most graceful squares in Montréal. It has a fountain and trees and is surrounded by 19th-century homes built in the large, comfortable style of the Second Empire. Originally a reservoir, these blocks became a park in 1879 and attracted upper-middle-class families and artists to the area. French Canadian poets were among the most famous creative people to occupy the houses back then, and the neighborhood is now home to painters, filmmakers, musicians, and writers. On the wall of 336 Square St-Louis you can see—

and read, if your French is good—a long poem by Michel Bujold. ✉ *Bordered by av. Laval and rue St-Denis.*

NEED A
BREAK?

On a pleasant sunny day there is no finer place to rest your feet than on one of the park benches near the fountain in Square St-Louis. There are plenty of take-out restaurants nearby if you want a coffee or a pastry.

🛈 **Université du Québec à Montréal.** Part of a network of provincial campuses set up by the provincial government in 1969, UQAM, which anchors the academic life of the surrounding Latin Quarter, has no traditional campus, but is housed in a series of massive, modern brick buildings that clog much of the three city blocks bordered by rues Sanguinet and Berri and boulevards de Maisonneuve and René-Lévesque. The splendid fragments of Gothic grandeur that you can see sprouting up among the modern brick hulks like flowers in a swamp are all that's left of the once magnificent Eglise St. Jacques. A more substantial religious monument that has survived right in UQAM's resolutely secularist heart is the Chapelle Notre-Dame-de-Lourdes (☞ *above*).

Parc du Mont-Royal (Mount Royal Park)

Parc du Mont-Royal (Mount Royal Park) is 494 acres of forest and paths in the heart of the city. It was designed by Frederick Law Olmsted, the celebrated architect of New York's Central Park. He believed that communion with nature could cure body and soul, and the park follows the natural topography and accentuates its features, in the English style. You can go skating on Beaver Lake in the winter, visit one of the two lookouts and scan the horizon. Horse-drawn transport is popular year-round: sleigh rides in winter and calèche rides in summer. On the eastern side of the hill stands the 100-foot steel cross that is the symbol of the city. Not far away from the park and perched on a neighboring crest of the same mountain is the Oratoire St-Joseph, a shrine that draws millions of tourists every year.

A Good Walk

Begin by taking the Métro's Orange Line to the Mont-Royal station and transfer to a No. 11 bus (be sure to get a transfer [*correspondance* in French] from a machine before you get on the Métro). The No. 11 drives right through the park on the Voie Camilien Houde. Get off at the **Obsérvatoire de l'Est** ㊱, a lookout that gives a spectacular view of the east end of the city and the St. Lawrence River. Climb the stone staircase at the end of the parking lot and follow the trails to the **Chalet du Mont-Royal** ㊲, a large, baronial building with a wide semicircular, flagstoned terrace in front of it overlooking downtown Montréal. The next stop is **Lac aux Castors** ㊳, or Beaver Lake, and there are at least three ways to get there. You can take the long way and walk down the steep flight of stairs at the east end of the terrace and then turn right to follow the gravel road that circles the mountain. The shortest way is to leave the terrace at the west end of the terrace and follow the crowds along the road. The middle way is to leave at the east end, but then to turn off the main road and follow one of the shaded paths that leads through the woods and along the southern ridge of the mountain. Lac aux Castors was reclaimed from boggy ground and so violates Olmstead's purist vision of a natural environment. But children like to float boats on it in summer, and it makes a fine skating rink in winter.

Across Chemin Remembrance from Lac aux Castors is what looks like one vast cemetery. It is in fact, two cemeteries—one Protestant and the other Catholic. The **Cimetière Mont-Royal** ㊴ is toward the east in a little valley that cuts off the noise of the city; it is the final resting place of Anna Leonowens, the real-life heroine of *The King and I*. The yellow-brick buildings and tower you can see on the north side of the mountain beyond Mount Royal Cemetery belong to the **Université de Montréal,** the second-largest French-language university in the world with nearly 60,000 students. If you're now humming "Getting to Know You," you'll probably change your tune to Canada's national anthem when you enter the **Cimetière Notre-Dame-des-Neiges** ⑥⑤, as the song's composer, Calixa Lavallée, is buried here.

Wander northwest through the two cemeteries, and you will eventually emerge on Chemin Queen Mary on the edge of a decidedly lively area of street vendors, ethnic restaurants, and boutiques. Walk west on Queen Mary across Chemin Côte-des-Neiges, and you come to Montréal's most grandiose religious monument, the **Oratoire St-Joseph** ⑥⑥. This huge domed church perched high on a ridge of Mont-Royal is the largest shrine in the world dedicated to the earthly father of Jesus. Across the street is the ivy-covered **Collège Notre Dame** ⑥⑦, where the oratory's founder, Brother André, worked as a porter. It's still an important private school, and one of the few in the city that still accepts boarders. Its students these days, however, include girls, a situation that would have shocked Brother André.

After visiting the church, retrace your steps to Chemin Côte-des-Neiges, and walk through the lively neighborhood to the Côte-des-Neiges station to catch the Métro home.

TIMING
Allot at least the better part of a day for this tour; longer if you plan on catching some rays or ice skating in the park.

Sights to See

⑥② **Chalet du Mont-Royal.** This large, baronial building with a wide semicircular, flagstoned terrace in front of it overlooks downtown Montréal. In the distance you can see Mont-Royal's sister mountains—Mont St-Bruno, Mont St-Hilaire, and Mont St-Grégoire. These isolated peaks—called the Montétrégies or Mountains of the King—rise quite dramatically from flat surrounding countryside. Be sure to take a look inside the chalet, especially at the murals that depict scenes from Canadian history. There's a snack bar in the back. ⊙ *Daily 9–5.*

⑥④ **Cimetière Mont-Royal.** This cemetery was established in 1852 by the Anglican, Presbyterian, Unitarian, and Baptist churches, and was laid out like a landscaped garden with monuments that are genuine works of art. Many prominent families have mausoleums and plots here, but the cemetery's most famous permanent guest is Anna Leonowens, who was governess to the children of the King of Siam and is the real-life model for the heroine of the musical *The King and I*. There are no tours of the cemetery. ⊠ *1297 Chemin de la Forêt.*

⑥⑤ **Cimetière Notre-Dame-des-Neiges.** This Catholic graveyard is the largest in the city, and the final resting place of hundreds of prominent artists, poets, intellectuals, politicians, and clerics. Among them is Calixa Lavallée, who wrote "O Canada." Many of the monuments and mausoleums—scattered along 55 kilometers (more than 30 miles) of paths and roadways—are the work of leading artists. There are no tours of the cemetery. ⊠ *4601 Côte-des-Neiges.*

⑥⑥ **Oratoire St-Joseph** (St. Joseph's Oratory). This huge church is the result of the persistence of a remarkable little man named Brother André, who was a porter in the school that his religious order ran. He dreamed of building a shrine dedicated to St. Joseph—Canada's patron saint—

and began in 1904 by building a little chapel. Miraculous cures were reported and attributed to St. Joseph's intercession, and Brother André's project caught the imagination of Montréal. The result is one of the most important shrines in North America. The oratory dome is one of the biggest in the world and the church has a magnificent setting. It's also home to Les Petits Chanteurs de Mont-Royal, the city's finest boys' choir. But alas, the interior is oppressive and drab. There's a more modest and quite undistinguished crypt church at the bottom of the structure, and right behind it is a room that glitters with hundreds of votive candles lit in honor of St. Joseph. The walls are festooned with crutches discarded by the cured. Right behind that is the simple tomb of Brother André, who was beatified in 1982. Brother André's heart is displayed in a glass case upstairs in a small museum depicting events in his life. From early December through February the oratory features a display of crèches (nativity scenes) from all over the world. High on the mountain beside the main church is a beautiful garden, commemorating the passion of Christ with life-sized representations of the 14 traditional Stations of the Cross. Carillon, choral, and organ concerts are held weekly at the oratory during the summer. To visit the church you can either climb the more than 300 steps to the front door (many pilgrims do so on their knees, pausing to pray at each step) or you can take the shuttle bus that runs from the front gate. ⊠ *3800 Chemin Queen Mary, near Côte-des-Neiges Métro station,* ☎ *514/733–8211.* ☉ *Sept.–May, daily 6 AM–9:30 PM; June–Aug., daily 6 AM–10 PM.*

Parc Olympique (Olympic Park) and Jardin Botanique (Botanical Garden)

Olympic Park and Botanical Garden are in the east end of the city. You can reach them via the Pie-IX or Viau Métro stations (the latter is nearer the stadium entrance).

The giant, mollusk-shaped Stade Olympique (Olympic Stadium) and the leaning tower that supports its roof are probably the preeminent symbols of modern Montréal—they dominate the skyline of the eastern end of the city. But the area has a lot more to recommend it than just the stadium complex: Montréal's world-class Jardin Botanique (Botanical Garden) are nearby, as is Parc Maisonneuve and the world's largest museum, the Insectarium, dedicated to bugs (visit at the right time, and you can even taste a few delicacies like deep-fried bumblebees).

There are daily guided tours of the entire complex, which leave from the **Tourist Hall** (☎ 514/252–8687) in the base of the Tower. The tours at 12:40 and 3:40 are in English and the ones at 11 and 2 are in French.

A Good Walk

Numbers in the text below correspond to numbers in the margin and on the maps.

Start with a ride on the Métro's Green Line and get off at the Viau station, which is only a few steps from the main entrance to the 70,000-seat **Stade Olympique** ⑱, built for the 1976 summer games. A trip to the top of the **Tour Olympique** ⑲, or Olympic Tower, the world's tallest tilting structure, on the funicular is very popular with visitors; a two-level cable car can whisk 90 people up the exterior of the 890-foot tower. On a clear day you can see up to 80 kilometers (50 miles) from the tower-top observatory. Under the base of the tower is the **Centre Aquatique** ⑳ (☎ 514/252–4622), the Aquatic Center, a complex of six swimming pools that's a good place for a refreshing dip.

Right next to the tower is what used to be the Velodrome, where the Olympic bicycle races were held. It has been converted into the very popular **Biodôme** ⑦, where you can explore both a rain forest and an arctic landscape. Continuing your back-to-nature experience, cross rue Sherbrooke to the north of the Olympic Park (or take the free shuttle bus) to reach the **Jardin Botanique** ⑦. This park, with 181 acres of gardens in summer and 10 exhibition greenhouses open all year, is the second-largest attraction of its kind in the world (after England's Kew Gardens). It includes the **Insectarium** ⑦ and the 5-acre **Montréal-Shanghai Lac de Rêve** ⑦, or Montréal-Shanghai Dream Lake Garden, an elegant Ming-style garden.

After you've looked at the flowers and the bugs, return to boulevard Pie IX, which runs along the eastern border of the gardens. The name of this main traffic artery (and the adjoining Métro station) puzzles thousands of tourists every year. The street is named for the 19th-century pope, Pius IX, or Pie IX in French. It's pronounced Pee-neuf, however, which isn't at all how it looks from an English-speaker's standpoint.

Walk south, crossing rues Rachel and Sherbrooke, to the **Musée des Arts Décoratifs** ⑦ on the west side of rue Sherbrooke. This exhibit of furniture and home decoration is in one of the best examples of Beaux-Arts architecture in Montréal.

TIMING

To see all the sights at a leisurely pace, you'll need a full day.

Sights to See

Numbers in the margin correspond to points of interest on the Olympic Park and the Botanical Garden map.

⑦ **Biodôme.** Not everyone thought it was a great idea to change a bicycle-racing stadium into a natural-history exhibit, but the result is one of the city's most popular attractions, with both residents and visitors. It combines four ecosystems—the boreal forest, tropical forest, polar world, and St. Lawrence River—under one climate-controlled dome. Visitors follow protected pathways through each environment, observing indigenous flora and fauna of each ecosystem. A word of warning: the tropical forest really is tropical. If you want to stay comfortable, dress in layers. ⊠ *4777 av. Pierre-de-Coubertin,* ☎ *514/868–3000.* ⊡ *$9.50.* ⊙ *June 18–Sept. 9, daily 9–8; Sept. 10–June 17, daily 9–6.*

⑦ **Jardin Botanique** (Botanical Garden). The garden was founded in 1931, and has more than 26,000 species of plants. The poisonous plant garden is a perennial favorite. Visitors can see a traditional tea ceremony in the Japanese Garden, which also has one of the best bonsai collections in the West. The 5-acre **Montréal-Shanghai Dream Lake Garden** is the largest Ming-style garden outside Asia, with seven elegant pavilions and a 30-foot rockery built around a reflecting pool. The **Insectarium**, a bug-shape building, houses more than 250,000 insect specimens. ⊠ *4101 rue Sherbrooke Est,* ☎ *514/872–1400.* ⊡ *May 15–Oct. 15 $6.50; combined ticket for Biodôme and Botanical Garden $14.75; Oct. 16–May 14 free.* ⊙ *Daily 9–6. Metro: Pie-IX.*

⑦ **Musée des Arts Décoratifs** (Montréal Museum of Decorative Arts). Stroll into this elegant Beaux-Arts building and you step back into another age. The Château Dufresne comprises two adjoining mansions built in 1916 for a pair of prosperous brothers, shoe manufacturers Marius and Oscar Dufresne. It is decorated much as it was when the Dufresnes lived there, with a Moorish smoking room and a Louis XVI drawing room. Some of the rooms have unusual allegorical murals. ⊠ *2929 rue Jeanne-d'Arc,* ☎ *514/259–2575,* ⊡ *$3.* ⊙ *Wed.–Sun., 11–5.*

Aquatic
Center, **70**
Biodôme, **71**
Botanical
Garden, **72**
Insectarium, **73**
Montréal
Museum of
Decorative
Arts, **75**
Montréal-
Shanghai
Dream Lake
Garden, **74**
Olympic
Stadium, **68**
Olympic
Tower, **69**

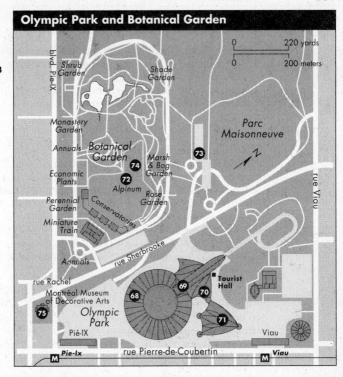

Olympic Park and Botanical Garden

68 Stade Olympique (Olympic Stadium). The stadium, built for the 1976 summer games, is beautiful to look at but not very practical. It's hard to heat and the retractable fabric roof, supported by the tower, has never worked properly. Nevertheless, it's home to the National League's Expos and is used for things like Montréal's annual car show. ⌧ *4141 av. Pierre-de-Coubertin,* ☎ *514/252–8687.*

Les Iles (The Islands)

Expo '67—the world fair staged to celebrate the centennial of the Canadian federation—was the biggest party in Montréal's history, and it marked a defining moment in the city's evolution as a modern metropolis. That party was held on two islands in the middle of the St. Lawrence River—Ile Ste-Hélène, which was formed by nature, and Ile Notre-Dame, which was created by humans out of the stone rubble excavated for Montréal's Métro. The two islands are still a playground—the Parc des Iles has a major amusement park with one of the biggest roller coasters in the world, acres of flower gardens, a beach with clean filtered water, and the wildly successful Casino de Montréal. There's history, too, at the Old Fort where soldiers in colonial uniforms display the military skills of ancient wars. In winter, you can skate on the old Olympic rowing basin or slide down iced trails on an inner tube. You can get information on most of the activities and attractions at Parc des Iles by phoning (☎ 514/872–6222).

A Good Walk

Start at the Ile Ste-Hélène station on the Métro's Yellow Line. The first thing you'll see when you emerge will be the huge geodesic dome that houses **Biosphere,** an environmental exhibition center. From the Biosphere walk to the northern shore and then east through the Parc des Iles to the **Old Fort,** now a museum of colonial life and a parade ground. Just east of the Old Fort past the Pont Jacques-Cartier (Jacques Cartier Bridge) is **La Ronde,** an amusement park.

Now cross over to the island's southern shore and walk back along the waterfront to the Cosmos Footbridge that leads to Ile Notre-Dame. On the way you'll pass the Restaurant Hélène de Champlain, which probably has the prettiest setting of any restaurant in Montréal, and the military cemetery of the British garrison stationed on Ile Ste-Hélène from 1828 to 1870.

Ile Notre-Dame is laced by a network of canals and ponds and the grounds are brilliant with flower gardens left from the 1980 Floralies Internationales flower show. Most of the Expo '67 buildings are gone, the victims of time and weather. One that has remained, however, is the fanciful French Pavilion, now the very successful **Casino de Montréal** and site of Nuances, one of the city's best restaurants. A five-minute walk west of the Casino is the Lac de l'Ile Notre-Dame, site of **Plage de l'Ile Notre Dame,** Montréal's only beach. In mid-June, Ile Notre-Dame is the site of the Molson Grand Prix du Canada, a top Formula I international auto race at the **Circuit Gilles Villeneuve.**

After your walk you can either return to the Métro or walk back to the city via the Pont de la Concorde and the Parc de la Cité du Havre to Vieux-Montréal. If you walk, you'll see what looks like an updated version of a Hopi cliff dwelling. This irregular pile of prefabricated concrete blocks is **Habitat '67,** a private apartment complex, designed by Moshe Safdie and built as an experiment in housing for Expo.

TIMING

This is a comfortable two-hour stroll, but the Biosphere and the Old Fort (try to time your visit to coincide with a drill display by the colonial troops of the Fraser Highlanders and the Compagnie Franche de la Marine) deserve at least an hour each, and you should leave another half hour to admire the flowers. Children will want to spend a whole day at La Ronde, but the best time to go is in the evening when it's cooler. Try to visit the casino during a weekday when the crowds are at their thinnest.

Sights to See

Biosphere. This center, in the huge geodesic dome designed by Buckminster Fuller as the American Pavilion at Expo '67, successfully brings fun to an earnest project—heightening awareness of the St. Lawrence River system and its problems. ⊠ *Ile St-Hélène,* ☎ *514/283-5000.* ⌑ *$6.50.* ⊙ *June 1–Sept. 30 daily 10–8; Oct. 1–May 31, Tues.–Sun., 10–6.*

Casino de Montréal. When the provincial government decided to get into the casino business, it elected to pursue the elegance of Monte Carlo rather than the flash of Las Vegas. It trained its croupiers in politeness as well as math and instituted a strict dress code. The dramatic interior glitters with glass and modern murals, the views of the city skyline across the river are stunning, and the three restaurants are all good. In fact, Nuances is among the city's best (☞ Dining, *below*). The minimum age to enter is 18 and the dress code—no jeans, shorts, or sneakers—is strictly enforced. ⊠ *1 av. du Casino, Ile Notre-Dame,* ☎ *514/392-2746 or 800/665-2274.* ⌑ *Free.* ⊙ *Daily 11 AM–3 AM.*

☼ **La Ronde.** This world-class amusement park has Ferris wheels, boat rides, simulator-style rides, and the second-highest roller coaster in the world. It is also the site of the annual Benson & Hedges International Fireworks Competition, one of the city's most popular festivals, which takes place every weekend in June and July. You can buy a ticket, which includes an amusement park pass, to watch the display from a reserved seat, but thousands of Montrealers take their lawn chairs and blankets down to the Vieux-Port or across the river to the park along the South Shore and watch the show for nothing. ☎ *514/935–5161 or 800/361–8020; fireworks in the U.S., 800/678–5440; fireworks in Canada, 800/361–4595.* ☒ *$24.75, grounds only (no rides) $13.* ☉ *May 11–June 20, daily 10–9; June 21–Sept. 2, daily 11–11; days of fireworks displays 10 AM–midnight.*

🦢 **Old Fort.** In summer the grassy parade square of this fine stone fort comes alive with the crackle of musket fire as the volunteer members of French and British colonial forces show off their skills. The French are represented by the Compagnie Franche de la Marine and the British by the kilted 78th Fraser Highlanders, one of the regiments that participated in the conquest of Québec in 1759. The fort itself, built to protect Montréal from American invasion, is now Stewart Museum at the Fort, which tells the story of colonial life in Montréal through displays of old firearms, maps, and uniforms. The fort is also the site of Le Festin du Gouverneur (☞ Dining, below) a re-creation of a 17th-century banquet. The two companies of colonial soldiers raise the flag every day at 11 am, practice their maneuvers at 1 pm, put on a combined dispaly of precision drilling and musket fire at 2:30, and lower the flag at 5. Children can participate. ☎ *514/861–6701.* ☒ *$5.* ☉ *Summer, Wed.–Mon. 10–6; winter, Wed.–Mon. 10–5.*

Plage de l'Ile Notre-Dame. This strip of sand is often filled to capacity in summer. The swimming beach is an oasis, with clear, filtered lake water, and an inviting stretch of lawn and trees. Lifeguards are on duty; there is a shop that rents swimming and boating paraphernalia, and there are picnic areas and a restaurant. ☒ *$3.* ☉ *Daily.*

DINING

Montréal has more than 4,500 restaurants of every price range, representing more than 75 ethnic groups. When you dine out, you can, of course, order à la carte, choosing each course yourself. But many of the better restaurants offer a table d'hôte menu as well, a kind of two- to four-course package deal selected by the chef. It's usually cheaper, often offers interesting special dishes, and may also take less time to prepare. If you want to splurge with your time and money, indulge yourself with the *menu de dégustation,* a five- to seven-course dinner executed by the chef. It usually includes soup, salad, fish, sherbet (to refresh the taste buds), a meat dish, dessert, and coffee or tea. At the city's finest restaurants, such a meal for two, along with a good bottle of wine, can easily cost close to $200 and last three or four hours; done well, it's worth every cent and every second.

A word about language. Menus in many restaurants are bilingual, but some are in French only. If you don't understand what a dish is, don't be shy about asking; a good server will be delighted to explain. If you feel brave enough to order in French, remember that in French an entrée is an appetizer and what English-speakers call an entrée is a *plat principal,* or main dish.

Chinese

$$–$$$ ✕ **Chez Chine.** The restaurant sits beside a miniature lake full of fat goldfish and is crossed by little stone bridges that zig and zag to fool evil spirits; there's also a huge skylight and a waterfall. The impressive menu has a whole page of specialties for shark-fin fans, along with such delicacies as a clay pot full of sautéed beef slices that have been stir-fried with fresh

Beaver Club, **20**
Bens, **22**
Bocca d'Oro, **29**
Bonaparte, **11**
Café Stash, **12**
Chez Better, **10**
Chez Chine, **18**
Chez Clo, **9**
Chez Delmo, **17**
Gibby's, **13**
Guy and Dodo
Morali, **21**
Hélène de
Champlain, **14**
Katsura, **26**
La Sucrerie de la
Montagne, **1**
Le Café de Paris, **25**
Le Passe-Partout, **30**
Le Taj, **24**
Les Halles, **28**
Les Trois Tilleuls, **16**
L'Express, **7**
Magnan, **31**
Maison Kam Fung, **19**
Milos, **3**
Moishe's, **5**
Nuances, **15**
Pizzaiole, **2, 3, 27**
Sawatdee Thai, **32**
Schwartz's, **8**
Toqué, **6**
Wilensky's Light
Lunch, **4**
Zen, **23**

Montréal Dining

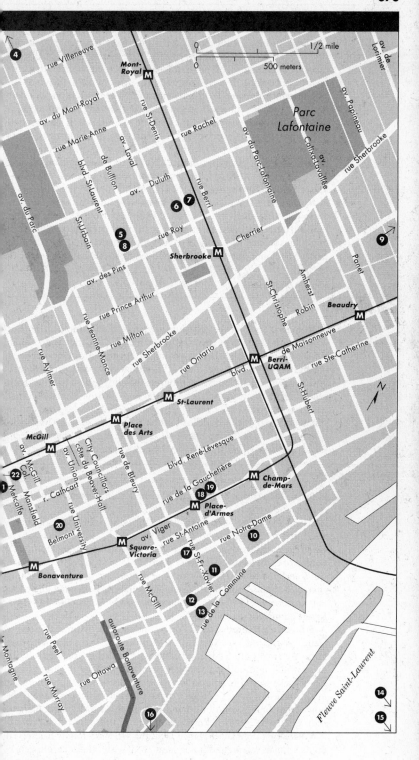

ginger, green onions, and oyster sauce. ✉ *Holiday Inn Centre-Ville, 99 rue Viger Ouest,* ☏ *514/878–9888. AE, D, DC, MC, V.*

$$–$$$ ✕ **Zen.** This mod establishment has a prix-fixe menu that should not be missed. Called the "Zen Experience," the meal is a kind of all-you-can-eat extravaganza, except that instead of helping yourself to a buffet of precooked dishes, you are presented with a menu of 45 magnificently prepared Szechuan items and asked to select one at a time until you can't possibly eat any more. If that doesn't suit your fancy, for the same price you can try the Chinese fondue, which features delicate Chinese cooking with some Thai, Malaysian, and Indonesian dishes mixed in for variety. Try the fillet of chicken with crispy spinach or the chicken with black bean sauce. This is very fine Chinese cuisine. ✉ *Le Westin Mont-Royal, 1050 rue Sherbrooke Ouest,* ☏ *514/499– 0801. Reservations essential. AE, DC, MC, V.*

$$ ✕ **Maison Kam Fung.** This bright, airy restaurant offers the most reliable dim sum lunch in Chinatown. Every day from 10 to 3, waiters push a parade of trolleys through the restaurant, carting treats like firm dumplings stuffed with pork and chicken, stir-fried squid, and delicate pastry envelopes filled with shrimp. Evening meals include delicacies like roast suckling pig. ✉ *1008 rue Clark,* ☏ *514/878–2888. Reservations not accepted for dim sum. AE, MC, V.*

Continental

$$$ ✕ **Nuances.** The Québec government wanted the Casino de Montréal ★ on Ile Notre-Dame to be classy rather than flashy, and the casino's main restaurant is stunning. Diners sit amidst burnished rosewood paneling and have a magnificent view of Montréal. Start with sautéed duck foie gras with exotic fruits and progress to lightly grilled red tuna with vegetables marinated in balsamic vinegar and olive oil. Even dishes that have been approved by the Québec Heart and Stroke Foundation sound exciting, like the saddle of rabbit pot-au-feu served with mushrooms. ✉ *1 av. de Casino,* ☏ *514/392–2708. Reservations essential. Jacket and tie. AE, DC, MC, V. No lunch weekends.*

Delicatessens

$ ✕ **Bens.** On the menu of this large, efficient deli, all the items with "Bens" in the name are red or are covered in red: "Bens Cheesecake" is smothered in strawberries; "Bens Ice Cold Drink" is the color of electric cherry juice; and the specialty, the "Big Ben Sandwich," is two slices of rye bread enclosing a seductive, pink pile of juicy smoked meat (Montréal's version of corned beef). The decor is strictly '50s, with yellow and green walls and institutional furniture. The waiters are often wisecracking characters but are, nonetheless, incredibly efficient. Beer, wine, and cocktails are served. ✉ *990 blvd. de Maisonneuve Ouest,* ☏ *514/844–1000. Reservations not accepted. MC, V.*

$ ✕ **Schwartz's Delicatessen.** Its proper name is the Montreal Hebrew Delicatessen, but everyone calls it Schwartz's. The sandwiches are huge; the steaks are tender and come with grilled liver appetizers. To drink you'll find nothing stronger than a Coke. The furniture looks like it was rescued from a Salvation Army depot and the waiters are briskly efficient. Don't ask for a menu (there isn't one) and avoid the lunch hour unless you don't mind long lines. ✉ *3895 blvd. St-Laurent,* ☏ *514/842–4813, Reservations not accepted. No credit cards.*

$ ✕ **Wilensky's Light Lunch.** Since 1932 the Wilensky family has served up its special: salami and bologna on a "Jewish" (kaiser) roll, generously slathered with mustard. You can also get hot dogs or a chopped-egg sandwich, which comes with a pickle and an old-fashioned soda fountain drink like a cherry or pineapple cola (there's no liquor license).

The regulars at the counter are among the most colorful in Montréal—a visit here is a must. This neighborhood haunt was a setting for the film *The Apprenticeship of Duddy Kravitz*, from the novel by Mordecai Richler. The service does not prompt one to linger, but the prices make up for it. ⊠ *34 rue Fairmount Ouest*, ☎ *514/271–0247. Reservations not accepted. No credit cards. Closed weekends.*

French

$$$$ ✕ **Beaver Club.** Early fur traders started the Beaver Club in a shack during Montréal's colonial days. In the 19th century it became a social club for the city's business and political elite, and it still has the august atmosphere of a men's club. Today, it's a gourmet French restaurant and open to anyone with a reservation. The luncheon table d'hôte often includes an exotic dish, such as terrine of duckling with pistachios and onion, and always includes one or two health-conscious selections. The restaurant also specializes in such meaty dishes as roast prime rib of beef au jus. The waitstaff are veterans, and the service is as excellent as the food. ⊠ *La Reine Elizabeth hotel, 900 blvd. René-Lévesque Ouest*, ☎ *514/861–3511. Reservations essential. Jacket and tie. AE, D, DC, MC, V.*

$$$$ ✕ **Les Halles.** This restaurant took its name from the celebrated Parisian market, and the mirrors and murals of the decor reflect the market theme. The wine cellar is exceptional. The menu shows a lot of imagination without ignoring the classics: main dishes like Grapefruit Marie-Louise with scallops and lobster or roasted duck with pears sit comfortably beside the chef's ventures into nouvelle cuisine, such as his lobster with ginger and coconut. The desserts are classic, delicious, and remarkably fresh. The Paris-Brest, a puff pastry with praline cream inside, is one of the best in town. ⊠ *1450 rue Crescent*, ☎ *514/844–2328. Reservations essential. AE, DC, MC, V. Closed Sun. and some holidays. No lunch Mon. or Sat.*

$$$$ ✕ **Les Trois Tilleuls.** Just 30 minutes southeast of town, you can lunch or dine on delectable food right on the Rivière Richelieu. This small, romantic inn, one of the prestigious Relais et Châteaux chain, has a terrace and a large, airy dining room with beautiful sunset views. The chef specializes in cream of onion soup, sweetbreads, and game dishes. ⊠ *290 rue Richelieu, Saint Marc sur Richelieu*, ☎ *514/584–2231. Reservations essential. AE, DC, MC, V.*

$$$ ✕ **Guy and Dodo Morali.** This comfortable room with pale yellow walls
★ and lots of art is in the very exclusive Cours Mont-Royal shopping plaza. In summer, dining spills out onto a little terrace on rue Metcalfe. Guy's cooking is classic French with a splash of modern flair; his menu is 70% seafood. His daily table d'hôte menu is the best bet, with openers such as excellent lobster bisque followed by beef Wellington (a house specialty), poached salmon, or fillet of halibut with leeks. Desserts are exquisite—try the *tatan*, apples and caramel with crème anglaise. ⊠ *Les Cours Mont-Royal, 1444 rue Metcalfe*, ☎ *514/842–3636. Reservations essential. AE, D, DC, MC, V.*

$$$ ✕ **Hélène de Champlain.** The food here is good if unadventurous (rack of lamb, filet of sole amandine), but people come for the setting. The restaurant is in the middle of the park on Ile Ste-Hélène, with views over the river and the city. The large dining room with its fireplace and antique furnishings is delightful. ⊠ *Ile Ste-Hélène near Métro station*, ☎ *514/395–2424. Reservations essential. AE, DC, MC, V.*

$$$ ✕ **Le Café de Paris.** Patrons sit at large, well-spaced tables in a room ablaze with flowers and with light streaming through the French windows. The Ritz garden, with its picturesque duck pond, is open for summer dining alfresco. The menu opens with a selection of fresh caviar.

You can then choose from such classics as escalope de veau Viennoise or steak tartare. At meal's end the waiter will trundle over the dessert cart; the royale chocolat and the *îles flottant* (puffs of soft meringue in custard) are favorites. ⌧ *Ritz-Carlton, 1228 rue Sherbrooke Ouest,* ☎ *514/842–4212. Reservations essential. Jacket required. AE, D, DC, MC, V.*

$$$ ✕ **Le Passe-Partout.** New York–born James MacGuire might make the
★ best bread in Montréal—moist but airy with a tight, crispy crust. He and his wife, Suzanne Baron-Lafrenière, sell this delicacy, along with homemade pâtés and terrines, in a storefront bakery next door to their restaurant. The handwritten menu is short and changes according to mood and availability, but each dish is a gem. You might start with smoked salmon, a potage of curried sweet potatoes, or perhaps a venison terrine. Entrées include swordfish steak served with a purée of red cabbage or a loin of veal with poached cucumbers and house-made noodles. ⌧ *3857 blvd. Décarie (5-min walk south from Ville-Marie Métro),* ☎ *514/487–7750. Reservations required. AE, DC, MC, V. No lunch Sat.–Mon., no dinner Sun.–Wed.*

$$$ ✕ **Toqué.** This is both the zaniest and most fashionable restaurant in
★ Montréal. Its name means "a bit crazy." Its appeal lies not just in its market-fresh ingredients whipped into dazzling combinations and colors, but also in the funky and eccentric ambience. The decor is a mix of florid red velvet, plain gray, and electric yellow that somehow works. The young and innovative chef-owner, Normand Laprise, and partner Christin LaMarche are among the best chefs in the city. The menu often features tournedos de saumon, smoked salmon, and warm foie gras, all flavored with fresh ingredients like red peppers, thinly shredded leeks, celery roots, and Québec goat cheese. The portions don't look big but they are surprisingly filling. ⌧ *3842 rue St-Denis,* ☎ *514/499–2084. Reservations essential. MC, V.*

$$–$$$ ✕ **L'Express.** This favorite Paris-style bistro is often crammed with popular media figures who come here to be seen—a task made easier by the mirrored walls. The atmosphere is smoky, and the noise level peaks on weekend evenings. The cuisine is always impeccable, the service is fast, and the prices are very good. The steak tartare with French fries, the salmon with sorrel, and the calves' liver with tarragon are marvelous. Jars of gherkins, fresh baguettes, and cheeses aged to perfection make the pleasure last longer. L'Express has one of the best and most original wine cellars in town. ⌧ *3927 rue St-Denis,* ☎ *514/845–5333. Reservations essential. AE, DC, MC, V.*

$ ✕ **Bonaparte.** In this wonderful little restaurant in the heart of Vieux-
★ Montréal, piped-in Mozart serenades diners surrounded by exposed brick walls. The traditional French dishes here have a light touch. You could start with a wild-mushroom ravioli seasoned with fresh sage and move on to a lobster stew flavored with vanilla and served with a spinach fondue, or a roast rack of lamb in a Port wine sauce. Lunch is a particularly good value. ⌧ *443 rue St-François-Xavier,* ☎ *514/844–4368. Reservations essential. AE, D, DC, MC, V. No lunch Sat.*

Greek

$$$$ ✕ **Milos.** Nets, ropes, floats, and lanterns—the usual cliché symbols of the sea—hang from Milos's walls and ceilings. The real display, however, in the refrigerated cases and on the beds of ice in the back by the kitchen, is fresh fish from all over the world: octopus, squid, shrimp, crabs, oysters, and sea urchins. The main dish at Milos is usually fish—pick whatever looks freshest—grilled over charcoal and seasoned with parsley, capers, and lemon juice. It's done to a turn and is achingly delicious. The fish are priced by the pound, and you can order one large fish to serve two or more. You'll also find lamb, steaks, chicken, cheeses, and olives. Milos is a healthy walk from Métro Laurier. You can also take Bus 51 from the same Métro stop and ask the driver to let you off at avenue du Parc; Milos is halfway up the block to the right. ⊠ *5357 av. du Parc,* ☎ *514/272–3522. Reservations essential. AE, D, DC, MC, V. No lunch Sat.*

Indian

$$–$$$ ✕ **Le Taj.** The cuisine of the north of India is produced here, less spicy and more refined than that of the south. The tandoori ovens seal in the flavors of the grilled meat and fish. Vegetarian dishes include the *taj-thali,* made of lentils, chili *pakoras,* basmati rice, and *saag panir*— spicy white cheese with spinach. A nine-course buffet is served daily at lunch for under $10, and in the evening there's an "Indian feast" for $20. The desserts—pistachio ice cream or mangoes—are often decorated with pure silver leaves. The Taj has a gift shop that sells Indian delicacies and objets d'art, as well as some of the ingredients used in the preparation of Taj dishes. ⊠ *2077 rue Stanley,* ☎ *514/845–9015. Reservations essential. AE, MC, V.*

Italian

$$$ ✕ **Bocca d'Oro.** This restaurant next to Métro Guy has a huge menu. One pasta specialty is *tritico di pasta:* one helping each of spinach ravioli with salmon and caviar, shellfish marinara, and spaghetti primavera. Also recommended is the *pasta mistariosa*—no cream, no butter, no tomatoes, but delicious nonetheless. With dessert and coffee, the waiters bring out a bowl of walnuts for you to crack at your table. The two-floor dining area is inexplicably decorated with a huge display of golf pictures, and Italian pop songs play in the background. The staff is extremely friendly and professional; if you're in a hurry, they'll serve your meal in record time. ⊠ *1448 rue St-Mathieu,* ☎ *514/933–8414. Reservations essential. AE, DC, MC, V. Closed Sun.*

$$ ✕ **Pizzaiole.** Pizzaiole brought the first wood-fired pizza ovens to Montréal, and it's still the best in the field. Whether you choose a simple tomato-cheese or a ratatouille on a whole-wheat crust—there are about 30 possible combinations—all the pizzas are made to order and brought to your table piping hot. The calzone is worth the trip. ⊠ *1446-A rue Crescent,* ☎ *514/845–4158;* ⊠ *5100 rue Hutchison,* ☎ *514/274–9349. AE, DC, MC, V.*

Japanese

$$$–$$$$ ✕ **Katsura.** This cool, elegant Japanese restaurant introduced sushi to Montréal and is the haunt of businesspeople who equate raw food with power. The sushi chefs create an assortment of raw seafood delicacies, as well as their own delicious invention, the cone-shaped Canada roll (smoked salmon and salmon caviar) at the sushi bar in the rear. The service is excellent, but if you sample all the sushi, the tab can be exorbitant. ⊠ *2170 rue de la Montagne,* ☎ *514/849–1172. Reservations essential. AE, DC, MC, V. No lunch weekends.*

Polish

$$–$$$ ✕ **Café Stash.** On chilly nights many Montrealers turn to Café Stash for sustenance—for roast pork or duck, hot borscht, pierogis, or cabbages and sausage—in short, for all the hearty specialties of a Polish kitchen. Diners sit on pews from an old chapel at refectory tables from an old convent. ⊠ *200 rue St-Paul Ouest,* ☎ *514/845–6611. AE, MC, V.*

Québécois

$$$$ ✕ **La Sucrerie de la Montagne.** On the road to Rigaud, toward Ottawa, maple syrup flows from carafes year-round and seasons plates of pork and beans, *tourtière* (meat pie flavored with cloves), ham, omelet soufflés, and crepes cooked over wood fires at this old-fashioned sugar hut. Pierre Faucher, the owner of this immense sugar cabin, who looks more like a lumberjack than a restaurateur, greets the Sunday passersby as well as the buses overflowing with tourists in the middle of July. An old-fashioned general store sells Québec handicrafts and maple syrup. ✉ *300 rang St-Georges, Rigaud (Rte. 40, Exit 17),* ☎ *514/451–5204. Reservations essential. AE, MC, V.*

$$ ✕ **Chez Clo.** Deep in the heart of east-end Montréal in a neighborhood where seldom is heard an English word, lies that rarest of Montréal culinary finds—authentic Québécois food. A meal here could start with a bowl of the best pea soup in the city, followed by a slab of *tourtière,* a mound of mashed potatoes, another of carrots and turnips, and a bowl of gloopy gravy on the side. And the best is yet to come. Desserts include bread pudding, egg pudding, and several flavors of *renversées* (upside-down cakes). But the restaurant is most famous for its *pudding au chomeur* (literally, pudding for the unemployed), a kind of shortcake smothered in a sauce thick with brown sugar. The service is noisy and friendly and the clientele mostly local. ✉ *3199 rue Ontario Est,* ☎ *514/522–5348. No credit cards.*

Sausages

$ ✕ **Chez Better.** The rustic fieldstone walls of historic Maison Sauvegarde create a fitting ambience for this North American branch of a popular European sausage house. Although the decor—exposed stone walls, casement windows, and dimmed lighting—is upscale, the limited nature of the menu keeps prices down, to only $3.95 in the case of the "Better Special," a satisfying sandwich of one mild sausage on freshly baked bread. It's a convenient refueling stop for visitors touring Vieux-Montréal, only a few steps from Place Jacques-Cartier. This Notre-Dame restaurant is the most elegant of the five "Betters." ✉ *160 rue Notre-Dame Est,* ☎ *514/861–2617;* ✉ *5400 chemin Côte-des-Neiges;* ✉ *1310 blvd. de Maisonneuve;* ✉ *4382 blvd. St-Laurent;* ✉ *1430 rue Stanley. Reservations essential. AE, MC, V.*

Seafood

$$$ ✕ **Chez Delmo.** Chez Delmo was founded at this address on rue Notre-Dame in 1910. Today, its location, halfway between the courts and the stock exchange, means that lunchtime finds it crammed with legal types gobbling oysters and fish. In the back is a more relaxed and cheerful dining room. A good first course is the seafood salad, a delicious mix of shrimp, lobster, crab, and artichoke hearts on a bed of Boston lettuce, sprinkled with a scallion vinaigrette. The poached salmon with hollandaise is a nice slab of perfectly cooked fish served with potatoes and broccoli. The service is efficient and low-key. ✉ *211–215 rue Notre-Dame Ouest,* ☎ *514/849–4061. Reservations essential. AE, DC, MC, V. Closed Sun., 2 wks in midsummer, and Christmas week.*

Steak

$$$ ✕ **Gibby's.** While the extensive menu here is rich in items like broiled
★ lobster, Dover sole meunière, and Cajun-blackened grouper, it was Gibby's first-class steaks—some say the best in the city—that made this magnificent restaurant famous. Gibby's also boasts its own on-site bak-

ery and makes its own ice cream. The thick gray stone walls and fireplaces here date to 1825, and the attention to service and detail also seems to belong to another age. ⊠ *298 Pl. d'Youville,* ☎ *514/282–1837. AE, D, DC, MC, V.*

$$$ ✕ **Moishe's.** The steaks here are big and marbled, and the Lighter brothers still age them in their own cold rooms for 21 days before charcoal grilling them, just the way their father did when he opened Moishe's more than 50 years ago. There are other things on the menu, such as lamb, veal sweetbreads, and grilled Arctic char—but people come for the beef. There's an exquisite selection of single-malt Scotches. ⊠ *3961 blvd. St-Laurent,* ☎ *514/845–3509. Reservations essential. AE, DC, MC, V. No lunch.*

$ ✕ **Magnan.** Women finally got free run (they were restricted to the upstairs dining room) of this tavern in working-class Pointe St-Charles in 1988, but the atmosphere remains decidedly and defiantly masculine. The decor is upscale warehouse and the half-dozen television sets are noisily stuck on professional sports. You can't beat the roast beef and the huge, industrial-strength steaks that range from 6 to 22 ounces. The tavern is right on the belt of parkland and bicycle paths that line the Lachine Canal, and is a great place to refuel after a strenuous pedal from downtown. It also has excellent beer from several local microbreweries on tap. ⊠ *2602 rue St-Patrick,* ☎ *514/935–9647. Reservations essential. AE, DC, MC, V.*

Thai

$$ ✕ **Sawatdee Thai.** The seedy stretch of rue Notre-Dame running west from avenue Atwater is one of the last places you'd expect to find a charming little restaurant decorated with exquisite Thai art and serving terrific Thai food. *Tom yam gay* is a spicy hot-and-sour chicken soup with lemongrass. *Som Tum* is a salad of papaya, dried shrimp, chili peppers, and lime juice. ⊠ *3453 rue Notre-Dame Ouest,* ☎ *514/ 938–8188. Reservations essential. AE, MC, V.*

LODGING

If you arrive in Montréal without a hotel reservation, the information booths at either airport can provide you with a list of hotels and room availability. You must, however, make the reservation yourself. Alternatively, there is a room reservation service at Info-touriste (☞ Contacts and Resources, *below*), which can find you a room in one of 80 hotels, motels, and bed-and-breakfasts.

Downtown

$$$$ ⊞ **Bonaventure Hilton International.** This large Hilton occupies the top
★ three floors of the Place Bonaventure exhibition center. From the outside the massive building is uninviting, but you step off the elevator into an attractive reception area flanked by an outdoor swimming pool (heated year-round) and 2½ acres of gardens. Also on this floor is Le Castillon restaurant, known for its three-course, 55-minute businessperson's lunch. All rooms have sleek modern furniture, pastel walls, and TVs in the bathrooms. The Bonaventure has excellent access to the Métro and the Underground City. ⊠ *1 Pl. Bonaventure, H5A 1E4,* ☎ *514/878–2332 or 800/267–2575,* ℻ *514/028–1442. 393 rooms. 3 restaurants, minibars, room service, pool, business services, shops. AE, D, DC, MC, V.*

$$$$ ⊞ **Hotel Inter-Continental Montréal.** This luxury hotel on the edge of
★ Vieux-Montréal is part of the Centre de Commerce Mondiale, a block-long retail and office development. Rooms are in a modernly built 24-

Auberge de Jeunesse Internationale de Montréal, **5**

Auberge de la Fontaine, **15**

Auberge Les Passants du Sans Soucy, **25**

Bonaventure Hilton International, **20**

Château Versailles, **3**

Days Inn Old Montréal, **26**

Delta Montréal, **17**

Holiday Inn Centre-Ville, **23**

Hotel Inter-Continental Montréal, **24**

Hôtel de la Montagne, **8**

Hôtel du Fort, **2**

Hôtel du Parc, **14**

Hôtel Radisson des Gouverneurs de Montréal, **21**

Hôtel Thrift Lodge, **27**

Howard Johnson Hôtel Plaza, **16**

Le Centre Sheraton, **7**

Le Marriott Château Champlain, **11**

Le Meridien, **22**

Le Nouvel Hôtel, **4**

Le Reine Elizabeth (Queen Elizabeth), **19**

Le Westin Mont-Royal, **12**

Loews Hôtel Vogue, **9**

McGill Student Apartments, **13**

Ritz-Carlton Kempinski, **11**

Université de Montréal Residence, **1**

YMCA, **10**

YWCA, **6**

Montréal Lodging

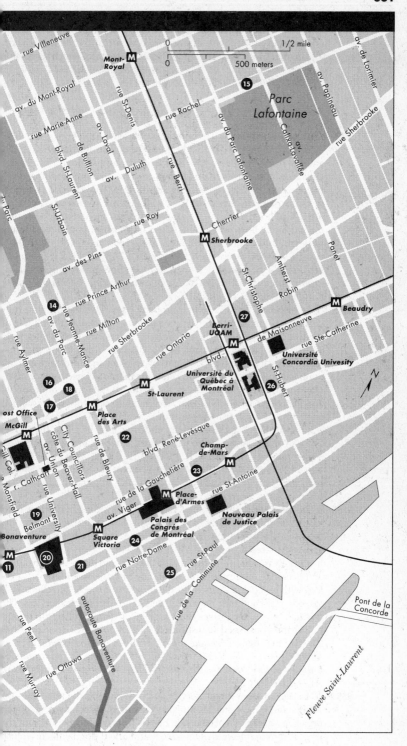

rue Villeneuve

av. du Mont-Royal

rue Marie-Anne

de Buillon

blvd. St-Laurent

St-Urbain

rue Villeneuve

Mont-Royal Ⓜ

rue St-Denis

av. Laval

Duluth

av.

rue Roy

av. des Pins

rue Rachel

Ⓜ **Sherbrooke**

Cherrier

av. du Parc Lafontaine

Ⓜ ⑮

Parc Lafontaine

av. Collax-tovaillée

av. Papineau

av. de Lormier

rue Sherbrooke

Panel

rue Prince Arthur

⑭

rue Jeanne-Mance

rue Milton

av. du Parc

rue Sherbrooke

rue Ontario

⑯
⑱

⑰

Ⓜ St-Laurent

Ⓜ **Place des Arts**

ost Office

McGill
Ⓜ

Gill Col.

r. Cathcart

av. Union

côte du Beaver-Hall

City Councillors

rue de Bleury

rue Aylmer

Ⓜ **Berri-UQAM**

Ⓜ
blvd.

Université du Québec à Montréal

⑳ ⑫

blvd. René-Lévesque

Champ-de-Mars
Ⓜ

⑳ ㉓

rue St-Antoine

㉗

de Maisonneuve

rue Ste-Catherine

St-Christophe

Amherst

Robin

Beaudry Ⓜ

Université Concordia Univesity

St-Hubert

㉖

Ⓜ **Place-d'Armes**

rue de la Gauchetière

av. Viger

Palais des Congrés de Montréal

Nouveau Palais de Justice

Belmont

Mansfield

rue University

⑲

Bonaventure
Ⓜ
⑪

⑳

㉑

Ⓜ **Square Victoria**

㉔

rue Notre-Dame

㉕

rue St-Paul

rue de la Commune

rue St-Antoine

rue Peel

rue Ottawa

rue Murray

autoroute Bonaventure

Pont de la Concorde

Fleuve Saint-Laurent

0 _____ 1/2 mile
0 _____ 500 meters

story brick tower with fanciful turrets and pointed roofs. They're large, with lush carpets, pastel walls, heavy drapes, and big windows overlooking either downtown or Vieux-Montréal and the waterfront. The main lobby is home to Le Continent Restaurant, which serves fine international cuisine. ⊠ *360 rue St-Antoine Ouest, H2Y 3X4,* ☎ *514/987–9900 or 800/327–0200; in the U.S. and Canada, 800/361–3600;* FAX *514/847–8550. 335 rooms, 22 suites. 2 restaurants, room service, indoor pool, sauna, health club, concierge, meeting facilities. AE, D, DC, MC, V.*

$$$$ 🏨 **Le Centre Sheraton.** This hotel is a favorite with celebrities. In a huge 37-story complex well placed between the downtown business district and the restaurant-lined streets of Crescent and Bishop, it offers services to both the business and tourist crowds. Rooms have coffee makers, irons, and ironing boards. The elite, 10-story Towers section is geared toward business travelers. The Sheraton caters to conventions. The rooms are typical hotel modern—beige, comfortable, and unremarkable, but the bar in the busy lobby is in a pleasant forest of potted trees, some of them 30 feet tall. ⊠ *1201 blvd. René-Lévesque Ouest, H3B 2L7,* ☎ *514/878–2000 or 800/325–3535,* FAX *514/878–3958. 784 rooms, 40 suites. 2 restaurants, 2 bars, indoor pool, beauty salon, sauna, health club with whirlpool and sauna, baby-sitting, business services, parking (fee). AE, D, DC, MC, V.*

$$$$ 🏨 **Le Meridien.** This Air France property rises 12 stories from the center of the Complexe Desjardins, a boutique-rich mall in the middle of the Underground City. The hotel caters to those who want ultramodern style like blonde wood and leather chairs in a huge lobby with patterned stone floors and potted plants overlooking a glassed-in swimming pool; a stainless-steel-and-glass elevator that looks like a space module to whisk guests from the ground floor to the fourth-floor lobby; and big rooms with lots of that sleek modern furniture with rounded edges and shiny finish. For instance, within Le Café Fleuri French restaurant there's a chicer, pricier enclave called Le Club. If you feel like a stroll, you can head to Chinatown, a five-minute walk away. ⊠ *4 Complexe Desjardins, C.P. 130, H5B 1E5,* ☎ *514/285–1450 or 800/543–4300,* FAX *514/285–1243. 572 rooms, 28 suites. 3 restaurants, piano bar, indoor pool, exercise room, sauna, whirlpool, baby-sitting, business services. AE, D, DC, MC, V.*

$$$$ 🏨 **Le Reine Elizabeth.** Le Reine Elizabeth, or Queen Elizabeth, is built
★ like a battleship—massive and gray. This Canadian Pacific hotel sits on top of the Gare Centrale train station in the very heart of the city across the street from Place Ville-Marie. The lobby is a bit too much like a railway station—hordes march this way and that—to be attractive and personal, but upstairs the rooms are modern, spacious, and spotless, with lush pale carpets, striped Regency wallpapers, and chintz bedspreads. The Penthouse floors—20 and 21—have business services. The hotel is home to the Beaver Club (☞ Dining, *above*), a flagship restaurant that is considered an institution. Conventions are a specialty here. ⊠ *900 blvd. René-Lévesque Ouest, H3B 4A5,* ☎ *514/861–3511 or 800/441–1414,* FAX *514/954–2256. 1,020 rooms. 2 restaurants, 4 lounges, indoor pool, health club, children's programs, beauty salon. AE, D, DC, MC, V.*

$$$$ 🏨 **Le Westin Mont-Royal.** Service and hospitality make this establish-
★ ment stand out among Montréal's best hotels. Its concierge desk can organize anything. The clientele here is primarily corporate, and the large rooms are decorated to serve that market: floral chintzes, plush carpeting, and English traditional furnishings. One of the city's best Chinese restaurants is the Zen (☞ Dining, *above*), downstairs. ⊠ *1050 rue Sherbrooke Ouest, H3A 2R6,* ☎ *514/284–1110 or 800/228–3000,* FAX *514/845–3025. 300 rooms, 28 suites. Restaurant, lounge.*

minibar, room service, pool, health club, whirlpool, 2 saunas. AE, D, DC, MC, V.

$$$$ ⊞ **Loews Hôtel Vogue.** The Vogue opened in late 1990, transforming
★ a drab office tower into a chic, elegant hotel with tall windows and a
facade of polished rose granite and deep aqua trim. It is in the heart
of downtown, right across the street from Ogilvy department store.
The lobby's focal point, the L'Opéra Bar, has an expansive bay window overlooking the trendy rue de la Montagne. Room furnishings are
upholstered with striped silk, and the beds are draped with lacy duvets. Fax machines and multiline telephones in rooms appeal to business travelers; the bathrooms—with whirlpool baths, televisions, and
phones—appeal to everyone. The Société Café on the lobby level is a
favorite among downtowners. ⊠ *1425 rue de la Montagne, H3G
1Z3,* ☎ *514/285–5555 or 800/465–6654,* ℻ *514/849–8903. 126
rooms, 16 suites. Restaurant, bar, exercise room. AE, D, DC, MC, V.*

$$$$ ⊞ **Ritz-Carlton Kempinski.** This property was opened in 1912 by lo-
★ cals who wanted a hotel where their rich European friends could indulge their champagne-and-caviar tastes. Since then, many earthshaking
events have occurred here, including the marriage of Elizabeth Taylor
and Richard Burton. Power meals are the rule at the elegant Le Café
de Paris (☞ Dining, *above*). Guest rooms are a successful blend of Edwardian style—some suites have working fireplaces—with such modern accessories as electronic safes. Careful and personal attention are
hallmarks of the Ritz-Carlton's service: your shoes get shines, there's
fresh fruit in your room, and everyone calls you by name. Even if you're
not a guest, stop by the Ritz's Hotel Courtyard during the summer for
afternoon tea and to see the duck pond, a Ritz tradition. At press time,
the hotel was in the middle of a multiphase restoration. ⊠ *1228 rue
Sherbrooke Ouest, H3G 1H6,* ☎ *514/842–4212 or 800/223–6800,*
℻ *514/842–3383. 201 rooms, 39 suites. 3 restaurants, bar, piano bar,
room service, barbershop. AE, DC, MC, V.*

$$$ ⊞ **Delta Montréal.** The Delta has the most complete exercise and pool
facility in Montréal and an extensive business center. The hotel's pub-
lic areas are spread over two stories and are decorated to look a bit
like a French château, with a huge baronial chandelier and thick, gold
patterned carpets. Rooms are big with plush broadloom, pastel walls,
mahogany-veneer furniture, and huge windows that overlook the
mountain or downtown. The jazz bar serves lunch on weekdays. ⊠
475 av. President-Kennedy, H3A 1J7, ☎ *514/286–1986 or 800/268–
1133,* ℻ *514/284–4306. 453 rooms, 10 suites. 2 restaurants, bar, in-
door and outdoor pools, sauna, health club, aerobics, 2 squash courts,
whirlpool, recreation room, video games, children's programs, busi-
ness services. AE, DC, MC, V.*

$$$ ⊞ **Holiday Inn Centre-Ville.** This Chinatown hotel is full of surprises,
★ from the two pagodas on the roof to the waterfall and fish pond in the
Chinese garden in the lobby. The hotel is one of the city's most charming, and its restaurant, Chez Chine (☞ Dining, *above*), is one of the
best Chinese restaurants in Montréal. There's an executive floor with
all the usual business facilities. The hotel has a pool and a small exercise room, but guests also have access to a plush private health and
leisure club downstairs with a whirlpool, saunas, a billiard room, and
a bar. The hotel is catercorner to the Palais des Congrès and a 5-
minute walk from the Centre de Commerce Mondiale. ⊠ *99 av. Viger
Ouest, H2Z 1E9,* ☎ *514/878–9888 or 800/465–4329,* ℻ *514/878–
6341. 325 rooms. Restaurant, lobby bar, pool, exercise room, business services. AE, D, DC, MC, V.*

$$$ ⊞ **Hôtel de la Montagne.** Upon entering the reception area you'll be
★ greeted by a naked, butterfly-winged nymph who rises out of a foun-
tain; an enormous crystal chandelier hangs from the ceiling. The decor

resembles Versailles rebuilt with a dash of Art Nouveau, although management prefers to describe it as a mix of Early American and Rococo. The rooms are tamer, large, and comfortable. There's a piano bar and a rooftop terrace, and a tunnel connects the hotel to Thursday's/Les Beaux Jeudis—a popular singles bar, restaurant, and dance club. The clientele is a bilingual mixture of French-speaking Montrealers stopping by for a drink and Torontans in town on business. If you're staying elsewhere, the reception area is at least worth a visit. ⊠ *1430 rue de la Montagne, H3G 1Z5,* ☎ *514/288–5656 or 800/361–6262,* 𝖥𝖠𝖷 *514/288–9658. 135 rooms. 2 restaurants, bar, pool, concierge. AE, D, DC, MC, V.*

$$$ 🏨 **Le Marriott Château Champlain.** In the heart of downtown Montréal, at the southern end of Place du Canada, is this 36-floor skyscraper with distinctive half moon–shape windows. The decor inside is formal, with only 20 rooms per floor. The floor-to-ceiling windows give the rooms a Moorish feel, but the furniture is elegantly French and the bedspreads are brightly patterned. Underground passageways connect the Champlain with the Bonaventure Métro station and Place Ville-Marie. ⊠ *1050 rue de la Gauchetière, H3B 4C9,* ☎ *514/878–9000 or 800/200–5909,* 𝖥𝖠𝖷 *514/878–6761. 616 rooms, 33 suites. Restaurant, bar, indoor pool, sauna, health club, no-smoking rooms. AE, DC, MC, V.*

$$–$$$ 🏨 **Auberge de la Fontaine.** The decor of this small hotel in the heart
★   of the trendy Plateau Mont-Royal district sounds wild—contrasting purple and bare-brick walls, a red molding separating yellow walls from a green ceiling, dark green doors with mauve frames—but the hotel is restful and delightful. Its 21 rooms are scattered over three floors in two turn-of-the-century residences. Some of them have whirlpool baths and a few have private balconies. Guests can use the little ground-floor kitchen and take whatever they like from its fridge full of snacks. The hotel is right on one of the city's bicycle paths and just across the street from Parc Lafontaine. ⊠ *1301 rue Rachel Est, H2J 2K1,* ☎ *800/597– 0597 or 514/597–0166,* 𝖥𝖠𝖷 *514/597–0496. 21 rooms with bath. Meeting room. CP. AE, DC, MC, V.*

$$–$$$ 🏨 **Hôtel du Fort.** All rooms here have good views of the city, the river, or the mountain, and have hair dryers, microwaves, refrigerators, and coffee makers, as well as comfortable desks with extra phone lines for modems and faxes. It's in the west end of downtown in a residential neighborhood known as Shaughnessy Village, close to shopping at the Faubourg Ste-Catherine and Square Westmount, and just around the corner from the Centre Canadien d'Architecture. Rates include Continental breakfast served in the charming Louis XV Lounge, which doubles as a bar in the evening. There is no restaurant on the premises, but the hotel is linked to Complexe du Fort where there are two good restaurants—Le Fuchsia and Café Suprême. ⊠ *1390 rue du Fort, H3H 2R7,* ☎ *514/938–8333 or 800/565–6333,* 𝖥𝖠𝖷 *514/938–2078. 127 rooms. Exercise room. CP. AE, DC, MC, V.*

$$–$$$ 🏨 **Hôtel du Parc.** This hotel's greatest virtue is its location. It's an L-shaped brick tower that faces northwest over Parc du Mont-Royal, just half a block away. The McGill University campus is a 5-minute walk to the west and the nightlife of rue Prince Arthur is just six blocks south. The hotel sits on top of a shopping mall with many stores and movie theaters. The hotel itself is a briskly efficient operation that caters to corporate clients. The rooms are large, and the decor is modern with lots of blonde wood and pastel shades. The lobby is dominated by a large and comfortable bar. ⊠ *3625 av. du Parc, H2X 3P8,* ☎ *514/288– 6666 or 800/448–8355; in Canada, 800/363–0735;* 𝖥𝖠𝖷 *514/288– 2469. 358 rooms, 20 suites. Restaurant, bar, café, no-smoking floors,*

2 outdoor pools, 1 indoor pool, tennis court, health club, squash. AE, D, DC, MC, V.

$$ 🏨 **Auberge Les Passants du Sans Soucy.** This gem is the only inn in ★ Vieux-Montréal. The building, on rue St-Paul behind the Basilique Notre-Dame, is a former fur warehouse dating to 1836; the foundations date to 1684. The lobby is also an art gallery that opens onto the street. Behind it are a living room and a dining room separated by a fireplace that crackles with burning hardwood in winter and lit by two skylights. The suite is on the ground floor, with a sitting room window overlooking the street. The rest of the rooms—all with private baths and discreetly hidden television sets—are on the second floor. This is one of the most romantic city hostelries you'll find anywhere, with brass beds, bare stone walls, exposed beams, soft lighting, whirlpool baths, and lots of fresh-cut flowers. But it's also a practical place for businesspeople, with fax machines at the front desk, and only a short walk from the financial district. ⊠ *171 rue St. Paul Ouest, H2Y 1Z5,* ☎ *514/842–2634,* FAX *514/842–2912. 8 rooms, 1 suite. CP. AE, DC, MC, V.*

$$ 🏨 **Château Versailles.** This charming hotel is unassuming, classy, and ★ not too expensive. It occupies a row of four converted mansions on rue Sherbrooke Ouest near Métro Guy-Concordia. The owners have decorated it with antique paintings, tapestries, and furnishings; some rooms have ornate moldings and plaster decorations on the walls and ceilings. All rooms have king-size beds and curtains and bedspreads with colorful Victorian prints. Across the street, at 1808 rue Sherbrooke, is a former apartment hotel that the Villeneuve family added as an annex to the original town houses. Called La Tour Versailles, it has 107 larger, more modern rooms—at the same reasonable price. There is a fine French restaurant, the Champs-Elysées, in La Tour, and a breakfast room in the Château. The staff is extremely helpful and friendly. ⊠ *1659 rue Sherbrooke Ouest, H3H 1E3,* ☎ *514/933–3611 or 800/361–3664; in Canada, 800/361–7199;* FAX *514/933–7102. 70 rooms in Château; 105 rooms, 2 suites in La Tour. Restaurant, breakfast room. AE, DC, MC, V.*

$$ 🏨 **Days Inn Old Montréal.** This is a moderately priced hotel near the restaurants and nightlife of rue St-Denis. Rooms have brightly colored bedspreads, modern furniture, and in-room movies. The restaurant, Il Cavaliere, serves Italian food and is popular with locals. The hotel is next to the Université du Québec à Montréal; the Berri-UQAM Métro stop is a block away. ⊠ *1199 rue Berri, H2L 4C6,* ☎ *514/845–9236 or 800/932–5985,* FAX *514/849–9855. 154 rooms. Restaurant, no-smoking floors, 3 meeting rooms. AE, DC, MC, V.*

$$ 🏨 **Hôtel Radisson des Gouverneurs de Montréal.** Abutting the stock exchange, this property rises above a three-story atrium-reception area and is attractive to convention crowds. It's near Place Bonaventure, the western fringe of Vieux-Montréal, and the Square Victoria Métro (accessible via an underground passage). There's an exclusive floor for higher-paying guests and a shopping arcade on the underground level. The Tour de Ville on the top floor is the city's only revolving restaurant, and its bar has live jazz nightly. Chez Antoine, an art nouveau–style bistro, serves gourmet salads and sandwiches. ⊠ *777 rue University, H3C 3Z7,* ☎ *514/879–1370 or 800/361–8155,* FAX *514/879–1761. 550 rooms, 23 suites. 2 restaurants, bar, indoor pool, steam room, health club. AE, DC, MC, V.*

$$ 🏨 **Howard Johnson Hôtel Plaza.** This medium-size, medium-price hotel, next to the McGill campus, caters to businesspeople and families. There are exercise machines and a spa with sauna, and the lobby is decorated in Art Deco style with dark-green leather furniture, brass trim, and marble tables. Rooms have chintz furniture and brass lamps. There are also several two-story suites with tall, dramatic windows overlooking downtown. The restaurant, La Découverte, is decorated with brass and marble and has bay windows overlooking the street and a terrace for outdoor dining. The Hôtel Plaza is handy to downtown business and shopping areas. ⊠ *475 rue Sherbrooke Ouest, H3A 2L9,* ☎ *514/842–3961 or 800/446–4656,* FAX *514/842–0945. 194 rooms. Restaurant, café, sauna, exercise room. AE, DC, MC, V.*

$$ ⊞ **Le Nouvel Hôtel.** In its four towers this hotel has a mix of brightly colored and functional studios and 2½-room apartments. It is near the restaurants and bars on rues Crescent, de la Montagne, and Bishop, six blocks from the heart of downtown, and two blocks from the Guy-Concordia Métro station. ⊠ *1740 blvd. René-Lévesque Ouest, H3H 1R3,* ☎ *514/931–8841 or 800/363–6063,* FAX *514/931–3233. 126 rooms, 60 2½-room units. Restaurant, bar, pool. AE, DC, MC, V.*

$ ⊞ **Hôtel Thrift Lodge.** This hotel is adjacent to the Terminus Voyageur bus station (buses park directly beneath one wing of the hotel), and some of the bus-station aura has rubbed off on the place: It's a little dingy. But if you're stumbling after a long bus ride and want somewhere to stay *now*, the Roussillon's rooms are large and clean, the service is friendly, and the price is right. It's also handy to the Berri-UQAM Métro station. ⊠ *1600 rue St-Hubert, H2L 3Z3,* ☎ *514/849–3214,* FAX *514/849–9812. 147 rooms. Restaurant. AE, MC, V.*

$ ⊞ **YMCA.** This clean Y is downtown, next to Peel Métro station. Men should book at least two days in advance; women should book seven days ahead because there are fewer rooms with showers for them. Anyone staying summer weekends must book at least a week ahead. There is a full gym facility and a typical Y cafeteria. ⊠ *1450 rue Stanley, H3A 2W6,* ☎ *514/849–8393,* FAX *514/849–8017. 331 rooms, 429 beds. Cafeteria, health club. AE, MC, V.*

$ ⊞ **YWCA.** Very close to dozens of restaurants, the Y is right downtown, one block from rue Ste-Catherine. Although men can eat at the café, the overnight facilities and health club are for women only. If you want a room with any amenities you must book in advance; not all of the rooms come with a sink and bath. ⊠ *1355 blvd. René-Lévesque, H3G 1P3,* ☎ *514/866–9941,* FAX *514/861–1603. 107 rooms. Café, pool, sauna, aerobics, exercise room, shops. MC, V.*

McGill University Area

$ ⊞ **Auberge de Jeunesse Internationale de Montréal.** This youth hostel is in the heart of downtown just a two-minute walk from Windsor Station and the Centre Molson, home of the Montréal Canadiens. It charges $16 per person, per night, for members, and $18 for Canadian nonmembers. Other nonmembers have to buy a membership ($25). Rooms sleep 3–10 people (same sex); some rooms are available for couples and families. There are kitchen facilities and lockers for valuables. Reserve early during summer. ⊠ *1030 rue Mackay, H3G 2H1,* ☎ *514/843–3317,* FAX *514/934–3251. 263 beds. Coin laundry. DC, MC, V.*

$ ⊞ **McGill Student Apartments.** From mid-May to mid-August, when McGill is on summer recess, you can stay in its dorms on the grassy, quiet campus in the heart of the city. Nightly rates are $28 students, $36.75 nonstudents (single rooms only). As a visitor, you may use the campus swimming pool and gym facilities for a fee. The university cafeteria is also open during the week, serving breakfast and lunch. ⊠ *3935 rue University, H3A 2B4,* ☎ *514/398–6367,* FAX *514/398–6770. 1,000 rooms. MC, V.*

Université de Montréal Area

$ 🏨 **Université de Montréal Residence.** The university's student housing accepts visitors from early May to late August. It's on the other side of Mont-Royal from downtown and Vieux-Montréal, but is right next to the Edouard Monpetit Métro station. The rooms have phones for local calls; common lounges have microwaves and TVs. For a fee, visitors may use the campus sports facilities. Nightly rates are $21 per night and $100 per week for students, and $31 per night and $141 per week for nonstudents. ⌧ 2350 blvd. Edouard-Montpetit, H3C 3J7, ☎ 514/343–6531, FAX 514/343–2353. 750–800 rooms. AE, MC, V.

NIGHTLIFE AND THE ARTS

The entertainment section of the *Gazette*, the English-language daily paper, is a good place to find out about upcoming events in Montréal. The Friday Preview section has an especially good list of all events at the city's concert halls, theaters, clubs, dance spaces, and movie houses. Other publications listing what's on include the *Mirror, Hour, Scope,* and *Voir* (in French), distributed free at restaurants and other public places. You can also phone **Info-Arts (Bell)** (☎ 514/790–2787) for events information.

For tickets to major pop and rock concerts, shows, festivals, and hockey and baseball games, go to the individual box offices or call **Admission** (☎ 514/790–1245 or 800/361–4595) or **Ticketmaster** (☎ 514/790–1111) for tickets to Théâtre St-Denis. Place des Arts tickets may be purchased at its box office underneath the Salle Wilfrid-Pelletier, next to the Métro station.

The Arts

Dance

Traditional and contemporary dance companies thrive in Montréal, though many take to the road or are on hiatus in the summer. **Ballets Classiques de Montréal** (☎ 514/866–1771) performs mostly classical programs. **Les Grands Ballets Canadiens** is the leading Québec company (☎ 514/849–8681 or 514/849–0269). **Ouest Vertigo Danse** (☎ 514/251–9177) stages innovative, postmodern performances. **Montréal Danse** (☎ 514/845–2031). **LaLaLa Human Steps** (☎ 514/277–9090) is an avant-garde, exciting powerhouse of a company. **Les Ballets Jazz de Montréal** (☎ 514/982–6771) experiments with new musical forms. **Margie Gillis Fondation de Danse** (☎ 514/845–3115) gives young dancers and choreographers opportunities to develop their art. **Tangente** (☎ 514/525–1860) is a nucleus for many of the more avant-garde dance troupes. When not on tour, many of these artists can be seen at Place des Arts or at any of the **Maisons de la Culture** (☎ 514/872–6211) performance spaces around town. Montréal's dancers have a downtown performance and rehearsal space, the **Agora Dance Theatre** (⌧ 840 rue Chérrier Est, ☎ 514/525–1500), affiliated with the Université de Montréal dance faculty. Every other September (that is, in the odd-numbered years, such as 1997), the **Festival International de Nouvelle Danse** brings "new" dance to various venues around town. Tickets for this event always sell quickly.

Music

The **Orchestre Symphonique de Montréal** (☎ 514/842–9951) has gained world renown under the baton of Charles Dutoit. When not on tour, its regular venue is the Salle Wilfrid-Pelletier at the Place des Arts. The orchestra also gives Christmas and summer concerts in the

Basilique Notre-Dame and pop concerts at the Arena Maurice Richard in Olympic Park. Also check the *Gazette* listings for its free summertime concerts in Montréal's city parks. Montréal's other orchestra, the **Orchestre Métropolitain de Montréal** (☎ 514/598–0870), also stars at Place des Arts most weeks during the October–April season. McGill University's **Pollack Concert Hall** (☎ 514/398–4547) is the site of concerts, notably by the **McGill Chamber Orchestra.** The city is home to one of the best chamber orchestras in Canada, I Musici de Montréal (☎ 514/982–6037). **L'Opéra de Montréal** (☎ 514/985–2258) stages four productions a year at Place des Arts.

The **Montréal Forum** (⊠ 2313 rue Ste-Catherine Ouest, ☎ 514/932–2582 or 800/678–5440) has 20,000 seats. **Stade Olympique** (⊠ Parc Olympique, ☎ 514/252–8687), much larger than the Forum, hosts rock and pop concerts. The 2,500-seat **Théâtre St-Denis** (⊠ 1594 rue St-Denis, ☎ 514/849–4211) is the second-largest auditorium in Montréal (after Salle Wilfrid-Pelletier in Place des Arts). Sarah Bernhardt and many other famous actors have graced its stage. The **Spectrum** (⊠ 318 rue Ste-Catherine Ouest, ☎ 514/861–5851) is an intimate concert hall.

Theater

French-speaking theater lovers will find a wealth of dramatic productions. There are at least 10 major companies in town, some that have an international reputation. **Théâtre de Quat'Sous** (⊠ 100 av. des Pins Est, ☎ 514/845-7277) performs modern, experimental, and cerebral plays. **Théâtre du Nouveau Monde** (⊠ 84 rue Ste-Catherine Ouest, ☎ 514/866–8667) is the North American temple of French classics. **Théâtre du Rideau Vert** (⊠ 4664 rue St-Denis, ☎ 514/844–1793) specializes in modern French repertoire. Anglophones have less to choose from. **Centaur Theatre** (⊠ 453 rue St-François-Xavier, ☎ 514/288–3161), the best-known English theatrical company, stages Beaux-Arts–style productions in the former stock exchange building in Vieux-Montréal. English-language plays can also be seen at the **Saidye Bronfman Centre** (⊠ 5170 chemin de la Côte Ste-Catherine, ☎ 514/739–2301 or 514/739–7944), a multidisciplinary institution that is a focus of cultural activity for Montréal as a whole and for the Jewish community in particular. The center was a gift from the children of Saidye Bronfman in honor of their mother's lifelong commitment to the arts. The Mies van der Rohe–inspired building was originally designed by Mrs. Bronfman's daughter, Montréal architect Phyllis Lambert. Many of its activities, such as gallery exhibits, lectures on public and Jewish affairs, performances, and concerts, are free to the public. The center, is home to the **Yiddish Theatre Group,** one of the few Yiddish companies performing today in North America. Michel Tremblay is Montréal's premier playwright, and all of his plays are worth seeing, even if in the English translation. Touring companies of Broadway productions can often be seen at the **Théâtre St-Denis** (⊠ 1594 rue St-Denis, ☎ 514/849–4211), as well as at Place des Arts (☎ 514/842–2112)—especially during the summer months.

Nightlife

Comedy

The **Comedy Nest** (⊠ 1740 blvd. René-Lévesque Ouest, ☎ 514/932–6378) has shows by name performers, up-and-comers, and new talent.

Discos

What was the glitziest disco in town, **Metropolis** (⊠ 59 rue Ste-Catherine Est, ☎ 514/288–2020), now has occasional theme evenings for a young, primarily French-speaking crowd. Most popular is Toro Toro, an evening of Latin dance the first Friday of every month. **Club 737** (✉ 1 Place Ville Marie, ☎ 514/397–0737) on top of Place Ville-Marie does the disco number every Thursday, Friday, and Saturday night. This has become very popular with the upscale, mid-20s to mid-30s crowd. The view is magnificent and there is an open-air rooftop bar to cool off. The **Zoo** (✉ 3556 blvd. St-Laurent, ☎ 514/848–6398) is *the* place for the beautiful people. **Hard Rock Café** (✉ 1458 rue Crescent, ☎ 514/987–1420). **Thursday's** (✉ 1449 rue Crescent, ☎ 514/288–5656) is a popular disco.

Folk

Hurley's Irish Pub (✉ 1225 rue Crescent, ☎ 514/861–4111) attracts some of the city's best Celtic musicians and dancers. An enthusiastic crowd sings along with Québécois performers at the **Deux Pierrots Boîte aux Chansons** (✉ 104 rue St-Paul Est, ☎ 514/861–1270).

Jazz

Montréal has a very active local jazz scene. The best-known club is Vieux-Montréal's **L'Air du Temps** (✉ 191 rue St-Paul Ouest, ☎ 514/842–2003). This small, smoky club presents 90% local talent and 10% international acts from 5 PM on into the night. Downtown, duck into **Biddle's** (✉ 2060 rue Aylmer, ☎ 514/842–8656), where bassist Charles Biddle holds forth most evenings when he's not appearing at a local hotel. Biddle's serves pretty good ribs and chicken. You might also try the **Quai des Brumes Dancing** (✉ 4481 rue St-Denis, ☎ 514/499–0467).

The annual **Festival International de Jazz de Montréal** (Montréal International Jazz Festival) brings together 2,000 musicians from 20 countries who enjoy more than 400 concerts over 11 days, from the end of June to the beginning of July. Festival dates for 1997 are June 26 to July 6. The biggest of the big names have played, including B.B. King, Buddy Guy, Etta James, Al Jareau, Charlie Haden, and Pat Metheny. And 75% of concerts are presented free of charge on the outdoor stages of the festival site: four city blocks that are closed to traffic. In addition to jazz, you can hear blues, Latin rhythms, gospel, Cajun, and world music as you wander from stage to stage. **Bell Info-Jazz** (☎ 514/871–1881 or 888/515–0515) answers all queries about the festival and about travel packages. Leave your name and address and they'll send you a program. You can charge tickets over the phone (☎ 514/790–1245 or 800/678–5440; in Canada, 800/361–4595).

Rock

Rock clubs seem to spring up, flourish, then fizzle out overnight. **Club Soda** (✉ 5240 av. du Parc, ☎ 514/270–7848), the granddaddy of them all, sports a neon martini glass complete with neon effervescence outside. Inside it's a small hall with a stage, three bars, and room for about 400 people. International rock acts play here, as does local talent. It's also a venue for the comedy and jazz festivals. The club is open only for shows. Phone the box office to find out what's on. **Déjà Vu** (✉ 1224 rue Bishop, ☎ 514/866–0512), a rock club with a nostalgia theme, is popular with young English-speakers. **L'Ours Qui Fume** (✉ 2019 rue St-Denis, ☎ 514/845–6998), or the Smoking Bear, is loud, raucous, and very Francophone.

OUTDOOR ACTIVITIES AND SPORTS

Most Montrealers would probably claim they hate winter, but the city is rich in cold-weather activities—skating rinks, cross-country ski trails, toboggan runs, and even a downhill ski run. In summer, there are ten-

nis courts, miles of bicycle trails, golf courses, and two lakes on the island for boating and swimming.

Participant Sports

Bicycling

The island of Montréal—except for Mont-Royal itself—is quite flat,
and there are more than 20 cycling paths in the metropolitan area. Bikes
are welcome on the first and last cars of Métro trains during non-rush
hours. Ferries at the Vieux-Port will take you to Ile Ste-Hélène and the
south shore of the St. Lawrence River. You can rent 10-speed bicycles
at **Cyclo-Touriste at the Centre Info-Touriste** (⊠ 1001 sq. Dorchester,
☏ 514/393–1528). One of the most interesting paths follows the **Lachine Canal** (1825) from Vieux-Montréal to the shores of Lac St.-
Louis in suburban Lachine. Along the way you can stop at the bustling
Atwater Farmer's Market (⊠ 110 av. Atwater) to buy the makings of
a picnic. In Lachine you can visit the **Fur Trade at Lachine Historic Site**
(⊠ 1255 blvd. St-Joseph, Lachine, ☏ 514/637–7433). **Parks Canada**
(☏ 514/283–6054 or 514/637–7433) conducts guided cycling tours
along the Lachine Canal every summer weekend.

Golf

For a complete listing of the many golf courses in the Montréal area,
call **Tourisme-Québec** (☏ 514/873–2015 or 800/363–7777).

Hunting and Fishing

The lakes and rivers around Montréal teem with fish, and a number
of guides offer day trips, but you'll need a provincial license first. For
complete information, call **Tourisme-Québec** (☏ 514/873–2015 or
800/363–7777).

Ice Skating

There are at least 195 outdoor and 21 indoor rinks in the city. There
are huge ones on Ile Ste-Héléne and at the Vieux-Port. Call the **Parks
and Recreation Department** (☏ 514/872–6211) for further information. There is year-round skating in the **Amphithéatre Bell** (☏ 514/395–
0555, Ext. 237) in Le 1000 Rue de la Gauchetière.

Jogging

Montréal became a runner's city following the 1976 Olympics. There
are paths in most city parks, but for running with a panoramic view,
head to the dirt track in **Parc du Mont-Royal** (take rue Peel, then the
steps up to the track).

Rafting

French settlers built Montréal where they did because they couldn't get
their boats safely past the Lachine Rapids—which means Montréal is
one of the few cities in the world where you can get in a boat at a downtown wharf and be crashing through Class V white water minutes later.
For more than a decade, Jack Kowalski has been taking thrill-seekers
on a 45-minute voyage through the rapids in big, sturdy aluminum jet
boats. He supplies heavy-water gear, but it's impossible to stay dry—
or have a bad time. He also offers speed-lovers a half-hour trip around
the islands in smaller, 10-passenger boats that can go 60 miles an hour.
Reservations are required; trips are narrated in French and English. ⊠
*Lachine Rapids Tours Ltd., 105 rue de la Commune (Quai de l'Hor-
loge or Clock Tower Pier),* ☏ 514/284–9607. ☞ *$48.* ☉ *5 trips through
rapids May–Sept., daily at 10, noon, 2, 4, and 6.*

Skiing

CROSS-COUNTRY

Trails crisscross most of the city's parks, including Parc des Iles, Maisonneuve, and Mont-Royal. Parc Angrignon in the nearby suburb of LaSalle is good for skiers as well, but the best is probably the 900-acre **Cap St-Jacques Regional Park** in suburban Pierrefonds on the west end of Montréal Island.

DOWNHILL

For the big slopes you'll have to go northwest to the Laurentians (☞ Chapter 10), or south to the Eastern Townships (☞ Chapter 10), an hour or two away by car. There is a small slope in Parc du Mont-Royal. Pick up the "Ski-Québec" brochure at **Tourisme-Québec** offices (☎ 514/873–2015 or 800/363–7777).

Squash

Reserve court time three days ahead at **Nautilus Centre St-Laurent Côte-de-Liesse Racquet Club** (✉ 8305 chemin Côte-de-Liesse, ☎ 514/739–3654).

Swimming

There is a large indoor pool at the Olympic Park's **Centre Aquatique** (Métro Viau, ☎ 514/252–4622) and at **Centre Sportif et des Loisirs Claude-Robillard** (✉ 1000 av. Emile Journault, ☎ 514/872–6900). The outdoor pool on Ile Ste-Hélène is an extremely popular (and crowded) summer gathering place, open June–Labor Day. The city-run beach at Ile Notre-Dame is the only natural swimming hole in Montréal (☎ 514/872–6211).

Tennis

There are public courts in the Jeanne-Mance, Kent, Lafontaine, and Somerled parks. For details, call the **Parks and Recreation department** (☎ 514/872–6211).

Windsurfing and Sailing

Sailboards and small sailboats can be rented at **L'Ecole de Voile de Lachine** (✉ 2105 blvd. St-Joseph, Lachine, ☎ 514/634–4326) and the **Société du Parc des Iles** (☎ 514/872–6093).

Spectator Sports

Baseball

The National League's **Montréal Expos** (☎ 514/253–3434 or 800/463–9767) play at the Olympic Stadium from April through September.

Cycling

Le Tour de l'Ile de Montréal (☎ 514/521–8356) has made the *Guinness Book of World Records* for attracting the greatest number of participants. More than 30,000 amateur cyclists participate in "North America's most important amateur cycling event" each June, wending their way 70 kilometers (38 miles) through the streets and parks of Montréal.

Grand Prix

The annual **Molson Grand Prix du Canada** (☎ 514/392–0000 or 514/392–4731), which draws top Formula 1 racers from around the world, takes place every June at the **Gilles Villeneuve Race Track** on Ile Notre-Dame.

Hockey

The **Montréal Canadiens,** winners of 23 Stanley Cups, meet National Hockey League rivals at the Centre Molson (✉ 1250 rue de la Gauchetière Ouest, ☎ 514/932–2582), which opened in spring 1996.

SHOPPING

Montrealers *magasinent* (go shopping) with a vengeance, so it's no surprise that the city has 160 multifaceted retail areas encompassing some
7,000 stores.

The law allows shops to stay open weekdays 9–9 and weekends 9–
5. However, many merchants close Monday–Wednesday evenings and
on Sunday. You'll find many specialty service shops closed on Monday, particularly in predominantly French neighborhoods. Stores in designated tourist zones, such as Vieux-Montréal, remain open on Sunday.

Just about all stores, with the exception of some bargain outlets and
a few selective art and antiques galleries, accept major credit cards. Buying with plastic usually gets you the best daily exchange rate on the
Canadian dollar. If you're shopping with cash, buy your Canadian money
at a bank or exchange bureau beforehand. Most purchases are subject
to a federal goods and services tax (GST) of 7% as well as a provincial tax of 8%.

Montréal Specialties

Visitors usually reserve at least one day to hunt for either exclusive fashions along rue Sherbrooke or bargains at the Vieux-Montréal flea
market. But there are specific items that the wise shopper seeks out in
Montréal.

Fine English bone china, crystal, and woolens are more readily available and cheaper in metropolitan stores than in their U.S. equivalents,
thanks to Canada's tariff status as a Commonwealth country.

CHINA AND CRYSTAL

Collectors of china and crystal will find reasonable prices at **Caplan
Duval** (⊠ Cavendish Mall, Côte-St-Luc, ☎ 514/483–4040; ⊠ Plaza
Côte-des-Neiges, Montréal, ☎ 514/345–0000), which has an over-
whelming variety of patterns.

FUR

Montréal is one of the fur capitals of the world. Close to 85% of
Canada's fur manufacturers are based in the city, as are many of their
retail outlets. Many of them are clustered along rue Mayor and rue de
Maisonneuve between rue Bleury and rue Aylmer. **McComber** (⊠ 402
blvd. de Maisonneuve Ouest, ☎ 514/845–1167) has been in business
for 100 years and its present owner has a flair for mink designs.
Shuchat (⊠ 418 blvd. de Maisonneuve Ouest, ☎ 514/849–2113) has
been in the same family for more than 40 years and has a pleasant showroom full of the latest fashions. **Grosvenor** (⊠ 400 blvd. de Maisonneuve Ouest, ☎ 514/288–1255) caters more to the wholesale trade,
but has several showrooms where customers can view its decidedly European styles. **Alexandor** (⊠ 2055 rue Peel, ☎ 514/288–1119), is nine
blocks west of the main fur trade area and its storefront showroom
caters to the downtown trade. **Birger Christensen at Holt Renfrew** (⊠
1300 rue Sherbrooke Ouest, ☎ 514/842–5111) is perhaps the most
exclusive showroom of the lot with prices to match.

If you think you might be buying fur, it is wise to check with your country's customs officials before leaving to find out which animals are considered endangered and cannot be imported. Do the same if you think
you might be buying Inuit carvings, many of which are made of whale-
bone and ivory and cannot be brought into the United States.

Centre-Ville

Downtown is Montréal's largest retail district. It takes in rue Sherbrooke, boulevard de Maisonneuve, rue Ste-Catherine, and the side streets between them. Because of the proximity and variety of shops, it's the best shopping bet for visitors in town overnight or over a weekend. The area bounded by rues Sherbrooke and Ste-Catherine, and rues de la Montagne and Crescent has antiques and art galleries in addition to designer salons. Rue Sherbrooke is lined with an array of art and antiques galleries. Rue Crescent is a tempting blend of antiques, fashions, and jewelry displayed beneath colorful awnings.

Complexe Desjardins

Complexe Desjardins (⊠ blvd. René-Lévesque and rue Jeanne Mance) is filled with splashing fountains and exotic plants, which give it a Mediterranean joie de vivre, even when it's below freezing outside. To get here take the Métro to the Place des Arts and follow the tunnels to Desjardins's multitiered atrium mall. The roughly 80 stores include budget outlets like Le Château for clothing as well as the exclusive Jonathan Roche Monsieur for men's fashions.

Department Stores

Eaton (⊠ 677 rue Ste-Catherine Ouest, ☎ 514/284–8411) is the city's leading department store and part of Canada's largest chain. Founded in Toronto by Timothy Eaton, the first Montréal outlet appeared in 1925. It now sells everything—from fashions and furniture to meals in the Art Deco top-floor restaurant and zucchini loaves in the basement bakery. Everything, that is, except tobacco. Timothy was a good Methodist and his descendants honor his principles.

La Baie—The Bay in English—(⊠ 585 rue Ste. Catherine Ouest) has been a department store since 1891. It was originally named Morgan's, but in 1960 it was bought by the Hudson Bay Company and acquired its present name. La Baie is known for its duffel coats and its Hudson Bay red-, green-, and white-striped blankets. It also sells the typical department store fare.

Exclusive **Holt Renfrew** (⊠ 1300 rue Sherbrooke Ouest, ☎ 514/842–5111), is known for its furs. The city's oldest store, it was established in 1837 as Henderson, Holt and Renfrew Furriers, and made its name supplying coats to four generations of British royalty. When Queen Elizabeth II married Prince Phillip in 1947, Holt's created a priceless Labrador mink as a wedding gift. Holt's carries the exclusive and pricey line of furs by Denmark's Birger Christensen, as well as the haute-couture and prêt-à-porter collections of Yves St-Laurent.

A kilted piper regales shoppers at **Ogilvy** (⊠ 1307 rue Ste-Catherine Ouest, ☎ 514/942–7711) every day at noon. An institution with Montrealers since 1865, the once-homey department store has undergone a miraculous face-lift. Fortunately, it preserved its delicate pink glass chandeliers and still stocks traditional apparel by retailers like Aquascutum and Jaeger. The store has been divided into individual designer boutiques selling pricier lines than La Baie or Eaton. It used to be Ogilvy's (just as Eaton used to be Eaton's) before Québec's French-only sign laws made apostrophes illegal.

Faubourg Ste-Catherine

A good place to start is the **Faubourg Ste-Catherine** (⊠ 1616 rue Ste-Catherine Ouest, at rue Guy), a vast bazaar abutting the Grey Nuns' convent grounds. There are three levels of clothing and crafts boutiques, as well as food counters and kiosks. You can pick up Québec maple syrup at a street-level boutique or a fine French wine for about $30 at the government-run Société d'Alcools du Québec. Prices at most stores here are generally reasonable, especially if you're sampling the varied ethnic cuisine of the snack counters.

Les Cours Mont-Royal

Les Cours Mont-Royal (⊠ 1550 rue Metcalfe) is *très élégant*. It's linked to both the Peel and McGill Métro stations and caters to expensive tastes, but even bargain hunters find it an intriguing spot for window shopping. Beware: The interior layout can be disorienting.

Les Promenades de la Cathédrale

The unusual location of **Les Promenades de la Cathédrale** (⊠ rues Ste-Catherine Ouest and University) makes it a sightseeing adventure as well as a shopping destination: It's directly beneath stately Christ Church Cathedral, the seat of Montréal's Anglican (Episcopalian) bishop. Les Promenades, which is connected to the McGill Métro station, has Canada's largest Linen Chest outlet, with hundreds of bedspreads and duvets draped over revolving racks plus aisles of china, crystal, linen, and silver. It's also home to the Anglican Church's Diocesan Book Room, which sells an unusually good and ecumenical selection of books as well as tasteful religious objects.

Place Bonaventure

Place Bonaventure (⊠ rues de la Gauchetière and University), is one of Canada's largest commercial exhibition centers. It's directly above the Bonaventure Métro station and has a mall with some 120 stores, including the trendy Au Coton and Bikini Village and the practical Bata Shoes. There are also a number of fun shops: Ici-Bas for outrageous hose, Le Rouet for handicrafts, and Miniatures Plus for exquisite dolls' furniture and tiny gifts.

Place Montréal Trust

Place Montréal Trust (⊠ 1600 rue McGill College, at rue Ste-Catherine Ouest) is the lively entrance to an imposing glass office tower. Shoppers, fooled by the aqua and pastel decor, may think they have stumbled into a California mall. Prices at the 110 outlets range from hundreds (for designs by Alfred Sung, haute couture at Gigi, or men's fashions at Rodier) to only a few dollars (for sensible cotton T-shirts or steak-and-kidney pies at the outpost of famed British department store Marks & Spencer). This shopping center is linked to the McGill Métro station.

Place Ville-Marie

Weatherproof shopping began in 1962 beneath the 42-story cruciform towers of **Place Ville-Marie** (⊠ blvd. René-Lévesque and rue Université). It's linked to the Bonaventure Métro station via Place Bonaventure, Central Station, and Le Reine Elizabeth and to the McGill station via the Centre Eaton, another major downtown shopping mall reached by taking the corridor from Centre Eaton south to Place Ville-Marie. Renovations opened Place Ville-Marie to the light, creating a more cheerful ambience.

Stylish women head to Place Ville-Marie's 100-plus retail outlets for the clothes (haute couture at Tristan & Iseut and Cactus). The upscale department store Holt Renfrew has an outlet here, and traditionalists will love Aquascutum. More affordable clothes shops include Dalmys and Reitmans. For shoes, try Mayfair, Brown's, François Villon, and French.

Notre-Dame Ouest

The place for antiquing is Notre-Dame Ouest, beginning at rue Guy and continuing west to avenue Atwater (a five-minute walk south from the Lionel-Groulx Métro station). Once a shabby strip of run-down secondhand stores, this area has blossomed beyond its former nickname of Attic Row. It now has the highest concentration of antiques, collectibles, and curiosity shops in Montréal. Collectors can find Canadian pine furniture—armoires, cabinets, spinning wheels, rocking chairs—for reasonable prices here. Consider a Sunday tour, beginning with brunch at **Salon de Thé Ambiance** (⊠ 1874 rue Notre-Dame Ouest, ☎ 514/939–2609), a charming restaurant that also sells antiques. Try **Antiquités Landry** (⊠ 1726 rue Notre-Dame Ouest, ☎ 514/937–7040) for solid pine furnitrue. **Viva Gallery** (⊠ 1970 rue Notre-Dame Ouest, ☎ 514/952–3200) specializes in Asian antiques. **Héritage Antique Métropolitain** has elegant English and French furniture. **Deuxième** (⊠ 1880 rue Notre-Dame Ouest, ☎ 514/933–8560) sells a fascinating jumble of objects from every age,

Rue Chabanel

And now for something completely different. **Rue Chabanel,** in the north end of the city, is the soul of Montréal's extensive garment industry. Every Saturday, from about 8:30 to 1, many of the manufacturers and importers in the area open their doors to the general public. At least, they do if they feel like it. What results is part bazaar, part circus, and often all chaos—but quite friendly chaos. When Montrealers say "Chabanel," they mean the eight-block stretch just west of boulevard St-Laurent. The factories and shops there are tiny—dozens of them are crammed into each building. The goods seem to get more stylish and more expensive the farther west you go. For really cheap leather goods, sportswear, children's clothes, and linens, try the shops at 99 rue Chabanel. For more deluxe options, drop into 555 rue Chabanel. The manufacturers and importers here have their work areas on the upper floors and have transformed the mezzanine into a stylish mall with bargains in men's suits, winter coats, knitted goods, and very stylish leather jackets. A few places on Chabanel accept credit cards, but bring cash, anyway. It's easier to bargain if you can flash bills, and if you pay cash, the price will often "include the tax."

Rue Wellington

Two sturdy institutions that bear witness to the working-class origins of much of Montréal's English-speaking population anchor the ends of this lively thoroughfare crammed with bargain clothing stores, grocery stores, and tanning salons near the de l'Eglise Métro station in the Verdun neighborhood. **Muirs** (⊠ 3651 rue Wellington, ☎ 514/768–2422), which supplies haggis for dozens of Robert Burns dinners every January, is a tiny shop decorated in early-Depression that makes and sells Scottish meat pies, potato scones, sausage rolls, egg custards, shortbread, and Empire biscuits (jam-filled, glazed cookies that are to die for). **Stilwells** (⊠ 5123 rue Wellington, ☎ 514/766–4481) has been at the same seedy little shopfront since 1926, making chocolate creams, truffles, peanut brittle, and the best humbugs (a striped hard candy that tastes of carmelized sugar and mint) in the known universe. (The place closes down every July and August because, the Stilwells say, chocolate doesn't set worth a darn in summer. But rumor has it they spend those months on a huge yacht called the S.S. *Humbug*.) The sparkling, modern **Chez Gaumond** (⊠ 3725 rue Wellington, ☎ 514/768–2564) is one of the best pastry shops on Montréal Island, with a wonderful array of desserts, cakes, pâtés, and homemade ice cream and sherbet. If you get peckish looking at all this food, try the Peruvian specialties at **Villa Wellington** (⊠ 4701 rue Wellington, ☎ 514/768–0102) or, for something a bit grander, the excellent Italian food at **Casa Rossi** (⊠ 5145 rue Wellington, ☎ 514/761–2578).

Square Westmount and Avenue Greene

Square Westmount (⊠ rue Ste-Catherine Ouest and av. Greene) has some of the city's finest shops (and the most luxurious public washrooms on the island), which is hardly surprising—it serves the mountainside suburb of Westmount, home to executives and former prime ministers. Humbler types can get there easily by taking the Métrovia to the Atwater station, and following the tunnel to Square Westmount. **Collange** (☎ 514/933–4634) sells lacy lingerie. **Ma Maison** (☎ 514/933–0045) stocks quality housewares. **Hugo Nicholson** (☎ 514/937–1937) sells exclusive fashions for men and women. The very elegant **Marché de Westmount** has an array of gourmet boutiques that sell pastries, cheeses, pâtés, fruits, cakes, chocolates, etc. You can assemble your own picnic and eat it at one of the little tables scattered among the stalls. If all this tires you out, you can stop in at the **Spade Westmount** (☎ 514/933–9966) for a massage. The square opens onto **avenue Greene,** two flower-lined blocks of restored redbrick row houses full of boutiques, restaurants, and shops. **Double Hook** (⊠ 1235A av. Greene, ☎ 514/932–5093) sells only Canadian books. And try the **Coach House** (⊠ 1325 av. Greene, ☎ 514/937–6191) for antique silverware.

Upper Boulevard St-Laurent and Avenue Laurier Ouest

Upper boulevard St-Laurent—which runs roughly from avenue du Mont-Royal north to rue St-Viateur and climbs the mountain to rue Bernard—has blossomed into one of Montréal's chicest *quartiers*. It's not entirely surprising, given that much of this area lies within or adjacent to Outremont, an enclave of wealthy Francophone Montrealers, with restaurants, boutiques, nightclubs, and bistros catering to the upscale visitor. **Scandale** (⊠ 3639 blvd. St-Laurent, ☎ 514/842–4707) has designs for the very hip as well as great lingerie and a second-hand clothes store. **J. Schrecter** (⊠ 4350 blvd. St-Laurent, ☎ 514/845–4231) had been supplying work duds for blue-collar workers for decades when the grunge look suddenly made the store trendy.

Shoppers flock to the two blocks of avenue Mont-Royal just east of boulevard St-Laurent for a series of shops that sell secondhand clothes and recycled clothes (things like housecoats chopped into sassy miniskirts). **Scarlett O'Hara** (⊠ 254 av. Mont-Royal Est, ☎ 514/844–9435) started the whole trend. **Eva B** (⊠ 2013 blvd. St-Laurent, ☎ 514/849–8246) sells new clothes as well as used. **Hatfield & McCoy** (⊠ 156 av. Mont-Royal Est, ☎ 514/982–0088) recycles clothes from the '30s, '40s and '50s.

Avenue Laurier Ouest, from boulevard St-Laurent to chemin de la Côte-Ste-Catherine, is roughly an eight-block stretch; you'll crisscross it many times as you explore its fashionable and trendy shops, which carry everything from crafts and clothing to books and paintings. **Tilley Endurables** (⊠ 158 av. Laurier Ouest, ☎ 514/272–7791) sells the famous Canadian-designed Tilley hat and other easy-care travel wear. **Boutique Gabriel Filion** (⊠ 1127 av. Laurier Ouest, ☎ 514/274–0697) sells interesting imported toys and a marvelous array of dolls, doll clothes, stuffed animals, and music boxes. For Asian and African crafts, try **Artefact** (⊠ 102 av. Laurier Ouest, ☎ 514/278–6575).

Vieux-Montréal

Despite Vieux-Montréal's abundance of garish souvenir shops, a shopping spree there can be worthwhile. Both rues Notre-Dame and St-Jacques, from rue McGill to Place Jacques-Cartier, are lined with low to moderately priced fashion boutiques and shoe stores. **Tripps** (⊠ 389 rue Notre-Dame Ouest, ☎ 514/845–1979), a pioneer clothes discounter, sells boxes full of end-of-the-line, brand-name goods in its huge, cluttered shop. **Desmarais et Robitaille** (⊠ 60 rue Notre-Dame Ouest, ☎ 514/845–3194), a store that supplies churches with vestments and liturgical aids, has Québécois carvings and handicrafts as well as tasteful religious articles. **Rue St-Paul** also has some interesting shops and art galleries. **Drags** (⊠ 367 rue St-Paul Est, ☎ 514/866–0631) is crammed with fragments of military uniforms and loads of clothes, shoes, hats, and accessories from the '30s and '40s. **L'Empreinte Coopérative** (⊠ 272 rue St-Paul Est, ☎ 514/861–4427) has a fine collection of Québec handicrafts. **Rita R. Giroux** (⊠ 206 rue St-Paul Ouest, ☎ 514/8444714) makes flamboyant dried flower creations. At the **Cerf Volanterie** (⊠ 224 rue St-Paul Ouest, ☎ 514/845–7613), Claude Thibaudeau makes sturdy, gloriously colored kites that he signs and guarantees for three years. The **Galerie Art & Culture** (⊠ 227 rue St-Paul Ouest, ☎ 514/843–5980) specializes in Canadian landscapes. **Galerie des Arts Relais des Epoques** (⊠ 234 rue St-Paul Ouest, ☎ 514/844–2133) sells some fascinating work by contemporary Montréal painters.

The Vieux-Port hosts a sprawling flea market, the **Marché aux Puces.** Dealers and pickers prowl through the huge hangar searching for secondhand steals and antique treasures. ⊠ *King Edward Pier,* ☉ *May 5–28, Fri. and Sun. 11–9, Sat. 11–10; May 31–Aug. 27, Wed., Thurs., and Sun. 11–9, Sat. 11–10; July and Aug., Tues. 11–9.*

MONTRÉAL A TO Z

Arriving and Departing

By Bus

For information about the following three companies, contact Terminus Voyageur (☞ *below*). **Greyhound** has coast-to-coast service and serves Montréal with buses arriving from and departing for various cities in North America. **Vermont Transit** serves Montréal via Boston, New York, and other points in New England. **Voyageur** and **Voyageur-Colonial** service destinations primarily within Québec and Ontario. The city's downtown bus terminal, **Terminus Voyageur** (⊠ 505 blvd. de Maisonneuve Est, ☎ 514/842–2281), connects with the Berri-UQAM Métro station.

By Car

Montréal is accessible from the rest of Canada via the Trans-Canada Highway, which enters the city from the east and west via Routes 20 and 40. The New York State Thruway (I–87) becomes Route 15 at the Canadian border, and then it's 47 kilometers (30 miles) to the outskirts of Montréal. U.S. I–89 becomes two-lane Route 133, which eventually joins Route 10, at the border. From I–91 from Massachusetts, you must take Routes 55 and 10 to reach Montréal. At the border you must clear Canadian Customs, so be prepared with proof of citizenship and your vehicle's ownership papers. On holidays and during the peak summer season, expect waits of a half hour or more at the major crossings.

Once you're in Québec, the road signs will be in French, but they're designed so you shouldn't have much trouble understanding them. The speed limit is posted in kilometers; on highways the limit is 100 kph (about 62 mph). There are extremely heavy penalties for driving while intoxicated, and drivers and front-seat passengers must wear over-the-shoulder seat belts. Gasoline is sold in liters (3¾ liters equal 1 U.S. gallon), and lead-free is called *sans plomb*. If you're traveling in winter, remember that your car may not start on extra-cold mornings unless it has been kept in a heated garage. All Montréal parking signs are in French, so brush up on your *gauche* (left), *droit* (right), *ouest* (west), and *est* (east).

Montréal police have a diligent tow-away and fine system for cars double-parked or stopped in no-stopping zones in downtown Montréal during rush hours and business hours. A parking ticket will cost between $35 and $40. If your car is towed away while illegally parked, it will cost an additional $35 to retrieve it. Be especially alert during winter: Montréal's snow-clearing crews are the best in the world and a joy to watch in action after a major blizzard—but they're ruthless in dealing with any parked cars that get in their way. If they don't tow them, they'll bury them. New York, Maine, and Ontario residents should drive with extra care in Québec: Traffic violations in the province are entered on their driving records back home (and vice versa).

And if you drive in the city, remember two things: Québec law forbids you to turn right on a red light and Montrealers are notorious jaywalkers.

By Plane

Montréal is served by two airports. **Dorval International,** 22½ kilometers (14 miles) west of the city, handles domestic and most U.S. flights. **Mirabel International,** 54½ kilometers (34 miles) northwest of the city, is a hub for the rest of the international trade.

Air Canada (☎ 514/393–3333 or 800/361–8620) offers nonstop service from New York, Miami, and Tampa and from Boston via its connector airline, Air Alliance. Direct service is available from Los Angeles and San Francisco. **American Airlines** (☎ 800/433–7300) has nonstop service from Chicago with connections from the rest of the United States. **Canadian Airlines International** (☎ 514/847–2211 or 800/426–7000; in Canada, 800/363–7530) has a nonstop charter from Fort Lauderdale and direct or connecting service from Hawaii and Los Angeles. **Delta Air Lines** (☎ 514/337–5520 or 800/221–1212; in Québec Province, 800/361–1970) has nonstops from Boston, Hartford, Connecticut, and Miami and connecting service from most major U.S. cities. **USAir** (☎ 800/428–4322) has services from Philadelphia and Pittsburgh.

Flying time from New York is 1½ hours; from Chicago, two hours; from Los Angeles, 6½ hours (with a connection).

A **taxi** from Dorval to downtown will cost $25, from Mirabel about $56. All taxi companies in Montréal must charge the same rates by law. It is best to have Canadian money with you, because the exchange rate for U.S. dollars is at the driver's discretion. **Autobus Connaisseur** (☎ 514/934–1222) is a much cheaper alternative to taxis into town from Mirabel and Dorval. **Shuttle service** from Mirabel to the terminal next to the **Gare Centrale** (✉ 777 rue de la Gauchetière) is frequent and costs only $14.50. The shuttle from Dorval runs about every half hour and stops at Le Centre Sheraton, Le Château Champlain, Le Reine Elizabeth, and the Voyageur terminal. It costs $9. If you know you are going to use the bus to go back to either airport, you can save $8 by buying a round-trip ticket. Connaisseur also runs a shuttle between Dorval and Mirabel.

By Train

The Gare Centrale (Central Station), on rue de la Gauchetière between rues University and Mansfield (behind Le Reine Elizabeth), is
the rail terminus for all trains from the United States and from other
Canadian provinces. It is connected by underground passageway to the
Bonaventure Métro station.

Budget cuts killed **Amtrak's** (☎ 800/878–7245) overnight *Montrealer*
from Washington and New York, but the *Adirondack* still leaves New
York's Penn Station every morning for the 10½–hour trip through the
spectacular scenery of upstate New York to Montréal. It has a snack
car but no dinner service or sleepers. A round-trip ticket is usually cheaper
than two one-way fares.

VIA Rail (☎ 514/871–1331 or 800/561–3949; in Québec Province,
800/361–5390) connects Montréal with all the major cities of Canada,
including Québec City, Halifax, Ottawa, Toronto, Winnipeg, Edmonton, and Vancouver.

Getting Around

By Bus and Métro

Public transportation is easily the best and cheapest way to get around.
The Métro (subway) is clean, quiet (it runs on rubber wheels), and safe,
and it's heated in winter and cooled in summer. Métro hours on the
Orange, Green, and Yellow lines are weekdays 5:30 AM–12:58 AM, Saturday 5:30 AM–1:28 AM, and Sunday 5:30 AM–1:58 AM. The Blue Line
runs daily from 5:30 AM to 11 PM. Trains run as often as every three
minutes on the most crowded lines—Orange and Green at rush hours.
The Métro is also connected to the 29 kilometers (18 miles) of the Underground City, so you may not need to go outside during bad weather.
Each of the 65 Métro stops has been individually designed and decorated; Berri-UQAM has stained glass, and at Place d'Armes a small collection of archaeological artifacts is exhibited. The stations between
Snowdon and Jean-Talon on the Blue Line are worth a visit, particularly Outremont, with its glass-block design. Each station connects with
one or more bus routes, which cover the rest of the island. The STCUM
(Société de Transport de la Communauté Urbaine de Montréal) ad-
ministers both the Métro and the buses, so the same tickets and transfers are valid on either service. You should be able to get within a few
blocks of anywhere in the city on one fare. At press time rates were:
single ticket, $1.85; six tickets, $7.75; monthly pass, $44.50. Visitors
can buy a day pass for $5 or a three-day pass for $12. They're available at most major hotels and at Info-Touriste.

Free maps may be obtained at Métro ticket booths. Try to get the *Carte
Réseau* (system map); it's the most complete. Transfers from Métro to
buses are available from the dispenser just beyond the ticket booth inside the station. Bus-to-bus and bus-to-Métro transfers may be obtained
from the bus driver. For more information on reaching your destination call the **Société de Transport de la Communauté de Montréal**
(☎ 514/288–6287).

By Taxi

Taxis in Montréal all run on the same rate: $2.25 minimum and $1 a
kilometer. They're usually reliable, although they may be hard to find
on rainy nights after the Métro has closed. Each carries on its roof a white
or orange plastic sign that is lit when available and off when occupied.

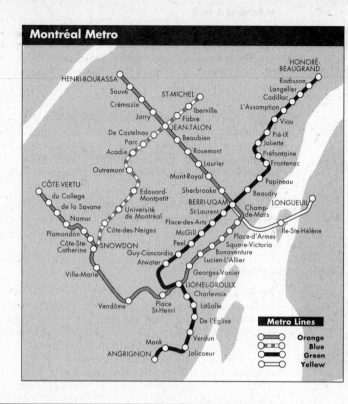

Montréal Metro

Metro Lines
Orange
Blue
Green
Yellow

Contacts and Resources

Car Rentals
Avis (☎ 514/866–7906 or 800/321–3652). **Budget** (☎ 514/938–1000). **Discount** (☎ 514/286–1554). **Dollar** (☎ 514/990–0074 or 800/800–4000). **Hertz** (☎ 514/842–8537 or 800/263–0678). **Tilden** (☎ 514/878–2771 or 800/387–4747). **Via Route** (☎ 514/521–5221).

Consulates
United States (⊠ 1155 rue St-Alexandre, ☎ 514/398–9695). Open weekdays 8:30–4:30. **United Kingdom** (⊠ 1000 rue de la Gauchetière Ouest, ☎ 514/866–5863). Open weekdays 9–5.

Doctors and Dentists
The U.S. Consulate cannot recommend specific doctors and dentists but does provide a list of various specialists in the Montréal area. Call in advance (☎ 514/398–9695) to make sure the consulate is open.

Dental clinic (☎ 514/342–4444) open 24 hours, Sunday emergency appointments only. **Montréal General Hospital** (☎ 514/937–6011). **Québec Poison Control Centre** (☎ 800/463–5060). **Touring Club de Montréal–AAA, CAA, RAC** (☎ 514/861–7111).

Emergencies
Dial 911 to reach the **police, fire,** and **ambulance.**

English-Language Bookstores
Coles (⊠ 1171 rue Ste-Catherine Ouest, ☎ 514/849–8825). **Double Hook** (⊠ 1235A av. Greene, ☎ 514/932–5093) sells only Canadian books. **Paragraphe** (⊠ 2065 rue Mansfield, ☎ 514/845–5811) has a café.

Guided Tours

BOAT

Amphi Tour Ltée (☎ 514/386–1298) offers a unique tour of Vieux-Mont-réal and the Vieux-Port on both land and water in an amphibious bus. The one-hour tours run from May to October. **Bateau-Mouche** (☎ 514/849–9952) runs four harbor excursions and an evening supper cruise every day from May to October. The boats are reminiscent of the ones that cruise the canals of the Netherlands—wide-beamed and low-slung, with a glassed-in passenger deck. Boats leave from the Jacques Cartier Pier at the foot of Place Jacques-Cartier in the Vieux-Port (Métro Champs-de-Mars).

CALÈCHE RIDES

Open horse-drawn carriages—fleece-lined in winter—leave from Place Jacques-Cartier, Square Dorchester, Place d'Armes, and rue de la Commune. An hour-long ride costs about $50 (☎ 514/653–0751).

ORIENTATION

Gray Line (☎ 514/934–1222) has nine different tours of Montréal in the summer and one tour during the winter. It offers pickup service at the major hotels, or you may board the buses at Info-Touriste (⊠ 1001 sq. Dorchester). **Murray Hill Trolley Buses** (☎ 514/871–4733) follow a 14-stop circuit of the city. Passengers can get off and on as often as they like and stay at each stop as long as they like. There's pickup service at major hotels.

Late-Night Pharmacies

Many pharmacies are open until midnight, including the following two. **Jean Coutu** (⊠ 501 Mont-Royal Est, ☎ 514/521–3481; ⊠ 5510 Côtes-des-Neiges, ☎ 514/344–8338). **Pharmaprix** (⊠ 1500 rue Ste-Catherine Ouest, ☎ 514/933–4744; ⊠ 5157 rue Sherbrooke Ouest, ☎ 514/484–3531). **Pharmaprix** (⊠ Promenades du Musée; ⊠ 5122 Côtes-des-Neiges, ☎ 514/738–8464; ⊠ 901 rue Ste-Catherine Est, ☎ 514/842–4915) is open 24 hours.

Lodging Reservations

Bed and Breakfast à Montréal represents more than 50 homes in downtown and in the elegant neighborhoods of Westmount and Outremont. Singles run $40–$55; doubles $55–$85. ⊠ *Marian Kahn, Box 575, Snowdon Station, H3X 3T8,* ☎ *514/738–9410,* FAX *514/735–7493.*

Downtown B&B Network represents 75 homes and apartments, mostly around the downtown core and along rue Sherbrooke, that have one or more rooms available for visitors. Singles are $25–$40, doubles $35–$55. Even during the height of the tourist season, this organization has rooms open. ⊠ *Bob Finkelstein, 3458 av. Laval (at rue Sherbrooke), H2X 3C8,* ☎ *514/289–9749 or 800/267–5180.*

There is a room reservation service at **Info-Touriste** (☎ 800/665–1528), which can find you a room in one of 80 hotels, motels, and bed-and-breakfasts.

Passes

The Montréal museum pass allows you access to 19 major museums, including most of the ones mentioned in this chapter. A day pass costs $15, a three-day pass $28; family passes are $30 for one day and $60 for three days. They are available at museums or **Centre Info-Touriste** (⊠ 1001 sq. Dorchester).

Travel Agencies

American Express (⊠ 1141 blvd. de Maisonneuve Ouest, ☎ 514/284–3300). **Canadian Automobile Club** (⊠ 1180 rue Drummond, ☎ 514/

861–5111). **Vacances Tourbec** (✉ 595 blvd. de Maisonneuve Ouest,
☎ 514/842–1400). **Voyages Campus** (✉ McGill University, 3480 rue
McTavish, ☎ 514/398–0647).

Visitor Information

Centre Info-Touriste (✉ 1001 sq. Dorchester, ☎ 514/873–2015 or
800/363–7777) on Square Dorchester is open June 10–Labor Day, daily
8:30–7:30, and Labor Day–June 9, daily 9–6. A second branch (✉
174 rue Notre-Dame Est, at pl. Jacques-Cartier, ☎ 514/873–2015) is
open Labor Day–mid-May, daily 9–1 and 2–5, and mid-May–Labor
Day, daily 9–7.

9 Québec City

Québec City, which enjoys one of the most beautiful natural settings in North America, perched on a cliff above a narrow point in the St. Lawrence River, is the capital of, as well as the oldest municipality in, Québec province.

By Alice H.
Oshins

Updated by
Donna
Nebenzahl

NO EXCURSION TO FRENCH-SPEAKING Canada is complete without a visit to exuberant, romantic Québec City, which enjoys one of the most beautiful natural settings in North America. The well-preserved Vieille Ville (Old City) is small and dense, steeped in four centuries of history and French tradition. Here you can explore 17th- and 18th-century buildings, the ramparts that once protected the city, and numerous parks and monuments. The Québec government has completely restored many of the centuries-old buildings of Place Royale, one of the oldest districts on the continent. Because of its immaculate preservation as the only fortified city remaining in North America, UNESCO has designated the Vieille Ville a World Heritage Site.

Perched on a cliff above a narrow point in the St. Lawrence River, Québec City is the oldest municipality in Québec province. In the 17th century the first French explorers, fur trappers, and missionaries came here to establish the colony of New France. Today it still resembles a French provincial town in many ways; its family-oriented residents have strong ties to their past. More than 95% of its metropolitan population of 650,000 are French-speaking.

In 1535 French explorer Jacques Cartier first came upon what the Algonquin Indians called "Kebec," meaning "where the river narrows." New France, however, was not actually founded in the vicinity of what is now Québec City until 1608, when another French explorer, Samuel de Champlain, recognized the military advantages of the location and set up a fort. On the banks of the St. Lawrence, on the spot now called Place Royale, this fort developed into an economic center for fur trade and shipbuilding. Twelve years later, Champlain realized the French colony's vulnerability to attacks from above and expanded its boundaries to the top of the cliff, where he built the fort Château St-Louis on the site of the present-day Château Frontenac.

During the early days of New France, the French and British fought for control of the region. In 1690, when an expedition led by Admiral Sir William Phipps arrived from England, Comte de Frontenac, New France's most illustrious governor, defied him with the statement, "Tell your lord that I will reply with the mouth of my cannons."

The French, preoccupied with scandals at the courts of kings Louis XV and Louis XVI, gave only grudging help to their possessions in the New World. The French colonists built walls and other military structures and had the advantage of the defensive position on top of the cliff, but they still had to contend with Britain's naval supremacy. On September 13, 1759, the British army, led by General James Wolfe, scaled the colony's cliff and took the French troops led by General Louis-Joseph Montcalm by surprise. The British defeated the French in a 20-minute battle on the Plains of Abraham, and New France came under British rule.

The British brought their mastery of trade to the region. During the 18th century, Québec City's economy prospered because of the success of the fishing, fur-trading, shipbuilding, and timber industries. Wary of new invasions, the British continued to expand upon the fortifications left by the French. They built a wall encircling the city and a star-shape citadel, both of which mark the city's urban landscape today. The constitution of 1791 established Québec City as the capital of Lower Canada until the 1840 Act of Union that united Upper and Lower Canada and made Montréal the capital. The city remained under British rule until 1867, when the Act of Confederation united several

Canadian provinces (Québec, Ontario, New Brunswick, and Nova Scotia) and established Québec City as capital of the province of Québec.

In the mid-19th century, the economic center of eastern Canada shifted west from Québec City to Montréal and Toronto. Today government is Québec City's main business: About 30,000 civil-service employees work and live in the area. Office complexes continue to spring up outside the older part of town; modern malls, convention centers, and imposing hotels now cater to an established business clientele.

Pleasures and Pastimes

Dining
Québec City reveals its French heritage most obviously in its cuisine. You'll discover a French touch in the city's numerous cafés and brasseries and in the artful presentation of dishes at local restaurants. This is the best place in the province to sample French-Canadian cuisine, composed of robust, uncomplicated dishes that make use of the region's bounty of foods, including fowl and wild game (quail, caribou, venison), maple syrup, and various berries and nuts. Because Québec has a cold climate for a good portion of the year, it has a traditionally heavy cuisine, with such specialties as *cretons* (pâtés), *tourtière* (meat pie), and *tarte au sucre* (maple-syrup pie).

Most dining establishments usually have a selection of dishes à la carte, but you'll often discover more creative specialties by opting for the table d'hôte, a two- to four-course meal chosen daily by the chef. At dinner, many restaurants will offer a *menu de dégustation,* a five- to seven-course dinner of the chef's finest creations. If you're budget-conscious, try the more expensive establishments at lunchtime. Lunch usually costs about 30% less than dinner, and many of the same dishes are available. Lunch is usually served 11:30 through 2:30; dinner, 6:30 until about 11. You should tip about 15% of the bill.

CATEGORY	COST*
$$$$	over $30
$$$	$20–$30
$$	$10–$20
$	under $10

*per person, excluding drinks, service, 7% federal sales tax, and 6.5% provincial sales tax

Lodging
With more than 35 hotels within its walls and countless family-run bed-and-breakfasts, Québec City has a range of lodging options. Landmark hotels stand as prominent as the city's most historic sites; modern high rises outside the ramparts offer spectacular views of the Old City. Visitors can immerse themselves in the city's historic charm by staying in one of the many old-fashioned inns where no two rooms are alike.

Be sure to make a reservation if you visit during peak season (May through September) or during the Winter Carnival, in February. During busy times, hotel rates usually rise 30%. From November through April, many lodgings offer discount weekend packages and other promotions.

CATEGORY	COST*
$$$$	over $140
$$$	$85–$140
$$	$50–$85
$	under $50

*All prices are for a standard double room, excluding 7% federal sales tax, 6.5% provincial sales tax, and an optional service charge.

Metropolitan Québec City

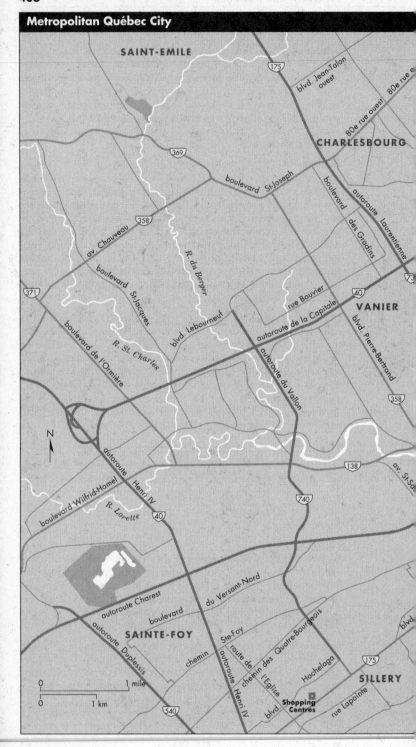

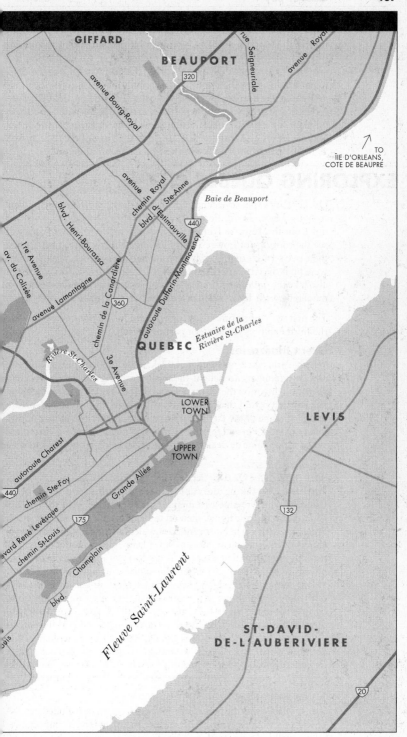

GIFFARD

BEAUPORT

320

rue Seigneuriale

avenue Royal

avenue Bourg-Royal

avenue

chemin Royal

chemin Ste-Anne

blvd d'Estimauville

TO
ÎLE D'ORLEANS,
COTE DE BEAUPRE

Baie de Beauport

blvd. Henri-Bourassa

1re Avenue

av. du Colisée

avenue Lamontagne

chemin de la Canardière

360

autoroute Dufferin-Montmorency

440

QUEBEC

Estuaire de la
Rivière St-Charles

Rivière St-Charles

3e Avenue

LEVIS

LOWER
TOWN

autoroute Charest

UPPER
TOWN

440

chemin Ste-Foy

Grande Allée

svard René Levêsque

175

chemin St-Louis

132

Champlain

blvd.

Fleuve Saint-Laurent

ouis

ST-DAVID-
DE-L'AUBERIVIERE

20

Walking

Québec City is a wonderful place to wander on foot. From Parc Mont-morency (Montmorency Park), you can see the Laurentian Mountains jutting majestically above the St. Lawrence River. Even more impressive vistas are revealed if you walk along the walls or climb to the city's highest point, Cap Diamant (Cape Diamond). You can spend days investigating the narrow cobblestone streets of the historic Old City, visiting historic sites or browsing for local arts and crafts in the boutiques of quartier Petit-Champlain. Strolling the Promenade des Gouverneurs and the Plains of Abraham, you are offered a view of the river as well as the Laurentian foothills and the Appalachian mountains.

EXPLORING QUÉBEC CITY

Québec City's split-level landscape divides the Upper Town on the cape from the Lower Town, along the shores of the St. Lawrence. If you look out from the Terrasse Dufferin boardwalk in Upper Town, you will see the rooftops of Lower Town buildings directly below. Separating these two sections of the city is steep and precipitous rock, against which were built the city's more than 25 *escaliers* (staircases). Today you can also take the *funiculaire* (funicular), a cable car that climbs and descends the cliff between Terrasse Dufferin and the Maison Jolliet in Lower Town.

The first two tours primarily focus on the oldest sections of town, while the third explores the modern part of the city.

Great Itineraries

Whether you take a weekend or a week, there's enough history, scenery, and entertainment to delight the most seasoned traveler. A weekend visitor might enjoy the historic sights of the Old City, strolling along ancient streets and the boardwalk by the river in the evening before dining at some of the city's fine restaurants. A week-long stay allows you to wander beyond the city proper, and might include a visit to the shrine of Ste-Anne de Beaupré or to the quiet splendor of Ile d'Orléans.

IF YOU HAVE 3 DAYS

Walk through the Quartier Petit-Champlain, Place Royale, and the Vieux Port. Start by taking the funicular from Terrasse Dufferin to the Quartier, which resembles a quaint riverside village. Visit the Maison Chevalier, a historic home; then on to Place Royale, the earliest site of French civilization in North America which, in the summer, has a wide variety of entertainment. Stop at Notre-Dame-des-Victoires church, its magnificent high altar sculpted in the form of a castle. On rue Dalhousie, visit Explore, a multimedia sound and light show. Further along, at number 85, the Musée de la Civilization has an assortment of dynamic exhibitions that can easily occupy a visitor for part of a day. A visit to the Vieux Port, just beyond the Musée, provides a window on the maritime activities of yesteryear. The Old Port interpretation center and the fascinating l'Ilot des Palais, an archaeological dig, are both worth a visit. Visit the antique shops on rue St-Paul and, at the foot of côte de la Montagne, walk down escalier Casse-cou (breakneck stairs) and take the funicular back up to Terrasse Dufferin.

IF YOU HAVE 5 DAYS

Vieux Québec was the first North American city to be included on UNESCO's prestigious World Heritage list. To understand its importance, take a walking tour starting at the Tourist Information Bureau at 60 rue d'Auteuil, then go south in the direction of St-Louis. Near the St-Louis gate, you can visit the Poudrière de l'Esplanade, a former powderhouse and initiation center on the fortifications. Farther along rue St-Louis, find rue Donnacona, the site of the museum and chapel of the Ursulines order, who arrived in Québec in 1639. In the museum, thematic exhibits evoke the daily life of the sisters while the chapel preserves its original 1723 interior decor. The mortal remains of the founder, Blessed Marie de l'Incarnation, rest in the adjacent oratory. The Anglican Cathedral of the Holy Trinity on rue des Jardins is modeled after London's St. Martin-in-the-Fields and houses numerous precious objects. Back along St-Louis, visit Place d'Armes, under the French regime a site for military parades and public speeches, and admire the majestic Chateau Frontenac to the south. Then it is on to the Terrasse Dufferin, where you can visit some of the sites listed in the two-day tour.

IF YOU HAVE 7 DAYS

A full week provides an opportunity to view the impressive fortifications in Québec, since the city was, in the 17th, 18th, and 19th centuries, instrumental in the ultimate defense of all northeastern America. Begin at the Citadelle, a national historic site atop Cap Diamant. Visit the star-shaped fortifications and then walk along the Fortifications of Québec, a rampart of nearly 4½ kilometers (3 miles) that encircles the old city. Other outdoor sites worth a visit are Artillery Park and Battlefield Park, home of the famous Plains of Abraham and the Musée du Québec, just a few steps from the Wolfe Monument. The Terrasse Earl Grey offers a splendid view of the river, and you can stroll the Promenade des Gouverneurs, which runs along the edge of the cliff to Terrasse Dufferin. Pick up some of the shorter tours at that point and, if time permits, save a day to visit the destination of 1.5 million pilgrims annually, the Basilica of Ste-Anne-de-Beaupré, taking the route of the historic avenue Royale or Route 360. Or enjoy the farms and woodlands of Ile d'Orléans, a 15-minute drive from Vieux Québec, connected to the mainland by a bridge.

Haute-Ville (Upper Town)

Numbers in the margin correspond to points of interest on the Upper and Lower Towns map.

The most prominent buildings of Québec City's earliest European inhabitants, who set up political, educational, and religious institutions, stand here. Upper Town became the political capital of the colony of New France and, later, of British North America. Historic buildings with thick stone walls, large wood doors, glimmering copper roofs, and majestic steeples fill the heart of the city.

A Good Walk

Start where rue St-Louis meets rue du Fort at **Place d'Armes** ①, a large plaza bordered by government buildings. To your right is the colony's former treasury building, **Maison Maillou,** interesting for its 18th-century architecture. A little farther along, at number 25, is **Maison Kent,** where the capitalization of Québec was signed in 1759. South of Place d'Armes's towers Québec City's most celebrated landmark, **Château** ★ **Frontenac** ②, an imposing green-turreted castle once the administrative and military headquarters of New France and now a hotel. As you head to the boardwalk behind the Frontenac, notice the glorious bronze **statue of Samuel de Champlain,** standing where he built his residence.

Walk south along the boardwalk called the **Terrasse Dufferin** ③ for a panoramic view. At the boardwalk's western tip begins the **Promenade des Gouverneurs,** which skirts along the cliff and leads up to the Citadelle and Québec's highest point, Cap Diamant (Cape Diamond).

As you pass to the southern side of the Frontenac, you will come to a small park called **Jardin des Gouverneurs** ④. From the north side of

410

Antiques district, **27**

Basilique Notre-Dame-
de-Québec, **11**

Cavalier du Moulin, **5**

Château Frontenac, **2**

Couvent des
Ursulines, **6**

Edifice Price, **9**

Eglise Notre-Dame-des-
Victoires, **20**

Explore, **24**

Holy Trinity Anglican
Cathedral, **7**

Hôtel Clarendon, **8**

Jardin des
Gouverneurs, **4**

Lévis-Québec
Ferry, **23**

Maison Chevalier, **18**

Maison Louis-
Jolliet, **16**

Maison Montcalm, **28**

Maison des Vins, **21**

Monastère des
Augustines de l'Hôtel-
Dieu de Québec, **12**

Musée de la
Civilisation, **25**

Musée du Fort, **15**

Parc de l'Artillerie, **29**

Parc Mont-
morency, **14**

Place d'Armes, **1**

Place de Paris, **22**

Place Royale, **19**

Rue du Petit-
Champlain, **17**

Rue du Trésor, **10**

Séminaire du
Québec, **13**

Terrasse Dufferin, **3**

Vieux-Port de
Québec, **26**

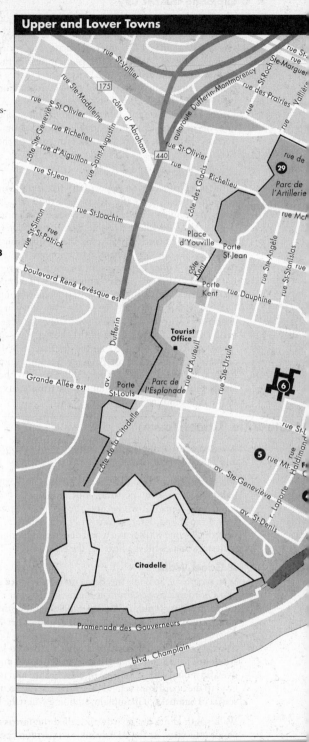

Upper and Lower Towns

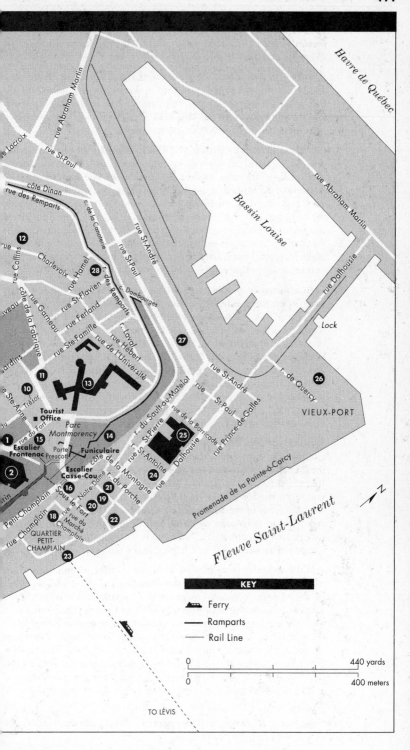

Havre de Québec

rue Abraham Martin

rue St-Paul

e Lacroix

côte Dinan

rue des Remparts

Bassin Louise

rue St-André

rue Abraham Martin

rue Dalhousie

12

rue Collins

Charlevoix

rue Hamel

28

côte de la Canoterie

rue St-Paul

c. Dambourges

rue St-André

Lock

rue St-Flavien

côte de la Fabrique

rue Carneau

rue Ferland

rue Ste-Famille

rue Hébert

Loyol

rue de l'Université

27

r. de Quercy

ardins

rdins

rue Ste-Anne

11

13

rue du Sault-au-Matelot

rue St-André

26

VIEUX-PORT

10

e Ste-Anne

Trésor

Tourist Office ■

Parc Montmorency

r. du Sault-au-Matelot

rue de la Barricade

rue St-André

St-Paul

1

rue du Fort

15

14

St-Pierre

25

rue Prince-de-Galles

Escalier Frontenac

Porte Prescott

Funiculaire

côte de la Montagne

rue St-Antoine

24

rue Dalhousie

2

Escalier Casse-Cou

16

Notre-Dame

r. du Porche

Promenade de la Pointe-à-Carcy

Petit-Champlain

Sous le Fort

21

19

rue du Fort

18

20

rue du Marché Champlain

22

Fleuve Saint-Laurent

rue Champlain

QUARTIER PETIT-CHAMPLAIN

23

N

KEY
🚢 Ferry
▬ Ramparts
— Rail Line

0 ——————— 440 yards

0 ——————— 400 meters

TO LÉVIS

the park follow rue Mont Carmel until you come to another small park landscaped with flower beds interlaced with footpaths, **Cavalier du Moulin** ⑤. After 1693, it was used as protective fortifications in the event of enemy attack.

Retrace your steps down rue Mont Carmel, turn left on rue Haldimand and left again on rue St-Louis; then make a right and follow rue du Parloir until it intersects with a tiny street called rue Donnacona where ★ you'll find the **Couvent des Ursulines** ⑥, a private school that houses a museum and has a lovely chapel next door.

On the nearby rue des Jardins, you'll see the **Holy Trinity Anglican Cathedral** ⑦ a dignified church with precious objects on display. Next come two buildings interesting for their Art Deco details: the **Hôtel Clarendon** ⑧ just east of the Cathedral, on the corner of rue des Jardins and rue Ste-★ Anne and, next door, the **Edifice Price** ⑨. Head back on rue Ste-Anne past the cathedral and continue straight until the street becomes a narrow, cobblestone thoroughfare lined with boutiques and restaurants. In summer, activity here starts early in the morning and continues until late at night. Stores stay open, artists paint, and street musicians perform as long as there is an audience, even if it's one o'clock in the morning.

Turn left onto the outdoor art gallery of **rue du Trésor** ⑩ and at its end, turn left on rue Buade. When you reach the corner of côte de la Fabrique, you'll see the **Basilique Notre-Dame-de-Québec** ⑪, which has a somberly ornate interior. The basilica marks the beginning of Québec City's **Latin Quarter,** which extends to the streets northwest of the ☞ Seminaire de Québec—rue Buade, rue des Remparts, côte de la Fabrique, and côte du Palais—as far as rue St-Jean. This district was dubbed the Latin Quarter because Latin was once a required language course at the seminary and was spoken among the students. Although Latin is no longer compulsory and Québec Seminary–Laval University has moved to a larger campus in Ste-Foy, students still cling to this neighborhood.

Head down côte de la Fabrique and turn right when it meets rue Collins. The cluster of old stone buildings sequestered at the end of the street is the **Monastère des Augustines de l'Hôtel-Dieu de Québec** ⑫. Retrace your steps on Collins Street and côte de la Fabrique. When you reach rue Ste-Famille on the left, you will find the wrought-iron entrance gates of the **Séminaire du Québec** ⑬. Head north across the courtyard to the **Musée de l'Amérique Française** (Museum of North American Francophones). Next, you can visit Québec Seminary's **Chapelle Extérieure** (Outer Chapel), at the seminary's west entrance.

Exit the seminary from the east at rue de l'Université and head south to côte de la Montagne, where **Parc Montmorency** ⑭ straddles the hill between Upper Town and Lower Town. This park marks the spot where Canada's first wheat was grown in 1618 and where the colony's first legislation was passed in 1694 in a building no longer standing. Walk through the park and cross côte du Montagne to the **Escalier Frontenac** (Frontenac Stairway), which leads to the north end of the Terrasse Dufferin. Turn right at the top for the 30-minute recap of the six sieges of Québec City at the **Musée du Fort** ⑮. As you leave the museum, head southeast to the funicular booth along Terrasse Dufferin.

TIMING

This tour should take the better part of a day. Lunchtime should find you at the Basilique Notre-Dame.

Sights to See

⑪ **Basilique Notre-Dame-de-Québec** (Our Lady of Québec Basilica). This basilica has the oldest parish in North America, dating from 1647. It's been rebuilt three times: in the early 1700s, when François de Montmorency Laval was the first bishop; in 1759, after cannons at Lévis fired upon it during the siege of Québec; and in 1922, after a fire. The basilica's somberly ornate interior includes a canopy dais over the episcopal throne, a ceiling of clouds decorated with gold leaf, richly colored stained-glass windows, and a chancel lamp that was a gift of Louis XIV. The large and famous crypt was Québec City's first cemetery; more than 900 people are interred here, including 20 bishops and four governors of New France. The founder of the city, Samuel de Champlain, is believed to be buried near the basilica: Archaeologists have been searching for his tomb since 1950. ⊠ *16 rue Bade,* ☎ *418/692–2533.* ☞ *Free.* ⊙ *Oct.–May, daily 7–4:30; June–Sept., daily 8–6.*

❺ Cavalier du Moulin. A small park landscaped with flower beds interlaced with footpaths, the Cavalier du Moulin is the former site of a stone windmill that became part of the French fortifications. The windmill was strategically placed so that its cannons could destroy the Cap-Diamant Redoubt (near Promenade des Gouverneurs) and the St-Louis Bastion (near St-Louis Gate) in the event that New France was captured by the British. ⊠ *Between rue St. Louis and av. Ste.-Geneviève.* ☞ *Free.* ⊙ *May–Nov., daily 7 AM–9 PM.*

Centre Marie-de-l'Incarnation. Next to the Musée des Ursulines (☞ *below*), is this bookstore with an exhibit on the life of the Ursulines' first superior, who came from France and cofounded the convent. ⊠ *10 rue Donnacona,* ☎ *418/692–1569.* ☞ *Free.* ⊙ *Feb.–Nov., Tues.–Sat. 10–11:30 and 1:30–4:30, Sun. 1:30–4:30.*

Chapelle des Ursulines (Ursuline Chapel). On the grounds of the Couvent des Ursulines (☞ *below*), is this little chapel where French General Montcalm was buried after he died in the 1759 battle. The exterior was rebuilt in 1902, but the interior contains the original chapel, which took sculptor Pierre-Noël Levasseur from 1726 to 1736 to complete. The votive lamp was lit in 1717 and has never been extinguished. ⊠ *12 rue Donnaconna.* ☞ *Free.* ⊙ *May–Oct., Tues.–Sat. 10–11:30 and 1:30–4:30, Sun. 12:30–4:30.*

★ ❷ Château Frontenac. This imposing green-turreted castle with its slanting copper roof, Québec City's most celebrated landmark, was once the administrative and military headquarters of New France. It owes its name to the Comte de Frontenac, governor of the French colony between 1672 and 1698. Looking at the magnificence of the château's location, you can see why Frontenac said, "For me, there is no site more beautiful nor more grandiose than that of Québec City."

Samuel de Champlain, who founded Québec City in 1608, was responsible for Château St-Louis, the first structure to appear on the site of the Frontenac; it was built between 1620 and 1624 as a residence for colonial governors. In 1784, Château Haldimand was constructed here, but it was demolished in 1892 to make way for Château Frontenac (☞ Lodging, *below*). The latter was built as a hotel in 1893, and it was considered to be remarkably luxurious at that time: Guest rooms contained fireplaces, bathrooms, and marble fixtures, and a special commissioner traveled to England and France in search of antiques for the establishment. The hotel was designed by New York architect Bruce Price, who also worked on Québec City's Gare du Palais (rail station) and other Canadian landmarks, such as Montréal's Windsor Station. The Frontenac was completed in 1925 with the addition of a 20-story central tower. Owned by Canadian Pacific Hotels, it has accumulated a star-studded guest roster, including Queen Elizabeth, Madame Chiang Kai-shek, Ronald Reagan, and François Mitterrand, as well as

Franklin Roosevelt and Winston Churchill, who convened here in 1943 and 1944 for two wartime conferences. ⊠ *1 rue des Carrières,* ☎ *418/692–3861.*

❻ **Couvent des Ursulines** (Ursuline Convent). The site of North America's oldest teaching institution for girls, still a private school, was founded in 1639 by two French nuns. The convent has many of its original walls still intact. On its property are a museum (☞ Musée des Ursulines, *below*) and a chapel (☞ Chapelle des Ursulines, *above*) that you may visit. Next door is an interesting bookstore (☞ Centre Marie-de-l'Incarnation, *above*). ⊠ *12 rue Donnacona.*

★ ❾ **Edifice Price** (Price Building). The city's first skyscraper, the 15-story Art Deco Edifice Price, was built in 1929 and served as headquarters of the Price Brothers Company, the lumber firm founded in Canada by Sir William Price. Today the building is owned by the provincial government and houses the offices of Québec City's mayor. Don't miss the interior: Exquisite copper plaques depict scenes of the company's early pulp and paper activities, while the two artfully carved maple-wood elevators are '30s classics. It is next door to the Hôtel Clarendon (☞ *below*). ⊠ *65 rue Ste-Anne.*

❼ **Holy Trinity Anglican Cathedral.** This stone church dates from 1804 and was one of the first Anglican cathedrals built outside the British Isles. Its simple and dignified facade is reminiscent of London's St. Martin-in-the-Fields. The cathedral's land was originally given to the Recollet fathers (Franciscan monks from France) in 1681 by the king of France for a church and monastery. When Québec came under British rule, the Recollets made the church available to the Anglicans for services. Later, King George III of England ordered construction of the present cathedral, with an area set aside for members of the royal family. A portion of the north balcony still remains exclusively for the use of the reigning sovereign or her representative. The church houses precious objects donated by George III; wood for the oak benches was imported from the Royal Forest at Windsor. The cathedral's impressive rear organ has more than 2,500 pipes. ⊠ *31 rue des Jardins,* ☎ *418/692–2193.* ☐ *Free.* ☉ *May–June, daily 9–5; July and Aug., daily 9–9; Sept. and Oct., weekdays 10–4; Nov.–May, offices only; Sun. services in English 8:30 and 11 AM and in French 9:30 AM.*

❽ **Hôtel Clarendon.** One of Québec City's finest Art Deco structures is the Clarendon, Québec's oldest hotel (☞ Lodging, *below*). Although the Clarendon dates from 1866, it was reconstructed in its current Art Deco style—geometric patterns of stone and wrought iron decorating its interior—in 1930. ⊠ *57 rue Ste-Anne, at rue des Jardins,* ☎ *418/ 692–2480.*

❹ **Jardin des Gouverneurs** (Governors' Park). This small park on the southern side of the Frontenac is home to the **Wolfe-Montcalm Monument**, a 50-foot obelisk that is unique because it pays tribute to both a winning (English) and a losing (French) general. The monument recalls the 1759 battle on the Plains of Abraham, which ended French rule of New France. British General James Wolfe lived only long enough to hear of his victory; French General Louis-Joseph Montcalm died shortly after Wolfe with the knowledge that the city was lost. During the French regime, the public area served as a garden for the governors who resided in Château St-Louis. On the south side of the park is **avenue Ste-Geneviève,** lined with well-preserved Victorian houses dating from 1850 to 1900 that have been converted to quaint old-fashioned inns.

Maison Maillou. The colony's former treasury building typifies the architecture of New France with its sharply slanted roof, dormer windows, concrete chimneys, shutters with iron hinges, and limestone walls. Built between 1736 and 1753, it stands at the end of ☞ **rue du Trésor**. Maison Maillou now houses the Québec City Chamber of Commerce and is not open for tours. ⊠ *17 rue St-Louis.*

⑫ **Monastère des Augustines de l'Hôtel-Dieu de Québec** (Augustine Monastery). Augustine nuns arrived from Dieppe, France, in 1639 with a mission to care for the sick in the new colony; they established the first hospital north of Mexico, the **Hôtel-Dieu hospital,** the large building west of the monastery. The **Musée des Augustines** (Augustine Museum) is in hospital-like quarters with large sterile corridors leading into a ward that has a small exhibit of antique medical instruments, such as a pill-making device from the 17th century. Upon request, the Augustines also offer guided tours of the **chapel** (1800) and the cellars used by the nuns as a shelter, beginning in 1659, during bombardments by the British. ⊠ *32 rue Charlevoix,* ☎ *418/692–2492.* ☞ *Free.* ☼ *Tues.–Sat. 9:30–noon and 1:30–5, Sun. 1:30–5.*

Musée de l'Amérique Française. Housed in a former student residence of the Québec Seminary–Laval University (☞ Séminaire du Québec, *below*), this museum focuses on the history of the French presence in North America. There are more than 400 landscape and still-life paintings dating from as long ago as the 15th century, rare Canadian money that was used in colonial times, and scientific instruments acquired through the centuries for the purposes of research and teaching. A former chapel has been renovated and is used for exhibits and cultural activities. The museum was expected to close during the summer of 1996 and reopen in October 1996 after extensive renovations. ⊠ *9 rue Université,* ☎ *418/692–2843.* ☞ *$3, free Tues.* ☼ *Tues.–Sun. 10–5.*

Musée des Ursulines (Ursuline Museum). Within the walls of the Couvent des Ursulines (☞ *above*) is this former residence of one of the convent's founders, Madame de la Peltrie. It offers an informative perspective on 120 years of the Ursulines' life under the French regime, from 1639 to 1759. For instance, you'll discover that because the Ursulines were without heat in winter, their heavy clothing sometimes weighed as much as 20 pounds. You'll also see why it took an Ursuline nun nine years of training to attain the level of a professional embroiderer; the museum contains magnificent pieces of ornate embroidery, such as altar frontals with gold and silver threads intertwined with precious jewels. ⊠ *12 rue Donnacona,* ☎ *418/694–0694.* ☞ *$3.* ☼ *Feb. 7–Dec. 1, Tues.–Sat. 9:30–noon and 1:30–5, Sun. noon–5.*

NEED A BREAK? At the neon-lit **Bistro Taste-Vin** (⊠ 32 rue St-Louis, ☎ 418/692–4191), on the corner of rue des Jardins and rue St-Louis, sample delicious salads, pastries, and desserts.

⑮ **Musée du Fort** (Fort Museum). This museum's sole exhibit is a sound-and-light show that reenacts the region's most important battles, including the Battle of the Plains of Abraham and the 1775 attack by American generals Arnold and Montgomery. ⊠ *10 rue Ste-Anne,* ☎ *418/692–2175.* ☞ *$5.50.* ☼ *June–Aug., daily 10–6; Apr.–May, Sept. and Oct., daily 10–5; Nov.–Mar., weekdays 11–noon and 1:45–3:30, weekends 11–5; English presentation every hr on the hr.*

❶ **Place d'Armes.** For centuries, this square atop a cliff has been a gathering place for parades and military events. Upper Town's most central location, the Place is bordered by government buildings; at its west side is the majestic **Ancien Palais de Justice** (Old Courthouse), a Renaissance-style building from 1887. The Place stands on land that was occupied by a church and convent of the Recollet missionaries (Franciscan monks), who in 1615 were the first order of priests to arrive in New France. The Gothic-style fountain at the center of Place d'Armes pays tribute to their arrival. ⊠ *rue St. Louis and rue du Fort.*

🔟 **Rue du Trésor.** The road colonists took on their way to pay rent to the king's officials is now a narrow alley where hundreds of colorful prints, paintings, and other artworks are on display. You won't necessarily find masterpieces here, but this walkway is a good stop for a souvenir sketch or two. On this street is the **Québec Experience,** a multimedia sound-and-light show that takes you into the heart of Québec's history, from the first explorers until modern days. ⊠ *8 rue du Trésor,* ☎ *418/694–4000.* ☜ *$6.50.* ⊙ *Mid-May–mid-Oct., daily 10–10; mid-Oct.–mid-May, daily 10–5.*

🔞 **Séminaire du Québec** (Québec Seminary). Behind these gates lies a tranquil courtyard surrounded by austere stone buildings with rising steeples; these structures have housed classrooms and student residences since 1663. The seminary was founded by François de Montmorency Laval, the first bishop of New France, to train priests of the new colony. In 1852 the seminary became Université Laval (Laval University), the first Catholic university in North America. The university eventually outgrew these cramped quarters; in 1946 it moved to a larger, modern campus in the suburb of Ste-Foy. The **Musée du Séminaire** offers guided tours of the seminary during the summer. The small Roman-style chapel, **Chapelle Extérieure** (Outer Chapel), at the west entrance of Québec Seminary, was built in 1888 after fire destroyed the first chapel, which dated from 1750. ⊠ *2 Côte de la Fabrique,* ☎ *418/694–1020.*

🔟 **Terrasse Dufferin.** The Terrasse, a wide boardwalk with an intricate wrought-iron guardrail, allows a panoramic view of the St. Lawrence River, the town of Lévis on the opposite shore, Ile d'Orléans, and the Laurentian Mountains. It was named for Lord Dufferin, governor of Canada between 1872 and 1878, who had this walkway constructed in 1878. At its western end begins the **Promenade des Gouverneurs,** which skirts the cliff and leads up to Québec's highest point, Cap Diamant, and also to the Citadelle (☞ *below*).

Basse-Ville (Lower Town)

New France first began to flourish in the streets of Lower Town along the banks of the St. Lawrence River. These streets became the colony's economic crossroads, where furs were traded, ships came in, and merchants established their residences.

Despite the status of Lower Town as the oldest neighborhood in North America, its narrow and time-worn thoroughfares have a new and polished look. In the 1960s, after a century of decay as the commercial boom moved west and left Lower Town abandoned, the Québec government committed millions of dollars to restore the district to the way it had been during the days of New France. Today modern boutiques, restaurants, galleries, and shops catering to tourists occupy the former warehouses and residences.

A Good Walk

Begin this tour on the northern tip of rue du Petit-Champlain at **Maison Louis-Jolliet** ⑯, the lower station of the funicular. You can also wander down the **Escalier Casse-Cou** (Breakneck Steps) instead of taking the funicular from the Upper to the Lower towns. Heading south on **rue du Petit-Champlain** ⑰, the city's oldest street, you'll notice the cliff on the right that borders this narrow thoroughfare, with Upper Town on the heights above. At the point where rue du Petit-Champlain intersects with boulevard Champlain, make a U-turn to head back north on rue Champlain. One block farther, at the corner of rue du Marché-Champlain, you'll find **Maison Chevalier** ⑱, an old stone house. Walk east to rue Notre-Dame, which leads directly to **Place Royale** ⑲, formerly the heart of New France. The small stone church at the south side of the Place Royale is the **Eglise Notre-Dame-des-Victoires** ⑳, the oldest church in Québec. Then, on the northwest corner of the square, look for the cool, dark, and musty cellars of the **Maison des Vins** ㉑, a wine store.

On the east side of Place Royale, take rue de la Place, which leads to an open square, **Place de Paris** ㉒ At this point of the tour you may conveniently catch the 15-minute **Lévis–Québec ferry** ㉓ to the opposite shore of the St. Lawrence River for the view. Back on the Québec side of the river, stop at **Explore** ㉔, a sound-and-light show. Continue north on rue Dalhousie until you come to the **Musée de la Civilisation** ㉕, devoted to Québecois culture and civilization. Head east toward the river to the **Vieux-Port de Québec** ㉖, at one time the busiest on the continent. The breezes here from the St. Lawrence provide a cool reprieve on a hot summer's day, and you can browse through the **Marché du Vieux-Port** (Farmer's Market). You are now in the ideal spot to explore Québec City's **antiques district** ㉗.

Walk west along rue St-Paul and turn left onto a steep brick incline called côte Dambourges; when you reach côte de la Canoterie, take the stairs back on the cliff to rue des Remparts. Continue approximately a block west along rue des Remparts until you come to the last building in a row of purple houses, **Maison Montcalm** ㉘, the former home of General Montcalm. Continue west on rue des Remparts and turn left on côte du Palais and then immediately right on rue de l'Arsenal,
★ which brings you to the **Parc de l'Artillerie** ㉙, a complex of 20 military, industrial, and civilian buildings.

TIMING

A morning of strolling will take you to two of the city's most famous squares, Place Royale and Place de Paris. Take the time for a brisk 15-minute ferry ride to Lévis and back and you'll be ready for a mid-morning snack. After the Explore light show, tour the Musée de la Civilisation before a late lunch in the antiques district. After browsing along rue St-Paul, explore Parc de l'Artillerie and its adjoining buildings.

Sights to See

㉗ **Antiques district.** Antiques shops cluster along rue St-Pierre and rue St-Paul. Rue St-Paul was once part of a business district where warehouses, stores, and businesses abounded. After World War I, shipping and commercial activities plummeted; low rents attracted antiques dealers. Today numerous cafés, restaurants, and art galleries have turned this area into one of the town's more fashionable sections.

⑳ **Eglise Notre-Dame-des-Victoires** (Our Lady of Victory Church). The oldest church in Québec was built on the site of Samuel de Champlain's first residence, which also served as a fort and trading post. The church was built in 1688 and was restored twice. Its name comes from two French victories against the British: one in 1690 against Admiral William Phipps and another in 1711 against Sir Hovendon Walker. The interior contains copies of paintings by such European masters as Van Dyck, Rubens, and Boyermans; its altar resembles the shape of a fort. A scale model suspended from the ceiling represents *Le Brezé*, the boat that transported French soldiers to New France in 1664. The side chapel is dedicated to Ste-Geneviève, the patron saint of Paris. ⊠ *Pl. Royale*, ☎ *418/692–1650*. ▱ *Free.* ☉ *Daily 9–4:30, Sat. 9–4, except during Mass (Sun. 9:30, 11, and noon; May–Oct., Sat. 7 PM), marriages, and funerals; Oct.–mid-May, Tues.–Sat. 9–4:30.*

Escalier Casse-Cou. The steepness of the city's first iron stairway, an ambitious 1893 design by Charles Baillairgé, a city architect and engineer, is ample evidence of how it got its name. It was built on the site of the original 17th-century stairway that linked Upper Town and Lower Town during the French regime. Today, shops, quaint boutiques, and restaurants are at various levels.

㉔ Explore. This 30-minute sound-and-light show uses high-tech visual art to relive the story of the founding of the city. Sail up the St. Lawrence River with Jacques Cartier and Samuel de Champlain to Québec and witness their first encounter with native Indians. ⊠ *63 rue Dalhousie,* ☎ *418/692–2063.* ☞ *$5.50.* ☉ *May–Sept., daily 10–6; Apr., May, Oct., and Nov., daily 10–5; Dec., daily 11–3.*

㉓ Lévis–Québec ferry. En route to the opposite shore of the St. Lawrence River, you get a striking view of Québec City's skyline, with the Château Frontenac and the Québec Seminary high atop the cliff. The view is even more impressive at night. ⊠ *Rue Dalhousie, 1 block south of Place de Paris,* ☎ *418/644–3704,* ☞ *$1.25.* ☉ *1st ferry leaves at 6:30 AM; crossings every ½ hr 7:30 AM–6:30 PM, every hr 7:30 PM–2:30 AM; final crossing 3:45 AM.*

NEED A
BREAK?

Café du Monde (⊠ 57 rue Dalhousie, ☎ 418/692–4455), with an impressive view of the St. Lawrence River, specializes in brunch on Saturday and Sunday. Croissants, sausages, waffles with maple syrup, and *moules et frites* (mussels with French fries) are popular.

⑱ Maison Chevalier. This old stone house was built in 1752 for shipowner Jean-Baptiste Chevalier; the house's style, of classic French inspiration, clearly reflects the urban architecture of New France. Fire walls, chimneys, vaulted cellars, and original wood beams and stone fireplaces are some of its noteworthy features. ⊠ *50 rue du Marché-Champlain,* ☎ *418/643–2158.* ☞ *Free.* ☉ *Mid-June–Sept., daily 10–6.*

㉑ Maison des Vins. In this former warehouse dating from 1689, the Québec Société des Alcools sells more than 1,000 kinds of rare and vintage wines, which range in price from $10 to $1,000. ⊠ *1 Pl. Royale,* ☎ *418/643–1214.* ☉ *Tues. and Wed. 9:30–5:30, Thurs. and Fri. 9:30–9, Sat. 9:30–5.*

⑯ Maison Louis-Jolliet. Built in 1683, this house, now a souvenir shop at the lower station of the funicular, was used by the first settlers of New France as a base for further westward explorations. A monument commemorating Louis Jolliet's discovery of the Mississippi River in 1672 stands in the park next to the house. At the north side of the house is Escalier Casse-Cou (☞ *above*), the city's first iron stairway. ⊠ *16 rue du Petit-Champlain,* ☎ *418/692–1132.*

㉘ Maison Montcalm. This was the home of French General Louis-Joseph Montcalm from 1758 until the capitulation of New France. A plaque dedicated to the general is on the right side of the house. ⊠ *rue des Remparts between rues Hamel and St. Flavien.*

㉕ Musée de la Civilisation (Civilization Museum). Wedged into the foot of the cliff, this spacious museum with a striking limestone and glass facade has been artfully designed by architect Moshe Safdie to blend into the city landscape. Its campanile echoes the shape of church steeples throughout the city. The museum has innovative, entertaining, and sometimes playful exhibits devoted to aspects of Québec's culture and civilization. Several of the shows, with their imaginative use of artwork, video screens, computers, and sound, will appeal to both adults and children. Its thematic approach, which focuses on participation and interaction, also extends to exhibits of an international nature. ✉ *85 rue Dalhousie,* ☎ *418/643–2158.* 💲 *$6; free Tues. in winter.* 🕐 *June 24–Sept. 2, daily 10–7; Sept. 3–June 23, Tues.–Sun. 10–5, Wed. 10–9.*

㉙ Parc de l'Artillerie (Artillery Park). This national historic park is a complex of 20 military, industrial, and civilian buildings, so situated to guard the St. Charles River and the Old Port. Its earliest buildings served as headquarters for the French garrison and were taken over in 1759 by the British Royal Artillery soldiers. The defense complex was used as a fortress, barracks, and cartridge factory during the American siege of Québec in 1775 and 1776. The area served as an industrial complex providing ammunition for the Canadian army from 1879 until 1964. One of the three buildings you can visit is a former **powder magazine,** which in 1903 became a shell foundry. The building houses a detailed model of Québec City in 1808, rendered by two surveyors in the office of the Royal Engineers Corps. Sent to Britain in 1813, it was intended to show British officials the strategic importance of Québec so that more money would be provided to expand the city's fortifications. The model details the city's houses, buildings, streets, and military structures. The powder magazine is open daily 10–5, and admission is $2.75. The **Dauphin Redoubt,** named in honor of the son of Louis XIV (the heir apparent), was constructed from 1712 to 1748. It served as a barracks for the French garrison until 1760, when it became an officers' mess for the Royal Artillery Regiment. It's open late June–early September, daily 10–5. The **Officers' Quarters,** a dwelling for Royal Artillery officers until 1871 when the British army departed, is now a museum for children, with shows on military life during the British regime. The Officers' Quarters are open late June–early September, daily 10–5. ✉ *2 rue d'Auteuil,* ☎ *418/648–4205.*

㉒ Place de Paris. This square, a newcomer to these historic quarters, is dominated by a black-and-white geometric sculpture, *Dialogue avec l'Histoire* (Dialogue with History), a gift from France positioned on the site where the first French settlers landed. ✉ *rue Dalhousie.*

⑲ Place Royale. This cobblestone square is encircled by the former homes of wealthy merchants, which have steep Normandy-style roofs, dormer windows, and several chimneys. Until 1686 the area was called Place du Marché, but its name was changed when a bust of Louis XIV, *"le Roi Soleil"* (the Sun King), was erected at its center. During the late 1600s and early 1700s, when Place Royale was continually under threat of attacks from the British, the colonists progressively moved to higher and safer quarters atop the cliff in Upper Town. Yet after the French colony fell to British rule in 1759, Place Royale flourished again with shipbuilding, logging, fishing, and fur trading. ✉ *Place Royale Information Centre, 215 Marche Finlay,* ☎ *418/646–3167.* 🕐 *June 3–Sept. 29.*

⑰ Rue du Petit-Champlain. This street was the main street of a former harbor village, with trading posts and the homes of rich merchants. Today it has pleasant boutiques and cafés. Natural-fiber weaving, Inuit carvings, hand-painted silks, and enameled copper crafts are some of the local specialties that are good buys here.

㉖ Vieux-Port de Québec (Old Port of Québec). The old harbor dates from the 17th century, when ships first arrived from Europe bringing supplies and settlers to the new colony. At one time this port was among the busiest on the continent: Between 1797 and 1897, Québec shipyards turned out more than 2,500 ships, many of which passed the 1,000-ton mark. The port saw a rapid decline after steel replaced wood and the channel to Montréal was deepened to allow larger boats to reach a good port upstream. In 1984, the 72-acre port was restored with a $100 million grant from the federal government; today it encompasses several parks. You can stroll along the riverside promenade, where merchant and cruise ships are docked. At the port's northern end, where the St. Charles meets the St. Lawrence, a lock protects the marina in the Louise basin from the generous Atlantic tides that reach even this far up the St. Lawrence. In the northwest section of the port, an exhibition center, **Port de Québec in the 19th Century** (✉ 100 rue St-André, ☎ 418/648–3300), presents the history of the port in relation to the lumber trade and shipbuilding. Admission to the center is $2.50, and it is open May–August, daily 10–5; September–October, daily noon–4; and October–May by reservation. At the port's northwestern tip is the **Marché du Vieux-Port** (Old Port Market), where farmers sell their fresh produce. The market is open May–Oct., daily 8–8.

Outside the Walls

Numbers in the margin correspond to points of interest on the Outside the City Walls map.

In the 20th century, Québec City grew into a modern metropolis outside the historic confines of the city walls. Yet beyond the walls lies a great deal of the city's military history, in the form of its complex fortifications and battlements.

A Good Walk

★ Start close to St-Louis Gate at **Parc de l'Esplanade** ㉚, the site of a former military drill and parade ground. Esplanade Park is also the starting point for walking the city's 4½ kilometers (3 miles) of walls; in summer, guided tours begin here. From the **Powder Magazine** in the park, head south on côte de la Citadelle, which leads directly to the **Citadelle** ㉛, the largest fortified base in North America still occupied by troops. Retrace your steps down côte de la Citadelle to Grande Allée. Continue west until you come to the Renaissance-style **Parliament Buildings** ㉜, which mark Parliament Hill, headquarters of the provincial government. Across from the Parliament on the south side of Grande Allée is the **Manège Militaire**, a turreted granite armory built in 1888, four years after the Parliament Buildings. Also designed by Taché, it is still a drill hall for the 22nd Regiment.

Continue along **Grande Allée** ㉝, Québec City's version of the Champs-Elysées, with its array of trendy cafés, clubs, and restaurants. If you turn left on Place Montcalm, you'll be facing the **Montcalm Monument** ㉞. Continue south on Place Montcalm to one of North America's largest and most scenic parks, **Parc des Champs-de-Bataille** ㉟, or Battlefields Park. This 250-acre area of gently rolling slopes offers unparalleled views of the St. Lawrence River. Within the park and just west of the Citadelle are the **Plains of Abraham** ㊱, the site of the famous 1759 battle that decided the fate of New France.

Take avenue Laurier, which runs parallel to Battlefields Park, a block west until you come to a neatly tended garden called **Parc Jeanne d'Arc** ㊲. If you continue west on avenue Laurier, you'll see a stone oval defense tower, **Tour Martello no. 2** ㊳; on the left, toward the south end of the park, stands **Tour Martello no. 1** ㊴. Continue a block west on rue de Bernières and then follow avenue George V along the outskirts of Battlefields Park until it intersects with avenue Wolfe-Montcalm. You'll come to the tall **Wolfe Monument** ㊵, which marks the place where the British general died. Turn left on avenue Wolfe-Montcalm for a leisurely stroll through the **Musée de Québec** ㊶. From the museum head north on avenue Wolfe-Montcalm, turning right on Grande Allée and walk-

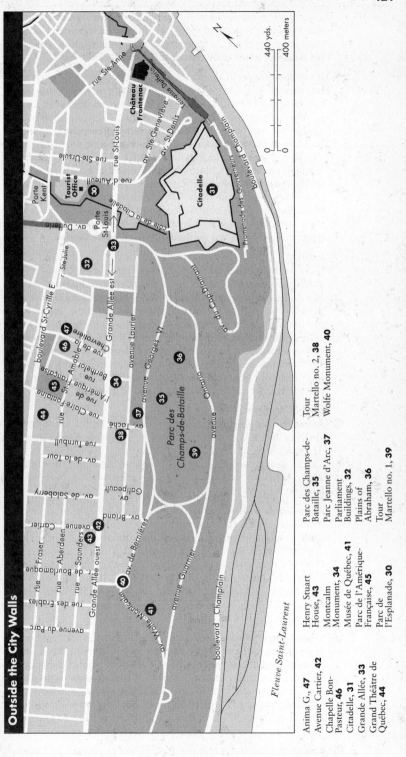

Outside the City Walls

Anima G., **47**
Avenue Cartier, **42**
Chapelle Bon-
  Pasteur, **46**
Citadelle, **31**
Grande Allée, **33**
Grand Théâtre de
  Québec, **44**

Henry Stuart
  House, **43**
Montcalm
  Monument, **34**
Musée de Québec, **41**
Parc de l'Amérique-
  Française, **45**
Parc de
  l'Esplanade, **30**

Parc des Champs-de-
  Bataille, **35**
Parc Jeanne d'Arc, **37**
Parliament
  Buildings, **32**
Plains of
  Abraham, **36**
Tour
  Martello no. 1, **39**

Tour
  Martello no. 2, **38**
Wolfe Monument, **40**

ing a block to avenue Cartier. Head north on **avenue Cartier** ㊷ to indulge in the pleasures offered by the many good restaurants, clubs, and cafés lining the block. At the corner of avenue Cartier is the **Henry Stuart House** ㊸, home to the same family from 1918 to 1987.

If you continue north along avenue Cartier, the first major intersection is boulevard René-Lévesque Est. Turn right and walk two blocks to the concrete modern building of the **Grand Théâtre de Québec** ㊹, a center for the city's performing arts. High-waving flags east of the Grand Théâtre are displayed in the **Parc de l'Amérique-Française** ㊺, dedicated to places in North America with a French-speaking population. Take rue Claire-Fontaine a block south, turn left on rue St-Amable, and then left again on rue de la Chevrotière. On the west side of the street you'll see the **Chapelle Bon-Pasteur** ㊻, which is surrounded by modern office complexes. Across rue de la Chevrotière is the entrance of **Edifice Marie-Guyart**, whose observation tower, **Anima G.** ㊼, allows a great view. Two sights not in walking distance are the **Aquarium du Québec** (Québec Aquarium) and the **Jardin Zoologique du Québec.**

TIMING

If the weather is fine, take in Esplanade Park and the Citadelle in the morning, with time out for a 30-minute tour of the Parliament Buildings (call ahead; reservations are required). Then stroll the Grande Allée to the scenic and sprawling Battlefields Park, site of the famous Plains of Abraham. Take some time before lunch to visit the Musée de Québec and, if you want to eat outdoors, stop at the Halles Petit-Cartier to pick up some bread and cheese. Visit the Henry Stuart House, built in 1849 and now designated a historic monument. Spend a little more time on avenue Cartier, then visit the Grand Théâtre du Québec or, if you prefer, continue exploring the Plains of Abraham.

Sights to See

㊼ **Anima G.** This observation gallery is on top of Edifice Marie-Guyart, Québec City's tallest office building. The gray, modern concrete tower, 31 stories high, has by far the best view of the city and the environs. There's an express elevator. ⊠ *1037 rue de la Chevrotière,* ☏ *418/644–9841.* 🎫 *Free.* ☉ *Late Jan.–early Dec., weekdays 10–4, weekends and holidays 1–5.*

🅒 **Aquarium du Québec.** About 10 kilometers (6 miles) from the city center, this aquarium contains more than 300 species of marine life, including reptiles, exotic fish, and seals from the lower St. Lawrence River. A wooded picnic ground makes this spot ideal for a family outing. The Québec City transit system, Société de Transport de la Communauté Urbaine de Québec, or STCUQ (☏ 418/627–2511), runs buses 13 and 25 here. ⊠ *1675 av. des Hôtels, Ste-Foy,* ☏ *418/659–5264; reservations, 418/659–5266.* 🎫 *$7.50.* ☉ *Daily 9–5; seals are fed and put on a show at 10:15 and 3:15.*

㊻ **Chapelle Bon-Pasteur** (Bon-Pasteur Chapel). This slender church with a steep sloping roof was designed by Charles Baillargé in 1868. Its ornate baroque-style interior has carved wood designs painted elaborately in gold leaf. The chapel houses 32 religious paintings done by the nuns of the community from 1868 to 1910. Classical concerts are performed here between October and June. ⊠ *1080 rue de la Chevrotière,* ☏ *418/641–1069 or 418/648–9710.* 🎫 *Free.* ☉ *July and Aug., Tues.–Sun. 1:30–4; Sept.–June by reservation; musical artists' Mass Sun. 10:45.*

㉛ **Citadelle** (Citadel). Built at the city's highest point, on Cap Diamant, the Citadelle is the largest fortified base in North America still occupied by troops. The 25-building fortress was intended to protect the port, prevent the enemy from taking up a position on the Plains of Abraham, and provide a last refuge in case of an attack. Having inherited incomplete fortifications, the British sought to complete the Citadelle to protect themselves against retaliations from the French. By the time the Citadelle was completed in 1832, the attacks against Québec City had ended. Since 1920 the Citadelle has served as a base for the Royal 22nd Regiment. Firearms, uniforms, and decorations from the 17th century are displayed in the **Royal 22nd Regiment Museum,** in the former powder house, built in 1750. If weather permits, you can watch the Changing of the Guard, an elaborate ceremony in which the troops parade before the Citadelle resplendent in red coats and black fur hats. Admission is by guided tour only. ✉ *1 côte de la Citadelle,* ☎ *418/648–2815.* 🎫 *$4.50.* ⏲ *Mid-Mar.–Apr., daily 10–3; May and June, daily 9–4; July–early Sept., daily 9–6; Sept., daily 9–4; Oct., daily 10–3, Nov.–early Feb. and mid-Feb.–mid-Mar., groups only (reservations required); early Feb.–mid-Feb., daily 11–3; Changing of the guard mid-June–Labor Day, daily 10 AM. Tattoo July and Aug., Tues., Thurs., and weekends 6 PM.*

㉝ Grande Allée. One of the city's oldest streets, Grande Allée was the route people took from outlying areas to sell their furs in town. Now there are trendy cafés, clubs, and restaurants here. The street actually has four names: in the old city, it is rue St-Louis; outside the walls, Grande Allée; farther west, chemin St-Louis; and farther still, boulevard Laurier.

㊹ Grande Théâtre de Québec. Opened in 1971, the theater incorporates two main halls, both named for 19th-century Canadian poets. The Grande Salle of Louis-Frechette, named for the first Québec poet and writer to be honored by the French Academy, holds 1,800 seats and is used for concerts, opera, and theater. The Petite Salle of Octave-Crémazie, used for experimental theater and variety shows, derives its name from the poet who stirred the rise of Québec nationalism in the mid-19th century.

As the complex was being constructed, Montréal architect Victor Prus commissioned Jordi Bonet, a Québec sculptor, to work simultaneously on a three-wall mural. The themes depicted in the three sections are death, life, and liberty. Bonet wrote "La Liberté" on one wall to symbolize the Québécois' struggle for freedom and cultural distinction. The theater has a full repertory in winter, but no shows in summer. ✉ *269 blvd. René-Lévesque Est,* ☎ *418/646–0609.* ⏲ *Guided tours (reservations required) daily 9–5.*

㊸ Henry Stuart House. Built in 1849, this English-style cottage was home to the Stuart family from 1918 to 1987 when it was designated a historic monument by the Ministry of Culture. Its decor has remained unchanged since 1930. Most of the furniture was imported from England in the second half of the 19th century. ✉ *82 Grande Allée Ouest,* ☎ *418/647–4347.* 🎫 *$5.* ⏲ *June–Aug., Wed.–Mon. 11–5; Sept.–May, Thurs. and Sun. 11–5 or by reservation.*

NEED A
BREAK?

Halles Petit-Cartier (✉ 1191 av. Cartier, ☎ 418/688–1630), a food mall, has restaurants and shops that sell French delicacies—cheeses, pastries, breads, vegetables, and candies.

. . . .

ⓒ **Jardin Zoologique du Québec.** This zoo is especially scenic because of the DuBerger River, which traverses the grounds. About 250 animal species live here, including bears, wildcats, primates, and birds of prey. There are farm animals and horse-drawn carriage rides, and you can cross-country ski here in winter. The zoo is 11 kilometers (7 miles) west of Québec City on Route 73. Québec City transit (☎ 418/627–2511) operates Bus 801 here. ✉ *9141 av. du Zoo, Charlesbourg,* ☎ *418/622–0313.* 🎫 *$4.50 June–Oct.; Nov.–May $4.50 weekends, free weekdays.*

③④ Montcalm Monument. France and Canada joined together to erect this monument honoring Louis-Joseph Montcalm, who claimed his fame by winning four major battles in North America—but his most famous battle was the one he lost, when the British conquered New France on September 13, 1759. Montcalm was north of Québec City at Beauport when he learned that the British attack was imminent. He quickly assembled his troops to meet the enemy and was wounded in battle in the leg and stomach. Montcalm was carried into the walled city, where he died the next morning. ⊠ *Pl. Montcalm.*

④① Musée de Québec (Québec Museum). This neoclassical beaux-arts showcase has more than 18,000 traditional and contemporary pieces of Québec art. The portraits by artists well known in the area, such as Ozias Leduc (1864–1955) and Horatio Walker (1858–1938), are particularly notable. This museum's very formal and dignified building in Battlefields Park was designed by Wilfrid Lacroix and erected in 1933 to commemorate the tricentennial of the founding of Québec. The museum has renovated the original building, incorporating the space of an abandoned prison dating from 1867. A hallway of cells, with the iron bars and courtyard still intact, has been preserved as part of a permanent exhibition of the prison's history. ⊠ *1 av. Wolfe-Montcalm,* ☎ *418/643–2150.* ⊡ *$4.75; free Wed.* ☉ *June–Aug., Thurs.–Tues. 10–5:45, Wed. 10–9:45; Sept.–May, Tues. and Thurs.–Sun. 11–5:45, Wed. 11–8:45.*

④⑤ Parc de l'Amérique-Française. Inaugurated in 1985 by former Québec premier, the late René Lévesque, the park is dedicated to places in North America with a French-speaking population. Flags are flown from Acadia, British Columbia, Louisiana, Manitoba, Saskatchewan, and Ontario, but Québec's own Fleur de Lys leads the way. Blue and white, the colors of Sun King Louis XIV, constitute a reminder of Québec's French origins, culture, and language. ⊠ *rues St. Amable and Claire-Fontaine.*

③⓪ Parc de l'Esplanade (Esplanade Park). In the 19th century, this was a clear space surrounded by a picket fence and poplar trees. Today you'll find the **Poudrière de l'Esplanade** (Powder Magazine), which the British constructed in 1820; it houses a model depicting the evolution of the wall surrounding the Old City. The French began building ramparts along the city's natural cliff as early as 1690 to protect themselves from British invaders. The colonists had trouble convincing the French government back home, though, to take the threat of invasion seriously, and by 1759, when the British invaded for control of New France, the walls were still incomplete; the British, despite attacks by the Americans during the War of Independence and the War of 1812, took a century to finish them. ⊠ *Powder Magazine, 100 rue St-Louis,* ☎ *418/ 648–7016.* ⊡ *$2.50.* ☉ *Daily 10–5.*

③⑦ Parc Jeanne d'Arc (Joan of Arc Park). This park, bright with colorful flowers, has an equestrian statue of Jeanne d'Arc as its focal point. A symbol of courage, the statue stands in tribute to the heroes of 1759 near the place where New France was lost to the British. The park also commemorates the Canadian national anthem, "O Canada"; it was played here for the first time on June 24, 1880. ⊠ *avs. Laurier and Taché.*

③② Parliament Buildings. The Parliament Buildings, erected between 1877 and 1884, are the seat of L'Assemblée Nationale (the National Assembly) of 125 provincial representatives. Québec architect Eugène-Étienne Taché designed the classic and stately buildings in the late 17th-century Renaissance style of Louis XIV, with four wings set in a square around an interior court. In front of the Parliament, statues pay tribute to important figures of Québec history: Cartier, Champlain, Frontenac,

Wolfe, and Montcalm. There's a 30-minute tour (in English or French) of the President's Gallery, the Legislative Council Chamber, and the National Assembly Chamber, which is green, white, and gold—colors that correspond to the House of Commons in both London and Ottawa. ⊠ *Av. Dufferin and Grande Allée Est, door 3,* ☎ *418/643–7239.* ⌧ *Free.* ☼ *Guided tours (reservations required) Jan.–May and Sept.–Nov., weekdays 9–5; late June–Aug., daily 9–5.*

㊱ Plains of Abraham. This park is the site of the famous 1759 battle that decided the fate of New France. It was named after the river pilot Abraham Martin. People cross-country ski here in winter. The interpretation center is open year-round. A bus serves as shuttle and guided tour, with commentary in French and English, around the Plains of Abraham, making 11 stops. Call Pavillon Baillargé, Musée de Québec (☎ 418/648–4071) for departure times. ⌧ *Tour $1.* ☼ *Tours Mid-June–1st Mon. in Sept., daily 10–6.*

Tour Martello nos. 1 and 2 (Martello Towers 1 and 2). Of the 16 Martello towers in all of Canada, four were built in Québec City because the British government feared an invasion after the American Rev-
㊴ olution. **Tour Martello no. 1** (⊠ South end of Parc Jeanne d'Arc), which exhibits the history of the four structures, was built between 1802 and
㊳ 1810. **Tour Martello no. 2** (⊠ av. Taché and av. Laurier), which has an astronomy display, was built in the early 19th century to slow an enemy approach. **Tour no. 3** guarded westward entry to the city, but it was demolished in 1904. **Tour no. 4** is on rue Lavigueur overlooking Rivière St-Charles (St. Charles River) but is not open to the public.

㊵ Wolfe Monument. This tall monument marks the place where the British general died. Wolfe landed his troops about 3 kilometers (less than 2 miles) from the city's walls; the 4,500 English soldiers scaled the cliff and opened fire on the Plains of Abraham. Wolfe was mortally wounded in battle and was carried behind the lines to this spot. ⊠ *Rue de Bernières and av. Wolfe-Montcalm.*

DINING

$$$$ ✕ **A la Table de Serge Bruyère.** This restaurant has put Québec on the
★ map of great gastronomic cities. The city's most famous culinary institution serves classic French cuisine presented with plenty of crystal, silver, and fresh flowers and with relentless attention to detail. Only one sitting is offered each night. Opened in 1980 by the late chef Serge Bruyère, native of Lyon, France, the restaurant is now run by Henriette Barré. The *menu gourmand* is a five-course meal for about $50. Specialties include scampi in puff pastry with fresh tomatoes, scallop stew with watercress, and duckling supreme with blueberry sauce. The 1843 Livernois building now includes a cafe, a food store, and a catering service—all serving food from Bruyère's celebrated kitchen. If the main restaurant is out of your price range, **A la Petite Table** is less formal and less expensive, with such dishes as seafood terrine and pork with tarragon sauce. ⊠ *1200 rue St-Jean,* ☎ *418/694–0618. Reservations essential. Jacket required. AE, DC, MC, V.*

$$$$ ✕ **Café de la Paix.** An evening spent at this local favorite takes you back to a dining experience in Paris circa 1930. The tables could not get closer or the lights dimmer amid the Art Deco extravagance of lamps in Venetian glass, wood sculpted in geometric patterns, and stained-glass windows. The food is on a par with other fine restaurants in the city, but there are hints that the chefs are relying on their reputations (the restaurant dates from 1952). The table d'hôte includes such tasty dishes as pheasant with peaches. Salmon comes with four sauces: rasp-

426

Dining

A la Table de Serge Bruyère, **22**

Aux Anciens Canadiens, **28**

Café de la Paix, **27**

Café Suisse, **36**

Casse-Crêpe Breton, **19**

Chez Temporel, **24**

Gambrinus, **37**

La Fenouillère, **1**

L'Apsara, **13**

L'Astral, **7**

Le Café de la Terrasse, **34**

Le Cochon Dingue, **33**

Le Commensal, **17**

Le Graffiti, **6**

Le Marie Clarisse, **35**

Le Paris Brest, **9**

Le Saint-Amour, **14**

L'Echaudé, **39**

Les Frères de la Côte, **21**

Paparazzi, **4**

Portofino Bistro Italiano, **23**

Lodging

Auberge St. Antoine, **38**

Château Bonne Entente, **2**

Château Frontenac, **34**

Château de la Terrasse, **32**

Germain de Près, **3**

Hilton International Québec, **12**

Hôtel Clarendon, **26**

Hôtel Loews Le Concorde, **8**

Hôtel Manoir Victoria, **18**

Hôtel Marie Rollet, **25**

Hôtel Radisson Gouverneurs Québec, **11**

L'Auberge du Quartier, **5**

L'Auberge St-Louis, **29**

Le Château de Pierre, **30**

L'Hôtel du Théâtre, **16**

L'Hôtel du Vieux Québec, **20**

Manoir d'Auteuil, **15**

Manoir des Remparts, **40**

Manoir Lafayette, **10**

Manoir Sainte-Geneviève, **31**

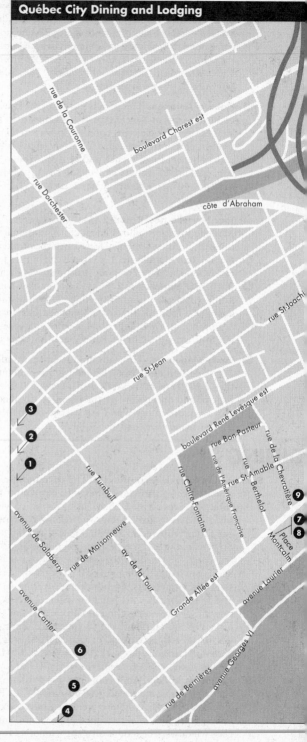

Québec City Dining and Lodging

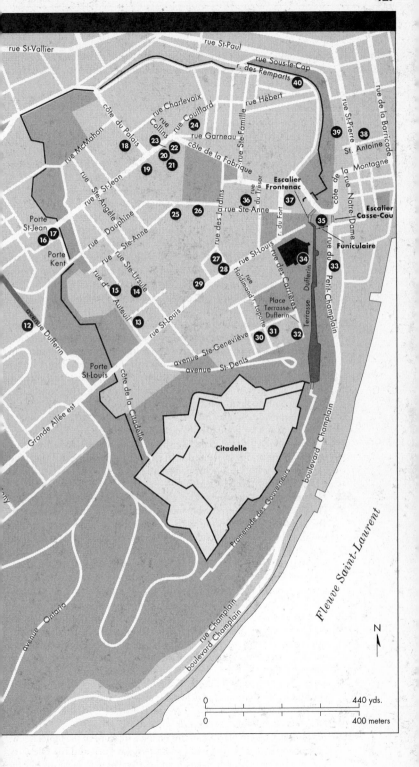

rue St-Vallier

rue St-Paul

rue Sous-le-Cap

r. des Remparts **40**

rue Hébert

rue de la Barricade

côte du Palais

rue Charlevoix

rue Couillard

rue St-Pierre

18

rue McMahon

rue Collins

24

rue Garneau

rue Ste-Famille

39

38

St. Antoine

23

22

côte de la Fabrique

côte de la Montagne

20

21

19

rue St-Jean

rue Ste-Angèle

rue des Jardins

36

rue du Trésor

Escalier Frontenac

37

rue de la Notre-Dame

Escalier Casse-Cou

Dauphine

25

26

rue Ste-Anne

35

Porte St-Jean

16 **17**

rue Ste-Anne

Funiculaire

Porte Kent

rue Ste-Ursule

27

rue St-Louis

34

rue du Petit-Champlain

33

rue d'Auteuil

15 **14**

29

rue des Carrières

28

12

13

rue St-Louis

rue Haldimand-Laporte

Place Terrasse-Dufferin

avenue Dufferin

rue St-Louis

30 **31**

32

Terrasse

Dufferin

Porte St-Louis

avenue Ste-Geneviève

avenue St-Denis

côte de la Citadelle

Grande Allée est

boulevard Champlain

Citadelle

avenue Ontario

Promenade des Gouverneurs

rue Champlain

boulevard Champlain

Fleuve Saint-Laurent

N

0   440 yds.

0   400 meters

berry vinegar, hollandaise, tarragon, and mustard. The meat entrées, including filet mignon and leg of lamb, are also recommended. You choose your dessert from a cart; try the fresh fruit and the chocolate truffle cake. The service is prompt and attentive. ⊠ *44 rue des Jardins,* ☎ *418/692–1430. Reservations essential. AE, DC, MC, V. No lunch Sun. in winter.*

$$$$ ✕ **La Fenouillère.** Here, in a bright wood room, views of the Pierre Laporte bridge can accompany your dinner. Chef Yvon Godbout has served a constantly rotating table d'hôte since 1986, going out of his way to offer seasonal products. The house specialty is salmon, but you may want to ask for the lamb, as it is done to a turn, and very popular among the restaurant's regular customers. ⊠ *Hotel Best Western Aristocrate, 3100, chemin St-Louis, Ste-Foy,* ☎ *418/653–3886. AE, DC, MC, V.*

$$$$ ✕ **Le Marie Clarisse.** Wood-beam ceilings, stone walls, sea-blue decor, and a lit fireplace make this dining spot one of the coziest in town. In an ancient building on the bottom of Escalier Casse-Cou near Place Royale, Le Marie Clarisse is well known for its unique seafood dishes, such as halibut with nuts and honey and scallops with port and paprika. Occasionally, the menu includes a good game dish, such as caribou with curry. The *menu du jour* has about seven entrées to choose from; dinner includes soup, salad, dessert, and coffee. ⊠ *12 rue du Petit-Champlain,* ☎ *418/692–0857. Reservations essential. AE, DC, MC, V. No lunch Sat. Closed Sun.*

$$$$ ✕ **Le Saint-Amour.** This restaurant has all the makings of a true haute-
★ cuisine establishment without the pretentious atmosphere. A light and airy atrium, with a retractable roof for outdoor dining in summer, creates a relaxed dining ambience. Chef Jean-Luc Boulay returns regularly to France for inspiration; his studies pay off in such specialties as stuffed quail in port sauce and salmon with chive mousse. Sauces here are light, with no flour or butter. The *menu de decouvert* has nine courses, and the *menu de dégustation* has seven. If you plan to order one of these menus, it's a good idea to mention it when you make your reservation. The chef's true expertise shines in his diverse dessert menu—try the crème brûlée sweetened with maple syrup or the royal chocolate cake made with caramelized hazelnuts. ⊠ *48 rue Ste-Ursule,* ☎ *418/694–0667. AE, DC, MC, V.*

$$$ ✕ **Aux Anciens Canadiens.** This establishment is named for a book by
★ Philippe-Aubert de Gaspé, who once resided here. The house, dating from 1675, has five dining rooms with different themes. The *vaisselier* (dish room) is bright and cheerful, with colorful antique dishes, a fireplace, and an antique stove. Come for the authentic French Canadian cooking; hearty specialties include duck in maple glaze and caribou with blueberry wine sauce. The restaurant also serves the best caribou (a local beverage made with sweet red wine and whiskey, known for its kick) drink in town. ⊠ *34 rue St-Louis,* ☎ *418/692–1627. AE, DC, MC, V.*

$$$ ✕ **Gambrinus.** This comfortable and convenient restaurant near rue
★ du Trésor and the Château Frontenac serves excellent Continental cuisine in two elegant, mahogany-paneled, plant-filled dining rooms with windows facing the street. The reliable menu includes a range of meat, fish, and pasta entrées, with such specialties as rack of lamb with herbs and caribou medallions. The table d'hôte is a good bet and provides generous portions and delectable desserts. Service here is unrushed and thoroughly professional. ⊠ *15 rue du Fort,* ☎ *418/692–5144. AE, DC, MC, V. No lunch weekends.*

$$$ ✕ **L'Astral.** This circular restaurant on the 29th floor of the Hôtel Loews Le Concorde revolves high above Battlefields Park and the Old City. The food is not the best in town and the service can be slow, but the views are excellent. The modern and uninspired decor does not detract from the view, either; there's no room for anything besides the dining

tables next to large windows. On Saturday nights, a vast buffet—organized around a theme such as Mediterranean food—is served. Sunday brunch consists of more than 30 items. ⊠ *1225 Pl. Montcalm,* ☎ *418/647–2222. AE, DC, MC, V.*

$$$ ✕ **Le Graffiti.** A good alternative to Old City dining, this restaurant housed in a modern gourmet food mall serves the cuisine of Provence. It's a romantic setting, with dark mahogany-paneled walls and large bay windows that look out onto the passersby along avenue Cartier. The distinctive seasonal menu includes such dishes as scampi spiced with basil and red pepper, and chicken liver mousse with pistachios. There's a reasonably priced table d'hôte. ⊠ *1191 av. Cartier,* ☎ *418/529–4949. AE, DC, MC, V.*

$$$ ✕ **Le Paris Brest.** This busy restaurant on Grande Allée serves a gre-
★   garious crowd attracted to its tastefully prepared French dishes. Its angular halogen lighting and soft yellow walls add a fresh, modern touch to this historic building. Traditional fare, such as *escargots au Pernod* (snails with Pernod) and steak tartare, are presented artistically. Popular dishes include lamb with *herbes de Provence* and beef Wellington. À la carte and main-course dishes are accompanied by a generous side platter of vegetables. Wine prices range from $22 to $250. ⊠ *590 Grande Allée Est,* ☎ *418/529–2243. AE, DC, MC, V.*

$$$ ✕ **Portofino Bistro Italiano.** By joining two 18th-century houses, owner James Monti has created a cozy restaurant with a bistro flavor. The room is distinctive: burnt sienna walls, a wood pizza oven set behind a semicircular bar, deep blue tablecloths and chairs. Service in this lively restaurant is excellent. Not to be missed: the thin-crust pizza and its accompaniment of oils flavored with pepper and oregano, and *pennini al'arrabiata*—tubular pasta with a spicy tomato sauce. Don't miss the homemade *tiramisù*—ladyfingers dipped in espresso with a whipped cream and mascarpone-cheese filling. There's a fixed price meal of the day, and from 3 to 7 PM the restaurant serves a beer and pizza meal for $9.95. ⊠ *54 rue Couillard,* ☎ *418/692–8888. Reservations essential. AE, D, DC, MC, V.*

$$ ✕ **Café Suisse.** This large chalet close to Place d'Armes serves Swiss cuisine, including 25 different varieties of fondue—the Gruyère and the chocolate fondues are especially recommended. Another popular item is *raclette*, a dish with melted cheese, served with bread, potatoes, onions, pickles, and ham. The spacious chalet looms three stories high with clichéd murals of alpine scenes. In the summer, there are umbrella-shaded café tables outside. ⊠ *32 rue Ste-Anne,* ☎ *418/694–1320. AE, DC, MC, V.*

$$ ✕ **L'Apsara.** The Cambodian family that owns this restaurant near the St-Louis Gate excels at using both subtle and tangy spices to create unique flavors. It's ideal if you're seeking a reprieve from French fare. Decor combines Western and Eastern motifs, with flowered wallpaper, Oriental art, and small fountains. Innovative dishes from Vietnam, Thailand, and Cambodia include such starters as *fleur de pailin* (a rice paste roll filled with fresh vegetables, meat, and shrimp) and *mou sati* (pork kebabs with peanut sauce and coconut milk). The assorted miniature Cambodian pastries are delicious with tea served from a little elephant container. ⊠ *71 rue d'Auteuil,* ☎ *418/694–0232. AE, MC, V.*

$$ ✕ **Le Café de la Terrasse.** This restaurant in the landmark Château Frontenac does not share the hotel's opulence, but it does have a view of Terrasse Dufferin and the St. Lawrence River. Standard but dependable Continental dishes are served à la carte and at buffets throughout the day. Between 2:30 and 5 PM you can have tea, complete with watercress sandwiches and pastries. ⊠ *Château Frontenac, 1 rue Car-rières,* ☎ *418/692–3861. AE, DC, MC, V.*

$$ ✕ **Le Commensal.** At Le Commensal, diners serve themselves from an
★ outstanding informal vegetarian buffet (plates are weighed to deter-
mine the price). Hot and cold dishes running the gamut of health-con-
scious cooking include stir-fry tofu and ratatouille (vegetables in mild
sauce with couscous). In a mix of modern and ancient atmospheres,
the restaurant has plenty of space. ✉ *860 rue St-Jean,* ☎ *418/647–
3733. AE, DC, MC, V.*

$$ ✕ **L'Echaudé.** This chic black-and-white bistro attracts a mix of business
★ and tourist clientele because of its location between the financial and an-
tiques districts in Lower Town. The modern decor consists of a stark dining area with a mirrored wall and a stainless-steel bar where you dine
atop high stools. Lunch offerings include *cuisse de canard confit* (duck
confit) with French fries and fresh seafood salad. The three-course
brunch for Sunday antiques shoppers includes giant croissants and a tan-
talizing array of desserts. ✉ *73 Sault-au-Matelot,* ☎ *418/692–1299. Reservations essential. AE, DC, MC, V. No dinner Sun. or Mon. Sept.–May.*

$$ ✕ **Paparazzi.** An Italian restaurant a 15-minute drive west of the Old
City, Paparazzi has a sleek, bistro ambience—bare wood tables, halo-
gen lighting, and wrought-iron accents. Its food competes with that of
many of the finer dining establishments in town, but without the high
prices. The imaginative menu changes twice a year. Specialties include
pizza paparazzi, with wild mushrooms, fresh tomatoes, and a mix of
cheeses. The dessert list is interesting. ✉ *1365 av. Maguire, Sillery,* ☎
418/683–8111. AE, DC, MC, V.

$ ✕ **Casse-Crêpe Breton.** Crepes in generous proportions are served in
this diner-style restaurant on rue St-Jean. From a menu of 15 fillings,
pick your own chocolate or fruit combinations, or design a larger
meal with cheese, ham, and vegetables. The tables surround three
round hot plates at which you watch your creations being made.
Crêpes made with two to five fillings cost under $5. ✉ *1136 rue St-
Jean.* ☎ *418/692–0438. No credit cards.*

$ ✕ **Chez Temporel.** Tucked behind rue St-Jean and côte de la Fabrique,
★ this homey café is an experience *très français.* The aroma of fresh cof-
fee fills the air. The rustic decor incorporates wooden tables, chairs,
and benches, and a tiny staircase winds to an upper level. Croissants
are made in-house; the staff will fill them with Gruyère and ham or
anything else you want. Try the equally delicious croque-monsieur and
quiche Lorraine. ✉ *25 rue Couillard,* ☎ *418/694–1813. No credit cards.*

$ ✕ **Le Cochon Dingue.** Across the street from the ferry in Lower Town
is the boulevard Champlain location of this chain, a cheerful café
(whose name translates to "The Crazy Pig"), with sidewalk tables and
indoor dining rooms, which artfully blend the chic and the antique.
Black-and-white checkerboard floors contrast with ancient stone walls.
Café fare includes dependably tasty homemade quiches, thick soups,
and such desserts as fresh raspberry tart and maple-sugar pie. ✉ *46
blvd. Champlain,* ☎ *418/692–2013;* ✉ *46 blvd. René Lévesque,* ☎
418/523–2013; ✉ *1326 ave. Maguire, Sillery,* ☎ *418/684–2013. AE,
DC, MC, V.*

$ ✕ **Les Frères de la Côte.** This pizza house, despite being in the heart
of the tourist district, is a favorite for many locals. The friendly, bois-
terous atmosphere flows from its doors into the foyer, where you will
find hundreds of snapshots documenting happy dining experiences. There
are 17 kinds of pizza and a full range of other dishes—pasta with blue
cheese, lamb with *herbes de Provence,* or grilled spicy Italian sausage
with fries. For dessert, try the apple pie with orange caramel glaze and
cream. When it comes time to leave, don't overlook the tempting bas-
ket of homemade bread for sale. ✉ *1190 rue St-Jean,* ☎ *418/692–
5445. AE, MC, V.*

LODGING

$$$$ ☆ 🏨 **Château Frontenac.** Towering above the St. Lawrence River, the Château Frontenac is Québec City's most renowned landmark. Its public rooms—from the intimate piano bar to the 700-seat ballroom reminiscent of the Versailles Hall of Mirrors—have the opulence of years gone by, and almost all the guest rooms have excellent views. Reserve well in advance, especially from the end of June to mid-October. An extensive renovation was completed in 1993, in time for the hotel's 100th birthday. The Frontenac has one of the finer restaurants in town, Le Champlain, where classic French cuisine is served by waiters dressed in traditional French costumes. ⊠ *1 rue des Carrières, G1R 4P5,* ☎ *418/692–3861 or 800/441–1414,* 🅵🅰🆇 *418/692–1751. 610 rooms. 2 restaurants, bar, snack bar, indoor pool, health club, hair salon, art gallery. AE, DC, MC, V.*

$$$$ 🏨 **Hilton International Québec.** Just outside St-Jean Gate, the Hilton rises from the shadow of Parliament Hill. It has spacious facilities and efficient services and hosts groups as well as tourists. The lobby, which can be chaotic at times, has a bar and an open-air restaurant. The hotel, next to the Parliament Buildings, is in the middle of the activity of the Winter Carnival and is connected to a mall, Place Québec, which has 40 shops. Standard yet ultramodern rooms have tall windows; those on upper floors have fine views of the Old City. Guests on executive floors are offered a free breakfast and an open bar from 5 to 6 PM. ⊠ *3 Pl. Québec, G1K 7M9,* ☎ *418/647–2411 or 800/445–8667,* 🅵🅰🆇 *418/647–6488. 565 rooms, 36 suites. Restaurant, piano bar, outdoor pool, sauna, health club. AE, D, DC, MC, V.*

$$$$ ☆ 🏨 **Hôtel Loews Le Concorde.** When Le Concorde was built in 1974, the shockingly tall concrete structure aroused controversy because it supplanted 19th-century Victorian homes. Yet for visitors, it is especially convenient for city touring and nightlife. Inside the hotel there's almost as much going on as at the cafés and restaurants along the nearby Grande Allée; Le Concorde houses the revolving restaurant L'Astral (☞ Dining, *above*), a sidewalk café, and a bar. Rooms have good views of Battlefields Park and the St. Lawrence River, and nearly all have been redone in modern decor combined with traditional furnishings. Amenities for business travelers have expanded; one of the VIP floors is reserved for female executives. ⊠ *1225 Pl. Montcalm, G1R 4W6,* ☎ *418/647–2222 or 800/463–5256; in the U.S., 800/235– 6397;* 🅵🅰🆇 *418/647–4710. 424 rooms. 2 restaurants, bar, outdoor pool, sauna, health club. AE, D, DC, MC, V.*

$$$$ 🏨 **Hôtel Radisson Gouverneurs Québec.** Opposite the Parliament Buildings, this large, full-service establishment is part of a Québec chain. Its light and spacious rooms have luminous pastel decor, wood furniture, and marble bathrooms. VIP floors were designed to lure the business traveler, but there is also plenty of room for tourists. The hotel occupies the first 12 floors of a tall office complex; views of the Old City are limited to the higher floors. ⊠ *690 blvd. René-Lévesque Est, G1R 5A8,* ☎ *418/647–1717 or 800/333–3333,* 🅵🅰🆇 *418/647–2146. 377 rooms with bath. Restaurant, piano bar, outdoor pool, sauna, health club. AE, D, DC, MC, V.*

$$$ 🏨 **Auberge Saint-Antoine.** This charming little find is within comfortable walking distance of all the old town's attractions. Although modernly built, it seems much older because it is installed in an old maritime warehouse and has a generally rustic atmosphere. Each room is styled differently; all have a combination of antiques and contemporary pieces. Some have river views; others have terraces. ⊠ *10 rue St-Antoine, G1K 4C9,* ☎ *418/692–2211 or 800/267–0525,* 🅵🅰🆇 *418/692–1177. 29 rooms. CP. AE, MC, V, DC.*

$$$ ▥ **Château Bonne Entente.** This sprawling resort is 10 minutes from the airport and 20 minutes from the walled city. It's commonly called "The Other Château," the country cousin of the urban Frontenac. A private mansion until 1940, it has evolved into a popular spot for the well heeled. In the newest wing, rooms are decorated in contemporary style with fine wood, plush carpeting, and all the modern amenities. Other rooms have antiques and a rustic atmosphere. The property encompasses 11 acres of land, with separate cottage rooms behind the main complex. ✉ *3400 chemin Ste-Foy, Ste-Foy G1X 1S6,* ☎ *418/653–5221 or 800/463–4390,* FAX *418/653–3098. 109 rooms, 50 cottages. Restaurant, bar, pool, health club, tennis, badminton, volleyball, fishing, ice-skating. AE, D, DC, MC, V.*

$$$ ▥ **Germain des Près.** One of the newly popular hotels for the business crowd is in Ste-Foy, close to Place Laurier and with easy access to Québec City and the airports. Its ultramodern rooms—in black and white or black and tan—have white comforters on the beds. ✉ *1200 av. Germain-des-Près, Ste-Foy, G1V 3M7,* ☎ *418/658–1224,* FAX *418/658–8846. 126 rooms with shower or bath. Restaurant, business services, meeting room. AE, DC, MC, V.*

$$$ ▥ **Hôtel Clarendon.** Built in 1870 and considered the oldest hotel in Québec, the Clarendon has been entirely refurbished in its original Art Deco and Art Nouveau styles. Most rooms have excellent views of old Québec. ✉ *57 rue Ste-Anne, G1R 3X4,* ☎ *418/692–2480 or 800/463–5250,* FAX *418/692–4652. 96 rooms with bath. Restaurant, café, air-conditioning, meeting rooms. AE, D, DC, MC, V.*

$$$ ▥ **Hôtel Manoir Victoria.** This European-style hotel with an excellent fitness center is well situated near the train station. Its discreet, old-fashioned entrance gives way to a large, wood-paneled foyer. A substantial buffet breakfast is included in some packages. ✉ *4 Côte du Palais, G1R 4H8,* ☎ *418/692–1030,* FAX *418/692–3822. 145 rooms and suites. Restaurant, bistro, meeting rooms, health club, indoor pool, sauna, beauty salon. AE, D, DC, MC, V.*

$$$ ▥ **Hôtel Marie Rollet.** This intimate little inn in the heart of Old Québec, built in 1876 by the Ursulines Order, is an oasis of warm woodwork and antique charm. Two rooms have working fireplaces. A rooftop terrace has a garden view. ✉ *81 rue Ste-Anne, G1R 3X4,* ☎ *418/694–9271. 10 rooms with bath. Indoor parking. MC, V.*

$$$ ▥ **Le Château de Pierre.** Built in 1853, this tidy Victorian manor on a picturesque street has kept its English origins alive. The high-ceilinged halls have ornate chandeliers and Victorian rooms are imaginatively decorated with floral themes; some have either a balcony, fireplace, or vanity room. Several rooms in the front have bay windows with a view of Governor's Park. ✉ *17 av. Ste-Geneviève, G1R 4A8,* ☎ *418/694–0429,* FAX *418/694–0153. 15 rooms. AE, MC, V.*

$$$ ▥ **L'Hôtel du Théâtre.** There's much history that accompanies this hotel in the Capitole Building just outside the St-Jean Gate. In 1903 it opened as an avant-garde theater, then it was a movie house before closing in the 1980s. In 1992 it came back to life, following a $15 million restoration that transformed it into an exclusive 40-room lodging, an Italian bistro, and an elaborate 1920s cabaret-style dinner theater, Théâtre Capitole (☞ Nightlife and the Arts, *below*). A glitzy showbiz theme is prevalent throughout the hotel, with stars on carpets, doors, and keys. Rooms are small and simple, highlighted with a few rich details. Ceilings are painted within sculpted moldings with a blue-and-white sky motif and beds have white down-filled comforters. ✉ *972 rue St-Jean, G1R 1R5,* ☎ *418/694–4040 or 800/363–4040,* FAX *418/694–1916. 40 rooms. Restaurant, bar, theater. AE, DC, MC, V.*

$$$ ⊞ **L'Hôtel du Vieux Québec.** In the heart of the Latin Quarter on rue St-Jean, this brick hotel is surrounded by striking historic structures. Once an apartment building, it still has the long-term visitor in mind. The interior design is simple, with sparsely furnished but comfortable rooms decorated in pastel colors. Many rooms have kitchens (dishes and cooking utensils can be rented for $10); some have air-conditioning. ⊠ *1190 rue St-Jean, G1R 1S6,* ☎ *418/692–1850,* ℻ *418/692–5637. 38 units with bath. AE, MC, V.*

$$$ ⊞ **Manoir d'Auteuil.** Originally a private home, this lodging is one of
★ the more lavish manors in town. At press time it was undergoing a renovation that will reinstate many of its former Art Deco and Art Nouveau details. An ornate sculpted iron banister wraps around four floors; guest rooms have detailed trimmings and blend modern design with the Art Deco structure. Each room is different; one room was formerly a chapel, and another has a tiny staircase leading to its bathroom. Of special interest is the room with blue bathroom—the shower has seven showerheads. Some rooms look out onto the wall between the St-Louis and St-Jean gates. ⊠ *49 rue d'Auteuil, G1R 4C2,* ☎ *418/694–1173,* ℻ *418/694–0081. 16 rooms with bath. Breakfast room. CP. AE, DC, MC, V.*

$$$ ⊞ **Manoir Ste-Geneviève.** This quaint and elaborately decorated hotel dating from 1880 stands near the Château Frontenac, on the southwest corner of the Jardin des Gouverneurs. A plush Victorian ambience is created with fanciful wallpaper and rooms decorated with precious stately English manor furnishings, such as marble lamps, large wooden bedposts, and velvet upholstery; you'll feel as if you are staying in a secluded country inn. Service here is personal and genteel. Some rooms have air-conditioning. ⊠ *13 av. Ste-Geneviève, G1R 4A7,* ☎ ℻ *418/694–1666. 9 rooms with bath. No credit cards.*

$$ ⊞ **Château de la Terrasse.** Although this four-story inn may not have the same charm as others in the city, it does have something that many lack: a view of the St. Lawrence River from rooms in the front. While the interior hints at having once possessed a refined and elegant decor, with its high ceilings and stained glass lining the large bay windows, the furnishings these days are plain and unremarkable. ⊠ *6 Pl. Terrasse Dufferin, G1R 4N5,* ☎ *418/694–9472,* ℻ *418/694–0055. 18 rooms. Breakfast room. AE, MC, V.*

$$ ⊞ **L'Auberge du Quartier.** This small, amiable inn in a house dating
★ from 1852 benefits from a personal touch. The cheerful rooms are modestly furnished but well maintained. A suite of rooms on the third floor can accommodate a family at a reasonable cost. A 20-minute walk west from the Old City, L'Auberge du Quartier is convenient to avenue Cartier and Grande Allée nightlife; joggers can use Battlefields Park across the street. ⊠ *170 Grande Allée Ouest, G1R 2G9,* ☎ *418/525–9726. 14 rooms with bath. Breakfast room, free parking. CP. AE, DC, MC, V.*

$$ ⊞ **L'Auberge St-Louis.** If you're looking for convenience, this inn's central location on the main street of the city can't be beat. A lobby resembling a European pension and tall staircases lead to small guest rooms with comfortable but bare-bones furniture. Six budget rooms are on the fourth floor. The service here is friendly. ⊠ *48 rue St-Louis, G1R 3Z3,* ☎ *418/692–2424,* ℻ *418/692–3797. 27 rooms, 14 with bath. MC, V.*

$$ ⊞ **Manoir Lafayette.** In 1882, this gray stone building was a lavish, private home; over a century later, it is a simple hotel. Considering the location on Grande Allée—a street crowded with restaurants and trendy bars—the clean, comfortable accommodations are reasonably priced. The lobby is open and welcoming, with floral sofas surrounding a fireplace and television. Rooms in the newer wing—although fresher—resemble those in the old part: All are quite small, with high ceilings, wooden furniture, floral bedspreads and drapes, televisions, and phones. Rooms facing Grande Allée may be noisy; older rooms cost a little less. ⊠ *661 Grande Allée Est, G1R 2K4,* ☎ *418/522–2652 or 800/363–8203,* FAX *418/522–4400. 67 rooms. Bistro, baby-sitting. AE, DC, MC, V.*

$ 🏨 **Manoir des Remparts.** There's nothing fancy about this hotel on a residential street bordering the north side of Québec City's natural cliff. Guest rooms with private bath have telephone and TV. ⊠ *3½ rue des Remparts, G1R 3R4,* ☎ *418/692–2056,* FAX *418/692–1125. 36 rooms. Breakfast room. CP. AE, DC, MC, V.*

NIGHTLIFE AND THE ARTS

For a place its size, Québec City has a wide variety of cultural institutions, from the reputed Québec Symphony Orchestra to several small theater companies. The arts scene changes significantly depending on the season. From September to May, a steady repertory of concerts, plays, and performances is presented in theaters and halls around town. In summer, indoor theaters close to make room for outdoor stages.

For arts and entertainment listings in English, consult the *Québec Chronicle-Telegraph,* published on Wednesday. The French-language daily newspaper, *Le Soleil,* has listings on a page called "Où Aller à Québec" ("Where to Go in Québec"). *Voilà Québec* and *Hospitalité Québec* are bilingual quarterly entertainment guides distributed free in tourist information areas. Also, *Voir,* a weekly devoted to arts listings and reviews, appears on the street every Thursday.

Tickets for most shows can be purchased through **Billetech,** with outlets at the Grand Théâtre de Québec (⊠ 269 blvd. René-Lévesque Est, ☎ 418/643–8131), Bibliothèque Gabrielle-Roy (☎ 418/691–7400), Colisée (☎ 418/691–7211), Théâtre Périscope (☎ 418/529–2183), Palais Montcalm (☎ 418/670–9011), Salle Albert-Rousseau (☎ 418/659–6710), La Baie department store, (⊠ Pl. Laurier, 2nd level, ☎ 418/627–5959), and Provigo supermarkets. Hours vary and in some cases tickets must be bought at the outlet.

The Arts

Dance

Grand Théâtre de Québec (⊠ 269 blvd. René-Lévesque Est, ☎ 418/643–8131) presents a dance series with both Canadian and international companies. Dancers also appear at Bibliothèque Gabrielle-Roy, Salle Albert-Rousseau, and the Palais Montcalm (☞ Theater, *below*).

Film

Most theaters present French films and American films dubbed into French. Two popular theaters are **Cinéma de Paris** (⊠ 966 rue St-Jean, ☎ 418/694–0891) and **Cinéma Place Charest** (⊠ 500 rue du Pont, ☎ 418/529–9745). **Cinémas Ste-Foy** (⊠ Pl. Ste-Foy, Ste-Foy, ☎ 418/656–0592) almost always shows films in English. **Le Clap** (⊠ 2360 chemin Ste.-Foy, Ste-Foy, ☎ 418/650–2527) has a repertoire of foreign, offbeat, and art films. **Imax Theatre,** (⊠ Galeries de la Capitale, 5401 blvd. des Galeries, Galeries de la Capitale, ☎ 418/627–4629 or 800/643–4629) has extra-large-screen movies.

Music

L'Orchestre Symphonique de Québec (Québec Symphony Orchestra) is Canada's oldest. It performs at Louis-Frechette Hall in the **Grand Théâtre de Québec** (⊠ 269 blvd. René-Lévesque Est, ☎ 418/643–8131).

Tickets for children's concerts at the **Joseph Lavergne auditorium** and classical concerts at the **Salle de l'Institut** (⊠ 42 rue St-Stanislaus) must be purchased in advance at the **Bibliothèque Gabrielle-Roy** (⊠ 350 rue St-Joseph Est, ☎ 418/691–7400).

Popular music concerts are often booked at the **Colisée de Québec** (⊠ Parc de l'Exposition, 2205 av. du Colisée, Parc de l'Exposition, ☎ 418/691–7211).

Theater

All theater productions are in French. The following theaters schedule shows from September through April.

Grand Théâtre de Québec (⊠ 269 blvd. René-Lévesque Est, ☎ 418/643–8131) is a theater where classic and contemporary plays are staged by the leading local theater company, le Théâtre du Trident (☎ 418/643–5873). **Palais Montcalm** (⊠ 995 Pl. d'Youville, ☎ 418/670–9011), a municipal theater outside St-Jean Gate, presents a broad range of productions. A diverse repertory, from classical to comedy, is staged at **Salle Albert-Rousseau** (⊠ 2410 chemin Ste-Foy, Ste-Foy, ☎ 418/659–6710). **Théâtre Capitole** (⊠ 972 rue St-Jean, ☎ 418/694–4444), a restored turn-of-the-century cabaret-style theater, offers a broad repertory of classical and pop music, plays, and comedy shows. **Théâtre de la Bordée** (⊠ 1143 rue St-Jean, ☎ 418/694–9631) presents small-scale productions. **Théâtre Périscope** (⊠ 2 rue Crémazie Est, ☎ 418/529–2183), a multipurpose theater, stages about 200 shows a year, including performances for children.

SUMMER THEATER

Place d'Youville. During the summer, open-air concerts are presented here, just outside St-Jean Gate.

Nightlife

Nightlife in Québec City is centered on the clubs and cafés of rue St-Jean, avenue Cartier, and Grande Allée. In winter, evening activity is livelier toward the end of the week, beginning on Wednesday. But as warmer temperatures set in, the café-terrace crowd emerges, and bars are active seven days a week. Most bars and clubs stay open until 3 AM.

Bars and Lounges

Le Pub Saint-Alexandre (⊠ 1087 rue St-Jean, ☎ 418/694–0015), a popular English-style pub, was formerly a men-only tavern. It's a good place to look for your favorite brand of beer—there are approximately 200 kinds, 20 on tap. You'll find mainly yuppies at **Vogue** and **Sherlock Holmes** (⊠ 1170 d'Artigny, ☎ 418/529–9973), two bars stacked one atop the other. Sherlock Holmes is a pub-restaurant downstairs; for dancing, try Vogue upstairs.

Discos

There's a little bit of everything—live rock bands to loud disco—at **Chez Dagobert** (⊠ 600 Grande Allée Est, ☎ 418/522–0393), a large and popular club. **Merlin** (⊠ 1179 av. Cartier, ☎ 418/529–9567), a second-story disco with an English pub below, is packed nightly.

Folk, Jazz, and Blues

Maison de la Chanson (⊠ Théâtre Petit Champlain, 78 rue du Petit-Champlain, ☎ 418/692–2613) is an excellent spot for contemporary Québec music. French-Canadian folk songs fill **Chez Son Père** (⊠ 24 St-Stanislas, ☎ 418/692–5308), a smoky pub on the second floor of an old building in the Latin Quarter. Singers perform nightly. At **Le d'Auteuil** (⊠ 35 rue d'Auteuil, ☎ 418/692–2263), a converted church across from Kent Gate, rhythm and blues, jazz, and blues emanate. The first jazz bar in Québec City, **L'Emprise at Hôtel Clarendon** (⊠ 57 rue

Ste-Anne, ☎ 418/692–2480), is the preferred spot for enthusiasts. The Art Deco decor sets the mood for Jazz Age rhythms.

OUTDOOR ACTIVITIES AND SPORTS

Two parks are central to Québec City: the 250-acre Battlefields Park, with its panoramic views of the St. Lawrence River, and Cartier-Brébeuf Park, which runs along the St. Charles River. Both are favorite spots for such outdoor sports as jogging, biking, and cross-country skiing. Scenic rivers and mountains close by (no more than 30 minutes by car) make this city ideal for the sporting life. For information about sports and fitness, contact **Québec City Tourist Information Office** (⊠ 60 rue d'Auteuil, G1R 4C4, ☎ 418/692–2471) or **Québec City Bureau of Parks and Recreation** (⊠ 65 rue Ste-Anne, 5th floor, G1R 3X5, ☎ 418/691–6278).

Participant Sports

Bicycling

Bike paths along rolling hills traverse Battlefields Park, at the south side of the city. For a longer ride over flat terrain take the path north of the city skirting the St. Charles River; this route can be reached from rue St-Roch, rue Prince Edouard, and Pont Dorchester (Dorchester Bridge). Paths along the côte de Beaupré, beginning at the confluence of the St. Charles and St. Lawrence rivers, are especially scenic. They begin northeast of the city at rue de la Verandrye and boulevard Montmorency or rue Abraham-Martin and Pont Samson (Samson Bridge) and continue 10 kilometers (6 miles) along the coast to Montmorency Falls.

You can rent bicycles by the day at **Auberge de la Paix** (⊠ 31 rue Couillard, ☎ 418/694–0735).

Boating

Lakes in the Québec City area have facilities for boating. Take Route 73 north of the city to St-Dunstan de Lac Beauport, then take Exit 157, boulevard du Lac, to **Lac Beauport** (☎ 418/849–2821), one of the best nearby resorts. Boats and boards can be rented at **Campex** (⊠ 8 chemin de l'Orée, Lac Beauport, ☎ 418/849–2236) for canoeing, kayaking, and windsurfing.

Dogsledding

Learn how to mush in the forest with **Adventure Nord-Bec** (⊠ 665 rue St. Aimé, St. Lambert de Lévis GOS 2WO, ☎ 418/889–8001), 20 minutes from the city. Overnight camping trips are available.

Fishing

Permits are needed for hunting and fishing in Québec. They are available from the **Ministry of Wildlife and the Environment** (⊠ Pl. de la Capitale, 150 blvd. René-Lévesque Est, ☎ 418/643–3127). The ministry also publishes a pamphlet on fishing regulations that is available at tourist information offices.

Réserve Faunique des Laurentides (☎ 418/848–2422) is a wildlife reserve with good lakes for fishing, approximately 48 kilometers (30 miles) north of Québec City via Route 73.

Golf

The Québec City region has 18 golf courses, and several are open to the public. Reservations during summer months are essential. **Club de Golf de Cap Rouge** (⊠ 4600 rue St-Felix, ☎ 418/653–9381) in Cap Rouge, with 18 holes, is one of the courses closest to Québec City. **Club de Golf de Beauport** (⊠ 3533 rue Clemenceau, ☎ 418/663–1578), a nine-hole course, is 20 minutes by car via Route 73 North. **Parc du Mont Ste-Anne** (⊠ Rte. 360, C.P. 653 Beaupré, ☎ 418/827–3778), a half-hour drive north of Québec, has one of the best 18-hole courses in the region.

Health and Fitness Clubs

One of the city's most popular health clubs is **Club Entrain** (⊠ Pl. de la Cité, 2600 blvd. Laurier, ☎ 418/658–7771). Facilities include a weight room with Nautilus, a sauna, a whirlpool, aerobics classes, and squash courts. Nonguests at **Hôtel Radisson des Gouverneurs** (⊠ 690 blvd. René-Lévesque Est, ☎ 418/647–1717) can use the health club facilities, which include weights, a sauna, a whirlpool, and an outdoor heated pool, for a $5 fee. **Hilton International Québec** (⊠ 3 Pl. Québec, ☎ 418/647–2411) has a smaller health club with weights, a sauna, and an outdoor pool available to nonguests for a $10 fee. **YMCA du Vieux-Québec** (⊠ 650 av. Wilfred Laurier, ☎ 418/522–0800) has facilities that include squash, badminton, a health club, volleyball, and access to a pool for a $2.28 fee. Pool facilities cost $2.25 at the **YWCA** (855 av. Holland, ☎ 418/683–2155).

Hiking and Jogging

The Parc Cartier-Brébeuf, north of the Old City along the banks of the St. Charles River, has about 13 kilometers (8 miles) of hiking trails. For more mountainous terrain, head 19 kilometers (12 miles) north on Route 73 to Lac Beauport. For jogging, Battlefields Park, Parc Cartier-Brébeuf, and Bois-de-Coulonge park in Sillery are the most popular places in the area.

Horseback Riding

Jacques Cartier Excursions (⊠ 978 av. Jacques-Cartier Nord, Tewkesbury, ☎ 418/848–7238), also known for rafting, offers summer and winter horseback riding. An excursion includes an hour of instruction and three hours of riding; the cost is $49 on weekends and $35 weekdays in spring and fall, and $55 on weekends and $39 on weekdays in winter. Reservations are required.

Horticulture

Visitors who enjoy gardening will delight in the botanical **Jardin Roger-Van den Hende.** Included is a water garden, more than 2,000 plant species from North and South America, Europe, and Asia and a collection of trees, small shrubs, and remarkable rhododendrons. The Metrobus and buses 11 and 16 run to the gardens. ⊠ *Pavillon de l'Environtron, 2480 blvd. Hochelaga, Ste-Foy G1K 7P4* ☎ *418/656–3410.* 🎫 *Free.* ☉ *May–Oct., daily 9 AM–8 PM.*

Villa Bagatelle is an interpretation center on the villas and garden estates of Sillery. Its English garden, where you can have tea, has more than 350 varieties of indigenous and exotic plants. ⊠ *1563 chemin St-Louis, Sillery G1S 1G1,* ☎ *418/688–8074.* 🎫 *$2.* ☉ *Mar.–Dec., Tues.–Sun., 11–5.*

Ice Canoeing

Hey, if people windsurf on the ice, why not canoe? This exhilarating sport entails propelling the vessel (a cross between a canoe and a rowboat) over the uneven ice of the St. Lawrence, dipping and sliding and rocking and dragging until you (hopefully) get to open water, at which time you jump in the boat and row. When you return, just hop on the nearest iceberg. To propel the boat on the ice, you straddle it, one knee in a padded rest inside, the other leg pushing like a skateboard. The professional guides at **Le Mythe des Glaces** (⊠ 737 Blvd. du Lac, Charlesbourg, G1H 7B1, ☎ 418/849–6131) will suit you up from head to toe. Half-day, full-day, and overnight trips are available. This sport is not for the unfit.

Rafting

Jacques Cartier River, about 48 kilometers (30 miles) northwest of Québec City, provides good rafting.

Jacques Cartier Excursions (⊠ 978 av. Jacques-Cartier Nord, Tewkesbury, G0A 4P0, ☎ 418/848–7238) offers rafting trips on the Jacques Cartier River. Tours originate from Tewkesbury, a half-hour drive from Québec City, from May through September. A half-day tour costs $30. A full day is $68 on weekends, $49 on weekdays. Wet suits are $15 extra. In winter, snow-rafting excursions are available and include a two-hour sleigh ride and all-day mountain sliding in river rafts. The total cost is $49. Reservations are required.

Nouveau Monde, Adventure–O–Max (⊠ 960 av. Jacques-Cartier Nord, Tewkesbury, ☎ 418/848–4144 or 800/267–4144) has excursions on the Jacques Cartier River from mid-May through September. A 3-hour excursion costs $44, a two-day package $99. Reserve one month in advance for weekends, two weeks in advance for weekdays.

Skating

The ice-skating season runs December through March. There is a 4-kilometer (2½ mile) stretch for skating along the St. Charles River, between the Dorchester and Lavigueur bridges, January through March, depending on the ice. Rentals and changing rooms are nearby. ⊠ *Marina St-Roch,* ☎ *418/691–7188.* ◷ *Skating weekdays noon–10, weekends 10–10.*

Place d'Youville, just outside St-Jean Gate, has an outdoor skating rink open from November to April. From December to March, try the Patinoire de la Terrasse adjacent to the Chateau Frontenac (☎ 418/692–2955). Open from 11 AM to 11 PM, skates can be rented for $4 daily. Nighttime skating can also be done at **Village des Sports** (⊠ 1860 blvd. Valcartier, St-Gabriel-de-Valcartier, ☎ 418/844–3725).

Skiing
You can ski cross-country on many trails; Battlefields Park on Québec City's south side, which you can reach from Place Montcalm, has scenic marked trails. Thirty-two ski centers in the Quebec area offer 1,700 kilometers (1,050 miles) of groomed trails and heated shelters; for information, call **Regroupement des stations de ski de fond** (☎ 418/653–5875). Lac Beauport, 19 kilometers (12 miles) north of the city, has more than 20 marked trails (250 kilometers, or 155 miles); contact **Les Sentiers du Moulin** (⊠ 99 chemin du Moulin, ☎ 418/849–9652). **Parc du Mont Ste-Anne** (⊠ Rte. 360, C.P. 400 Beaupré, G0A 1E0, ☎ 418/827–4561), which is 40 kilometers (25 miles) northeast of Québec City, has 215 kilometers (133 miles) of cross-country trails. **Le Centre de Randonnée à Skis de Duchesnay** (⊠ 143 rue de Duchesnay, St-Catherine-de-Jacques-Cartier, ☎ 418/875–2147), just north of Québec City, has 11 marked trails totaling 125 kilometers (77 miles).

Four alpine ski resorts, all with night skiing, are within a 30-minute drive of Québec City. **Station Mont Ste-Anne** (⊠ Rte. 360, C.P. 400 Beaupré G0A 1E0, ☎ 418/827–4561; lodging, 800/463–1568) is the largest resort in eastern Canada, with 50 downhill trails, 12 lifts, and a gondola. **Station Touristique Stoneham** (⊠ 1420 av. du Hibou, Stoneham G0A 4P0, ☎ 418/848–2411) is known for its long, easy slopes with 25 downhill runs and 10 lifts. Two smaller alpine centers can be found at Lac Beauport: 15 trails at **Mont St-Castin** (⊠ 82 chemin du Tour du Lac, Box 1129, Lac Beauport G0A 2C0, ☎ 418/849–6776 or 418/849–1893) and 25 trails at **Le Relais** (⊠ 1084 blvd. du Lac, Lac Beauport G0A 2C0, ☎ 418/849–1851).

Upon request and for a fee, most major hotels arrange ski-bus service for guests. **Visite Touristique de Québec** (☎ 418/653–9722) offers a bus service to Mont Ste-Anne and Stoneham. It leaves from major hotels in Québec City and from the information center in Ste-Foy daily between 7:30 AM and 8:30 AM and returns from the slopes at 4 PM. It costs $9 each way; $15 round-trip. Telephone for reservations.

Brochures about ski centers in Québec are available at the Québec Tourism and Convention Bureaus or by calling 800/363–7777.

Snow Slides

At **Glissades de la Terrasse,** adjacent to the Château Frontenac, a wooden toboggan takes you down a 700–foot snow slide. ☎ *418/692–2955.* ⊡ *$1 per ride.* ☉ *Daily 11 AM–11 PM.*

Visitors to **Village des sports** can use inner tubes or carpets on the two 300-foot snow slides, or join 6–12 others for a snow raft ride down one of seven groomed trails. ⊠ *1860 blvd. Valcartier, St-Gabriel-de-Valcartier,* ☎ *418/844–3725.* ⊡ *Rafting and sliding $16.50 per day, with skating $18.50.* ☉ *Weekdays 10–10, weekends 10 AM–10:30 PM.*

Tennis

At **Montcalm Tennis Club** (⊠ 901 blvd. Champlain, Sillery, ☎ 418/687–1250), south of Québec City in Sillery, four indoor and seven outdoor courts are open daily from 8 AM to 10 PM. At **Tennisport** (⊠ 6280 blvd. Hamel, Ancienne Lorette, ☎ 418/872–0111) there are 11 indoor tennis courts, two squash courts, seven raquetball courts, and eight badminton courts.

Winter Carnival

One of the highlights of the winter season in Québec is the **Québec Winter Carnival** (⊠ 290 rue Joly, GIL 1N8, ☎ 418/626–3716), famous for its joie de vivre. The whirl of activities over 3 weekends in January and/or February includes night parades, a snow-sculpture competition, and a canoe race across the St. Lawrence River. You can participate in or watch every activity imaginable in the snow from dogsledding to ice climbing. Dates for 1997 are January 31 to February 16.

Spectator Sports

Tickets for sporting events can be purchased at **Colisée de Québec** (⊠ Québec Coliseum, 2205 av. du Colisée, ☎ 418/691–7211) or through **Billetech** (☞ Nightlife and the Arts, *above*).

Harness Racing

There's horse racing at **Hippodrome de Québec.** ⊠ *Parc de l'Exposition,* ☎ *418/524–5283.* ⊡ *$2.50 grandstand, $5 club house; half price Mon., Tues., and Fri. nights, when Montréal and Ontario races are shown only on TV.*

SHOPPING

Shopping is European-style on the fashionable streets of Québec City. The boutiques and specialty shops clustered along narrow streets (such as rue du Petit-Champlain, and rue Buade and rue St-Jean in the Latin Quarter) have one of the most striking historic settings on the continent.

Prices in Québec City tend to be on a par with those in Montréal and other North American cities, so you won't have much luck hunting for bargains. When sales occur, they are usually listed in the French daily newspaper, *Le Soleil*.

Stores are generally open Monday through Wednesday 9:30–5:30, Thursday and Friday until 9, Saturday until 5, and Sunday noon–5. In summer, shops may be open seven days a week, and most have later evening hours.

Department Stores

Large department stores can be found in the malls of the suburb of Ste-Foy, but some have outlets inside Québec City's walls.

Holt Renfrew & Co., Ltd. (⊠ Pl. Ste-Foy, Ste-Foy, ☎ 418/656–6783), one of the country's more exclusive stores, carries furs, perfume, and tailored designer collections for men and women. **La Baie** (⊠ Pl. Laurier, Ste-Foy, ☎ 418/627–5959) is Québec's version of the Canadian Hudson's Bay Company conglomerate, founded in 1670 by Montréal trappers Pierre Radisson and Medard de Groseillers; the company established the first network of stores in the Canadian frontier. Today, La Baie carries both men's and women's clothing and household wares. **Simons** (⊠ 20 côte de la Fabrique, ☎ 418/692–3630), one of Québec City's oldest family stores, used to be its only source for fine British woolens and tweeds; now the store also has a large selection of designer clothing, linens, and other household items.

Food and Flea Markets

At **Marché du Vieux-Port,** farmers from the Québec countryside sell fresh produce in the Old Port near rue St-André, from May through October, 8–8.

Rue du Trésor hosts a flea market near the Place d'Armes that features sketches, paintings, and etchings by local artists. Fine portraits of the Québec City landscape and region are plentiful. Good, inexpensive souvenirs also may be purchased here.

Shopping Centers

Place Québec (⊠ 5 Pl. Québec, ☎ 418/529–0551), the mall closest to the Old City, is a multilevel shopping complex and convention center with 40 stores; it is connected to the Hilton International Hotel. **Halles Petit-Cartier** (⊠ 1191 av. Cartier, ☎ 418/688–1630), off Grande Allée and a 15-minute walk from St-Louis Gate, is a food mall for gourmets, with everything from utensils to petits fours.

The following shopping centers are approximately a 15-minute drive west along Grande Allée. **Place Ste-Foy** (⊠ 2450 blvd. Laurier, Ste-Foy, ☎ 418/653–4184) has 125 specialty stores. Next door to Place Ste-Foy is **Place de la Cité** (⊠ 2600 blvd. Laurier, Ste-Foy, ☎ 418/657–6920), with 125 boutiques. The massive **Place Laurier** (⊠ 2700 blvd Laurier, Ste-Foy, ☎ 418/653–9318) has more than 350 stores.

Quartier Petit-Champlain (☎ 418/692–2613) in Lower Town is a pedestrian mall with some 40 boutiques, local businesses, and restaurants. This popular district is the best area to find native Québec arts and crafts, such as wood sculptures, weaving, ceramics, and jewelry. Try **Pot-en-Ciel** (⊠ 27 rue du Petit-Champlain, ☎ 418/692–1743) for ceramics. **Pauline Pelletier** (⊠ 38 rue du Petit-Champlain, ☎ 418/692–4871) has porcelain.

Specialty Stores

Antiques

Québec City's antiques district is on rue St-Paul and rue St-Pierre, across from the Old Port. French Canadian, Victorian, and Art Deco furniture, along with clocks, silverware, and porcelain, are some of the rare collectibles that can be found here. Authentic Québec pine furniture, characterized by simple forms and lines, is becoming increasingly rare and costly.

L'Héritage Antiquités (⊠ 110 rue St-Paul, ☎ 418/692–1681) specializes in precious Québécois furniture from the 18th century. **Antiquités Zaor** (⊠ 112 rue St-Paul, ☎ 418/692–0581), the oldest store on rue St-Paul, is still the best place in the neighborhood to find excellent English, French, and Canadian antiques.

Art

Aux Multiples Collections (⊠ 43 rue Buade, ☎ 418/692–4298) has Inuit art and antique wood collectibles. **Galerie Brousseau et Brousseau** (⊠ Château Frontenac, 1 rue des Carrières, ☎ 418/694–1828) has Inuit art. **Galerie Madeleine Lacerte** (⊠ 1 côte Dinan, ☎ 418/692–1566), in Lower Town, sells contemporary art and sculpture.

Books

English-language books are difficult to find in Québec. One of the city's first bookstores, **Librairie Garneau** (⊠ 24 côte de la Fabrique, ☎ 418/692–4262), near City Hall, carries mostly volumes in French. **La Maison Anglaise** (⊠ Pl. de la Cité, Ste-Foy, ☎ 418/654–9523), has English-language titles only, specializing in fiction. **Librairie du Nouveau-Monde** (⊠ 103 rue St-Pierre, ☎ 418/694–9475), stocks general-interest titles in French and English. **Librairie Smith** (⊠ Pl. Laurier, blvd. Laurier, ☎ 418/653–8683) is popular.

Clothing

François Côté Collections (⊠ 35 rue Buade, ☎ 418/692–6016) is a chic boutique with fashions for men. **La Maison Darlington** (⊠ 7 rue Buade, ☎ 418/692–2268) carries well-made woolens, dresses, and suits for women by fine names in couture. **Louis Laflamme** (⊠ 1192 rue St-Jean, ☎ 418/692–3774) has a large selection of stylish men's clothes.

Crafts

Les Trois Colombes Inc. (⊠ 46 rue St-Louis, ☎ 418/694–1114) sells handmade items on two floors filled with such goods as clothing made from handwoven fabric, Indian and Inuit carvings, jewelry, pottery, and paintings.

Fur

The fur trade has been an important industry here for centuries. Québec City is a good place to purchase high-quality furs at fairly reasonable prices. Since 1894, one of the best furriers in town has been **Jos Robitaille** (⊠ 1500 des Taneurs, ☎ 418/681–7297). The department store **J. B. Laliberté** (⊠ 595 rue St-Joseph Est, ☎ 418/525–4841) also carries furs.

Gifts

Collection Lazuli (⊠ 774 rue St-Jean, ☎ 418/525–6528; ⊠ Pl. de la Cité, Ste. Foy, ☎ 418/652–3732) offers a good choice of unusual art objects and international jewelry.

Jewelry

Joaillier Louis Perrier (⊠ 48 rue du Petit-Champlain, ☎ 418/692–4633) has Québec-made gold and silver jewelry. Exclusive jewelry can also be found at **Zimmermann** (⊠ 46 côte de la Fabrique, ☎ 418/692–2672).

SIDE TRIPS

Côte de Beaupré and Montmorency Falls

As legend tells it, when explorer Jacques Cartier first caught sight of the north shore of the St. Lawrence River in 1535, he exclaimed, *"Quel beau pré!"* ("What a lovely meadow!"), because the area was the first inviting piece of land he had spotted since leaving France. Today this fertile meadow, first settled by French farmers, is known as Côte de Beaupré (Beaupré Coast), stretching 40 kilometers (25 miles) northeast from Québec City to the famous pilgrimage site of Ste-Anne-de-Beaupré. The impressive Montmorency Falls are midway between these two points.

Montmorency Falls, as they cascade down the side of a 274-foot cliff, are one of the most beautiful sights in the province. These falls are 50% higher than Niagara Falls, which is wider. More than half a million people each year make spiritual pilgrimages to the monumental and inspiring basilica at Ste-Anne-de-Beaupré, along the historic route 360 or chemin Royal, that winds its way from Beauport to St-Joachim. Ste. Anne is the patron saint of those in shipwrecks.

Montmorency Falls

As it cascades over a cliff into the St. Lawrence River, the Montmorency River (named for Charles de Montmorency, who was a governor of New France) is one of the most beautiful sights in the province. The falls, at 274 feet, are higher than Niagara Falls. During very cold weather, the falls's heavy spray freezes and forms a giant loaf-shape ice cone (hill) known to Québécois as the Pain du Sucre (Sugarloaf); this phenomenon attracts sledders and sliders from Québec City. Ice climbers come scale the falls; a school trains novices for only a few days to make the ascent. In the warmer months, a park in the river's gorge leads to an observation terrace that is continuously sprayed by a fine drizzle from water pounding onto the cliff rocks. The top of the falls can be observed from avenue Royale.

The park is also a historic sight. The British general Wolfe, on his way to conquer New France, set up camp here in 1759. In 1780, Sir Frederick Haldimand, then the governor of Canada, built a summer home—now a good restaurant called Manoir Montmorency—on top of the cliff. Prince Edward, Queen Victoria's father, rented this villa from 1791 to 1794. Unfortunately, the structure burned several years ago; what now stands is a re-creation. ☎ 418/663–2877. 🎟 *Free, parking $6.* ☽ *May–mid-June, daily 8:30–6; mid-June–July, daily 9 AM–11 PM; Aug., daily 9–9; Sept. and Oct., daily 9–6; Nov.–May, weekends 8:30–4:30.*

NEED A
BREAK?

Restaurant Baker (✉ 8790 av. Royale, Château-Richer, ☎ 418/824–4478), on the way to Ste-Anne-de Beaupré on Route 360, is a good, old-fashioned rustic restaurant that serves such hearty traditional French Canadian dishes as meat pie, pea soup, pâtés, and maple-sugar pie.

Basilique Ste-Anne-de-Beaupré

The monumental and inspiring **Basilique Ste-Anne-de-Beaupré** (Ste-Anne-de-Beaupré Basilica) is in a small town with the same name. The basilica has become a popular attraction as well as an important shrine: More than half a million people visit the site each year.

The French brought their devotion to St. Anne with them when they sailed across the Atlantic to New France. In 1650, Breton sailors caught in a storm vowed to erect a chapel in honor of this patron saint at the exact spot where they landed. The present-day neo-Roman basilica constructed in 1923 was the fifth to be built on the site where the sailors first touched ground.

According to local legend, St. Anne was responsible over the years for saving voyagers from shipwrecks in the harsh waters of the St. Lawrence. Tributes to her miraculous powers can be seen in the shrine's various mosaics, murals, altars, and ceilings. A bas-relief at the entrance depicts St. Anne welcoming her pilgrims, and ceiling mosaics represent her life. Numerous crutches and braces posted on the back pillars have been left by those who have felt the saint's healing powers.

The basilica, which is in the shape of a Latin cross, has two granite steeples jutting from its gigantic structure. Its interior has 22 chapels and 18 altars, as well as round arches and numerous ornaments in the Romanesque style. The 214 stained-glass windows by Frenchmen Auguste Labouret and Pierre Chaudière, finished in 1949, tell a story of salvation through personages who were believed to be instruments of God over the centuries. Other features of the shrine include intricately carved wood pews decorated with various animals and several smaller altars (behind the main altar) that are dedicated to different saints.

The original, 17th-century wood chapel in the village of Ste-Anne-de-Beaupré was built too close to the St. Lawrence and was swept away by river flooding. In 1676, the chapel was replaced by a stone church that was visited by pilgrims for more than a century, but this structure was also demolished in 1872. The first basilica, which replaced the stone church, was destroyed by a fire in 1922. The following year architects Maxime Rosin from Paris and Louis-N. Audet from Québec province designed the basilica that now stands. Tours are given daily in summer at 1 and begin at the information booth at the southwest corner of the courtyard outside the basilica. ⊠ *10,018 av. Royale, Ste-Anne-de-Beaupré,* ☎ *418/827–3781.* 🎫 *Free.* ☉ *Reception booth mid-May–mid-Oct., daily 8:30–7:30; guided tours Sept.–mid-May can be arranged by calling in advance.*

Across from the basilica on avenue Royale is the **Commemorative Chapel,** designed by Claude Bailiff and built in 1878. The memorial chapel was constructed on the location of the transept of a stone church built in 1676 and contains the old building's foundations. Among the remnants housed here are the old church's bell dating from 1696, an early 18th-century altar designed by Vezina, a crucifix sculpted by François-Noël Levasseur in 1775, and a pulpit designed by François Baillargé in 1807.

Beaupré Coast Interpretation Center, in the old mill Petit-Pré, built in 1695, has displays on the history and development of the region. ⊠ *7007 av. Royale, Château-Richer,* ☎ *418/824–3677.* 🎫 *$1.* ☉ *Late June–Labor Day, daily 9–noon and 1–5.*

Côte de Beaupré A to Z

ARRIVING AND DEPARTING

By Car. To reach Montmorency Falls, take Route 440 (Dufferin-Montmorency Autoroute) northeast from Québec City approximately 9½ kilometers (6 miles) to the exit for Montmorency Falls. To drive directly to Ste-Anne-de Beaupré, continue northeast on Route 440 for approximately 29 kilometers (18 miles) and exit at Ste-Anne-de-Beaupré.

An alternative way to reach Ste-Anne-de-Beaupré is to take Route 360 or avenue Royale. Take Route 440 from Québec City, turn left at d'Estimauville, and right on boulevard Ste-Anne until it intersects with Route 360. Also called "le chemin du Roi" (the King's Road), this panoramic route is one of the oldest in North America, winding 30 kilometers (20 miles) along the steep ridge of the Côte de Beaupré. The road borders 17th- and 18th-century farmhouses, historic churches, and Normandy-style homes with half-buried root cellars. Route 360 goes past the Ste-Anne-de-Beaupré Basilica.

GUIDED TOURS

Companies such as **Gray Line** (☎ 418/653–9722, FAX 418/653–9834), which charge $13–$80 per tour, and **Maple Leaf Sightseeing Tours** (☎ 418/649–9226), lead day excursions along the Côte de Beaupré, with stops at Montmorency Falls and the Ste-Anne-de-Beaupré Basilica.

Beau Temps, Mauvais Temps (✉ 22 rue du Quai, Suite 101, Ste-Pétronille, Ile d'Orléans, ☎ 418/828–2275) offers guided bus tours of the Côte de Beaupré.

Ile d'Orleans

Ile d'Orléans, an island slightly downstream in a northeasterly direction from Québec City, exemplifies the historic charm of rural Québec province with its quiet, traditional lifestyle. A drive around the island will take you past stone churches that are among the oldest in the region and centuries-old houses amid acres of lush orchards and cultivated farmland. Horse-drawn carriages are still a means of transport. Ile d'Orléans is also an important marketplace that provides fresh produce daily for Québec City; roadside stands on the island sell a variety of local products, such as crocheted blankets, woven articles, maple syrup, homemade breads and jams, and fruits and vegetables. The island is known for its superb fruits, and you won't find better strawberries anywhere else in the province. There are about two dozen spots where you can pick your own.

The island was discovered at about the same time as Québec City in 1535. Explorer Jacques Cartier noticed an abundance of vines on the island and called it the "Island of Bacchus," after the Greek god of wine. In 1536, Cartier renamed the island in honor of the duke of Orléans, son of the king of France, François I. Long considered part of the domain of Côte de Beaupré, the island was not given its seignorial autonomy until 1636.

Ile d'Orléans, about 9 kilometers (5½ miles) wide and 34 kilometers (21 miles) long, is now composed of six small villages. These villages have sought over the years to remain relatively private residential and agricultural communities; the island's bridge to the mainland was built only in 1935.

Numbers in the margin correspond to points of interest on the Ile d'Orléans map.

Ste-Pétronille

Start your tour heading west on chemin Royal to Ste-Pétronille, the first village to be settled on the island. Founded in 1648, the community was chosen in 1759 by British General James Wolfe for his headquarters. With 40,000 soldiers and a hundred ships, the English bombarded French-occupied Québec City and Côte de Beaupré.

During the late 19th century, the English population of Québec developed Ste-Pétronille into a resort village. This region is considered by many to be the island's most beautiful, not only because of the spectacular views it offers of Montmorency Falls and Québec City but also for the stylish English villas and exquisitely tended gardens that can be seen from the roadside.

After crossing the bridge to the island, and turning right on chemin Royal, on the left at 20 chemin Royal is the **Plante family farm,** where

It helps to be pushy in airports.

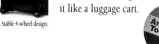

Introducing the revolutionary new TransPorter™ from American Tourister.® It's the first suitcase you can push around without a fight. TransPorter's™ exclusive four-wheel design lets you push it in front of you with almost no effort–the wheels take the weight. Or pull it on two wheels if you choose. You can even stack on other bags and use it like a luggage cart.

Stable 4-wheel design.

TransPorter™ is designed like a dresser, with built-in shelves to organize your belongings. Or collapse the shelves and pack it like a traditional suitcase. Inside, there's a suiter feature to help keep suits and dresses from wrinkling. When push comes to shove, you can't beat a TransPorter.™ For more information on how you can be this pushy, call 1-800-542-1300.

Shelves collapse on command.

 **Making travel less primitive.®**

©1996 American Tourister®

Use your MCI Card®

for the easy way to

call when traveling

MCI. Calling Card

415 555 1234 2244
J.D. SMITH

Convenience on the road

- Your MCI Card® number is your
  home number, guaranteed.

- Pre-programmed to
  speed dial to your home.

- Call from any phone in
  the U.S.

1 - 8 0 0 - 7 5 4 - 8 9 4 1

http://www.mci.com

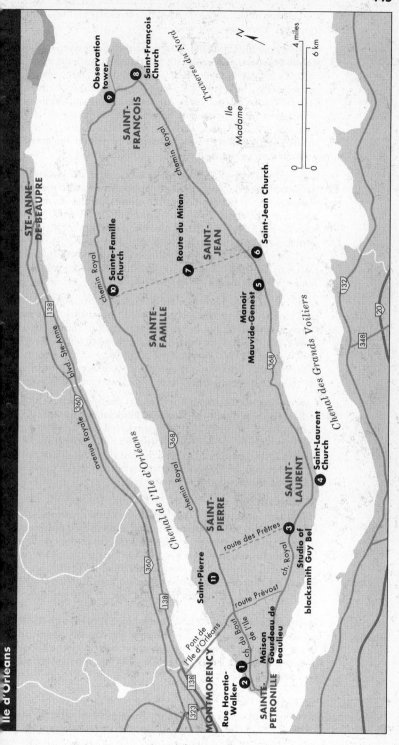

you can stop to pick apples (in season) or buy some of the island's fresh fruits and vegetables.

Coming from the Plante family farm, farther along on the right is the **①** **Maison Gourdeau de Beaulieu** (⊠ 137 chemin Royal), the island's first home, built in 1648 for Jacques Gourdeau de Beaulieu, who was the first seigneur of Ste-Pétronille. Today this white house with blue shutters is still privately owned by his descendants. Remodeled over the years, it now incorporates both French and Québécois styles. Its thick walls and dormer windows are characteristic of Breton architecture, but its sloping bell-shape roof, designed to protect buildings from large amounts of snow, is typically Québécois.

Coming from Maison Gordeau de Beaulieu, after you descend an incline, **②** turn right beside the river on the tiny street called **rue Horatio-Walker,** named after the turn-of-the-century painter known for his landscapes of the island. Walker lived on this street from 1904 until his death in 1938. At 11 and 13 rue Horatio-Walker are his home and workshop. During the summer, his paintings are exhibited in the workshop. Designed by Harry Staveley, the home is a good example of English Arts & Crafts architecture. To tour the house, contact Beau Temps, Mauvais Temps (☎ 418/828–2275).

Farther along chemin Royal, at the border of Ste-Pétronille and St-Laurent, look for a large boulder in the middle of nowhere. The **roche Maranda** (to the left, just before the intersection of chemin Royal and route Prévost), named for the owner of the property where the rock was discovered in the 19th century, is one of the oldest such rock formations in the world. When the glaciers melted in 9,000 BC, such rocks as this one rolled down with glacial water from the Laurentians onto lower land.

Continue east along chemin Royal, and as you approach the village of **③** St-Laurent, you'll find the **studio of blacksmith Guy Bel** (⊠ 2200 chemin Royal, ☎ 418/828–9300), a talented and well-known local artisan who has done ironwork restoration for Québec City. He was born in Lyon, France, and studied there at the Ecole des Beaux Arts. In summer, you can watch him hard at work; his stylish candlesticks, mantels, and other ironworks are for sale.

St-Laurent

St-Laurent, founded in 1679, is one of the island's maritime villages. Until as late as 1935, residents here used boats as their main means of transportation. Next to the village's marina stands the tall, inspiring **④** **St-Laurent Church.** It was built in 1860 on the site of an 18th-century church that, because of its poor construction, had to be torn down. One of the church's procession chapels is a miniature stone replica of the original. ⊠ 1532 chemin Royal. 🎟 Free. ☉ Summer, daily.

NEED A BREAK? **Moulin de Saint-Laurent** (⊠ 754 chemin Royal, ☎ 418/829–3888) is an early 18th-century stone mill where you can dine in the herb-and-flower garden out back. Scrumptious snacks, such as quiches, bagels, and salads, are available at the café-terrace. The restaurant is closed November–April.

St-Jean

If you continue on chemin Royal, you'll come to the southernmost point of the island, St-Jean, a village whose inhabitants were once river pilots and navigators. Most of its small, homogeneous row homes were built between 1840 and 1860. Being at sea most of the time, the sailors did not need large homes and plots of land as did the farmers. The island's sudden drop in elevation is most noticeable in St-Jean.

5 St-Jean's beautiful Normandy-style manor, **Manoir Mauvide-Genest,** was built in 1734 for Jean Mauvide—surgeon to Louis XV—and his wife, Marie-Anne Genest. Most notable about this house, which still has its original thick walls, ceiling beams, and fireplaces, is the degree to which it has held up over the years, in spite of being targeted by English guns during the 1759 siege of Québec City. The home is a pleasure to roam; all rooms are furnished with original antiques from the 18th and 19th centuries. It also offers an exhibit on French architecture and a downstairs restaurant that serves French cuisine. ✉ *1451 chemin Royal,* ☎ *418/829–2630.* ⏲ *June–Aug., daily 10–5; Sept.–mid-Oct., weekends by reservation.*

6 At the opposite end of the village, you'll see **St-Jean Church,** a massive granite structure with large red doors and a towering steeple built in 1749. The church bears a remarkable resemblance to a ship; it is big and round and appears to be sitting right on the St. Lawrence River. Paintings of the patron saints of seamen line the interior walls. The church's cemetery is also intriguing, especially if you can read French. Back in the 18th century, piloting the St. Lawrence was a dangerous profession; the boats could not easily handle the rough currents. The cemetery tombstones recall the tragedies of lives lost in these harsh waters. ✉ *2001 chemin Royal,* ☎ *418/829–3182.* 🎫 *Free.* ⏲ *Summer, daily.*

7 As you leave St-Jean, chemin Royal mounts the incline and crosses **route du Mitan.** In old French, *mitan* means "halfway." This road, dividing the island in half, is the most direct route from north to south. It is also the most beautiful on the island, with acres of tended farmland, apple orchards, and maple groves. If you're running out of time and want to end the tour here, take route du Mitan, which brings you to St-Pierre and the bridge to the mainland.

St-François

When you come to 17th-century farmhouses separated by sprawling open fields, you know you've reached the island's least-toured and most rustic village, St-François. At the eastern tip of the island, this community was originally settled mainly by farmers. St-François is also the perfect place to visit one of the island's *cabanes à sucre* (maple-sugaring huts) found along chemin Royal. Stop at a hut for a tasting tour; sap is gathered from the maple groves and boiled until it turns to syrup. When it is poured on ice, it tastes like a delicious toffee. The maple syrup season is late March through April.

8 Straight on chemin Royal is **St-François Church,** built in 1734 and one of eight provincial churches dating from the French regime. At the time the English seized Québec in 1759, General Wolfe knew St-François to be among the better strategic points along the St. Lawrence. Consequently, he stationed British troops here and used the church as a military hospital. In May 1988, a fatal car crash set the church on fire and, most of the interior treasures were lost.

9 About a mile down the road from the St-François Church is a picnic area with a wood **observation tower** situated for perfect viewing of the majestic St. Lawrence at its widest point, 10 times as wide as it is near Québec City. During the spring and autumn months, you can observe wild Canada geese here.

Ste-Famille

Heading west now on chemin Royal, you'll come to one of the island's earliest villages, Ste-Famille, which was founded in 1661. The scenery is exquisite here; there are abundant apple orchards and strawberry fields with views of Côte de Beaupré and Mont Ste-Anne in the distance. But the village also has plenty of artificial historic charm; it has the area's highest concentration of stone houses dating from the French regime.

⑩ Take a quick look at **Ste-Famille Church,** which was constructed in 1749, later than some of the others on the island. This impressive structure is the only church in the province to have three bell towers at the front. Its ceiling was redone in the mid-19th century with elaborate designs in wood and gold. The church also holds a famous painting, *L'Enfant Jésus Voyant la Croix,* done in 1670 by Frère Luc (Father Luc), who was sent from France to decorate churches in the area. ⊠ *3915 chemin Royal.* 🎫 *Free.* ☉ *Summer, daily.*

St-Pierre

⑪ The village after Ste-Famille on the northwest side of the island, **St-Pierre,** was established in 1679. Its church, dating from 1717, is the oldest on the island. **St-Pierre Church** is no longer open for worship, but it was restored during the 1960s and is open to tourists. Many of its original components are still intact, such as benches with compartments below, where hot bricks and stones were placed to keep people warm during winter services. ⊠ *1243 chemin Royal.* 🎫 *Free.* ☉ *Summer, daily.*

Because St-Pierre is situated on a plateau with the island's most fertile land, the village has long been the center of traditional farming industries. The best products grown here are potatoes, asparagus, and corn, and the many dairy farms have given the village a renowned reputation for butter and other dairy products. At 2370 chemin Royal is the **former home of Felix Leclerc,** one of the many artists who have made the island their home. Leclerc, the father of Québécois folk singing, lived here until he died in August 1988.

If you continue west on chemin Royal, just up ahead are the bridge back to the mainland and Route 440.

DINING AND LODGING

$$$ ✕ **L'Atre.** After you park your car, you'll be driven in a 1954 Chevy to the 17th-century Normandy-style house furnished with Québécois pine antiques. True to the establishment's name, which means "hearth," all the traditional dishes are cooked and served from a fireplace. The menu emphasizes hearty fare, such as beef Bourguignon and tourtière with maple-sugar pie for dessert. La Grande Fête (the Big Feast) is a nine-course dinner that costs about $60. Halfway through the meal guests visit the attic for a nip of maple-syrup liqueur. ⊠ *4403 chemin Royal, Ste-Famille,* ☎ *418/829–2474. Reservations essential. AE, MC, V. Closed Nov.–Apr.*

$$–$$$ ✕⌂ **La Goéliche.** This 1890 rustic Victorian country inn stands just steps away from the St. Lawrence River. Québécois antiques decorate light and spacious rooms with their original wood floors. Rooms have telephones; half look out across the river to Québec City. The first rule of this classic French kitchen is that only the freshest ingredients from the island's farms can be used. Lunch is a moderately priced à la carte selection of salads, quiches, and omelets. The evening's menu is more expensive and features such specialties as quail with red vermouth and chicken with pistachio mousseline. The desserts, such as maple syrup mousse with strawberry syrup, have a regional flavor. The romantic dining room has windows overlooking the St. Lawrence River. ⊠ *2 chemin du Quai, Ste-Pétronille,* ☎ *418/828–2248,* ℻ *418/828–2745. 24 rooms. 2 restaurants. AE, MC, V.*

$$ ✕🏠 **Auberge le Chaumonot.** This medium-size hotel in rural St-François is right near the St. Lawrence River's widest point. The inn's large bay windows capitalize on the view of the river and neighboring islands, but the decor is uninspired, with simple wood furniture of the island. The service here is efficient and friendly. The restaurant serves Continental cuisine, with table d'hôte and à la carte menus. ✉ *425 chemin Royal, St-François, G0A 3S0,* ☎ *418/829–2735. 8 rooms with bath. Restaurant, air-conditioning, pool. AE, MC, V. Closed Nov.–Apr.*

Ile d'Orléans A to Z

ARRIVING AND DEPARTING

By Car. Ile d'Orléans has no public transportation; cars are the only way to get to and around the island, unless you take a guided tour (☞ Guided Tours, *below*). Parking on the island is never a problem; you can always stop and explore the villages on foot. The main road, chemin Royal (Route 368), extends 67 kilometers (40 miles) through the island's six villages; street numbers along chemin Royal begin at No. 1 for each municipality.

From Québec City, take Route 440 (Dufferin-Montmorency Autoroute) northeast. After a drive of about 10 kilometers (6 miles) take the bridge, Pont de l'Ile d'Orléans, to the island.

B&B RESERVATION SERVICE

You can get to know the island by staying at one of its 30 B&Bs. Reservations are necessary. The price for a room, double occupancy, runs about $45–$90. **Beau Temps, Mauvais Temps** (☎ 418/828–2275) is a referral service for these accommodations.

EMERGENCIES

Centre Médical (✉ 1015 Rte. Prévost, St-Pierre, ☎ 418/828–2213) is the only medical clinic on the island.

GUIDED TOURS

Beau Temps, Mauvais Temps (✉ 22 rue du Quai, Suite 101, Ste-Pétronille, ☎ 418/828–2275) leads guided walking tours of three villages: Ste-Pétronille, St-Jean, and St-Laurent. River excursions departing from St-Laurent are available from mid-May–mid-September.

Québec City touring companies, including **Maple Leaf Sightseeing Tours** (☎ 418/649–9226), **Gray Line** (☎ 418/653–9722, FAX 418/653–9834) and **Visite Touristiques de Québec** (☎ 418/653–9722) offer full- and half-day bus tours of the western tip of the island, combined with sightseeing along the Côte de Beaupré.

Any of the offices of the **Québec City Region Tourism and Convention Bureau** (☞ Québec City A to Z, *below*) can provide information on tours and accommodations on the island.

VISITOR INFORMATION

Beau Temps, Mauvais Temps has a tourist office in Ste-Pétronille. ✉ *22 rue du Quai, Suite 101, Ste-Pétronille,* ☎ *418/828–2275.* ☻ *May–Oct., weekdays 8:30–4; Nov.–Apr., leave message on answering machine.*

The island's **Chamber of Commerce** operates a tourist information kiosk situated at the west corner of côte du Pont and chemin Royal. ✉ *490 côte du Pont, St-Pierre,* ☎ *418/828–9411.* ☻ *June–Sept., daily 8:30–7, Oct.–May, daily 8:30–noon, 1–4.*

QUÉBEC CITY A TO Z

Arriving and Departing

By Bus

Voyageur Inc. provides regular service from Montréal to Québec City daily, departing hourly 6 AM–9 PM, with an additional bus at 11 PM. The cost of the three-hour ride is $35 one way, round-trip is double that; but a round-trip costs $52.13 if you return within 10 days and do not travel on Friday. Senior citizens travel for $26.46 each way, good for any day. You can purchase tickets only at the terminal.

BUS TERMINALS

Montréal: Terminus Voyageur (⊠ 505 blvd. de Maisonneuve Est, ☎ 514/842–2281). **Québec:** Downtown Terminal (⊠ 320 rue Abraham-Martin, ☎ 418/525–3000); Ste-Foy Terminal (⊠ 2700 blvd. Laurier, ☎ 418/651–7015).

By Car

Montréal and Québec City are linked by Autoroute 20 on the south shore of the St. Lawrence River and by Autoroute 40 on the north shore. On both highways, the ride between the two cities is about 240 kilometers (150 miles) and takes some three hours. U.S. I–87 in New York, U.S. I–89 in Vermont, and U.S. I–91 in New Hampshire connect with Autoroute 20. Highway 401 from Toronto also links up with Autoroute 20.

Driving northeast from Montréal on Autoroute 20, follow signs for Pont Pierre-Laporte (Pierre-Laporte Bridge) as you approach Québec City. After you've crossed the bridge, turn right onto boulevard Laurier (Route 175), which becomes the Grande Allée leading into Québec City.

It is necessary to have a car only if you are planning to visit outlying areas. The narrow streets of the Old City leave few two-hour metered parking spaces available. However, there are several parking garages at central locations in town, with rates running approximately $10 a day. Main garages are at City Hall, Place d'Youville, Edifice Marie Guyart, Complex G, Place Québec, Château Frontenac, Québec Seminary, rue St-Paul, and the Old Port.

By Plane

Québec City has one airport, **Jean Lesage International Airport,** in the suburb of Ste-Foy, about 19 kilometers (12 miles) from downtown. Few U.S. airlines fly directly to Québec City. You usually have to stop in Montréal, Toronto, or Ottawa and take one of the regional and commuter airlines, such as Air Canada's **Air Alliance** (☎ 418/692–0770 or 800/361–8620) or **Canadian Airlines International** (☎ 418/692–1031). **Air Alliance** has a daily direct flight between Newark, New Jersey, and Québec City.

BETWEEN THE AIRPORT AND QUÉBEC CITY

The ride from the airport into town should be no longer than 30 minutes. Most hotels do not have an airport shuttle, but they will make a reservation for you with a bus company. If you're not in a rush, a shuttle bus offered by Maple Leaf Sightseeing Tours (☞ *below*) is convenient and half the price of a taxi.

By Bus. Maple Leaf Sightseeing Tours (⊠ 240 3e rue, ☎ 418/649–9226) has a shuttle bus that runs from the airport to hotels and costs under $10 one-way. Reservations are necessary for the trip to the airport.

By Car. If you're driving from the airport, take Route 540 (Autoroute Duplessis) to Route 175 (blvd. Laurier), which becomes Grande Allée and leads right to the Old City. The ride is about 30 minutes and may be only slightly longer (45 minutes or so) during rush hours (7:30–8:30 AM into town, and 4–5:30 PM leaving town).

By Limousine. Private limo service is expensive, starting at $50 for the ride from the airport into Québec City. Try **Groupe Limousine A-1** (⊠ 361, rue des Commissaires Est, ☎ 418/523–5059). **Maple Leaf Sightseeing Tours** (⊠ 240 3e rue, ☎ 418/649–9226) acts as a referral service for local companies offering car service.

By Taxi. Taxis are always available immediately outside the airport exit near the baggage claim area. Two local taxi firms are **Taxi Québec** (⊠ 975 8e av., ☎ 418/522–2001) and **Taxi Coop de Québec** (⊠ 496 2e av., ☎ 418/525–5191), the largest company in the city. A ride into the city costs about $25.

By Train

VIA Rail (☎ 418/692–3940; 800/361–5390 in Québec province), Canada's passenger rail service, runs trains from Montréal to Québec City four times daily on weekdays, three times a day on Saturday, and twice on Sunday. The trip takes less than three hours, with a stop in Ste-Foy. Tickets must be purchased in advance at any VIA Rail office or travel agent. The basic one-way rate is about $40, but it may be reduced to $23 at certain times of year (not including Friday, Sunday, or holidays). Reservations must be made and tickets bought at least five days in advance. First-class service costs about $70 each way, and includes early boarding and a three-course meal with wine.

The train arrives in Québec City at the 19th-century **Gare du Palais** (⊠ 450 rue de la Gare du Palais, ☎ 418/524–6452), in the heart of the Old City.

Getting Around

Walking is the best way to explore the city. The Old City measures 11 square kilometers (about 4 square miles), and most historic sites, hotels, and restaurants are within the walls or a short distance outside. City maps are available at tourist information offices.

By Bus

The city's transit system, **Société de Transport de la Communauté Urbaine de Québec (STCUQ)** (☎ 418/627–2511) runs buses approximately every 15 or 20 minutes that stop at major points around town. The cost is $1.85; you'll need exact change. Bus tickets are available for $1.50 ($3.75 for day pass) at major convenience stores. All buses stop in Lower Town at Place Jacques-Cartier or outside St-Jean Gate at Place d'Youville in Upper Town. Transportation maps are available at tourist information offices.

By Ferry

The **Québec–Lévis ferry** (☎ 418/644–3704, ⤳ $1.25) makes a 15-minute crossing of the St. Lawrence River to the town of Lévis. The first ferry leaves daily at 6:30 AM from the pier at rue Dalhousie, across from Place Royale. Crossings run every half hour from 7:30 AM until 6:30 PM, then hourly until 2:30 AM, with a final crossing at 3:45 AM.

By Horse-Drawn Carriage

Hire a calèche on rue d'Auteuil between the St-Louis and Kent gates from **André Beaurivage** (☎ 418/687–9797), **Balades en Calèche** (☎ 418/624–3062), or **Promenades en Calèche** (☎ 418/683–9222). The cost is about $50 without tax or tip for a 45-minute tour of the Old City. Some drivers talk about Québec's history and others don't; if you want a storyteller, ask in advance.

By Limousine

Groupe Limousine A-1 (⊠ 361 rue des Commissaires Est, ☎ 418/523–5059) has 24-hour service.

By Taxi

Taxis are stationed in front of major hotels and the Hôtel de Ville (City Hall), along rue des Jardins, and at Place d'Youville outside St-Jean Gate. For radio-dispatched cars, try **Taxi Coop de Québec** (☎ 418/525–5191) and **Taxi Québec** (☎ 418/522–2001). Passengers are charged an initial $2.25, plus $1 for each kilometer.

Contacts and Resources

B&B Reservation Service

Québec City has a large number of B&B and hostel accommodations. To guarantee a room during peak season, be sure to reserve in advance. **Québec City Tourist Information** (⊠ 60 rue d'Auteuil, G1R 4C4, ☎ 418/692–2471, ☉ June–Sept. 5, daily 8:30–8; Sept. 5–Oct. 9, daily 8:30–5:30; Oct. 10–Apr. 15, weekdays 9–5, Apr. 17–May, weekdays 8:30–5:30) has B&B listings.

Car Rentals

Hertz Canada (Québec City Airport: ☎ 418/871–1571; Vieux-Québec, ⊠ 44 Côte du Palais, ☎ 418/694–1224 or 800/654–3131), **Via Route** (⊠ 2605 Hamel Blvd., ☎ 418/682–2660), **Tilden** (Airport: ☎ 418/871–1224, ⊠ 295 St. Paul St., ☎ 418/694–1727).

Consulate

The **U.S. Consulate** (⊠ 2 Pl. Terrasse Dufferin, ☎ 418/692–2095) faces the Governor's Park near the Château Frontenac.

Dentists and Doctors

Clinique Dentaire Darveau, Dablois and Tardis (⊠ 1175 rue Lavigerie, Edifice Iberville 2, Room 100, Ste-Foy, ☎ 418/653–5412) is open Monday and Tuesday 8–8, Wednesday and Thursday 8–5, and Friday 8–4.

Hôtel-Dieu Hospital (⊠ 11 côte du Palais, ☎ 418/691–5042) is the main hospital inside the Old City. **Hale Hospital** (⊠ 1250 chemin Ste-Foy, ☎ 418/683–4471) is opposite St. Sacrament Church.

Emergencies

Distress Center (☎ 418/683–2153). **24-hour Poison Center** (☎ 418/656–8090). **Police and fire** (☎ 911 or 418/691–6911). **Provincial police** (☎ 418/623–6262).

English-Language Bookstore

La Maison Anglaise (⊠ Pl. de la Cité, Ste-Foy, ☎ 418/654–9523).

Guided Tours

EXCURSIONS

Le Bateau Mouche (⊠ 132 rue St-Pierre, No. 100, ☎ 418/692–4941 or 800/361–0130) offers 90-minute boat trips four times a day and a three-hour dinner cruise from mid-May to mid-October. **Croisières AML Inc.** (⊠ Pier Chouinard, 10 rue Dalhousie, across the street from the funicular, ☎ 418/692–1159) runs cruises on the St. Lawrence River aboard the MV *Louis-Jolliet*. One- to three-hour cruises from May through mid-October cost $19.

ORIENTATION

Tours cover such sights as Québec City, Montmorency Falls, and Ste Anne-de-Beaupré; combination city and harbor cruise tours are also available. Québec City tours operate year-round; other excursions to outlying areas may operate only in summer.

Tickets for **Gray Line** bus tours (✉ 720 rue des Rocailles; departure from Château Frontenac terrace, ☎ 418/622–7420) can be purchased at most major hotels or at the kiosk at Terrasse Dufferin at Place d'Armes. Tours run year-round and cost $13–$70. **Maple Leaf Sightseeing Tours** (✉ 240 3e rue, ☎ 418/649–9226) offers guided tours in a minibus. Call for a reservation, and the company will pick you up at your hotel. Prices are $20–$91. **Visite Touristique de Québec** (✉ C.P. 246, ☎ 418/653–9722) gives tours (in English or French) in a panoramic bus, and charges $20–$35. Smaller companies offering tours include **La Tournée du Québec Inc.** (☎ 418/836–8687) and **Fleur de Lys** (418/831–0188).

Late-Night Pharmacy
Pharmacie Brunet (✉ Les Galeries Charlesbourg, 4266 1re av., north of Québec City in Charlesbourg, ☎ 418/623–1571) is open daily, 24 hours a day.

Opening and Closing Times
Most **banks** are open Monday through Wednesday 10–3 and close later on Thursday and Friday. **Bank of Montréal** (✉ Pl. Laurier, 2700 blvd. Laurier, Ste-Foy, ☎ 418/525–3786) is open on Saturday 9:30–2. For currency exchange, **Echange de Devises Montréal** (✉ 12 rue Ste-Anne, Québec, ☎ 418/694–1014) is open September–mid-June, daily 9–5, and mid-June–Labor Day, daily 8:30–7:30.

Museum hours are typically 10–5, with longer evening hours during summer months. Most are closed on Monday.

Shopping hours are Monday through Wednesday 9:30–5:30, Thursday and Friday 9:30–9, Saturday 9:30–5, and Sunday noon–5. Stores tend to stay open later during summer months.

In winter, many attractions and shops change their hours; visitors are advised to call ahead.

Road Conditions
☎ 418/643–6830 (Nov.–Apr.).

Travel Agency
Inter-Voyage (✉ 1095 rue de l'Amérique Francâise, ☎ 418/524–1414) is on the first floor of the Édifice Bon Pasteur (Bon Pasteur Building), near the Parliament. It's open weekdays 8:30–5.

Visitor Information
Québec City Region Tourism and Convention Bureau has two tourist information centers, both of which are open year-round:

Québec City (✉ 60 rue d'Auteuil, ☎ 418/692–2471). The office is open June–early September, daily 8:30–8; early September–mid-October, daily 8:30–5:30; mid-October–mid-April, weekdays 9–5; and mid-April–May, weekdays 8:30–5:30.

Ste-Foy (✉ 3005 blvd. Laurier, near Québec and Pierre-Laporte bridges, ☎ 418/651–2882). The office is open June–August, daily 8:30–8; September–mid-October, daily 8:30–6; mid-October–mid-April, daily 9–5; and mid-April–May, daily 8:30–6.

Québec Government Tourism Department (✉ 12 rue Ste-Anne [Place d'Armes], ☎ 418/643–2280 or 800/363–7777). The office is open fall–winter, daily 9–5, and summer, daily 8:30–7:30.

10 Province of Québec

*The Laurentians, l'Estrie,
the Gaspé Peninsula*

*Québec is set apart by its strong French
heritage, a matter not only of language
but of customs, religion, and political
structure. Defining the land outside the
cities are innumerable lakes, streams,
and rivers; farmlands and villages;
great mountains, such as the
Laurentians with their ski resorts, and
deep forests; and a rugged coastline
along the Gulf of St. Lawrence.*

By Dorothy
Guinan

Updated by
Donna
Nebenzahl

AMONG THE PROVINCES OF CANADA, Québec is set apart by its strong French heritage, a matter not only of language but of customs, religion, and political structure. Québec covers a vast area—almost one-sixth of Canada's total—although the upper three-quarters is only sparsely inhabited. Most of the population lives in the southern cities, especially Montréal (☞ Chapter 8) and Québec City (☞ Chapter 9). Outside the cities, however, you'll find serenity and natural beauty in the province's innumerable lakes, streams, and rivers; in its farmlands and villages; in its great mountains and deep forests; and in its rugged coastline along the Gulf of St. Lawrence. Though the winters are long, there are plenty of winter sports to while away the cold months, especially in the Laurentians, with its many ski resorts.

The first European to arrive in Québec was French explorer Jacques Cartier, in 1534; another Frenchman, Samuel de Champlain, arrived in 1603 to build French settlements in the region, and Jesuit missionaries followed in due course. Louis XIV of France proclaimed Canada a crown colony in 1663, and the land was allotted to French aristocrats in large grants called seigneuries. As tenants, known as habitants, settled upon farms in Québec, the Roman Catholic church took on an importance that went beyond religion. Priests and nuns also acted as doctors, educators, and overseers of business arrangements between the habitants and between French-speaking fur traders and English-speaking merchants. An important doctrine of the church in Québec, one that took on more emphasis after the British conquest of 1759, was "survivance," the survival of the French people and their culture. Couples were told to have large families, and they did—up until the 1950s families with 10 or 12 children were the norm.

Québec's recent threats to secede from the Canadian union are part of a long-standing tradition of independence. Although the British won control of Canada in the French and Indian War, which ended in 1763, Parliament passed the Québec Act in 1774, which ensured the continuation of French civil law in Québec and left provincial authority in the hands of the Roman Catholic church. In general, the law preserved the traditional French-Canadian way of life. Tensions between French and English-speaking Canada continued throughout the 20th century, however, and in 1974 the province proclaimed French its sole official language, much the same way the provinces of Manitoba and Alberta had taken steps earlier in the century to make English their sole official language. In 1990 the Canadian government failed to add Québec's signature to changes it had brought about in the Canadian Constitution, and in 1992 failed to have its proposed constitutional changes accepted by the Canadian population in a referendum. Today Québec is part of the Canadian union and a signatory to its constitution, but it has not accepted the changes made in that document during the 1980s. Trying to engage French or English-speaking Canadians in a conversation on politics or the constitution, however, usually brings yawns.

Being able to speak French can make your visit to the province more pleasant—many locals do not speak English. If you don't speak French, arm yourself with a phrase book or at least a knowledge of some basic phrases. It's also worth your while to sample the hearty traditional Québécois cuisine, for this is a province where food is taken seriously.

Lower Québec

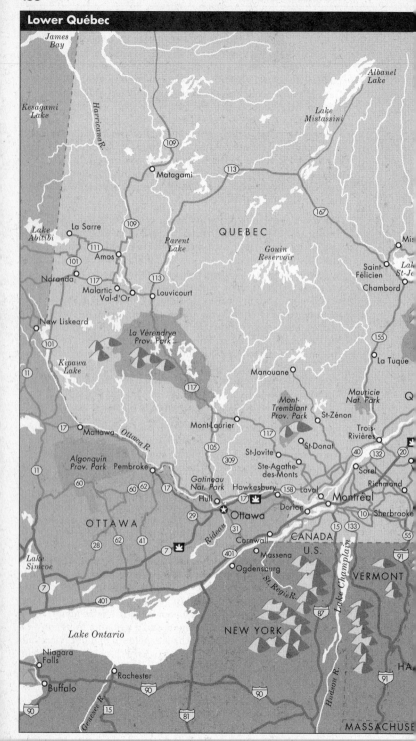

James Bay

Kesagami Lake

Lake Mistassini

Albanel Lake

(109)

Matagami

(113)

Parent Lake

QUEBEC

Gouin Reservoir

(167)

La Sarre

Lake Abitibi

(111)

Amos

(101)

(109)

Saint-Félicien

Lake St-Je

Mis

Noranda

(117)

(113)

Malartic

Val-d'Or

Louvicourt

Chambord

New Liskeard

La Vérendrye Prov. Park

(101)

(155)

Kipawa Lake

(11)

(117)

Manouane

La Tuque

Mauricie Nat. Park

Q

(17)

Mattawa

Ottawa R.

Mont-Tremblant Prov. Park

St-Zénon

Algonquin Prov. Park

Pembroke

Mont-Laurier

(117)

St-Donat

Trois-Rivières

(11)

(60)

(105)

(309)

St-Jovite

(40)

(132)

(20)

R

(60)

(62)

(17)

Gatineau Nat. Park

Ste-Agathe-des-Monts

Sorel

Richmond

Hawkesbury

(158)

Laval

Hull

(17)

Dorion

Montréal

(10)

Sherbrooke

(29)

Ottawa

(15)

(133)

(55)

(31)

Cornwall

CANADA

OTTAWA

(28)

(62)

(41)

(7)

Rideau

(401)

Massena

U.S.

(91)

Lake Simcoe

Ogdensburg

St. Regis R.

VERMONT

(7)

Ontario Lake

Niagara Falls

(87)

NEW YORK

HA

Buffalo

Rochester

(90)

(90)

Genesee R.

(15)

(81)

Hudson R.

Lake Champlain

(91)

MASSACHUSE

(90)

Pleasures and Pastimes

Dining

Whether you enjoy a croissant and espresso at a sidewalk café or order *poutine* (a streetwise mix of homemade French fries—*frites*—and curd cheese and gravy) from a fast-food emporium, you won't soon forget your meals in Québec. There is no such thing as simply "eating out" in the province; restaurants are an integral slice of Québec life.

Outside Montréal and Québec City, you can find both good value and classic cuisine. Cooking in the province tends to be hearty, with such fare as cassoulet, *tourtières* (meat pies), onion soup, and apple pie heading up menus. In the Laurentians, chefs at some of the finer inns have attracted international followings. Local blueberries and maple syrup find their way into a surprising number of dishes.

Granby and its environs are one of Québec's foremost regions for traditional Québécois cuisine, here called *la fine cuisine estrienne*. Specialties include such mixed-game meat pies as *cipaille* and sweet, salty dishes like ham and maple syrup. Actually, maple syrup—on everything and in all its forms—is a mainstay of Québécois dishes. L'Estrie is one of Québec's main maple-sugaring regions.

In addition to maple sugar, the flavorings cloves, nutmeg, cinnamon, and pepper—spices used by the first settlers—have never gone out of style here, and local restaurants make good use of them in their distinctive dishes. The full country experience of l'Estrie includes warm hospitality at area lodges and inns.

Early reservations are essential. Monday or Tuesday is not too soon to book weekend tables at the best provincial restaurants.

CATEGORY	COST*
$$$$	over $35
$$$	$25–$35
$$	$15–$25
$	under $15

per person, excluding drinks, service, 7% federal tax, and 6.5% provincial tax

Fishing

There are more than 60 outfitters (also known as innkeepers) in the northern Laurentians area, where provincial parks and game sanctuaries abound. Pike, walleye, and lake and speckled trout are plentiful just a three-hour drive north of Montréal. Outfitters provide the dedicated angler with accommodations and every service wildlife and wilderness enthusiasts could possibly require. Open year-round in most cases, their lodging facilities range from the most luxurious first-class resorts to log cabins. As well as supplying trained guides, all offer services and equipment to allow neophytes or experts the best possible fishing in addition to boating, swimming, river rafting, windsurfing, ice fishing, cross-country skiing, hiking, or just relaxing amid the splendor of this still spectacularly unspoiled region.

Lodging

Weary travelers have a full spectrum of accommodation options in Québec: from large resort hotels in the Laurentians and Relais & Châteaux properties in l'Estrie to shared dormitory space in rustic youth hostels near the heart of Gaspé.

CATEGORY	COST*
$$$$	over $125
$$$	$90–$125
$$	$50–$90
$	under $50

Prices are for a standard double room, excluding 10% service charge, 7% federal tax.

River Rafting

Rivière Rouge in the Laurentians rates among the best in North America, so it's not surprising that this river has spawned a miniboom in the sport. Just an hour's drive north of Montréal, the Rouge cuts across the rugged Laurentians through canyons and alongside beaches. From April through October, the adventurous can experience what traversing the region must have meant in the days of the voyageurs, though today's trip, by comparison, is much safer and more comfortable. For outfitter information, see Contacts and Resources at the end of this chapter.

Skiing

CROSS-COUNTRY

Cross-country skiing is popular throughout the Laurentians from December to the end of March, especially at Val David, Val Morin, and Ville l'Estérel. Each has a cross-country ski center and at least a dozen groomed trails.

L'Estrie has more than 900 kilometers (560 miles) of cross-country trails. Three inns—Manoir Hovey, Auberge Hatley, and the Ripplecove Inn—offer the Skiwippi, a week-long package of cross-country treks from one inn to another. The network covers some 32 kilometers (20 miles) of l'Estrie.

DOWNHILL

L'Estrie is a scenic and increasingly popular ski center. Although it is still less crowded and commercialized than the Laurentians, it boasts ski hills on four mountains that dwarf anything the Laurentians have to offer, with the exception of lofty Mont-Tremblant. And, compared to those in Vermont, ski-pass rates are still a bargain. Owl's Head, Mont-Orford, Mont-Sutton, and Bromont have interchangeable lift tickets.

Charlevoix has three main ski areas, with excellent facilities for both the downhill and cross-country skier.

Sugar Huts

Every March the combination of sunny days and cold nights causes the sap to run in the maple trees. *Cabanes à sucre* (sugar huts) go into operation boiling the sap collected from the trees in buckets (now, at some places, complicated tubing and vats do the job). The many commercial shacks scattered over the area host "sugaring offs" and tours of the operation, including the tapping of maple trees, the boiling of the sap in vats, and *tire sur la neige,* when hot syrup is poured over cold snow to give it a taffy consistency just right for "pulling" and eating. A number of cabanes offer hearty meals of ham, baked beans, and pancakes, all drowned in maple syrup. We recommend two cabanes near Sherbrooke.

Exploring Québec

There are two major attractions beyond the city limits of Montréal: l'Estrie (the Eastern Townships), where city folk retreat in summer, and Les Laurentides (the Laurentians), where they escape in winter.

The Laurentians have thousands of miles of unspoiled wilderness and world-famous ski resorts, which can be visited for a weekend, a week, or, for the avid skier, a two-week stay to enjoy the great outdoors. In l'Estrie, rolling hills and farmland make it a major vacation area in both winter and summer, with outdoor activities on ski slopes and lakes and in their provincial parks. Charlevoix is often called the Switzerland of Québec because of its landscape, and the knobby Gaspé Peninsula is where the St. Lawrence River meets the Gulf of St. Lawrence.

Great Itineraries

IF YOU HAVE 2 DAYS

Visit the **Basses Laurentides,** or lower Laurentians, which begin almost immediately outside Montréal. Include in your visit one of the historic seigneuries in the region, or buy renowned Oka cheese from the Cistercian Abbey at **Oka.**

IF YOU HAVE 5 DAYS

Add the **Hautes Laurentides,** or Upper Laurentians, to the two-day itinerary, and enjoy the natural surroundings at **St-Jérome**'s Parc Régional de la Rivière-du-Nord and the quaint resort area of **St-Sauveur-des-Monts.**

IF YOU HAVE 10 DAYS

Summer or winter, your visit can begin in the bustling ski town of **St-Sauveur-des-Monts** and end as far away as **Mont-Tremblant.** For the first-time visitor, the hills and resorts around **Morin Heights, Val Morin,** and **Val David,** up to **Ste-Agathe,** form a pleasant hodgepodge of villages, hotels, and inns. If you have kids in tow, drop in to Val David for a visit to the Santa Claus Village, the summer residence of old St. Nick. Your final destination might be **Parc Mont-Tremblant,** a vast wildlife sanctuary of more than 500 lakes and rivers.

When to Tour Québec

The Laurentians are mainly a winter ski destination, but Montréalers can drive up to enjoy the fall foliage or engage in spring skiing and still get home before dark. The only slow periods are early October, when there is not much to do, and June, when there is plenty to do but the area is beset by blackflies.

LES LAURENTIDES

The Laurentians are divided into two major regions—les Basses Laurentides (the Lower Laurentians) and les Hautes Laurentides (the Upper Laurentians). But don't be fooled by the designations; they don't signify great driving distances.

Avid skiers might call Montréal a bedroom community for the Laurentians; just 56 kilometers (35 miles) to the north, they are home to some of North America's best-known ski resorts. The Laurentian range is ancient, dating to the Precambrian era (more than 600 million years ago). These rocky hills are relatively low, worn down by glacial activity, but they include eminently skiable hills, with a few peaks above 2,500 feet. World-famous Mont-Tremblant, at 3,150 feet, is the tallest.

The P'tit Train du Nord made it possible to easily transport settlers and cargo to the Upper Laurentians. It also opened them up to skiing by the turn of the century. Before long, trainloads of skiers replaced settlers and cargo as the railway's major trade. The Upper Laurentians soon became known worldwide as the number-one ski center in North America—a position they still hold today. Initially a winter weekend getaway for Montréalers who stayed at boardinghouses and fledgling resorts while skiing its hills, the Upper Laurentians began attracting an international clientele, especially with the advent of the Canadian National Railway's special skiers' train, begun in 1928. (Its competitor, the Canadian Pacific Railway, jumped on the bandwagon soon after, doubling the number of train runs bringing skiers to the area.)

Ski lodges, originally private family retreats for wealthy city dwellers, were accessible only by train until the 1930s, when the highway was built. Once the road opened up, cottages became year-round family retreats. Today, there is an uneasy alliance between the longtime cottagers and resort-driven entrepreneurs. Both recognize the other's historic role in developing the Upper Laurentians, but neither espouses the other's cause. At the moment, commercial development seems to be winning out. A number of large hotels have added indoor pools and spa facilities, and efficient highways have brought the country closer to the city—45 minutes to St-Sauveur, 1½–2 hours to Mont-Tremblant.

The Lower Laurentians start almost immediately outside Montréal. Considered the birthplace of the Laurentians, this area is rich in historic and architectural landmarks. Beginning in the mid-17th century, the governors of New France, as Québec was then called, gave large concessions of land to its administrators, priests, and top-ranking military, who became known as seigneurs. In the Lower Laurentians, towns like Terrebonne, St-Eustache, Lac-des-Deux-Montagnes, and Oka are home to the manors, mills, churches, and public buildings these seigneurs had built for themselves and their habitants—the inhabitants of these quasi-feudal villages.

The resort vacation area truly begins at St-Sauveur-des-Monts (Exit 60) and extends as far north as Mont-Tremblant, where it turns into a wilderness of lakes and forests best visited with an outfitter. Laurentian guides planning fishing and hunting trips are concentrated around St-Donat near Parc Mont-Tremblant.

To the first-time visitor, the hills and resorts around St-Sauveur, Ste-Marguerite Station, Morin Heights, Val Morin, and Val David, up to Ste-Agathe, form a pleasant hodgepodge of villages, hotels, and inns that seem to blend one into another.

La Seigneurie de Terrebonne

Numbers in the margin correspond to points of interest on the Laurentians map.

❶ *30 km (20 mi) north of Montréal. From Montréal take blvd. Pie-IX to the bridge of the same name then Highway 25 N. Exit at Terrebonne to Hwy. 440.*

La Seigneurie de Terrebonne, one of the most famous seigneuries, is on l'Ile-des-Moulins, about 20 minutes from Montréal.

Governor Frontenac gave the land to Sieur André Daulier in 1673. Terrebonne was maintained by a succession of seigneurs until 1832, when Joseph Masson, the first French-Canadian millionaire, bought it. He and his family were the last seigneurs de Terrebonne; their reign ended in 1883.

Today, Terrebonne offers visitors a bona fide glimpse of the past. Now run by the Corporation de l'Ile-des-Moulins rather than a French aristocrat, the seigneurie's mansions, manors, and buildings have all been restored. Take a walk through Terrebonne's historical center and then stop at the **Centre d'Interprétation Historique de Terrebonne Museum.**

462

The Laurentians

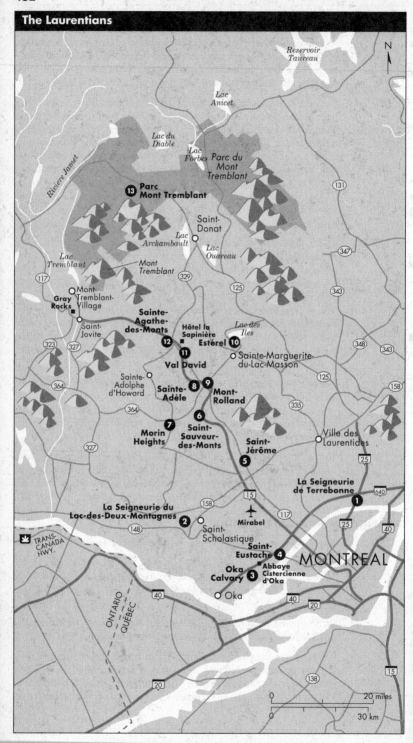

It features three exhibits: the Seigneurial Regime; the water, saw, flour, and wool mills of the region that gave the island its name; and the beginning of the Industrial Revolution in Terrebonne. ⊠ *Blvd. des Braves and rue St-Pierre*, ☎ *514/471–0619.* ◻ *Free.* ☉ *Mid-May–late June, Tues.–Sun. 1–5; late June–early Sept., Tues.–Sun. 10–8.*

La Seigneurie du Lac-des-Deux-Montagnes

➋ *30 km (20 mi) west of Montréal. Take Hwy. 13 or 15 North out of Montréal to Hwy. 640 West. Exit from Hwy. 640 West at Hwy. 148. Take this road into the town of St-Scholastique.*

La Seigneurie du Lac-des-Deux-Montagnes, in St-Scholastique, is 40 minutes from Montréal. It was allotted to the Sulpician priests in 1717. Already appointed the seigneurs of the entire island of Montréal, the priests used this as the base from which to establish an Amerindian mission. A highlight of the seigneury is the Sulpicians' seignorial manor on rue Belle-Rivière, erected between 1802 and 1808. The manor was part of the set for the late Claude Jutra's acclaimed film, *Kamouraska*, based on the novel by Québec's prize-winning author Anne Hébert.

Dining and Lodging

$$$ ✕▥ **Hotel du Lac Carling.** This new hotel caters to the athletic crowd: In addition to its sports center, there's a golf course next door, and there's cross-country skiing and downhill skiing nearby. The rooms are done in a rustic theme, and a stay includes breakfast and supper in their award-winning restaurant, the Lis. ⊠ *Rte. 327, Pinehill, Brownsburg, 21 km/13 mi north of St-Scholastique J0V 1A0*, ☎ *514/533–9211 or 800/661–9211*, 𝔽𝔸𝕏 *514/533–9197. 100 rooms. Restaurant, bar, pool, sauna, exercise room, racquetball, squash. EP, MAP. AE, DC, MC, V.*

Oka Calvary

➌ *12 km (8 mi) southeast of La Seigneurie du Lac-des-Deux-Montagnes.*

To promote piety among the Amerindians, the Sulpicians erected the Oka Calvary (Stations of the Cross) between 1740 and 1742. Three of the seven chapels are still maintained, and every September 14 since 1870, Québécois pilgrims have congregated here from across the province to participate in the half-hour ceremony that proceeds on foot to the Calvary's summit. A sense of the divine is inspired as much by the magnificent view of Lac-des-Deux-Montagnes as by religious fervor.

In 1887, the Sulpicians gave about 865 acres of their property near the Oka Calvary to the Trappist monks, who had arrived in New France in 1880 from Bellefontaine Abbey in France. Within 10 years they had built their monastery, the **Abbaye Cistercienne d'Oka,** and they transformed this land into one of the most beautiful domains in Québec. The abbey is one of the oldest in North America. Famous for creating Oka cheese, the Trappists established the Oka School of Agriculture, which operated until 1960. Today, the monastery is a noted prayer retreat. The gardens and chapel are open to visitors. ⊠ *1600 chemin d'Oka*, ☎ *514/ 479–8361.* ◻ *Free.* ☉ *Chapel daily 8–12:15 and 1–8; gardens and boutique weekdays 9:30–11:30 and 1–4:30, Sat. 9–4.*

Kanestake, a Mohawk Indian reserve near Oka, made headlines during the summer of 1990 when a 78-day armed standoff between Mohawk Warriors (the reserve's self-proclaimed police force) and Canadian and provincial authorities took place. The Mohawks of Kanestake said they opposed the expansion of the Oka golf course, claiming the land was stolen from them 273 years before. When the standoff ended peacefully, the golf course was not expanded. As was the case when Indians opposed logging in British Columbia during the early 1990s, the Canadian media turned the affair into a cause célèbre. But the Oka incident, like the others, has since died down.

St-Eustache

❹ *25 km (16 mi) northeast of Oka Calvary.*

St-Eustache is another must for history buffs. One of the most important and tragic scenes in Canadian history took place here: the 1837 Rebellion. Since the British conquest of 1759, French Canadians had been confined to preexisting territories while the new townships were allotted exclusively to the English. Adding to this insult was the government's decision to tax all imported products from England, which made them prohibitively expensive. The result? In 1834, the French Canadian Patriot party defeated the British party locally. Lower Canada, as it was then known, became a hotbed of tension between the French and English, with French resistance to the British government reaching an all-time high. Rumors of rebellion were rife, and in December 1837, some 2,000 English soldiers led by General Colborne were sent in to put down the "army" of North Shore patriots by surrounding the village of St-Eustache. Jean-Olivier Chénier and his 200 patriots took refuge in the local church, which Colborne's cannons bombed and set afire. Chénier and 80 of his comrades were killed during the battle, and more than 100 of the town's houses and buildings erected during the seignorial regime were looted and burned down by Colborne's soldiers. Traces of the bullets fired by the English army cannons are visible on the facade of St-Eustache's church at 123 rue St-Louis. Most of the town's period buildings are open to the public. For a guided tour or for a free brochure that serves as a good walking-tour guide, visit the town's **Arts and Cultural Services Center** (✉ 235 rue St-Eustache, ☎ 514/974–5000, Ext. 282). Tours are offered from April until November.

NEED A BREAK?	Before heading north, stop at **Pâtisserie Grande-Côte** (✉ 367A chemin de la Grande-Côte, ☎ 514/473–7307) to sample the wares of St-Eustache's most famous bakery and pastry shop.

St-Jérôme

❺ *25 km (16 mi) north of St-Eustache.*

Rivaling St-Eustache in Québec's historic folklore is St-Jérôme, in the Upper Laurentians. Founded in 1834, it is today a thriving economic center and cultural hub. It first gained prominence in 1868 when Curé Antoine Labelle became pastor of this parish on the shores of Rivière du Nord. Curé Labelle devoted himself to opening up northern Québec to French Canadians. Between 1868 and 1890, he founded 20 parish towns—an impressive achievement given the harsh conditions of this vast wilderness. But his most important legacy was the famous P'tit Train du Nord railway line, which he persuaded the government to build in order to open St-Jérôme to travel and trade.

Follow St-Jérôme's **promenade,** a 4-kilometer-long (2½-mile-long) boardwalk alongside the Rivière du Nord from rue de Martigny bridge to rue St-Joseph bridge for a walk through the town's history. Descriptive plaques en route highlight episodes of the Battle of 1837. The **Centre d'Exposition du Vieux-Palais** housed in St-Jérôme's old courthouse has changing exhibits of contemporary art, featuring mostly Québec artists.

✉ *185 rue du Palais,* ☎ *514/432–7171.* ☞ *Free.* ☉ *Tues.–Fri. noon–5, weekends 1–5.*

Parc Régional de la Rivière-du-Nord was created as a nature retreat. Trails through the park lead to the spectacular **Wilson Falls** (*chutes*). The **Pavillon Marie-Victorin** has summer weekend displays and workshops devoted to nature, culture, and history. You can hike, bike, cross-country ski, snowshoe, or snow slide; bike and ski rentals are available. ✉ *1051 blvd. International (R.R. 2),* ☎ *514/431–1676.* ☞ *$3 per car.* ☉ *fall–spring, daily 9–5; summer, daily 9–7.*

St-Sauveur-des-Monts

6 *25 km (16 mi) north of St-Jérôme.*

St-Sauveur-des-Monts is the focal point for area resorts. It has gone from a 1970s sleepy Laurentian village of 4,000 residents that didn't even have a traffic light to a thriving year-round town attracting some 30,000 cottagers and visitors on weekends. Its main street, rue Principale, once dotted with quaint French restaurants, now boasts *brochetteries*, and the narrow strip is so choked in summertime with cars and tourists that it has earned the sobriquet "Crescent Street of the North," borrowing its name from the well-known, action-filled street in Montréal. Despite all this development, St-Sauveur has managed to maintain some of its charming, rural character.

For those who like their vacations—winter or summer—lively and activity-filled, St-Sauveur is the place where the action rolls nonstop. In winter, skiing is the main thing. (Mont-St-Sauveur, Mont-Avila, Mont-Gabriel, and Mont-Olympia all offer special season passes and programs, and some ski-center passes can be used at more than one center in the region.) From Mont-St-Sauveur to Mont-Tremblant, the area's ski centers (most situated in or near St-Sauveur, Ste-Adèle, Ste-Agathe, and St-Jovite) offer night skiing. All have ski instructors—many are members of the Canadian Ski Patrol Association.

Just outside St-Sauveur, the Mont-St-Sauveur **Water Park** and tourist center will keep children occupied with slides, a giant wave pool, a shallow wading pool, snack bars, and more. The rafting river attracts the older, braver crowd; the nine-minute ride follows the natural contours of steep hills and requires about 12,000 gallons of water to be pumped per minute. The latest attraction is tandem slides where plumes of water flow through figure-eight tubes. ✉ *350 rue St-Denis,* ☎ *514/871–0101 or 800/363–2426.* ☞ *Full day $22, half-day $17, evening (after 5) $9; cost includes access to all activities.* ☉ *June 3–June 21, daily 10–4; June 22–Aug. 25, daily 10–7; Aug. 26–Sept. 2, daily 11–6.*

Dining

$$$ ✕ **Auberge St-Denis.** This classic Québec inn has a fine restaurant serving French cuisine; game is a specialty. Artfully presented dishes are served in one of three dining rooms, one with a huge stone fireplace. Try the *arrivage de gibier,* an assortment of wild game with an exotic fruit sauce. ✉ *61 St-Denis,* ☎ *514/227–4602. Reservations essential. AE, DC, MC, V.*

Nightlife

Les Vieilles Portes (✉ 185 rue Principale, ☎ 514/227–2662) is a popular pub where you can relax, order your favorite beer, and have a bite to eat.

Shopping

Rue Principale has shops, fashion boutiques, and outdoor café terraces decorated with bright awnings and flowers. Housed in a former bank,

Solo Mode (⊠ 239B rue Principale, ☎ 514/227–1234) carries such international labels as Byblos. **Les Factoreries St-Sauveur** (⊠ 100 rue Guindon, Exit 60 from Hwy. 15, ☎ 514/227–1074) is a factory outlet mall with 12 boutiques. Canadian, American, and European manufacturers sell a variety of goods at reduced prices, from designer clothing to household items.

Morin Heights

❼ *10 km (6 mi) west of St-Sauveur-des-Monts.*

The town's architecture and population reflect its English settlers' origins, and most residents are English-speaking. Morin Heights has escaped the overdevelopment of St-Sauveur but still offers the visitor a good range of restaurants, bookstores, boutiques, and crafts shops to explore. During the summer months, windsurfing, swimming, and canoeing on the area's two lakes are popular pastimes.

There's a new spin on an old sport at **Ski Morin Heights** (⊠ Exit 60, Autoroute 15 N, ☎ 514/227–2020 or 800/661–3535), where snowboarding is the latest craze. Although it doesn't have overnight accommodations, Ski Morin Heights has a 44,000-square-foot chalet with hospitality services and sports-related facilities, eateries, après-ski activities, a pub, and a day-care center. There are special ski-lesson programs for children ages 2 and up.

In the summer, vacationers head for the region's golf courses (two of the more pleasant are the 18-hole links at Ste-Adèle and Mont-Gabriel), campgrounds at Val David, Lacs Claude and Lafontaine, and beaches; in the fall and winter, they come for the foliage as well as alpine and Nordic skiing.

The Arts
Théâtre Morin Heights (☎ 514/226–1944) presents productions at a local elementary school during summer. Popular musicals, lighthearted comedies, mysteries, and children's plays are in the repertoire. Reservations are a must.

Lodging
$$ 🏠 **Auberge Swiss Inn.** This moderately priced inn is within 4 kilometers (2½ miles) of Ski Morin Heights, and is a bargain to boot. The Swiss-style chalet exudes coziness, with wood paneling and a fireplace lounge. ⊠ *796 Rte. St-Adolphe, J0R 1H0,* ☎ *514/226–2009,* FAX *514/226–5709. 10 rooms. Restaurant, lounge, boating, cross-country skiing. MC, V.*

Ste-Adèle

❽ *12 km (7 mi) north of Morin Heights.*

The busy town of Ste-Adèle is full of gift and Québec-crafts shops, boutiques, and restaurants. It also has an active nightlife, including a few discos.

The reconstructed **Village de Seraphin**'s 20 small homes, grand country house, general store, and church recall the settlers who came to Ste-Adèle in the 1840s. This award-winning historic town also has a train tour through the woods. ⊠ *Hwy. 117,* ☎ *514/229–4777.* ⊒ *$8.75.* ☉ *Late May–late June and early Sept.–mid-Oct., weekends 10–5; late June–early Sept., daily 10–5.*

Dining and Lodging

$$$$ ✕ **La Clef des Champs.** This family-owned hillside restaurant, with its gourmet French cuisine and cozy, romantic atmosphere, is tucked away among trees and faces a mountain. Elegant dishes include *noisette d'agneau en feuilleté* (lamb in pastry) and poached salmon in red wine sauce. Top off your meal with the *gâteau aux deux chocolats* (two-chocolate cake). ✉ *875 chemin Ste-Marguerite,* ☎ *514/229–2857. AE, DC, MC, V. Closed Mon. Oct.–May, except holidays.*

$$$$ ✕🏠 **L'Eau à la Bouche.** This elegant inn has superb service, luxurious
★ appointments, and a terrace with a flower garden. The auberge faces Le Chantecler's ski slopes, so skiing is literally at the door. Tennis, sailing, horseback riding, and a golf course are nearby. The highly recommended restaurant superbly marries nouvelle cuisine and traditional Québec dishes. The care and inventiveness of chef-proprietor Anne Desjardins is extraordinary. Try the marinated salmon and smoked scallops on a bed of julienned cucumber with a blend of mustards, or a warm salad of quail breast, with an emulsion of olive oil and citrus fruit. ✉ *3003 blvd. Ste-Adèle, J0R 1L0,* ☎ *514/229–2991,* ℻ *514/229–7573. 25 rooms. Restaurant, pool. EP, MAP. AE, DC, MC, V.*

$$$$ 🏠 **Le Chantecler.** This Montréaler favorite on Lac Ste-Adèle is nestled at the base of a mountain with 22 downhill ski runs. Skiing is the obvious draw—trails begin almost at the hotel entrance. The condominium units, hotel rooms, and chalets all have a rustic appeal, furnished with Canadian pine. ✉ *1474 chemin Chantecler, C.P. 1048, J0R 1L0,* ☎ *514/229–3555; in Québec, 800/363–2420;* ℻ *514/229–5593. 300 rooms, 20 suites. Restaurant, indoor pool, spa, golf course, beach, tennis, boating. EP, MAP. AE, D, DC, MC, V.*

$$ 🏠 **Auberge aux Croissants.** This inn at the foot of the Laurentian Mountains is only a five-minute drive from Mont-St-Sauveur. Although most rooms have no TV or telephone, such conveniences are found in one of the two cozy lounges, and an impressive buffet-breakfast is included with the price of the room. One room has a whirlpool bath. ✉ *750 chemin Ste-Marguerite, J0R 1L0,* ☎ *514/229–3838. 13 rooms, 1 suite. 2 lounges, outdoor pool. MC, V.*

Outdoor Activities and Sports

GOLF

Club de Golf Chantecler (✉ Exit 67, 2520 chemin du Golf, ☎ 514/229–3742) has 18 holes.

Mont-Rolland

❾ *3 km (2 mi) east of Ste-Adèle.*

Mont-Rolland is the jumping-off point for the Mont-Gabriel ski area, about 16 kilometers (10 miles) to the northeast.

Dining and Lodging

$$$ ✕🏠 **Auberge Mont-Gabriel.** At this deluxe resort spread out on a 1,200-acre estate, you can relax in one of the cozy, modern rooms with a view of the valley or be close to nature in one of the log cabins with fireplaces. The dining is superb here. Tennis, golf, and ski-week and -weekend packages are available. ✉ *Autoroute 15 (Exit 64), J0R 1G0,* ☎ *514/229–3547 or 800/668-5253,* ℻ *514/229–7034. 127 rooms, 10 suites. Restaurant, indoor and outdoor pools, 18-hole golf course, 6 tennis courts. EP, MAP. AE, DC, MC, V.*

Nightlife

If live music is what you want, head to **Bourbon Street** (⊠ 2045 Rte. 117, ☎ 514/229–2905).

Outdoor Activities and Sports

DELTAPLANING

If white-water rafting isn't adventure enough, there is always delta-planing, in which human and machine become one. The **Vélidelta Free-Flying School** (⊠ C.P. 631, ☎ 514/229–6887) offers lessons on free-flying, and the more advanced tricks of the trade you'll need to earn the required deltaplane pilot's license, including flight maneuvers, speed, and turns. Equipment is provided. You can choose a one-day initiation flying lesson, or a four-day course.

SKIING

Ski Mont-Gabriel (☎ 514/227–1100) has 12 superb downhill trails primarily for intermediate and advanced skiers. The most popular runs are the Tamarack and the O'Connell trails for advanced skiers and Obergurgl for intermediates.

Estérel

❿   *12 km (7 mi) north of Mont-Rolland.*

The permanent population of the town of Estérel is a mere 80 souls. But visitors to **Hotel l'Estérel,** a resort off Autoroute 370, at Exit 69, near Ste-Marguerite Station, swell that number into the thousands. Founded in 1959 on the shores of Lac Dupuis, this 5,000-acre domain was bought by Fridolin Simard from Baron Louis Empain. Named Estérel by the baron because it evoked memories of his native village in Provence, Hotel l'Estérel soon became a household word for holiday vacationers in search of a first-class resort area.

Lodging

$$$$ 🏨 **Hôtel l'Estérel.** If this all-inclusive resort were in the Caribbean, it would probably be run by Club Med, given the nonstop activities. Comfortable rooms offer a view of either the lake or the beautiful flower gardens. ⊠ *39 blvd. Fridolin Simard, J0T 1E0, ☎ 514/228–2571 or 800/363–3623, 𝖥𝖠𝖷 514/228–4977. 135 rooms. Restaurant, indoor pool, exercise room, tennis courts, 18-hole golf course, beach, marina, downhill and cross-country skiing, ice-skating disco. EP, MAP. AE, DC, MC, V.*

Val David

⓫   *18 km (11 mi) west of Estérel.*

Val David is a rendezvous for mountain climbers, ice scalers, dogsledders, hikers, and summer or winter campers.

🌣   Children know Val David for its **Santa Claus Village.** This is Santa Claus's summer residence, where children can sit upon Santa's knee and speak to him in either French or English. On the grounds is a petting zoo, with goats, sheep, horses, and colorful birds. Bumper boats and games are run here, as well. ⊠ *987 rue Morin, ☎ 819/322–2146. 🌣 $7. ☺ Late May–early June, weekends 10–6; early June–late Aug., daily 10–6.*

Dining and Lodging

$$$$ ✕🏨 **Hôtel La Sapinière.** Comfortable accommodations are offered in this homey, dark brown frame hotel with its bright country flowers. The rooms, with country-style furnishings and pastel floral accents, come with such luxurious little extras as thick terry-cloth bathrobes and hair dryers. Relax in front of a blazing fire in one of several cozy lounges.

The property is best known for its fine dining room and wine cellar. ⊠ *1244 chemin de la Sapinière, J0T 2N0,* ☎ *819/322–2020 or 800/567–6635,* ℻ *819/322–6510. 70 rooms. Dining room, lounge. MAP. AE, DC, MC, V.*

Shopping

Val David is a haven for artists, many of whose studios are open to the public. The **Atelier Bernard Chaudron, Inc.** (⊠ 2449 chemin de l'Ile, ☎ 819/322–3944), sells hand-shaped and hammered lead-free pewter objets d'art.

Ste-Agathe-des-Monts

⑫ *5 km (3 mi) north of Val David, 96 km (60 mi) northwest of Montréal.*

Overlooking Lac des Sables is Ste-Agathe-des-Monts, the largest commercial center for ski communities farther north.

The **Village du Mont-Castor,** about 1 kilometer (½ mile) north of Ste-Agathe-des-Monts, is an attractive re-creation of a turn-of-the-century Québécois village; more than 100 new homes have been built here in the traditional fashion of full-length logs set *pièce sur pièce* (one upon the other).

Dining and Lodging

$$–$$$ ✕ **Chatel Vienna.** Run by Eberhards Rado and his wife, who is also
★ the chef, this Austrian restaurant serves Viennese and other Continental dishes in a lakeside setting. You may want to try the prize-winning home-smoked trout, served with an herb and spice butter and garden-fresh vegetables. You may also opt for a variety of schnitzels, a sauerkraut plate, or venison. Try the hot spiced wine, Czech pilsner beer, or dry Austrian and other international white wines. A Sunday buffet brunch tempts the palate with approximately 35 dishes and is served from 11:30 until 2 for under $20. ⊠ *6 rue Ste-Lucie,* ☎ *819/326–1485. Reservations essential. MC, V.*

$$–$$$ ✕ **Chez Girard.** Excellent French cuisine is the hallmark of this restaurant-auberge on the shores of Lac des Sables. The airy dining room has windows facing the lake and pastel colors that create a soft, romantic atmosphere. Some of the house specialties include *saumon au champagne* (salmon with champagne), rack of lamb with *herbes de Provence,* ostrich patand *magret de canard.* A Sunday brunch is offered for $16.95. ⊠ *18 rue Principale Ouest,* ☎ *819/326–0922. Reservations essential. AE, DC, MC, V.*

$$$ 🏨 **Auberge du Lac des Sables.** A favorite with couples, this inn offers a quiet, relaxed atmosphere in a country setting with a magnificent view of Lac des Sables. All rooms have contemporary decor and a balcony. ⊠ *230 St-Venant, J8C 2Z7,* ☎ *819/ 326–3994,* ℻ *819/326–9159. 19 rooms. Dining room. CP. MC, V.*

$ 🏕 **Au Parc des Campeurs.** This lively resort area attracts campers with this spacious campground. ⊠ *Tour du Lac and Rte. 329, J8C 1M9,* ☎ *819/324–0482 or 800/561–7360.*

Outdoor Activities and Sports

BOATING

The *Alouette* touring launch (⊠ Municipal dock, rue Principal, ☎ 819/326–3656) has guided tours of Lac des Sables. Sailing is the favorite summer sport, especially during the "24 Heures de la Voile," a weekend sailing competition (☎ 819/326–0457) that takes place each year in June.

Mont-Tremblant

25 km (16 mi) north of Ste-Agathe-des-Monts.

Mont-Tremblant, one of Canada's best-known ski resorts, is also car-racing country. Racing champion Jackie Stewart has called Mont-Tremblant "the most beautiful racetrack in the world." The **Formula 2000 "Jim Russell Championships"** of the Canadian Car Championships (☎ 819/425–2739) take place here on weekends in June, July, August, and September.

⑬ The mountain and the hundreds of square miles of wilderness beyond it constitute **Parc Mont-Tremblant.** Created in 1894, this was once the home of the Algonquin Indians, who called this area Manitonga Soutana, meaning "mountain of the spirits." Today it is a vast wildlife sanctuary of more than 500 lakes and rivers protecting about 230 species of birds and animals, including moose, deer, bear, and beaver. In the winter, its trails are used by cross-country skiers, snowshoers, and snowmobile enthusiasts. Moose hunting is allowed in season, and camping and canoeing are the main summer activities.

Dining and Lodging

$$$–$$$$ ✕▥ **Club Tremblant.** Across the lake from Station Mont-Tremblant, this hotel was built as a private retreat in the 1930s by a wealthy American. The original large, log-cabin lodge is furnished in colonial style, with wooden staircases and huge stone fireplaces. The rustic but comfortable main lodge has excellent facilities and a dining room serving four-star cuisine. Both the main lodge and the 122-unit deluxe condominium complex—fireplaces, private balconies, kitchenettes, and split-level design de rigueur—built just up the hill from the lodge, offer magnificent views of Mont-Tremblant and its ski hills. There is a golf course nearby. ✉ *av. Cuttle, J0T 1Z0,* ☎ *819/425–2731,* ㎫ *819/425–9903. 121 rooms. Restaurant, indoor pool, exercise room, swimming, fishing, boating, tennis. EP, MAP. AE, MC, V.*

$$–$$$$ ✕▥ **Auberge du Coq de Montagne.** Owners Nino and Kay Faragalli have earned a favorable reputation for their auberge on Lac Moore. The cozy, family-run inn is touted for its friendly service, great hospitality, and modern accommodations. Kudos have also been garnered for the great Italian cuisine served up nightly, which also draws a local crowd; reservations are essential. Year-round facilities and activities, on-site or nearby, include canoeing, kayaking, sailboarding, fishing, badminton, tennis, horseback riding, skating, and skiing. ✉ *2151 chemin Principale, C.P. 208, J0T 1Z0,* ☎ *819/425–3380 or 800/895–3380,* ㎫ *819/425–7846. 16 rooms. Restaurant, sauna, exercise room, beach. MAP in winter; EP, MAP in summer. AE, MC, V.*

$$$–$$$$ ▥ **Station Mont-Tremblant.** On 14-kilometer-long (9-mile-long) Lac
   ★   Tremblant, this is the northernmost resort that is easily accessible in the Upper Laurentians. Accommodations include a rustic lodge and modern condo units with kitchenettes. The partying is lively in winter, with lots of après-ski bars in the hotel and in the immediate area. ✉ *3005 chemin Principale, J0T 1Z0,* ☎ *819/425–8711 or 800/461–8711,* ㎫ *819/681–5590. Restaurant, bars, golf course, tennis courts, horseback riding, beach, swimming, windsurfing, sailing, dance club. EP, MAP. AE, MC, V.*

$$–$$$$ ▥ **Gray Rocks.** This sprawling wood hotel is the oldest ski resort in the Laurentians and has its own private mountain ribboned by 20 ski runs. The modern chalets and condominium units overlook Lac Ouimet. Some of the rooms share baths. Winter ski packages, including cross-country skiing, are good value for the money, as are the summer tennis packages. A private airstrip and seaplane anchorages are available. ⊠ *Rte. 327 N, 525 rue Principale, J0T 1Z0,* ☎ *819/425–2771 or 800/567–6767,* FAX *819/425–3474. 306 rooms. Restaurant, indoor pool, health club, horseback riding, spa, 22 tennis courts, children's programs. EP, MAP. AE, MC, V.*

$$$ 🏨 **Auberge Villa Bellevue.** This equally venerable and less expensive alternative to Gray Rocks (☞ *below*) is on Lac Ouimet. Supporting its reputation as a family resort, the inn invites children under 18 who share a room with their parents to stay free and pay for meals only during the summer. In winter, weekend packages include transportation to nearby Mont-Tremblant. The hotel has a list of local baby-sitters, and offers a full summer program of children's activities. Accommodations range from hotel rooms to chalets and condominiums. ⊠ *845 rue Principale, J0T 1Z0,* ☎ *819/425–2734 or 800/567–6763,* FAX *819/425–9360. 86 rooms, 14 suites. Restaurant, indoor pool, tennis courts, exercise room, beach, sailing, windsurfing, waterskiing, children's programs. EP, MAP. AE, DC, MC, V.*

Outdoor Activities and Sports

SKIING

With the longest vertical drop (2,131 feet) in eastern Canada, **Mont-Tremblant** (☎ 819/425–8711 or 819/681–2000) offers 74 downhill trails, 10 lifts, and 90 kilometers (56 miles) of cross-country trails. Downhill beginners favor the 6-kilometer (3-mile) Nansen trail; intermediate skiers head for the Beauchemin run. Experts choose the challenging Flying Mile on the south side and Duncan and Expo runs on the mountain's north side. The speedy Duncan Express is a quadruple chair lift.

L'ESTRIE

L'Estrie (also known as the Eastern Townships) refers to the area in the southeast corner of the province of Québec, bordering Vermont, New Hampshire, and Maine. Its northern Appalachian hills, rolling down to placid lakeshores, were first home to the Abenaki natives, long before "summer people" built their cottages and horse paddocks here. The Abenaki are gone, but the names they gave to the region's recreational lakes remain—Memphremagog, Massawippi, Mégantic.

L'Estrie was populated by United Empire Loyalists fleeing the Revolutionary War and, later, the newly created United States of America, to continue living under the English king in British North America. It's not surprising that l'Estrie is reminiscent of New England with its covered bridges, village greens, white church steeples, and country inns. The Loyalists were followed, around 1820, by the first wave of Irish immigrants—ironically, Catholics fleeing their country's union with Protestant England. Some 20 years later the potato famine sent more Irish pioneers to the townships.

The area became more Gallic after 1850, as French Canadians moved in to work on the railroad and in the lumber industry. Around the turn of the century, English families from Montréal and Americans from the border states discovered the region and began summering at cottages along the lakes. During the Prohibition era, the area attracted even more cottagers from the United States. Lac Massawippi became a favorite summer resort of wealthy families whose homes have since been converted into gracious inns.

Today the summer communities fill up with equal parts French and English visitors, though the year-round residents are primarily French. Nevertheless, the locals are proud of both their Loyalist heritage and Québec roots. They boast of "Loyalist tours" and Victorian gingerbread homes and in the next breath direct visitors to the snowmobile museum in Valcourt, where, in 1937, native son Joseph-Armand Bombardier built the first *moto-neige* (snowmobile) in his garage. (Bombardier's inventions were the basis of one of Canada's biggest industries, supplying New York City and Mexico City with subway cars and other rolling stock.)

Over the past two decades, l'Estrie has developed from a series of quiet farm communities and wood-frame summer homes to a thriving all-season resort area. In winter, skiers flock to eight downhill centers and some 90 kilometers (56 miles) of cross-country trails. By early spring, the sugar huts are busy with the new maple syrup. L'Estrie's southerly location makes this the balmiest corner of Québec, notable for its spring skiing. In summer, boating, swimming, sailing, golfing, and bicycling take over. And every fall the inns are booked solid with "leaf peepers" eager to take in the brilliant foliage.

Granby

Numbers in the margin correspond to points of interest on the L'Estrie (Eastern Townships) and Montérégie map.

⑭ *80 km (50 mi) east of Montréal.*

Granby is the gateway to l'Estrie. This town is best known for its zoo, ★ ☝ the **Jardin Zoologique de Granby.** It houses some 800 animals from 225 species. There are two rare snow leopards here on loan from Chicago's Lincoln Park Zoo and New York's Bronx Zoo. The complex includes amusement park rides and souvenir shops as well as a playground and picnic area. ✉ *347 rue Bourget,* ☎ *514/372–9113.* ✉ *$15.* ☉ *Late May–early Sept., daily 9:30–5; Sept., weekends 9–5.*

Granby is also the townships' gastronomic capital. Each October, the month-long Festival Gastronomique attracts more than 10,000 *gastronomes* who use the festival's "gastronomic passport" to sample the cuisines at several dining rooms. To reserve a passport, contact **Festival Gastronomique de Granby et Région** (✉ 650 rue Principle, J2G 8L4, ☎ 514/378–7272).

Dining and Lodging

$$$–$$$$ ✕▥ **Hostellerie les Trois Tilleuls.** This romantic little inn on a quiet coun-
★ try road is a lovely spot to hole up and investigate the surrounding Montérégie region, or to return to after a hard day exploring the big city—Montréal is 20 minutes away. The rooms are modern, and well equipped with hair dryers and magnifying mirrors; each has a balcony or terrace facing the lovely Rivière Richelieu just outside. Packages are available for theatergoers and cross-country skiers, among others. Montréalers come to savor the cuisine of chef Jean-Francois Methot—and in the hopes of taking home one of his recipes. ✉ *290 Richelieu, St-Marc-sur-Richelieu, JOL 2EO,* ☎ *514/584–2231 or 800/263–2230; in Québec, 800/856–7787;* ℻ *514/584–3146. 24 rooms, 1 suite. Restaurant, bar, pool, 2 tennis courts, meeting rooms. AE, DC, MC, V.*

Outdoor Activities and Sports

BIKING
Cyclists will find outdoor bliss on the paved l'Estriade path, which links Granby to Waterloo, and the Montérégiade between Granby and Farnham, both 21 km (13 miles) long.

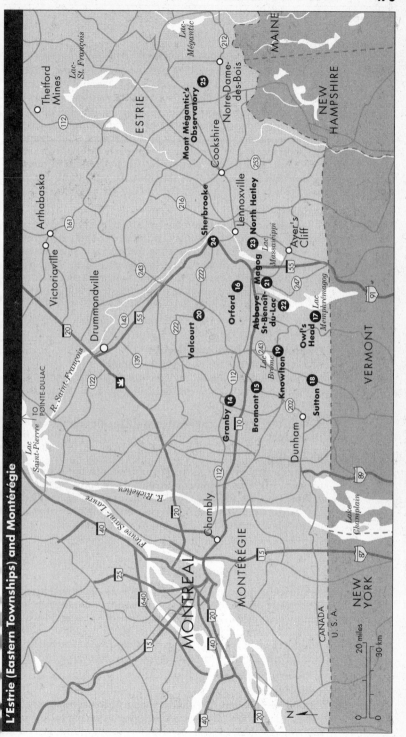

L'Estrie (Eastern Townships) and Montérégie

Bromont

⑮   *8 km (5 mi) south of Granby.*

Bromont, closest to Montréal, is as lively at night as during the day. It offers the only night skiing in l'Estrie and a slope-side disco, Le Bromontais, where the après-ski action continues into the night. Bromont and Orford are *stations touristiques* (tourist centers), meaning that they offer a wide range of activities in all seasons—boating, camping, golf, horseback riding, swimming, tennis, water parks, trail biking, canoeing, fishing, hiking, cross-country and downhill skiing, and snowshoeing. As the former Olympic equestrian site, Bromont is horse country, and every year in late June it holds a riding festival (☏ 514/534–3255). **Bromont Aquatic Park** (✉ Exit 78 from Autoroute 10, ☏ 514/534–2200) is a water-slide park.

Lodging

$$$–$$$$ 🏨 **Le Château Bromont Resort Spa.** Massages, electropuncture, algae wraps, facials, and aromatherapy are just a few of the pampering services at this European-style resort spa. Rooms are large and comfortable, with contemporary furniture, but those facing the Atrium are a little somber. L'Equestre Bar, named for Bromont's equestrian interests, has a cocktail hour and live entertainment. ✉ *90 rue Stanstead, J0E 1L0,* ☏ *514/534–3433, 800/304–3433,* ℻ *514/534–0514. 147 rooms. Restaurant, bar, indoor pool, sauna, spa, hot tubs, squash, racquetball, badminton. EP, MAP. AE, D, DC, MC, V.*

Outdoor Activities and Sports

BIKING, CANOEING, AND HORSEBACK RIDING

Base de Plein Air Davignon (✉ 319 chemin Gale, ☏ 514/534–2277 or 800/363–8952) rents mountain bikes, canoes, and horses.

SKIING

Bromont (☏ 514/534–2200), which has 22 trails, was the site of the 1986 World Cup.

Shopping

Factory outlet shopping is gaining popularity in l'Estrie—especially in Bromont, where **Les Versants de Bromont** (✉ 120 blvd. Bromont, Exit 78 from Hwy. 10, ☏ 819/843–8300) houses 27 boutiques. Shoppers can save between 30% and 70% on items carrying such national and international labels as Liz Claiborne, Vuarnet, and Oneida.

Orford

⑯   *25 km (16 mi) northeast of Bromont.*

Orford's regional park is the site of an annual arts festival highlighting classical music, pops, and chamber orchestra concerts. Since 1951, thousands of students have come to the **Orford Arts Center** (✉ Box 280, ☏ 819/843–3981; in Canada May–Aug., 800/567–6155) to study and perform classical music in the summer. Canada's internationally celebrated Orford String Quartet originated here. Festival Orford also includes jazz and folk music.

Lodging

$$$ 🏨 **Auberge Estrimont.** An exclusive complex in cedar combining hotel rooms, condos, and larger chalets, Auberge Estrimont is close to ski hills, riding stables, and golf courses. Every room, whether in the hotel or in an adjoining condo unit, has a fireplace and a private balcony. ✉ *44 av. de l'Auberge, C.P. 98, Orford-Magog J1X 3W7,* ☏ *819/843–1616 or 800/567–7320,* ℻ *819/843–4909. 76 rooms, 7 suites. Restau-*

*rant, bar, indoor and outdoor pools, hot tub, sauna, tennis, exercise
room, squash, racquetball. AE, DC, MC, V.*

Outdoor Activities and Sports
SKIING

Mont-Orford Ski Area (☎ 819/843–6548), at the center of a provincial park, offers plenty of challenges for alpine and cross-country
skiers, from novices to veterans. It has 41 trails and the steepest drop
of all area ski resorts.

Owl's Head

🄗 *25 km (16 mi) south of Magog.*

Owl's Head Ski Area (☎ 514/292–3342) is a mecca for skiers looking for fewer crowds. It has 27 trails and a 4-kilometer (2½-mile) intermediate run, the longest in l'Estrie. Aside from superb skiing, Owl's
Head has tremendous scenery. From the trails you can see nearby Vermont and Lac Memphrémagog. (You might even see the lake's legendary
sea dragon, said to have been sighted around 90 times since 1816.)

Sutton

🄘 *40 km (25 mi) southwest of Magog.*

Sutton is a well-established community with crafts shops, cozy eateries, and bars (La Paimpolaise is a favorite among skiers).

The Arts
Arts Sutton (✉ 7 rue Academy, ☎ 514/538–2563) is a long-established
mecca for the visual arts.

Lodging

$$–$$$ 🏨 **Auberge la Paimpolaise.** This auberge is right on Mont-Sutton, 50
feet from the ski trails. Nothing fancy is offered, but the location is hard
to beat. Rooms are simple, comfortable, and clean, with a woodsy appeal. All-inclusive weekend ski packages are available. A complimentary
breakfast is served. ✉ *615 rue Maple, J0E 2K0,* ☎ *514/538–3213 or
800/263–3213,* FAX *514/538–3970. 28 rooms. EP, MAP. AE, MC, V.*

Outdoor Activities and Sports
BICYCLING

Vélo Sutton (✉ 33 rue Principale Nord, ☎ 819/538–2561) rents
bicycles.

GOLF

Reservations must be made in advance at **Les Rochers Bleus** (✉ 550
Rte. 139, ☎ 514/538–2324), an 18-hole course.

SKIING

Mont-Sutton (☎ 514/538–2339), where you pay to ski by the hour,
has 53 trails. This ski area attracts a diehard crowd of mostly Anglophone skiers from Québec. It's also one of the area's largest resorts,
with trails that plunge and wander through pine, maple, and birch trees
slope-side.

Knowlton

🄙 *15 km (9 mi) northeast of Sutton.*

Along the shore of Lac Brome is the village of Knowlton, a pleasant
place to shop for antiques and gifts. In summer check to see what's
★   playing at Knowlton's popular **Théâtre Lac Brome** (☞ *below*). In win-

ter many Montréalers come here to ski at **Glen Mountain** (✉ off Rte. 243, ☎ 514/243–6142).

The Arts

Théâtre Lac Brome (☎ 514/243–0361) is an English-language theater company that stages productions of classic Broadway and West End hits. The 175-seat, air-conditioned theater is behind Knowlton's popular pub of the same name.

Valcourt

㉘   *32 km (20 mi) north of Knowlton.*

Valcourt is the birthplace of the inventor of the snowmobile, so it follows that this is a world center for the sport, with more than 1,500 kilometers (1,000-plus miles) of paths cutting through the woods and meadows. The **Musée Joseph-Armand Bombardier** displays this innovator's many inventions. ✉ *1001 av. Joseph-Armand Bombardier, ☎ 514/532–5300.* ➿ *$5.* ☉ *Late June–Aug., daily 10–5:30; Sept.–late June, Tues.–Sun. 10–5.*

Lodging

$$$ ▣ **L'Auberge du Lac St-Pierre.** This small, modern hotel on the lake
★   near Trois Rivières, halfway between Montréal and Québec City, has high ratings for cuisine and accommodations. The luxurious rooms are done in soothing pastels, with televisions, telephones, and whirlpool baths in many. Lake views from the dining room, the conservatory, and many of the guest rooms add to the tranquillity. It's an ideal stop on a tour of southern Québec. ✉ *Box 10, 1911 rue Notre-Dame (Rte. 138), Pointe-du-Lac (about 160 km/100 mi north of Valcourt) G0X 1Z0, ☎ 819/377–5971 or 888/377–5971, ℻ 819/377–5579. 30 rooms. Restaurant, pool, tennis court, business services, meeting rooms. EP, MAP. AE, DC, MC, V.*

Magog

㉙   *32 km (20 mi) south of Valcourt.*

At the northern tip of Lac Memphrémagog, a large body of water reaching into northern Vermont, lies the bustling resort town of Magog. A once sleepy village, the town has grown into a four-season resort destination. Two sandy beaches, great bed-and-breakfasts, hotels and restaurants, boating, ferry rides, bird-watching, sailboarding, aerobics, horseback riding, and snowmobiling are just some of the activities offered.

The streets downtown are lined with century-old homes and churches, some of which have been converted into stores, galleries, and theaters.

NEED A   **La Source** (✉ 420 rue Principale Ouest, ☎ 819/843–0319) is a small
BREAK?   tearoom with an array of cheeses, pâtés, and Swiss chocolates.

Dining and Lodging

$$ ✕ **Auberge de l'Étoile Sur-le-lac.** This popular restaurant serves three meals a day in casual surroundings. Its somber interior, decorated in dark colors, is brightened by the windows facing Lac Memphrémagog. House specialties include wild game and Swiss fondue. ✉ *1150 rue Principale Ouest, ☎ 819/843–6521. Reservations essential. AE, DC, MC, V.*

$$$ ✕▣ **Ripplecove Inn.** The Ripplecove vies with the Hatley and Hovey inns for best in the region. Its accommodations, service, and dining room are consistently excellent. The English pub–style room combines classical and French cuisine in such dishes as *petit timbale de sole e* *saumon fumé a l'algue nori* (timbale of sole and smoked salmon with seaweed), and the *gateau de foie de volaille a la creme de porto* (gateau of chicken livers in a port-flavored sauce). ✉ *700 chemin Ripplecove, C.P. 246, Ayer's Cliff (11 km/7 mi south of Magog) J0B 1CO,* ☎ *819/838–4296 or 800/668–4296,* FAX *819/838–5541. 25 rooms with bath. Restaurant, 2 beaches, pool, windsurfing, sailing, cross-country skiing, meeting facilities. MAP. AE, MC, V.*

$$$–$$$$ ⊡ **Centre de Santé Eastman.** This four-season resort offers respite to the bone-weary and bruised skier. Accommodations are in three houses: the rustic Maison Canadienne, the country-style Volet Bleu, and the modern Pavillon Kaufman. There are holistic spa treatments, massage, and stretch workouts. Top off an already healthy day with fine vegetarian cuisine or light seafood and chicken dishes in the dining room. ✉ *895 chemin Diligence, Eastman (15 km/9 mi west of Magog) J0E 1P0,* ☎ *514/297–3009 or 800/665–5272,* FAX *514/297–3370. 19 rooms. Dining room, spa, cross-country skiing. MAP. AE, MC, V.*

$$$ ⊡ **Club Azur.** Fireplaces warm these condominiums, many of which have kitchens. The units accommodate from two to eight people. ✉ *81 rue des Jardins, R.R. 4, J1X 5X8,* ☎ *819/868–6681 or 800/823–6681,* FAX *819/868–4484. Indoor and outdoor pool, badminton, 3 tennis courts, ice-skating, cross-country skiing. MC, V.*

Nightlife and the Arts

Théâtre le Vieux Clocher (✉ 64 rue Merry Nord, ☎ 819/847–0470) presents pop and rock concerts, and occasionally French plays.

Magog is lively after dark, with a variety of bars, cafés, bistros, and great restaurants to suit every taste and pocketbook. **La Grosse Pomme** (✉ 270 rue Principale Ouest, ☎ 819/843–9365) is a multilevel complex with huge video screens, dance floors, and restaurant service. An outdoor summer terrace has live entertainment. **Au Chat Noir** (✉ 266 rue Principale Ouest, ☎ 819/843–4337) features jazz music, dinner theater, and dancing. **The Auberge Orford** (✉ 20 rue Merry Sud, ☎ 819/843–9361) is another outdoor summer terrace that doesn't stop. There's often live entertainment.

Shopping

Stroll along Magog's **rue Principale** for a look at boutiques, art galleries, and crafts shops with local artisans' work. **Amandine** (✉ 499 rue Principale Ouest, ☎ 819/847–1346) is a lovely gift shop with unusual dishes, bath items, and Belgian chocolates.

Abbaye St-Benoît-du-Lac★

㉒ *21 km (13 mi) west of Magog. From Magog to St-Benoît, take the road to Austin and then follow the signs for the side road to the abbey.*

This abbey's slender bell tower juts up above the trees like a fairy-tale castle. Built on a wooded peninsula in 1912 by the Benedictines, the abbey is home to some 60 monks, who sell apples and apple cider from their orchards as well as distinctive cheeses: Ermite, St-Benoît, and ricotta. Gregorian masses are sung daily and are open to the public (☎ 819/843–4080). The abbey was once known as a favorite retreat for some of Québec's best-known politicians.

North Hatley

㉓ *15 km (9 mi) east of Magog.*

North Hatley, the town on the tip of Lac Massawippi, is home to **The Pilsen** (☎ 819/842–2971), Québec's earliest microbrewery. Although the beer is no longer brewed on-site, the Pilsen still serves Massawippi pale ale on tap. The pub also has great food, loads of atmosphere, and a convivial crowd year-round.

The Arts

★ **The Piggery** (✉ Box 390, ☎ 819/842–2432 or 819/842–2431), a theater that was once a pig barn, reigns supreme in l'Estrie cultural life. The venue is renowned for its risk taking, often presenting new plays by Canadian playwrights and even experimenting with bilingual productions. The season runs June–August.

Naive Arts Contest (✉ Galerie Jeannine-Blais, 100 rue Main, ☎ 819/842–2784) shows the work of more than 100 painters of naive art from some 15 countries. This show takes place every two years; the next year is 1998.

L'Association du Festival du Lac Massawippi (☎ 819/563–4141) presents an annual antiques and folk-arts show in July. The association also sponsors a series of classical music concerts performed at the Eglise Ste-Catherine in North Hatley, on Sundays starting in late April and continuing through June.

Dining and Lodging

$$$$ ✕▥ **Manoir Hovey.** Overlooking the perfectly pristine Lac Massawippi, ★ this retreat has the ambience of a private estate, while offering the activities of a resort. Built in 1900, Hovey Manor resembles George Washington's home at Mount Vernon, Virginia. Each wallpapered room has personality, with a mix of antiques and newer wood furniture, richly printed fabrics, and lace trimmings; many have fireplaces and private balconies. The dining room serves exquisite Continental and French cuisine; if in season, try warm roulades of Swiss chard with spring lamb, preserved apricots, and roasted hazelnuts or grilled tenderloin of beef marinated with juniper berries and a sauce of tarragon and horseradish. Dinner, breakfast, and most sports facilities are included in room rates. ✉ C.P. 60, J0B 2C0, ☎ 819/842–2421 or 800/661–2421 FAX 819/842–2248. 40 rooms, 1 suite, 1 4-bedroom cottage. Dining room, 2 bars, pool, tennis court, 2 beaches, ice fishing, mountain bikes, cross-country skiing, library, meeting rooms. MAP. AE, DC, MC, V.

$$$ ✕▥ **Auberge Hatley.** Chef Alain Labrie specializes in regional dishes at this restaurant/inn, which has three times been voted the best in Québec. The menu changes seasonally, but the rich foie gras and *canard de Barbarie* are recommended if available. The antique yellow room has a panoramic view of Lake Massawippi; linger over your coffee or sip your selection from the wine cellar, which has more than 3,000 bottles. Guest rooms in this 1903 country manor are charmingly decorated; some have a whirlpool and a fireplace. ✉ 325 chemin Virgin, C.P. 330, J0B 2C0, ☎ 819/842–2451, FAX 819/842–2907. 25 rooms. Restaurant. MAP. AE, DC, MC, V. Closed last 2 wks in Nov.

Sherbrooke

❷❹ *16 km (10 mi) north of North Hatley.*

The region's unofficial capital and largest city is Sherbrooke, named in 1818 for Canadian Governor General Sir John Coape Sherbrooke. Founded by Loyalists in the 1790s along the St-François River, it has a number of art galleries, including the **Musée des Beaux-Arts de Sherbrooke** (✉ 174 rue du Palais, ☎ 819/821–2115). This gallery is open Tuesday and Thursday–Sunday 1–5 and Wednesday 1–9. Admission is $2; the charge is waived on Wednesday evening. The **Sherbrooke Touris**

Information Center (✉ 48 rue Dépôt, ☎ 819/564–8331) conducts city tours from late June through early September. Call for reservations.

The Arts

The **Centennial Theatre** (☎ 819/822–9692) at Bishop's University in Lennoxville, 5 kilometers (3 miles) south of Sherbrooke, presents a roster of international, Canadian, and Québécois jazz, classical, and rock concerts, as well as dance, mime, and children's theater.

Dining and Lodging

$$ ✕ **La Falaise St-Michel.** Chef and part-owner Patrick Laigniel offers up French cuisine in a warm redbrick and wood room that takes off any chill even before you sit down. A large selection of wines complements the table d'hôte. ✉ *Rue Webster and Wellington North, behind Banque National,* ☎ *819/346–6339. AE, DC, MC, V.*

$$ ✕ **Restaurant au P'tit Sabot.** Specialties include dishes featuring wild boar, quail, and bison. The cozy room is a pleasant refuge from the bustle of Sherbrooke's main drag. With a piano in the corner, pink decor, and room for only 35 patrons, a romantic atmosphere prevails. ✉ *1410 rue King Ouest,* ☎ *819/563–0262. AE, DC, MC, V.*

$ 🏠 **Bishop's University.** If you are on a budget, this is a great place to stay. The prices can't be beat, and the location near Sherbrooke is good for touring. The university's grounds are lovely, with a river cutting through the campus and its golf course. Much of the architecture is reminiscent of stately New England campuses. Visit the university's 136-year-old chapel, and also look for the butternut tree, an endangered species in l'Estrie. Facilities include a sports complex with an Olympic-size indoor pool and tennis courts. Reservations for summer guests are accepted as early as September, so it's a good idea to book in advance. ✉ *Rue College, Lennoxville (5 km/3 mi south of Sherbrooke) J1M 1Z7,* ☎ *819/822–9651,* 🆑 *819/822–9615. 564 beds. Indoor pool, tennis courts, exercise room. MC, V. Closed Sept.–mid May.*

Sugar Huts

There are two sugar huts near Sherbrooke that give tours of their maple-syrup producing operations in the spring: It's best to call before visiting. **Erablière Patoine** (✉ 1105 chemin Beauvoir, ☎ 819/563–7455) is in Fleurimont. **Bolduc** (✉ 525 chemin Lower, ☎ 819/875–3022) is in Cookshire.

Mont-Mégantic's Observatory

㉕ *74 km (46 mi) east of Sherbrooke.*

Both amateur stargazers and serious astronomers are drawn to this site, in a beautifully wild and mountainous part of l'Estrie. The observatory is at the summit of l'Estrie's second-highest mountain (3,601 feet), whose northern face records annual snowfalls rivaling any in North America. The observatory is a joint venture by the Université de Montréal and Université Laval. Its powerful telescope allows resident scientists to observe celestial bodies 10 million times smaller than the human eye can detect. There's a welcome center, called the Astrolab, on the mountain's base, where visitors can view an exhibition, a multimedia show, and learn about the night sky. ✉ *189 Route du Parc, Notre-Dame-des-Bois,* ☎ *819/888–2822.* 🎟 *Astrolab $8, night tour to summit $8.* ☉ *Astrolab late June–Labor Day, daily 10–6; night tour to summit late June–Labor Day, daily 8 PM.*

Dining and Lodging

$$$ ⊡ **Aux Berges de l'Aurore.** Although this tiny bed-and-breakfast has attractive furnishings and spectacular views, as it sits at the foot of Mont-Mégantic, the draw here is the inn's cuisine. The award-winning restaurant has a five-course meal with ingredients supplied from the inn's huge fruit, vegetable, and herb garden, as well as wild game from the surrounding area: boar, fish, hare, and quail. ⊠ *51 chemin de l'Observatoire, Notre-Dame-des-Bois,* ☏ *819/888–2715. MC, V. Closed Jan.–May.*

CHARLEVOIX

Stretching along the St. Lawrence River's north shore, east of Québec City from Ste-Anne-de-Beaupré to the Saguenay River, Charlevoix embraces mountains rising from the sea and a succession of valleys, plateaus, and cliffs cut by waterfalls, brooks, and streams. The roads wind into villages of picturesque houses and huge tin-roof churches.

New France's first historian, the Jesuit priest François-Xavier de Charlevoix, gave his name to the region. Charlevoix (pronounced sharle-vwah) was first explored by Jacques Cartier, who landed in 1535, although the first colonists didn't arrive until well into the 17th century. They developed a thriving shipbuilding industry, specializing in the sturdy schooner they called a *goelette,* which they used to haul everything from logs to lobsters up and down the coast in the days before rail and paved roads. Shipbuilding has been a vital part of the provincial economy until recent times, though wrecked and forgotten goelettes are visible from many beaches in the region.

Ste-Anne-de-Beaupré

Numbers in the margin correspond to points of interest on the Charlevoix map.

❷❻ *33 km (20 mi) east of Québec City.* Charlevoix begins in the tiny town of Ste-Anne-de-Beaupré (named for Québec's patron saint). Each year more than a million pilgrims visit the region's most famous religious
★ site, the **Basilique Ste-Anne-de-Beaupré** (☞ Chapter 9), which is dedicated to the mother of the Virgin Mary.

At the **Cap Tourmente Wildlife Reserve,** about 8 kilometers (5 miles) northeast of Ste-Anne-de-Beaupré, more than 100,000 greater snow geese gather every October and May.

Outdoor Activities and Sports

SKIING

Parc du Mont-Ste-Anne (☞ Chapter 9), outside Québec City, is on the World Cup downhill ski circuit. **Le Massif** (⊠ 1350 rue Principale, C.P 47, Petite Rivière St-François, ☏ 418/632–5876) is a three-peak ski resort that has the province's highest vertical drop—2,500 feet.

WHALE-WATCHING

Whale-watching cruises (in St-Joachim, ☏ 418/827–3776) are highly recommended. You can, on occasion, spot whales, seals, and dolphins from ferries and from land, so nature lovers are encouraged to bring their binoculars.

Baie-St-Paul

❷❼ *60 km (37 mi) northeast of Ste-Anne-de-Beaupré.*

Baie-St-Paul, Charlevoix's earliest settlement after Beaupré, is popular with hang gliders and artists. Here, the high hills circle a wide plain

Charlevoix

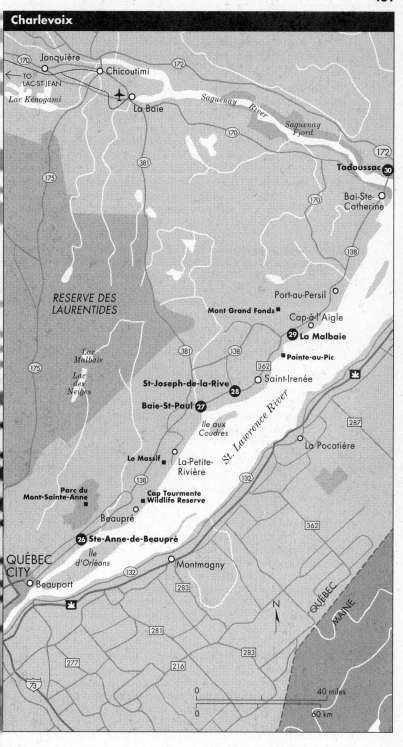

To LAC-ST-JEAN

Jonquière

Chicoutimi

Lac Kénogami

La Baie

Saguenay River

Saguenay Fjord

Tadoussac

Bai-Ste-Catherine

RESERVE DES LAURENTIDES

Port-au-Persil

Mont Grand Fonds

Cap-à-l'Aigle

La Malbaie

Lac Malbaie

Lac des Neiges

St-Joseph-de-la-Rive

Saint-Irenée

Pointe-au-Pic

Baie-St-Paul

Ile aux Coudres

St. Lawrence River

La Pocatière

Le Massif

La-Petite-Rivière

Parc du Mont-Sainte-Anne

Cap Tourmente Wildlife Reserve

Beaupré

Ste-Anne-de-Beaupré

QUÉBEC CITY

Beauport

Île d'Orléans

Montmagny

QUÉBEC

MAINE

N

0   40 miles

0   60 km

holding the village beside the sea. Many of Québec's greatest landscapists portray the area, and their work is on display year-round at the **Centre d'Art Baie-St-Paul** (⊠ 4 rue Ambroise-Fafard, ☎ 418/435–5654), and the **Centre d'Exposition de Baie-St-Paul** (⊠ 23 rue Ambroise-Fafard, ☎ 418/435–3681).

Dining and Lodging

$$$ ✕ **Auberge la Maison Otis.** Try creative Québec-oriented French cuisine like *ballotine de faisan* (pheasant), stuffed with quail and served in a venison sauce followed by a delicious assortment of cheeses. The restaurant is a 150-year-old Norman-style house, elegantly decorated in pastel pink, centered around a huge stone fireplace. ⊠ *23 rue St-Jean-Baptiste,* ☎ *418/435–2255. MC, V.*

$$ ✕ **Mouton Noir.** French cuisine is served amid flowers on the terrace in the summer or in a cozy rustic setting in the winter. You'll always find a varied menu, with pasta, fish, and meat, for very reasonable prices. ⊠ *43 rue Ste-Anne,* ☎ *418/435–3075. AE, MC, V.*

$$$$ 🏠 **Auberge la Maison Otis.** This inn offers calm and romantic accommodations in three buildings, including an old stone house, in the ★   center of the village. Some of the 30 country-style rooms have whirlpools, fireplaces, and antique furnishings. Summer lunches are served amid flowers on an outdoor terrace. Skiing and ice-skating are possible nearby. ⊠ *23 rue St-Jean-Baptiste, G0A 1B0,* ☎ *418/435–2255,* FAX *418/435–2464. 30 rooms with bath, 4 suites. Restaurant, lounge, piano bar, air-conditioning, indoor pool, sauna, health club. MAP available. AE, MC, V.*

En Route   From Baie-St-Paul, you can take the open, scenic coastal drive (Route 362) or the faster Route 138 to Pointe-au-Pic, La Malbaie, and Cap-à-l'Aigle. This section of Route 362 has memorable views of rolling hills—green, white, or ablaze with fiery hues, depending on the season—meeting the broad expanse of the "sea" as the locals like to call the St. Lawrence estuary.

St-Joseph-de-la-Rive

28   *15 km (9 mi) northeast of Baie-St-Paul.*

A secondary road leads sharply down into St-Joseph-de-la-Rive, with its line of old houses hugging the mountain base on the narrow shore road. The town is host to peaceful inns and inviting restaurants, such as l'Auberge sous les Pins (⊠ 362 rue F.A. Savard, Box 4, G0A 3Y0, ☎ 418/635–2583), which means "inn under the pines." Nearby Papeterie St-Gilles (⊠ 304 rue F.A. Savard, ☎ 418/635–2430) produces unusual handcrafted stationery, using a 17th-century process. Across rue F.A. Savard from Papeterie St-Gilles is the small **Exposition Maritime** (Maritime Museum), which commemorates the days of the St. Lawrence goelettes.

OFF THE   **ILE AUX COUDRES** – From St-Joseph you can catch a ferry (☎ 418/438–
BEATEN PATH   2743) to Ile aux Coudres, an island where Jacques Cartier's men gathered *coudres* (hazelnuts) in 1535. Since then, the island has produced many a goelette, and former captains now run several small inns. Large inns feature folk-dance evenings. Many visitors like to bike around the 16-kilometer (10-mile) island taking in windmills, inns, water mills, and old schooners, as well as boutiques selling paintings and local handicrafts, such as household linen.

Lodging

$$ 🛏 **Hôtel Cap-aux-Pierres.** This hotel provides top-notch accommoda-
★ tions in both a traditionally Canadian main building and a motel sec-
tion open in the summer only. About a third of the rooms have river
views. The restaurant serves a mix of Québec standards and nouvelle
cuisine, and entertainment includes folk dancing on summer Saturday
evenings. ✉ *246 rue Principale, La Baleine, Ile aux Coudres, G0A 2A0,*
☎ *418/438–2711 or 800/463–5250,* 🖷 *418/438–2127. 98 rooms.*
Restaurant, bar, indoor and outdoor pool. MAP. AE, DC, MC, V.

La Malbaie

㉙ *35 km (22 mi) northeast of St-Joseph.*

La Malbaie is one of the most elegant and historically interesting re-
sort towns in the province. It was known as Murray Bay in an earlier
era when wealthy Anglophones summered here and in the neighbor-
ing villages of Pointe-au-Pic and Cap-à-l'Aigle. Once called the "sum-
mer White House," this area became popular with both American and
Canadian politicians in the late 1800s when Ottawa Liberals and
Washington Republicans partied decorously through the summer with
members of the Québec judiciary. William Howard Taft built the first
of three summer residences in Pointe-au-Pic in 1894, when he was the
American civil governor of the Philippines. He became the 27th pres-
ident of the United States in 1908, and later chief justice of the Supreme
Court. Locals still fondly remember the Tafts and the parties they
threw in their elegant summer homes.

Now many Taft-era homes serve as handsome inns, guaranteeing an old-
fashioned coddling, with such extras as breakfast in bed, gourmet
meals, whirlpools, and free shuttles to the ski areas in winter. Many serve
lunch and dinner to nonresidents, so you can tour the area going from
one gourmet's delight to the next. The cuisine, as elsewhere in Québec,
is genuine French, rather than a hybrid invented for North Americans.

Musée de Charlevoix traces the region's history as a vacation spot in
a series of exhibits and is developing an excellent collection of local
paintings and folk art. ✉ *1 rue du Havre, Pointe-au-Pic (3 km/2 mi
south of La Malbaie),* ☎ *418/665–4411.*

The **Casino de Charlevoix,** styled after European casinos, welcomes vis-
itors year-round. The minimum age is 18. ✉ *183 av. Richelieu,* ☎ *418/
665–5300 or 800/965–5355.* ⊘ *Sun.–Thurs. 10 AM–2 AM, Fri. and
Sat. 10 AM–3 AM.*

The Arts

Domaine Forget is a music and dance academy that presents concerts
on summer evenings by international-caliber musicians, many of whom
are teaching or learning at the school. The Domaine also functions as
a stopover for traveling musicians, who take advantage of its rental
studios. The season runs from the beginning of May through August.
✉ *St-Irenée (15 km/9 mi south of La Malbaie),* ☎ *418/452–8111 or
418/452–2535,* 🖷 *418/452–3503.*

Dining and Lodging

$$$$ ✕ **Auberge des 3 Canards.** This inn has made a name for itself in the
region, not only for its accommodations but also for its award-winning
restaurant. The menu may include *gratin d'escargots aux bluets* (snails
with a blueberry and grapefruit sauce baked au gratin) as an appetizer,
and stuffed pheasant—the breasts smothered in mustard sauce and the
legs seasoned with spicy maple sauce—as a main course. Homemade
desserts include *Pomme de l'Ile aux Coudres*—cheese-topped apples with

a touch of honey. Meals are elegantly presented in a rustic setting. The warmth of the natural wood contrasts with the pale and deep blue touches throughout. ⊠ *49 côte Bellevue, Pointe-au-Pic (3 km/2 mi south of La Malbaie)*, ☎ *418/665–3761. AE, MC, V.*

$$$–$$$$ ✕ **Auberge sur la Côte.** Simple white tablecloths, natural wood, and stone walls create a rustic setting for fine French cuisine. A house specialty is *agneau de Charlevoix*, lamb seasoned with lemon and thyme, served with fresh vegetables. Lunch is served in summer only, but the dining room is open in the evening year-round. ⊠ *205 chemin des Falaises, La Malbaie*, ☎ *418/665–3972. AE, MC, V.*

$$$$ ⊞ **Auberge la Pinsonnière.** An atmosphere of country luxury prevails,
★ and each room is decorated differently; some have fireplaces, whirlpools, and king-size four-poster beds. Rooms offer a commanding view of Murray Bay on the St. Lawrence River. ⊠ *124 rue St-Raphael, Cap-à-l'Aigle (3 km/2 mi south of La Malbaie), G0T 1B0*, ☎ *418/665–4431*, FAX *418/665–7156. 21 rooms, 6 suites. 2 restaurants, 3 lounges, indoor pool, sauna, tennis court, beach, spa. MAP. AE, MC, V.*

$$$$ ⊞ **Hôtel Manoir Richelieu.** The Manoir Richelieu, an imposing castle nestled amid trees on a cliff overlooking the St. Lawrence River, has been offering first-class accommodations to vacationers for centuries. It was founded in 1776 as a haven for wealthy travelers. Although still rich in elegance and charm, the resort has adapted to the needs of today's visitor and is now an affordable vacation spot. Whale-watching and snowmobile packages are available. ⊠ *181 rue Richelieu, Pointe-au-Pic (3 km/2 mi south of La Malbaie), G0T 1M0*, ☎ *418/665–3703 or 800/463–2613*, FAX *418/665–3093. 372 rooms. Restaurant, indoor and outdoor pools, sauna, golf course, tennis courts, cross-country skiing, snowmobiling. AE, DC, MC, V.*

$$ ⊞ **Les Studios du Domaine.** This unique retreat at the foot of the Charlevoix Mountains facing the St. Lawrence River is a music and dance academy in the summer but is open to tourists during the winter season. Studio apartments, each with one or two bedrooms, and a kitchenette are available for reasonable prices. In the summer, weekly concerts are open to the public, and Les Studios also offers a Sunday brunch complete with a musical ensemble. Golf, cross-country and downhill skiing, and the Charlevoix casino are all nearby. Concerts are held June–August on Wednesday, Friday, and Saturday at 8:30; admission is $20 per person. Sunday brunch is served 11–2 and costs $22 per person. ⊠ *398 chemin les Bains, St-Irenée (15 km/9 mi sout of La Malbaie), G0T 1V0*, ☎ *418/452–3535*, FAX *418/452–3503. 28 apartments. MC, V.*

Outdoor Activities and Sports

GOLF

Club de Golf de Manoir Richelieu (⊠ 181 av. Richelieu, Pointe-au-Pic ☎ 418/665–2526 or 800/463–2613) has 18 holes.

SKIING

Mont-Grand Fonds (⊠ 1000 chemin des Loisirs, ☎ 418/665–0095) has 14 slopes and 125 kilometers (80 miles) of cross-country trails.

Tadoussac

⓿ *71 km (44 mi) north of La Malbaie.*

The road, the views, and the villages continue all the way up to Baie Ste-Catherine, which shares the view up the magnificent Saguenay Fjord with the small town of Tadoussac. Jacques Cartier made a stop at this point in 1535, and it became an important meeting site for fur traders in the French Territory until the mid-19th century. Whale-watching excursions and cruises of the fjord now depart from Tadoussac as well as from Chicoutimi, farther up the deep fjord. As the Saguenay River flows from Lac St-Jean south toward the St. Lawrence, it has a dual character: Between Alma and Chicoutimi, the once rapidly flowing river has been turned into hydroelectric power; in its lower section, it becomes wider and deeper and flows by steep mountains and cliffs, en route to the St. Lawrence. The white beluga whale breeds in the lower portion of the Saguenay in summer, and in the confluence of the fjord and the seaway are many marine species, which attract other whales, such as pilot, finback, humpback, and blues.

Sadly, the beluga is an endangered species; the whales, along with 27 species of mammals and birds and 17 species of fish, are being threatened by pollution in the St. Lawrence River. This has inspired a $100 million project funded by both the federal and provincial governments. An 800-square-kilometer (496-square-mile) marine park (☎ 418/235–4703) at the confluence of the Saguenay and St. Lawrence rivers has been created to protect its fragile ecosystem in the hope of reversing some of the damage already done.

Outdoor Activities and Sports

WHALE-WATCHING

Croisières Navimex Canada, Inc. (✉ 25 Pl. Marché Champlain, Suite 400, Québec City G1K 4H2, ☎ 418/692–4643), offers three-hour whale-watching cruises ($30) and 4½-hour dinner cruises on the Saguenay Fjord ($40). Cruises depart from Baie-Ste-Catherine, Tadoussac, and Rivière du Loup (the departure from Rivière du Loup costs an additional $5).

THE GASPÉ PENINSULA

Jutting into the stormy Gulf of St. Lawrence like the battered prow of a ship, the Gaspé Peninsula remains an isolated region of unsurpassed wild beauty, an area where the land ends. Sheer cliffs tower above broad beaches, and tiny coastal fishing communities cling to the shoreline. Inland rise the Chic-Choc Mountains, eastern Canada's highest, the realm of woodland caribou, black bear, and moose. Townspeople in some Gaspé areas speak mainly English.

Jacques Cartier landed on the Gaspé in 1534, but it wasn't until the early 1800s that the first settlers arrived. Today, the area still seems unspoiled and timeless, a blessing for travelers dipping and soaring along the spectacular coastal highways or venturing on river-valley roads to the interior. Geographically, the peninsula is among the oldest lands on earth. A vast, mainly uninhabited forest covers the hilly hinterland. Local tourist officials can be helpful in locating outfitters and guides to fish and hunt large and small game. The Gaspé's four major parks—Port Daniel, Forillon, Causapscal, and Gaspé—cover a total of 2,292 square kilometers (885 square miles).

The Gaspé was on Jacques Cartier's itinerary—he first stepped ashore in North America in the town of Gaspé—but Vikings, Basques, and Portuguese fisherfolk had come long before. The area's history is told in countless towns en route. Acadians, displaced by the British from New Brunswick in 1755, settled Bonaventure; Paspébiac still has a gunpowder shed built in the 1770s to help defend the peninsula from American ships; and United Empire Loyalists settled New Carlisle in 1784.

Carleton

Numbers in the margin correspond to points of interest on the Gaspé Peninsula map.

 201 km (125 mi) southeast of Mont-Joli.

Gaspé Peninsula

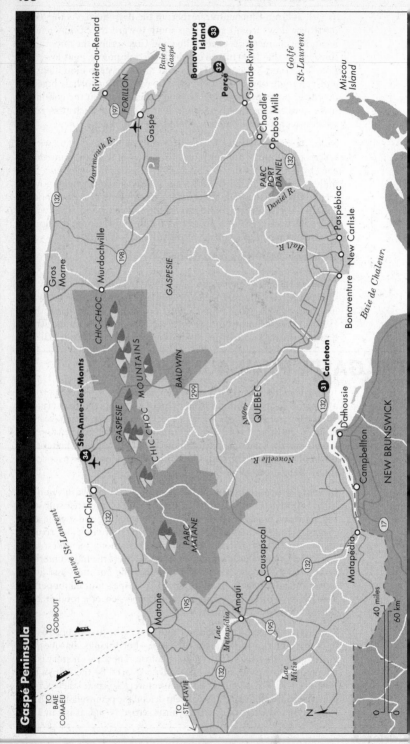

The **Notre Dame Oratory** on Mont-St-Joseph dominates this French-speaking city. The view from this point, almost 2,000 feet above Baie de Chaleurs, is spectacular on a clear day.

Dining and Lodging

$$–$$$ ✕🖪 **Motel Hostelerie Baie-Bleue.** This motel is snuggled up against a mountain beside the Baie des Chaleurs and offers great views. Daily guided bus tours leave from the hotel June–September. The large restaurant, La Seignerie, has been recognized for excellence. Chef Simon Bernard prepares regional dishes, especially seafood. The table d'hôte won't break your budget and the wine list is extensive and well chosen. ⊠ *482 blvd. Perron, Rte. 132, G0C 1J0,* ☎ *418/364–3355 or 800/463–9099,* FAX *418/364–6165. 95 rooms. Restaurant, pool, tennis courts, beach. AE, MC, V.*

Outdoor Activities and Sports

WATER SPORTS

Windsurfers and sailors enjoy the breezes around the Gaspé; there are windsurfing marathons in Baie-des-Chaleurs each summer.

Percé

㉜ *193 km (120 mi) east of Carleton.*

The most famous sight in the region is the huge fossil-embedded rock off the town of Percé that the sea "pierced" thousands of years ago. The largest colony of gannets in the world summers off Percé on

★ **㉝** **Bonaventure Island.**

Dining and Lodging

$ ✕ **La Sieur de Pabos.** Boasting the best seafood in the province, this rustic restaurant overlooks Pabos Bay, south of Chandler, about 40 kilometers (25 miles) south of Percé. The chef suggests *crêpe de la seigneurie,* a seafood crepe with a delicately seasoned white sauce. ⊠ *325 Rte. 132, Pabos Mills,* ☎ *418/689–2281. AE, MC, V.*

$$–$$$ 🖪 **La Bonaventure-sur-Mer Hotel.** The waterfront location with views of Percé Rock and Bonaventure Island makes up for the motel-standard decor. Some motel units have kitchenettes. ⊠ *Rte. 132, C.P. 339, G0C 2L0,* ☎ *418/782–2166. 90 rooms. Dining room, beach. AE, DC, MC, V. Closed Nov.–May.*

$$–$$$ 🖪 **La Normandie Hotel/Motel.** All but four rooms of this split-level motel face the ocean, with views of Percé Rock and Bonaventure Island. The location in the center of town puts shops and restaurants within walking distance; a beach and a municipal pool are also nearby. Third-floor rooms are more spacious. ⊠ *221 Rte. 132 Ouest, C.P. 129, G0C 2L0,* ☎ *418/782–2112 or 800/463–0820. 45 rooms. Restaurant, lounge, sauna, exercise room. EP, MAP. AE, DC, MC, V. Closed Nov.–Apr.*

$$ 🖪 **La Côte Surprise Motor Hotel.** Most of the rooms of this motel have views of Percé Rock and the village. Decor is standard in both motel and second-floor hotel units, but the private balconies and terraces are a plus. ⊠ *Rte. 132, C.P. 339, G0C 2L0,* ☎ *418/782–2166,* FAX *418/782–5323. 36 rooms. Dining room, snack bar, lounge. AE, D, DC, MC, V. Closed Oct.–May.*

Ste-Anne-des-Monts

㉝ *282 km (175 mi) northwest of Percé.*

The region boasts Québec's longest ski season and highest peaks. Ste-Anne-des-Monts, on the north shore of the peninsula, offers the only heli-skiing east of the Rockies, with deep powder, open bowl, and glade skiing clear into June on peaks that rise to 2,700 feet. Other centers operate from mid-November through May.

Dining and Lodging

$$ ✕ **Cabillaud.** In this bright restaurant, chef Yvan Belzile serves the local specialty—seafood—as well as his own—duck. This is a good place to unwind with a wine from their fine selection and a view of the ever-present ocean. ⊠ *268 rue Notre-Dame Est, Cap-Chat,* ☎ *418/786–2480. MC, V.*

$$ ▥ **Gite du Mont-Albert.** In Gaspé Provincial Park, this property is 40 kilometers (25 miles) south of Ste-Anne, nestled in the middle of the Chic-Choc Mountains. It's a perfect retreat for hiking, bicycling, horseback riding, or salmon fishing on the Ste-Anne River. ⊠ *Rte. 299, C.P. 1150, G0E 2G0,* ☎ *418/763–2288 or 888/270-4483. 48 rooms. Dining room, bar. AE, MC, V.*

QUÉBEC A TO Z

Arriving and Departing

By Bus
Most major bus lines in the province connect with **Voyageur** (☎ 514/842–2281).

By Car
The major highways are Autoroute des Laurentides 15, a six-lane highway from Montréal to the Laurentians; Autoroute 10 East from Montréal to l'Estrie; U.S. 91 from New England, which becomes Autoroute 55 as it crosses the border to l'Estrie; and Highway 138, which runs from Montréal along the north shore of the St. Lawrence River.

By Plane
Most airlines fly into either of Montréal's airports (Mirabel or Dorval) or Québec City's airport (☞ Chapters 8 and 9).

By Train
Regular **VIA Rail** (800/665–0200) passenger service connects all the province with Montréal and Québec City and offers limited service to the Gaspé Peninsula.

Getting Around

Québec
BY BUS
Most bus traffic to the outer reaches of the province begins at the bus terminal in downtown Québec City (⊠ 225 blvd. Charest Est, ☎ 418/524–4692).

BY CAR
The province has fine roads, along which drivers insist on speeding. Road maps are available at any of the numerous seasonal or permanent Québec tourist offices (call 800/363–7777 for the nearest location). Major entry points are Ottawa/Hull, U.S. 87 from New York State south of Montréal, U.S. 91 from Vermont into l'Estrie area, and the Trans-Canada Highway just west of Montréal.

The Laurentians
BY BUS
Frequent bus service is available from the **Terminus Voyageur** (⊠ 505 blvd. de Maisonneuve Est, ☎ 514/842–2281) in downtown Montréal. **Limocar Laurentides'** service (☎ 514/435–8899) departs regularly for

L'Annonciation, Mont-Laurier, Ste-Adèle, Ste-Agathe-des-Monts, and St-Jovite, among other stops en route. Limocar also has a service to the Basses Laurentides (Lower Laurentians) region, departing from the Laval bus terminal at the Métro Henri-Bourassa stop in north Montréal, stopping in many towns, and ending in St-Jérôme.

BY CAR

Autoroute des Laurentides 15, a six-lane highway, and the slower but more scenic secondary road, Route 117, lead to this resort country. Try to avoid traveling to and from the region on Friday evening or Sunday afternoon, as you're likely to sit for hours in bumper-to-bumper traffic.

L'Estrie

BY BUS

Buses depart daily from the **Terminus Voyageur** in Montréal (⌧ 505 blvd. de Maisonneuve Est, ☎ 514/842–2281), to Granby, Lac-Mégantic, Magog, and Sherbrooke.

BY CAR

Take Autoroute 10 East from Montréal; from New England take U.S. 91, which becomes Autoroute 55 as it crosses the border at Rock Island.

Gaspé Peninsula

BY CAR

Take the Trans-Canada Highway northeast along the southern shore of the St. Lawrence River to just south of Rivière-du-Loup, where you pick up the 270-kilometer (150-mile) Route 132, which hugs the dramatic coastline. At Ste-Flavie, follow the southern leg of Route 132. Note that the entire distance around the peninsula is 848 kilometers (527 miles).

Contacts and Resources

Camping

For information on camping in the province's private trailer parks and campgrounds, write for the free publication "Québec Camping," available from **Tourisme Québec** (⌧ 12 rue Ste-Anne, Québec City G1X 3X2, ☎ 418/643–2280). Inquiries about camping in Québec's three national parks should be directed to **Parks Canada Information Services** (⌧ 3 rue Buade, Box 6060, Haute Ville, Québec City G1R 4V7, ☎ 418/648–4177).

Emergencies

Dial 911 to reach the **police, fire,** and **ambulance.**

Fishing

More than 20 outfitters are members of the Laurentian tourist association; several recommendations follow. **Pourvoirie des 100 Lacs Nords** (☎ 514/444–4441). **Lac Beauregard Outfitters** (⌧ Mont-Laurier, ☎ 819/326–0269). **Pourvoirie Boismenu** (⌧ Lac-du-Cerf, ☎ 819/597–2619). Before setting off into the wilds, consult the **Fédération des Pourvoyeurs du Québec** (⌧ Québec Outfitters Federation, 2485 blvd. Hamel, Québec City G1P 2H9, ☎ 418/527–5191) or ask for its list of outfitters available through tourist offices.

Don't forget: Fishing requires a permit, available from the regional offices of the **Ministère du Loisir, de la Chasse et de la Pêche** (⌧ 6255 av. 13, Montréal H1X 3E6, ☎ 514/374–2417), or inquire at any Laurentians sporting-goods store displaying an "authorized agent" sticker.

Guest Farms

Agricotours (✉ 4545 av. Pierre de Coubertin, C.P. 1000, Succursale M, Montréal H1V 3R2, ☎ 514/252–3138), the Québec farm-vacation association, can provide lists of guest farms in the province.

Mountain Climbing

Perhaps the best way to view the scenery of the Upper Laurentins is to mountain climb. The **Fédération Québécoise de la Montagne** (✉ 4545 rue Pierre-de-Coubertin, C.P. 1000, Succursale M, Montréal H1V 3R2, ☎ 514/252–3004) can give you information about this sport, as can the region's tourist offices.

Nature Tours

The **Montréal Zoological Society** (✉ 2055 rue Peel, Montréal H3A 1V4, ☎ 514/845–8317) is a nature-oriented group that offers lectures, field trips, and weekend excursions. Tours include whale watching in the St. Lawrence estuary, and hiking and bird-watching in national parks throughout Québec, Canada, and the northern United States.

River Rafting

Four companies specializing in white-water rafting at Rivière Rouge are on-site at the trip's departure point near Calumet. (Take Route 148 past Calumet; turn onto chemin de la Rivière Rouge until you see the signs for the access road to each rafter's headquarters.) **Aventures en Eau Vive** (☎ 819/242–1916), **Nouveau Monde** (☎ 819/242–7238), **Propulsion** (☎ 800/461–3300), and **W-3 Rafting** (☎ 514/334–0889) all offer four- to five-hour rafting trips and provide transportation to and from the river site, as well as guides, helmets, life jackets, and, at the end of the trip, a much-anticipated meal. Most have facilities on-site or nearby for dining, drinking, camping, bathing, swimming, hiking, and horseback riding.

Skiing

For information about ski conditions, telephone the **Maison du Tourisme des Laurentides** (☎ 800/463–9777) and ask for the ski report.

Snowmobiling

Point de Vue Canada (✉ 1227 av. St-Hubert, Suite 200, Montréal H2L 3Y8, ☎ 514/843–8161) offers snowmobile tours in the Laurentians, in Charlevoix, and as far north as the James Bay region. The group also has such adventure packages as "The Magic of the Nunavik Arctic," a weeklong adventure in Québec's Grand Nord, where participants spend one night in an igloo, travel on dogsleds, and go ice fishing.

Visitor Information

QUÉBEC

Tourism Québec (✉ 12 rue Ste-Anne, Québec City, G1R 3X2, ☎ 418/643–2280 or 800/363–7777) can provide information on provincial tourist bureaus throughout the province.

THE LAURENTIANS

The major tourist office is the **Maison du Tourisme des Laurentides** (✉ 14142 rue de Lachapelle, R.R. 1, St-Jérôme J7Z 5T4, ☎ 514/436–8532 or 800/561–6673), just off the Autoroute des Laurentides 15 at Exit 39. The office is open mid-June–Aug., daily 8:30–8; Sept.–mid-June, Sat.–Thurs. 9–5, Fri. 9–7.

Year-round regional tourist offices are in the towns of Labelle, Mont-Laurier, Mont-Tremblant, St-Antoine, St-Sauveur-des-Monts, St-Jovite, Ste-Adèle, Ste-Agathe-des-Monts, Val David, and Piedmont. **Seasonal tourist offices** (mid-June–Labor Day) are in Bois Briand, Grenville,

Lachute, L'Annonciation, Ste-Marguerite-du-Lac-Masson, Notre-Dame-du-Laus, and St-Adolphe-Howard.

Year-round regional provincial tourist offices are in the towns of Bromont, Danville, Eastman, Granby, Lac Mégantic, Magog, Sherbrooke, Sutton, Mansonville, and Waterloo. **Seasonal tourist offices** (June–Labor Day) are in Coaticook, La Patrie, Pike River, East Angus, Eaton-Corner, Freliohsburg, Lac Brome, and Stanstead. Seasonal bureaus' schedules are irregular, so contact the **Association Touristique de l'Estrie** (⊠ 25 Brocage, Sherbrooke, J1L 2J4, ☎ 819/820–2020) before visiting. This association also provides lodging information.

11 New Brunswick

New Brunswick is where the great Canadian forest, sliced by sweeping river valleys and modern highways, meets the Atlantic. To the north and east, the gentle, warm Gulf Stream washes quiet beaches. Besides the seacoast, there are pure inland streams, pretty towns, and historic cities. The province's dual heritage (35% of its population is Acadian French) provides added spice.

By Colleen
Whitney
Thompson

Updated by
Ana Watts

NEW BRUNSWICK IS WHERE the great Canadian forest, sliced by sweeping river valleys and modern highways, meets the sea. It's an old place in New World terms, and the remains of a turbulent past are still evident in some of its quiet nooks. Near Moncton, for instance, bees gather nectar, and wild strawberries perfume the air of the grassy slopes of Fort Beausejour, where, in 1755, one of the last battles for possession of Acadia took place—the English finally overcoming the French. The dual heritage of New Brunswick (35% of its population is Acadian French) provides added spice. If you decide to stay in both Acadian and Loyalist regions, a trip to New Brunswick can seem like two vacations in one.

More than half the province is surrounded by coastline—the rest nestles into Québec and Maine, creating slightly schizophrenic attitudes in border towns. The dramatic Bay of Fundy, which has the highest tides in the world, sweeps up the coast of Maine, around the enchanting Fundy Isles at the southern tip of New Brunswick and on up the province's rough and intriguing south coast. To the north and east, the gentle, warm Gulf Stream washes quiet beaches.

New Brunswick is still largely unsettled—85% of the province is forested. Inhabitants have chosen the easily accessible area around rivers, ocean, and lakes, leaving most of the interior to the pulp companies. For years this Cinderella province has been virtually ignored by tourists who whiz through to better-known Atlantic destinations. New Brunswick's residents can't seem to decide whether this makes them unhappy or not. Money is important in the economically depressed maritime area, where younger generations have traditionally left home for higher-paying jobs in Ontario and "the West." But no one wishes to lose the special characteristics of this still unspoiled province.

This attitude is a blessing in disguise to motorists who do leave the major highways to explore 2,240 kilometers (1,400 miles) of spectacular seacoast, pure inland streams, pretty towns, and historical cities. The custom of hospitality is so much a part of New Brunswick nature that tourists are perceived more as welcome visitors than paying guests. Even cities often retain a bit of naïveté. It makes for a charming vacation, but don't be deceived by ingenuous attitudes. Most residents are products of excellent school and university systems, generally travel widely, live in modern cities, and are well versed in world affairs.

Pleasures and Pastimes

Beaches

There are two kinds of saltwater beaches in New Brunswick: warm-m-m-m-m and c-c-c-c-cold. The warm beaches are along the Northumberland Strait and Gulf of St. Lawrence on the east coast. Here it's sand castles, salt water, and sunscreen all the way, with a little beach volleyball on the side. You'll always find enough people for a game at Parlee Beach in Shediac. If sand and solitude are more your style, try Koughibouguac National Park and its 26 kilometers (16 miles) of beaches and dunes.

The cold beaches are on the Bay of Fundy, on the province's southern coast. The highest tides in the world (a **vertical** difference of as much as 48 feet!) have carved some spectacular caves, crevices, and cliffs. There are some sandy beaches, and hardy souls do swim in the "invigorating" salt water. But the Fundy beaches are more for adventurers who want to investigate aquatic wildlife on the flats at low tide, hound rocks, hunt fossils, or jump off a cliff! (There's a rappelling outfitter at Cape Enrage.)

Bicycling

Byroads, lanes, and rolling secondary highways run through small towns, along the ocean, and into the forest. Set out on your own, or try a guided adventure with a specialist tour operator. B&Bs frequently have bicycles for hire and Tourism New Brunswick has listings and free cycling maps.

Dining

Cast your line just about anywhere in New Brunswick and you catch fish 'n chips, clams 'n chips, and scallops 'n chips. If you want the seafood but not the batter, you'll need a longer line. Better restaurants in the cities have other possibilities, as do better accommodation dining rooms. New Brunswick has never been famous for sophisticated dining, but things are improving. Saint John, Moncton, and some communities along the Acadian Peninsula offer some interesting options, and resort communities like St. Andrews and Caraquet have consistently good catches.

Silver salmon, once a spring staple when set nets were allowed, is still available but quite costly. Most salmon served in restaurants is farm-reared. Lobster, a favorite maritime dish, is available in most restaurants, but is not always cheap. The custom of the residents is to buy it fresh from the fishermen or shore outlets and devour it in huge quantities. Because of the cool waters, New Brunswick shellfish is especially tasty. Look for oysters, scallops, clams, crab, and mussels. And be sure to try the purple seaweed called dulse, which the natives eat like potato chips. To be truly authentic, accompany any New Brunswick–style feast with hearty Moosehead beer, brewed in Saint John and one of the province's well-known exports.

In the spring, once the ice has left streams and rivers, a provincial delicacy—the fiddlehead fern—is picked from their banks. Eaten as a vegetable (boiled, drenched with lemon, butter, salt, and pepper), fiddleheads have something of an artichoke taste and go well with spring's bony fish, shad, and gaspereaux.

CATEGORY	COST*
$$$	$20–$40
$$	$10–$20
$	under $10

per person, excluding drinks, service, and 11% sales tax

Fishing

Dotted with freshwater lakes, crisscrossed with fish-laden rivers, and bordered by 1,129 kilometers (700 miles) of seacoast, this province is one of Canada's natural treasures. Sports people are drawn by the excellent bass fishing and such world-famous salmon rivers as the Miramichi, the Restigouche, and the Nashwaak. Commercial fishermen often take visitors line fishing for groundfish. A freshwater fishing license for out-of-province visitors costs $30 for the season, $20 for 7 days, or $15 for 3 days and allows you to fish without a guide and for everything but salmon (☞ New Brunswick A to Z, *below*).

Golf

There are 36 excellent golf courses in New Brunswick. Many provide sparkling views of the sea. Greens fees run about $20–$25, $15 for some nine-hole courses; visitors are generally welcome. For a list of golf courses, contact Tourism New Brunswick (☞ New Brunswick A to Z, *below*).

Lodging

New Brunswick has a number of officially designated Heritage Inns—historically significant establishments built in the 19th century. Their accommodations run the gamut from elegant to homey; many have antique china and furnishings or other charming touches.

Hotels and motels in and around Saint John and Fredericton are adequate and friendly. Accommodations in Saint John are at a premium in summer, so reserve ahead to ensure a place to stay.

CATEGORY	COST*
$$$	over $60
$$	$45–$60
$	under $45

All prices are for a standard double room, excluding 10% service charge.

Nightlife and the Arts

New Brunswick's nightlife is most vibrant in the three southern cities: Saint John, Moncton, and Fredericton. Live music—from Celtic to jazz to blues—can be heard in many pubs.

Theatre New Brunswick, a professional troup based in Fredericton, takes five productions on the road throughout the province during its October to May season.

The Beaverbrook Art Gallery in Fredericton, with canvasses from the finest contemporary New Brunswick artists to the old masters, is the designated Provincial Gallery. It also plays host annually to several prestigious visiting exhibitions.

Shopping

There are a lot of very creative New Brunswickers. Fine art galleries around the province proudly display and sell their paintings and sculptures. Craft galleries, shops, and fairs are brimming with beautiful jewelry, glass, pottery, clothing, furniture, and leather goods. Some of the province's better bookstores even have sections devoted to New Brunswick authors, both literary and popular.

St. Andrews is a mecca for those seeking fine gifts and crafts. Saint John's Prince William Street is part of a delightful heritage area brimming with crafts and antiques. Nearby Brunswick Square is home to some unique and better-chain boutiques. The Saint John City market is delightful and delicious, as is Fredericton's Saturday morning Boyce Farmer's Market. The capital city's alleys are just as fruitful as the streets if you're looking for crafts, treasures, and a bit of haute couture. Moncton's five big malls and Price Club store make it a popular shopping center for the maritime region.

Winter Sports

New Brunswick can get as much as 16 feet of snow each year, so winter fun often lasts well into spring. Dogsledding is taking off, ice-fishing communities pop up on just about any river that freezes, and you can always find someone to go tobogganing, skating, or snowshoeing with you.

CROSS-COUNTRY SKIING

A perfect province for cross-country skiing, New Brunswick has groomed trails at such provincial and national parks as Mactaquac Provincial Park near Fredericton, Fundy National Park in Alma, and Kouchibouguac National Park between Moncton and Bathurst. Many communities and small hotels offer groomed trails, but it's also possible to set off on your own in almost every section of the province.

DOWNHILL SKIING

New Brunswick downhill ski areas usually operate from mid-December through April. There are four ski hills—Farlagne, Crabbe, Poley, and Sugarloaf.

SNOWMOBILING

Smowmobiling has boomed in New Brunswick. With more than 6,000 kilometers (4,000 miles) of groomed, marked, and serviced snowmobile trails and dozens of snowmobile clubs hosting special events, this area is as exciting as the Arctic without the travel hassles.

EXPLORING NEW BRUNSWICK

In recent years New Brunswick has led much of the world onto the Information Highway, but all that has done little to change its settlement patterns. The population still clings to the original highways—rivers and oceans. In fact, the Saint John River in the west, and the Fundy and Acadian Coasts in the south and east, essentially encompass the province.

The Saint John River is a world-class river where people engage in world-class endeavours. Much of the river valley scenery is panoramic—gently rolling hills and sweeping forests with just enough rocky gorges to keep it interesting. The French, English, Scots, and Danes who settled along it have ensured its culture is equally intriguing.

The Fundy Coast is phenomenal. Yachts, fishing boats, and tankers bob on the waves at high tide, then sit high and dry on the ocean floor when it goes out. The same tides force the mighty Saint John River to reverse its flow. You'll even find a "magnetic" hill that seems to defy gravity. The southwestern shores have spawned more than their share of world-class artists, authors, actors, and musicians. Maybe it's the Celtic influence; maybe it's the fog.

Along the Acadian Coast the water is warm, the sand is fine, and the accent is acutely French—except in the middle. Where the Miramichi River meets the sea there is an island of English, Irish, and Scottish tradition that is unto itself. Many practical people in this region find their livelihood in the forests, in the mines, and on the sea. But with phantom ships and fictional communities, some of the things you encounter along this coast may not be as they seem.

Numbers in the text below correspond to numbers in the margin and on the maps.

Great Itineraries

IF YOU HAVE 3 DAYS

You really should concentrate on one region if you only have a few days. Otherwise, because distances are so great, you would spend all your time driving and have no time to stop and enjoy the scenery, history, culture, and fun. The Saint John River valley is best seen by following the well-marked River Valley Scenic Drive from **Edmundston** ⑦ to **Saint John** ⑪–㉕—a trip of about 380 kilometers (240 miles).

This beautiful journey begins with the vibrant colors and classical music in the botanical gardens at **Les Jardins Park Complex** just outside Edmundston. The drive from Edmundston to 🔝 **Fredericton** ①– ⑤ is about 275 kilometers (170 miles) and offers—in addition to panoramic pastoral and river scenery—a mighty waterfall, a floral clock, and the longest covered bridge in the world. With its Gothic cathedral, Victorian architecture, art galleries, museums, libraries, Provincial Archives, theater company, universities, venerable legislature, and idyllic riverfront pathways, Fredericton is one of the most beautiful and culturally rich provincial capitals in the country. Walk through the historic downtown and don't miss nearby **Kings Landing Historical Settlement** ⑥, a faithful depiction of life on the river in the last century.

The drive from Fredericton to 🖼 **Saint John** ⑪–㉕ is just over 100 kilometers (66 miles) and passes through the village of **Gagetown** ⑩, a must-see for those who love art and history. Saint John is Canada's oldest incorporated city and celebrates its impressive heritage with great enthusiasm. Its artistic community is legendary and its industrial influence is second to none in the province. The result is a modern city with an eclectic blend of culture and ingenuity, sports and entertainment.

IF YOU HAVE 6 DAYS

You can easily explore two regions of the province in six days. To the River Valley region (with one night in 🖼 **Fredericton** ①–⑤ and the next in 🖼 **Saint John** ⑪–㉕) you can add the Fundy Coastal area: Here again it is easily seen by following the well-marked Fundy Coastal Drive. Visit 🖼 **St. Andrews By-the-Sea** ㉗, where art, history, nature, golf courses, and seafood abound. A whale-watching tour, which might entail a ferry ride to either **Grand Manan** ㉘ or **Deer Island** ㉚, is well worth the time and distance. Humpbacks love to perform for whale-watchers, and privileged viewers have spotted the rare right whales.

Route 1 winds about 100 kilometers (66 miles) along the coast past Saint John to **St. Martins,** about 45 kilometers (30 miles) on Route 111. Here nothing much has changed since the days when stout men built even stouter wooden ships. Follow the Fundy Coastal Route signs inland, over hill and dale to **Hampton** (back on Route 1) and up the Kennebecasis River Valley to **Sussex.** The Fundy Coastal Route soon heads back for the bay through Fundy National Park, but travelers would do better to stay on the Trans-Canada Highway for another 75 kilometers (50 miles) and stop in 🖼 **Moncton** ㉝ for two nights. This cosmopolitan city is a microcosm of New Brunswick in that English and French flow with equal ease. It is also a vibrant center of Acadian French culture and education, a great place to shop, and has several atttractions for children.

Moncton is also a good starting point for touring the rest of the Bay of Fundy. Drive 80 kilometers (50 miles) down the coast to Alma, the entrance to **Fundy National Park** ㉛. Here hikers, golfers, and nature lovers will find everything they want. On the way back to Moncton are: **Cape Enrage** with its rappelling, canoeing, and hiking opportunities; and **Hopewell Cape,** where the Fundy Tides have sculpted gigantic flowerpots that turn into islands at high tide.

Up the coast from Moncton you'll find marshlands created by an efficient dyking system brought to North America by the Acadians. In **Memramcook** the struggle of the Acadian people is dramatically documented. **Sackville,** at the very tip of the Bay, is the end of the 325-kilometer (200-mile) journey. The ivy-covered halls of the university here overlook a renowned waterfowl park.

IF YOU HAVE 10 DAYS

With up to 10 days to explore New Brunswick you can see it all—the Acadian Coast as well as the Saint John River valley and the Bay of Fundy coast.

For this tour, you'll follow the Acadian Coastal Drive, another officially designated provincial tourist route that is well marked from **Aulac** to **Campbellton,** a distance of about 400 kilometers (250 miles). But 🖼 **Shediac,** about 30 kilometers (20 miles) north of Moncton, is the place

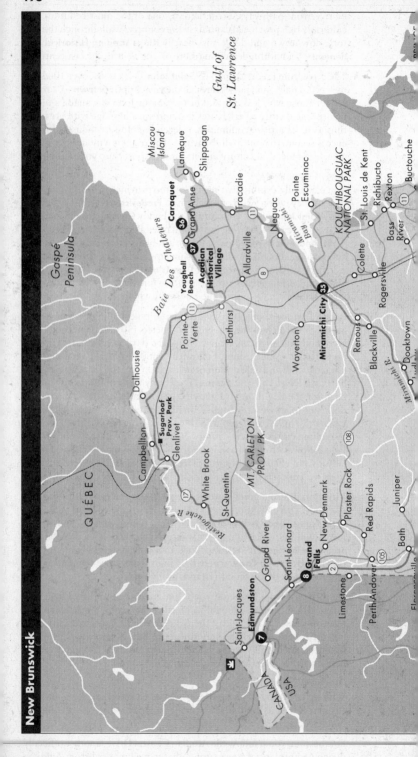

New Brunswick

Gulf of St. Lawrence

Miscou Island
Lamèque
Shippagan

Caraquet
36
Grand Anse
Tracadie

37
Youghall Beach
Acadian Historical Village
Allardville
Neguac
Pointe Escuminac

(11)

Miramichi Bay

KOUCHIBOUGUAC NATIONAL PARK
St. Louis de Kent
Richibucto
Rexton
(11)
Buctouche

Bass River

Pointe Verte
Bathurst
Wayerton
Miramichi River
(8)
35
Miramichi City
Colette
Rogersville

Baie Des Chaleurs

Dalhousie

Renous
Blackville
Doaktown
Miramichi R.

Campbellton
Sugarloaf Prov. Park
Glenlivet
(17)
White Brook
St-Quentin
MT. CARLETON PROV. PK.
(108)

QUÉBEC

Gaspé Peninsula

Restigouche R

Grand River
Saint-Léonard
New Denmark
Plaster Rock
Red Rapids
Juniper

Saint-Jacques
Edmundston
7
8
Grand Falls
(2)
Limestone
Perth-Andover
(105)
Bath

CANADA
USA

Florenceville

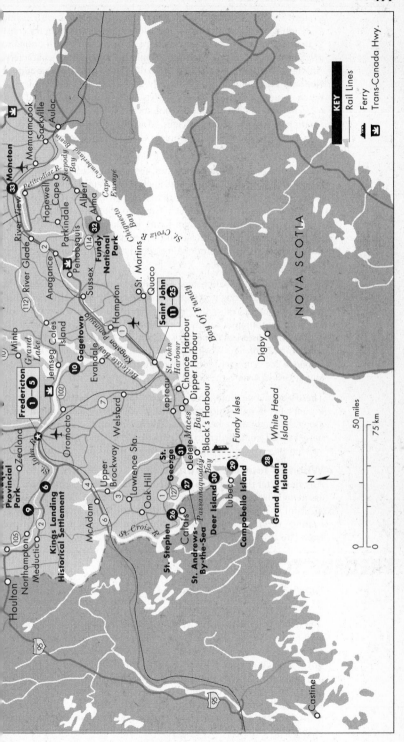

KEY
— Rail Lines
Ferry
Trans-Canada Hwy.

NOVA SCOTIA

50 miles
75 km

Fredericton 1–5
Saint John 11–25
Gagetown 10

Moncton 33
Memramcook
Sackville
Aulac
River View
River Glade
Anagance
Hopewell Cape
Parkindale
Penobsquis
Albert
Alma 32
Cape Enrage
Fundy National Park 114
Sussex
St. Martins
Hampton
Quaco
Chignecto Bay
Shepody Bay
Cumberland Basin
Petitcodiac R.
St. Croix R.

Minto
Grand Lake
Jemseg
Coles Island
Evandale
Welsford
Kingston Peninsula
Belleisle Bay
St. John Harbour
Lepreau
Maces Bay
Chance Harbour
Dipper Harbour
Bay of Fundy

Northampton
Meductic
Houlton
Zealand
Oromocto
John R.
Upper Brockway
McAdam
Oak Hill
Lawrence Sta.
St. George 31
Letete
Black's Harbour
Fundy Isles
White Head Island
Grand Manan Island 28

Kings Landing Historical Settlement
Provincial Park 9
6

St. Stephen 26
Calais
St. Andrews-By-the-Sea 27
Passamaquoddy Bay
Deer Island 30
Campobello Island
Lubec 29

St. Croix R.

Castine

Digby

N

to start. Shediac is famous for lobsters and for Parlee Beach with its fine sand and warm salt water. About 35 kilometers (25 miles) up the coast in **Bouctouche** is La Pays de la Sagouine, a theme park with dramatic presentations of author Antonine Maillet's most famous characters. Another 30 kilometers (20 miles) north is unspoiled **Kouchibouguac National Park,** which protects nearly 250 kilometers (160 miles) of beaches, forests, and peat bogs. The coastal drive from the national park to ⚏ **Miramichi City** ㉟, about 75 kilometers (50 miles), follows a fascinating network of fishing villages. Most of the communities are Acadian, but as you approach Miramichi City, English dominates again.

Incorporating the former towns of Chatham and Newcastle and several small villages and communities, the city of Miramichi is rich in history, tradition, and folklore. Here English, Irish, and Scottish influences have mutated to form a culture the likes of which doesn't exist anywhere else on the globe. Miramichi City also celebrates the salmon that spawn in the mighty Miramichi River, which reaches from this coast into some of the richest forests in the province. A stopover in one of the city's motels will position you perfectly to begin your exploration of the Acadian Peninsula.

It is only about 120 kilometers (75 miles) from Miramichi City to ⚏ **Caraquet** ㊱, but it might as well be a million. The entire peninsula is so different from the rest of the province it is like a trip to a foreign country: This is a romantic land with a dramatic history and an artistic flair. The **Acadian Historical Village** ㊲ is a faithful re-creation of the traditional Acadian way of life. World-famous musicians travel to the **Island of Lamèque** each summer for the International Festival of Baroque Music; and at **Grand Anse** is the only Pope's Museum in North America.

There's more fine dining in and around the city of **Bathurst,** about 65 kilometers (40 miles) along the coast. If you opt for a moonlight stroll along the sandy shore here, beware the phantom ship. By the time you have traveled from Shediac to Bathurst, about 300 kilometers (200 miles), you have seen the most interesting sites on the Acadian Coastal Drive.

When to Tour New Brunswick

Any time after the first of July and continuing into September, you are assured full bloom at Les Jardins, outside Edmundston. Whales are more plentiful in the Bay of Fundy after the first of August. Festivals celebrating everything from jazz to salmon are held around the province from late spring until early fall.

FREDERICTON

Numbers in the margin correspond to points of interest on the New Brunswick map.

The small inland city of Fredericton spreads itself on a broad point of land jutting into the Saint John River. Its predecessor, the early French settlement of St. Anne's Point, was established in 1642, during the reign of the French governor Villebon, who made his headquarters at the junction of the Nashwaak and the Saint John rivers. Settled by Loyalists and named for Frederick, second son of George III, the city serves as the seat of government for New Brunswick's 728,500 residents. Wealthy and scholarly Loyalists set out to create a gracious and beautiful place, and thus even before the establishment of the University of New Brunswick, in 1785, the town served as a center for liberal arts and sciences. It remains a gracious and beautiful place as well as a center of education, arts, and culture. The river, once the only highway to Fredericton, is now a focus of recreation. The streets are shaded

Beaverbrook
Art Gallery, **3**

Christ Church
Cathedral, **5**

Military
Compound
(parade
grounds,
Guard House,
Soldiers'
Barracks), **1**

Provincial
Legislature, **4**

York-Sunbury
Museum, **2**

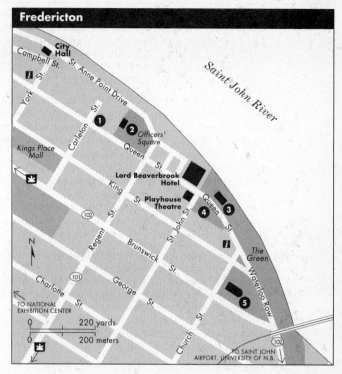

Fredericton

by leafy plumes of ancient elms. Downtown Queen Street runs parallel with the river, and its blocks enclose historic sites and attractions. Most major sites are within walking distance of each other.

❶ The **Military Compound** extends two blocks along Queen Street, at the corner of Carleton Street. The buildings have been restored, and visitors are welcome to tour the Guard House and Soldiers' Barracks; soldiers from the British 15th Regiment will be your guide. Redcoats stand guard; in summer a changing-of-the-guard ceremony takes place in Officer's Square at 11 and 7. ⊠ *Queen St. at Carleton St.,* ☎ *506/453–3747.* 🎫 *Free.* ☉ *Early June–Labor Day, daily 10–6; Sept.–June, group tours by appointment.*

Within the Military Compound stands the **John Thurston Clark Building**—an outstanding example of Second Empire architecture. On the main floor is the **National Exhibition Centre.** You'll have fun with the scintillating displays of arts, crafts, history, science, and technology. Upstairs you'll find the **Sports Hall of Fame,** which celebrates the surprising array of locals who have made sports history, most notably Ron Turcotte, who won horse racing's Triple Crown on the immortal Secretariat. The Hall of Fame's collection of original charcoal portraits of honored members is the largest of its kind in Canada. ⊠ *503 Queen St.,* ☎ *506/453–3747.* 🎫 *Free.* ☉ *Both attractions May–Labor Day, daily 10–6, or by appointment; Labor Day–Apr., Tues.–Sun. noon–5, or by appointment.*

❷ Officer's Quarters houses the **York-Sunbury Museum,** a living picture of the community from the time when only natives inhabited the area, through the pioneer days, to the immediate past. It also contains the shellacked remains of one of Fredericton's legends, the puzzling Coleman Frog. This giant frog, allegedly discovered in nearby Killarney Lake by late hotelier Fred Coleman, supposedly weighed 42 pounds soaking wet at the time of its death (by a dynamite charge set by unorthodox fishermen). Coleman had the frog stuffed and displayed it for years in the lobby of his hotel. Take a look and judge for yourself—the frog just keeps on smiling. ⊠ *Officer's Sq., Queen St.,* ☎ *506/455–6041.* ☞ *$1.* ☉ *May–Labor Day, Mon.–Sat. 10–6 (also July and Aug., Mon. and Fri. 10–9 and Sun. noon–6); Labor Day–mid-Oct., weekdays 9–5, Sat. noon–4; mid-Oct.–Apr., Mon., Wed., and Fri. 11–3, or by appointment.*

The late Lord Beaverbrook, former New Brunswick resident and multimillionaire British peer and newspaper magnate, showered gifts upon

❸ his native province. One of them is the **Beaverbrook Art Gallery,** displaying works by local and internationally acclaimed painters. Salvador Dalí's gigantic canvas *Santiago el Grande* is here as well as canvasses by Reynolds, Turner, Hogarth, Gainsborough, the Canadian Group of Seven, and even Andy Warhol. The gallery has the largest collection in any public institution of the works of Cornelius Krieghoff, famed Canadian landscape painter of the early 1800s. ⊠ *703 Queen St.,* ☎ *506/458–8545.* ☞ *$3.* ☉ *July and Aug., weekdays 9–6, weekends 10–5; Sept.–June, Tues.–Fri. 9–5, Sat. 10–5, Sun. noon–5.*

❹ The interior chamber of the **Provincial Legislature** reflects the taste of the late Victorians. The chandeliers are brass and the prisms are Waterford. The portraits of King George III and Queen Charlotte are replicas of paintings by Sir Joshua Reynolds. There is a free-standing staircase, and a volume of Audubon's *Birds of America* on display. ⊠ *Queen St.,* ☎ *506/453–2527.* ☞ *Free.* ☉ *Legislature tours early June–late Aug., daily 9–8; early Sept.–June, weekdays 9–4; Library weekdays 8:15–5.*

❺ **Christ Church Cathedral,** one of Fredericton's prides, is situated where Queen Street becomes Waterloo Row. Completed in 1853, the gray stone building is an excellent example of decorated Gothic architecture and the first new cathedral foundation built on British soil since the Norman Conquest. Inside you'll see a clock known as "Big Ben's little brother," the test run for London's famous timepiece, designed by Lord Grimthorpe. Free tours are given June–August, daily 9–9.

★ ❻ ☾ To understand New Brunswick's background and history, visit **Kings Landing Historical Settlement,** about 30 kilometers (19 miles) west of Fredericton. This reconstructed village—more than 60 buildings, including homes, an inn, a forge, a store, a church, a school, working farms, and a sawmill—illustrates life in the central Saint John River valley between 1790 and 1900. Winding country lanes, creaking wagons, old houses, and freshly baked bread pull you back a century or more. The costumed staff is friendly and informative. The Tap Room of Kings Head Inn is a congenial spot to try a draft of cold beer or a mug of frosty cider; the restaurant upstairs serves tasty, old-fashioned traveler's fare. After a hearty meal of King George III's roast beef or Mrs. Long's chicken-vegetable pie, drop by the General Store. It's the heart of the community, and the genial storekeeper makes everyone feel welcome. ⊠ *Trans-Canada Hwy.,* ☎ *506/363–5090.* ☞ *$7.50.* ☉ *June–mid-Oct., daily 10–5.*

Dining and Lodging

$$ ✕ **Luna Steakhouse.** Specialties include huge Caesar salads, garlic bread, escargots, brochettes, and Italian food. In fine weather you can dine on an outdoor terrace. Inside, the stucco walls and dark arches make a cozy environment. ⊠ *168 Dundonald St.,* ☎ *506/455–4020. AE, DC, MC, V.*

$$ ✕ **Mei's Chinese Restaurant.** In this family operation downtown, mother Mei does all the cooking. She serves a variety of Chinese cui-

sine including Szechaun, Cantonese, and Taiwanese; dumplings are a house specialty. A Japanese sushi bar is available with an 8-hour reservation. The decor is basic. This is a very popular spot for lunch Monday to Friday. ⊠ *73 Carlton St.,* ☎ *506/454–2177. AE, MC, V. No lunch weekends.*

$–$$ ✕ **Bar B Q Barn.** Special children's menus and barbecued ribs and chicken are the standards; the blackboard lists plenty of other daily dinner specials, such as salmon, scallops, and chili. This popular spot has a convenient downtown location, and is great for winding down; the bar serves fine martinis. ⊠ *540 Queen St.,* ☎ *506/455–2742. AE, DC, MC, V.*

$$$ 🏨 **Howard Johnson Motor Lodge.** This HoJo is on the north side of the river and at the north end of the Princess Margaret Bridge. It has a terrace bar in a pleasant interior courtyard overlooked by the balconies of many of the rooms. Guest-room decor is standard for the chain. ⊠ *Trans-Canada Hwy., Box 1414, E3B 5E3,* ☎ *506/472–0480 or 800/596–4656,* 🖷 *506/472–0170. 116 rooms. Restaurant, bar, indoor pool, tennis courts, exercise room. AE, DC, MC, V.*

$$$ 🏨 **Lord Beaverbrook Hotel.** A central location is this modern, seven-story hotel's main attraction. Some rooms have whirlpools or minibars. There is a veranda overlooking the river off the main dining room, and the bar is lively. ⊠ *659 Queen St., E3B 5A6,* ☎ *506/455–3371 or 800/561–7666,* 🖷 *506/455–1441. 168 rooms. 2 restaurants, bar, no-smoking rooms, indoor pool. AE, DC, MC, V.*

$$$ 🏨 **Sheraton Inn Fredericton.** Within walking distance of downtown, this big hotel with elegant country decor has sunset views over the river from the restaurant and many of the modern rooms. The restaurant has a pleasant outdoor terrace. The gift shop carries topnotch crafts. ⊠ *225 Woodstock Rd., E3B 2H8,* ☎ *506/457–7000 or 800/325–3535,* 🖷 *506/457–4000. 223 rooms. Restaurant, bar, minibars, indoor pool, outdoor pool, sauna, hot tub, exercise room. AE, DC, MC, V.*

$$–$$$ 🏨 **Carriage House Inn.** This Heritage mansion has lovely bedrooms furnished with Victorian antiques. Homemade breakfast, complete with homemade maple syrup for the fluffy pancakes, is served in the solarium. Breakfast is included in the rates. ⊠ *230 University Ave., E3B 4H7,* ☎ *506/452–9924 or 800/267–6068,* 🖷 *506/458–0799. 6 rooms with bath, 4 rooms share bath. MC, V.*

Guided Tours

Heritage Tour Guide Service (☎ 506/459–5950) leads bus tours of Fredericton. Guides dressed in 18th-century costume from the **Calithumpians** (☎ 506/457–1975) theater company give free historical walks from City Hall.

Nightlife and the Arts

The Arts

Theatre New Brunswick (⊠ 686 Queen St., ☎ 506/458–8344) performs in the Playhouse and tours the province. Top musicians and other performers usually appear at the **Aitken Center** (⊠ Rte. 102, ☎ 506/453–5054) on the University of New Brunswick campus near Fredericton.

Nightlife

Fredericton has lively nightlife, with lots of live music in downtown pubs, especially on the weekends. Just wander down **King Street** until you hear your kind of music. **Dolan's Pub** (⊠ 349 King St., ☎ 506/454–7474) has Celtic and folk-style entertainment. **The Lunar Rogue** (⊠ 625 King St., ☎ 506/450–2065) has an old-world pub atmosphere.

Outdoor Activities and Sports

Rowing

Shells, canoes, and kayaks can be rented by the hour, day, or week at the **Aquatic Center** (☎ 506/462–6021), which also arranges guided tours.

Skiing

Crabbe Mountain Winter Park (✉ Box 20187, Kings Place Postal Outlet, Fredericton, E3B 7A2, ☎ 506/463–8311) is in Lower Hainesville (about 55 km/40 miles west of Fredericton). There are 14 trails (nearly half with snowmaking capabilities), a vertical elevation of 853 feet, snowboard and ski rentals, instruction, baby-sitting, and a lounge and restaurant.

Shopping

New Brunswick is famous for its crafts, and mammoth **crafts markets** are held occasionally in Fredericton and every Labor Day weekend in Mactaquac Park (☞ Saint John River Valley to Saint John, *below*). For sale are pottery, blown glass, pressed flowers, metal flowers, turned wood, leather, quilts, and other fine items, many made by members of the New Brunswick Craft Council.

Aitkens Pewter (✉ 65 Regent St., ☎ 506/453–9474) specializes in beautiful pewter goblets, belt buckles, and jewelry. **Mulhouse Country Classics** (✉ Trans-Canada Hwy., ☎ 506/459–8859) is a gem for crafts, Tilley Endurable clothing, and handmade furniture. Excellent men's shoes can be bought at **Hartt's Shoe Factory** (✉ 401 York St., ☎ 506/458–8358). **The Linen Closet** (✉ 397 King St., ☎ 506/450–8393) sells lace, exquisite bedding, and bathroom accessories.

SAINT JOHN RIVER VALLEY TO SAINT JOHN

The Saint John River forms 120 kilometers (75 miles) of the border with Maine and rolls down to Saint John, New Brunswick's largest and Canada's oldest, city. Gentle hills of rich farmland and the blue sweep of the water make this a pretty drive. The Trans-Canada Highway (Route 2) follows the banks of the river for most of its winding 403-kilometer (250-mile) course.

At the northern end of the valley, near the border with Québec, you'll find yourself in the mythical Republic of Madawaska. In the early 1800s the narrow wedge of land was coveted by Québec on one side and New Brunswick on the other; the United States claimed it as well. Seeking to retain it for New Brunswick, Governor Sir Thomas Carleton found it easy to settle with Québec. He rolled dice all night with the governor of British North America at Québec, who happened to be his brother. Sir Thomas won at dawn—by one point. Settling with the Americans was more difficult. The border had always been disputed, and even the lumbermen engaged in combat. Finally, in 1842, the British flag was hoisted over Madawaska county. One old-timer, tired of being asked to which country he belonged, replied, "I am a citizen of the Republic of Madawaska." So began the republic, which exists today with its own flag (an independent eagle on a field of white) and a coat of arms.

Edmundston

❼ *275 km (171 mi) northwest of Fredericton.*

Edmundston, the unofficial capital of Madawaska, has always de-pended on the wealth of the deep forest around it. Even today, Ed-mundston looks to the Fraser Company pulp mills as the major source of employment. It was in these woods that the legend of Paul Bunyan was born. Tales spread to Maine and even to the West Coast. The Foire Brayonne festival, held annually during the last week of July, is proud to claim the title of the biggest festival outside of Québec's Winter Car-nival. It is certainly one of the most lively and vibrant cultural events in New Brunswick, offering concerts by acclaimed artists as well as local musicians and entertainers who enliven the Arts and Crafts Square.

Nearby St. Jacques is home to New Brunswick's **Botanical Garden.** Roses, rhododendrons, alpine flowers, and dozens of annuals and perennials bloom in the eight gardens while Mozart, Handel, Bach, or Vivaldi plays in the background. Two arboretums have coniferous and deciduous trees and shrubs. ⊠ *Main St., St. Jacques, 5 mi northwest of Edmunston,* ☎ *506/739–6335.* ☞ *$4.75.* ☼ *Mid-May–mid-Oct., daily 9–dusk.*

Outdoor Activities and Sports

SKIING

Mont Farlagne (⊠ Box 61, Edmundston, E3V 3K7, ☎ 506/735–8401) in Saint-Jacques, near Edmundston, offers 17 trails on a verti-cal drop of 182 meters (600 feet). Its 4 lifts can handle 4,000 skiers per hour, and there is night skiing on 6 trails. Snowboarding and a tube slide add to the fun. There are equipment rentals, instruction, and a lounge with live music.

Grand Falls

❽ *50 km (30 mi) south of St. Jacques.*

Although Grand Falls is largely French-speaking, English becomes more prevalent as you move down the Saint John River valley. At Grand Falls, the Saint John throws itself over a high cliff, squeezes through a narrow rocky gorge, and emerges as a wider river. The result is a mag-nificent cascade, whose force has worn strange round wells in the rocky bed—some as much as 16 feet in circumference and 30 feet deep. From the Gorge Walk, which starts at the tourist information center ($2), you'll see the holes and the magnificent stream up close. According to Indian legend, a young maiden named Malabeam led her Iroquois captors to their deaths over the foaming cataract rather than guide them to her village. Local history is depicted at the **Grand Falls Historical Museum.** ⊠ *209 Sheriff St.,* ☎ *506/473–5265.* ☞ *Free.* ☼ *July and Aug., Mon.–Sat. 9–5, Sun. 2–5; Sept.–June, by appointment.*

Shopping

The studio and store of the **Madawaska Weavers** (⊠ Main St., St-Léonard, north of Grand Falls, ☎ 506/423–6341) has handwoven items known the world over. Handsome skirts, stoles, and ties are some of the items for sale.

En Route   Stop in **Florenceville** for a look at the small but reputable **Andrew and Laura McCain Gallery** (⊠ McCain St., ☎ 506/392–5249), which has launched the career of many a New Brunswick artist. The Trans-Canada Highway is intriguingly scenic, but if you're looking for less crowded highways and typical small communities, cross the river to Route 105 at Hartland, via the **longest covered bridge** in the world—1,282 feet in length.

Mactaquac Provincial Park

☾ ❾ *197 km (123 mi) south of Grand Falls.*

Within Mactaquac Provincial Park is Mactaquac Pond, whose exis
tence is attributed to the building of the hydroelectric dam that has caused
the upper Saint John River to flood as far up as Woodstock. Park fa
cilities include an 18-hole golf course, two beaches with lifeguards, two
marinas, supervised craft activities, and a dining room. There are 300
campsites; reservations are advised for high season. ⊠ *Rte. 105 at Mac
taquac Dam,* ☎ *506/363–3011.* ☜ *$3.50 per vehicle in summer, free
off-season.* ⊙ *Overnight camping mid-May–Thanksgiving, day an
evening activities early Sept.–mid-May.*

En Route   From Fredericton to Saint John you have a choice of two routes. Route
7 cuts away from the river to run straight south for its fast 109 kilome
ters (68 miles). Route 102 leads along the Saint John River through en
gaging communities. You don't have to decide until you hit **Oromocto**
the site of the Canadian Armed Forces Base, **Camp Gagetown** (not to
be confused with the pretty town of Gagetown farther downriver), the
largest military base in Canada. Prince Charles completed his helicopter
training here. The base has an interesting military museum. ⊠ *Building
A5,* ☎ *506/422–2630.* ☜ *Free.* ⊙ *July and Aug., weekdays 9–5, week
ends and holidays noon–5; Sept.–June, weekdays 8:30–noon and 1–4*

Gagetown

🔟   *50 km (30 mi) southeast of Fredericton.*

Gagetown, a pleasant historic community, bustles with artisans' stu
dios and the summer sailors who tie up at the marina. The gingerbread
trimmed **Tilley House** takes you back to Canada's beginnings. Once the
home of Sir Leonard Tilley, one of the Fathers of the Confederation
it now houses the **Queens County Museum.** ⊠ *Front St.,* ☎ *506/488–
2966.* ☜ *$1.* ⊙ *Mid-June–mid-Sept., daily 10–5.*

Shopping

Flo Grieg's (⊠ Front St., ☎ 506/488–2074) carries superior pottery
Claremont House B&B (⊠ Tilley Rd., ☎ 506/488–2825) displays un
usual batik items and copper engravings. **Loomcrofters** (⊠ Loomcrof
La. off Main St., ☎ 506/488–2400) is a good choice for handwoven
items.

OFF THE
BEATEN PATH
From Gagetown you can ferry across the river to Jemseg and continue
to **Grand Lake Provincial Park** (☎ 506/385–2919), which offers freshwater swimming off the sandy beaches of Grand Lake. At Evandale (farther south) you can ferry to Belleisle Bay and the beautiful **Kingston
Peninsula,** with its mossy Loyalist graveyards and pretty churches.

Saint John

⓫   *70 km (40 mi) south of Gagetown.*

As you travel past farms, churches, and homes and public buildings
you'll begin to get a feeling for how old New Brunswick really is, and
nowhere more so than in Saint John. It was the first incorporated cit
in Canada and has that weather-beaten quality common to so man
antique seaport communities. Although sometimes termed a blue-col
lar town because so many of its residents work for Irving Oil, its gen
teel Loyalist heritage lingers; you sense it in the grand old buildings
the ladies' teas at the old Union Club, and the beautifully restored down
town harbor district.

In 1604, two Frenchmen, Samuel de Champlain and Sieur de Monts
landed here on Saint John the Baptist Day to trade with the natives

Nearly two centuries later, in May of 1785, 3,000 Loyalists escaping from the Revolutionary War poured off a fleet of ships to found a city amid the rocks and forests. From those beginnings, Saint John has emerged as a thriving industrial port.

Up until the early 1980s, the buildings around Saint John's waterfront huddled together in forlorn dilapidation, their facades crumbling and blurred by a century of grime. A surge of civic pride sparked a major renovation project that reclaimed these old warehouses as part of an enchanting waterfront development.

The city has spawned many of the province's major artists—Jack Humphrey, Millar Brittain, and Fred Ross—along with such Hollywood notables as Louis B. Mayer, Donald Sutherland, and Walter Pidgeon. There's also a large Irish population that emerges in a jubilant Irish Festival every March. In July, costumed residents reenact the landing of the Loyalists during the Loyalist City Festival.

Numbers in the margin correspond to points of interest on the Downtown Saint John map.

12 You can easily explore Saint John's town center and harbor area on foot. Get your bearings on **King Street,** the town's old main street, where sidewalks are paved with red brick and lit with old-fashioned lamps.

13 **Market Slip** (by the water at the end of King Street) is where the Loyalists landed in 1783 and is the site of **Barbour's General Store** (☎ 506/658–2939), a 19th-century shop. The scents of tobacco, pickles, smoked fish, and peppermint sticks mingle with the tangy, unforgettable aroma of dulse, an edible seaweed. Beside the store is a 19th-century red schoolhouse, now a tourist information center. Skywalks and underground passages lead from Market Square to City Hall, the Delta Hotel, and Brunswick Square, an adjoining shopping mall. Adjoining

★ **14** Market Slip is **Market Square,** with historic exhibits, shops, restaurants, and cafés.

15 The **New Brunswick Museum** has three floors of natural and human history galleries. The full-size suspended right whale model and skeleton are impossible to miss. Hike through time on a geologic trail, meet the industries that made the province, and see fine art from New Brunswick and around the world. Ongoing events and activities as well as the Family Discovery Centre ensure there is something for everyone. ✉ *Market Sq.,* ☎ *506/643–2300.* ✍ *$5.50, free Wed. 6–9.* ☉ *Mon. and Tues. 9–6, Wed.–Fri. 9–9, Sat. 10–6, Sun. noon–5.*

16 **Old City Market,** built in 1876, occupies a full city block between Germain and Charlotte Streets. Its temptations include fresh-cooked lobster, great cheeses, dulse, and other inexpensive snacking along with much friendly chatter.

17 The imposing **Old Loyalist House,** built in 1810 by Daniel David Merritt, a wealthy Loyalist merchant, is distinguished by its authentic period furniture and eight fireplaces. ✉ *120 Union St.,* ☎ *506/652–3590.* ✍ *$2.* ☉ *June–Sept., Mon.–Sat. 10–5, Sun. 2–5, or by appointment; Oct.–May, by appointment.*

18 The **Old Loyalist Burial Grounds,** off Sydney Street, between King and East Union streets, is like a history book published in stone. Fully restored, it is a delightful spot. At the northeast corner of **King Square,**

19 you'll find a strange mass of metal on the ground. It is actually a great lump of melted stock from a neighboring hardware store that was demolished in Saint John's Great Fire of 1877, in which hundreds of buildings were destroyed.

King Square, **19**

King Street, **12**

Market Slip, **13**

Market Square, **14**

New Brunswick Museum, **15**

Old City Market, **16**

Old Courthouse, **20**

Old Loyalist Burial Grounds, **18**

Old Loyalist House, **17**

Trinity Church, **21**

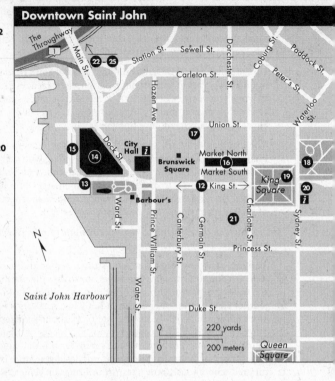

Downtown Saint John

20. The **Old Courthouse,** at the corner of King and Sydney streets, has a spiral staircase, built of tons of unsupported stones that ascends seemingly by miracle for three stories. You can see the staircase year-round during business hours, except when court is in session. *Free.*

21. **Trinity Church** (⊠ 115 Charlotte St., ☎ 506/693–8558) dates from 1877, when it was rebuilt after the Great Fire. Inside, over the west door, note the coat of arms—a symbol of the monarchy—rescued from the council chamber of the colony at Massachusetts Bay. The coat of arms was deemed a worthy refuge and given a place of honor in the church.

Dining and Lodging

$$$ ✕ **Top of the Town.** This dining room at Keddy's Fort Howe Hotel has a spectacular view of the harbor and city and a sophisticated menu. Local seafood is creatively prepared; Fundy scallops are a specialty, and the Maritime Mix—mussels, herring, and lobster—is the favorite of seafood lovers. There is live dinner music nightly, except Sunday. ⊠ *Main and Portland Sts.,* ☎ *506/657–7320. Reservations essential. AE, DC, MC, V.*

$$ ✕ **Mexicali Rosa's.** For a franchise, this restaurant has a lot of character. The decor is essentially Santa Fe–style, with adobe arches and so forth. The specialty is California-Mexican food, which is heavy on sauces, as opposed to Tex-Mex, which concentrates more on meats. Guests waiting to be seated can order a fine margarita in the large lounge. The chimichangas are with good reason the most popular dish. ⊠ *8 Prince William St.,* ☎ *506/652–5252. AE, DC, MC, V.*

$–$$ ✕ **Grannan's.** Seafood brochette with scallops, shrimp, and lobster tail ★ sautéed at your table in a white-wine and mushroom sauce, and a "Captain's Platter" for two, with salmon, halibut, scallops, lobster, jumbo shrimp, oysters, and steamed clams and mussels, are two of the specials in this nautically decorated restaurant. The desserts, including ba-nanas Foster flambéed at your table, are memorable. Dining spills over onto the sidewalk in summer, and there are three lively bars con-nected to the restaurant. ⊠ *1 Market Sq.,* ☎ *506/634–1555. AE, DC, MC, V. No lunch Sun.*

$–$$ ✕ **Incredible Edibles.** Here you can enjoy down-to-earth food—biscuits, garlic-laden hummus, salads, pastas, and desserts—in cozy rooms or, in summer, on the outdoor terrace. The menu also includes beef and chicken dishes. You'll get a good cup of coffee here, too. ⊠ *42 Princess St.,* ☎ *506/633–7554. AE, DC, MC, V. Closed Sun.*

$$$ ✕🏨 **Saint John Hilton.** Part of the Market Square complex, this Hilton is furnished in Loyalist decor; guest rooms overlook the harbor or the town. Mellow antiques furnish corners of the Turn of the Tide dining room and the medieval-style Great Hall, which hosts banquets. A pedestrian walkway system connects this 12-story property to uptown shops, restaurants, bars, a library, museum, and a civic center for con-certs and sporting events. The large Turn of the Tide restaurant has terrific views of the harbor. Although the dining is pleasant at all times, the best meal of the week is the Sunday buffet, with a long table full of dishes from the exotic to the tried-and-true. ⊠ *1 Market Sq., E2L 4Z6,* ☎ *506/693–8484 or 800/561–8282,* ℻ *506/657–6610. 197 rooms. Restaurant, bar, pool. AE, DC, MC, V.*

$$$ ✕🏨 **Shadow Lawn Country Inn.** This charming village inn is in an af-
★ fluent suburb, with tree-lined streets and palatial houses, ten minutes from Saint John. Tennis, golf, horseback riding, and a yacht club are nearby. The inn has nine old-fashioned bedrooms, some with fire-places. The dining room is open to the public for breakfast (Continental breakfast is included in the room rate), lunch, and dinner. Specialties include salmon Florentine and chicken Grand Marnier. ⊠ *Box 41, Rothe-say Rd., E2E 5A3,* ☎ *506/847–7539 or 800/561–4166,* ℻ *506/849–9238. 9 rooms. Restaurant. CP. AE, DC, MC, V.*

Nightlife

Taverns and lounges, usually with music of some kind, provide lively nightlife. Top musical groups, noted professional singers, and other performers regularly appear at **Harbour Station** (⊠ 99 Station St., ☎ 800/267–2800). **O'Leary's Pub** (⊠ 46 Princess St., ☎ 506/634–7135) is in the middle of the Trinity Royal Preservation Area and spe-cializes in old-time Irish fun complete with Celtic performers; on Wednesdays though, Brent Mason, a well-known neo-folk artist, starts the evening with a set then turns the mike over to the audi-ence. **Sherlock's** (⊠ 7 Market Sq., ☎ 506/633–7470) is next to Loy-alist Plaza outside Market Square. The scene really heats up here after midnight with contemporary and retro music spun by a DJ. **Grannan's** (☞ Dining and Lodging, *above*), a restaurant, also have a lively bar scene. **Spirits** (⊠ 1 Market Sq., ☎ 506/634–1555) is a colorful nightclub.

Outdoor Activities and Sports

BOAT TOURS
Harbor tours are offered by **Partridge Island Tours** (☎ 506/693–2598) and **DMK Marine Tours** (☎ 506/635–4150).

KAYAKING
Kayaking along the Fundy coast has become very popular. **Eastern Out-doors** (⊠ Brunswick Sq., ☎ 506/634–1530 or 800/565–2925) has sin-gle and double kayaks, lessons, tours, and white-water rafting on the world-famous Reversing Falls Rapids.

Carleton
Martello
Tower, **24**

Cherry Brook
Zoo, **25**

Fort Howe, **22**

Reversing Falls
Rapids, **23**

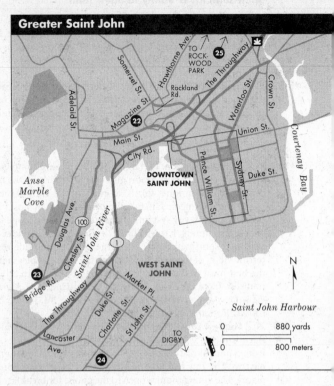

Greater Saint John

WALKING TOURS

Free guided walking tours begin in Market Square at Barbour's General Store. For information call the **Saint John Tourist and Convention Center** (☎ 506/658–2990).

Shopping

Prince William Street provides interesting browsing in antiques shops and crafts boutiques. **House of Tara** (⊠ 72 Prince William St., ☎ 506/634–8272) is wonderful for fine Irish linens and woolens. **Brunswick Square** (⊠ King and Germain Sts., ☎ 506/658–1000) has many top-quality boutiques. **Old City Market,** between Charlotte and Germain streets, bustles Monday–Saturday and always stocks delicious local specialties, such as maple syrup and lobster.

Side Trips

Numbers in the margin correspond to points of interest on the Greater Saint John map.

You will need a car to reach these four sights in greater Saint John.

㉒ **Fort Howe** (⊠ Rockland Rd. and Magazine St.) is a reconstructed fortress atop a cliff overlooking the harbor and affords fine views from its walls (it's not open for tours). It is near the site of Fort LaTour, a French stronghold resolutely defended by Madame LaTour from her absent husband's fur-trading rival. Finally surrendering on the condition that the lives of her men would be spared, the unfortunate woman was betrayed and forced to watch them all put to death. She died shortly after of a broken heart it is said—a romantic fate befitting her former profession as star of the Paris stage. To get here from downtown Saint John drive north on Prince William Street, along Dock Street, across the viaduct and up Main Street, then watch for signs on your right. The fort is in the park on your right.

㉓ Twice daily at the **Reversing Falls Rapids,** the strong Fundy Tides rise faster than the river can empty, and the tide water attempts to push the river water back upstream. When the tide ebbs, the river once again pours over the rock ledges and the rapids appear to reverse themselves. To learn more about the phenomenon watch the excellent and free film shown at the **Reversing Falls Tourist Bureau** (✉ Rte. 100, Reversing Falls Bridge, ☎ 506/658–2937). A pulp mill on the bank is less scenic, and the stench it occasionally sends out is one of the less-than-charming parts of a visit.

㉔ **Carleton Martello Tower,** like Fort Howe, is a great place to survey the harbor. The tower was built during the war of 1812 as a precaution against American attack. The guides will tell you about the spartan life of a soldier living in the stone fort, and an audiovisual presentation outlines its role in the defense of Saint John during World War II. ✉ *Charlotte Extension W,* ☎ *506/636–4011.* 🎟 *Free.* ☉ *June–mid-Oct., daily 9–5.*

㉕ **Cherry Brook Zoo** houses Siberian tigers, wildebeests, and other exotic species. ✉ *R.R. 1, Sandy Point Rd.,* ☎ *506/634–1440.* 🎟 *$4.75.* ☉ *Daily 10–dusk.*

THE FUNDY COAST

Bordering the chilly and powerful tidal Bay of Fundy is some of New Brunswick's loveliest coastline. A tour of the region will take you from the border town of St. Stephen, through tiny fishing villages and past rocky coves, to Fundy National Park, where the world's most extreme tides rise and fall twice daily. The Fundy Isles—Grand Manan Island, Deer Island, and Campobello—are havens of peace that have lured harried mainlanders for generations.

St. Stephen

㉖ *107 km (66 mi) west of Saint John.*

Numbers in the margin correspond to points of interest on the New Brunswick map.

St. Stephen, on the Maine border, is a mecca for chocoholics, who converge on the small town during the Chocolate Festival held the first week in August. "Choctails," chocolate puddings and cakes, and even complete chocolate meals should come as no surprise when you realize that it was here that the chocolate bar was invented. Sample Ganong's famed, hand-dipped chocolates at the factory store, the **Ganong Chocolatier.** ✉ *73 Milltown Blvd.,* ☎ *506/465–5611.* ☉ *July and Aug., weekdays 9–8, Sat. 9–5, Sun. noon–5; Sept.–Dec., Mon.–Sat., Sun. noon–5; Jan.–mid-May, Mon.–Sat. 9–5.*

Follow the Ledge Road to **Crocker Hill Studios,** on the banks of the St. Croix River. Walk down the garden path to the artists' studio with its paintings and carved decoys. It is surrounded by a fragrant, tranquil herb garden. Relax on one of the comfortable garden benches and watch the osprey and eagles soar over the river, and seals make their way upstream on the incoming tide. ☎ *506/466–4251.* 🎟 *$3.* ☉ *June–Sept., daily 10–5; Oct.–June, by appointment.*

St. Andrews-By-the-Sea

㉗ *29 km (18 mi) southeast of St. Stephen.*

St. Andrews-By-the-Sea is one of North America's prettiest and least-spoiled resort towns. Long the summer place of the affluent (mansions ring the town), St. Andrews retains its year-round population of fishermen, and little has changed in the past two centuries. Of the town's

550 buildings, 280 were erected before 1880; 14 have survived from the 1700s. Some Loyalists even brought their homes with them piece by piece from Castine, Maine, across the bay, when the war didn't go their way.

Pick up a walking-tour map at the tourist information center at 46 Reid Avenue (next to the arena) and follow it through the pleasant streets. A particular gem is the **Court House** (⊠ 123 Frederick St., ☎ 506/529-4248), which is still active. Within these old stone walls is the **Old Gaol**, home of the county's archives. Tours are given weekdays 9–5. **Greenock Church,** at the corner of Montegue and Edward streets, owes its existence to a remark someone made at an 1822 dinner party about the "poor" Presbyterians not having a church of their own. Captain Christopher Scott, who took exception to the slur, spared no expense on the building, which is decorated with a carving of a green oak tree in honor of Scott's birthplace, Greenock, Scotland. Also along Water Street are numerous antiques shops and artists' studios.

NEED A
BREAK?
The porch of the **Shiretown Inn** (⊠ 218 Water St., ☎ 506/529-8877) is a perfect place to relax with a snack.

The **Ross Memorial Museum** has a fine antiques collection. ⊠ *188 Montague St., ☎ 506/529-1824. ☞ Free. ☺ Late May–June and early October, Mon.–Sat. 10–4:30; July–Sept., Mon.–Sat. 10–4:30, Sun. 1:30–4:30; shoulder seasons, Tues.–Sat. 10–4:30.*

The **Huntsman Aquarium and Museum** houses marine life and displays including some very entertaining seals. ⊠ *Brandy Cove Rd., ☎ 506/529-1202. ☞ $4. ☺ May–mid-Oct., Tues.–Sat. 10–4:30; July and Aug., Tues.–Sat. 10–4:30, Sun. 1:30–4:30.*

Dining and Lodging

$$-$$$ ╳ **L'Europe.** You may be amused by the cheerful decor in this intimate restaurant, in particular the whimsical objets d'art reflecting the tastes of the German owners. The food is European—some French, Swiss, German dishes, and so on, with particular attention given to seafood. All meals are served with delicious homemade Black Forest bread and pâté. ⊠ *48 King St., ☎ 506/529-3818. Reservations essential. V. No lunch. Closed Mon. and Oct.–early May.*

$$$ ╳▥ **The Algonquin Resort.** The wraparound veranda of this grand old hotel overlooks wide lawns, and the bellmen wear kilts, setting a mood of relaxed elegance. An extension added 50 rooms and three suites to the property; the rooms in the addition are larger than those in the original hotel and have air-conditioning, two queen-size beds, and kitchenettes with microwave, refrigerator, coffee maker, and toaster. The suites have huge fireplaces. Rooms in the original hotel all have TVs. The dining room is noted for its buffets. In good weather, meals are served on the veranda. ⊠ *Rte. 127, E0G 2X0, ☎ 506/529-8823 or 800/563-4299,* ☏ *506/529-4194. 250 rooms. 2 restaurants, 2 bars, outdoor pool, 2 golf courses, tennis. AE, DC, MC, V. Closed winter.*

Outdoor Activities and Sports

GOLF
Algonquin Golf Club (☎ 506/529-3062).

Shopping

The Sea Captain's Loft (⊠ Water St., ☎ 506/529-3190) specializes in English and New Brunswick woolens, English bone china, and marvelous wool yarn. **Cottage Craft** (⊠ Town Sq., ☎ 506/529-3190) employs knitters year-round to make mittens and sweaters from their specially dyed wool. **Tom Smith's Studio** (✉ Water St., ☎ 506/529–4234) is highly regarded for Asian *raku* pottery.

Grand Manan Island

㉘ *Two hours by car ferry from Black's Harbour.*

Grand Manan, the largest of the three Fundy Islands, is also the farthest away from the mainland; you might see spouting whales, sunning seals, or a rare puffin on the way over. Circular herring weirs dot the island's coastal waters, and fish sheds and smokehouses lie beside long wharfs that reach out to bobbing fishing boats. Place names are romantic—Swallowtail, Southern Head, Seven Days Work, and Dark Harbour. It's easy to get around—only about 32 kilometers (20 miles) of road lead from the lighthouse at Southern Head to the one at Northern Head. Grand Manan attracted John James Audubon, that human encyclopedia of birds, in 1831. The puffin is the island's symbol. Whale-watching expeditions can be booked at the Marathon Inn and the Compass Rose (☞ Dining and Lodging *and* Whale Watching, *below*), and scuba diving to old wrecks is popular.

Dining and Lodging

$$–$$$ ✕🏨 **Marathon Inn.** Perched on a hill overlooking the harbor, this gracious mansion built by a sea captain has guest rooms furnished with antiques. About half the rooms have private baths, the others share. Whale- and bird-watching cruises can be arranged for those wishing to explore. The restaurant specializes in seafood. ✉ *Box 129, North Head, E0G 2M0,* ☎ *506/662–8488. 28 rooms. Restaurant, 2 lounges, pool, 2 tennis courts. MC, V.*

$$ ✕🏨 **Compass Rose.** Lovely guest rooms, with comfortable turn-of-the-century furnishings, are available in the two old houses that have been combined into this small, English-style country inn. All the rooms share baths. It is conveniently near the ferry landing, and whale-watching tours can be arranged. A full English breakfast is included in the room rate. Morning and afternoon teas, lunch, and dinner are also served. ✉ *North Head, E0G 2M0,* ☎ *506/662–8570. 8 rooms with shared bath. Dining room. MC, V.*

Outdoor Activities and Sports

TOURS

More than 240 species of seabirds nest on Grand Manan Island, which is a paradise for painters, nature photographers, hikers, and whale watchers. Any of these activities can be arranged by calling **Tourism New Brunswick** (✉ Box 12345, Fredericton, E3B 5C3, ☎ 506/453–2170 or 800/561–0123).

WHALE-WATCHING

One New Brunswick experience that is difficult to forget is the sighting of a huge humpback, right whale, finback, or minke. **Ocean Search** (✉ Marathon Inn, North Head, ☎ 506/662–8488) has whale-watching tours.

Campobello Island

★ **㉙** *45 min ferry ride from Deer Island. By road, drive to St. Stephen, cross the border to Maine, drive about 80 km (50 mi) down Route 1 then Route 190 to Lubec.*

Neatly manicured, preening itself in the bay, Campobello Island has always had a special appeal to the wealthy and the famous. It was here that the Roosevelt family spent their summers. The **home of Franklin Delano Roosevelt,** former president of the United States, is now maintained as a lovely museum in his honor. In the center of Roosevelt International Park, a joint project of the Canadian and American governments, President Roosevelt's home was also the setting for the movie *Sunrise at Campobello*. ⊠ *Roosevelt Park Rd.,* ☎ *506/752–2922.* ⊡ *Free.* ☉ *House late May–mid-Oct., daily 10–6; grounds daily.*

The island's **Herring Cove Provincial Park** has camping facilities and a nine-hole golf course. ⊠ *Welshpool,* ☎ *506/752–7010.*

Dining and Lodging

$$ 🏠 **Owen House.** Mellow with history, this 200-year-old home, now a bit worn, was built by Admiral Owen, who fancied himself ruler of the island. Its gracious old rooms have hosted such luminaries as actress Greer Garson, who stayed here (in a room with a fireplace in the bathroom) when filming *Sunrise at Campobello*. Breakfasts are wonderful—pancakes come topped with local berries. ⊠ *Welshpool, E0G 3H0,* ☎ *506/752–2977. 3 rooms. MC, V.*

$$ ✕🏠 **Lupine Lodge.** Originally a vacation home built by the Adams family (friends of the Roosevelts) around the turn of the century, these three attractive log buildings set on a bluff overlooking the Bay of Fundy are now a modern guest lodge. Nature trails connect it to Herring Cove Provincial Park. Two of the cabins comprise the guest rooms; the third houses the dining room, which specializes in simple but well-prepared local seafood. ⊠ *Box 2, Welshpool, E0G 3H0,* ☎ *506/752–2555. 10 rooms, 1 suite. Restaurant, lounge. MC, V.*

Deer Island

③⓪ *40 min. by free ferry ride from Letete, 13 km (8 mi) south of St. George.*

On Deer Island you'll enjoy exploring the fishing wharves, such as those at **Chocolate Cove.** At **Deer Point** you can walk through a small nature park while waiting for the toll ferry to nearby Campobello Island. If you listen carefully, you may be able to hear the sighing and snorting of **"the Old Sow,"** the second largest whirlpool in the world. If you can't hear it, you'll be able to see it, just a few feet offshore. Exploring the island takes only a few hours; it's 12 kilometers (7½ miles) long, varying in width from almost 5 kilometers (3 miles) to a few hundred feet at some points.

Lodging

$$ 🏠 **45th Parallel Motel and Restaurant.** Deer Island has only one motel—fortunately, it's clean and comfortable. A full breakfast is complimentary, and everything from lobster to pizza is available at the informal restaurant. Three of the rooms have kitchenettes. Pets are welcome. ⊠ *Fairhaven, E0G 1R0,* ☎ *506/747–2231. 10 rooms. Restaurant. AE, MC, V.*

$$ 🏠 **West Isles World B&B.** This white frame house overlooks the cove and offers three snug rooms with an informal country feel; the big upstairs bedroom has a water view. A full breakfast is included in the room rate. One room has a private bath, the other two share. The owners will arrange whale-watching cruises for you. ⊠ *Lord's Cove, E0G 2J0* ☎ *506/747–2946. 3 rooms. No credit cards.*

Outdoor Activities and Sports

WHALE-WATCHING

Cline Marine Tours (☎ 506/529–2287) offers scenic and whale-watching tours.

St. George

③ *40 km (25 mi) east of St. Stephen, 60 km (40 mi) west of Saint John.*

St. George is a pretty town with some excellent bed-and-breakfasts, one of the oldest Protestant graveyards in Canada, and a fish ladder running up the side of a dam.

Lodging

$$–$$$ 🏨 **Granite Town Hotel.** Although this hotel was built in 1991, it has an old-country-inn feeling to it. The decor is subtle, with pine and washed-birch woodwork prominent. Light blues and pinks dominate in the rooms. One side of the building overlooks an apple orchard, the other sits just atop the bank of the Maguadavic River. A Continental breakfast is available but is not included in the room rate; there is a barbecue available for summertime use. Two of the rooms have whirlpool baths. ⊠ *15 Main St., E0G 2Y0,* ☎ *506/755–6415,* FAX *506/755–6009. 32 rooms. Restaurant, bar, boating, bicycles, laundry. AE, D, DC, MC, V.*

Outdoor Activities and Sports

SAILING

Fundy Yacht Sales and Charter (⊠ Rte. 2, Dipper Harbour, Lepreau, E0G 2H0, ☎ 506/634–1530 or 800/565–2925) charters sailboats.

En Route The peaceful, hidden fishing villages of **Maces Bay, Dipper Harbour,** and **Chance Harbour** are much the same as they have been for centuries. At Dipper Harbour, you can rent sea kayaks and canoes, arrange for whale-watching and deep-sea fishing, or buy a lobster roll to munch on while strolling the long sun-warmed wharfs. **St. Martins,** about 45 km (30 miles) east of Saint John, has a rich shipbuilding heritage, whispering caves, miles of beaches, spectacular tides, and a cluster of covered bridges.

Alma

135 km (84 mi) northeast of Saint John.

★ ☙ **③** Alma is the small seaside town that services Fundy National Park. Here you'll find great lobster and the local specialty, sticky buns. **Fundy National Park** is a 206-square-kilometer (80-square-mile) microcosm of New Brunswick's inland and coastal climates. Stand on a sandstone ledge above a dark-sand beach and watch the bay's phenomenal tide rise or fall. ⊠ *Box 40, E0A 1B0,* ☎ *506/887–6000.* 🎟 *$3.25 in summer.*

Outdoor Activities and Sports

GOLF

The **Fundy National Park Golf Club** (☎ 506/887–2970) is nestled near cliffs overlooking the restless Bay of Fundy; deer grazing on the course are one of its hazards.

SKIING AND SNOWMOBILING

Poley Mountain Ski Area (⊠ Box 1097, Sussex, E0E 1P0, ☎ 506/433–3230) is 10 kilometers (6 miles) from Sussex. Its 13 trails, half-pipe, and snowboard park mean there's fun for everyone on this 660-foot vertical drop. Poley is also on the groomed Fundy Snowmobile Trail between Saint John and Moncton, so it's a handy spot to refuel.

En Route The coast road (Route 114) from Alma to Moncton winds through covered bridges and along rocky coasts, past such photogenic spots as the wild driftwood-cluttered beach at **Cape Enrage** and **Hopewell Cape,** home of the famous Giant Flowerpots—rock formations carved by the Fundy Tides.

The 180-foot cliffs at Cape Enrage are ideal for rappelling, a relatively new sport in New Brunswick. By using state-of-the-art ropes, harnesses, and high-tech safety clips for control, it is actually a family sport, although special arrangements have to be made for children who weigh less than 70 pounds. **Cape Enrage Adventures** (⊠ Site 5, R.R. 1; off season, ☎ 506/856–6081; mid-May–mid Sept., 506/887–2273) charges $30 per person for three hours with as many descents as time allows.

MONCTON AND THE ACADIAN PENINSULA

The white sands and gentle tides of the Northumberland Strait and Baie des Chaleurs are as different from the rocky cliffs and powerful tides of the Bay of Fundy as the Acadians are from the Loyalists. This tour takes you from the burgeoning city of Moncton with its glamourous women and high-tech industries, past sandy dunes, and through Acadian fishing villages.

Moncton

③ *80 km (50 mi) north of Alma.*

A friendly town, often called the Gateway to Acadia because of its mix of English and French and its proximity to the Acadian shore, Moncton has a pretty downtown where wisely placed malls do a booming business.

This city has long touted two natural attractions, the Tidal Bore and the Magnetic Hill. You may be disappointed if you've read too much tourist hype. In days gone by, before the harbor mouth filled with silt, the **Tidal Bore** was indeed an incredible sight, a high wall of water that surged in through the narrow opening of the river to fill red mud banks to the brim. It still moves up the river, and the moving wave is worth waiting for, but it's nowhere near as lofty as it used to be, except sometimes in the spring when the tides are very high. Bore Park on Main Street is the best vantage point; viewing times are posted there.

★ ☺ ③ **Magnetic Hill** creates a bizarre optical illusion. If you park your car in neutral at the designated spot, you'll seem to be coasting uphill without power. ⊠ *north of Moncton off Trans-Canada Hwy. (watch for signs).* ☉ *Victoria Day in May–Labor Day, daily 8–8 daily.* ▨ *2$.*

An excellent family water-theme park, **Magic Mountain,** is adjacent to Magnetic Hill. ⊠ *north of Moncton off Trans-Canada Hwy.,* ☎ *506/857–9283.* ▨ *$17.25.* ☉ *Mid-June–July 1 and mid-Aug.–Labor Day, daily 10–6; July–mid-Aug., daily 10–8.*

Among Moncton's notable artificial attractions is the **Acadian Museum,** at the University of Moncton, whose remarkable collection of artifacts reflects 300 years of Acadian life in the Maritimes. ⊠ *Clement Cormier Bldg., Univ. of Moncton,* ☎ *506/858–4088.* ▨ *Free.* ☉ *June–Sept., weekdays 10–5, weekends 1–5; Oct.–May, Tues.–Fri. 1–4:30, weekends 1–4.*

Dining and Lodging

$$ ✕ **Cy's Seafood Restaurant.** This restaurant, decorated in dark wood
★ and brass, has been serving generous portions for decades. Though renowned for its seafood casserole, the restaurant also offers reliable scallop, shrimp, and lobster dishes. You can see the Tidal Bore from the windows. ⊠ *170 Main St.,* ☎ *506/857–0032. AE, DC, MC, V.*

$$ ✕ **Fisherman's Paradise.** In spite of the enormous dining area, which seats more than 350 people, this restaurant serves memorable à la carte seafood dishes in an atmosphere of candlelight and wood furnishings. The children's menu and such down-home specials as lobster-bake make this a good spot for families. ⊠ *375 Dieppe Blvd.,* ☏ *506/859–4388. AE, DC, MC, V.*

$$$ 🏨 **Best Western Crystal Palace.** Moncton's newest hotel has theme rooms (want to be Ali Baba or Elvis for a night?) and, for families, an indoor pool and a miniature wonderland of rides, midway stalls, and coin games. Champlain Mall is just across the parking lot. ⊠ *499 Paul St.,* ☏ *506/858–8584 or 800/528–1234,* FAX *506/858–5486. 115 rooms. Restaurant, indoor pool. AE, D, DC, MC, V.*

$$$ 🏨 **Hotel Beausejour.** Moncton's finest hotel, conveniently located
★ downtown, has friendly service. The lobby is elegant and the decor of the guest rooms echoes the city's Loyalist and Acadian roots. L'Auberge, the main hotel restaurant, has a distinct Acadian flavor. The Windjammer dining room is more formal, modeled after the opulent luxury liners of the turn of the century, and reservations are required. ⊠ *750 Main St.,* ☏ *506/854–4344; in Canada and the U.S., 800/441–1414; in the Maritimes and Québec, 800/561–2328;* FAX *506/858–0957. 314 rooms. 2 restaurants, bar, café, pool. AE, DC, MC, V.*

$$–$$$ 🏨 **Chez Françoise.** This lovely old mansion with a wraparound veranda
★ has been decorated in Victorian style, with hardwood floors and antiques. There are 10 guest rooms (six with private baths) in this house; another building across the street houses an additional 10 (four with baths). Front rooms in the main house have water views. The dining room, open to the public for dinner, serves excellent traditional French cuisine with an emphasis on seafood. ⊠ *93 Main St., Shediac (30 km/20 mi northeast of Moncton),* ☏ *506/532–4233. 20 rooms. Restaurant, bar. AE, DC, MC, V. Closed Jan.–May 1.*

$$–$$$ 🏨 **Marshlands Inn.** In this white clapboard inn, a welcoming double
★ living room with fireplace sets the informal, country atmosphere. Bedrooms are furnished with sleigh beds or four-posters, but some also have such modern touches as air-conditioning and in-room telephones. Most rooms also have private baths, four share. ⊠ *Box 1440, Sackville (53 km/33 mi north of Moncton) E0A 3C0,* ☏ *506/536–0170,* FAX *506/536–0721. 21 rooms. Restaurant. AE, DC, MC, V.*

Nightlife and the Arts

THE ARTS

Top musicians and other performers appear at the **Colosseum** (☏ 506/857–4100).

NIGHTLIFE

Moncton's downtown really rocks at night. **Au Deuxième** (⊠ Main St., ☏ 506/383–6192) has live music on the weekends, mostly Francophone artists. **Ziggy's** (⊠ 730 Main St., ☏ 506/858–8844) offers dance and party music and lots of fun promotions. **Club Cosmopolitain** (⊠ 700 Main St., ☏ 506/857–9117) is open Wednesday through Sunday for rockin' 'n' rollin'. Its **Caveau Bar** has live jazz Fridays 5–9. **Chevy's** (⊠ 939 Mountain Rd., ☏ 506/858–5861) boasts Moncton's biggest dance floor.

Outdoor Activities and Sports

CANOEING AND HIKING

Cape Enrage Adventures (⊠ Site 5, R.R. 1; off season, ☏ 506/856–6081; mid-May–mid Sept., 506/887–2273) leads coastal wilderness canoeing and hiking trips.

Shopping

Five spacious malls and numerous pockets of shops in downtown Moncton make it one of the best places to shop in New Brunswick. Among the crafts to look for are the yarn portraits of La Sagouine, "the old sage" of Buctouche. The sayings of the old Acadian woman, as she does her daily chores, were made famous in Antonine Maillet's novel *La Sagouine.*

En Route Along the coast from Moncton on Route 11 you'll find the salty shores of such unique Acadian communities as **Shediac, Cocagne, Buctouche,** and **Rexton,** with their warm sand dunes, lobster feeds, lighthouses, weathered wharves, and sea-stained churches. The friendliness of the Acadians makes this trip a joy. The white, dune-edged beaches of

★ **Kouchibouguac National Park** (⊠ Off Rte. 11, Kent County, ☎ 506/876–2443) are some of the finest on the continent. Admission to the park is $3 mid-May–mid-October. There are 249 campsites; reservations are not accepted.

Miramichi City

③⑤ *150 km (95 mi) north of Moncton.*

The fabled Miramichi region is one of lumberjacks and fishermen. Celebrated for its salmon rivers and the ebullient nature of its residents (Scottish, English, Irish, and a smattering of French and Indian), this is a land of stories, folklore, and lumber kings. Sturdy wood homes dot the banks of Miramichi Bay at Miramichi City (where the politician and British media mogul Lord Beaverbrook grew up and is buried).

The **Miramichi Salmon Museum** provides a look at the endangered Atlantic salmon and at life in noted fishing camps along the rivers. ⊠ *297 Main St., Doaktown, 80 km (50 mi) southwest of Miramichi City,* ☎ *506/365–7787.* ⊙ *June–Sept. daily 9–5.* 🖭 *$4.*

The **Woodmen's Museum,** with artifacts that date from the 1700s to the present, is in what looks like two giant logs set on more than 60 acres of land. The museum portrays a lumberman's life through displays, but its tranquil grounds are excuse enough to visit. There are picnic facilities and camping sites. ⊠ *Rte. 8, Boiestown, 110 km (66 mi) southwest of Miramichi City,* ☎ *506/369–7214.* 🖭 *$5.* ⊙ *May–Sept. daily 9–5.*

Lodging

$$$ 🏨 **Pond's Chalet Resort.** You'll get a traditional fishing-camp experience here in a lodge and chalets set among trees overlooking a salmon river. The accommodations here in Ludlow, 15 kilometers (9 miles) northwest of Boiestown, are comfortable but not luxurious. The dining room in the lodge turns out reliable but undistinguished food. ⊠ *Ludlow E0C 1N0 (watch for signs on Rte. 8),* ☎ *506/369–2612,* 🖷 *506/369–2293. 10 rooms in lodge, 14 cabins. Bar, dining room. AE, DC, MC, V.*

$$–$$$ 🏨 **Wharf Inn.** Here in Miramichi country, the staff is friendly and the restaurant serves excellent salmon dinners. This low-rise modern building has two wings; guest rooms in the executive wing have extra amenities. ⊠ *Jane St.,* ☎ *506/622–0302,* 🖷 *506/622–0354. 70 rooms. Restaurant, bar, patio lounge, no-smoking rooms, indoor pool. AE, DC, MC, V.*

Outdoor Activities and Sports

DOGSLEDDING

Miramichi Four Seasons Outfitters (⊠ Box 705, R.R. 2, ☎ 506/622–0089) offers custom packages for all levels.

Rocky coastline and inland highland trails offer hiking opportunities for both experienced and casual trekkers. **Miramichi Four Seasons Outfitters** (⊠ Box 705, R.R. 2, ☎ 506/622–0089) leads hiking tours.

Caraquet

36 *118 km (73 mi) north of Miramichi City.*

Caraquet, on the Acadian Peninsula, is perched along the Baie des Chaleurs, with Québec's Gaspé Peninsula beckoning across the inlet.

★ ♨ **37** The pièce de résistance of the Acadian Peninsula is, without doubt, the **Acadian Historical Village**, 10 kilometers (6 miles) west of Caraquet. As Kings Landing (near Fredericton) depicts the early English settlement, this village re-creates an early Acadian community between 1780 and 1890. Summer days are wonderfully peaceful: the chapel bell tolls, ducks waddle and quack under a footbridge, wagons creak, and the smell of hearty cooking wafts from cottage doors. Costumed staff act as guides, and a restaurant serves old-Acadian dishes. ⊠ *Rte. 11,* ☎ *506/726–2600.* ▣ *$8.* ☉ *June–Labor Day, daily 10–6; Sept., daily 10–5.*

Lodging

$$$ 🏨 **Aylesford Inn.** Truly a find, this friendly inn in a Victorian man-
★ sion in Campbellton, near the Québec border and Sugarloaf Provincial Park, has guest rooms handsomely furnished with Eastlake and Canadian-pine antiques. Large gardens and verandas have views of the Restigouche River. Excellent dinners are served to guests (quail and frogs' legs are featured entrées), and full breakfasts are included in the room rate. Nonguests are welcome for afternoon tea. ⊠ *8 MacMillan Ave., E3N 1E9,* ☎ *506/759–7672. 6 rooms. Dining room, croquet. AE, MC, V.*

$–$$ 🏨 **Hotel Paulin.** The word *quaint* really fits this property. Each pretty room has its own unique look, with old pine dressers and brass beds, and the colors are as bright and cheerful as the seaside town. About half the rooms have private baths. An excellent small dining room specializes in fresh fish cooked to perfection. ⊠ *143 blvd. St-Pierre W, E1W 1B6* ☎ *506/727–9981. 9 rooms, 1 suite. Dining room. MC, V.*

Outdoor Activities and Sports

SKIING
Sugarloaf Provincial Park (⊠ Box 629, Atholville, E0K 1A0, ☎ 506/789–2366) is in Campbellton, 180 kilometers (112 miles) north of Caroquet. The eight ski trails on this 507-foot vertical drop accommodate all levels of skiers. There are also 25 kilometers (16 miles) of cross-country ski trails, snowshoeing, tobogganing, sliding, and skating. Ski instruction and equipment rentals are available, and there are a lounge and a cafeteria.

NEW BRUNSWICK A TO Z

Arriving and Departing

By Car Ferry
There are car ferries from Prince Edward Island and Nova Scotia. **Marine Atlantic** (☎ 902/794–5700) has a car-and-passenger ferry from Digby, Nova Scotia, which takes 2½ hours. For reservations in the United States, call 800/341–7981. The trip from Prince Edward Island takes 30–45 minutes; reservations are not required.

By Plane
Air Canada and its regional carrier **Air Nova** (☎ in the U.S., 800/776–3000; in Canada, 800/563–5151) serve New Brunswick in Saint John, Moncton, Fredericton, Bathurst, and St-Léonard, and fly to the Atlantic provinces from Montréal, Toronto, and Boston.

Canadian Airlines International operates through **Air Atlantic** (☎ in the U.S., 800/426–7000; in Canada, 800/665–1177) in Saint John, Fredericton, Moncton, Charlo, and Miramichi, and serves the Atlantic provinces, Montréal, Ottawa, and Boston.

By Train
VIA Rail (☎ 800/562–3952) offers passenger service three times a week from Moncton to Montréal and Halifax. Bus connections are available to Prince Edward Island and Newfoundland from Moncton.

Getting Around

By Bus
SMT Eastern Ltd. (☎ 506/859–5100) runs buses within the province and connects with most major bus lines.

By Car
New Brunswick has an excellent highway system with numerous facilities. The Trans-Canadian Highway, marked by a maple leaf, is the same as Route 2. The only map you'll need is the one available at the tourist information centers listed below. Major entry points are at St. Stephen, Houlton, Edmundston, and Cape Tormentine from Prince Edward Island, and Aulac from Nova Scotia.

Contacts and Resources

Bicycling
Covered Bridge Bicycle Tours (✉ Dept. F, Box 693, Main Post Office, Saint John E2L 4B3, ☎ 506/849–9028) leads bike trips in the province.

Emergencies
Dial 911 for medical, fire, and police emergencies anywhere in New Brunswick.

Fishing
New Brunswick Fish and Wildlife (☎ 506/453–2440) can give you information on sporting licenses and tell you where the fish are.

Hiking
For general trail information, contact Eric Hadley at the **New Brunswick Trails Council** (✉ Department of Natural Resources and Energy, Box 6000, Fredericton E3B 5H1, ☎ 506/453–2383).

Hospitals
Dr. Everett Chalmers Hospital (✉ 700 Priestman St., Fredericton, ☎ 506/452–5400). **Moncton City Hospital** (✉ 135 MacBeath Ave., Moncton, ☎ 506/857–5111). **Dr. Georges Dumont Hospital** (✉ 330 Archibald St., Moncton, ☎ 506/862–4000). **Saint John Regional Hospital** (✉ Tucker Park Rd., Saint John, ☎ 506/648–6093). **Chaleur Regional Hospital** (✉ 1750 Sunset Dr., Bathurst, ☎ 506/548–8961). **Campbellton Regional Hospital** (✉ 189 Lilly Lake Rd., Campbellton, ☎ 506/789–5000). **Edmundston Regional Hospital** (✉ 275 Hébert Blvd., ☎ 506/739–2211). **Miramichi Regional Hospital** (✉ 500 Main St., Chatham Head, Miramichi, ☎ 506/623–3000).

Snowmobiling

For information on snowmobiling in New Brunswick contact the **New Brunswick Federation of Snowmobile Clubs** (⊠ Box 536, Miramichi E1V 3T7, ☎ 506–325–2627).

Visitor Information

Tourism New Brunswick (⊠ Box 12345, Fredericton E3B 5C3, ☎ 506/453–2170 or 800/561–0123) can provide information on the seven provincial tourist bureaus. Also helpful are information services of the cities of **Bathurst** (☎ 506/548–0410), **Campbellton** (☎ 506/789–2367), **Fredericton** (☎ 506/452–9508), **Moncton** (☎ 506/853–3590), and **Saint John** (☎ 506/658–2990).

12 Prince Edward Island

In the Gulf of St. Lawrence north of Nova Scotia and New Brunswick, Prince Edward Island seems too good to be true, with its crisply painted farmhouses, manicured green fields rolling down to sandy beaches, the warmest ocean water north of Florida, lobster boats in trim little harbors, and a vest-pocket capital city, Charlottetown, packed with architectural heritage.

PRINCE EDWARD ISLAND SEEMS too good to be true, with its crisply painted farmhouses, manicured green fields rolling down to sandy beaches, the warmest ocean water north of Florida, lobster boats in trim little harbors, and a vest-pocket capital city packed with architectural heritage.

By Silver Donald Cameron

Updated by Julie V. Watson

When you experience Prince Edward Island, you'll understand instantly that it was no accident that Lucy Maud Montgomery's novel of youth and innocence, *Anne of Green Gables,* was framed against this land. What may have been unexpected, however, was how the story burst on the world in 1908 and is still selling untold thousands of copies every year. After potatoes and lobsters, Anne is the island's most important product.

Anne is everywhere on the island: At the Confederation Centre of the Arts in Charlottetown you can often peruse Montgomery's original handwritten manuscript; even on cars throughout the province you'll see the freckled redhead, as the government stamped her face on the province's license plates. But Anne's fame stretches beyond Prince Edward Island and Cavendish—fondly referred to as Anne's land. She attracts international attention, especially from the Japanese, with whom she is hugely popular.

Those visitors who have come because of Anne usually leave having fallen in love with her island. Outside the tourist mecca of Cavendish, the island seems like an oasis of peace in a world of turmoil. Here you'll find fishing ports, crossroads villages, small family farms. You can choose full-service resorts and gourmet restaurants, or bed-and-breakfasts and lobster suppers. You can opt for a farm vacation or take a deep-sea fishing cruise.

When you're in Charlottetown see the musical *Anne of Green Gables.* Have dinner first—there are great little places within a few blocks of the theater.

Pleasures and Pastimes

The Arts
The arts, particularly writing and the theater, are an integral part of the Island. The highlights of the island's theater season are the productions that take place during the summer. The grandest is the Charlottetown Festival, which happens from June through mid-September at the Confederation Centre of the Arts. Other productions in Summerside, Georgetown, and Victoria each have their own unique charm. Dinner theater has a large following and takes place in Charlottetown, Summerside, and Mont-Carmel. Concerts and musical festivals abound on the island, especially in summer. Live traditional Celtic music, with fiddling and step-dancing, can be heard almost any day of the week.

Beaches
Prince Edward Island is ringed by beaches, and few of them are heavily used. Ask a dozen islanders to recommend their favorites. Bothwell Beach, near Souris, says one—miles of singing sands, utterly deserted. West Point, says a second—lifeguards, restaurant nearby, showers at the provincial park. Greenwich, near St. Peter's Bay, another suggests—a half-hour walk through magnificent wandering dunes brings you to an endless empty beach.

Bicycling
Prince Edward Island is popular with bike-touring companies for its moderately hilly roads and stunning scenery. Level areas can be found

over most of the island, especially east of Charlottetown to Montague and along the north shore. However, shoulderless, narrow, secondary roads in some areas and summer's car traffic can be challenging for cyclists. A 9-kilometer (6-mile) path near Cavendish campground loops around marsh, woodland, and farmland. Cycling trips are organized throughout the province, and Prince Edward Island's visitor services can recommend tour operators. Bicycles can be rented in Charlottetown and Cavendish.

Dining

On Prince Edward Island, wholesome, home-cooked fare is a matter of course. Talented chefs are found about the Island ensuring fine cuisine in each region. The service is friendly—though a little laid back at times—and the setting is generally informal. Seafood is usually good anywhere on the island, with top honors being given to lobster and any dish using local produce.

Look for lobster suppers, offered both commercially and by church and civic groups. These meals feature lobster, rolls, salad, and mountains of sweet, home-baked goodies. Regular suppers are held daily in New London, New Glasgow, St. Ann's Church in Hope River, and Fisherman's Wharf in North Rustico from mid-May through September. Check the local papers, bulletin boards at local grocery stores, or Visitor Information Centres for community suppers.

CATEGORY	COST*
$$$$	over $35
$$$	$25–$35
$$	$15–$25
$	under $15

per person, excluding drinks, service, 10% sales tax, and 7% GST

Fishing

Prince Edward Island has some of the best brook-trout fishing in eastern Canada, as well as excellent deep-sea fishing off the island's northeast coast. Charter boats leave daily in summer from the fishing ports of Cove Head, North Lake, and North Rustico, for very elusive tuna and rich mackerel fishing; there are more than 20 boat charters to choose from. Clam digging is possible in many less-populated coastal areas around the island. Ask at the Visitor Information Centres about open areas.

Golf

Prince Edward Island's 11 beautiful courses with scenic vistas offer a diversity that would be hard to duplicate in such a small geographic area. Golfing is virtually hassle-free: Tee times are easily booked any day of the week, rates are inexpensive, and courses uncrowded, particularly in the fall.

Hiking

Hiking within the lush scenic areas of Prince Edward Island National Park and provincial parks is encouraged with marked trails. Much of the trail system follows abandoned railway lines that are being upgraded to provide quality surfaces great for walking or cycling to hiking trails. Confederation Trail, a provincial linear trail system, will eventually allow users to travel 350 kilometers (217 miles) within the province (half of the trail is now completed). Or, pull over near a beach, take off your shoes, wiggle your toes in the sand, and listen to the sound of the surf and the cry of the gulls as you explore miles of coastal nature.

Lodging

Prince Edward Island offers a variety of accommodations at a variety of prices, from full-service resorts and luxury hotels to moderately priced motels, cottages, and lodges, to farms that take guests. Lodgings in summer should be booked early, especially if you are planning a long stay.

CATEGORY	COST*
$$$$	over $75
$$$	$55–$75
$$	$40–$55
$	under $40

All prices are for a standard double room, excluding 10% provincial sales tax and 7% GST.

Exploring Prince Edward Island

Prince Edward Island has been described as "two long sandbars with a potato field in the middle." It is indeed a rich agricultural region surrounded by beautiful sand beaches, delicate dunes, and stunning red sandstone cliffs. The rural landscape tends to become more rolling as you drive from west to east; even so, you are never more than 15 minutes from a beach or waterway.

The province is very irregular in shape, with deep inlets and tidal streams almost dividing it into three nearly equal parts, known locally by their county names of Kings, Queens, and Prince (east to west). The land in the east and central sections consists of gentle hills, which create a rolling landscape that can tax bicyclists. Even though consistently hilly, the land never rises to a height of more than 500 feet above sea level. To the west, from Summerside to North Cape, the land is flatter.

Great Itineraries

Visitors often tour the island in a loop: taking the ferry from New Brunswick to Bordon, seeing Anne country and the PEI National Park, and departing by ferry from Wood Island to Nova Scotia. To more deeply experience the island's character, stray to the wooded hills of the east—to compact, bustling Montague, straddling its river; or to the estuarine maze of Murray Harbour. Or go west to superb, almost-private beaches, the Acadian parishes of Egmont Bay and Tignish, and the silver-fox country around Summerside. Even if you're in a rush, it won't take long to get off the beaten path: In most places you can cross the island, north to south, in half an hour or so. Any of the four tours detailed in this chapter can be completed in one day, however, we suggest extending them to two or three days. Charlottetown is primarily a walking tour, while the others follow the major scenic highways—Blue Heron Drive, Kings Byway, and Lady Slipper Drive. There are plenty of chances to get out of the car, go fishing, hit the beach, photograph wildflowers, or just watch the sea roll in.

Numbers in the text correspond to numbers in the margin and on the Prince Edward Island and Charlottetown maps.

IF YOU HAVE 1 DAY

Leaving **Charlottetown** ①–⑨ on Route 2 west, take Route 15 north to **Brackley Beach.** This puts you onto a scenic drive marked with signs depicting a blue heron. This drive is approximately 85 miles in length, allowing plenty of time for sightseeing, shopping, and dining. Route 6 west will take you to **Rustico** and **Cavendish** ⑪, areas that have numerous crafts shops, restaurants, and entrances to **PEI National Park** ⑩. Cavendish is the home of the fictional character Anne of Green Gables created by Lucy Maud Montgomery. Green Gables is open to the public and is part of the National Park complex. This area has enough shops and attractions for a full day, or if you prefer to keep exploring, continue west on Route 6, where charming tearooms and museums vie with fishing wharfs and scenic vistas for your attention. Blue Heron Trail joins Route 20, where you'll find the **Anne of Green Gables Museum** at Silver Bush; it offers a glimpse of the life of author Lucy Maud Montgomery in the early 1900s, with a farm, wagon rides, and a family atmosphere. Continue west, then south on Route 20 and rejoin Route 2 south until turning onto Route 1 east and back to Charlottetown.

IF YOU HAVE 3 DAYS

Leaving Charlottetown early in the day, follow Route 1 east to **Wood Islands,** where it links with Route 4. This puts you onto the Kings Byway Scenic Drive, marked with signs featuring a king's crown. Continue on to **Murray River** or **Montague** for a seal-watching tour, and spend the afternoon at **Brudenell Provincial Park,** where you can go canoeing, swimming, golfing, or hiking. Overnight in ⊞ **Bay Fortune.** The next day, a picnic lunch will be the perfect wrap-up to a morning spent at Basin Head Fisheries Museum in **Basin Head.** Continue east on Kings Byway to East Point for a stop at the lighthouse, which marks the most easterly point on the Island. When you leave the lighthouse you will proceed west along the north shore. Proceed to the eastern entrance of the PEI National Park; overnight in ⊞ **Brackley Beach.** Spend day three in the National Park, then follow Route 15 south back to Charlottetown.

When to Tour Prince Edward Island

Prince Edward Island is primarily a summer destination for families with children. Many family attractions operate from late June to early September only. Adults might like to visit in the shoulder seasons (May, September, and October). Fall is an excellent time for hiking and golfing. Winters are unpredictable, but can be harsh. Among the most overlooked island attractions are cross-country skiing, snowmobiling, and ice-skating on ponds—usually excellent from January through March. Nightlife is limited in winter months. Prince Edward Island is not subject to rush hour; in fact the only time that "town" really gets busy is on a rainy day.

CHARLOTTETOWN

56 km (35 mi) east of Borden.

Sheltered on an arm of the Northumberland Strait, Prince Edward Island's oldest city is named for the stylish consort of King George III. Charlottetown, the largest community on the island, is a small city (population 30,000) with generous, gingerbread-clad Victorian houses and tree-shaded squares. It is often called "the Cradle of Confederation," a reference to the 1864 conference held here that led to the union of Nova Scotia, New Brunswick, Ontario, and Québec in 1867, and eventually, to Canada itself.

Charlottetown's main activities center on government, tourism, and private commerce. While new suburbs were springing up around it, the core of Charlottetown remained unchanged, and the waterfront has been restored to recapture the flavor of earlier eras. Today the waterfront includes the Prince Edward Hotel; an area known as Peake's Wharf and Confederation Landing Park, with informal restaurants and handicraft and retail shops; and a marked walking path. You can easily explore the downtown on foot in a couple of hours. Irene Rogers's *Charlottetown: The Life in Its Buildings* gives much detail about the architecture and history of downtown Charlottetown.

With the exception of the Charlottetown Driving Park, this tour of Charlottetown can be easily walked in a half day to full day, depending on your predilection to stop and smell the roses.

① Charlottetown's historic redbrick core is the setting for the modern, concrete **Confederation Centre of the Arts,** opened in 1964 as a tribute to the Fathers of Confederation. The Confederation Centre houses a 1,100-seat theater, a memorial hall, a gift shop with Canadian crafts, an art gallery and museum, and restaurant and catering facilities. From June to September the center's **Charlottetown Festival** offers excellent professional theater, including the annual musical adaptation of *Anne of Green Gables.* ✉ *Queen St. between Grafton and Richmond Sts.,* ☎ *902/628–1864; box office, 902/566–1267;* FAX *902/566–4648.* ◷ *Sept.–June, daily 9–5; hrs extended June–Sept.*

★ ② The Georgian-style **Province House National Historic Site,** the meeting place of the provincial legislature, is next door to the Confederation Centre. The three-story sandstone building, completed in 1847, contains the Confederation Chamber, where representatives of the 19th-century colonies met to discuss creating a union. Rooms, restored to their 1864 condition, and the legislative chamber are open to the public. Displays and a slide presentation portray the historic meeting. ✉ *Richmond St.,* ☎ *902/566–7626.* ◱ *Donation accepted.* ◷ *Sept.–June, weekdays 9–5; July and Aug., daily 9–8.*

③ Two churches near Province House are noteworthy. **St. Paul's Angli-**
④ **can Church** (✉ 101 Prince St.) was erected in 1747, making it the oldest Protestant church on the island. **St. Dunstan's Basilica** (✉ Great George St.) is the seat of the Roman Catholic diocese on the island. Known for its twin Gothic spires and fine Italian carvings, it is one of Canada's largest churches.

NEED A BREAK? The **Merchantman Pub** (✉ 23 Queen St., ☎ 902/892-9150), in a historic building just steps from the waterfront walking path, is a cozy spot.

⑤ **Confederation Landing Park** is at the bottom of Great George Street on the water. The waterfront walking path, or **Peake's Wharf,** is a popular spot, with restaurants, crafts shops, and boardwalks. You can walk along the waterfront from Peake's to Victoria Park—a wonderful summer evening stroll.

⑥ The **All Saints Chapel** in **St. Peter's Cathedral** (✉ Rochford Sq.) contains murals by Robert Harris, the famous Canadian portrait painter. The chapel was designed in 1888 by his brother W. C. "Willy" Harris, the most celebrated of the island's architects, and the designer of many historic homes and buildings.

⑦ At the southern tip of the city is the beautiful 40-acre **Victoria Park,** overlooking Charlottetown Harbour, a perfect place to stroll, picnic, or watch a baseball game. Next to the park, on a hill between groves of white birches, is the white colonial **Government House,** built in 1835 as the official residence of the province's lieutenant-governors. The house is not open to the public. ✉ *Park, Lower Kent St.* ◷ *Daily sunrise–sunset.*

⑧ **Beaconsfield Historic House,** a gracious Victorian mansion, is near the entrance to Victoria Park. Designed by architect W. C. Harris and built in 1877, this is one of the island's finest residential buildings. On site are a gift shop and bookstore. Special events such as theatrical and musical performances, socials, and lectures are held regularly. ✉ *2 Kent St.,* ☎ *902/368–6600.* ◱ *$2.50.* ◷ *June–Labor Day, daily 10–5; Labor Day–June, Tues.–Sun. 1–5.*

Prince Edward Island

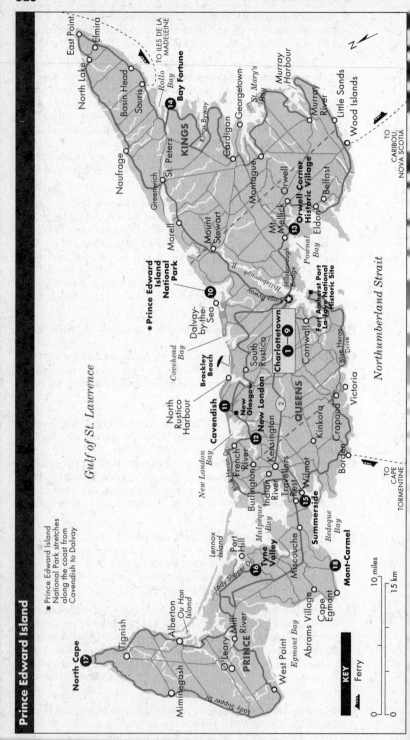

* Prince Edward Island National Park stretches along the coast from Cavendish to Dalvay.

Gulf of St. Lawrence

Northumberland Strait

TO ILES DE LA MADELEINE

TO CARIBOU, NOVA SCOTIA

TO CAPE TORMENTINE

East Point
Elmira
North Lake
Basin Head
Souris
Naufrage
Rollo Bay
14 Bay Fortune
Greenwich
St. Peters
Kings Byway
KINGS
Georgetown
Cardigan
St. Mary's Bay
Murray Harbour
Murray River
Little Sands
Wood Islands
Montague
Orwell
13 Orwell Corner Historic Village
Mt. Mellick
Eldon
Belfast
Mount Stewart
Morell
Pownal Bay
Hillsborough R.
Kings Byway
Hillsborough Bridge
Prince Edward Island National Park
10
Dalvay-by-the-Sea
Conehead Bay
Brackley Beach
★ Charlottetown **1–9**
Fort Amherst Port La Joye National Historic Site
Cornwall
North Rustico Harbour
South Rustico
QUEENS
Blue Heron Drive
New London Bay
11 **Cavendish**
New Glasgow
12 New London
Kensington
(2)
Kinkora
Victoria
Crapaud
Borden
Blue Heron Dr.
French River
Burlington
Indian River
Travellers Rest
Wilmot
15
Summerside
Bedeque Bay
Malpeque Bay
Lennox Island
Port Hill
16 **Tyne Valley**
Miscouche
18 **Mont-Carmel**
Lady Slipper Dr.
Ou Hon Island
Alberton
Tignish
O'Leary
Mill River
Cape Egmont
Egmont Bay
Abrams Village
West Point
PRINCE
Lady Slipper Dr.
Mimenegash
North Cape
17

10 miles
15 km

KEY
Ferry

Beaconsfield, **8**
Charlottetown Driving Park, **9**
Confederation Centre of the Arts, **1**
Confederation Landing Park, **5**
Province House, **2**
St. Dunstan's Basilica, **4**
St. Paul's Anglican Church, **3**
St. Peter's Cathedral, **6**
Victoria Park, **7**

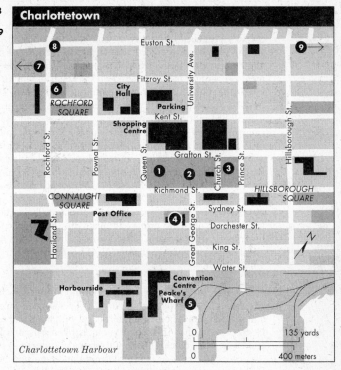

Charlottetown

❾ The **Charlottetown Driving Park,** at the eastern end of the city, is the home of a sport that is dear to the hearts of islanders—harness racing. Standardbred horses are raised on farms throughout the island, and harness racing on the ice and on country tracks has been popular for generations. In fact, there are more horses per capita on the island than in any other province of Canada. ⊠ *Kensington Rd.,* ☎ *902/892–6823.* ⛶ *$2.* ⊘ *Races Jan.–May, once per wk; June, July, and most of Aug., 3 nights per week; Old Home Week (mid-Aug.), Mon.–Sat. twice daily.*

The Arts

The **College of Piping and Celtic Performing Arts of Canada** (⊠ Summerside, ☎ 902/436–5377) presents Friday night *ceilidhs* (dances with live traditional entertainment) at the **Benevolent Irish Hall** (⊠ Charlottetown, ☎ 902/892–2367) and Sunday concerts of classical, sacred, and traditional music at **St. Mary's Church** (☎ 902/836–3733) in Indian River, between Charlottetown and Summerside.

Dining and Lodging

$$$$ ✕ **The Selkirk.** The island's most sophisticated dining room has an extensive, imaginative menu and special theme nights. Service and ambience match the chefs' excellence, and a pianist plays in the evenings. Few other island eateries can compete with the expertly presented gourmet delights served here. Local fare is the specialty. ⊠ *Prince Edward Hotel, 18 Queen St.,* ☎ *902/566–2222 or 800/441–1414. Reservations essential. AE, DC, MC, V.*

$$$ ✕ **Culinary Institute of Canada.** Students at this internationally acclaimed school cook and present lunch and dinner during the school year as part of their training. Here's an opportunity to enjoy excellent food and top service at reasonable prices. Call for schedule and reservations. ⊠ *Kent St.,* ☎ *902/566–9550. Reservations essential. MC, V. Closed May–Sept.*

$$–$$$ ★ ✕ **Claddagh Room Restaurant.** You'll find some of the best seafood in Charlottetown here. The "Galway Bay Delight," one of the Irish owner's specialties, is a savory combination of fresh scallops and shrimp sautéed with onions and mushrooms, flambéed in Irish Mist, and doused with fresh cream. A pub upstairs has live Irish entertainment every night in summer and on weekends in winter. ✉ *131 Sydney St.,* ☎ *902/892–9661. Reservations essential. AE, DC, MC, V.*

$$ ✕ **Off Broadway.** Popular with Charlottetown's young professional set is this cozy spot that began modestly as a crepe-and-soup joint. You can still make a meal of the lobster or chicken crepe and the spinach or Caesar salad that's served with it, but now the restaurant also has a fairly inventive menu of Continental entrées. The old-fashioned private booths won't reveal your indiscretions—including your indulgence in dessert. ✉ *125 Sydney St.,* ☎ *902/566–4620. Reservations essential. AE, MC, V.*

$ ✕ **Little Christo's.** Hand-tossed gourmet pizzas like cordon bleu with roasted pine nuts and primavera make this the favorite spot in town for true aficionados. Soup, salad, pasta, and sandwiches round out the menu of this charming restaurant. ✉ *411 University Ave.,* ☎ *905/566–4000. MC, V.*

$$$–$$$$ ★ ✕ **Dundee Arms.** Depending on your mood, you can choose to stay in either a 1960s motel or a 1904 inn. The motel is simple, modern, and neat; the inn is homey and furnished with brass and antiques. The Griffin Room, the inn's dining room, is filled with antiques, copper, and brass. The French Continental cuisine includes fresh seafood. Specialties include rack of lamb, chateaubriand, and poached or grilled fillet of salmon in a light lime-dill sauce. ✉ *200 Pownal St., C1A 3W8,* ☎ *902/892–2496,* FAX *902/368–8532. 16 rooms, 2 suites. Restaurant, pub. CP. MC, V.*

$$$$ ★ **The Charlottetown.** This five-story, redbrick hotel with white pillars and a circular driveway is just two blocks from the center of Charlottetown. The rooms have the latest amenities but retain the hotel's old-fashioned flavor, with antique-reproduction furnishings. The grandeur and charm of the Confederation Dining Room will take you back to the elegance of a previous era. ✉ *Kent and Pownal Sts., Box 159, C1A 7K4,* ☎ *902/894–7371,* FAX *902/368–2178. 107 rooms, 2 suites. Bar, dining room, indoor pool, sauna. AE, DC, MC, V.*

$$$$ ★ **Prince Edward Hotel.** A member of the Canadian Pacific chain of hotels and resorts, the Prince Edward has all the comforts and luxuries of its first-rate counterparts—from whirlpool baths in some suites to a grand ballroom and conference center. Guest rooms are modern, and two-thirds of the units in this 10-story hotel overlook the developed Charlottetown waterfront. ✉ *18 Queen St., Box 2170, C1A 8B9,* ☎ *902/566–2222 or 800/441–1414,* FAX *902/566–2282. 178 rooms, 33 suites. 2 restaurants, bar, indoor pool, sauna, exercise room. AE, DC, MC, V.*

$–$$$ **Blue Heron Hideaways.** The MacAndrews, the owners, are a film producer and a journalist who run these executive-style cottages, a luxury beach house, and a honeymoon cottage just 15 minutes from downtown Charlottetown in Blooming Point. The private beach has sand dunes and much wildlife, and it's a great place for windsurfing. An outboard motorboat and gas barbecues are available for guest use. Weekly rentals only are available from early June through mid-October. ✉ *Meadowbank, R.R. 2, Cornwall, C0A 1H0,* ☎ *902/566–2427,* FAX *902/368–3798. 1 2-bedroom cottage, 2 3-bedroom cottages, 1 waterfront cottage with bunkhouse, 1 6-bedroom oceanfront house with guest house. Pool, windsurfing, boating. No credit cards.*

$$ ⊞ **Sherwood Motel.** This family-oriented motel is about 5 kilometers (3 miles) north of downtown Charlottetown on Route 15. The friendly owners offer help in reserving tickets for events and planning day trips. Don't be daunted by the Sherwood's proximity to the airport—the motel sees very little traffic. Most rooms have kitchenettes. ⊠ *R.R. 9, Winsloe C1E 1Z3,* ☎ *902/892–1622 or 800/567–1622. 30 rooms with bath. MC, V.*

$ ⊞ **Court Bed and Breakfast.** In a residential area 2 kilometers (1¼ miles) from downtown, this two-story bed-and-breakfast with a welcoming red door offers large, simple, comfortable rooms and a full, hearty breakfast, including ham, eggs, bacon, muffins, and fresh fruits in season. ⊠ *68 Hutchinson Ct., C1A 8H7,* ☎ *902/894–5871. 2 rooms with shared bath. No credit cards. Closed Sept.–Apr.*

BLUE HERON DRIVE

Circling the island's center segment and roughly outlining Queens County, Blue Heron Drive is 190 kilometers (114 miles) long. It takes its name from the great blue heron, a stately water bird that migrates to Prince Edward Island every spring to nest in the shallow bays and marshes. The highway marker is a white square with a blue border and a blue heron in the center.

From Charlottetown, Blue Heron Drive follows Route 15 north to the north shore, then winds along Route 6 through north-shore fishing villages, spectacular white-sand beaches of Prince Edward Island National Park and Cabot Provincial Park, through Anne of Green Gables country, and finally along the south shore, with its red sandstone seascapes and historic sites. This drive circles some of the island's most beautiful landscapes and best beaches, but its northern section around picturesque Cavendish and the Green Gables farmhouse is also cluttered with tourist traps. If you're looking for unspoiled beauty, you'll have to look beyond the fast-food outlets, tacky gift shops, and expensive carnival-type attractions and try to keep in your mind's eye the island's simpler days.

Prince Edward Island National Historic Park

❿   *24 km (15 mi) north of Charlottetown.*

Prince Edward Island National Historic Park stretches for about 40 kilometers (25 miles) along the north shore of the island, from Cavendish to Dalvay, on the Gulf of St. Lawrence. The park is blessed with nature's broadest brush strokes—sky and sea meet red sandstone cliffs, rolling dunes, and long stretches of sand. Beaches invite you to swim, picnic, or take a quiet walk. Trails lead through woodlands and along streams and ponds. Among more than 200 species of birds are the northern phalarope, Swainson's thrush, and the endangered piping plover. The park **visitor centers** in Cavendish and Brackley provide information on activities and events in the park. The three campgrounds—in Cavendish, Rustico Island, and Stanhope—have toilets, showers, electrical hookups, and a coin laundry. ☎ *902/672–6350. ☉ Park summer, daily; visitor center June–Oct., daily 10–6.*

NEED A
BREAK?
   Three grand old hotels gracing the eastern end of the park all provide pleasant spots for a quiet break. At **Shaw's Hotel, Stanhope-by-the-Sea,** and **Dalvay-by-the-Sea** you can get good food in an extra-special setting. The latter was built in the 1890s as a summer home by an oil magnate and is now operated by the hotel as a resort lodge. Or go down to the wharf in **Covehead,** where you can get fresh seafood straight from

the boat. Take it home or eat it on the spot: Fishermen will cook it to your liking.

Dining and Lodging

$$$$ ⛲ **Dalvay-by-the-Sea.** Just within the borders of the Prince Edward Island National Park is this Victorian house, built in 1896 as a private summer home. Now a popular inn and restaurant, Dalvay-by-the-Sea has Victorian-style rooms furnished with antiques and reproductions. Guests can sip cocktails or tea on the porch while admiring the inn's gardens, Dalvay Lake, or the nearby beach. ⊠ *Rte. 6, Grand Tracadie, near Dalvay Beach, Box 8, York C0A 1P0,* ☎ *902/672–2048; in winter, 902/672–2546. 31 rooms, 2 cottages. Restaurant, bar, driving range, 2 tennis courts, windsurfing, boating. MAP. AE, MC, V. Closed mid-Sept.–mid-June.*

Outdoor Activities and Sports

GOLF

The course at **Stanhope Golf and Country Club** (☎ 902/672–2842) is one of the most challenging and most scenic on the island. It's a few kilometers (a couple of miles) west of Dalvay, off Route 6, along beautiful Covehead Bay.

SEA KAYAKING

Sea kayaking with **Outside Expeditions** (⊠ Prince Edward Island National Park, ☎ 800/207–3899) can be geared to suit the beginner or experienced paddler. Tours are all fully catered.

Cavendish

❶ *18 km (11 mi) west of South Rustico.*

Cavendish is the most visited Island community outside of Charlottetown, due to the heavy influx of visitors to Green Gables, the PEI National Park, and the amusement-park style attractions in the area. This is the mecca for families with children who appreciate the entertainment, which ranges from bumper-car rides to water slides and pristine sandy beaches.

★ **Green Gables House** is the green-and-white farmhouse that is the setting for Lucy Maud Montgomery's first and most famous novel, *Anne of Green Gables.* The book was published in 1908, and it became one of the most popular children's books ever written. It's about a young orphan girl adopted by a strict but kindly brother and sister who live on a Prince Edward Island farm. The story has so caught the imagination of readers that hundreds of thousands of visitors from around the world visit Green Gables every summer. The house, once owned by Montgomery's cousins, is organized to reflect the story. ⊠ *In Prince Edward Island National Park,* ☎ *902/673–6350.* 💲 *$2.75.* ⊙ *Mid-May–late June, daily 9–5; late June–Aug., daily 9–8; Sept.–Oct., daily 9–5.*

Dining and Lodging

$$–$$$ ✕ **Dunes Cafe.** This stunning café is an integral part of a pottery stu-
★ dio, art gallery, artisans outlet, and outdoor gardens. Elegant, soaring, wood ceilings add to a spacious setting that seats more than 80 people on two levels, as well as on an outside deck overlooking the dunes and marshlands of Covehead Bay. The chef specializes in local seafood and island lamb, and dishes use locally grown, fresh produce, much of which comes from the café's own gardens. ⊠ *Rte. 15, Brackley Beach,* ☎ *902/672–2586. Reservations essential. AE, MC, V. Closed Nov.–May. No dinner weekdays June, Sept., or Oct.*

$$$–$$$$ ✕🏠 **Shaw's Hotel and Cottages.** Each room is unique in this 1860s
★ hotel with antique furnishings, floral-print wallpapers, and hard-
wood floors. Half the cottages have fireplaces. This country elegance
doesn't come cheap; Shaw's is one of the most expensive hotels on the
Island, but guests have the opportunity for activities such as sailing (on
small vessels) and windsurfing. If you'd like, include in your room rate
a home-cooked breakfast and dinner in the Shaw's dining room. ⊠
Rte. 15, Brackley Beach C1E 1Z3, ☎ *902/672–3000,* FAX *902/672–
6000. 20 rooms, 18 cottages, 2 suites. Restaurant, bar, beach, boat-
ing, playground. AE, MC, V. Closed late Sept.–May except for 6
cottages.*

$$$ ✕🏠 **Bay Vista Motor Inn.** This clean, friendly motel caters to families.
Parents can sit on the outdoor deck and admire the New London Bay
panorama while keeping an eye on their children in the motel's large
playground. Almost all of the rooms have views of the bay. Fiddles 'n
Vittles is a great place to eat with the family. ⊠ *R.R. 1, Breadalbane,
Cavendish C0A 1E0; in winter,* ⊠ *R.R. 1, North Wiltshire C0A 1Y0;
book reservations at RR 2, Hunter River, PEI C0A 1N0,* ☎ *902/963–
2225. 28 rooms, 2 efficiencies. Restaurant, pool, golf, boating, fishing, playground. AE, MC, V. Closed late Sept.–mid-June.*

Outdoor Activities and Sports

GOLF

Green Gables Course (☎ 902/963–2488) is a scenic Scottish-style
"links" course.

Shopping

The Dunes Studio and Gallery (⊠ Rte. 15, Brackley Beach, ☎ 902/672–
2586) is the island's most visually stunning shop and museum, featuring
the work of leading local artists, as well as craftspeople from around
the world. The production pottery studio is open for viewing, as is a
rooftop water garden. There's a café on the premises and the view—
a panorama of saltwater bays, sand dunes, gentle rolling hills, and the
Gulf of St. Lawrence—is wonderful.

New London

🔟 *11 km (7 mi) southwest of Cavendish.*

The **Lucy Maud Montgomery Birthplace** is the modest white house
where the famous author was born in 1874. Among memorabilia on
display are her wedding dress and personal scrapbooks. ⊠ *Rte. 6,* ☎
902/886–2596. 🎫 *$1.* ⊙ *June and early–mid-Sept., daily 9–5; July
and Aug., daily 9–7; mid-Sept.–mid-Oct., daily 9–5.*

NEED A Home baking is the specialty at **Kitchen Witch Tea Room & Eatery** (⊠
BREAK? Rte. 234, Long River, between New London and Woodleigh, ☎
902/886–2294), a country tearoom where you can have your tea-leaf
reading done by the resident "witch." Prices are reasonable and there's
an antiques and crafts shop on the premises. The Kitchen Witch is open
mid-May–September.

En Route Some of the most beautiful scenery on the island is on Blue Heron Drive
along the north shore. Along the way you will pass close to **Woodleigh**
(⊠ Rte. 234, ☎ 902/836–3401), a town with miniature castles. The
Anne of Green Gables Museum is in Silver Bush (⊠ Rte. 20, ☎
902/886–2884). Blue Heron Drive follows the coastline south to the
other side of the island through rolling farmland by the shores of
Malpeque Bay, almost into Summerside. Across Malpeque Bay is
Lennox Island, the largest Micmac Indian reserve in the province. The
head of Malpeque Bay almost meets Bedeque Bay, nearly cutting the

island in two. At Carleton, Blue Heron Drive intersects with Route 1, the main highway between Charlottetown and Borden and the terminus for the New Brunswick ferries. At the waterfront you'll see the ongoing construction of the bridge, which is to span the 14½ kilometers (9 miles) of the Northumberland Straight. When the bridge is completed in the summer of 1997 it will replace the car ferry. Prior to the late 1800s (when ferry service began) passengers and mail were taken across the straight in iceboats, which were alternately pushed, pulled, and rowed, even in horrendous winter weather. A memorial pays tribute to the crews of those ships. Paralleling the coast, Blue Heron Drive continues past a fine Harris church at Crapaud to Victoria. **Victoria** is a picturesque fishing village with antiques, art galleries, handicraft shops, and live summer theater in the historic **Victoria Playhouse** (☎ 902/658–2025). The drive from Victoria to Rocky Point passes through the Argyle Shore to **Fort Amherst Port-La-Joye National Historic Site** (✉ Rte. 19, ☎ 902/675–2220), at the mouth of Charlottetown Harbour. This pretty spot, with its lighthouse, is the location of the first European settlement on the island, established in 1720 during French rule. You can picnic on the site while watching boats and cruise ships sail into the harbor. There's an audiovisual display in the visitor center. The site is open mid-June–Labor Day, daily 10–6.

THE KINGS BYWAY

The Kings Byway follows the coastline of Kings County for 375 kilometers (225 miles) on the eastern end of the island. The route passes woodlots, patchwork-quilt farms, fishing villages, and historic sites in this green and tranquil section of the province. Starting at Charlottetown, take Route 1 east and follow Kings Byway counterclockwise.

Orwell Corner Historic Village

★ **⑬** *27 km (17 mi) west of Charlottetown.*

The Orwell Corner Historic Village re-creates a 19th-century rural settlement. It's a living farm museum, employing methods used by Scottish settlers in the 1800s, including handsome draft horses. The village contains a beautifully restored 1864 farmhouse, school, church, community hall, blacksmith, and barns. On Wednesdays in the summer the village hosts musical evenings (*ceilidhs*) featuring traditional Scottish fiddle music by local musicians. Other special events occur year-round. ✉ Rte. 1, ☎ 902/651–2013. ☞ $3. ☉ *Late June–Labor Day, Tues.–Sun. 9–5; mid-May–late June and Labor Day–late Oct., Tues.–Fri. 10–3.*

The **Sir Andrew MacPhail Homestead** has an interpretive center and gardens that explain and reflect life in the early 20th century. This 140-acre property with walking trails commemorates the life of MacPhail, a local author and historian. ✉ *Off Rte. 1 (north from Orwell Village 1 mi to gravel road), Orwell,* ☎ *in summer, 902/651–2789; in winter, 902/659–2735.* ☞ *Donations accepted.* ☉ *June and Sept., Tues.–Sun. 10–5; July–Aug., extended hrs.*

☾ **Ben's Lake Trout Farm** is an enjoyable attraction for the whole family, but especially loved by aspiring young anglers. Not only are you almost guaranteed a fish, but the staff will clean it and supply the barbecue and picnic table for a great meal. To get back to Route 1, reverse the route. ✉ *Rte. 24 (follow gravel road from Sir Andrew McPhail Homestead to Rte. 24; turn right), Bellevue,* ☎ *902/838–2706.* ☞ *Free.* ☉ *Apr.–Oct.*

En Route   One of the island's most historic churches, **St. John's Presbyterian,** is
in **Belfast,** just off Route 1 on Route 207. This pretty white church,
on a hill against a backdrop of trees, was built by settlers from the Isle
of Skye who were brought to the island in 1803 by Lord Selkirk.
Route 1 passes **Wood Islands,** the terminus for the Northumberland
Ferries service to Nova Scotia. Ferries operate while Northumberland
Strait is free of ice, generally from May through December. The eastern coastline is dotted with fishing villages and long uncrowded beaches.
St. Mary's Bay, inside Panmure Island, has excellent windsurfing behind a long protected beach. Seal-watching and bird-watching boat tours
are available at seductive **Montague,** the business hub of eastern Prince
Edward Island.

Bay Fortune

⑭   *38 km (23 mi) north of Georgetown.*

Bay Fortune, a little-known scenic village, has been a secret refuge of
well-heeled Americans for two generations, and is home to the wonderful Inn at Bay Fortune, with old-time style and panache.

Dining and Lodging

$$$$ ✕🏠 **Inn at Bay Fortune.** This enticing, unforgettable getaway, the for-
★   mer summer home of a Broadway playwright, and more recently of
actress Colleen Dewhurst (Marilla in *Anne of Green Gables*), is now
a charming inn overlooking Fortune Harbour and Northumberland
Straight. You'll find superb dining, cooking classes from a top chef,
and a taste of genteel living. Superb local fresh-caught and -harvested
ingredients are served in an ambience reminiscent of a bygone era. A
full breakfast is included in room rates. ⊠ *Rte. 310, R.R. 4, C0A 2B0,*
☎ *902/687–3745; off-season, 203/633–4930. 11 rooms with bath.
Closed late Oct.–mid-May.*

En Route   In early summer you can see whole fields of blue, white, pink, and purple wild lupines sloping down to red cliffs and blue sea, and the view
from the hill overlooking the town of **Souris,** on the northeastern
coast, is especially lovely. At Souris, a car ferry links Prince Edward
Island with the Québec-owned Magdalen Islands. The Souris area is
noted for its fine traditional musicians. An outdoor Scottish concert
at Rollo Bay in July, with fiddling and step-dancing, attracts thousands
every year. In **Basin Head,** at the **Basin Head Fisheries Museum** (⊠ Off
Rte. 16, ☎ 902/357–2966; off-season, 902/368–6600), which is spectacularly located on a bluff overlooking Northumberland Straight,
boats, gear, and photographs depict the life of an inshore fisherman.
There's an aquarium, a smokehouse, a cannery, and coastal-ecology
exhibits. The museum is open June and September, Wednesday–Friday
10–3; July and August, daily 10–5; admission is $3. Walk over the
cast-iron bridge by the museum. The exquisite, silvery beach stretches
northeast for miles, backed by high, grassy dunes. Scuff your feet in
the sand: It will squeak, squawk, and purr at you. These are known
locally as the **"singing sands,"** a phenomenon found in only a few locations worldwide. There are changing rooms, locker rentals, and a
canteen here. In **Elmira,** The **Elmira Railway Museum** (⊠ Rte. 16A,
☎ 902/357–2481) recounts the development and history of the 19th-
and early 20th-century Prince Edward Island railway. Artifacts, maps,
and photos are on display. The museum is open mid-June–Labor Day,
Tuesday–Sunday 9–5; admission is $1.50. Numerous detailed books
depicting the mysteries and tales of life at sea are available in the gift
shop of the **East Point Lighthouse** (⊠ Rte. 16). An especially good stop
for photographers and those interested in fishing communities is **North
Lake,** several kilometers (a few miles) from Basin Head. For even more

extensive dune scenery, follow Route 2 to St. Peter's Bay, and Rout?
313 to Greenwich, where you can take a half-hour walk through beige
dunes to reach the superb beach.

LADY SLIPPER DRIVE

This drive—named for the delicate lady's slipper orchid, the province'
official flower—winds along the coast of the narrow, indented west
ern end of the island through very old and very small villages, which
still adhere to a traditional way of life. Many of these hamlets are in
habited by Acadians, descendants of the original French settlers. The
area is known for its oysters and Irish moss, but most famously for it?
potato farms: The province is a major exporter of seed potatoes world
wide, and half the crop is grown here.

Summerside

⑮ *71 km (44 mi) west of Charlottetown.*

Summerside is the second-largest community on the island. A self-guided
walking tour, arranged by the **Summerside Tourism Office** (⊠ Rte. 1A
☎ 800/463–4734), is a pleasant excursion through the leafy streets
with their spacious houses. Some of these homes are known as "fo?
houses"; silver foxes were first bred in captivity in western Prince Ed
ward Island, and for several decades Summerside was the headquar
ters of a virtual gold rush based on fox ranching. For more history and
walking-tour brochures, stop in at the **International Fox Museum and
Hall of Fame.** ⊠ *286 Fitzroy St.,* ☎ *902/436–2400 or 902/436–1589*
🖾 *$1 donation accepted.* ☉ *May–Sept., Mon.–Sat. 9–6.*

The **Eptek National Exhibition Centre,** on the waterfront, has a spaciou?
main gallery with changing history and fine arts exhibits from all part
of Canada. This contemporary structure is named for the Micmac word
for "warm spot." ⊠ *130 Water St.,* ☎ *902/888–8373,* FAX *902/888–*
8375. 🖾 *$2.*

The **Prince Edward Island Sports Hall of Fame,** this province's physi
cal tribute to its outstanding athletes and builders, is in the **Wyatt Cen
tre** on Summerside's waterfront, adjacent to the Eptek Centre. This large
complex houses sporting memorabilia, photographs, and portraits o?
the 105-plus inductees, as well as rare archival material and an action
area for visitors to test their own athletic prowess. Under construction
is a performing arts, heritage, and cultural center. ⊠ *130 Water St.*
☎ *902/436–2246.*

The eight-day **Summerside Lobster Carnival,** held every July, include?
livestock exhibitions, harness racing, fiddling contests, and lobste?
suppers.

Lodging

$$$ 🏨 **Loyalist Country Inn.** At the waterfront, this traditional inn with Vic
torian decor is centrally located. Ten rooms have whirlpool baths. ⊠
195 Harbour Dr., C1N 5B2, ☎ *902/436–3333 or 800/361–2668,* FAX
902/436–4304. 51 rooms. Dining room, tavern, exercise room, indoo?
pool, sauna, tennis court. AE, DC, MC, V.

$$–$$$ 🏨 **Quality Inn Garden of the Gulf.** Close to downtown Summerside
this clean motel is a convenient place to stay. The nine-hole golf cours?
on the property slopes to Bedeque Bay. ⊠ *618 Water St. E, C1N 2V5*
☎ *902/436–2295 or 800/265–5551,* FAX *902/436–6277. 77 room?*
6 suites. Restaurant, bar, coffee shop, indoor and outdoor pool?
9-hole golf course. AE, DC, MC, V.

En Route   In **Mistouche,** the Acadian Museum of Prince Edward Island (✉ Rte. 2, ☎ 902/436–6237) has a permanent exhibition on Acadian life as well as an audiovisual presentation depicting the history and culture of island Acadian people. There are 30,000 genealogical cards listing Acadian descent. The museum is open weekdays year-round, 9:30–5, and late June–Labor Day, Saturday 9:30–5 and Sunday 1–5. Relatively few visitors travel west of Summerside, which is unfortunate for them and fortunate for you. Route 2 goes straight as an arrow through the drab plain of the Miscouche Swamp. Avoid this route by following the Lady Slipper signs from Miscouche to **Port Hill,** where you may visit the **Green Park Shipbuilding Museum and Historic House** (✉ Rte. 12, ☎ 902/831–2206). The house was originally the home of shipbuilder James Yeo, Jr. This 19th-century mansion is topped by a cupola, from which Yeo observed his nearby shipyard through a spyglass. The modern museum building, in what has become a provincial park, details the history of the shipbuilder's craft, which is brought to life at a re-created shipyard with carpenter and blacksmith shops. The park also provides an opportunity for some welcome R&R, with picnic tables and camping facilities, as well as swimming in the river (there may not be a lifeguard on duty). The house and museum are open mid-June–Labor Day, Tuesday–Sunday 9–5; admission is $2.50.

Tyne Valley

⑯   *8 km (5 mi) south of Port Hill.*

The tiny community of Tyne Valley has some of the finest food on Prince Edward Island, as well as an annual summer Oyster Festival.

Dining and Lodging

$$–$$$$ ✕ **Seasons In Thyme.** The island's ambience of gracious living is per-
★   sonified in this charming country restaurant. The owner-chef Stefan Czapalay has 27 potato dishes at his fingertips, allowing him to cater to industry officials visiting to check the quality of the island's famous seed potatoes. In recognition of his varied clientele he utilizes the freshest local ingredients from farm and sea in dishes ranging from the most sophisticated to the most casual. The food is excellent, the atmosphere casual, and the produce organic. ✉ *Rte. 178, C0B 2C0,* ☎ *902/831–2124. Reservations essential. AE, MC, V.*

$$$$ 🏨 **Rodd's Mill River Resort and Conference Centre.** With activities ranging from night skiing and tobogganing to golfing, this is truly an all-season resort. An international dogsled-racing weekend is a popular winter event. Ask about year-round family-weekend packages. ✉ *Box 399, O'Leary C0B 1V0,* ☎ *902/859–3555 or 800/565–7633,* FAX *902/859–2486. 87 rooms, 3 suites. 2 bars, dining room, 2 indoor pools, sauna, golf course, tennis court, exercise room, squash, windsurfing, boating, bicycles, ice-skating, cross-country skiing, tobogganing, pro shop. AE, MC, V. Closed Nov.–early Dec., Apr.*

$$ 🏨 **Doctor's Inn Bed & Breakfast.** This charming, beautifully landscaped village home is a joy in summer, with its garden of herbs and flowers. In winter the inn attracts cross-country skiers—there's plenty of opportunity to gather 'round the woodstove or fireplace and share good conversation over a warm drink. At the dining room table, which seats up to eight, enjoy good meals based on what is available from local fishermen and farmers and from the inn's own organic gardens. Dinner is by reservation only and costs $35 per person. For the horticulturally inclined, there are free tours of the inn's gardens. ✉ *Rte. 167, C0B 2C0,* ☎ *902/831–3057. 2 rooms share bath. CP. V.*

Outdoor Activities and Sports

GOLF

Mill River Provincial Golf Course (☎ 902/859–2238) in Mill River Provincial Park is among the most scenic and challenging courses in eastern Canada.

Shopping

Shoreline Sweaters (⊠ Lady Slipper Dr., ☎ 902/831–2950), sometimes known as Tyne Valley Studio, is where Lesley Dubey produces sweaters with a unique Fair Isle–style lobster pattern, and sells local crafts May to September.

En Route   Everything in **Tignish,** an Acadian community, seems to be cooperative, including the supermarket, insurance company, fish plant, service station, and credit union. The imposing **parish church of St. Simon and St. Jude Parish House** (⊠ 315 School St., ☎ 902/882–2049), across from Dalton Square, has a superb Tracker pipe organ, one of the finest such instruments in eastern Canada, and is often used for recitals by world-renowned musicians.

North Cape

★ ⑰   *14 km (9 mi) north of Tignish.*

In North Cape, the island narrows to a north-pointing arrow of land with an imposing lighthouse. At low tide you can walk out onto one of the longest reefs in the world, a great spot to find tidal pools teeming with marine life. If you feel you are being watched, you probably are: Look offshore to where the seals gather for some prime people-watching! The curious structures near the reef are wind turbines at the **Atlantic Wind Test Site,** set up on this breezy promontory to evaluate the feasibility of electrical generation by wind power. The **Interpretive Centre and Aquarium** has information about marine life, local history, and wind energy. ⊠ *End of Rte. 12,* ☎ *902/882–2991.* ☞ *$2.* ☉ *July–Aug., daily 9–9; mid-May–June and Sept.–Oct., daily 10–6.*

Dining

$$ ✕ **Wind & Reef.** This restaurant serves good seafood, such as Island clams, mussels, and lobster, as well as steaks, prime rib, and chicken. There's a breathtaking view of the Gulf of St. Lawrence and Northumberland Strait. ⊠ *End of Rte. 12,* ☎ *902/882–3535. MC, V. Closed Oct.–May.*

En Route   Near North Cape, just off Lady Slipper Drive on the western side of the island, is the very popular natural rock formation called "Elephant Rock." You may see draft horses in the fields or working in the surf. They are "moss horses," used in harvesting a versatile and valuable sea plant known as Irish moss. In **Mininegash,** visit the **Irish Moss Interpretive Centre** (⊠ Rte. 14, ☎ 902/882–4313) and find out how much Irish moss there was in your last ice cream cone. Then take time for some Seaweed Pie (also from Irish moss) at the adjacent **Seaweed Pie Cafe** and search for souvenirs at **Sea Side Crafts.** The Interpretive Centre is open late June–September, weekdays 9–5. At the southern tip of the western shore is **West Point,** with a tiny fishing harbor, campsites, supervised beach, and what one visitor has called an "insanely friendly" community. **West Point Lighthouse** (⊠ Rte. 14, ☎ 902/859–3605) is more than 120 years old and is the tallest on the island. When the lighthouse was automated, the community took over the building and converted it into an inn and museum, with a gift shop and an excellent moderately priced restaurant attached. The lighthouse is open mid-May–mid-October, daily 8–9:30; admission to the museum is $1.65. Lady Slipper Drive meanders from West Point back to Summerside.

through **Région Evangeline,** the main Acadian district of the island. At **Cape Egmont,** stop for a look at the **Bottle Houses,** the work of a retired carpenter: two tiny houses and a chapel built entirely out of glass bottles mortared together like bricks.

Mont-Carmel

🔞 *84 km (52 mi) southeast of West Point.*

This community has a magnificent brick church overlooking Northumberland Strait. The **Acadian Pioneer Village** has a church, school, blacksmith shop, store, restaurant (where you can sample authentic Acadian dishes), and modern accommodations. ⊠ *Rte. 11,* ☎ *902/854–2227.* 🎟 *$2.* ⊙ *Mid-June–mid-Sept., daily 10–7.*

The Arts

La Cuisine à Mémé (⊠ Rte. 11, ☎ 902/854–2227), a French dinner theater, serves a buffet and has typical Acadian entertainment, such as step-dancing and fiddle music.

PRINCE EDWARD ISLAND A TO Z

Arriving and Departing

By Car

A bridge connecting Prince Edward Island with New Brunswick is due to open in July 1997. Known locally as the "Fixed Link," the bridge will have a toll approximately the same as the ferry service it replaces (☞ *below*). It will take approximately 15 minutes to drive across Northumberland Straight.

By Ferry

Two car-ferry services serve Prince Edward Island. **Marine Atlantic** (☎ 902/794–5700 or 902/855–2030) sails between Cape Tormentine, New Brunswick, and Borden, year-round, crossing daily between 6:30 AM and 1 AM. It will continue to operate until the replacement bridge is opened (July 1997). The crossing takes about 45 minutes and costs approximately $20 per car round-trip plus $8.50 per adult. No reservations are accepted. **Northumberland Ferries** (☎ 902/566–3838; in the Maritimes, 800/565–0201) sails between Caribou, Nova Scotia, and Wood Islands, from May to mid-December. The crossing takes about 75 minutes, and the round-trip costs approximately $27.25 per automobile and $7.75 per adult. This ferry service will continue after the bridge opens. Reservations are not accepted, and no fares are collected inbound; you pay only on leaving the island.

By Plane

Charlottetown Airport is 5 kilometers (3 miles) north of town. **Air Canada/Air Nova** (☎ 902/892–1007 or 800/776–3000) and **Canadian Airlines International/Air Atlantic** (☎ 902/892–4581 or 800/665–1177) offer daily service to major cities in eastern Canada and the United States via Halifax. **Prince Edward Air** (☎ 902/566-4488) is available for private charters.

Getting Around

By Car

There are more than 3,700 kilometers (2,300 miles) of paved road in the province, including the three scenic coastal drives called Lady Slipper Drive, Blue Heron Drive, and Kings Byway. The adventurous will enjoy exploring the designated "Heritage Roads," which consist of red clay, the native soil base. These unpaved roads meander through un-

developed areas of rural Prince Edward Island, where you're likely to
see lots of wildflowers and birds. A four-wheel-drive vehicle is not nec
essary, but in spring and when the weather is bad the mud can get quite
deep and roads become impassable.

Contacts and Resources

Emergencies
Police and **fire,** dial 0.

Golf
For a publication listing courses, contact **Golf Prince Edward Island** (⊠
Box 2653, Charlottetown C1A 8C3, ☎ 800/463–4734).

Guided Tours
The island has about 20 sightseeing tours, including double-decker bu
tours, cycling tours, harbor cruises, and walking tours. Most tou
companies are in Charlottetown and offer excursions around the city
and to the beaches. For a listing of current tour companies contac
Tourism PEI (⊠ Box 940, Charlottetown, C1A 7M5, ☎ 800/463–4734
FAX 902/368–4438).

Hiking
Island Nature Trust and Island Trails (⊠ Ravenwood, Box 265, Char
lottetown C1A 7K4, ☎ 902/894–7535, FAX 902/628–6331) publishe
a nature trail map of the island, available for $4.50.

Hospital
Queen Elizabeth Hospital (⊠ Riverside Dr., Charlottetown, ☎ 902/566-
6200).

Shopping
Information on crafts outlets and varieties is provided by the **Prince
Edward Island Crafts Council** (⊠ 156 Richmond St., Charlottetown C1/
1H9, ☎ 902/892–5152).

Visitor Information
For prices and information before your trip, contact the **Prince Edward
Island Department of Economic Development & Tourism** (⊠ Quality Ser
vice Division, Box 940, Charlottetown C1A 7M5, ☎ 902/368–444
or 800/463–4623, FAX 902/368–4438). The department publishes an
excellent annual "Visitor's Guide," and maintains eight **Visitor Infor
mation Centres** (VICs) on the island. The main VIC is in Charlotte
town (⊠ Oak Tree Pl., University Ave., ☎ 902/368–4444 o
902/463–4623, FAX 902/368–4438) and is open mid-May–October, daily
November–mid-May, weekdays.

13 Nova Scotia

This little province on the Atlantic Coast, compact and distinctive, has a capital city, Halifax, the same size as Christopher Marlowe's London. The days when Nova Scotians were prosperous shipwrights and merchants trading with the world left Victorian mansions in all the salty little ports that dot the coastline and created a uniquely Nova Scotian outlook: worldly, approachable, and sturdily independent.

By Silver
Donald
Cameron

Updated by
Julie V. Watson

INFINITE RICHES IN A LITTLE ROOM," wrote Elizabethan playwright Christopher Marlowe. He might have been referring to Nova Scotia, Canada's second-smallest province, which packs an impossible variety of cultures and landscapes into an area half the size of Ohio.

Nova Scotia's landscapes echo every region of Canada. Mountain clefts in Cape Breton Island could pass for crannies in British Columbia. Stretches of the Tantramar Marshes are as board-flat as the prairies. The glaciated interior, spruce-swathed and peppered with lakes, closely resembles the Canadian Shield in northern Manitoba. The apple blossoms in the Annapolis Valley are as glorious as those in Niagara, and parts of Halifax could masquerade as downtown Toronto. A massive Catholic church in a tiny French village recalls Québec. The warm salt water and long sandy beaches of Prince Edward Island are also found on the mainland side of Northumberland Strait, and the brick-red mud flats of the Bay of Fundy echo their counterparts in New Brunswick. Neil's Harbour looks just like a Newfoundland outport—and sounds like one, too.

As with the land, so with the people. The Micmac Indians have been here for 10,000 years. The French came to the Annapolis Basin in 1605. In the 1750s, cockneys and Irish settled in Halifax and "Foreign Protestants"—chiefly Germans—in Lunenburg. By then Yankees from New England were putting down roots in Liverpool, Cape Sable Island, and the Annapolis Valley. In the 1780s they were joined by thousands of "Loyalists"—many of them black—displaced by the American Revolution. Soon after, the Scots poured into northern Nova Scotia and Cape Breton, evicted from the Highlands by their landlords' preference for sheep. The last wave of immigrants, in the 1890s, became steelworkers and coal miners in Cape Breton; they came from Wales, the West Indies, Poland, Ukraine, and the Middle East. They're all Nova Scotians, and they're all still here, eating their own foods and worshiping in their own churches. Infinite riches abound: Gaelic street signs in Pugwash and Mabou, French masses in Cheticamp and Point de l'Eglise, black gospel choirs in Halifax, Micmac handcrafts in Eskasoni, onion dome churches in Sydney, sauerkraut in Lunenburg, and Yankee Puritanism in Clark's Harbour.

This is a little buried nation, compact and distinctive, with a capital city the same size as Marlowe's London. Before Canada was formed in 1867, Nova Scotians were prosperous shipwrights and merchants trading with the world. Who created Cunard Lines? A Haligonian, Samuel Cunard. Those days brought democracy to the British colonies, left Victorian mansions in all the salty little ports that dot the coastline, and created a uniquely Nova Scotian outlook: worldly, approachable, and sturdily independent.

Pleasures and Pastimes

Beaches
The province is one big seashore. The warmest beaches are found on the Northumberland Strait shore and include Heather Beach, Caribou, and Melmerby, all in provincial parks. The west coast of Cape Breton and the Bras d'Or Lake also offer fine beaches and warm salt water.

Bird-Watching
One of the highest concentrations of bald eagles in North America is in Cape Breton, along the Bras d'Or Lake and in Cape Breton Highlands National Park. July and August are the best eagle-watching

times. MacNabs Island, in Halifax harbor, has a large osprey population. The Bird Islands, off the coast of Cape Breton, are home to a variety of seabirds, including the rare Atlantic puffin.

Dining

Skilled chefs find their abilities enhanced by the availability of ingredients such as succulent blueberries, crunchy apples, wild mushrooms, home-raised poultry, quality beef, fresh-from-the-sea lobster, cultivated mussels, Digby scallops, and the famous Atlantic salmon. The quality of ingredients comes from the closeness of the harvest. Agriculture, fisheries (both wild harvest and aquaculture) are never far from the doorstep of the food and hospitality industry.

Helping travelers discover for themselves the best tastes of this beautiful province, the Nova Scotian culinary industry has formed an organization called the Taste of Nova Scotia. It pulls together the producers and the preparers, setting quality standards to ensure that patrons at member restaurants receive authentic Nova Scotian food. Look for their symbol: a golden oval porthole framing food and a ship.

CATEGORY	COST*
$$$$	over $50
$$$	$35–$50
$$	$15–$35
$	under $15

per person, excluding drinks, service, 7% GST, and 11% sales tax on meals costing more than $3

Fishing

Nova Scotia has more than 9,000 lakes and 100 brooks; practically all lakes and streams are open to anglers. The catch includes Atlantic salmon (June–September), brook and sea trout, bass, rainbow trout, and shad. You can get a nonresident fishing license from any Department of Natural Resources office in the province and at most sporting-goods stores. South of Shelburne, from Barrington to Digby, is the most prosperous fishing region in the province.

Fossil Hunting and Rock Hounding

The shoreline along the Bay of Fundy contains some of the oldest rocks and fossils in the world. Fossilized trees, insects, plants, and ferns can be seen at the famous fossil cliffs of Joggins on Chignecto Bay. The Minas Basin near Parrsboro has dinosaur fossils as well as semiprecious stones such as agate and amethyst. Rock hounds are welcome to gather what they find along the beaches, but a permit from the Nova Scotia Museum is required to dig along the cliffs. Organized rock hounding tours are available in Joggins and Parrsboro.

Lodging

Nova Scotia's strength lies within a sprinkling of first-class resorts that have retained the traditional feel, top country inns where a dedication to fine dining with an emphasis on local products and high-level accommodation rule, and a smattering of exceptional corporate hotels. Bed-and-breakfasts, particularly those in smaller towns, are often exceptional. Most of the resorts and many B&Bs are seasonal.

In addition to the reliable chains, Halifax and Dartmouth have a number of excellent hotels; reservations are necessary year-round and can be made by calling Check In (☞ Contacts and Resources *in* Nova Scotia A to Z, *below*). Expect to pay considerably more in the capital district than elsewhere.

CATEGORY	COST*
$$$$	over $80
$$$	$65–$80
$$	$45–$65
$	under $45

All prices are for a standard double room, excluding 10% service charge.

Music

Talented musicians abound in Nova Scotia, ranging from traditional fiddlers to folk singers and rock bands. Names to watch for include the Rankin Family, the Barra MacNeills, the Minglewood Band, Sam Moon, Rita MacNeil, David MacIsaac, Scott Macmillan, and such traditional fiddlers as Buddy MacMaster, Ashley MacIsaac, Sandy MacIntyre, Lee Cremo, and Jerry Holland.

Shopping

Antiques, gifts, and crafts are especially popular in Cape Breton, but shops selling these items appear in numbers throughout the province. You'll find everything from blacksmithing in East Dover and silversmithing in Waverley to leaded glass ornaments in Purcells Cove, hooked rugs in Cheticamp, woolens in Yarmouth, wooden toys in Middletown, pewter in Wolfville, and pottery in Arichat.

Although the government is reviewing its policy on sales tax refunds, at present you may claim a refund of Nova Scotia's 11% sales tax (nonrefundable on accommodations, meals, and alcohol) paid on goods you transport home. Refund claims must be filed within 90 days of leaving Nova Scotia and must be in excess of $15. Refunds of the national Goods and Services Tax must be applied for separately.

Exploring Nova Scotia

On the eastern edge of North America, Nova Scotia is astonishing in its variety. Along the eastern coast, the North Atlantic breaks on rocky shores and beaches of fine, white sand. To the west the world's largest tides ebb and flow along the Bay of Fundy. Inland, dense forests and country roads weave among hundreds of inland lakes and rivers. The rugged terrain continues in central Nova Scotia and Cape Breton where there are spectacular cliffs.

Great Itineraries

This great province by the sea naturally divides itself into regions that can be explored in two to five days. Some visitors to the province do a whirlwind drive around, taking in Cape Breton Island, for example, in just a day. But it's better to "do" one region well and have a relaxed, enjoyable visit than to just brush the surface. Any of the routes detailed in the sections on the South Shore and Annapolis Valley, Northern Nova Scotia, or Cape Breton Island can be enjoyed in two to three days from Halifax and Dartmouth. If you have more time you will enjoy lingering or linking up two or more tours.

Numbers in the text correspond to numbers in the margin and on the Novia Scotia and Halifax maps.

IF YOU HAVE 3 DAYS

Explore the South Shore and Annapolis Valley, taking in the Lighthouse Route and Evangeline Trail. The loop beginning and ending in Halifax (via Route 3, 103, or 333, the scenic road around the shore) is a distance of approximately 850 kilometers (510 miles) with no side trips. Leaving Halifax, we suggest you spend the morning in **Peggy's Cove**, a picturesque fishing village surrounded by bare granite and coastal barrens. Explore **Mahone Bay** and travel on to **Lunenburg** ⑯, where the Old Town has been designated a National Historic District. Make sure you take in the Fisheries Museum before continuing on Route 3 or 103 to ⊞ **Shelburne** for an overnight stay. Begin day two with a visit to **Yarmouth** ⑱ and travel on to **Digby** for a lunch of scallops. **Annapolis Royal** ㉑, with its gardens, historic sites, and harborfront boardwalk, is a lovely spot for an afternoon, although children may prefer to visit Upper Clements amusement park in Clementsport. Travel on to ⊞ **Wolfville** for an overnight stay. The next day check tide times and plan a drive to the shore of Minas Basin, where the tides are the highest in the world. A leisurely drive will put you back in Halifax by late afternoon.

IF YOU HAVE 5 DAYS

Cape Breton Island with its lush natural areas, wonderful small towns, and spectacular National Park is perfect for a five-day tour. Follow the coastal route (described in the following pages), which takes you on a west-to-east loop from the Canso Strait Causeway. Overnight in ⊞ **Margaree Harbour** ㉜ so that you can enjoy the Cabot Trail and **Cape Breton Highlands National Park** (☞ **Chéticamp** ㉝) for a full day. These are not roads that the uninitiated should drive at night or when they are overtired. Also spend your second night in Margaree Harbour, and on your third day, seek out orchids, photograph spectacular scenery, walk the trails to hidden waterfalls, or go whale-watching (whale-watching opportunities abound on the northeastern side of the peninsula). An overnight in ⊞ **Sydney** ㉟, with its casino for evening entertainment, will position you for a daylong visit to Fortess of Louisbourg National Historic Site, the largest historic restoration in Canada, and the town of **Louisbourg** ㊳, which has an interesting shipwreck museum. Take Route 4 back to Canso Causeway through **Big Pond,** home of singer Rita McNeil, and loop around Bras d'Or Lake to Iona. An overnight in ⊞ **Iona** ㊱ will allow time for a visit to the Alexander Graham Bell Museum in **Baddeck** ㉟ before returning to Canso.

When to Tour Nova Scotia

The best time of year to visit Nova Scotia is mid-June to mid-September; in fact, many resorts, hotels, and attractions are only open during July and August. Nova Scotia, particularly the Cape Breton area, is a very popular destination in the fall due to the spectacular changing of the leaves. Whale-watching, wildlife cruises, and sea kayaking outfitters generally operate from July to mid-September. Most golf courses stay open from June until late September, and some into October. Skiing (both downhill and cross-country) is popular at a variety of locations including Kejimkujik and Cape Breton Highlands from mid-December to early April.

HALIFAX AND DARTMOUTH

The Halifax and Dartmouth metro area surrounds the second-largest natural harbor in the world, Halifax Harbour. It bustles with activity day and night, and flavors the rest of the city with its presence. Pubs, shops, museums, parks, and public gardens buzz with activity. Jazz, street performers, outdoor festivals, and cultural and sporting events abound. Galleries, concerts, theater, and fine dining combine to make the twin cities a destination for any season with a mix of big-city life and small-town charm.

Depending on your tendency to stop and study or sit back and savor the moment, the following walking tours can take from a half to a full day. You can drive from sight to sight, but parking is a problem, and you will miss out on much of the flavor of the city. You can either drive or take the ferry from Halifax to Dartmouth.

Halifax

1137 km (707 mi) northeast of Boston; 275 km (171 mi) southeast of Moncton, New Brunswick.

Salty and urbane, learned and plain-spoken, Halifax is large enough to have the trappings of a capital city, yet small enough to retain the warmth and convenience of a small town.

❶ Begin your walking tour at **Purdy's Wharf** (⊠ Lower Water St.), twin office towers shaped like milk cartons with feet, standing right in the harbor. Much of downtown Halifax is connected by overhead walkways, making it convenient for executives in Purdy's Wharf to get around without venturing outdoors. Take the walkway to the Sheraton (☞ Dining and Lodging, *below*), built low to match the historic ironstone buildings next door. If you're feeling lucky, step inside and try your luck at the waterfront casino.

★ **❷** Next door to the Sheraton are the warehouses of **Historic Properties,** dating from the early 19th century when trade and war made Halifax prosperous. They were built by such raffish characters as Enos Collins, who did business in the Collins Bank building. A privateer, smuggler, and shipper whose vessels defied Napoléon's blockade to bring American supplies to the Duke of Wellington, Collins was also a prime mover in the Halifax Banking Company, which evolved into the **Royal Bank of Canada,** the country's largest bank. Look up and to the right. There's the Royal Bank's office tower, three blocks away. When Collins died in 1871, at 99, he was said to be the richest man in Canada. The buildings have been taken over by quality shops and restaurants, boisterous pubs, and chic offices.

❸ The **Maritime Museum of the Atlantic** is in a restored chandlery and warehouse. The exhibits include small boats once used around the coast, as well as displays describing Nova Scotia's proud sailing heritage, from the days when the province, on its own, was one of the world's foremost shipbuilding and trading nations. Other exhibits concern the Halifax Explosion of 1917, shipwrecks, and lifesaving. ⊠ *1675 Lower Water St.,* ☎ *902/424–7490 or 902/424–7491,* ℻ *902/424–0612.* ☉ *June–mid-Oct., Mon. and Wed.–Sat. 9:30–5:30, Tues. 9:30–8, Sun. 1–5:30; mid-Oct.–May, Wed.–Sat. 9:30–5, Tues. 9:30–8, Sun. 1–5.*

The **wharves** outside the Maritime Museum are favorite berths for visiting transatlantic yachts and sail-training ships; at any time you may find South American and European square-riggers, classic yachts, and even Viking long ships.

❹ The **Brewery Market** (⊠ between Hollis and Lower Water Sts.) is a sprawling ironstone complex that was once Keith's Brewery (named for Alexander Keith, a 19th-century brewer) but now houses offices, restaurants, and a farmers' market. This area is a favored haunt of Haligonians on Saturday morning.

Take the elevator at the office-end of the Brewery Market, and emerge on Hollis Street. Turn left, past several elegant Victorian town houses—notably **Keith Hall** (⊠ 1475 Hollis St.)—once the executive offices of the brewery. Turn right on Bishop Street and right again on Barrington Street, Halifax's main downtown thoroughfare. The stone mansion on your right is **Government House,** the official residence of Nova Scotia's lieutenant-governor, built from 1799 to 1805 for Sir John Wentworth, the Loyalist governor of New Hampshire, and his racy wife

Fanny. Thomas Raddall's novel *The Governor's Lady* tells their story. The house is not open to the public.

NEED A
BREAK?

In summer the front lawn of the Halifax City Regional Library (✉ 5381 Spring Garden Rd.) is crowded with people listening to street singers and snacking on French fries bought from **Bud the Spud,** a chip-wagon parked at the curb. Surrounding the lawn are plenty of opportunities for a more substantial take-out lunch.

6 At the **Halifax Public Gardens,** the statues of Robbie Burns and Sir Walter Scott face one another from across Spring Garden Road. The gardens were first laid out in 1753. Gravel paths wind among ponds, trees, and flower beds, revealing an astonishing variety of plants from all over the world. The centerpiece is a filigreed bandstand erected in 1887 for Queen Victoria's Golden Jubilee. ✉ *Bounded by Sackville, Summer, and S. Park Sts. and Spring Garden Rd.*

7 At the **Nova Scotia Museum of Natural History,** one block north of the Public Gardens, one can discover the natural wonders of Nova Scotia by standing next to a whale skeleton or visiting the life-size models of dinosaurs that once lived nearby. There'a also an exciting Micmac and archaeology gallery. The museum is most easily recognized by the huge fiberglass model of the tiny northern spring peeper (a frog), which "clings" to the side of the building May–October. ✉ *1747 Summer St.,* ☎ *902/424–7353,* FAX *902/424–0560.* ✎ *$3.* ☉ *Mid-May–Oct., Mon.–Tues. and Thurs.–Sun. 9:30–5:30, Wed. 9:30–8; Nov.–mid-May, Tues. and Thurs.–Sun. 9:30–5, Wed. 9:30–8.*

★ **8** **Citadel Hill,** topped by its star-shape fort, is between the Halifax Commons (a grassy expanse of green space with playing fields and playgrounds) and the compact downtown. The Citadel was the heart of the city's fortifications, and was linked to smaller forts and gun emplacements on the harbor islands and on the bluffs above the harbor entrance. It is now a National Historic Site, with kilted soldiers drilling in front of the **Army Museum,** once the barracks. A cannon is fired every day at noon, and there are audiovisual programs and special events offered several times throughout the year. ✉ *Citadel Hill,* ☎ *902/426–5080.* ✎ *Mid-June–Labor Day $2.* ☉ *July–Labor Day, daily 9–6; Labor Day–mid-June, daily 10–5.*

Pause over the view from the Citadel, and take in the details: the spiky downtown crowded between the hilltop and the harbor; the wooded islands at the harbor's mouth; and the naval dockyard under the Angus L. MacDonald Bridge, the nearer of the two bridges connecting Halifax with its sister city of Dartmouth.

9 **St. Paul's Church** (1749) is Canada's oldest Protestant church, Britain's first overseas cathedral, and the burial site of many colonial notables. Inside, on the north end, a piece of metal is embedded in the wall. It is a fragment of the *Mont Blanc,* one of the two ships whose collision caused the Halifax Explosion of December 6, 1917, the greatest human-caused explosion prior to Hiroshima. The blast flattened a square mile of the North End and left 2,000 dead, another 2,000 seriously injured, and 6,000 homeless. ✉ *Between Barrington and Argyle Sts.* ☉ *Sept.–May, weekdays 9–4:30; June–Aug., Mon.–Sat. 9–4:30. Services on Sun. 8:30 AM, 10:30 AM, 7:30 PM.*

10 The **Grand Parade,** where musicians perform at noon on fine summer days, faces City Hall. From here, look uphill: The tall, stylish brick building is the **World Trade and Convention Centre** and is attached to the 10,000-seat **Halifax Metro Centre**—the site of hockey games, rock

Nova Scotia

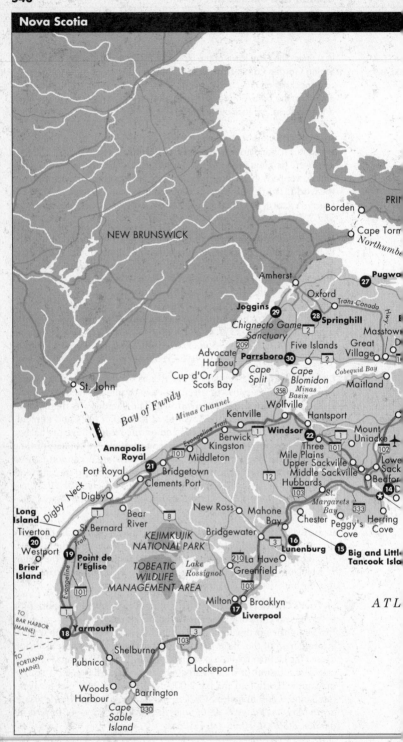

NEW BRUNSWICK

Borden

Cape Torm

Northumbe

PRIN

27 Pugwa

Amherst

Oxford *Trans-Canada*

Joggins **29**

28 **Springhill**

Chignecto Game Sanctuary

Masstow

[2]

Five Islands

Great Village

D

Advocate Harbour

Parrsboro **30**

[209]

[2]

Cape Split

Cape Blomidon

Cobequid Bay

Cup d'Or / Scots Bay

Minas Basin

Maitland

St. John

Bay of Fundy

[358]

Wolfville

Hantsport

Minas Channel

Kentville

Evangeline Trail

Berwick

Kingston

Mount Uniacke

Windsor **22**

[101]

Three Mile Plains

Annapolis Royal

[101]

21

Bridgetown

Middleton

Upper Sackville

Middle Sackville

Lowe Sack

[102]

Port Royal

Clements Port

Hubbards

[12]

[103]

Bedfor

14

D

Digby

Bear River

[8]

New Ross

Mahone Bay

St. Margarets Bay

Chester

Peggy's Cove

[333]

Long Island

Tiverton

20

Westport

St. Bernard

Evangeline Trail

KEJIMKUJIK NATIONAL PARK

Bridgewater

[3]

Lunenburg **16**

Herring Cove

15 **Big and Little Tancook Isla**

Brier Island

19 **Point de l'Eglise**

TOBEATIC WILDLIFE MANAGEMENT AREA

Lake Rossignol

[210] La Have

Greenfield

A T L

[101]

[103]

Evangeline

Milton

Brooklyn

17

Liverpool

TO BAR HARBOR (MAINE)

[1]

18 **Yarmouth**

[3]

[103]

Shelburne

TO PORTLAND (MAINE)

Pubnica

Lockeport

Woods Harbour

Barrington

Cape Sable Island

[330]

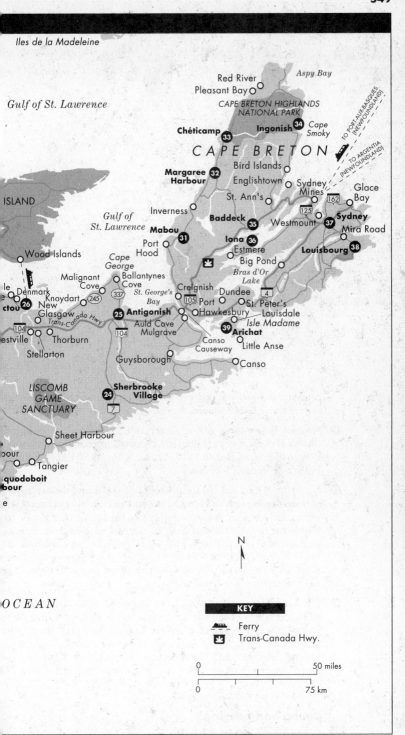

Iles de la Madeleine

Gulf of St. Lawrence

Aspy Bay

Red River
Pleasant Bay ○

**CAPE BRETON HIGHLANDS
NATIONAL PARK**

Chéticamp ❸❸ **Ingonish** ❸❹ *Cape
Smoky*

C A P E   B R E T O N

Bird Islands ○

**Margaree
Harbour** ❸❷ Englishtown ○ Sydney
Mines ○

ISLAND

*Gulf of
St. Lawrence*

St. Ann's ○

Glace
Bay ○

Inverness ○ **Baddeck**
❸❺ Westmount ○ [162]

[125]

Sydney ○

Mabou ○ ❸❶ **Iona** ❸❻ Mira Road ○

Wood Islands ○

Port ○
Hood

Estmere ○
Big Pond ○

Louisbourg ❸❽

*Cape
George*

Malignant
Cove ○

Ballantynes
Cove ○

Creignish ○ Dundee ○ *Bras d'Or
Lake*

[4]

*St. George's
Bay*

[105] Port ○ St. Peter's ○

le ○
○ Denmark
ctou ❷❻

Knoydart ○ [245]

[337]

Hawkesbury ○ Louisdale ○

New ○
Glasgow ○
Trans-Canada Hwy.

❷❺ **Antigonish** ○ *Isle Madame*

estville ○
○ ○ Thorburn

[104]

Auld Cove
Mulgrave ○

❸❾ **Arichat**

Little Anse ○

Stellarton ○

Canso
Causeway

Guysborough ○

Canso ○

*LISCOMB
GAME
SANCTUARY*

**Sherbrooke
Village**
❷❹

[7]

Sheet Harbour ○

bour

○ ○ Tangier

**quodoboit
bour**

e

O C E A N

*TO PORT-AUX-BASQUES
(NEWFOUNDLAND)*

*TO ARGENTIA
(NEWFOUNDLAND)*

N

KEY

Ferry
Trans-Canada Hwy.

0 _____ 50 miles

0 _____ 75 km

550

Anna Leonowens Gallery, **13**

Art Gallery of Nova Scotia, **12**

Brewery Market, **4**

Citadel Hill, **8**

Government House, **5**

Grand Parade, **10**

Halifax Public Gardens, **6**

Historic Properties, **2**

Maritime Museum of the Atlantic, **3**

Nova Scotia Museum of Natural History, **7**

Province House, **11**

Purdy's Wharf, **1**

St. Paul's Church, **9**

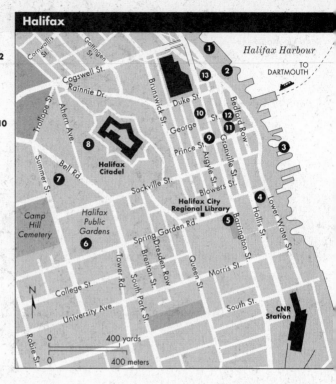

concerts, and political conventions. Farther to the right are the office towers above **Scotia Square,** the leading downtown shopping mall.

⓫ **Province House** is "a gem of Georgian architecture," according to Charles Dickens. The provincial legislature still meets in this lovely sandstone building, erected in 1819. ⊠ *Hollis St.,* ☎ *902/424–5982.* ☞ *Free.* ⊙ *Weekdays 9–6, Sat. 9–4.*

⓬ Across from Province House at Cheapside you'll find the **Art Gallery of Nova Scotia,** with an extensive permanent collection of over 4,000 works, including an internationally recognized collection of folk art. Within the historic building are galleries of Canadian Art, ceramics, international art, and more. ⊠ *1741 Hollis St., at Cheapside,* ☎ *902/424–7542,* FAX *902/424-0750.* ☞ *$2.50.* ⊙ *June–Aug., Tues., Wed., and Fri. 10–5, Thurs. 10–9, weekends noon–5; Sept.–May, Tues.–Fri. 10–5, weekends noon–5.*

⓭ The **Anna Leonowens Gallery** often shows the most challenging exhibits in Halifax. The gallery is named for the founder of the Nova Scotia College of Art and Design, a remarkable Victorian woman who served the King of Siam as governess and wrote a book about the experience; Rodgers and Hammerstein eventually turned it into the Broadway production of *The King and I,* starring Yul Brynner and Gertrude Lawrence. ⊠ *1891 Granville St.,* ☎ *902/494–8223.* ☞ *Free.* ⊙ *Tues.–Fri. 11–5, Sat. noon–4.*

Dining and Lodging

$$$ ✕ **MacAskill's Restaurant.** Experience a continuing tradition of Nova Scotian hospitality in this romantic dining room overlooking beautiful Halifax Harbor. Award-winning chefs will delight you with a unique selection of seafood dishes prepared with only the finest, freshest fish available. Specialties include pepper steak, flambéed table

side. ⊠ *88 Alderney Dr., Dartmouth Ferry Terminal Bldg.,* ☎ *902/466–3100. AE, DC, MC, V.*

$$–$$$ ✕ **Salty's on the Waterfront.** This restaurant gets the prize for the best
★ location in the city: It overlooks Privateer's Wharf and the entire harbor. Request a table with a window view, and save room for their famous dessert, called "Cadix" (chocolate mousse over praline crust). The **Salty Dog Bar & Grill** on the ground level is less expensive, and serves lunches outside on the wharf in summer. ⊠ *1869 Upper Water St.,* ☎ *902/423–6818. Reservations essential. AE, DC, MC, V.*

$$ ✕ **Da Maurizio.** At this popular northern Italian restaurant in the
★ Brewery Center, try the homemade pastas, ravioli stuffed with duck or rabbit, grilled fish and meats, and the only risotto in town. The brewery has enormously high ceilings—15 and 20 feet—and stone-and-brick walls adorned with paintings and masks of a Venetian carnival theme. Fresh flowers are placed at linen-draped tables set with gleaming silver. ⊠ *1496 Lower Water St.,* ☎ *902/423–0859. Reservations essential. AE, MC, V. Closed Sun. No lunch Sat.*

$$ ✕ **Old Man Morias.** Greek music, tapestries, and archways set the
★ mood for authentic Greek specialties at this turn-of-the-century Halifax town house. Sample the fried squid and fried cheese appetizers, lamb on a spit, or moussaka. ⊠ *1150 Barrington St.,* ☎ *902/422–7960. Reservations essential. AE, DC, MC, V. Closed Sun.–Tues. No lunch.*

$–$$ ✕ **Privateer's Warehouse.** History surrounds you in this 200-year-old building, where three restaurants share the early 18th-century stone walls and hewn beams, serving food in descending order of elegance. **Upper Deck Waterfront Fishery & Grill** (☎ *902/422–1289*), where you can experience a nautical setting with great views of the harbor, specializes in Nova Scotian cuisine such as oysters, and lobsters straight from their holding tank. **Middle Deck Pasta Works & Beverage Co.** (☎ *902/426–1500*) has a bistro-style, relaxed atmosphere and serves innovative pastas and traditional cuisine; there's also a children's menu. **Lower Deck Good Time Pub** (☎ *902/426–1501*) is a boisterous bar with long trestle tables, a patio, and lots of hand-holding and singing; fish-and-chips and other pub food is served. ⊠ *Historic Properties, Lower Water St. AE, DC, MC, V.*

$ ✕ **Satisfaction Feast.** This small, vegetarian restaurant is informal, friendly, and usually packed at lunchtime. The food is simple and wholesome; try the fresh whole-wheat bread and one of the daily curries. ⊠ *1581 Grafton St.,* ☎ *902/422–3540. MC, V.*

$$$$ ✕🏨 **Hotel Halifax.** This first-class Canadian Pacific hotel has spacious, attractive rooms, the majority with a panoramic view of the harbour. An aboveground pedway network provides easy access to the Scotia Square shopping mall and Historic Properties. The **Crown Bistro** has a unique blend of elegant dishes and lighter fare. **Sam Slicks,** a cozy piano bar, has nightly entertainment and serves great food. ⊠ *1990 Barrington St., B3J 1P2,* ☎ *902/425–6700 or 800/441–1414,* FAX *902/425–6214. 279 rooms, 21 suites. Restaurant, piano bar, indoor pool, hot tub, sauna, exercise room. AE, DC, MC, V.*

$$$$ ✕🏨 **Prince George Hotel.** Contemporary mahogany furnishings in
★ this luxurious and understated business-oriented hotel include writing desks. Chef Stephen Huston attracts both visitors and locals to Georgio's, where specialties are pasta and seafood with an international flavor. The hotel is conveniently connected by underground tunnel to the World Trade and Convention Centre. ⊠ *1725 Market St., B3J 3N9,* ☎ *902/425–1986 or 800/565–1567 in Canada. 207 rooms, 9 suites. Restaurant, bar, café, pub, pool, hot tub, exercise room, concierge. AE, DC, MC, V.*

$$$$ 🏨 **Cambridge Suites.** This hotel, in a convenient location, has th
motto, "A suite for the price of a room." Choose from among thre
suite sizes; all have sitting room and kitchenette. ⊠ 1583 Brunswic
St., B3J 3P5, ☎ 902/420–0555 or 800/565–1263, FAX 902/420–9379
200 minisuites and 1-bedrooms. Restaurant, bar, kitchenettes, whirlpoo.
hot tub, sauna, exercise room. CP. AE, D, MC, V.

$$$$ 🏨 **Halliburton House Inn.** Halifax's only four-star registered Heritag
property, this hotel is an elegant renovation of three 19th-centur
town houses. Comfortable rooms are furnished with period antiques
lending a homey ambience. Several suites have fireplaces. ⊠ 518
Morris St., B3J 1B3, ☎ 902/420–0658, FAX 902/423–2324. 24 room
with bath, 3 suites. Dining room, library. CP. AE, DC, MC, V.

$$$$ 🏨 **Sheraton Halifax.** The convenient location, in Historic Properties
contributes to the elegance of this waterfront hotel. Other assets in
clude an indoor pool with a summer sun deck. Halifax's only casin
is in the lobby. ⊠ 1919 Upper Water St., B3J 3J5, ☎ 902/421–170
or 800/325–3535, FAX 902/422–5805. 335 rooms, 19 suites. Restau
rant, bar, health club, room service, dock, concierge, meeting rooms
casino. AE, DC, MC, V.

$$$ 🏨 **Inn on the Lake.** A great value in a quiet, relaxing location, this smal
country club–style hotel is on 5 acres of parkland on the edge of Fa
River Lake, 10 minutes from Halifax and the airport. ⊠ Box 29, Wa
verly, B0N 2S0, ☎ 902/861–3480, FAX 902/861–4883. 34 rooms, 1.
suites. Restaurant, lounge, parking, beach, airport shuttle. AE, MC, V

Nightlife and the Arts

THE ARTS

Halifax has a dynamic and growing film industry, which presents cur
rent work during the **Atlantic Film Festival,** held in Halifax the thir
week in September. The festival also showcases feature films, TV
movies, and documentaries made elsewhere in the Atlantic Provinces
Wormwood's Dog and Monkey Cinema (⊠ 2112 Gottingen St., ☎
902/422–3700) shows Canadian, foreign-language, and experimen
tal films.

Scotia Festival of Music (☎ 902/429–9469) presents internationally rec
ognized classical musicians in concerts and master classes each Ma
and June. The **Atlantic Jazz Festival** takes place in mid-July.

Canada's oldest professional repertory theater, the **Neptune Theatre** (⊠
5216 Sackville St., ☎ 902/429–7300), presents a full season each
summer and winter of performances from classics to contemporary Cana
dian drama. The **Atlantic Fringe Festival** presents 40 shows in eight venue
during the first week of September. The **Historic Feast Company** (☎
902/420–1840) presents shows set in the 19th century at Historic Prop
erties Thursday, Friday, and Saturday evenings. **Grafton Street Dinne
Theatre** (⊠ 1741 Grafton St., ☎ 902/425–1961) performs Wednes
day through Saturday.

NIGHTLIFE

The multilevel entertainment center in Historic Properties, **Privateer'
Warehouse** (☎ 902/422–1289), is a popular nighttime hangout. A
the ground-level **Lower Deck** tavern you can quaff a beer to Celtic music
Cheers (⊠ 1743 Grafton St., ☎ 902/421–1655), with bands and en
tertainment nightly, is a popular spot. **O'Carroll's** (⊠ 1860 Uppe
Water St., ☎ 902/423–4405) has a restaurant, oyster bar, and loung
where you can hear live Irish music nightly.

Shopping

The Spring Garden Road area has two stylish shopping malls, with shop
selling everything from designer clothing to fresh pasta. **Jennifer of Nova**

Scotia (⊠ 5635 Spring Garden Rd., ☏ 902/425–3119) sells locally made jewelry, pottery, wool sweaters, and soaps. You can find fine crafts in Historic Properties and the Barrington Inn complex, near the waterfront, at such shops as **Pewter House** (⊠ 1875 Granville St., ☏ 902/423–8843) and the **Stornoway** (⊠ 1873 Granville St., ☏ 902/422–9507). The **Plaid Place** (⊠ 1903 Barrington Pl., ☏ 902/429–6872) has a dazzling array of tartans and Highland accessories. The **Wool Sweater Outlet** (⊠ 1870 Hollis St., ☏ 902/422–9209) sells wool and cotton sweaters at good prices.

Dartmouth

25 km (16 mi) northeast of Halifax.

Dartmouth, Nova Scotia's second city, was first settled by Quaker whalers from Nantucket. The 23 lakes within Dartmouth's boundaries provided the Micmacs with a canoe route to the province's interior and to the Bay of Fundy. A 19th-century canal system connected the lakes for a brief time, but today there are only ruins, which have been partially restored as heritage sites.

⑭ The **Black Cultural Centre for Nova Scotia,** in Westphal (a neighborhood of Dartmouth), is in the heart of the oldest black community in the area. The museum, library, and educational complex is dedicated to the preservation of the history and culture of blacks in Nova Scotia, who first arrived here in the 1600s. ⊠ *Rte. 7 at Cherrybrooke Rd.,* ☏ *902/434–6223.* ⊡ *$2.* ☉ *Weekdays 9–5; also, June–Sept. Sat. 10–4.*

Lodging

$$$$ ☒ **Ramada Renaissance.** In Dartmouth's Burnside Industrial Park, this luxury hotel is aimed at the business traveler as well as families. There is a 108-foot indoor water slide. ⊠ *240 Brownlow Ave., B3B 1X6,* ☏ *902/468–8888; in Canada, 800/561–3733;* FAX *902/468–8765. 178 rooms, 30 suites. Restaurant, bar, room service, pool, hot tub, sauna, exercise room, meeting rooms. AE, DC, MC, V.*

THE SOUTH SHORE AND ANNAPOLIS VALLEY

Mainland Nova Scotia is a long, narrow peninsula; no point in the province is more than 56 kilometers (35 miles) from salt water. The South Shore is on the Atlantic side, the Annapolis Valley on the Fundy side, and though they are less than an hour apart by car, the two destinations seem like different worlds.

The South Shore is rocky coast, island-dotted bays, fishing villages, and shipyards; the Annapolis Valley is lumber, farms, vineyards, and orchards. The South Shore is German, French, and Yankee; the Valley is stoutly British. The South Shore is Lutheran, Catholic, and Puritan. The sea is everywhere on the South Shore; in the Valley the sea is blocked from view by a ridge of mountains.

Route 103, Route 3, and various secondary roads form the province's designated Lighthouse Route, which leads from Halifax down the South Shore. It touches the heads of several big bays and small harbors, revealing an ever-changing panorama of shoreline, inlet, and island. Charming little towns are spaced out every 50 kilometers (30 miles). The Lighthouse Route ends in Yarmouth and the Evangeline Trail begins, winding along the shore of St. Mary's Bay, through a succession of Acadian villages collectively known as the French Shore. The villages blend seamlessly into one another for about 32 kilometers (nearly

20 miles), each one, it seems, with its own wharf, fish plant, and enor mous Catholic church. This tour mostly focuses on the towns along Route 1, but you should follow the side roads whenever the inclina tion strikes; the South Shore rewards slow, relaxed exploration.

The Annapolis Valley runs northeast like a huge trench, flat on the bot tom, sheltered on both sides by the long ridges of the North and South mountains. Occasional roads over the South Mountain lead to the South Shore; short roads over the North Mountain lead to the Fundy shore The rich soil of the valley bottom supports dairy herds, hay, grain, root vegetables, tobacco, and fruit. Apple blossom season (late May and early June) and during the fall harvest are the loveliest times to visit The major impression of the region is one of tranquillity: lush farm land and a settled agricultural society.

Peggy's Cove

48 km (30 mi) southwest of Halifax.

Peggy's Cove, on Route 333, stands at the mouth of the bay facing the open Atlantic. The cove, with its houses huddled around the narrow slit in the boulders, is probably the most photographed village in Canada. It also has the only Canadian post office located in a light house (open April–November). Be careful exploring the bald, rocky shore. Incautious visitors have been swept to their deaths by the tow ering surf that sometimes breaks here.

Dining and Lodging

$$$ ✕🏠 **Dauphinee Inn.** On the shore of Hubbards Cove, about 6 miles before Chester, this charming country inn has first-class accommoda tions and an excellent restaurant. Try its Hot Rocks, a very social din ing concept where you cook on a hot slab of South Shore granite. Very enjoyable, and healthy, with a selection of fresh veggies, and seafood, beef, or chicken to experiment with. Dine on the deck overlooking the cove, savor the view, and feel the tensions roll off your shoulders. Take a walk down to the shore, via the herb garden. There are opportuni ties for bicycling, bird-watching, and deep-sea fishing nearby. ✉ *167 Shore Club Rd., Hubbard B0J 1T0 (Exit 6 off Rte. 103),* ☎ *902/857– 1790 or 800/567–1790,* ℻ *902/857–9555. 6 rooms, 2 suites. Restau rant, lounge, boating, fishing. AE, D, DC, MC. Closed Nov.–Apr.*

Chester

79 km (49 mi) west of Peggy's Cove.

Chester, with just over 1,100 people, is the first stop on Lunenburg County's Mahone Bay. The bay has literally hundreds of islands and, according to locals, there is one for every day of the year. In summer Chester swells with its well-established population of U.S. visitors and Haligonians and with the sailing and yachting community. In mid-Au gust the town celebrates **Chester Race Week,** the largest regatta in At lantic Canada.

The **Ross Farm Museum** is a restored 19th-century living museum that illustrates the evolution of agriculture from 1600 to 1925 and has the types of animals found on a farm of the 1800s—draft horses, oxen, and older breeds or types of animals—not the genetically developed, purebred animals of today. At the Pedlar's Shop you can purchase items made on the premises. ✉ *Rte. 12, New Ross (20-min drive inland from Chester),* ☎ *902/689–2210.* ⊡ *$3.* ☉ *June–mid-Oct., daily 9:30–5:30; winter programs Jan.–mid-Mar., but call ahead.*

⓯ A passenger-only ferry runs from the dock in Chester to the scenic **Big and Little Tancook Island,** 8 kilometers (5 miles) out in Mahone Bay. Reflecting its part-German heritage, Big Tancook claims to make the best sauerkraut in Nova Scotia. There are good walking trails here. The boat runs four times daily Monday–Thursday; six times daily Friday; and twice daily on Saturday and Sunday. The 45-minute trip costs $1.

Dining

$ ✕ **The Galley.** Decked out in nautical bric-a-brac and providing a spectacular view of the ocean, this restaurant has a pleasant, relaxed atmosphere. Try the seafood chowder, live lobster from their in-house pound, and homemade desserts. ⊠ *Rte. 3, 115 Marina Rd., Marriots Cove (Exit 8 off Rte. 103, 3 km west of Chester),* ☎ *902/275–4700. Reservations essential. AE, D, MC, V. Closed mid-Dec.–mid-Mar.*

En Route The town of **Mahone Bay** presents a dramatic face to visitors: Three tall wooden churches—of different denominations—stand side by side, their images reflected in the harbor. Once a shipbuilding community, Mahone Bay is now a crafts center.

Lunenburg

★ ⓰ *9½ km (6 mi) south of the town of Mahone Bay.*

Lunenburg is a feast of Victorian-era architecture, wooden boats, steel draggers (a fishing boat that operates a trawl), historic inns, and good restaurants. In the center of town is a **national historic district.** The fantastic old school on the hilltop is the region's finest remaining example of Second Empire architecture, an ornate style that began in France.

Lunenburg is home port to *Bluenose* and *Bluenose II,* the great racing schooner and its replica. The *Bluenose,* depicted on the back of the Canadian dime, was built in 1921. It was the undefeated champion of the North Atlantic fishing fleet and winner of four international schooner races. *Bluenose II,* a replica of the original schooner, built in 1963, is open to visitors through the Fisheries Museum (☞ *below*) when in port.

The **Fisheries Museum of the Atlantic,** part of the Nova Scotia Museum, is in a renovated fish-plant building and adjacent wharf and includes the last of the Grand Bank schooners, the *Theresa E. Connor,* a steel stern trawler, *Cape Sable,* and an aquarium. There is a gift shop, a theater, and a restaurant within the museum. ⊠ *68 Bluenose Dr.,* ☎ *902/634–4794.* 🖀 *$6.* ☉ *June–mid-Oct., daily 9:30–5:30; off-season, weekdays by appointment only.*

The **Houston North Gallery** represents both trained and self-taught Nova Scotian artists and Inuit (Eskimo) soapstone carvers and printmakers. The gallery, in a large converted house, overlooks the harbor and is near the Fisheries Museum. ⊠ *110 Montague St.,* ☎ *902/634–8869.* ☉ *Feb.–Dec., Mon.–Sat. 10–6, Sun. 1–6.*

Lodging

$$–$$$ 🏨 **Boscawen Inn.** Antiques and fireplaces decorate this elegant mansion built in 1888 in the center of town. Afternoon tea is served in the drawing rooms or on the balcony of this inn that has views of the town's harbor. McLachlan House, an annex, has harbor-view suites. ⊠ *Box 1343, 150 Cumberland St., B0J 2C0,* ☎ *902/634–3325,* 𝐅𝐀𝐗 *902/634–9293. 21 rooms. AE, MC, V.*

$$–$$$ 🏨 **Pelham House Bed & Breakfast.** Close to downtown, this sea captain's home, ca. 1906 and decorated to period throughout, has a large collection of books and periodicals about the sea, sailing, and wooden boats. Sit back and relax on the veranda overlooking the harbour. Full

breakfast and afternoon tea are included in the room rate. ✉ *Box 358, 224 Pelham St., B0J 2C0,* ☎ *902/634–7113,* FAX *902/634–7114. 3 rooms with bath. Business services.*

En Route **Bridgewater** is the main market town of the South Shore and is home to the **DesBrisay Museum** (✉ 130 Jubilee Rd., ☎ 902/543–4033), which explores the nature and people of Lunenburg County and presents exhibits on art, science, technology, and history from museums around the world. The gift shop carries books by local authors and art and crafts by local artisans. The museum accepts donations and is open mid-May to September, Monday to Saturday 9 to 5, Sunday 1 to 5; and October to mid-May, Tuesday to Sunday 1 to 5, Wednesday 1 to 9.

Liverpool

⑰ *46 km (29 mi) south of Bridgewater.*

Liverpool, on the estuary of the Mersey River, was settled around 1760 by New Englanders and is now a fishing and paper-milling town. During the American Revolution and the War of 1812, Liverpool was a privateering center; later, it became an important shipping and trading port. In the center of town is the **Simeon Perkins House,** built in 1766, which was the home of a prominent early settler who kept an extensive and revealing diary. ✉ *109 Main St.,* ☎ *902/354–4058.* ✎ *Free.* ☉ *June–mid-Oct., Mon.–Sat. 9:30–5:30, Sun. 1–5:30.*

The Perkins diary was used extensively by Thomas Raddall, whose internationally successful novels and stories are sometimes set in and around Liverpool. *His Majesty's Yankees* (1944) is a vivid account of a local family's deeply divided loyalties during the American Revolution, when many Nova Scotians sympathized with the rebels.

OFF THE BEATEN PATH

KEJIMKUJIK NATIONAL PARK – This is a 381-square-kilometer (147-square-mile) inland wilderness about 45 minutes from Liverpool in the interior of the western part of the province. Kejimkujik has many lakes with well-marked canoe routes that have primitive campsites. Nature trails are marked for hikers, boat rentals are available, and there's freshwater swimming. One precaution: Check for ticks after hiking in the deep woods. Kejimkujik also operates the Seaside Adjunct near Port Joli on the Atlantic shore that protects one of the last undeveloped tracts of coastline on the Eastern Seaboard. There are two mile-long beaches, both reached by hiking trails (no visitor services; day use only). ✉ Rte. 8 from Liverpool or Annapolis Royal, Maitland Bridge, ☎ 902/682-2772. ✎ $4 per vehicle per day, 4-day pass $9, annual pass $25, camping $8.50–$13 per day.

Outdoor Activities and Sports

The Mersey is the oldest documented canoe route on the continent; it drains Lake Rossignol, Nova Scotia's largest freshwater lake. The interior of the province here is almost entirely unsettled and is ideally explored by canoe. There is good trout and salmon fishing here. For canoe and fishing outfitters, go into the town of Greenfield, on Route 210, off Route 8.

En Route The high noon of **Shelburne** occurred right after the Revolution, when 16,000 Loyalists briefly made it one of the largest communities in North America. Today it is a fishing and shipbuilding town situated on a superb harbor at the mouth of the Roseway River. Many of its homes date back to the Loyalists, including the **Ross-Thomson House** (✉ 9 Charlotte La., ☎ 902/875–3141), which is open June to mid-October, daily 9:30–5:30 (call for winter hours). In Barrington, the **Barrington**

Woolen Mill (⊠ Rte. 3., ☎ 902/637–2185), built in 1882, displays machinery and has exhibits that explain how wool is woven into bolts of twills and flannels, blankets, and suitings. On its grounds are the **Old Meeting House**, a national historic site; the **Seal Island Light Museum**, with its 1906 Fresnel beacon; and the **Western Counties Military Museum**. The mill and its museums are open mid-June to September, Monday to Saturday 9:30–5:30, Sunday 1:30–5:30. Admission is free. **Cape Sable Island,** connected to the mainland via a bridge, has a 13-mile loop that includes Nova Scotia's southernmost extremity. Like Barrington, Cape Sable Island is a Yankee community, as common family names attest; everyone seems to be named "Smith" or "Nickerson." Interestingly, there is a bewildering variety of small evangelical churches, which presumably reflects the Puritan enthusiasm for irreconcilable disagreements over fine points of doctrine. The largest community on Cape Sable is **Clark's Harbour** (locally pronounced "Cla'k's Ha'bah." The famous Cape Islander fishing boat was developed here. By now you will have seen hundreds of examples of them: Sitting high on the water, with its pilothouse forward and its high, flaring bow and low stern, the Cape Islander is Nova Scotia's standard inshore fishing boat.

Pubnico

48 km (30 mi) west of Barrington.

Upon reaching Pubnico you enter the Acadian milieu; from here to Digby the communities are mostly French-speaking. Favorite local fare includes *fricot,* a stew made mostly of vegetables that sometimes has rabbit meat; and rappie pie, made of meat or poultry with potatoes from which much of the starch has been removed.

You'll no doubt notice that there are no fewer than seven Pubnicos: Lower West Pubnico, Middle West Pubnico, and West Pubnico, all on the west shore of Pubnico Harbour; three East Pubnicos on the eastern shore; and just plain Pubnico, at the top of the harbor. These towns were founded by Phillipe Muis D'Entremont, and they once constituted the only barony in French Acadia. He was a prodigious progenitor: To this day, many of the people in the Pubnicos are D'Entremonts, and most of the rest are D'Eons or Amiraults.

You'll also notice the Acadian flag, tricolored with a gold star representing *stella maris,* the star of the sea. The star guides the Acadians during troubled times, which have been frequent. In 1755, after residing for a century and a half in Nova Scotia, chiefly in the Annapolis Valley, the Acadians were expelled by the British—an event that inspired Longfellow's famous *Evangeline.* Some eluded capture and others slowly crept back, and many settled in New Brunswick and along this shore of Nova Scotia.

Yarmouth

❸ *82 km (51 mi) north of Barrington.*

Yarmouth is the largest town (with some 8,500 inhabitants) in southern Nova Scotia, the biggest port west of Halifax, and the point of entry for travelers arriving by ferry from Maine. The ferries are a major reason for Yarmouth's prosperity, as they pull in much revenue by providing quick, inexpensive access for merchants and consumers going to the Boston market for fish, pulpwood, boxes and barrels, knitwear, Irish moss, Christmas trees, and berries.

NEED A
BREAK?   Ask locals in Yarmouth where to go for seafood and they'll tell you, "down 't' **Harris's Quick 'n' Tasty** (⊠ Rte. 1, Dayton, ☎ 902/742–

3467). Specialties include good, old-fashioned food such as rappie pie and lobster cooked up more ways than you can imagine.

In the 19th century Yarmouth was an even bigger shipbuilding center, and its location put the port on all the early steamship routes. The award-winning **Yarmouth County Museum,** in a late-19th-century church, does a fine job of unraveling the region's history with its displays of period furniture, costumes, tools, and toys, as well as a significant collection of ship models and paintings. Also in the building is a research library and archives, where local history and genealogy are documented. ⊠ 22 Collins St., ☎ 902/742–5539. ☜ $2. ⊙ June–mid-Oct., Mon.–Sat. 9–5, Sun. 2–5; mid-Oct.–May, Tues.–Sun. 2–5.

The **Firefighters Museum of Nova Scotia,** one block from the waterfront, is surprisingly interesting. It presents the evolution of fire fighting through its displays of equipment from the leather bucket to the chemical spray. ⊠ 451 Main St., ☎ 902/742–5525. ☜ $1. ⊙ June, Mon.–Sat. 9–5; July and Aug., Mon.–Sat. 9–9, Sun. 10–5; Sept., Mon.–Sat. 9–5; Oct.–May, weekdays 10–noon and 2–4.

Point de l'Eglise

🔟 *70 km (44 mi) north of Yarmouth.*

Point de l'Eglise (Church Point) is the site of **Université Ste-Anne** (⊠ Church Point, ☎ 902/769–2114), the only French-language institution among Nova Scotia's 17 degree-granting colleges and universities. Founded in 1891, this small university is a focus of Acadian studies and culture in the province.

St. Mary's Church (⊠ Church Point, ☎ 902/769–2832), finished in 1905, is the tallest and largest wooden church in North America, at 190 feet long and 185 feet high. The steeple requires 40 tons of rock ballast to keep it steady in the ocean winds. A small museum in the church is open July to mid-October 9:30–5:30; admission is $1; and tours are given by appointment.

Dining and Lodging

$$ ╳🏨 **Manor Inn.** With superior rooms and good food in pleasant surroundings, this colonial mansion beside Doctors Lake on Route 1 is a nice find. There are four settings and price ranges to choose from: coach-house units, lakeside or rose-garden motels, or the main estate. Steak and lobster are the specialties in the dining room; reservations are required. ⊠ Box 56, Rte. 1, Hebron, B0W 1X0 (Rte 1., 5 mi northeast of Yarmouth), ☎ 902/742–2487, ℻ 902/742–8094. 53 rooms. 2 dining rooms, 2 bars, outdoor café, pool, hot tub, tennis court. AE, DC, MC, V.

$$$$ 🏨 **Rodd Grand Hotel.** This hotel is centrally located, just minutes from the ferry terminal. ⊠ Box 220, 417 Main St., B5A 4B2, ☎ 902/742–2446 or 800/565–7633, ℻ 902/742–4645. 138 rooms with bath. Restaurant, lounge, pool, whirlpool, health club. AE, DC, MC, V.

En Route **St. Bernard,** a few miles north of Point de l'Eglise, marks the end of the French Shore. It has an impressive granite Gothic church that seats 1,000 people. Building started in 1910 and took 40 years to complete. **Digby Neck,** the other side of St. Mary's Bay from St. Bernard, is a long basalt peninsula. To explore it, drive on to Digby and follow Route 217.

ong Island and Brier Island

20 *10-minute ferry ride between East Ferry and Tiverton ($1).*

Digby Neck is extended seaward by two narrow islands, Long Island and Brier Island; on the far side is the mouth of the Bay of Fundy. An important stop on the "Atlantic Flyway," the islands are an excellent spot for bird-watching, and because the surrounding waters are rich in plankton they attract a variety of whales, including fins, humpbacks, minkes, and right whales, as well as harbor porpoises.

Ferries going between the islands have to crab sideways against the ferocious Fundy tidal streams that course back and forth through the narrow gaps. The ferries operate hourly, 24 hours a day, and are free to pedestrians ($1 for cars). One of the boats is called *Joshua Slocum* and the other is *Spray;* the former is named for Westport's most famous native, and the latter for the 36-foot oyster sloop that he rebuilt and in which from 1894 to 1896 he became the first man to circumnavigate the world single-handedly. At the southern tip of Brier Island is a **cairn** commemorating the voyage.

Outdoor Activities and Sports

Pirate's Cove Whale Cruises (⊠ Rte. 217, Tiverton, Long Island, ☎ 902/839–2242) operates whale-watching cruises from June through October. The fare is $33.

Digby

35 km (22 mi) north of Point de l'Eglise.

Digby is the terminus of the ferry service from St. John, New Brunswick, and an important fishing port with several good restaurants and a major resort, The Pines (☞ *below*). The town is on an otherwise-landlocked Annapolis Basin, into which the Annapolis River flows after its long course through the valley that bears its name. It's particularly famous for its scallops and for smoked herring known as "Digby Chicks." For a real treat go down to the wharf and visit seafood retailers: They'll cook up the delicious scallops and lobster that you buy.

OFF THE BEATEN PATH   **BEAR RIVER –** This jewel of a village is called the "Switzerland of Nova Scotia." It has a large arts-and-crafts community and an **Ethnographic Museum** (⊠ 18 Chute Rd., ☎ 902/467–3762) devoted to folk costumes and artifacts from exotic lands. ⊠ *15 km (10 mi) inland from Digby.*

Dining and Lodging

$$$$ ✕🖭 **Pines Resort Hotel.** Complete with fireplaces, sitting rooms, a bistro, dining room, and a view of Annapolis Basin, this elegant property offers myriad amenities. Seafood with a French touch is served daily in the restaurant, and the lounge is perfect for quiet relaxation. ⊠ *Box 70, Shore Rd., B0V 1A0,* ☎ *902/245–2511 or 800/667–4637,* FAX *902/245–6133. 144 rooms. Restaurant, bar, pool, sauna, 18-hole golf course, 2 tennis courts, health club, walking trails. AE, D, DC, MC. Closed mid-Oct.–May.*

En Route   **Upper Clements Park,** a theme park that celebrates Nova Scotia's crafts and heritage and has a variety of rides and attractions, including a water slide, carousel, and roller coaster. ⊠ *Rte. 1, Clementsport,* ☎ *902/532–7557; in Atlantic Provinces, 800/565–7275.* 🎫 *Free, but visitors pay for rides.* ☉ *Mid-May–mid-Oct.*

Annapolis Royal

★ ❷ *29 km (18 mi) north of Digby.*

On the Annapolis River, Annapolis Royal was Nova Scotia's first capital (for both the French and English until 1749) and first military base. Local businesses (or the tourist information center, in the Annapolis Royal Tidal Power Building) can provide *Footprints with Footnotes,* a self-guided walking tour of the town; guided tours leave from the lighthouse on St. George Street, daily at 10 and 2:30. This town is well supplied with imposing mansions, particularly along the upper end of St. George Street.

Here you'll find the **Fort Anne National Historic Site,** which was fortified in 1643; the present structures are the remains of the fourth fort erected here and garrisoned by the British, as late as 1854. The officers' quarters are now a museum, with exhibits on the site's history. This is Canada's oldest National Historic Site. ✉ *Waterfront,* ☎ *902/532–2397 or 902/532–2321.* ☞ *Grounds free, museum $2.50.* ☉ *Mid-May–mid-Oct., daily 9–6; mid-Oct.–mid-May, by appointment.*

Don't miss the **Annapolis Royal Historic Gardens,** 10 acres of magnificent theme gardens connected to a wildlife sanctuary maintained by Ducks Unlimited. ✉ *441 St. George St.,* ☎ *902/532–7018.* ☞ *$3.50.* ☉ *Mid-May–mid-Oct., daily 8–dusk.*

The **Annapolis Royal Tidal Power Project** was designed to test the feasibility of generating electricity from tidal energy. This pilot project is the only tidal generating station in North America and one of only three operational sites in the world. The interpretive center explains the process with guided tours. ✉ *¼ mi from Annapolis Royal on causeway that crosses Annapolis River to Granville Ferry,* ☎ *902/532–5454.* ☞ *Free.* ☉ *Mid-May–mid-June, daily 9–5:30; mid-June–Aug., daily 9–8; Sept.–mid-Oct., daily 9–5:30.*

Lodging

$$$ 🏨 **Auberge Wandlyn Royal Anne Motel.** This modern, no-frills motel has a pleasant, quiet setting on 20 acres of land. ✉ *Box 628, Rte. 1, B0S 1A0,* ☎ *902/532–2323,* ℻ *902/532–7277. 30 rooms. Restaurant, whirlpools, sauna, meeting rooms. AE, DC, MC, V.*

$$ 🏨 **Moorings Bed & Breakfast.** Built in 1881, this tall, beautiful home overlooking Annapolis Basin has a fireplace, tin ceilings, antiques, contemporary art, and an extra-long bathtub. ✉ *Box 118, Granville Ferry B0S 1K0,* ☎ ℻ *902/532–2146. 2 rooms with bath, 1 room shares bath. V.*

Port Royal

8 km (5 mi) downriver from Annapolis Royal on the opposite bank.

Port Royal is one of the oldest European settlements in Canada. It was founded in 1605 by Sieur deMonts, with Samuel de Champlain as his geographer. DeMonts's habitation has been reconstructed and is now the **Port Royal National Historic Site,** a French fur-trading post. Here, amid the hardships of the New World, North America's first social club—the Order of Good Cheer—was founded, and the first theatrical presentation written and produced. ✉ *Rte. 1 to Granville Ferry, left 12 km (8 mi),* ☎ *902/532–2898.* ☞ *$2.50.* ☉ *Mid-May–mid-Oct., daily 9–6.*

En Route Like the South Shore, the Valley is punctuated with pleasant small towns, each with a generous supply of extravagant Victorian homes and churches. For most visitors, the Valley towns, each with its own distinction, go by like charming milestones. The Gallery at Saratoga in **Bridgetown** has the paintings of Kenneth Tolmie, whose works reveal Valley scenes and hang in many leading galleries, including the National Gallery of Canada. Kentville, New Minas, Greenwich, and Wolfville run into one another almost like the towns of the French Shore; their more than 12,000 residents form the Valley's largest urban cluster. In **Kentville, Agriculture Canada** (Rte. 1, ☎ 902/678–1093) maintains an important research station on horticulture and poultry; the grounds are beautiful, and free guided tours can be arranged from June through August, weekdays 8–4:30. At Greenwich, take Route 358 to Cape Blomidon via Port Williams and Canning for a spectacular view of the Valley and the Bay of Fundy from the **Lookoff.** Cape Blomidon itself rises 760 feet from the Bay. Continue to **Scots Bay,** where rock shelves contain ribbons of amethyst, jasper, and carnelian. A popular hiking trail leads from the end of Route 358 to the dramatic cliffs of Cape Split. Follow Route 358 back to Route 101 through Wolfeville to **Grand Pré,** which was once a major Acadian site. A small stone church, at the Grand Pré National Historic Site (☎ 902/542–3631) is open mid-May to mid-October, daily 9–6. It commemorates Longfellow's hero in *Evangeline,* and houses an exhibit on the 1755 deportation of the Acadians from the Valley.

Windsor

㉒ *25 km (16 mi) southeast of Wolfville.*

Windsor, the last of the Valley towns, was settled in 1703 as an Acadian community. **Fort Edward**—one of the assembly points for the expulsion of the Acadians—still stands as the only remaining colonial blockhouse in Nova Scotia. ⊠ *Exit 6 off Rte. 1; 1st left at King St.; left again up the street facing the fire station,* ☎ *902/542–3631.* ☉ *Mid-June–Labor Day, daily 10–6.*

Flora Macdonald, the Scottish heroine who helped Bonnie Prince Charlie escape to France, spent the winter of 1779 in Windsor while her husband was posted at the fort. Windsor is also the home of Judge Thomas Chandler Haliburton—lawyer, politician, historian, and humorist. His best-known work, *The Clockmaker,* pillories Nova Scotian follies from the viewpoint of a Yankee clock peddler, Sam Slick, whose witty sayings are still commonly used. **Haliburton House Museum,** on a manicured 25-acre estate, now belongs to the Nova Scotia Museum. ⊠ *414 Clifton Ave.,* ☎ *902/798–2915.* ☉ *June–Oct. 15, Mon.–Sat. 9:30–5:30, Sun. 1–5:30.*

The tide's average rise and fall at Windsor is over 40 feet, and you can see the tidal bore (the leading edge of the incoming tide) rushing up the Meander River and sometimes reaching a height of 3 feet. The local tourist office (☎ 902/798–2690) can tell you estimated tide times.

Uniacke Estate Museum Park, in Mount Uniacke, has a summerhouse built about 1815 for Richard John Uniacke. During the American Revolution, Uniacke, who was fighting on the rebel side, was captured just across the Bay of Fundy. The young Irishman became attorney-general and advocate-general to the Admiralty Court, where his fees in one three-year period during the War of 1812 amounted to the stupendous sum of £50,000. Some of that money went into Uniacke House, a superb example of colonial architecture, on spacious grounds near a lake. The house is preserved in its original condition with many authentic furnishings. ⊠ *758 Main Rd., 30 km (18 mi) east of Windsor,* ☎ *902/866–2560.* ⊠ *Free.* ☉ *June–Oct. 15, Mon.–Sat. 9:30–5:30, Sun. 1–5:30.*

En Route Route 101 cuts across the peninsula through gypsum hills to **Bedford,** at the head of Bedford Basin. Once a tony summer resort, Bedford is now a favored suburb of Halifax. Follow the Bedford Highway to Halifax. If you take Windsor Street downtown, you will be following the 18th-century route between Windsor and Halifax—a proper conclusion to a memorable tour.

NORTHERN NOVA SCOTIA

The area that lies between Halifax and Cape Breton Island includes the rugged coastline on the Atlantic and the gentler Bay of Fundy and Northumberland Strait. We suggest you travel on into Cape Breton before completing that loop. Fishing villages, sandy beaches, and remote cranberry barrens range along the eastern shore. The salt marshes, Scottish clans, and feasts of lobster along Northumberland Strait give way to mills, rolling hills, hiking trails, and farms as you move inland. A land of high tides, million-year-old fossils, and semiprecious stones borders the Bay of Fundy. Walk on the bottom of the sea when the mighty Fundy tide recedes, or ride the tidal bore when it comes rushing back.

This tour takes in parts of three of the official Scenic Trails, including Marine Drive (315 kilometers, or 189 miles), the Sunrise Trail (316 kilometers, or 190 miles), and the Glooscap Trail (365 kilometers, or 219 miles). Any one leg of the routes could be done comfortably as an overnight trip from Halifax; for the whole tour, allow at least three or four days.

Pick up Route 7 at Dartmouth. The Eastern Shore—the Atlantic coast east of Halifax-Dartmouth—is perhaps the most scenic and unspoiled stretch of coastline in mainland Nova Scotia. Because it is unspoiled, of course, the Eastern Shore's facilities are relatively few and simple. The road winds along a deeply indented, glaciated coastline of rocky waters interspersed with pocket beaches, long narrow fjords, and fishing villages. Take the time to prowl the side roads and discover your own favorite rock pools and islets—there are plenty to find.

Musquodoboit Harbour

23 *45 km (28 mi) east of Dartmouth.*

Musquodoboit Harbour, with about 930 residents, is a substantial village at the mouth of the Musquodoboit River. The river itself offers good trout and salmon fishing, and the village touches on two slender and lovely harbors. One of the Eastern Shore's best beaches, **Martinique Beach,** is about 12 kilometers (8 miles) south of the village, and other fine beaches are at Clam Bay and Clam Harbour, several kilometers (a few miles) east of Martinique.

Lodging

$$–$$$ ⊞ **Salmon River House.** About 35 minutes east of Dartmouth, where Route 7 crosses the Salmon River, is this unpretentious white-frame inn, on 30 acres and providing glorious views. The home has a sun room and one room with a waterbed and whirlpool bath. ⊠ *9931 #7 Hwy., Salmon River Bridge, B0J 1P0,* ☎ *902/889–3353 or 800/565–3353,* FAX *902/889–3653. 6 rooms with bath or shower. Dining room, boating, fishing. MC, V.*

Ship Harbour

43 km (25 mi) east of Musquodoboit Harbour.

In Ship Harbour, the provincial Department of Fisheries has developed the **Aquaculture Demonstration Centre** (⊠ Rte. 7, ☎ 902/845–2991), with a small interpretive center on the hatchery. The Centre is open May–September, weekdays 9–3; admission is free. As you travel a bit farther, take note of the strings of white buoys in Ship Harbour, marking one of North America's largest cultivated mussel farms. Another side of the fishery can be seen at the **Fisherman's Life Museum at Jeddore Oyster Pond,** where a homestead and small farm illustrate the way of life of an inshore fisherman and his family circa 1900. ⊠ *58 Navy Pool Loop,* ☎ *902/889–2053.* ☞ *Free.* ☉ *June–Oct. 15, Mon.–Sat. 9:30–5:30, Sun. 1–5:30.*

En Route   This part of the shore experienced a small gold rush during the first part of this century, complete with a 1936 mine disaster. A small local museum (⊠ Rte. 224, ☎ 902/384–2653) in **Moose River Gold Mines,** about 30 kilometers (19 miles) north of Tangier, commemorates the period. It's open July and August, Monday–Saturday 10–6, Sunday 1–6; admission is free.

Don't fail to stop in **Tangier** for some delicious smoked salmon, eel, or mackerel from **Willy Krauch's Danish Smokehouse** (⊠ Rte. 7, ☎ 902/772–2188). It is open year-round, weekdays 8–6 and weekends 10–5. **Sheet Harbour** is the major service center for the Eastern Shore, with a bank, hospital, accommodations, and campgrounds.

Sherbrooke Village

★ ㉔   *83 km (52 mi) north of Sheet Harbour.*

Sherbrooke Village, although it has fewer than 400 residents, is the Shore's leading tourist center. The St. Mary's River, which flows through the hamlet, is one of Nova Scotia's best salmon rivers, and much of the village itself has been rebuilt by the Nova Scotia Museum to its late 19th-century character, with a blacksmith shop, water-powered sawmill, horse-drawn wagons, tearooms, and stores. Twenty-five buildings have been restored on their original sites for the living history village. ⊠ *Rte. 7,* ☎ *902/522–2400.* ☞ *$4.* ☉ *June–mid-Oct., daily 9:30–5:30.*

En Route   From Sherbrooke you'll have to decide in which direction you wish to go. Marine Drive continues up the shore through wild, harsh, lovely country rarely visited by tourists. To see Nova Scotia unbuttoned, as it were, follow the Drive over to **Canso,** and pick up the Trans-Canada Highway via Guysborough. You will find few tourist attractions, although Canso itself has a stirring history and a National Historic Site; in this part of the province you'll come closer to traditional Nova Scotian ways of life than you will anywhere else.

The alternative is to stay on Route 7, which turns inland up the St. Mary's River through spruce woods and rolling farmland to Antigonish, an hour's drive away. The drive takes you from the Atlantic to the Northumberland Strait, part of the Gulf of St. Lawrence: from cold water and rocky shores to warm water and broad sandy beaches. If water sports are your thing, this is your shore: There are miles of wonderful beaches all along Northumberland Strait.

Antigonish

㉕ *62 km (39 mi) north of Sherbrooke Village.*

Antigonish is the home of **St. Francis Xavier University,** a center for Gaelic studies and for the cooperative movement. Antigonish is also a **cathedral** town and has a population of about 5,200.

Dining

$$ ✕ **Lobster Treat Restaurant.** This cozily decorated brick, pine, and stained-glass restaurant was once a two-room schoolhouse. The varied menu includes fresh seafood, chicken, pastas, and bread and pie baked on the premises. Because of its relaxed atmosphere and children's menu, families enjoy coming here. ✉ *241 Post Rd. (Trans-Canada Hwy.),* ☎ *902/863–5465. AE, DC, MC, V. Closed Nov.–mid-Apr.*

En Route Follow Route 337, the Sunrise Trail, for a glorious drive along St George's Bay with its many good swimming beaches, before the road abruptly climbs 1,000 feet up and over to **Cape George.** There's a little take-out shop on the wharf at **Ballantyne's Cove,** a tiny artificial harbor near the tip of Cape George, that has some of the best best fish-and-chips in Nova Scotia. Grab an order and enjoy the views.

After following the Cape, high above the sea, the road runs along Northumberland Strait through lonely farmlands and tiny villages, such as Arisaig and Lismore. If, after hearing those names, you have any doubt about the Scottish origin of the people, they will be laid to rest by a stone cairn in Lismore that commemorates Bonnie Prince Charlie's Highland rebels, slaughtered by the English at Culloden in 1746.

Much of the rest of the road runs inland, but the turnoff to Merigomish leads into a maze of inlets, beaches, and islands that are well worth exploring. Either way you go, you'll eventually emerge at Route 104, the Trans-Canada Highway. Turn right 1½ kilometers (1 mile) later and follow the shore road to **Melmerby Beach**—a favorite local spot—and continue on to New Glasgow by a circuitous shoreside road. Alternatively, stay on the Trans-Canada to reach New Glasgow, a few kilometers (a couple of miles) away.

New Glasgow is one of five industrial towns on the three rivers that flow into Pictou Harbour. Combined, the five towns have a population of nearly 30,000, making this one of the largest urban centers in the province. New Glasgow is a steel-fabricating and manufacturing center, **Trenton** manufactures railway cars, and **Westville** and **Stellarton** are coal-mining towns.

Pictou

★ **㉖** *74 km (46 mi) west of Antigonish.*

For the visitor, the most interesting town by far is Pictou, somewhat sullied by a paper mill across the harbor, but nevertheless one of the most engaging communities in Nova Scotia. Lining its streets are typically Scottish-style stone cottage homes and public buildings, and there's a good selection of very attractive small hotels and restaurants Tour the **Grohmann** factory (✉ 116 Water St., ☎ 902/485–4224) for a glimpse of knife making. Using the main highway system, Pictou can be reached in about two hours from Halifax.

In 1773 the *Hector*—the nearest thing to a Canadian *Mayflower*—came to Pictou Harbour, inaugurating the torrent of Scottish immigration that permanently altered the character of the province and the nation. A replica of the *Hector* is under construction at the *Hector Heritage Quay* (☎ 902/485–8028).

Under the inspired leadership of such men as the pioneering educator Thomas McCulloch, Pictou quickly became a center of commerce, education, theological disputation, and radical politics. **McCulloch House,** a restored 1806 building with displays of McCulloch's scientific collection and such personal items as furniture, is preserved as part of the Nova Scotia Museum. ⌧ *Old Haliburton Rd.,* ☎ *902/485–4563.* 🖾 *Free.* ☉ *June–mid-Oct., Mon.–Sat. 9:30–5:30, Sun. 11:30–5:30.*

Dining and Lodging

$$–$$$ ✕🖬 **Braeside Inn.** Built in 1938, this inn, on a 5-acre hillside in the center of historic Pictou, has well-appointed accommodations and fine food. Beaches are nearby. The dining room specializes in fresh seafood dishes. ⌧ *Box 1810, 126 Front St., B0K 1H0,* ☎ *902/485–5046 or 800/613–7701,* 🖷 *902/485–1701. 20 rooms with bath. 2 dining rooms, meeting room. AE, MC, V.*

$$ 🖬 **Walker Inn.** A hospitable and energetic Swiss couple run this downtown inn in their brick Georgian-style town house, built in 1865. Every room is different. ⌧ *Box 629, 34 Coleraine St., B0K 1H0,* ☎ *902/485–1433. 10 no-smoking rooms with bath. Restaurant, library, meeting room. CP. AE, MC, V.*

En Route Leave Pictou on Route 6, the Sunrise Trail. The road runs beside an apparently endless string of beaches, with many summer homes plunked in the adjoining fields. **River John** is a good meal stop, especially during May, June, and July, when the community prepares lobster suppers, or in August, when chicken barbecues are on the menu. At Brule, take Route 326 for about 4 kilometers (2½ miles) to the **Sutherland Steam Mill** (⌧ Denmark off Rte. 326, ☎ 902/657–3365), which is open June–October 15, Monday–Saturday 9:30–5:30, Sunday 1–5:30. Inquire about steam-up days, when steam engine enthusiasts get together and fire up their engines. From the Sutherland Steam Mill turn right on Route 256 (at the intersection with Route 311) to reach the water-powered gristmill at **Balmoral Mills** (☎ 902/657–3016). Built in 1860, it's the oldest operating mill in Nova Scotia and one of five that once operated on this stream. It is now a museum with milling demonstrations and a picnic park on the grounds. It's open June–mid-October, Monday–Saturday 9:30–5:30, Sunday 1–5:30; demonstrations daily 10–noon and 2–4. **Tatamagouche,** a market center for farmers and fishermen, is beautifully situated on a ridge overlooking a small estuarine harbor. Beyond Tatamagouche, turn right to Malagash to find **Jost Vineyards** (⌧ Off Highway 104, on Rte. 6, ☎ 902/257–2636; in Atlantic Canada, 800/565–4567), one of three farm wineries in the province. Jost produces a surprisingly wide range of very acceptable, award-winning wines, including an ice wine that's making a name for the vineyard. Tours run at 3 PM daily, from mid-June through September.

Pugwash

㉗ *46 km (29 mi) west of Tatamagouche.*

Pugwash was the home of Cleveland industrialist Cyrus Eaton, at whose estate numerous Thinkers' Conferences brought together leading intellectual figures from the West and the Soviet Union during the 1950s and 1960s. Pugwash is still Scottish terrain, as the Gaelic street signs attest. The town is also the home of **Seagull Pewter** (⌧ Durham St., ☎ 902/243–2516) a husband-and-wife crafts operation that has grown into a $25 million business of exporting pewter vessels, picture frames, and other artifacts worldwide. The showroom fronts on the main highway.

En Route From Pugwash, a half-hour drive will take you to Amherst, through rolling hills and along the edge of Amherst Marsh, part of the Tantramar Marsh. The Tantramar covers most of the Isthmus of Chignecto, the narrow neck of land that joins Nova Scotia to the rest of North America, and it is said to be the largest marsh in the world. If you have not yet had your fill of sandy beaches, however, an attractive alternative route leads through Northport, Lorneville, and Tidnish Dock.

Amherst

44 km (28 mi) west of Pugwash.

Amherst stands on one of the glacial ridges that borders the Tantramar Marsh. It was once a thriving manufacturing center for many products, including pianos and furnaces. In 1917, en route from New York to Russia, the Communist leader Leon Trotsky was confined here for a month in a prisoner-of-war camp.

Dining and Lodging

$$$ ✕🏠 **Amherst Shore Country Inn.** This seaside country inn with a beau-
★   tiful view of Northumberland Strait has comfortable rooms, suites, and a seaside cottage fronting 600 feet of private beach. Incredibly well-prepared four-course dinners, featuring home-grown produce, are served at one daily seating (7:30, by reservation only). ⊠ *Lorneville (32 km, or 20 mi, from Amherst on Rte. 366), R.R. 2, Amherst, B4H 3X9,* ☎ *902/661–4800. 2 rooms, 6 suites, 1 rustic cottage. Dining room AE, DC, MC, V. Closed late Oct.–Apr.*

En Route From Amherst, a two-hour drive via Routes 104 and 102 will return you directly to Halifax. However, the Glooscap Trail from Amherst through Parrsboro to Truro is much more interesting and takes only about an hour longer. Relatively few tourists travel the latter route, which provides some of the most striking scenery in Nova Scotia. If you opt for the Glooscap Trail, there are several roads that connect Amherst and Parrsboro.

Springhill

28 *42 km (26 mi) southeast of Amherst.*

Route 2 leads through the coal-mining town of Springhill, the site of the famous mine disaster immortalized in the folk song "The Ballad of Springhill" by Peggy Seeger and Ewen McColl. Today the public is invited to tour a real coal mine, the **Spring Hill Miners Museum.** ⊠ *Black River Rd, off Rte. 2,* ☎ *902/597–3449.* 🕐 *Mid-May–mid-Oct.* 🎟 *$4*

Springhill is the hometown of singer Anne Murray, whose career is celebrated in the **Anne Murray Centre.** ⊠ *Main St.,* ☎ *902/597–8614.* 🎟 *$5.* 🕐 *May–Oct., daily 9–5.*

En Route Routes 2 and 302 offer the most direct passage to Parrsboro, running through tall hills and farmland to join Route 2 at Southampton. An alternative—and better—option is to take the Glooscap Trail, which branches off via Route 242 to Joggins.

Joggins

29 *40 km (25 mi) west of Springhill.*

Joggins has coal-age fossils embedded in 150-foot sandstone cliffs. Visit the **Joggins Fossil Centre,** where you can learn about the region's geological and archaeological history. Also, guided tours of the fossil cliffs are available, but departure times depend on the tides. ⊠ *30 Main St.*

☎ 902/251–2727. ✉ *Centre $3.50, tour $10.* ☉ *June–Sept., daily 9–6:30.*

En Route   From Joggins, the Glooscap Trail runs along the shore of Chignecto Bay through Shulie and Sand River to Apple River. You are now on the Bay of Fundy, the third coastline of this tour, where stupendous volumes of water rushing into a narrow shelving bay create the world's highest tides; they sometimes reach heights of 50 feet.

En Route   **Advocate Harbour** was named by Champlain for his friend Marc Lescarbot, who was a lawyer, or "avocat." Built on flat shore land with a tall ridge backdrop and a broad harbor before it, Advocate is eerily beautiful. **Cap d'Or,** a piece of land that juts out and divides the waters of the main Bay of Fundy from the narrow enclosure of the Minas Basin, has a spectacular lighthouse. As the tides change, fierce riptides create stunning waves. The view from the ridge down to the lighthouse is superb; the view from the lighthouse itself is almost equally magnificent, but the road down is rather primitive and should be attempted only in four-wheel-drive vehicles. **Spencer's Island** (not really an island) is a 19th-century shipbuilding community on Route 209. A cairn commemorates the construction of the famous *Mary Celeste*, which was found in 1872 sailing in the mid-Atlantic without a crew; she had been abandoned at sea with the table still set for dinner.

Parrsboro

③⓪   *45 km (28 mi) east of Spencer's Island.*

Parrsboro, a center for rock hounds and fossil hunters, is the main town on this shore, and hosts the **Rockhound Roundup** every August. Among the exhibits and festivities are geological displays, concerts, and other special events. The **Fundy Geological Museum** (✉ 6 Two Island Rd., ☎ 902/254–3814) stimulates geologists' interests year-round with exhibits from pre-Jurassic to present; admission is $3. Parrsboro is an appropriate setting for the museum since it's not far from the Minas Basin area, the site where some of the oldest dinosaur fossils in Canada were found. Two-hundred-million-year-old dinosaur fossils are displayed here, alongside exhibits of amethysts, agates, zeolites, and other mineral, plant, and animal relics that have washed out of nearby cliffs; hunting for them is a favorite pastime of the town's visitors. The museum offers workshops on jewelry-making and walking tours to nearby geological sites, led by the museum curator.

If you still haven't gotten your fill of dinosaurmania, check out the "World's Smallest Dinosaur footprints," on display at the **Parrsboro Rock and Mineral Shop and Museum** (✉ 39 Whitehall Rd., ☎ 902/254–2981), run by Eldon George.

Although fossils have become Parrsboro's claim to fame, this harbor town was also a major shipping and shipbuilding port, and its history is described at the **Ottawa House Museum-by-the-Sea.** Ottawa House, which has a striking location overlooking the Bay of Fundy, was the summer home of Sir Charles Tupper, a former premier of Nova Scotia who was briefly prime minister of Canada. ✉ *Whitehall Rd.,* ☎ *902/254–2376.* ✉ *$1.* ☉ *July–early Sept., daily 10–8.*

The 125-foot-high **Hidden Falls** is almost 5 kilometers (about 3 miles) from Parrsboro. The gift shop here is a jumble of antique furniture, books, crockery, and bric-a-brac that warrants a visit. ✉ *Rte. 2,* ☎ *902/254–2505.* ✉ *Free.* ☉ *Mid-May–Nov.*

The Arts

Parrsboro's professional **Ship's Company Theatre** (☎ 902/254–2003)
has a summer season of plays based on historical events of the region,
performed aboard the MV *Kipawo*, a former Minas Basin ferry.

Five Islands

24 km (15 mi) east of Parrsboro.

Among the most beautiful scenic areas along Route 2 is Five Islands,
which, according to Micmac legend, was created when the god Glooscap
threw handfuls of sod at Beaver. **Five Islands Provincial Park** (☎
902/254–2980), on the shore of Minas Bay, has a campground, a beach,
hiking trails, and some interpretation of the region's unusual geology.

Lodging

$$–$$$ 🏠 **Shady Maple B&B.** Here's a unique property: a working farm where
you can breakfast on fresh eggs and the farm's own maple syrup,
jams, and jellies. Enjoy the smoke-free rooms and sun-dried bed linen,
and take a dip in the pool. One of the three rooms is a deluxe suite
with a waterbed. Full breakfast included. ✉ *R.R. 1, Masstown,
B0M 1G0,* ☎ *902/662–3565,* ℻ *902/662–3565. 3 rooms. Pool.
MC, V.*

CAPE BRETON ISLAND

The highways and byways of the Island of Cape Breton are some of
the most spectacular drives in North America. Wind through the Cape
Breton Highlands National Park where you climb mountains and
plunge back down to the sea in a matter of minutes, as you skirt the
rugged coastal headlands. Visit villages where ancient dialects can still
be heard. Explore a fortress where period players bring history alive.
This is a place where heritage is alive, where the atmosphere is maritime, and where inventors Marconi and Bell share the spotlight with
coal miners and singers like Rita MacNeil.

If Halifax is the heart of Nova Scotia, Cape Breton is its soul, complete with soul music: flying fiddles, boisterous rock, velvet ballads.
Cape Breton musicians—weaned on Scottish jigs and reels—are among
Canada's finest, and you can hear them all over the island, all summer long, at dozens of local festivals and concerts.

Allow three or four days for this meandering tour of approximately
710 kilometers (about 420 miles) that begins by entering the island via
the Canso Causeway on Route 104. Turn left at the rotary, and take
Route 19, the Ceilidh Trail (129 kilometers, or 72 miles), which winds
along the mountainside, with fine views across St. George's Bay to Cape
George. This western shoreline of Cape Breton faces the Gulf of St.
Lawrence, and is famous for its sandy beaches and warm salt water.

Mabou

31 *13 km (8 mi) northeast of Port Hood.*

Mabou has been called "the prettiest village in Canada," and it is also
perhaps the most Scottish, with its Gaelic signs and a deep tradition
of Scottish music and dancing. This is the hometown of national
recording and performing artists, such as John Allan Cameron and the
Rankin Family; stop at a local gift shop and pick up some tapes to play
as you drive down the long fjord of Mabou Harbour to **Mabou Mines**.
The mines is a place so hauntingly exquisite that you expect to meet
the *sidhe,* the Scottish fairies, capering on the hillsides. Within these

hills is some of the finest hiking in the province, and above the land fly bald eagles, plentiful in this region. Inquire locally or at the tourist office on Margaree Forks for information about trails. The Ceilidh Trail winds on through green wooded glens and hidden farms.

Lodging

$$$ ☷ **Glenora Inn & Distillery.** This friendly inn is home of North America's only single malt whisky distillery. Sample a "wee dram" of their own whiskey—billed as Canada's first legal moonshine—as you dine. Stop in for a distillery tour even if you don't stay overnight. From November through April, rooms are available by reservation only. ⊠ *Glenville (Rte. 19 between Mabou and Inverness), B0E 1X0,* ☎ *902/258–2662. 29 rooms. Restaurant, lounge, gift shop. AE, MC, V.*

En Route The road continues past **Inverness,** a fishing port and former coal-mining town with many services, and on to **Broad Cove,** the site of one of the most venerable Cape Breton Scottish concerts, held annually in late July. The road forks at **Dunvegan,** the home of Alastair MacLeod, whose powerful short stories pierce deeply into the life of these Scottish communities. Look for his collections *The Lost Salt Gift of Blood* or *As Birds Bring Forth the Sun* for a better understanding of the region.

Take Route 219 at Dunvegan, following the coast through **Chimney Corner** and **Whale Cove.** One of the beaches near Chimney Corner has "sonorous sands": When you step on the sand or drag a foot through it, it squeaks and moans.

Margaree Harbour

㉜ *28 km (18 mi) north of Inverness.*

The Margaree River is a cultural dividing line: South of the river the settlements are Scottish, up the river they are largely Irish, and north of the river they are Acadian French.

The Ceilidh Trail joins the Cabot Trail at Margaree Harbour at the mouth of the Margaree River, a famous salmon-fishing stream and a favorite canoe route. Stop at the schooner *Marion Elizabeth,* now the Schooner Village restaurant and free museum, with many small shops and a good selection of books about Cape Breton. On the grounds is writer Farley Mowat's schooner *Happy Adventure,* featured in his book *The Boat That Wouldn't Float.* ⊠ *At the bridge, no phone.*

Dining and Lodging

$$$ ✕☷ **Normaway Inn.** This secluded 1920s inn, nestled on 250 acres in the hills of the Margaree Valley at the beginning of the Cabot Trail, has distinctive rooms and cabins, most with wood stoves and screened porches; some have hot tubs. Take advantage of the traditional entertainment or films featured nightly, and the weekly square dances in the "Barn." The inn is known for its gourmet country cuisine. ⊠ *Box 326, Egypt Rd., 2 mi off Cabot Trail, B0E 2C0,* ☎ *902/248–2987 or 800/565–9463,* ⅆ *902/248–2600. 9 rooms, 19 cabins. Restaurant, tennis court, hiking, bicycles, travel services. MC, V. Closed mid-Oct.–mid-June.*

$–$$ ☷ **Heart of Hart's B&B Inn.** This 100-year-old rural farmhouse is within walking distance of the village. The theme is "very country," with wood stove, antiques, colonial colored glass, and an array of flowers in the gardens. A full breakfast is included in the room rate and four-course country dinners are served by reservation to in-house guests Wednesday through Sunday. ⊠ *Cabot Trail, B0E 2H0,* ☎ *902/248–2765,* ⅆ *902/248–2606. 5 rooms. Travel services. MC, V.*

En Route The Cabot Trail crosses the river and runs along the shore through Bel
Côte and **Cap Le Moine.** Don't miss Joe Delaney's whimsical scarecrov
farm and gift shop at Cap Le Moine (⊠ Cabot Trail, ☎ 902/235–2108
Most of the harbors on this bold, straight coast are the estuaries c
small rivers, with treacherous sandbars at their mouths. Stop at **Friar'
Head** and look over the cliff: The tiny cleft in the rocks below was lon
used as a fishing harbor.

Chéticamp

❸❸ *26 km (14 mi) north of Margaree Harbour.*

Chéticamp, an Acadian community, has the best harbor and the larges
settlement on the shore. With its tall silver steeple towering over the vil
lage, it stands exposed on a wide lip of flat land below a range of bal
green hills, behind which lies the high plateau of the Cape Breton High
lands. Chéticamp is famous for its hooked rugs, available at many loca
gift shops. The **Dr. Elizabeth LeFort Gallery and Museum** displays art
facts and fine hooked embroidery work, rugs, and tapestries. ⊠ *Les Tro*
Pignons, ⌷ *$2.* ☉ *May–Oct., weekdays 9–5; July–Aug. 9–6.*

★ At the outskirts of Chéticamp begins **Cape Breton Highlands Nationc
Park,** a 950-square-kilometer (361-square-mile) wilderness of woode
valleys, plateau barrens, and steep cliffs that stretches across the north
ern peninsula of Cape Breton from the Gulf Shore to the Atlantic. Th
highway through the park is magnificent, as it rises to the tops of th
coastal mountains and descends through tight switchbacks to the sea
For wildlife watchers there's much to see, including moose, eagle, dee
bear, fox, and bobcat. ☎ *902/285–2535, in winter, 902/285–2270*
⌷ *May–Oct. $6 per party per day, 4-day pass $18, seasonal pass $30*
Nov.–Apr. free (includes use of Cabot Trail lookouts within park
roadside exhibits, walking trails, picnic areas); camping $13–$19.

Outdoor Activities and Sports

Chéticamp is known for its whale-watching cruises, which depart i
June, once daily, and in July and August, three times daily from th
government wharf. **Whale Cruisers Ltd.** (☎ 902/224–3376 or 800/813-
3376) is one of the reliable charter companies in the area. Cruises cos
$25 for adults.

En Route **Pleasant Bay** is a tiny village in a cleft of the mountains, where the Grand
Anse River reaches the sea. A spur road creeps along the cliffs to Re
River, beyond which is **Gampo Abbey**—the only Tibetan Buddhis
monastery in America—on a broad flat bench of land high above th
sea. The most northerly tip of the island is not part of the Nationa
Park; turn off to discover **Bay St. Lawrence** and **Meat Cove,** in an am
phitheater of bare green hills, looking northward to the killer islan
of **St. Paul's,** site of more than 60 charted shipwrecks. Whale-watch
ing cruises are available June through August, three times daily, throug
Whale Watch Bay St. Lawrence in Bay St. Lawrence (in summer, ☎
902/383–2981; in winter, 902/492–0325). The cost is $22.

The main road reenters the park near **Cabot's Landing,** the long sand
beach in Aspy Bay where Cape Breton folks believe that John Cabc
made his landfall in 1497; this theory, however, is vigorously denie
in Newfoundland. **Dingwall,** in the center of the bay, is an archetypa
fishing village; so are White Point, New Haven, and Neil's Harbou.

ngonish

34 *113 km (70 mi) northeast of Chéticamp.*

Ingonish, one of the leading holiday destinations on the island, is actually several villages on two bays, divided by a long narrow peninsula called Middle Head. Each bay has a sandy beach, and Middle Head is home to the provincially owned **Keltic Lodge,** a first-class hotel and resort complex located within the national park. It offers a wide range of activities, among them cross-country skiing, golfing on the world-class Highlands Links, swimming, and hiking. The lodge is open June–October and January–March. Downhill ski facilities are also nearby. Stop at **Lynn's Craft Shop and Art Gallery** (Cabot Trail, ☎ 902/285–2735), which offers the work of noted local artist Christopher Gorey and others. The gallery is open May–October.

En Route From Ingonish, the road snakes up Cape Smokey and along the face of the mountains, offering spectacular views from high above the sea. **Wreck Cove** is the headquarters of *Cape Breton's Magazine,* an award-winning oral-history publication whose homespun appearance belies its essential sophistication. Look for it on newsstands throughout the island.

En Route Notice the small islands on the far side of the mouth of St. Ann's Bay: These are the **Bird Islands,** breeding grounds for Atlantic puffins, black guillemots, razor-billed auks, and cormorants. Boat tours are available from **Bird Islands Boat Tour** (☎ 902/674–2384) in Big Bras d'Or (landing on the islands is forbidden, however). The road turns into a ferry wharf. Take the short ferry ride to **Englishtown,** home of the celebrated Cape Breton Giant, Angus MacAskill. Ferries run 24 hours a day, and the fare is 50¢. The **Giant MacAskill Museum** (⌧ Rte. 312, ☎ 902/929–2106) holds artifacts and the remains of the 7'9" man. It's open May–October, daily 9–6; admission is $1. **South Gut St. Ann's** is home to North America's only **Gaelic College** (☎ 902/295–3441). Its Great Hall of the Clans depicts Scottish history and has an account of the Great Migration. The college offers courses in Gaelic language and literature, Scottish music and dancing, weaving, and other Scottish arts. There's also a Scottish gift shop. In the first week of August Gaelic College hosts the Gaelic Mod, a weeklong festival of games, theater, and music.

Baddeck

35 *20 km (13 mi) south of South Gut St. Ann's.*

Baddeck, the most highly developed tourist center in Cape Breton, has more than 1,000 motel beds, a golf course, many fine gift shops, and numerous restaurants. Baddeck is the main town on the **Bras d'Or Lake,** a vast, warm, almost-landlocked inlet of the sea, which occupies the entire center of Cape Breton. The coastline of the Lake is more than 967 kilometers (600 miles) long, and people sail yachts from all over the world to cruise their serene, unspoiled coves and islands. Bald eagles have become so plentiful around the lake that they are now exported to the United States to restock natural habitats. Four of the largest communities along the shore are Micmac Indian reserves.

Baddeck's attractions include the **Centre Bras d'Or Festival of the Arts,** which offers live music and drama every evening during the summer. The annual **regatta** of the Bras d'Or Yacht Club is held in the first week of August. Sailing tours and charters are available locally, as are bus tours along the Cabot Trail. A free ferry (passengers only) shuttles be-

tween the government wharf and the sandy **beach,** by the lighthouse
at Kidston Island.

The **Alexander Graham Bell National Historic Site** is the most com
prehensive collection of Bell's artifacts, mementos, and photograph
in the world. Three exhibit halls tell the story of Bell's incredible life
and work, including the invention of the telephone. The site is a trib
ute to the genius and compassion of the great inventor who spent hi
summers here and is buried on the mountaintop above his mansio
(which is still owned by his family). People of all ages will find a visi
here an entertaining and educational experience; inquire about specia
summer programs. Picnic facilities are available on these beautifu
grounds. ⊠ *Chebucto St.,* ☎ *902/295–2069, TTY 902/295–1512.*
$2.25. ⊘ *July and Aug., daily 9–8; Sept., daily 9–6; Oct.–June (re
duced service), daily 9–5.*

Dining and Lodging

$$$$ ✕🖼 **Inverary Inn Resort.** On the shores of the magnificent Bras d'O
Lake, this resort has stunning views and a lot of activities for the
money. Choose from cozy pine-paneled cottages, modern hotel units
or the elegant 100-year-old main lodge. There's boating and swimming
and close proximity to the village, but the resort remains tranquil. Fam
ilies will appreciate the on-site children's playground and the choice
of dining in the Lakeside Cafe or the elegant main dining room. ⊠ *Bo:
190, Rte. 205 and Shore Rd., B0E 1B0,* ☎ *902/295–2674,* FAX *902/295–
5660. 137 rooms. Restaurant, café, indoor pool, sauna, 3 tennis courts
chapel. AE, D, MC, V.*

En Route   From Baddeck, continue along the lake shore on Trans-Canada 10.
to Exit 6, which leads to **Little Narrows,** then take the ferry to the
Washabuck Peninsula and Route 223 to **Estmere** and **Iona.** Ferries run
24 hours a day, and the fare is 25¢.

Iona

㊱   *56 km (35 mi) south of Baddeck.*

Iona is the site of the **Nova Scotia Highland Village,** set high on a moun
tainside, with a spectacular view of Bras d'Or Lake and the narrov
Barra Strait. The village's 10 historic buildings were assembled from
all over Cape Breton to depict Highland Scots' way of life from thei
origins in the Hebrides to the present day. Among the participants a
this living-history museum are a smith in the blacksmith shop and
clerk in the store. ⊠ *Rte. 233,* ☎ *902/725–2272.* 🎫 *$4.* ⊘ *Recep
tion desk and museum, mid-June–mid-Sept., Mon.–Sat. 9–5, Sun. 11–
6; reception desk also mid-Sept.–mid-June, weekdays 9–5.*

Dining and Lodging

$$ ✕🖼 **Highland Heights Inn.** The rural surroundings, the Scottish home
style cooking served near the dining room's huge stone fireplace, an
the view of the lake substitute nicely for the Scottish Highlands. Th
inn is on a hillside beside the Nova Scotia Highland Village, overlookin;
the village of Iona, where some residents still speak the Gaelic languag
of their ancestors. Enjoy the salmon (or any fish in season), fresh-bake
oat cakes, and homemade desserts. ⊠ *Box 19, Rte. 223,* ☎ *902/725–
2360,* FAX *902/725–2800. 26 rooms. Dining room. D, MC, V. Close
mid-Oct.–mid-May.*

En Route   The Barra Strait Bridge joins Iona to Grand Narrows. A few kilome
ters (about 2 miles) from the bridge, bear right toward East Bay. (▶
you miss this turn, don't worry; you'll have just as scenic a drive alon;
St. Andrews Channel.) The East Bay route runs through the Micma

village of **Eskasoni,** the largest native community in the province. This is one of the friendliest villages, with a fascinating cultural heritage.

Sydney

③⑦ *60 km (37 mi) northeast of Iona.*

East Bay becomes a prosperous outer suburb of Sydney, the heart of Nova Scotia's second largest urban cluster. "Industrial Cape Breton" encompasses villages, unorganized districts, and a half-dozen towns—most of which sprang up around the coal mines, which fed the steel plant at Sydney. These are warmhearted, interesting communities with a diverse ethnic population, including Ukrainians, Welsh, Poles, Lebanese, West Indians, Italians; most residents descended from the miners and steelworkers who arrived a century ago when the area was booming. Sydney is also the only significantly industrialized district in Atlantic Canada, and it has suffered serious environmental damage.

Sydney has the island's only real airport, its only university, and a lively entertainment scene that specializes in Cape Breton music. The **University College of Cape Breton** (⊠ 1250 Grand Lake Rd., ☎ 902/539–5300) has many facilities for the public, such as the **Boardmore Playhouse** and the island's only public **art gallery.**

Sydney is also a popular departure point: Fast ferries leave from North Sydney for Newfoundland, and scheduled air service to Newfoundland and the French islands of St. Pierre and Miquelon departs from Sydney Airport.

Dining and Lodging

$$$ ✕🏨 **Delta Sydney.** This hotel is on the harbor, beside the yacht club, and close to the center of town. The attractively decorated guest rooms each have a view of the harbor. The intimate dining room specializes in seafood and Continental cuisine. ⊠ *300 Esplanade, B1P 6J4;* ☎ *902/562–7500 or 800/887–1133; in Canada, 800/268–1133;* ℻ *902/562–3023. 152 rooms. Restaurant, lounge, indoor pool, sauna, exercise room. AE, DC, MC, V.*

$$ ✕ **Joe's Warehouse.** For excellent food in the heart of town, stop here, where the specialties include local seafood and prime rib. In summer, when the patio is open, the restaurant seats 200 people. After dinner head downstairs for live music and dancing at Smooth Herman's. ⊠ *424 Charlotte St.,* ☎ *902/539–6686. AE, DC, MC, V.*

Nightlife and the Arts

The **Cape Breton Summertime Revue,** based in Sydney, performs an annual original revue of music and comedy that tours Nova Scotia during June and August. Many leading fiddlers appear at the **Big Pond Concert** in mid-July. At the **Sheraton Casino** (⊠ 625 George St., ☎ 902/563–7777), try the slot machines, roulette, or gaming tables, or enjoy live entertainment in the lounge. Glace Bay's opulent old opera house, the **Savoy Theatre** (⊠ Union St., ☎ 902/842–1577) is the home of the summer-long Festival on the Bay.

Louisbourg

③⑧ *33 km (21 mi) southeast of Sydney.*

★ **Fortress of Louisbourg National Historic Park,** the most remarkable site in Cape Breton, is about 30 minutes from Sydney. After the French were forced out of mainland Nova Scotia in 1713, they established their headquarters here, in a walled and fortified town on a low point of land at the mouth of Louisbourg Harbour. The fortress was twice captured, once by New Englanders and once by the British; after the second siege, in 1758, it was razed to the ground. Its capture essentially ended the French Empire in America. A quarter of the original town has been rebuilt on its foundation, just as it was in 1744, before the first siege. Costumed actors re-create the lives and activities of the original inhabitants; you can watch a military drill, see nails and lace being made, and eat food prepared from 18th-century recipes in the town's two inns. Plan on spending at least half a day. Louisbourg tends to be chilly, so pack a warm sweater or windbreaker. ⊠ *Rte. 22,* ☎ *902/733–2280 or 800/565–9464.* ☞ *$7.50.* ⊘ *June and Sept., daily 9:30–5; July and Aug., daily 9–6.*

There's a railway museum at the **Sydney and Louisburg Historical Society.** This restored 1895 railway station exhibits the history of the S&L Railway, railway technology, and marine shipping. Rolling stock includes a baggage car, coach, and caboose. ⊠ *7336 Main St.,* ☎ *902/733–2720.* ☞ *Free.* ⊘ *June–Sept., weekdays 9–5; July and Aug., daily 9–7.*

Atlantic Statiquarium is a marine museum devoted largely to underwater treasure. ⊠ *7523 Main St.,* ☎ *902/733–2721.* ☞ *$2.50.* ⊘ *June–Sept., daily 10–8.*

En Route To return, retrace your tracks, via Route 22, Route 125, and Route 4 to East Bay; continue down the east side of the Bras d'Or Lake. **Big Pond,** 40 kilometers (25 miles) west of Sydney, is comprised of just a few houses on the side of Route 4. One of them is the home of singer/songwriter Rita MacNeil, who operates a tearoom in a tranquil setting with seating indoors and out. Stop in for Rita's special blend of tea and home-baked goodies such as oatcakes. A display room contains Rita's awards and memorabilia. A gift shop stocks tapes, CDs, customized merchandise, and local crafts. Route 4 continues along the lake, sometimes close to the shore and sometimes high in the hills. From St. Peter's to Port Hawkesbury the population is largely Acadian French. At **St. Peter's** the Atlantic Ocean is connected with the Bras d'Or Lake by the century-old St. Peter's Canal, still heavily used by pleasure craft and fishing vessels. The town is a service center for the surrounding region, and has a marina, hotels, restaurants, and a liquor store. From St. Peter's, Route 247 leads through the Acadian villages of **Grand Greve** and L'Ardoise to a fine beach at **Point Michaud.** The road onward along the Bras d'Or Lake travels through pretty Acadian villages along the twisting channel of St. Peter's Inlet, with many coves and islands, and then along the main body of the lake to **Dundee,** where there's a large resort (⊠ Dundee Resort, R.R. #2, West Bay, B0E 3K0, ☎ 902/345–2649 or 800/565–1774, ℻ 902/345–2697) with a spectacular hilltop golf course overlooking the island-studded waters of West Bay. The alternative route, equally engaging, leads along the Atlantic coast, through coves and islands past **River Tillard** and **River Bourgeois** to **Louisdale.**

Turn off on Route 320 for **Isle Madame,** a 27-square-kilometer (10-square-mile) island named for Madame de Maintenon, second wife of Louis XIV. Route 320 leads through the villages of **Poulamon** and **D'Escousse,** and overlooks the protected waterway of Lennox Passage, with its spangle of islands. Route 206 meanders through the low hills to a maze of land and water at West Arichat. Together, the two routes encircle the island, meeting at Arichat, the principal town of Isle Madame.

Arichat

39 *43 km (27 mi) south of Dundee.*

Arichat was once the seat of the local Catholic diocese. **Notre Dame de l'Assumption church,** built in 1837, still retains the grandeur of its former cathedral status. Its **bishop's palace,** the only one in Cape Breton, is now a law office. The two cannons overlooking the harbor were installed after the town was sacked by John Paul Jones, founder of the U.S. Navy, during the American Revolution. The town was an important shipbuilding and trading center during the 19th century, and some fine old houses from that period still remain, along with the 18th-century **LeNoir Forge,** a restored French 18th-century stone blacksmith shop. ⊠ *Rte. 320, off Rte. 4,* ☎ *902/226–9364;* ⊙ *May–Sept., weekdays 9–5, Sat. 10–3.*

With its rocky red bluffs, cobble shores, tiny harbor, and brightly painted houses, **Little Anse** is particularly attractive to artists and photographers. A dead-end road leads here from Arichat, past the Acadian villages of Petit de Grat and Sampson's Cove.

NOVA SCOTIA A TO Z

Arriving and Departing

By Bus

Greyhound Lines (☎ 800/231–2222) from New York, and **Voyageur Inc.** (☎ 613/238–5900) from Montréal, connect with **Scotia Motor Tours** or **SMT** (☎ 506/458–6000) through New Brunswick, which links (rather inconveniently) with **Acadian Lines Limited** (☎ 902/454–8279), which provides inter-urban services within Nova Scotia.

By Car

The Trans-Canada Highway reaches Nova Scotia through New Brunswick. Entering the province at Amherst, it becomes Route 104. To reach Halifax, pick up Route 102 at Truro. To reach Cape Breton, continue east on Route 104.

Throughout Nova Scotia, the highways numbered from 100 to 199 are all-weather, limited-access roads, with 100-kilometer-per-hour (62-mile-per-hour) speed limits. The last two digits usually match the number of an older trunk highway along the same route, numbered from 1 to 99. Thus, Route 102, between Halifax and Truro, matches the older Route 2, between the same towns. Roads numbered from 200 to 399 are secondary roads that usually link villages. Unless otherwise posted, the speed limit on these and any roads other than the 100-series highways is 80 kilometers per hour (50 miles per hour).

Most highways in the province lead to Halifax and Dartmouth. Routes 3/103, 7, 2/102, and 1/101 terminate in the twin cities.

By Ferry

Three car ferries connect Nova Scotia with Maine and New Brunswick. **Marine Atlantic** (☎ 902/794–5700 or 800/341–7981) sails from Bar Harbor, Maine, and **Prince of Fundy Cruises** (☎ 800/341–7540) from Portland; both arrive in Yarmouth. From Saint John, New Brunswick, to Digby, Nova Scotia, ferry service is provided by **Marine Atlantic** (☎ 800/341–7981; in Canada, 800/565–9470).

Marine Atlantic also operates ferries between New Brunswick and Prince Edward Island, and between Cape Breton and Newfoundland (☎ 902/794–5700, 709/772–7701, or 800/341–7981). Between May and December, **Northumberland Ferries** (☎ 902/566–3838; in Nova

Scotia and Prince Edward Island, 800/565–0201) operate between Caribou, Nova Scotia, and Wood Islands, Prince Edward Island.

By Plane

The **Halifax International Airport** is 40 kilometers (25 miles) northeast
of downtown Halifax. **Sydney Airport** is 13 kilometers (8 miles) east
of Sydney.

Air Canada (☎ 902/429–7111 or 800/776–3000) provides regular,
daily service to Halifax and Sydney, Nova Scotia, from New York,
Boston, Toronto, Montréal, and St. John's, Newfoundland. **Canadian
Airlines International** (☎ 800/527–8499) has service to Halifax via
Toronto and Montréal. **Air Nova** (☎ 902/429–7111 or 800/776–
3000) and **Air Atlantic** (☎ 800/426–7000; in Canada, 800/665–1177)
provide regional service to both airports with flights to Toronto, Montréal, and Boston. **Northwest Air Link** offers service from Boston to Halifax. **KLM** (☎ 902/455–8282) provides three weekly flights between
Halifax and Amsterdam, with connections to the United Kingdom and
continental Europe.

Visiting pilots will find aviation-related information for the flying
tourist from the **Aviation Council of Nova Scotia** (✉ Box 100, Debert,
Nova Scotia B0M 1G0, ☎ 902/895–1143). A publication, *Air Tourist
Information: Canada* is available on request from the **Aeronautical In-
formation and Publications Office** (✉ Ministry of Transport, Place de
Ville, Tower C, Ottawa, Ontario K1A 0N5).

BETWEEN THE AIRPORT AND CITY CENTER
Limousine and taxi service, as well as car rentals, are available at Halifax, Sydney, and Yarmouth airports. Airport bus service to most Halifax and Dartmouth hotels costs $20 round-trip, $12 one-way. Regular
taxi fare is $35 each way, but if you book in advance with **Aero Cab**
(☎ 902/445–3393) the fare is $26 if you pay cash, slightly more with
a credit card (MC, V). The trip takes 30–40 minutes.

By Train

VIA Rail (☎ 800/561–3949) provides service from Montréal to Halifax via Moncton, in New Brunswick, and Amherst and Truro, in Nova
Scotia. **Amtrak** (☎ 800/872–7245) from New York City makes connections in Montréal.

Getting Around

Halifax
Walking and biking are excellent ways to get around and see the city,
especially on weekdays when parking in the downtown area can be a
problem. A pleasant alternative, however, is to take one of the rick-
shaws, available downtown during summer.

BY BUS
Metro Transit (☎ 902/421–6600) provides bus service throughout the
cities of Halifax and Dartmouth, the town of Bedford, and (to a limited
extent) the county of Halifax. The base fare is $1.30; exact change only.

BY FERRY
Metro Transit (☎ 902/421–6600) runs three passenger ferries from the
Halifax Ferry Terminal on the hour and half hour from 6:30 AM to 11:57
PM. During the weekday commuter rush, ferries cross continuously to
the Woodside Terminal from 6:52 AM to 10:04 AM and 3:37 PM to 6:19
PM only. Ferries also operate on Sundays during the summer (June–September). Free transfers are available from the ferry to the bus system (and
vice versa). The fare for a single crossing is $1.10, and is well worth it
considering you get an up-close view of both waterfronts.

Rates begin at about $2.50 and increase based on mileage and time. A crosstown trip should cost $5–$6, depending on traffic. Hailing a taxi can be difficult, but there are taxi stands at major hotels and shopping malls. Most Haligonians simply phone for a taxi service; try **Aero Cab** (☎ 902/445–3393).

Elsewhere in Nova Scotia

BY BUS
There are a number of small, regional bus services; however, connections are not always convenient. Outside of Halifax there are no innercity bus services. For information, call **Nova Scotia Visitors Services** (☎ 800/565–0000).

BY CAR
The recommended mode of travel within the province is by car. As you explore Nova Scotia, be on the lookout for the 10 designated "Scenic Travelways" that appear throughout the province and are easily identified by roadside signs with icons that correspond with trail names. These routes, as well as tourist literature (maps and the provincial *Travel Guide*) published in accordance with this scheme, have been developed by the Nova Scotia Economic Renewal Agency. **Nova Scotia Visitor Information Centres** (☎ 800/565–0000) provide information and reservation services.

BY PLANE
Internal air travel is very limited. **Air Nova** (☎ 902/429–7111 or 800/776–3000) and **Air Atlantic** (☎ 800/426–7000; in Canada, 800/665–1177) provide regional service to other provinces and to Sydney.

Contacts and Resources

Bicycling
Bicycle Tours in Nova Scotia ($7) is published by **Bicycle Nova Scotia** (⊠ Box 3010, 5516 Spring Garden Rd., Halifax B3J 3G6, ☎ 902/425–5450). **Backroads** (⊠ 1516 5th St., Suite Q333, Berkeley, CA 94710, ☎ 510/527–1555 or 800/245–3874) offers five- and six-day bike trips in the province.

Bird-Watching
Nova Scotia is located on the "Atlantic Flyway" and is an important staging point for migrating species. An excellent, beautifully illustrated book, *Birds of Nova Scotia,* by Robie Tufts, is a must on every ornithologist's reading list.

Canoeing
Nova Scotia is seamed with small rivers and lakes, by which the Micmac Indians roamed both Cape Breton and the peninsula. Especially good canoe routes are within Kejimkujik National Park. The publication *Canoe Routes of Nova Scotia* and a variety of route maps are available from the **Nova Scotia Government Bookstore** (⊠ Box 637, 1700 Granville St., Halifax B3J 2T3, ☎ 902/424–7580). Canoeing information is also available from **Canoe NS** (⊠ Box 3010S, Halifax B3J 3G6, ☎ 902/425–5450, Ext. 316; ℻ 902/425–5606).

Car Rentals
Halifax is the most convenient place from which to begin your driving tour of the province. The following list details city and airport venues of rental-car agencies. **Avis** (⊠ 5600 Sackville St., ☎ 902/423–6303; airport, ☎ 902/873–3523). **Budget** (⊠ 1558 Hollis St., ☎ 902/421–1242; airport, ☎ 902/873–3509). **Hertz** (⊠ Halifax Sheraton, ☎ 902/421–1763; airport, ☎ 902/873–3700). **Thrifty** (⊠ 6930 Lady Ham-

mond, ☎ 902/422–4455; airport, ☎ 902/873–3527). **Tilden** (✉ 1130 Hollis St., ☎ 902/422–4433; airport, ☎ 902/873–3505).

Emergencies

Dial **"0"** for operator in emergencies; check the front of the local phone book for specific medical services.

Guided Tours

There are more than 20 tour operators specializing in specific areas, modes of transportation, tour topics, and types of groups. For information, and to connect with the tour company most suited to your needs, contact **Nova Scotia Tourism** (☎ 800/565–0000).

BOAT TOURS

Murphy's on the Water (☎ 902/420–1015) sails various vessels: *Harbour Queen I*, a paddle wheeler; *Haligonian III*, an enclosed motor launch; *Stormy Weather I*, a 40-foot Cape Islander (fishing boat); and *Mar II*, a 75-foot sailing ketch. All operate from mid-May to late October, from berths at 1751 Lower Water Street on Cable Wharf, next to the Historic Properties in Halifax. Costs vary, but a basic tour of the Halifax Harbour ranges from $10 to $15.

BUS TOURS

Both **Gray Line Sightseeing** (☎ 902/454–8279) and **Cabana Tours** (☎ 902/423–6066) run coach tours through Halifax, Dartmouth, and Peggy's Cove. **Halifax Double Decker Tours** (☎ 902/420–1155) offer two-hour tours on double-decker buses that leave daily from Historic Properties in Halifax.

Hiking

The province has a wide variety of trails along the rugged coastline and inland through forest glades, which enable you to experience otherwise inaccessible scenery, wildlife, and vegetation. *Hiking Trails of Nova Scotia* ($12.95) is available through **Gooselane Editions** (✉ 469 King St., Fredericton, New Brunswick, E3R 1E5, ☎ 506/450–4251).

Reservation Service

Nova Scotia has a computerized system called **Check In** (☎ 902/425–5781 or 800/565–0000; in the continental U.S., 800/341–6096; in Maine, 800/492–0643), which provides information and makes reservations with more than 700 hotels, motels, inns, campgrounds, and car-rental agencies. Check In also represents most properties in Prince Edward Island and some in New Brunswick.

Shopping

For refund forms and information, contact the **Provincial Tax Commission** (✉ Tax Refund Unit, Box 755, Halifax B3J 2V4, ☎ 902/424–5946; in Nova Scotia, 902/424–6708).

Snowmobiling

Visiting snowmobilers can get information on trails, activities, clubs, and dealers through the **Snowmobile Association of Nova Scotia** (✉ Box 3010 South, Halifax B3J 3G6, ☎ 902/425–5450).

Visitor Information

Nova Scotia Tourism (✉ Box 130, Halifax B3J 2M7, ☎ 902/424–5000 or 800/341–6096; in Canada, 800/565–0000; FAX 902/420–1286) publishes a range of literature, including an exhaustive annual travel guide. **Nova Scotia Tourism Information Centre** (✉ Old Red Store at Historic Properties, Halifax, ☎ 902/424–4247) and **Tourism Halifax** (✉ City Hall, Duke and Barrington Sts., ☎ 902/421–8736 or 902/421–2842) are open mid-June–Labor Day, daily 9–6; Labor Day–mid-June, weekdays 9–4:30.

14 Newfoundland and Labrador

Canada's easternmost province, Newfoundland, was a center of the world's cod fishing industry for 400 years until the supply nearly ran out in 1992. In summer, Newfoundland's stark cliffs, bogs, and meadows become a riot of wildflowers and greenery, and the sea is dotted with boats and buoys. St. John's, the capital, is a classic harbor city.

By Margaret
M. Kearney

Updated by
Ed Kirby

NEWFOUNDLAND WAS THE FIRST PLACE explorers John Cabot (1497) and Gaspar Corte-Real (1500) touched down in the New World. Exactly where they went no one knows, for neither survived a second voyage. But while he was here, Cabot reported that he saw fish in the water so thick you could dip your basket in anywhere and catch as much as you wanted. Within a decade of the explorers' discovery, St. John's had become a crowded harbor. Fishing boats from France, England, Spain, and Portugal vied for a chance to catch Newfoundland's lucrative cod, which was to subsequently shape the province's history and geography.

At one time there were 700 hard-working settlements or "outports" dotting Newfoundland's coast, most devoted to catching, salting, and drying the world's most plentiful fish. Today, only about 400 of these settlements survive. Newfoundland's most famous resource has become so scarce that a partial fishing moratorium was declared in 1992 and extended in 1993. While the province waits for the cod to return, some 25,000 fishers and processors are going to school or looking for other work instead of fishing.

Newfoundland and Labrador became part of Canada in 1949. For almost 400 years previous, however, the people had survived the vagaries of a fishing economy on their own, until the Great Depression forced the economy to go belly-up. After 40-some years of Confederation with Canada, the economy of the province has improved considerably, but the people are still of independent mind: Newfoundlanders regard themselves as North America's first separatists and maintain a unique language and lifestyle as well as their own customs.

Visitors to Newfoundland find themselves straddling the centuries. Old accents and customs are common in small towns and outports, yet the major cities of St. John's on the east coast and Corner Brook on the west coast of the island of Newfoundland are very much part of the 20th century. Regardless of where you visit—an isolated outport or lively Water Street—you're sure to interact with some of the warmest, wittiest people in North America. Strangers have always been welcome in Newfoundland, since the days when locals brought visitors in from out of the cold, warmed them by the fire, and charmingly interrogated them for news of events outside the province.

Before you can shoot the breeze, though, you'll have to acclimate yourself to the language: It's English all right, but provincial dialects are strong and vary from place to place. Newfoundland is one of two provinces in Canada with their own dictionaries. Prince Edward Island is the other, but its book has only 873 entries. The *Dictionary of Newfoundland English* has more than 5,000 words, mostly having to do with fishery, weather, and scenery. To get started, you can practice with the name of the province—it's *New'fund'land,* with the accent on "land." However, only "livyers" ever get the pronunciation exactly right.

Pleasures and Pastimes

Dining

John Cabot and Sir Humphrey Gilbert raved about "waters teeming with fish." Today, despite the fishing moratorium, seafood is still an excellent value in Newfoundland and Labrador. Many restaurants offer seasonal specialties featuring a wide variety of traditional wild and cultured species. Although cod may still be available, it may not be locally harvested. It will still, however, be traditionally prepared—

panfried, baked, or poached. Try cod tongues, salt cod, and fish and brewis (it is cod of course!). Aquaculture species like steelhead trout, salmon, mussels, and sea scallops are available in better restaurants. Cold-water shrimp, snow crab, lobster, redfish, grenadier, halibut, and turbot are also good seafood choices.

Two other foods you shouldn't leave without trying are partridgeberries and bakeapples. Partridgeberries are a small, lush-tasting berry, called the mountain cranberry in the U.S., and locally they are used for just about everything—pies, jams, cakes, pancakes, and even as a sauce for turkey and game. Bakeapples in the wild are a low-growing berry that looks like a yellow raspberry—you'll see them ripening in bogs in August throughout Newfoundland and Labrador. Enterprising pickers sell them by the side of the road in jars. If the ones you buy are hard, wait a few days and they'll ripen into rich-tasting fruit. They're popular on ice cream or spread on fresh homemade bread. In Scandinavia they're known as cloudberries and are made into a liqueur.

You may also hear Newfoundlanders talk about the herb they call summer savory. Newfoundlanders are so partial to this peppery herb that they slip it into most stuffings and stews. Growers in the province ship the product all over the world, and Newfoundlanders visiting relatives living outside the province are usually asked to "bring the savory."

Only the large urban centers across the province, especially St. John's and Corner Brook, have gourmet restaurants. Fish is a safe dish to order just about everywhere—even in the lowliest take-out. You'll be agreeably surprised by the quality of the meals along the Trans-Canada Highway: Restaurants in the Irving Gas Station chain, for example, offer thick homemade soups with dumplings, and Sunday dinners that draw in local customers for miles around. Don't be shy about trying some of the excellent meals offered in the province's expanding network of "hospitality homes," where home cooking goes hand in hand with the warm welcome for which Newfoundlanders are famous.

CATEGORY	COST*
$$$$	over $50
$$$	$35–$50
$$	$20–$35
$	under $20

per person, excluding drinks, service, 12% provincial sales tax, and 7% federal Goods and Services tax.

Fishing
Newfoundland has over 200 salmon rivers—60 percent of all salmon rivers in North America—and thousands of trout streams. Angling in these unpolluted waters is a fisherman's dream. The feisty Atlantic salmon is king of the game fish. Top salmon rivers in Newfoundland include the Gander, Humber, and Exploits, while Labrador's top-producing waters are the Sandhill, Michaels, Flowers, and Eagle Rivers. Lake trout, brook trout, and landlocked salmon are other favourite species. In Labrador, northern pike and Arctic char can be added to that list.

Hiking
Many provincial and both national parks in Newfoundland and Labrador have hiking and nature trails. Coastal and woods trails radiate from most small communities. However, you can never be sure how far the trail will go unless you ask a local. Be careful: Landmarks are few, the weather is changeable, and it is surprisingly easy to get lost. Many small communities now also have formal walking trails.

Lodging

Newfoundland and Labrador offer lodgings that range from modestly priced "hospitality homes," which you can find through local tourist offices, to luxury accommodations. In between, visitors can choose from affordable, basic lodging and mid-priced hotels. In remote areas, visitors should be prepared to find very basic lodgings. However, the lack of amenities is usually made up for by the home-cooked meals and the great hospitality that you'll encounter.

CATEGORY	COST*
$$$	over $100
$$	$60–$90
$	under $60

All prices are for a standard double room, excluding service charge.

Exploring Newfoundland and Labrador

Tours in this chapter divide the province into the island of Newfoundland, beginning with St. John's and the Avalon Peninsula, and move west. Labrador is considered as a whole, with suggested driving and train excursions.

Great Itineraries

Numbers in the text below correspond to numbers in the margin and on the maps.

IF YOU HAVE 3 DAYS

Pick either the west or east coast of Newfoundland. On the west coast, after arriving by ferry at **Port-aux-Basques** ③①, drive through the Codroy Valley, heading north to the **Gros Morne National Park** ㉒ and its fjords, and overnight in ⊟ **Rocky Harbour** ㉙ or ⊟ **Woody Point** ㉓. The next day, visit **L'Anse aux Meadows National Historic Site** ㉗, where the Vikings built a village a thousand years ago; here there are reconstructions of the dwellings, plus a Viking boat tour. Then overnight at ⊟ **Cape Onion** or ⊟ **St. Anthony** ㉘.

On the east coast, the ferry docks at Argentia. Explore the Avalon Peninsula beginning in ⊟ **St. John's** ②, where you should spend your first night. The next day, visit **Cape Spear** ①, the most easterly point in North America, and the **Witless Bay Ecological Reserve** ③ for seabirds, whales, and icebergs. Overnight in ⊟ **Placentia** ⑨ and spend your third day at **Cape St. Mary's Ecological Reserve** ⑪, known for its gannets.

IF YOU HAVE 6 DAYS

On Newfoundland's west coast, add southern Labrador to your list. A ferry takes you from St. Barbe to Blanc Sablon on the Québec-Labrador border. Drive 60 miles to **Red Bay** ㉞ to explore the remains of a 17th-century Basque whaling station then head to **Point Amour** to see Canada's second tallest lighthouse. Overnight at ⊟ **L'Anse au Clair** ㉜. Return through Gros Morne National Park and explore ⊟ **Corner Brook** ㉙, where you should stay overnight. The next day, explore the **Port au Port Peninsula,** home of Newfoundland's French-speaking population.

On the east coast add ⊟ **Trinity** ⑭ to your must-see list, and overnight there or in ⊟ **Clarenville** ⑫. The north shore of **Conception Bay** is where you will find many picturesque villages. Overnight in ⊟ **Harbour Grace** ⑧ or ⊟ **Cupids** ⑦, where you can explore the home of famed Arctic explorer Capt. Bob Bartlett. Several half-day, full-day, and two-day excursions are possible from St. John's, and in each direction a different personality of the region unfolds.

In addition to the places already mentioned on the west coast, take a drive into central Newfoundland and visit the villages of **Notre Dame Bay.** Overnight in ⛴ **Twillingate** ⑳. Catch a ferry to offshore islands like ⛴ **Fogo** or the ⛴ **Change Islands.** Accommodations are available in both towns, but book ahead.

On the east coast add the **Burin Peninsula** and a trip to France to your itinerary. Yes, France. You can reach the French territory of ⛴ **St-Pierre and Miquelon** ⑰ by passenger ferry from **Fortune.** Explore romantic **Grand Bank** ⑯, named for the famous fishing area just offshore, and climb Cook's Lookout in ⛴ **Burin** ⑱, where Captain James Cook kept a lookout for smugglers from St-Pierre. Smuggling still thrives in some communities.

When to Tour Newfoundland and Labrador

Depending on the time of year you visit, your experiences will be dramatically different. In spring icebergs float down from the north, and fin, pilot, minke, and humpback whales hunt for food along the coast. Their preferred cuisine is capelin, a small, smeltlike fish that moves in schools and spawns on Newfoundland's many pebble beaches. During the summer, temperate days turn Newfoundland's stark cliffs, bogs, and meadows into a riot of wildflowers and greenery; and the sea is dotted with boats and buoys marking traps and nets. Fall is a favored season: The weather is usually fine; cliffs and meadows are loaded with berries; and the woods are alive with moose, caribou, partridges, and rabbits, to name just a few residents. In the winter, the forest trails hum with the sound of snowmobiles and ATVs hauling wood home or taking the fishers to their favorite lodges and lakes.

The tourist season runs from June through September, when the province is awash with festivals, fairs, concerts, plays, and crafts shows. The temperature hovers between 75 and 85 degrees, and gently cools off in the evening, providing a good night's sleep.

Numbers in the margin correspond to points of interest on the New-foundland and Labrador map.

NEWFOUNDLAND

St. John's

When Sir Humphrey Gilbert sailed into St. John's to establish British colonial rule for Queen Elizabeth in 1583, he found Spanish, French, and Portuguese fishermen actively working the harbor. As early as 1627, the merchants of Water Street—then known as "the lower path"—were doing a thriving business buying fish, selling goods, and supplying booze to soldiers and sailors. Today the city still encircles the snug, punch-bowl harbor that helped establish its reputation.

★ ❶ True early birds can begin their tour of the area at daybreak by filling up a thermos of coffee, getting some muffins, and driving on Route 11 to **Cape Spear,** so they can be among the first to watch the sun come up over North America. Songbirds begin their chirping in the dim light of dawn and whales feed directly below the cliffs, providing an unforgettable start to the day.

Cape Spear Lighthouse (☎ 709/772–5367), Newfoundland's oldest such beacon, has been lovingly restored to its original form and furnishings and is open to visitors, daily 10–6 from early June through Labor Day. Admission is $2.25.

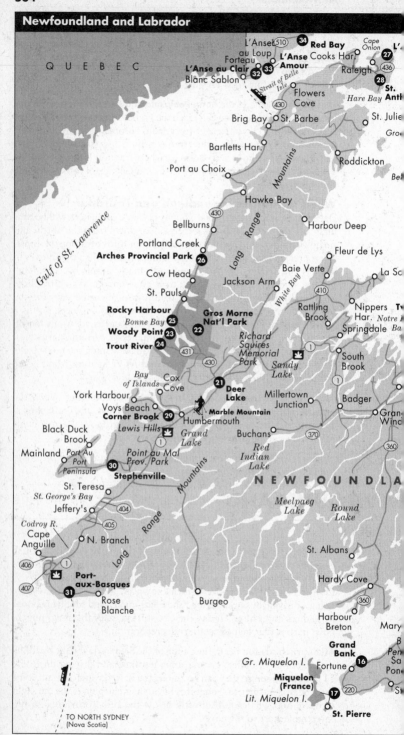

QUEBEC

L'Anse 510 **34 Red Bay** Cape Onion L'
au Loup **27**
Forteau **L'Anse** Cooks Har. Raleigh 436
L'Anse au Clair **32** **33** **Amour** **28**
Blanc Sablon Strait of Belle Isle **St. Anth**

Flowers Cove Hare Bay
430
Brig Bay St. Barbe St. Julie
Gro

Bartletts Har. Roddickton
Be
Port au Choix

Hawke Bay Harbour Deep

Bellburns
430
Portland Creek Fleur de Lys
Arches Provincial Park **26** Baie Verte La Sc
Cow Head
Jackson Arm
St. Pauls 410
Rattling Nippers **Tw**
Rocky Harbour **25** Brook Har. Notre
Bonne Bay **Gros Morne** Springdale Ba
Woody Point **23** **22** **Nat'l Park**
Trout River **24** Richard South
431 Squires Brook
Memorial
430 Park Sandy 1
Lake
Cox **21** South
Bay Cove **Deer** 1
of Islands **Lake** Millertown
York Harbour **Marble Mountain** Junction Badger
Voys Beach Humbermouth
Corner Brook **29** Buchans 370 **Gran**
Black Duck Lewis Hills Grand Red 360 **Winc**
Brook Lake Indian
Mainland Port Au Point au Mal Lake
Port Prov. Park **NEWFOUNDLA**
Peninsula **30**
St. Teresa **Stephenville** Meelpaeg Round
St. George's Bay Lake Lake
Jeffery's 404
Range
Codroy R. 405
Cape Mountains St. Albans
Anguille N. Branch
406 Hardy Cove
407 1 **Port-** 360
aux-Basques **31** Rose Burgeo
Blanche Harbour
Breton Mary

Grand **B**
Gr. Miquelon I. **Bank** **16** **Pen**
Fortune Sa
Miquelon Pon
(France) **17** 220
Lit. Miquelon I. S

St. Pierre

TO NORTH SYDNEY
(Nova Scotia)

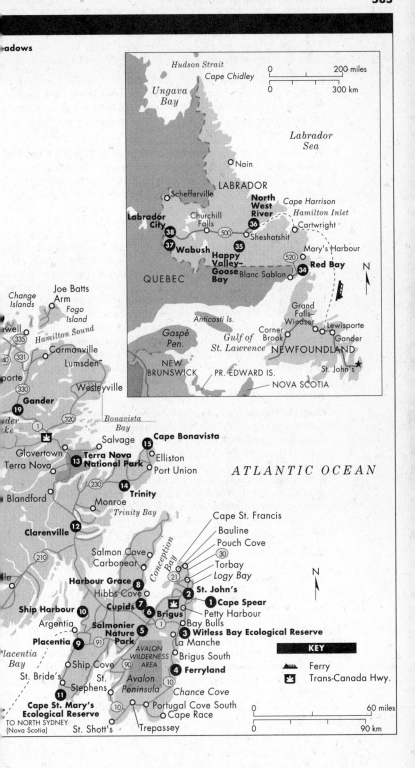

adows

Hudson Strait
Cape Chidley
Ungava Bay

Labrador Sea

0 — 200 miles
0 — 300 km

Nain

Schefferville

LABRADOR

North West River
Cape Harrison
Hamilton Inlet

Labrador City
Churchill Falls
Cartwright

38 **37** Wabush (500) **36** Sheshatshit

35 Happy Valley–Goose Bay
(520) Mary's Harbour

QUEBEC
Blanc Sablon **34** Red Bay

N

Grand Falls–Windsor

Change Islands
Joe Batts Arm
Fogo Island

Gaspé Pen.
Anticosti Is.
Gulf of St. Lawrence
Corner Brook
Lewisporte
Gander

ewell
Hamilton Sound
(335)

NEW BRUNSWICK
PR. EDWARD IS.
NEWFOUNDLAND

(40) (331)
Carmanville
Lumsden

NOVA SCOTIA

St. John's

orte
(330)
Wesleyville

Gander **19**
der (1) (320)
ke
Bonavista Bay

Salvage
Cape Bonavista
15
Elliston
Port Union

ATLANTIC OCEAN

Glovertown
Terra Nova
Terra Nova National Park **13**

Blandford
(230)
Monroe
14 **Trinity**
Trinity Bay

Clarenville **12**

Cape St. Francis
Bauline
Pouch Cove

(210)
Salmon Cove
Carbonear
(30)

Conception Bay
(21)
Torbay
Logy Bay

le
Harbour Grace **8**
Hibbs Cove
2 **St. John's**

Ship Harbour **10**
Cupids **7**
6
Brigus
(1)
1 Cape Spear
Petty Harbour

Argentia
Salmonier Nature Park
5
Bay Bulls
3 Witless Bay Ecological Reserve
La Manche

Placentia **9**
(91)
Brigus South

lacentia Bay
Ship Cove
4 Ferryland
St. Bride's
St. Stephens
AVALON WILDERNESS AREA
Avalon Peninsula
Chance Cove

11
Cape St. Mary's Ecological Reserve
(90)
(10)

TO NORTH SYDNEY
(Nova Scotia)
St. Shott's
(10)
Portugal Cove South
Cape Race
Trepassey

KEY

⚓ Ferry
⬇ Trans-Canada Hwy.

0 — 60 miles
0 — 90 km

❷ Those who are less ambitious may wish to begin exploring **St. John's** a little later in the day, when the Tourist Chalet on the waterfront is open. This is an old converted railway caboose, staffed from May through October. ✉ *Harbour Dr.,* ☎ *709/576–8514.* ⊙ *May–Oct., daily 9–7.*

Whichever way you look—left or right—you'll see the always-fascinating array of ships that tie up along **Harbour Drive.** Walk the harbor front, a favorite route in St. John's, to the **Battery,** a tiny, still-active fishing village perched precariously at the base of steep cliffs between hill and harbor.

★ You can either walk or drive from the Battery to **Signal Hill National Historic Site.** To walk, take the well-maintained 5-kilometer (3-mile) walking path that leads along the cliff edge, through the Narrows, and zigzags through the park. To drive, take steep Signal Hill Road. In spite of its height, Signal Hill was difficult to defend: Throughout the 1600s and 1700s it changed hands with every attacking French, English, and Dutch force. A wooden palisade encircles the summit of the hill, indicating the boundaries of the old fortifications. En route to the hill is the **Park Interpretation Centre,** with exhibits describing St. John's history. **Gibbet Hill,** the rocky knob immediately to the west of the Interpretation Centre, got its name—a gibbet is a post with a projecting arm for hanging—because a miscreant was once hung there and left dangling as a deterrent to other would-be lawbreakers. From the top of the hill it's a 500-foot drop to the narrow harbor entrance below. **Cabot Tower,** at the summit of Signal Hill, was constructed in 1897 to commemorate the 400th anniversary of Cabot's landing in Newfoundland. ✉ *Cabot Tower,* ☎ *709/772–5367.* 🎫 *Free.* ⊙ *Labor Day–early June, daily 9–5; mid-June–Labor Day, daily 8:30–8, guides available on summer weekends.*

Quidi Vidi Village is an authentic fishing community whose history goes back to the beginning of St. John's. To get there, if you're driving, go down from Signal Hill, make a right turn at Quidi Vidi Road, and continue to the right, down Forest Road. If you are walking, paths lead from the summit and the Interpretation Centre to the village. **Quidi Vidi Battery** is a small redoubt that has been restored to the way it appeared in 1812 and is staffed by costumed interpreters who will tell you about the hard, unromantic life of a soldier of the empire. ✉ *Near entrance to village harbor,* ☎ *709/729–2460 or 709/729–2977.* 🎫 *Free.* ⊙ *July–early Sept., daily 10–5:30.*

Quidi Vidi Lake, to the west of Quidi Vidi Village, is encircled by a leisurely path, popular with walkers and joggers. It's the site of the **Royal St. John's Regatta,** the oldest continuing sporting event in North America, which has taken place since at least 1826. Weather permitting, the regatta takes place on the first Wednesday in August.

From Quidi Vidi Lake, follow the **Rennies River Trail** (4½ kilometers, or 3 miles) that cuts through the city along a wooded stream and ends at the only public fluvarium in North America, the **Newfoundland Freshwater Resource Center,** where you can observe spawning brown and brook trout in their natural habitat through underwater windows. Feeding time for the fish, frogs, and eels is 4 PM daily. ✉ *Pippy Park,* ☎ *709/754–3474.* 🎫 *$2.75.* ⊙ *July and Aug., daily 9–5; guided tours at 11, 1, and 3. Sept.–June,* ⊙ *Mon.–Tues. and Thurs.–Sat. 9–4:30; Sun. noon–4:30.*

To get back downtown from the fluvarium, retrace your steps along the Rennies River Trail by foot, or drive down Prince Philip Drive and turn right onto Portugal Cove Road. This runs into New Cove Road—follow this and turn right onto King's Bridge Road. Go straight through the light at Cavendish Square and turn right onto Duckworth Street, from where you can turn left down one of several side streets onto Water Street. As you walk around St. John's, you'll notice the diversity of architectural styles due to two major fires: one in 1846 and another in 1892. The 1892 fire stopped where George and Water streets intersect, at **Yellowbelly Corner.** This junction was so-named because in the 19th century it was a gathering spot for Irish immigrants from Wexford who wore yellow sashes to distinguish themselves from their Waterford rivals.

Look west on Water Street, where the block still resembles a typical Irish market town of the 1840s. To the east, Victorian-style architecture predominates, with curved mansard roofs typical of the popular Second Empire style. After the 1892 fire the city's elite moved to **Circular Road,** in the center of the city, out of reach of future fires, and built a string of impressive and highly ornamented Victorian mansions, which bear witness to the sizable fortunes made in the old days from the humble cod.

While you're downtown, take a look at the churches of St. John's, rich in architectural history. All these churches usually schedule summer tours. The **Basilica Cathedral of St. John the Baptist** (⊠ Military Rd., ☎ 709/754–2170), with a commanding position above Military Road, overlooks the older section of the city and the harbor. The land was granted to the church by young Queen Victoria, and the edifice was built with stones from both Ireland and Newfoundland. From the basilica you can see the **Anglican Cathedral of St. John the Baptist** (⊠ 22 Church Hill, ☎ 709/726–5677), one of the finest examples of Gothic Revival architecture in North America. Near the cathedral is the imposing **Gower Street United Church** (⊠ Gower St., ☎ 709/753–7286), with its redbrick facade and green turrets. The **St. Thomas (Old Garrison) Church** (⊠ Bottom of Military Rd., adjacent to Hotel Newfoundland, ☎ 709/576–6632) is where the English soldiers used to worship during the early and mid-1800s.

The **Commissariat House,** just around the corner from St. Thomas church, has been restored to the way it appeared when it was the residence and office of the British garrison's supply officer in the 1830s. Interpreters dress in period costume. ⊠ *King's Bridge Rd.,* ☎ *709/729–2460 or 709/729–6730.* ⊙ *Summer, daily.*

The **Memorial University Botanical Garden** is a 110-acre garden and natural area at Oxen Pond with four pleasant walking trails and many gardens, including rock gardens and scree, a Newfoundland heritage-plants bed, ericaceous borders, peat and woodland beds, a wildlife garden, an alpine house, wildfire cottage and vegetable gardens, an herb wall, and native plant collections. The environmental education programs include seasonal indoor exhibits, and wildflower and bird-watching walks. ⊠ *306 Mt. Scio Rd., Pippy Park,* ☎ *709/737–8590.* ☞ *$1.* ⊙ *May, June, and Sept.–Nov., Wed.–Sun. 10–5; July and Aug., Fri.–Mon. and Wed. 10–5, Tues. and Thurs. 10–8.*

Bowring Park, an expansive Victorian park, was donated to the city by the wealthy Bowring family in 1911. It resembles the famous inner city parks of London, after which it was modeled. Dotting the grounds are artfully designed ponds, ducks to feed, and rustic bridges; there's also a statue of Peter Pan. ⊠ *Waterford Bridge Rd.* ☞ *Free.*

Dining and Lodging

$$$ ✕ **The Cellar.** This restaurant, in a historic building on the waterfront, ★ gets rave reviews for its innovative Continental cuisine featuring the best local ingredients. Menu selections include blackened fish dishes and *tiramisù* for dessert. ✉ *Baird's Cove, between Harbour and Water Sts.,* ☎ *709/579–8900. Reservations essential. AE, MC, V.*

$$$ ✕ **Stone House.** In one of St. John's most historic buildings, a restored
★ 19th-century stone cottage, this dining room serves imported game and Newfoundland specialties. ✉ *8 Kennas Hill,* ☎ *709/753–2380. AE, DC, MC, V.*

$$–$$$ ✕ **Hungry Fishermen.** Salmon, scallops, halibut, mussels, cod, and shrimp top the menu here. Non-fish eaters can choose veal, chicken, or the five-onion soup. This restaurant in a 19th-century historic building overlooking a courtyard has great sauces; desserts change daily and are homemade. ✉ *Murray Premesis, 5 Beck's Cove, off Water St.,* ☎ *709/726–5790. AE, D, DC, MC, V.*

$$$ ✕🏨 **Hotel Newfoundland.** St. John's residents gather here for special
★ occasions. It's noted for its Sunday and evening buffets, charming rooms that overlook St. John's harbor, atrium, and the fine cuisine of the Cabot Club. ✉ *Box 5637, Cavendish Sq., A1C 5W8,* ☎ *709/726–4980,* 🅵🅰🅷 *709/726–2025. 267 rooms, 20 suites. Restaurant. AE, DC, MC, V.*

$$–$$$ ✕🏨 **Delta St. John's.** In this convention hotel in downtown St. John's,
★ rooms overlook the harbor and the city. The restaurant, Brazil Square, is noted for its breakfast and noon buffets. ✉ *120 New Gower St., A1C 6K4,* ☎ *709/739–6404,* 🅵🅰🅷 *709/570–1622. 276 rooms, 9 suites. Restaurant. AE, DC, MC, V.*

$$ ✕🏨 **Quality Hotel by Journey's End Motel.** This hotel overlooks St. John's harbor. Like other Journey's Ends, it offers clean, comfortable rooms at a reasonable price. The hotel's restaurant, Rumplestiltskins, has a splendid view and an unpretentious menu. ✉ *Hill O'Chips, A1C 6B1,* ☎ *709/754–7788,* 🅵🅰🅷 *709/754–5209. 162 rooms. Restaurant. AE, DC, MC, V.*

$$ 🏨 **Compton House Bed & Breakfast.** In a charming, restored historic
★ St. John's residence in the west end of the city, this inn is professionally run and beautifully decorated. Twelve-foot ceilings and wide halls give the place a majestic feeling, and rooms done in pastels and chintzes add an air of coziness. The location, within walking distance of downtown St. John's, is ideal. ✉ *26 Waterford Bridge Rd., A1E 1C6,* ☎ *709/739–5789. 4 rooms, 2 suites. AE, MC, V.*

$$ 🏨 **Prescott Inn.** Local art decorates the walls of this house, the city's
★ most popular bed-and-breakfast. It has been modernized, tastefully blending the new and the old. Downtown, it's central to shopping and attractions. ✉ *17–21 Military Rd., A1C 2C3,* ☎ *709/753–6036,* 🅵🅰🅷 *709/579–7774. 15 rooms, 7 suites. MC, V.*

$ 🏨 **Gower Street House Bed & Breakfast.** This gracious former home of the late photographer Elsie Holloway has been designated by the Newfoundland Historic Trust as a point of interest. It's also an ideal setting for paintings by prominent local artists. The downtown location is within walking distance of all the city's main attractions. A full breakfast is included in the room rate. ✉ *180 Gower St., A1C 1P9,* ☎ *709/754–0047 or 800/563–3959,* 🅵🅰🅷 *709/754–5721. 4 rooms. Lounge, access to laundry. MC, V.*

Nightlife and the Arts

THE ARTS

The province has an unusually active arts community. Most major towns have an arts and culture center, which has theater, ballet, and concerts by local, national, and international artists. The **Resource Centre for the Arts** (✉ LSPU Hall, 3 Victoria St., ☎ 709/753–4531) is one of the country's oldest and most innovative experimental theaters. In addition to a busy fall and winter season, the center enjoys a busy summer, with cabarets, outdoor concerts, plays, and alternative concerts.

Newfoundlanders love a party, and from the cities to the smallest towns they celebrate their history and unique culture throughout the summer with festivals and events. The **Newfoundland and Labrador Folk Festival** (☎ 709/576–8508), held in St. John's in early August, is the province's best-known traditional music festival. **The Newfoundland International Irish Festival** (☎ 709/754–0700), held in Mount Pearl each July, features international performers and a Leprechaun Festival for the kids.

NIGHTLIFE

It has been a long-standing claim (since at least the 1700s) that St. John's has more bars per mile than any city in North America. Each establishment has its own personality. **Erin's Pub** (✉ 186 Water St., ☎ 709/722–1916) is famous for its Irish music. The **Blarney Stone** (✉ 342 Water St., 2nd floor, ☎ 709/754–1798) also has Irish music. **George Street,** downtown, a beautifully restored street of pubs and restaurants, often has open-air concerts.

Shopping

ANTIQUES

Murray's Antiques (✉ 414 Blackmarsh Rd., ☎ 709/579–7344) is renowned for silver, china, and fine mahogany and walnut furniture. **Livyers** (✉ 202 Duckworth St., ☎ 709/726–5650) carries locally crafted furniture and is a great spot for digging through books, prints, and maps.

ART

St. John's has a dozen commercial and public art galleries, nearly all of which carry works by local artists. Newfoundland's unique landscape, portrayed realistically or more experimentally, is a favorite subject. **The Art Gallery of Newfoundland and Labrador** (✉ Allandale Rd. and Prince Philip Dr., ☎ 709/737–8209) is the province's largest public gallery and exhibits historical and contemporary Canadian arts and crafts with an emphasis on Newfoundland and Labrador artists and artisans. The gallery is closed Monday. The **Emma Butler Gallery** (✉ 111 George St., ☎ 709/739–7111) sells a large selection of Newfoundland art including works by David Blackwood and Christopher Pratt. **Christina Parker Fine Art** (✉ 7 Plank Rd., ☎ 709/753–0580) represents local and national artists in all media, including painting, sculpture, drawing, and fine art prints. Several galleries have reasonably priced work aimed at the visitor market.

BOOKS

Most bookstores have a prominent section devoted to local history, fiction, and memoirs. **Word Play** (✉ 221 Duckworth St., ☎ 709/726–9193 or 800/563–9100) carries a wide selection of magazines and books of general interest to visitors.

HANDICRAFTS

St. John's has more than its fair share of fine crafts shops. **NONIA** (Newfoundland Outport Nurses Industrial Association, ✉ 286 Water St., ☎ 709/753–8062) was founded in 1920 to give Newfoundland women in the outports an opportunity to earn money to support nursing services in these remote communities. Their reputation for fierce independence was as colorful as their reputation for turning homespun wool into exquisite clothing. Today the shop continues to sell these fine homespun articles as well as lighter and more modern handmade items. **The Salt Box** (✉ 194 Duckworth St., ☎ 709/753–0622) sells local crafts and specializes in pottery. **The Cod Jigger** (⊠ 245 Duckworth St., ☏ 709/726–7422) carries handmade wool sweaters, socks, and mitts a well as Newfoundland's unique Grenfell coats. **The Devon House Craf Gallery** (⊠ 59 Duckworth St., ☏ 709/753–2749) is owned by the New foundland and Labrador Crafts Development Association and carrie only juried crafts. **The Newfoundland Weavery** (⊠ 177 Water St., ☏ 709/753–0496) sells rugs, prints, lamps, books, crafts, and other gifts

MUSIC
Fred's Records (⊠ 198 Duckworth St., ☏ 709/753–9191) has the bes selection of local recordings, as well as other music.

Avalon Peninsula

On the southern half of the peninsula are small Irish hamlets separated by large tracts of wilderness. You can travel part of the peninsula's south ern coast one or two days, depending on how much time you have Quaint coastal towns line the road, and the natural sites are beauti ful. At the intersection of Routes 90 and 91, in Salmonier, you need to decide whether to continue north toward Salmonier Nature Park and on to Conception Bay, or to head west then south to Route 100 to Cape St. Mary's Ecological Reserve (☞ *Route 100: The Cape Shore, below*). Each option takes about three hours. On the former route, we end our tour in Salmon Cove; if you plan to travel on to Bay de Verde at the northern tip of the peninsula, and down the other side of the peninsula on Route 80 along Trinity Bay, consider turning in for the night in the Harbour Grace–Carbonear area. Otherwise turn around and follow the same route back.

Witless Bay Ecological Reserve
❸ *29 km (18 mi) south of St. John's.*

The wildness of this coast is usually what's most striking to visitors, and La Manche and Chance Cove—both now-abandoned communities turned provincial parks—attest to the bounty of natural resources of the region. But nowhere are those resources more on display than in the Wit less Bay Ecological Reserve, a strip of water and three offshore islands between Bay Bulls and Tors Cove. Sometimes referred to as "the Serengeti of the northwest Atlantic," the reserve is the summer home of millions of seabirds that nest on the islands. The birds, and the humpback and minke whales who tarry here before continuing north to the summer grounds in the Arctic, feed on the billions of capelin that swarm inshore to spawn. Here, too, is an excellent place to see icebergs. The best views are from tour boats that operate in the reserve. For information contact **Parks and Natural Areas Division** (☏ 709/729–2421). ⊠ *Rte. 10.*

En Route   Although a visit to many of the hamlets along the way from Witless Bay to Ferryland will fulfill any search for prettiness, a few favorites are exceptional. La Manche and Brigus South have especially attractive settings and strong traditional flavors.

Ferryland
❹ *43½ km (27 mi) south of Witless Bay Ecological Reserve.*

A major ongoing archaeological dig at Ferryland has uncovered the early 17th-century colony of Lord Baltimore, who abandoned the Colony of Avalon after a decade for the warmer climes of Maryland. The site includes an archaeology laboratory and exhibit center. ⊠ *Rte. 10, The Pool; (seasonal);* ☏ *709/432–2767.* ☞ *Free.* ☉ *June–Oct., daily 9–8.*

En Route   In springtime, between Chance Cove and Portugal Cove South, in a stretch of land about 58 kilometers (36 miles) long, hundreds of caribou and their calves gather on the wide barrens near the road. Although the graceful animals are there during other times of the year, their numbers are few and it's difficult to spot them because they blend in so well with the scenery.

Salmonier Nature Park

5 *14½ km (9 mi) north of the intersection of routes 90 and 91.*

Visitors can see many of the animal species that are indigenous to the province here. The park is a 3,000-acre wilderness reserve area and has an enclosed 100-acre exhibit that allows up-close viewing. ⊠ *Salmonier Line, Rte. 90,* ☎ *709/729–6974 or 709/229–7078.* ☞ *Free.* ⊙ *June 6–Sept. 2, daily noon–7; other times by appointment.*

En Route From Salmonier Nature Park to Brigus, take Route 90, which passes through the scenic Hawkes Hills, before meeting up with the Trans-Canada Highway (Route 1). Turn off at the Holyrood Junction (Route 62) and follow Route 70, which skirts Conception Bay.

Brigus

6 *19 km (12 mi) off Route 1 and Route 70.*

This beautiful village is best known as the birthplace of Capt. Bob Bartlett, the famed Arctic explorer who accompanied Admiral Peary on polar expeditions during the first decade of this century. His home, **Hawthorne Cottage,** is one of the few surviving examples of the picturesque cottage style, with a veranda decorated with ornamental wooden fretwork. It dates from 1830 and is a National Historic Site. ☎ *709/753–9262; in summer,* ☎ *709/528–4004.* ☞ *$2.25.* ⊙ *Early June–mid-Oct., daily.*

This town also has a wonderful public garden, winding lanes, a teahouse, and **Ye Old Stone Barn Museum,** which display photos and artifacts of the town's history, especially its connection with the fishery. ⊠ *4 Magistrate's Hill,* ☎ *709/528–3298.* ☞ *$1.* ⊙ *June–Labor Day, daily; Sept. and Oct., weekends.*

Cupids

7 *5 km (3 mi) north of Brigus.*

Cupids is the oldest English colony in Canada, founded in 1610 by John Guy to whom the town erected a monument. In 1995 archaeologists began unearthing the long-lost site of the original colony, and some of these artifacts are on display in the community museum, **Cupids Archaeological Site.** ⊠ *United Church Hall, Main Rd.,* ☎ *709/596–1906.* ☞ *Free.* ⊙ *June–Aug., daily 9–4:30.*

Harbour Grace

8 *16 km (10 mi) north of Hibbs Cove.*

Harbour Grace was once the headquarters of Peter Easton, a 17th-century pirate. Beginning in 1919, this town was the departure point for many attempts to fly the Atlantic. Amelia Earhart left Harbour Grace in 1932 to become the first woman to fly solo across the Atlantic. Several handsome stone churches and buildings remain as evidence of the town's pride.

Route 100: The Cape Shore

Placentia

9 *48 km (30 mi) south of Route 1.*

Placentia was the French capital of Newfoundland in the 1600s. Trust the French to select a beautiful place for a capital! **Castle Hill National Historic Site,** just north of town, is on what remains of the French fortifications. The visitor's center has a "life at Plaisance" exhibit that shows the life and hardships endured by early English and French settlers. ⊠ *Off Rte. 100,* ☎ *709/227–2401.* 🖃 *$2.25.* ☉ *June–Labor Day, daily 8:30–8; Labor Day–May, daily 8:30–4:30.*

Ship Harbour
❿ *34 km (21 mi) north of Placentia.*

Ship Harbour is an isolated, edge-of-the-world place that has the curious distinction of being the home of the free world. Off Route 102, amid the splendor of Placentia Bay, an unpaved road leads to a monument marking the historic Atlantic Charter. It was on a ship in these waters where, in 1941, Roosevelt and Churchill signed the charter and formally announced the "Four Freedoms," which still shape the politics of the world's most successful democracies: freedom of speech, freedom of worship, freedom from want, and freedom from fear.

Cape St. Mary's Ecological Reserve
★ ⓫ *65 km (40 mi) south of Placentia.*

Cape St. Mary's Ecological Reserve is the most southerly nesting site in the world for gannets and common and thick-billed murres. A paved road takes you within a mile of the seabird colony. Visit the interpretation center—guides are on site during the summer—then walk to within 100 feet of the colony of nesting gannets, murres, black-billed kittiwakes, and razorbills. You'll also be able to enjoy some of the most dramatic coastal scenery in Newfoundland. For information contact the **Parks and Natural Areas Division** (☎ 709/729–2421).

Clarenville and the Bonavista Peninsula

Clarenville
⓬ *189 km (118 mi) northwest of St. John's.*

Clarenville is about two hours from St. John's via the Trans-Canada Highway (Route 1) and is the departure point for two different excursions: the Discovery Trail and Terra Nova National Park. If history and quaint towns interest you, begin the tour in Clarenville, the starting point for Route 230A—the **"Discovery Trail."** The route goes as far as the town of Bonavista, one of John Cabot's reputed landing spots in 1497.

★

LODGING

$$ 🏨 **Holiday Inn.** There are no surprises at this chain member; rooms are standard Holiday Inn fare. ⊠ *Box 967, A0E 1J0,* ☎ *709/466–7911,* FAX *709/466–3854. 64 rooms. Restaurant, bar. AE, DC, MC, V.*

Terra Nova National Park
⓭ *24 km (15 mi) northwest of Clarenville.*

If you're interested in rugged terrain, golf, fishing, and camping, Terra Nova National Park, on the exposed coastline that adjoins Bonavista Bay, is the place to be. If you are a golfer, you can play on one of the most beautiful courses in Canada, the course at the eponymously named lodge in the park, and the only one where a salmon river cuts through the 18-hole course. Call 709/543–2626 for a reservation. fees run between $24 and $30 per person, depending on the season. The park also has attractive campsites, whale-watching tours, and nature walks. ⊠ *Trans-Canada Hwy., Glovertown,* ☎ *709/533–2801 or 709/533–2802,* FAX *709/533–2706.* 🖃 *Park and vehicle permit $6 daily, 4-day pass $18, seasonal pass $30 ($20 before June 22).* ☉ *June–Aug., daily 10–9; Sept.–May, Mon.–Fri. 8–4:30.*

Trinity

14 *71 km (44 mi) northeast of Clarenville. Take Rte. 230 to Rte. 239.*

Trinity is one of the jewels of Newfoundland. The village's picturesque views, winding lanes, and snug houses are the main attraction, and several homes have been turned into museums and inns. In the 1700s Trinity competed with St. John's as a center of culture and wealth. Its more contemporary claim to fame, however, is that its intricate harbor was a favorite anchorage for the British navy, and it was here that the smallpox vaccine was introduced to North America by a local rector. An information center with costumed interpreters is open daily from July to September.

THE ARTS

Rising Tide Theatre (☎ 709/738–3256) stages the **Summer in the Bight** festival. Outdoor Shakespeare productions, dinner theater, and back-porch dramas and comedies fill the bill.

GUIDED TOURS

Rising Tide Theatre (☎ 709/738–3256) conducts walking tours (Wednesday, Saturday, and Sunday at 2) of the town that are more theater than tour, led by actors in period costumes.

Cape Bonavista

15 *16 km (10 mi) north of Port Union.*

Cape Bonavista is a popular destination because of its association with **Cabot's landing.** In 1997 the town will be the focal point for a year of celebrations (☎ 800/563–6353) marking the 500th anniversary of Cabot's landing, including a visit by a replica of Cabot's ship, ***Matthew.*** The **lighthouse** on the point has been restored to the 1870 period condition. The **Mockbeggar Property** teaches about the life of a well-to-do outport merchant in the years immediately before Confederation. ⊠ *Off Rte. 230,* ☎ *709/729–2460 or 709/468–7300.* 🎫 *Free.* ☉ *Late June–early Sept., daily 10–5:30.*

Burin Peninsula, Gander, and Notre Dame Bay

The journey down to the Burin Peninsula is a three- to four-hour drive from the intersection of Routes 230 and 1 through the sometimes incredible landscapes along Route 210. The peninsula's history is tied to the rich fishing grounds of the Grand Banks, which established this area as a center for European fishery as early as the 1500s. By the early 1900s, one of the world's largest fishing fleets was based on the Burin Peninsula. Today its inhabitants still operate the fishery in the modern trawlers that harvest the Grand Banks. Marystown is the peninsula's commercial center.

Grand Bank

16 *53 km (33 mi) southwest of Marystown on Rte. 220.*

Grand Bank, one of the most beautiful communities on the Atlantic seaboard, has a fascinating fishing history. For details about the town's past visit the **Southern Newfoundland Seamen's Museum,** in a sail-shape building. ⊠ *Marine Dr.,* ☎ *709/832–1484.* 🎫 *Free.* ☉ *May–Oct., weekdays 9–5, weekends 2–5.*

St-Pierre and Miquelon

17 *55 min. ferry ride from Fortune.*

Just south of Grand Bank is Fortune, where you can catch the ferry to France's only territory in North America—the islands of St-Pierre and Miquelon. These islands are the place to go if you crave French cuisine or a bottle of perfume. Shopping and eating are both popular pastimes, and if you plan to stay overnight, consider the Hotel Robert on St-Pierre. Visitors traveling to the islands should carry proof of citizenship; people from outside the United States and Canada will have to show valid visas and passports. A passenger ferry operated by **Lloyd G. Lake Ltd.** (☎ 709/832–2006) leaves Fortune daily at 2:15 PM from mid-June to late September; the crossing takes 55 minutes. The ferry leaves St-Pierre at 1 PM daily, and the round-trip costs $55 per person. The ferry operated by **St-Pierre Tours** (☎ 709/722–4103 or 709/832–0429) crosses daily from Fortune to St-Pierre from May 1 to September 30, and weekly from October to early December.

Burin

18 *45 km (28 mi) north of St. Lawrence.*

Following Route 220 will take you around the peninsula to the old town of Burin, a community built amid intricate cliffs and coves. This was an ideal setting for pirates and privateers who used to lure ships into the rocky, dead-end areas in order to plunder them. Captain Cook was among those who watched for smugglers from "Cook's Lookout" on a hill that still bears his name. Also in Burin are the **Heritage House** and **Heritage II** museums; considered two of the best community museums in Newfoundland, they give you a sense of what life was like in the past. Heritage II features a display on the 1929 tidal wave that struck Burin. ☎ 709/891–2217, ☜ *Free.* ☉ *Mon. and Tues. 9–5, Wed.–Sun. 9–9.*

Gander

19 *170 km (106 mi) northwest of Goobies.*

Gander, a busy center with 12,000 people, is the home of Gander International Airport. During World War II it was chosen by the Canadian and U.S. Air Forces as a major strategic air base because of its favorable weather and secure location. After the war, the airport became an international hub, and young islanders would hang around to see the stars come and go, among them Zsa Zsa Gabor and Tyrone Power. Now, like all modern airports, it's tightly secured. Gander has many hotels and still makes a good base for your travels. The **Aviation Exhibition** in the airport's Domestic Passenger's Lounge (☎ 709/256–6667) traces Newfoundland's role in the history of air travel. It's open 24 hours, 7 days a week.

DINING AND LODGING

$$ ✕🏨 **Albatross Motel.** This motel has a deserved reputation as an at-
★   tractive place to stop off for a meal. Try the cod au gratin—you won't find it this good anywhere else. Rooms are basic and clean. ⊠ *Box 450, A1V 1W8,* ☎ *709/256–3956,* 🖷 *709/651–2692. 103 rooms, 3 suites. Restaurant. AE, DC, MC, V.*

Twillingate

20 *31 km (19 mi) north of Boyd's Cove.*

The inhabitants of this charming old fishing village make their living from the sea and have been doing so for nearly two centuries. Every year on the last weekend in July, the town hosts the **Fish, Fun and Folk Festival,** where all different kinds of fish are cooked every kind of way. Twillingate is also one of the best places on the island to see **icebergs**, and is known to the locals as "Iceberg Alley." These majestic and dangerous mountains of ice are awe-inspiring to see while they're grounded in early summer.

OFF THE   **CHANGE ISLANDS AND FOGO ISLAND** – You can take a ferry from
BEATEN PATH   Farewell (take Route 340 to Route 335, which takes you through scenic coastal communities) to either Change Islands or Fogo Island. These is-

lands give you the impression of a place frozen in time. Clapboard homes are precariously perched on rocks or built on small lots surrounded by vegetable gardens. As you walk the roads, watch for moose and herds of wild Newfoundland ponies who spend their summers grazing and enjoying the warm breeze off the ocean.

he Great Northern Peninsula

Deer Lake
㉑ *208 km (130 mi) from Grand Falls-Windsor.*

Deer Lake was once just another small town on the Trans-Canada Highway, but the opening of Gros Morne National Park in the early '70s and a first-class paved highway passing right through to St. Anthony changed all that. Today, with an airport and car rentals available, Deer Lake is a good starting point for a fly-drive vacation.

DINING AND LODGING

$$ ✕🏨 **Deer Lake Motel.** The guest rooms here are clean and comfortable, and the food in the café is basic, home-cooked fare. You'll find the seafood dishes exceptionally well prepared. ✉ *Box 820, A0K 2E0,* ☎ *709/635–2108,* 🖷 *709/635–3842. 54 rooms, 2 suites. Café. AE, DC MC, V.*

En Route From Deer Lake take Route 430 to Route 422 to **Sir Richard Squires Memorial Park.** Natural and unspoiled, it contains one of the most interesting salmon fishing areas in Newfoundland. This drive will also take you through **Cormack,** one of the best farming regions on the island.

Gros Morne National Park
★ **㉒** *46 km (29 mi) north of Deer Lake. Travel north on Rte. 40 and pick up the Viking Trail.*

Because of its geological uniqueness and immense splendor, this park has been named a UNESCO World Heritage Site. Among the more breathtaking visions are the expanses of wild orchids in springtime. There is an excellent **interpretation center** (☎ 709/458–2417), which has displays and videos about the park. Camping and hiking are popular recreations, and boat tours are available. It takes at least two days to see Gros Morne properly. Scenic **Bonne Bay,** a deep, mountainous fjord, divides the park in two. You can drive around the perimeter of the fjord on Route 430 going north.

㉓ In the south of the park is **Woody Point,** a charming community of old houses and imported Lombardy poplars. Until it was bypassed by the now-defunct railway, the community was the commercial capital of Newfoundland's west coast. Rising behind Woody Point are the **Tablelands,** a unique rock massif that was once an ancient seabed. Its rocks are toxic to most plant life, and Ice Age conditions linger in the form of persistent snow and moving rock glaciers.

Follow Route 431 to scenic **Trout River Pond** and the once isolated **㉔** and still unusual community of **Trout River.** The **Green Gardens Trail,** a four- to five-hour hike, is along the way and it's one you'll remember for your lifetime, but be prepared to do a bit of climbing on your return journey. The trail passes through the Tablelands barrens and descends sharply down to a fairy-tale coastline of eroded cliffs, sea stacks, and lush green meadows.

㉕ On the northern side of the park, along coastal Route 430, is **Rocky Harbour,** with a wide range of services and a luxurious indoor public pool—the perfect thing to soothe tired limbs after a strenuous day.

The most popular attraction in the northern portion of Gros Morne is the boat tour of **Western Brook Pond,** which is reached by a leisurely 45-minute walk from the main highway through an interesting mix of bog and woods. Cliffs rise 2,000 feet on both sides of the gorge, and high waterfalls tumble over ancient rocks. If you have strong legs and are in good shape, another natural attraction is the 10-mile hike up **Gros Morne Mountain,** at 2,644 feet the second-highest peak in Newfoundland. Weather permitting, your labor will be rewarded by a unique arctic landscape and spectacular views. The park's coast in the north offers visitors an unusual mix of sand beaches, rock pools, and trails through tangled dwarf forests known locally as "tuckamore." Sunsets, seen from **Lobster Point Lighthouse,** are spectacular. Keep an eye out for whales and visit the lighthouse museum, devoted to the history of the area.

Arches Provincial Park

26 *20 km (13 mi) north of Gros Morne National Park.*

Arches Provincial Park is a geological curiosity where the action of undersea current millions of years ago cut a succession of caves through a bed of dolomite that was later raised above sea level by tectonic upheaval.

En Route   Continuing north, parallel to the Gulf of St. Lawrence, you'll find yourself refreshingly close to the ocean and the wave-tossed beaches: Stop to breathe the fresh sea air and listen to the breakers. The Long Range Mountains to your right reminded Jacques Cartier, who saw them in 1534, of the long, rectangular-shape farm buildings of his home village in France. Small villages are interspersed with rivers where salmon and trout grow to be "liar-size." The remains of the Maritime Archaic Indians and Dorset Eskimos have been found in abundance along this coast, and there's an interesting interpretation center (☎ 709/623–3522 or 709/623–2608) at Port au Choix.

L'Anse aux Meadows

★ **27** *210 km (130 mi) northeast of Arches Provincial Park.*

L'Anse aux Meadows National Historic Site, a UNESCO World Heritage Site, was discovered in 1960 by a Norwegian team, Helge and Anne Stine Ingstad. Most believe the remains of the long sod houses here were built around 1000 as the site of Norseman Lief Erikson's colony in the New World. The Canadian Parks Service has established a marvelous **visitor center** and has meticulously reconstructed some of the sod huts. With fires burning inside and sheepskins about, one gets a sense of centuries past. ⊠ *Rte. 436,* ☎ *709/623–2601 or 709/623–2608.* 🎫 *Free.* ☉ *Mid-June–Labor Day, daily 9–8.*

DINING AND LODGING

$ ✕🏠 **Tickle Inn at Cape Onion.** This refurbished, century-old fisherman's house on the beach is probably the most northerly residence on the island of Newfoundland. Guests often gather around the Franklin stove in the parlor after a day of exploring the area meadows, hills, and coast, or taking a trip to the Viking settlement at L'Anse aux Meadows (about 45 kilometers, or 73 miles, away). ⊠ *R.R. 1, Box 62, Cape Onion, A0K 4J0; June–Sept.,* ☎ *709/452–4321; Oct.–May, 709/739–5503.* *4 rooms share bathrooms. Dining room. CP, MAP available. MC, V.*

$ 🏠 **Valhalla Lodge Bed & Breakfast.** Adjacent to the Viking site, this B&B is comfortable and inviting. Note the interesting fossils in the rock fireplace in the dining room. Hot breakfasts are available, and other meals can be had on request. ⊠ *Gunner's Cove, Griquet A0K 2X0; in summer,* ☎ *709/623–2018; in winter, 709/896–5519.* *6 rooms. V.*

St. Anthony
28 *16 km (10 mi) south of L'Anse aux Meadows.*

The northern part of the Great Northern Peninsula served as the model for the Pulitizer-prize winning novel *The Shipping News* by E. Annie Proulx. St. Anthony is a beautiful town settled around a natural harbor on the eastern side of the Great Northern Peninsula near its tip. Take a trip out to the **lighthouse**—you may see an iceberg or two floating by.

The **Grenfell Mission,** the huge hospital adjacent to Charles S. Curtis Memorial Hospital, attests to the work done by Sir Wilfred Grenfell, a British medical missionary, who established nursing stations and co-operatives and provided medical services to the scattered villages of northern Newfoundland and the south coast of Labrador in the early 1900s. The main foyer of the hospital has a decorative **tile mural** that's worth a visit. **Grenfell House,** the home of Sir Wilfred and Lady Grenfell, has been restored to period condition and can also be visited. ⊠ *On west side of town on hill overlooking harbor,* ☎ *709/454–2281.* 🖃 *$2.* ☉ *Mid-May–mid-Oct., daily 10–8; winter, by appointment.*

Don't leave without visiting the **Grenfell Handcraft** store (☎ 709/454–3576). Importing craftspeople to train the villagers to become self-sufficient in a harsh environment was one of Grenfell's aims. A windproof cloth that villagers turned into well-made parkas came to be known as Grenfell cloth. Beautiful clothes fashioned out of Grenfell cloth have quality and style not found anywhere else and are available for sale here.

The West Coast

Corner Brook
29 *50 km (31 mi) southwest of Deer Lake.*

Corner Brook is Newfoundland's second largest city and the hub of the west coast of the island. Mountains fringe three sides of the city, and there are beautiful views of the harbor and the Bay of Islands. Corner Brook is also home to one of the largest paper mills in the world. Every July the city hosts the **Hangashore Folk Festival,** where you can go to hear some great traditional Canadian and Newfoundland music.

If you plan to explore the west coast, Corner Brook is a convenient hub and point of departure. It is only three hours from the Port-aux-Basques ferry and is an attractive and active city. The town enjoys more clearly defined seasons than most of the rest of the island, and in summer there are many pretty gardens to enjoy.

The north and south shores of the **Bay of Islands** have fine paved roads—Route 440 on the north shore and Route 450 on the south—and both are a scenic half-day drive. On both roads, farming and fishing communities exist side by side. Take a camera with you—the scenery is breathtaking, with farms, mountains, and pockets of brilliant wildflowers.

DINING AND LODGING
$$ ✕🏠 **Best Western Mamateek Inn.** Rooms are more modern than at the
★ Glynmill Inn (☞ *below*). The dining room, which serves good Newfoundland home-cooked food, is known for its exquisite view of the city. Sunsets seen from here are remarkable. ⊠ *Box 787, Rte. 1, A2H 6G7,* ☎ *709/639–8901 or 800/563–8600,* 🖳 *709/639–7567. 55 rooms. Restaurant. AE, MC, V.*

$$ ✕🏠 **Glynmill Inn.** This charming inn has the feel of old England. It was
★ once the staff house for the visiting top brass of the mill. Rooms are cozy and the dining room serves basic and well-prepared Newfound-

land seafood, soups, and specialty desserts made with partridgeberrie￼ There's also a popular steak house in the basement. ⊠ *Box 550, 1 Cob￼ La., A2H 6E6,* ☎ *709/634–5181; in Canada, 800/563–4400;* ℻￼ *709/634–5106. 82 rooms. 2 restaurants. AE, MC, V.*

$$ ⊞ **Holiday Inn.** There's nothing extraordinary here, aside from the con￼ venience of being located right in town. The outdoor pool is heate￼ and some of the rooms have minibars. The restaurant is average, asid￼ from good seasonal fish dishes. ⊠ *48 West St., A2H 2Z2,* ☎ *709/634￼ 5381,* ℻ *709/634–1723. 103 rooms. Restaurant, lounge, minibars￼ pool. AE, DC, MC, V.*

$–$$ ⊞ **Comfort Inn by Journey's End Motel.** This is a comfortable, mod￼ ern motel with an attractive interior (the dominating colors are dust￼ rose and blue) and beautiful views of either the city or the Bay Island￼ ⊠ *Box 1142, 41 Maple Valley Rd., A2H 6T2,* ☎ *709/639–1980,* ℻￼ *709/639–1549. 81 rooms. Restaurant. AE, MC, DC, V.*

OUTDOOR ACTIVITIES AND SPORTS

The **Marble Mountain Ski Resort** (☎ 709/637–7600), just east of th￼ city, has the highest slopes and the most snowfall in eastern North Amer￼ ica and is growing rapidly. There's a large day lodge, ski shop, da￼ care center, and restaurant at the mountain summit.

Stephenville
㉚ *77 km (48 mi) south of Corner Brook.*

Harmon Air Force Base is in Stephenville, which is best known for i￼ summer festival. The peninsula was largely settled by the French￼ who brought their way of life and language to this small corner c￼ Newfoundland.

THE ARTS

The **Stephenville Festival** (☎ 709/643–5756) is held throughout Jul￼ and into August. The festival is the province's major annual summe￼ theatrical event and features a well-produced mix of light musicals an￼ serious drama.

Port-aux-Basques
㉛ *70 km (44 mi) south of Stephenville.*

As you move farther down the Trans-Canada Highway toward Por￼ aux-Basques, Routes 404, 405, 406, and 407 will bring you into th￼ small Scottish communities of the Codroy Valley. Nestled in the va￼ ley are some of the finest salmon rivers and most productive farms i￼ the province, all of this against the backdrop of the Long Range Moun￼ tains and the Lewis Hills, from which gales strong enough to stop tra￼ fic hurl off the plateau and down to the coast. In J. T. Cheesema￼ Provincial Park and at Grand Bay West you can catch sight of the en￼ dangered Piping Plover, which nests in the sand dunes along this pa￼ of the coast.

LODGING

$$ ⊞ **St. Christopher's Hotel.** This clean, comfortable hotel has quiet, ai￼ conditioned rooms and good food. Rooms have satellite TV. ⊠ *Box 204￼ Caribou Rd., Port-aux-Basques, A0M 1C0,* ☎ *709/695–7034,* ℻￼ *709/695–9841. 58 rooms. Restaurant, meeting room. AE, DC, MC,* ￼

LABRADOR

Isolated from the rest of the continent, Labrador has remained one ￼ the world's truly wild places, and yet its two main centers of Labrad￼ City–Wabush and Happy Valley–Goose Bay offer all the amenities ava￼

able in larger, urban centers. Labrador is steeped in history, a place where the past invades the present, and life evolves as it did many years ago—a composite of natural phenomena, wilderness adventure, history, and culture.

Labrador's vast landscape—293,347 square kilometers (113,204 square miles) of land and 8,000 kilometers (5,000 miles) of coastline—is home to a small but richly diverse population with a history that in some cases stretches back thousands of years; in other cases, the mining towns of Labrador West for example, the history goes back less than four decades.

traits

32 The Straits were a rich hunting-and-gathering ground for the continent's earliest peoples. In **L'Anse au Clair,** anglers can try their luck for trout and salmon on the scenic Forteau and Pinware rivers. You can also walk the "Doctor's Path," where long ago Dr. Marcoux searched out herbs and medicinal plants in the days when hospitals and nursing stations were few and far between.

33 The elaborate **Maritime Archaic Indian burial site** discovered near **L'Anse Amour,** which is 19 kilometers (12 miles) east of L'Anse au Clair, is 9,000 years old. A plaque marks the site that is the oldest known aboriginal funeral monument in North America. The L'Anse Amour **lighthouse** was constructed in 1857 and is the second tallest lighthouse in Canada.

The **Labrador Straits Museum** provides an interesting glimpse into the history and lifestyle of the area. ⊠ *Rte. 510 between Forteau and L'Anse au Loup,* ☎ *709/927–5860.* 🖃 *$1.50.* ☉ *Summer, daily.*

★ **34** You must drive to the very end of Route 510 to visit the area's main attraction: **Red Bay,** the site of a 16th-century Basque whaling station and the province's newest UNESCO World Heritage Site. Basque whalers began harpooning migrating whales from flimsy boats in frigid waters a few years after Cabot's discovery of the coast in 1497. Between 1550 and 1600 Red Bay was the world's whaling capital. A visitor center (☎ 709/920–2197), which is open mid-June to early October, Monday through Saturday 8–8 and Sunday noon–8, interprets the Basque heritage through film and artifact. Between June and October, a boat will take you on a five-minute journey over to the site of excavations on Saddle Island.

Coastal Labrador

You can tour coastal Labrador aboard Marine Atlantic's (☎ 709/695–7081) car ferry from Lewisporte, Newfoundland. The trip takes 33 hours one-way, and two regularly scheduled return trips are made weekly. A second vessel, a coastal freighter, travels from St. Anthony, Newfoundland, to Nain, Labrador's northernmost settlement. This trip takes two weeks to complete. Both vessels carry all sorts of food and goods for people living along the coast. On the coastal freighter you'll stop at a number of summer fishing stations and coastal communities. Reservations are required.

35 **Happy Valley–Goose Bay** is the chief service center for coastal Labrador. The town was founded in the 1940s as a top-secret air base used to ferry fleets of North American–manufactured aircraft to Europe. It is still used as a low-level flying training base by the British, Dutch, and German air forces. **Snow Goose Mountain Ski Club** (☎ 709/896–5923) is between Happy Valley–Goose Bay and North West River.

Sheshatshit is the home of the Montagnais Innu Indians of Labrador. The spirit in which the Innu (Naskapi-Montagnais) people inhabited the interior for centuries can still be felt the moment you step outside the region's modern mining communities. **North West River,** which retains its frontier charm, was founded as a Hudson's Bay trading post and is the former Labrador headquarters of the International Grenfell Association.

Labrador West

Labrador West's subarctic landscape is challenging and unforgettable. Here are some of the world's best angling and wilderness adventure opportunities.

The best way to see this area is to ride the **Québec North Shore and Labrador Railway** (☎ 418/968–7805 or 709/944–8205), which leaves Sept Isles, Québec, three times a week in summer and twice a week in the winter. The seven- to eight-hour trip to Schefferville takes you through nearly 600 kilometers (350 miles) of virgin forest, spectacular water falls, and majestic mountains.

The modern town of **Wabush** has all the amenities of larger, urban centers, including accommodations, sports and recreational facilities, good shopping, live theater, and some of the finest hospitality you will find anywhere. The **Smokey Mountain Alpine Skiing Center** (☎ 709/944–3505), west of Wabush, is open mid-November–late April and has trails and slopes for both beginners and advanced skiers. **Labrador City** has all the facilities of Wabush.

NEWFOUNDLAND AND LABRADOR A TO Z

Arriving and Departing

By Car Ferry
Marine Atlantic (✉ Box 250, North Sydney, Nova Scotia B2A 3M3, ☎ 902/794–5700 or 709/772–7701, TTY 902/794–8109, FAX 902/564–7480) operates a car ferry from North Sydney, Nova Scotia, to Port aux-Basques, Newfoundland (crossing time is six hours); and, from June through October, from North Sydney to Argentia, twice a week (crossing time 12–14 hours). In all cases, reservations are required.

By Plane
The province's main airport for connections from all major North American and European destinations is St. John's. Airports in Newfoundland are at Stephenville, Deer Lake, St. Anthony, Gander, and St. John's; airports in Labrador are in Happy Valley–Goose Bay, Wabush, and Churchill Falls. **Air Canada** (☎ 800/776–3000; in Canada, 800/422–6232) flies into Newfoundland. The following are regional connectors. **Air Nova** (☎ 800/776–3000; in Newfoundland, 800/563–5151). **Interprovincial Airlines** (☎ 709/576–1666). **Air Labrador** (☎ 709/896–3387; in Newfoundland, 800/563–3042). **Air Atlantic** (☎ 800/563–8359; in Newfoundland, 709/576–0274).

By Train
Iron Ore Canada's Québec North Shore and Labrador Railway (☎ 418/962–9411) has service between Sept Isles, Québec, and Labrador City and Schefferville in Labrador.

Getting Around

Labrador

From the island of Newfoundland, you can fly to Labrador via St. John's, Gander, Deer Lake, or Stephenville. Route 500 links Labrador City with Happy Valley–Goose Bay via Churchill Falls. If you plan on doing any extensive driving in any part of Labrador, you should contact the **Department of Tourism, Culture and Recreation** (☎ 709/729–2830 or 800/563–6353) for advice on the best routes and road conditions. Conditions on this 526-kilometer (315-mile) unpaved wilderness road are best between June and October.

To explore the south coast of Labrador, catch the **ferry** at St. Barbe on Route 430 in Newfoundland to Blanc Sablon, Québec. From here you can drive to Red Bay along Route 510.

Summer travel is possible by car ferry through **Marine Atlantic** (☎ 800/341–7981; in Lewisporte, Newfoundland, ☎ 709/535–6876; in Happy Valley–Goose Bay, Labrador, 709/896–0041). The ship travels from Lewisporte in Newfoundland to Cartwright, on the coast of Labrador, and then through the Hamilton inlet to Happy Valley–Goose Bay. Reservations are required.

Newfoundland

DRL Coachlines (☎ 709/738–8088) runs a trans-island bus service. Buses leave at 8 AM from St. John's and Port-aux-Basques. Small buses known as outport taxis connect the major centers with surrounding communities.

Newfoundland has an excellent highway system, and all but a handful of secondary roads are paved. The province's roads are generally uncrowded, adding to the pleasure of driving. Traveling time along the Trans-Canada Highway from Port-aux-Basques to St. John's is about 13 hours, with time out for a meal in either Gander or Grand Falls-Windsor. The trip from Corner Brook to St. Anthony at the northernmost tip of the island is about five hours. The drive from St. John's to Grand Bank on the Burin Peninsula takes about four hours.

From St. John's to the north coast of the Avalon Peninsula, take Route 30 (Logy Bay Road) to Marine Drive. If you're heading for the southern coast, just south of St. John's pick up Route 10 and follow it toward Trepassey. Locals call this trip "going up the shore," even though it looks like you're traveling down on a map.

In winter some highways may close during and after severe snowstorms. For winter road conditions on the west coast and in Labrador, call the **Department of Works, Services, and Transportation** (in Deer Lake, ☎ 709/635–2162; in Grand Falls-Windsor and Central Newfoundland, 709/292–4300; in Clarenville, 709/466–7953; in St. John's, 709/729–2391).

Contacts and Resources

Emergencies

Dial **911** for medical emergencies and police.

Fishing

Seasonal and regulatory fishing information can be obtained from the **Department of Tourism, Culture and Recreation** (☎ 800/563–6353).

Guided Tours

ADVENTURE TOURS

Adventure touring in Newfoundland and Labrador is experiencing period of rapid growth. Local adventure tour operators offer se kayaking, ocean-diving, canoeing, wildlife viewing, mountain bikin white-water rafting, heli-hiking, and interpretive walks in the summe In winter, snowmobiling, heli-skiing, and caribou- and seal-watchin expeditions are popular. Before choosing an operator it's advisable contact the Department of Tourism, Culture and Recreation to mak sure you're calling a reputable outfit. **Eastern Edge Outfitters** (70 782–1465) leads east-coast sea-kayaking tours and gives white-wate kayaking instruction. **Gros Morne Adventure Guides** (709/458–272 or 709/686–2241) offers sea-kayaking up the fjords and land-locke ponds of Gros Morne National Park, as well as a variety of hikes an adventures in the area. **Tuckamore Lodge** (709/865–6361) in Ma Brook uses its luxurious lodge on the Great Northern Peninsula as base for viewing caribou, seabird colonies, whales, and iceberg **Labrador Scenic Ltd.** (709/497–8326) in North West River orga nizes tours through central and northern Labrador with an emphas on wildlife and Labrador's spectacular coast.

BOAT TOURS

South of St. John's, in Bay Bulls, **O'Brien's Bird Island Charters** (70 753–4850 or 709/334–2355) offers popular two-hour excursions fea turing whale-, iceberg-, and seabird-watching as well as cod jiggin **Gatherall's Sanctuary Boat Charters** (709/334–2887) is O'Brien main competitor. **Great Island Tours** (709/432–2272) charters a 3 foot boat on an hourly basis, accommodating up to 18 people.

On the Trinity–Bonavista Peninsula, **Ocean Contact Limited** (709/464 3269) is an established specialist in whale-watching and whale re search. Dr. Peter Beamish's book, *Dancing with Whales*, documen their interesting findings. **Island Rendezvous** (709/747–7253) o fers two days of boating and an overnight stay on Woody Island, Pl centia Bay. **Island View Boat Tours** (709/535–2258) promises a muss and lobster boil-up on the beach, an island treasure hunt, and a chanc to visit abandoned settlements and Indian sites in the Lewisporte are **Twillingate Island Boat Tours** (709/884–2242) specializes in icebe photography in the iceberg-rich waters around Twillingate. There an iceberg interpretation center right on the dock.

On the west coast, 2,000-foot-high cliffs and spectacular landlocke fjords are the main attraction. **Bontours** (709/458–2730) runs th best-known of the sightseeing trips—up Western Brook Pond in Gr Morne National Park. **Tableland Boat Tours** (709/451–2101) lea tours up Trout River Pond near the southern boundary of the par **Seal Island Boat Tours** (709/243–2376 or 709/243–2278) explor St. Paul's Inlet, an area of the park rich in seals, terns, and other ma rine and shore life.

BUS TOURS

McCarthy's Party (709/781–2244) in St. John's offers guided b tours across Newfoundland (May–October) in addition to a varie of charter services. **Fleetline Motorcoach Tours** (709/722–2608) Holyrood runs island-wide tours. Local tours are available for Por aux-Basques, the Codroy Valley, Corner Brook, the Bay of Islands, Gr Morne National Park, the Great Northern Peninsula, and St. John'

Hospitals

St. Clare's Mercy Hospital (154 Le Marchant Rd., St. John's, 70 778–3111). **Grace Hospital** (241 Le Marchant Rd., St. John

☎ 709/778–6222). **General Hospital** (✉ 300 Prince Philip Dr., St. John's, ☎ 709/737–6300). **George B. Cross Hospital** (✉ Manitoba Dr., Clarenville, ☎ 709/466–3411). **James Paton** (✉ 125 Trans-Canada Hwy., Gander, ☎ 709/651–2500). **Western Memorial** (✉ Brookfield Ave., Corner Brook, ☎ 709/637–5000). **Charles S. Curtis Memorial Hospital** (✉ West St., St. Anthony, ☎ 709/454–3333). **Captain William Jackman Hospital** (✉ 410 Booth Ave., Labrador City, ☎ 709/944–2632).

Visitor Information

The Department of Tourism, Culture and Recreation (✉ Box 8730, St. John's A1B 4K2, ☎ 709/729–2830) distributes brochures and maps from its offices in the Confederation Building, West Block, St. John's. The province also maintains a **tourist information line** (☎ 800/563–6353), which operates year-round, 24 hours a day.

From June until Labor Day, a network of **Visitor Information Centres,** open daily 9–9, dots the province. These centers carry up-to-date information on events, accommodations, shopping, and crafts stores in their area. There are in-season visitor information booths at the airports in Gander and St. John's. The city of St. John's operates a complete information center in a restored railway carriage next to the harbor.

15 Wilderness Canada

Northwest Territories, Yukon

Life above the 60th parallel in the mountainous, river-threaded Yukon and the flat, lake-dotted Northwest Territories is strange and wonderful. The landscape is austere and beautiful in ways unlike anywhere else in North America: the tundra plains that reach to the Arctic Ocean, the remote ice fields of the St. Elias Mountains, white-water rivers snaking through mountain ranges and deep canyons. This is also the last region of North America where native peoples have managed to sustain traditional cultures relatively undisturbed.

y Peter Oliver

pdated by
osemary
llerston
Northwest
erritories) and
na Sebert
he Yukon)

LET IT BE STATED AS SIMPLY AS POSSIBLE: Life in Canada's far north is strange. Strange as in weird, strange as in wonderful, strange as in uncommon. The inherent strangeness of the world north of the 60th parallel—the latitudinal line separating Canada's provinces and the Yukon and the Northwest Territories—is perceptible in empirical, practical, and mysterious ways.

Consider examples from life in the heart of strangeness:

In recent years, diamond discoveries have created barren outposts out on the tundra. The people in these camps depend for survival on airplanes, as do many small communities all over the Arctic. Other residents of the far north may drive hundreds of miles to a major city to stock up on groceries. In many cases, it is easier to hunt caribou or moose than it is to go shopping for vegetables.

Seasons become so overlapped in the few, non-winter months that summer wildflowers have not finished blooming by the time the foliage picks up its fall color. In winter, a network of highways, built entirely upon ice and hard-packed snow, opens up to automotive traffic large areas inaccessible in summer. So cold are the snow and ice that they lose their slipperiness, and thus make pretty good pavement. Bridges over rivers are also built of ice, and northerners must learn to prepare for "break-up" and "freeze-up"—the few weeks in spring and fall when ice bridges are unstable but when rivers are still too frozen for ferries to operate. Unprepared travelers will sometimes fork over $700 or more for a helicopter to sling their cars across a river. This underscores the fact that, in a region where bush pilots are held in high regard, air transport is the way to go. In a plane with pontoons, an uncountable number of lakes means an uncountable number of watery runways. As the Mayor of Yellowknife once said, "We get on planes here just like a New Yorker gets in a taxi."

If a single strange element of life in the far north stands out, it is the quality of light. In mid-summer, sunrise and sunset merge, and north of the Arctic Circle, they don't happen at all. And when night does come—so belatedly in summer that it is a way of life to draw shades tightly during sunlit evenings to simulate night— there is the mystical voodoo show of the Northern Lights.

The Yukon and the Northwest Territories make up 1,456,375 square miles, almost three times the size of Alaska and half the size of the rest of the United States. There are cities—Whitehorse in the Yukon, and Yellowknife in the Northwest Territories—but there are many more communities that more than likely are accessible only by plane.

Most of the region is climatically classified as semiarid, much of it covered by the vast granite spread of the Canadian Shield. But because water evaporates and ice melts so slowly in Arctic climes, there is an abundance of water. That water is mostly in the form of lakes and ponds in the flatter Northwest Territories and in the form of rivers in the mountainous Yukon. A good deal of it, of course, remains ice; the glaciers of the St. Elias Mountains in the Yukon's Kluane National Park, topped by 19,550-foot Mt. Logan, create the largest nonpolar ice field in the world.

This is wilderness and the wildlife loves it. A migrating caribou herd exceeding 80,000 is not uncommon, and that's a number to keep in perspective: It represents the entire human census of the region. Indeed, people are profoundly outnumbered by nonhuman mammals: bears (black, grizzly, polar), Dall sheep, wolves, wolverines, moose, bison and, of course, caribou. Humans are also outnumbered by fish and birds. Bald eagles are a common sight, as are the flocks of migratory water-fowl that spend their summers here.

The Klondike Gold Rush of 1896 is legendary, of course, but it was relatively short-lived (though gold continues to be mined profitably by companies in the Yukon). At the beginning of the 20th century, mining entered a new era—gold miners could no longer get rich from "just digging in the ground," as they had during the gold rush. Mechanization took over, and only the large operators who could afford the expensive machinery remained. Most of the gold rushers packed up their money bags and abandoned the Klondike for good.

Reason number one to visit: the landscape is austere and beautiful in ways unlike anywhere else in North America. Consider the tundra plains that reach to the Arctic Ocean, the remote ice fields of the St. Elias Mountains, white-water rivers snaking through mountain ranges and deep canyons, the glacially sculpted ranges of Baffin Island. Reason number two: all of that wildlife. Fishermen regularly throw back trout weighing 10 pounds, because a fish that size is considered in these parts to be too puny.

And perhaps less obviously, reason number three: people. This is the last region of North America where native peoples have managed to sustain traditional cultures relatively undisturbed. The main tribal groups are seven nations of Athapaskan peoples and the Inland Tlingit in the Yukon, and the Dene and Inuit peoples of the Northwest Territories. Many of these people still go about their lives much as their ancestors did centuries before them, although helped today by such 20th-century basics as electricity and motor-driven machinery.

Signs on government buildings are often inscribed in as many as eight official languages—English, French, and various native languages. One of those languages, Slavey, is so difficult to learn that it was used in coding during World War II. Native people in the far north are wielding increasing influence in governmental affairs. In recent years, large tracts of land have been ceded to native groups in land-claims settlements. And in 1999, the Northwest Territories will be split in two, separating the principal lands of the Dene and the Inuit. (The new Inuit territory is to be called *Nunavut,* or "our land.") The Dene call their region *Denendeh,* which means the same thing; this portion of the Territories is known for now as the Western Arctic.

A visit to the far north does not happen without commitment and preparation. Lodging under $100 a night is the exception, unless you camp, and what you get for the price is unlikely to be fancy digs. Having to rely on planes to get from one place to the next does not come cheaply. Guides and outfitters can be expensive, too, but their fees aren't out of line with the general cost of living in the far north, and their travel packages often end up saving you money.

Visitors must be willing to abide possible discomforts and inconveniences. Mosquitoes and blackflies rule the north during summer and early fall, and anyone without a good insect repellent is in for big trouble. Packing gloves and insulated clothing in August might seem excessive, but such are the necessities of traveling in a world where it's not uncommon for summertime temperatures to drop from above 70°F to well below freezing in a single day. And life doesn't always proceed with clockwork precision; a frontier quality still pervades much of the far north, meaning that a lot of business is conducted on an ad-hoc, by the-bootstraps basis. Visiting the far north can be daunting, difficult, frightening, and even dangerous, but for those who prepare themselves for the commitment, it can be nothing short of exhilarating.

leasures and Pastimes

Cross-Country Skiing

In a world covered by snow eight months out of the year, cross-country skiing opportunities are obviously plentiful. The best time for skiing, however, is from mid-March until the snow melts (the precise time varying according to the latitude and elevation), when days are longer and warmer. While short outings on skis are possible almost anywhere in the north, perhaps the most interesting extended excursions are in the Kluane area and the Arctic North. A number of backcountry lodges have begun opening in April and May for ski-touring enthusiasts.

Dining

Cooking in the far north rarely reaches grand epicurean standards, but it can have a distinctive character, making wide use of local foods. This means that in some places and at certain times of year, a caribou steak or a moose burger may be easier to find than a fresh salad. Once outside the main cities, be prepared for limited choices; the dining room of your hotel or lodge may well be your *only* choice. But if the far north is not necessarily a gastronomic paradise, it is surprising and certainly admirable what some chefs are able to concoct given the limitations on ingredients.

CATEGORY	COST*
$$$$	over $25
$$$	$18–$25
$$	$10–$18
$	under $10

per person, excluding drinks, service, and 7% GST

Dogsledding

Before there were planes and snowmobiles, dogsleds were the vital means of transportation in the far north. The Yukon Quest International Dogsled Race, along the Yukon River from Whitehorse to Fairbanks or Fairbanks to Whitehorse, takes place every year in mid-February. Destination/start points alternate annually. Top mushers compete for the $100,000 purse in this 1,000-mile trek that is touted to be the "toughest dogsled race in the world."

Fishing

Fishing in wilderness Canada is a way of life, a means of sustenance for a good many native residents. What sustains the native people of the north is also what attracts sports fishers: fish in large quantities and of considerable proportions. Farther south on the continent, an eight-pound trout might be considered a trophy fish, but in the far north it would be rejected as not much more than a sardine. Lake trout between 30 and 70 pounds are not unusual. The most common catches in the far north are Arctic char, grayling, pike, lake trout, and whitefish.

Numerous outfitters throughout the region can guide fishers on day trips or short excursions; your best bet is to check with a regional tourist office for outfitter recommendations. Day trips from Yellowknife to Great Slave Lake are especially easy to arrange. Some lakes and streams are accessible by road in the Yukon and in the Northwest Territories. However, the more typical fishing adventure in the far north involves flying for several days to a remote lodge.

Golf

Golf in the far north can be truly bizarre. For example, golfers at th
Yellowknife public golf course carry mats of artificial turf with the
because there are no grass fairways. Wherever your ball lands, yo
put down the mat, place the ball on it, and make your shot. The
is also a local rule about what to do should a raven steal your bal
What this ought to tell you is that golf is not a featured reason
come to the far north, although there are reasonable facsimiles of tra
ditional golf courses in Whitehorse and Dawson City. If, howeve
you want to take northern golf to its bizarre extreme, Adventu
Canada stages a golf "tournament" each April at the North Pole. Th
greens fees may be the world's highest: The cost of the eight-day tri
exceeds $10,000.

Hiking

While the landscape can be spectacular, the going can be rough. Marke
trails are relatively few, and sometimes the only trails to follow are tho
beaten down by wild animals. The four general areas that are best fe
hiking are Baffin Island, Kluane National Park, the Chilkoot Trail, ar
the mountains along the Dempster Highway.

The 100-kilometer (60-mile) backpacking hike through Baffin Island
Aksayook Pass is a trek through a world of mountains, fjords, ar
glaciers. The going is rugged and remote, but at least there is a tra
something that can't be said for the region's other classic trek: the 13(
kilometer (80-mile) hike from Tanquary Fjord to Lake Hazen c
Ellesmere Island. The trip runs above 80 degrees north latitude, so the
is considerable travel over ice plateaus and glaciers.

The trail system of Kluane National Park is the most extensive in th
far north. It's possible to make a five-day backpacking trip on marke
trails, with opportunities for off-trail scrambling on mountaintops a
fording good views of the park's big peaks and glaciers in the distanc
Be aware that Kluane is *serious* bear country, and all precautio
should be strictly followed.

The Chilkoot Trail offers a three- to five-day historic backpacking tr
through some spectacular scenery. Hikers begin their journey in Dy
on the Alaskan coast and ascend through rain forest, across alpine tu
dra, and into boreal forest. Along the way are the scattered shove
and graves of gold rushers who traveled this route a century ago.

Lodging

Lodging prices in the far north are generally higher than you mig
find elsewhere in Canada. In many communities, a lodge or hotel ma
be the only show in town, so if you don't like the price, you don't ha
much choice. In addition, the shortness of the tourism season forc
lodging proprietors to try to make ends meet in two or three mont
of active vacation business. Although you might think you're payi
a good chunk of change for pretty ordinary accommodations, consid
too, the lack of quality building materials in many areas and the pr
hibitive costs of construction. In months other than July and Augu
expect better deals—room prices reduced 50% or more—but few
choices, because many places are closed from September to June.

Territorial, or public, campgrounds are found along all roads in th
north, and are open from the spring thaw until the fall freeze. Visito
centers throughout the region can provide information on speci
campground locations and facilities as well as permits. Note: It is a
visable to boil or filter all water, even water that has been designate
as "drinking water" at a campground.

CATEGORY	COST*
$$$$	over $150
$$$	$120–$150
$$	$80–$120
$	under $80

All prices are for a standard double room (or equivalent, where not applicable), excluding gratuities and 7% GST.

Mountaineering

In the far north, the question is not so much what to climb but how to access the mountain. The major peaks of Kluane National Park, Mt. St. Elias, and particularly Canada's highest peak, Mt. Logan, are tops in the mountaineering world but can only be reached by helicopter or plane. In addition, all climbing parties must receive authorization from the Superintendent of Kluane National Park. The effect has been to weed out inexperienced climbers, and there have been far fewer serious accidents in Kluane than in Alaska, where many major peaks, most notably Mt. McKinley, are relatively close to public roads.

For serious rock climbers, the Cirque of the Unclimbables, located in Nahanni National Park, presents an obvious challenge. This breathtaking cathedral of rock towers rising as much as 3,000 vertical feet does not entirely live up to its name, but the few who have made successful ascents here can be counted among the most proficient rock climbers in the world. Perhaps the biggest problem posed by this cirque is that it is nearly as unreachable as it is unclimbable.

Shopping

Native arts and crafts are the most compelling reason to go shopping in the far north. (Products not made in the territories are generally much less expensive elsewhere.) You may find that prices are best when buying directly from artists or craftspeople in local communities; however, buying from galleries or stores in the cities provides at least some guarantee of authenticity. Soapstone carvings, clothing, and moose- or caribou-hair tuftings (hair sewn onto velvet or hide and cut and shaped into pictures of flowers or animals) are among the most popular items to purchase. Be aware before buying, however, that some products, such as those made from hides or materials from endangered species, may not be brought into the United States. In many cases—such as a polar-bear rug—the import problem is obvious, but not in all cases; for example, jewelry made of walrus ivory may be confiscated at the border.

Water Sports

Without question, river travel is one of the best ways to experience the wilderness of the far north; these roads of water provide access to remote areas. Canoes of various configurations are the preferred means of travel, although for some rivers—particularly those with considerable white water—rafts or kayaks may be used.

The major rivers, such as the Liard, Mackenzie, and Yukon, pass through nodes of civilization, while others, such as the Bonnet Plume, Snake, Firth, Keele, and Mountain rivers, run through long stretches of uninhabited wilderness. If you decide on an unguided trip, outfitters can provide both the necessary gear as well as transportation to and from the river.

It would be difficult to single out one river as *the* river to run in the far north. However, the South Nahanni in Nahanni National Park as the best known, would be the logical choice. Two-week canoe trips can start from Rabbit Kettle Lake at the park's northwestern extreme, but require portage around Virginia Falls. Eight- to 12-day canoe or raft trips put in below Virginia Falls. White water along the way is mini-

mal, so previous canoeing or rafting experience is not essential. Tw(
other rivers that are considered classics by river runners are the Alsel
and the Tatshenshini, which run primarily through British Columbia
although they begin in the Kluane region of the Yukon.

The Keele River and the Natla River run through the Mackenzi(
Mountains and may be preferred by canoeists seeking a more remot(
white-water experience. The wide, turbulence-free Yukon River is con
sidered one of the easiest rivers to run; the Big Salmon, with consid
erably more white water, is preferred by canoeists seeking more technica
challenge; the Takhini River, with a mix of gentle stretches and whit(
water, provides one of the best day trips from Whitehorse.

For experienced canoeists and kayakers, the Arctic coast holds a wealtl
of possibilities. The Coppermine River, a fairly easy-flowing rive
through the tundra, is a worthy destination, if for no better reason thar
a visit to Bloody Fall, the site of a 1771 massacre of Inuit by guides o
the Northwest Passage explorer, Samuel Hearne. There is also a 16
kilometer (10-mile) hiking trail along the river from the communit
of Kugluktuk (formerly Coppermine) to Bloody Fall.

One other water-borne adventure to consider is sailing on Great Slav(
Lake. (For those unsure of their navigation skills, hiring a skipper i
recommended, since many of the lake's small bays are still uncharted.
The lake's East Arm, a two- to three-day sail from Yellowknife, is prim(
cruise country, with dramatic cliffs rising from narrow bays.

Exploring Wilderness Canada

Great Itineraries

The idea of exploring all of Canada's far north in a single trip is ar
absurdity. It would be comparable to trying to visit Florida, New En
gland, and the Rocky Mountains on the same vacation, only with fa
fewer roads to travel. Size is only one problem; expense is another. Food
gas, and lodging are typically priced higher than in other parts o
Canada, but the big cost is transportation, especially in those vast, road
less areas where you'll need to depend on air travel. This is not to sa
it is difficult to get from one place to another; in fact, the number o
charter plane operators and the number of expert bush pilots able t(
land a float plane on a little more than a mud puddle make getting aroun(
easier than you might think. But the costs of traveling by small plane
can add up with dizzying speed.

Thus, the best strategy for exploring the far north is to be selective
Focus on a specific area (e.g., Baffin Island, the Nahanni region, Daw
son City) and/or an activity (e.g., fishing, wildlife viewing). Specific trave
plans can save hundreds, even thousands, of dollars. The choices fal
roughly into four categories: visiting the main cities (Dawson City, White
horse, Yellowknife); excursions from the main cities; adventures in th(
backcountry wilderness; and adventures in the Arctic north. The citie
of Whitehorse and Yellowknife are probably the least interesting ele
ments. There are points of cultural and historical interest in each, an(
almost everyone who visits the region ends up spending some time ii
either city. However, it makes little sense to come this far and not ven
ture beyond the city limits.

YUKON

Anyone expecting to see a lot of the Yukon will need to spend a con
siderable amount of time in a car or a considerable amount of mone
on airfare. If you can afford the time, seven days is a good start to get
ting to know the territory, but you could easily spend three weeks ex
ploring the backcountry beauty of just one region.

The stories and events surrounding the Klondike Gold Rush attract many visitors to the territory. To fully explore the places and events of that time, a visit of seven days is a minimum. If a hike over the Chilkoot Trail is part of your plan, count on four days just for that leg of your trip; a stay of two weeks would be appropriate.

If backcountry adventure is more your style, guided hiking or canoeing trips run from 6 to 14 days. The Yukon is one of the premier wilderness adventure destinations in the world. A combination of hiking, biking, canoeing, rafting, and wildlife viewing ventures could keep you occupied for months.

If You Have 3 Days: Start your tour in ⛴ **Whitehorse;** see the S.S. *Klondike* National Historic Site, the MacBride Museum, and Miles Canyon. The next day, drive down Route 2 to picturesque **Carcross** and on to ⛴ **Skagway,** Alaska along the approximate route traversed by the Klondike Gold Rushers in 1898. You'll pass through a variety of landforms, including the Carcross Desert, the alpine tundra of the White Pass, and the coastal rain forest of the Alaskan Panhandle. On the morning of your third day, ride the historic White Pass & Yukon Route railway round-trip past blue glaciers and rushing waterfalls. After lunching in the Red Onion Saloon, and shopping, it's time to make the two-hour return trip to Whitehorse.

If You Have 5 Days: Start your trip as you would with the three-day itinerary, but on day three, drive 8 hours, from Skagway past Whitehorse to ⛴ **Dawson City.** On your fourth day, drive down Bonanza Creek Road to see Dredge #4 and the original claim where the discovery of gold was made in 1896. Also highly recommended are the readings at Robert Service's cabin, the Palace Grand Theatre, and Diamond Tooth Gertie's Gambling Hall. On your way back to ⛴ **Whitehorse** the next day, drive up the Dome Road just outside of Dawson. You'll get panoramic views of Dawson City, the Yukon River, the Klondike River Valley, and Bonanza Creek.

If You Have 10 Days: A 10-day itinerary allows travelers who are interested in a wilderness experience to travel into the backcountry. A Klondike Gold Rush itinerary could be a hike over the **Chilkoot Trail** (four days) in addition to traveling to ⛴ **Skagway,** ⛴ **Whitehorse,** and ⛴ **Dawson.** If river scenery and wildlife viewing is more of an interest, a canoe trip down the Thirty-Mile section of the Yukon River, from Whitehorse to Carmacks, might fit the bill.

Some of the planet's best hiking is possible in **Kluane National Park.** A ten-day itinerary could take you as far back as the Donjek Glacier into the heart of Kluane's ethereal wilderness. People wanting to stay on the Yukon's roadways could venture up the Dempster Highway, past the Arctic Circle to ⛴ **Inuvik** in the Northwest Territories, an adventurous four-day extension to the five-day itinerary above.

Backcountry travelers should be advised: the Yukon's wilderness truly remains wild. If you are an inexperienced hiker (or canoeist) you should take a guided excursion into the backcountry. Even a hike over the Chilkoot Trail, which is monitored by the U.S. and Canadian Parks Services, is extremely rigorous.

NORTHWEST TERRITORIES

The following are memorable experiences for those who don't have a lot of time, but would like a taste of the north. Note that these trips involve flying, not driving. For short time spans, it's the only way to go.

If You Have 3 Days: You can jet north from Edmonton or Calgary across the Arctic Circle to ⛴ **Inuvik,** to see the amazing Mackenzie Delta, Tuk-

toyaktuk, and the Beaufort Sea. With two nights in Inuvik, you'll als
have time for a flying tour over the giant estuary (where belugas rom
in summer) to **Herschel Island,** a bird sanctuary that used to be the haur
of 19th-century whalers.

If You Have 5 Days: Fly up to ⚑ **Yellowknife** in late March for Cari
bou Carnival and the Canadian Championship Dog Derby. Bring you
warmest duds: it's still winter then, even though northerners think it
spring. But the sun's out, the ice sculptures sparkle, and everybody ha
loads of fun in a warm community atmosphere. You can book
dogsled ride on Great Slave Lake, go snowshoeing or ice-fishing, han
around the pub, and cheer the dog mushers on.

If You Have 7 Days: Head for ⚑ **Baffin Island,** the heart of Canada
newest political entity, Nunavut. You can fly to Iqaluit from Montréa
or Edmonton, via ⚑ **Yellowknife.** Depending when you go, you ca
book a jaunt by dogsled or snowmobile to see icebergs up close, tr
sea-kayaking or hike the tundra in search of wildflowers. Fly with
regional airline to ⚑ **Pangnirtung,** where you can watch artists a
work and drink in the serene beauty of Pang Fjord. This is the gate
way to **Auyuittuq National Park;** you won't have time for a full-scal
backpacking expedition, but outfitters will arrange a quick introduc
tory tour. Baffin is the true Arctic, inhabited for thousands of years b
the Inuit, and haunting relics of past cultures can be seen at Kekerte
and Qaummaarviit historic parks.

When to Tour Wilderness Canada

June through August is the high season for visiting the far north. Fo
the other nine months of the year, many businesses and outfitters clos
up shop, as much for lack of business as the length of winter. How
ever, many northerners say that April, when daylight lengthens, win
ter begins its recession, and such snow sports as skiing and dogsleddin
are still possible, is a good month to visit. September is another choic
month, when the fall colors are brilliant and ducks, geese, and animal
such as caribou begin their migrations. And as harsh—and dark—a
other months are, they can be prime time for visitors fascinated by th
spectral displays of the Northern Lights.

WHITEHORSE

Whitehorse began as an encampment near the White Horse Rapids o
the Yukon River. It was a logical layover point for gold rushers in th
late 1890s—most coming north along the Chilkoot Trail from Alaska—
who headed north toward Dawson to seek their fortune. Today's cit
of more than 22,000 residents is the Yukon's center of commerce, com
munication, and transportation, and is the seat of the territorial gov
ernment. It is not, however, a city of any great architectural distinction
Visitors should regard Whitehorse as a base camp, from which to ven
ture out to explore other parts of the Yukon. There are, however, a
few points of interest in Whitehorse that can fill a well-spent day o
two of exploring.

The logical place to start touring Whitehorse is the **Whitehorse Infor
mation Centre,** centrally located at Steele Street and Third Avenue. Thi
is the best place to pick up information on local lodging, restaurants
shops, attractions, and special events. ✉ *302 Steele St., Suite 101,* ☎
403/667–7545, FAX *403/667–4507.* ☉ *Daily 8:30–5, extended hour.
in summer.*

The **MacBride Museum** is your best general introduction to the spiri
and heritage of the Yukon. Over 5,000 square feet of exhibits displa

artifacts, natural history specimens, historic photographs, maps, diagrams, and heritage buildings from prehistory to the present. Exhibits provide a historical overview of the Yukon, from early exploration to the present, covering the trapping era and the gold rush. The museum has the largest public collection of Yukon gold in Canada. ⊠ *1st Ave. and Wood St.,* ☎ *403/667–2709,* ℻ *403/633–6607.* ▧ *$3.50.* ☉ *Mid-May–Labor Day, daily 10–6.*

The **Waterfront Walkway** along the Yukon River will take you past a few stops of interest. Your walk starts just east of the MacBride Museum entrance on 1st Avenue. Traveling upstream (south) you'll go by the old White Pass & Yukon Route building on Main Street. Two blocks down from Main is the **Yukon Visitor Information Centre** where you can pick up information on all Yukon sights and services and see the free 20-minute slide show on the geology and history of the region. ⊠ *Lambert St. and 2nd Ave.,* ☎ *407/667–2915,* ℻ *403/667–7669.* ☉ *Mid-May–mid-Sept., daily 8–8.*

Just south of the Yukon Visitor Information Centre is the **Yukon Territorial Government Building.** This is worth a quick visit to see the **Yukon Permanent Art Collection,** a display of works by Yukon artists depicting northern landscapes and lifestyles. ⊠ *2nd Ave. and Hanson St.,* ☎ *403/667–5811.* ▧ *Free.* ☉ *Weekdays 8:30–5.*

★ The **S.S. Klondike,** a national historic site, is through Rotary Park. The 35-foot stern-wheeler was built in 1929, sank in 1936, and was rebuilt in 1937. In the days when the Yukon River was the transportation link between Whitehorse and Dawson, the *Klondike* was the largest boat plying the river. Today it is dry-docked and has been restored to its 1930s glory. ⊠ *S. Access Rd. and 2nd Ave.,* ☎ *403/667–4511.* ▧ *$3.* ☉ *May–Sept., daily 9–6:30.*

If you're in Whitehorse during late summer, it's possible to take in one of nature's great endurance records: the longest Chinook (King) salmon migration in the world. The **Whitehorse Rapids Dam and Fish Ladder** has interpretive displays, display tanks of freshwater fish, and a viewing platform of the fish ladder. The best time to visit is August, when between 150 and 2,100 salmon use the ladder to bypass the dam. ⊠ *End of Nisutlin Dr.,* ☎ *403/633–5965.* ▧ *Free.* ☉ *June–Labor Day, daily; hours vary, so call ahead.*

Miles Canyon, a ten-minute drive south of Whitehorse, is both picturesque and historic. Although the dam below it now makes the canyon seem relatively tame, it was this perilous stretch of water that determined the location of Whitehorse as the starting point for river travel north. You can hike on trails along the canyon. Or experience the canyon as Jack London did when he was a pilot on these turbulent waters during the gold rush by taking a two-hour cruise aboard the **M.V. Schwatka.** ⊠ *Schwatka Lake, 2 mi south of downtown Whitehorse on Miles Canyon Rd.,* ☎ *403/668–4716,* ℻ *403/633–5574.* ▧ *$17.* ☉ *Cruises early–mid-June and mid-Aug.–early Sept., daily at 2; mid-June–mid-Aug., daily at 2 and 7.*

The **Yukon Transportation Museum** displays artifacts and exhibits of the Yukon's unusual transportation legacy, from snowshoes to cars, dogsleds to airplanes. ⊠ *Mi 915.4, Alaska Hwy.,* ☎ *403/668–4792.* ▧ *$3.50.* ☉ *Late May–Labor Day, daily 10–6.*

At **Takhini Hot Springs,** off the Klondike Highway, there's swimming in the spring-warmed water (suits and towels are available for rental), horseback riding, and areas for picnicking. ⊠ *Km 9.6 on Takhini Hot*

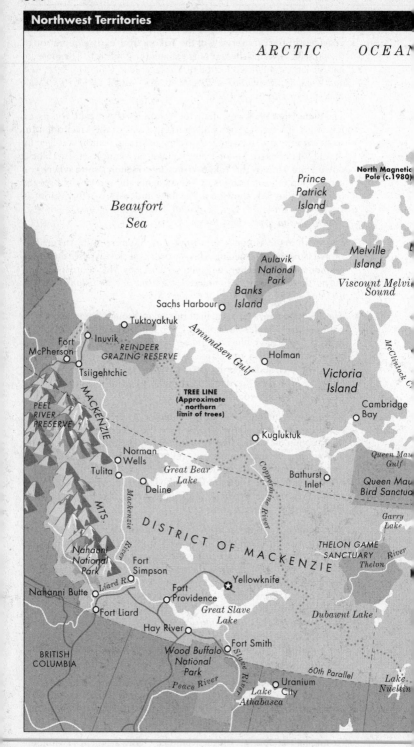

ARCTIC   OCEAN

North Magnetic Pole (c.1980)

Beaufort Sea

Prince Patrick Island

Melville Island

Aulavik National Park

Viscount Melvi Sound

Sachs Harbour *Banks Island*

Tuktoyaktuk

Amundsen Gulf

Fort McPherson Inuvik *REINDEER GRAZING RESERVE*

Tsiigehtchic

Holman

McClintock C

Victoria Island

TREE LINE (Approximate northern limit of trees)

Cambridge Bay

Kugluktuk

PEEL RIVER PRESERVE

MACKENZIE

Norman Wells

Tulita *Great Bear Lake*

Deline

Coppermine River

Bathurst Inlet

Queen Mau Gulf

Queen Mau Bird Sanctua

MTS.

DISTRICT OF MACKENZIE

Garry Lake

THELON GAME SANCTUARY *River*

Thelon

Mackenzie River

Nahanni National Park

Fort Simpson

Yellowknife

Nahanni Butte *Liard R.*

Fort Providence

Fort Liard

Great Slave Lake

Dubawnt Lake

Hay River

BRITISH COLUMBIA

Wood Buffalo National Park

Fort Smith

Slave River

60th Parallel

Lake Nuelti

Peace River

Uranium City

Lake Athabasca

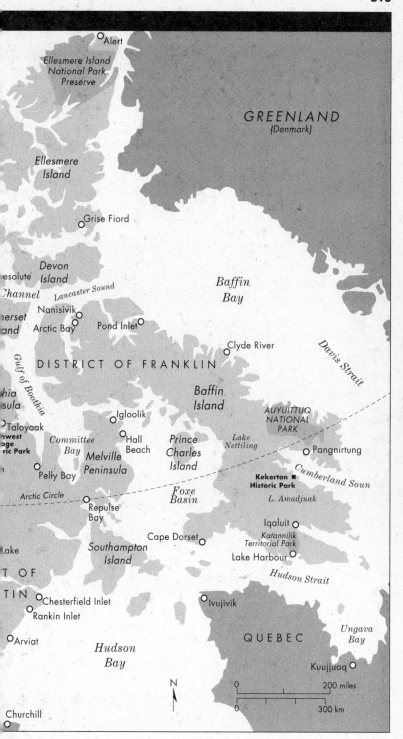

Alert

Ellesmere Island
National Park
Preserve

GREENLAND
(Denmark)

Ellesmere
Island

Grise Fiord

Devon
Island

esolute

Channel

Lancaster Sound

Baffin
Bay

Nanisivik

herset
and

Arctic Bay

Pond Inlet

Clyde River

Davis Strait

Gulf of Boothia

DISTRICT OF FRANKLIN

hia
sula

Baffin
Island

AUYUITTUQ
NATIONAL
PARK

Igloolik

Taloyoak

nwest
age
ric Park

Committee
Bay

Hall
Beach

Melville
Peninsula

Prince
Charles
Island

Lake
Nettling

Pangnirtung

Cumberland Soun

Pelly Bay

Kekerton ■
Historic Park

Arctic Circle

Foxe
Basin

Repulse
Bay

L. Amadjuak

Iqaluit

Cape Dorset

Southampton
Island

Katannilik
Territorial Park

Lake Harbour

Hudson Strait

Lake

T OF
TIN

Chesterfield Inlet

Rankin Inlet

Ivujivik

Ungava
Bay

Arviat

Hudson
Bay

QUEBEC

Kuujjuaq

N

0   200 miles

0   300 km

Churchill

The Yukon

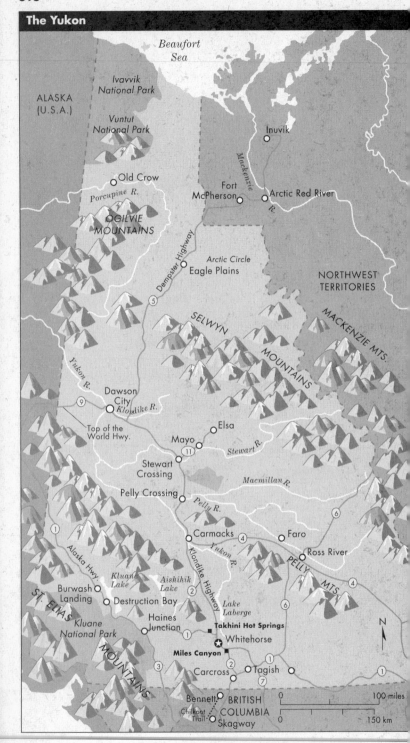

Beaufort
Sea

ALASKA
(U.S.A.)

*Ivavvik
National Park*

*Vuntut
National Park*

Inuvik

Old Crow

Porcupine R.

Mackenzie

Fort
McPherson

Arctic Red River

OGILVIE
MOUNTAINS

Dempster Highway

Arctic Circle

Eagle Plains

NORTHWEST
TERRITORIES

5

SELWYN

MOUNTAINS

MACKENZIE MTS.

Yukon R.

Dawson
City

Klondike R.

9

Elsa

Top of the
World Hwy.

Mayo

Stewart R.

11

Stewart
Crossing

Macmillan R.

Pelly Crossing

Pelly R.

6

1

Carmacks

4

Faro

Ross River

Yukon R.

PELLY

MTS

4

Alaska Hwy.

*Kluane
Lake*

*Aishihik
Lake*

2

Burwash
Landing

Destruction Bay

ST. ELIAS

Klondike Highway

*Lake
Laberge*

6

*Kluane
National Park*

Haines
Junction

1

Takhini Hot Springs

MOUNTAINS

★ Whitehorse

Miles Canyon

1

3

2

Carcross

Tagish

1

7

N

Bennett

Chilkoot
Trail

BRITISH

COLUMBIA

Skagway

0		100 miles

0		150 km

Springs Rd., 10 km (6 mi) north of Whitehorse, ☏ 403/633–2706. ☉
Summer, daily 7 AM–10 PM; call for winter hrs.

The **Yukon Wildlife Preserve** offers a fail-safe way of photographing
rarely spotted animals in a natural setting. Visitors might spot elk, caribou, mountain goats, musk oxen, bison, and mule deer and Dall,
mountain, and Stone sheep. Two-hour tours can be arranged only
through Gray Line. ⊠ *Gray Line Yukon, 208G Steele St., ☏ 403/668–*
3225. ☝ $21. ☉ Tour mid-May–mid-Sept., daily.

Dining and Lodging

$$$$ ✕ **The Cellar.** The fact that the tables have tablecloths immediately makes
this restaurant high-class in the Whitehorse dining scene. Indeed, The
Cellar, in the cellar of the Edgewater Hotel, with its high-back Victorian chairs, approaches the standards of an elegant dining room elsewhere in the world. Seafood, such as Alaska king crab, and prime rib
highlight the menu. This may be the only restaurant in the far north
where a jacket is advised. The Gallery upstairs serves breakfast and
lunch on a much more casual basis. ⊠ *101 Main St., Edgewater Hotel,*
☏ *403/667–2572. Reservations essential. AE, DC, MC, V.*

$$$–$$$$ ✕ **Angelo's Restaurant on Top.** Angelo's has the best views of any restau-
★ rant in town. Classic Greek and Italian cuisine is complemented by such
local delicacies as king salmon, Alaskan halibut, and king crab. The
calamari is especially wonderful—it's the subject of local debate what
chef John Tsambouris's secret is. Prices are a bit high, but you're cer-
tain to have a good dining experience. ⊠ *202 Strickland St., ☏*
403/668–6266. Reservations essential. MC, V. No lunch.

$$ ✕ **Chocolate Claim.** Besides handmade chocolates and truffles, the
★ chefs at "The Claim" produce delectable soups and baked goods that
run the gamut from the exotic, like fragrant Thai soups, to homespun
surprises, such as pumpkin cheesecake. The company is always interesting, the sandwiches are highly recommended, and the coffee is the
best in town. It's too bad "The Claim" isn't open for dinner. ⊠ *305*
Strickland St., ☏ 403/667–2202. V. No dinner.

$$ ✕ **No Pop Sandwich Shop.** The white-brick exterior promises all of
the atmosphere of a laundromat, but inside, the dining room—with
straight-edge pine furniture and walls adorned with the work of local
artists—is downright cozy. A small terrace in back with a tree rising
through the roof adds character to dining al fresco. People wander in
and out at all hours for take-out orders, a cup of coffee, or a full, sit-
down dinner. Rack of lamb and Arctic char are among the rotating
dinner specials; fresh-baked pastries are good any time of day. ⊠ *312*
Steele St., ☏ 403/668–3227. MC, V.

$–$$ ✕ **Talisman Cafe.** The pine furniture may be typical of the far north,
but the menu is all over the map, from veggie burgers to Middle East-
ern dishes such as tabbouleh. The dining experience here is comfortable and low-key. The take-out service provides well-prepared salads
and fresh-baked goods. ⊠ *2112 2nd Ave., ☏ 403/667–2736. MC, V.*

$$$$ ▥ **Inconnu Lodge.** Within the spectrum of rustic backcountry lodges,
Inconnu Lodge is a statement in relative luxury. The fly-in lodge on the
shores of McEvoy Lake, about 320 kilometers (200 miles) northeast of
Whitehorse, provides accommodations in modern log cabins. The principal activities are fishing and heli-hiking, although the lodge also arranges canoe trips on nearby rivers. Wildlife is plentiful, as attested by
the considerable taxidermy displayed in the lodge living room. The lodge
also acts as a jumping-off point for canoe and climbing trips into Nahanni National Park. Rates for five-day packages, including trans-

portation to and from Whitehorse, are about $2,600 U.S. ⊠ *Box 4730, Y1A 4N6,* ☎ FAX *403/667–4070. 5 duplex cabins sleep 20.*

$$$$ 🏨 **Oldsquaw Lodge.** The original lodge was built from materials salvaged from the Canol Trail by wildlife biologists. Those beginnings point to much of what the present-day lodge is all about: a place from which to access the Canol Trail, and a place dedicated primarily to wildlife viewing. The basic lodge program consists of daily hikes (in some cases helicopter assisted) on the open tundra in search of wildlife ranging from grizzly bears to falcons. The lodge also arranges mountain-biking trips on the Canol Trail and cross-country skiing in spring. Lodging is in six outlying cabins. Rates for weekly packages begin at $2,000 per person. ⊠ *Bag Service 2711, Y1A 4K8,* ☎ FAX *403/668–6732. 6 cabins sleep 12.*

$$$ 🏨 **Westmark Whitehorse Hotel.** If it weren't for all the tour-bus baggage to trip over in the hallways, this would be a fine place to stay. Rooms are attractively decorated with dark-wood furnishings and include such nice touches as coffee makers. The hotel can even boast its own vaudeville show, the *Frantic Follies*, a revue playing heavily on Gold Rush themes. The restaurant can get crowded. There's a gift shop and a travel agency on the premises. ⊠ *2nd Ave. and Wood St., Box 4250, Y1A 3T3,* ☎ *403/668–4700 or 800/544–0970,* FAX *403/668–2789. 176 rooms, 5 suites. Restaurant, lounge, barbershop, beauty salon. AE, DC, MC, V.*

$$ 🏨 **Edgewater Hotel.** This small hotel on a quiet end of Main Street is a good alternative to the Westmark for those trying to avoid the tour-bus bustle. The lobby is small and the passageway to the rooms is a bit narrow and awkward, but the rooms are large, modernly furnished, and quiet. They are also somewhat on the dark side, but when daylight stretches well into the night, this might be an asset. ⊠ *101 Main St., Y1A 2A7,* ☎ *403/667–2572,* FAX *403/668–3014. 28 rooms, 2 suites. Restaurant, lounge. AE, DC, MC, V.*

$$ 🏨 **High Country Inn.** This inn offers the budget traveler the best value in Whitehorse, without a large compromise in comfort. All of the rooms are clean, well maintained, and nicely decorated in light, pastel colors. There are economy singles, suites, and deluxe suites with kitchenettes. Some of the rooms are small or strangely laid out, so it's worth taking a look at what's available before you commit. The lobby, restaurant, and lounge are cozy and the location is close to the S.S. *Klondike* and the public swimming pool. ⊠ *4051 4th Ave., Y1A 1H1* ☎ *403/667–4471 or 800/554–4471,* FAX *403/667–5457. 110 units. Restaurant, lounge, laundry. AE, DC, MC, V.*

Outdoor Activities and Sports

Golf

Mountain View Golf Course (⊠ Range Rd., Box 5883, ☎ 403/633–6020), an 18-hole, par 72 course that's open May through September, has real grass and greens.

Shopping

Native-made clothing (and other products) is available at **Yukon Native Products** (⊠ 4230 4th Ave., ☎ 403/668–5955). **Murdoch's Gem Shop** (⊠ 207 Main St., ☎ 403/668–7403) is the Yukon's largest manufacturer of gold-nugget jewelry. **Northern Images** (⊠ 311 Jarvis St., ☎ 403/668–5739) sells a variety of native crafts and artwork, from sculpture to moose-hair tuftings to clothing, and has stores in several Canadian cities, including Whitehorse and Yellowknife. **Yukon Gallery** (⊠ 2093 2nd Ave., ☎ 403/667–2391) sells the works of Yukon artists and craftspeople including limited-edition art prints and original sculptures and paintings.

SIDE TRIPS FROM WHITEHORSE

The options for travelers leaving Whitehorse are north to Dawson, south to Skagway, Alaska, east to Watson Lake, and west to the Kluane region. No matter in which direction you head, expect to encounter considerable bus and RV traffic during the summer; the Yukon ranks with Alaska as one of the great road-touring regions of North America.

Watson Lake

Perhaps the least inspiring of the four options is the 450-kilometer (280-mile) trip east to Watson Lake. Its principal raison d'être is as gateway city to the Yukon for travelers heading northwest along the Alaska Highway. One notable point of interest, however, is the **Signpost Forest**; during the construction of the Alaska Highway in 1942, a homesick U.S. soldier put up a sign indicating the name of his hometown as well as the mileage and direction. Since then, other visitors have followed suit, to the tune of more than 29,000 signs.

Lodging

\$\$–\$\$\$ **Big Horn Hotel.** The Big Horn, downtown, is Watson Lake's newest and nicest hotel. Large rooms are creatively decorated with forest draperies and bedspreads and wooden headboards. The whirlpool suites are especially decadent, without being prohibitively expensive. ✉ *Box 157, Alaska Hwy., Y0A 1C0,* ☎ *403/536–2020,* FAX *403/536–2021. 29 rooms. Coin laundry. AE, MC, V.*

\$\$ **Watson Lake Hotel.** On the western edge of Watson Lake, this hotel provides basic services and clean, neat guest rooms at reasonable prices, either in the hotel itself or in motel units. Three units have kitchenettes. Log walls and exposed-stone accents add to the comfortable, rustic atmosphere. ✉ *Box 370, Y0A 1C0,* ☎ *403/536–7781,* FAX *403/536–2724. 47 units, 1 suite. Dining room, lounge, sauna, laundry. AE, DC, MC, V.*

Kluane National Park

About 160 kilometers (100 miles) west of Whitehorse is **Haines Junction,** the main gateway to Kluane National Park. Kluane (pronounced kloo-AH-nee) is one of the most extraordinary national parks in the world, home to the largest nonpolar ice mass in the world as well as Canada's highest mountain, **Mt. Logan** (19,550 feet). **Glaciers** up to 100 kilometers (60 miles) long, several kilometers (a couple of miles) wide, and 2 kilometers (1 mile) deep stretch from the huge ice fields of the interior. Kluane combines with neighboring Wrangell–St. Elias National Park in Alaska and Tatshenshini Provincial Park in British Columbia to form the largest expanse of contiguous national-park land in the world.

Few visitors, other than experienced mountaineers, get a full sense of Kluane's most extraordinary terrain; no roads or trails lead into the interior. A helicopter or fixed-wing flight over the Kluane ice fields is well worth the price on a clear day. Expect to pay approximately $100 per person—fixed-wing flights are slightly cheaper, but they can't offer the maneuverability of a helicopter flight. Many visitors content themselves with exploring the front ranges, which have impressive mountains with abundant wildlife—Dall sheep, black bears, and grizzly bears are the most noteworthy species. There is also a network of hiking trails—rare in the far north—facilitating everything from half-day hikes to multiday backpacking excursions.

Kluane visitors should start at **Kluane National Park Headquarters** (⊠ Box 5495, Haines Junction, ☎ 403/634–2251, FAX 403/634–2686). A free, 25-minute slide presentation provides an excellent introduction to the region's geology, flora, and fauna. The Kluane mountains comprise the most earthquake-prone zone in Canada, with an average of 1,000 tremors, most barely perceptible, recorded each year. Staff at the headquarters can also give you valuable information about the condition of the many hiking trails—including any recent bear sightings.

Be sure to drop in on the **Kluane Park Adventure Center** (⊠ Box 5383, Whitehorse, ☎ 403/633–5470 or 800/661–0469), next to the Mountain View Restaurant on the Alaska Highway, in summer. The center is a one-stop booking service for accommodations and a variety of activities, including flight-seeing, river rafting, trail rides, and nature walks, and rents canoes and bikes as well.

To hike in the park, head either south on Haines Road from the park headquarters to **Kathleen Lake** or north on the Alaska Highway to the **visitors' center at Sheep Mountain** (⊠ Mile 1019, Alaska Hwy., ☎ 403/634–2251). Most marked hiking trails follow lake shorelines or glacially carved river basins and are relatively easy to negotiate. Day hikers should check at the Haines Junction visitors' center (☞ Contacts and Resources, *below*) for a summer schedule of guided hikes. More ambitious hikers can backpack from the Sheep Mountain visitors' center up the Slims River valley to the toe of the Kaskawulsh Glacier, a 27-kilometer (16-mile) jaunt. Short of backcountry scrambling, this is as close as hikers can get to Kluane's glacier country. Be sure to pick up a tent-camping permit and free food-storage canisters at the visitors' center; keep in mind that this is bear country, and all bear precautions—especially storing food in canisters—must be taken. Horse-packing trips are also possible in the Slims River valley; check at the Kluane Park Adventure Center for information on outfitters. The backcountry registration fee for Kluane is $10.75 per party.

Dining and Lodging

$$$–$$$$ ✗🍴 **Raven Motel.** The Raven, Haines Junction's finest dining and lodging establishment, has fresh rooms, tastefully designed in a European style and unbelievably, room service. Dining in the restaurant on the second floor is a delight for the eyes and the palate. Fresh local salmon and lake trout, homemade pasta, juicy steaks, and fresh herbs will satisfy your tasebuds as the beautiful mountain views of Kluane's Front Ranges delight your eyes. ⊠ *Box 5470, Alaska Hwy., Haines Junction, Y0B 1L0,* ☎ *403/634–2500,* FAX *403/634–2517. 12 rooms. CP. MC, V.*

$–$$ ✗🍴 **Cozy Corner.** The name is anything but original, yet there is a genuine coziness about this small motel and café. The rooms are unusually large—big enough for a bed and sofa bed—although the bathrooms are surprisingly small. Some of the rooms' small windows have views of the front ranges of Kluane National Park. As for the adjoining Cozy Corner Cafe, it's the sort of roadhouse where you order eggs for breakfast, burgers for lunch or dinner, and coffee at any time of day, served up with lots of homespun friendliness. ⊠ *Alaska Hwy. and Haines Rd., Box 5406, Haines Junction, Y0B 1L0,* ☎ *403/634–2511,* FAX *403/634–2119. 12 rooms. AE, MC, V.*

Skagway, Alaska

This excursion from Whitehorse takes you through an interesting succession of geological zones along Route 2, which runs south out of th

Yukon into British Columbia and on to Alaska. This is the approximate route traversed by the Klondike Gold Rushers in 1898. Heading out of Carcross, the highway gradually ascends to the summit of the White Pass—an area of stark alpine tundra vegetation and impressive mountain scenery. Near the town of **Carcross,** 74 kilometers (46 miles) from Whitehorse, is the **Carcross Desert,** a small expanse of, indeed, desert, attesting to the aridity of the climate; it is affectionately known as the smallest desert in the world. Carcross is one of the Yukon's most picturesque towns, so be sure to spend a few minutes walking along the shores of **Bennett Lake** where thousands of gold rush stampeders landed after a rough journey on the windy waters. You'll also pass through the alpine tundra of the White Pass and the coastal rain forest of the Alaskan Panhandle. By the time the road begins descending steeply into Skagway, the landscape changes dramatically to a heavily vegetated world of glacially carved fjords.

Skagway was once controlled by the notorious "Soapy" Smith but now hosts cruise ships traveling up the Alaskan coast. Shops, museums, restored buildings, and historic re-creations will keep you entertained. When you walk down Broadway today, the scene is not appreciably different from what the prospectors saw in the days of 1898.

There are two alternatives to driving through this area. One is the **White Pass & Yukon Route,** a combined bus-and-rail trip between Whitehorse and Skagway. The train travels 1¾ hours to Frasier, British Columbia, then a bus completes the trip to Whitehorse in another 2½ hours. A three-hour round-trip is also available, starting and ending in Skagway. Nobody ever regrets a ride on this historic railway past blue glaciers and rushing waterfalls (even if they do grumble about the price before taking the trip). ⊠ *Box 435, Skagway, AK 99840,* ☎ *907/983–2217 or 800/343–7373,* FAX *907/983–2734)* ⊠ *One-way, $95 US; round-trip $75 U.S.* ☉ *Departures mid-May–mid-Sept., daily.*

Another alternative is backpacking on the 54-kilometer (33-mile) **Chilkoot Trail** between Skagway and Bennett, British Columbia. Although the trail never actually reaches the Yukon, it is vitally linked with Yukon history: during the Klondike Gold Rush, prospectors trekked over Chilkoot Pass to Bennett, where they built their own boats and sailed across Bennett and Tagish lakes to the headwaters of the Yukon River. Those boats that weren't wrecked in Miles Canyon or the White Horse or Five Finger rapids eventually arrived in Dawson City.

Dining and Lodging

$$ ✕⌂ **Golden North Hotel.** Alaska's most historic hotel was built in
★ 1898 in the heyday of the gold rush—golden dome and all—and has been lovingly restored to reflect that period. Pioneer Skagway families have contributed gold-rush furnishings to each of the hotel's rooms, and the stories of those families are posted on the walls of each unit. Popular choices in the Golden North Restaurant include sourdough pancakes for breakfast; soups, salads, and sandwiches for lunch; salmon or other seafood for dinner. ⊠ *Box 343, 3rd Ave. and Broadway, Skagway, AK 99840,* ☎ *907/983–2294,* FAX *907/983–2755. 32 rooms. Restaurant, lobby lounge. AE, DC, MC, V.*

$$ ✕⌂ **Skagway Inn Bed & Breakfast.** Each room in this downtown inn
★ has a Victorian motif with antiques and cast-iron beds; some have mountain views. The building was constructed in 1897 and is thus one of Skagway's oldest. The inn's summer-only restaurant, Lorna's at the Skagway Inn, is considered by many to be Skagway's finest. Owner and chef Lorna McDermott is a graduate of Le Cordon Bleu. ⊠ *Box 500, 7th Ave. and Broadway, Skagway, AK 99840,* ☎ *907/983–2289,* FAX *907/983–2713. 12 rooms. Restaurant. D, MC, V.*

Dawson City

Dawson City was the epicenter of gold fever at the turn of the century. Preservationists have done an admirable job of not only restoring many of the city's historic buildings but also enforcing a zoning code that requires newly built structures to adopt facades conforming to a turn-of-the-century look. If it weren't for the presence of cars and camera-toting tourists strolling along Dawson's streets in summer, you might just feel like you had entered the Gold Rush era.

Dawson really got its start at the gold-mining sites just east of town. Huge mounds of rock and slag along the roadside attest to the considerable amount of earth turned over in search of precious metal. The most famous of many mining sites is **Bonanza Creek,** 2 kilometers (1¼ miles) east of Dawson, which produced several million-dollar claims in the days when gold went for $16 an ounce. In fact, the creek is so rich in minerals that it is still being mined today. Those who want to try their luck at gold-panning can rent the necessary gear for $5 at **Claim 33** (⊠ Mile 7, Bonanza Creek Rd., ☎ 403/993–5804). You're guaranteed some gold, but don't expect to strike it rich.

Well worth a visit is **Dredge No. 4,** 16 kilometers (10 miles) up Bonanza Creek Road from Claim 33. During the summer, daily tours are conducted through the dredge, which was used to dig up the creek bed during the height of Bonanza Creek's largesse. ⊠ Klondike National Historic Sites, ☎ 403/993–5462. ☎ $2.25; pass for all Klondike National Historic Sites, $5.40. ☉ June–Aug., daily.

The **Visitor Reception Centre** at Front and King streets (⊠ Box 389, Dawson City, ☎ 403/993–5566 FAX 403/993–6415) is an excellent source of information on everything from historical minutiae to lodging availability. Walking tours and historic presentations take place daily.

Built in 1899, the **Palace Grand Theatre** was show-time central during the Gold Rush days, staging everything from opera to vaudeville. It was restored in the 1970s by the Canadian Parks Service, and today is the home of the **Palace Revue,** a musical show based on Gold Rush history. ⊠ King St. between 2nd and 3rd Aves., ☎ 403/993–5575. ☎ $13–16. ☉ Show mid-May–mid-Sept., Wed.–Mon. at 8 PM.

The construction of the **Old Post Office** in 1900 was a symbolic affirmation of Dawson's permanence as a legitimate city rather than a boomtown of opportunism. The post office today effectively captures an aura of Dawson life at the turn of the century, and philatelists may want to purchase commemorative stamps. ⊠ 3rd Ave. and King St., ☎ Free. ☉ June–Sept., daily noon–5.

The **Dawson City Museum** chronicles the Gold Rush and includes exhibits on the material culture of the local Han native people, steam locomotives, and the paleontology of the region. The genealogical library is invaluable to visitors trying to trace relatives who traveled to Dawson during the gold rush. ⊠ Box 333, 5th Ave. between Mission and Turner Sts., ☎ 403/993–5291. FAX 403/993–5839. ☎ $3.50. ☉ Mid-May–early Sept., daily 10–6.

Within a block of one another are the former homes of Jack London and Robert Service, the two writers most closely associated with the Yukon Territory's history. Regular readings of the writers' works are held at each home. **Jack London** is best known for such Yukon-inspired novels as The Call of the Wild and White Fang. ⊠ Jack London Interpretive Center, 8th Ave. and 1st St., ☎ 403/993–5575. ☎ Free. ☉ Late May–mid-Sept., daily 10–6.

Robert Service, primarily a poet, has been dubbed "Bard of the Klondike." ☒ *Robert W. Service Cabin, 8th Ave. and Hanson St.,* ☎ *403/993–5462.* ☜ *$2.25; pass for all Klondike National Historic Sites $5.40.* ☉ *June–mid-Sept., daily 9–5.*

If you want a firsthand feel for river travel, board the **Yukon Queen,** docked along Front Street, which makes the 173-kilometer (108-mile) trip westward to Eagle, Alaska in approximately five hours. One-way travelers may opt to return to Dawson by bus. ☒ *Box 420, Dawson City,* ☎ *403/993–5599; 208G Steele St., Whitehorse,* ☎ *403/668–3225 or 800/544–2206.* ☜ *One-way $85, round-trip $138.* ☉ *Departures mid-May–mid-Sept., daily.*

★ **Diamond Tooth Gertie's Gambling Hall** offers a glimpse at the frolicking times of the Gold Rush. "Gertie" and her cancan dancers put on shows nightly while grizzled miners sit at the poker table. Gamblers can enjoy real slot machines, blackjack, red dog, and roulette. Note: no minors are permitted. ☒ *4th Ave. and Queen St.,* ☎ *403/993–5575.* ☜ *$4.75.* ☉ *Mid-May–mid-Sept., daily 7 PM–2 AM.*

Dining and Lodging

$$$ ✕ **Jack London Grill.** This restaurant in the Downtown Hotel is one of the most attractive dining rooms in Dawson. The decor evokes the urbane atmosphere of a turn-of-the-century men's club, with dark-wood siding reaching halfway up walls adorned by framed mirrors and prints. Steaks are served in three sizes. For Dawson diners looking for a touch of civility and formality, this is a good choice. ☒ *Downtown Hotel, 2nd Ave. and Queen St.,* ☎ *403/993–5346. AE, DC, MC, V.*

$$$ ✕ **Marina's.** You'd think being so far north, you'd be inspired to order something more interesting than pizza. But the fact of the matter is, Marina's thick-crusted pizzas are first-rate and reasonably priced. There are other entrées, but it's the pizza that makes Marina's so popular with locals and visitors alike. Because of the location across from the Westmark, the dining room can fill up if there's a bus tour in town (and in the summer, there usually are a few). ☒ *5th Ave. between Princess and Harper Sts.,* ☎ *403/993–6800. MC, V.*

$$ ✕ **Klondike Kate's.** The line at Klondike Kate's can sometimes get a
★ little intimidating, but the food is extremely good. The Cajun blackened salmon is especially noteworthy, and the linguine pesto and smoked local king salmon are also standouts. A large, covered, outdoor deck is an airy, casual spot for a meal on a warm summer's day or evening. The main decorative statement on the deck is a large map of the world, onto which guests are invited to stick pins to mark their hometowns. ☒ *3rd Ave. and King St.,* ☎ *403/993–6527. V.*

$$ ✕ **River West Food and Health.** River West serves up homemade soups, hearty sandwiches, and coffee drinks made with organic coffee beans. "The best coffee in Dawson" is a boast River West lives up to, and after a night on the town, the health food atmosphere alone can have a purifying effect. The smoked salmon bagel is not only delectable—it's a bargain. ☒ *Front and York Sts.,* ☎ *403/993–6339. V.*

$$–$$$ ☷ **Triple J Hotel.** This "hotel" does indeed come in three parts: a main hotel, a separate motel, and several outlying cabins. The motel, little more than a large mobile home, is not worth considering. The cabins, which include kitchenettes, are a nice choice; their small porches and bright flowers out front exude a homey quality. But the best choice is one of the spacious, upstairs rooms, quaintly decorated in pseudo-antiques. Though they may be a bit dark, this can be an asset at this latitude in summer. The kitchen is one of the better hotel kitchens; you can order your pizza to go, or stay in the outdoor seating area. ☒ *Box*

359, 5th Ave. and Queen St., Y0B 1G0, ☎ 403/993–5323, 800/661–0405, or 800/764–3555; FAX 403/993–5030. 47 units. Restaurant lounge. AE, MC, V. Closed late Oct.–mid-Apr.

$$–$$$ 🏨 **Westmark Inn.** Like its counterpart in Whitehorse, this Westmark is a nice hotel that suffers from tour-bus overload. Rooms are clean, modern, and spacious if not particularly distinctive. The operative concept here is to create the familiar basic-American-hotel-room comforts behind a turn-of-the-century facade dictated by Dawson zoning codes. ⊠ *Box 420, 5th Ave. and Harper St., Y0B 1G0, ☎ 403/993–5542 or 800/544–0970, FAX 403/993–5623. 131 rooms. Restaurant, lounge, coin laundry. AE, DC, MC, V. Closed mid-Sept.–mid-May.*

$$ 🏨 **Downtown Hotel.** This hotel consists of a main building of 35 units which is open all year, and an annex of 25 units open only in summer across the street from the main hotel. The rooms in the main complex are marginally better. This hotel operates an airport shuttle service, which is especially valuable as there are no taxis in Dawson. ⊠ *Box 780, 2nd Ave. and Queen St., Y0B 1G0, ☎ 403/993–5346, 800/661–0514, or 800/765–4653; FAX 403/993–5076. 60 rooms. Dining room, lounge, hot tub, meeting rooms, airport shuttle. AE, DC, MC, V.*

$–$$ 🏨 **Dawson City Bunkhouse.** While accommodations in the Bunkhouse are spare (no TVs or room phones), they are comfortable and clean. Some rooms have private baths; others share public washrooms. For budget-minded travelers, this is the best deal in town. ⊠ *Front and Prince Sts., Bag 4040, Y0B 1G0, ☎ 403/993–6164, FAX 403/993–6051. 32 rooms. MC, V. Closed Labor Day–May.*

Nightlife and the Arts

THE ARTS

The **Dawson City Music Festival** (⊠ Dawson City Music Festival Association, Box 456, Y0B 1G0, ☎ 403/993–5584), featuring a variety of musicians from Alaska, Yukon, and the rest of Canada, is held each July. This is one of the most popular events in the north, so tickets can be extremely difficult to get. Write to the festival association in spring to request tickets.

NIGHTLIFE

The way that many Dawson visitors spend the evening (not to mention a few dollars) is at the gambling tables of **Diamond Tooth Gertie's Gambling Hall.** Short shows are staged throughout the evening, but gambling, with Klondike flair (croupiers are dressed in period costumes), is the main attraction. ⊠ *4th Ave. and Queen St., ☎ 403/993–5575. 🎟 $4.75. ⏱ Mid-May–mid-Sept., daily 7 PM–2 AM.*

The **Canteen Show** is a fun-filled re-creation of the 1940s U.S.O. show that entertained soldiers during the war years and the construction of the Alaska Highway. ⊠ *Gold Rush Inn, 411 Main St., ☎ 403/668–4500. 🎟 $16.50. ⏱ Performances June–Aug., daily.*

Outdoor Activities and Sports

RUNNING

A Labor Day weekend event that often draws a big crowd and the enthusiastic participation of Dawson City residents is the **Great Klondike Outhouse Race** (contact the Klondike Visitors Association, ☎ 403/993–5575), in which runners pull home-built "outhouses" on wheels through the streets of Dawson.

Top of the World Highway

The 108-kilometer (67-mile) trip west along the Top of the World Highway to the Yukon/Alaska border provides expansive vistas. The road partially lives up to its name, set as it is along ridge lines and high-mountain

tain shoulders, but the dirt-and-gravel surface (which creates plenty of dust thanks to RV traffic) can hardly be called a highway. The northernmost border crossing on land between Canada and the United States is along this route; the U.S. side is in Polar Creek, Alaska—population: two.

Dempster Highway

The 766-kilometer (476-mile) journey north to Inuvik on the Dempster Highway is a much more adventurous and ambitious undertaking than driving the Top of the World Highway. The only public highway in Canada to cross the Arctic Circle, it passes through a tundra landscape that is severe, mountainous, and ever changing. In its southern extreme, the highway passes first by the rugged Tombstone Mountains and then into the more rounded ranges of the Ogilvie Mountains. The route crosses Eagle Plains (approximately halfway between Dawson and Inuvik and a good stopping point for gas and supplies) before reaching the **Arctic Circle,** where a sign marks the point of crossing, providing a photo opportunity. From here, the highway passes through the Richardson Mountains and enters the flatlands surrounding the Mackenzie River Delta before reaching Inuvik (☞ *below*). This is certainly one of *the* great wilderness drives in North America, but because there are no services for 370 kilometers (230 miles) between the junction of the Dempster and Klondike highways and Eagle Plains, travelers should be prepared to cope with possible emergencies. If you prefer someone else to do the driving, contact **Gold City Tours** (⌧ Box 960, Dawson City, Y0B 1G0, ☎ 403/993–5175, ℻ 403/993–5261), which has summer bus service between Dawson and Inuvik.

YELLOWKNIFE

Yellowknife is not necessarily a city of great architectural, cultural, or historical distinction, but it does provide a few elements of interest. Originally established in 1934 after the discovery of gold, Yellowknife has since grown into the hub of government, transportation, and communication in the Northwest Territories.

In the **Old Town,** small houses and industrial buildings crowd around rocky knolls. Note the many structures perched on hard granite; those who have built on less solid foundations have often seen their homes contorted or wrecked by the shifting permafrost. The **Bush Pilots' Memorial,** which honors both the daring pilots who helped open the north and today's pilots, who are vital to the north's economy, is atop a knoll in the Old Town. Around the **Float Plane Base** there are piles of plastic bags, which are mining samples flown in from outlying prospectors' camps; the discovery of diamonds northwest of Yellowknife in recent years has spurred a modest boom in speculation.

NEED A
BREAK?
Drop in at the **Unicorn Pub and Steak Loft** (⌧ 5022 47th St., ☎ 403/669–9852) for Guiness and Harp on tap, English lunches, and Saturday brunch.

★ Yellowknife's most noteworthy geographical feature is **Great Slave Lake.** Day trips and extended excursions on the lake are offered by a number of companies.

The **Prince of Wales Northern Heritage Centre,** on the shore of Frame Lake, is just a few minutes from downtown. It houses extensive displays of northern artifacts as well as exhibits on exploration and settlement. The aviation section, documenting the north's history of flight, is especially worthwhile, as are exhibits devoted to the search for the Northwest Passage. ⊠ *Opposite City Hall,* ☎ *403/873–7551.* 🎟 *Free.* ☉ *June–Aug., daily 10:30–5; Sept.–May, Tues.–Fri. 10:30–5, weekends noon–5.*

N'dilo Cultural Village provides an excellent, hands-on opportunity to experience the culture and native life of the north. Village activities include leather tanning, fish drying, and carving, and visitors are encouraged to participate in native games and drum dances, as well as sample traditional native foods. ⊠ *Eastern end of Latham Island,* ☎ *403/873–2869.* 🎟 *$16.* ☉ *May–Aug., daily.*

Dining and Lodging

$$$$ ✕ **Factor's Club.** This big, airy dining room in the Explorer Hotel (☞ *below*) is highlighted by a central, circular hearth, and includes on its menu such unusual northern delicacies as musk ox chops. Dinners are pricey, but lunches and Sunday brunch are bargains. ⊠ *48th St. and 49th Ave.,* ☎ *403/873–3535 or 800/661–0892. AE, MC, V.*

$$$ ✕ **Bistro on Franklin.** The descent of the narrow stairs leading into the Bistro's basement setting feels vaguely ominous—more like heading down to check out the boiler room rather than going out to dinner. But the dining area brings relief: an attractive, unpretentious room with a small bar. Low lighting, tablecloths, and dinner waiters in bow ties lend a touch of formality to an otherwise casual place. Chicken and pasta dishes are excellent, including the chicken pesto pasta, a boneless breast of chicken in a pesto cream sauce, served with fettuccine; fish dishes such as Arctic char are less reliable. ⊠ *4910 Franklin Ave.,* ☎ *403/873–3991. MC, V.*

$$$ ✕ **Sweetgrass Cafe.** A warm, sophisticated atmosphere is highlighted by Navajo-influenced design touches (the Navajo are closely related to the northern Dene). The menu is eclectic, imaginative, and especially strong on unusual sauces to accompany appetizers like deep-fried Brie and char cakes, and such entrées as caribou tenderloin, lamb chops, Arctic char, and the chef's pasta of the day. ⊠ *5022 47th St.,* ☎ *403/873–9640. AE, MC, V.*

$$ ✕ **Bullock's Fish and Chips.** A good alternative to the nearby Wildcat Cafe when that becomes overcrowded, Bullock's has log-cabin walls and rough-hewn furniture that provide a warm, rustic atmosphere. The dining room has only five or six tables and the kitchen is effectively part of the dining room. As for the specialty of the house, the name tells all. ⊠ *4 Lessard Dr.,* ☎ *403/873–3474. V.*

$$ ✕ **Wildcat Cafe.** The Wildcat is an institution as much as a restaurant, the sort of place that everybody who comes to town eventually visits. It has been around since 1937; the low-slung, log structure and split log tables and benches inside lend to the aura of life at the frontier's edge. This is a place where strangers are expected to share tables. The food, ranging from fresh fish to vegetarian chili to caribou burgers, is excellent and modestly priced. Many people drop in at the Wildcat for coffee and desserts—mostly fresh-baked delectables. ⊠ *Doornbo's La. and Wiley Rd.,* ☎ *403/873–8850. MC, V.*

$ ✕ **Split Pea.** There is nothing fancy about Split Pea: It's primarily a take-out place. But it's a good spot to pick up sandwiches or fresh-baked muffins for those on the go. ⊠ *5000 Franklin Ave.,* ☎ *403/873–5510. No credit cards.*

$$$$ 🏨 **Bathurst Inlet Lodge.** Perhaps the most popular destination in the central Arctic, particularly for ornithologists, is this lodge, a lone outpost on the tundra shores of the inlet. Traveling by plane, boat, and foot from the lodge, guests typically spot musk oxen, Arctic foxes, wolves falcons, and eagles. In late spring, as many as half a million migrating caribou pass this way. Outings from the lodge include a hike (after a short airplane transfer) to **Wilberforce Falls,** the highest waterfall north of the Arctic Circle, where the Hood River cuts spectacularly through a series of gorges. In addition to week-long naturalist tours, the lodge also outfits canoe or raft trips on nearby rivers and bays. Fees start at about $2,300 per person for a 1-week stay, including flights to and from Yellowknife. ⊠ *Box 820, 3618 McAvoy Rd., Yellowknife X1A 2N6,* ☎ *403/873–2595. 15 rooms in lodge, 15 cabins. V. Closed early Aug.–late June.*

$$$$ ⊞ **Blachford Lake Lodge.** Many fishing lodges in the far north provide a minimum of services (unless patrons request otherwise) for guests seeking to keep vacation costs down. Blachford Lake Lodge is a good example of the genre. Guests are flown to and from the remote lodge (less than a half-hour flight from Yellowknife), where they stay in cabins and have the use of boats to venture out on the small lake. Guests are expected to bring and prepare their own food, as well as bring their own bedding and fishing tackle. The result is a cost that is generally under $120 per person per day (including the flights to and from the lodge), and less for groups—modest by fly-in fishing standards. The lodge is also open in winter for ice-fishing, snowmobiling, and dogsledding. ⊠ *Box 1568, X1A 2P2,* ☎ *403/873–3303,* ℻ *403/920–4013. 6 cabins sleep 14. V.*

$$$$ ⊞ **Frontier Lodge.** On the southeastern shore of Great Slave Lake, Frontier Lodge is typical of a full-service fishing lodge. Guests are housed in attractive, if spare, outlying cabins and in the main lodge, and breakfast and dinner are served daily around a big table in the main lodge. Guides take guests to the best fishing waters on the Great Slave as well as adjoining rivers and lakes, and lake trout exceeding 25 pounds are landed regularly. This is a lodge strictly dedicated to fishing; aside from reading or watching wolves feeding on dinner scraps, there is not much else to do except appreciate the lakeside wilderness setting. Packages, including flights to and from Yellowknife, begin at $250 per day per person. ⊠ *Box 32008, Edmonton, Alberta T6K 4C2,* ☎ *403/465–6843 or 403/370–3501,* ℻ *403/466–3874. 8 buildings with shared baths and a capacity of 35 people. Sauna, shop, meeting facilities. Closed mid-Sept.–mid-June. MAP. No credit cards.*

$$$ ⊞ **Explorer Hotel.** Atop a promontory overlooking Yellowknife, the Explorer is best recommended for its views of the city and surrounding bays of Great Slave Lake. Rooms are large and decorated with run-of-the-mill brown-veneer furniture, but they are bright and clean. ⊠ *Box 7000, X1A 2R3,* ☎ *403/873–3531; in Canada, 800/661–0892;* ℻ *403/873–2789. 127 rooms, 2 suites. 2 restaurants, lounge, airport shuttle. AE, MC, V.*

$$$ ⊞ **Yellowknife Inn.** This is the oldest hotel in a city where there isn't much that could be called old. It has a tradition of trying to be all things to all people, including, until the 1993 completion of a legislative building, home to the Northwest Territories legislative assembly. Rooms in the front are preferable, with large bathrooms, pastel upholstery, and dark, varnished cabinetry. Rooms in the back are rougher around the edges, geared more toward mining speculators and the like than the tourist crowd. The hotel's Mackenzie Lounge, with dark-wood paneling that lends it a clubby feel, is a nice place to meet for a pre-dinner drink. ⊠ *Box 490, X1A 2N4,* ☎ *403/873–2600,* ℻ *403/873–2602. 150 rooms, 7 suites. Restaurant, lounge, shops, airport shuttle. CP. AE, DC, MC, V.*

$$ ⊞ **Igloo Inn.** Don't expect much more here than a motel-style room at a decent price. Rooms are on the small side and have the basics—bed, bathroom, TV; many have kitchenettes. The Igloo is a perfectly good

choice for budget-minded travelers laying over for a night before head-
ing off to more adventurous ports of call in the territorial outback. ⊠
Box 596, X1A 2R3, ☎ *403/873–8511,* FAX *403/873–5547. 44 rooms.
Restaurant. AE, MC, V.*

$–$$ 🏨 **Blue Raven.** The Blue Raven is the best of the several good bed-and-
breakfast options in Yellowknife. Attractively set on a bluff at the edge
of Old Town and overlooking the Great Slave Lake, this is a good place
for those who like their Continental breakfast—served in a common
room—with a view. Rooms are small, modern, clean, and quiet, set
apart from one another by the home's three-story configuration. ⊠ *37B
Otto Dr., X1A 2T9,* ☎ *403/873–6328. 1 room with bath, 2 rooms
share a bath. CP. No credit cards.*

Nightlife and the Arts

Folk on the Rocks (⊠ Society for the Encouragement of Northern Talent, Box 326, X1A 2N3, ☎ 403/920–7806), folk music festival, is usually held on a mid-July weekend. The event attracts folk musicians from
throughout North America, as well as Dene and Inuit performers.

Raven Mad Daze (⊠ Yellowknife Chamber of Commerce, ☎ 403/920–
4944) takes place during summer solstice (the third week in June), when
the sun's still out at midnight. Sidewalk sales, street vendors, concerts,
and dances are part of the fun.

Outdoor Activities and Sports

Boating
Sail North (⊠ Box 2497, X1A 2P8, ☎ 403/873–8019) rents boats and
takes people on outings on crewed boats on Great Slave Lake. The **M.S.
Norweta** (⊠ N.W.T. Marine Group, 17 England Crescent, ☎ 403/873–
2489) offers short outings, dinner cruises, and multiday cruises to the
legendary East Arm of Great Slave Lake.

Shopping

Clothing
In a world where warm clothing is essential, parkas, mukluks, cari-
bou-hide mittens, and the like are a fashion statement. **Polar Parkas**
(⊠ 5023 49th St., ☎ 403/873–3343) is the best place in Yellowknife
to buy native-made parkas.

Native Arts and Crafts
One of the best and most reasonably priced stores for soapstone sculpture is **Webster Galleries** (⊠ 5016 50th St., ☎ 403/873–5876), devoted exclusively to northern artists working with northern materials
(many northern artists use soapstone imported from Brazil). **Northern
Images** (⊠ YK Centre, 49th St. and 50th Ave., ☎ 403/873–5944) sells
a variety of native crafts and artwork, from sculpture to moose-hair
tuftings to clothing, and has stores in several Canadian cities, including Whitehorse and Yellowknife. The **Arctic Art Gallery** (⊠ 4801
Franklin Ave., ☎ 403/873–5666) has a selection of carvings, lithographic
prints, and original paintings.

SIDE TRIPS FROM YELLOWKNIFE

Yellowknife is a transportation hub for outlying areas in the western
Arctic. Sports lovers can set out from Yellowknife for backcountry lodges
on the shores of Great Slave Lake or on one of the thousands of smaller
lakes that, along with their barren rock underpinnings and scrub
growth, are the principal geological constituents of the far north's in-

terior. For driving excursions from Yellowknife, you can pass through Wood Buffalo National Park and Fort Smith to the south, and through Fort Liard to the west. This is not, generally speaking, rousingly scenic driving. Long stretches of road cutting through the low-lying, subarctic bush are highlighted by occasional waterfalls or the sight of wildlife near or on the highway.

Alexandra Falls

Of the scenic waterfalls along the road between Yellowknife and Fort Smith, the most dramatic is Alexandra Falls, a few kilometers south of the town of Hay River, on Route 1 at the junction of Routes 1 and 2, where the Hay River majestically drops 108 feet over limestone cliffs.

Wood Buffalo National Park

The area where you're most likely to spot wildlife is Wood Buffalo National Park, straddling the Alberta/Northwest Territories border. Covering 44,807 square kilometers (17,026 square miles), this is the largest national park in Canada. Much of the terrain—a flat land of bogs, swamps, salt plains, sink holes, and meandering streams and rivers—is essentially inaccessible to visitors. This is not a world that people would think of spending much time in, but wildlife and insects (i.e., swarms of mosquitoes and blackflies) think otherwise. It is home, not surprisingly, to the world's largest free-roaming bison herd (about 5,000 total), and it is also a summer nesting ground for many bird species, including bald eagles, peregrine falcons, and the exceedingly rare whooping crane. The park's reception center in Fort Smith can provide additional information, and park rangers lead interpretive programs and hikes during July and August. ⊠ *Superintendent, Wood Buffalo National Park, Box 750, Fort Smith, Northwest Territories X0E 0P0,* ☎ *403/872–2349.*

Nahanni National Park

The principal reason to head west from Yellowknife is to visit Nahanni National Park. The Mackenzie and Liard rivers, which join forces at Fort Simpson, are the region's approximate geographical dividers, separating the low-lying bush of the east and the mountains to the west. This separation is perhaps most dramatically appreciated at **Blackstone Territorial Park,** with its views across the Liard River to the front ranges of the Nahanni Mountains. Blackstone is about as close as road-bound travelers can come to Nahanni National Park. Access to Nahanni National Park is possible only by helicopter or plane; inside the park, canoes and rafts are the principal means of travel. Perhaps the
★ most impressive feature in the park is **Virginia Falls,** more than 410 feet high and about 656 feet wide—a thunderous wall of white water cascading around a central spire of rock. **Simpson Air** (⊠ Box 260, Fort Simpson, Northwest Territories X0E 0N0, ☎ 403/695–2505) is one of several plane and helicopter services that offer sightseeing trips to Virginia Falls. A well-maintained park campground near the falls facilitates overnight excursions. For a complete listing of air services, contact the park headquarters. Several canoe and raft outfitters also guide trips on the Nahanni River. ⊠ *Nahanni National Park Reserve, Box 348-EG, Fort Simpson, X0E 0N0,* ☎ *403/695–3151.*

Outdoor Activities and Sports

BOATING

Two reliable outfitters that lead guided trips in Nahanni National Park are **Nahanni River Adventures** (⊠ Box 4869, Whitehorse, Yukon Territory Y1A 4N6, ☎ 403/668–3180) and **Nahanni Wilderness Ad-**

ventures (✉ Box 4, Site 6, R.R. 1, Didsbury, Alberta T0M 0W0, ☎ 403/637–3843).

MOUNTAINEERING

Simpson Air (✉ Box 260, Fort Simpson, Northwest Territories X0E 0N0, ☎ 403/695–2505) can shuttle climbers into the Cirque of the Unclimbables in Nahanni National Park from Fort Simpson. **Inconnu Lodge** (☞ Dining and Lodging *in* Whitehorse, *above*) can fly in climbers from the Yukon side; expect to pay handsomely for the service.

THE ARCTIC NORTH

One doesn't "tour" the Arctic North in the usual sense of the word. Rather, the concept is more expeditionary: Choose a community—such as Inuvik, Rankin Inlet, Iqaluit, or Pangnirtung—as a base camp from which to make day or extended side trips. Lodging and transportation in the Arctic North tend to be expensive even by high-end northern standards, so that having a well-defined travel plan is critical to staying within a budget. Trip organizers and outfitters can be particularly helpful in tailoring a travel program to meet particular interests and budgets. Keep in mind that the prime Arctic travel season tends to be very short: Many visitor services and tour organizers operate only in July and August.

Inuvik

Like Yellowknife, Inuvik, a commercial and transportation center of the western Arctic, is less a destination than it is a hub from which to reach out to other Arctic points of interest. The most compelling aspects of the region, dominated by the sprawling Mackenzie River Delta, are wildlife and culture.

The Arts

The **Great Northern Arts Festival** (✉ Box 2921, X0E 0T0, ☎ 403/979–3536) in July features displays, workshops, demonstrations, and performances.

Dining and Lodging

$$$–$$$$ ✕🏨 **Finto Inn.** The Finto is typical of far-northern lodging—decent motel-style rooms in a two-story, square structure resembling a big box that might have been flown in by a helicopter sling and dropped on the spot. The wood siding somewhat softens the harsh edges. Elegance in accommodations is not a reason to stay at the Finto, but the inn's restaurant—The Peppermill—is; it's generally considered Inuvik's best and is listed among the top 500 in Canada. The dining room overlooks green meadows and blue water; the menu features local foods, such as Arctic char and musk ox, but the German chef lends a European influence as evidenced in the Weiner schnitzel, Cordon Bleu dishes, and the German sauces. Home-baked breads are especially good. Four of the rooms have kitchenettes; all have satellite TV. The inn is on the outskirts of Inuvik, at the junction of the Marine Bypass and Mackenzie Road. ✉ *Box 1925, Inuvik X0E 0T0,* ☎ *403/979–2647,* 𝖥𝖠𝖷 *403/979–3442. 44 rooms. Restaurant. AE, DC, MC, V.*

SIDE TRIPS IN THE ARCTIC NORTH

Tuktoyaktuk

If you're interested primarily in the culture of the north, Tuktoyaktuk, a small Inuvialuit (western Inuit) community a short flight north of Inuvik, is the place to experience the interesting blend of ancient culture with modern influences. Tours of Tuktoyaktuk—Inuit-owned land in accordance with recent land-claim settlements—are conducted by In-uvialuit guides (☞ Guided Tours *in* Contacts and Resources, *below*).

Banks Island and Herschel Island

Although wildlife—particularly migrant birds—is abundant through-out the Mackenzie River Delta area, Banks Island and Herschel Island are destinations of particular interest. Banks Island is best known for its large herd of musk oxen. Herschel Island is today a park, although at the turn of the century it was the site of considerable whaling ac-tivity. It remains an excellent base for sighting beluga and bowhead whales and is known for abundant bird life, Arctic fox and polar bear dens, and wildflowers that grow from the seemingly barren tundra (☞ Guided Tours *in* Contacts and Resources, *below*).

Baffin Island

Even northerners accustomed to the unique beauty of the Arctic wilder-ness speak of Baffin Island in tones of awe. It is a world of junctures: where mountains meet sea, where the climates of summer and winter may be experienced on the same day, where summer flowers bloom on green, tundra meadows amid ice-locked surroundings. It remains a stronghold of Inuit tradition despite the ever-increasing influences of modern culture. At least 3,000 years ago, the Thule, ancestors of the Inuit, migrated to the Canadian Arctic across the frozen Bering Sea. Later, whaling became a prime means of sustenance, both for Inuit and European hunters, and many Baffin communities have exhibits or mu-seums that chronicle whaling life. Baffin tours start at the southeast-ern end of the island on Frobisher Bay in **Iqaluit,** which, like Inuvik and Yellowknife, is a point of reference and departure rather than a destination in itself. It is the transportation, communication, and gov-ernment center of Canada's eastern Arctic, and will be the capital of Nunavut when the territorial division comes about in 1999.

From Iqaluit, visitors must choose a medium of travel: land or sea. In winter, of course, the land and sea merge under ice and snow, and April and May are the ideal months for those interested in cross-country ski-ing, dogsledding, or snowmobiling. Those who journey into the Baf-fin wilderness should have an adventurous spirit and a willingness to abide life in a world with virtually none of the trappings of civiliza-tion. While some tour organizers offer general sightseeing tours of the region, Baffin is best appreciated by those inclined (and physically fit enough) to rough it.

Sea kayaking is popular in summer in the bays and fjords of Baffin, populated by whales, narwhals, walruses, and seals. The jewel of Baf-★ fin, however, is **Auyuittuq National Park,** where rivers and glaciers have cut deep fjords and have carved out **Aksayook Pass** (formerly Pang-nirtung Pass) between Cumberland Sound to the south and Davis Strait to the north. The 60-kilometer (37-mile) pass is surrounded by jagged peaks exceeding 6,600 feet that jut up from glacial ice (glacial melt provides the water supply supporting the brief burst of summer wildflowers on the tundra lowlands). A marked trail leads through the pass, and in summer, backpacking groups regularly make the five- to seven-day journey. There are emergency shelters along the route, but this is still a trip only for those properly prepared and physically fit, given the length of the trip and the vagaries of climatic changes, even in mid-summer. All park visitors should sign up with a trip organizer and/or check in at the park headquarters in Pangnirtung for informa-tion on hiking in the park. For more information, contact **Parks Canada**

(✉ Eastern Arctic District, Box 1720, Iqaluit, Northwest Territories
X0A 0H0, ☎ 819/979–6277). ✉ *Park headquarters.* ☉ *July and
Aug., weekdays 8:30–noon, 1–5, and 6–10; weekends 1–5 and 6–
10; Sept.–June, weekdays 8:30–5.*

OFF THE
BEATEN PATH

ELLESMERE ISLAND NATIONAL PARK – Even more adventurous visitors can
head north from Baffin to this park, above 80 degrees north latitude.
Ellesmere—like Baffin, a land of mountains and glaciers—is intriguing
as much for its climate as its landscape. Technically a "polar desert," the
island, with an annual precipitation of about 2½ inches, is one of the
driest places in the northern hemisphere; yet, because of the water-re-
taining effects of ice, parts of the island can support plant and wildlife.
For more information, contact **Parks Canada** (✉ Eastern Arctic District,
Box 1720, Iqaluit, Northwest Territories X0A 0H0, ☎ 819/979–6277).

Dining and Lodging

$$$ ✕🏨 **Discovery Lodge Hotel.** The lobby area of this hotel is brightened
by skylights. An oddity here is that some rooms have trapezoidal beds,
wider at the top than the bottom. The Granite Room, with its gran-
ite-slab tabletops, is perhaps the best restaurant in Iqaluit, notewor-
thy for its use of local ingredients, including Arctic char, Baffin Island
shrimp, and scallops. ✉ *Box 387, Iqaluit X0A 0H0,* ☎ *819/979–4433,*
FAX *819/979–6591. 51 rooms, 1 suite. Dining room, lounge, laundry,
airport shuttle. AE, DC, MC, V.*

$$$ ✕🏨 **Frobisher Inn.** In its brochure, the inn promotes itself as being "part
of an integrated, climate-controlled, indoor shopping and high-rise apart-
ment complex." So much for the rustic charm of the far north. Rooms
are boxlike and simply adorned with veneer-wood furnishings. Rooms
in the front offer good views of Frobisher Bay and Iqaluit. There's no
airport shuttle, but the inn will reimburse you for the taxi ride. The
dining room specializes in Canadian Arctic cuisine. ✉ *Box 610, Iqaluit
X0A 0H0,* ☎ *819/979–2222,* FAX *819/979–0427. 48 rooms. Dining
room, lounge, pool, sauna, laundry. AE, MC, V.*

Outdoor Activities and Sports

RUNNING

The **Midnight Sun Marathon** (contact Linda Brunner, Strathcona Mineral Services Ltd., 20 Toronto St., Toronto, Ontario M5C 2B8, ☎
416/869–0772) takes place in early July at Nanisivik, on the north end
of Baffin Island; it is a series of four races ranging from 10 to 84 kilometers (6 to 52 miles).

WILDERNESS CANADA A TO Z

Arriving and Departing

By Bus

Greyhound Lines of Canada (✉ 10234 103rd St., Edmonton, Alberta
T5J 0Y9, ☎ 403/421–4211) provides service from Edmonton to Hay
River, Northwest Territories. Greyhound also has service from Edmonton
or Vancouver to Whitehorse in the Yukon.

By Car

It hardly bears saying that getting to the Yukon or the Northwest Territories by car calls for a good deal of driving. The best route into the
region is the Alaska Highway (Route 97 in British Columbia), accessible from Edmonton via Routes 43, 34, and 2 and from Vancouver
via Route 1. After Fort Nelson, British Columbia, Routes 7, 1, and 3
lead to Yellowknife; the Alaska Highway (Route 1 in the Yukon) continues on to Whitehorse. The good news is that with so few roads in

the region, it's difficult to make a wrong turn. The distance from Vancouver to Whitehorse is more than 2,400 kilometers (1,500 miles). Be aware that as you drive farther north, gas stations are few and gas is expensive—in some cases exceeding 70¢ a liter, or roughly U.S. $2.40 a gallon. With relatively little lodging along the way, you might want to embark on the trip in a camper or recreational vehicle.

By Plane

Whitehorse International Airport is the major airport for the Yukon and is located 5 kilometers (3 miles) from downtown Whitehorse. **Yellowknife Airport,** the main facility for the Northwest Territories, is 5 kilometers (3 miles) northeast of the city center. Many smaller settlements—notably Cambridge Bay, Inuvik, Rankin Inlet, and Iqaluit—have regular as well as charter passenger service.

Air Canada (☎ 800/776–3000; in MI and NY, 800/387–2710; in ID and WA, 800/663–9100) is one of two major air carriers with connecting service from the United States to points in the Northwest Territories and the Yukon; it has better connections in the east than Canadian Airlines, but does not have service to the Yukon. Air Canada's service in the Northwest Territories is provided in conjunction with its affiliate, **NWT Air** (☎ 403/920–2500 or 800/661–0789).

Canadian Airlines (☎ 800/426–7000), the other major carrier with connecting service from the United States, has better connections in the west than Air Canada. Canadian Airlines affiliate, **Canadian North** (☎ 800/426–7000) is responsible for most of the connecting service throughout the far north. Canadian Airlines also has a scheduling agreement with **American Airlines** (☎ 800/433–7300) for connections from the United States. For the eastern Northwest Territories, **First Air** (☎ 613/839–1247 or 800/267–1247) offers extensive service from Montréal and Ottawa.

By Train

There is no regular rail service into the Yukon or the Northwest Territories. The **White Pass & Yukon Route** (✉ Box 435, Skagway, AK 99840, ☎ 907/983–2217 or 800/343–7373, ℻ 907/983–2734) runs trains between Skagway, Alaska, and Fraser, British Columbia, during the summer, primarily for the astonishing mountain scenery.

Getting Around

By Bus

Frontier Coachlines (✉ 328 Old Airport Rd., Yellowknife, Northwest Territories X1A 3T3, ☎ 403/873–4892) offers service connecting Fort Smith, Hay River, and Yellowknife. In the Yukon, **Alaska Direct Transport and Bus Line** (✉ 4051 4th Ave., Whitehorse, Yukon Territory Y1A 1H1, ☎ 403/668–4833, ℻ 403/667–7411) provides scheduled service from Whitehorse to many Alaskan communities and to Haines Junction, Dawson City, Burwash Landing, and Beaver Creek in the Yukon. **Alaskon Express** (✉ 208-G Steele St., Whitehorse, Yukon Territory Y1A 2C4, ☎ 403/668–3225, ℻ 403/667–4494 or 800/544–2206) has service between Whitehorse and cities in Alaska from mid-May to mid-September. **Gold City Tours** (✉ Box 960, Dawson City, Yukon Territory Y0B 1G0, ☎ 403/993–5175, ℻ 403/993–5261) schedules summer service for the Dempster Highway. **Norline Coaches** (✉ 34 MacDonald Rd., Whitehorse, Yukon Territory Y1A 4L2, ☎ 403/633–3864, ℻ 403/633–3849) provides service between Dawson City and Whitehorse. **North West Stage Lines** (✉ Box 4932, 108 Lambert St., Whitehorse, Yukon Territory Y1A 4S2, ☎ 403/668–7240, ℻ 403/668–4650) provides service to Haines Junction, Destruction Bay, and Beaver Creek, in the Yukon.

By Car

In general, exploring by car is a more sensible idea in the Yukon than in the Northwest Territories. The only part of the Northwest Territories with any kind of highway network is the southwest, where the roads are paved from the Alberta border to Fort Providence, and again near Yellowknife. Farther north and west, they are hard-packed gravel. Many highways in the Yukon are paved, the scenery along the way considerable, and roadside services more extensive.

Anyone traveling by car in the far north should take precautions. Distances from one service area to the next typically exceed 160 kilometers (100 miles), so make sure to monitor your fuel gauge. At least one good spare tire is essential, and many residents of the region carry more, especially when traveling long distances on unpaved roads. Another common practice is to cover headlights, grills, and even windshields with plastic shields or wire mesh to protect against flying gravel. It is advisable to carry extra parts (air filter, fan belt, and fluids). Be sure your vehicle has good suspension, even if you plan to stick to the major highways; shifting permafrost regularly damages paved roads, and ruts and washboard occasionally appear on unpaved roads, especially after periods of bad weather.

Winter driving requires extra precautionary measures. Many a far-north resident can tell you a tale about overnighting on the road and waiting out fierce weather. Take along emergency survival gear, including ax, shovel, flashlight, plenty of matches, kindling (paper or wood) to start a fire, sleeping bag, rugged outerwear, and food. Also, you should have a properly winterized car, with light engine oil and transmission fluid, a block heater, tire chains, and good antifreeze.

One other thing to think about: in the Northwest Territories there are several river crossings without real bridges. In summer, you ride a free ferry; in winter you cross on ice bridges. However, there are the seasons known as "freeze-up" and "break-up," in fall and spring, respectively, when ice bridges aren't solid but rivers are too frozen for ferries to run. For daily ferry reports in summer, call: for Routes 1 and 3, ☎ 403/695–2018 or 800/661–0751; for the Dempster Highway, ☎ 403/979–2678 or 800/661–0752. For winter road conditions, call: for Routes 1 through 7, ☎ 403/874–2208 or 800/661–0750; for the Dempster Highway, ☎ 403/979-2678 or 800/661–0752. For Yukon Highway information, call 403/667–8215.

By Plane

Once outside the Yukon and the southwest section of the Northwestern Territories, flying is pretty much the only way to get around in wilderness Canada. Canadian North, First Air, and NWT Air (☞ Arriving and Departing by Plane, *above*) have regularly scheduled service within the territories. All airlines listed also offer charter air service, an option worth considering for groups of four or more and usually the only option for getting to and from remote wilderness areas. Check with regional tourist offices for other charter services operating locally and regionally. **Alkan Air** (✉ Box 4008, Whitehorse, Yukon Territory Y1A 3S9, ☎ 403/668–2107 or 800/661–0432, FAX 403/667–6117) operates primarily in the Yukon. **Air North** (✉ Box 4998, Whitehorse, Yukon Territory Y1A 4S2, ☎ 403/668–2228, FAX 403/667–6224) also operates primarily in the Yukon. **Air Nunavut** (✉ Box 1239, Iqaluit, Northwest Territories X0A 0H0, ☎ 819/979–2900, FAX 819/979–2425), **Buffalo Airways** (✉ Box 1479, Hay River, Northwest Territories X0E 0R0, ☎ 403/874–3333, FAX 403/874–3572), **North-Wright Air** (✉ Bag Service 2200, Norman Wells, Northwest Territories X0E 0V0, ☎ 403/587–2288 or 800/661–0702, FAX 403/587–2962), and **Ptarmigan**

Airways (✉ Box 100, Yellowknife, Northwest Territories X1A 2N1, ☎ 403/873–4461 or 800/661–0808, FAX 403/873–5209) operate primarily in the Northwest Territories. For a copy of the *Air Tourism Guide to the NWT,* call 800/661–0788.

Contacts and Resources

Car Rental

Rental agencies in both Whitehorse and Yellowknife typically rent trucks and four-wheel-drive vehicles in addition to cars. **Budget** (☎ 800/268–8900) has locations at both the Whitehorse and Yellowknife airports. **Tilden** (☎ 800/387–4747) also has locations at both the Whitehorse and Yellowknife airports. **Avis** (☎ 800/879–2847) rents at the Yellowknife airport. **Norcan** (☎ 800/661–0445) rents at the Whitehorse airport.

Emergencies

For emergency services in either the Northwest Territories or the Yukon, dial 0 for the operator and explain the nature of the emergency. You will then be connected with the police, fire department, or medical service, as needed. You may also call a toll-free emergency number, 403/667–5555 for the Royal Canadian Mounted Police or 403/667–3333 for medical assistance, from anywhere in the Yukon. In Whitehorse, dial 911 for emergencies.

It's a good idea when traveling in the far north—especially in remote wilderness areas and if unescorted by a guide or outfitter—to give a detailed itinerary to someone at home or to the police, to facilitate emergency rescue.

Guided Tours

For a complete list of tour operators, contact **Tourism Yukon** or, in the Northwest Territories, the **Department of Economic Development and Tourism,** or write to **NWT Tourism Information** (☞ *below*).

ORIENTATION

Arctic Tour Company (✉ 181 Mackenzie Rd., Box 2021, Inuvik, Northwest Territories X0E 0T0, ☎ 403/979–4100, FAX 403/979–2259) offers various Inuvik-based day and multiday trips in the area of the Mackenzie River Delta, between Dawson and Inuvik, and between Yellowknife and Inuvik. **Atlas Tours** (✉ Box 4340, Whitehorse, Yukon Territory Y1A 3T5, ☎ 403/668–3161 or 800/663–6122, FAX 403/668–7143) offers cruises, cruise-coach tours, and motor-coach tours throughout the Yukon, Alaska, and Western Arctic. **Gray Line Yukon** (✉ 208-G Steele St., Whitehorse, Yukon Territory Y1A 2C4, ☎ 403/668–3225, FAX 403/667–4494) offers package tours to Dawson City and Alaska as well as Yukon River cruises and sightseeing tours of the Yukon Wildlife Preserve near Whitehorse. **Holland America Westours** (✉ 300 Elliott Ave. W, Seattle, WA 98119, ☎ 206/281–3535, FAX 206/281–0631) offers bus tours through the Yukon and Alaska as well as combined cruise-ship/bus tours that link in Skagway, Alaska. **Rainbow Tours** (✉ 212 Lambert St., Whitehorse, Yukon Territory Y1A 1Z4, ☎ 403/668–5598 or 800/661–0468, FAX 403/668–5595) runs tours by van throughout the Yukon. **Raven Tours** (✉ Box 2435, Yellowknife, North Territories X1A 2P8, ☎ 403/873–4776, FAX 403/873–4856) offers a variety of tours in the Northwest Territories, including tours of Yellowknife and Northern Lights tours in winter. **NWT Air** (☞ Arriving and Departing by Plane, *above*), working with local operators and outfitters, also features an extensive tour program throughout the Northwest Territories.

SPECIAL-INTEREST

Outdoor activities and sports are really the essence of visiting the far north. In most cases, you'll have to sign up with an outfitter or tour operator, or fly into a wilderness lodge. Even those who prefer self-guided adventures may find the assistance of an outfitter helpful or necessary in planning an itinerary and getting transportation into and out of the wilderness. Keep in mind that the scope of possibilities is enormous and that most outfitters are flexible; plan ahead and use your imagination in working with an outfitter to develop a program that best meets your interests and physical abilities.

Access Yukon (⊠ 212 Lambert St., Whitehorse, Yukon Territory Y1A 1Z4, ☎ 403/668–1233 or 800/661–0468, FAX 403/668–5595) offers river trips, canoe rentals, heli-hiking, camper and 4X4 rentals, trail riding, sightseeing, wilderness lodges, and transportation throughout the Yukon. **Adventure Canada** (⊠ 2426 Goodison Ave., Mississauga, Ontario L5B 2AL, ☎ 800/363–7566, FAX 905/270–8343) is particularly active in arranging trips to the Arctic North, including excursions to the North Pole. Backpacking, dogsledding, canoeing, and wildlife viewing are among the activities featured. **Arctic Edge/TransArctic Tours** (⊠ Box 4850, Whitehorse, Yukon Territory Y1A 4N6, ☎ 403/633–5470 or 800/661–0469, FAX 403/633–3820): Arctic Edge specializes in active adventures from cross-country skiing to canoeing, and TransArctic Tours focuses more on wildlife viewing and cultural tours. Most of the twin company's trips are in the Yukon. **Arctic Waterways** (⊠ Number 41, 1355 Citadel Dr., Port Coquitlam, British Columbia V3C 5X6, ☎ 800/681–6659 or 604/944–5500) is one of several outfitters who guide trips on the Coppermine River. **Black Feather Wilderness Adventures** (⊠ 1960 Scott St., Ottawa, Ontario K1Z 8L8, ☎ 613/722–9717, FAX 613/722–0245) is one of the largest adventure-travel companies in Canada, leading backpacking trips in Auyuittuq National Park on Baffin Island, canoeing and hiking trips in Nahanni National Park, and canoe trips on rivers in the Mackenzie Mountains. They can also arrange cycling trips. **Canadian North Outfitting** (⊠ Box 3100, 87 Mills St., Almonte, Ontario K0A 1A0, ☎ 613/256–4057) leads six-day trips, supported by dogsleds, in the wilderness of Baffin Island. **Canadian River Expeditions** (⊠ #37 9571 Emerald Dr., Whistler, British Columbia V0N 1B9, ☎ 604/938–6651, FAX 604/938–6621) offers 6- to 12-day wilderness and natural history expeditions on the Tatshenshini, Alsek, and Firth rivers in the Yukon. **Ecosummer Canada Expeditions** (⊠ 1516N Duranleau St., Vancouver, British Columbia V6H 3S4, ☎ 604/669–7741) leads guided backpacking trips on Baffin Island and Ellesmere Island. In the Yukon, **Kanoe People** (⊠ Box 5152, Whitehorse, Yukon Territory Y1A 4S3, ☎ 403/668–4899, FAX 403/668–4891) arranges guided and unguided canoe trips, from a half day to two weeks, for several rivers. **Kluane Adventures** (⊠ Box 5396, Haines Junction, Yukon Territory Y0B 1L0, ☎ FAX 403/667–1099 or 403/634–2282) specializes in backpacking, canoeing, and fly-in fishing trips in the Kluane area. The company is affiliated with **Dalton Trail Lodge** (⊠ Box 5466, Haines Junction, Yukon Territory Y0B 1L0, ☎ FAX 403/667–1099 or 403/634–2282), a drive-in lodge 50 kilometers (30 miles) south of Haines Junction, which oversees fishing, horseback riding, and photography programs. **Qimmiq Adventures** (⊠ Box 1181, Yellowknife, Northwest Territories X1A 2N8, ☎ 403/920–7533) offers both lodge-based tours and winter-camping tours in the Yellowknife area between February and April. **Subarctic Wildlife Adventures** (⊠ Box 685, Fort Smith, Northwest Territories X0E 0P0, ☎ 403/872–2467, FAX 403/872–2126) specializes primarily in wildlife-viewing tours in the Northwest Territories, but also offers canoeing, hiking, and dogsledding.

One tour of note is the 1,600-kilometer (1,000-mile) cruise along the Mackenzie River, from Yellowknife to Inuvik (or vice versa) aboard the M.S. *Norweta,* a 100-foot cruise ship. The 10-day cruise includes many stops, as well as return air transportation to the city of departure. Contact **N.W.T. Marine Group** (✉ 17 England Crescent, Yellowknife, Northwest Territories X1A 3N5, ☎ FAX 403/873–2489).

Hiking
For a trail map and background information on the Chilkoot Trail, contact **Parks Canada** (✉ Yukon National Historic Sites, Room 205, 300 Main St., Whitehorse, Yukon Territory Y1A 2B5, ☎ 403/667–3910).

Hospitals and Clinics
Limited medical services, with staff on call 24 hours a day, are available at nursing stations in all communities. Major hospitals are as follows. **Yellowknife** (✉ Stanton Regional Hospital, ☎ 403/920–4111). **Fort Smith** (✉ Fort Smith Health Care Centre, ☎ 403/872–2713). **Hay River** (✉ H. H. Williams Memorial Hospital, ☎ 403/874–6512). **Inuvik** (✉ Inuvik Regional Hospital, ☎ 403/979–2955). **Iqaluit** (✉ Baffin Regional Hospital, ☎ 819/979–5231). **Watson Lake** (✉ Watson Lake Hospital, ☎ 403/536–4444). **Whitehorse** (✉ Whitehorse General Hospital, ☎ 403/667–8700).

Hunting
Nonresident hunters are required to sign up with a guide. For information on bag limits, fees, and hunting regulations in the Northwest Territories, contact the **Department of Renewable Resources** (✉ Government of the Northwest Territories, Box 1320, Yellowknife, Northwest Territories X1A 2L9, ☎ 403/873–7200 or 800/661–0788, FAX 403/920–2801). In the Yukon, contact the **Yukon Department of Renewable Resources** (✉ Fish and Wildlife Branch, Box 2703, Whitehorse, Yukon Territory Y1A 2C6, ☎ 403/667–5221, FAX 403/667–2691).

Late-Night Pharmacies
Pharmacies are located in major settlements of the Yukon and Northwest Territories, but late-night service is rarely available; after hours, contact the nearest hospital or nursing station (☞ Hospitals and Clinics, *above*). If you have a preexisting medical condition requiring special medication, be sure you are well supplied; getting unusual prescriptions filled can be difficult or impossible.

Lodging Reservations Services
Inns North (✉ Arctic Cooperatives Ltd., Hotel Division, 1645 Inkster Blvd., Winnipeg, Manitoba R2X 2W1, ☎ 204/697–1625, FAX 204/697–1880) is an organization of native-operated hotels throughout the far north that may be particularly helpful to visitors planning travels in some of the region's smaller communities. The **Northern Network of Bed and Breakfasts** (✉ Box 94-T, Dawson City, Yukon Territory Y0B 1G0, ☎ FAX 403/993–5648) publishes a brochure with more than 80 listings in the Northwest Territories and the Yukon as well as Alaska and British Columbia.

RV Rentals
Ambassador Motor Home & Recreational Services Ltd. (✉ Box 4147, 37 Boswell Crescent, Whitehorse, Yukon Territory Y1A 3S9, ☎ 403/667–4130, FAX 403/633–2195) offers one-way rentals between British Columbia, Alberta, and the Yukon. **CanDream Inc.** (✉ 110 Copper Rd., Whitehorse, Yukon Territory Y1A 2Z6, ☎ 403/668–3610, FAX 403/668–3795). **Klondike Recreational Rentals** (✉ Box 5156, Whitehorse, Yukon Territory Y1A 4S3, ☎ 403/668–2200 or 800/665–4755, FAX 403/668–6567). **Frontier Rentals** (✉ Box 1088-EG, Yel-

lowknife, Northwest Territories X1A 2N7, ☎ 403/873–5413, FAX 403/873–5417).

Sailing

Sail North (✉ Box 2497, Yellowknife, Northwest Territories X1A 2P8, ☎ 403/873–8019) charters 26- to 42-foot sloops, both skippered and unskippered.

Visitor Information

NORTHWEST TERRITORIES

For general information and a copy of the Northwest Territories "Explorers' Guide," contact the **Department of Economic Development and Tourism** (✉ Government of the Northwest Territories, Yellowknife, Northwest Territories X1A 2L9, ☎ 403/873–7200 or 800/661–0788, FAX 403/873–0294). You may also write to **NWT Tourism Information** (✉ Box 1320-EX, Yellowknife, Northwest Territories, X1A 2L9). For more detailed information, regional tourist offices may be of further help.

The Northwest Territories is divided into six designated tourism regions, each with its own regional association. For the Arctic coastal region, contact the **Arctic Coast Tourism Association** (✉ Box 91-EG, Cambridge Bay, Northwest Territories X0C 0C0, ☎ 403/983–2224, FAX 403/983–2302). For Baffin and Ellesmere islands, contact the **Baffin Tourism Association** (✉ Box 1450-EG, Iqaluit, Northwest Territories X0A 0H0, ☎ 819/979–6551, FAX 819/979–1261). For the southwest, contact the **Big River Tourism Association** (✉ Box 185-EG, Hay River, Northwest Territories X0E 0R0, ☎ 403/874–2422, FAX 403/874–6020). For the Keewatin region, which includes the western coast of Hudson Bay, contact **Travel Keewatin** (✉ Box 328-EG, Rankin Inlet, Northwest Territories X0C 0G0, ☎ 819/645–2618, FAX 819/645–2320). For the Nahanni River area and the west, contact **Nahanni-Ram Tourism Association** (✉ Box 177-EG, Fort Simpson, Northwest Territories X0E ONO, ☎ 403/695–3182, FAX 403/695–2511). For Yellowknife and its environs, contact the **Northern Frontier Visitors Association** (✉ Box 1107-EG, 4807 49th St., Yellowknife, Northwest Territories X1A 3T5, ☎ 403/873–3131, FAX 403/873–3654). For the Great Bear Lake and Mackenzie Mountain area, contact the **Sahtu Tourism Association** (✉ Box 115-EG, Norman Wells, Northwest Territories X0E 0V0, ☎ 403/587–2054, FAX 403/587–2935). For the far northwest, contact the **Western Arctic Tourism Association** (✉ Box 2600-EG, Inuvik, Northwest Territories X0E 0T0, ☎ 403/979–4321, FAX 403/979–2434).

YUKON

Tourism Yukon (✉ Box 2703, Whitehorse, Yukon Territory Y1A 2C6, ☎ 403/667–5340, FAX 403/667–3546) is the publisher of the Yukon "Vacation Guide" and the central source of information for the entire area. Tourism Yukon also operates six regional information centers that are open mid-May to mid-September. **Beaver Creek** (✉ Km 1,934 [Mi 1,202] on Alaska Hwy., ☎ 403/862–7321). **Carcross** (✉ Old Train Depot, ☎ 403/821–4431). **Dawson City** (✉ Front and King Sts., ☎ 403/993–5566). **Haines Junction** (✉ Kluane National Park Headquarters, ☎ 403/634–2345). **Watson Lake** (✉ Rtes. 1 and 4, ☎ 403/536–7469). **Whitehorse** (✉ 2nd Ave. and Lambert St., ☎ 403/667–2915).

bbaye Cistercienne d'Oka, 463

bbaye St.-Benoit-du-Lac, 477

cadian Historical Village, 519

cadian Museum (Moncton), 516

cadian Museum of Prince Edward Island, 537

cadian Pioneer Village, 539

dvocate Harbour, 567

frican Lion Safari, 321

gawa Canyon, 329

ksayook Pass, 631

lberta, 165, 166–169, 225. ☞ Also Calgary; Canadian Rockies; Edmonton

lberta Government Centre, 184

lberta Legislature Building, 184

ldred Building, 348

lexander Graham Bell National Historic Site, 572

lexander Henry (icebreaker), 300

lexandra Falls, 629

lgonquin Logging Museum, 307

lgonquin Park, 307

llen Sapp Gallery, 210

lma, 515–516

methyst Mine Panorama, 331

mherst, 566

mherstburg, On., 311–312

mphithéâtre Bell, 356

musement parks
Calgary, 173
dmonton, 188
Montréal, 370–371
New Brunswick, 516
Nova Scotia, 559
Ontario province, 306, 316
outhern Alberta, 181
oronto, 233
ancouver, 31

ncien Palais de Justice, 415–416

ndrew and Laura McCain Gallery, 505

nglican Cathedral of St. John the Baptist, 587

nima G (office building), 422

nna Leonowens Gallery, 550

nnapolis Royal, 560

nnapolis Royal Historic Gardens, 560

nnapolis Valley, 553–554

nne of Green Gables Museum, 533

Anne Hathaway's Cottage, 73, 75

Anne Murray Centre, 566

Anne Tannenbaum Gallery School, 242

Antigonish, 564

Aquarium du Québec, 422

Aquariums
New Brunswick, 512
Prince Edward Island, 538
Québec City, 422
Vancouver, 28–29
Victoria, 76

Arches Provincial Park, 596

Arichat, 575

Army Museum, 547

Art Gallery of Hamilton, 320

Art Gallery of Nova Scotia, 550

Art Gallery of Ontario, 242

Art Gallery of Windsor, 312

Arts and crafts, 6, 88, 134, 221, 589, 628

Assiniboine Park, 214

Assiniboine Zoo, 214

Asulkan Valley trail, 156

Athabasca Falls, 144

Athabasca Glacier, 139

Atlantic Statiquarium, 574

Atlantic Wind Test Site, 538

ATMs, xvi, xxx–xxxi

Auyuittuq National Park, 631–632

Avalon Peninsula, 590–591

Aviation Exhibition, 594

B

Backcountry lodges, 121

Baddeck, 571–572

Baffin Island, 631–632

Baie-St-Paul, 480, 482

Balmoral Mills, 565

Bamfield, 90

Banff, 124–125, 129–134, 165

Banff Centre, 129

Bannf National Park, 137

Bannf Park Museum, 125

Banff Springs Hotel, 125

Bank of Canada Currency Museum, 292

Bank of Commerce Building, 239

Bank of Commerce Tower, 239

Bank of Montréal building (Montréal), 347

Bank of Nova Scotia and Scotia Plaza, 239

Banks Island, 631

Barrie, On., 303–304

Barrie Raceway, 303

Barrington Woolen Mill, 556–557

Basilica Cathedral of St. John the Baptist, 587

Basilique Notre-Dame de Montréal, 7, 349–350

Basilique Notre-Dame-de-Québec, 412–413

Basilique Ste-Anne-de-Beaupré, 7, 442–443, 480

Basin Head, 535

Basin Head Fisheries Museum, 535

Basketball, 53–54

Bata Shoe Museum Collection, 247

Bathurst, 500, 521

Batoche National Historic Site, 209

Bay building, 239

Bay Fortune, 535–536

Bay of Islands, 597

B.C. Sports Hall of Fame and Museum, 32

BCE Place, 239

Beaconsfield Historic House, 527

Bear River, 559

Beaver Creek trail, 222

Beaverbrook Art Gallery, 502

Bedford, 562

Belfast (Prince Edward Island), 535

Bell Homestead, 322

Bellevue, 300

Berg Lake, 145

Better Business Bureau, xi

Bethune Memorial House, 305

Bibliothèque National du Québec, 361

Big and Little Tancook Islands, 555

Big Nickel Mine, 333

Big Pond, 545

Biodôme, 368

Biology Museum, 206

Biosphere, 370

Bird-watching, 542–543, 571, 577

Black Creek Pioneer Village, 247–248

Black Cultural Center for Nova Scotia, 553

Blacksmiths' studios, 335, 446

Blackstone Territorial Park, 629

Blue Heron Drive, 531–534

Bluma Appel Theatre, 267

Boat tours
British Columbia, 114
Edmonton, 193
Montréal, 401
New Brunswick, 509
Newfoundland and Labrador, 602
Niagara Falls, 315

Nova Scotia, 578
Ontario, 304–305
Ottawa, 298
Prince Edward Island, 540
Québec Province, 469
Queen Charlotte Islands, 114
Sault Ste. Marie, 329
Vancouver, 64
wilderness Canada, 636–637
Winnipeg, 224
Boat travel
British Columbia, 111
Victoria, 84
Bonanza Creek, *622*
Bonaventure Island, *487*
**Books and movies on
    Canada,** *xxii–xxiii*
**Botanical Garden
    (Montréal),** *8, 368*
Botanical Garden (New
    Brunswick), *505*
Bottle Houses, *539*
Bow Pass, *138*
Bracebridge, *306*
Brandon, *221*
Brantford, On., *322*
Bridgewater, *556*
Brier Island, *559*
Briqus, *591*
British Columbia, *66–115.*
    ☞ *Also* Vancouver Island
**British Columbia Forest
    Museum,** *88*
British Columbia Rockies,
    154–161
Brockton Point, *27*
Broken Group Islands, *91–
    92*
Bromont, *474*
Brook trail, *156*
Buctouche, *518*
Bugaboo Recreation Area,
    119, 155
Burgess Shale site, *146*
Burin Peninsula, *593–594*
Burns Building, *172*
Bus travel, *xi*
British Columbia, 111, 112
Calgary, 182–183
Canadian Rockies, 161, 163
Edmonton, 193
Montréal, 397, 399
New Brunswick, 520
Newfoundland, 601, 602
Nova Scotia, 575, 576, 577
Ontario province, 298
Prairie Provinces, 225
Québec Aity, 450, 451, 488
Québec province, 488–489
Regina, 204
Saskatoon, 211
Toronto, 278, 280
Vancouver, 61, 62–63
Vancouver Island, 112
Victoria, 84
Whistler, 60
wilderness Canada, 632, 633
Winnipeg, 224
Business hours, *xxiii–xxiv*

Butchart Gardens, *7, 84*
**Butterfly World Vancouver
    Island,** *92*
Byrnes Block building, *26*
Bytown Museum, *292*
Byward Market, *292*

C

Cabot Tower, *586*
**Calaway Park
    (amusements),** *173*
Calgary, *xxxv, 169, 171–
    183*
**Calgary Centre for the
    Performing Arts,** *171–172*
**Calgary Chinese Cultural
    Centre,** *172*
Calgary Public Building, *172*
Calgary Tower, *172*
**Calgary Zoo, Botanical
    Gardens and Prehistoric
    Park,** *173–174*
Camcorders, *xxiv*
Cameras, *xxiv*
Cameron Lake, *153*
Camp Gagetown, *506*
Campbell House, *243*
Campbell River, *94–96*
Campbellton, *497, 521*
Camping, *3*
*Canadian Rockies, 118–119,
    163–164*
Ontario, 285–286, 337
Québec Province, 489
Campobello Island, *513–514*
Canada Olympic Park, *174*
**Canadian Country Music Hall
    of Honor,** *186*
Canadian Craft Museum, *23*
**Canadian Imperial Bank of
    Commerce** (CIBC)
    building, *21*
**Canadian Museum of
    Civilization,** *292, 294*
Canadian Museum of Nature,
    294
**Canadian Museum of Rail
    Travel,** *148*
Canadian Opera Company,
    268
Canadian Pacific Station, *23*
**Canadian Permanent Trust
    building,** *239–240*
Canadian Rockies, *116–165*
Canadian Stage Company,
    267
Canmore, *148–149*
**Cannington Manor Historic
    Park,** *203*
Canso, *563*
Cape Bonavista, *593*
**Cape Breton Highlands
    National Park,** *8, 570*
Cape Breton Island, *568–575*
Cape Enragé, *515–516*
Cape George, *564*
Cape Sable Island, *557*
Cape Scott Provincial Park,
    96

Cape Shore, *591–592*
Cape Spear, *583*
**Cape St. Mary's Ecological
    Reserve,** *592*
Capilano Salmon Hatchery,
    32
**Capilano Suspension Bridge
    and Park,** *32*
**Cap Tourmente Wildlife
    Reserve,** *480*
Car rentals, *xi, xxiv*
Car travel, *xiv, xxvii*
British Columbia, 111, 112
Calgary, 182, 183
Canadian Rockies, 162, 163
Côte de Beaupré, 443–444
Edmonton, 193
Gulf Islands, 112
Ile d'Orléans, 449
Montréal, 397–398
New Brunswick, 520
*Newfoundland and Labrador,
    600, 601*
Nova Scotia, 575, 577
Ontario province, 298, 336
Prairie Provinces, 225
*Prince Edward Island, 539–
    540*
Québec City, 450, 488
Québec province, 488, 489
Regina, 203
Saskatoon, 211
Toronto, 278–279, 280
Vancouver, 61, 63
Victoria, 112
Whistler, 60
*wilderness Canada, 632–633,
    634*
Winnipeg, 223
Caraquet, *519*
Carcross, *621*
Carleton, *485, 487*
Carleton Martello Tower, *511*
Casa Loma, *248*
Casinos, *50–51, 178, 191,
    199, 220, 370, 483, 573*
Cathedral Grove, *92*
Cathedral Provincial Park,
    109–110
Cave and Basin Centre Pool,
    125, 129
**Cave and Basin National
    Historic Site,** *125, 129*
Cavendish, *532–533*
Centennial Centre, *214–215*
Centennial Museum, *197*
**Central B.C. Railway and
    Forest Industry Museum,**
    103
Centre d'Art Baie-St-Paul,
    482
**Centre de Commerce Mondia
    de Montréal,** *350*
**Centre d'Exposition de Baie-
    St-Paul,** *482*
**Centre d'Exposition du
    Vieux-Palais,** *464–465*
**Centre d'Histoire de
    Montréal,** *350*

entre d'Interprétation
  Historique de Terrebonne
  Museum, *461, 463*
entre Marie-de-
  l'Incarnation, *413*
entre Molson, *356, 358*
entreville (amusement
  park), *233*
halet du Mont-Royal, *366*
hance Harbour, *515*
hange Islands, *594–595*
hanging of the Guard
  ceremony, *295*
hapelle Bon-Pasteur, *422*
hapelle des Ursulines, *413*
hapelle Extérieure, *416*
hapelle Notre-Dame-de-
  Bonsecours, *350*
hapelle Notre-Dame-de-
  Lourdes, *362*
harlevoix, *480–485*
harlottetown, *526–527,
  529–531*
harlottetown Driving Park,
  529
harlottetown Festival, *527*
hâteau Frontenac, *413–
  414*
hateau Lake Louise, *134*
hâteau Ramezay, *350*
hermainus, *88*
herry Brook Zoo, *511*
hester, *554–555*
héticamp, *570*
hildren, traveling with, *xi–
  xii, xxiv–xxv*
hildren's Village, *237*
hilkoot Trail, *621*
hinese Times Building, *26*
hinese Cultural Center, *25*
hinese Freemasons Building,
  26
hocolate Cove, *514*
hrist Church Cathedral
  (Montréal), *358*
hrist Church Cathedral
  (New Brunswick), *502*
hrist Church Cathedral
  (Vancouver), *23*
hurches
  ôte de Beaupré, 442–443
  e d'Orleans, 446, 447, 448
  lanitoba, 216
  layne Island, 97
  *ontréal, 349–350, 354, 358,
    359, 360, 362*
  *ew Brunswick, 502, 508,
    512*
  ewfoundland, 587
  ova Scotia, 547, 558, 575
  ntario, 304, 322, 334–335
  *rince Edward Island, 527,
    529, 535, 538*
  *uébec City, 412–413, 414,
    415, 417, 422, 443*
  uébec province, 464, 477
  ancouver, 23
urchill, *223*
mitière Mont-Royal, *366*

Cimetière Notre-Dame-des-
  Neiges, *366*
Cinémathèque Québecoise,
  362, 364
Cinesphere (films), *237*
Citadelle, *422–423*
Clarenville, *592*
Clifton Hill, On., *316*
Climate, *xxxiv–xxxvi*
CN Tower, *236*
Coast Mountain Circle, *56*
Cobourg, *301–302*
Cocagne, *518*
Cochrane, On., *334*
Commemorative Chapel, *443*
Commerce Court, *240*
Commonwealth Air Training
  Plan Museum, *221*
Comox, *93–94*
Complexe Desjardins, *358,
  393*
Confederation Centre of the
  Arts, *527*
Confederation Landing Park,
  527
Confederation Square
  (Ontario), *294*
Connaught Drive, *139*
Cormack, *595*
Corner Brook, *597–598*
County Museum, *301*
Courtenay, *93–94*
Couvent des Ursulines, *414*
Côte de Beaupré, *442–444*
Craigdarroch Castle, *75*
Cranbrook, *160*
Crocker Hill Studios, *511*
Crowsnest Pass, *119, 153*
Crysler's Farm Battlefield
  Memorial Park, *299*
Crystal Gardens, *75*
Cullen Gardens and
  Miniature Village, *278*
Cupids, *591*
Curling, *4, 200*
Currency exchange, *xvi,
  xxxi*
Customs, *xii, xxv–xxvi*
Customs Examining
  Warehouse (Vancouver),
  24
Cypress Hills Provincial Park,
  202

D

Dalnavert House, *215*
Dartmouth, *545–546, 553*
Dauphine Redoubt, *419*
Dawson City, *622–624*
Dawson City Museum, *622*
Deadman's Island, *27*
Deane House, *174*
Deer Island, *514*
Deer Lake, *549*
Della Falls, *93*
Dempster Highway, *625*
Denman Island, *93*
DesBrisay Museum, *556*
Design Exchange, *240*

Devil's Punch Bowl, *221*
Devonian Gardens, *172*
Diefenbaker Canada Centre,
  206
Digby, *559*
Digby Neck, *558*
Dinosaur Provincial Park, *180*
Dipper Harbour, *515*
Disabilities & accessibility,
  xii–xiii, xxvi
Discount & deals, *xiii–xiv,
  xxvi–xxvii*
Discovery Trail, *592*
Dr. Sun Yat-sen Gardens, *26*
Dogsledding, *286, 337, 436,
  495, 518, 607*
Dominion Bank building, *240*
Dominion Carillonneur, *295*
Doon Heritage Crossroads,
  323
Dorset, On., *306*
Drumheller, *179–180*
Duck Lake, *210*
Duncan, *87–88*
Dundee, *574*
Dundurn Castle, *320*
Duties, *xxv–xxvi*

E

Eastend, *202–203*
Eastend Fossil Research
  Station, *202–203*
East Point Lighthouse, *535*
Eaton Centre (Toronto),
  243, 275
Eaton's Department Store,
  298, 354, 393
Echo Dale Regional Park,
  181
Ed Jones Haida Museum, *102*
Edifice Price, *414*
Edmonton, *xxxv, 183–194*
Edmonton Art Gallery, *184*
Edmonton Convention Centre,
  186
Edmonton Public Library,
  186
Edmonton Space and
  Sciences Centre, *186*
Edmundston, *504–505*
Elgin Theatre, *268*
Église Notre-Dame-des-
  Victoires, *417*
Elk Island National Park, *192*
Ellesmere Island National
  Park, *632*
Elmira, *535*
Elmira Railway Museum, *535*
Emerald Lake, *122, 146*
Emergencies
  British Columbia, 113
  Calgary, 183
  Canadian Rockies, 163
  Edmonton, 193
  Ile d'Orléans, 449
  Labrador, 601
  Montréal, 400
  New Brunswick, 520
  Newfoundland, 601

Northwest Territories, 635
Nova Scotia, 578
Ontario, 337
Ottawa, 298
Prince Edward Island, 540
Québec province, 489
Regina, 204
Saskatoon, 211
Toronto, 281
Vancouver, 64, 113
Victoria, 85, 113
Whistler, 61
Winnipeg, 224
Yukon, 635
Emily Carr Institute of Art and Design, 30
English Bay, 28
Ermatinger Stone House, 329
Estérel, 468
Estevan, 203
Ethnographic Museum, 559
Explore (diorama), 418
Exposition Maritime, 482

F

Fairmont Hot Springs, 159–160
Falcon Lake, 222
Far Enough Farm, 233
Father Pandosy's Mission, 107
Fernie, 161
Ferryland, 590–591
Ferry service, xiv
British Columbia, 112, 114
New Brunswick, 519
Newfoundland and Labrador, 600
Nova Scotia, 575–576
Prince Edward Island, 539
Québec City, 418, 451
Vancouver, 61–62, 63
Vancouver Island, 112
Firefighters Museum of Nova Scotia, 558
First Canadian Place, 240
Fisheries Museum of the Atlantic, 555
Fisherman's Life Museum at Jeddore Oyster Pond, 563
Five Islands, 568
Five Islands Provincial Park, 568
Floe Lake, 138, 145
Florenceville, 505
Fogo Island, 594–595
Forestry Farm Park and Zoo, 205
Forks, 216
Forks National Historic Site, 215–216
Fort Amherst Port-La-Joye National Historic Site, 534
Fort Anne National Historic Site, 560
Fort Battleford National Historic Site, 210–211
Fort Calgary Interpretive Center, 174

Fort Carlton Provincial Historic Park, 210
Fort Edmonton Park, 187
Fort Erie, On., 308
Fort George, 318
Fort Henry, 300
Fort Howe, 510
Fort Macleod, 182
Fort Macleod Museum, 182
Fort Malden, On., 311
Fortress of Louisbourg National Historic Park, 573–574
Fort St. Joseph, 332
Fort Steele, 160
Fort Steele Heritage Town, 160
Fort Walsh National Historic Park, 202
Fort Wellington, 299
Fort Whoop-Up, 181
Fort Whyte Center for Environmental Education, 216
Forum (concerts), 237
Fossils, 543, 566–567
François Baby House: Windsor's Community House, 312
Frank Slide Interpretive Center, 153–154
Fraser-Ft. George Regional Museum, 103
Fredericton, 500–504, 521
Fundy Geological Museum, 567
Fundy National Park, 515
Fun Mountain Water Slide Park, 216

G

Gabriola Island, 89
Gaelic College, 571
Gage Park, 320
Gagetown, 506
Gallery of Inuit Art, 241
Gander, 594
Ganges, 98
Garden of the Provinces, 294
Gardens
British Columbia, 110
Calgary, 172, 173–174, 181
Edmonton, 187
Montréal, 368
New Brunswick, 505
Newfoundland, 587
Nova Scotia, 547, 560
Ontario, 316, 320
Québec City, 437
Toronto, 278
Vancouver, 26, 33, 34
Victoria, 75, 84
Garibaldi Provincial Park, 56
Gaspé Peninsula, 485–488, 489
Gay and lesbian travelers, xiv
George-Étienne Cartier Museum, 352

George R. Gardiner Museum of Ceramic Art, 248
Gibbet Hill, 586
Gibraltar Lighthouse, 233
Gimli, 222–223
Gimli Historical Museum, 222–223
Glacier National Park, 155–156, 165
Glen Mountain, 476
Glenbow Museum, 172–173
Goat Haunt, 153
Golden, 155
Gold Rush Trail, 103–104
Gordon Snelgrove Gallery, 206
Gordon MacMillan Southam Observatory, 33
Government House (Nova Scotia), 546–547
Government House (Regina), 196
Gower Street United Church, 587
Graham Island, 101
Grain Academy, 175
Granby, 472
Grand Bank, 593
Grand Beach Provincial Park, 222
Grand Falls, 505
Grand Falls Historical Museum, 505
Grand Lake Provincial Park, 506
Grand Manan Island, 513
Grand Marais, 222
Grand Séminaire de Montréal, 358–359
Grand Théâtre de Québec, 423
Grange house, The, 242
Granville Island, 29–31
Granville Island Public Market, 30–31
Granville Island Water Park, 31
Grasslands National Park, 203
Gravenhurst, 305
Green Gables House, 532
Greenhouse and Plant Conservatory, 316
Green Park Shipbuilding Museum and Historic House, 537
Greenock Church, 512
Grenfell House, 597
Gros Morne National Park, 595–596
Grouse Mountain (Vancouver), 32
Gryphon Theatre, 303
Guest farms, 490
Guest ranches, 121, 150–151
Gulf Islands, 96–100, 111, 112, 113
Gull Harbour, 223

H

R. MacMillan Planetarium, 33
Haines Junction, 619
Haliburton, 305–306
Haliburton House Museum, 561
Halifax, xxxv, 545–547, 550–553, 576–577
Halifax Public Gardens, 547
Hamilton, On., 320–322, 338
Happy Valley-Goose Bay, 599
Harbour Grace, 591
Harrison Hot Springs, 110
Hart House, 250
Hazleton, 103
Head-Smashed-In Buffalo Jump, 182
Hecla Island, 223
Hecla Provincial Park, 223
Helicopter travel, 84
Heli-skiing, 60, 133, 159, 163, 164
Hell's Gate, 109
Helmcken House, 75–76
Henderson Lake Park, 181
Henry Moore Sculpture Centre, 242
Henry Stuart House, 423
Heritage Highway, 299–302
Heritage House and Herritage House II museums, 594
Heritage Park, 174
Herring Cove Provincial Park, 514
Herschel Island, 631
Hockey Hall of Fame, 240
Holidays, xxiii–xxiv
Holy Trinity Anglican Cathedral, 414
Homestead Antique Museum, 180
Hopewell Cape, 515
Hornby Island, 93
Horne Lake Caves Provincial Park, 93
Hotels, xv, xxix
Houseboat communities, 29
Houses, historic
British Columbia, 106
Calgary, 174
Île d'Orléans, 446, 447
Montréal, 353
New Brunswick, 502, 506, 507
Newfoundland and Labrador, 587, 597
Nova Scotia, 550, 556, 565
Ontario province, 300, 301–302, 305, 311, 312, 322, 329
Prince Edward Island, 527, 532, 537
Québec City, 418, 423
Saskatchewan, 203
Toronto, 242, 243
Victoria, 75
Winnipeg, 215

Huntsman Aquarium and Museum, 512
Huntsville, 307
Huron Indian Village, 304
Huronia Museum and Gallery of Historic Huronia, 304

I

Icefield Centre, 139
Icefields Parkway, 138–139
Île aux Coudres, 482
Illecillewaet Campground, 156
Île d'Orléans, Q.P., 444–449
Images du Futur, 352
Indian arts and crafts, 55–56
British Columbia, 101
Canadian Rockies, 134
Ontario, 287
Québec City, 441
Indian Battle Park, 181
Ingonish, 571
Insectarium, 368
Inside Passage, 100
Institut de Tourisme et d'Hôtellerie du Québec, 369
Insurance, xiv–xv, xxviii–xxix
International Fox Museum and Hall of Fame, 536
International Hockey Hall of Fame, 300
Inuvik, 630
Invermere, 158–159
Iona, 572–573
Iqaluit, 631
Irish Moss Interpretive Centre, 538
Isle Madame, 574

J

Jack Miner's Bird Sanctuary, 310–311
Jardin Zoologique de Granby, 472
Jardin Zoologique du Québec, 423
Jasper, 139–143, 165
Jasper Aquatic Center, 140
Jasper National Park, 137–138, 143–145
Jasper Tramway, 140
Jasper-Yellowhead Museum, 140
Joggins Fossil Center, 566–567
John R. Park Homestead and Conservation Area, 311
Johnstone Strait, 95
John Thurston Clark Building, 501
Jumbo statue, 309

K

Kakabeka Falls, 332
Kalamalka Lake Provincial Park, 106

Kamloops, 104–106
Kamloops Wildlife Park, 105
Kananaskis Country, 149–151, 165
Kananaskis Lake, 122
Kananaskis Village, 150
Kanestake, 463–464
Kathleen Lake, 620
Keene, On., 302
Kejimkujik National Park, 556
Kelowna, 107–108
Kettle Valley Steam Railway, 108
Kids Only Market, 31
Kilby Historic Store and Farm, 110
Kimberley, 160–161
Kinbasket Lake, 122
Kings Byway, 534–536
King's Landing Historical Settlement, 502
Kingston, On., 299–301, 338
Kingsville, 310–311
Kinney Lake, 145
Kinsmen Park, 205
Kitchener, On., 322–324, 338
Kitimat, 103
Kluane National Park, 619–620
Knowlton, 475–476
Knox College, 251
Kootenay National Park, 138, 145–146, 165
Kouchibouguac National Park, 518
'Ksan, 103
'Ksan Museum, 103

L

Les Laurentides, 460–471, 488–489, 490–491
L'Estrie region, 471–480, 489, 491
La Malbaie, 483–484
La Ronde (amusement park), 370–371
La Seigneurie de Terrebonne, 461, 463
Labrador, 579–583, 598–603
Labrador Straits Museum, 599
Lac Beauvert, 122
Lady Slipper Drive, 536–539
Lake Annette, 122
Lake Edith, 122
Lake Louise, 122, 134–137, 165
Lake O'Hara, 122, 138, 146–147
Lake Windermere, 122
Lang Pioneer Village, 302
Language, xxix
L'Anse Amour, 599
L'Anse au Clair, 599
L'Anse aux Meadows National Historic Site, 596

Le Centre Canadien d'Architecture, *359*

Leclerç, Felix (home), *448*

Lévis-Québec ferry, *418*

Lennox Island, *533–534*

LeNoir Forge, *575*

Le 1000 rue de la Gauchetière (skating rink), *356*

Legislative building (Regina), *196*

Legislative Building (Winnipeg), *216*

Lethbridge, *181–182*

Library of Parliament, *295*

Liberty Square building (Vancouver), *32–33*

Limousines, *452*

Lions Gate Bridge, *28*

Little Anse, *575*

Little Current-Howland Centennial Museum, *332–333*

Little Stone School House, *206*

Liverpool, *556–557*

Lodging, *xv, xxix–xxxx.* ☞ *Also Hotels*

apartment and villa rental, *xv, xxix*

B&Bs, *xxix–xxx*

dorms, *xxx*

farm holidays, *xv*

home exchange, *xv, xxx*

hosteling, *xxx*

London, On., *326–327*

London and Port Stanley Railroad, *309*

London Museum of Archaeology, *326*

London Regional Art and Historical Museum, *326*

Long Beach, *91*

Long Island, *559*

Louisbourg, *573–574*

Lower Fort Garry, *222*

Lumberman's Arch, *28*

Lunenburg, *555–556*

M

Mabou, *568–569*

Macaulay Heritage Park, *301*

MacBride Museum, *612–613*

Maces Bay, *515*

Mackenzie Art Gallery, *196*

Mactaquac Provincial Park, *505–506*

Magic Mountain (water theme park), *516*

Magnetic Hill, *516*

Magog, *476–477*

Mahone Bay, *555*

Maid of the Mist boats, *315*

Mail service, *xxx*

Maison Chevalier, *418*

Maison de la Sauvegarde, *348*

Maison des Vins, *418*

Maison Gourdeau de Beaulieu House, *446*

Maison Louis-Jolliet, *418*

Maison Maillou, *409*

Maison Montcalm, *418*

Maligne Canyon, *144*

Maligne Lake, *138, 144*

Manitoba, *166–169, 225–226.* ☞ *Also Winnipeg*

Manitoba Children's Museum, *216*

Manitoba Museum of Man and Nature, *214–215*

Manitoba Planetarium, *214–215*

Manitou Beach, *211*

Manitoulin Island, *332–333*

Manitou Springs Mineral Spa, *211*

Manoir Mauvide-Genest, *447*

Maple Creek, *201–202*

Maple Leaf Quay, *236*

Maple Syrup, *6*

Margaree Harbour, *569–570*

Marine Building, *23*

Marine Museum at the Great Lakes of Kingston, *300*

Marineland, *316*

Maritime Museum, *33*

Maritime Museum of British Columbia, *76*

Maritime Museum of the Atlantic, *546*

Martello Towers, *425*

Martinique Beach, *562*

Martyr's Shrine, *304*

Mary Queen of the World Cathedral, *359*

Massey College, *251*

Massey Hall, *267*

Mayne Island, *97–98*

McCord Museum of Canadian History, *359*

McGill University, *359*

McMichael Canadian Art Collection, *248*

Medication, *xxxii*

Medicine Hat, *180–181*

Medicine Lake, *144*

Meewasin Valley Centre and Trail, *205*

Memorial University Botanical Gardens, *587*

Mennonite Heritage Village, *222*

Metro Toronto Zoo, *248–249*

Metropolitan Toronto Reference Library, *248*

Midland, On., *304, 338*

Miette Hot Springs, *138, 144–145*

Miles Canyon, *613*

Military compound, *501*

Ministry of Natural Resources Interpretive Centre, *335*

Minolta Tower, *316*

Minter Gardens, *110*

Miquelon, *593–594*

Miramichi City, *518–519*

Miramichi Salmon Museum, *518*

Miscouche, *537*

Mister Rudolph's Funland, *306*

Mohawk Church, *322*

Monastère des Augustines de l'Hôtel-Dieu de Québec, *415*

Monasteries

Québec City, *415*

Québec province, *463, 477*

Moncton, *516–518, 521*

Money matters, *xvi, xxx–xxxi*

Mont-Carmel, *539*

Mont-Mégantic's Observatory, *479–480*

Montague, *535*

Montcalm Monument, *424*

Montgomery, Lucy Maud, *533*

Montmorency Falls, *442*

Montréal, *xxxvi, 339–402*

avenue Greene, *396*

avenue Laurier Ouest, *396*

boulevard St-Laurent, *361, 396*

Centre-Ville, *353–360, 393–394*

Champs de Mars, *348*

Chinatown, *358*

Faubourg Ste-Catherine, *393–394*

Les Cours Mont-Royal, *395*

Les Promenades de la Cathédrale, *394*

Marché Bonsecours, *348*

Notre-Dame Ouest, *394–395*

Parc Lafontaine, *364*

Parc du Mont-Royal, *365–367*

Parc Olympique, *367–369*

Place Bonaventure, *354, 394*

Place d'Armes, *352–353*

Place des Arts, *360*

Place du Canada, *360*

Place Jacques-Cartier, *353*

Place Montréal Trust, *394*

Place Royale, *348*

Place Vauquelin, *348*

Place Ville-Marie, *354, 394*

Pointe-à-Callière, *353*

Quartier Latin, *360*

rue Chabanel, *395*

rue Duluth, *362*

rue Prince Arthur, *364*

rue St-Paul, *348*

rue St-Sulpice, *348*

rue Wellington, *395–360*

Square Dorchester, *360*

Square St-Louis, *364–365*

Square Westmount, *396*

Vieux-Montréal, *347–353, 393*

Montréal-Shanghai Lac de Rêve, *368*

Mont Rolland, *467–468*

Mont-Sutton, *475*

Mont Tremblant, *470–471*

Morin Heights, *466*

Moose Factory Island, *334–335*

Moose Jaw, *200–201*
Moose Jaw Art Museum, *201*
Moose Mountain Provincial
  Park, *203*
Moose River Gold Mines, *563*
Moosonee, *335*
Moraine Lake, *122, 135*
Morin Heights, *466*
Mountain bicycling
  Canadian Rockies, 118
Mt. Edith Cavell, *138, 144*
Mt. Golden Hinde, *93*
Mt. Logan, *619*
Mt. Maxwell Provincial Park,
  98–99
Mt. Norquay, *118, 133*
Mt. Revelstoke National Park,
  156–157, 165
Mt. Robson, *119, 145*
Municipal Building, *173*
Museum of Anthropology, *33*
Museum of Antiquities, *206*
Museum of Contemporary
  Photography, *294*
Museum of Northern British
  Columbia, *101*
Museum of the Regiments,
  174
Musée d'Archéologie Pointe-
  à-Callière, *352*
Musée d'Art Contemporain,
  359
Musée des Arts Décoratifs,
  368
Musée de Charlevoix, *483*
Musé des Hospitalières, *364*
Musée de L'Amérique
  Française, *415*
Musée de la Civilisation,
  418–419
Musée de Québec, *424*
Musée des Augustines, *415*
Musée des Beaux-Arts de
  Montréal, *359–360*
Musée des Beaux-Arts de
  Sherbrooke, *478*
Musée des Ursulines, *415*
Musée du Fort, *415*
Musée du Séminaire, *416*
Musée Joseph-Armand
  Bombardier, *476*
Musée Juste pour Rire, *364*
Museums
  Alberta, 179–180, 182, 192
  British Columbia, 101, 102,
    103
  Calgary, 172–173, 174, 179–
    180
  Canadian Rockies, 125, 140,
    148, 158, 182
  Edmonton, 187
  Labrador, 599
  Manitoba, 214–215, 216,
    222–223
  Montréal, 352, 350, 359–360,
    364, 368
  New Brunswick, 501–502,
    505, 507, 512, 516, 518
  Newfoundland, 593, 594

  Nova Scotia, 546, 547, 554,
    555, 556, 557, 558, 559,
    561, 566, 567, 571
  Ontario province, 285, 292,
    294, 295, 299, 300, 301,
    304, 305, 307, 308, 311–
    312, 315, 318, 323, 326,
    332–333
  Prince Edward Island, 527,
    533, 535, 536, 537
  Québec City, 415, 416, 418–
    419, 423, 424
  Québec province, 461, 463,
    476, 478, 482, 483
  Saskatchewan, 197, 201, 202
  Saskatoon, 205–206, 210
  Toronto, 230, 240, 243, 247,
    250
  Vancouver, 23, 24, 32, 33, 34
  Vancouver Island, 87, 88
  Victoria, 76
  wilderness Canada, 612–613,
    622
  Winnipeg, 216
Musquodoboit Harbour, *562*
Muttart Conservatory, *187*

N

Nahanni National Park, *8,*
  629–630
Naikoon Provincial Park, *102*
Nanaimo, *88–89*
Nanaimo District Museum, *88*
National Archives of Canada,
  294
National Arts Center, *294*
National Aviation Museum,
  294
National Exhibition Center,
  501
National Gallery of Canada,
  294–295
National Library of Canada,
  294
National Museum of Science
  and Technology, *295*
Native Canadian art, *6*
Native Heritage Centre, *88*
Natural Sciences Museum,
  206
Nature Centre, *210*
Naval Museum of Alberta,
  174
Navy Yard Park, *311*
N'dilo Cultural Village, *626*
Net Loft building
  (Vancouver), *31*
New Brunswick, *492–521*
New Brunswick Museum,
  507
Newcastle Island, *89*
Newfoundland, *579–598,*
  600–603
New London, *533–534*
Niagara Apothecary, *318*
Niagara Falls, On., *313–*
  317, 338
Niagara Falls Museum, *315*
Niagara Glen, *315*

Niagara Historical Society
  Museum, *318*
Niagara-on-the-Lake, *318–*
  320
Niagara Peninsula, *320*
Niagara Spanish Aero Car,
  315
Nikka Yuko Japanese
  Gardens, *181*
Nine O'Clock Gun, *27*
Nitobe Memorial Garden, *33*
Norquay Road, *129*
North American Black
  Historical Museum, *311–*
  312
North Battleford, *210–211*
North Cape, *538–539*
North Hatley, *477–478*
Northwest Territories, *604–*
  612, 635–638
Notre Dame Oratory, *487*
Nova Scotia, *541–578*
Nova Scotia Museum of
  Natural History, *547*
NPC School of Horticulture,
  315

O

O'Keefe Centre, *267*
O'Keefe Historic Ranch, *106*
Officer's Quarters, *419*
Ogilvy Department Store,
  355, 393
Oka Calvary (Stations of
  the Cross), *463–464*
Okanagan Game Farm, *108*
Okanagan Valley, *104–111*
Old Courthouse Building,
  326
Old Fort, *371*
Old Fort Erie, *308*
Old Fort William, *331*
Old Loyalist Burial Grounds,
  507
Old Loyalist House, *507*
Old School House Gallery
  and Art Centre, *93*
Old Sow (whirlpool), *515*
Old Strathcona Foundation,
  187
Old Strathcona Historic Area,
  187
Old Strathcona Model and
  Toy Museum, *187*
Old Timer's Museum, *202*
Olympic Hall of Fame, *174*
Olympic Saddledome, *175*
Ontario, *283–338*
Ontario College of Art and
  Design Gallery, *246*
Ontario Legislative Building,
  249
Ontario Place
  (entertainment complex),
  237
Ontario Science Centre, *249*
Oratoire St-Joseph, *366–*
  367
Orford, *474–475*

Orillia, *305*
Oromocto, *506*
Orwell Corner Historic Village, *534–535*
Ottawa, *xxxvi, 290–299*
Ottawa House Museum-by-the-Sea, *567*
Ouimet Canyon, *330–331*
Owl's Head, *475*

P

Packing for Canada, *xxxi–xxxii*
Pacific Rim National Park, *7, 91–92*
Pacific Space Centre, *33*
Pacific Undersea Gardens, *76*
Palais de Justice (Montréal), *352*
Palais des Congrès de Montréal Convention Centre, *356*
Panorama, *158, 159*
Parc Mont-Tremblant, *470*
Parc Régional de la Rivière-du-Nord, *465*
Parks, national and provincial, *5*
Alberta, *192*
British Columbia, *98–99, 102, 106, 109–110*
Canadian Rockies, *137–138, 143–147, 152–154, 155–156*
Manitoba, *207, 223*
New Brunswick, *505–506, 514, 515, 518, 519*
Newfoundland and Labrador, *586, 592, 595–596*
Nova Scotia, *556, 568, 573–574*
Ontario, *299, 301, 302, 307, 309–310, 323*
Prairie Provinces, *180*
Prince Edward Island, *531–532*
Québec province, *465*
Saskatchewan, *201, 202, 203, 210*
Vancouver Island, *88, 91–92, 93, 96*
Whistler, *56*
wilderness Canada, *619–620, 629–630, 631–632*
Parksville, *92–93*
Parliament Building (Ottawa), *295*
Parliament Buildings (Québec City), *424–425*
Parliament Buildings (Victoria), *76*
Parrsboro, *567–568*
Parry Sound, *304–305*
Passports, *xvi, xxxii–xxxiii*
Path of Discovery Tour, *333–334*
Patricia Lake, *122, 140*
Peace Tower, *295*
Peggy's Cove, *544*

Pelee Island, *310*
Penetanguishene, *304*
Penticton, *108–109*
Percé, *487*
Perry's Victory and International Peace Monument, *310*
Peter Lougheed Provincial Park, *149*
Peterborough, On., *302, 338*
Peterborough Lift and Lock Visitor Center, *302*
Petroglyph Provincial Park (Vancouver Island), *88*
Petroglyphs Provincial Park, On., *302*
Photography, *xvi*
Picton, On., *301*
Pictou, *564–565*
Pilsen Brewery, *477–478*
Pioneer Village and Museum, *201*
Placentia, *591–592*
Plage de l'Ile Notre-Dame, *371*
Plains of Abraham, *7, 425*
Plane travel, *x–xi, xxii*
Alberta, *225*
British Columbia, *111, 113*
Calgary, *182*
Canadian Rockies, *162*
cutting costs, *xxii*
discounts, *xiii*
domestic flights, *x–xi*
Edmonton, *193*
flight insurance, *xxviii*
Manitoba, *225*
Montréal, *398*
New Brunswick, *520*
Newfoundland and Labrador, *600*
Nova Scotia, *576, 577*
Ontario province, *298, 336*
Prairie Provinces, *225*
Prince Edward Island, *539*
Québec City, *450–451*
Québec province, *488*
Regina, *203–204*
Saskatchewan, *225*
Saskatoon, *211*
Toronto, *279*
Vancouver, *62, 64*
Victoria, *84*
wilderness Canada, *633, 634–635*
Winnipeg, *224*
Planetariums and observatories
Calgary, *174*
Québec province, *479*
Vancouver, *33*
Winnipeg, *214–215*
Point de l'Eglise, *558*
Point Pelee National Park, *309–310*
Port Alberni, *90*
Port-aux-Basques, *598*
Port Colborne, *308*

Port Colborne Historical and Marine Museum, *308*
Port de Québec in the 19th Century, *420*
Port Dover, On., *309*
Port Hardy, *96*
Port Hill, *537*
Port Royal, *560–561*
Port Royal National Historic Site, *560*
Port Stanley, On., *309*
Post Office building (Vancouver), *24*
Post Office Extension (Vancouver), *24*
Poudrière de l'Esplanade, *424*
Powell River, *94*
Power Plant (arts center), *237*
Prairie Provinces, *166–226*
Prehistoric Park, *180*
Prime minister's residence, *295–296*
Prince Albert, *210*
Prince Albert Historical Museum, *210*
Prince Albert National Park, *210*
Prince Edward, *301*
Prince Edward Island, *522–540*
Prince Edward Island National Park, *8, 531–532*
Prince George, *103*
Prince George Native Art Gallery, *103*
Prince of Wales Northern Heritage Centre, *625–626*
Prince Rupert, B.C., *100–101*
Prospect Point, *28*
Province House, *550*
Province House National Historic Site, *527*
Provincial Legislature (New Brunswick), *502*
Provincial Museum of Alberta, *187*
Provincial Parliament Buildings, *249*
Pubnico, *557*
Pugwash, *565*
Pump House Steam Museum, *300*
Purcell Wilderness, *158*
Purdy's Wharf, *546*
Pyramid lake, *121–122, 140*

Q

Qualicum Beach, *93*
Québec City, *xxxvi, 403–453*
avenue Cartier, *422*
Basse-Ville (lower town), *416–420*
Cavalier du Moulin park, *413*

Escalier Casse-Cou, 418
Grande Allée, 423
Haute-Ville (upper town), 409–416
Jardin des Gouverneurs, 414
Parc de l'Amérique-Française, 424
Parc de l'Artillerie, 419
Parc de l'Esplanade, 424
Parc des Champs-de-Bataille, 420
Parc Jeanne d'Arc, 424
Parc Montmorency, 412
Place d'Armes, 415–416
Place de Paris, 419
Place Royale, 419
Promenade des Gouverneurs, 416
rue du Petit-Champlain, 419
rue du Trésor, 416
Terrasse Dufferin, 416
Québec Experience, 416
Québec province, 454–491
Queen Charlotte Islands, 101–103, 112, 113
Queen Charlotte Islands Museum, 102
Queen Elizabeth Park, 34
Quidi Vidi Lake, 586

R

Radium Hot Springs, 157–158
Rail travel. ☞ Train travel
Rathtrevor Provincial Park, 92
Red Bay, 599
Red Deer, 192
Red Rock Canyon, 152
Regina, 194, 196–204
Reptile World, 180
Revelstoke, 122, 157
Revelstoke Dam, 156–157
Reversing Falls Rapids, 511
Rexton, 518
Ride Niagara, 315
Rideau Hall, 296
Rideau Locks, 296
Riding Mountain National Park, 223
Riverside Amusement Park, 181
Robson Bight, 95
Rock hounding, 543
Rock and Roll Heaven, 26
Rodeos, 5
Roderick Haig-Brown Conservation Area, 105
Rogers Pass, 155–156
Roosevelt, Franklin (home of), 513–514
Rosebrugh Building, 250
Rosedale, 110–111
Ross Farm Museum, 554
Ross Memorial Museum, 512
Ross-Thomson House, 556
Rowing, 273, 504
Royal Alexandra (theater), 267

Royal 22nd Regiment Museum, 423
Royal Bank building (Toronto), 240
Royal Bank building (Vancouver), 21
Royal Bank Plaza, 240–241
Royal Botanical Gardens, 320
Royal British Columbia Museum, 76
Royal Canadian Mint, 216
Royal Canadian Mounted Police Training Academy, 197
Royal London Wax Museum, 76
Royal Military College of Canada, 300
Royal Ontario Museum, 250
Royal St. John's Regatta, 586
Royal Saskatchewan Museum, 197
Royal Tyrrell Museum of Paleontology, 179–180
Roy Thomson Hall, 266–267
Ruckle Provincial Park, 99
Running, 624, 632

S

S.S. Klondike National Historic Site, 613
Sackville, 497
Safety, xvi, 164
Ste-Agathe-des-Monts, 469
Ste-Adèle, 466–467
St. Andrews-by-the-Sea, 511–513
Ste-Anne-de-Beaupre, 480
Ste-Anne-des-Monts, 487–488
St. Anthony, 597
St. Bernard, 558
St. Boniface Cathedral, 216
St. Boniface Museum, 216
St. Dunstan's Basilica, 527
St-Eustache, 464
Ste-Famille, 447–448
Sainte-Famille Church, 448
Ste-Foy, 453
St. Francis Xavier University, 564
St-François, 447
St. George's, 354
St. George, 515
St. Jacobs, On., 324–325
St-Jean, 446–447
St-Jean Church, 447
St-Jérôme, 464–465
Saint John, 506, 511, 521
St. John's, Newf., 583, 586–590
St. John's Presbyterian, 535
St-Joseph-de-la-Rive, 482–483
St. Joseph Island, 332
Ste-Laurent, 446
St. Lawrence Centre for the Arts, 267

Sainte-Marie among the Hurons, 304
St. Martins, 515
St. Mary Magdalene Church, 97
St. Mary's Church (Charlottetown), 529
St. Mary's Church (Pointe de l'Eglise), 558
St. Patrick's Basilica, 360
St. Paul's Anglican Church, 527
St. Paul's Church, 547
St. Peter's Cathedral, 527
St. Peter's Canal, 574
Ste-Pétronille, 444, 446
St-Pierre (Ile d'Orléans), 448
St-Pierre, (Newfoundland), 593–594
St-Sauveur-des-Monts, 465–466
St. Simon and St. Jude Parish House, 538
St. Stephen, 511
St. Thomas, On., 309
St. Thomas Anglican Church, 334–335
St. Thomas (Old Garrison) Church, 587
Salmonier Nature Park, 591
Salt Spring Island, 98–100
Sam Kee Building, 26
Santa Claus Village, 468
Santa's Village, 306
Saskatchewan, 166–169, 226
Saskatchewan Landing Provincial Park, 201
Saskatchewan Science Centre, 197
Saskatoon Prairieland Exhibition Grounds, 205
Saskatoon, 204–212
Sault Ste. Marie, On., 327, 329–330, 338
Science Centre and Planetarium, 174
Science North, 333
Science World, 34
Scuba diving, xvii, 5, 122
Seal Island Light Museum, 557
Séminaire de Québec, 416
Seagram Museum, 323
Seigneurie du Lac-des-Deux-Montagnes, 463
Senior citizens, xvi–xvii, xxxiii
Serpent Mounds Provincial Park, 302
Shaw Festival, 318–319
Shediac, 518
Sheep Mountain, 620
Shelburne, 556
Sherbrooke, 478–479
Sherbrooke Village, 563
Sheshatshit, 600
Ship Harbour (Newfoundland), 592

Ship Harbour (Nova Scotia), *563*

Sigmund Samuel Canadiana Collections, *250*

Signal Hill National Historic Site, *586*

Signpost Forest, *619*

Simeon Perkins House, *556*

Singing sands phenomenon, *535*

Sir Andrew MacPhail Homestead, *534*

Sir Richard Squires Memorial Park, *595*

Sir Winston Churchill Square, *186*

Siwash Rock, *28*

Skagway, Alaska, *620–621*

SkyDome, *237*

Skyline Trail, *138*

Skylon Tower, *316*

Sleigh riding, *272*

Snowcat skiing, *71, 115*

Snowmobile, *287, 306, 338, 490, 496, 515, 521, 578*

Soccer, *53, 274*

Soo Locks, *329*

Sooke, *87*

Sound and Light Show, *295*

Southern Newfoundland Seamen's Museum, *593*

South Moresby National Park Reserve, *102*

Southwestern Ontario Heritage Village, *311*

Sparks Street Pedestrian Mall, *296*

Spiral Tunnels, *146*

Spirit Sands, *221*

Sports Hall of Fame, *501*

Spray Lakes Reservoir, *122*

Springhill, *566*

Spring Hill Miners Museum, *566*

Spruce Woods Provincial Heritage Park, *221*

Squash, *391*

Sri Lankan Gem Museum, *24*

Stade Olympique, *369*

Stampede Park, *175*

Stanley Park, *26–29*

Steinbach, *222*

Stephen Leacock Memorial Home, *305*

Stephenville, *598*

Stockade Barracks and Hospital Museum, *299*

Storybook Gardens, *326*

Stratford, On., *325–326*

Stratford Festival, *325*

Strathcona Provincial Park, *93*

Student travel, *xvii, xxxiii*

Sudbury, On., *333–334*

Sugar huts, *459, 479*

Sulfur Mountain Gondola, *125*

Summerside, *536–537*

Supreme Court, *296*

Sutton, *475*

Swift Current, *201*

Swimming, *121–122, 371, 391*

Sydney, *573*

Sydney and Louisburg Historical Society, *574*

T

Tablelands, *595*

Table Rock Scenic Tunnels, *315*

Tadoussac, *484–485*

Takakkaw Falls, *146*

Takhini Hot Springs, *613, 617*

Tangier, *563*

Taxes, *xxxi*

Taxis

Calgary, *183*

Edmonton, *193*

Montréal, *399*

Nova Scotia, *577*

Ottawa, *298*

Québec City, *452*

Regina, *204*

Saskatoon, *211*

Toronto, *280*

Vancouver, *53*

Victoria, *84*

Winnipeg, *224*

Telegraph Cove, *95*

Telephone Historical Center, *187*

Telephones, *xxxiii*

Terra Nova National Park, *592*

Terrace, *103*

Theater Plus, *267*

Théâtre St-Denis, *361*

Thompson Gallery, *239*

Thunder Bay, On., *331, 338*

Thunderbird Park, *75*

Tidal Bore, *516*

Tilley House, *506*

Timmins, *335–336*

Tipping, *xxxiii*

Tobogganing, *272*

Tofino, *91*

Tonquine Valley, *138*

Top of the World Highway, *624–625*

Toronto, On., *xxxvi, 227– 282*

Bloor-Yorkville area, *274– 275*

Central Toronto, *242–246*

Chinatown, *243*

City Halls, *246*

Financial District, *237–241*

Harbourfront, *233, 236–237, 274*

Kensington market, *243, 246*

North-central Toronto, *246– 251*

Queen Street West, *274*

Queen's Park, *249*

Queen's Quay Terminal, *237, 274*

Spadina Avenue, *246, 274*

Toronto Islands, *232–233*

Underground City, *241, 274*

Yorkville, *251*

Toronto-Dominion Bank, *21*

Toronto-Dominion Centre, *241*

Toronto Islands, *232–233*

Toronto Mendelssohn Choir, *267*

Toronto Stock Exchange building, *241*

Toronto Symphony, *267*

Totem poles, *28*

Tour Olympique, *367*

Tour operators, *xvii–xix, xxxiii–xxxiv*

Trader's Bank building, *241*

Train travel, *xix–xx, xxxiv*

Alberta, *225*

British Columbia, *113*

Canadian Rockies, *162*

Manitoba, *225*

Montréal, *399*

New Brunswick, *520*

Newfoundland and Labrador, *600*

Nova Scotia, *576*

Prairie Provinces, *225*

Ontario province, *298, 336*

Québec City, *451*

Québec province, *488*

Saskatchewan, *225*

Toronto, *279*

Vancouver, *62, 63*

Whistler, *61*

Winnipeg, *224*

Trans-Canada Waterslides, *110*

Transportation Museum, *311*

Travel agencies, *xx*

Traveler's checks, *xxxi*

Trent-Severn Waterway, *302*

Trinity, *593*

Trinity Church, *508*

Tuktoyaktuk, *630–631*

Tunnel Mountain Drive, *129*

Twillingate, *594*

Tyne Valley, *537–538*

U

U.S. Government travel briefings, *xx, xxxiv*

Ucluelet, *90*

Ukrainian Cultural Heritage Village, *192*

Ukrainian Museum of Canada, *205–206*

Uniacke Estate Museum Park *561*

Union Station, *241*

Université du Québec à Montréal, *365*

Université Ste-Anne, *558*

University College, *250–251*

University College of Cape Breton, *573*

University of Saskatchewan, *206*

University of Toronto, *250–261*

Upper Canada Village, *299*

Upper Hot Springs, *125*

V

Val David, *468–469*

Valcourt, *476*

Valley Zoo, *187*

Val Marie, *203*

Van Dusen Botanical Garden, *34*

Vancouver, *xxxvi, 14–65*
  Blood Alley, *25–26*
  Canada Place Pier, *21, 23*
  Cathedral Place, *20*
  Chinatown and Gastown, *24–26*
  East Indian district, *54*
  Gaoler's Mews, *25–26*
  Greater Vancouver, *31–34*
  Granville Island, *29–31*
  Italian community, *54*
  Japantown, *54*
  Pacific Space Centre, *33*
  Queen Elizabeth Park, *34*
  Robson to the Waterfront, *20–24*
  Sinclair Centre, *24*
  Stanley Park, *26–29*

Vancouver Art Gallery, *24*

Vancouver Club, *24*

Vancouver Island, *85–96, 112, 113*

Vancouver Aquarium, *27*

Vancouver Museum, *34*

VAT refunds, *xxxi*

Vegreville, *192*

Vermillion Crossing, *145–146*

Vermilion Lakes Drive, *129*

Vermilion Pass, *145*

Vernon, *106*

Victoria Hall, *301–302*

Victoria, B.C. *73–85, 112*

Victoria, Prince Edward Island, *534*

Victoria Park, *527*

Vieux Séminaire, *353*

Vieux-Port-de-Montréal, *353*

Vieux-Port de Québec, *419–420*

Village by the Grange, *246*

Village de Seraphin, *466*

Village du Mont-Castor, *469*

Virginia Falls, *629*

Visas, *xvi, xxxii–xxxiii*

Visitor information, *xx*

W

Wanuskewin Heritage Park, *209*

Wasagaming, *223*

Wascana Waterfowl Park Display Ponds, *197*

Waskasoo Park, *192*

Waskesiu, *210*

Waterfalls
  Canadian Rockies, *144, 146*
  Côte de Beaupré, *442*
  New Brunswick, *505, 511*
  Niagara Falls, *313–317*
  Nova Scotia, *567*
  Ontario, *329, 332*
  Vancouver Island, *93*
  wilderness Canada, *629*

Waterloo, On., *322–324*

Water Park, *465*

Waterton/Glacier International Peace Park, *152*

Waterton Lakes National Park, *152–154, 165*

Watson Lake, *619*

Wawa, On., *330*

Weather information, *xx–xxi*

Welland, On., *308*

West Coast Trail, *92*

West Dock, On., *310*

West Edmonton Mall, *187*

Western Counties Military Museum, *557*

Western Development Museum, *201, 206, 210*

West Hawk Lake, *222*

West Point, *538*

Whale watching, *6*
  British Columbia, *71, 114*
  New Brunswick, *513, 514*
  Nova Scotia, *559, 570*
  Québec province, *480, 485*
  Victoria, *83*

Whistler, *56–61*

Whitby, *278*

Whitehorse, *612–613, 617–619*

Whitemud Drive Amusement Park, *188*

White River, On., *330*

Whiteshell Provincial Park, *222*

White Water Park, *316*

Whyte Museum, *125*

Wikwemikong, On., *333*

Wilderness Canada, *604–638*

Wild Waters Waterslide Park, *188*

William Hawrelak Park, *188*

William Watson Lodge, *150*

Willistead Manor, *312*

Wilson Falls, *465*

Winch Building (Vancouver), *24*

Windermere Lake, *158*

Windermere Valley Pioneer Museum, *158*

Windsor (Nova Scotia), *561–562*

Windsor, On., *312–313, 338*

Windsor Station, *354*

Wine Region, On., *318–327*

Wineries, *107, 318*

Winnipeg, *212–224*

Winnipeg Art Gallery, *216–217*

Winnipeg Commodity Exchange, *217*

Winter Carnival, *439*

Winter Garden Theatre, *268*

Wiring funds, *xvi, xxxi*

Witless Bay Ecological Reserve, *590*

Wolfe Monument, *425*

Wolfville, *545*

Wood Buffalo National Park, *629*

Woodland Indian Cultural Educational Centre, *322*

Woodleigh, *533*

Woodmen's Museum, *518*

Woodside National Historic Park, *323*

Woody Point, *595*

Y

Yarmouth, *557–558*

Yellowknife, *625–628*

Yoho National Park, *138, 146–147, 165*

York-Sunbury Museum, *501–501*

Young People's Theatre, *268*

Youville Stables, *349*

Yukon Territorial Government Building, *613*

Yukon Territory, *604–611*

Yukon Permanent Art Collection, *613*

Yukon Transportation Museum, *613*

Yukon Wildlilfe Preserve, *617*

Z

Zoos
  Calgary, *173–174*
  Edmonton, *187*
  Manitoba, *214*
  New Brunswick, *511*
  Québec City, *423*
  Québec province, *472*
  Saskatchewan, *205*
  Toronto, *248–249*

Escape to ancient cities and

journey to exotic islands with

CNN Travel Guide, a wealth of valuable advice. Host

Valerie Voss will take you to

all of your favorite destinations,

including those off the beaten

path. Tune-in to your passport to the world.

CNN TRAVEL GUIDE
SATURDAY 12:30 PMET   SUNDAY 4:30 PMET

CNN®

WHEREVER YOU TRAVEL, *H*ELP IS NEVER FAR AWAY.

From planning your trip to providing travel assistance along the way, American Express® Travel Service Offices are always there to help.

Canada

American Express Travel Service
Canada Trust Tower, Main Floor
421-7th Avenue S.W.
Calgary
403/261-5982

American Express Travel Service
American Express Place
101 McNabb Street
Markham
905/474-8350

American Express Travel Service
Centre Eaton, Metro Level
705 St. Catherine Ouest
Montreal
514/282-0445

American Express Travel Service
1141 De Maisonneuve West
Montreal
514/284-3300

Matthews Travel
International Inc. (R)
4685 Queen Street
Niagara Falls
905/354-5649

American Express Travel Service
Constitution Square
350 Albert Street, Suite 1620
Ottawa
613/783-8626

American Express Travel Service
Royal York Hotel, #133-134
100 Front Street West
Toronto
416/363-3883

American Express Travel Service
666 Burrard Street
Vancouver
604/669-2813

Travel

http://www.americanexpress.com/travel

**American Express Travel Service Offices are
found in central locations throughout Canada.**